CONTRACTS

CASES AND THEORY OF CONTRACTUAL OBLIGATION

Second Edition

■ ■ ■

by

Carter G. Bishop
Professor of Law
Suffolk University Law School

Daniel D. Barnhizer
Professor of Law & Bradford Stone Faculty Scholar
Michigan State University College of Law

AMERICAN CASEBOOK SERIES®

WEST ACADEMIC PUBLISHING

Mat #41653659

American Casebook Series is a trademark registered in the U.S. Patent and Trademark Office.

© 2008 Thomson/West
© 2015 LEG, Inc. d/b/a West Academic
    444 Cedar Street, Suite 700
    St. Paul, MN 55101
    1-877-888-1330

West, West Academic Publishing, and West Academic are trademarks of West Publishing Corporation, used under license.

Printed in the United States of America

ISBN: 978-1-62810-110-2

ACKNOWLEDGMENTS

This second edition would not have been possible without the support and assistance of many others. Louis Higgins at West Academic Publishing provided insights and comments for changes to this second edition. Brittney Kern, Timothy Lee, and Jacqueline Kittel provided invaluable research assistance, proof reading and editorial support.

SUMMARY OF CONTENTS

TABLE OF CONTENTS

TABLE OF CASES

The principal cases are in bold type.

TABLE OF UNIFORM
COMMERCIAL CODE CITATIONS

xxix

TABLE OF
RESTATEMENT (FIRST)
OF CONTRACTS CITATIONS

TABLE OF RESTATEMENT (SECOND) OF CONTRACTS CITATIONS

TABLE OF SCHOLARLY AUTHORITIES

CONTRACTS

CASES AND THEORY OF
CONTRACTUAL OBLIGATION

Second Edition

CHAPTER 1

INTRODUCTION TO CONTRACT LAW STUDY & JURISPRUDENCE

■ ■ ■

Contracts are ubiquitous. Nearly everyone forms or deals with a contract every day. The simplest transaction involves multiple layers of contracts between the parties themselves and between everyone else who made that transaction possible. Importantly, this often involves lawyers at one or more stages of the process of getting goods or services from those who can supply them to those who can pay for them. Your studies in contract law will prepare you to provide legal services, advice, and counsel in assisting your clients in ordering their dealings with other actors in the market.

In light of the multitude of parties involved in most transactions, this text assumes that contract law is best understood from the perspective of the primary two parties to the particular contract *and* in the context of the larger social contract. In this sense, every contract is part of a larger social compact within the legal system from which disappointed contracting parties may ultimately seek enforcement. Without a legal system to enforce contracts as made by the parties, the contract is no better than the moral obligation of the parties.

In truth, contract law is unlike other law school subjects because it remains, to a large degree, that last domain of private ordering and private "lawmaking." In many ways, contract law begins with the proposition that the parties seek to create a legal relationship that each party believes will maximize its welfare. For many reasons, contract law seeks to enforce those privately created obligations.

But the parties' capacity to establish legally binding obligations between themselves necessarily affects the interests of other members of society. If the legal system enforced every promise, then the parties to the contract could displace literally all other public law legal doctrines. Contract law and the normative case for private ordering do not extend to such libertarian and even anarchic extremes. Consequently, much of contract law concerns identifying the boundaries of private ordering, how did these boundaries develop, and are the boundaries flexible as societal mores change over time? These larger questions make the study of

1

contracts both contextually and socially meaningful and constitute the larger jurisprudence of contract law.

A. THE JURISPRUDENCE OF CONTRACT LAW

This chapter provides an overview of the sociological, economic, and philosophical theories and influences that generated the body of law you are learning today. In many ways, the theories considered in this chapter are part of a broader discussion over the proper relationship between the individual and the state. On the one hand, contract law is often described as a body of private law that provides individuals with "freedom of contract" to arrange their affairs with others as they see fit. On the other hand, the state, which is ultimately responsible for enforcement of these private agreements, may have an interest in intervening in such contracts to prevent contract law from allowing one party to take undue advantage of another. In this sense, the state essentially provides "freedom from contract" in situations where circumstances render private autonomy meaningless or where private orderings systemically harm the public interest.

The story of contract law is best understood as jurisprudential evolution with multiple paths and variant outcomes. The modern common law of contracts began in the early Seventeenth Century, split into two separate legal regimes (law and equity), and was later transplanted whole cloth to the United States (and the original colonies). In the United States, jurisdictions experimented with alternative responses to new contract enforcement problems, and state variations reflect different views of these policy matters.

As you read the following text, consider the sociological and economic circumstances that accompanied the jurisprudential development of contract law. Contract can be a great engine for individual freedom or a tool for economic oppression by the state or by other economic actors. Importantly, each of the jurisprudential developments discussed below can justify expansions or restrictions of individual freedom. The strategically oriented lawyer must consider not only how law and jurisprudence can support obtaining a current objective, but also how it might support a loss of individual liberty or harm to society in the future.

1. WHY STUDY JURISPRUDENCE IN CONTRACT LAW?

Although it is not impossible to study and learn contract law without a background in the philosophy of law, such a background greatly enhances one's understanding of the subject matter. Without jurisprudence, the study of law is merely mechanical acquisition of rote doctrines. The student records the law without truly understanding it as an integrated whole. While this strategy may suffice for much of law practice, it is unlikely to produce the kind of legal thinking that separates great lawyers from good ones.

Jurisprudence generally—and contract jurisprudence specifically—attempts to provide a justification or an explanation for the law. These accounts take two different forms: (1) descriptive or positive accounts, and (2) normative accounts. A positive jurisprudence explains what the law "is." A normative account explains what the law "ought" to be.

At the simplest level, descriptive or positive accounts of the law attempt to address the question, "how does the law really work?" The actual workings of the legal system are complex, and the myriad interactions between legal actors generate unforeseen consequences as the law is applied. Consider, for example, the unconscionability doctrine discussed in Chapter 5 that permits courts to overturn contracts deemed to be unduly harsh or oppressive, particularly when one of the parties is a poor, unsophisticated consumer and the other party is a large, successful business entity. Although the law on its face appears to protect the interests of the poor consumer, the broader consequences of that doctrine might cause businesses to refuse to continue doing business in certain communities or to raise their prices to reflect the increased risks that their contracts will not be upheld. Descriptive jurisprudence attempts to explain not only how various legal rules work and fit together on paper, but also the consequences those rules produce when actually applied in the real world. As one commentator notes, "[n]o set of legal institutions or prescriptions exists apart from the narratives that locate it and give it meaning. For every constitution there is an epic, for each decalogue there is a scripture. Once understood in the context of the narratives that give it meaning, law becomes not merely a system of rules to be observed, but a world in which we live." Robert M. Cover, "*Nomos* and Narrative," 97 Harv. L. Rev. 4, 4–5 (1983).

Descriptive jurisprudence also attempts to make the law "transparent." See Stephen A. Smith, Contract Theory 24 (2004) ("Law is transparent to the extent that the reasons legal actors give for doing what they do are their real reasons. By contrast, law is not transparent if the real reasons are hidden."). In many cases, what legal actors say they are doing or the reasons they give for their actions fail to accord with what they are actually doing or with the real consequences of a legal rule. For example, the parol evidence rule, addressed in Chapter 4, ostensibly prohibits the introduction of certain forms of evidence of contract terms where the parties have reduced their contract to a complete and final written expression of their intent. But empirical studies of actual applications of the parol evidence rule suggest that courts tend to base their applications of the rule upon the apparent *status* of the parties rather than the definiteness of any writing between them. See Robert Childres & Stephen J. Spitz, "Status in the Law of Contract," 47 N.Y.U. L. Rev. 1, 2,

30–31 (1972) ("a court's interpretation and enforcement of a contract frequently depends upon the status of the parties," rather than strict application of formal legal rules). A good descriptive account of the law identifies such mismatches and non-transparent applications of the law.

In contrast to descriptive or positive statements about the law, normative jurisprudence provides an account of the way the law "ought" to be. Thus, normative jurisprudence might tackle the question, "are the current rules relating to the enforceability of some promises as contracts justifiable?" Such justifications may be offered in terms of morality, economic efficiency, rationality, psychology, anthropology, principles of natural law, justice, or some other standard. Normative jurisprudence may also begin from the proposition that the current state of the law is unjustified in order to argue how the law ought to change so as to become justifiable.

So why is an awareness of basic American jurisprudence necessary to your study of contract law? First, jurisprudence can explain the background forces that drive judicial reasoning. In many cases, a court's jurisprudence governs how that court will choose among and interpret the legal rules that might apply to the case at bar. For example, in *Ocean Accident & Guarantee Corp. v. Industrial Comm'n of Arizona*, 32 Ariz. 275, 257 P. 644 (1927), the court adopted a strongly "Realist" jurisprudence to justify upholding a state workers' compensation statute similar to statutes that other courts had struck down as contrary to contract, labor, antitrust, and constitutional law. For this court, such abstract legal principles should be subordinate to the social reality that individual employees had little freedom of choice with respect to contract terms offered by their employers.

> Many of the other states were engaged in discussing the advisability of adopting some form of [Workers'] Compensation Law, and in their natural desire to avoid the objections which caused the New York statute to be held unconstitutional, worded their acts accordingly. But of even greater influence on these acts was the fact that most men, and particularly most lawyers, were still governed by the old school of economics of which Adam Smith, Ricardo, Malthus, and Mills were shining lights, and in which the doctrine of laissez faire was considered to be the rule which the state should observe in regard to the relation of employer and employee. It was under the influence of these ideas that the fellow-servant rule and that of assumption of risk were applied to an industrial civilization for which they were utterly unfitted, and it was gravely insisted by bench, bar, and the leaders of society that the individual working man, without money, friends, or influence, must be 'protected' in his right to contract freely with his employer, by this time generally a corporation with immense resources, and no personal touch with or interest in its employees;

which considered labor as a mere commodity to be bought at the cheapest possible price, used till worn out, and then scrapped like any other worn-out tool. Our enlightened modern thought realizes that an equality of bargaining power between two such unequal parties is impossible, and has attempted to equalize the balance through the labor unions and state regulation of industry; but old ideas die hard, and the pathways of progress are strewn with the fragments of legislation designed for this purpose but wrecked on the insistence of court after court that the state must not interfere with the 'free right of contract.' The eight-hour day, protection for women and children in industry, and every reform which has lightened the burden and brightened the life of the workman has had to fight its way up against this insistence on applying a philosophy which was perhaps just enough at one time, to a civilization which has outgrown it as the grown man has the swaddling clothes of the babe. Id. at 645 (emphasis added).

The *Ocean Accident & Guarantee* opinion was contrary to the then-extant legal rules regarding the sanctity of contracts between employer and employee and freedom of contract doctrine prohibitions against legislatures and courts intervening to alter the terms freely chosen by the parties. But the decision can be explained as a strong example of the jurisprudence of the Legal Realists, a school of thought that began around the end of the nineteenth century and reached its pinnacle in the New Deal era. According to the Legal Realists, law—including doctrines relating to individual freedom of contract—should be based upon and responsive to social realities, not upon abstract concepts of what the law requires. Existing legal rules at the time generally disfavored judicial interventions into employment contracts, despite that those rules had been developed in a much more agrarian, decentralized economy. With the rapid industrialization, urbanization, and concentration of capital in the hands of large corporate employers, the *Ocean Accident & Guarantee* court rejected strict application of freedom of contract rules in favor of new rules that recognized that there was no good reason to respect the terms of employment contracts if those contracts were imposed upon individual workers who had no real freedom of choice.

In contrast, the Michigan Supreme Court has issued a series of opinions that can only be explained in terms of a "Formalist" or "Neoformalist" jurisprudence and that explicitly reject many of the doctrines developed by more Realist courts. In *Wilkie v. Auto–Owners Ins. Co.*, 469 Mich. 41, 664 N.W.2d 776 (2003), for example, the court analyzed the reasonable expectations doctrine that other jurisdictions had developed in response to the apparent gross disparities of bargaining power between individual insureds and insurance companies. In its strongest form, the reasonable expectations doctrine asserts that insureds—like the employees in *Ocean Accident & Guarantee*—have no bargaining power to negotiate the terms of their insurance contracts, and thus, do not really consent to those terms. Consequently, the reasonable expectations doctrine permits courts to disregard the plain terms of insurance contracts and instead enforce what the court determines to be the reasonable expectations of the insured. See, e.g., *C & J Fertilizer, Inc. v. Allied Mutual Ins. Co.*, 227 N.W.2d 169 (Iowa 1975) (burglary insurance contract that plainly conditioned right to insurance on presence of marks of forcible entry on exterior of building was nonetheless contrary to reasonable expectations of insured, and contract would be reformed to eliminate exterior marks requirement). The Michigan Supreme Court in *Wilkie* rejected the reasonable expectations doctrine as antithetical to principles of freedom of contract and the rule of law:

> This approach, where judges divine the parties' reasonable expectations and then rewrite the contract accordingly, is contrary to the bedrock principle of American contract law that parties are free to contract as they see fit, and the courts are to enforce the agreement as written absent some highly unusual circumstance, such as a contract in violation of law or public policy. . . . The notion, that free men and women may reach agreements regarding their affairs without government interference and that courts will enforce those agreements, is ancient and irrefutable. It draws strength from common-law roots and can be seen in our fundamental charter, the United States Constitution, where government is forbidden from impairing the contracts of citizens, art. I, § 10, cl. 1.[1] . . . It is, in short, an unmistakable and ineradicable part of the legal fabric of our society. Few have expressed the force of this venerable axiom better than the late Professor Arthur Corbin, of Yale Law School, who wrote on this topic in his definitive study of contract law, Corbin on Contracts, as follows:

> One does not have "liberty of contract" unless organized society both forbears and enforces, forbears to penalize him for making his bargain and enforces it for him after it is made. . . .

> In contrast to this legal pedigree extending over the centuries, the rule of reasonable expectations is of recent origin. Moreover, it is antagonistic to this understanding of the rule of law, and is, accordingly, in our view, invalid as an approach to contract interpretation. Wilkie, 664 N.W.2d at 782.

When read in conjunction with *Ocean Accident & Guarantee*, the choice between the former rule and the *Wilkie* rule appears entirely arbitrary until placed in jurisprudential context. Specifically, the *Wilkie*

---

[1] "No state shall . . . pass any . . . Law impairing the Obligation of Contracts. . . . "

court has clearly adopted a jurisprudence that favors enforcement of the strict terms of a contract, certainty of legal rules, and individual autonomy even if that freedom of contract leads to harsh results in some cases. This Formalist jurisprudence explains why the *Wilkie* court rejected the reasonable expectations doctrine.

Correlatively, familiarity with the jurisprudence of contract also implicates an ability to advocate for changes in the law. As the *Wilkie* court notes, the reasonable expectations doctrine developed only recently in the 1970s in response to scholars such as W. David Slawson and Robert Keeton, who argued for a change in then-extant legal rules requiring strict enforcement of insurance contracts. See W. Slawson, "Standard Form Contracts and Democratic Control of Lawmaking Power," 84 Harv. L. Rev. 529 (1971) and R. Keeton, "Insurance Law Rights At Variance With Policy Provisions," 83 Harv. L. Rev. 961 (1970). Over time, as courts and scholars observed the uncertainty and unpredictability of insurance contract enforcement created by the reasonable expectations doctrine, the strength of the individual autonomy and formalist critiques eventually convinced at least one jurisdiction to reject that doctrine.

2. OVERVIEW OF AMERICAN CONTRACT LAW JURISPRUDENCE

A broad overview of American contract jurisprudence promotes a better understanding of the various components. Importantly, there are an innumerable number of different philosophies of law. The following is intended only as a survey of a few of the major schools of jurisprudence that have influenced the development of American contract law doctrines over the last two hundred years, including Legal Realism and Formalism, Critical Legal Studies and Law & Economics, Behavioral Decision Theory, and Legal Positivism and Natural Law. This overview is necessarily oversimplified, both in that it cannot cover even a significant portion of the schools of legal thought that have addressed contract jurisprudence, and in that there are many divisions even within these broader categories.

a. Legal Realism and Formalism

Legal Realism and Formalism lie at the heart of important questions of American contract jurisprudence, and for many reasons each can only be understood in terms of the other. Historically, the two schools overlapped. The Formalist or Classical model of contract jurisprudence coalesced in the decades following the Civil War and peaked in the first two decades of the twentieth century. The Legal Realists arguably had their roots in the last decades of the nineteenth century. See e.g., Oliver Wendell Holmes, The Common Law 1–2 (1881) ("The life of the law has not been logic: it has been experience. The felt necessities of the time, the prevalent moral and political theories, intuitions of public policy, avowed or unconscious, even the prejudices which judges share with their fellow-men, have had a good deal more to do than the syllogism in determining the rules by which men should be governed."). The Realist school developed significantly with a series of articles and addresses by Roscoe Pound between 1908 and 1910 (discussed below) and experienced its heyday in the period between World Wars I and II. More importantly, these schools still inform and impact the most basic jurisprudential inquiries of modern times. See e.g., American Legal Realism xiv (William W. Fisher III, et al., eds. 1993) (". . . Legal Realism continues to exert an important influence on modern American legal scholarship through its capacity to set the agenda—to define the questions that need answering."); John E. Murray, Jr., "Contract Theories and the Rise of Neoformalism," 71 Fordham L. Rev. 869, 870 (2002) ("More recent academic literature advocates a return to formalism, a so-called neoformalism.").

Formalism, as the name suggests, ostensibly comprised an approach to legal rules generally (and contract rules specifically) that assumed that: (1) rules are certain, (2) rules are knowable, (3) rules can guide individual choices, and (4) rules can constrain judicial discretion. In addition to this philosophy of rules, Classical Formalism emphasized a preference for bright-line rules, strong doctrines of individual autonomy, and judicial restraint from interference in private contracts. For the Formalists, a relatively simple, general proposition of law could provide a court all of the tools necessary to decide the concrete contracts disputes brought before it.

As the *Wilkie* case suggests, there is much to be said in favor of a formalist approach. Simple, clear, bright-line rules communicate ex ante to individuals regarding how they should structure their interactions with others to take advantage of legal benefits—such as the ability to make an agreement that is enforceable by resort to legal process and sanctions—and to avoid unpleasant legal results, such as an unenforceable contract or criminal sanctions for fraud. Likewise, Formalism assumes that courts can reliably discern which bright-line rules apply to a given situation and how those rules govern that situation.

Although not a sine qua non of formalist jurisprudence, the school is also often associated with "scientism"—the idea that basic precepts and axioms of law and legal reasoning can be "discovered" by thorough analysis of individual legal decisions, such as cases and statutes. See, e.g., Christopher Columbus Langdell, A Selection of Cases on the Law of Contracts vi (1871) ("Law, considered as a science, consists of certain principles or doctrines. To have such a master of these as to be able to apply them with constant facility and certainty to the ever-tangled skein of human affairs, is what constitutes a true lawyer; and hence to acquire that mastery should be the business of every earnest student of law."). Once such foundational principles are discovered, they should yield general rules that will control judicial discretion in deciding future specific cases.

Legal formalism arguably reached its pinnacle, at least with respect to contract law and freedom of contract doctrines, in the 1905 case of *Lochner v. New York*, 198 U.S. 45 (1905). At issue was a New York statute that, among other things, prohibited bakery employees from working more than sixty hours per week. The majority, relying upon general principles of private autonomy and freedom of contract, determined that the statute violated the 14th Amendment prohibition against the state depriving "any person of life, liberty, or property without due process of law." See *id.* at 53. Justice Oliver Wendell Holmes famously dissented:

> Some of these laws embody convictions or prejudices which judges are likely to share. Some may not. But a Constitution is not intended to embody a particular economic theory, whether of paternalism and the organic relation of the citizen to the state or of laissez faire. It is made for people of fundamentally differing views, and the accident of our finding certain opinions natural and familiar, or novel, and even shocking, ought not to conclude our judgment upon the question whether statutes embodying them conflict with the Constitution of the United States.

> General propositions do not decide concrete cases. The decision will depend on a judgment or intuition more subtle than any articulate major premise. But I think that the proposition just stated, if it is accepted, will carry us far toward the end. Every opinion tends to become a law. I think that the word 'liberty,' in the 14th Amendment, is perverted when it is held to prevent the natural outcome of a dominant opinion, unless it can be said that a rational and fair man necessarily would admit that the statute proposed would infringe fundamental principles as they have been understood by the traditions of our people and our law. It does not need research to show that no such sweeping condemnation can be passed upon the statute before us. A reasonable man might think it a proper measure on the score of health. Men whom I certainly could not pronounce unreasonable would uphold it as a first installment of a general regulation of the hours of work. Whether in the latter aspect it would be open to the charge of inequality I think it unnecessary to discuss. Id. at 75–76 (Holmes, J., dissenting).

The Legal Realist movement developed as a reaction against the perceived formalism of the late-nineteenth and early-twentieth century courts. In contrast to the Formalists, the Legal Realists were much more dubious of the power of rules to guide individual action and predictably constrain judicial discretion. More formalist scholars and judges mocked this skepticism regarding the certainty, predictability, and knowability of rules "as the proposition that how a judge decides a case on a given day depends primarily on what he or she had for breakfast." American Legal

Realism xiv (William W. Fisher III, et al., eds. 1993). But to the Realists, classical formalist judges engaged in a "mechanical jurisprudence" that applied abstract principles of law to concrete cases without any attempt to address the social reality underlying those cases. See e.g., Roscoe Pound, "Mechanical Jurisprudence," 8 Colum. L. Rev. 605 (1908). Thus, for Pound, the majority decision in *Lochner* and similar cases ignored social realities in favor of deciding concrete cases based upon purely abstract conceptions of legal doctrines such as "liberty of contract":

> The conception of liberty of contract, in particular, has given rise to rules and decisions which, tested by their practical operation, defeat liberty. . . . The conception of freedom of contract is made the basis of a logical deduction. The Court does not inquire what the effect of such a deduction will be, when applied to the actual situation. It does not observe that the result will be to produce a condition precisely the reverse of that which the conception originally contemplated. . . . deductions from this and like conceptions . . . have given us rules which, when applied to the existing commercial and industrial situation, are wholly inadequate. Id. at 616.

See also Felix S. Cohen, "Transcendental Nonsense and the Functional Approach," 35 Colum. L. Rev. 809, 809 (1935) (caricaturing classical formalists as attempting to work in "a special heaven reserved for the theoreticians of the law [where] one met, face to face, the many concepts of jurisprudence in their absolute purity, freed from all entangling alliances with human life.").

In place of this rigid and abstract conceptualism in which the cases of actual parties were supposedly forced into rigid molds required by formal rules, the Legal Realists advocated what Pound called a "sociological jurisprudence" in which legal decision makers such as legislatures and courts would create and apply something akin to what Karl Llewellyn eventually described as "singing rules." See Karl N. Llewellyn, "On the Good, the True, the Beautiful, in Law," 9 U. Chi. L. Rev. 224, 250 (1941) ("Only the rule which shows its reason on its face has ground to claim maximum chance of *continuing* effectiveness. . . . the singing rule with purpose and with reason clear, whose nature, whose very possibility, the Formal Perpendicular has led our legal thinkers to forget—almost to deny."). For the Realists, rules and legal decisions under those rules should reflect social reality and be responsive to the social facts on the ground instead of attempting to fit a dynamic and ever-changing society into the formal law.

The importance of the Formalists and the Realists to the study of contract law cannot be understated. Practically every course on the study of contracts—indeed, most of the generally accepted cannon of what contracts scholars, lawyers, and judges deem to comprise "contract law"—reflects, to some extent, Christopher Columbus Langdell's original formulation of the subject. Formalism purportedly presented classical contract law as an internally integrated, consistent, and coherent body of interrelated doctrines that could determine an answer in any dispute arising out of a private agreement. Although the Realists successfully poked many holes in this façade, the classical structure still provides an excellent pedagogical organization for the teaching of contract law—so long as students recognize that it is merely a convenient structure for communicating basic concepts. Similarly, vestiges of formalist scientism still provide the baseline vocabulary for researching and investigating legal principles, such as the West Key Number and Headnote system with which you will become intimately familiar as you undertake your own legal research. See Charles J. Ten Brink, "A Jurisprudential Approach to Teaching Legal Research," 39 New Eng. L. Rev. 307 (2005).

On the other hand, Legal Realism arguably informs every important legal question—if the abstract blackletter rules and doctrines do not clearly and unambiguously resolve the dispute (and they usually do not, at least in litigated cases), what choices among rules will best promote preferred policies? More importantly, many of the most important jurisprudential developments of the Twentieth and Twenty-First Centuries developed from the insights of Legal Realism. Besides the major schools discussed below, we are necessarily skipping many of these other developments. For example, Stewart Macaulay's and Ian MacNeil's work on relational contracts—the insight that contract law may be more about relationships over time than about the terms the parties happened to use at the moment of contracting—is based in part on their attempts to understand how contracting parties actually understood their relationship. See, e.g., Stewart Macaulay, "Private Legislation and the Duty to Read—Business Run by IBM Machine, the Law of Contracts and Credit Cards," 19 Vand. L. Rev. 1051 (1966); Ian R. Macneil, "Relational Contract: What We Do and Do Not Know,"1985 Wis. L. Rev. 483. Likewise, the substantial increase in empirical legal studies over the past twenty years also reflects a desire to understand how law works in the real world. These and other jurisprudential developments are worth an entire course in themselves.

b. Critical Legal Studies and Law & Economics

As the leading lights of the Legal Realist school were absorbed into the Roosevelt New Deal administration, the courts, and retirement, scholars with different agendas competed to assume the mantle of successor to the Realists. The two most important immediate successors were the Critical Legal Studies movement and the cross-disciplinary Law & Economics school.

The Critical Legal Studies school (CLS or Crits) adopted an explicitly nihilistic and Marxist approach to jurisprudence. See John E. Murray, Jr., "Contract Theories and the Rise of Neoformalism," 71 Fordham L. Rev. 869, 873 (2002). "Though it describes all legal reasoning as myth, its principal target is contract law because the social institutions of contract and property constitute the mechanism of the market system." *Id.*

The defining characteristics of CLS lie in two propositions. The first builds upon the rule skepticism of the Realists. While the Formalists might say that given sufficient information it might be possible to construct rules that would constrain judicial discretion in every case, the Legal Realists argued that most or all rules have some gray areas in which judges must make discretionary choices (and impliedly that those choices should further socially beneficial policies). CLS takes this rule skepticism to the point of arguing that *all* rules are *always* indeterminate. A rule is said to be indeterminate if it does not constrain judicial discretion regarding how to decide a case arising under that rule. A rule may be indeterminate because it is vague or ambiguous or because other rules conflict with the first rule. Thus, a rule stating "vehicles are prohibited in public parks" may be indeterminate with respect to whether a bicycle or skateboard is a "vehicle" or with respect to whether an ambulance may enter the park on an emergency call. See H.L.A. Hart, The Concept of Law 121–127 (1961). A CLS scholar, however, would argue that the legal decision maker can *always* find an ambiguity, exception, or counter-rule for any proposition of law, and thus, can always claim to have based her decisions upon legitimate legal rules. Thus, as in the case of *Batsakis v. Demotsis*, which you will encounter in Chapter 2, the court enforced a contract under which the defendant agreed to pay $2,500 in exchange for a loan worth only $25 under the theory that the parties had entered a valid contract. Another court, however, might adopt a counter-rule, such as the proposition that a contract is unenforceable if it was entered under duress (the borrower was attempting to escape from Greece during World War II) or if it was unconscionable (the "interest rate" on the loan was absurdly high). CLS scholars used such examples of conflicting rules and counter-rules to argue that the whole of contract law was indeterminate, and that legal decisions are wholly unconstrained. See e.g., Roberto Mangabeira Unger, "The Critical Legal Studies Movement," 96 Harv. L. Rev. 561 (1983).

The second major proposition of the CLS school argues that while rules are indeterminate, legal decision makers tend to render decisions for the purpose of maintaining in power those who are currently in power. See *id.* at 624 (providing example of family law rules as mechanism for maintaining power hierarchy established by settled conceptions of family). The *Wilkie* and *Lochner* cases discussed above would arguably be examples of this phenomenon, as both appeal to formalist principles to support a facially neutral rule that, nonetheless, primarily benefits established economic interests.

The problem with absolute rule skepticism and nihilism, of course, is that eventually one runs out of things to be skeptical and nihilistic about, and CLS was no exception—after a burst of scholarship in the 1970s and 1980s, CLS has more or less vanished from the jurisprudential scene. But while CLS did not directly influence judicial or legislative decision making, CLS should not be discounted as irrelevant. More than any other school of jurisprudence, CLS focuses upon critiquing the status quo and constantly inquiring whether that status quo represents a relatively neutral position governed by the rule of law or instead represents the interests of the established power hierarchy. This skepticism toward "settled" law might promote the ability of lawyers to discern systemic injustices that others accept as normal. Possibly as a result of this focus on skeptical inquiry, a number of other "Critical" schools of jurisprudence, such as Critical Race Theory and Feminist Legal Theory, developed following the death of CLS and continue to push constantly at the relationships between law and the members of the society subject to that law. See, e.g., Blake D. Morant, "Critical Perspectives of Traditional Contract Doctrines," in Larry A. DiMatteo, et al., Visions of Contract: Rationality, Bargaining, and Interpretation 206 (2007) ("These movements debunk the objectivity of law, expose the disproportionate effects of established legal orders on traditionally disadvantaged groups, and, to some degree, establish the need to reform the law to ensure that these groups are treated fairly.").

Contemporaneously with the development of CLS, the 1970s also saw the development of an intentionally cross-disciplinary school of jurisprudence known as Law & Economics. Although many scholars had previously discussed some aspects of law in economic terms, Richard Posner, a judge on the Seventh Circuit U.S. Court of Appeals and professor at the University of Chicago law school, is often credited as the driving force behind this intellectual movement with the publication of his seminal treatise, Economic Analysis of Law (1973). In this jurisprudence, legal scholars and economists attempted to explore whether non-market legal rules and institutions, as well as decisions by participants in those systems, could be analyzed in economic terms. "The economic analysis of law is primarily concerned with using economic methods as theoretical constructs for analyzing, in economic terms, the rules and laws adopted by a particular society." Robin Paul Malloy, Law and Economics: A Comparative Approach to Theory and Practice 3 (1990). Importantly, the economic analysis of law can be pursued under many different economic theories— an economist steeped in a Marxist or socialist tradition will apply a very different set of economic principles than a free-market, capitalist economist would apply to the same set of observed facts. See *id.* at 2.

Unlike CLS, which largely focuses on the rule skepticism branch of Legal Realism, Law & Economics tends to be more concerned with whether law and legal rules advance social or individual welfare. This project depends upon two foundational principles. First, the economic analysis of law presumes that individuals are to some extent "rational." That is, individuals presented with two or more options choose among those options based upon whichever option will make them better off post hoc. Individuals may be assumed to be perfectly rational or "boundedly" rational to some extent. See e.g., Gregory Mitchell, "Why Law and Economics' Perfect Rationality Should Not Be Traded for Behavioral Law and Economics' Equal Incompetence," 91 Geo. L.J. 67, 68 (2002) ("A fundamental assumption within the law and economics movement is that 'individuals are rational maximizers of their satisfactions in their nonmarket as well as their market behavior.' "); Russell Korobkin, "Bounded Rationality, Standard Form Contracts, and Unconscionability," 70 U. Chi. L. Rev. 1203, 1206 (2003) ("Because buyers are boundedly rational rather than fully rational decision makers, when making purchasing decisions they take into account only a limited number of product attributes and ignore others.").

Second, Law & Economics attempts to predict whether positive and normative accounts of the law are "efficient," that is whether the law aids or interferes with individuals' and society's attempts to maximize utility or welfare. As with the rationality assumption, there are multiple possible standards for evaluating efficiency. One common measure of efficiency is "Pareto efficiency." A rule or transaction promotes Pareto efficiency if it makes at least one party better off and no party worse off. Thus, assume A and B contract for the sale and purchase of a batch of widgets at $50 that would be worth $60 on the open market. Before delivery, a third-party C offers A $80 for the widgets if they are delivered immediately. A rule that permits X to breach the original contract with Y provided she pays Y for damages caused by the breach would be Pareto efficient. Z would receive desperately needed widgets, Y would receive $10 in damages from X (the added cost of replicating the breached contract on the open market), and X would net an additional $20 over the value of the original transaction. If there is no alternative rule or transaction that can make any party better off without also making any party worse off, the situation is said to be "Pareto optimal." Other models of efficiency, such as Kaldor–Hicks efficiency and wealth maximization, deem rules or transactions efficient if the net welfare gains—measured in terms of utility or money value—from the rule or transaction exceed the net costs imposed upon other parties by the rule or transaction.

c.   Behavioral Decision Theory

Law & Economics' assumption that individuals are rational maximizers of their utility—however measured—on its face is arguably absurd. See Robert A. Prentice, "Chicago Man, K-T Man, and the Future of Behavioral Law and Economics," 56 Vand. L. Rev. 1663, 1666–67 (2003) ("In the past decade it has become clear . . . that people simply do not make decisions as modeled by traditional law and economics. A 'mountain of experiments' performed in psychology and related disciplines . . . demonstrate that people tend to deviate systematically from rational norms when they make decisions."); Gregory Mitchell, "Why Law and Economics' Perfect Rationality Should Not Be Traded for Behavioral Law and Economics' Equal Incompetence," 91 Geo. L.J. 67, 70–71 (2002) ("Research from psychology and behavioral economics studies reveals that human judgment and decision making necessarily rely on imperfect psychological mechanisms that cause systematic departures from rationality."). Partly in response to the perceived deficiencies of the Law & Economics rationality models, cross-disciplinary work in what has variously been called Law & Psychology, Behavioral Decision Theory, Legal Decision Theory, and Behavioral Law and Economics has attempted to craft a model of decision-making behavior by legal actors that reflects experimental evidence of systemic irrationalities.

At the heart of Behavioral Decision Theory (BDT) is the proposition that human beings generally make decisions on the basis of "heuristics"— mental rules of thumb—that, although they help individuals avoid high costs of information gathering and analysis, contribute to a well-defined set of biases and irrationalities that more sophisticated parties can exploit. See e.g., Cass R. Sunstein, "Introduction," in Behavioral Law and Economics 3 (Cass R. Sunstein, ed.) (2000). Although it is impossible to review completely all of the experimentally observed biases and heuristics, a few examples are worth noting as particularly relevant to the study of contract law. First, individuals are subject to an over-optimism bias in which they tend to under-estimate risks and assume, even if a product or transaction has a known chance of failure, that the risks cannot happen to them. Thus, in the context of a consumer purchasing passage on a cruise ship, individuals tend to discount the presence of a clause governing the forum or jurisdiction where a dispute must be filed because they assume that all will go well with the cruise and there will not be any dispute.

Second, the status quo bias represents the tendency of individuals to irrationally favor the current state of affairs over superior alternatives. The old adage, "a bird in the hand is worth two in the bush," potentially provides an example of this phenomenon, depending on the likelihood of successfully capturing both of the bush-bound birds. If the probability of capturing both birds exceeds 50% (plus the transaction costs of the capture effort), then the adage is false. The status quo bias, however, suggests that individuals will demand an extra premium over and above the expected value of a transaction to induce them to move from the status quo.

A third cognitive distortion—framing effects—occurs when individuals shift their preferences among alternatives depending on how those alternatives are presented. Thus, it may make a difference in a consumer's choice whether to use a credit card or cash for a particular transaction if the choice is framed as a "5% cash discount" or a "5% credit surcharge." See *id.* at 6. Likewise, a seller who successfully frames her standard form terms as the anchor or default position from which further negotiations should commence is more likely to obtain those terms than if the parties began bargaining without such a set of default terms. See Russell Korobkin, "Inertia and Preference in Contract Negotiation: The Psychological Power of Default Rules and Form Terms," 51 Vanderbilt L. Rev. 1583 (1998). Obviously, each of these distortions challenges a system of contract predicated upon the voluntary rational consent of the parties.

d. Legal Positivism and Natural Law—Instrumentalist and Non-Instrumentalist Views of Law

The final two categories in this survey of jurisprudence concern themselves primarily with the legitimization of law rather than with issues of the ability of rules to guide decision making or the interaction between legal rules and social realities. As discussed above, "positive" accounts of the law attempt to describe what the law *is*—Legal Positivism, in turn, stands for the proposition that a law is valid and justified because it is the command of the sovereign. The obligation of members of a society to obey the laws arises by virtue of the fact that those laws were properly issued by a sovereign with the capacity to enforce those laws. See, e.g., John Austin, The Province of Jurisprudence Determined 1–8 (1832) ("The matter of jurisprudence is positive law: law, simply and strictly so called: or law set by political superiors to political inferiors."). For positivists, the moral justification of a law or set of laws is unrelated to the validity or binding nature of those laws, a proposition classically formulated as the separation of what law *is* from what law *ought to be.*

In contrast, Natural Law theory holds that human laws are justified only to the extent those laws comport with standards that are external and superior to those human standards.

> Natural law theory was initially premised upon the belief that there is a "set of universal prescriptions whose prescriptive force is a function of the rationality which all human beings share in virtue of their common humanity." The universal prescriptions found in natural law theory can be divinely inspired or based upon secularly formulated standards. Numerous external standards have been offered through the years including morality, politics,

and economics. Larry A. DiMatteo, "The History of Natural Law Theory: Transforming Embedded Influences Into A Fuller Understanding of Modern Contract Law," 60 U. Pitt. L. Rev. 839, 861–62 (1999) (quoting Joseph Boyle, Natural Law and the Ethics of Tradition, in Natural Law Theory 4 (Robert P. George ed., 1992)).

Under a natural law jurisprudence, these external standards may be religious or secular.

The problem for Natural Law theorists, of course, is that there exists no convenient, universally accepted compilation of the "black letter" natural law. Absent such an unimpeachable source, Natural Law theory in the West has struggled since the time of Plato and Aristotle to identify the content of the natural law sufficiently that it could be communicated among and between individuals. See Aristotle, Rhetoric, bk. I, ch. 13, at (W. Rhys Roberts trans.) (The Franklin Library ed. 1981) ("Universal law is the law of Nature. For there really is, as every one to some extent divines, a natural justice and injustice that is binding on all men, even on those who have no association or covenant with each other."). While some versions of the natural law find the source of that law in divine revelation and commands, many natural law theorists—both secular and religious— hold that human beings may determine the content of the natural law by exercise of their capacities for observation of the world and for reasoning from those specific observations to general propositions that are universally just and correct. See e.g., Lloyd L. Weinreb, "A Secular Theory of Natural Law," 72 Fordham L. Rev. 2287, 2287–88 (2004) ("Is there any theory of natural law, any viewpoint or world view unaided by faith, that is properly called natural law? And second, if there is, is it worth our attention? My answer to both questions is yes."); St. Thomas Aquinas, Summa Theologica I–II, Q. 91, art. 2 (Fathers of the English Dominican Province trans., Benziger Bros., Inc. 1947) ("[T]he rational creature is subject to Divine providence in the most excellent way, in so far as it partakes of a share of providence, by being provident both for itself and for others. Wherefore it has a share of the Eternal Reason, whereby it has a natural inclination to its proper act and end: and this participation of the eternal law in the rational creature is called the natural law.").

The importance of the Legal Positivism and Natural Law to the study of contracts does not lie primarily in their content, although both schools are critical to contract jurisprudence. See Larry A. DiMatteo, Equitable Law of Contracts: Standards and Principles 240–43 (2001) ("Classical contract theory's role is the recognition of the existing rules of contract, an essentially positivistic inquiry. Many of the norms and rationales that underlie these rules, however, stem from natural law philosophy."). Rather, these approaches to contracts jurisprudence provide examples of the critically difficult choice facing every lawyer regarding how they approach their study and practice of the "Law."

The defining philosophy of Peter Parker, alter ego of Marvel comic book superhero Spiderman, is encapsulated in the proposition that, "With great power comes great responsibility." Although such sentiments often seem corny or sentimental to our cynical, post-modern ears, the continued vitality of the rule of law depends on how lawyers—as agents of that law—choose to carry out their responsibilities to the law. As Brian Tamanaha has observed, the law may be viewed from either an instrumental or a non-instrumental perspective. See Brian Z. Tamanaha, Law as a Means to an End: Threat to the Rule of Law 215–26 (2006). The non-instrumental perspective views law in terms similar to those proposed by Natural Law theory: there exist limits and standards that govern the operation of law that give it content, meaning, restraint, and make the law worthy of being followed. See *id.* at 215. A non-instrumental approach to the law recognizes that there is a core of justice that transcends the noise of conflicting political positions and strivings. In contrast, the instrumental view, like some branches of Legal Positivism, sees law as a tool for achieving particular desires that has no special worth or content in and of itself.

Each of these positions has important consequences for how lawyers deal with the immense powers they are developing as agents of the law. The non-instrumentalist perspective emphasizes the need to respect the law as an institution in itself. To some extent, instrumental views of the law promote the ability of special interests to exclude others from accessing contract law, as with the Jim Crow-era restrictions on the rights of African–Americans to contract and participate in other forms of private expression and earlier restrictions on the rights of women to contract and own or alienate property. Where law is seen not as an institution, but rather as merely a mechanism through which those in power can impose their political preferences upon those out of power, law no longer deserves respect. In essence, it is possible that strongly instrumentalist approaches to legal action can "break" a system of laws and cause the disintegration of a community of shared legal values.

On the other hand, as the Legal Realists observed, a purely non-instrumental view of the law risks ossifying legal thinking and forcing society to conform its behavior to legal rules solely because they are the rules, regardless of the justice or injustice of the matter. Similarly, even in the most strongly non-instrumentalist system—such as a theocratic regime dictating the substance of contract rules as divine revelation—there will always be a power group at the top of the regime that is aware to some extent of the instrumentalist possibilities of law and is willing to use their power over the law to achieve particular ends.

At the end of the day, you—as lawyers—are developing and earning an awesome power to manipulate and preserve the law. With that power comes often-conflicting responsibilities to preserve the law as an institution and to advocate for changes to the law where necessary to represent the interests of your clients or constituencies. From your authors' perspective, this tension is particularly important in the field of contract law. Contract is what permits individuals and businesses to express themselves in terms of their personal and corporate identities, goals, and desires. A person who lacks access to the ability to contract with others is denied the fundamental human right of self-determination. You have a duty to respect and preserve the law of contract to the extent it continues to advance that right, but at the same time to critique and advocate against that law where it is arbitrary and unjust. Ultimately, the only defense against the excesses of unadulterated non-instrumentalism or instrumentalism, and the only means of resolving this tension, is an awareness of the fact that both positions exist independent of the facts of each case and controversy and that lawyers must constantly guard against both positions at their extremes.

CHAPTER 2

ENFORCEABILITY OF PROMISES: THE NATURE OF LEGAL DUTY & OBLIGATION

■ ■ ■

The early building blocks of a contract are the most important. In these early beginnings are found the promise (the nucleus of the contract), its meaning, whether the law will enforce it, and the secret as to whether one of the parties might later undo the contract. The eye of the storm is the free will or intent of the parties, sometimes expressed, sometimes implied from conduct, and less seldom presumed by law. The heart and soul of the contract is the promise.

The materials below explore whether a promise was made and, if so, whether a legal theory exists to make it binding. By making a promise, persons impose obligations upon themselves. Charles Fried, Contract As Promise 1 (1981). But will the law enforce the promise if the maker has a change of heart? Of course, the parties might simply perform their promise according to its terms regardless of whether the law would compel performance or award damages for a failure.

Organizing and marshaling legal process to enforce the promise is a higher order question and one the law has struggled with, in various forms and by divergent societies, over centuries. Not surprisingly, Canon Law has always recognized the moral obligation to keep a promise. Secular law has not always followed the same path. Discovering that path is an adventure of sorts. In England alone, the early seeds will take us to William the Conqueror and the Norman Conquest in 1066. Roman law recognized a form of contract obligation under the doctrine of *obligatio* nearly 1500 years ago. Of course, still earlier promises were made and broken according to the needs of commerce.

Anglo-American contract law shares a common history and path. At the most basic level, theories of contract obligation connect the philosophy of law to contract and beyond. Autonomy and free will are the foundation of American society. As you read and study the materials in this chapter, you will begin to recognize the tension between the free will of private autonomy and the need of society to regulate free will to channel it into a collective good. Disagreement is rare as to whether private autonomy is a positive good. Disagreement is common as to whether society must intervene, even as to the simple question of whether a contract breaker is accountable in law.

But what are the supposed doctrinal limits of "freedom of contract"? Roman law applied the doctrine of *jus dispositivum*, that is, the application of contract law depends on the intent of the parties or on their failure to state their intent. In the latter case, the parties to a contract will be supposed to have intended the consequences envisioned by common law. Anglo-American contract law however has never truly been in a state of such freedom. Rather, it is a system of relatively greater autonomy for the parties compared to other schemes such as regulatory or statutory ordering. Roscoe Pound, "Liberty of Contract," 18 Yale L. J. 454, 482 (1909) and Samuel Williston, "Freedom of Contract," 6 Cornell L. Q. 365, 373 (1921).

Post–Civil War American jurisprudence generally focused on systematizing and organizing contract law into an internally coherent framework that we recognize today as classical contract theory. By the end of the nineteenth century and beginning of the twentieth century, however, classical contract theory had come to embody a strong emphasis on individualism and *laissez-faire* economic theory. These attitudes reached their pinnacle in a series of cases in which courts struck down state statutes regulating contractual matters such as minimum wages and maximum hours as an unconstitutional interference with individual freedom of contract rights under the due process clause of the Fourteenth Amendment. The leading case in this respect—*Lochner v. New York*, 198 U.S. 45 (1905)—elevated liberty of contract to the status of a fundamental property right, and the time between the beginning of the twentieth century and the mid-1930s is still known as the "*Lochner*-era." Morton J. Horwitz, The Transformation of American Law 1870–1960 36 (1992).

The trend waned as courts slowly developed limitations of "freedom of contract" to promote fairness, public policy, and public good. In a famous dissenting opinion in *Lochner*, Justice Oliver Wendell Holmes observed that "freedom of contract" must be limited in order to preserve the doctrine. Evolving principles of economic and social democracy gradually overshadowed "freedom of contract" rhetoric with "freedom from contract" ideals. Edwin A. Patterson, "An Apology for Consideration," 58 Columbia L. Rev. 929, 949 (1958) (attributed as the source of the phrase "freedom from contract"). "Freedom from contract" is now firmly established in contract law as evidenced by a 2004 symposium at the University of Wisconsin Law School devoted to the topic.

With this background, the making of a promise, without more, does not create a legal duty to perform that promise. In the language of classical contract law, the term "contract" is a surrogate for a promise made enforceable by some other legal doctrine, such as the receipt of consideration, reliance by the other party, or benefit received by the maker before the promise was made. Only then will the contract itself have been legally formed, which in turn creates a legal duty in the maker to perform the promises made therein. Importantly, every contractual promise, and hence every legal duty, has two aspects. At once, the promise creates a duty to perform according to its terms and a correlative right to that same performance in the beneficiary of the promise. Wesley Newcomb Hohfeld, "Some Fundamental Legal Conceptions as Applied in Judicial Reasoning," 23 Yale L. J. 16, 28–30 (1913) (suggesting far broader correlatives: "right" signifies one's affirmative claim against another, as distinguished from "privilege," one's freedom from the right or claim of another).

This chapter concerns itself with the elements associated with the making of a contract. The next chapter then undertakes similar work to examine the traditional "offer and acceptance" exchange mechanism to express formation. While a few contracts involve a singular promise, the vast majority consider mutual exchanges of promises of future performance (offer and acceptance). Given that the term "promise" is used in a technical legal sense rather than a colloquial sense, the materials consider how that term has evolved in legal doctrine. Next, given that most students are aware of the notions of "freedom of contract," the materials explore the precise nature of the actual contractual intent necessary to form a contract. Does the formation of contract require a "meeting of the minds" of the parties? Finally, since the making of a promise, without more, does not create a legal duty to perform that promise, exactly what more is required? These materials explore the strengths and weaknesses of the most significant legal theories developed over centuries for enforcing legal obligations created by contract.

A. THE NATURE OF PROMISE—A COMMITMENT

Unfortunately, the words "contract" and "promise" are often used colloquially to refer to the same thing. They are not the same in the eyes of the law. While the term "contract" generally refers to a promise or set of promises that the law will enforce, the term "promise" carries no such meaning. Compare Restatement (Second) of Contracts § 1 with § 2(1). While the making of a promise may create a moral obligation to honor its terms, the law requires more. Nonetheless the existence of an enforceable contract depends critically upon the existence of some promise. No promise means no contract, even with the presence of various enforcement doctrines. The existence of a promise itself is an essential nucleus of every contract. While the law could have chosen many definitions of a promise, the one selected requires that the maker's words and conduct convey some commitment to act, or refrain from acting, in the future. See Restatement (Second) of Contracts § 2(1). The term thus implies some present intention with regard to the maker's future conduct.

KING V. TRUSTEES OF BOSTON UNIVERSITY

Supreme Judicial Court of Massachusetts
420 Mass. 52, 647 N.E.2d 1196 (1995)

ABRAMS, Justice.

A jury determined that Dr. Martin Luther King, Jr., made a charitable pledge to Boston University (BU) of certain papers he had deposited with BU. The plaintiff, Coretta Scott King, in her capacity as administratrix of the estate of her late husband, and in her individual capacity, appeals from that judgment. The plaintiff sued BU for conversion, alleging that the estate and not BU held title to Dr. King's papers, which have been housed in BU's library's special collection since they were delivered to BU at Dr. King's request in July, 1964.

The case was submitted to the jury on theories of contract, charitable pledge, statute of limitations, and laches. In response to special questions the jury determined that Dr. King made a promise to give absolute title to his papers to BU in a letter signed by him and dated July 16, 1964, and that the promise to give the papers was enforceable as a charitable pledge supported by consideration or reliance. The jury also determined that the letter promising the papers was not a contract. The jury accordingly did not reach BU's additional statute of limitations and laches defenses. The trial judge denied the plaintiff's motion for judgment notwithstanding the verdict or for a new trial. The plaintiff appealed. We granted the plaintiff's application for direct appellate review. We affirm.

I. *Facts.* In reviewing the judge's denial of the plaintiff's motion for directed verdict on the affirmative defense of charitable pledge, we summarize the evidence in a light favorable to the nonmoving party, BU. . . . In 1963, BU commenced plans to expand its library's special collections. Once plans for construction of a library to house new holdings were firm, the newly appointed director of special collections, Dr. Howard Gotlieb, began his efforts to obtain Dr. King's papers. Dr. King, an alumnus of BU's graduate school program, was one of the first individuals BU officials sought to induce to deposit documents in the archives.

Around the same time, Dr. King was approached regarding his papers by other universities, including his undergraduate alma mater, Morehouse College. Mrs. King testified that, although her late husband thought "Boston seemed to be the only place, the best place, for safety," he was concerned that depositing his papers with BU would evoke criticism that he was "taking them away from a black institution in the South." However, the volatile circumstances during the 1960s in the South led Dr. King to deposit some of his papers with BU pursuant to a letter, which is the centerpiece of this litigation and is set forth herewith:

563 Johnson Ave. NE
Atlanta, Georgia
July 16, 1964

Boston University Library
725 Commonwealth Ave.
Boston 15, Massachusetts

Dear Sirs:

On this 16th day of July, 1964, I name the Boston University Library the Repository of my correspondence, manuscripts and other papers, along with a few of my awards and other materials which may come to be of interest in historical or other research.

In accordance with this action I have authorized the removal of most of the above-mentioned papers and other objects to Boston University, including most correspondence through 1961, at once. It is my intention that after the end of each calendar year, similar files of materials for an additional year should be sent to Boston University.

All papers and other objects which thus pass into the custody of Boston University remain my legal property until otherwise indicated, according to the statements below. However, if, despite scrupulous care, any such materials are damaged or lost while in custody of Boston University, I absolve Boston University of responsibility to me for such damage or loss.

I intend each year to indicate a portion of the materials deposited with Boston University to become the absolute property of Boston University as an outright gift from me, until all shall have been thus given to the University. In the event of my death, all such materials deposited with the University shall become from that date the absolute property of Boston University.

SINCERELY YOURS,

/S/ MARTIN LUTHER KING, JR.

At issue is whether the evidence at trial was sufficient to submit the question of charitable pledge to the jury. BU asserts that the evidence was sufficient to raise a question of fact for the jury as to whether there was a promise by Dr. King to transfer title to his papers to BU and whether any such promise was supported by consideration or reliance by BU. We agree.

II. *Evidence of an enforceable charitable pledge.*[3] Because the jury found that BU had acquired rightful ownership of the papers via a charitable pledge, but not a contract, we review the case on that basis. We note at the outset that there is scant Massachusetts case law in the area of charitable pledges and subscriptions.

A charitable subscription is "an oral or written promise to do certain acts or to give real or personal property to a charity or for a charitable purpose." See generally E. L. Fisch, D. J. Freed, & E. R. Schacter, Charities and Charitable Foundations § 63, at 77 (1974). To enforce a charitable subscription or a charitable pledge in Massachusetts, a party must establish that there was a promise to give some property to a charitable institution and that the promise was supported by consideration or reliance. Congregation Kadimah Toras-Moshe v. DeLeo, 405 Mass. 365, 367 & n. 3, 540 N.E.2d 691 (1989), and cases cited therein.[4] See In re Morton Shoe Co., 40 B. R. 948 (Bankr. D. Mass. 1984) (discussing Massachusetts law of charitable subscriptions).

The jurors were asked two special questions regarding BU's affirmative defense of rightful ownership by way of a charitable pledge: (1) "Does the letter, dated July 16, 1964, from Martin Luther King, Jr., to [BU], set forth a promise by Dr. King to transfer ownership of his papers to [BU]?"; and (2) "Did [BU] take action in reliance on that promise or was that promise supported by consideration?" In determining whether the case

---

[3] The terms "subscription" and "pledge" are frequently used interchangeably. . . . We note that, because of the bailor-bailee relationship between the donor and charitable institution, the transaction here technically is a charitable pledge. See R. A. Brown, Personal Property § 15.1, at 469 (3d ed. 1975) (defining a pledge as "a bailment of personal property to secure an obligation of the of the bailor").

[4] In Congregation Kadimah Toras-Moshe v. DeLeo, 405 Mass. 365, 540 N.E.2d 691 (1989), the Congregation sued the estate of a decedent who had made an oral gratuitous promise to give $25,000 to the synagogue. The Congregation planned to spend the $25,000 on renovation of a storage room in the synagogue into a library. The oral promise was never memorialized in a writing or consummated by delivery before the decedent died intestate. Noting that "[a] hope or expectation, even though well founded, is not equivalent to either legal detriment or reliance," id. at 366–367, 540 N.E.2d 691, we affirmed the judgment of the trial court that the oral charitable subscription was not enforceable because it was oral, not supported by consideration, and without evidence of reliance.

By requiring that a promise to make a charitable subscription be supported by consideration or reliance, we declined to adopt the standard for enforceable charitable subscriptions set forth in the Restatement (Second) of Contracts § 90 (1981). See id. at 368, 540 N.E.2d 691. Section 90(1), as modified for charitable subscriptions by subsection (2), provides that, "[a] promise which the promisor should reasonably expect to induce action or forbearance on the part of the promisee or a third person . . . is binding if injustice can be avoided only by enforcement of the promise. . . ." We noted that, although § 90 thus dispenses with a strict requirement of consideration or reasonable reliance for a charitable subscription to be enforceable, the official comments to the Restatement make clear that consideration and reliance remain relevant to whether the promise must be enforced to avoid injustice. Id. See Arrowsmith v. Mercantile-Safe Deposit & Trust Co., supra 313 Md. at 353–354, 545 A.2d 674 (rejecting argument that court should adopt Restatement [Second] of Contracts § 90[2]); Jordan v. Mount Sinai Hosp. of Greater Miami, Inc., supra at 108 ("Courts should act with restraint in respect to the public policy arguments endeavoring to sustain a mere charitable subscription. To ascribe consideration where there is none, or to adopt any other theory which affords charities a different legal rationale than other entities, is to approve fiction").

properly was submitted to the jury, we consider first, whether the evidence was sufficient to sustain a conclusion that the letter contained a promise to make a gift and second, whether the evidence was sufficient to support a determination that any promise found was supported by consideration or reliance.

III(A). *Evidence of a promise to make a gift.* The plaintiff argues that the terms of the letter promising "to indicate a portion of the materials deposited with [BU] to become the absolute property of [BU] as an outright gift . . . until all shall have been thus given to [BU]," could not as a matter of basic contract law constitute a promise sufficient to establish an inter vivos charitable pledge because there is no indication of a bargained-for exchange which would have bound Dr. King to his promise. The plaintiff asserts that the above-quoted excerpt (hereinafter "first statement") from the letter merely described an unenforceable "unilateral and gratuitous mechanism by which he might" make a gift of the papers in the future but by which he was not bound. In support of her position that Dr. King did not intend to bind himself to his statement of intent to make a gift of the papers he deposited with BU, the plaintiff points to the language which appears above the promise to make gifts of the deposited papers that "[a]ll papers and other objects which thus pass into the custody of [BU] remain my legal property until otherwise indicated, according to the statements below." According to the plaintiff, because of Dr. King's initial retention of legal ownership, BU could not reasonably rely on the letter's statements of intent to make a gift of the papers. We do not agree.

The letter contains two sentences which might reasonably be construed as a promise to give personal property to a charity or for a charitable purpose. The first statement, quoted above, is that Dr. King intended in subsequent installments to transfer title to portions of the papers in BU's custody until all the papers in its custody became its property. The second statement immediately follows the first, expressing an intent that "[i]n the event of [Dr. King's] death, all . . . materials deposited with [BU] shall become from that date the absolute property of [BU]" (hereinafter "second statement"). BU claims that these two sentences should be read together as a promise to make a gift of all of the papers deposited with it at some point between the first day of deposit and at the very latest, on Dr. King's death.

Before analyzing the first and second statements, we note the considerations governing our review. A primary concern in enforcing charitable subscriptions, as with enforcement of other gratuitous transfers such as gifts and trusts, is ascertaining the intention of the donor. See, e.g., Fuss v. Fuss (No. 2), 373 Mass. 445, 449, 368 N.E.2d 276 (1977) ("The effect of a purported transfer will be determined by the design of the original transaction as understood by the principal actors"); Stryker v. Kennard, 339 Mass. 373, 377, 159 N.E.2d 71 (1959) ("It is familiar law that in construing a trust instrument the intention of the settlor must be ascertained from the entire instrument, giving due weight to all its language, considered in the light of the attendant circumstances known to the settlor at the time of execution. The intent ascertained in this manner must prevail unless a positive rule of law forbids"). If donative intent is sufficiently clear, we shall give effect to that intent to the extent possible without abandoning basic contractual principles, such as specificity of the donor's promise, consideration, and reasonableness of the charity's reliance. DeLeo, supra 405 Mass. at 368 n. 5, 540 N.E.2d 691. In determining the intention of Dr. King as expressed in the letter and the understanding BU had of that letter, we look first to the language of the letter, in its entirety, but also consider the circumstances and relationship of the parties with respect to the papers.

III(A)(1). *First statement.* Regarding the first statement, the plaintiff contends that it is not a promise but a mere statement of intent to do something in the future. See, e.g., Phoenix Spring Beverage Co. v. Harvard Brewing Co., 312 Mass. 501, 506, 45 N.E.2d 473 (1942) ("A promise made with an understood intention that it is to be not legally binding, but only expressive of a present intention is not a contract"). We might agree that the first statement could induce nothing more than a "hope or mere expectation" on BU's part, if the statement were considered in a vacuum. Cf. Pappas v. Bever, 219 N.W.2d 720, 722 (Iowa 1974) ("The language of the pledge form in this case, standing alone, shows nothing more than a statement of intention. There is no evidence the pledge was intended to be obligatory" [emphasis added]). However, our interpretation of that first statement is strongly influenced by the bailor-bailee relationship the letter unequivocally establishes between Dr. King and BU.

A bailment is established by "delivery of personalty for some particular purpose, or on mere deposit, upon a contract, express or implied, that after the purpose has been fulfilled it shall be redelivered to the person who delivered it, or otherwise dealt with according to his directions, or kept until he reclaims it, as the case may be." 9 S. Williston, Contracts § 1030 (3d ed. 1967), quoting State v. Warwick, 48 Del. 568, 576, 108 A.2d 85 (1954). See Stuart v. D.N. Kelley & Son, 331 Mass. 76, 77–78, 117 N.E.2d 160 (1954), quoting D.A. Schulte, Inc. v. North Terminal Garage Co., 291 Mass. 251, 256, 197 N.E. 16 (1935) ("A bailment is essentially a consensual transaction arising out of a contract express or implied . . . and there must be an acceptance by the bailee of the goods forming the subject matter of the bailment before there can be any bailment"). The terms of the letter establish a bailment in which certain "correspondence, manuscripts and other papers, along with a few of [Dr. King's] awards" were placed in "the custody of [BU]." The bailed papers were to "remain [Dr. King's] legal property until otherwise indicated." By accepting delivery of the papers, BU assumed the duty of care as bailee set forth in the letter, that of "scrupulous care." Stuart, supra 331 Mass. at 78, 117 N.E.2d 160, quoting D.A. Schulte, Inc., supra ("It is plain the law does not thrust upon one the liabilities of a bailee without his knowledge or consent, and equally obvious that while an acceptance may be implied the law will not infer such until there is something to show notice or knowledge of the alleged bailee that the goods are in fact in his possession").

Generally there will be a case for the jury as to donative intent if property allegedly promised to a charity or other eleemosynary institution is placed by the donor in the custody of the donee.[5] The bailor-bailee relationship established in the letter could be viewed by a rational factfinder as a security for the promise to give a gift in the future of the bailed property, and thus as evidence in addition to the statement in the letter of an intent of the donor to be bound. Furthermore, while we have been unwilling to abandon fundamental principles of contract law in determining the enforceability of charitable subscriptions, see DeLeo, supra 405 Mass. at 368 n. 4, 540 N.E.2d 691, second par. (declining to adopt Restatement [Second] of Contracts rule that charitable subscriptions enforceable without consideration or reliance where justice so requires), we do recognize that the "meeting of minds" between a donor and a charitable institution differs from the understanding we require in the context of enforceable arm's-length commercial agreements. Charities depend on donations for their existence, whereas their donors may give personal property on conditions they choose, with or without imposing conditions or demanding consideration. In re Field's Will, 15 Misc. 2d 950, 951, 181 N.Y.S. 2d 922 (1959), 11 A.D. 2d 774, 204 N.Y.S. 2d 947 (1960) ("Charitable subscription agreements can rarely be regarded as part of a bargaining agreement that provide for a quid pro quo"). In combination with the letter and in the context of a disputed pledge to a charity, the bailment of Dr. King's letters provided sufficient evidence of donative intent to submit to the jury the questions whether there was a promise to transfer ownership

So judge is arguing BU is a charity?

---

[5] We do not suggest that bailment of property allegedly promised to a bailee-charity creates an irrebuttable presumption of donative intent on the part of the bailor. Nor do we suggest that we would weigh bailment more heavily than evidence that the parties agreed to conditions or terms of a bailment that express a lack of donative intent.

Intent is our primary concern and a bailment may be evidence of donative intent. However, a bailor and a bailee-charity may agree to a contractual bailment in terms that make clear that the bailed property is not being pledged as a future gift or that the bailed property may remain in the custody of the charity or become the charity's property only if certain conditions are met. Cf. De Cicco v. Barker, 339 Mass. 457, 458, 159 N.E.2d 534 (1959) ("It is generally held that an engagement ring is in the nature of a pledge, given on the implied condition that the marriage shall take place. If the contract to marry is terminated without fault on the part of the donor he may recover the ring"). In sum, we consider the terms of any valid express or implied agreement to determine intent. Fuss v. Fuss (No. 2), 373 Mass. 445, 449, 368 N.E.2d 276 (1977) ("The effect of a purported transfer will be determined by the design of the original transaction as understood by the principal actors").

of the bailed property and whether there was consideration or reliance on that promise.[6]

III(A)(2). *Second statement*. The parties agree that a testamentary transfer of the papers by means of the July 16, 1964, letter would be invalid because the letter did not comply with the Statute of Wills. G.L. c. 191, § 1 (1992 ed.) (requiring testamentary dispositions to be subscribed by two or more competent witnesses). However, "[t]he statute of wills . . . does not prevent an owner of property from stipulating by contract for the disposition of his property at the time of his death." Hale v. Wilmarth, 274 Mass. 186, 189, 174 N.E. 232 (1931). See Roberts v. Roberts, 419 Mass. 685, 690 n. 7, 646 N.E.2d 1061 (1995), quoting National Shawmut Bank v. Joy, 315 Mass. 457, 471, 53 N.E.2d 113 (1944). The parties dispute whether the statement of intent to transfer title on Dr. King's death comports with the Statute of Frauds for contracts to make testamentary dispositions. G.L. c. 259, § 5 (1992 ed.). General Laws c. 259, § 5, provides in relevant part: "No agreement to make a will of real or personal property or to give a legacy or make a devise shall be binding unless such agreement is in writing signed by the person whose executor or administrator is sought to be charged, or by some person by him duly authorized." *who?*

The plaintiff contends that the intent that BU have absolute title to the papers in its possession from Dr. King's death forward was a disposition effective on death of the donor and was invalid because it was not in conformity with the strict formalities imposed on contracts to make testamentary dispositions under G.L. c. 259, § 5. Although the letter was a writing signed by Dr. King, the plaintiff asserts that the second statement does not satisfy the Statute of Frauds because it did not contain all the terms of an enforceable agreement. We do not agree. The Statute of Frauds was not applicable because the letter was not a contract to make a will, but rather was a promise to give BU absolute title to all papers in its possession either at some future point in Dr. King's life or on his death.

is this King or BU.

they are calling it a promise

BU argues that, even if the Statute of Frauds were to apply, the letter was a writing signed by the promisor and the evidence was sufficient to assure that the risk of fraud or deceit would not increase by enforcing the agreement. As we noted above, the first statement of intent to make gifts

---

[6]   The jury could have found on that evidence alone that the first statement in the letter expressing an intent to give all papers in BU's custody to it at some future date was not a mere statement of future intent when the bailment relationship is considered. However, there was evidence in addition to the bailor-bailee relationship which justified submission of the special questions on whether there was a charitable pledge to the jury. First, there was evidence the papers would be appraised (for Dr. King's) tax purposes. Second, as promised in the letter, Dr. King delivered additional papers after the initial boxes of papers were delivered. This evidence could be considered by a jury in determining whether Dr. King intended to be bound by his promise. Thus, the trial judge did not err in submitting to the jury the first special question on charitable pledge. There was evidence which the jury could weigh in determining whether the statement of intent to give a gift of portions of the papers was an expression of an intent to be bound.

during his lifetime of the bailed papers could have been interpreted by the jury as a promise to give gifts on which BU reasonably relied or for which BU rendered consideration. The second statement that papers not yet transferred to BU but in its custody at the time of Dr. King's death could have been interpreted by the jury as a statement of the latest date on which Dr. King intended to make a gift to BU of the bailed property. Such an interpretation states all terms of an enforceable agreement. Thus, the Statute of Frauds governing contracts to make testamentary dispositions would be satisfied.

III(B). *Evidence of consideration or reliance.* The judge did not err in submitting the second question on charitable pledge, regarding whether there was consideration for or reliance on the promise, to the jury. "It may be found somewhat difficult to reconcile all the views which have been taken, in the various cases that have arisen upon the validity of promises, where the ground of defense has been that they were gratuitous and without consideration." Ives v. Sterling, 6 Met. 310, 315 (1843). There was evidence that BU undertook indexing of the papers, made the papers available to researchers, and provided trained staff to care for the papers and assist researchers. BU held a convocation to commemorate receipt of the papers. Dr. King spoke at the convocation. In a speech at that time, he explained why he chose BU as the repository for his papers.

As we explained above, the letter established that so long as BU, as bailee, attended the papers with "scrupulous care," Dr. King, as bailor, would release them from liability for "any such materials . . . damaged or lost while in [its] custody." The jury could conclude that certain actions of BU, including indexing of the papers, went beyond the obligations BU assumed as a bailee to attend the papers with "scrupulous care" and constituted reliance or consideration for the promises Dr. King included in the letter to transfer ownership of all bailed papers to BU at some future date or at his death. Trustees of Amherst Academy v. Cowls, 6 Pick. 427, 431 (1828) ("It seems that an actual benefit to the promisor, or an actual loss or disadvantage to the promisee, will be a sufficient consideration to uphold a promise deliberately made. Whether the consideration received is equal in value to the sum promised to be paid, seems not to be material to the validity of a note . . . "); Ives, supra at 317–319; Ladies' Collegiate Inst. v. French, 16 Gray 196, 202 (1860).

The issue before us is not whether we agree with the jury's verdict but whether the case was properly submitted to the jury. We conclude that the letter could have been read to contain a promise supported by consideration or reliance; "[t]he issue [of whether transfer of ownership to BU was transferred by way of a charitable pledge by Dr. King] was, therefore, properly submitted to the jury, and their verdicts, unless otherwise untenable, must stand." Carr v. Arthur D. Little, Inc., 348 Mass. 469, 474,

204 N.E.2d 466 (1965) (evidence sufficient as matter of contract law to raise question of fact for jury as to existence of common employment). . . .

Judgment affirmed.

NOTES AND QUESTIONS

1.   *Existence of a promise.* Boston University's entire case depends upon whether Dr. King made a "promise" to give permanently to the University the papers in its temporary possession. Restatement (Second) of Contracts § 2 defines a promise by reference to a "commitment." Other similar definitions exist, but all require the existence of a commitment or assurance of some future conduct. See *Baehr v. Penn-O-Tex Oil Corp.*, 258 Minn. 533, 104 N.W.2d 661 (1960) ("Although the definition of contract does not help much in determining what expressions shall be held to impose legal obligations, it does direct attention to a promise as the starting point of inquiry. Both in popular and legal usage, a promise is an assurance, in whatever form of expression given, that a thing will or will not be done. While we must take care to distinguish between statements meant to express merely present intention and those meant to give an assurance as to a future event, this involves no more than the common difficulty of seeking precise meaning in the usually imprecise, and often careless, expressions of ordinary colloquy."). Do you agree that Dr. King made such an assurance? What evidence was critical to the court's determination? How do you view that same evidence? Was Dr. King's promissory intent a question of fact or law? What is the importance of that distinction for purposes of appellate review?

 2 factor right. *only deals w/ LAW*

2.   *Opinion or prediction of future events.* Courts often distinguish between expressions of intent to make a prediction or express an opinion, neither of which constitutes a promise, and an assurance as to a future event. Do you think the distinction is helpful to properly exclude some language from becoming promissory? See *Anderson v. Backlund*, 159 Minn. 423, 199 N.W. 90 (1924) (landlord statement to tenant to induce lease was a mere weather prediction and not a promise: "Never mind the water, John. I will see there will be plenty of water, because it never failed in Minnesota yet"); *Hawkins v. McGee*, 84 N.H. 114, 146 A. 641 (1929) (physician's response to a question regarding duration of hospital visit was a prediction and not a promise: "Three or four days, not over four; then the boy can go home . . ."); and *Basch v. George Washington University*, 370 A.2d 1364 (D.C. Ct. App. 1977) (language in university bulletin regarding future tuition a mere expression of intent to continue current tuition: "Every effort will be made to keep tuition increases within these limits. However, it is not possible to project future economic data with certainty, and circumstances may require an adjustment in this estimate"). Is the distinction between commitment and prediction clear? Restatement (Second) of Contracts § 2, *cmt. f.*   *usually?*

3.   *UCC & CISG approach to promise.* The UCC governs a contract for the sale of goods whereas the common law of contract as generally referenced in the Restatement (Second) of Contracts governs all other contract matters.

As a result, Dr. McGee's promise was governed by common law and not the UCC. The UCC does not explicitly utilize the concept of promise and contract, although it incorporates the common law by reference. UCC § 1–103 (unless displaced by specific UCC provisions, the principles of law and equity supplement all provisions of the UCC). Accordingly, the terms "promise" and "contract" are most likely to have the same meanings under the UCC as under the common law. Indeed, UCC § 2–204 purports to expand the notion of when a contract is formed or made. Under that section, a contract may be made in any manner to show agreement, including conduct by both parties that recognizes the existence of the contract.

Like the UCC, the CISG governs a contract for the sale of goods, but only when the contracting parties have places of business in different countries that have adopted the CISG. CISG, art. 1(1). As a result, the UCC governs the sale of goods between two businesses located in the United States. In contrast, the CISG would apply, for example, to a sale of goods between a U.S. and a Canadian corporation. However, unlike the UCC, the CISG does not generally apply to a sale of goods purchased for personal, family, or household use. CISG art. 2(a). But the language of the CISG is more similar to common law than the UCC. See CISG arts. 14–24.

4. *Jurisprudential analysis of Dr. King's teachings and contract law.* Can you find evidence of Dr. King's message of peace, justice, and hope in the stark rules of contract law? For a comprehensive analysis of Dr. King's work and its plausible intersections with contract law maxims, ancient to modern, see Blake D. Morant, "The Teachings of Dr. Martin Luther King, Jr., and Contract Theory: An Intriguing Comparison," 50 Ala. L. Rev. 63 (1998).

5. *Promises and morality.* The act of promising creates a moral obligation in the promisor to fulfill his promise. What is the source of that moral obligation? As noted above, one possible answer is based upon objective moral principles existing independent of human society. Thus, the Canon Law rule that promises should be performed derives from religious principles that breaking a promise—a kind of deceit—is objectively sinful according to moral rules established by God. Such objective moral principles may also be discerned from observations of the world in general, or of human beings and human societies in particular. For example, as Lloyd Weinreb states, "We are looking for a place in the description of the world as it is that in and of itself implicates normative conclusions; that is, we are looking for a locus of the normative in nature. The only phenomenon that meets that description—as opposed to the view that nothing can meet it—is persons, regarded as bearers of rights." Lloyd L. Weinreb, *A Secular Theory of Natural Law*, 72 Ford. L. Rev. 2287, 2290 (2004). These objective theories of morality thus base any normative duty to fulfill promises upon essential characteristics of human beings.

Alternatively, human social institutions may positively describe and define moral obligations to keep promises. Under such positive theories of morality, we may have an obligation to perform our promises because society deems it "just" or "right" to do so. Alternatively, positive theories of morality may impose such an obligation because doing so promotes the ability of other actors in society to rely on our promises and thus increases overall social welfare. In other words, the social practice of promising includes a positive moral judgment that we should keep our promises.

Thomas Scanlon addresses the question of whether the moral obligation to keep one's promises depends upon an existing social practice creating a positive duty of promise-keeping or is independent of social practices by supposing a transaction in the hypothetical "state of nature." See Thomas Scanlon, *Promises and Practices*, 19 Philosophy and Pub. Aff. 199 (1990). Assume you are alone on a desert island. Hunting one day, you accidentally throw your spear across a deep, uncrossable stream. From across the stream, another hunter—whom you have never met before and will never meet again— has accidentally thrown his boomerang across the stream to land at your feet. Through a series of gestures, you cause him to believe that you will throw back his boomerang if he throws you the spear. If the other hunter throws your spear, what moral obligation do you have to return the boomerang? See id.

Scanlon proposes two sources for a moral obligation to keep one's promises. First, "breaking a promise is a wrong that depends essentially on the existence of a social practice of agreement-making." Id. at 199. Under this justification, however, your failure to return the boomerang is not morally wrong because by definition a state of nature exists between you and the other hunter such that you have no shared social practice of agreement making. Id. at 200.

On the other hand, the wrong involved in promise-breaking behavior may be based upon the principle that it is morally improper to create an expectation in another person—whether through the social institution of promising or by some other mechanism—with the intent to disappoint that expectation. Id. at 203. In other words, the wrong implicated by promise-breaking is the unjustified manipulation of another person to expect that, if he undertakes an act desired by the promisor, the promisor will reciprocate with an act desired by the promisee. Id.

6.   *Non-promissory theories of obligation.* Promises are not the only mechanisms by which two parties may create well-defined moral obligations of future performance with each other. In a famous study of social and economic practices among Trobriand Islanders in the early twentieth century, for example, Bronislaw Malinowski described a system of obligation based upon displays of generosity and gift-giving that impose strong, socially recognized duties upon gift recipients to reciprocate at some later date. Thus, Malinowski relates a gift- and reciprocity-based trading relationship between fishing villagers and farming villagers. According to Malinowski, this relationship was both economic and legal—"a system of mutual obligations which forces the fisherman to repay whenever he has received a gift from his inland partner, and vice versa." Bronislaw Malinowski, Crime and Custom in Savage Society 22–23 (Rowman & Littlefield Publishers, Inc. 1989) (1926).

Marcel Mauss describes a similar system of reciprocal obligations in the potlatch systems of Native American tribes of the Pacific Northwest. See Marcel Mauss, The Gift: Forms and Functions of Exchange in Archaic Societies 31–41 (Ian Cunnison trans., 1966) (1950). In the potlatch system, an individual's or group's prestige and honor often depend upon displays of generosity and gift-giving that demonstrate their wealth and good fortune. See id. Recipients generally may not refuse a proffered gift—to do so generally insults the offeror and causes the recipient to suffer a loss of prestige and social standing. See id. at 39–40. Finally, the recipient must reciprocate with a future gift and faces social sanctions for failure to reciprocate ranging from a loss of status to loss of freedom. See id. at 40–41. Similarly, business relations among Chinese businesspeople provide a modern example of this phenomenon. Chinese business relations are often defined as much by a system of reciprocal favors, gifts, and friendship—called "guanxi"—as they are by specific contract terms and negotiations.

7.   *Aftermath*. Following the death of Coretta Scott King in 2006, the King family sought to auction a separate collection of Dr. King's papers. Ultimately, however, the collection was purchased for $32 million by a group of Atlanta business and civil leaders who desired to ensure that the collection would remain in the South and open to future researchers. Shaila Dewan, "The Deal That Let Atlanta Retain Dr. King's Papers," New York Times, June 27, 2006, at A11.

When reading and analyzing the cases dealing with promises to make gifts, consideration, and reliance upon promises, keep in mind that in these situations the extra-legal social sanctions that may be leveled against a promise-breaker may often be more serious than legal remedies for breach. It is no accident that many of the seminal cases addressing the existence and enforceability of promises arise only after the promisor has died and the promisor's executor attempts to avoid the promise.

B. UNDERSTANDING CONTRACTUAL INTENT: THE OBJECTIVE THEORY OF CONTRACTS

As a contract value, private autonomy requires deference to the intent of the parties. So one could easily imagine a genuine judicial search for the true subjective intent of each party to the contract. Under this "will theory," a contract can form when and only if the parties have a "meeting of the minds." Compare Lon L. Fuller, "Consideration and Form," 41 Colum. L. Rev. 799 (1941) and Duncan Kennedy, "From the Will Theory To The Principle of Private Autonomy: Lon Fuller's 'Consideration and Form,' " 100 Colum. L. Rev. 94 (2000). It is easy enough when each party subjectively agrees on identical contract terms. But what happens when the subjective intents of the two parties differ, and there is literally no "meeting of the minds"? This is particularly important in two specific contractual contexts—(1) whether the parties have formed a contract, and (2) if a contract exists, whose terms control? The formation problem is considered in this chapter, while the choice of terms is considered in the next.

As to the formation question, will contract law make and enforce a contract when one of the parties had no intent to form a contract? In such cases, there is no "meeting of the minds." If so, what legal theory justifies such an approach? On the one hand, respect for private autonomy suggests that no contract has formed because one party lacked the necessary intent to agree. On the other hand, fairness principles lead to the conclusion that courts should enforce the parties' contract because justice and fairness to the other party overrides that subjective intent. Modern contract law attempts to resolve the tension between these competing interests through the doctrine of "objective theory of contracts." But how successful is that theory and at what cost to the true intent of the parties?

According to the modern formulation of the objective theory of contracts, a maker's "legal intent" is determined not from the promisor's actual, true, secret, or subjective intent, but rather from objective manifestations of the promisor's intent. Specifically, the objective theory of contracts requires courts to examine the promisee's discernable reasonable understanding of the maker's words or conduct. Restatement (Second) of Contracts § 2(1). The law switches the vantage point of legal intent from the promisor to the promisee and in so doing prefers an objective reconstruction of the promisee's understanding over the promisor's actual subjective intent. Since the recipient's understanding must be "reasonable" in order to be respected and preferred to the maker's actual intent, the doctrine suggests that the maker's legal intent is "objectively" determined.

Of course, even this characterization of the promisor's intent is somewhat misleading. The true genius of the doctrine does not ascribe a mythical intent to the promisor. Rather, the objective theory doctrine attempts to determine the promisor's legal intent from words and conduct communicated to the promisee. The doctrine merely changes the referent for determining legal intent. Restatement (Second) of Contracts § 2(1) , *cmt. b.* Consequently, the promisor is legally bound by the intent fairly communicated to the recipient, even if the inferred intent was not actually, or subjectively, what the promisor intended. This disconnect between actual and inferred intent caused Judge Learned Hand* to observe:

> A contract has, strictly speaking, nothing to do with the personal,
> or individual, intent of the parties. A contract is an obligation
> attached by the mere force of law to certain acts of the parties,

---

* Learned Hand (1872–1961) was one of the most famous American jurists not to serve on the United States Supreme Court. In 1909 he was appointed to the U.S. District Court for the Southern District of New York and elevated to the U.S. Court of Appeals for the Second Circuit in 1924 where he served until retirement in 1951. His most famous contributions embrace economics and the law and include the "calculus of negligence" used to determine whether a legal duty of care has been breached. See United States v. Carroll Towing, 159 F.2d 169 (2nd Cir. 1947).

usually words, which ordinarily accompany and represent a known intent. If, however, it were proved by twenty bishops that either party, when he used the words, intended something else than the usual meaning which the law imposes upon them, he would still be held, unless there were some mutual mistake, or something else of the sort. Of course, if it appear by other words, or acts, of the parties, that they attribute a peculiar meaning to such words as they use in the contract, that meaning will prevail, but only by virtue of the other words, and not because of their unexpressed intent.—Hotchkiss v. National City Bank of New York, 200 F. 287, 293 (S.D.N.Y. 1911).

Judge Hand's description of the objective theory of contract is widely accepted. Nonetheless, the unfortunate phrase "meeting of the minds" continues to appear even in modern judicial opinions as a loose but inaccurate respect to the value of private autonomy.

While the modern contours of the objective theory of contracts are now reasonably clear, its doctrinal roots are less certain. In a preeminent article critiquing the central policy themes in contract law as generally inadequate to fully explain contract law outcomes, Professor Morris Cohen observed of the "will theory" in contracts:

According to the classical view, the law of contracts gives expression to and protects the will of the parties, for the will is something inherently worthy of respect. . . . [t]he first essential is the agreement of the wills, or the meeting of the minds. . . . [a] line of objection can be found in the incompatibility of the classical theory with the consequences that the law attaches to an offer.— Morris R. Cohen, "The Basis of Contract," 46 Harv. L. Rev. 553, 575 (1933).

Other legal history scholars have argued the subjective "meeting of the minds" standard was the law of contract but modern law shifted from that view for various compelling reasons. Lawrence Friedman argued the objective theory was developed by late nineteenth-century scholars to reduce business risks and enhance predictability. Lawrence M. Friedman, Contract Law in America 87 (1965). Similarly, Morton Horwitz argued the transformation occurred as part of a larger societal shift from fairness and justice to objective market values. Morton J. Horwitz, The Transformation of American Law 1780–1860 (1977). Grant Gilmore argued that the "objective theory" was created by Oliver Wendell Holmes, Jr. Grant Gilmore, The Death of Contract 12 (1974). More recently, Professor Joseph Perillo argued all three accounts were flawed and that the theory in various forms has been part of contract law from the beginning. Joseph M. Perillo, "The Origins of the Objective Theory of Contract Formation and Interpretation," 69 Fordham L. Rev. 427 (2000).

Whether a modern invention or a consistently applied principle from the beginnings of contract, the objective theory of contracts is alive and well. But like many legal doctrines, practical applications at the margins of the theory create difficult judgments.

LUCY V. ZEHMER

Supreme Court of Appeals of Virginia
196 Va. 493, 84 S.E.2d 516 (1954)

BUCHANAN, J., delivered the opinion of the court.

This suit was instituted by W. O. Lucy and J. C. Lucy, complainants, against A. H. Zehmer and Ida S. Zehmer, his wife, defendants, to have specific performance of a contract by which it was alleged the Zehmers had sold to W. O. Lucy a tract of land owned by A. H. Zehmer in Dinwiddie county containing 471.6 acres, more or less, known as the Ferguson farm, for $50,000. J. C. Lucy, the other complainant, is a brother of W. O. Lucy, to whom W. O. Lucy transferred a half interest in his alleged purchase.

The instrument sought to be enforced was written by A. H. Zehmer on December 20, 1952, in these words: 'We hereby agree to sell to W. O. Lucy the Ferguson Farm complete for $50,000.00, title satisfactory to buyer,' and signed by the defendants, A. H. Zehmer and Ida S. Zehmer.

The answer of A. H. Zehmer admitted that at the time mentioned W. O. Lucy offered him $50,000 cash for the farm, but that he, Zehmer, considered that the offer was made in jest; that so thinking, and both he and Lucy having had several drinks, he wrote out 'the memorandum' quoted above and induced his wife to sign it; that he did not deliver the memorandum to Lucy, but that Lucy picked it up, read it, put it in his pocket, attempted to offer Zehmer $5 to bind the bargain, which Zehmer refused to accept, and realizing for the first time that Lucy was serious, Zehmer assured him that he had no intention of selling the farm and that the whole matter was a joke. Lucy left the premises insisting that he had purchased the farm.

Depositions were taken and the decree appealed from was entered holding that the complainants had failed to establish their right to specific performance, and dismissing their bill. The assignment of error is to this action of the court.

W. O. Lucy, a lumberman and farmer, thus testified in substance: He had known Zehmer for fifteen or twenty years and had been familiar with the Ferguson farm for ten years. Seven or eight years ago he had offered Zehmer $20,000 for the farm which Zehmer had accepted, but the agreement was verbal and Zehmer backed out. On the night of December 20, 1952, around eight o'clock, he took an employee to McKenney, where Zehmer lived and operated a restaurant, filling station and motor court.

While there he decided to see Zehmer and again try to buy the Ferguson farm. He entered the restaurant and talked to Mrs. Zehmer until Zehmer came in. He asked Zehmer if he had sold the Ferguson farm. Zehmer replied that he had not. Lucy said, 'I bet you wouldn't take $50,000.00 for that place.' Zehmer replied, 'Yes, I would too; you wouldn't give fifty.' Lucy said he would and told Zehmer to write up an agreement to that effect. Zehmer took a restaurant check and wrote on the back of it, 'I do hereby agree to sell to W. O. Lucy the Ferguson Farm for $50,000 complete.' Lucy told him he had better change it to 'We' because Mrs. Zehmer would have to sign it too. Zehmer then tore up what he had written, wrote the agreement quoted above and asked Mrs. Zehmer, who was at the other end of the counter ten or twelve feet away, to sign it. Mrs. Zehmer said she would for $50,000 and signed it. Zehmer brought it back and gave it to Lucy, who offered him $5 which Zehmer refused, saying, 'You don't need to give me any money, you got the agreement there signed by both of us.'

The discussion leading to the signing of the agreement, said Lucy, lasted thirty or forty minutes, during which Zehmer seemed to doubt that Lucy could raise $50,000. Lucy suggested the provision for having the title examined and Zehmer made the suggestion that he would sell it 'complete, everything there,' and stated that all he had on the farm was three heifers.

Lucy took a partly filled bottle of whiskey into the restaurant with him for the purpose of giving Zehmer a drink if he wanted it. Zehmer did, and he and Lucy had one or two drinks together. Lucy said that while he felt the drinks he took he was not intoxicated, and from the way Zehmer handled the transaction he did not think he was either.

December 20 was on Saturday. Next day Lucy telephoned to J. C. Lucy and arranged with the latter to take a half interest in the purchase and pay half of the consideration. On Monday he engaged an attorney to examine the title. The attorney reported favorably on December 31 and on January 2 Lucy wrote Zehmer stating that the title was satisfactory, that he was ready to pay the purchase price in cash and asking when Zehmer would be ready to close the deal. Zehmer replied by letter, mailed on January 13, asserting that he had never agreed or intended to sell.

Mr. and Mrs. Zehmer were called by the complainants as adverse witnesses. Zehmer testified in substance as follows:

He bought this farm more than ten years ago for $11,000. He had had twenty-five offers, more or less, to buy it, including several from Lucy, who had never offered any specific sum of money. He had given them all the same answer, that he was not interested in selling it. On this Saturday night before Christmas it looked like everybody and his brother came by there to have a drink. He took a good many drinks during the afternoon and had a pint of his own. When he entered the restaurant around eight-thirty Lucy was there and he could see that he was "pretty high." He said to Lucy, "Boy, you got some good liquor, drinking, ain't you?" Lucy then offered him a drink. "I was already high as a Georgia pine, and didn't have any more better sense than to pour another great big slug out and gulp it down, and he took one too."

After they had talked a while Lucy asked whether he still had the Ferguson farm. He replied that he had not sold it and Lucy said, "I bet you wouldn't take $50,000.00 for it." Zehmer asked him if he would give $50,000 and Lucy said yes. Zehmer replied, "You haven't got $50,000 in cash." Lucy said he did and Zehmer replied that he did not believe it. They argued "pro and con for a long time," mainly about "whether he had $50,000 in cash that he could put up right then and buy that farm."

Finally, said Zehmer, Lucy told him if he didn't believe he had $50,000, "you sign that piece of paper here and say you will take $50,000.00 for the farm." He, Zehmer, "just grabbed the back off of a guest check there" and wrote on the back of it. At that point in his testimony Zehmer asked to see what he had written to "see if I recognize my own handwriting." He examined the paper and exclaimed, "Great balls of fire, I got 'Firgerson' for Ferguson. I have got satisfactory spelled wrong. I don't recognize that writing if I would see it, wouldn't know it was mine."

After Zehmer had, as he described it, "scribbled this thing off," Lucy said, "Get your wife to sign it." Zehmer walked over to where she was and she at first refused to sign but did so after he told her that he "was just needling him [Lucy], and didn't mean a thing in the world, that I was not selling the farm." Zehmer then "took it back over there . . . and I was still looking at the dern thing. I had the drink right there by my hand, and I reached over to get a drink, and he said, 'Let me see it.'" He reached and picked it up, and when I looked back again he had it in his pocket and he dropped a five dollar bill over there, and he said, "Here is five dollars payment on it." . . . I said, "Hell no, that is beer and liquor talking. I am not going to sell you the farm. I have told you that too many times before."

Mrs. Zehmer testified that when Lucy came into the restaurant he looked as if he had had a drink. When Zehmer came in he took a drink out of a bottle that Lucy handed him. She went back to help the waitress who was getting things ready for next day. Lucy and Zehmer were talking but she did not pay too much attention to what they were saying. She heard Lucy ask Zehmer if he had sold the Ferguson farm, and Zehmer replied that he had not and did not want to sell it. Lucy said, "I bet you wouldn't take $50,000 cash for that farm," and Zehmer replied, "You haven't got $50,000 cash." Lucy said, "I can get it." Zehmer said he might form a company and get it, "but you haven't got $50,000.00 cash to pay me tonight." Lucy asked him if he would put it in writing that he would sell him this farm. Zehmer then wrote on the back of a pad, "I agree to sell the Ferguson Place to W. O. Lucy for $50,000.00 cash." Lucy said, "All right, get your wife to sign it." Zehmer came back to where she was standing and said, "You want to put your name to this?" She said "No," but he said in an undertone, "It is nothing but a joke," and she signed it.

She said that only one paper was written and it said: "I hereby agree to sell," but the "I" had been changed to "We." However, she said she read what she signed and was then asked, "When you read 'We hereby agree to sell to W. O. Lucy,' what did you interpret that to mean, that particular phrase?" She said she thought that was a cash sale that night; but she also said that when she read that part about "title satisfactory to buyer" she understood that if the title was good Lucy would pay $50,000 but if the title was bad he would have a right to reject it, and that that was her understanding at the time she signed her name.

On examination by her own counsel she said that her husband laid this piece of paper down after it was signed; that Lucy said to let him see it, took it, folded it and put it in his wallet, then said to Zehmer, "Let me give you $5.00," but Zehmer said, "No, this is liquor talking. I don't want to sell the farm, I have told you that I want my son to have it. This is all a joke." Lucy then said at least twice, "Zehmer, you have sold your farm," wheeled around and started for the door. He paused at the door and said, "I will bring you $50,000.00 tomorrow. . . . No, tomorrow is Sunday. I will bring it to you Monday." She said you could tell definitely that he was drinking and she said to her husband, "You should have taken him home," but he said, "Well, I am just about as bad off as he is."

The waitress referred to by Mrs. Zehmer testified that when Lucy first came in "he was mouthy." When Zehmer came in they were laughing and joking and she thought they took a drink or two. She was sweeping and cleaning up for next day. She said she heard Lucy tell Zehmer, "I will give you so much for the farm," and Zehmer said, "You haven't got that much." Lucy answered, "Oh, yes, I will give you that much." Then "they jotted down something on paper . . . and Mr. Lucy reached over and took it, said let me see it." He looked at it, put it in his pocket and in about a minute he left. She was asked whether she saw Lucy offer Zehmer any money and replied, "He had five dollars laying up there, they didn't take it." She said Zehmer told Lucy he didn't want his money "because he didn't have enough money to pay for his property, and wasn't going to sell his farm." Both of them appeared to be drinking right much, she said.

She repeated on cross-examination that she was busy and paying no attention to what was going on. She was some distance away and did not see either of them sign the paper. She was asked whether she saw Zehmer put the agreement down on the table in front of Lucy, and her answer was this: "Time he got through writing whatever it was on the paper, Mr. Lucy reached over and said, 'Let's see it.' He took it and put it in his pocket," before showing it to Mrs. Zehmer. Her version was that Lucy kept raising his offer until it got to $50,000.

The defendants insist that the evidence was ample to support their contention that the writing sought to be enforced was prepared as a bluff or dare to force Lucy to admit that he did not have $50,000; that the whole matter was a joke; that the writing was not delivered to Lucy and no binding contract was ever made between the parties.

It is an unusual, if not bizarre, defense. When made to the writing admittedly prepared by one of the defendants and signed by both, clear evidence is required to sustain it.

In his testimony Zehmer claimed that he "was high as a Georgia pine," and that the transaction "was just a bunch of two doggoned drunks bluffing to see who could talk the biggest and say the most." That claim is inconsistent with his attempt to testify in great detail as to what was said and what was done. It is contradicted by other evidence as to the condition of both parties, and rendered of no weight by the testimony of his wife that when Lucy left the restaurant she suggested that Zehmer drive him home. The record is convincing that Zehmer was not intoxicated to the extent of being unable to comprehend the nature and consequences of the instrument he executed, and hence that instrument is not to be invalidated on that ground. 17 C.J.S., Contracts, § 133 b., p. 483; Taliaferro v. Emery, 124 Va. 674, 98 S.E. 627. It was in fact conceded by defendants' counsel in oral argument that under the evidence Zehmer was not too drunk to make a valid contract.

The evidence is convincing also that Zehmer wrote two agreements, the first one beginning 'I hereby agree to sell.' Zehmer first said he could not remember about that, then that "I don't think I wrote but one out." Mrs. Zehmer said that what he wrote was "I hereby agree," but that the "I" was changed to "We" after that night. The agreement that was written and signed is in the record and indicates no such change. Neither are the mistakes in spelling that Zehmer sought to point out readily apparent.

The appearance of the contract, the fact that it was under discussion for forty minutes or more before it was signed; Lucy's objection to the first draft because it was written in the singular, and he wanted Mrs. Zehmer to sign it also; the rewriting to meet that objection and the signing by Mrs. Zehmer; the discussion of what was to be included in the sale, the provision for the examination of the title, the completeness of the instrument that was executed, the taking possession of it by Lucy with no request or suggestion by either of the defendants that he give it back, are facts which furnish persuasive evidence that the execution of the contract was a serious business transaction rather than a casual, jesting matter as defendants now contend.

On Sunday, the day after the instrument was signed on Saturday night, there was a social gathering in a home in the town of McKenney at which there were general comments that the sale had been made. Mrs. Zehmer testified that on that occasion as she passed by a group of people, including Lucy, who were talking about the transaction, $50,000 was mentioned, whereupon she stepped up and said, "Well, with the high-price whiskey you were drinking last night you should have paid more. That was cheap." Lucy testified that at that time Zehmer told him that he did not want to "stick" him or hold him to the agreement because he, Lucy, was too tight and didn't know what he was doing, to which Lucy replied that he was not too tight; that he had been stuck before and was going through with it. Zehmer's version was that he said to Lucy: "I am not trying to claim it wasn't a deal on account of the fact the price was too low. If I had wanted to sell $50,000.00 would be a good price, in fact I think you would get stuck at $50,000.00." A disinterested witness testified that what Zehmer said to Lucy was that "he was going to let him up off the deal, because he thought he was too tight, didn't know what he was doing. Lucy said something to the effect that 'I have been stuck before and I will go through with it.' "

If it be assumed, contrary to what we think the evidence shows, that Zehmer was jesting about selling his farm to Lucy and that the transaction was intended by him to be a joke, nevertheless the evidence shows that Lucy did not so understand it but considered it to be a serious business transaction and the contract to be binding on the Zehmers as well as on himself. The very next day he arranged with his brother to put up half the money and take a half interest in the land. The day after that he employed an attorney to examine the title. The next night, Tuesday, he was back at Zehmer's place and there Zehmer told him for the first time, Lucy said, that he wasn't going to sell and he told Zehmer, "You know you sold that place fair and square." After receiving the report from his attorney that the title was good he wrote to Zehmer that he was ready to close the deal.

Not only did Lucy actually believe, but the evidence shows he was warranted in believing, that the contract represented a serious business transaction and a good faith sale and purchase of the farm.

In the field of contracts, as generally elsewhere, "We must look to the outward expression of a person as manifesting his intention rather than to his secret and unexpressed intention. 'The law imputes to a person an intention corresponding to the reasonable meaning of his words and acts.' " First Nat. Bank v. Roanoke Oil Co., 169 Va. 99, 114, 192 S.E. 764, 770.

At no time prior to the execution of the contract had Zehmer indicated to Lucy by word or act that he was not in earnest about selling the farm. They had argued about it and discussed its terms, as Zehmer admitted, for a long time. Lucy testified that if there was any jesting it was about paying $50,000 that night. The contract and the evidence show that he was not expected to pay the money that night. Zehmer said that after the writing was signed he laid it down on the counter in front of Lucy. Lucy said Zehmer handed it to him. In any event there had been what appeared to be a good faith offer and a good faith acceptance, followed by the execution and apparent delivery of a written contract. Both said that Lucy put the writing in his pocket and then offered Zehmer $5 to seal the bargain. Not until then, even under the defendants' evidence, was anything said or done to indicate that the matter was a joke. Both of the Zehmers testified that when Zehmer asked his wife to sign he whispered that it was a joke so Lucy wouldn't hear and that it was not intended that he should hear.

The mental assent of the parties is not requisite for the formation of a contract. If the words or other acts of one of the parties have but one reasonable meaning, his undisclosed intention is immaterial except when an unreasonable meaning which he attaches to his manifestations is known to the other party. Restatement of the Law of Contracts, Vol. I, § 71, p. 74.

> . . . The law, therefore, judges of an agreement between two persons exclusively from those expressions of their intentions which are communicated between them. . . . —Clark on Contracts, 4 ed., § 3, p. 4.

An agreement or mutual assent is of course essential to a valid contract but the law imputes to a person an intention corresponding to the reasonable meaning of his words and acts. If his words and acts, judged by a reasonable standard, manifest an intention to agree, it is immaterial what may be the real but unexpressed state of his mind. 17 C.J.S., Contracts, § 32, p. 361; 12 Am. Jur., Contracts, § 19, p. 515.

So a person cannot set up that he was merely jesting when his conduct and words would warrant a reasonable person in believing that he intended a real agreement, 17 C.J.S., Contracts, § 47, p. 390; Clark on Contracts, 4 ed., § 27, at p. 54.

Whether the writing signed by the defendants and now sought to be enforced by the complainants was the result of a serious offer by Lucy and a serious acceptance by the defendants, or was a serious offer by Lucy and an acceptance in secret jest by the defendants, in either event it constituted a binding contract of sale between the parties.

Defendants contend further, however, that even though a contract was made, equity should decline to enforce it under the circumstances. These circumstances have been set forth in detail above. They disclose some drinking by the two parties but not to an extent that they were unable to understand fully what they were doing. There was no fraud, no misrepresentation, no sharp practice and no dealing between unequal parties. The farm had been bought for $11,000 and was assessed for taxation at $6,300. The purchase price was $50,000. Zehmer admitted that it was a good price. There is in fact present in this case none of the grounds usually urged against specific performance.

Specific performance, it is true, is not a matter of absolute or arbitrary right, but is addressed to the reasonable and sound discretion of the court. First Nat. Bank v. Roanoke Oil Co., supra, 169 Va. at p. 116, 192 S.E. at p. 771. But it is likewise true that the discretion which may be exercised is not an arbitrary or capricious one, but one which is controlled by the established doctrines and settled principles of equity; and, generally, where a contract is in its nature and circumstances unobjectionable, it is as much a matter of course for courts of equity to decree a specific performance of it as it is for a court of law to give damages for a breach of it. Bond v. Crawford, 193 Va. 437, 444, 69 S.E. 2d 470, 475.

The complainants are entitled to have specific performance of the contracts sued on. The decree appealed from is therefore reversed and the cause is remanded for the entry of a proper decree requiring the defendants to perform the contract in accordance with the prayer of the bill.

Reversed and remanded.

NOTES AND QUESTIONS

1. *Specific performance remedy.* The *Lucy* court granted the plaintiffs' request for specific performance. This means that the court ordered the Zehmers to convey the Ferguson farm in return for the agreed $50,000 sale price. In the American common law system, an injured party may seek specific performance to remedy a breach of contract only where damages for the breach are not adequate to protect the expectancy interest. Restatement (Second) of Contracts § 359(1). Because every parcel of land is typically unique, money damages would not enable the Lucy brothers to procure an adequate substitute parcel. Thus, in actions for breach of a contract for the sale of an interest in real property, courts typically presume that specific performance is the appropriate remedy. Restatement (Second) of Contracts § 360(b). The presumption is reversed, however, in contracts for the sale of personal property such as automobiles or commodities because in most such cases a buyer can be made whole through payment of money damages and purchase of substitute goods from another seller. In contracts for the sale of goods, for example, UCC § 2–716(1) provides that the court may order specific performance only where "the goods are unique or in other proper circumstances." And in contracts for personal services, such as an employment agreement, specific performance is never available. Restatement (Second) of Contracts § 367(a).

2. *The joke defense.* The Zehmers' principal defense was that the Lucy brothers were not entitled to a contract breach remedy because there was no contract to breach. While it is clear that the Lucy brothers subjectively intended to purchase the farm, the Zehmers argued they did not intend to sell the Ferguson farm. Even though Mr. Zehmer stated an early intent to sell, he contended he was joking. Assuming that to be true, is it relevant? If not, why?

"Joke" promises continue to raise problems for the jokers, the courts, and the humorless. In *Leonard v. Pepsico, Inc.*, 88 F.Supp.2d 116 (S.D.N.Y. 1999), a self-described member of "the 'Pepsi Generation'" viewed a television commercial explaining a Pepsico, Inc. promotion for "Pepsi Stuff." Viewers were invited to purchase and drink Pepsi products to collect "Pepsi Points" which could be redeemed for various articles of merchandise emblazoned with the Pepsi logo. After showing a teenager wearing a Pepsi t-shirt worth 75 Pepsi Points and donning a leather jacket (1450 Pepsi Points) and sunglasses (175 Pepsi Points), the commercial concluded with the teenager entering the cockpit of a Harrier fighter jet and opining "Sure beats the bus." The following words appeared on the screen: "HARRIER FIGHTER 7,000,000 PEPSI POINTS." Leonard later noticed that other Pepsi Stuff promotional materials provided the option of purchasing additional Pepsi Points for 10 cents apiece. With the help of some acquaintances, he submitted an order form, fifteen Pepsi Points, and a check for $700,008.50 (to purchase the remaining 6,999,985 points) to Pepsi, claiming a right to receive the promised Harrier jet. Pepsi executives informed him that the Harrier jet "offer" was a joke.

Leonard did not get the joke, and he filed suit against Pepsico. The court was singularly unreceptive to claims that the commercial had seriously promised to award a Harrier fighter jet in exchange for approximately $700,000 worth of Pepsi Points, holding, *inter alia*, that a reasonable person would have understood that Pepsico's purported "offer" of a Harrier jet was a joke. "In light of the obvious absurdity of the commercial, the Court rejects plaintiff's argument that the commercial was not clearly in jest." Id. at 128–30.

3.   *Mrs. Zehmer's role.* The Ferguson farm belonged to Mr. and Mrs. Zehmer. After Mr. Zehmer agreed to sell the farm, Lucy demanded that Mrs. Zehmer sign as well. She initially refused and only agreed after her husband told her it was a joke and that that the farm would not be sold. Does the court properly analyze the intent issue from her perspective? If not, why not?

4.   *Role of assignment.* As Mr. Zehmer expected, Lucy did not have the resources to purchase the farm. To fund the purchase, apparently Lucy "assigned" one-half of his $50,000 contract right to his brother for $25,000. A party to a contract is usually defined by reference to the persons who execute the contract. Lucy's brother was therefore not a "party" to the contract. Nonetheless, this third party brother he obtained rights to enforce the contract from Lucy. How can this be so? Contract rights are the property of the parties to the contract. Like any other permissible transfer of property or property rights, a valid assignment of a contract right transfers legal ownership of the contract right to the assignee and simultaneously extinguishes the assignor's rights in the transferred property. Restatement (Second) of Contracts § 317(1). As a result, the assignee brother owned part of whatever rights that his brother owned prior to the assignment and therefore joined the lawsuit against the Zehmers. Chapter 10 on The Rights and Duties of Third Parties discusses this issue in greater detail.

5. *Intoxication and voidable contracts.* A voidable contract is one in which at least one of the parties has the power either to avoid or to ratify the legal relations of the contract. Restatement (Second) of Contracts § 7. An intoxicated person enters only a voidable contract if the other party had reason to know that the intoxicated party was unable to understand the transaction. Restatement (Second) of Contracts § 16. Thus, an intoxicated person has the power to avoid or ratify a contract made while intoxicated. Zehmer testified he was as "high as a Georgia pine" and that he and Lucy were "two doggoned drunks bluffing." The court did not accept this explanation. If the court had accepted the argument, how would you characterize the resulting contract? Why do you think the common law takes such an approach? Contracts may be avoidable on many grounds, all challenging the quality of the assent of one or both of the parties to the contract. Why would the law in such cases make the contract voidable rather than simply not a contract at all? These concepts are explored in more detail in Chapter 8 on Contracts Unenforceable By Election.

6. *Will theory and contract damages.* It has been suggested that it is impossible to separate the law of contract damages from the general law of contracts. For this reason, Professor Fuller suggested that to move from reliance damages to expectancy damages is to move from undoing harm (Aristotelian corrective justice) to satisfaction for mere disappointment (Aristotelian distributive justice). Lon L. Fuller and William R. Perdue, "The Reliance Interest in Contract Damages (Part) I.," 46 Yale L. J. 52, 53–56 (1936). Does the objective theory of contracts undermine the theoretical support for expectancy damages?

C. ENFORCING PROMISES: LEGAL THEORIES OF OBLIGATION

It is one thing for parties to make an agreement intending it to control the matters expressed therein. It is an entirely different matter to ask the law and the courts to enforce the agreement in the event one party fails to perform as promised. Understanding this distinction helps explain why the law and courts require a proper reason to enforce any promise or exchange of promises.

Systems of contract have relied upon many different mechanisms to distinguish enforceable from unenforceable promises. Ancient Roman law, for example, provided that private parties could form binding legal obligations by following a ritual oral recitation and response called *stipulatio*. Under this formula, the promisor phrased the proposed contract obligations in the form of a question: "Do you promise [to perform or refrain from performing specified acts and obligations]?" The promisee completed the contractual form by responding, "I promise." The resulting oral contract was enforceable, even in the absence of witnesses or written evidence of the exchange.

what constitutes "sealed"?

Likewise, until the turn of the twentieth century, courts generally recognized promises in a sealed written document—"promises under seal"—as enforceable obligations at common law. Although many jurisdictions have attempted to limit or abolish the legal effectiveness of the seal, Restatement (Second) of Contracts § 95(1) still provides that a written promise that identifies the parties, and is both sealed and delivered, is enforceable at common law in the absence of a statutory provision to the contrary. See Eric Mills Holmes, "Stature and Status of a Promise Under Seal as a Legal Formality," 29 Willamette L. Rev. 617, 637–63 (1993) (surveying state statutes abolishing, modifying, and promoting use of a seal to create enforceable obligations).

Today, courts primarily rely upon three bases for determining the enforceability of promises. The first, consideration, makes promises enforceable only when they are made in the context of a bargained-for exchange of legal detriments. The second, promissory estoppel, provides for enforcement of promises upon which the promisee reasonably relies, despite the absence of consideration. Finally, courts may order restitution to avoid "unjust enrichment" in cases where one party to a transaction confers a benefit upon the other party for which the recipient should pay. Each of these three mechanisms will be addressed in detail below.

Importantly, the reasons for enforceability do not always yield the same result. This means that while a promise might not be enforceable under one theory (such as consideration), it may nonetheless be enforceable under an alternative theory (e.g., promissory estoppel or restitution). Regardless of the reason for enforcing the obligation, no one can deny the importance of enforcement of promises and obligations, and thus the role of contract, in civilized society. Indeed, Sir Henry Maine observed that ". . . the movement of the progressive societies has hitherto been a movement from Status to Contract as individual autonomy has replaced the family" as the unit of which civil law takes account. Sir Henry Maine, Ancient Law 163–164 (1864).

A primary role and function of the law is to define obligations. Obligations are descriptions of relationships between the parties. An obligation includes both the legal duty imposed by law on one person and its correlative legal right to enforcement in favor of another person. Obligation can arise from many sources including public law and private law. Public law generally considers the relationship between individuals and government. Public law may find its source in constitutions and statutes (e.g., constitutional law, criminal law, and administrative law). Private law generally considers the relationship between individuals and their property. This law of private ordering generally finds its source in statutes and the common law (e.g., tort law and contract law).

In this context, the law of contracts specifically considers that aspect of private law through which a private agreement between the parties creates a legal obligation that will be enforced by public courts and executives. The agreement itself is the source of the legal obligation, and defines the legal duty of one party and the correlative right of the other. In contracts, the law purposes to determine when and under what circumstances one or both parties can marshal public resources to enforce (by state-legitimized violence if necessary) a legal obligation created by the making of a promise to do or not to do (refrain or forbearance) something in the future.

Since the parties create the obligation by way of their agreement, there is a natural tension in the role of the law between enforcing only their respective individual free wills or intervening in the contract to protect broader public interests, such as judicial economy or prohibitions on the use of courts to enforce inequitable contracts. This presents a tension between the "will theory" of contracts and doctrines such as the "objective theory" of contracts that impose obligations other than by a free will referent. While free-market and individual rights adherents argue that societal controls of private contracts might appear unwarranted, other scholars have asserted that the free market inadequately reflects the tastes and interests of society in many legal contexts. Contract law is no exception. The materials below explore the principal doctrines utilized by law over time to enforce promises and create contractual obligations.

1. OBLIGATION BY REASON OF AN AGREEMENT SUPPORTED BY CONSIDERATION

Perplexing and long the bane of every law student, consideration is nonetheless the dominant and leading theory of contract obligation and the way by which most promises are made enforceable. The theory of consideration is not a new problem. See, e.g., Karl N. Llewellyn, "On the Complexity of Consideration: A Foreword," 41 Colum. L. Rev. 777 (1941). Making a promise enforceable creates two correlative legal concepts. The promisor becomes legally obligated (duty) to perform the promise exactly as made. In turn, the promisee becomes legally entitled (right) to that performance. The promisor and promisee become the two parties to the contract. What is it about consideration that creates this powerful legal result? According to the Restatement (Second) of Contracts, the bargain between the two parties holds the secret. Under the bargain concept of consideration, the law will enforce a promise made in an exchange when the promisor seeks and receives something in return for the promise. Restatement (Second) of Contracts § 71(1)–(2).

Function of Consideration. Consideration, like all other mechanisms for making enforceable promises, is a tool that helps ensure that the power of the state will not be brought to bear to enforce a promise that was never made, that the parties did not intend to be legally binding, that would produce unjust results, or that is contrary to the public interest. In a world without consideration, the hazards of mistaken or perjured testimony could influence a jury to enforce a promise falsely alleged. Also, the law might be reduced to enforcement of promises impulsively made without due deliberation. Aside from these process objections, enforcement of gratuitous promises may not be the proper object of sufficient societal importance to merit enforcement. The preeminent statement of the function of consideration to address some of these concerns was provided by Professor Lon L. Fuller, "Consideration and Form," 41 Colum. L. Rev. 799, 800–801 (1941). First, Fuller observed that consideration has an *evidentiary function*. Consideration, by requiring the parties to engage in a bargained-for exchange of legal detriments, creates the conditions under which the parties' transaction causes real-world effects. A court or fact finder may evaluate these effects as evidence that the parties made an enforceable promise.

Second, consideration serves a *cautionary function*. By requiring the parties to engage in a legal ritual such as the exchange of considerations, the doctrine supposedly provides a cautionary check against parties making unconsidered or unintended promises.

Third, the *channeling function* of consideration recognizes that the requirements the doctrine imposes upon the creation of enforceable promises channels or guides their behavior in recognizable and repeatable patterns. Courts and fact finders in a common law context thus know to look for the actions typically associated with a bargained-for exchange of legal detriments. As Fuller notes, this channeling function, like other formal requirements, "relieve[s] the judge of an inquiry *whether* a legal transaction was intended, and—in case different forms are fixed for different legal transactions—*which* was intended." See id.

Not all scholars agree with Professor Fuller. Some modern scholars have been skeptical of the function of the form notion. See Andrew Kull, "Reconsidering Gratuitous Promises," 21 J. Legal Studies 39, 51–55 (1992) (questioning whether absence of consideration should conclusively resolve unenforceability) and Duncan Kennedy, "From Will Theory to the Principle of Private Autonomy," 100 Colum. L. Rev. 94 (2000). Others might simply argue that all serious promises should be legally enforceable because such promises create a moral obligation. See Celia Taylor, "My Modest Proposal," 18 St. Thomas L. Rev. 117 (2005).

History of Consideration. While every society and legal system likely has had some mechanism for creating legally binding promissory obligations between private parties, the first antecedents of modern common law contract doctrine developed rather late and probably not before the Norman Conquest in 1066. Medieval English law provided several distinct "writs" or "forms of action" by which parties could create and enforce discrete types of private promissory obligations. The forms of action that most resembled modern contract law included the writ of covenant and the writ of debt. Medieval "contract" law distinguished between common law writs of covenant and debt to enforce legal rights somewhat similar to those arising under contract law.

The writ of covenant permitted a promisee to recover unliquidated damages for a wrongful or tortious breach of a covenant (medieval term for a formal agreement under seal). However, several limitations imposed on the action rendered it less useful, including the requirement that the action could only be brought on a written instrument properly sealed. In addition, consequential damages—those indirectly caused by a breached promise— were not recoverable. Liquidated damage clauses ameliorated the latter limitation, but the seal formality made the action useful primarily in significant transactions among those able to afford the costs of the required formalities.

The writ of debt was more functional because it was not limited to formal agreements. However, the action only permitted recovery of a fixed sum. Also, it was not promissory in nature. Rather, the writ of debt was restorative, and thus the writ generally required the plaintiff to establish the debt creation by some quid pro quo. Most importantly, breaching promisors could avoid their debt obligations through a process known as a "wager of law." The alleged debtor could elect either to have a jury hear the case or to wage his case. In the latter instance, the defendant in effect pleaded no debt and offered to prove the defense by an oath that nothing was owed. On the day of the "trial," the debtor was required to appear with a number of "oath-helpers" (also called "compurgators"), and all would then swear an oath on the Bible attesting that the debtor did not owe the debt. See A.W. Brian Simpson, A History of the Common Law of Contract—The Rise and Fall of The Action of Assumpsit 138 (1996 Reprint).

Due to these infirmities, the common law action in *assumpsit* gradually displaced the writs of covenant and debt to eventually become the remedy for breach of promise. See A.W. Brian Simpson, A History of the Common Law of Contract—The Rise and Fall of The Action of Assumpsit 1–17 (1996 Reprint); James B. Ames, "The History of Assumpsit (Part I–Express Assumpsit)," 2 Harv. L. Rev. 1 (1888).

The action in assumpsit (literally, "to assume") originated as a special form of a writ or action of trespass around the fourteenth century. The trespass action resembled the modern action of tort. Originally, the trespass action addressed public wrongs but eventually extended to cover private wrongs in the form of "trespass on the case." Such actions eventually became known as an action in assumpsit because the pleading alleged the defendant voluntarily assumed the obligation. As originally conceived, the action for assumpsit was only available for misfeasance (defective performance) but not nonfeasance (failure to perform). (Nonfeasance was only actionable under a writ of covenant (and subject to its infirmities)). Courts grafted further exceptions onto this distinction eventually allowing an action for assumpsit to address nonfeasance as well (around the sixteenth century). As a result, assumpsit eventually subsumed the action for covenant.

The transition was not always easy however. Where an action could be brought in debt or assumpsit, defendant debtors objected to the assumpsit characterization because it did not permit wager of law. *Slade's Case*, 76 Eng. Rep. 1074 (1602) definitively settled this dispute by holding that plaintiffs could elect either action. As a practical result, *Slade's Case* thus ended the medieval wager of law institution as plaintiffs routinely elected the more favorable assumpsit form of action. See Jackson, "The Scope of the Term 'Contract,'" 53 L. Q. Rev. 525, 529 (1937). But while *Slade's Case* eliminated the problem of perjured defendants escaping their obligations through wager of law, it opened the door for a new problem of perjured plaintiffs. Because assumpsit permitted a purported promisee to bring an action to enforce any informal exchange of promises, an unscrupulous plaintiff could potentially recover upon a fraudulent claim that the defendant had entered a binding agreement. The English parliament responded to this problem by protecting particular classes of contracts—most notably contracts for the sale of an interest in real property—by adopting the Statute of Frauds in 1677. As discussed in another chapter, the Statute of Frauds required many contracts to be in writing in order to be enforced against the party charged (defendant).

While infirmities plagued the actions of covenant (written and under seal) and debt (debt certain and wager of law), assumpsit was not subject to the same conditions. Nonetheless, over time, the action for assumpsit acquired its own limitations. Most notably, the plaintiff had to plead the factors the defendant considered in making the promise. The pleading of such "considerations" eventually developed into a formal requirement and condition to the action. As case law developed, courts began to distinguish between "adequate" and "inadequate" considerations to support the assumpsit action. Early indicia of adequate considerations included detriment to the promisee (linked to the harm suffered by the plaintiff in the trespass action) and benefit to the promisor (linked to the quid pro quo by the defendant in a debt action).

Through the course of the next three centuries, "consideration" became the touchstone for determining whether or not a promise would be enforced. A promise without consideration was a *nudum pactum* (unenforceable). The emphasis shifted, however, from the search for detriment to the promisee or benefit to the promisor to a "bargained-for exchange."

The Roman lawyers had coined the well-known tag "quid pro quo" as the marker for an enforceable promise. The element of a trade or bargain implicit in that tag became the requirement for a finding of consideration. The notion of consideration was important because of its theoretical justification for the difference between promises that were enforceable and those that were not.

In practice, the notion was rarely important. The most basic form of contract is the barter—exchange of something for something else. Here the exchange requirement is clearly satisfied. The more complex form of contract, the promise to do something in return for another's promise to do something else, a form which covers most familiar commercial transactions, equally clearly is based on a bargained-for exchange.

Most consideration questions involve situations where there was an apparent bargained-for exchange, but the promise on one side lacked any value. The *Batsakis* case below illustrates the strong disinclination of judges to open up the factual issue of whether the exchange was fair to both parties. The value of the exchange is generally a matter of judgment for the contracting parties except in the most extreme cases. Where there is at least the appearance of consideration in an exchange, courts generally refuse to recognize consideration where one of the parties gives a consideration that is truly valueless or where the consideration is illusory. Thus, in *Fiege v. Boehm*, 210 Md. 352, 123 A.2d 316 (1956), where the alleged father of an illegitimate child contracted with the mother to provide support for the child, the court found the alleged father's promise to be enforceable even though subsequently discovered evidence established that he could not have been the child's father. It was sufficient for enforceability that both parties had engaged in good faith in a bargained-for exchange.

The shift from assumpsit involved a fundamentally significant change with respect to remedy for breach of the promise. Assumpsit involved, essentially, a restitutionary approach to remedy. The receiver of goods, for instance, having received the goods, ought to pay their value in the event of nonperformance of the return promise to pay. Following the decision in *Slade's Case*, a bilateral exchange of promises each involving the doing of something in the future became enforceable. But here, when one of the promisors defaulted, there was no basis for restitutionary relief. The loss involved had to be measured by a new standard, the value of the benefit that would have been received had the promise been performed. The rewarding of the lost "expectancy" became the norm. See Restatement (Second) of Contracts § 347.

a.   The Donor-Promise Principle

One of the most important historical roles for the doctrine of consideration preserves the distinction between enforceable promises and unenforceable promises to make a gift. Unenforceable gratuitous promises, not supported by consideration, are referred to as the "donor-gift" or "donative-promise" principle. The case below explores this doctrine.

DOUGHERTY V. SALT

Court of Appeals of New York
227 N.Y. 200, 125 N.E. 94 (1919)

Action from Supreme Court, Appellate Division, Second Department.

Action by Charles Napoleon Dougherty, an infant, by Susan M. Teves, his guardian, against Emma L. Salt, as executrix of the last will and testament of Helena M. Dougherty, deceased. From a judgment of the second department of the Appellate Division of the Supreme Court (184 App. Div. 910, 170 N. Y. Supp. 1076), reversing a judgment of the Trial Term, which set aside a verdict of the jury in favor of plaintiff and dismissed the complaint, and reinstating the verdict and directing judgment thereon, the defendant appeals. Judgment of Appellate Division reversed, and judgment of Trial Term modified by granting a new trial.

CARDOZO, J.* The plaintiff, a boy of eight years, received from his aunt, the defendant's testatrix, a promissory note for $3,000, payable at her death or before. Use was made of a printed form, which contains the words 'value received.' How the note came to be given was explained by the boy's guardian, who was a witness for his ward. The aunt was visiting her nephew.

> When she saw Charley coming in, she said, "Isn't he a nice boy?" I answered her, Yes; that he is getting along very nice, and getting along nice in school; and I showed where he had progressed in school, having good reports, and so forth, and she told me that she was going to take care of that child; that she loved him very much. I said, "I know you do, Tillie, but your taking care of the child will be done probably like your brother and sister done, take it out in talk." She said, "I don't intend to take it out in talk; I would like to take care of him now." I said, "Well, that is up to you." She said, "Why can't I make out a note to him?" I said, "You can, if you wish to." She said, "Would that be right?" And I said, "I do not know,

---

* Benjamin Nathan Cardozo (1870–1938) opinions are praised for prose but often criticized as verbose and not helpful in setting forth legal principles. See Grant Gilmore, The Death of Contract 63 (1974) (referring to Cardozo as a "master of judicial ambiguity"). Cardozo was a judge on the New York Court of Appeals, that state's highest court, from 1914–1932, and the Chief Judge, from 1926–1932. In 1932, President Hoover appointed Judge Cardozo to the United States Supreme Court to replace the seat vacated by then-retiring Justice Oliver Wendell Holmes, Jr. Albert J. Cardozo (1828–1885), his father, was also a justice on the New York Court of Appeals until he resigned in 1872 because of a judicial corruption scandal. See Grant Gilmore, The Death of Contract 69 (1974) (". . . Cardozo contract opinions, scattered over his long tenure . . . might be called an expansive theory of contract. Courts should make contracts wherever possible, rather than the other way around. Missing terms can be supplied. If an express promise is lacking, an implied promise can be easily found. In particular Cardozo delighted in weaving gossamer spider webs of consideration.").

but I guess it would; I do not know why it would not." And she said, "Well, will you make out a note for me?" I said, "Yes, if you wish me to," and she said, "Well, I wish you would."

A blank was then produced, filled out, and signed. The aunt handed the note to her nephew, with these words:

You have always done for me, and I have signed this note for you. Now, do not lose it. Some day it will be valuable.

The trial judge submitted to the jury the question whether there was any consideration for the promised payment. Afterwards, he set aside the verdict in favor of the plaintiff, and dismissed the complaint. The Appellate Division, by a divided court, reversed the judgment of dismissal, and reinstated the verdict on the ground that the note was sufficient evidence of consideration.

We reach a different conclusion. The inference of consideration to be drawn from the form of the note has been so overcome and rebutted as to leave no question for a jury. This is not a case where witnesses, summoned by the defendant and friendly to the defendant's cause, supply the testimony in disproof of value. Strickland v. Henry, 175 N. Y. 372, 67 N. E. 611. This is a case where the testimony in disproof of value comes from the plaintiff's own witness, speaking at the plaintiff's instance. The transaction thus revealed admits of one interpretation, and one only. The note was the voluntary and unenforceable promise of an executory gift. Harris v. Clark, 3 N. Y. 93, 51 Am. Dec. 352; Holmes v. Roper, 141 N. Y. 64, 66, 36 N. E. 180. This child of eight was not a creditor, nor dealt with as one. The aunt was not paying a debt. She was conferring a bounty. Fink v. Cox, 18 Johns. 145, 9 Am. Dec. 191. The promise was neither offered nor accepted with any other purpose. "Nothing is consideration that is not regarded as such by both parties." [Philpot v. Gruninger, 14 Wall. 570, 577, 20 L. Ed. 743]. . . . A note so given is not made for "value received," however its maker may have labeled it. The formula of the printed blank becomes, in the light of the conceded facts, a mere erroneous conclusion, which cannot overcome the inconsistent conclusion of the law. Blanshan v. Russell, 32 App. Div. 103, 52 N. Y. Supp. 963, affirmed on opinion below 161 N. Y. 629, 55 N. E. 1093. . . . The plaintiff through his own witness, has explained the genesis of the promise, and consideration has been disproved. Neg. Instr. Law, § 54 (Consol. Laws, c. 38).

We hold, therefore, that the verdict of the jury was contrary to law, and that the trial judge was right in setting it aside. He went too far, however, in dismissing the complaint. He might have dismissed it if he had reserved his ruling on the defendant's motion for a nonsuit or for the direction of a verdict. Code Civ. Proc. §§ 1185, 1187. Instead of reserving his ruling, he denied the motion absolutely. Upon the return of the verdict, he should have granted a new trial.

A new trial was also necessary because of error in rejecting evidence. The defendant attempted to prove that the signature to the note was forged. The court refused to hear the evidence, because forgery had not been pleaded as a defense. The answer did deny the execution of the note. The evidence of forgery was admissible under the denial. Schwarz v. Oppold, 74 N. Y. 307;. . . .

The judgment of the Appellate Division should be reversed, and the judgment of the Trial Term modified by granting a new trial, and, as modified, affirmed, with costs in all courts to abide the event.

HISCOCK, C. J., and CHASE, COLLIN, HOGAN, CRANE, and ANDREWS, JJ., concur.

Judgment accordingly.

NOTES AND QUESTIONS

1.   *Matter of law.* In *Dougherty*, Cardozo treated the matter of consideration as a question of law and not appropriate for the jury. Such an interpretation grants the court more control over the jury by simply deciding matters itself under established legal doctrine when a factual question is not presented. In fact, the trial court erroneously submitted the question to the jury, which held the note was enforceable. Having submitted the question to the jury, the trial judge exercised a later power by deciding as a matter of law the jury verdict was in error or contrary to the law. Cardozo determined that the question should not have been submitted in the first place. What is the legal standard governing this question?

2.   *Testamentary transfers.* Aunt Helen "Tillie" Dougherty made the $3,000 note payable to her nephew Charles Napoleon Dougherty upon her death. Do you suppose that if she had administered her own estate she would have paid the $3,000? If so, what does this tell you about why Emma Salt (executrix of Tillie Dougherty's estate) did not pay the amount? Instead of making a promissory note payable from her estate, why not simply provide for her nephew in her will and eliminate the note? In the law of testamentary disposition, consideration is irrelevant. Indeed, most testamentary transfers are pure gifts. However, a person may change their will at any time. How could Tillie Dougherty ensure that the payment would be made, but only after her death?

3.   *The donative-promise principle.* As illustrated in *Dougherty*, the donative-promise principle provides that an unrelied-upon promise is not enforceable. Professor Melvin Eisenberg makes a persuasive argument that the principle has importance beyond the traditional role of protecting against false claims: ". . . first, that the world of gift would be impoverished if simple donative promises were placed into the world of contract, and second, that in the absence of special circumstances, like reliance, where a donative promise is based on affected considerations, normally the promisee is morally obligated to release a repenting promisor." Melvin A. Eisenberg, "The World of Contract

and the World of Gift," 85 Cal. L. Rev. 821, 823 (1997). See Roy Kreitner, "The Gift Beyond the Grave: Revisiting the Question of Consideration," 101 Colum. L. Rev. 1876 (2001) (arguing that a principal role of consideration serves to center contract law upon its promissory roots, enhance free will, and reduce the role of the state in ordering the affairs of individuals); Celia R. Taylor, "No Regrets in Reading Professor Farnsworth's Contribution," 68 Geo. Wash. L. Rev. 377 (2000) (book review of E. Allan Farnsworth, Changing Your Mind: The Law of Regretted Decisions (1998)).

4. *False and nominal consideration.* The promissory note specifically recited that it was made in return for "value received." Based upon the testimony of the guardian, Cardozo treated the recitation as essentially false. Nothing was in fact sought or given in return for Tillie Dougherty's promise. This remains the law today. Even if the parties paid an actual dollar as nominal consideration, that payment would be treated the same as the false recital of consideration—not truly bargained for. Restatement (Second) of Contracts § 71, *cmt. b* ("Moreover, a mere pretense of bargain does not suffice, as where there is a false recital of consideration or where the purported consideration is merely nominal").

5. *An argument for enforcement.* Why not make at least some types of donative promises legally enforceable? Roman law, for example, provided for enforcement of unremunerated promises in several contexts without any element of exchange or quid pro quo. Thus, two types of bailment contracts—the *depositum* (a deposit of personal property with another for a period of time) and the *commodatum* (a loan of the use of an asset under which the possessor kept income generated by the asset)—were both enforceable, as was the *mutuum*, a loan of money requiring repayment of principal only. Modern European Civil Codes retain similar institutions. See John P. Dawson, Gifts and Promises: Continental and American Law Compared 2–10 (1978). But while Roman law expressly recognized the validity of specific categories of donative promises, it also maintained strong prohibitions on gifts and gift promises in one specific type of transaction—gifts between spouses. These prohibitions may have developed out of concern for protecting vulnerable spouses or preventing diversion of family assets. See id.

6. *Promissory certainty.* Suppose that attempts to distinguish enforceable from unenforceable donative promises on the basis of transaction type—i.e., commercial bargains, charitable subscriptions, or intrafamilial gift promises—fail. American contract law expressly distinguishes between a donative promise to make a gift in the future (generally unenforceable) and actual delivery of the gift (generally enforceable). This rule means that promisors lack the ability to make enforceable gift promises, despite that they may in some situations desire to provide their promisees with some evidence of their sincerity. See E. Allan Farnsworth, "Promises and Paternalism," 41 Wm. & Mary L. Rev. 385, 390 (2000). While this principle may, as Farnsworth observed, protect profligate promisors, it is also undeniably paternalistic and seems to fly in the face of a countervailing principle that contract law should

seek to give effect to the wills of the parties to the contract. See id. at 392–400; see also Ian Ayres & Gregory Klass, Insincere Promises (2005).

b.   The Peppercorn Principle and the Equivalency Theory

Under normal circumstances, the consideration doctrine only requires that the promisor seek or bargain with the promisee for the return consideration in exchange for the promise. Restatement (Second) of Contracts §§ 71(1)–(2). This notion reflects the idea that the court uses the consideration doctrine merely to enforce the promise, not to police imbalances in the value of items in the exchange itself. But historical consideration doctrine is not totally isolated from fairness determinations. These two features of the doctrine of consideration present two inconsistent notions.

On the one hand, consideration doctrine is confined to form. It is blind to questions of fairness. On the other hand, consideration doctrine might refuse legal enforcement to an unfair exchange in extreme cases. The ancient doctrine that mere "inadequacy" of consideration is not a bar to enforcement affirms the first proposition and refutes the second. Justification for the "inadequacy" doctrine might be found in *laissez-faire* principles. See Note, "The Peppercorn Theory of Consideration and the Doctrine of Fair Exchange in Contract Law," 35 Colum. L. Rev. 1090 (1935). But ignoring the equitable limitations of consideration doctrine simply places greater pressure on other contract doctrines to do the work left undone by consideration. Specifically, if formal consideration creates an enforceable contract, other doctrines, such as unconscionability, public policy, duress, mistake, and others, must be used to police against gross unfairness in the exchange. Are such ex post measures effective or do they simply encourage ex ante coercive conduct by enforcing the contract in the first instance? See Oren Bar-Gill & Omri Ben-Shahar, "Credible Coercion," 83 Tex. L. Rev. 717 (2005) (arguing that late relief only encourages coercion in the first instance and therefore exacerbates the resulting harm).

Since consideration is the dominant theory of obligation, this tension raises serious concerns for contract law. In the cases to follow, try to determine if the doctrine of fair exchange has been fairly applied. In each case, try to assess the values of the items involved in the exchange.

HAMER V. SIDWAY
Court of Appeals of New York
124 N.Y. 538, 27 N.E. 256 (1891)

Appeal from an order of the general term of the supreme court in the fourth judicial department, reversing a judgment entered on the decision of the court at special term in the county clerk's office of Chemung county on the 1st day of October, 1889. The plaintiff presented a claim to the executor of William E. Story, Sr., for $5,000 and interest from the 6th day of February, 1875. She acquired it through several mesne assignments from William E. Story, 2d. The claim being rejected by the executor, this action was brought. It appears that William E. Story, Sr., was the uncle of William E. Story, 2d., that at the celebration of the golden wedding of Samuel Story and wife, father and mother of William E. Story, Sr., on the 20th day of March, 1869, in the presence of the family and invited guests, he promised his nephew that if he would refrain from drinking, using tobacco, swearing, and playing cards or billiards for money until he became 21 years of age, he would pay him the sum of $5,000. The nephew assented thereto, and fully performed the conditions inducing the promise. When the nephew arrived at the age of 21 years, and on the 31st day of January, 1875, he wrote to his uncle, informing him that he had performed his part of the agreement, and had thereby become entitled to the sum of $5,000. The uncle received the letter, and a few days later, and on the 6th day of February, he wrote and mailed to his nephew the following letter:

Buffalo, Feb. 6, 1875.
W. E. Story, Jr.-

Dear Nephew:

Your letter of the 31st ult. came to hand all right, saying that you had lived up to the promise made to me several years ago. I have no doubt but you have, for which you shall have five thousand dollars, as I promised you. I had the money in the bank the day you was twenty-one years old that I intend for you, and you shall have the money certain. Now, Willie, I do not intend to interfere with this money in any way till I think you are capable of taking care of it, and the sooner that time comes the better it will please me. I would hate very much to have you start out in some adventure that you thought all right and lose this money in one year. The first five thousand dollars that I got together cost me a heap of hard work. You would hardly believe me when I tell you that to obtain this I shoved a jack-plane many a day, butchered three or four years, then came to this city, and, after three months' perseverance, I obtained a situation in a grocery store. I opened this store early, closed late, slept in the fourth story of the building in a room 30 by 40 feet, and not a human being in the building but myself. All this I done to live as cheap as I could to save something. I don't want you to take up with this kind of fare. I was here in the cholera season of '49 and '52, and the deaths averaged 80 to 125 daily and plenty of small-pox. I wanted to go home, but Mr. Fisk, the gentleman I was working for, told me if I left then, after it got healthy, he probably would not want me. I stayed. All the money I have saved I know just how I got it. It did not come to me in any mysterious way, and the reason I speak of this is that money got in this way stops longer with a fellow that gets it with hard knocks than it does when he finds it. Willie, you are twenty-one, and you have many a thing to learn yet. This money you have earned much easier than I did, besides acquiring good habits at the same time, and you are quite welcome to the money. Hope you will make good use of it. I was ten long years getting this together after I was your age. Now, hoping this will be satisfactory, I stop. One thing more. Twenty-one years ago I bought you 15 sheep. These sheep were put out to double every four years. I kept track of them the first eight years. I have not heard much about them since. Your father and grandfather promised me that they would look after them till you were of age. Have they done so? I hope they have. By this time you have between five and six hundred sheep, worth a nice little income this spring. Willie, I have said much more than I expected to. Hope you can make out what I have written. Today is the seventeenth day that I have not been out of my room, and have had the doctor as many days. Am a little better to day. Think I will get out next week. You need not mention to father, as he always worries about small matters.

Truly yours,
W. E. STORY.

P. S. You can consider this money on interest.

The nephew received the letter, and thereafter consented that the money should remain with his uncle in accordance with the terms and conditions of the letter. The uncle died on the 29th day of January, 1887, without having paid over to his nephew any portion of the said $5,000 and interest.

PARKER, J. (*after stating the facts as above.*)

The question which provoked the most discussion by counsel on this appeal, and which lies at the foundation of plaintiff's asserted right of recovery, is whether by virtue of a contract defendant's testator, William E. Story, became indebted to his nephew, William E. Story, 2d, on his twenty-first birthday in the sum of $5,000. The trial court found as a fact that on the 20th day of March, 1869, ". . . . William E. Story agreed to and with William E. Story, 2d, that if he would refrain from drinking liquor using tobacco, swearing, and playing cards or billiards for money until should become twenty-one years of age, then he, the said William E. Story, would at that time pay him, the said William E. Story, 2d, the sum of $5,000 for such refraining, to which the said William E. Story, 2d, agreed," and that he "in all things fully performed his part of said agreement." The defendant contends that the contract was without consideration to support it, and therefore invalid. He asserts that the promisee, by refraining from the use of liquor and tobacco, was not harmed, but benefited; that that which he did was best for him to do, independently of his uncle's promise,— and insists that it follows that, unless the promisor was benefited, the contract was without consideration,-a contention which, if well founded, would seem to leave open for controversy in many cases whether that which the promisee did or omitted to do was in fact of such benefit to him as to leave no consideration to support the enforcement of the promisor's agreement. Such a rule could not be tolerated, and is without foundation in the law. The exchequer chamber in 1875 defined "consideration" as follows: "A valuable consideration, in the sense of the law, may consist either in some right, interest, profit, or benefit accruing to the one party, or some forbearance, detriment, loss, or responsibility given, suffered, or undertaken by the other." Courts "will not ask whether the thing which forms the consideration does in fact benefit the promisee or a third party, or is of any substantial value to any one. It is enough that something is promised, done, forborne, or suffered by the party to whom the promise is made as consideration for the promise made to him" Anson, Cont. 63. "In general a waiver of any legal right at the request of another party is a sufficient consideration for a promise." Pars. Cont. "Any damage, or suspension, or forbearance of a right will be sufficient to sustain a promise." 2 Kent, Comm. (12th Ed.). Pollock in his work on Contracts, (page 166,) after citing the definition given by the exchequer chamber, already quoted, says: "The second branch of this judicial description is really the most important one. 'Consideration' means not so much that one party is profiting as that the other abandons some legal right in the present, or limits his legal freedom of action in the future, as an inducement for the promise of the first." Now, applying this rule to the facts before us, the promisee used tobacco, occasionally drank liquor, and he had a legal right to do so. That right he abandoned for a period of years upon the strength of the promise of the testator that for such forbearance he would give him $5,000. We need not speculate on the effort which may have been required to give up the use of those stimulants. It is sufficient that he restricted his lawful freedom of action within certain prescribed limits upon the faith of his uncle's agreement, and now, having fully performed the conditions imposed, it is of no moment whether such performance actually proved a benefit to the promisor, and the court will not inquire into it; but, were it a proper subject of inquiry, we see nothing in this record that would permit a determination that the uncle was not benefited in a legal sense. Few cases have been found which may be said to be precisely in point, but such as have been, support the position we have taken. In Shadwell v. Shadwell, 9 C. B. (N. S.) 159, an uncle wrote to his nephew as follows:

My Dear Lancey:

I am so glad to hear of your intended marriage with Ellen Nicholl, and, as I promised to assist you at starting, I am happy to tell you that I will pay you 150 pounds yearly during my life and until your annual income derived from your profession of a chancery barrister shall amount to 600 guineas, of which your own admission will be the only evidence that I shall receive or require.

Your affectionate uncle,

CHARLES SHADWELL.

It was held that the promise was binding, and made upon good consideration. In Lakota v. Newton, (an unreported case in the superior court of Worcester, Mass.,) the complaint averred defendant's promise that "if you [meaning the plaintiff] will leave off drinking for a year I will give you $100," plaintiff's assent thereto, performance of the condition by him, and demanded judgment therefor. Defendant demurred, on the ground, among others, that the plaintiff's declaration did not allege a valid and sufficient consideration for the agreement of the defendant. The demurrer was overruled. In Talbott v. Stemmons, 12 S. W. Rep. 297, (a Kentucky case, not yet officially reported,) the step-grandmother of the plaintiff made with him the following agreement: "I do promise and bind myself to give my grandson Albert R. Talbott $500 at my death if he will never take another chew of tobacco or smoke another cigar during my life, from this date up to my death; and if he breaks this pledge he is to refund double the amount to his mother." The executor of Mrs. Stemmons demurred to the complaint on the ground that the agreement was not based on a sufficient consideration. The demurrer was sustained, and an appeal taken therefrom to the court of appeals, where the decision of the court below was reversed. In the opinion of the court it is said that "the right to use and enjoy the use of tobacco was a right that belonged to the plaintiff, and not forbidden by law. The abandonment of its use may have saved him money, or contributed to his health; nevertheless, the surrender of that right caused the promise, and, having the right to contract with reference to the subject matter, the abandonment of the use was a sufficient consideration to uphold the promise." Abstinence from the use of intoxicating liquors was held to furnish a good consideration for a promissory note in Lindell v. Rokes, 60 Mo. 249. The cases cited by the defendant on this question are not in point. In Mallory v. Gillett, 21 N. Y. 412; Belknap v. Bender, 74 N. Y. 446; and Berry v. Brown, 107 N. Y. 659, 14 N. E. Rep. 289, the promise was in contravention of that provision of the statute of frauds which declares void all promises to answer for the debts of third persons unless reduced to writing. In Beaumont v. Reeve, Shir. Lead. Cas. 7, and Porterfield v. Butler, 47 Miss. 165, the question was whether a moral obligation furnishes sufficient consideration to uphold a subsequent express promise. In Duvoll v. Wilson, 9 Barb. 487, and Wilbur v. Warren, 104 N. Y. 192, 10 N. E. Rep. 263, the proposition involved was whether an executory covenant against encumbrances in a deed given in consideration of natural love and affection could be enforced. In Vanderbilt v. Schreyer, 91 N. Y. 392, the plaintiff contracted with defendant to build a house, agreeing to accept in part payment therefor a specific bond and mortgage. Afterwards he refused to finish his contract unless the defendant would guaranty its payment, which was done. It was held that the guaranty could not be enforced for want of consideration; for in building the house the plaintiff only did that which he had contracted to do. And in Robinson v. Jewett, 116 N. Y. 40, 22 N. E. Rep. 224, the court simply held that 'the performance of an act which the party is under a legal obligation to perform cannot constitute a consideration for a new contract.' It will be observed that the agreement which we have been considering was within the condemnation of the statute of frauds, because not to be performed within a year, and not in writing. But this defense the promisor could waive, and his letter and oral statements subsequent to the date of final performance on the part of the promisee must be held to amount to a waiver. Were it otherwise, the statute could not now be invoked in aid of the defendant. It does not appear on the face of the complaint that the agreement is one prohibited by the statute of frauds, and therefore such defense could not be made available unless set up in the answer. Porter v. Wormser, 94 N. Y. 431, 450. This was not done.

In further consideration of the questions presented, then, it must be deemed established for the purposes of this appeal that on the 31st day of January, 1875, defendant's testator was indebted to William E. Story, 2d, in the sum of $5,000; and, if this action were founded on that contract, it would be barred by the statute of limitations, which has been pleaded, but on that date the nephew wrote to his uncle as follows: "Dear Uncle: I am 21 years old today, and I am now my own boss; and I believe, according to agreement, that there is due me $5,000. I have lived up to the contract to the letter in every sense of the word." A few days later, and on February 6th, the uncle replied, and, so far as it is material to this controversy, the reply is as follows: "Dear Nephew: Your letter of the 31st ult. came to hand all right, saying that you had lived up to the promise made to me several years ago. I have no doubt but you have, for which you shall have $5,000, as I promised you. I had the money in the bank the day you was 21 years old that I intend for you, and you shall have the money certain. Now, Willie, I don't intend to interfere with this money in any way until I think you are capable of taking care of it, and the sooner that time comes the better it will please me. I would hate very much to have you start out in some adventure that you thought all right, and lose this money in one year. * * * This money you have earned much easier than I did, besides acquiring good habits at the same time; and you are quite welcome to the money. Hope you will make good use of it. * * * W. E. STORY. P. S. You can consider this money on interest" The trial court found as a fact that 'said letter was received by said William E. Story, 2d, who thereafter consented that said money should remain with the said William E. Story in accordance with the terms and conditions of said letter.' And further, 'that afterwards, on the 1st day of March, 1877, with the knowledge and consent of his said uncle, he duly sold, transferred, and assigned all his right, title, and interest in and to said sum of $5,000 to his wife, Libbie H. Story, who thereafter duly sold, transferred, and assigned the same to the plaintiff in this action.' We must now consider the effect of the letter and the nephew's assent thereto. Were the relations of the parties thereafter that of debtor and creditor simply, or that of trustee and *cestui que trust?* If the former, then this action is not maintainable, because barred by lapse of time. If the latter, the result must be otherwise. No particular expressions are necessary to create a trust. Any language clearly showing the settler's intention is sufficient if the property and disposition of it are definitely stated. Lewin, Trusts, 55. A person in the legal possession of money or property acknowledging a trust with the assent of the *cestui que trust* becomes from that time a trustee if the acknowledgment be founded on a valuable consideration. His antecedent relation to the subject, whatever it may have been, no longer controls. 2 Story, Eq. Jur., ß 972. If before a declaration of trust a party be a mere debtor, a subsequent agreement recognizing the fund as already in his hands, and stipulating for its investment on the creditor's account, will have the effect to create a trust. Day v. Roth, 18 N. Y. 448. It is essential that the letter, interpreted in the light of surrounding circumstances, must show an intention on the part of the uncle to become a trustee before he will be held to have become such; but in an effort to ascertain the construction which should be given to it we are also to observe the rule that the language of the promisor is to be interpreted in the sense in which he had reason to suppose it was understood by the promisee. White v. Hoyt, 73 N. Y. 505, 511. At the time the uncle wrote the letter he was indebted to his nephew in the sum of $5,000, and payment had been requested. The uncle, recognizing the indebtedness, wrote the nephew that he would keep the money until he deemed him capable of taking care of it. He did not say, 'I will pay you at some other time,' or use language that would indicate that the relation of debtor and creditor would continue. On the contrary, his language indicated that he had set apart the money the nephew had 'earned,' for him, so that when he should be capable of taking care of it he should receive it with interest. He said: 'I had the money in the bank the day you were 21 years old that I intend for you, and you shall have the money certain.' That he had set apart the money is further evidenced by the next sentence: 'Now, Willie, I don't intend to interfere with this money in any way until I think you are capable of taking care of it.' Certainly the uncle must have intended that his nephew should understand that the promise not 'to interfere with this money' referred to the money in the bank, which he declared was not only there when the nephew became 21 years old, but was intended for him. True, he did not use the word 'trust,' or state that the money was deposited in the name of William E. Story, 2d, or in his own name in trust for him, but the language used must have been intended to assure the nephew that his money had been set apart for him, to be kept without interference until he should be capable of taking care of it, for the uncle said in substance and in effect: "This money you have earned much easier than I did. . . . You are quite welcome to. I had it in the bank the day you were 21 years old, and don't intend to interfere with it in any way until I think you are capable of taking care of it; and the sooner that time comes the better it will please me." In this declaration there is not lacking a single element necessary for the creation of a valid trust, and to that declaration the nephew assented. The learned judge who wrote the opinion of the general term seems to have taken the view that the trust was executed during the life-time of defendant's testator by payment to the nephew, but, as it does not appear from the order that the judgment was reversed on the facts, we must assume the facts to be as found by the trial court, and those facts support its judgment. The order appealed from should be reversed, and the judgment of the special term affirmed, with costs payable out of the estate. All concur.

NOTES AND QUESTIONS

1. *Origin of the "peppercorn doctrine."* The "peppercorn doctrine" apparently originated in 2 Blackstone Commentaries on the Laws of England 440 (5th Ed. 1773) ("[I]n case of leases, always reserving a rent, though it be but a peppercorn [such] . . . considerations will, in the eyes of the law, convert the gift . . . into a contract."). This usage overlaps with the doctrine of nominal consideration. Restatement (Second) of Contracts § 71, *cmt. b* ("Moreover, a mere pretense of bargain does not suffice, as where there is a false recital of consideration or where the purported consideration is merely nominal"). See Comment, "The Peppercorn Reconsidered: Why a Promise to Sell Blackacre for Nominal Consideration Is Not Binding, But Should Be," 97 Nw. U. L. Rev. 1809 (2003).

2. *Restatement approach.* The Restatement (Second) of Contracts § 79, *comment a* reiterates the principle that if the requirement of consideration is met, there is no additional requirement of a gain, advantage, or benefit to the promisor, or a loss, disadvantage, or detriment to the promisee. Moreover, equivalence in the exchange is also not required: ". . . it has sometimes been said that consideration must consist of a 'benefit to the promisor' or a 'detriment to the promisee' . . . [b]ut experience has shown that these are not essential elements of a bargain or of an enforceable contract, and they are negated as requirements . . . [t]his Section makes that negation explicit."

3. *The trust as an alternative to unenforceable donative promises.* After holding that the nephew's acts of forbearance were adequate consideration for the promised $5,000, the *Hamer v. Sidway* court concludes its opinion with a discussion of the law of trusts. "A trust . . . is a fiduciary relationship with respect to property, subjecting the person by whom the title to the property is

held to equitable duties to deal with the property for the benefit of another person, which arises as a result of a manifestation of an intention to create it." Restatement (Second) Trusts § 2 (1959). As E. Allan Farnsworth notes, a simple declaration by a donor that he holds certain specified property owned by the donor "in trust" for a beneficiary creates an enforceable equitable obligation on the part of the donor-trustee to deal with that property for the benefit of the beneficiary under the terms of the trust. E. Allan Farnsworth, "Promises and Paternalism," 41 Wm. & Mary L. Rev. 385, 399–400 (2000). Importantly, creation of a trust does not require any consideration—the trust obligation arises from the expressly declared intention of the trustee to create the trust. Restatement (Second) Trusts § 2 (1959).

4.   *Contract, trust, and the statute of limitations.* Note that in *Hamer v. Sidway*, the existence of a valid trust under which the uncle would hold the $5,000 was not necessary to the court's initial finding of an enforceable contract. Why did the court find it necessary to examine whether the uncle had also created a trust?

5.   *Legality of the promisee's detriment.* The *Hamer* case makes much of the fact that the promisee's detriment must be "legal." So, for example, what happens if the uncle promises to pay his nephew for refraining from doing that which is illegal, such as using illegal drugs? Is such a promise supported by consideration? Restatement (Second) of Contracts § 72 provides that "any performance which is bargained for is consideration." Thus, even if refraining from illegal activity was bargained for, it would constitute consideration. See Restatement (Second) of Contracts § 72, *cmt. d* ("Nor does the Section require that the consideration or the promise be lawful."). Of course, if the uncle sought a promise from the nephew to do something illegal as opposed to refrain from doing something illegal, the contract would not be enforceable under the public policy concepts discussed in Chapter 7 (illegal contracts). However, the distinction does mean that even a promise to do something illegal is supported by adequate consideration—it simply is not enforceable by the courts.

BATSAKIS V. DEMOTSIS

Texas Court of Civil Appeals
226 S.W.2d 673 (1949)

McGILL, Justice.

This is an appeal from a judgment of the 57th judicial District Court of Bexar County. Appellant was plaintiff and appellee was defendant in the trial court. The parties will be so designated.

Plaintiff sued defendant to recover $2,000 with interest at the rate of 8% per annum from April 2, 1942, alleged to be due on the following instrument, being a translation from the original, which is written in the Greek language:

Peiraeus
April 2, 1942

Mr. George Batsakis
Konstantinou Diadohou #7
Peiraeus

Mr. Batsakis:

I state by my present (letter) that I received today from you the amount of two thousand dollars ($2,000.00) of United States of America money, which I borrowed from you for the support of my family during these difficult days and because it is impossible for me to transfer dollars of my own from America.

The above amount I accept with the expressed promise that I will return to you again in American dollars either at the end of the present war or even before in the event that you might be able to find a way to collect them (dollars) from my representative in America to whom I shall write and give him an order relative to this. You understand until the final execution (payment) to the above amount an eight per cent interest will be added and paid together with the principal.

I thank you and I remain yours with respects.

The recipient,
(Signed) Eugenia The Demotsis.

Trial to the court without the intervention of a jury resulted in a judgment in favor of plaintiff for $750.00 principal, and interest at the rate of 8% per annum from April 2, 1942 to the date of judgment, totaling $1163.83, with interest thereon at the rate of 8% per annum until paid. Plaintiff has perfected his appeal.

The court sustained certain special exceptions of plaintiff to defendant's first amended original answer on which the case was tried, and struck therefrom paragraphs II, III and V. Defendant excepted to such action of the court, but has not cross-assigned error here. The answer, stripped of such paragraphs, consisted of a general denial contained in paragraph I thereof, and of paragraph IV, which is as follows:

IV. That under the circumstances alleged in Paragraph II of this answer, the consideration upon which said written instrument sued upon by plaintiff herein is founded, is wanting and has failed to the extent of $1975.00, and defendant pleads specially under the verification hereinafter made the want and failure of consideration stated, and now tenders, as defendant has heretofore tendered to plaintiff, $25.00 as the value of the loan of money received by defendant from plaintiff, together with interest thereon.

Further, in connection with this plea of want and failure of consideration defendant alleges that she at no time received from plaintiff himself or from anyone for plaintiff any money or thing of value other than, as hereinbefore alleged, the original loan of 500,000 drachmae. That at the time of the loan by plaintiff to defendant of said 500,000 drachmae the value of 500,000 drachmae in the Kingdom of Greece in dollars of money of the United States of America, was $25.00, and also at said time the value of 500,000 drachmae of Greek money in the United States of America in dollars was $25.00 of money of the United States of America. The plea of want and failure of consideration is verified by defendant as follows.

The allegations in paragraph II which were stricken, referred to in paragraph IV, were that the instrument sued on was signed and delivered in the Kingdom of Greece on or about April 2, 1942, at which time both plaintiff and defendant were residents of and residing in the Kingdom of Greece, and

[Defendant] avers that on or about April 2, 1942 she owned money and property and had credit in the States of America, but was then and there in the Kingdom of Greece in straitened financial circumstances due to the conditions produced by World War II and could not make use of her money and property and credit existing in the United States of America. That in the circumstances the plaintiff agreed to and did lend to defendant the sum of 500,000 drachmae, which at that time, on or about April 2, 1942, had the value of $25.00 in money of the United States of America. That the said plaintiff, knowing defendant's financial distress and desire to return to the United States of America, exacted of her the written instrument plaintiff sues upon, which was a promise by her to pay to him the sum of $2,000.00 of United States of America money.

Plaintiff specially excepted to paragraph IV because the allegations thereof were insufficient to allege either want of consideration or failure of consideration, in that it affirmatively appears therefrom that defendant received what was agreed to be delivered to her, and that plaintiff breached no agreement. The court overruled this exception, and such action is assigned as error. Error is also assigned because of the court's failure to enter judgment for the whole unpaid balance of the principal of the instrument with interest as therein provided.

Defendant testified that she did receive 500,000 drachmas from plaintiff. It is not clear whether she received all the 500,000 drachmas or only a portion of them before she signed the instrument in question. Her testimony clearly shows that the understanding of the parties was that plaintiff would give her the 500,000 drachmas if she would sign the instrument. She testified:

Q. Who suggested the figure of $2,000.00?

A. That was how he asked me from the beginning. He said he will give me five hundred thousand drachmas provided I signed that I would pay him $2,000.00 American money.

The transaction amounted to a sale by plaintiff of the 500,000 drachmas in consideration of the execution of the instrument sued on, by defendant. It is not contended that the drachmas had no value. Indeed, the judgment indicates that the trial court placed a value of $750.00 on them or on the other consideration which plaintiff gave defendant for the instrument if he believed plaintiff's testimony. Therefore the plea of want of consideration was unavailing. A plea of want of consideration amounts to a contention that the instrument never became a valid obligation in the first place. National Bank of Commerce v. Williams, 125 Tex. 619, 84 S.W. 2d 691.

Mere inadequacy of consideration will not void a contract. 10 Tex. Jur., Contracts, Sec. 89, p. 150; Chastain v. Texas Christian Missionary Society, Tex. Civ. App., 78 S.W. 2d 728, loc. cit. 731(3), Wr. Ref.

Nor was the plea of failure of consideration availing. Defendant got exactly what she contracted for according to her own testimony. The court should have rendered judgment in favor of plaintiff against defendant for the principal sum of $2,000.00 evidenced by the instrument sued on, with interest as therein provided. We construe the provision relating to interest as providing for interest at the rate of 8% per annum. The judgment is reformed so as to award appellant a recovery against appellee of $2,000.00 with interest thereon at the rate of 8% per annum from April 2, 1942. Such judgment will bear interest at the rate of 8% per annum until paid on $2,000.00 thereof and on the balance interest at the rate of 6% per annum. As so reformed, the judgment is affirmed.

Reformed and affirmed.

NOTES AND QUESTIONS

1.   *Terminology—"Want" or "failure" of consideration.* Eugenia Demotsis argued her promise to repay should not be enforced because there was no consideration. Did George Batsakis make a loan of 500,000 drachmae in return for her promise to repay $2,000? If so, did she obtain what she sought?

2. *Inadequacy of consideration.* Eugenia Demotsis also argued that at that the time of the loan and her promise, 500,000 drachmae were worth only $25, and therefore her promise to repay $2,000 was not supported by consideration. What is the court's view of this question? Restatement (Second) of Contracts § 79(b) specifically provides that if the bargain was sought, the consideration doctrine does not impose an additional requirement of equivalence in values. *Comment c* states that ordinarily the parties are free to fix their own values on the matters exchanged in a contract. Valuation is remitted to the parties because they are better able to evaluate the particular and peculiar circumstances associated with the transaction. However, *comment e* provides that "gross inadequacy of consideration" may be relevant in the application of other contract rules such as fraud, mistake, misrepresentation, duress, or undue influence. Do you think gross inadequacy was the basis of her argument? If so, why did the lawyer fail to make those arguments? Apparently concerned with the fairness of the transaction, the trial court reduced the promise to $750. But on appeal the $2,000 promise was reinstated. Why did the appeal court reinstate the promise of $2,000? One contracts commentator argues the case unjustly enforces a promise made under duress. See Charles Fried, Contract as Promise 109–111 (1981). Do you agree?

3. *Doctrine of fair exchange.* Contract law's theoretical resistance to balancing the equities under the consideration doctrine presents a serious problem. Given that consideration is the leading theory of contract obligation, its failure to promote fairness is a serious flaw. Is the flaw real or illusory? In *Krell v. Codman*, 28 N.E. 578, 154 Mass. 454 (1891), Oliver Wendell Holmes, then a judge on the Massachusetts Supreme Judicial Court, observed that "we presume that, in the absence of fraud, oppression, or unconscionableness, the courts would not inquire into the amount of such consideration." Thus, since early times, the application of the inadequacy doctrine discussed in the note above has been tempered through a judicial application of fairness. It is therefore more accurate to suggest that the adequacies of consideration will not be balanced in the absence of a reason to do so. When such a reason arises, the inadequacies of the considerations will be very important in determining whether an enforceable contract exists. Removing consideration removes a theory of obligation. Is this the same as attacking a valid contract supported by valid consideration on the basis of "fraud, oppression, or unconscionableness?"

You should see at this early point in your study that no contract at all (because of the failure of consideration) is a different species of legal problem than an otherwise valid contract that is not enforceable (because of some formation difficulty). Some have argued that the objectification of classical contract law moved the law away from fairness. Others argue that fairness has always been a part of consideration theory and application. Compare Morton J. Horwitz, "The Historical Foundations of Modern Contract Law," 87 Harv. L. Rev. 917, 923 (1974) ("The most important aspect of the eighteenth century conception of exchange is an equitable limitation on contractual obligation.

Under the modern will theory, the extent of contractual obligation depends upon the convergence of individual desires. The equitable theory, by contrast, limited and sometimes denied contractual obligation by reference to the fairness of the underlying exchange.") with A. W. B. Simpson, "The Horwitz Thesis and the History of Contracts," 46 U. Chi. L. Rev. 533, 542 (1979) ("It is my view that the differences Horwitz claims to have discovered between eighteenth-century and early nineteenth-century contract law are, for the most part, illusory.").

4.   *International civil law doctrine of fair exchange.* The doctrine of fair exchange has roots in civil law as well. For an international view of the doctrine of fair exchange, see John P. Dawson, "Economic Duress and the Fair Exchange in French and German Law," 11 Tulane L. Rev. 345 (1937) (arguing economic duress cannot be divorced from the doctrine of fair exchange).

5.   *Policing inadequacy of consideration.* A famous Columbia Law Review Note—"The Peppercorn Theory of Consideration and the Doctrine of Fair Exchange in Contract Law," 35 Colum. L. Rev. 1090, 1090–92 (1935)— addresses whether courts do (or should) use consideration doctrine to police the fairness of a bargain. Consideration, according to the Note, can be described by two inconsistent theories. On the one hand, consideration is merely a formal requirement—if it exists, courts should not inquire further into whether the consideration given in exchange for another promise or performance is or is not "fair." If consideration is not present on one side of an exchange, the resulting promise must be enforced under some alternative theory of obligation (such as promissory estoppel or unjust enrichment) or held to be unenforceable altogether. See id.

Alternatively, consideration may be used to assure a "fair exchange." As the note observes, while courts routinely claim that they cannot inquire as to the adequacy or fairness of the consideration, they also routinely do so under the guise of doctrines such as duress and fraud. See id.

The doctrine of consideration provides fertile ground for evaluating the competing approaches of the Formalist and Realist schools discussed in Chapter 1. On the one hand, as an abstract rule, the requirement that promises be supported by a consideration to be legally enforceable appears to be one that courts can apply easily, definitively, and at low cost. In evaluating whether consideration exists, a court need only ask whether the promise is supported by a bargained-for exchange, and they do not need to spend time and resources evaluating the value of each party's consideration. Thus, the Formalist rule that courts only hold promises unenforceable where there has been a *failure* of consideration, but will not inquire into the *adequacy* of consideration, provides an apparently bright-line rule that can govern any case.

But strict adherence to bright-line legal rules, such as the consideration doctrine, will always produce apparently harsh results at the margins. It must always be remembered that judges are human beings and will react to such harshness in several ways. First, they may apply the abstract rule despite such harsh results, perhaps decrying the harshness of the rule and hoping for a legislative change. Second, a court might also attempt explicitly to ignore or change the abstract rule with respect to the current case, thus creating a new rule to govern similar situations. Finally, a court can pretend to apply the abstract rule but reach a result other than that required by strict application of the rule. As noted in the quote from "The Peppercorn Theory of Consideration," for example, courts have often asserted that they do not police the *adequacy* of the purported considerations between the parties. But in reality, judges also often twist consideration doctrine where necessary to achieve the "correct" result. This is particularly the case when the plaintiff is particularly sympathetic—occasionally described as the "widows & orphans problem"—or when the disparity in considerations between the parties suggests that one of the parties may have engaged in fraud, duress, or other oppressive conduct. What benefits or problems can you describe with respect to each of these approaches?

c. The Past Consideration Doctrine

The bargain requirement of consideration requires the maker of a promise to seek something in return. When the promise trails the benefit, it is grounded in the past and thus does not seek anything in the future. Such "trailing promises" present troubling questions in classical contract law. A trailing promise, like a gratuitous promise, is not enforceable, even if motivated by understandable gratitude. Trailing promises are arguably more pernicious than problems under the *Dougherty v. Salt* donative-promise principle. While the context of a gratuitous promise under the donative-promise principle is likely to be family, the context of a trailing promise is likely to be commercial. The promises are likely generated under different contexts because gratitude for past conduct extends far beyond the family relationship to, as the next case illustrates, the work environment and other commercial contexts. The promisee's "expectation" of performance is significantly elevated in these circumstances. Does the law take this into account? In other circumstances, promissory estoppel serves as an equitable back-up to failed consideration cases—particularly in the commercial context where the likelihood of reliance is elevated. But promissory estoppel, like consideration, is forward looking. The promisor's motivation for making a promise is irrelevant. As a result, trailing promises will, by definition, both fail to provide consideration and fail to satisfy the promissory estoppel requirements, as classically defined. Consideration is lacking because the promisee's promise or performance was not sought as it has already passed. With promissory estoppel, the promisee's detrimental reliance was not induced by the promisor's promise because the promise occurs after the act is performed. (It is impossible to do an act in reliance on a promise that has not yet been made.) In both cases, the promise or conduct of the promisee precedes the promise and therefore cannot be based upon that promise.

Given promissory estoppel's historical role in filling in for failed consideration cases, one might expect the doctrine to be more lenient. In the case to follow, determine if the employer's promise to pay retirement benefits preceded or lagged the employee retirement decision. If the latter, at least the act of retiring might not satisfy the rigors of promissory estoppel-based "reliance" but what of later reliance? Is promissory estoppel frozen in time or can a promise, once made, continue to induce other forms of reliance?

HAYES V. PLANTATIONS STEEL COMPANY

Supreme Court of Rhode Island
438 A.2d 1091 (1982)

SHEA, Justice.

The defendant employer, Plantations Steel Company (Plantations), appeals from a Superior Court judgment for the plaintiff employee, Edward J. Hayes (Hayes). The trial justice, sitting without a jury, found that Plantations was obligated to Hayes on the basis of an implied-in-fact contract to pay him a yearly pension of $5,000. The award covered three years in which payment had not been made. The trial justice ruled, also, that Hayes had made a sufficient showing of detrimental reliance upon Plantations' promise to pay to give rise to its obligation based on the theory of promissory estoppel. The trial justice, however, found in part for Plantations in ruling that the payments to Hayes were not governed by the Employee Retirement Income Security Act, 29 U.S.C.A. §§ 1001–1461 (West 1975), and consequently he was not entitled to attorney's fees under § 1132(g) of that act. Both parties have appealed.

We reverse the findings of the trial justice regarding Plantations' contractual obligation to pay Hayes a pension. Consequently we need not deal with the cross-appeal concerning the award of attorney's fees under the federal statute.

Plantations is a closely held Rhode Island corporation engaged in the manufacture of steel reinforcing rods for use in concrete construction. The company was founded by Hugo R. Mainelli, Sr., and Alexander A. DiMartino. A dispute between their two families in 1976 and 1977 left the DiMartinos in full control of the corporation. Hayes was an employee of the corporation from 1947 until his retirement in 1972 at age of sixty-five. He began with Plantations as an "estimator and draftsman" and ended his career as general manager, a position of considerable responsibility. Starting in January 1973 and continuing until January 1976, Hayes received the annual sum of $5,000 from Plantations. Hayes instituted this action in December 1977, after the then company management refused to make any further payments.

Hayes testified that in January 1972 he announced his intention to retire the following July, after twenty-five years of continuous service. He decided to retire because he had worked continuously for fifty-one years. He stated, however, that he would not have retired had he not expected to receive a pension. After he stopped working for Plantations, he sought no other employment.

Approximately one week before his actual retirement Hayes spoke with Hugo R. Mainelli, Jr., who was then an officer and a stockholder of Plantations. This conversation was the first and only one concerning payments of a pension to Hayes during retirement. Mainelli said that the company "would take care" of him. There was no mention of a sum of money or a percentage of salary that Hayes would receive. There was no formal authorization for payments by Plantations' shareholders and/or board of directors. Indeed, there was never any formal provision for a pension plan for any employee other than for unionized employees, who benefit from an arrangement through their union. The plaintiff was not a union member.

Mr. Mainelli, Jr., testified that his father, Hugo R. Mainelli, Sr., had authorized the first payment "as a token of appreciation for the many years of (Hayes's) service." Furthermore, "it was implied that that check would continue on an annual basis." Mainelli also testified that it was his "personal intention" that the payments would continue for "as long as I was around."

Mainelli testified that after Hayes's retirement, he would visit the premises each year to say hello and renew old acquaintances. During the course of his visits, Hayes would thank Mainelli for the previous check and ask how long it would continue so that he could plan an orderly retirement.

The payments were discontinued after 1976. At that time a succession of several poor business years plus the stockholders' dispute, resulting in the takeover by the DiMartino family, contributed to the decision to stop the payments.

The trial justice ruled that Plantations owed Hayes his annual sum of $5,000 for the years 1977 through 1979. The ruling implied that barring bankruptcy or the cessation of business for any other reason, Hayes had a right to expect continued annual payments.

The trial justice found that Hugo Mainelli, Jr.'s statement that Hayes would be taken care of after his retirement was a promise. Although no sum of money was mentioned in 1972, the four annual payments of $5,000 established that otherwise unspecified terms of the contract. The trial justice also found that Hayes supplied consideration for the promise by voluntarily retiring, because he was under no obligation to do so. From the words and conduct of the parties and from the surrounding circumstances, the trial justice concluded that there existed an implied contract obligating the company to pay a pension to Hayes for life. The trial justice made a further finding that even if Hayes had not truly bargained for a pension by voluntarily retiring, he had nevertheless incurred the detriment of foregoing other employment in reliance upon the company's promise. He specifically held that Hayes's retirement was in response to the promise and held also that Hayes refrained from seeking other employment in further reliance thereon.

The findings of fact of a trial justice sitting without a jury are entitled to great weight when reviewed by this court. His findings will not be disturbed unless it can be shown that they are clearly wrong or that the trial justice misconceived or overlooked material evidence. Lisi v. Marra, R.I., 424 A.2d 1052 (1981); Raheb v. Lemenski, 115 R.I. 576, 350 A.2d 397 (1976). After careful review of the record, however, we conclude that the trial justice's findings and conclusions must be reversed.

Assuming for the purpose of this discussion that Plantations in legal effect made a promise to Hayes, we must ask whether Hayes did supply the required consideration that would make the promise binding? And, if Hayes did not supply consideration, was his alleged reliance sufficiently induced by the promise to estop defendant from denying its obligation to him? We answer both questions in the negative.

We turn first to the problem of consideration. The facts at bar do not present the case of an express contract. As the trial justice stated, the existence of a contract in this case must be determined from all the circumstances of the parties' conduct and words. Although words were expressed initially in the remark that Hayes "would be taken care of," any contract in this case would be more in the nature of an implied contract. Certainly the statement of Hugo Mainelli, Jr., standing alone is not an expression of a direct and definite promise to pay Hayes a pension. Though we are analyzing an implied contract, nevertheless we must address the question of consideration.

Contracts implied in fact require the element of consideration to support them as is required in express contracts. The only difference between the two is the manner in which the parties manifest their assent. J. Koury Steel Erectors, Inc. v. San-Vel Concrete Corp., R.I., 387 A. 2d 694 (1978); Bailey v. West, 105 R.I. 61, 249 A.2d 414 (1969). In this jurisdiction, consideration consists either in some right, interest, or benefit accruing to one party or some forbearance, detriment, or responsibility given, suffered, or undertaken by the other. See Dockery v. Greenfield, 86 R.I. 464, 136 A.2d 682 (1957); Darcey v. Darcey, 29 R.I. 384, 71 A. 595 (1909). Valid consideration furthermore must be bargained for. It must induce the return act or promise. To be valid, therefore, the purported consideration must not have been delivered before a promise is executed, that is, given without reference to the promise. Plowman v. Indian Refining Co., 20 F. Supp. 1 (E.D. Ill. 1937). Consideration is therefore a test of the enforceability of executory promises, Angel v. Murray, 113 R.I. 482, 322 A.2d 630 (1974), and has no legal effect when rendered in the past and apart from an alleged exchange in the present. Zanturjian v. Boornazian, 25 R.I. 151, 55 A. 199 (1903).

In the case before us, Plantations' promise to pay Hayes a pension is quite clearly not supported by any consideration supplied by Hayes. Hayes had announced his intent to retire well in advance of any promise, and therefore the intention to retire was arrived at without regard to any promise by Plantations. Although Hayes may have had in mind the receipt of a pension when he first informed Plantations, his expectation was not based on any statement made to him or on any conduct of the company officer relative to him in January 1972. In deciding to retire, Hayes acted on his own initiative. Hayes's long years of dedicated service also is legally insufficient because his service too was rendered without being induced by Plantations' promise. See Plowman v. Indian Refining Co., supra.

Clearly then this is not a case in which Plantations' promise was meant to induce Hayes to refrain from retiring when he could have chosen to do so in return for further service. 1 Williston on Contracts, § 130B (3d ed., Jaeger 1957). Nor was the promise made to encourage long service from the start of his employment. Weesner v. Electric Power Board of Chattanooga, 48 Tenn.App. 178, 344 S.W.2d 766 (1961). Instead, the testimony establishes that Plantations' promise was intended "as a token of appreciation for (Hayes's) many years of service." As such it was in the nature of a gratuity paid to Hayes for as long as the company chose. In Spickelmier Industries, Inc. v. Passander, 172 Ind. App. 49, 359 N.E.2d 563 (1977), an employer's promise to an employee to pay him a year-end bonus was unenforceable because it was made after the employee had performed his contractual responsibilities for that year.

The plaintiff's most relevant citations are still inapposite to the present case. Bredemann v. Vaughan Mfg. Co., 40 Ill. App. 2d 232, 188 N.E.2d 746 (1963), presents similar yet distinguishable facts. There, the appellate court reversed a summary judgment granted to the defendant employer, stating that a genuine issue of material fact existed regarding whether the plaintiff's retirement was in consideration of her employer's promise to pay her a lifetime pension. As in the present case, the employer made the promise one week prior to the employee's retirement, and in almost the same words. However, Bredemann is distinguishable because the court characterized that promise as a concrete offer to pay if she would retire immediately. In fact, the defendant wanted her to retire. Id. 188 N.E. 2d at 749. On the contrary, Plantations in this case did not actively seek Hayes's retirement. DiMartino, one of Plantations' founders, testified that he did not want Hayes to retire. Unlike Bredemann, here Hayes announced his unsolicited intent to retire.

Hayes also argues that the work he performed during the week between the promise and the date of his retirement constituted sufficient consideration to support the promise. He relies on Ulmann v. Sunset-McKee Co., 221 F.2d 128 (9th Cir. 1955), in which the court ruled that work performed during the one-week period of the employee's notice of impending retirement constituted consideration for the employer's offer of a pension that the employee had solicited some months previously. But there the court stated that its prime reason for upholding the agreement was that sufficient consideration existed in the employee's consent not to compete with his employer. These circumstances do not appear in our case. Hayes left his employment because he no longer desired to work. He was not contemplating other job offers or considering going into competition with Plantations. Although Plantations did not want Hayes to leave, it did not try to deter him, nor did it seek to prevent Hayes from engaging in other activity.

Hayes argues in the alternative that even if Plantations' promise was not the product of an exchange, its duty is grounded properly in the theory of promissory estoppel. This court adopted the theory of promissory estoppel in East Providence Credit Union v. Geremia, 103 R.I. 597, 601, 239 A.2d 725, 727 (1968) (quoting 1 Restatement Contracts § 90 at 110 (1932)) stating:

A promise which the promisor should reasonably expect to induce action or forbearance of a definite and substantial character on the part of the promisee and which does induce such action or forbearance is binding if injustice can be avoided only by enforcement of its promise.

In East Providence Credit Union this court said that the doctrine of promissory estoppel is invoked "as a substitute for a consideration, rendering a gratuitous promise enforceable as a contract." Id. To restate the matter differently, "the acts of reliance by the promisee to his detriment (provide) a substitute for consideration." Id.

Hayes urges that in the absence of a bargained-for promise the facts require application of the doctrine of promissory estoppel. He stresses that he retired voluntarily while expecting to receive a pension. He would not have otherwise retired. Nor did he seek other employment.

We disagree with this contention largely for the reasons already stated. One of the essential elements of the doctrine of promissory estoppel is that the promise must induce the promisee's action or forbearance. The particular act in this regard is plaintiff's decision whether or not to retire. As we stated earlier, the record indicates that he made the decision on his own initiative. In other words, the conversation between Hayes and Mainelli which occurred a week before Hayes left his employment cannot be said to have induced his decision to leave. He had reached that decision long before.

An example taken from the restatement provides a meaningful contrast:

> 2. A promises B to pay him an annuity during B's life. B thereupon resigns profitable employment, as A expected that he might. B receives the annuity for some years, in the meantime becoming disqualified from again obtaining good employment. A's promise is binding. 1 Restatement Contracts § 90 at 111 (1932).

In Feinberg v. Pfeiffer Co., 322 S.W.2d 163 (Mo.App.1959), the plaintiff-employee had worked for her employer for nearly forty years. The defendant corporation's board of directors resolved, in view of her long years of service, to obligate itself to pay "retirement privileges" to her. The resolution did not require the plaintiff to retire. Instead, the decision whether and when to retire remained entirely her own. The board then informed her of its resolution. The plaintiff worked for eighteen months more before retiring. She sued the corporation when it reduced her monthly checks seven years later. The court held that a pension contract existed between the parties. Although continued employment was not a consideration to her receipt of retirement benefits, the court found sufficient reliance on the part of the plaintiff to support her claim. The court based its decision upon the above restatement example, that is, the defendant informed the plaintiff of its plan, and the plaintiff in reliance thereon, retired. Feinberg presents factors that also appear in the case at bar. There, the plaintiff had worked many years and desired to retire; she would not have left had she not been able to rely on a pension; and once retired, she sought no other employment.

However, the important distinction between Feinberg and the case before us is that in Feinberg the employer's decision definitely shaped the thinking of the plaintiff. In this case the promise did not. It is not reasonable to infer from the facts that Hugo R. Mainelli, Jr., expected retirement to result from his conversation with Hayes. Hayes had given notice of his intention seven months previously. Here there was thus no inducement to retire which would satisfy the demands of § 90 of the [R]estatement. Nor can it be said that Hayes's refraining from other employment was "action or forbearance of a definite and substantial character." The underlying assumption of Hayes's initial decision to retire was that upon leaving the defendant's employ, he would no longer work. It is impossible to say that he changed his position any more so because of what Mainelli had told him in light of his own initial decision. These circumstances do not lead to a conclusion that injustice can be avoided only by enforcement of Plantations' promise. Hayes received $20,000 over the course of four years. He inquired each year about whether he could expect a check for the following year. Obviously, there was no absolute certainty on his part that the pension would continue. Furthermore, in the face of his uncertainty, the mere fact that payment for several years did occur is insufficient by itself to meet the requirements of reliance under the doctrine of promissory estoppel.

For the foregoing reasons, the defendant's appeal is sustained and the judgment of the Superior Court is reversed. The papers of the case are remanded to the Superior Court.

NOTES AND QUESTIONS

1. *Searching for a theory of obligation.* The trial court determined that the company employer, through an officer, made a promise to pay a pension and that Hayes supplied consideration for the promise by voluntarily retiring, because he was under no obligation to do so. The trial court focused on the promisee's motivation for its retirement decision. Is such motivation relevant to the consideration question? The Supreme Court applies the bargain theory of consideration, which requires that the company seek the retirement. Restatement (Second) § 71(1)–(2). If the conduct is sought, no further inquiry is normally justified to determine the adequacy of the consideration. Restatement (Second) of Contracts § 79. Why did the Supreme Court determine the company did not seek the retirement? Did it improperly conflate the employer's motive (why it sought the retirement) with whether it sought the retirement? Restatement (Second) of Contracts § 81. The Court also determined that the continued employment for one week after the promise was made was not consideration. It distinguished another case that involved a covenant not to compete. What is the relevance of the covenant? If the employer sought the employee's continued employment for another week, the employment should satisfy the doctrine unless the Court is secretly applying an "inadequacy" test. Do you think the company sought one more week of continued employment? Assuming for the moment that consideration does not exist, was the Supreme Court's analysis correct regarding promissory estoppel? Why did the Court reject the promissory estoppel argument? As the Court suggests, promissory estoppel requires "substantial reliance." Why would a fairness doctrine like promissory estoppel require substantial reliance when the adequacy of consideration is never measured? Are those theories inconsistent?

2. *Pernicious problem.* For the reasons mentioned before the case, the past consideration doctrine creates problems not inherent in the donor-promise principle. Promissory estoppel would protect a promisee's future reliance or change in position under that doctrine even if the conduct was not bargained for under consideration theory. However, the past consideration doctrine precludes the application of even promissory estoppel, at least in cases involving temporally immediate reliance. Is the reliance confined to the decision to retire? While it might be expected that a promise to pay retirement benefits for life might induce retirement, might it also induce other later forms

of reliance? The promise was made in 1972, and the first payment made in January 1973, with like payments made in 1974, 1975, and 1976. Hayes was 65 in 1972 and was about 68 when the payments stopped. Are there other acts Hayes may have taken or foregone that could have constituted reliance? What is the significance of the Court's finding that Hayes visited the plant once a year and would ask about his check: " . . . how long it would continue so that he could plan an orderly retirement . . . ?" Does this indicate that Hayes did not "expect" his retirement to result from the promise? In addition to lack of reliance, is this lack of expectancy a valid reason for denying relief? Edward Yorio and Steve Thel, "The Promissory Basis of Section 90," 101 Yale L. J. 111, 158 (1991).

d.   Gratuitous Conditional Promises

Distinguishing bargained-for consideration from conditional promises is an onerous task. An offer is a conditional promise—a promise that will become enforceable only upon an acceptance of the terms of the offer that supplies the necessary bargained-for consideration. We say an offer is conditional in the sense that nothing happens between the parties until the condition of acceptance is satisfied. Upon acceptance, the promise stated in the offer becomes enforceable. But an offer may also include other conditions, beyond acceptance, that must be satisfied before a contract will form or before the contract promises must be performed.

Just as a promisor can make a "gratuitous absolute promise," the promisor may also impose conditions to make a "gratuitous conditional promise." In both cases, the promise is unenforceable because the promisor made a donative promise and did not seek anything in return. Of course, the contrary is also true. It is possible to make an enforceable absolute promise and an enforceable conditional promise.

The difficulty involves distinguishing the "gratuitous conditional promise" from its enforceable counterpart, the "enforceable conditional promise." The basis for this distinction involves both the objective theory of contract discussed in *Lucy v. Zehmer*, above, and the doctrine of consideration. The standard asks whether a reasonable person would understand that the promisor objectively intended performance of the condition to be a gift or consideration for a return promise or performance. In this context, the court attempts to determine whether, by attaching the condition to the promise, the maker of the promise "seeks" performance of the condition or rather "intends" the condition as a mere necessary attachment to the enjoyment of the otherwise gift (gratuitous promise). By its very nature, the statement of a condition imparts a seeking of sorts because it is normally phrased in an "if/then" fashion. However, the matter is seldom that simple. Interpretative difficulties are an expectable externality of the consideration doctrine. This is especially true when the consideration doctrine is interpreted through the lens of the objective theory of contracts. The intent that controls is not the subjective intent of the maker. Rather, what matters is the objective understanding of a reasonable person standing in the position of the recipient. As you read the materials to follow, keep in mind Williston's famous "tramp" illustration. "If a benevolent man says to a tramp, 'If you go around the corner to the clothing shop there, you may purchase an overcoat on my credit,' no reasonable person would understand that the short walk was requested as the consideration for the promise; rather, the understanding would be that in the event of the tramp going to the shop the proprietor would make him a gift." Williston on Contracts § 7.18 (4th Ed. 2006). The walk to the shop could, in some cases, be consideration—the tramp has a right not to change position and doing so would constitute a legally cognizable detriment. But a reasonable person would recognize that the promisor did not ask for the tramp to move in exchange for the promise of the coat. Rather, a reasonable person, considering all the surrounding facts and circumstances from the tramp's viewpoint, would understand that the promisor objectively intended the promise as a gift subject only to the tramp's walking to the shop to take delivery. See id.

In the following case, try to determine whether the maker of the promise bargained for the terms of the condition.

KIRKSEY V. KIRKSEY

Alabama Supreme Court
8 Ala. 131 (1845)

Assumpsit by the defendant, against the plaintiff in error. The question is presented in this Court, upon a case agreed, which shows the following facts:

The plaintiff was the wife of defendant's brother, but had for some time been a widow, and had several children. In 1840, the plaintiff resided on public land, under a contract of lease, she had held over, and was comfortably settled, and would have attempted to secure the land she lived on. The defendant resided in Talladega county, some sixty, or seventy miles off. On the 10th October, 1840, he wrote to her the following letter:

Dear sister Antillico—

Much to my mortification, I heard, that brother Henry was dead, and one of his children. I know that your situation is one of grief, and difficulty. You had a bad chance before, but a great deal worse now. I should like to come and see you, but cannot with convenience at present. . . . I do not know whether you have a preference on the place you live on, or not. If you had, I would advise you to obtain your preference, and sell the land and quit the country, as I understand it is very unhealthy, and I know society is very bad. If you will come down and see me, I will let you have a place to raise your family, and I have more open land than I can tend; and on the account of your situation, and that of your family, I feel like I want you and the children to do well.

Within a month or two after the receipt of this letter, the plaintiff abandoned her possession, without disposing of it, and removed with her family, to the residence of the defendant, who put her in comfortable houses, and gave her land to cultivate for two years, at the end of which time he notified her to remove, and put her in a house, not comfortable, in the woods, which he afterwards required her to leave.

A verdict being found for the plaintiff, for two hundred dollars, the above facts were agreed, and if they will sustain the action, the judgment is to be affirmed, otherwise it is to be reversed.

ORMOND, J.

The inclination of my mind, is, that the loss and inconvenience, which the plaintiff sustained in breaking up, and moving to the defendant's, a distance of sixty miles, is a sufficient consideration to support the promise, to furnish her with a house, and land to cultivate, until she could raise her family. My brothers, however think, that the promise on the part of the defendant, was a mere gratuity, and that an action will not lie for its breach. The judgment of the Court below must therefore be reversed, pursuant to the agreement of the parties.

NOTES AND QUESTIONS

1. *The relevancy of motive.* The maker of an enforceable promise must seek the consideration in the exchange, but the reasons or motive for doing so are legally irrelevant. Restatement (Second) of Contracts §§ 71(1)–(2) and 81. The motive doctrine makes the evaluation of the gratuitous conditional promise particularly difficult. Therefore, it is useful to understand there is usually considerable overlap between the reason the promisor seeks the consideration and that it was in fact sought.

2. *Gender bias.* Can the decision in *Kirksey* be explained on the basis of gender bias against women? See Amy H. Kastely, "Cogs or Cyborgs?: Blasphemy and Irony in Contract Theories," 90 Nw. L. Rev. 132 (1995). One feminist critique of consideration doctrine observes that "self-interested bargaining remains the privileged form of interaction." Marjorie Maguire Schultz, "The Gendered Curriculum: Of Contracts and Careers," 77 Iowa L. Rev. 55, 64 (1991). In contrast, donative promises "often arise out of relations of trust and interpersonal intimacy." Id. As a consequence, "[b]ecause women place substantially greater priority on an ethic of care and concern for persons than do men, women might design a different hierarchy of promissory enforceability than the one currently having the status of received truth in first-year contracts courses." Id. Do you agree or disagree with Professor Schultz's critique? Is it possible to create a truly neutral law of contract with

respect to gender, race, ethnicity, sexual orientation, and other personal attributes? What does your answer say about the legitimacy of contract law as an institution for creating enforceable obligations between and among individual members of differently situated social groups?

3.   *The true story. Kirksey* is cited often, but its brevity leaves much to question. A few facts help make the case even more interesting. "Antillico" was really Angelico and married to Henry Kirksey who died in August 1840. Henry and Angelico had fourteen children, nine of whom traveled with her upon her brother-in-law's invitation. Her brother-in-law was Isaac Kirksey who lived in Talladega, Alabama and had married Angelico's sister Mary Connolly in 1821. Mary died after eighteen years of marriage to Isaac, but he re-married six months before his invitation to Angelico.

Isaac's offer to Angelico was not altruistic. He intended her to occupy public land as a placeholder so that he could subsequently purchase it at a substantial discount from the government for only $200. A subsequent change in those laws barred his purchase but permitted Angelico and her children to buy the land at the discounted price. Isaac evicted her so he could block her purchase and buy the land for himself. She sued alleging damages equal to the discounted $200 purchase price that the trial court awarded her. Isaac purchased the land she had occupied. After the appeal, she paid Isaac's costs and eventually moved away to live with her son. She died penniless. Isaac died in 1865, a wealthy man. See William R. Castro and Val D. Ricks, " 'Dear Sister Antillico . . . ': The Story of Kirksey v. Kirksey," 94 Geo. L. J. 321 (2006).

4.   *Another theory of obligation.* The *Kirksey* case demonstrates that the traditional theory of consideration will not make a gratuitous conditional promise enforceable. The next section explores the utilization of a party's expected reliance to enforce an unbargained-for promise. As you prepare to review these cases, consider whether Antillico Kirksey relied on her brother-in-law's promise and if so whether that fact alone should encourage the law to make his promise enforceable. Was her reliance substantial? Should he have anticipated her reliance? Note, however, that this case was decided before the theory of promissory estoppel evolved.

2.   OBLIGATION BY REASON OF RELIANCE: THE PROMISSORY ESTOPPEL DOCTRINE

Like tort law, contract law attempts to promote as a major policy goal the protection of an injured contract party from the harm caused by the other party's breach. The primary mechanism of such protection is an award of damages designed to "undo" the harm. In tort law, an award of monetary damages attempts to "return" the plaintiff to a status equal to that before the tort. The contract law correlative is reliance damages designed to put the injured party in status equal to that prior to entering the contract. Restatement (Second) of Contracts § 344(b). Contract damages are inseparable from the larger body of motives and policies that constitute the general law of contracts. Lon L. Fuller and William R.

Perdue, "The Reliance Interest in Contract Damages (Part) I.,"46 Yale L. J. 52 (Part I) and 373 (Part II), 53–56 (1936). But simply awarding reliance damages for a breach of a contract is quite different from using reliance of a promise to "create" the liability. Chapter 6 considers the matter of measuring damages, including reliance damages, when a contract is breached. In this section, we explore the extended concept of using reliance to create a legal remedy—to create a contract when other theories of liability such as consideration might fail. Contract law uses the doctrine of promissory estoppel to make a promise binding where the promisee has detrimentally relied on a promise that otherwise lacks consideration. See Warren A. Seavey, "Reliance upon Gratuitous Promises or Other Conduct," 64 Harv. L. Rev. 913, 925 (1951) (estoppel basically a tort doctrine).

Promissory estoppel, in its pure form, appears to be a modern legal invention with specific doctrinal roots in Restatement (First) of Contracts § 90. But in reality, this reliance-based theory of enforceable promises is closely connected to a similar doctrine known as equitable estoppel. Like many equitable notions, the doctrine of equitable estoppel has been a feature of Anglo-American law from the beginning. See *Dickerson v. Colgrove,* 100 U.S. 578, 580 (1879) ("The estoppel here relied upon is known as an equitable estoppel, or estoppel *in pais*. The law upon the subject is well settled. The vital principle is that he who by his language or conduct leads another to do what he would not otherwise have done, shall not subject such person to loss or injury by disappointing the expectations upon which he acted.").

The doctrine of equitable estoppel presented both protection and disappointment. While protecting reliance, the doctrine required the representation of a past or present fact. Historically, statements of present and future intention were not addressed because they were subject to change, reliance was less warranted, and the law was less likely to therefore equitably charge the cost of the reliance to the maker. Enter promissory estoppel. While a few early cases appeared to simply "extend" the doctrine of equitable estoppel to cases of probable promissory-based reliance, the subject became fixed legal doctrine in 1932 with the adoption of the Restatement (First) of Contracts § 90. See e.g., Seavey v. Drake, 62 N.H. 393 (1882) (a reliance expenditure "constitutes, in equity, a consideration for the promise and the promise will be enforced" in equity). With a few minor changes, in 1979 the Restatement (Second) of Contracts continued the doctrine in force. See Benjamin F. Boyer, "Promissory Estoppel: Principal from Precedent," 50 Mich. L. Rev. 639 (Part I) and 873 (Part II) (1952). Thus, what began as a twentieth century doctrine is now firmly in place in contract jurisprudence.

In fact, the development of promissory estoppel as a significant independent legal doctrine led one prominent legal writer to suggest the doctrine's tort-like reliance-based features would soon swallow all of contract law. See Grant Gilmore, The Death of Contract 95–98 (1974) ("I have occasionally suggested . . . that a desirable reform in legal education would be to merge the first-year courses in Contracts and Torts into a single course which we could call Contorts.").

Has promissory estoppel replaced or at least overwhelmed the doctrine of consideration you just patiently learned? See Charles L. Knapp, "Reliance in the Revised Restatement: The Proliferation of Promissory Estoppel," 81 Colum. L. Rev. 52 (1981) and Note, "Contracts, Promissory Estoppel," 20 Va. L. Rev. 214, 218 (1933) (principal objection to promissory estoppel is that it eschews classical consideration doctrine). Specifically, does promissory estoppel only apply when consideration is absent? Early cases suggested the doctrine of promissory estoppel should be limited to noncommercial situations. See Grant Gilmore, The Death of Contract 73 (1974) and *James Baird Co. v. Gimbel Bros.,* 64 F.2d 344, 346 (2d Cir. 1933) (Hand, J.). We begin our journey in just such a context. But be advised. Some argue persuasively that promissory estoppel has not had this "doomsday effect" and indeed is sparingly applied. See Robert A. Hillman, "Questioning the 'New Consensus' on Promissory Estoppel: An Empirical and Theoretical Study," 98 Colum. L. Rev. 580 (1998) (arguing the doctrine is sparingly applied and rarely successful in court in cases lacking reliance).

a.   Noncommercial Promises

Courts first developed and applied the promissory estoppel doctrine in cases involving promises without consideration upon which the promisee reasonably and detrimentally relied. Promises between family members are much more likely to be gratuitous than those in a commercial context. Family members are more likely to make gifts to other family members than unrelated commercial parties. As a result and not surprisingly, the first true proving ground for the Restatement (First) of Contracts § 90 determined whether to enforce the family gift promise, apparently directly contravening the donor-promise principle.

RICKETTS V. SCOTHORN

Supreme Court of Nebraska
57 Neb. 51, 77 N.W. 365 (1898)

SULLIVAN, J.

In the district court of Lancaster county the plaintiff, Katie Scothorn, recovered judgment against the defendant, Andrew D. Ricketts, as executor of the last will and testament of John C. Ricketts, deceased. The action was based upon a promissory note, of which the following is a copy:

May the first, 1891.

I promise to pay to Katie Scothorn on demand, $2,000, to be at 6 per cent. per annum.

J. C. Ricketts.

In the petition the plaintiff alleges that the consideration for the execution of the note was that she should surrender her employment as bookkeeper for Mayer Bros., and cease to work for a living. She also alleges that the note was given to induce her to abandon her occupation, and that, relying on it, and on the annual interest, as a means of support, she gave up the employment in which she was then engaged. These allegations of the petition are denied by the administrator. The material facts are undisputed. They are as follows: John C. Ricketts, the maker of the note, was the grandfather of the plaintiff. Early in May—presumably on the day the note bears date—he called on her at the store where she was working. What transpired between them is thus described by Mr. Flodene, one of the plaintiff's witnesses:

> A.   Well, the old gentleman came in there one morning about nine o'clock, probably a little before or a little after, but early in the morning, and he unbuttoned his vest, and took out a piece of paper in the shape of a note; that is the way it looked to me; and he says to Miss Scothorn, "I have fixed out something that you have not got to work any more." He says, none of my grandchildren work, and you don't have to.
>
> Q.   Where was she?
>
> A.   She took the piece of paper and kissed him, and kissed the old gentleman, and commenced to cry.

It seems Miss Scothorn immediately notified her employer of her intention to quit work, and that she did soon after abandon her occupation. The mother of the plaintiff was a witness, and testified that she had a conversation with her father, Mr. Ricketts, shortly after the note was executed, in which he informed her that he had given the note to the plaintiff to enable her to quit work; that none of his grandchildren worked, and he did not think she ought to. For something more than a year the plaintiff was without an occupation, but in September, 1892, with the consent of her grandfather, and by his assistance, she secured a position as bookkeeper with Messrs. Funke & Ogden.

On June 8, 1894, Mr. Ricketts died. He had paid one year's interest on the note, and a short time before his death expressed regret that he had not been able to pay the balance. In the summer or fall of 1892 he stated to his daughter, Mrs. Scothorn, that if he could sell his farm in Ohio he would pay the note out of the proceeds.

He at no time repudiated the obligation. We quite agree with counsel for the defendant that upon this evidence there was nothing to submit to the jury, and that a verdict should have been directed peremptorily for one of the parties.

The testimony of Flodene and Mrs. Scothorn, taken together, conclusively establishes the fact that the note was not given in consideration of the plaintiff pursuing, or agreeing to pursue, any particular line of conduct. There was no promise on the part of the plaintiff to do, or refrain from doing, anything. Her right to the money promised in the note was not made to depend upon an abandonment of her employment with Mayer Bros., and future abstention from like service. Mr. Ricketts made no condition, requirement, or request. He exacted no quid pro quo. He gave the note as a gratuity, and looked for nothing in return. So far as the evidence discloses, it was his purpose to place the plaintiff in a position of independence, where she could work or remain idle, as she might choose. The abandonment of Miss Scothorn of her position as bookkeeper was altogether voluntary. It was not an act done in fulfillment of any contract obligation assumed when she accepted the note. The instrument in suit, being given without any valuable consideration, was nothing more than a promise to make a gift in the future of the sum of money therein named.

Ordinarily, such promises are not enforceable, even when put in the form of a promissory note. Kirkpatrick v. Taylor, 43 Ill. 207; Phelps v. Phelps, 28 Barb. 121. . . . But it has often been held that an action on a note given to a church, college, or other like institution, upon the faith of which money has been expended or obligations incurred, could not be successfully defended on the ground of a want of consideration. Barnes v. Perine, 12 N. Y. 18; Philomath College v. Hartless, 6 Or. 158. . . .

In this class of cases the note in suit is nearly always spoken of as a gift or donation, but the decision is generally put on the ground that the expenditure of money or assumption of liability by the donee on the faith of the promise constitutes a valuable and sufficient consideration. It seems to us that the true reason is the preclusion of the defendant, under the doctrine of estoppel, to deny the consideration. Such seems to be the view of the matter taken by the supreme court of Iowa in the case of Simpson Centenary College v. Tuttle, 71 Iowa, 596, 33 N. W. 74, where Rothrock, J., speaking for the court, said:

> Where a note, however, is based on a promise to give for the support of the objects referred to, it may still be open to this defense [(want of consideration)], unless it shall appear that the donee has, prior to any revocation, entered into engagements, or made expenditures based on such promise, so that he must suffer loss or injury if the note is not paid. This is based on the equitable principle that, after allowing the donee to incur obligations on the

faith that the note would be paid, the donor would be estopped from pleading want of consideration.

And in the case of Reimensnyder v. Gans, 110 Pa. St. 17, 2 Atl. 425, which was an action on a note given as a donation to a charitable object, the court said: "The fact is that, as we may see from the case of Ryerss v. Trustees, 33 Pa. St. 114, a contract of the kind here involved is enforceable rather by way of estoppel than on the ground of consideration in the original undertaking." It has been held that a note given in expectation of the payee performing certain services, but without any contract binding him to serve, will not support an action. Hulse v. Hulse, 84 E. C. L. 709. But when the payee changes his position to his disadvantage in reliance on the promise, a right of action does arise. McClure v. Wilson, 43 Ill. 356; Trustees v. Garvey, 53 Ill. 401.

Under the circumstances of this case, is there an equitable estoppel which ought to preclude the defendant from alleging that the note in controversy is lacking in one of the essential elements of a valid contract? We think there is. An estoppel in pais is defined to be "a right arising from acts, admissions, or conduct which have induced a change of position in accordance with the real or apparent intention of the party against whom they are alleged." Mr. Pomeroy has formulated the following definition: "Equitable estoppel is the effect of the voluntary conduct of a party whereby he is absolutely precluded, both at law and in equity, from asserting rights which might, perhaps, have otherwise existed, either of property, of contract, or of remedy, as against another person who in good faith relied upon such conduct, and has been led thereby to change his position for the worse, and who on his part acquires some corresponding right, either of property, of contract, or of remedy." 2 Pom. Eq. Jur. 804. According to the undisputed proof, as shown by the record before us, the plaintiff was a working girl, holding a position in which she earned a salary of $10 per week. Her grandfather, desiring to put her in a position of independence, gave her the note, accompanying it with the remark that his other grandchildren did not work, and that she would not be obliged to work any longer. In effect, he suggested that she might abandon her employment, and rely in the future upon the bounty which he promised. He doubtless desired that she should give up her occupation, but, whether he did or not, it is entirely certain that he contemplated such action on her part as a reasonable and probable consequence of his gift. Having intentionally influenced the plaintiff to alter her position for the worse on the faith of the note being paid when due, it would be grossly inequitable to permit the maker, or his executor, to resist payment on the ground that the promise was given without consideration. The petition charges the elements of an equitable estoppel, and the evidence conclusively establishes them. If errors intervened at the trial, they could not have been prejudicial. A verdict for the defendant would be unwarranted.

The judgment is right, and is affirmed.

NOTES AND QUESTIONS

1. *Estoppel in pais and promissory estoppel compared.* The court mentions the doctrine of estoppel in pais or equitable estoppel, not promissory estoppel. Whereas promissory estoppel has a more recent history dating to Restatement (First) of Contracts § 90 in 1932, equitable estoppel's origins are much more ancient. See, e.g., *Dickerson v. Colgrove,* 100 U.S. 578, 580 (1879). When applicable, equitable estoppel doctrinally requires the representation of a past or existing "fact" by a maker who is thereafter prevented (estopped) from denying the making of the representation if denial would result in injury or loss to a person who relied on the representation. Representations of present or future intention are "promissory," and recipients of such types of statements are not protected in their reliance on those statements. Historically, representations regarding intention were regarded as too uncertain and likely to change for the law to hold the maker accountable for reliance by the recipient. "Promissory" estoppel on the other hand fills that gap and extends the range of legally protected reliance from fact to promise. Returning to *Ricketts,* do you think the court applied the doctrine of equitable estoppel or promissory estoppel? To understand the difference, focus on Katie Scothorn's reliance. What did she rely on, a promise of future conduct or a representation of past or existing fact?

2. *Promissory estoppel, equitable estoppel, and fundamental legal conceptions.* The doctrines of promissory estoppel and equitable estoppel illustrate an important distinction between legal "rights" and legal "privileges." Both legal and non-legal discourse often use terms such as "rights," "powers," "privileges," "duties," and "liabilities" indiscriminately. This, in turn, often leads to confusion in attempting to describe the legal relations that exist between parties and in attempting to assign legal consequences to those relations.

Wesley Newcomb Hohfeld published only seven articles during his short lifetime, but his work ranks as one of the most important jurisprudential developments in the last century. Two of his articles—"Some Fundamental Legal Conceptions as Applied in Judicial Reasoning," 23 Yale L. J. 16 (1913) and "Fundamental Legal Conceptions as Applied in Judicial Reasoning," 26 Yale L. J. 710 (1917)—provide the first complete and systematic taxonomy and analysis of legal relations, and his analytic method is still used to describe legal relations today.

As noted by the editor of the compilation of Hohfeld's scholarship, revised from his notes after his death in 1918, Hohfeld developed his system not as an abstract method for conceiving of philosophical and jurisprudential issues, but rather as a practical tool for correctly describing and analyzing concrete, real-world legal problems:

> In the opinion of the present writer one of the greatest messages
> which the late Wesley Newcomb Hohfeld during his all too short life

gave to the legal profession was this, that an adequate analytical jurisprudence is an absolutely indispensable tool in the equipment of the properly trained lawyer or judge—indispensable, that is, for the highest efficiency in the discharge of the daily duties of his profession. It was Hohfeld's great merit that he saw that, interesting as analytical jurisprudence is when pursued for its own sake, its chief value lies in the fact that by its aid the correct solution of legal problems becomes not only easier but more certain. In this respect it does not differ from any other branch of pure science. We must hasten to add . . . that no one saw more clearly than he that while the analytical matter is an indispensable tool, it is not an all-sufficient one for the lawyer. On the contrary, he emphasized over and over again . . . that analytical work merely paves the way for other branches of jurisprudence, and that without the aid of the latter satisfactory solutions of legal problems cannot be reached.— Walter Wheeler Cook, "Hohfeld's Contributions to the Science of Law," 28 Yale L.J. 721, 721–22 (1919).

Hohfeld's system first distinguishes four related and previously ambiguous legal concepts: rights, privileges, powers, and immunities. Hohfeld then defines each of these concepts in terms of what he calls their "jural opposites" (no pair can exist together) and their "jural correlatives" (each pair must always exist together):

Jural Opposites:	right	privilege	power	immunity
(never together)	no-right	duty	disability	liability

Jural Correlatives:	right	privilege	power	immunity
(always together)	duty	no-right	liability	disability

For Hohfeld, the concept of a legal "right" is intimately related and can only be defined in connection with its jural correlative "duty." "In other words, if X has a right against Y that he shall stay off the former's land, the correlative (and equivalent) is that Y is under a duty toward X to stay off the place." Wesley Newcomb Hohfeld, "Some Fundamental Legal Conceptions as Applied in Judicial Reasoning," 23 Yale L. J. 13, 30–32 (1913). Thus, in the context of contracts, if A makes an enforceable promise to convey Whiteacre to B, the resulting contract gives B a "right" to receive Whiteacre from A and imposes a correlative "duty" on A to transfer Whiteacre to B. In the case of a promissory estoppel, Scothorn's reasonable reliance on Ricketts's promise of a demand note for $2000 at 6% interest created a right in Scothorn to enforce the note and an equivalent duty in Ricketts to pay interest and, if demanded, the principal. In common parlance, promissory estoppel operates as a "sword" by which one who reasonably relies upon another's promise may bring a cause of action to enforce that promise.

In contrast, the next set of correlatives—privilege/no-right—better describes the equitable estoppel principles that the *Ricketts v. Scothorn* court attempted to stretch to cover the situation before it. For Hohfeld, in the sale of Whiteacre from A to B described above, after the sale B as the owner of Whiteacre has the *privilege* of entering on and occupying that property. And A—the former owner—has *no right* (e.g., no legal claim) against B for B's occupation of land owned by B. That is, A cannot sue to have B removed from land that B owns because B is privileged against such claims by A. See Wesley Newcomb Hohfeld, "Some Fundamental Legal Conceptions As Applied in Judicial Reasoning," 23 Yale L. J. 16, 32–33 (1913).

Equitable estoppel, as noted, bars a person who makes a representation of past or existing fact from denying that fact if it would injure another who has reasonably relied on that representation. A common example of equitable estoppel in the commercial real estate acquisition process is the use of "estoppel statements." Prospective purchasers of commercial real estate often buy properties (like shopping malls and office buildings) subject to leases by commercial tenants. To value the property accurately and manage their future risks, the prospective purchaser may demand that every tenant sign an estoppel statement advising the prospective purchaser that the tenant either has legal claims against the property or does not have such claims. When the purchaser buys the property in reliance on a tenant's statement that, as of the purchase date, the tenant does not have any legal claims against the property, the tenant is later estopped from asserting pre-purchase claims to the detriment of the relying purchaser. In Hohfeldian terms, we can say that the purchaser has a "privilege" of relying on the tenant's representation, and the tenant has a corresponding "no-right" to alter that representation to the purchaser's detriment. In contrast to the "sword" of promissory estoppel, equitable estoppel operates as a "shield" under which the purchaser may assert a privilege against a tenant's pre-purchase legal claim, while the tenant has no-right to assert such a claim.

WRIGHT V. NEWMAN

Supreme Court of Georgia
266 Ga. 519, 467 S.E.2d 533 (1996)

CARLEY, Justice.

Seeking to recover child support for her daughter and her son, Kim Newman filed suit against Bruce Wright. Wright's answer admitted his paternity only as to Newman's daughter and DNA testing subsequently showed that he is not the father of her son. The trial court nevertheless ordered Wright to pay child support for both children. As to Newman's son, the trial court based its order upon Wright's "actions in having himself listed on the child's birth certificate, giving the child his surname and establishing a parent-child relationship. . . ." According to the trial court, Wright had thereby:

allow[ed] the child to consider him his father and in so doing
deterr[ed Newman] from seeking to establish the paternity of the
child's natural father [,] thus denying the child an opportunity to
establish a parent-child relationship with the natural father.

We granted Wright's application for a discretionary appeal so as to
review the trial court's order requiring that he pay child support for
Newman's son.

Wright does not contest the trial court's factual findings. He asserts
only that the trial court erred in its legal conclusion that the facts
authorized the imposition of an obligation to provide support for Newman's
son. If Wright were the natural father of Newman's son, he would be legally
obligated to provide support. OCGA § 19–7–2. Likewise, if Wright had
formally adopted Newman's son, he would be legally obligated to provide
support. OCGA § 19–8–19(a)(2). However, Wright is neither the natural
nor the formally adoptive father of the child and "the theory of 'virtual
adoption' is not applicable to a dispute as to who is legally responsible for
the support of minor children." Ellison v. Thompson, 240 Ga. 594, 596, 242
S.E. 2d 95 (1978).

Although Wright is neither the natural nor the formally adoptive
father of Newman's son and the theory of "virtual adoption" is inapplicable,
it does not necessarily follow that, as a matter of law, he has no legal
obligation for child support. A number of jurisdictions have recognized that
a legally enforceable obligation to provide child support can be "based upon
parentage or contract. . . ." (Emphasis supplied.) Albert v. Albert, 415 So.
2d 818, 819 (Fla. App. 1982). See also Anno., 90 A.L.R. 2d 583 (1963).
Georgia is included among those jurisdictions. Foltz v. Foltz, 238 Ga. 193,
194, 232 S.E. 2d 66 (1977). Accordingly, the issue for resolution is whether
Wright can be held liable for child support for Newman's son under this
state's contract law.

There was no formal written contract whereby Wright agreed to
support Newman's son. Compare Foltz v. Foltz, supra. Nevertheless, under
this state's contract law,

> [a] promise which the promisor should reasonably expect to induce
> action or forbearance on the part of the promisee or a third person
> and which does induce such action or forbearance is binding if
> injustice can be avoided only by enforcement of the promise. The
> remedy granted for breach may be limited as justice requires.

OCGA § 13–3–44(a). This statute codifies the principle of promissory
estoppel. Insilco Corp. v. First Nat. Bank of Dalton, 248 Ga. 322(1), 283
S.E.2d 262 (1981). In accordance with that principle,

> [a] party may enter into a contract invalid and unenforceable, and
> by reason of the covenants therein contained and promises made

in connection with the same, wrongfully cause the opposite party to forego a valuable legal right to his detriment, and in this manner by his conduct waive the right to repudiate the contract and become estopped to deny the opposite party any benefits that may accrue to him under the terms of the agreement. [Cits.]

Pepsi Cola Bottling Co. of Dothan, Ala., Inc. v. First Nat. Bank of Columbus, 248 Ga. 114, 116–117(2), 281 S.E.2d 579 (1981).

The evidence authorizes the finding that Wright promised both Newman and her son that he would assume all of the obligations and responsibilities of fatherhood, including that of providing support. As the trial court found, this promise was evidenced by Wright's listing of himself as the father on the child's birth certificate and giving the child his last name. Wright is presumed to know "the legal consequences of his actions. Since parents are legally obligated to support their minor children, [he] accepted this support obligation by acknowledging paternity." Marshall v. Marshall, 386 So. 2d 11, 12 (Fla. App. 1980). There is no dispute that, at the time he made his commitment, Wright knew that he was not the natural father of the child. Compare NPA v. WBA, 8 Va. App. 246, 380 S.E.2d 178 (1989). Thus, he undertook his commitment knowingly and voluntarily. Moreover, he continued to do so for some 10 years, holding himself out to others as the father of the child and allowing the child to consider him to be the natural father.

The evidence further authorizes the finding that Newman and her son relied upon Wright's promise to their detriment. As the trial court found, Newman refrained from identifying and seeking support from the child's natural father. Had Newman not refrained from doing so, she might now have a source of financial support for the child and the child might now have a natural father who provided emotional, as well as financial, support. If, after 10 years of honoring his voluntary commitment, Wright were now allowed to evade the consequences of his promise, an injustice to Newman and her son would result. Under the evidence, the duty to support which Wright voluntarily assumed 10 years ago remains enforceable under the contractual doctrine of promissory estoppel and the trial court's order which compels Wright to discharge that obligation must be affirmed. See Nygard v. Nygard, 156 Mich. App. 94, 401 N.W.2d 323 (1986); Marshall v. Marshall, supra; In re Marriage of Johnson, 88 Cal. App. 3d 848, 152 Cal. Rptr. 121 (1979); Hartford v. Hartford, 53 Ohio App. 2d 79, 7 O.O. 3d 53, 371 N.E.2d 591 (1977).

Judgment affirmed

All the Justices concur, except BENHAM, C.J., who dissents.

SEARS, Justice, concurring.

I concur fully with the majority opinion. I write separately only to address the dissenting opinion's misperception that Newman has not relied upon Wright's promise to her detriment.

It is an established principle in Georgia that a promise which the promisor should reasonably expect to induce action or forbearance on the part of the promisee or a third person and which does induce such action or forbearance is binding if injustice can be avoided only by enforcement of the promise. This doctrine, known as "promissory estoppel," prevents a promisor from reneging on a promise, when the promisor should have expected that the promisee would rely upon the promise, and the promisee does in fact rely upon the promise to her detriment. Sufficient consideration to enforce a contractual promise pursuant to promissory estoppel may be found in any benefit accruing to the promisor, or any reliance, loss, trouble, disadvantage, or charge imposed upon the promisee.

Bearing these principles in mind, and as explained very well in the majority opinion, it is clear that Wright's commitment to Newman to assume the obligations of fatherhood as regards her son are enforceable. Specifically, it is abundantly clear that Wright should have known that Newman would rely upon his promise, especially after he undertook for ten years to fulfill the obligations of fatherhood. In this regard, it could hardly have escaped Wright's notice that Newman refrained from seeking to identify and obtain support from the child's biological father while Wright was fulfilling his commitment to her. Moreover, Newman did in fact rely upon Wright's promise, to her detriment when, ten years after he undertook the obligations of fatherhood, Wright reneged on his promise.

Promissory estoppel requires only that the reliance by the injured party be *reasonable*. In this case, it cannot seriously be argued that Newman's reliance was anything other than reasonable, as she had absolutely no indication that Wright would ever renege, especially after he fulfilled his promise for such a long time. Moreover, contrary to the dissent's implicit assertion, promissory estoppel does not require that the injured party exhaust all other possible means of obtaining the benefit of the promise from any and all sources before being able to enforce the promise against the promisor. In this regard, it is illogical to argue that Newman, after reasonably relying upon Wright's promise for ten years, can now simply seek to determine the identity of the biological father and collect support from him. First, there is nothing in the case law that requires Newman to do so before being entitled to have Wright's promise enforced. Second, this requirement would be an imposing, if not an impossible, burden, and would require Newman not only to identify the father (if possible), but also to locate him, bring a costly legal action against him, and to succeed in that action. Imposing this requirement would effectively penalize Newman for no reasons other than (1) her reasonable reliance upon a promise that was not kept, and (2) for allowing herself to be dissuaded by Wright from seeking the identity of the biological father. As noted, nowhere does the case law support imposing such a requirement, and none of the facts in this case support doing so now.

Finally, there can be no doubt that, unless Wright's promise to Newman is enforced, injustice will result. Given the approximately ten years that have passed since the child's birth, during which time Wright, for all purposes, *was* the child's father, it likely will be impossible for Newman to establish the identity of the child's biological father, bring a successful paternity action, and obtain support from that individual. Consequently, if Wright is allowed to renege on his obligation, Newman likely will not receive any support to assist in the cost of raising her son, despite having been promised the receipt of such by Wright. Furthermore, an even greater injustice will be inflicted upon the boy himself. A child who has been told by any adult, regardless of the existence of a biological relationship, that he will always be able to depend upon the adult for parenting and sustenance, will suffer a great deal when that commitment is broken. And when a child suffers under those circumstances, society-at-large suffers as well.[5]

Because Wright's promise is capable of being enforced under the law, and because I believe that Wright's promise must be enforced in order to prevent a grave miscarriage of justice, I concur fully in the majority opinion.

BENHAM, Chief Justice, dissenting.

I respectfully dissent. While I agree with the majority opinion's statement that liability for child support may be based on promissory estoppel in a case where there is no statutory obligation or express contract, I first note that this issue was not brought by either of the parties. Further, there is a critical element that must be shown for promissory estoppel to apply. In addition to making a showing of expectation and reasonable reliance, a person asserting liability on the theory of promissory estoppel must show that she relied on the promise to her detriment. Nickell v. IAG Federal Credit Union, 213 Ga.App. 516, 445 S.E.2d 335 (1994); Lake Tightsqueeze, Inc. v. Chrysler First Financial Services Corp., 210 Ga.App. 178, 435 S.E.2d 486 (1993). The majority states that Newman and her son incurred detriment by refraining from identifying and seeking support from the child's natural father. However, the record is completely bereft of any evidence that Newman met her burden of proof as to promissory

---

[5] Wright is also morally obligated to provide support for Newman's son. Merely because an obligation may not be capable of legal enforcement, one is not necessarily free to act in any way that he might choose. In addition to our legal duties, we are also bound by a consciousness of duty that is based upon fundamental values such as honor, truth, and responsibility. The "non-legal" obligations that we undertake are no less sacrosanct merely because they may not be capable of legal enforcement. The moral (as opposed to the legal) dilemma faced by Wright lies within his conscience, heart, and soul. He need have looked no further than there to determine what he must do in this case.

estoppel, and the majority fails to state how she is prevented from now instituting a child support action against the natural father. Newman has not alleged, nor does the record reveal, that she does not know the identity of the natural father, nor does she show that the natural father is dead or unable to be found. Consequently, Newman has not shown that she is now unable to do what she would have had to do ten years ago—seek support from the natural father.

In fact, Wright contends, and Newman does not refute, that Newman severed the relationship and all ties with Wright when the child was approximately three years old. For approximately the next five years, until the child was eight, Newman and Wright did not communicate. Only for the past two years has Wright visited with the child. Importantly, Wright contends that during the past seven years he did not support the child. Thus, taking Wright's undisputed contentions as true, any prejudice incurred by Newman because of the passage of ten years in time is not due to Wright's actions, since, at least for the past seven years, Newman has been in the same situation—receiving no support payments from Wright. Thus, although Wright may be morally obligated to support the ten-year-old child, he is not legally obligated to do so because Newman has failed to show that she or the child incurred any detriment by Wright's failure to fulfill his promise made ten years ago.

For the foregoing reasons, I dissent.

NOTES AND QUESTIONS

1.   *Express and implied promises as bases for promissory estoppel.* Wright did not make an express promise to Newman to support her child. Rather, the court implied his factual promise to do so was implied from his conduct including his listing himself as the father on the birth certificate and giving the child his last name. Given the outcome of the case, the absence of an express promise was not fatal. Should promissory estoppel be any different than an implied-in-fact contract in this regard? Is conduct rather than words any less likely to trigger justified reliance?

2.   *Remedy limited as justice requires.* The *Wright* majority opines that an "injustice" would result if Wright were permitted to evade child support obligations. Likewise, Restatement (Second) of Contracts § 90(1) provides that a promise that satisfies the other elements of promissory estoppel "is binding if *injustice* can be avoided only by enforcement of the promise," and that "[t]he remedy may be limited as *justice* requires." (emphasis added).

The meaning of "justice" has fascinated philosophers, politicians, and scholars for thousands of years. The ancient Greek philosopher, Aristotle, framed the general outlines of the debate over what it means to be "just" 2,500 years ago. Aristotle divided the idea of justice into two separate concepts—distributive justice and commutative justice. Distributive justice encompassed the idea that each member of society deserves a certain proportion of the society's wealth and resources. Under Aristotle's conception of distributive justice, "[e]ach citizen receives a share of whatever there is to be divided. It is the mathematics of dividing a pie. Aristotle noted that there is no one correct principle for determining the share each person should receive. Rather, a particular society will adopt a principle consistent with its political regime." James Gordley, "Equality in Exchange," 69 Cal. L. Rev. 1587, 1589 (1981).

In contrast, commutative or corrective justice represented the principle that courts should correct inequalities resulting from transactions—including interactions such as physical torts, theft, and contracts—between individuals:

> This, then, is what the just is—the proportional; the unjust is what violates the proportion. Hence, one term becomes too great, the other too small, as indeed happens in practice; for <u>the man who acts unjustly has too much, and the man who is unjustly treated too little, of what is good</u>.—Aristotle, Nichomachean Ethics, Bk. V, Ch. 3, ln 1131ᵇ25–26 (W.D. Ross trans. 1908).

For Aristotle, injustice in an interaction between two parties was determined—at least in part—by the equality of the exchange between them. Where the exchange was unequal, that inequality was an issue to be corrected, if possible, by application of commutative justice because it violated the principle of proportionality. "Commutative justice . . . follows an arithmetic proportion. It is concerned not with sharing resources, but with preserving each citizen's share. Therefore the party who has lost resources to another has a claim for the amount necessary to restore his original position. . . . To paraphrase Aristotle only slightly, commutative justice operates on the principle that no one should gain by another's loss." James Gordley, "Equality in Exchange," 69 Cal. L. Rev. 1587, 1589 (1981).

> But the justice in transactions is a sort of equality indeed, and the injustice a sort of inequality; not according to that kind of proportion, however, but according to arithmetical proportion. For it makes no difference whether a good man has defrauded a bad man or a bad man a good one . . . ; the law looks only to the distinctive character of the injury, and treats the parties as equal, if one is in the wrong and the other is being wronged, and if one inflicted injury and the other has received it. <u>Therefore, this kind of injustice being an inequality, the judge tries to equalize it</u>; for in the case also in which one has received and the other has inflicted a wound, . . . the suffering and the action have been unequally distributed; <u>but the judge tries to equalize things by means of the penalty, taking away from the gain of the assailant</u>. Aristotle, Nichomachean Ethics, Bk. V, Ch. 4, ln. 1131b32—1132ª14 (W.D. Ross trans. 1908) (emphasis added).

How does the Aristotelian notion of justice square with the idea of justice presented in the promissory estoppel context? What other conceptions of "justice" could be used to describe a court's inquiry under Restatement (Second) of Contracts § 90? Keep these issues in mind as you read the cases in the following section dealing with issues of "unjust enrichment."

3. *Codifying the common law.* In the last two centuries, many states, like Georgia, reduced the common law to statutory form in a presumed attempt to make the law more stable and more widely accessible. Does codification alter the role of the courts? See generally Nathan M. Crystal, "Codification and the Rise of the Restatement Movement," 54 Wash. L. Rev. 239 (1979).

Notably, most states have rejected by statute contract actions for breach of a promise to marry. See, e.g., Mass. Gen. Stat. ch. 207 § 47A. Such statutes are often referred to as "heart balm" balm statutes because they ban law actions based on a broken heart. Prior common law often enforced a promise by a man but not by a woman who retained the right to change her mind.

b. Contract and Family Law

Some of the most intractable issues in contract law arise from within family relationships. Intra-familial transactions—gifts, promises, contracts, torts, crimes, etc.—often occur in the context of strong emotional exchanges and in an atmosphere of informality. Additionally, social and family pressures may provide strong incentives to make, keep, or break promises improvidently. Some of these promises, as in *Hamer v. Sidway* and *Ricketts v. Scothorn*, merely involve monetary obligations that, while significant to the parties involved, have no overreaching social considerations. But other promises in the family context, as discussed in *Wright v. Newman*, carry profound social implications far outside of contract law.

c. Charitable Subscriptions

Charitable subscriptions represent unique policy questions arguably not present with other forms of promises. Unlike promises within the family setting, such promises raise important public policy issues regarding charitable support. Unfortunately, like promises in a family context, promises to make a gift to a charity are no more likely to be supported by a consideration. As a result, if consideration were the sole test, many if not most such promises would not be legally binding. Fortunately, most donors simply keep their promises and legal enforcement is not necessary. In rare cases, this is not the case. In those cases, promissory estoppel will become the most likely candidate to enforce the promise.

Unfortunately, promissory estoppel has its own practical defects in the charitable subscription context. Most commonly, unless the gift is of enormous size and importance, the charitable organization cannot prove reliance on any specific promise. In these circumstances, Restatement (Second) of Contracts § 90(2) becomes vitally important as it eliminates the need to show reliance. As noted in *King v. Trustees of Boston University*, very few states have followed the rule suggested in that subsection. This simply means that the charitable pledge usually stands on an equal footing with other unbargained-for gratuitous promises—not enforceable unless the charity can establish reliance.

ALLEGHENY COLLEGE V. NATIONAL CHAUTAUQUA COUNTY BANK

New York Court of Appeals
246 N.Y. 369, 159 N.E. 173 (1927)

CARDOZO, C. J.

The plaintiff, Allegheny College, is an institution of liberal learning at Meadville, Pa. In June, 1921, a "drive" was in progress to secure for it an additional endowment of $1,250,000. An appeal to contribute to this fund was made to Mary Yates Johnston, of Jamestown, New York. In response thereto, she signed and delivered on June 15, 1921, the following writing:

Estate Pledge, Allegheny College Second Century Endowment.

Jamestown, N. Y., June 15, 1921.

In consideration of my interest in Christian education, and in consideration of others subscribing, I hereby subscribe and will pay to the order of the treasurer of Allegheny College, Meadville, Pennsylvania, the sum of five thousand dollars; $5,000.

This obligation shall become due thirty days after my death, and I hereby instruct my executor, or administrator, to pay the same out of my estate. This pledge shall bear interest at the rate of ___ per cent. per annum, payable annually, from ___ till paid. The proceeds of this obligation shall be added to the Endowment of said Institution, or expended in accordance with instructions on reverse side of this pledge.

Name: Mary Yates Johnston,
Address: 306 East 6th Street, Jamestown, N.Y.
Dayton E. McClain, Witness,
T. R. Courtis, Witness, To authentic signature.

On the reverse side of the writing is the following endorsement:

In loving memory this gift shall be known as the Mary Yates Johnston memorial fund, the proceeds from which shall be used to educate students preparing for the ministry, either in the United States or in the Foreign Field.

This pledge shall be valid only on the condition that the provisions of my will, now extant, shall be first met.

Mary Yates Johnston.

The subscription was not payable by its terms until 30 days after the death of the promisor. The sum of $1,000 was paid, however, upon account in December, 1923, while the promisor was alive. The college set the money aside to be held as a scholarship fund for the benefit of students preparing for the ministry. Later, in July, 1924, the promisor gave notice to the college that she repudiated the promise. Upon the expiration of 30 days following her death, this action was brought against the executor of her will to recover the unpaid balance.

The law of charitable subscriptions has been a prolific source of controversy in this state and elsewhere. We have held that a promise of that order is unenforceable like any other if made without consideration. Hamilton College v. Stewart, 1 N. Y. 581; Presbyterian Church v. Cooper, 112 N. Y. 517, 20 N. E. 352, 3 L. R. A. 468, 8 Am. St. Rep. 767. . . . On the other hand, though professing to apply to such subscriptions the general law of contract, we have found consideration present where the general law of contract, at least as then declared, would have said that it was absent. Barnes v. Perine, 12 N. Y. 18; Presbyterian Soc. v. Beach, 74 N. Y. 72. . . .

A classic form of statement identifies consideration with detriment to the promisee sustained by virtue of the promise. Hamer v. Sidway, 124 N. Y. 538, 27 N. E. 256, 12 L. R. A. 463, 21 Am. St. Rep. 693. . . . So compendious a formula is little more than a half truth. There is need of many a supplementary gloss before the outline can be so filled in as to depict the classic doctrine. "The promise and the consideration must purport to be the motive each for the other, in whole or at least in part. It is not enough that the promise induces the detriment or that the detriment induces the promise if the other half is wanting." Wisconsin & Michigan R. Co. v. Powers, 191 U. S. 379, 386, 24 S. Ct. 107, 108 (48 L. Ed. 229); McGovern v. City of New York, 234 N. Y. 377, 389, 138 N. E. 26, 25 A. L. R. 1442. . . . If A promises B to make him a gift, consideration may be lacking, though B has renounced other opportunities for betterment in the faith that the promise will be kept.

The half truths of one generation tend at times to perpetuate themselves in the law as the whole truth of another, when constant repetition brings it about that qualifications, taken once for granted, are disregarded or forgotten. The doctrine of consideration has not escaped the common lot. As far back as 1881, Judge Holmes in his lectures on the Common Law (page 292), separated the detriment, which is merely a consequence of the promise from the detriment, which is in truth the motive or inducement, and yet added that the courts "have gone far in obliterating this distinction." The tendency toward effacement has not lessened with the years. On the contrary, there has grown up of recent days a doctrine that a substitute for consideration or an exception to its ordinary requirements can be found in what is styled "a promissory estoppel." Williston, Contracts, §§ 139, 116. Whether the exception has made its way in this state to such an extent as to permit us to say that the general law of consideration has been modified accordingly, we do not now attempt to say. Cases such as Siegel v. Spear & Co., 234 N. Y. 479, 138 N. E. 414, 26 A. L. R. 1205, and De Cicco v. Schweizer, 221 N. Y. 431, 117 N. E. 807, L. R. A. 1918E, 1004, Ann. Cas. 1918C, 816, may be signposts on the road. Certain, at least, it is that we have adopted the doctrine of promissory estoppel as the equivalent of consideration in connection with our law of charitable subscriptions. So long as those decisions stand, the question is not merely whether the enforcement of a charitable subscription can be squared with the doctrine of consideration in all its ancient rigor. The question may also be whether it can be squared with doctrine of consideration as qualified by the doctrine of promissory estoppel.

We have said that the cases in this state have recognized this exception, if exception it is thought to be. Thus, in Barnes v. Perine, 12 N. Y. 18, the subscription was made without request, express or implied, that the church do anything on the faith of it. Later, the church did incur expense to the knowledge of the promisor, and in the reasonable belief that the promise would be kept. We held the promise binding, though consideration there was none except upon the theory of a promissory estoppel. In Presbyterian Society v. Beach, 74 N. Y. 72, a situation substantially the same became the basis for a like ruling. So in Roberts v. Cobb, 103 N. Y. 600, 9 N. E. 500, and Keuka College v. Ray, 167 N. Y. 96, 60 N. E. 325, the moulds of consideration as fixed by the old doctrine were subjected to a like expansion. Very likely, conceptions of public policy have shaped, more or less subconsciously, the rulings thus made. Judges have been affected by the thought that 'defenses of that character' are 'breaches of faith towards the public, and especially towards those engaged in the same enterprise, and an unwarrantable disappointment of the reasonable expectations of those interested.' W. F. Allen, J., in Barnes v. Perine, supra, p. 24; and cf. Eastern States League v. Vail, 97 Vt. 495, 505, 124 A. 568, 38 A. L. R. 845, and cases there cited. The result speaks for itself irrespective of the motive. Decisions which have stood so long, and which are supported by so many considerations of public policy and reason, will not be overruled to save the symmetry of a concept which itself came into our law, not so much from any reasoned conviction of its justice, as from historical accidents of practice and procedure. 8 Holdsworth, History of English Law, 7 et seq. The concept survives as one of the distinctive features of our legal system. We have no thought to suggest that it is obsolete or on the way to be abandoned. As in the case of other concepts, however, the pressure of exceptions has led to irregularities of form.

It is in this background of precedent that we are to view the problem now before us. The background helps to an understanding of the implications inherent in subscription and acceptance. This is so though we may find in the end that without recourse to the innovation of promissory estoppel the transaction can be fitted within the mould of consideration as established by tradition.

The promisor wished to have a memorial to perpetuate her name. She imposed a condition that the "gift" should "be known as the Mary Yates Johnston Memorial Fund." The moment that the college accepted $1,000 as a payment on account, there was an assumption of a duty to do whatever acts were customary or reasonably necessary to maintain the memorial fairly and justly in the spirit of its creation. The college could not accept the money and hold itself free thereafter from personal responsibility to give effect to the condition. Dinan v. Coneys, 143 N. Y. 544, 547, 38 N. E. 715; Brown v. Knapp, 79 N. Y. 136. . . . More is involved in the receipt of such a fund than a mere acceptance of money to be held to a corporate use. Cf. Martin v. Meles, 179 Mass. 114, 60 N. E. 397. . . . The purpose of the founder would be unfairly thwarted or at least inadequately served if the college failed to communicate to the world, or in any event to applicants for the scholarship, the title of the memorial. By implication it undertook, when it accepted a portion of the "gift," that in its circulars of information and in other customary ways when making announcement of this scholarship, it would couple with the announcement the name of the donor. The donor was not at liberty to gain the benefit of such an undertaking upon the payment of a part and disappoint the expectation that there would be payment of the residue. If the college had stated after receiving $1,000 upon account of the subscription, that it would apply the money to the prescribed use, but that in its circulars of information and when responding to prospective applicants it would deal with the fund as an anonymous donation, there is little doubt that the subscriber would have been at liberty to treat this statement as the repudiation of a duty impliedly assumed, a repudiation justifying a refusal to make payments in the future. Obligation in such circumstances is correlative and mutual. A case much in point is New Jersey Hospital v. Wright, 95 N. J. Law, 462, 464, 113 A. 144, where a subscription for the maintenance of a bed in a hospital was held to be enforceable by virtue of an implied promise by the hospital that the bed should be maintained in the name of the subscriber. Cf. Board of Foreign Missions v. Smith, 209 Pa. 361, 58 A. 689. A parallel situation might arise upon the endowment of a chair or a fellowship in a university by the aid of annual payments with the condition that it should commemorate the name of the founder or that of a member of his family. The university would fail to live up to the fair meaning of its promise if it were to publish in its circulars of information and elsewhere the existence of a chair or a fellowship in the prescribed subject, and omit the benefactor's name. A duty to act in ways beneficial to the promisor and beyond the application of the fund to the mere uses of the trust would be cast upon the promisee by the acceptance of the money. We do not need to measure the extent either of benefit to the promisor or of detriment to the promisee implicit in this duty. "If a person chooses to make an extravagant promise for an inadequate consideration, it is his own affair." 8 Holdsworth, History of English Law, p. 17. It was long ago said that "when a thing is to be done by the plaintiff, be it never so small, this is a sufficient consideration to ground an action." Sturlyn v. Albany, 1587, Cro. Eliz. 67, quoted by Holdsworth, supra; cf. Walton Water Co. v. Village of Walton, 238 N. Y. 46, 51, 143 N. E. 786. The longing for posthumous remembrance is an emotion not so weak as to justify us in saying that its gratification is a negligible good.

We think the duty assumed by the plaintiff to perpetuate the name of the founder of the memorial is sufficient in itself to give validity to the subscription within the rules that define consideration for a promise of that order. When the promisee subjected itself to such a duty at the implied request of the promisor, the result was the creation of a bilateral agreement. Williston, Contracts, §§ 60a, 68, 90, 370; Brown v. Knapp, supra; Grossman v. Schenker, supra; Williams College v. Danforth, 12 Pick. (Mass.) 541, 544; Ladies Collegiate Institute v. French, 16 Gray (Mass.) 196, 200. There was a promise on the one side and on the other a return promise, made, it is true, by implication, but expressing an obligation that had been exacted as a condition of the payment. A bilateral agreement may exist though one of the mutual promises be a promise "implied in fact," an inference from conduct as opposed to an inference from words. Williston, Contracts, §§ 90, 22a; Pettibone v. Moore, 75 Hun, 461, 464, 27 N. Y. S. 455. We think the fair inference to be drawn from the acceptance of a payment on account of the subscription is a promise by the college to do what may be necessary on its part to make the scholarship effective. The plan conceived by the subscriber will be mutilated and distorted unless the sum to be accepted is adequate to the end in view. Moreover, the time to affix her name to the memorial will not arrive until the entire fund has been collected. The college may thus thwart the purpose of the payment on account if at liberty to reject a tender of the residue. It is no answer to say that a duty would then arise to make restitution of the money. If such a duty may be imposed, the only reason for its existence must be that there is then a failure of 'consideration.' To say that there is a failure of consideration is to concede that a consideration has been promised, since otherwise it could not fail. No doubt there are times and situations in which limitations laid upon a promisee in connection with the use of what is paid by a subscriber lack the quality of a consideration, and are to be classed merely as conditions. Williston, Contracts, § 112; Page, Contracts, § 523. "It is often difficult to determine whether words of condition in a promise indicate a request for consideration or state a mere condition in a gratuitous promise. An aid, though not a conclusive test in determining which construction of the promise is more reasonable is an inquiry whether the happening of the condition will be a benefit to the promisor. If so, it is a fair inference that the happening was requested as a consideration." Williston, supra, § 112. Such must be the meaning of this transaction unless we are prepared to hold that the college may keep the payment on account, and thereafter nullify the scholarship which is to

There is consideration?

preserve the memory of the subscriber. The fair implication to be gathered from the whole transaction is <u>assent</u> to the condition and the assumption of a duty to go forward with performance. De Wolf Co. v. Harvey, 161 Wis. 535, 154 N. W. 988. . . . Cf. Corbin, Offer and Acceptance, 26 Yale L. J. 169, 177, 193; McGovney, Irrevocable Offers, 27 Harv. L. R. 644; Sir Frederick Pollock, 28 L. Q. R. 100, 101. The subscriber does not say: I hand you $1,000, and you may make up your mind later, after my death, whether you will undertake to commemorate my name. What she says in effect is this: I hand you $1,000, and if you are unwilling to commemorate me, the time to speak is now.

There is consideration, therefore no need to worry about estoppel?

The conclusion thus reached makes it needless to consider whether, aside from the feature of a memorial, a promissory estoppel may result from the assumption of a duty to apply the fund, so far as already paid, to special purposes not mandatory under the provisions of the college charter (the support and education of students preparing for the ministry)–an assumption induced by the belief that other payments sufficient in amount to make the scholarship effective would be added to the fund thereafter upon the death of the subscriber. Ladies Collegiate Institute v. French, 16 Gray (Mass.) 196; Barnes v. Perine, 12 N. Y. 18, and cases there cited.

The judgment of the Appellate Division and that of the Trial Term should be reversed, and judgment ordered for the plaintiff as prayed for in the complaint, with costs in all courts.

KELLOGG, J. (dissenting).

The Chief Judge finds in the expression, "In loving memory this gift shall be known as the Mary Yates Johnston Memorial Fund," an offer on the part of Mary Yates Johnston to contract with Allegheny College. The expression makes no such appeal to me. Allegheny College was not requested to perform any act through which the sum offered might bear the title by which the offeror states that it shall be known. The sum offered was termed a "gift" by the offeror. Consequently, I can see no reason why we should strain ourselves to make it, not a gift, but a trade. Moreover, since the donor specified that the gift was made, "In consideration of my interest in Christian education, and in consideration of others subscribing," considerations not adequate in law, I can see no excuse for asserting that it was otherwise made in consideration of an act or promise on the part of the donee, constituting a sufficient quid pro quo to convert the gift into a contract obligation. To me the words used merely expressed an expectation or wish on the part of the donor and failed to exact the return of an adequate consideration. But if an offer indeed was present, then clearly it was an offer to enter into a unilateral contract. The offeror was to be bound provided the offeree performed such acts as might be necessary to make the gift offered become known under the proposed name. This is evidently the thought of the Chief Judge, for he says: "She imposed a condition that the 'gift' should be known as the Mary Yates Johnston Memorial Fund." In other words, she proposed to exchange her offer of a donation in return for acts to be performed. Even so, there was never any acceptance of the offer, and therefore no contract, for the acts requested have never been performed. The gift has never been made known as demanded. Indeed, the requested acts, under the very terms of the assumed offer, could never have been performed at a time to convert the offer into a promise. This is so for the reason that the donation was not to take effect until after the death of the donor, and by her death her offer was withdrawn. Williston on Contracts, § 62. Clearly, although a promise of the college to make the gift known, as requested, may be implied, that promise was not the acceptance of an offer which gave rise to a contract. The donor stipulated for acts, not promises.

"In order to make a bargain it is necessary that the acceptor shall give in return for the offer or the promise exactly the consideration which the offeror requests. If an act is requested, that very act and no other must be given. If a promise is requested, that promise must be made absolutely and unqualifiedly." Williston on Contracts, § 73. "It does not follow that an offer becomes a promise because it is accepted; it may be, and frequently is, conditional, and then it does not become a promise until the conditions are satisfied; and in case of offers for a consideration, the performance of the consideration is always deemed a condition." Langdell, Summary of the Law of Contracts, § 4.

It seems clear to me that there was here no offer, no acceptance of an offer, and no contract. Neither do I agree with the Chief Judge that this court "found consideration present where the general law of contract, at least as then declared, would have said that it was absent" in the cases of Barnes v. Perine, 12 N. Y. 18, Presbyterian Society v. Beach, 74 N. Y. 72, and Keuka College v. Ray, 167 N. Y. 96, 60 N. E. 325. In the Keuka College Case an offer to contract, in consideration of the performance of certain acts by the offeree, was converted into a promise by the actual performance of those acts. This form of contract has been known to the law from time immemorial (Langdell, § 46), and for at least a century longer than the other type, a bilateral contract (Williston, § 13). It may be that the basis of the decisions in Barnes v. Perine and Presbyterian Society v. Beach, supra, was the same as in the Keuka College Case. See Presbyterian Church of Albany v. Cooper, 112 N. Y. 517, 20 N. E. 352, 3 L. R. A. 468, 8 Am. St. Rep. 767. However, even if the basis of the decisions be a so-called "promissory estoppel," nevertheless they initiated no new doctrine. A so-called "promissory estoppel," although not so termed, was held sufficient by Lord Mansfield and his fellow judges as far back as the year 1765. Pillans v. Van Mierop, 3 Burr. 1663. Such a doctrine may be an anomaly; it is not a novelty. Therefore I can see no ground for the suggestion that the ancient rule which makes consideration necessary to the formation of every contract is in danger of effacement through any decisions of this court. To me that is a cause for congratulation rather than regret. However, the discussion may be beside the mark, for I do not understand that the holding about to be made in this case is other than a holding that consideration was given to convert the offer into a promise. With that result I cannot agree and, accordingly, must dissent.

POUND, CRANE, LEHMAN, and O'BRIEN, JJ., concur with CARDOZO, C. J. KELLOGG, J., dissents in opinion, in which ANDREWS, J., concurs.

Judgment accordingly.

NOTES AND QUESTIONS

1.   *Famous but controversial opinion.* The *Allegheny College* case is quite famous primarily for the fame of its author who determined in the case that the donor did not simply make a gift. Rather Mary Yates Johnson bargained for certain conduct on the part of the college. Can you find the peppercorn? For various views on this case, see Joshua P. Davis, "Cardozo's Judicial Craft and What Cases Come to Mean," 68 N.Y.U. L. Rev. 777 (1993); Brady Coleman, "Lord Denning & Justice Cardozo: The Judge as Poet-Philosopher," 32 Rutgers L. J. 485 (2001); Curtis Bridgeman, "Allegheny College Revisited: Cardozo, Consideration, and Formalism in Context," 39 U. C. Davis L. Rev. 149 (2005); and Lawrence A. Cunningham, "Cardozo and Posner: A Study in Contracts," 36 Wm. & Mary L. Rev. 1379 (1995).

2.   *New York courts and promissory estoppel.* One reason Cardozo did not embrace promissory estoppel is that the New York Court of Appeals had not then (nor has it yet) adopted the doctrine. While the Second Circuit has adopted the doctrine, as have several lower state courts in New York, the Court of Appeals has yet to do so. See Arthur B. Schwartz, "The Second Circuit Estopped: There Is No Promissory Estoppel in New York," 19 Cardozo L. Rev. 1201 (2000).

3.   *Unilateral and bilateral contracts.* The *Allegheny College* case discusses the difference between unilateral (Kellogg) and bilateral (Cardozo) contracts that are explored in the next chapter. Based on the intent of the maker of an offer (a promise conditioned upon acceptance), the promisee might accept the offer in one of two ways: full performance of the requested acts (unilateral contract) or merely by making a counter promise to perform those acts in the future (bilateral contract). Acceptance makes the offer binding. Acceptance does not occur in a unilateral contract until those acts are fully performed. In contrast, acceptance in a bilateral contract occurs at the time of the return promise. The unilateral contract doctrine therefore presents serious issues of unprotected promisee reliance. Cardozo conceptualized the transaction as bilateral while the Kellogg dissent conceptualized it as unilateral. Why might this make a difference in outcome? In the bilateral form, the donor promise must find consideration in a bargained-for counter promise. Did Allegheny College make a promise to establish a memorial fund? Did Mary

Yates Johnston seek such a promise in return for her pledge promise? Where and how does Cardozo find the counter promise? In express words or implied from conduct? If from conduct, exactly what conduct?

4.   *Regretted decisions.* Mary Yates Johnston made the $5,000 pledge in a signed pledge document and later paid $1,000 even though payment was not due until death. Later still, she changed her mind and repudiated the pledge. After her death, Allegheny College sued the bank that administered her estate but refused to honor the repudiated pledge. What was or should be the effect of her partial performance in making the remainder of the pledge enforceable?

5.   *Role of* Allegheny College v. National Chautauqua County Bank *in prompting the adoption of promissory estoppel.* Justice Cardozo was a staunch supporter of the ALI efforts to restate contracts. See Mike Townsend, "Cardozo's *Allegheny College* Opinion: A Case Study in Law as an Art," 33 Hous. L. Rev. 1103, 1119 (1996). *Allegheny College* predates Restatement (First) of Contracts and was cited in the reporter's notes as a primary reason to include Section 90. See Arthur L. Corbin, "Mr. Justice Cardozo and the Law of Contracts," 48 Yale. L. J. 426, 431–437 (1939). As a testament to the influence of Cardozo, he was also credited with the linkage between *Palsgraf v. Long Island R.R. Co.*, 248 N.Y. 339, 162 N.E. 99 (1928) and Restatement Torts § 281. But because of Cardozo's debate surrounding the case at the ALI meetings before it came to the New York Court of Appeals, he took no part in the decision. See William L. Prosser, "*Palsgraf* Revisited," 52 Mich. L. Rev. 1, 4–5 (1953).

6.   *Assuming § 90(2) applied.* Would the outcome have been different under Restatement (First) of Contracts § 90? Under Restatement (Second) of Contracts § 90(2)?

7.   *Policy grounds for enforcement or non-enforcement of charitable subscriptions.* Few courts have explicitly adopted Restatement (Second) of Contracts § 90(2) and thus eliminated the necessity of proving either consideration or reliance to make a charitable pledge enforceable. See *Salsbury v. Northwestern Bell Telephone Co.*, 221 N.W.2d 609 (Iowa 1974). Other jurisdictions, however, have enforced charitable subscriptions on other grounds such as public policy. See, e.g., *Jewish Fed. of Cent. New Jersey v. Barondess*, 234 N.J.Super. 526, 560 A.2d 1353, 1353–54 (1989); see also E. Allan Farnsworth, "Promises and Paternalism," 41 Wm. & Mary L. Rev. 385, 403–04 (2000).

8.   *Is contract based upon promise or reliance?* One of the enduring jurisprudential questions raised by the development of promissory estoppel doctrine over the last century asks whether the "core" of contract law—the justification for enforcement of promises—depends upon the moral obligation to keep one's promises or upon the need to protect the reasonable reliance of the promisee. Professor Charles Fried, the leading proponent of the "contract as promise" position, for example, bases his argument that contract is grounded in the institution of promising upon principles of individual autonomy and trust. See Charles Fried, Contract as Promise 16–17 (1981).

Fried argues that the institution of promising is a moral institution. Individuals are morally bound to perform their promises because those individuals "intentionally invoked a convention whose function it is to give grounds—moral grounds—for another to expect the promised performance." Id.

In contrast, Grant Gilmore, among others, has argued at length that Restatement (Second) of Contracts § 90 opens the door to make reliance, not promise, the basis for contract enforcement. See Grant Gilmore, The Death of Contract 90 (1974) ("A remarkable passage in the *Restatement (Second) of Contracts* § 90 Commentary explains how most 'contracts' cases, if not all of them, can be brought under § 90 so that resort to § 75 and consideration theory will rarely, if ever, be necessary. By passing through the magic gate of § 90, it seems, we can rid ourselves of all the technical limitations of contract theory.").

Such unitary theories of contract law, however, are often imprecise. Some scholars have offered a third, pluralist view on whether individualistic promissory principles or social interests in protecting reasonable reliance best captures the core of contract doctrine. Robert Hillman, for instance, notes that "the modern contract law paradigm encompasses numerous norms and many dimensions." Robert A. Hillman, The Richness of Contract Law: An Analysis and Critique of Contemporary Theories of Contract Law 40–41 (1998). Neither Fried's contract-as-promise principle nor Gilmore's "death-of-contract" can "adequately capture[ ] the institution of contract because each emphasizes one view of the other. In reality, freedom of contract and fairness principles share the contract law spotlight." Id.

Which of these three views of contract do you find most *normatively* compelling?

d. Commercial Promises

The justification for applying promissory estoppel to commercial rather than gratuitous promises is less clear. Early empirical studies established that promissory estoppel doctrine had a future for enforcement of promises in the commercial context. Stanley D. Henderson, "Promissory Estoppel and Traditional Contract Doctrine," 78 Yale L. J. 343 (1969) and Charles L. Knapp, "Reliance in the Revised Restatement: The Proliferation of Promissory Estoppel," 81 Colum. L. Rev. 52 (1981). But those heralded reports were soon challenged by a series of later empirical studies suggesting that the nature and context of the promise determined the availability of promissory estoppel, not the presence or absence of reliance. Daniel A. Farber and John H. Matheson, "Beyond Promissory Estoppel: Contract Law and the 'Invisible Handshake,'" 52 U. Chi. L. Rev. 903 (1983); Randy E. Barnett, "The Death of Reliance," 46 J. Legal Educ. 518 (1996); and Edward Yorio and Steve Thel, "The Promissory Basis of Section 90," 101 Yale L. J. 111 (1991). Not long thereafter promissory estoppel doctrine returned to its historical roots in an empirical study concluding (i) bargain theory and not promissory estoppel was the primary basis of legal obligation, (ii) reliance and not the promise was the central tenet of promissory estoppel, and (iii) reliance damages as opposed to expectancy remedies were normative in promissory estoppel cases. Robert A. Hillman, "Questioning the 'New Consensus' On Promissory Estoppel: An Empirical and Theoretical Study," 98 Colum. L. Rev. 580 (1998).

This storied journey will never be complete because promissory estoppel is a doctrine grounded in equity. Where does the pendulum swing in the context of gratuitous versus commercial promises? It appears that while commercial promissory estoppel claims are frequent, successes are rare. One scholar described the reduced utility of the doctrine in commercial context as a product of judicial sympathy designed to minimize the business risk of promissory estoppel liability in the context of waivers and notices. Successful claims are narrowly allowed and only when the commercial promisee successfully articulates an "enforcement promise" rather than more traditional "performance reliance." The former requires a reasonable belief in legal enforceability of the promise, whereas the latter only requires a reasonable belief that the promise will be performed. Sidney W. DeLong, "The New Requirement of Enforcement Reliance in Commercial Promissory Estoppel: Section 90 as Catch-22," 1997 Wis. L. Rev. 943 (1997).

3. OBLIGATION BY REASON OF UNJUST ENRICHMENT: THE RESTITUTION DOCTRINE

For purposes of contract law, obligation may arise *ex delicto* (e.g., from a tort), *ex contractu* (from a contract), or from a body of common law known in America as "restitution" or alternatively as *quasi ex contractu* ("quasi contract"). Restitution as a term generally implies the restoration of something to its rightful owner. Obligation from restitution does not arise from tort or contract (despite the reference to quasi contract) but simply by virtue of the plaintiff's unjust enrichment of the defendant. In these cases, any person unjustly enriched at the expense of another must make restitution to the other person. Restatement (First) Restitution § 1. Unlike tort and contract law, recovery under restitution is not based upon the plaintiff's "loss" but on the defendant's "gain." Because it is an independent branch of law, recovery does not depend upon the existence of an independent tort or breach of contract.

The legal term "restitution" is an American invention stemming from the Restatement of Restitution first published by the ALI in 1937 (now in the third edition process). By design, this specific terminology was used to replace earlier and more general English and American law terms including *quantum meruit, quasi-contract,* and *implied-in-law contracts.* The other terms were indefinite, misleading, and otherwise inadequate to the task. For the most part, terms like *quasi-contract* and *implied-in-law contract* create the mistaken impression that the action is based on or connected to the breach of a valid contract. It is not. The restitution action exists regardless of and independent from any contractual relationship that might or might not exist between the parties. See Warren A. Seavey and Austin W. Scott, "Restitution," 54 L. Q. Rev. 29, 38 (1938).

Notwithstanding the clarity and unity purposes of the term "restitution," its use has not been uniformly adopted. Indeed, modern cases still commonly use the terms *quantum meruit*, *quasi-contract*, and *implied-in-law contracts*. One commentator describes the usefulness of the alternative terminology in terms of maintaining the idea that restitution imposes contract-like obligations: "[A]lthough the contract implied is a fictitious contract because there is no consent, the liability is so analogous to a contract that some of the rules relating to a true contract must be applied to determine whether in the circumstances it is possible to impose it." W. S. Holdsworth, "Unjustifiable Enrichment," 55 L. Q. Rev. 37, 42 (1939).

Adding to the confusion, a true contract may be formed either according to express statements of the parties ("express contract") or even implied from their course of conduct ("implied-in-fact contract"). Despite the differences for determining formation assent, the distinction between express and implied-in-fact contracts has no legal consequences. Both are contracts differing only in the method of manifesting assent.

The discussion of *Slade's Case*, 76 Eng. Rep. 1074 (1602), *supra*, makes clear that the case was responsible for the future development and unification of contract law under the assumpsit action. At about that time, assumpsit actions were divided into two classes—special assumpsit and indebitatus assumpsit. The two forms required distinct pleading. Indebitatus assumpsit required merely that the plaintiff merely "allege" a debt due and a promise to repay. In contrast, special assumpsit required very specific pleading with many pitfalls. Because of this difference, indebitatus assumpsit evolved into the more generally used and more flexible actions, especially after *Slade's Case*. Through use, standardized pleading forms referred to as "common counts" developed to cover specific situations including the recovery of the reasonable value of (i) goods delivered ("quantum valebat") and (ii) services rendered ("quantum meruit").

In each case, the promise to pay reasonable sums for the goods or services delivered or rendered was simply a legal fiction or a promise implied by law. An express promise did not exist and was not necessary to the count. Indeed, the count was based on notions of natural justice. As noted by Lord Mansfield in *Moses v. Macferlan*, 2 Burr. 1005 (1760):

If the defendant be under an obligation, from the ties of natural justice, to refund; the law implies a debt, and gives this action, founded in the equity of the plaintiff's case, as it were upon a contract ("quasi ex contractu," as the Roman law expresses it).

The common law counts for quantum valebat and quantum meruit thus began the evolution of the modern law of implied-in-law contracts or quasi-contracts. Regardless of terminology, such "contracts" are simply not contracts at all.

As noted, recovery in restitution requires the defendant to disgorge any gain received from the plaintiff, thus returning the defendant to the status quo that existed before execution of the contract. The gain or benefit conferred may be in the form of property or services. Most of the difficult common law cases consider under what circumstances the provider of services is entitled to restitution for the value of services conferred upon another person.

Cases considering required restitution for the value of services not requested by the benefited party are even more difficult. In these situations, the law of restitution attempts to balance the right of the provider of the services to restitution against the right of the enriched party to be free from unwarranted intervention (without request) in its affairs. This balance is captured in the restitution concepts of the "officious intermeddler" or "volunteer," both of which deny restitution relief to the the service provider. See Restatement (First) Restitution § 2.

Under what circumstances might a person confer a benefit upon another without the request of the other party? Three common examples are gratuitous transactions, emergency services, and self-interested transactions. The gratuitous or altruistic intermeddler confers a benefit upon another as a gift and without any expectation of repayment. Restitution provides no remedy for this intermeddler any more than restitution provides a remedy of the return of gifts. While the gratuitous intermeddler has enriched the recipient, the enrichment was not unjust since there is no injustice in making or receiving a gift. For this reason, restitution cases between family members are seldom successful—in the absence of express contractual intent, courts presume that family members transfer goods or services to other family members with donative intent. Cases not involving family members normally involve business promotional activities and the like. While these situations make more difficult cases, they are likewise are seldom successful. In most cases, the plaintiff's original altruism vanishes once the introduction proves profitable.

The second group of cases involves emergency services necessary for the preservation or protection of the defendant's life or property rendered without request of the defendant. Again benefit exists, but is it compensable under restitution theory? These cases are related to the first group because the occupation of the service provider is often crucial to the outcome. Persons in the business of rendering the type of services involved generally are not presumed to have rendered the services altruistically. Thus, in the famous case of *Cotnam v. Wisdom*, 83 Ark. 601, 104 S.W. 164 (1907), Wisdom, a medical doctor, performed emergency medical services on the victim of a street car accident. The victim never regained consciousness and subsequently died despite Wisdom's services, and Wisdom sued for payment. The court awarded restitution in favor of Wisdom, basing the recovery on the value of Wisdom's professional medical services. In contrast, others not in the business of rendering such services are mostly treated as good Samaritans and not entitled to restitution.

A final group of cases involve persons who seek to promote their own self-interest through the rendition of services (expect compensation), but who confer the unsolicited benefit on strangers. This is perhaps the most vexing problem. The enriched party will argue the benefit was forced upon them without choice or request whereas the plaintiff will argue enrichment occurred nonetheless and equity should not allow retention without payment. See generally, John P. Dawson, "The Self-Serving Intermeddler," 87 Harv. L. Rev. 1409 (1974).

Finally, even when a court awards restitution, measuring the value of the benefit to the defendant is a delicate and confusing matter. It is not the market value of the services to the plaintiff that matters (the loss) but the market value of those services to the defendant that is crucial (the unjust enrichment gain). Proving that value itself is a source of confusion. See Candace S. Kovacic, "A Proposal to Simplify Quantum Meruit Litigation," 35 Am. U. L. Rev. 547 (1946).

Restitution's historical connection to contract law perpetuates the use of that term or concept in settings where a promise does exist. To avoid confusion, it is important to distinguish three categories of cases that implicate the term restitution:

- **Category I**—Non-Contractual Restitution (No Promise)
  - As discussed in the prior section, a party uses this category of restitution to recover unjust enrichment of the other party in the absence of a promise to return that benefit. It is a doctrine in equity and not contract law.
- **Category II**—Promissory Restitution (Promise But Trails Enrichment)
  - This category is addressed in this section. Unlike the unjust enrichment restitution theory of obligation, promissory restitution always involves a promise. However, the promise follows receipt of the benefit by the promisor and thus is not enforceable by traditional

contractual obligation theories explored earlier in this chapter. Since the promise was made after the promisor received the benefit, it neither "sought" the benefit (no consideration under Restatement (Second) § 71(1)), nor expected it in the form of reasonable reliance (no promissory estoppel under Restatement (Second) § 90(1)). Consideration and promissory estoppel theory do not support contractual recovery for promises made in connection with a benefit already received. In the case of consideration, the benefit was not given in exchange for a return promise or benefit. Similarly, in the case of promissory estoppel, the benefit was not given in reliance upon a promise because at the time the promisee conferred of the benefit no promise had been made.

While consideration and promissory estoppel doctrines might characterize the promise as purely gratuitous, an important difference exists where the benefit was conferred with the expectation of repayment. Unlike pure gifts where the donor does not expect repayment, the party in these cases expects repayment. Nonetheless, unjust enrichment restitution theory normally does not provide a remedy because the enrichment was "officious." But in some cases, the promisor follows receipt of the benefit with a promise of repayment for that benefit received in the past. Accordingly, these "intermediary" failed restitution and contractual claims seize the trailing promise as a theory of obligation to enforce the promise "where necessary to prevent injustice." Restatement (Second) of Contracts § 86. Like promissory estoppel, justice is used to determine whether the promise is binding, but unlike promissory estoppel, the court must normally choose to either enforce the promise as made or not. For example, this theory of obligation does not expressly permit the court to fashion a narrower remedy if the promise would not otherwise be enforceable to prevent injustice. Compare Restatement (Second) of Contracts § 90(1) ("The remedy granted for breach may be limited as justice requires."). However, justice might prevent the promise from being binding where, for example, the value of the promise is highly disproportionate to the value of the benefit received (Restatement (Second) of Contracts) § 86(2)(b)) or where the benefit was conferred as a gift and not simply officiously (Restatement (Second) of Contracts § 86(2)(a)).

- **Category III**—Contractual Restitution (Contract Defense or Breach)

    o   In many cases to follow in later chapters, a promise is made and supported by a "peppercorn of apparent consideration." "Restitution" will also often be available in such cases. But unlike the above two categories, an enforceable contract existed, supported by consideration or by promissory estoppel. The restitution remedy in these situations is truly contract-based because it emanates from a true contract. In most instances, a court may only choose how to measure the restitution remedy, not whether the remedy is otherwise available under a justice theory. Compare Restatement (Second) of Contracts §§ 86 and 90. Measurement is restricted to a choice between the marketplace replacement cost of the benefit received versus the increase in value of the promisor's property interests. Restatement (Second) § 371. This restitution remedy might arise in several situations, including a total breach of the contract (Restatement (Second) § 373), the party in breach confers a greater benefit than the non-breaching party's loss (Restatement (Second) § 374), enforcement of the contract is barred because it is not in writing (Restatement (Second) of Contracts § 375), the contract is voidable because of some formation deficiency (Restatement (Second) of Contracts § 376), and a supervening event after the contract is formed makes further performance impracticable or the purpose of the contract is otherwise frustrated (Restatement (Second) of Contracts § 377). As might be expected, restitution in contract cases is limited by various equitable considerations such as election among remedies and delay. See Restatement (Second) of Contracts §§ 378–385. This third category of restitution-styled remedies appears throughout the remainder of this casebook in nearly every chapter.

The task in each case is simple. The difficulty is restricted to identifying the proper category of restitution. If restitution is sought where no promise was made at all, Category I controls. If restitution is sought on the basis of a promise made after a benefit was received and is therefore not supported by consideration or promissory estoppel, Category II controls. However, in most situations in this casebook, where restitution is sought on the basis of a failed promise supported by consideration, Category III controls.

Promises grounded in the past are not favored by classical contract doctrine and are traditionally not enforced because of some infirmity in the bargaining process. Courts normally invoke doctrines such as "moral obligation" and "past consideration" to prevent enforcement of a promise. As discovered in the restitution section, restitution theory will not always provide a remedy for enrichment. An altruistic or gratuitous intermeddler cannot recover under restitution when the enrichment was fairly conferred as a gift without expectation of repayment. An officious intermeddler will be denied recovery when appropriate to protect the enriched party from unrequested and unwarranted intrusion. As discussed in the consideration section, a promise made for a past benefit fails under the consideration doctrine because the promisee did not seek the promise in exchange for the previously rendered benefit. And in the context of reliance, justified reliance is not a basis for enforcement because there was no existing promise at the time the benefit was conferred. As a consequence, classic contract law, at least as grounded in consideration, reliance, and restitution theories, fails to provide any basis to enforce a promise made for a benefit previously conferred.

Perhaps the best enforcement cases involve those situations where the trailing promise itself causes a reconsideration of a failed restitution case absent the promise. Exactly what is the nature and purpose of such promise that purports to rebalance the restitution equities? What are its limits? Without the promise, restitution theory fails to provide a remedy. With the promise, consideration and reliance theories fail to provide a remedy. The enforcement secret lies in the combination of the moral overtones attaching to all promissory conduct, especially when made in recognition of a prior benefit received.

Proper limitation can be discovered in distinguishing gratuitous intermeddlers from officious intermeddlers. While the latter might expect more hope, purely gratuitous transactions should expect less favor. The Restatement (Second) § 86 adopts this position, but as with many contract doctrines, the law is easier to state abstractly than to apply fairly. See generally, Stanley D. Henderson, "Promises Grounded in the Past: The Idea of Unjust Enrichment and the Law of Contracts," 57 Va. L. Rev. 1115 (1971) and Steve Thel and Edward Yorio, "The Promissory Basis of Past Consideration," 78 Va. L. Rev. 1045 (1992).

A claim in restitution and a claim in promissory restitution are different. A pure restitution claim may be advanced even though a contract does not exist. A claim in promissory restitution advances even in the absence of an independent restitution claim and even in the absence of an independent theory of obligation based on consideration or reliance. As a result, a claim in promissory restitution is an independent theory of obligation. Like consideration and reliance, promissory restitution seeks to enforce the promise itself as opposed to a restitution remedy designed to force the enriched party to make restitution to the plaintiff based on the value of unjust enrichment.

The point to remember when reading the following cases is that a true contract does not exist because the benefit was not requested and the promisee did not actually—objectively or subjectively—assent. Instead, one party provided a benefit, and the beneficiary made a return promise that trailed the receipt of the benefit. As a result, any recovery may not be based upon a theory of contract breach—the claim must be based upon equity and justice inherent in restitution theory. As you read the next series of cases, evaluate the restitution claim independent of the promissory action. Also, determine if enforcement of the trailing promise emasculates the doctrine of past consideration.

MILLS V. WYMAN

Supreme Judicial Court of Massachusetts
20 Mass. 207 (1825)

This was an action of *assumpsit* brought to recover a compensation for the board, nursing, etc., of Levi Wyman, son of the defendant, from the 5th to the 20th of February, 1821. The plaintiff then lived at Hartford, in Connecticut; the defendant, at Shrewsbury, in this county. Levi Wyman, at the time when the services were rendered, was about 25 years of age, and had long ceased to be a member of his father's family. He was on his return from a voyage at sea, and being suddenly taken sick at Hartford, and being poor and in distress, was relieved by the plaintiff in the manner and to the extent above stated. On the 24th of February, after all the expenses had been incurred, the defendant wrote a letter to the plaintiff, promising to pay him such expenses. There was no consideration for this promise, except what grew out of the relation which subsisted between Levi Wyman and the defendant, and Howe J., before whom the cause was tried in the Court of Common Pleas, thinking this not sufficient to support the action, directed a nonsuit. To this direction the plaintiff filed exceptions.

The opinion of the Court was read, as drawn up by PARKER, C. J.

General rules of law established for the protection and security of honest and fair-minded men, who may inconsiderately make promises without any equivalent, will sometimes screen men of a different character from engagements which they are bound in *foro conscientiæ* to perform. This is a defect inherent in all human systems of legislation. The rule that a mere verbal promise, without any consideration, cannot be enforced by action, is universal in its application, and cannot be departed from to suit particular cases in which a refusal to perform such a promise may be disgraceful.

The promise declared on in this case appears to have been made without any legal consideration. The kindness and services towards the sick son of the defendant were not bestowed at his request. The son was in no respect under the care of the defendant. He was twenty-five years old, and had long left his father's family. On his return from a foreign country, he fell sick among strangers, and the plaintiff acted the part of the good Samaritan, giving him shelter and comfort until he died. The defendant, his father, on being informed of this event, influenced by a transient feeling of gratitude, promises in writing to pay the plaintiff for the expenses he had incurred. But he has determined to break this promise, and is willing to have his case appear on record as a strong example of particular injustice sometimes necessarily resulting from the operation of general rules.

It is said a moral obligation is a sufficient consideration to support an express promise; and some authorities lay down the rule thus broadly; but upon examination of the cases we are satisfied that the universality of the rule cannot be supported, and that there must have been some preexisting obligation, which has become inoperative by positive law, to form a basis for an effective promise. The cases of debts barred by the statute of limitations, of debts incurred by infants, of debts of bankrupts, are generally put for illustration of the rule. Express promises founded on such preexisting equitable obligations may be enforced; there is a good consideration for them; they merely remove an impediment created by law to the recovery of debts honestly due, but which public policy protects the debtors from being compelled to pay. In all these cases there was originally a *quid pro quo;* and according to the principles of natural justice the party receiving ought to pay; but the legislature has said he shall not be coerced; then comes the promise to pay the debt that is barred, the promise of the man to pay the debt of the infant, of the discharged bankrupt to restore to his creditor what by the law he had lost. In all these cases there is a moral obligation founded upon an antecedent valuable consideration. These promises therefore have a sound legal basis. They are not promises to pay something for nothing; not naked pacts; but the voluntary revival or creation of obligation which before existed in natural law, but which had been dispensed with, not for the benefit of the party obliged solely, but principally for the public convenience. If moral obligation, in its fullest sense, is a good substratum for an express promise, it is not easy to perceive why it is not equally good to support an implied promise. What a man ought to do, generally he ought to be made to do, whether he promise or refuse. But the law of society has left most of such obligations to the *interior* forum, as the tribunal of conscience has been aptly called. Is there not a moral obligation upon every son who has become affluent by means of the education and advantages bestowed upon him by his father, to relieve that father from pecuniary embarrassment, to promote his comfort and happiness, and even to share with him his riches, if thereby he will be made happy? And yet such a son may, with impunity, leave such a father in any degree of penury above that which will expose the community in which he dwells, to the danger of being obliged to preserve him from absolute want. Is not a wealthy father under strong moral obligation to advance the interest of an obedient, well disposed son, to furnish him with the means of acquiring and maintaining a becoming rank in life, to rescue him from the horrors of debt incurred by misfortune? Yet the law will uphold him in any degree of parsimony, short of that which would reduce his son to the necessity of seeking public charity.

Without doubt there are great interests of society which justify withholding the coercive arm of the law from these duties of imperfect obligation, as they are called; imperfect, not because they are less binding upon the conscience than those which are called perfect, but because the wisdom of the social law does not impose sanctions upon them.

A deliberate promise, in writing, made freely and without any mistake, one which may lead the party to whom it is made into contracts and expenses, cannot be broken without a violation of moral duty. But if there was nothing paid or promised for it, the law, perhaps wisely, leaves the execution of it to the conscience of him who makes it. It is only when the party making the promise gains something, or he to whom it is made loses something, that the law gives the promise validity. And in the case of the promise of the adult to pay the debt of the infant, of the debtor discharged by the statute of limitations or bankruptcy, the principle is preserved by looking back to the origin of the transaction, where an equivalent is to be found. An exact equivalent is not required by the law; for there being a consideration, the parties are left to estimate its value; though here the courts of equity will step in to relieve from gross inadequacy between the consideration and the promise.

These principles are deduced from the general current of decided cases upon the subject, as well as from the known maxims of the common law. The general position, that moral obligation is a sufficient consideration for an express promise, is to be limited in its application, to cases where at some time or other a good or valuable consideration has existed.

A legal obligation is always a sufficient consideration to support either an express or an implied promise; such as an infant's debt for necessaries, or a father's promise to pay for the support and education of his minor children. But when the child shall have attained to manhood, and shall have become his own agent in the world's business, the debts he incurs, whatever may be their nature, create no obligation upon the father; and it seems to follow, that his promise founded upon such a debt has no legally binding force.

The cases of instruments under seal and certain mercantile contracts, in which considerations need not be proved, do not contradict the principles above suggested. The first import a consideration in themselves, and the second belong to a branch of the mercantile law, which has found it necessary to disregard the point of consideration in respect to instruments negotiable in their nature and essential to the interests of commerce. . . .

It has been attempted to show a legal obligation on the part of the defendant by virtue of our statute, which compels lineal kindred in the ascending or descending line to support such of their poor relations as are likely to become chargeable to the town where they have their settlement. But it is a sufficient answer to this position, that such legal obligation does not exist except in the very cases provided for in the statute, and never until the party charged has been adjudged to be of sufficient ability thereto. We do not know from the report any of the facts which are necessary to create such an obligation. Whether the deceased had a legal settlement in this commonwealth at the time of his death, whether he was likely to become chargeable had he lived, whether the defendant was of sufficient ability, are essential facts to be adjudicated by the court to which is given jurisdiction on this subject. The legal liability does not arise until these facts have all been ascertained by judgment, after hearing the party intended to be charged.

For the foregoing reasons we are all of opinion that the nonsuit directed by the Court of Common Pleas was right, and that judgment be entered thereon for costs for the defendant.

NOTES AND QUESTIONS

1.   *Restitution claim.* Assume that Mills did not sue on the contract but rather brought a claim for restitution against Levi's father. Did Mills confer any benefit on the father? If so, was the benefit conferred gratuitously or officiously? How do your answers to the restitution claim affect your resolution of a contract claim under promissory restitution under Restatement (Second) of Contracts §§ 86(1) and 86(2)(a)?

2.   *Antecedent consideration doctrine.* Chapter 7 discusses contracts that are unenforceable at law simply because the contract is not in writing and signed by the party to be charged. *Mills* refers to three other cases where a contract is not enforceable by law: infancy, statute of limitation, and bankruptcy. Historically, these cases all involve a special form of "past consideration"—the existence of a true antecedent contract supported by legal consideration. Unlike normative past consideration cases where a true contract and consideration never existed, these cases utilize the fresh promise to "revive" the prior enforceable promise. This use of morality to effect a policy of enforcing promises to protect socially recognized moral duties is traditionally absorbed in the so-called "moral obligation" exception to the past consideration doctrine. The case cites the three principal examples of this doctrine: debts barred by time, debts discharged in bankruptcy, and obligations of minors. All three now have roots in the Restatement (Second) of Contracts.

Debts barred by time. Early common law did not set a time limitation on bringing a cause of action, but early seventeenth century English statutes stated an action must generally be brought within six years of the cause of such action. All states now have various statutes expressing similar limitations depending on the type of contract. See, e.g., Mass. Gen. Laws Ann. tit. 260 § 2 (six years). The parties to a contract commonly specify a shorter period of limitations. When the debt does become barred by the applicable period of limitations, neither party may maintain an action upon that debt, unless the obligor or debtor makes a fresh promise regarding payment of some or all of the debt. Restatement (Second) of Contracts § 82(1) provides that a promise to pay all or a part of an antecedent debt is binding if the debt would still be enforceable but for a statute of limitations, a law that bars claims after a specified period of time. Contract claims traditionally mature ("accrue") on the date of the breach and not on the earlier date of the making of the contract. For example, UCC § 2–725 states a basic four-year statute of limitations with respect to the sale of goods. Many states now govern this matter by statute and often increase the common law requirements such as requiring the promise to be in writing. See Restatement (Second) of Contracts § 110(4) and Mass. Gen. Laws Ann. tit. 260 § 13. A promise to pay a debt barred by a statute of limitation may, of course, be an express promise. Restatement (Second) of Contracts § 82(2) also provides that such a promise may be "implied" from the conduct of the obligor including: (i) an obligor's voluntary acknowledgement to the obligee admitting the present existence of the antecedent debt; (ii) an obligor's voluntary transfer of money or property to the obligee to pay interest, to pay a portion of the principal, or to operate as security for a future payment; or (iii) an obligor's statement that the statute of limitations will not be pleaded as a defense to an obligee's suit to enforce the fresh promise. The Restatement version expresses the rule in absence of a statute. Many states now govern this matter by statute and often increase the common law requirements such as requiring the promise to be in writing. See Restatement (Second) of Contracts § 110(4) and Mass. Gen. Laws Ann. tit. 260 § 13.

Debts barred by federal bankruptcy law. Federal bankruptcy law generally defers to state law to determine whether a promise to pay a debt discharged in bankruptcy is enforceable. 11 U.S.C.A. § 524(c) (specific requirements exist for affirmation prior to discharge). Unlike promises to pay a claim barred by time, only an express promise to pay all or a part of a debt discharged creates a "moral consideration," and courts will not imply such promises from the obligor's conduct. Restatement (Second) of Contracts § 83.

Obligations of minors. Chapter 8 considers the topic of "voidable" contracts generally, a concept that applies to minor contracts as well as a number of others. Generally, a voidable contract is one in which at least one of the parties has the power to either affirm or disaffirm (rescind) the contract. Restatement (Second) of Contracts § 7. Restatement (Second) of Contracts § 85 provides that a promise to perform a voidable duty (one incurred under a voidable contract) is binding. In other words, a promise to perform a voidable duty is treated as an affirmance of the contract. However, if the promise is made when the party is still a minor, it would again be subject to disaffirmance. The topic of voidable contracts is treated extensively in Chapter 8.

3.   *Commentary.* Historical research into the background of *Mills v. Wyman* discovered a few surprises. First, Mills ran a boarding house and

sought paying customers. Second, it seems the young Levi Wyman did not die as suggested in the case. Third, it appears the referenced February 24, 1821 letter stating a promise to pay for past services was not clearly a promise at all: "I received a line from you relating to my Son Levi's sickness and requesting me to come up and see him, but as the going is very bad I cannot come up at the present, but I wish you to take all possible care of him and if you cannot have him at your house I wish you to remove him to some convenient place and if he cannot satisfy you for it I will." See Geoffrey R. Watson, "In the Tribunal of Conscience: Mills v. Wyman Reconsidered," 71 Tul. L. Rev. 1749, 1760–1761 (1997).

WEBB V. McGOWIN

Court of Appeal of Alabama
27 Ala.App. 82, 168 So. 196 (1935)

BRICKEN, Presiding Judge.

This action is in assumpsit. The complaint as originally filed was amended. The demurrers to the complaint as amended were sustained, and because of this adverse ruling by the court the plaintiff took a non-suit, and the assignment of errors on this appeal are predicated upon said action or ruling of the court.

A fair statement of the case presenting the questions for decision is set out in appellant's brief, which we adopt.

On the 3d day of August, 1925, appellant while in the employ of the W.T. Smith Lumber Company, a corporation, and acting within the scope of his employment, was engaged in clearing the upper floor of mill No. 2 of the company. While so engaged he was in the act of dropping a pine block from the upper floor of the mill to the ground below; this being the usual and ordinary way of clearing the floor, and it being the duty of the plaintiff in the course of his employment to so drop it. The block weighed about 75 pounds.

As appellant was in the act of dropping the block to the ground below, he was on the edge of the upper floor of the mill. As he started to turn the block loose so that it would drop to the ground, he saw J. Greeley McGowin, testator of the defendants, on the ground below and directly under where the block would have fallen had appellant turned it loose. Had he turned it loose it would have struck McGowin with such force as to have caused him serious bodily harm or death. Appellant could have remained safely on the upper floor of the mill by turning the block loose and allowing it to drop, but had he done this the block would have fallen on McGowin and caused him serious injuries or death. The only safe and reasonable way to prevent this was for appellant to hold to the block and divert its direction in falling from the place where McGowin was standing and the only safe way to divert it so as to prevent its coming into contact with McGowin was for appellant to fall with it to the ground below. Appellant did this, and by holding to the block and falling with it to the ground below, he diverted the course of its fall in such way that McGowin was not injured. In thus preventing the injuries to McGowin appellant himself received serious bodily injuries, resulting in his right leg being broken, the heel of his right foot torn off and his right arm broken. He was badly crippled for life and rendered unable to do physical or mental labor.

On September 1, 1925, in consideration of appellant having prevented him from sustaining death or serious bodily harm and in consideration of the injuries appellant had received, McGowin agreed with him to care for and maintain him for the remainder of appellant's life at the rate of $15 every two weeks from the time he sustained his injuries to and during the remainder of appellant's life; it being agreed that McGowin would pay this sum to appellant for his maintenance. Under the agreement McGowin paid or caused to be paid to appellant the sum so agreed on up until McGowin's death on January 1, 1934. After his death the payments were continued to and including January 27, 1934, at which time they were discontinued. Thereupon plaintiff brought suit to recover the unpaid installments accruing up to the time of the bringing of the suit.

The material averments of the different counts of the original complaint and the amended complaint are predicated upon the foregoing statement of facts.

In other words, the complaint as amended averred in substance: (1) That on August 3, 1925, appellant saved J. Greeley McGowin, appellee's testator, from death or grievous bodily harm; (2) that in doing so appellant sustained bodily injury crippling him for life; (3) that in consideration of the services rendered and the injuries received by appellant, McGowin agreed to care for him the remainder of appellant's life, the amount to be paid being $15 every two weeks; (4) that McGowin complied with this agreement until he died on January 1, 1934, and the payments were kept up to January 27, 1934, after which they were discontinued.

The action was for the unpaid installments accruing after January 27, 1934, to the time of the suit.

The principal grounds of demurrer to the original and amended complaint are: (1) It states no cause of action; (2) its averments show the contract was without consideration; (3) it fails to allege that McGowin had, at or before the services were rendered, agreed to pay appellant for them; (4) the contract declared on is void under the statute of frauds.

The averments of the complaint show that appellant saved McGowin from death or grievous bodily harm. This was a material benefit to him of infinitely more value than any financial aid he could have received. Receiving this benefit, McGowin became morally bound to compensate appellant for the services rendered. Recognizing his moral obligation, he expressly agreed to pay appellant as alleged in the complaint and complied with this agreement up to the time of his death; a period of more than 8 years.

Had McGowin been accidentally poisoned and a physician, without his knowledge or request, had administered an antidote, thus saving his life, a subsequent promise by McGowin to pay the physician would have been valid. Likewise, McGowin's agreement as disclosed by the complaint to compensate appellant for saving him from death or grievous bodily injury is valid and enforceable.

Where the promisee cares for, improves, and preserves the property of the promisor, though done without his request, it is sufficient consideration for the promisor's subsequent agreement to pay for the service, because of the material benefit received. . . .

In Boothe v. Fitzpatrick, 36 Vt. 681, the court held that a promise by defendant to pay for the past keeping of a bull which had escaped from defendant's premises and been cared for by plaintiff was valid, although there was no previous request, because the subsequent promise obviated that objection; it being equivalent to a previous request. On the same principle, had the promisee saved the promisor's life or his body from grievous harm, his subsequent promise to pay for the services rendered would have been valid. Such service would have been far more material than caring for his bull. Any holding that saving a man from death or grievous bodily harm is not a material benefit sufficient to uphold a subsequent promise to pay for the service, necessarily rests on the assumption that saving life and preservation of the body from harm have only a sentimental value. The converse of this is true. Life and preservation of the body have material, pecuniary values, measurable in dollars and cents. Because of this, physicians practice their profession charging for services rendered in saving life and curing the body of its ills, and surgeons perform operations. The same is true as to the law of negligence, authorizing the assessment of damages in personal injury cases based upon the extent of the injuries, earnings, and life expectancies of those injured.

In the business of life insurance, the value of a man's life is measured in dollars and cents according to his expectancy, the soundness of his body, and his ability to pay premiums. The same is true as to health and accident insurance.

It follows that if, as alleged in the complaint, appellant saved J. Greeley McGowin from death or grievous bodily harm, and McGowin subsequently agreed to pay him for the service rendered, it became a valid and enforceable contract.

It is well settled that a moral obligation is a sufficient consideration to support a subsequent promise to pay where the promisor has received a material benefit, although there was no original duty or liability resting on the promisor. . . . State ex rel. Bayer v. Funk, 105 Or. 134, 199 P. 592, 209 P. 113, 25 A.L.R. 625, 634; . . . . In the case of State ex rel. Bayer v. Funk, supra, the court held that a moral obligation is a sufficient consideration to support an executory promise where the promisor has received an actual pecuniary or material benefit for which he subsequently expressly promised to pay.

The case at bar is clearly distinguishable from that class of cases where the consideration is a mere moral obligation or conscientious duty unconnected with receipt by promisor of benefits of a material or pecuniary nature. Park Falls State Bank v. Fordyce, supra. Here the promisor received a material benefit constituting a valid consideration for his promise.

Some authorities hold that, for a moral obligation to support a subsequent promise to pay, there must have existed a prior legal or equitable obligation, which for some reason had become unenforceable, but for which the promisor was still morally bound. This rule, however, is subject to qualification in those cases where the promisor, having received a material benefit from the promisee, is morally bound to compensate him for the services rendered and in consideration of this obligation promises to pay. In such cases the subsequent promise to pay is an affirmance or ratification of the services rendered carrying with it the presumption that a previous request for the service was made. . . .

Under the decisions above cited, McGowin's express promise to pay appellant for the services rendered was an affirmance or ratification of what appellant had done raising the presumption that the services had been rendered at McGowin's request.

The averments of the complaint show that in saving McGowin from death or grievous bodily harm, appellant was crippled for life. This was part of the consideration of the contract declared on. McGowin was benefited. Appellant was injured. Benefit to the promisor or injury to the promisee is a sufficient legal consideration for the promisor's agreement to pay. Fisher v. Bartlett, 8 Greenl. (Me.) 122, 22 Am.Dec. 225; State ex rel. Bayer v. Funk, supra.

Under the averments of the complaint the services rendered by appellant were not gratuitous. The agreement of McGowin to pay and the acceptance of payment by appellant conclusively shows the contrary.

The contract declared on was not void under the statute of frauds (Code 1923, ß 8034). The demurrer on this ground was not well taken. 25 R.C.L. 456, 457 and 470, ß 49. . . .

From what has been said, we are of the opinion that the court below erred in the ruling complained of; that is to say, in sustaining the demurrer, and for this error the case is reversed and remanded.

Reversed and remanded.

SAMFORD, Judge (concurring).

The questions involved in this case are not free from doubt, and perhaps the strict letter of the rule, as stated by judges, though not always in accord, would bar a recovery by plaintiff, but following the principle announced by Chief Justice Marshall in Hoffman v. Porter, Fed. Cas. No. 6,577, 2 Brock. 156, 159, where he says, "I do not think that law ought to be separated from justice, where it is at most doubtful," I concur in the conclusions reached by the court.

NOTES AND QUESTIONS

1. *Restitution claim.* Assume that Webb did not sue on the contract but rather brought a claim for restitution against McGowin. Did Webb confer any benefit on McGowin? If so, was the benefit conferred gratuitously or officiously? How do your answers to the restitution claim affect your resolution of a contract claim under promissory restitution under Restatement (Second) of Contracts §§ 86(1) and 86(2)(a)?

2. *Part performance.* In Webb, the promisor made monthly payments on his promise for years until he passed away. By contrast, in Mills, the father never made any payments on the promise. Is there or should there be any legal relevance to such actual payments?

3. *Modern rule.* Mills, Webb, and Restatement (Second) of Contracts § 86 purport to suggest at least two rules (and possibly three) for the same issue. Which is correct? Another way of asking the question is to ask whether the restatement section published by the ALI is a true "restatement" of the law or rather a forecast of what some hope the law will become. Most contracts casebooks, including this one, take reasonable care in the first chapter discussing "sources of the law" to make clear that restatement provisions are not an accurate statement of the law and may not even state the majority view. In some instances, a restatement provision may reflect confusion in cases and use that confusion to articulate a hopeful outcome. In the case of Restatement (Second) of Contracts § 86, it appears the rule is followed although not often cited. See generally, Gregory E. Maggs, "Ipse Dixit: The Restatement (Second) of Contracts and the Modern Development of Contract Law," 66 Geo. Wash. L. Rev. 508, 520 (1998).

4. *Promise "is binding to the extent necessary to prevent injustice."* Restatement (Second) of Contracts § 86(1) thus states a "limitation" on the

enforcement of such a promise. Restatement (Second) of Contracts § 90(1) (promissory estoppel) states a similar limitation, but the language is different: ".... is binding if injustice can be avoided only by enforcement of the promise." Do you suppose that the language difference is accidental and meaningless? If not, what difference does the language convey?

5.   *Remedy.* In addition to the comparative "binding" nature of the promises under the two provisions, Restatement (Second) of Contracts § 90(1) also states that when binding, the remedy for breach of the now binding promise may be limited as justice requires. This language is designed to allow a Court some flexibility in designing a remedy for breach. However, the remedy for breach of a Restatement (Second) of Contracts § 86 trailing promise is not so flexible. Restatement (Second) of Contracts § 86(2)(b) does state that a promise is not binding to the extent that the value of the promise is disproportionate to the benefit. But this appears to present a Court with an "either or" choice as opposed to sliding scale flexibility. Why the different approach?

The "value" and "benefit" measures to determine disproportionality are ancient concepts. The two concepts purport to compare and contrast the value of what was received with the increase in wealth created thereby. This would be reflected in the reasonable value of the performer's services contrasted with the increase in the wealth of the enriched party. See Restatement (Second) of Contracts § 371. In *Maglica v. Maglica,* 66 Cal.App.4th 442, 78 Cal.Rptr.2d 101 (1998), an unmarried couple cohabitated as if married for over twenty years. Together they built a hugely successful business around the "Mag" flashlight. After the relationship failed, Claire sued Anthony on several theories including *quantum meruit.* The jury awarded her $84 million in damages based upon the value by which he had benefited. The case was reversed on appeal when the court determined the measure must be based only upon the much lower reasonable replacement cost of her services—what similar services could have been purchased for in the open market. Do you agree with the market replacement cost or the increase in value measure? Many contract problems are exacerbated in family contracts. See Michelle Oberman, "Sex, Lies, and the Duty to Disclose," 47 Ariz. L. Rev. 871 (2005) (rejecting the doctrine of caveat emptor in a family relationship).

Some commentators argue that a Court should also be able to award damages based solely on the reliance interest in a restitution case. See John P. Dawson, "Restitution Without Enrichment," 61 B.U. L. Rev. 563 (1981) and Jeffrey L. Harrison, "A Case for Loss Sharing," 56 Cal. L. Rev. 573 (1983). Others argue the cases cited in support of such a doctrine are mostly implied-in-fact contracts where a reliance remedy is clearly available. See Andrew Kull, "Rationalizing Restitution," 83 Cal. L. Rev. 1191, 1200 (1995).

CHAPTER 3

REACHING AGREEMENT THROUGH THE PROCESS OF OFFER AND ACCEPTANCE

■ ■ ■

A. INTRODUCTION

The previous chapter explored three theories of legal obligation used to make a promise binding or to imply a promise-like obligation through operation of law. This chapter focuses on the leading theory of obligation—consideration in the context of a bargain.

Even as the modern and historical leading theory of contract legal obligation, the doctrine of consideration has not been static. Early common law history provided that "consideration" for a promise arose from the ashes of the doctrine of assumpsit and required either the promisee to relinquish something in exchange for the promise that constituted a detriment to the promisee or a benefit to the promisor. In *Hamer v. Sidway,* 124 N.Y. 538, 543, 27 N.E. 256 (1891), Justice Parker quoted an earlier English case:

> A valuable consideration, in the sense of the law, may consist either in some right, interest, profit, or benefit accruing to the one party, or some forbearance, detriment, loss, or responsibility given, suffered, or undertaken by the other.

Either promisee detriment or promisor benefit would do. Later, as part of an early attempt to develop a theory of contract from developing case law in the Langdellian vision, Oliver Wendell Holmes, Jr.,* stated a new "bargain theory" of consideration where detriment and benefit might provide some evidence of consideration but were no longer legally important:

> It is said that any benefit conferred by the promisee on the promisor, or any detriment incurred by the promisee, may be consideration. It is also thought that every consideration may be

---

* Oliver Wendell Holmes, Jr. (1841–1935) became the editor of the American Law Review in 1870 and in 1881 published the first edition of his legendary work The Common Law. In 1882 he became a professor of law at Harvard Law School and a justice on the Supreme Judicial Court of Massachusetts. Holmes was promoted to Chief Justice in 1899. In 1902, he was appointed to the U.S. Supreme Court where his tenure was marked by pithy but often quoted opinions.

reduced to a case of the latter sort, using the word "detriment" in a somewhat broad sense. . . .

It appears to me that it has not always been sufficiently borne in mind that the same thing may be a consideration or not, as it is dealt with by the parties. . . .

. . . It is hard to see the propriety of erecting any detriment which an instrument may disclose or provide for, into a consideration, unless the parties have dealt with it on that footing. In many cases a promisee may incur a detriment without thereby furnishing consideration. The detriment may be nothing but a condition precedent to performance, as where a man promises another to pay him five hundred dollars if he breaks his leg. . . .

It is said that consideration must not be confounded with motive. It is true that it must not be confounded with what may be the prevailing or chief motive in actual fact. A man may promise to paint a picture for five hundred dollars, while his chief motive may be a desire for fame. A consideration may be given and accepted, in fact, solely for the purpose of making a promise binding. But, nevertheless, it is the essence of a consideration, that, by terms of the agreement, it is given and accepted as the motive or inducement for furnishing the consideration. The root of the whole matter is the relation of reciprocal conventional inducement, each for the other, between consideration and promise. Oliver Wendell Holmes, Jr., The Common Law 289–294 (1881).

"The Common Law" is a comprehensive work by Holmes to articulate a general theory of liability embracing both criminal and the civil law. P. S. Atiyah, "The Legacy of Holmes Through English Eyes," 63 B. U. L. Rev. 341 (1983). Whether restating common law precedents or proposing new doctrine, the Holmes "bargain theory" of consideration shifted focus from the benefit-detriment analysis to the requirement that consideration must be bargained for. Grant Gilmore, The Death of Contract 21–22 (1974). Of course, by eliminating the requirement that consideration involve a detriment or benefit, some previously enforceable promises became unenforceable and vice versa. Commercial promises remained largely unaffected because they satisfied both tests. See Karl N. Llewellyn, "Our Case-Law of Contract: Offer and Acceptance, II," 48 Yale L. J. 779, 784 & 787 (1939) and Mark B. Wessman, "Should We Fire the Gatekeeper? An Examination of the Doctrine of Consideration," 48 U. Miami L. Rev. 45, 66–67 (1993). But the bargain theory rarely permits enforcement of purely gratuitous family promises because the promisor seeks little or nothing in exchange. Importantly, the bargain theory shifted the court's focus away from the substance of the transaction to an inquiry into the process by which the parties arrived at the exchange. Blind to detriment and benefit, new doctrines like promissory estoppel thus became necessary to police the fairness of the non-bargain promise. Melvin A. Eisenberg, "The Principles of Consideration," 67 Cornell L. Rev. 640, 642 (1982). Indeed, the harshness of the literal doctrine may help to explain why some courts continue to use the term "consideration" more broadly to serve the ends of justice. Melvin A. Eisenberg, "The Responsive Model of Contracts Law," 36 Stanford L. Rev. 1107, 1116–1117 (1984).

So, how well do the restatements of contracts adopt the Holmes "bargain theory?" As it turns out, nearly perfectly. Restatement (First) of Contracts § 75 defines consideration for a promise as an act or promise bargained for and given in exchange for the promise. There is no mention of benefit or detriment.

Restatement (Second) of Contracts elevates all this to an art form through a specific declaration that neither benefit or detriment is required. Restatement (Second) § 3 defines a "bargain" as an agreement to exchange promises or performances. Restatement (Second) of Contracts § 71(1) states that to constitute consideration for a promise, the return promise or performance must be "bargained for." Restatement (Second) of Contracts § 71(2) provides a promise or performance is bargained for in this context if it is "sought" and given in exchange for the promise. To complete the circle, Restatement (Second) of Contracts § 79(a) provides that if the promisor sought the return promise or act in exchange for making the promise, there is no additional requirement of promisor benefit or promisee detriment. As a consequence, Restatement (Second) of Contracts § 79(b) confirms that there is also no requirement in equivalence in the values exchanged despite the great potential for unfairness in the exchange itself. The courts simply refuse—at least overtly—to police the fairness of the bargain, in terms of equality of exchange. Karl Llewellyn, "What Price Contract?—An Essay in Perspective," 40 Yale L. J. 704, 717 (1931).

The bargain theory has yet one more layer of complexity. As Judge Jerome Frank observed, the bargain theory creates problems for courts attempting to apply the objective theory of contracts. Concurring in a judgment invalidating a release signed by an injured employee in favor of the employer, Judge Frank observed:

> In the early days of this century a struggle went on between the respective opponents of two theories of contracts, (a) the "actual intent" theory—or "meeting of the minds" or "will" theory—and (b) the so-called "objective" theory. Without doubt, the first theory had been carried too far: Once a contract has been validly made, the courts attach legal consequences to the relation created by the contract, consequences of which the parties usually never dreamed—as, for instance, where situations arise which the parties had not contemplated. As to such matters, the "actual

intent" theory induced much fictional discourse which imputed to parties intention they plainly did not have.

But the objectivists also went too far. They tried (1) to treat virtually all the varieties of contractual arrangements in the same way, and (2), as to all contracts in all their phases, to exclude, as legally irrelevant, consideration of the actual intention of the parties or either of them, as distinguished from the outward manifestation of that intention. The objectivists transferred from the field of torts that stubborn anti-subjectivist, the "reasonable man"; so that, in part at least, advocacy of the "objective" standard in contracts appears to have represented a desire for legal symmetry, legal uniformity, a desire seemingly prompted by aesthetic impulses. Whether (thanks to the "subjectivity" of the jurymen's reactions and other factors) the objectivists' formula, in its practical workings, could yield much actual objectivity, certainty, and uniformity may well be doubted. At any rate, the sponsors of complete "objectivity" in contracts largely won out in the wider generalizations of the Restatement of Contracts and in some judicial pronouncements. *Ricketts v. Pennsylvania R. Co.*, 153 F.2d 757, 760–762 (2nd Cir. 1946).

The objective theory of contracts was well entrenched in Restatement (First) of Contracts because Samuel Williston, a leading proponent of objective theory along with Oliver Wendell Holmes, Jr. and Learned Hand, drafted the restatement as its reporter. Nonetheless, as Judge Frank carefully notes in his full concurring opinion, an expansive reading of the objective theory will often form a contract in unwarranted circumstances. Such harsh or absurd results under the objective theory thus merit a reversion to the subjective intent or "meeting of the minds" doctrine. Herein lies the secret to the balance between subjective and objective theory. Each theory necessarily overlaps with the other, and neither carries the argument in every circumstance.

B. MUTUAL MISUNDERSTANDING & OBJECTIFICATION

The concept of mutual assent requires *consensus ad item,* meaning assent to the same terms and bargain. What happens when two parties attach different meaning to the same terms? Contract law provides for two different legal responses: (1) determine whose meaning prevails; or (2) determine that the parties failed to form an enforceable contract. The former response is the subject of Chapter 4. In the latter case, no contract ever came into being because the parties did not adequately assent to the same terms. Such cases are most often referred to as mutual misunderstandings. While it is tempting to categorize the latter under the doctrine of mistake, contract law usually reserves that category for mistake of facts in existence at the time the contract is made. The mistake, if any, in such cases concerns a belief about the other party's understanding, not an external fact.

In the following famous case, determine what each party believed, whether each belief was in accordance with true facts, and whether the court prefers one meaning over the other or simply determines that no contract was formed. What rules do you think should apply to determine whether the court should prefer one party's meaning (mutual assent) or neither (no mutual assent)? Most important, what does the case have to offer concerning our newly minted objective theory of contracts?

RAFFLES V. WICHELHAUS

Court of Exchequer (England)
2 Hurlstone & Coltman; 159 Eng. Rep. 375 (1864)

Jan. 20, 1864.—To a declaration for not accepting Surat cotton which the defendant bought of the plaintiff "to arrive ex 'Peerless' from Bombay," the defendant pleaded that he meant a ship called the "Peerless" which sailed from Bombay in October, and the plaintiff was not ready to deliver any cotton which arrived by that ship, but only cotton which arrived by another ship called the "Peerless," which sailed from Bombay in December. Held, on demurrer, that the plea was a good answer. . . .

Declaration. For that it was agreed between the plaintiff and the defendants, to wit, at Liverpool, that the plaintiff should sell to the defendants, and the defendants buy of the plaintiff, certain goods, to wit, 125 bales of Surat cotton, guaranteed middling fair merchant's Dhollorah, to arrive ex "Peerless" from Bombay; and that the cotton should be taken from the quay, and that the defendants would pay the plaintiff for the same at a certain rate, to wit, at the rate of 17¼ d. per pound, within a certain time then agreed upon after the arrival of the said goods in England.— Averments: that the said goods did arrive by the said ship from Bombay in England, to wit at Liverpool, and the plaintiff was then and there ready, and willing and offered to deliver the said goods to the defendants, etc. Breach: that the defendants refused to accept the said goods or pay the plaintiff for them.

Plea. That the said ship mentioned in the said agreement was meant and intended by the defendants to be the ship called the "Peerless," which sailed from Bombay, to wit, in October; and that the plaintiff was not ready and willing and did not offer to deliver to the defendants any bales of cotton which arrived by the last mentioned ship, but instead thereof was only ready and willing and offered to deliver to the defendants 125 bales of Surat cotton which arrived by another and different ship, which was also called the "Peerless," and which sailed from Bombay, to wit, in December.

Demurrer, and joinder therein.

Milward, in support of the demurrer.—The contract was for the sale of a number of bales of cotton of a particular description, which the plaintiff was ready to deliver. It is immaterial by what ship the cotton was to arrive, so that it was a ship called the "Peerless." The words "to arrive ex 'Peerless,'" only mean that if the vessel is lost on the voyage, the contract is to be at an end. [POLLOCK, C.B. It would be a question for the jury whether both parties meant the same ship called the "Peerless."] That would be so if the contract was for the sale of a ship called the "Peerless"; but it is for the sale of cotton on board a ship of that name. [POLLOCK, C.B. The defendant only bought that cotton which was to arrive by a particular ship. It may as well be said, that if there is a contract for the purchase of certain goods in warehouse A., that is satisfied by the delivery of goods of the same description in warehouse B.] In that case there would be goods in both warehouses; here it does not appear that the plaintiff had any goods on board the other "Peerless."

[MARTIN, B. It is imposing on the defendant a contract different from that which he entered into. Pollock, C.B. It is like a contract for the purchase of wine coming from a particular estate in France or Spain, where there are two estates of that name.] The defendant has no right to contradict by parol evidence a written contract good upon the face of it. He does not impute misrepresentation or fraud, but only says that he fancied the ship was a different one. Intention is of no avail, unless stated at the time of the contract. [POLLOCK, C.B. One vessel sailed in October and the other in December.] The time of sailing is no part of the contract.

Mellish (Cohen with him), in support of the plea.—There is nothing on the face of the contract to show that any particular ship called the "Peerless" was meant; but the moment it appears that two ships called the "Peerless" were about to sail from Bombay there is a latent ambiguity, and parol evidence may be given for the purpose of showing that the defendant meant one "Peerless," and the plaintiff another. That being so, there was no consensus ad idem, and therefore no binding contract. He was then stopped by the Court.

PER CURIAM—There must be judgment for the defendants.

Judgment for the defendants.

POLLOCK, C.B., MARTIN, B., and PIGOTT, B.

NOTES AND QUESTIONS

1. *Stopped by the Court.* Mellish and Cohen, successful counsel for the defendant purchaser Wichelhaus, were interrupted by the Court with a declaration of a judgment for the defendants. The plaintiff-seller, Raffles, alleged that the contract provided for a sale of cotton to arrive on a ship named

"Peerless" sailing from Bombay and that when the ship and cotton arrived in December, Wichelhaus refused the shipment in breach of the contract. Wichelhaus did not deny any of these facts but pleaded that he "meant and intended" a ship named Peerless sailing from Bombay and arriving in October. Raffles demurred, thus conceding that Wichelhaus meant and intended a different ship, but arguing that Wichelhaus's subjective understanding had no legal relevancy. Why would Milward, counsel for the Raffles, think this irrelevant? The term "ex Peerless" has a special commercial meaning. Normally, it means that if the ship is lost at sea, the seller assumes the risk of loss and that the buyer has no cause of action for the failure to deliver. See UCC § 2–322 (delivery "ex ship" is not restricted to a particular ship). How and why does the Court make or assume that the "identity" of the ship was then fundamentally important to the contract? Was Milward's puzzled and desperate shift to parol (oral) evidence a factor? It certainly provided Mellish the opportunity to argue no "meeting of the minds" by using the phrase *consensus ad idem* (literally, agreement as to the same thing). See Grant Gilmore, The Death of Contract 42 (1974).

2.   *Holmes's famous lectures.* In his famous successive series lectures published in *The Common Law*, Oliver Wendell Holmes, Jr. discussed *Raffles* in a section titled "Contract—III. Void and Voidable." According to Holmes, "a contract fails to be made when it seems to have been [void], or, having been made, can be rescinded by one side or the other, and treated as if it had never been [voidable]." Holmes then proceeds to treat *Raffles* as a correctly decided "void" contract by reference to the objective theory of contracts:

> It is commonly said that such a contract is void, because of mutual mistake as to the subject-matter, and because therefore the parties did not consent to the same thing. But this way of putting it seems to me misleading. The law has nothing to do with the actual state of the parties' minds. In contract, as elsewhere, it must go by externals, and judge parties by their conduct. If there had been but one "Peerless," and the defendant had said "Peerless" by mistake, meaning "Peri," he would have been bound. The true ground of the decision was not that each party meant a different thing from the other, as is implied by the explanation which has been mentioned, but that each said a different thing. The plaintiff offered one thing, the defendant expressed his assent to another. Oliver Wendell Holmes, Jr., The Common Law 309 (1881).

Not all agree with Holmes's conceptualization of the case. Professor Gilmore argues Holmes's "objectification" of *Raffles* was contrary to the popular view and inaccurately shifted focus away from the actual intent of the parties. See Grant Gilmore, The Death of Contract 46–47 (1974); Charles M. Yablon, "Grant Gilmore, Holmes, and the Anxiety of Influence," 90 Nw. U. L. Rev. 236 (1995). Indeed, Holmes first applied his objective theory to explain tort and criminal law and only later extended the theory to contract law. See Patrick J. Kelley, "A Critical Analysis of Holmes's Theory of Contract," 75 Notre Dame L. Rev. 1681 (2000). Nonetheless, many commentators use the case as an example of a failure of the meeting of the minds. See Keith A. Rowley, "You Asked for It, You Got It . . . Toy Yoda: Practical Jokes, Prizes, and Contract Law," 3 Nev. L. J. 526, 533 (2003) and Val D. Ricks, "American Mutual Mistake: Half-Civilian Mongrel, Consideration Reincarnate," 58 La. L. Rev. 663, 674 (1998).

3. *Fair-to-middling. Raffles* has become such an important case that one noted scholar suggested: "No student of the law of contract could regard his education as complete without either reading the case in the reports themselves or, more commonly, acquiring some acquaintance with the case from one of the abbreviated, and sometimes garbled, accounts which appear in legal casebooks or hornbooks." A. W. Brian Simpson, "Contracts for Cotton to Arrive: The Case of Two Ships *Peerless*," 11 Cardozo L. Rev. 287, 287–288 (1989). While at first blush it might seem preposterous that *two* ships with the name *Peerless* might sail the high seas at the same time, it appears there were as many as *eleven*. Simpson, at 295. Decreasing quality gradations of cotton included "fine," "good," "good fair," "fair," "middling," and "ordinary." The cotton grade in *Raffles* was apparently a half-grade "fair-to-middling." Simpson, at 317.

4. *Economic analysis.* Economic analysis, as applied to contract law, seeks to enhance the utility of contracting as a method of organizing economic activity. These rules might suggest that ambiguities such as found in *Raffles* be resolved against the party seeking to enforce the contract. This analysis forces the parties to draft carefully or bear the risk of a language failure. In essence, the ambiguity is resolved against the party who seeks to rely on it—the profferer—and has become known as the doctrine of *contra proferentem.* See Richard A. Posner, "The Law and Economics of Contract Interpretation," 83 Tex. L. Rev. 1581, 1590 (2005). In the world of insurance law, the doctrine of *contra proferentem* tilts issues of interpretation towards the insured because the insurer drafts the insurance policy, and then seeks to rely on its own language after a dispute arises.

5. *Modern restatement approach.* Restatement (Second) of Contracts § 20 considers the situation in *Raffles*. According to Restatement (Second) of Contracts § 20(1), mutual assent does not exist (and therefore no contract) where the parties attach materially different meanings to their manifestations and neither party is at fault for failing to understand the other party's interpretation. If one is at fault, the contract is operative in accordance with the innocent party's understanding. Restatement (Second) of Contracts § 20(2). How would *Raffles* be decided under this formulation? Are other factors now relevant? If so, why? Of course, it is perfectly conceivable (likely?) that Raffles preferred the Wichelhaus interpretation (October Peerless) to no contract at all. Why does the law prefer a "no contract" solution when it is obvious that both parties intended a contract on similar terms? Would a better solution involve a "no retraction" doctrine that does not allow Wichelhaus to retract the promise to purchase cotton? Does the no contract solution simply sanction economic opportunism by allowing Wichelhaus to escape a bad bargain? See

Omri Ben-Shahar, "Contracts Without Consent: Exploring a New Basis for Contractual Liability," 152 U. Pa. L. Rev. 1829, 1857 (2004).

6.   *CISG and objective theory.* CISG art. 8(2) states the familiar objective theory of contracts in that statements or conduct are to be interpreted according to the understanding of a reasonable person. However, CISG art. 8(2) applies only if art. 8(1) does not apply. CISG art. 8(1) provides that statements and conduct are to be interpreted according to the maker's actual intent where the other party knew or could not have been unaware of what that intent was. Notwithstanding the confusing language, CISG art. 8(1) does not dictate a return to the will theory of contract. Consistent with common law, objective theory fails only when there is no preponderance of evidence favoring one interpretation over another. Accordingly, *Raffles* would indeed be decided in the same way under the objective theory and under the CISG because neither party knew or could not have been unaware of the other party's intent. See John E. Murray, Jr., "An Essay on the Formation of Contracts and Related Matters Under the United Nations Convention on Contracts for the International Sale of Goods," 8 J. L. & Com. 11, 47 (1988).

C. THE THEORY OF OFFER AND ACCEPTANCE

The combination of the Holmesian bargain theory of consideration and the objectification of contractual intent require a difficult analysis. How does contract law merge the two doctrines and move from theory to practice? The most important innovation in this regard is the doctrine of "mutual assent" and the ensuing language of offer and acceptance. The doctrine of "mutual assent" was present in both restatements. Mutual assent analysis, like bargain theory, shifts analysis from the nature of the underlying transaction to an expression of assent to the common terms of the deal. The theory of mutual assent is generally designed to carry the burden of expression of the objective theory of contract formation. See Samuel Williston, "Mutual Assent In the Formation of Contracts," 14 Ill. L. Rev. 85 (1919) and Clarke B. Whittier, "The Restatement of Contracts and Mutual Assent," 17 Cal. L. Rev. 441 (1929). Assent in general refers to a consent to the terms of the contract. Edwin W. Patterson, "Compulsory Contracts in the Crystal Ball," 43 Colum. L. Rev. 731, 740 (1943).

Restatement (Second) of Contracts § 17(1) provides that formation of a contract requires a bargain in which there is a manifestation of mutual assent to the exchange and a consideration. Manifestation requires that the mutual assent be communicated to the other party and may be in words or conduct. Restatement (Second) of Contracts §§ 18, 19. However, mutual assent ordinarily takes the form of an offer and acceptance to the same terms or exchange. Restatement (Second) of Contracts §§ 22, 23. Predictably, both an offer and acceptance are defined by reference to the objective theory of contracts. Restatement (Second) of Contracts §§ 24, 50. Consistent with the Holmesian bargain theory, the "offer and acceptance" language of the exchange is also modern nineteenth century invention. A.W.B. Simpson, "Innovation in Nineteenth Century Contract Law," 91 L. Q. Rev. 247, 258 (1975).

You might reasonably anticipate that while the "offer and acceptance" terminology is useful, it is not always adopted or followed by the parties. Contract negotiations are often long and detailed. Any attempt to identify specific moments of offer and acceptance is likely to be quite frustrating— especially when the parties do not phrase their words or conduct in precise terminology of offer and acceptance. For this reason, the Uniform Commercial Code specifically abandons the offer and acceptance focus by stating that a contract for sale of goods may be made in any manner sufficient to show agreement including conduct by both parties recognizing the existence of a contract. UCC § 2–204 and UCC § 2–206.

The most important nineteenth century conceptualization of the offer and acceptance process is that the offer creates a "power of acceptance." Restatement (Second) of Contracts § 36. This formulation follows the paradigm established by Professor Hohfeld in an important early article regarding correlative legal relationships. See Wesley Newcomb Hohfeld, "Some Fundamental Legal Conceptions as Applied in Judicial Reasoning," 23 Yale L. J. 16 (1913). Under this conceptualization, when making an offer, the offeror creates in the offeree a "power" of acceptance. In so doing, the offeror subjects itself to a "liability"—a risk that the offeree will exercise the power of acceptance and impose a contract upon the offeror. The offeree's exercise of the power of acceptance transforms the power-liability relationship into a contractual right-duty relationship.

An important consequence of the offeror's ability to craft an offer is the doctrine that the offeror is the "master of the offer." Under this doctrine, the offeror has control over the conditions of acceptance. To exercise the power of acceptance (and form a contract), the offeree must perform precisely and completely all of the conditions of acceptance imposed by the offeror. Should the offer require the offeree to "don an Uncle Sam costume, climb a greased flagpole, and, upon reaching the gold ball at the top, whistle Yankee Doodle twice," then acceptance cannot be otherwise. See John E. Murray, "Contracts: A New Design for the Agreement Process," 53 Cornell L. Rev. 785 (1968).

For this reason, an important early question about an offer is what terms of acceptance are required by the offer. Generally, the offeror will be indifferent to the manner of acceptance and prefer merely knowledge of acceptance itself. For this reason, the Uniform Commercial Code does not emphasize the offer and acceptance mechanisms. See Karl N. Llewellyn, "Our Case-Law of Contract: Offer and Acceptance, II," 48 Yale L. J. 779 (1939).

As described in the Restatement (Second) of Contracts, the process of contract formation begins when one party advances beyond preliminary negotiations (§ 26) and makes an offer (§ 24) stating some or all of the terms discussed to that point. An "offer" is (i) the manifestation of the maker (offeror) to enter into a bargain (ii) so made as to justify another person (offeree) in understanding that (iii) his assent to that bargain will conclude the bargain. Restatement (Second) of Contracts § 24. The making of the offer creates a power of acceptance in another, and the party who possesses the power of acceptance may exercise that power and make the offeror's promises legally binding. Restatement (Second) of Contracts § 35.

The first part of the definition of offer emphasizes that an offer is a particular kind of promise made by the offeror. "Promise" is separately defined as a manifestation of an intention to act or refrain from acting in a specified manner "so made as to justify a promisee in understanding that a commitment has been made." Restatement (Second) of Contracts § 2(1). Thus, in order to rise to the level of an offer, the maker's words or conduct must first constitute a promise—a commitment to act or refrain from acting.

The offer is a special form of promise. Not all promises are offers. Specifically, a promise becomes an offer only when it indicates that the offeror is willing to enter a bargain on the terms of the offer and invites the offeree to assent and conclude a bargain on those terms. The requirement that the offer manifest willingness to enter a bargain and justify the offeree in "understanding that his assent to that bargain is invited and will conclude it" distinguishes offers from other types of promises such as a donative promise to make a gift in the future. In *Dougherty v. Salt*, for instance, nephew Charlie (or at least his guardian) clearly accepted the gift promise of $3000, but the acceptance could not form a bargain or a contract because Aunt Tillie's promise did not invite assent to a bargain. See Restatement (Second) of Contracts § 3 ("A bargain is an agreement to exchange promises or to exchange a promise for a performance or to exchange performances.").

The objective theory of contracts remains alive and well in this scheme. The definitions of both a promise and an offer specifically examine the recipient's objective and reasonable understanding of whether a promise or offer has been made. Compare Restatement (Second) of Contracts § 2(1) (promise) and § 24 (offer). Both rely on the same language: "[S]o made as to justify" another person "in understanding" that a promise or offer was made.

The distinction between promises and offers is important for enhancing understanding the promissory nature of all offers. No promise, no offer. By way of exclusion, this analytical approach fosters a more perfect exclusion of communications that fall short of offers because they simply are not promissory. On the inclusionary side, since offers are promissory in nature, it is quite feasible that the offeree might well rely on the promissory elements of the offer prior to formal acceptance. In such cases, the doctrine might protect the reliance even when consideration in the form of acceptance has not yet occurred. And, as the cases in Chapters 2 and 3 demonstrate, the gray areas between non-promissory statements, naked promises, and promises that actually create contractual or quasi-contractual liabilities are the source of many of the most interesting questions in contract law.

1. THE PROMISSORY NATURE OF AN OFFER

Restatement (Second) of Contracts § 24 defines an offer as the manifestation of the maker's "willingness to enter a bargain, so made as to justify another person in understanding that assent to the same bargain will conclude it." The offer is defined elsewhere as " . . . an act on the part of one person whereby he gives to another the legal power of creating an obligation called contract." Arthur L. Corbin, "Offer and Acceptance, And Some of the Resulting Legal Relations,"26 Yale L. J. 169, 171 (1917). These definitions clearly convey the message that an offer creates a power of acceptance in another person. The next section considers the power of acceptance in detail.

Strikingly, both definitions fail to mention the promissory characteristics of an offer. Restatement (First) of Contracts § 24 defined an offer as " . . . a promise which is in its terms conditional upon an act, forbearance or return promise being given in exchange for the promise or its performance." See George W. Goble, "Is An Offer A Promise," 22 Ill. L. Rev. 567 (1928); Samuel Williston, 22 Ill. L. Rev. 788 (1928) (response). The reason for the change in language in the two restatements was to shift emphasis to the creation of the power of acceptance, not to de-emphasize the promissory nature of an offer. Also, the language shift may also have been intended to include an isolated and seldom used category of non-promissory offers. See Restatement (Second) of Contracts § 24, *cmt. a;* George W. Goble, "The Non-Promissory Offer," 48 Nw. U. L. Rev. 590 (1953). Nonetheless, the promissory nature of an offer remains its central core: non-promissory words and acts cannot constitute an offer. See Williston on Contracts § 4.4 (4th Ed. 2006) and Restatement (Second) of Contracts § 55 (acceptance of non-promissory offers). As you read the next case, try to determine whether one of the parties made a promise capable of acceptance by the other party.

Buyer   Seller
OWEN V. TUNISON

Supreme Judicial Court of Maine
131 Me. 42, 158 A. 926 (1932)

BARNES, J.

This case is reported to the law court, and such judgment is to be rendered as the law and the admissible evidence require.

Plaintiff charges that defendant agreed in writing to sell him the Bradley block and lot, situated in Bucksport, for a stated price in cash, that he later refused to perfect the sale, and that plaintiff, always willing and ready to pay the price, has suffered loss on account of defendant's unjust refusal to sell, and claims damages.

From the record it appears that defendant, a resident of Newark, N. J., was, in the fall of 1929, the owner of the Bradley block and lot.

With the purpose of purchasing, on October 23, 1929, plaintiff wrote the following letter:

Dear Mr. Tunison:

Will you sell me your store property which is located on Main St. in Bucksport, Me. running from Montgomery's Drug Store on one corner to a Grocery Store on the other, for the sum of $6,000.00?

Nothing more of this letter need be quoted.

On December 5, following, plaintiff received defendant's reply, apparently written in Cannes, France, on November 12, and it reads:

In reply to your letter of Oct. 23rd which has been forwarded to me in which you inquire about the Bradley Block, Bucksport Me.

Because of improvements which have been added and an expenditure of several thousand dollars it would not be possible for me to sell it unless I was to receive $16,000.00 cash.

The upper floors have been converted into apartments with baths and the b'l'dg put into first class condition.

Very truly yours,
[Signed] R. G. Tunison.

Whereupon, and at once, plaintiff sent to defendant, and the latter received, in France, the following message:

Accept your offer for Bradley block Bucksport Terms sixteen thousand cash send deed to Eastern Trust and Banking Co Bangor Maine Please acknowledge.

Four days later he was notified that defendant did not wish to sell the property, and on the 14th day of January following brought suit for his damages.

Granted that damages may be due a willing buyer if the owner refuses to tender a deed of real estate, after the latter has made an offer in writing to sell to the former, and such offer has been so accepted, it remains for us to point out that defendant here is not shown to have written to plaintiff an offer to sell.

There can have been no contract for the sale of the property desired, no meeting of the minds of the owner and prospective purchaser, unless there was an offer or proposal of sale. It cannot be successfully argued that defendant made any offer or proposal of sale.

In a recent case the words, "Would not consider less than half" is held "not to be taken as an outright offer to sell for one-half." Sellers v. Warren, 116 Me. 350, 102 A. 40, 41.

Where an owner of millet seed wrote, "I want $2.25 per cwt. for this seed f. o. b. Lowell," in an action for damages for alleged breach of contract to sell at the figure quoted above, the court held: "He [(defendant)] does not say, 'I offer to sell to you.' The language used is general, and such as may be used in an advertisement, or circular addressed generally to those engaged in the seed business, and is not an offer by which he may be bound, if accepted, by any or all of the persons addressed." Nebraska Seed Co. v. Harsh, 98 Neb. 89, 152 N. W. 310, 311, and cases cited in note L. R. A. 1915F, 824.

Defendant's letter of December 5 in response to an offer of $6,000 for his property may have been written with the intent to open negotiations that might lead to a sale. It was not a proposal to sell.

Judgment for defendant.

NOTES AND QUESTIONS

1.   *Classifying the parties.* In most cases, a conversation or negotiation pattern will continue for some time with the prospective parties exchanging information and trying to determine if the purported transaction is beneficial. At some point in these discussions, one person must make a promissory statement based on the negotiations. That person is identified as the offeror or the maker of the offer. The person to whom the offer is communicated will most often be the offeree (or its agent).

2.   *Theory of obligation.* In *Owen,* it is easy to determine that Tunison owns land that Owen desires to purchase. Owen asserts that Tunison breached an enforceable promise to sell him the land. The court states that there could be no "contract" for the sale of the land unless there was first an "offer." Based on your readings from the previous chapter on theory of obligation, do you agree that a contract cannot be formed without an offer? Why do you suppose the term "offer" is used rather than the term "promise"? Does the term "offer" implicate a particular theory of obligation? Are there other theories of obligation to support a contract in this case?

3. *Failure of a promissory offer.* Do you agree with the court that Tunison failed to make an offer to sell? Tunison's responsive December 5 letter states "it would not be possible for me to sell it unless I was to receive $16,000.00 cash." Is this language promissory? Does it convey Tunison's commitment to sell on those terms or does it appear more to be language of discussion or statement of intention? A statement of intention is not promissory because it fails to convey a commitment. In theory, the difference is between "I intend to sell my land" and "I agree to sell my land." The latter is promissory whereas the former is not. Do you understand why?

4. *Magic words not required.* It is clear that Tunison need not phrase his words as an "offer" in order for the words to mean as much. However, given the fact that the word "offer" is well understood in commerce, the use of that word alone might well create an offer and power of acceptance in the other party, at least if that person reasonably understood the language to be an offer. The more common case is that specified in the case. While Tunison did not use the word "offer," notice that Owen used the word "accept." If Tunison's letter constituted an offer, is there room for doubt whether Owen made a promise to purchase on the terms of the offer? For a discussion of the importance of terminology in this context, see Comment, "The Language of Offer and Acceptance: Speech Acts and the Question of Intent," 74 Cal. L. Rev. 189 (1986).

5. *Advertisements versus offers.* It is important to distinguish offers, which manifest the offeror's intent to conclude a bargain upon acceptance, from advertisements and other preliminary negotiations, which usually operate as requests for offers or expressions of interest in beginning negotiations. See Restatement (Second) of Contracts § 26, *cmt. b.* It is possible for an advertiser to make an offer to the general public, or to a specified subset thereof, by clearly and unequivocally expressing an intention to enter a contract with those who accept, but the common law presumes the opposite in the absence of strong evidence of such intent. For example, in *Leonard v. Pepsico, Inc.,* 88 F. Supp. 2d 116, 122–23 (1999), Pepsico advertised a promotional program under which Pepsi consumers could earn "Pepsi Points" by purchasing Pepsi products (or purchasing points directly) and subsequently redeem those points for Pepsi merchandise. The court concluded the advertisements were not offers because they were not sufficiently definite and because the advertisements did not limit in any way the parties entitled to accept the purported offer. See id. In contrast, the court distinguished the case of Lefkowitz v. Great Minneapolis Surplus Store, 86 N.W.2d 689 (1957):

> In *Lefkowitz,* defendant had published a newspaper announcement stating: "Saturday 9 AM Sharp, 3 Brand New Fur Coats, Worth to $100.00, First Come First Served $1 Each." *Id.* at 690. Mr. Morris Lefkowitz arrived at the store, dollar in hand, but was informed that under defendant's "house rules," the offer was open to ladies, but not gentlemen. *See id.* The court ruled that because plaintiff had fulfilled all of the terms of the advertisement and the advertisement was

specific and left nothing open for negotiation, a contract had been formed.

In a 1994 article, Professor Melvin A. Eisenberg argued that the Restatement (Second) of Contracts § 26 view is not accurate. According to Professor Eisenberg, most people believe that an advertiser does intend to commit itself when advertising on a first-come, first-serve basis and that accordingly a majority of modern cases impose liability on advertisers. See Melvin A. Eisenberg, "Expression Rules in Contract Law and Problems of Offer and Acceptance," 82 Cal. L. Rev. 1127 (1994). Consider the last time you responded to an advertisement—did you believe that the advertisement was offering to sell you a good or service on specified terms or that the advertiser was merely inviting you to come and make an offer? Are there any reasons for retaining the presumption that advertisements are not offers even if that presumption is contrary to common understandings of consumers?

6. *Context, offers, and the probability of performance.* Ian Ayres and Gregory Klass observed that statements regarding intent to act or refrain from acting in the future—framed as offers or naked promises—convey both the existence or fact of that intent and the probability that the maker will fulfill that intent. See Ian Ayres and Gregory Klass, Insincere Promises: The Law of Misrepresented Intent 1–3 (2005) ("We accept that most of the law of contracts is best viewed as playing a supporting role in the way that promises create obligations and we believe that this is proper. . . . [P]romises also convey information about the promisor's intentions with respect to performance and, more generally, about the probability of her performance."). Consider their opening example: You sit down at a diner counter and tell the waiter, "I want two eggs over easy with hash browns and rye toast." See id. at 1–2. In that context, your statement impliedly asserts a conditional promise to pay the menu price if the waiter brings you the food you have ordered. See id. The statement—still in context—also provides additional information to an objective observer, such as your dietary preferences, and potentially your ability and willingness to pay, your socio-economic class and upbringing, and your understanding of the cultural institutions that permit you to order breakfast with that statement. See id.

Note that the breakfast order creates a contractual obligation to pay for the breakfast despite that it is framed in terms of your appetitive desires and does not make an explicit promise. What if, when ordering the breakfast, you fully intend to skip out without paying the bill? In that case, your statement "I want two eggs over easy . . . " can be both true and false. It is true in the sense that it correctly states your desire for breakfast, but it is false in the sense that you have implicitly made an offer to pay the menu price if served the specified meal while actually intending not to fulfill your end of the deal. In the latter sense, the statement is a lie and is actionable under the doctrine of promissory fraud. See Ian Ayres and Gregory Klass, Insincere Promises: The Law of Misrepresented Intent 3–6 (2005).

7. *Hohfeldian "powers," "liabilities," and the power of acceptance.* As discussed in Chapter 2, Wesley Newcomb Hohfeld revolutionized the manner in which legal scholars, among other disciplines, thought about the relationships between legal actors. See also Curtis Nyquist, "Teaching Wesley Hohfeld's Theory of Legal Relations," 52 J. Legal Educ. 238 (2002). Chapter 2 introduced the Hohfeldian correlatives of "right"/"duty" and "privilege"/"no-right." As noted, a "right" is a legal claim against the other party to a jural relationship, while a "duty" represents a legal obligation to the holder of the right. Likewise, a "privilege" represents freedom from a legal claim by another, while the correlative "no-right" indicates that the other party to the jural relationship has no legal claim against the holder of the privilege for exercising that privilege.

Hohfeld's analysis permits discussion of abstract legal relations in relatively precise terms. Rather than merely dividing all legal relations into a simple dichotomy of "rights" and "duties," Hohfeld's scheme provides for a much more detailed description of the relations between contracting parties. Consider how the Hohfeldian can describe the different legal relationships between two parties in an ordinary sale of land transaction. Before contracting, A—the owner of Whiteacre—generally has a "privilege" of entering into, using, improving, devising, and alienating that real property (absent exceptional circumstances not relevant in a course on contracts). A's privilege merely permits A to do these acts if she chooses, but does not imply any affirmative obligation to do so. Correlative of A's privilege, the rest of the world—including B, an interested buyer—has "no-right" to assert a legal claim against A for exercising her legal privilege.

Here, in the context of offer and acceptance, Hohfeld's discussion of the jural relation "power," its jural opposite "disability," and its jural correlative "liability" is particularly instructive in analyzing the relations between offeror and offeree. See Wesley Newcomb Hohfeld, "Some Fundamental Legal Conceptions as Applied in Judicial Reasoning," 23 Yale L. J. 16, 44–54 (1913). A "power," for Hohfeld, represented an ability to impose a legal obligation on another, while the correlative "liability" resided in the party subject to the exercise of the power. See id. The legal relationship between A and B continues as one of "privilege/no-right" until A makes an offer to sell Whiteacre to B for $1000. At that point, the parties have created a new legal relation in addition to the privilege/no-right relation. With the making of an offer, A has created a "power" of acceptance in B, and A is under a correlative "liability" to B to enter a contract if B exercises his power of acceptance. At the same time, A retains a "power" to revoke the offer at any time before acceptance, while B suffers a correlative "liability"—the contingent loss of the power to accept A's offer if A revokes. See id.

B's acceptance of A's offer erases the power/liability relationships created by the offer and replaces those relations with a right/duty relationship. At the making of the contract to sell Whiteacre for $1,000, B has a "right"—that is, an affirmative claim—against A for the delivery of Whiteacre under the terms of their contract. A is under a correlative "duty"—an affirmative obligation—to comply with the contract terms. And finally, fulfillment of the contract terms erases the right/duty relationship and creates a new privilege/no-right relationship, this time with B as the privilege holder with respect to Whiteacre and A holding no-right against B for exercising his privilege. See id.

2. THE CONDITION OF ACCEPTANCE

The existence of an offer creates a power of acceptance in the offeree. That power may be exercised by acceptance provided that the offer has not been terminated prior to acceptance. The next section considers the termination of the power of acceptance while the current section addresses how an offeree may exercise that power.

Restatement (Second) of Contracts § 35(1) provides that an offer creates in the offeree a continuing power to complete the circle of mutual assent by acceptance of the offer. Thus, it is clear that once an offer exists, that offer creates a power of acceptance in the offeree. Restatement (Second) of Contracts § 50(1) defines "acceptance" of an offer as the manifestation of assent to the terms of the offer made in a manner invited or required by the offer. An acceptance is defined elsewhere as ". . . the exercise of the power conferred by the offer, by the performance of some other act or acts." Arthur L. Corbin, "Offer and Acceptance, And Some of the Resulting Legal Relations," 26 Yale L. J. 169, 171 (1917).

The terms of the offer can control the manner of and conditions of acceptance. Indeed, Restatement (Second) of Contracts § 36(2) provides that the power of acceptance terminates with the non-occurrence of any conditions of acceptance under the terms of the offer. Recall from the previous chapter's discussion of gratuitous conditional promises that a condition of acceptance is related but distinct based on context and purpose. A condition of acceptance is a condition attached to the promise by the maker of the promise that renders the promise enforceable if, and only if, acceptance occurs in the manner invited by this offer.

INTERNATIONAL FILTER CO. v. CONROE GIN, ICE & LIGHT CO.

Commission of Appeals of Texas
277 S.W. 631 (1925)

NICKELS, J.

Plaintiff in error, an Illinois corporation, is a manufacturer of machinery, apparatus, etc., for the purification of water in connection with the manufacture of ice, etc., having its principal office in the city of Chicago. Defendant in error is a Texas corporation engaged in the manufacture of ice, etc., having its plant, office, etc., at Conroe, Montgomery county, Tex.

On February 10, 1920, through its traveling solicitor, Waterman, plaintiff in error, at Conroe, submitted to defendant in error, acting through Henry Thompson, its manager, a written instrument, addressed to defendant in error, which (with immaterial portions omitted) reads as follows:

Gentlemen:

We propose to furnish, f. o. b. Chicago, one No. two Junior (steel tank) International water softener and filter to purify water of the character shown by sample to be submitted. . . . Price: Twelve hundred thirty ($1,230.00) dollars. . . . This proposal is made in duplicate and becomes a contract when accepted by the purchaser and approved by an executive officer of the International Filter Company, at its office in Chicago. Any modification can only be made by duly approved supplementary agreement signed by both parties.

This proposal is submitted for prompt acceptance, and unless so accepted is subject to change without notice.

Respectfully submitted,
International Filter Co.
W. W. Waterman.

On the same day the "proposal" was accepted by defendant in error through notation made on the paper by Thompson reading as follows:

Accepted Feb. 10, 1920.

Conroe Gin, Ice & Light Co.,
By Henry Thompson, Mgr.

The paper as thus submitted and "accepted" contained the notation, "Make shipment by Mar. 10." The paper, in that form, reached the Chicago office of plaintiff in error, and on February 13, 1920, P. N. Engel, its president and vice president, indorsed thereon: "O. K. Feb. 13, 1920, P. N. Engel." February 14, 1920, plaintiff in error wrote and mailed, and in due course defendant in error received, the following letter:

Feb. 14, 1920.

Attention of Mr. Henry Thompson, Manager.

Conroe Gin, Ice & Light Co., Conroe, Texas. Gentlemen: This will acknowledge and thank you for your order given Mr. Waterman for a No. 2 Jr. steel tank International softener and filter, for 110 volt, 60 cycle, single phase current for shipment March 10th.

Please make shipment of the sample of water promptly so that we may make the analysis and know the character of the water before shipment of the apparatus. Shipping tag is enclosed, and please note the instructions to pack to guard against freezing.

Yours very truly,
International Filter Co.,
M. B. Johnson.

By letter of February 28, 1920, defendant in error undertook to countermand the "order," which countermand was repeated and emphasized by letter of March 4, 1920. By letter of March 2, 1920 (replying to the letter of February 28th), plaintiff in error denied the right of countermand, etc., and insisted upon performance of the "contract." The parties adhered to the respective positions thus indicated, and this suit resulted.

Plaintiff in error sued for breach of the contract alleged to have been made in the manner stated above. The defense is that no contract was made because: (1) Neither Engel's endorsement of "O. K.," nor the letter of February 14, 1920, amounted to approval "by an executive officer of the International Filter Company, at its office in Chicago." (2) Notification of such approval, or acceptance, by plaintiff in error was required to be communicated to defendant in error; it being insisted that this requirement inhered in the terms of the proposal and in the nature of the transaction and, also, that Thompson, when he indorsed "acceptance" on the paper stated to Waterman, as agent of plaintiff in error, that such notification must be promptly given; it being insisted further that the letter of February 14, 1920, did not constitute such acceptance or notification of approval, and therefore defendant in error, on February 28, 1920, etc., had the right to withdraw, or countermand, the unaccepted offer. Thompson testified in a manner to support the allegation of his statement to Waterman. There are other matters involved in the suit which must be ultimately determined, but the foregoing presents the issues now here for consideration.

The case was tried without a jury, and the judge found the facts in favor of defendant in error on all the issues indicated above, and upon other material issues. The judgment was affirmed by the Court of Civil Appeals, 269 S. W. 210.

Opinion.

We agree with the honorable Court of Civil Appeals upon the proposition that Mr. Engel's endorsement of "O. K." amounted to an approval "by an executive officer of the International Filter Company, at its office in Chicago," within the meaning of the so-called "proposal" of February 10th. The paper then became a "contract," according to its definitely expressed terms, and it became then, and thereafter it remained, an enforceable contract, in legal contemplation, unless the fact of approval by the filter company was required to be communicated to the other party and unless, in that event, the communication was not made.

We are not prepared to assent to the ruling that such communication was essential. There is no disposition to question the justice of the general rules stated in support of that holding, yet the existence of contractual capacity imports the right of the offeror to dispense with notification; and he does dispense with it "if the form of the offer," etc., "shows that this was not to be required." 9 Cyc. 270, 271; Carlill v. Carbolic Smoke Ball Co., 1 Q. B. 256 (and other references in note 6, 9 Cyc. 271). The case just cited, it seems to us, correctly states the rule:

> As notification of acceptance is required for the benefit of the person who makes the offer, the person who makes the offer may dispense with notice to himself if he thinks it desirable to do so, and I suppose there can be no doubt that where a person in an offer made by him to another person, expressly or impliedly intimates a particular mode of acceptance as sufficient to make the bargain binding, it is only necessary for the other person to whom such offer is made to follow the indicated method of acceptance; and if the person making the offer, expressly or impliedly intimates in his offer that it will be sufficient to act on the proposal without communicating acceptance of it to himself, performance of the condition is a sufficient acceptance without notification.

See, also, Fort v. Barnett, 23 Tex. 460, 464. The Conroe Gin, Ice & Light Company executed the paper for the purpose of having it transmitted, as its offer, to the filter company at Chicago. It was so transmitted and acted upon. Its terms embrace the offer, and nothing else, and by its terms the question of notification must be judged, since those terms are not ambiguous.

The paper contains two provisions which relate to acceptance by the filter company. One is the declaration that the offer shall "become a contract . . . when approved by an executive officer of the International Filter Company, at its Chicago office." The other is thus stated: "This proposal is submitted for prompt acceptance, and unless so accepted is subject to change without notice." The first provision states "a particular mode of acceptance as sufficient to make the bargain binding," and the filter company (as stated above) followed "the indicated method of acceptance." When this was done, so the paper declares, the proposal "became a contract." The other provision does not in any way relate to a different method of acceptance by the filter company. Its sole reference is to the time within which the act of approval must be done; that is to say, there was to be a "prompt acceptance," else the offer might be changed "without notice." The second declaration merely required the approval thereinbefore stipulated for to be done promptly; if the act was so done, there is nothing in the second provision to militate against, or to conflict with, the prior declaration that, thereupon, the paper should become "a contract."

A holding that notification of that approval is to be deduced from the terms of the last-quoted clause is not essential in order to give it meaning or to dissolve ambiguity. On the contrary, such a construction of the two provisions would introduce a conflict, or ambiguity, where none exists in the language itself, and defeat the plainly expressed term wherein it is said that the proposal "becomes a contract . . . when approved by an executive officer." There is not anything in the language used to justify a ruling that this declaration must be wrenched from its obvious meaning and given one which would change both the locus and time prescribed for the meeting of the minds. The offeror said that the contract should be complete if approval be promptly given by the executive officer at Chicago; the court cannot properly restate the offer so as to make the offeror declare that a contract shall be made only when the approval shall have been promptly given at Chicago and that fact shall have been communicated to the offeror at Conroe. In our opinion, therefore, notice of the approval was not required.

The letter of February 14th, however, sufficiently communicated notice, if it was required. The following authorities have been cited to the contrary . . . However, none of these authorities are exactly in point here. They involved the question of what was sufficient to evidence an acceptance of an offer, and not the question of the form of notice of acceptance. Here the fact of acceptance in the particular method prescribed by the offeror is established aliunde the letter. Engel's "O. K." indorsed on the paper at Chicago did that. The form of notice, where notice is required, may be quite a different thing from the acceptance itself; the latter constitutes the meeting of the minds, the former merely relates to that pre-existent fact. The rules requiring such notice, it will be marked, do not make necessary any particular form or manner, unless the parties themselves have so prescribed. Whatever would convey, by word or fair implication, notice of the fact would be sufficient. And this letter, we think, would clearly indicate to a reasonably prudent person, situated as was the defendant in error, the fact of previous approval by the filter company. If the Gin, Ice & Light Company had acted to change its position upon it as a notification of that fact, it must be plain that the filter company would have been estopped to deny its sufficiency.

There are other questions in the case which must be determined on the appeal. Those questions were pretermitted by the honorable Court of Civil Appeals because of its holdings that communication of notice of the filter's company's approval was necessary, that such notice was not given, the letter of February 14th being thought insufficient for that purpose, and that defendant in error, therefore, had the right to countermand the proposal as it did (rather, attempted to do) on February 28th.

We recommend that the judgment of the Court of Civil Appeals be reversed, and that the cause be remanded to that court for its disposition of all questions not passed upon by it heretofore and properly before it for determination.

CURETON, C. J.

Judgment of the Court of Civil Appeals reversed, and cause remanded to the Court of Civil Appeals for further consideration by that court, as recommended by the Commission of Appeals.

NOTES AND QUESTIONS

1. *Home office control.* International Filter Co., a Chicago company, made a "proposal" to sell Conroe Gin a water purification system for use in its Texas plant. The terms of the International proposal specifically provided that the proposal becomes a contract only when "approved by an executive officer" of International Filter. According to the clear terms of the proposal who had the power of acceptance, International Filter or Conroe Gin? By definition, the party with the power of acceptance is the offeree. Does the court agree with this analysis? Does this analysis provide a clue why the court referred to the International Filter "proposal" and the Conroe Gin "offer"? Given that International hired Waterman as its sale agent, why would it make a proposal to sell rather than an offer to sell?

2. *Notification requirement.* Conroe Gin argues that International Filter's acceptance was not effective because the acceptance was not timely communicated to Conroe Gin. To underscore its argument, Henry Thompson of Conroe Gin testified that he stated to Waterman of International Filter that the notification must be prompt. The court expressed two thoughts. First, the "offer" may dispense with the notification requirement. This comports with Restatement (Second) of Contracts § 56 that notice of acceptance must be communicated to the offeror unless the terms of the offer "manifests a contrary intention." The court also dismissed Conroe Gin's argument that International Filter's February 14 letter was timely notice. The offer had been signed by Conroe Gin on February 10 and was accepted by International Filter on February 13. Does the February 14 letter, received in "due course," seem timely to you? How was the Conroe Gin "offer" communicated to International Filter? Should the method of communicating the offer have any relevance to whether the acceptance was timely communicated? See Restatement (Second) of Contracts § 56, *comment b* (communication requires only reasonable diligence by the offeree which may be affected by a face-to-face communication).

3. *"F.O.B." and other bill of lading terms.* Sales contracts, purchase orders, invoices, and similar writings such as the proposal at issue here often contain shorthand shipment and destination terms defining the parties' rights and responsibilities with respect to the purchased goods. These shorthand terms can have significant impacts upon not only the cost of performance, but also upon allocating the risk of loss of goods during shipment (and thus the costs of obtaining insurance) between the parties. For example, "F.O.B."—meaning "free on board"—designates when and where the seller must deliver

goods to the buyer or to the carrier designated by the contract. See UCC § 2–319(1). Similarly, the term "ex-ship" specifies delivery at a named part of destination, and the "seller bears the risk of loss until the goods are properly unloaded from the ship." UCC § 2–322(1), (2). Thus, the term in *Raffles v. Wichelhaus*—"to arrive ex Peerless"—under the UCC would not merely specify the name of the ship upon which the goods were to be delivered, but also precisely define the responsibilities of the seller and buyer with respect to those goods.

The International Chamber of Commerce periodically publishes a list of accepted "Incoterms" (standing for "International Commercial Terms") that provide similar shorthand descriptions that commercial parties worldwide may incorporate into their contracts. See, e.g., International Chamber of Commerce, Incoterms 2010 (2010). The set of Incoterms rules effective January 1, 2011 includes terms familiar in UCC usage such as FAS ("Free Alongside Ship"), FOB ("Free On Board"), and CIF ("Cost, Insurance and Freight"), along with other common terms such as EXW ("Ex Works"), CIP ("Carriage and Insurance Paid To"), and DDP ("Delivered Duty Paid"). For a full explanation of the proper usage of the current Incoterms, see id.

3.   THE MAILBOX RULE

Contracting parties frequently negotiate at some distance and often conclude their offer and acceptance using mail, fax, voicemail, email, and other forms of asynchronous communication. Assuming an offer exists and was communicated by mail, when does acceptance of such an offer become effective—when the acceptance is deposited in the mail or only after actual receipt by the offeror? If acceptance is effective upon deposit in the mail, the offeror will be bound by an as yet unknown acceptance. If acceptance is effective only upon receipt by the offeror, the offeree will not know whether and when the offeror actually received the acceptance and thus whether the offeree is bound to a contract. In both cases, only a later third communication will verify whether a contract has been formed.

The common law "mailbox rule" resolves this question in favor of the offeree by making acceptance effective upon deposit in the mail. See Restatement (Second) of Contracts § 63 ("an acceptance made in a manner and by a medium invited by an offer is operative . . . as soon as put out of offeree's possession."). Thus, if the offeror "invites" acceptance by mail—either implicitly by mailing the offer to the offeree or expressly—the offeree accepts the offer by placing the acceptance in the mail. The Restatement rule does not apply, however, to acceptances of option contracts, which are only effective upon receipt.

This common law mailbox rule implies several important corollaries. First, the offeree is bound by a mailed acceptance just as much as the offeror. In some cases, the offeree may attempt to retrieve or reclaim the acceptance from the post office or other carrier. Alternatively, an offeree who mails an acceptance may make an "overtaking" rejection, such as by telephoning, telegraphing, faxing, or emailing a rejection to the offeror. In both cases, the attempted revocation is ineffective.

Second, in some cases the offeree may mail a rejection first before changing her mind and attempting to overtake the rejection with an acceptance. A mailed rejection is effective only upon receipt and consequently does not terminate the offeree's power of acceptance until it is actually received by the offeror. See Restatement (Second) of Contracts § 40. In that case, whether the contract is formed or not depends on which communication, the rejection or acceptance, reaches the offeror first. See id.

Third, while an offer creates a power of acceptance in the offeree and a power of revocation in the offeror, a revocation—like a rejection—is effective only upon receipt by the offeree. See Restatement (Second) of Contracts § 43 (power of acceptance terminates "when offeree receives from the offeror a manifestation" of intent not to enter proposed contract). Consequently, a mailed acceptance immediately extinguishes the offeror's power of revocation, even if the offeror communicates that revocation to the offeree while the acceptance is still in transit.

Electronic communications raise significant complications for application of the mailbox rule. Although asynchronous, electronic communications are potentially instantaneous and appear to eclipse the postal gap between mailing and receiving documents. Some would argue this means the mailbox rule should have no application to such communications. See E. Allan Farnsworth, Contracts § 3.22 at 172–173 (4th ed. 2004) ("The rule has no application to substantially instantaneous means of communication, such as telephone, telex, facsimile, and electronic mail."). Does this portend the demise of the mailbox rule? Should the mailbox dispatch rule be eliminated in favor of a receipt rule applicable to face-to-face communications? See Restatement (Second) of Contracts § 64 (acceptance in a "substantially instantaneous" medium is governed by rules applicable to acceptance where the parties are in presence of each other). Some argue that contrary to popular perception, internet mail is not universally instantaneous as traveling through a server might involve minutes, hours, and sometimes days. Such electronic communications are therefore not "substantially instantaneous." Accordingly, the mailbox rule should have continuing vitality. See Note, "Internet Electronic Mail: A Last Bastion for the Mailbox Rule," 25 Hofstra L. Rev. 971, 1000–01 (1997).

Many statutes abrogate the common law mailbox rule in specific contexts. Several statutory regimes have overlapping applicability to the mailbox rule and are part of a larger issue of when and how parties may manifest mutual assent electronically. The UCC governs any sale of goods, including those concluded electronically, but UCC § 2–206(1) generally provides that an offer may be accepted "in any manner and by any medium reasonable in the circumstances." This need not always be in the same medium as the offer was communicated. See John E. Murray, "Contracts: A New Design For The Agreement Process," 53 Cornell L. Rev. 785, 793 (1968). The Uniform Commercial Information Transaction Act ("UCITA") is the uniform commercial code for software licenses and computer information transactions, but it has been sparsely adopted in only a few states. UCITA §§ 102 and 103 governs computer information transactions which includes agreements to create, modify, transfer, or license computer information and thus includes both "clickwrap" agreements (software licensing agreements) and "shrinkwrap" agreements. UCITA § 203(4)(A) rejects the mailbox rule and adopts a receipt rule when an electronic offer is accepted by an electronic message. See generally Valerie Watnick, "The Electronic Formation of Contracts and the Common Law Mailbox Rule," 56 Baylor L. Rev. 175 (2004). The Uniform Electronic Transactions Act ("UETA") has been widely adopted. Its purpose is to remove barriers to electronic commerce by validating and effectuating electronic records and signatures. UETA § 7 provides that contract formation cannot be denied legal effect solely because an electronic record was used in formation. Nonetheless, the substantive rules of contracts remain unaffected and thus agreements are defined by reference to traditional rules. UETA § 2(1). UETA § 15 provides that an electronic record is deemed received when it enters an information processing system designated by the recipient. Unlike UCITA, acceptance is not defined but rather left to other law after describing when a record is deemed received.

In transnational sale of goods transactions, however, the applicable rule depends upon the applicability of the Convention on Contracts for the International Sale of Goods ("CISG"). The CISG governs contracts for the sale of goods between parties whose place of business are in different countries, provided one or both countries are signatories of that treaty. Article 18(2) provides that acceptance of offers governed by the CISG is effective only upon receipt and thus appears to reject the mailbox rule. Likewise, Article 16(1) provides that an otherwise revocable offer may be revoked if the revocation reaches the offeree before acceptance is dispatched. Therefore, unlike the mailbox rule, the CISG places the risk of loss of the acceptance on the offeree, not the offeror. See William S. Dodge, "Teaching the CISG in Contracts," 50 J. Legal Educ. 72, 81 (2000). For a discussion of rules in other countries and sales not governed by CISG, see Calvin W. Corman, "Formation of Contracts for the Sale of Goods," 42 Was. L. Rev. 347 (1967) (Asian Law Symposium).

4. ACCEPTANCE BY SILENCE

In general, an offeror is the "master of the offer". As such, the offeror may specify the persons entitled to exercise the power of acceptance and the form and timing of that exercise. Thus, as discussed later in this chapter, an offeror may state that an offer may only be accepted by performing some act or forebearance, or that the offeree must exercise the power of acceptance before a certain date or time. Similarly, an offer may state that a mailed acceptance is effective only upon receipt by the offeror, thus opting out of the mailbox rule default. But while the offeror's control over the terms of the offer and the form and timing of the acceptance is largely unfettered, the common law substantially restricts the situations in which the offeror may deem complete inaction or silence by the offeree to be an effective acceptance. The second restatement states that the offeree's silence and inaction constitute an acceptance in three situations:

(a)   Where an offeree takes the benefit of offered services with reasonable opportunity to reject them and reason to know that they were offered with the expectation of compensation.

(b)   Where the offeror has stated or given the offeree reason to understand that assent may be manifested by silence or inaction, and the offeree in remaining silent and inactive intends to accept the offer.

(c)   Where because of previous dealings or otherwise, it is reasonable that the offeree should notify the offeror if he does not intend to accept.

Restatement (Second) of Contracts § 69(1)(a)–(c). In Hohfeldian terms, an offer can and does create a power of acceptance in the offeree, with a corresponding and correlative liability in the offeror. But the election whether to exercise that power of acceptance remains solely within the offeree's discretion. By purporting to make silence or inaction an effective acceptance, the offeror is improperly attempting unilaterally to impose a duty on the offeree to act affirmatively to reject the offer. Thus, the general rule provides that an offeree who receives an offer purportedly acceptable by silence does not need to respond and that silence or inaction cannot be deemed an acceptance.

This general rule is subject to important caveats. First, in cases where the offer accompanies property of the offeror, silence or inaction by the offeree cannot create an acceptance, but the offeree cannot engage in "any act inconsistent with the offeror's ownership of [the] offered property." Restatement (Second) of Contracts § 69(2). For example, if an offeror sends a cookbook to an offeree and offers to sell the cookbook to the offeree for $50 unless the offeree returns the cookbook to the offeror, the offeree may leave the book in its packaging to gather dust in the corner. If the offeree exercises dominion or control over the cookbook, however, such as by opening the packaging and using the cookbook or giving it as a gift, that action is inconsistent with the offeror's ownership of the cookbook and implicitly acts as an acceptance. Second, while the offeror cannot deem silence or inaction to be an acceptance, an offeree may nonetheless reasonably and detrimentally rely upon the offeror's promise to deem silence to be an acceptance. An offeror in such a situation may be bound to a contract without notice of an acceptance.

As you read the following case, analyze how the rules relating to acceptance by silence accord with the objective theory of assent. Is it correct to say that an offeror may never unilaterally impose a duty to reject upon the offeree? Under what circumstances will it be reasonable for an offeror to conclude that an offeree's non-responsiveness indicates assent, rather than an alternative intent?

DAY V. CATON

Supreme Judicial Court of Massachusetts
119 Mass. 513 (1876)

. . . CONTRACT to recover the value of one half of a brick party wall built by the plaintiff upon and between the adjoining estates, 27 and 29 Greenwich Park, Boston.

At the trial in the Superior Court, before *Allen,* J., it appeared that, in 1871, the plaintiff, having an equitable interest in lot 29, built the wall in question, placing one half of it on the vacant lot 27, in which the defendant then had an equitable interest. The plaintiff testified that there was an express agreement on the defendant's part to pay him one half the value of the wall when the defendant should use it in building upon lot 27. The defendant denied this, and testified that he never had any conversation with the plaintiff about the wall; and there was no other direct testimony on this point.

The defendant requested the judge to rule that, "1. The plaintiff can recover in this case only upon an express agreement."

"2. If the jury find there was no express agreement about the wall, but the defendant knew that the plaintiff was building upon land in which the defendant had an equitable interest, the defendant's rights would not be affected by such knowledge, and his silence and subsequent use of the wall would raise no implied promise to pay anything for the wall."

The judge refused so to rule, but instructed the jury as follows: "A promise would not be implied from the fact that the plaintiff, with the defendant's knowledge, built the wall and the defendant used it, but it might be implied from the conduct of the parties. If the jury find that the plaintiff undertook and completed the building of the wall with the expectation that the defendant would pay him for it, and the defendant had reason to know that the plaintiff was so acting with that expectation and allowed him so to act without objection, then the jury might infer a promise on the part of the defendant to pay the plaintiff."

The jury found for the plaintiff; and the defendant alleged exceptions.

DEVENS, J.

The ruling that a promise to pay for the wall would not be implied from the fact that the plaintiff, with the defendant's knowledge, built the wall, and that the defendant used it, was substantially in accordance with the request of the defendant, and is conceded to have been correct. Chit. Con. (11th Am. ed.) 86. *Wells v. Banister,* 4 Mass. 514. *Knowlton v. Plantation No. 4,* 14 Maine 20. . . .

The defendant, however, contends that the presiding judge incorrectly ruled that such promise might be inferred from the fact that the plaintiff undertook and completed the building of the wall with the expectation that the defendant would pay him for it, the defendant having reason to know that the plaintiff was acting with that expectation, and allowed him thus to act without objection.

The fact that the plaintiff expected to be paid for the work would certainly not be sufficient of itself to establish the existence of a contract, when the question between the parties was whether one was made. *Taft v. Dickinson,* 6 Allen 553. It must be shown that, in some manner, the party sought to be charged assented to it. If a party, however, voluntarily accepts and avails himself of valuable services rendered for his benefit, when he has the option whether to accept or reject them, even if there is no distinct proof that they were rendered by his authority or request, a promise to pay for them may be inferred. His knowledge that they were valuable, and his exercise of the option to avail himself of them, justify this inference. *Abbot v. Hermon,* 7 Greenl. 118. *Hayden v. Madison,* 7 Greenl. 76. And when one stands by in silence and sees valuable services rendered upon his real estate by the erection of a structure, (of which he must necessarily avail himself afterwards in his proper use thereof,) such silence, accompanied with the knowledge on his part that the party rendering the services expects payment therefor, may fairly be treated as evidence of an acceptance of it, and as tending to show an agreement to pay for it.

The maxim, *Qui tacet consentire videtur,** is to be construed indeed as applying only to those cases where the circumstances are such that a party is fairly called upon either to deny or admit his liability. But if silence may be interpreted as assent where a proposition is made to one which he is bound to deny or admit, so also it may be if he is silent in the face of facts which fairly call upon him to speak. *Lamb v. Bunce,* 4 M. & S. 275. . . .

If a person saw day after day a laborer at work in his field doing services, which must of necessity enure to his benefit, knowing that the laborer expected pay for his work, when it was perfectly easy to notify him

---

*   Authors' note: "He who is silent is supposed to consent." Black's Law Dictionary (6th ed. 1990).

if his services were not wanted, even if a request were not expressly proved, such a request, either previous to or contemporaneous with the performance of the services, might fairly be inferred. But if the fact was merely brought to his attention upon a single occasion and casually, if he had little opportunity to notify the other that he did not desire the work and should not pay for it, or could only do so at the expense of much time and trouble, the same inference might not be made. The circumstances of each case would necessarily determine whether silence with a knowledge that another was doing valuable work for his benefit, and with the expectation of payment, indicated that consent which would give rise to the inference of a contract. The question would be one for the jury, and to them it was properly submitted in the case before us by the presiding judge.

Exceptions overruled.

NOTES AND QUESTIONS

1. *Question of law versus question of fact.* Note that the *Day* decision turns on an issue of fact for the jury—whether the facts and circumstances of the case sufficiently indicated that the defendant's silence and inaction communicated his assent to the offer. In what situations, if ever, would it be appropriate for a court to determine as a matter of law that the defendant's silence indicated assent?

2. *Inferring acceptance by silence or inaction from previous relations and dealings.* In *Hobbs v. Massasoit Whip Co.*, 158 Mass. 194, 33 N.E. 495 (1893), for example, the plaintiff sought to enforce a contract allegedly formed when he sent a batch of eel skins to the defendant, and the defendant took no action with respect to the skins, which eventually rotted in the defendant's care. While noting the rule that silence generally cannot be deemed an acceptance, the court nonetheless held that the prior relationship and dealings between the two parties made it reasonable for the plaintiff to assume a contract formed when the defendant failed to reject the skins:

> Standing alone, and unexplained, this proposition might seem to imply that one stranger may impose a duty upon another, and make him a purchaser, in spite of himself, by sending goods to him, unless he will take the trouble, and bear the expense, of notifying the sender that he will not buy. The case was argued for the defendant on that interpretation. But, in view of the evidence, we do not understand that to have been the meaning of the judge, and we do not think that the jury can have understood that to have been his meaning. The plaintiff was not a stranger to the defendant, even if there was no contract between them. He had sent eel skins in the same way four or five times before, and they had been accepted and paid for. On the defendant's testimony, it was fair to assume that if it had admitted the eel skins to be over 22 inches in length, and fit for its business, as the plaintiff testified and the jury found that they were, it would have

accepted them; that this was understood by the plaintiff; and, indeed, that there was a standing offer to him for such skins.

Id. at 495.

5. CONTRACTS OF ADHESION

Form contracts are sometimes referred to as "contracts of adhesion." This term was originally applied to life insurance policies. See Edwin W. Patterson, "The Delivery of a Life Insurance Policy," 33 Harv. L. Rev. 198, 222 (1919) ("The contract is drawn up by the insurer and the insured, who merely 'adheres' to it, has little choice as to its terms."). Of course today, the standard form contract is ubiquitous. One study of the construction industry determined that few items have a larger impact on construction costs than legal documents and form contracts. See William H. Hughes, Jr., "The AIA Form Construction and Design Agreements: A Departure From Typical Owner Expectations," 128 Ed. Law Rep. 953 (1998).

But if courts refused to enforce standard form contracts simply because the drafting party offers its terms on a take-it-or-leave-it basis, commercial contracting as we know it would come to a standstill. Standard form contracts provide substantial benefits in addition to their potential costs. Most importantly, standard form contracts reduce the costs of production and distribution for the seller of goods and services. Depending on the degree of competition faced by the seller, the savings may be shared with the purchaser or kept for the seller's own profit. See Friedrick Kessler, "Contracts of Adhesion—Some Thoughts About Freedom of Contract," 43 Colum. L. Rev. 629, 632 (1943).

The question then becomes one of balance. How should the law respond to questions of use and abuse? The problem with form contracts is that the parties specifically (and knowingly) consent to some terms, such as price or warranty, while the non-drafting party seldom even reads some terms and provisions. Thus, some terms are specifically assented to (making enforcement realistic) whereas other boilerplate provisions are seldom even read (making enforcement more problematic on assent grounds). The problems then can be reduced to the question of what to do about the objectionable provisions. Reject the entire agreement as not enforceable or create a legal method for attacking the objectionable terms while retaining the negotiated terms?

Karl N. Llewellyn, the principal architect of the Uniform Commercial Code, criticized the all-or-nothing approach of rejecting or accepting the agreement in whole. Llewellyn identified two different types of assent in standard form contracts. First, the apparently weaker party likely does give real assent to the transaction in general (e.g., "I need cell phone service.") and particular dickered terms of the transaction (e.g., "I want the white iPhone with 8 gigs of memory and a two-year service contract for

$112 per month."). Those terms are salient to both parties because while the provider knows all of the terms in its contract, the purchaser also is paying attention to these dickered terms.

Second, by signing the standard form contract, the purchaser also gives the appearance of assent to the boilerplate clauses, including such terms as arbitration, choice of law, choice of forum, severability, and integration clauses. The quality of assent in this second situation is different than for the dickered terms, and Llewellyn described it as a "blanket assent" as opposed to a specific assent. See Karl N. Llewellyn, The Common Law Tradition 370–71 (1960). For Llewellyn, the blanket assent was "to any not unreasonable or indecent terms the seller may have on his form, which do not alter or eviscerate the reasonable meaning of the dickered terms." Id.

Other commentators have argued that the problem of adhesive contracting practices is not as significant as traditional wisdom suggests. Some anecdotal evidence suggests that truly "pathological" adhesion contract terms are rare. See, e.g., John J.A. Burke, "Contract as Commodity: A Nonfiction Approach," 24 Seton Hall Legis. J. 285, 287–94 (2000) (noting 1999 study by the New Jersey Law Revision Commission that reported, inter alia, "Of the seventeen standard form contracts relating to goods in the sample, none contained especially onerous terms."). Similarly, economic theory suggests that oppressive terms should quickly disappear from efficient markets because even a small number of savvy consumers should be able to communicate their preferences for non-abusive terms to competing sellers and other consumers. See Robert A. Hillman & Jeffrey J. Rachlinski, "Standard Form Contracting in the Electronic Age," 77 N.Y.U. L. Rev. 429, 442–44 (2003). As a producer gains a reputation for imposing inefficient or oppressive terms upon its consumers, consumers in that market will take their business elsewhere. See id.

At the same time, however, producers in inefficient markets may continue to impose inefficient or oppressive terms on consumers because the pool of savvy consumers who would otherwise spot the oppressive terms is too small or because the costs of disseminating information about such inefficient practices to the marketplace are too high. See id. And, as some commentators have noted, producers have incentives to impose inefficient contract terms even in efficient markets. Russell Korobkin, for example, notes that consumers are "boundedly rational," meaning that they typically do not obtain and analyze every piece of available information regarding a choice before making that choice. See Russell Korobkin, "Bounded Rationality, Standard Form Contracts, and Unconscionability," 70 U. Chi. L. Rev. 1203, 1203 (2003). Instead, consumers limit their decision criteria to only a few salient product attributes. See id. Because producers typically have much greater information regarding their products—including their contract terms—they can compete by offering efficient terms with respect to salient attributes such as price and warranty, while offering inferior non-salient terms such as choice of law and arbitration clauses. See id. at 1206.

The problem for courts in assessing adhesion contracts lies in attempting to balance the private and societal benefits of contracts of adhesion, while at the same time protecting the weaker party from abuse. This balancing often implicates the role of assent of the weaker party in that deliberation. In that regard, Llewellyn's bifurcation of form contracts into two contracts is helpful: the negotiated terms contract and the boilerplate contract containing standard or form terms. The negotiated terms contract will be subjected to the classical contract rules governing contract formation, interpretation, and enforceability. The boiler-plate contract with non-negotiated terms will be subjected to a different standard. Under Llewellyn's view, merely that the non-drafter signed the form contract does not imply assent to those terms. Nonetheless, courts will enforce the form terms unless (i) the standard terms impair the fair meaning of the negotiated terms, or (ii) the terms are unfair or manifestly unreasonable. Keep in mind that not all standard contracts are contracts of adhesion and not all adhesion contracts are standardized. See W. David Slawson, "Standard Form Contracts and Democratic Control of Lawmaking Power," 84 Harv. L. Rev. 529, 549 (1971).

CARNIVAL CRUISE LINES, INC. V. SHUTE

United States Supreme Court
499 U.S. 585 (1991)

Justice BLACKMUN delivered the opinion of the Court.

In this admiralty case we primarily consider whether the United States Court of Appeals for the Ninth Circuit correctly refused to enforce a forum-selection clause contained in tickets issued by petitioner Carnival Cruise Lines, Inc., to respondents Eulala and Russel Shute.

I

The Shutes, through an Arlington, Wash., travel agent, purchased passage for a 7-day cruise on petitioner's ship, the *Tropicale*. Respondents paid the fare to the agent who forwarded the payment to petitioner's headquarters in Miami, Fla. Petitioner then prepared the tickets and sent them to respondents in the State of Washington. The face of each ticket, at its left-hand lower corner, contained this admonition:

SUBJECT TO CONDITIONS OF CONTRACT ON LAST PAGES
IMPORTANT! PLEASE READ CONTRACT—ON LAST PAGES
1, 2, 3 App. 15.

The following appeared on "contract page 1" of each ticket:

TERMS AND CONDITIONS OF PASSAGE CONTRACT TICKET

. . .

3. (a) The acceptance of this ticket by the person or persons named hereon as passengers shall be deemed to be an acceptance and agreement by each of them of all of the terms and conditions of this Passage Contract Ticket. . . .

8. It is agreed by and between the passenger and the Carrier that all disputes and matters whatsoever arising under, in connection with or incident to this Contract shall be litigated, if at all, in and before a Court located in the State of Florida, U.S.A., to the exclusion of the Courts of any other state or country. *Id.,* at 16.

The last quoted paragraph is the forum-selection clause at issue.

II

Respondents boarded the *Tropicale* in Los Angeles, Cal. The ship sailed to Puerto Vallarta, Mexico, and then returned to Los Angeles. While the ship was in international waters off the Mexican coast, respondent Eulala Shute was injured when she slipped on a deck mat during a guided tour of the ship's galley. Respondents filed suit against petitioner in the United States District Court for the Western District of Washington, claiming that Mrs. Shute's injuries had been caused by the negligence of Carnival Cruise Lines and its employees. *Id.,* at 4.

Petitioner moved for summary judgment, contending that the forum clause in respondents' tickets required the Shutes to bring their suit against petitioner in a court in the State of Florida. Petitioner contended, alternatively, that the District Court lacked personal jurisdiction over petitioner because petitioner's contacts with the State of Washington were insubstantial. The District Court granted the motion, holding that petitioner's contacts with Washington were constitutionally insufficient to support the exercise of personal jurisdiction. See App. to Pet. for Cert. 60a.

The Court of Appeals reversed. Reasoning that "but for" petitioner's solicitation of business in Washington, respondents would not have taken the cruise and Mrs. Shute would not have been injured, the court concluded that petitioner had sufficient contacts with Washington to justify the District Court's exercise of personal jurisdiction. 897 F.2d 377, 385–386 (CA 9 1990).*

---

* The Court of Appeals had filed an earlier opinion also reversing the District Court and ruling that the District Court had personal jurisdiction over the cruise line and that the forum-selection clause in the tickets was unreasonable and was not to be enforced. 863 F.2d 1437 (CA 9 1988). That opinion, however, was withdrawn when the court certified to the Supreme Court of Washington the question whether the Washington long-arm statute, Wash. Rev. Code § 4.28.185 (1988), conferred personal jurisdiction over Carnival Cruise Lines for the claim asserted by the See 872 F.2d 930 (CA 9 1989). The Washington Supreme Court answered the certified question in

Turning to the forum-selection clause, the Court of Appeals acknowledged that a court concerned with the enforceability of such a clause must begin its analysis with The Bremen v. Zapata Off-Shore Co., 407 U.S. 1, 92 S. Ct. 1907, 32 L. Ed. 2d 513 (1972), where this Court held that forum-selection clauses, although not "historically . . . favored," are "prima facie valid." Id., at 9–10, 92 S. Ct., at 1913. See 897 F.2d, at 388. The appellate court concluded that the forum clause should not be enforced because it "was not freely bargained for." Id., at 389. As an "independent justification" for refusing to enforce the clause, the Court of Appeals noted that there was evidence in the record to indicate that "the Shutes are physically and financially incapable of pursuing this litigation in Florida" and that the enforcement of the clause would operate to deprive them of their day in court and thereby contravene this Court's holding in *The Bremen*. 897 F.2d, at 389.

We granted certiorari to address the question whether the Court of Appeals was correct in holding that the District Court should hear respondents' tort claim against petitioner. 498 U.S. 807–808, 111 S. Ct. 39, 112 L. Ed. 2d 16 (1990). Because we find the forum-selection clause to be dispositive of this question, we need not consider petitioner's constitutional argument as to personal jurisdiction. See Ashwander v. TVA, 297 U.S. 288, 347, 56 S. Ct. 466, 483, 80 L. Ed. 688 (1936) (Brandeis, J., concurring) ("It is not the habit of the Court to decide questions of a constitutional nature unless absolutely necessary to a decision of the case," quoting Burton v. United States, 196 U.S. 283, 295, 25 S. Ct. 243, 245, 49 L. Ed. 482 (1905)).

III

We begin by noting the boundaries of our inquiry. First, this is a case in admiralty, and federal law governs the enforceability of the forum-selection clause we scrutinize. See Archawski v. Hanioti, 350 U.S. 532, 533, 76 S. Ct. 617, 619, 100 L. Ed. 676 (1956); The Moses Taylor, 4 Wall. 411, 427, 18 L. Ed. 397 (1867). . . . Second, we do not address the question whether respondents had sufficient notice of the forum clause before entering the contract for passage. Respondents essentially have conceded that they had notice of the forum-selection provision. Brief for Respondents 26 ("The respondents do not contest the incorporation of the provisions nor [sic] that the forum selection clause was reasonably communicated to the respondents, as much as three pages of fine print can be communicated"). Additionally, the Court of Appeals evaluated the enforceability of the forum clause under the assumption, although "doubtful," that respondents could be deemed to have had knowledge of the clause. See 897 F.2d, at 389, and n. 11.

---

the affirmative on the ground that the Shutes' claim "arose from" petitioner's advertisement in Washington and the promotion of its cruises there. 113 Wash. 2d 763, 783 P. 2d 78 (1989). The Court of Appeals then "re-filed" its opinion "as modified herein." See 897 F.2d, at 380, n. 1.

Within this context, respondents urge that the forum clause should not be enforced because, contrary to this Court's teachings in *The Bremen,* the clause was not the product of negotiation, and enforcement effectively would deprive respondents of their day in court. Additionally, respondents contend that the clause violates the Limitation of Vessel Owner's Liability Act, 46 U.S.C. App. § 183c. We consider these arguments in turn.

IV.A.

Both petitioner and respondents argue vigorously that the Court's opinion in *The Bremen* governs this case, and each side purports to find ample support for its position in that opinion's broad-ranging language. This seeming paradox derives in large part from key factual differences between this case and *The Bremen,* differences that preclude an automatic and simple application of *The Bremen*'s general principles to the facts here.

In *The Bremen,* this Court addressed the enforceability of a forum-selection clause in a contract between two business corporations. An American corporation, Zapata, made a contract with Unterweser, a German corporation, for the towage of Zapata's oceangoing drilling rig from Louisiana to a point in the Adriatic Sea off the coast of Italy. The agreement provided that any dispute arising under the contract was to be resolved in the London Court of Justice. After a storm in the Gulf of Mexico seriously damaged the rig, Zapata ordered Unterweser's ship to tow the rig to Tampa, Fla., the nearest point of refuge. Thereafter, Zapata sued Unterweser in admiralty in federal court at Tampa. Citing the forum clause, Unterweser moved to dismiss. The District Court denied Unterweser's motion, and the Court of Appeals for the Fifth Circuit, sitting en banc on rehearing, and by a sharply divided vote, affirmed. In re Complaint of Unterweser Reederei GmbH, 446 F.2d 907 (1971).

This Court vacated and remanded, stating that, in general, "a freely negotiated private international agreement, unaffected by fraud, undue influence, or overweening bargaining power, such as that involved here, should be given full effect." 407 U.S., at 12–13, 92 S. Ct. at 1914–1915 (footnote omitted). The Court further generalized that "in the light of present-day commercial realities and expanding international trade we conclude that the forum clause should control absent a strong showing that it should be set aside." Id., at 15, 92 S. Ct., at 1916. The Court did not define precisely the circumstances that would make it unreasonable for a court to enforce a forum clause. Instead, the Court discussed a number of factors that made it reasonable to enforce the clause at issue in *The Bremen* and that, presumably, would be pertinent in any determination whether to enforce a similar clause.

In this respect, the Court noted that there was "strong evidence that the forum clause was a vital part of the agreement, and [that] it would be unrealistic to think that the parties did not conduct their negotiations, including fixing the monetary terms, with the consequences of the forum clause figuring prominently in their calculations." *Id.,* at 14, 92 S. Ct., 1915 (footnote omitted). Further, the Court observed that it was not "dealing with an agreement between two Americans to resolve their essentially local disputes in a remote alien forum," and that in such a case, "the serious inconvenience of the contractual forum to one or both of the parties might carry greater weight in determining the reasonableness of the forum clause." Id., at 17, 92 S. Ct., at 1917. The Court stated that even where the forum clause establishes a remote forum for resolution of conflicts, "the party claiming [unfairness] should bear a heavy burden of proof." *Ibid.*

In applying *The Bremen,* the Court of Appeals in the present litigation took note of the foregoing "reasonableness" factors and rather automatically decided that the forum-selection clause was unenforceable because, unlike the parties in *The Bremen,* respondents are not business persons and did not negotiate the terms of the clause with petitioner. Alternatively, the Court of Appeals ruled that the clause should not be enforced because enforcement effectively would deprive respondents of an opportunity to litigate their claim against petitioner.

The Bremen concerned a "far from routine transaction between companies of two different nations contemplating the tow of an extremely costly piece of equipment from Louisiana across the Gulf of Mexico and the Atlantic Ocean, through the Mediterranean Sea to its final destination in the Adriatic Sea." Id., at 13, 92 S. Ct., at 1915. These facts suggest that, even apart from the evidence of negotiation regarding the forum clause, it was entirely reasonable for the Court in *The Bremen* to have expected Unterweser and Zapata to have negotiated with care in selecting a forum for the resolution of disputes arising from their special towing contract.

In contrast, respondents' passage contract was purely routine and doubtless nearly identical to every commercial passage contract issued by petitioner and most other cruise lines. See, e.g., Hodes v. S.N.C. Achille Lauro ed Altri-Gestione, 858 F.2d 905, 910 (CA3 1988), cert. dism'd, 490 U.S. 1001, 109 S. Ct. 1633, 104 L. Ed. 2d 149 (1989). In this context, it would be entirely unreasonable for us to assume that respondents—or any other cruise passenger—would negotiate with petitioner the terms of a forum-selection clause in an ordinary commercial cruise ticket. Common sense dictates that a ticket of this kind will be a form contract the terms of which are not subject to negotiation, and that an individual purchasing the ticket will not have bargaining parity with the cruise line. But by ignoring the crucial differences in the business contexts in which the respective contracts were executed, the Court of Appeals' analysis seems to us to have distorted somewhat this Court's holding in *The Bremen.*

In evaluating the reasonableness of the forum clause at issue in this case, we must refine the analysis of *The Bremen* to account for the realities of form passage contracts. As an initial matter, we do not adopt the Court of Appeals' determination that a nonnegotiated forum-selection clause in a form ticket contract is never enforceable simply because it is not the subject of bargaining. Including a reasonable forum clause in a form contract of this kind well may be permissible for several reasons: First, a cruise line has a special interest in limiting the fora in which it potentially could be subject to suit. Because a cruise ship typically carries passengers from many locales, it is not unlikely that a mishap on a cruise could subject the cruise line to litigation in several different fora. See *The Bremen*, 407 U.S., at 13, and n. 15, 92 S. Ct., at 1915, and n. 15; Hodes, 858 F.2d, at 913. Additionally, a clause establishing ex ante the forum for dispute resolution has the salutary effect of dispelling any confusion about where suits arising from the contract must be brought and defended, sparing litigants the time and expense of pretrial motions to determine the correct forum and conserving judicial resources that otherwise would be devoted to deciding those motions. See Stewart Organization, 487 U.S., at 33, 108 S. Ct., at 2246 (concurring opinion). Finally, it stands to reason that passengers who purchase tickets containing a forum clause like that at issue in this case benefit in the form of reduced fares reflecting the savings that the cruise line enjoys by limiting the fora in which it may be sued. Cf. Northwestern Nat. Ins. Co. v. Donovan, 916 F.2d 372, 378 (CA 7 1990).

We also do not accept the Court of Appeals' "independent justification" for its conclusion that *The Bremen* dictates that the clause should not be enforced because "[t]here is evidence in the record to indicate that the Shutes are physically and financially incapable of pursuing this litigation in Florida." 897 F.2d, at 389. We do not defer to the Court of Appeals' findings of fact. In dismissing the case for lack of personal jurisdiction over petitioner, the District Court made no finding regarding the physical and financial impediments to the Shutes' pursuing their case in Florida. The Court of Appeals' conclusory reference to the record provides no basis for this Court to validate the finding of inconvenience. Furthermore, the Court of Appeals did not place in proper context this Court's statement in *The Bremen* that "the serious inconvenience of the contractual forum to one or both of the parties might carry greater weight in determining the reasonableness of the forum clause." 407 U.S., at 17, 92 S. Ct., at 1917. The Court made this statement in evaluating a hypothetical "agreement between two Americans to resolve their essentially local disputes in a remote alien forum." *Ibid.* In the present case, Florida is not a "remote alien forum," nor—given the fact that Mrs. Shute's accident occurred off the coast of Mexico—is this dispute an essentially local one inherently more suited to resolution in the State of Washington than in Florida. In light of these distinctions, and because respondents do not claim lack of notice of the forum clause, we conclude that they have not satisfied the "heavy burden of proof," *ibid.,* required to set aside the clause on grounds of inconvenience.

It bears emphasis that forum-selection clauses contained in form passage contracts are subject to judicial scrutiny for fundamental fairness. In this case, there is no indication that petitioner set Florida as the forum in which disputes were to be resolved as a means of discouraging cruise passengers from pursuing legitimate claims. Any suggestion of such a bad-faith motive is belied by two facts: Petitioner has its principal place of business in Florida, and many of its cruises depart from and return to Florida ports. Similarly, there is no evidence that petitioner obtained respondents' accession to the forum clause by fraud or overreaching. Finally, respondents have conceded that they were given notice of the forum provision and, therefore, presumably retained the option of rejecting the contract with impunity. In the case before us, therefore, we conclude that the Court of Appeals erred in refusing to enforce the forum-selection clause.

IV.B.

Respondents also contend that the forum-selection clause at issue violates 46 U.S.C. App. § 183c. That statute, enacted in 1936, see ch. 521, 49 Stat. 1480, provides:

> It shall be unlawful for the . . . owner of any vessel transporting passengers between ports of the United States or between any such port and a foreign port to insert in any rule, regulation, contract, or agreement any provision or limitation (1) purporting, in the event of loss of life or bodily injury arising from the negligence or fault of such owner or his servants, to relieve such owner . . . from liability, or from liability beyond any stipulated amount, for such loss or injury, or (2) purporting in such event to lessen, weaken, or avoid the right of any claimant to a trial by court of competent jurisdiction on the question of liability for such loss or injury, or the measure of damages therefor. All such provisions or limitations contained in any such rule, regulation, contract, or agreement are hereby declared to be against public policy and shall be null and void and of no effect.

By its plain language, the forum-selection clause before us does not take away respondents' right to "a trial by [a] court of competent jurisdiction" and thereby contravene the explicit proscription of § 183c. Instead, the clause states specifically that actions arising out of the passage contract shall be brought "if at all," in a court "located in the State of Florida," which, plainly, is a "court of competent jurisdiction" within the meaning of the statute.

Respondents appear to acknowledge this by asserting that although the forum clause does not directly prevent the determination of claims against the cruise line, it causes plaintiffs unreasonable hardship in asserting their rights and therefore violates Congress' intended goal in enacting § 183c. Significantly, however, respondents cite no authority for their contention that Congress' intent in enacting § 183c was to avoid having a plaintiff travel to a distant forum in order to litigate. The legislative history of § 183c suggests instead that this provision was enacted in response to passenger-ticket conditions purporting to limit the shipowner's liability for negligence or to remove the issue of liability from the scrutiny of any court by means of a clause providing that "the question of liability and the measure of damages shall be determined by arbitration." See S. Rep. No. 2061, 74th Cong., 2d Sess., 6 (1936); H.R. Rep. No. 2517, 74th Cong., 2d Sess., 6 (1936). . . . There was no prohibition of a forum-selection clause. Because the clause before us allows for judicial resolution of claims against petitioner and does not purport to limit petitioner's liability for negligence, it does not violate § 183c.

V

The judgment of the Court of Appeals is reversed.

It is so ordered.

Justice STEVENS, with whom Justice MARSHALL joins, dissenting.

The Court prefaces its legal analysis with a factual statement that implies that a purchaser of a Carnival Cruise Lines passenger ticket is fully and fairly notified about the existence of the choice of forum clause in the fine print on the back of the ticket. See *ante,* at 1524. Even if this implication were accurate, I would disagree with the Court's analysis. But, given the Court's preface, I begin my dissent by noting that only the most meticulous passenger is likely to become aware of the forum-selection provision. I have therefore appended to this opinion a facsimile of the relevant text, using the type size that actually appears in the ticket itself. A careful reader will find the forum-selection clause in the 8th of the 25 numbered paragraphs.

Of course, many passengers, like the respondents in this case, see *ante,* at 1524, will not have an opportunity to read paragraph 8 until they have actually purchased their tickets. By this point, the passengers will already have accepted the condition set forth in paragraph 16(a), which provides that "[t]he Carrier shall not be liable to make any refund to passengers in respect of . . . tickets wholly or partly not used by a passenger." Not knowing whether or not that provision is legally enforceable, I assume that the average passenger would accept the risk of having to file suit in Florida in the event of an injury, rather than canceling—without a refund—a planned vacation at the last minute. The fact that the cruise line can reduce its litigation costs, and therefore its liability insurance premiums, by forcing this choice on its passengers does not, in my opinion, suffice to render the provision reasonable. Cf. Steven v. Fidelity & Casualty Co. of New York, 58 Cal. 2d 862, 883, 27 Cal. Rptr. 172, 186, 377 P. 2d 284, 298 (1962) (refusing to enforce limitation on liability in insurance policy because insured "must purchase the policy before he even knows its provisions").

* * *

I respectfully dissent.

NOTES AND QUESTIONS

1.   *Subsequent statutory amendment.* After the decision in *Carnival Cruise Lines v. Shute*, Congress amended U.S.C. § 183c in 1992 and again in 1993. The effect of the first amendment effectively overruled *Shute* with the 1993 amendment having the opposite effect. As a result, *Shute* remains good law. See *Compagno v. Commodore Cruise Line, Ltd.*, 1994 WL 462997 (E.D. La. 1994) (unreported opinion).

2.   *Llewellyn's analysis.* Did *Shute* adopt or apply Llewellyn's famous analysis? What were the negotiated terms of the form contract? What were the boiler-plate terms? Was the forum selection clause specifically negotiated? Under Llewellyn's analysis, the forum selection clause would be presumptively enforceable (from signature and "duty to read") unless the clause (i) impaired the meaning of the negotiated terms or (ii) was unfair. Which, if either, analysis did *Shute* apply?

3.   *Duty to read doctrine, objective theory of contracts, and adhesion contracts.* The "duty to read" doctrine is a product of the objective theory of contract. The doctrine suggests that when a person signs a contract, a reasonable person is entitled to believe that the party read the contract and assented to all its terms. Stated another way, a contract no longer requires true assent but rather only what the recipient of a manifestation may justifiably regard as assent. See Restatement (Second) of Contracts § 23. If an offeree, in total ignorance of the terms of an offer, acts or expresses an intent in a manner to justify the offeror in inferring assent to the terms of the offer, and a reasonable person in the position of the offeree should have known the act or expression would lead the offeror to so conclude, then a contract will be formed despite the offeree's actual ignorance of the terms of the offer. See Restatement (Second) of Contracts § 23, *comment b.* The most obvious example of such a manifestation involves the failure of an offeree to read a writing but signing the document under a mistaken belief as to its contents. In the absence of fraud, such a person is normally bound to the terms of the contract. The case for enforceability becomes stronger as the offeree is capable of reading and understanding the terms. See *Stanley A. Klopp, Inc. v. John Deere Co.*, 510 F. Supp. 807, 811 (E.D. Pa. 1981) ("The general rule is that absent an allegation of fraud or incompetence a person has a duty to read a contract before signing it and his failure to do so will not excuse his ignorance of its contents."). While the doctrine is phrased in terms of a "duty" to read, in Hohfeldian terms, there is in truth no positive duty nor correlative right. However, the simple failure to read a written document before signing can produce a forfeiture of the

privilege to assert that assent was not properly given. The person who signs may be bound by what was not read.

No doubt, strict application of the rule promotes market function, but is it fair to broadly apply the rule, especially to form and adhesion contracts where it is doubtful that many (if any) adhering parties actually read and assent to those contracts? See Stewart Macaulay, "Private Legislation and the Duty to Read—Business Run by IBM Machine, the Law of Contracts and Credit Cards," 19 Vand. L. Rev. 1051 (1966) (thorough policy discussion of the rule and its implications). Specifically, how does the signature on a contract of adhesion relate to Llewellyn's argument that boilerplate terms and clauses are seldom read and cannot be changed in any event? What about important clauses that the dominant party hides or buries in a long form contract? There may be circumstances where important terms arguably should not be binding because assent can not properly be presumed from a signature. As John Calamari comments, traditional contract law privileges and protects the sanctity of a written "integration" of the parties' agreement through rules that "exclude or minimize the true subjective intention of the parties." The so-called "duty to read," according to Calamari, developed at a time when it would have been reasonable to expect parties to read their written contracts before signing, before standard form contracts became the predominant contracting mechanism. See id. But in the modern mass market context, parties may reasonably believe they are not expected to read standardized agreements. See id; see John D. Calamari, "Duty To Read—A Changing Concept,"43 Fordham L. Rev. 341, 360–361 (1974):

Do you think Professor Calamari endorses Llewellyn's modified assent theory? If so, how do you reconcile the early will theory or subjective intent "meeting of the minds" theory view with the later nineteenth century objective theory? Is there yet another pendulum swing in contracts back to subjective intent? Stated another way, do you think that objectivists like Holmes and Williston would agree with realists like Llewellyn? See Alan M. White and Cathy Lesser Mansfield, "Literacy and Contract," 13 Stan. L. & Pol'y Rev. 233, 234 (2002) ("[J]udges and legislators continue to assume that consumers have the ability to read and understand, and do in fact read and understand, contract and disclosure documents. As a result, consumers are charged with the duty to read and know the contents of their contracts and are bound by them, no matter what actually has transpired between the consumer and the merchant or lender.").

4.   *Restatement approach.* Restatement (Second) of Contracts § 211(3) regarding standardized agreements provides that a term is not part of an agreement where "the other party has reason to believe that the party manifesting such assent would not do so if he knew that the writing contained a particular term." *Comment b* (assent to unknown terms) provides that "customers do not in fact ordinarily understand or even read the standard terms. They trust the good faith of the party using the form and to the tacit representation that like terms are being accepted regularly by others similarly situated. But they understand that they are assenting to the terms not read or

not understood, subject to such limitations as the law may impose." *Comment c* (review of unfair terms) provides that the "customer assents to a few terms, typically inserted in blanks on the printed form, and gives blanket assent to the type of transaction embodied in the standard form." *Comment f* (terms excluded) provides that "although customers typically adhere to standardized agreements and are bound by them without even appearing to know the standard terms in detail, they are not bound to unknown terms which are beyond the range of reasonable expectation." The latter quote would negate inclusion of the term under the duty to read either because the party including the term has reason to believe that the adhering party would not have accepted the agreement if that party had known the agreement contained that particular term. Where does this leave the doctrine of the duty to read, at least in form contracts? Does it adopt Llewellyn's no true assent to unreasonable boilerplate?

5.   *UCC duty to read.* The UCC does not state a separate and specific rule regarding the duty to read. As a result, the common law duty to read doctrine applies by virtue of UCC § 1–103.

6.   *Disclosure timing.* In many cases, the forum selection clause will be printed only on the passenger ticket neither mailed nor received at the time the contract was formed (time of acceptance). The passenger will therefore not have meaningful notice or an opportunity to shop for other cruise lines with more favorable forum clauses. Of course, since all cruise contracts include forum clauses, shopping is not meaningful in any event. Note, "Carnival's Got the Fun . . . and the Forum: A New Look at Choice-of-Forum Clauses and the Unconscionability Doctrine After *Carnival Cruise Lines, Inc. v. Shute*," 53 U. Pitt. L. Rev. 1025 (1992) (all cruise contracts include similar clauses). After this case, cruise lines are so confident in the validity of the forum selection clause that they will seek sanctions or a counterclaim breach of contract claim against parties who bring suit in a forum other than that contractually specified. Debra D. Burke, "Cruise Lines and Consumers: Troubled Waters," 37 Am. Bus. L. J. 689, 701 (2000).

7.   *Adhesion contracts and socio-economic context.* Legal scholars have for some time recognized that form contracts, particularly in the consumer contracting context, are somehow different from negotiated or dickered-for contracts. Roscoe Pound, for example, famously argued that contract rules created in the economic and social contexts of the nineteenth century—when contracting parties were supposedly presumed to operate from positions of relatively equal bargaining power—should not be used to invalidate legislation meant to police relations between contracting parties in a modern, industrial economy:

> Why do so many [courts] force upon legislation an academic theory of equality in the face of practical conditions of inequality? Why do we find a great and learned court in 1908 taking the long step into the past of dealing with the relation between employer and employee in railway transportation, as if the parties were individuals—as if they

were farmers haggling over the sale of a horse? Roscoe Pound, Liberty of Contract, 18 Yale L. J. 454, 454 (1908).

Do you accept Pound's implicit proposition that, while contract law presumptions that individuals were generally capable of protecting their own interests in dealing with others "worked" at some point in the past, it no longer works under current social and economic conditions?

8. *Contract as Thing and Contract as Product.* Legal scholars for some time have argued that adhesive standard form contracts between producers and consumers should be treated under a different legal regime than contract law. Arthur Allen Leff, for example, noted that in bargaining over the purchase of a car, the buyer and seller negotiate almost exclusively over color, size, configuration, and other attributes of the physical product. Only the contract is left unnegotiated.

Leff observed that regulators have three strategies for regulating the parties' interactions in this situation—(a) regulate the parties with respect to who can enter particular types of transactions; (b) regulate the deal making process, such as by requiring greater disclosure or waiting periods; or (c) regulate the contract terms as part of the product being sold. See id. at 148. Leff determined that in the consumer context, legislators could most effectively promote consumer welfare by regulating the contract terms as attributes of the product being sold.

Margaret Jane Radin similarly proposed that adhesion contracts should be treated as part of the product being sold, rather than as true contracts. For Radin, typical boilerplate terms are no different than physical attributes of the product—a consumer has equally little information about, and equally little ability to understand, the inner workings of a microchip as she does the inner workings of an arbitration clause. See Margaret Jane Radin, *Humans, Computers, and Binding Commitment*, 75 Ind. L. J. 1125, 1126 (2000) (discussing shift to contract as product paradigm). Are these arguments for regulating the "quality" of terms in consumer adhesion contracts through legislation rather than common law contract rules compelling? Why or why not?

9. *Adhesion contracts and "sticky" terms.* As noted, not all standard form contracts are adhesive, and not all adhesion contracts are offered on pre-printed standard forms. But standard form contracts are still well-suited for imposing adhesive terms on the offeree. One reason for this close connection may be that contracting parties tend to suffer from a psychological bias in favor of the first set of default terms offered. As Russell Korobkin notes, parties often irrationally give such terms greater weight than later-offered terms and require costly justifications for moving away from any of the default terms. "Parties are likely to favor default terms, in many instances, because these terms are often correlated with inaction (i.e., the default terms will be operative if the parties do nothing)." Russell Korobkin, "Inertia and Preference in Contract Negotiation: The Psychological Power of Default Rules and Form Terms," 51 Vand. L. Rev. 1583, 1586 (1998).

Does Korobkin's inertia theory explain why consumers sometimes fail to attempt to dicker over contracts that appear to be offered on a take-it-or-leave-it basis but would really be open to negotiation if consumers just asked? Are there any other reasons consumers might not attempt to negotiate in such situations?

10. *Social context and adhesion contracting.* Note that producers often have an incentive to *appear* to offer contract terms on a "take-it-or-leave-it" basis, when in reality they are willing to negotiate on at least some terms, such as price and warranty. In the anecdotal experience of many contracts and negotiation theory scholars, it is often remarkably easy to negotiate price terms for even the most mundane of consumer transactions. So why do consumers generally fail to attempt to dicker on potentially negotiable items such as price or warranty terms? Consider the social context in which consumers often execute significant adhesion contracts: car rental counters, a travel agent's office, signing a credit card transaction in the check-out line at Wal-Mart, an insurance agent's office, the first day of employment, over the phone with their real estate agent, etc. What social and psychological pressures are at work on consumers in such situations that would tend to prevent bargaining? Do you think that producers intentionally establish high-pressure situations to impair consumer willingness to bargain, or have those situations developed naturally as a result of the fast pace of the modern American economy? For an excellent analysis of these issues, see generally Robert A. Hillman & Jeffrey J. Rachlinski, "Standard Form Contracting in the Electronic Age," 77 N.Y.U. L. Rev. 429, 447–49 (2002).

D. TERMINATION OF THE POWER OF ACCEPTANCE

The existence of an offer creates a power of acceptance in the offeree. The offeree may exercise that power provided that the power of acceptance has not been previously terminated. This section considers the termination of the offeree's power of acceptance. Since the power may be exercised anytime prior to termination of the offer, many contract disputes center on the question of which occurred first, acceptance or termination. This struggle was introduced in the discussion of the mailbox rule but continues here in a more dramatic fashion. Unlike the mailbox rule where acceptance can occur without the knowledge of the offeror, acceptance or termination compete through notice and knowledge. This often allows a court to determine whether the affected party had a reasonable expectation that the power of acceptance remained available for exercise. In rare cases where notice or knowledge may not be possible (such as the death or supervening incapacity of one of the parties), the law constructs equitable default rules.

The idea that the offer creates a power of acceptance in the offeree is credited to Professor Hohfeld for his early work on legal relationships. See

Wesley Newcomb Hohfeld, "Some Fundamental Legal Conceptions as Applied in Judicial Reasoning," 23 Yale L. J. 16, 28–30 (1913) and John E. Murray, "Contracts: A New Design For The Agreement Process," 53 Cornell L. Rev. 785 (1968). Beyond peradventure, that "power" doctrine is incorporated into the fabric of Restatement (Second) of Contracts. Once the power is created, it must be exercised or terminated. If the offeree exercises the power of acceptance prior to termination, the parties have formed a contract. If, on the other hand, the power terminates before it is exercised, a contract cannot form. With no contract, the conditional promises made by the offer are not enforceable, at least by exercise of the power of acceptance.

The Restatement (Second) of Contracts § 36 sets forth two basic paradigms for the termination of the power. The first termination paradigm focuses on conduct by the offeror and offeree that acts to terminate the power of acceptance. Under Restatement (Second) of Contracts § 36(1), the power of acceptance may terminate before exercise in any of the following ways:

(a) rejection or counter-offer by the offeree, or

(b) lapse of time, or

(c) revocation by the offeror, or

(d) death or incapacity of the offeror or offeree.

Under this paradigm, the appropriate focus is on whether the parties' acts or failures to that indicate a lack of intent to enter into a contract.

The second method provides that the power is terminated by the nonoccurrence of any condition of acceptance stated in the offer. Conditions of acceptance permit the offeror to limit or specify the manner and time in which the offeree may accept the offer. Because of this ability to place conditions on acceptance, courts often refer to the offeror as the "master of the offer." This simply means the offeror may state any condition of acceptance desired, and a failure to comply will terminate the power of acceptance.

1. TERMINATION BY OFFEROR REVOCATION

Restatement (Second) of Contracts § 36(1)(c) provides that the power of acceptance terminates when the offeror revokes that power prior to its exercise by the offeree. Revocation terminates the offeree's power of acceptance upon receipt by the offeree and may be communicated directly or indirectly. See Restatement (Second) of Contracts §§ 42–43. But why is this so? Contract law could express the opposite rule that the offeror may not revoke the offer after communicating it to the offeree. Is the rule of revocability a rule of history, convenience, or logic? Several theories can be advanced to support a rule of revocability.

First, the contrary rule would contravene the bargain principle and consideration theory. The offer that creates the power of acceptance is not a contract in itself in part because it is, by definition, not bargained for. Thus, any promise by the offeror to make the offer irrevocable is merely a non-contractual gratuitous promise by the offeror. Consequently, consideration theory supports revocability. Stated another way, consideration theory of obligation does not exist to enforce a promise of irrevocability unless and until the offeror receives supporting consideration. (Notably, a promise to keep an offer open for a period of time that is supported by consideration creates an enforceable "option" to exercise the power of acceptance with respect to the offer.) The will theory might also be used to support revocability. Under this theory, there has been no subjective or objective "meeting of the minds" until mutual assent is expressed through the acceptance mechanism. Still another theory of fairness could be used to justify revocability. Unless and until the offeree exercises the power of assent, it would be unfair to bind the offeror without also binding the offeree. Why should the law permit the offeree to speculate on the terms of the offer while the offeror may not?

Perhaps because of a confluence of these reasons, American common law clings to the notion, historically justified, that an offer is revocable by the offeror until the offeree exercises the power of acceptance—even if the terms of the offer expressly state that the offer is not revocable. See Arthur L. Corbin, "Offer and Acceptance, And Some of the Resulting Legal Relations," 26 Yale L.J. 169, 185 (1917). Particularly where the offer states it is irrevocable, the notion that it is revocable unless the promise of irrevocability is supported by consideration should be perhaps no more surprising than the fact that a promise not supported by consideration is not binding. Of course, other theories of obligation including promissory estoppel might well justify enforcement, at least in cases where the offeree detrimentally relied on the promise of irrevocability.

On the other hand, given the moral obligation and perhaps predictable pattern that promises of irrevocability are likely to happen in the context of commercial promises where no gratuity was intended, a contrary rule might easily develop. For that reason, UCC § 2–205 provides that a written offer signed by a merchant giving assurances that it will be held open (e.g., is a "firm offer"), is irrevocable for a period not to exceed three months notwithstanding the absence of consideration.

In a concession to enforceability, CISG art. 16(2)(a) provides that an offer stating irrevocability is in fact irrevocable for the period stated. Thus, the CISG eliminates the UCC limitations concerning a signed writing and the three-month limit. It also eliminates the merchant requirement, but the CISG does not apply to sales of consumer goods. As you study the materials below, consider applications of the general rule and theories of obligation supporting irrevocability.

DICKINSON V. DODDS

Court of Appeal, Chancery Division (England)
(1875–1876) L.R. 2 Ch. D. 463 (1876)

BACON, Vice-Chancellor.

On Wednesday, the 10th of June, 1874, the Defendant John Dodds signed and delivered to the Plaintiff, George Dickinson, a memorandum, of which the material part was as follows:—

I hereby agree to sell to Mr. George Dickinson the whole of the dwelling-houses, garden ground, stabling, and outbuildings thereto belonging, situate at Croft, belonging to me, for the sum of £800.

As witness my hand this tenth day of June, 1874.

£800.   (Signed) John Dodds

P.S.—This offer to be left over until Friday, 9 o'clock, A.M. J. D. (the twelfth), 12th June, 1874.

(Signed) J. Dodds

The bill alleged that Dodds understood and intended that the Plaintiff should have until Friday 9 A.M. within which to determine whether he would or would not purchase, and that he should absolutely have until that time the refusal of the property at the price of £800, and that the Plaintiff in fact determined to accept the offer on the morning of Thursday, the 11th of June, but did not at once signify his acceptance to Dodds, believing that he had the power to accept it until 9 A.M. on the Friday.

In the afternoon of the Thursday the Plaintiff was informed by a Mr. Berry that Dodds had been offering or agreeing to sell the property to Thomas Allan, the other Defendant. Thereupon the Plaintiff, at about half-past seven in the evening, went to the house of Mrs. Burgess, the mother-in-law of Dodds, where he was then staying, and left with her a formal acceptance in writing of the offer to sell the property. According to the evidence of Mrs. Burgess this document never in fact reached Dodds, she having forgotten to give it to him.

On the following (Friday) morning, at about seven o'clock, Berry, who was acting as agent for Dickinson, found Dodds at the Darlington railway station, and handed to him a duplicate of the acceptance by Dickinson, and explained to Dodds its purport. He replied that it was too late, as he had sold the property. A few minutes later Dickinson himself found Dodds entering a railway carriage, and handed him another duplicate of the notice of acceptance, but Dodds declined to receive it, saying, "You are too late. I have sold the property."

It appeared that on the day before, Thursday, the 11th of June, Dodds had signed a formal contract for the sale of the property to the Defendant Allan for £800, and had received from him a deposit of £40.

The bill in this suit prayed that the Defendant Dodds might be decreed specifically to perform the contract of the 10th of June, 1874; that he might be restrained from conveying the property to Allan; that Allan might be restrained from taking any such conveyance; that, if any such conveyance had been or should be made, Allan might be declared a trustee of the property for, and might be directed to convey the property to, the Plaintiff; and for damages.

The cause came on for hearing before Vice-Chancellor *Bacon* on the 25th of January, 1876.

* * *

[Eds.—The text of the trial court opinion is omitted.]

There will be a decree for specific performance, with a declaration that Allan has no interest in the property; and the Plaintiff will be at liberty to deduct his costs of the suit out of his purchase-money.

From this decision both the Defendants appealed, and the appeals were heard on the 31st of March and the 1st of April, 1876. . . .

The arguments amounted to a repetition of those before the Vice-Chancellor. . . .

JAMES, L. J. The document, though beginning "I hereby agree to sell," was nothing but an offer, and was only intended to be an offer, for the Plaintiff himself tells us that he required time to consider whether he would enter into an agreement or not. Unless both parties had then agreed there was no concluded agreement then made; it was in effect and substance only an offer to sell. The Plaintiff, being minded not to complete the bargain at that time, added this memorandum—"This offer to be left over until Friday, 9 o'clock A.M., 12th June, 1874." That shows it was only an offer. There was no consideration given for the undertaking or promise, to whatever extent it may be considered binding, to keep the property unsold until 9 o'clock on Friday morning; but apparently Dickinson was of opinion, and probably Dodds was of the same opinion, that he (Dodds) was bound by that promise, and could not in any way withdraw from it, or retract it, until 9 o'clock on Friday morning, and this probably explains a good deal of what afterwards took place. But it is clear settled law, on one of the clearest principles of law, that this promise, being a mere nudum pactum, was not binding, and that at any moment before a complete acceptance by Dickinson of the offer, Dodds was as free as Dickinson himself. Well, that being the state of things, it is said that the only mode in which Dodds could assert that freedom was by actually and distinctly saying to Dickinson, "Now I withdraw my offer." It appears to me that there is neither principle nor authority for the proposition that there must be an express and actual withdrawal of the offer, or what is called a retraction. It must, to constitute a contract, appear that the two minds were at one, at the same moment of time, that is, that there was an offer continuing up to the time of the acceptance. If there was not such a continuing offer, then the acceptance comes to nothing. Of course it may well be that the one man is bound in some way or other to let the other man know that his mind with regard to the offer has been changed; but in this case, beyond all question, the Plaintiff knew that Dodds was no longer minded to sell the property to him as plainly and clearly as if Dodds had told him in so many words, "I withdraw the offer." This is evident from the Plaintiff's own statements in the bill.

The Plaintiff says in effect that, having heard and knowing that Dodds was no longer minded to sell to him, and that he was selling or had sold to some one else, thinking that he could not in point of law withdraw his offer, meaning to fix him to it, and endeavoring to bind him, "I went to the house where he was lodging, and saw his mother-in-law, and left with her an acceptance of the offer, knowing all the while that he had entirely changed his mind. I got an agent to watch for him at 7 o'clock the next morning, and I went to the train just before 9 o'clock, in order that I might catch him and give him my notice of acceptance just before 9 o'clock, and when that occurred he told my agent, and he told me, you are too late, and he then threw back the paper." It is to my mind quite clear that before there was any attempt at acceptance by the Plaintiff, he was perfectly well aware that Dodds had changed his mind, and that he had in fact agreed to sell the property to Allan. It is impossible, therefore, to say there was ever that existence of the same mind between the two parties which is essential in point of law to the making of an agreement. I am of opinion, therefore, that the Plaintiff has failed to prove that there was any binding contract between Dodds and himself.

MELLISH, L. J. I am of the same opinion. The first question is, whether this document of the 10th of June, 1874, which was signed by Dodds, was an agreement to sell, or only an offer to sell, the property therein mentioned to Dickinson; and I am clearly of opinion that it was only an offer, although it is in the first part of it, independently of the postscript, worded as an agreement. I apprehend that, until acceptance, so that both parties are bound, even though an instrument is so worded as to express that both parties agree, it is in point of law only an offer, and, until both parties are bound, neither party is bound. It is not necessary that both parties should be bound within the Statute of Frauds, for, if one party makes an offer in writing, and the other accepts it verbally, that will be sufficient to bind the person who has signed the written document. But, if there be no agreement, either verbally or in writing, then, until acceptance, it is in point of law an offer only, although worded as if it were an agreement. But it is hardly necessary to resort to that doctrine in the present case, because the postscript calls it an offer, and says, "This offer to be left over until Friday, 9 o'clock A.M." Well, then, this being only an offer, the law says, and it is a perfectly clear rule of law that, although it is said that the offer is to be left open until Friday morning at 9 o'clock, that did not bind Dodds. He was not in point of law bound to hold the offer over until 9 o'clock on Friday morning. He was not so bound either in law or in equity. Well, that being so, when on the next day he made an agreement with Allan to sell the property to him, I am not aware of any ground on which it can be said that that contract with Allan was not as good and binding a contract as ever was made. Assuming Allan to have known (there is some dispute about it, and Allan does not admit that he knew of it, but I will assume that he did) that Dodds had made the offer to Dickinson, and had given him till Friday morning at 9 o'clock to accept it, still in point of law that could not prevent Allan from making a more favorable offer than Dickinson, and entering at once into a binding agreement with Dodds.

Then Dickinson is informed by Berry that the property has been sold by Dodds to Allan. Berry does not tell us from whom he heard it, but he says that he did hear it, that he knew it, and that he informed Dickinson of it. Now, stopping there, the question which arises is this—If an offer has been made for the sale of property, and before that offer is accepted, the person who has made the offer enters into a binding agreement to sell the property to somebody else, and the person to whom the offer was first made receives notice in some way that the property has been sold to another person, can he after that make a binding contract by the acceptance of the offer? I am of opinion that he cannot. The law may be right or wrong in saying that a person who has given to another a certain time within which to accept an offer is not bound by his promise to give that time; but, if he is not bound by that promise, and may still sell the property to some one else, and if it be the law that, in order to make a contract, the two minds must be in agreement at some one time, that is, at the time of the acceptance, how is it possible that when the person to whom the offer has been made knows that the person who has made the offer has sold the property to someone else, and that, in fact, he has not remained in the same mind to sell it to him, he can be at liberty to accept the offer and thereby make a binding contract? It seems to me that would be simply absurd. If a man makes an offer to sell a particular horse in his stable, and says, "I will give you until the day after tomorrow to accept the offer," and the next day goes and sells the horse to somebody else, and receives the purchase-money from him, can the person to whom the offer was originally made then come and say, "I accept," so as to make a binding contract, and so as to be entitled to recover damages for the non-delivery of the horse? If the rule of law is that a mere offer to sell property, which can be withdrawn at any time, and which is made dependent on the acceptance of the person to whom it is made, is a mere nudum pactum, how is it possible that the person to whom the offer has been made can by acceptance make a binding contract after he knows that the person who has made the offer has sold the property to some one else? It is admitted law that, if a man who makes an offer dies, the offer cannot be accepted after he is dead, and parting with the property has very much the same effect as the death of the owner, for it makes the performance of the offer impossible. I am clearly of opinion that, just as when a man who has made an offer dies before it is accepted it is impossible that it can then be accepted, so when once the person to whom the offer was made knows that the property has been sold to some one else, it is too late for him to accept the offer, and on that ground I am clearly of opinion that there was no binding contract for the sale of this property by Dodds to Dickinson, and even if there had been, it seems to me that the sale of the property to Allan was first in point of time. However, it is not necessary to consider, if there had been two binding contracts, which of them would be entitled to priority in equity, because there is no binding contract between Dodds and Dickinson.

BAGGALLAY, J. A. I entirely concur in the judgments which have been pronounced.

JAMES, L. J. The bill will be dismissed with costs. . . .

NOTES AND QUESTIONS

1.   *Mellish promoted.* In the earlier *Raffles v. Wichelhaus* case, notice that Mellish was counsel for Wichelhaus, the purchaser of cotton. Between the date of that case in 1864 and the date of this case in 1875, Mellish became a law judge.

2.   *Intervening Allan purchase.* After Dodds made the offer to sell the property to Dickinson, but before the stated expiration of the offer, Dodds sold the property to Allan. Having been informed of the sale by his broker Berry, Dickinson nonetheless attempted to exercise the power of acceptance created in the written offer. How does the court view Dickinson's behavior? Notice the lower trial court held for Dickinson. Why? Restatement (Second) of Contracts § 42 provides that the power of acceptance is terminated when the offeree receives a manifestation of intent to no longer enter into a contract. Did Dodds make such an expression to Dickinson? Restatement (Second) of Contracts § 43 provides that the power of acceptance is also terminated when the offeror takes "definite action" inconsistent with a continuing interest to enter into a contract, and the offeree acquires "reliable information" to that effect. What "definite action" did Dodds take, and how did Dickinson acquire "reliable information" to that effect? *Comment d* indicates that "equivocal action" is not "definite action." If Berry told Dickinson that Dodds was "negotiating" to sell the property to Allan and that if he wanted the property he should hurry his acceptance, would the case be resolved differently? If so, would it make any difference to you that Dodds had sold the property to Allan, but that Dickinson had only learned of the negotiations? If not, do you think it provident that

contract law should base enforcement upon whether Dodds utters "revoke" immediately before or after Dickinson utters "accept"?

3.   *Evolution of the restatement rules.* The *Dickinson* case has been immortalized in limerick. Douglass G. Boshkoff, "Selected Poems on the Law of Contracts," 66 N.Y.U. L. Rev. 1533, 1536 (1991).

The lead case rule concerning indirect revocation was limited to cases involving a sale of land in the first restatement. See Restatement (First) of Contracts § 42. Apparently the rule was originally thought unsound. Arthur L. Corbin, "The Restatement of the Common Law by the American Law Institute," 15 Iowa L. Rev. 19, 36 (1929). Nevertheless, the rule was broadly adopted in the second restatement without the limitations. See Restatement (Second) of Contracts § 43.

4.   *Revocation versus withdrawal.* Lord Justice James mentions that the offer could be withdrawn or retracted (now revocation). Is there a difference between withdrawal and revocation? An offer must be communicated to the offeree in order to become effective as such. If an offer is mailed, but the offeror telephones the prospective offeree to negate the offer prior to when it was received or otherwise communicated, has the offer been withdrawn or revoked? Does an offeratory communication create a power of acceptance before it reaches the offeree? Does this difference explain the distinction between withdrawal and revocation?

5.   *Option contracts.* An option is simply an enforceable contract to keep an offer open. Thus, a promise to hold an offer open for a period of time, if supported by a consideration, is enforceable as an option contract. See Restatement (Second) of Contracts § 25. The promise is not revocable for the option period, and if the power of acceptance (option exercise) is not exercised prior to the termination of the stated time period, the consideration is forfeited to the offeror as compensation for keeping the contract subject matter off the market for that period. Because the "value" of making an offer irrevocable for a stated period of time is difficult to measure, freedom of contract defers heavily to the agreement of the parties. For the same reason, while the mere recital of consideration is ordinarily inadequate consideration if not actually paid, greater deference is given to such recitals in the context of written options. See Restatement (Second) of Contracts § 87(1). However, this rule was not found in the Restatement (First) of Contracts and has not been widely adopted by courts.

6.   *In abrogation of the common law rule.* Professor Melvin A. Eisenberg advances several arguments why the common law should enforce offers stated to be irrevocable. Most importantly, most offerors intend and most offerees understand such offers to be irrevocable. Thus, irrevocability complies with common commercial understanding. See Melvin A. Eisenberg, "The Revocation of Offers," 2004 Wis. L. Rev. 271, 283–287 (2004) (Freedom From Contract Symposium). In a responsive article, Professor Knapp challenges the wisdom of conflating implied promises to hold open with express promises and also the treatment of firm offers as options contracts. See Charles L. Knapp, "An Offer

You Can't Revoke," 2004 Wis. L. Rev. 309 (204) (Freedom From Contract Symposium). Would Dodds's offer have been legally irrevocable under Professor Eisenberg's theory? If you were the reporter for the Restatement (Third) of Contracts, would you articulate a common law firm offer rule?

7. *UCC and CISG firm offer rules.* As mentioned in the introduction, both the UCC and CISG provide that an offer stated to be irrevocable will retain some measure of irrevocability. The conditions of enforceability differ. Under UCC § 2–205, an offer stated to be irrevocable will be so only if the offer: (i) is made by a merchant, (ii) is included in a writing signed by the merchant, and (iii) makes an assurance it will be held open. If so, the offer is irrevocable, even if not supported by consideration, for a period not to exceed three months. CISG art. 16(2) requires only that the offer state it is irrevocable. The other UCC conditions are not imposed including the writing, signature, three-month duration, and merchant limitations. However, the CISG does not apply to consumer goods transactions. See CISG art. 2(a). In the language of UCC § 2–205, did Dodds make an "assurance" that the offer would be held open? An example of a clear assurance would include: "This offer is firm and will remain open for three months." In the language of CISG art. 16(2), did Dodds "state" the offer was irrevocable or would be held open for acceptance? As you can see, unlike the UCC, the CISG does not require an express "assurance." It need only state that the offer is irrevocable, which may be accomplished by simply stating a fixed time for acceptance. To understand the difference, if the offer merely stated it would expire after three days, would the offer be irrevocable under either or both authorities? See John E. Murray, Jr., "An Essay on the Formation of Contracts and Related Matters Under the United Nations Convention on Contracts for the International Sale of Goods," 8 J. L. & Com. 11, 23–27 (1988) and William S. Dodge, "Teaching the CISG in Contracts," 30 J. Legal Educ. 72, 80 (2000).

8. *Role of detrimental reliance.* As discussed in the above notes, a promise of irrevocability unsupported by consideration will not be enforceable as an option contract under traditional contract doctrine. What if the offeree nonetheless detrimentally relies on the promise? Provided the reliance was substantial and reasonably expected by the promisor, Restatement (Second) of Contracts § 87(2) will enforce the promise as an option contract "to the extent necessary to avoid injustice." Avoiding injustice normally requires the reliance to be detrimental. Reliance is detrimental when the promise reduces the action or forbearance, and the promisee is worse off than if the reliance had not occurred. Nevertheless, the reliance need not always result in an "economic" worsening. Other factors may also be considered even when, for example, a promisee-employee accepts a promotion. See, e.g., *Vasteler v. American Can Co.*, 700 F.2d 916 (3d Cir. 1983) (while promotion granted better pay, the same pay increase generates stress and emotional trauma). To the same general effect, see CISG art. 16(2)(b). Although the UCC does not state a specific reliance rule in this context, UCC § 1–103 clearly provides that estoppel and other doctrines of law and equity remain applicable to UCC questions "unless displaced by the particular provisions of this Act." Do you think UCC § 2–205

displaces reliance? Did Dickinson incur the detrimental reliance necessary to invoke these reliance doctrines? Do we know about his reliance? If not, why not?

9. *Government contracts.* Federal agencies must generally follow the Federal Acquisition Regulation ("FAR") in procuring services from the private sector. 5 C.F.R. § 300.506. FAR regulations generally provide that bidders on government contracts may withdraw or modify their bids by written notice, provided the notice is received not later than the exact time set for opening sealed bids. 48 C.F.R. § 14.303. After the bid is opened, it becomes irrevocable under federal bid procurement regulations. See W. Noel Keyes, Government Contracts § 14.34 (2000). By case law, those regulations are generally binding upon those who submit bids. See *Refining Associates, Inc. v. United States*, 109 F. Supp. 259 (Ct. Cl. 1953); Recent Case, "Contracts—Revocation of Offer—Bid Opened by United States May Not Be Withdrawn Before Acceptance Where Regulation Makes Bid Irrevocable After Opening," 66 Harv. L. Rev. 1312 (1953) and William Noel Keyes, "Consideration Reconsidered—The Problem of the Withdrawn Bid," 10 Stan. L. Rev. 441 (1958). State government contracts are generally governed by similar rules set by statute or regulation, although the variation is significant. See Michael L. Closen and Donald C. Weiland, "The Construction Industry Bidding Cases: Application of Traditional Contract, Promissory Estoppel, and Other Theories to the Relations Between General Contractors and Subcontractors," 13 J. Marshall L. Rev. 565, 571 (1980). The American Bar Association, through its Section of Public Contract Law, State and Local Procurement Division, Model Procurement Code Committee first promulgated a Model Procurement Code in 1979. It was later updated and a Model Code (2000) and Model Regulations (2002) are now available for state adoption. Approximately fifteen states have adopted the M.P.C. since its 1979 promulgation.

10. *Offer deposits.* Deposits often accompany an offer, such as an offer to purchase a home accompanied by a deposit. The offeror may ordinarily recover these deposits under restitution theory if the offer is not accepted. Occasionally, the parties may agree that the deposit secures performance of a promise not to revoke. Such a deposit is not consideration for the offer and does not make the offer binding or otherwise affect the power of the offeror to revoke. See Restatement (Second) of Contracts § 44. However, revocation will ordinarily result in forfeiture of the deposit in the form of liquidated damages. Provided the amount of forfeiture is reasonable under other contract rules, it will be enforced.

11. *Lapse of time and late acceptance.* The power to accept an offer terminates after the expiration of the time stated in the offer or, if none, after a reasonable time. Restatement (Second) of Contracts §§ 36(1)(b) and 41. What is reasonable is a question of fact. Factors affecting the determination of a reasonable time include the subject matter of the contract and the method of communicating the offer (face-to-face versus mail). A late acceptance will generally be treated as a counter-offer that may be accepted by the original

offeror. See Restatement (Second) of Contracts § 70. CISG art. 21(1) treats a late acceptance as effective provided the offeror promptly notifies the offeree.

2. TERMINATION BY OFFEREE REJECTION OR COUNTEROFFER

Like offeror revocation, offeree rejection similarly terminates the offeree's power of acceptance, at least unless the terms of the offer provide otherwise. Restatement (Second) of Contracts §§ 36(1)(a) and 38(1). Under objective theory, a communication operates as a rejection when the offeror has reasonable grounds for understanding that the offeree does not intend to accept the offer, even if communicated prior to the time the offer was to lapse. Restatement (Second) of Contracts § 38, *comment b*. An offeree may avoid the rejection classification by "manifesting an intent to take the offer under advisement." The basis for the rule is said to be to protect the likely reliance of the offeror following receipt of rejection. In such cases, the offeror is likely to engage in a substitute transaction on the theory that the prior transaction did not occur. However, actual reliance is not necessary. See Restatement (Second) of Contracts § 38, *comment a*.

The most likely difficulty occurs in determining whether a purported acceptance that varies the terms of the offer is an acceptance or a counteroffer. Restatement (Second) of Contracts § 36(1)(a) treats a counteroffer as first a rejection of the old offer and the making of a new offer. Of course, after a counteroffer, the old offer is no longer capable of being accepted. Therefore, a communication intended to be an acceptance could result in an unintended termination of the power of acceptance.

Common law traditionally makes the offeror the "master of the offer." To be effective, acceptance must be unconditional and on the precise terms of the offer. Stated another way, the acceptance must be the "mirror image" of the offer and must not vary the terms of the offer in any manner. Strictly applied, the mirror image rule would block any acceptance other than one effectively understood by the offeror as "I accept on your terms." The effect of any additional or different terms would constitute varying terms, a qualified acceptance, and normally not a valid acceptance.

For example, in the well-known case of *Poel v. Brunswick-Balke-Collender Co.*, 216 N.Y. 310, 110 N.E. 619 (1915), Poel made an offer to sell rubber on specified terms, and Brunswick-Balke-Collender Co. responded with a purported acceptance that added: "The acceptance of this order which in any event you must promptly acknowledge will be considered by us as a guaranty on your part of prompt delivery within the specified time." No performance by either party occurred for several months, during which the price of rubber rose. When the price suddenly fell, Poel proposed to make the sale, but Brunswick-Balke-Collender successfully argued a contract had not been formed because the additional language violated the mirror image rule by proposing additional terms. Restatement (Second) of Contracts § 39(1) provides that a counteroffer "proposes a substituted bargain differing from that proposed by the original offer." *Comment b* explains:

> *Qualified acceptance, inquiry or separate offer.* A common type of counteroffer is the qualified or conditional acceptance, which purports to accept the original offer but makes acceptance expressly conditional on assent to additional or different terms. See § 59. Such a counteroffer must be distinguished from an unqualified acceptance which is accompanied by a proposal for modification of the agreement or for a separate agreement. A mere inquiry regarding the possibility of different terms, a request for a better offer, or a comment upon the terms of the offer, is ordinarily not a counteroffer. Such responses to an offer may be too tentative or indefinite to be offers of any kind; or they may deal with new matters rather than a substitution for the original offer; or their language may manifest an intention to keep the original offer under consideration.

The comment makes a clear distinction between a counteroffer and other possible responses. The distinction lies in the promissory nature of the counteroffer. A rejection alone grants no prospect of another deal. The counteroffer makes a substitute proposal in the form of a new offer that confers a new power of acceptance on the original offeror/counterofferee. Thus, like an offer, a counteroffer must be promissory and is subject to the objective theory of contracts.

To complicate matters further, performance by the parties that proves the existence of a contract may obviate the normal rules of offer and acceptance. In such cases, the *existence* of a contract is not at issue. Rather, the parties in such situations typically dispute the *terms* of the purported agreement. When the terms of the offer and acceptance differ, but the parties perform without further discussion or agreement, what is the effect of the performance? Does that performance make a contract on the terms stated in the first offer, the counteroffer, or some combination? Stated another way, does performance without objection by the original offeror imply acceptance of the terms of the counteroffer? That is the view of the common law. An offeror who proceeds under a contract after receiving a counteroffer accepts the terms of the counteroffer by performance without objection. The reason? The maker of the counteroffer is entitled under the objective theory of contract to assume that its terms were accepted or performance would not have moved forward. See Restatement (Second) of Contracts § 19(1) (assent inferred from conduct) and *Princess Cruises, Inc. v. General Electric Co.*, 143 F.3d 828, 834 (4th Cir. 1998).

Where commercial parties often deal with each other through purchase order and order confirmation forms, each expressing common price and quantity terms but with many other additional or different terms, this play is often referred to as a "battle of the forms." In response to the problem, UCC § 2–207 was enacted. In your review of the case below, determine whether the statute follows the common law.

STEP-SAVER DATA SYSTEMS, INC. v. WYSE TECHNOLOGY

United States Court of Appeals, Third Circuit
939 F.2d 91 (1991)

WISDOM, Circuit Judge:

The "Limited Use License Agreement" printed on a package containing a copy of a computer program raises the central issue in this appeal. The trial judge held that the terms of the Limited Use License Agreement governed the purchase of the package, and, therefore, granted the software producer, The Software Link, Inc. ("TSL"), a directed verdict on claims of breach of warranty brought by a disgruntled purchaser, Step-Saver Data Systems, Inc. We disagree with the district court's determination of the legal effect of the license, and reverse and remand the warranty claims for further consideration. . . .

I.   FACTUAL AND PROCEDURAL BACKGROUND

The growth in the variety of computer hardware and software has created a strong market for these products. It has also created a difficult choice for consumers, as they must somehow decide which of the many available products will best suit their needs. To assist consumers in this decision process, some companies will evaluate the needs of particular groups of potential computer users, compare those needs with the available technology, and develop a package of hardware and software to satisfy those needs. Beginning in 1981, Step-Saver performed this function as a value added retailer for International Business Machine (IBM) products. It would combine hardware and software to satisfy the word processing, data management, and communications needs for offices of physicians and lawyers. It originally marketed single computer systems, based primarily on the IBM personal computer.

As a result of advances in micro-computer technology, Step-Saver developed and marketed a multi-user system. With a multi-user system, only one computer is required. Terminals are attached, by cable, to the main computer. From these terminals, a user can access the programs available on the main computer.[1]

---

[1]   In essence, the terminals are simply video screens with keyboards that serve as input-output devices for the main computer. The main computer receives data from all of the terminals and processes it appropriately, sending a return signal to the terminal. To someone working on

After evaluating the available technology, Step-Saver selected a program by TSL, entitled Multilink Advanced, as the operating system for the multi-user system. Step-Saver selected WY-60 terminals manufactured by Wyse, and used an IBM AT as the main computer. For applications software, Step-Saver included in the package several off-the-shelf programs, designed to run under Microsoft's Disk Operating System ("MS-DOS"), as well as several programs written by Step-Saver. Step-Saver began marketing the system in November of 1986, and sold one hundred forty-two systems mostly to law and medical offices before terminating sales of the system in March of 1987. Almost immediately upon installation of the system, Step-Saver began to receive complaints from some of its customers.[3]

Step-Saver, in addition to conducting its own investigation of the problems, referred these complaints to Wyse and TSL, and requested technical assistance in resolving the problems. After several preliminary attempts to address the problems, the three companies were unable to reach a satisfactory solution, and disputes developed among the three concerning responsibility for the problems. As a result, the problems were never solved. At least twelve of Step-Saver's customers filed suit against Step-Saver because of the problems with the multi-user system.

Once it became apparent that the three companies would not be able to resolve their dispute amicably, Step-Saver filed suit for declaratory judgment, seeking indemnity from either Wyse or TSL, or both, for any costs incurred by Step-Saver in defending and resolving the customers' law suits. The district court dismissed this complaint, finding that the issue was not ripe for judicial resolution. We affirmed the dismissal on appeal. Step-Saver then filed a second complaint alleging breach of warranties by both TSL and Wyse and intentional misrepresentations by TSL. The district court's actions during the resolution of this second complaint provide the foundation for this appeal.

On the first day of trial, the district court specifically agreed with the basic contention of TSL that the form language printed on each package containing the Multilink Advanced program ("the box-top license") was the complete and exclusive agreement between Step-Saver and TSL under § 2–202 of the Uniform Commercial Code (UCC).[6] Based on § 2–316 of the UCC,

---

one of the terminals of a properly operating multi-user system, the terminal appears to function as if it were, in fact, a computer. Thus, an operator could work with a word processing program on a terminal, and it would appear to the operator the same as working with the word processing program on a computer. The difference is that, with a set of computers, the commands of each user are processed within each user's computer, whereas with a multi-user system, the commands of all of the users are sent to the main computer for processing.

[3] According to the testimony of Jeffrey Worthington, an employee of Step-Saver, twenty to twenty-five of the purchasers of the multi-user system had serious problems with the system that were never resolved.

[6] All three parties agree that the terminals and the program are "goods" within the meaning of UCC § 2–102 & 2–105. Cf. Advent Sys. Ltd. v. Unisys Corp., 925 F.2d 670, 674–76 (3d Cir. 1991).

the district court held that the box-top license disclaimed all express and implied warranties otherwise made by TSL. The court therefore granted TSL's motion *in limine* to exclude all evidence of the earlier oral and written express warranties allegedly made by TSL. After Step-Saver presented its case, the district court granted a directed verdict in favor of TSL on the intentional misrepresentation claim, holding the evidence insufficient as a matter of law to establish two of the five elements of a prima facie case: (1) fraudulent intent on the part of TSL in making the representations; and (2) reasonable reliance by Step-Saver. The trial judge requested briefing on several issues related to Step-Saver's remaining express warranty claim against TSL. While TSL and Step-Saver prepared briefs on these issues, the trial court permitted Wyse to proceed with its defense. On the third day of Wyse's defense, the trial judge, after considering the additional briefing by Step-Saver and TSL, directed a verdict in favor of TSL on Step-Saver's remaining warranty claims, and dismissed TSL from the case.

The trial proceeded on Step-Saver's breach of warranties claims against Wyse. At the conclusion of Wyse's evidence, the district judge denied Step-Saver's request for rebuttal testimony on the issue of the ordinary uses of the WY-60 terminal. The district court instructed the jury on the issues of express warranty and implied warranty of fitness for a particular purpose. Over Step-Saver's objection, the district court found insufficient evidence to support a finding that Wyse had breached its implied warranty of merchantability, and refused to instruct the jury on such warranty. The jury returned a verdict in favor of Wyse on the two warranty issues submitted.

Step-Saver appeals on four points. (1) Step-Saver and TSL did not intend the box-top license to be a complete and final expression of the terms of their agreement. (2) There was sufficient evidence to support each element of Step-Saver's contention that TSL was guilty of intentional misrepresentation. (3) There was sufficient evidence to submit Step-Saver's implied warranty of merchantability claim against Wyse to the jury. (4) The trial court abused its discretion by excluding from the evidence a letter addressed to Step-Saver from Wyse, and by refusing to permit Step-Saver to introduce rebuttal testimony on the ordinary uses of the WY-60 terminal.

II. THE EFFECT OF THE BOX-TOP LICENSE

The relationship between Step-Saver and TSL began in the fall of 1984 when Step-Saver asked TSL for information on an early version of the

---

TSL and Step-Saver have disputed whether Pennsylvania or Georgia law governs the issues of contract formation and modification with regard to the Multilink programs. Because both Pennsylvania and Georgia have adopted, without modification, the relevant portions of Article 2 of the Uniform Commercial Code, see Ga. Code Ann. §§ 11–2–101 to 11–2–725 (1990); 13 Pa. Cons. Stat. Ann. §§ 2101–2725 (Purdon 1984), we will simply cite to the relevant UCC provision.

Multilink program. TSL provided Step-Saver with a copy of the early program, known simply as Multilink, without charge to permit Step-Saver to test the program to see what it could accomplish. Step-Saver performed some tests with the early program, but did not market a system based on it.

In the summer of 1985, Step-Saver noticed some advertisements in Byte magazine for a more powerful version of the Multilink program, known as Multilink Advanced. Step-Saver requested information from TSL concerning this new version of the program, and allegedly was assured by sales representatives that the new version was compatible with ninety percent of the programs available "off-the-shelf" for computers using MS-DOS. The sales representatives allegedly made a number of additional specific representations of fact concerning the capabilities of the Multilink Advanced program.

Based on these representations, Step-Saver obtained several copies of the Multilink Advanced program in the spring of 1986, and conducted tests with the program. After these tests, Step-Saver decided to market a multi-user system which used the Multilink Advanced program. From August of 1986 through March of 1987, Step-Saver purchased and resold 142 copies of the Multilink Advanced program. Step-Saver would typically purchase copies of the program in the following manner. First, Step-Saver would telephone TSL and place an order. (Step-Saver would typically order twenty copies of the program at a time.) TSL would accept the order and promise, while on the telephone, to ship the goods promptly. After the telephone order, Step-Saver would send a purchase order, detailing the items to be purchased, their price, and shipping and payment terms. TSL would ship the order promptly, along with an invoice. The invoice would contain terms essentially identical with those on Step-Saver's purchase order: price, quantity, and shipping and payment terms. No reference was made during the telephone calls, or on either the purchase orders or the invoices with regard to a disclaimer of any warranties.

Printed on the package of each copy of the program, however, would be a copy of the box-top license. The box-top license contains five terms relevant to this action:

(1) The box-top license provides that the customer has not purchased the software itself, but has merely obtained a personal, non-transferable license to use the program.

(2) The box-top license, in detail and at some length, disclaims all express and implied warranties except for a warranty that the disks contained in the box are free from defects.

(3) The box-top license provides that the sole remedy available to a purchaser of the program is to return a defective disk for

replacement; the license excludes any liability for damages, direct or consequential, caused by the use of the program.

(4) The box-top license contains an integration clause, which provides that the box-top license is the final and complete expression of the terms of the parties's agreement.

(5) The box-top license states: "Opening this package indicates your acceptance of these terms and conditions. If you do not agree with them, you should promptly return the package unopened to the person from whom you purchased it within fifteen days from date of purchase and your money will be refunded to you by that person."

The district court, without much discussion, held, as a matter of law, that the box-top license was the final and complete expression of the terms of the parties's agreement. Because the district court decided the questions of contract formation and interpretation as issues of law, we review the district court's resolution of these questions *de novo*.

Step-Saver contends that the contract for each copy of the program was formed when TSL agreed, on the telephone, to ship the copy at the agreed price.[9] The box-top license, argues Step-Saver, was a material alteration to the parties's contract which did not become a part of the contract under UCC § 2–207. Alternatively, Step-Saver argues that the undisputed evidence establishes that the parties did not intend the box-top license as a final and complete expression of the terms of their agreement, and, therefore, the parol evidence rule of UCC § 2–202 would not apply.[11]

TSL argues that the contract between TSL and Step-Saver did not come into existence until Step-Saver received the program, saw the terms of the license, and opened the program packaging. TSL contends that too many material terms were omitted from the telephone discussion for that discussion to establish a contract for the software. Second, TSL contends that its acceptance of Step-Saver's telephone offer was conditioned on Step-Saver's acceptance of the terms of the box-top license. Therefore, TSL argues, it did not accept Step-Saver's telephone offer, but made a counteroffer represented by the terms of the box-top license, which was accepted when Step-Saver opened each package. Third, TSL argues that, however the contract was formed, Step-Saver was aware of the warranty

---

[9]   See UCC § 2–206(1)(b). . . .

[11]   Two other issues were raised by Step-Saver. First, Step-Saver argued that the box-top disclaimer is either unconscionable or not in good faith. Second, Step-Saver argued that the warranty disclaimer was inconsistent with the express warranties made by TSL in the product specifications. Step-Saver argues that interpreting the form language of the license agreement to override the specific warranties contained in the product specification is unreasonable. . . . Because of our holding that the terms of the box-top license were not incorporated into the contract, we do not address these issues.

disclaimer, and that Step-Saver, by continuing to order and accept the product with knowledge of the disclaimer, assented to the disclaimer.

In analyzing these competing arguments, we first consider whether the license should be treated as an integrated writing under UCC § 2–202, as a proposed modification under UCC § 2–209, or as a written confirmation under UCC § 2–207. Finding that UCC § 2–207 best governs our resolution of the effect of the box-top license, we then consider whether, under UCC § 2–207, the terms of the box-top license were incorporated into the parties's agreement.

A.   DOES UCC § 2–207 GOVERN THE ANALYSIS?

As a basic principle, we agree with Step-Saver that UCC § 2–207 governs our analysis. We see no need to parse the parties's various actions to decide exactly when the parties formed a contract. TSL has shipped the product, and Step-Saver has accepted and paid for each copy of the program. The parties's performance demonstrates the existence of a contract. The dispute is, therefore, not over the existence of a contract, but the nature of its terms. When the parties's conduct establishes a contract, but the parties have failed to adopt expressly a particular writing as the terms of their agreement, and the writings exchanged by the parties do not agree, UCC § 2–207 determines the terms of the contract.

As stated by the official comment to § 2–207:

1.   This section is intended to deal with two typical situations. The one is the written confirmation, where an agreement has been reached either orally or by informal correspondence between the parties and is followed by one or more of the parties sending formal memoranda embodying the terms so far as agreed upon and adding terms not discussed. . . .

2.   Under this Article a proposed deal which in commercial understanding has in fact been closed is recognized as a contract. Therefore, any additional matter contained in the confirmation or in the acceptance falls within subsection (2) and must be regarded as a proposal for an added term unless the acceptance is made conditional on the acceptance of the additional or different terms.

Although UCC § 2–202 permits the parties to reduce an oral agreement to writing, and UCC § 2–209 permits the parties to modify an existing contract without additional consideration, a writing will be a final expression of, or a binding modification to, an earlier agreement only if the parties so intend. It is undisputed that Step-Saver never expressly agreed to the terms of the box-top license, either as a final expression of, or a modification to, the parties's agreement. In fact, Barry Greebel, the President of Step-Saver, testified without dispute that he objected to the terms of the box-top license as applied to Step-Saver. In the absence of evidence demonstrating an express intent to adopt a writing as a final expression of, or a modification to, an earlier agreement, we find UCC § 2–207 to provide the appropriate legal rules for determining whether such an intent can be inferred from continuing with the contract after receiving a writing containing additional or different terms.

To understand why the terms of the license should be considered under § 2–207 in this case, we review briefly the reasons behind § 2–207. Under the common law of sales, and to some extent still for contracts outside the UCC, an acceptance that varied any term of the offer operated as a rejection of the offer, and simultaneously made a counteroffer. This common law formality was known as the mirror image rule, because the terms of the acceptance had to mirror the terms of the offer to be effective. If the offeror proceeded with the contract despite the differing terms of the supposed acceptance, he would, by his performance, constructively accept the terms of the "counteroffer," and be bound by its terms. As a result of these rules, the terms of the party who sent the last form, typically the seller, would become the terms of the parties's contract. This result was known as the "last shot rule."

The UCC, in § 2–207, rejected this approach. Instead, it recognized that, while a party may desire the terms detailed in its form if a dispute, in fact, arises, most parties do not expect a dispute to arise when they first enter into a contract. As a result, most parties will proceed with the transaction even if they know that the terms of their form would not be enforced.[18] The insight behind the rejection of the last shot rule is that it would be unfair to bind the buyer of goods to the standard terms of the seller, when neither party cared sufficiently to establish expressly the terms of their agreement, simply because the seller sent the last form. Thus, UCC § 2–207 establishes a legal rule that proceeding with a contract after receiving a writing that purports to define the terms of the parties's contract is not sufficient to establish the party's consent to the terms of the writing to the extent that the terms of the writing either add to, or differ from, the terms detailed in the parties's earlier writings or discussions.[19] In the absence of a party's express assent to the additional or different terms of the writing, section 2–207 provides a default rule that the parties intended, as the terms of their agreement, those terms to which both

[18] As Judge Engel has written: "Usually, these standard terms mean little, for a contract looks to its fulfillment and rarely anticipates its breach. Hope springs eternal in the commercial world and expectations are usually, but not always, realized."

[19] As the Mead Court explained: "Absent the [UCC], questions of contract formation and intent remain factual issues to be resolved by the trier of fact after careful review of the evidence. However, the [UCC] provides rules of law, and section 2–207 establishes important legal principles to be employed to resolve complex contract disputes arising from the exchange of business forms. Section 2–207 was intended to provide some degree of certainty in this otherwise ambiguous area of contract law. In our view, it is unreasonable and contrary to the policy behind the [UCC] merely to turn the issue over to the uninformed speculation of the jury left to apply its own particular sense of equity." Mead Corp., 654 F.2d at 1206 (citations omitted).

parties have agreed,[20] along with any terms implied by the provisions of the UCC.

The reasons that led to the rejection of the last shot rule, and the adoption of section 2–207, apply fully in this case. TSL never mentioned during the parties's negotiations leading to the purchase of the programs, nor did it, at any time, obtain Step-Saver's express assent to, the terms of the box-top license. Instead, TSL contented itself with attaching the terms to the packaging of the software, even though those terms differed substantially from those previously discussed by the parties. Thus, the box-top license, in this case, is best seen as one more form in a battle of forms, and the question of whether Step-Saver has agreed to be bound by the terms of the box-top license is best resolved by applying the legal principles detailed in section 2–207.

B.   APPLICATION OF § 2–207

TSL advances several reasons why the terms of the box-top license should be incorporated into the parties's agreement under a § 2–207 analysis. First, TSL argues that the parties's contract was not formed until Step-Saver received the package, saw the terms of the box-top license, and opened the package, thereby consenting to the terms of the license. TSL argues that a contract defined without reference to the specific terms provided by the box-top license would necessarily fail for indefiniteness. Second, TSL argues that the box-top license was a conditional acceptance and counter-offer under § 2–207(1). Third, TSL argues that Step-Saver, by continuing to order and use the product with notice of the terms of the box-top license, consented to the terms of the box-top license.

1.   WAS THE CONTRACT SUFFICIENTLY DEFINITE?

TSL argues that the parties intended to license the copies of the program, and that several critical terms could only be determined by referring to the box-top license. Pressing the point, TSL argues that it is impossible to tell, without referring to the box-top license, whether the parties intended a sale of a copy of the program or a license to use a copy. TSL cites *Bethlehem Steel Corp. v. Litton Industries* in support of its position that any contract defined without reference to the terms of the box-top license would fail for indefiniteness.

From the evidence, it appears that the following terms, at the least, were discussed and agreed to, apart from the box-top license: (1) the specific goods involved; (2) the quantity; and (3) the price. TSL argues that the following terms were only defined in the box-top license: (1) the nature of the transaction, sale or license; and (2) the warranties, if any, available.

---

[20] The parties may demonstrate their acceptance of a particular term either "orally or by informal correspondence," UCC 2–207, comment 1, or by placing the term in their respective form.

TSL argues that these two terms are essential to creating a sufficiently definite contract. We disagree.

Section 2–204(3) of the UCC provides:

> Even though one or more terms are left open a contract for sale does not fail for indefiniteness if the parties have intended to make a contract and there is a reasonably certain basis for giving an appropriate remedy.

Unlike the terms omitted by the parties in *Bethlehem Steel Corp.,* the two terms cited by TSL are not "gaping holes in a multi-million dollar contract that no one but the parties themselves could fill." First, the rights of the respective parties under the federal copyright law if the transaction is characterized as a sale of a copy of the program are nearly identical to the parties's respective rights under the terms of the box-top license. Second, the UCC provides for express and implied warranties if the seller fails to disclaim expressly those warranties.[24] Thus, even though warranties are an important term left blank by the parties, the default rules of the UCC fill in that blank.

We hold that contract was sufficiently definite without the terms provided by the box-top license.

2. THE BOX-TOP LICENSE AS A COUNTER-OFFER?

TSL advances two reasons why its box-top license should be considered a conditional acceptance under UCC § 2–207(1). First, TSL argues that the express language of the box-top license, including the integration clause and the phrase "opening this product indicates your acceptance of these terms," made TSL's acceptance "expressly conditional on assent to the additional or different terms." Second, TSL argues that the box-top license, by permitting return of the product within fifteen days if the purchaser does not agree to the terms stated in the license (the "refund offer"), establishes that TSL's acceptance was conditioned on Step-Saver's assent to the terms of the box-top license, citing *Monsanto Agricultural Products Co. v. Edenfield.*[28] While we are not certain that a conditional acceptance analysis applies when a contract is established by performance,[29] we assume that it does and consider TSL's arguments.

---

[24] See, UCC § 2–312, 2–313, 2–314, & 2–315.

[28] 426 So.2d 574 (Fla. Dist. Ct. App. 1982).

[29] Even though a writing is sent after performance establishes the existence of a contract, courts have analyzed the effect of such a writing under UCC § 2–207. . . . The official comment to UCC § 2–207 suggests that, even though a proposed deal has been closed, the conditional acceptance analysis still applies in determining which writing's terms will define the contract: "2. Under this Article a proposed deal which in commercial understanding has in fact been closed is recognized as a contract. Therefore, any additional matter contained in the confirmation or in the acceptance falls within subsection (2) and must be regarded as a proposal for an added term unless the acceptance is made conditional on the acceptance of the additional or different terms."

To determine whether a writing constitutes a conditional acceptance, courts have established three tests. Because neither Georgia nor Pennsylvania has expressly adopted a test to determine when a written confirmation constitutes a conditional acceptance, we consider these three tests to determine which test the state courts would most likely apply.

Under the first test, an offeree's response is a conditional acceptance to the extent it states a term "materially altering the contractual obligations solely to the disadvantage of the offeror." Pennsylvania, at least, has implicitly rejected this test. In *Herzog Oil Field Service, Inc.,*[32] a Pennsylvania Superior Court analyzed a term in a written confirmation under UCC § 2–207(2), rather than as a conditional acceptance even though the term materially altered the terms of the agreement to the sole disadvantage of the offeror.[33]

Furthermore, we note that adopting this test would conflict with the express provision of UCC § 2–207(2)(b). Under § 2–207(2)(b), additional terms in a written confirmation that "materially alter [the contract]" are construed "as proposals for addition to the contract," not as conditional acceptances.

A second approach considers an acceptance conditional when certain key words or phrases are used, such as a written confirmation stating that the terms of the confirmation are "the only ones upon which we will accept orders."[34] The third approach requires the offeree to demonstrate an unwillingness to proceed with the transaction unless the additional or different terms are included in the contract.

Although we are not certain that these last two approaches would generate differing answers,[36] we adopt the third approach for our analysis because it best reflects the understanding of commercial transactions developed in the UCC. Section 2–207 attempts to distinguish between: (1)

---

[32] 391 Pa. Super. 133, 570 A. 2d 549 (Pa. Super. Ct. 1990).

[33] The seller/offeree sent a written confirmation that contained a term that provided for attorney's fees of 25 percent of the balance due if the account was turned over for collection.

[34] Note that even though an acceptance contains the key phrase, and is conditional, these courts typically avoid finding a contract on the terms of the counteroffer by requiring the offeree/counterofferor to establish that the offeror assented to the terms of the counteroffer. Generally, acceptance of the goods, alone, is not sufficient to establish assent by the offeror to the terms of the counteroffer. . . . If the sole evidence of assent to the terms of the counteroffer is from the conduct of the parties in proceeding with the transaction, then the courts generally define the terms of the parties's agreement under UCC § 2–207(3).

[36] Under the second approach, the box-top license might be considered a conditional acceptance, but Step-Saver, by accepting the product, would not be automatically bound to the terms of the box-top license. . . . Instead, courts have applied UCC § 2–207(3) to determine the terms of the parties's agreement. The terms of the agreement would be those "on which the writings of the parties agree, together with any supplementary terms incorporated under any other provisions of this Act." UCC § 2–207(3). Because the writings of the parties did not agree on the warranty disclaimer and limitation of remedies terms, the box-top license version of those terms would not be included in the parties's contract; rather, the default provisions of the UCC would govern.

those standard terms in a form confirmation, which the party would like a court to incorporate into the contract in the event of a dispute; and (2) the actual terms the parties understand to govern their agreement. The third test properly places the burden on the party asking a court to enforce its form to demonstrate that a particular term is a part of the parties's commercial bargain.

Using this test, it is apparent that the integration clause and the "consent by opening" language is not sufficient to render TSL's acceptance conditional. As other courts have recognized, this type of language provides no real indication that the party is willing to forego the transaction if the additional language is not included in the contract.

The second provision provides a more substantial indication that TSL was willing to forego the contract if the terms of the box-top license were not accepted by Step-Saver. On its face, the box-top license states that TSL will refund the purchase price if the purchaser does not agree to the terms of the license. Even with such a refund term, however, the offeree/counterofferor may be relying on the purchaser's investment in time and energy in reaching this point in the transaction to prevent the purchaser from returning the item. Because a purchaser has made a decision to buy a particular product and has actually obtained the product, the purchaser may use it despite the refund offer, regardless of the additional terms specified after the contract formed. But we need not decide whether such a refund offer could ever amount to a conditional acceptance; the undisputed evidence in this case demonstrates that the terms of the license were not sufficiently important that TSL would forego its sales to Step-Saver if TSL could not obtain Step-Saver's consent to those terms.

As discussed, Mr. Greebel testified that TSL assured him that the box-top license did not apply to Step-Saver, as Step-Saver was not the end user of the Multilink Advanced program. Supporting this testimony, TSL on two occasions asked Step-Saver to sign agreements that would put in formal terms the relationship between Step-Saver and TSL. Both proposed agreements contained warranty disclaimer and limitation of remedy terms similar to those contained in the box-top license. Step-Saver refused to sign the agreements; nevertheless, TSL continued to sell copies of Multilink Advanced to Step-Saver.

Additionally, TSL asks us to infer, based on the refund offer, that it was willing to forego its sales to Step-Saver unless Step-Saver agreed to the terms of the box-top license. Such an inference is inconsistent with the fact that both parties agree that the terms of the box-top license did not represent the parties's agreement with respect to Step-Saver's right to transfer the copies of the Multilink Advanced program. Although the box-top license prohibits the transfer, by Step-Saver, of its copies of the program, both parties agree that Step-Saver was entitled to transfer its copies to the purchasers of the Step-Saver multi-user system. Thus, TSL was willing to proceed with the transaction despite the fact that one of the terms of the box-top license was not included in the contract between TSL and Step-Saver. We see no basis in the terms of the box-top license for inferring that a reasonable offeror would understand from the refund offer that certain terms of the box-top license, such as the warranty disclaimers, were essential to TSL, while others such as the non-transferability provision were not.

Based on these facts, we conclude that TSL did not clearly express its unwillingness to proceed with the transactions unless its additional terms were incorporated into the parties's agreement. The box-top license did not, therefore, constitute a conditional acceptance under UCC § 2–207(1). . . .

4.   PUBLIC POLICY CONCERNS.

TSL has raised a number of public policy arguments focusing on the effect on the software industry of an adverse holding concerning the enforceability of the box-top license. We are not persuaded that requiring software companies to stand behind representations concerning their products will inevitably destroy the software industry. We emphasize, however, that we are following the well-established distinction between conspicuous disclaimers made available before the contract is formed and disclaimers made available only after the contract is formed. When a disclaimer is not expressed until after the contract is formed, UCC § 2–207 governs the interpretation of the contract, and, between merchants, such disclaimers, to the extent they materially alter the parties's agreement, are not incorporated into the parties's agreement.

If TSL wants relief for its business operations from this well-established rule, their arguments are better addressed to a legislature than a court. Indeed, we note that at least two states have enacted statutes that modify the applicable contract rules in this area, but both Georgia and Pennsylvania have retained the contract rules provided by the UCC.

C.   *THE TERMS OF THE CONTRACT*

Under section 2–207, an additional term detailed in the box-top license will not be incorporated into the parties's contract if the term's addition to the contract would materially alter the parties's agreement.[47] Step-Saver alleges that several representations made by TSL constitute express warranties, and that valid implied warranties were also a part of the parties's agreement. Because the district court considered the box-top license to exclude all of these warranties, the district court did not consider whether other factors may act to exclude these warranties. The existence

---

[47]   UCC § 2–207(2)(b).

and nature of the warranties is primarily a factual question that we leave for the district court, but assuming that these warranties were included within the parties's original agreement, we must conclude that adding the disclaimer of warranty and limitation of remedies provisions from the box-top license would, as a matter of law, substantially alter the distribution of risk between Step-Saver and TSL. Therefore, under UCC § 2–207(2)(b), the disclaimer of warranty and limitation of remedies terms of the box-top license did not become a part of the parties's agreement.

Based on these considerations, we reverse the trial court's holding that the parties intended the box-top license to be a final and complete expression of the terms of their agreement. Despite the presence of an integration clause in the box-top license, the box-top license should have been treated as a written confirmation containing additional terms. Because the warranty disclaimer and limitation of remedies terms would materially alter the parties's agreement, these terms did not become a part of the parties's agreement. We remand for further consideration the express and implied warranty claims against TSL. . . .

V. EVIDENTIARY RULINGS

We have carefully reviewed the record regarding the evidentiary rulings. For the reasons given on these two issues in the district court's memorandum opinion rejecting Step-Saver's motion for a new trial, we hold that the exclusion of the unsent letter and the refusal to permit rebuttal testimony on the issue of the ordinary uses of the WY-60 terminal did not constitute an abuse of discretion.

VI.

We will reverse the holding of the district court that the parties intended to adopt the box-top license as the complete and final expression of the terms of their agreement. We will remand for further consideration of Step-Saver's express and implied warranty claims against TSL. Finding a sufficient basis for the other decisions of the district court, we will affirm in all other respects.

NOTES AND QUESTIONS

1. *Renewal of terminated offer.* An offeror may revive an offer where the power has been terminated by offeree rejection, including by rejection by counter-offer. For example, a reply to a counter-offer at a lower price in the nature of "cannot reduce price" could reasonably be construed by the offeree as a renewal of the terms of the original offer now capable of acceptance. See *Livingstone v. Evans*, 4 D.L.R. 769 (1925) and Restatement (Second) of Contracts § 23, *illustration 6*.

2. *Option contract.* Under common law, a purported acceptance that varied the terms of the offer terminated the first offer and constituted a

counter-offer. But what is the effect of a counter-offer on an otherwise irrevocable offer in the form of an option contract? Will a counteroffer terminate the main offer even though it is otherwise irrevocable? Since the irrevocable offer is in fact an "option contract," the offer-acceptance loop is closed. Consequently, the counteroffer should not have a similar effect on an irrevocable offer. Restatement (Second) of Contracts § 37 essentially provides that neither counteroffer, rejection, death, nor incapacity of the offeror terminates the power of acceptance under an option contract. See also Michael J. Cozzillio, "The Option Contract: Irrevocable Not Irrejectable," 39 Cath. U. L. Rev. 491 (1990).

3. *The common law last shot rule versus UCC § 2–207. Step-Saver Data Systems* directly addresses the conflict between the Uniform Commercial Code's "battle of the forms" in sales of goods contexts and the last shot rule developed under the common law. As the court notes, the common law rule permits the parties to trade competing forms, treating each new form as a counteroffer to the last form. The first party to begin performance is deemed, as a consequence of the objective theory of contracts, to have accepted the terms of the last counteroffer—typically the terms contained on the last-transmitted form before acceptance.

In contrast, the battle of the forms rule adopted by the UCC is significantly more complex. UCC § 2–207 provides:

§ 2–207. Additional Terms in Acceptance or Confirmation.

(1) A definite and seasonable expression of acceptance or a written confirmation which is sent within a reasonable time operates as an acceptance even though it states terms additional to or different from those offered or agreed upon, unless acceptance is expressly made conditional on assent to the additional or different terms.

(2) The additional terms are to be construed as proposals for addition to the contract. Between merchants such terms become part of the contract unless:

(a) the offer expressly limits acceptance to the terms of the offer;

(b) they materially alter it; or

(c) notification of objection to them has already been given or is given within a reasonable time after notice of them is received.

(3) Conduct by both parties which recognizes the existence of a contract is sufficient to establish a contract for sale although the writings of the parties do not otherwise establish a contract. In such case the terms of the particular contract consist of those terms on which the writings of the parties agree, together with any supplementary terms incorporated under any other provisions of this Act.

4.   *Purposes of § 2–207.* Note that § 2–207 abrogates the common law system of offer, acceptance, counteroffer, and rejection. This may merely reflect the perception that real-world contracting practices typically do not lend themselves to easy division into the common law offer and acceptance paradigm. Often, parties doing business in the real world do not have a clear idea when they have made an offer or when that offer has been accepted. This is particularly true in the situations to which the drafters of UCC § 2–207 attempted to respond:

> 1.   [§ 2–207] is intended to deal with two typical situations. The one is the written confirmation, where an agreement has been reached either orally or by informal correspondence between the parties and is followed by one or both of the parties sending formal memoranda embodying the terms so far as agreed upon and adding terms not discussed. The other situation is offer and acceptance, in which a wire or letter expressed and intended as an acceptance or the closing of an agreement adds further minor suggestions or proposals such as "ship by Tuesday," "rush," "ship draft against bill of lading inspection allowed," or the like. A frequent example of the second situation is the exchange of printed purchase order and acceptance (sometimes called "acknowledgment") forms. Because the forms are oriented to the thinking of the respective drafting parties, the terms contained in them often do not correspond. Often the seller's form contains terms different from or additional to those set forth in the buyer's form. Nevertheless, the parties proceed with the transaction.

5.   *Definite and seasonable expression of acceptance.* What is the difference between a "definite and seasonable expression of acceptance" and a plain old "acceptance"? As comment 1 to § 2–207 clarifies, the former term is intended to encompass situations in which the parties have reached agreement on sufficient terms to create a contract, but the document transmitting the purported acceptance nonetheless varies the terms of the offer. See UCC § 2–207, *cmt.* 2 ("Under this Article a proposed deal which in commercial understanding has in fact been closed is recognized as a contract.").

6.   *Sales of goods contracts between merchants versus non-merchants.* Subsection (2) is one of a handful of places where Article 2 creates different rules for merchants and non-merchants. UCC § 2–104(1) defines "merchant" as:

> [A] person who deals in goods of the kind or otherwise by his occupation holds himself out as having knowledge or skill peculiar to the practices or goods involved in the transaction or to whom such knowledge or skill may be attributed by his employment of an agent or broker or other intermediary who by his occupation holds himself out as having such knowledge or skill.

The comments to Section 2–104 clarify that the Code addresses "merchants" in three contexts. First, §§ 2–201(2) (written confirmation between merchants exception to the statute of frauds), 2–205 (firm offers by merchants to hold an offer open for a period of time), 2–207 (battle of the forms), and 2–209 (modification) deal with persons familiar with "normal business practices which are or ought to be typical of and familiar to any person in business." UCC § 2–104, cmt. 2. The commentary further notes that "almost every person in business would, therefore, be deemed to be a 'merchant' " by virtue of holding themselves out as "having knowledge or skill peculiar to the practices . . . involved in the transaction. . . ." Id. In this context, the vast majority of business firms would be merchants, although the Code also observes that "these sections only apply to a merchant in his mercantile capacity; a lawyer or bank president buying fishing tackle for his own use is not a merchant." Id.

This position is not, however, absolute. For example, in *Forms World of Illinois, Inc. v. Magna Bank, N.A.*, 779 N.E.2d 917 (Ill. App. 3d 2002), the court held that a bank was not a merchant for purposes of the § 2–201(2) merchant exception to the statute of frauds because the bank was "a mere consumer of forms and printing . . . [and] does not resell these forms or hold itself out as a copy service to the general public." Id. at 921. Notably, the seller specifically argued in that case that § 2–104, cmt. 2 stated that banks can be deemed merchants, but the court rejected this argument, interpreting the comment "to mean that a bank can be deemed a merchant of goods in which it commonly deals." Id. Although the *Forms World* court's reasoning likely fails to reflect accurately the intent of the UCC drafters, the question whether business firms are merchants outside of their ordinary business activities remains open.

The second context involves UCC §§ 2–314 (implied warranty of merchantability), 2–402(2) (retention of possession by a merchant seller), and 2–403(2) (entrusting). In each of these situations, "merchant" is qualified to comprise only merchants who deal in goods of the kind at issue in the transaction.

The third context covers situations involving good faith, merchant buyers, risk of loss, and adequate assurances of performance under UCC §§ 2–103(1)(b), 2–327(1)(c), 2–603, 2–605, 2–509, and 2–609. "This group of sections applies to persons who are merchants under either the 'practices' or the 'goods' aspect of the definition of merchant." UCC § 2–104, cmt. 2.

7. *"Additional or different" versus "additional" terms: interpreting Subsections (1) and (2).* Note that while Subsection 1 refers to "additional or different" terms, Subsection (2) speaks only to "additional" terms. What possible problems can you foresee from a literal application of this statutory language?

8. *Proposals not included in the contract under § 2–207(2)(a)–(c).* Between merchants, additional terms are presumptively treated as incorporated into the parties' agreement unless one of the three enumerated exceptions applies: "(a) the offer expressly limits acceptance to the terms of the offer; (b) [the new terms] materially alter it; or (c) notification of objection to [the new terms] has already been given or is given within a reasonable time after notice of them is received." In light of these exceptions, what drafting

advice would you give to a client regarding the content of its form contract terms?

9.   *Acceptance expressly made conditional on assent to the additional or different terms and contracting by performance.* The final clause of § 2–207(1) provides that even a written form containing a definite and seasonable expression of acceptance cannot create a contract "unless acceptance is expressly made conditional on assent to the additional or different terms." If the receiving party begins performance despite the conditional acceptance term, has the party accepted the terms contained in the final form? In *Roto-Lith, Ltd. v. F. P. Bartlett & Co.*, 297 F.2d 497 (1st Cir. 1962), a seller of a quantity of food packaging emulsion replied to the buyer's purchase order with an "Acknowledgment" letter purporting to exclude all warranties, limit the buyer's damages to replacement cost only, and make the seller's acceptance conditional on acceptance of those terms. The buyer did not object to the new terms and later sought to recover damages for defects in the delivered products, contrary to the terms of the Acknowledgment. Focusing on the final clause in Subsection (1), the court held that "a response which states a condition materially altering the obligation solely to the disadvantage of the offeror is an 'acceptance . . . expressly . . . conditional on assent to the additional . . . terms.'" Id. at 500. The court then applied the last shot rule, apparently concluding that such a reply removed the parties' interaction from § 2–207 so that the first party to begin performing is deemed to have accepted the terms contained in the last form before performance.

The First Circuit Court of Appeals revisited this issue thirty-five years later in *Ionics, Inc. v. Elmwood Sensors, Inc.*, 110 F.3d 184 (1st Cir. 1997). In that case, two merchants sent separate forms, each purporting to limit acceptance solely to the terms contained therein. Expressly overruling *Roto-Lith*, the court held that a conditional acceptance by one party requires a court to determine the terms of the contract under Subsection (3).

> We hold, consistent with section 2–207 . . . , that where the terms in two forms are contradictory, each party is assumed to object to the other party's conflicting clause. As a result, mere acceptance of the goods by the buyer is insufficient to infer consent to the seller's terms under the language of subsection (1). Nor do such terms become part of the contract under subsection (2) because notification of objection has been given by the conflicting forms. See § 2–207(2)(c).

> The alternative result, advocated by Elmwood and consistent with Roto-Lith, would undermine the role of section 2–207. Elmwood suggests that "a seller's expressly conditional acknowledgment constitutes a counteroffer where it materially alters the terms proposed by the buyer, and the seller's terms govern the contract between the parties when the buyer accepts and pays for the goods." . . . Under this view, section 2–207 would no longer apply to cases in which forms have been exchanged and subsequent disputes reveal

that the forms are contradictory. That is, the last form would always govern.

The purpose of section 2–207, as stated in Roto-Lith, "was to modify the strict principle that a response not precisely in accordance with the offer was a rejection and a counteroffer." Roto-Lith, 297 F.2d at 500; see also Dorton v. Collins & Aikman Corp., 453 F.2d 1161, 1165–66 (6th Cir. 1972) (stating that section 2–207 "was intended to alter the 'ribbon-matching' or 'mirror' rule of common law, under which the terms of an acceptance or confirmation were required to be identical to the terms of the offer"). Under the holding advocated by Elmwood, virtually any response that added to or altered the terms of the offer would be a rejection and a counteroffer. We do not think that such a result is consistent with the intent of section 2–207. . . .

10. *Contracting by performance under Subsection (3).* As you saw in cases such as *Lucy v. Zehmer*, the objective theory of contracts creates a contract where both parties objectively manifest an intention to be bound to the terms of their agreement, even if they subjectively did not intend to enter that contract. In general, however, the parties themselves provided the basis for determining the terms of their agreement. How does § 2–207(3) determine the terms of the parties' contract? Does this process comport with the objective theory of contracts as described in previous cases, or have the UCC drafters created a new source of contractual liability?

11. *The Uniform Computer Information Transactions Act ("UCITA") and application of UCC Article 2 to software license contracts.* Assuming that the vast majority of software transactions only transfer a license to use the software, and not the software itself, are such transactions really "sales of goods" transactions governed under the UCC? In *i.Lan Systems, Inc. v. Netscout Service Level Corp.*, 183 F. Supp. 2d 328 (D. Mass. 2002), the court squarely addressed this issue and concluded that the question is disturbingly unsettled:

> Two bodies of contract law might govern the clickwrap license agreement: Massachusetts common law and the Uniform Commercial Code ("UCC") as adopted by Massachusetts. Article 2 of the UCC applies to "transactions in goods," UCC § 2–102, Mass. Gen. Laws ch. 106, § 2–102, but "unless the context otherwise requires 'contract' and 'agreement' are limited to those relating to the present or future sale of goods," id. § 2–106(1) (emphasis added). Indeed, the title of Article 2 is "Sales" and the definition of "goods" assumes a sale: "goods" is defined as "all things (including specially manufactured goods) which are movable at the time of identification to the contract for sale. . . ." Id. § 2–105(1). The purchase of software might seem like an ordinary contract for the sale of goods, but in fact the purchaser merely obtains a license to use the software; never is there a "passing of title from the seller to the buyer for a price," id. § 2–106(1). So is the purchase of software a transaction in goods?

Despite Article 2's requirement of a sale, courts in Massachusetts have assumed, without deciding, that Article 2 governs software licenses. . . .

Given the cases above, and others to the same effect, i.LAN argues that the UCC should govern the 1999 purchase order and clickwrap license agreement. NextPoint does not disagree with the idea that the UCC might apply to software purchases in general, but under NextPoint's theory of the case, the 1998 VAR agreement is most important to this dispute, and that agreement predominately concerns services, rather than the sale of goods. NextPoint, therefore, argues that the UCC should not govern any part of this dispute. See, e.g., Cambridge Plating Co. v. Napco, Inc., 991 F.2d 21, 24 (1st Cir.1993) (considering "predominate factor, thrust, or purpose" of contract). To the extent it matters—and given the facts of this case, it likely does not—the Court will examine the clickwrap license agreement through the lens of the UCC. Admittedly, the UCC technically does not govern software licenses, and very likely does not govern the 1998 VAR agreement, but with respect to the 1999 transaction, the UCC best fulfills the parties' reasonable expectations.

In Massachusetts and across most of the nation, software licenses exist in a legislative void. Legal scholars, among them the Uniform Commissioners on State Laws, have tried to fill that void, but their efforts have not kept pace with the world of business. Lawmakers began to draft a new Article 2B (licenses) for the UCC, which would have been the logical complement to Article 2 (sales) and Article 2A (leases), but after a few years of drafting, those lawmakers decided instead to draft an independent body of law for software licenses, which is now known as the Uniform Computer Information Transactions Act ("UCITA"). So far only Maryland and Virginia have adopted UCITA; Massachusetts has not. Accordingly, the Court will not spend its time considering UCITA. At the same time, the Court will not overlook Article 2 simply because its provisions are imperfect in today's world. Software licenses are entered into every day, and business persons reasonably expect that *some* law will govern them. For the time being, Article 2's familiar provisions—which are the inspiration for UCITA—better fulfill those expectations than would the common law. Article 2 technically does not, and certainly will not in the future, govern software licenses, but for the time being, the Court will assume it does.

The Uniform Computer Information Transactions Act ("UCITA"), which would provide a uniform scheme for regulating the terms of software licenses in much the same way as the UCC does for sales of goods, has been unfavorably received by state legislatures. Virginia and Maryland remain the only states that have adopted UCITA, while a handful of other states have adopted legislation to prohibit application of the model act's provisions to their residents.

Consequently, the ambiguity over whether software license agreements are contracts for the sale of goods under Article 2 of the UCC remains unresolved.

12. *"Money-Now-Terms-Later:* ProCD v. Zeidenberg, Hill v. Gateway2000 *and* Klocek v. Gateway. In a pair of (in)famous opinions, Judge Frank Easterbrook addressed contract formation in the context of a retail sale, payment and delivery followed by trailing terms. In *ProCD, Inc. v. Zeidenberg,* 86 F.3d 1447 (7th Cir. 1996), and *Hill v. Gateway2000, Inc.,* 105 F.3d 1147 (1997), Judge Easterbrook addressed two similar situations: a customer purchases a product such as software or a computer at a store or over the phone, pays, and receives the product. At home, the consumer opens the product that turns out to have additional documentation that includes:

- Additional terms such as a restrictive license or a mandatory arbitration term;

- A provision stating that if the consumer uses the product or fails to return it within a certain time then the consumer has agreed to the additional term; and

- An opportunity to reject the additional terms by returning the product and obtaining a refund.

In both cases, Judge Easterbrook concluded that "money-now-terms-later" with an opportunity to reject the trailing terms and return the goods for a refund was an enforceable method for creating a contract. More importantly, in both cases, Judge Easterbrook distinguished *Step-Saver* and rejected arguments that the transaction was governed by UCC § 2–207. "Step-Saver is a battle-of-the-forms case, in which the parties exchange incompatible forms and a court must decide which prevails. Our case has only one form; UCC § 2–207 is irrelevant." See *ProCD,* 86 F.3d at 1452; *Hill,* 105 F.3d at 1150 ("Plaintiffs tell us that *ProCD* came out as it did only because Zeidenberg was a 'merchant' and the terms inside ProCD's box were not excluded by the 'unless' clause. This argument pays scant attention to the opinion in *ProCD,* which concluded that, when there is only one form, 'sec. 2–207 is irrelevant.' "). For Judge Easterbrook, UCC § 2–207 addressed the problem of adding terms after a contract was formed, not whether and how a contract formed in the first place. "The question in *ProCD* was not whether terms were added to a contract after its formation, but how and when the contract was formed—in particular, whether a vendor may propose that a contract of sale be formed, not in the store (or over the phone) with the payment of money or a general 'send me the product,' but after the customer has had a chance to inspect both the item and the terms. *ProCD* answers 'yes,' for merchants and consumers alike." *Hill,* 105 F.3d at 1150.

Although a minority position, other courts have disagreed with Judge Easterbrook's money-now-terms-later contracting model. In *Klocek v. Gateway, Inc.,* 104 F.Supp.2d 1332 (2000), for instance, the court considered an arbitration contract similar to that in *Hill* (although with only five days to reject and return the computer instead of thirty days). The *Klocek* court rejected Judge Easterbrook's *Hill v. Gateway* and *ProCD, Inc. v. Zeidenberg* reasoning on several grounds. First, Easterbrook's characterization of the vendor as "master of the offer" in *ProCD* (83 F.3d at 1452) is contrary to the normal rule that in retail transactions the *purchaser* makes an offer to purchase (albeit on terms suggested by the vendor). Thus, Gateway's advertisements were properly considered as requests to receive offers, the buyer made an offer to purchase on the terms suggested in the advertisement, and Gateway accepted by performance when it took the purchaser's money in exchange for shipping the computer. Under this model, the contract formed at the time of payment or shipment and the additional terms sent afterwards would have no legal effect.

Second, *Klocek* also rejected the *ProCD* and *Hill* conclusions that UCC § 2–207 does not apply where there is only one form. To the contrary, nothing in § 2–207 requires more from one form—a definite and seasonable expression of acceptance or a written confirmation—and the comments to that section expressly note that it applies "where an agreement has been reached orally . . . and is followed by one or both of the parties sending formal memoranda embodying the terms so far agreed and adding terms not discussed." UCC § 2–207, cmt. 1.

Under § 2–207(2), *Klocek* concluded that the additional terms operated as mere proposals. Because the non-merchant buyer did not expressly accept the proposed additional terms, those terms (including the arbitration term) never became part of the contract. Consequently the parties never mutually agreed to submit their disputes to binding arbitration.

3.   TERMINATION BY DEATH OR INCAPACITY

The common law determines that the death or incapacity of the offeree terminates that person's power of acceptance. The general rule is that the offer is personal to the offeree and may not be exercised by, or transferred to, another. Restatement (Second) of Contracts §§ 29 and 52. Accordingly, the death or incapacity of the offeree terminates the power to accept the offer. Restatement (Second) § 36(1)(d). Application of this aspect of the termination rule generally is not problematic because the offeror generally cannot rely on an acceptance that has not occurred.

The death or incapacity of the offeror is more problematic. As a result, such an occurrence terminates the offeree's power of acceptance even though the offeree may have no knowledge of the offeror's death or incapacity. Despite the Restatement's adoption of the traditional rule, *comment a* criticizes that rule as an apparent "relic of the obsolete view that a contract requires a 'meeting of the minds.' " As it stands, the traditional rule of Restatement (Second) of Contracts § 36(1)(d) thus radically departs from the objective theory of assent. Clearly, under objective theory, the offeror should be bound because the offeree did not know and had no reason to know of the offeror's death or incapacity. The rule thus not only protects the offeror's estate in cases where the contract would not have been beneficial, but also prevents the estate from taking advantage of beneficial contracts. See Richard Craswell, "Offer, Acceptance, and Efficient Reliance," 48 Stan. L. Rev. 481, 515–516 (1996).

The first restatement included the rule on the theory that the contract rule should track the agency termination rule despite that few cases had adopted the rule. See Arthur L. Corbin, "Offer and Acceptance, and Some of the Resulting Legal Relations," 26 Yale L. J. 169, 198 (1917). The same paucity of cases stating the rule did not block the continuance of the rule in the second restatement. See E. Allan Farnsworth, "Ingredients in the Redaction of the Restatement (Second) of Contracts," 81 Colum. L. Rev. 1, 6 (1981). Moreover, the rule has been noted and criticized. See Merton L. Ferson, "Does the Death of an Offeror Nullify His Offer?," 10 Minn. L. Rev. 373, 381 (1926) and Herman Oliphant, "Duration and Termination of an Offer," 18 Mich. L. Rev. 201, 209 (1919). A notable case rejected the rule in the context of supervening incapacity of the offeror unknown to the offeree. See *Swift & Co. v. Smigel*, 115 N.J.Super. 391, 279 A.2d 895 (App. Div. 1971). Nonetheless, some support for the rule exists in the sense that the estate of a decedent offeror should not be bound to harsh expectancy damages on an unfavorable offer not accepted prior to death. See Melvin A. Eisenberg, "The Revocation of Offers," 2004 Wis. L. Rev. 271, 307 (2004). Indeed, Professor Val D. Ricks argues that while the rule may be a vestige of the will theory and the subjective meeting of the minds requirement, applications of the rule have largely reached just results. See Val D. Ricks, "The Death of Offers," 79 Ind. L. J. 667 (2004).

Finally, it is important to distinguish the effect of death or incapacity on an *offer* from the effect of such events on *contracts*. As discussed in Chapter 9, death or incapacity of a party to a contract generally does not terminate the contract unless that party was necessary for performance of the contract. Thus, death of a lender does not terminate a loan contract. In contrast, the incapacity of an actor would excuse non-performance of the actor's employment contract.

E. EFFECT OF PRE-ACCEPTANCE RELIANCE

In some cases, offerees rely upon offers before making the acceptance that would form a contract. Such pre-contract reliance typically occurs in three contexts: (1) unilateral contracts; (2) bilateral contracts; and (3) reliance on pre-contract negotiations. All are externalities of the bargain theory of consideration. The first, unilateral contracts, explores the vexing problem of offeree reliance in accepting an offer to form a unilateral contract. In such a contract, the offer seeks acceptance *only* by completion of the performance requested. Acceptance, therefore, occurs only when that performance is completed and not before. For example, a statement by A that "I offer to pay $1000 to the first person who paints my house" would be an offer to enter a unilateral contract. An offeree can accept that offer only by actually completing the requested house painting. While the offer remains unaccepted, the offeror remains free to revoke the offer at anytime prior to the completion of the performance. Thus, the offeror may choose to "waste" the offeree's partial performance of the acts required for acceptance by revoking the offer before the offeree can complete these acts. Continuing the house-painting offer example, if B decides to accept and paints ninety percent of the house, A may still attempt to revoke the offer at the last moment and thereby prevent acceptance.

The second context involves bilateral contracts, which involve promises on both sides of the transaction, rather than only a promise and performance. In some situations, the offeree relies on the offer to some extent before acceptance. Such pre-acceptance reliance commonly occurs, for instance, where a general contractor relies on bids received from potential subcontractors in preparing and submitting its own bid for the general contract. Early common law often permitted a subcontractor to withdraw or cancel its bid even after such reliance by the general contractor. In that case, the general contractor suffered prejudice. Where the general contractor bid was selected, the general contractor was prejudiced by having to replace the bid work with a more expensive bid and paying the difference between the original bid and the replacement cost out of its own profits.

The third context implicating pre-acceptance reliance arises from negotiations in which a party detrimentally relies on non-contractual promises or representations by the other party to the transaction. Negotiations do not form a contract until the parties manifest the necessary intent to form a contract. If the negotiating parties did not conclude a contract under early common law, how does the law protect a party relying on a representation made during those negotiations? In each context, consider how fairness should allocate the risk that a contract will not materialize. Should the losses simply be allocated to the party who suffered the loss, even if disproportionate to the other party's loss? Or should the law seek a method to allocate the loss to the party most responsible?

Consider also the importance of enforcement mechanisms in each of these three contexts. Consideration is rarely available before acceptance and thus does not justify enforcement. Similarly, restitution theory is not available because the reliance losses ordinarily do not create a benefit in the other party. As a result, promissory estoppel moves to center stage as the primary theory of obligation for enforcement of such promises. The application of that doctrine requires enforcement as justice requires. Make certain you see the "justice" (or the lack thereof) in the materials below.

1.   UNILATERAL CONTRACTS

Most promises to perform in the future are made in exchange for a return promise to perform in the future. Such promises—and the resulting contractual obligations—are said to be "executory." Since a promise exists on both sides, the contract is referred to as a bilateral contract in reference to the coupled promises. A bilateral contract is a true contract in the sense that both parties are legally bound to perform, thereby creating mutuality of obligation. The bargain exchange creates a contract at the moment the offeror's promise is accepted by a sought return promise in the form of acceptance. Most of the work of this course is focused on understanding bilateral contracts simply because most contracts are bilateral contracts.

There is another type of "contract" that is not bilateral, but rather unilateral. The unilateral moniker refers to the fact that only the offeror makes a promise in the form of an offer. The terms of the offer provide that it can only be accepted by "completing the requested performance." A promise to perform the act, the beginning of performance, or even the near completion of the performance will not do. Acceptance *only* occurs when the requested performance is completed. The power of acceptance remains a power for the duration of the requested performance.

Because the offer has not ripened into a contract by way of acceptance, the offeror is not bound until the moment of acceptance. Accordingly, under early common law, the offeror might revoke the offer anytime prior to the completed performance by the offeree. What justified this extraordinary result? Early common law assumed the equities were in balance because the offeree was under no promissory obligation to complete the performance merely by beginning the performance. Both the offeror and offeree were free until the requested performance was completed. In terms of the house painting example offered above, A remains free to withdraw the offer, just as B remains free to stop painting (or never start) at anytime before completion of the requested performance. Perhaps surprisingly, unilateral contracts in form pre-date bilateral contracts by about a century and paralleled the growth of the doctrine of consideration. Both forms of contract were recognized by the seventeenth century, but the lack of terminology caused the distinction to be overlooked for much of the early history of contract law. Williston on Contracts § 1.17 (4th ed. 2006).

The idea that a contract is created through the process of offer and acceptance was a nineteenth century innovation superimposed on the sixteenth century civil law concept of consideration. A. W. B. Simpson, "Innovation in Nineteenth Century Contract Law," 91 Law Q. Rev. 247, 258–259 (1975). Perhaps in an effort to develop symmetry with bilateral contracts, Christopher Columbus Langdell applied the early notions of offer and acceptance with equal force to unilateral contracts. Karl N. Llewellyn, "On the Good, the True, the Beautiful, in Law," 9 U. Chi. L. Rev.

224, 228 (1941). But the fit was never an easy one, despite the theoretical efforts of some as best described in this famous illustration:

> Suppose A says to B, "I will give you $100 if you walk across the Brooklyn Bridge," and B walks—is there a contract? It is clear that A is not asking B for B's *promise* to walk across the Brooklyn Bridge. What A wants from B is the *act* of walking across the bridge. When B has walked across the bridge there is a contract, and A is then bound to pay B $100. At that moment there arises a unilateral contract. A has bartered away his volition for B's act of walking across the Brooklyn Bridge.
>
> When an act is thus wanted in return for a promise, a unilateral contract is created when the act is done. It is clear that only one party is bound. B is not bound to walk across the Brooklyn Bridge, but A is bound to pay B $100 if B does so. Thus, in unilateral contracts, on one side we find merely an act, on the other side a promise. . . .
>
> Let us suppose that B starts to walk across the Brooklyn Bridge and has gone about one-half of the way across. At that moment A overtakes B and says to him, "I withdraw my offer." Has B then any rights against A? . . .
>
> What A wanted from B, and what A asked for, was the act of walking across the bridge. Until that was done, B had not given to A what A had requested. The acceptance by B of A's offer could be nothing but the act on B's part of crossing the bridge. It is elementary that an offeror may withdraw his offer until it has been accepted. . . . I. Maurice Wormser, "The True Conception of Unilateral Contracts," 26 Yale L. J. 136, 136–138 (1916). [Professor Wormser later recanted "clad in sackcloth" that the early common law result was indeed unfair to the partially performing offeree. 3 J. Leg. Educ. 145, 146 (1950)].

Professor Wormser noted that for some critics of this early unilateral contract rule such a result seemed unfair or "hard" upon B, who by that point would have detrimentally walked halfway across the bridge. In response, Professor Wormser argued that critics were ignoring the mutuality of the rights of both A and B to withdraw from the contract. Just as A would not be bound until B completed the walk, B also is free to cease performance at any time. Based upon this principle of mutuality, Prof. Wormser concluded that the early common law unilateral contract rule was "just, equitable and logical." See id. Do you agree with Professor Wormser? Is the early common law rule of unilateral contract "just, equitable and logical" merely because the offeree has an equal opportunity with the offeror to withdraw? Can you see cases of opportunistic behavior of the offeror capitalizing on an unsuspecting offeree by revoking an offer prior to the completion of the performance necessary to make a unilateral contract?

Notwithstanding Professor Wormser's defense, other contract scholars thought the rule ridiculously harsh to the offeree, particularly given that the power to revoke continued for so long. L. L. Fuller and William R. Perdue, Jr., "The Reliance Interest in Contract Damages: 2," 46 Yale L. J. 373, 410 (1937). Indeed, several alternative "fixes" for the problem were suggested. In varying degrees, the solutions effectively made the offer irrevocable once performance began. These included using the offeree's substantial reliance to trigger promissory estoppel, implying a second offer to keep the principal offer open, or simply making the offer irrevocable once the offeree began performance. Peter Meijes Tiersma, "Reassessing Unilateral Contracts: The Role of Offer, Acceptance and Promise," 26 U. C. Davis L. Rev. 1, 7 (1992).

In 1932, Restatement (First) of Contracts § 45 adopted the second approach. Under that section with the title mentioning "unilateral contracts," the beginning of the requested performance made the offer binding upon the offeror subject to the condition that the offeree fully rendered performance. The inequities resolved, scholarly attention turned to the basis of the unilateral-bilateral distinction. In particular, Karl Llewellyn, the architect of the Uniform Commercial Code, argued the conceptualization itself was preposterous and false. Llewellyn, and later other scholars, argued for abolishing the distinction outright and replacing it with the idea that any offer could be accepted by simple assent to the terms of the offer, including the beginning of performance. Where the offer clearly did not contemplate an agreement by acceptance, Llewellyn argued substantial reliance was adequate to make the offer binding, but not under a conception of an agreement by way of acceptance. Karl N. Llewellyn, "On Our Case-Law of Contract: Offer and Acceptance," 48 Yale L. J. 1, 33–35 [Part I] and 779, 816–818 [Part II] (1938) and Samuel J. Stoljar, "The False Distinction Between Bilateral and Unilateral Contracts,"64 Yale L. J. 515 (1955).

The Restatement (Second) of Contracts incorporated Llewellyn's criticism of the unilateral-bilateral distinction by abandoning that terminology. But the second restatement still maintained the mechanics of the acceptance by performance doctrine. Restatement (Second) of Contracts § 45 eliminated references to a "unilateral contract" in favor of an "option contract." A more faithful following of Llewellyn's argument of course can be found in UCC § 2–204(1), which provides that an agreement can be formed in any manner sufficient to show agreement, including conduct by both parties. Indeed, Restatement (Second) of Contracts § 50 and *comment b* provide that an offeree may accept an offer either by a promise or performance unless the offer specifically requires acceptance by performance. Robert Braucher, "Offer and Acceptance in the Second

Restatement," 74 Yale L. J. 302, 304 (1964) and Note, "The Restatement of Contracts Second and Offers to Enter into Unilateral Contracts," 29 U. Pitt. L. Rev. 546 (1968).

The paradigm of both restatements rested upon a single theory. The making of an offer for a unilateral contract stated two promises. The first and principal offer promise was "express" and required performance of the promise upon the satisfaction of the condition required for acceptance, i.e., full performance by the offeree. The second and subsidiary promise was "implied" and provided that the offer would become irrevocable upon the beginning of the requested offeree performance. Restatement (First) of Contracts § 45, *comment b* provides:

> The main offer includes as a subsidiary promise, necessarily implied, that if part of the requested performance is given, the offeror will not revoke his offer, and that if tender is made it will be accepted. Part performance or tender may thus furnish consideration for the subsidiary promises. Moreover, merely acting in justifiable reliance on an offer may in some cases serve as sufficient reason for making a promise binding (see § 90).

Have the Restatement (Second) of Contracts and the Uniform Commercial Code, through deference to scholars generally and Llewellyn in particular, buried once and for all the troubling unilateral-bilateral distinction? The answer seems to be, "clearly not." The simple truth is that, in many cases, an offeror clings to the notion that full performance is bargained for and nothing short thereof should create any obligation. Indeed, some argue that the innovation of the "unilateral contract" not only fits the marketplace, but also has allowed an equitable expansion of civil obligation to meet appropriate circumstances. Mark Pettit, Jr., "Modern Unilateral Contracts," 63 B. U. L. Rev. 551, 552 (1983). In some circumstances, the concept of a unilateral contract may be the only method to achieve fair results. James Gordley observes, for instance, that traditional unilateral contract doctrine "can also be fair when one party is not certain whether he can perform, or how much his performance will cost. He may not want to commit himself to succeed or to complete the job at a fixed price. The other party may not want to pay him merely for trying, or to pay cost plus." James Gordley, "The Common Law in the Twentieth Century: Some Unfinished Business," 88 Cal. L. Rev. 1815, 1857–58 (2000). Gordley notes in such contexts the fair contract rule recognizes these interests of the parties instead of artificially forcing them into a bilateral contract model. See id.

As you read the following materials, search for the implied promise of irrevocability. At the same time, search for the point when the reliance of the offeree rises to the level that it is fair or appropriate to treat the offeror's promise as irrevocable, even though the offeree may quit at any time. Which justification better resolves the problem of pre-acceptance reliance in this context?

PETTERSON V. PATTBERG

Court of Appeals of New York
248 N.Y. 86, 161 N.E. 428 (1928)

KELLOGG, J.

The evidence given upon the trial sanctions the following statement of facts: John Petterson, of whose last will and testament the plaintiff is the executrix, was the owner of a parcel of real estate in Brooklyn, known as 5301 Sixth avenue. The defendant was the owner of a bond executed by Petterson, which was secured by a third mortgage upon the parcel. On April 4, 1924, there remained unpaid upon the principal the sum of $5,450. This amount was payable in installments of $250 on April 25, 1924, and upon a like monthly date every three months thereafter. Thus the bond and mortgage had more than five years to run before the entire sum became due. Under date of the 4th of April, 1924, the defendant wrote Petterson as follows:

> I hereby agree to accept cash for the mortgage which I hold against premises 5301 6th Ave., Brooklyn, N. Y. It is understood and agreed as a consideration I will allow you $780 providing said mortgage is paid on or before May 31, 1924, and the regular quarterly payment due April 25, 1924, is paid when due.

On April 25, 1924, Petterson paid the defendant the installment of principal due on that date. Subsequently, on a day in the latter part of May, 1924, Petterson presented himself at the defendant's home, and knocked at the door. The defendant demanded the name of his caller. Petterson replied: "It is Mr. Petterson. I have come to pay off the mortgage." The defendant answered that he had sold the mortgage. Petterson stated that he would like to talk with the defendant, so the defendant partly opened the door. Thereupon Petterson exhibited the cash, and said he was ready to pay off the mortgage according to the agreement. The defendant refused to take the money. Prior to this conversation, Petterson had made a contract to sell the land to a third person free and clear of the mortgage to the defendant. Meanwhile, also, the defendant had sold the bond and mortgage to a third party. It therefore became necessary for Petterson to pay to such person the full amount of the bond and mortgage. It is claimed that he thereby sustained a loss of $780, the sum which the defendant agreed to allow upon the bond and mortgage, if payment in full of principal, less that sum, was made on or before May 31, 1924. The plaintiff has had a recovery for the sum thus claimed, with interest.

Clearly the defendant's letter proposed to Petterson the making of a unilateral contract, the gift of a promise in exchange for the performance of an act. The thing conditionally promised by the defendant was the reduction of the mortgage debt. The act requested to be done, in consideration of the offered promise, was payment in full of the reduced principal of the debt prior to the due date thereof. "If an act is requested, that very act, and no other, must be given." Williston on Contracts, § 73. "In case of offers for a consideration, the performance of the consideration is always deemed a condition." Langdell's Summary of the Law of Contracts, § 4. It is elementary that any offer to enter into a unilateral contract may be withdrawn before the act requested to be done has been performed. Williston on Contracts, § 60; Langdell's Summary, § 4; Offord v. Davies, 12 C. B. (N. S.) 748. A bidder at a sheriff's sale may revoke his bid at any time before the property is struck down to him. Fisher v. Seltzer, 23 Pa. 308, 62 Am. Dec. 335. The offer of a reward in consideration of an act to be performed is revocable before the very act requested has been done. Shuey v. United States, 92 U. S. 73, 23 L. Ed. 697; Biggers v. Owen, 79 Ga. 658, 5 S. E. 193; Fitch v. Snedaker, 38 N.Y. 248, 97 Am. Dec. 791. So, also, an offer to pay a broker commissions, upon a sale of land for the offeror, is revocable at any time before the land is sold, although prior to revocation the broker performs services in an effort to effectuate a sale. Stensgaard v. Smith, 43 Minn. 11, 44 N. W. 669, 19 Am. St. Rep. 205; Smith v. Cauthen, 98 Miss. 746, 54 So. 844.

An interesting question arises when, as here, the offeree approaches the offeror with the intention of proffering performance and, before actual tender is made, the offer is withdrawn. Of such a case Williston says:

> The offeror may see the approach of the offeree and know that an acceptance is contemplated. If the offeror can say "I revoke" before the offeree accepts, however brief the interval of time between the two acts, there is no escape from the conclusion that the offer is terminated.—Williston on Contracts, § 60b.

In this instance Petterson, standing at the door of the defendant's house, stated to the defendant that he had come to pay off the mortgage. Before a tender of the necessary moneys had been made, the defendant informed Petterson that he had sold the mortgage. That was a definite notice to Petterson that the defendant could not perform his offered promise, and that a tender to the defendant, who was no longer the creditor, would be ineffective to satisfy the debt. "An offer to sell property may be withdrawn before acceptance without any formal notice to the person to whom the offer is made. It is sufficient if that person has actual knowledge that the person who made the offer has done some act inconsistent with the continuance of the offer, such as selling the property to a third person." Dickinson v. Dodds, 2 Ch. Div. 463, headnote. To the same effect is Coleman v. Applegarth, 68 Md. 21, 11 A. 284, 6 Am. St. Rep. 417. Thus it clearly appears that the defendant's offer was withdrawn before its acceptance had been tendered. It is unnecessary to determine, therefore, what the legal situation might have been had tender been made before withdrawal. It is the individual view of the writer that the same result would follow. This would be so, for the act requested to be performed was the completed act of payment, a thing incapable of performance, unless assented to by the person to be paid. Williston on Contracts, § 60b. Clearly an offering party has the right to name the precise act performance of which would convert his offer into a binding promise. Whatever the act may be until it is performed, the offer must be revocable. However, the supposed case is not before us for decision. We think that in this particular instance the offer of the defendant was withdrawn before it became a binding promise, and therefore that no contract was ever made for the breach of which the plaintiff may claim damages.

The judgment of the Appellate Division and that of the Trial Term should be reversed, and the complaint dismissed, with costs in all courts.

LEHMAN, J. (dissenting).

The defendant's letter to Petterson constituted a promise on his part to accept payment at a discount of the mortgage he held, provided the mortgage is paid on or before May 31, 1924. Doubtless, by the terms of the promise itself, the defendant made payment of the mortgage by the plaintiff, before the stipulated time, a condition precedent to performance by the defendant of his promise to accept payment at a discount. If the condition precedent has not been performed, it is because the defendant made performance impossible by refusing to accept payment, when the plaintiff came with an offer of immediate performance.

> It is a principle of fundamental justice that if a promisor is himself the cause of the failure of performance either of an obligation due him or of a condition upon which his own liability depends, he cannot take advantage of the failure.—Williston on Contracts, § 677.

The question in this case is not whether payment of the mortgage is a condition precedent to the performance of a promise made by the defendant, but, rather, whether, at the time the defendant refused the offer of payment, he had assumed any binding obligation, even though subject to condition.

The promise made by the defendant lacked consideration at the time it was made. Nevertheless, the promise was not made as a gift or mere gratuity to the plaintiff. It was made for the purpose of obtaining from the defendant something which the plaintiff desired. It constituted an offer which was to become binding whenever the plaintiff should give, in return for the defendant's promise, exactly the consideration which the defendant requested.

Here the defendant requested no counter promise from the plaintiff. The consideration requested by the defendant for his promise to accept payment was, I agree, some act to be performed by the plaintiff. Until the act requested was performed, the defendant might undoubtedly revoke his offer. Our problem is to determine from the words of the letter, read in the light of surrounding circumstances, what act the defendant requested as consideration for his promise.

The defendant undoubtedly made his offer as an inducement to the plaintiff to "pay" the mortgage before it was due. Therefore, it is said, that "the act requested to be performed was the completed act of payment, a thing incapable of performance, unless assented to by the person to be paid." In unmistakable terms the defendant agreed to accept payment, yet we are told that the defendant intended, and the plaintiff should have understood, that the act requested by the defendant, as consideration for his promise to accept payment, included performance by the defendant himself of the very promise for which the act was to be consideration. The defendant's promise was to become binding only when fully performed; and part of the consideration to be furnished by the plaintiff for the defendant's promise was to be the performance of that promise by the defendant. So construed, the defendant's promise or offer, though intended to induce action by the plaintiff, is but a snare and delusion. The plaintiff could not reasonably suppose that the defendant was asking him to procure the performance by the defendant of the very act which the defendant promised to do, yet we are told that, even after the plaintiff had done all else which the defendant requested, the defendant's promise was still not binding because the defendant chose not to perform.

I cannot believe that a result so extraordinary could have been intended when the defendant wrote the letter. "The thought behind the phrase proclaims itself misread when the outcome of the reading is injustice or absurdity." See opinion of Cardozo, C. J., in Surace v. Danna, 248 N. Y. 18, 161 N. E. 315. If the defendant intended to induce payment by the plaintiff and yet reserve the right to refuse payment when offered he should have used a phrase better calculated to express his meaning than the words: "I agree to accept." A promise to accept payment, by its very terms, must necessarily become binding, if at all, not later than when a present offer to pay is made.

I recognize that in this case only an offer of payment, and not a formal tender of payment, was made before the defendant withdrew his offer to accept payment. Even the plaintiff's part in the act of payment was then not technically complete. Even so, under a fair construction of the words of the letter, I think the plaintiff had done the act which the defendant requested as consideration for his promise. The plaintiff offered to pay, with present intention and ability to make that payment. A formal tender is seldom made in business transactions, except to lay the foundation for subsequent assertion in a court of justice of rights which spring from refusal of the tender. If the defendant acted in good faith in making his offer to accept payment, he could not well have intended to draw a distinction in the act requested of the plaintiff in return, between an offer which, unless refused, would ripen into completed payment, and a formal tender. Certainly the defendant could not have expected or intended that the plaintiff would make a formal tender of payment without first stating that he had come to make payment. We should not read into the language of the defendant's offer a meaning which would prevent enforcement of the defendant's promise after it had been accepted by the plaintiff in the very way which the defendant must have intended it should be accepted, if he acted in good faith.

The judgment should be affirmed.

CARDOZO, C. J., and POUND, CRANE, and O'BRIEN, JJ., concur with KELLOGG, J.

LEHMAN, J., dissents in opinion, in which ANDREWS, J., concurs.

Judgments reversed, etc.

NOTES AND QUESTIONS

1.   *Willistonian view.* The majority opinion quotes from Williston on Contracts for the authority that an offer to enter into a unilateral contract is revocable at any time prior to acceptance, which, in turn, does not occur until the offeree completes the performance requested. However, along with Arthur Corbin, Samuel Williston was one of the architects of the Restatement (First) of Contracts, which includes section 45. How could Williston stand on both sides? The *Petterson* case was decided in 1928 and the first restatement was released in 1932. In the ensuing four years, Williston changed his view because "great injustice may arise" if the power to revoke continues. E. Allan Farnsworth, "Contracts Scholarship in the Age of Anthology," 85 Mich. L. Rev. 1406, 1453–1454 (1987). Restatement (First) of Contracts § 45 incorporates Williston's changed view:

> § 45. Revocation Of Offer For Unilateral Contract; Effect Of Part Performance Or Tender.

> If an offer for a unilateral contract is made, and part of the consideration requested in the offer is given or tendered by the offeree in response thereto, the offeror is bound by a contract, the duty of immediate performance of which is conditional on the full consideration being given or tendered within the time stated in the offer, or, if no time is stated therein, within a reasonable time.

It appears that Williston did change his view from that expressed in his treatise and relied upon as authority in *Petterson*.

2. *Implied subsidiary promise paradigm of the first restatement.* The first restatement provides that the making of an offer to enter into a unilateral contract (main promise) "implies by law" a second promise not to revoke the main promise once the offeree tenders performance (subsidiary promise). Must the offeree's reliance be substantial to make the offer irrevocable? The rule itself states that a mere "tender" to "begin" performance is adequate as further explained by the following comment:

> *Comment b.* Tender, however, is sufficient. Though not the equivalent of performance, nevertheless it is obviously unjust to allow so late withdrawal. There can be no actionable duty on the part of the offeror until he has received all that he demanded, or until the condition is excused by his own prevention of performance by refusing a tender; but he may become bound at an earlier day. The main offer includes as a subsidiary promise, necessarily implied, that if part of the requested performance is given, the offeror will not revoke his offer, and that if tender is made it will be accepted. Part performance or tender may thus furnish consideration for the subsidiary promises. Moreover, merely acting in justifiable reliance on an offer may in some cases serve as sufficient reason for making a promise binding (see § 90).

Under this view, beginning performance, or even offering to begin performance, may provide adequate consideration to render the implied subsidiary promise enforceable. Thus, a mere "tender" makes the offer irrevocable. A "tender" is generally defined as an offer of performance, whereas a "tender of performance" is more specifically defined as a demonstration of "readiness, willingness, and ability" to perform as requested. Did Petterson make a qualifying "tender of performance" before Pattberg revoked the offer? Given that the offeree has not made a promise to perform, may quit at any time, and has incurred minimal or no reliance, does the rule go too far? Is it fair to bind the offeror in such circumstances? How do you evaluate Petterson's preparations to perform?

3. *Option contract paradigm of the second restatement.* The second restatement provides that the making of an offer to enter into a unilateral contract (main promise) creates an "implied by law" option contract, and the beginning of performance "completes the manifestation of mutual assent and furnishes consideration for an option contract." See Restatement (Second) of Contracts § 45, *cmt d.* Does this paradigm differ from that expressed in the first restatement? Restatement (Second) of Contracts § 25 defines an "option contract" "as a promise which meets the requirements for the formation of a contract and limits the promisor's power to revoke an offer." Thus, although the first restatement is expressed in terms of an "implied subsidiary promise" not to revoke and the second restatement in terms of an "implied option contract," given the definition of an option contract, there does not appear to be any substantive difference in approaches. What is the reason for the switch in approaches? One answer may be that the second restatement introduced the concept of an "option contract," and this expression simply completed the

symmetry given that the value of the option contract notion was to preserve the offer. Note, "The Restatement of Contracts Second and Offers to Enter into Unilateral Contracts," 29 U. Pitt. L. Rev. 546, 548–549 (1968). Restatement (First) of Contracts § 24 included an "option" concept in the definition of an offer: "An offer is also a contract, commonly called an option, if the requisites of a formal or an informal contract exist." It appears the change from the "option" to "option contract" terminology was simply clarifying. Robert Braucher, "Offer and Acceptance in the Second Restatement," 74 Yale L. J. 302, 306 (1964).

Compared to the first restatement, does the second restatement alter the nature or increase the degree of reliance necessary to make the subsidiary promise or option contract enforceable? The following Restatement (Second) of Contracts § 45 and comment is instructive:

§ 45. Option Contract Created By Part Performance Or Tender.

(1) Where an offer invites an offeree to accept by rendering a performance and does not invite a promissory acceptance, an option contract is created when the offeree tenders or begins the invited performance or tenders a beginning of it.

Comment f. Preparations for performance. What is begun or tendered must be part of the actual performance invited in order to preclude revocation under this Section. Beginning preparations, though they may be essential to carrying out the contract or to accepting the offer, is not enough. Preparations to perform may, however, constitute justifiable reliance sufficient to make the offeror's promise binding under § 87(2).

In many cases what is invited depends on what is a reasonable mode of acceptance. See § 30. The distinction between preparing for performance and beginning performance in such cases may turn on many factors: the extent to which the offeree's conduct is clearly referable to the offer, the definite and substantial character of that conduct, and the extent to which it is of actual or prospective benefit to the offeror rather than the offeree, as well as the terms of the communications between the parties, their prior course of dealing, and any relevant usages of trade.

Would your answer to the question of whether Petterson tendered performance before Pattberg revoked change from the first to the second restatement? The second restatement adds the phrase "tenders a beginning of performance." What is intended by this phrase?

What is the relevance of the majority determination that: "Before a tender of the necessary moneys had been made, the defendant informed Petterson that he had sold the mortgage." How then does the majority opinion conceptualize the tender of performance when it is the payment of money? What is the effect of the continuing language: "It is unnecessary to determine, therefore, what the legal situation might have been had tender been made before withdrawal. It is the individual view of the writer that the same result would follow. This would be so, for the act requested to be performed was the completed act of payment, a thing incapable of performance, unless assented to by the person to be paid." Is this remark what is referred to as *obiter dictum*? For an analysis of *Petterson* under the first and second restatements, see Note, "The Restatement of Contracts Second and Offers to Enter into Unilateral Contracts," 29 U. Pitt. L. Rev. 546 (1968).

4.   *Mutuality of obligation.* Restatement (Second) of Contracts 79(c) provides that if the requirement of consideration is met, there is no additional requirement of mutuality of obligation. *Comment f* further provides that the concept of mutuality of obligation is frequently and erroneously used to suggest that in the positive form "both parties must be bound or neither is bound." In the negative form, if one party is not bound for any reason, then the other party is not bound. *Comment f* then provides an example of a unilateral contract where mutuality of obligation is not present and thus the doctrine is not universally true. In a unilateral contract, the contract itself is not formed until the offeree completes performance that constitutes acceptance of the offer. At that point, the offeree lacks any further obligation. As a result, the doctrine of mutuality of obligation has no application to unilateral contracts. Any vitality or doctrinal meaning must then depend upon its meaning in the context of a bilateral contract where the parties have exchanged promises. But there too the doctrine has been discredited. An early but important article argued the doctrine was overly broad and failed to account or explain why contract law recognized the right of one party to maintain an action while another could not (voidable contracts): (i) infant contracts, (ii) incapacity contracts, (iii) fraud, (iv) duress, (v) illegality, and (vi) Statute of Frauds. Herman Oliphant, "Mutuality of Obligation in Bilateral Contracts at Law," 25 Colum. L. Rev. 705, 706 (1925).

Some argue that the mutuality doctrine is nearly inextricably connected to the doctrine of consideration. This view states the doctrine in broad "obligation" terms rather than narrower "consideration" terms (as merely one way of making an obligation) and has confused the application of the doctrine. Joseph M. Perillo, Calamari and Perillo on Contracts § 4.12(b) (5th Ed. 2003) and Arthur D. Austin, "Mutuality of Obligation: A Multi-Dimensional Doctrine for All Seasons," 30 Ohio St. L. J. 61 (1969). Early applications of the mutuality doctrine were connected to early formulations of consideration under the benefit-detriment analysis. Under this explanation, one is assumed to bargain for an enforceable promise. And if the promise is not enforceable against one party, that party may not enforce the reciprocal promise. This defensive aspect of the doctrine, as well as others, is captured separately under the second restatement. See, e.g., Restatement (Second) of Contracts § 73 (pre-existing legal duty rule stating that the performance of a legal duty is not consideration). Others argue that the mutuality of obligation and consideration doctrines stand together. Accordingly, if the mutuality of obligation doctrine is eliminated, the consideration doctrine should be eliminated. Val D. Ricks, "In Defense of Mutuality of Obligation: Why 'Both Should Be Bound, Or Neither,'" 78 Neb. L. Rev. 491, 547 (1999). In either event, with the "bargain theory" shift away from benefit-detriment to a bargained-for exchange analysis, both the necessity and application of the mutuality doctrine have been broadly reduced. Reconsider the facts of *Lucy v. Zehmer*. If Lucy had refused to perform, could Zehmer have sued successfully for specific performance?

5.   *Williston's jurisprudence.* Samuel Williston, Reporter for the first restatement, remains one of the most important figures in American jurisprudence. For many years, scholars from the Legal Realist school of jurisprudence and its later adherents characterized his work as pure classical formalism, divorced from social and policy considerations. See Mark L. Movsesian, "Rediscovering Williston," 62 Wash. & Lee L. Rev. 207, 209–10 & nn. 16–17 (2005) (noting, inter alia, Grant Gilmore's characterization of Williston as "a plodding scrivener," Lawrence M. Friedman's assertion that Williston's contribution to social and legal thought comprised volumes of "heavy void," and Morton J. Horowitz's claim that Williston's work promoted inequalities of bargaining power). But as Mark Movsesian observes in his excellent intellectual history of Williston's work, the contemporary account does not bear up on reexamination of Williston's writings. Movsesian agrees that Williston was clearly a formalist who emphasized "the importance of coherent general principles, clear rules, and logical analysis." Id. But Williston was a pragmatist—for him formalism promoted "simplicity, predictability, and comprehensibility" in the law. Id. And Williston also recognized that, in some cases, practical concerns could override strict adherence to formalist principles. See id. " 'Law is made for man; he chides,' not man for the law.' " Id.

2.   BILATERAL CONTRACTS

Classical contract law provides that an offer to enter into a bilateral contract is revocable by the offeror at anytime before the offeree's acceptance. Restatement (Second) of Contracts § 36(1)(c). Moreover, unlike an offer to enter into a unilateral contract that cannot be accepted until the offeree completes the requested performance, an offer to enter into a bilateral contract can be immediately accepted simply by communicating acceptance. Accordingly, it would appear that opportunities for offeree reliance are minimal. Nonetheless, the context may dictate otherwise. In bid cases, a general contractor normally seeks subcontractor bid-offers to be included in the general contractor's bid on the general contract. Upon receipt of multiple offers, the general contractor normally selects the lowest qualified bid and incorporates that bid in the general bid submitted on the project. If the general contractor's bid is accepted, the general contractor communicates acceptance to the subcontractor whose bid-offer may then be accepted.

The difficulty occurs with honest mistakes in the subcontractor bid. Under classical contract law, if the subcontractor discovers the error in its bid-offer prior to when the general contractor accepts the bid, the subcontractor remains free to revoke because acceptance has not occurred. The difficulty with this approach is that the general contractor may have already submitted the erroneous subcontractor bid as part of its general bid. By contract or statute, most sealed bids for general contracts for government work are binding unless revoked in writing prior to the bid opening date. If the bid opening date has passed and the general contractor's bid has been accepted, the general contractor will be responsible for the subcontractor mistake if the subcontractor revokes prior to the general accepting its bid.

The first two cases below explore the use of promissory estoppel to shift the risk of the mistake back to the subcontractor by making the subcontractor bid irrevocable after its use by the general contractor. Like the option contract solution for unilateral contracts, this is a one-sided bargain ("One Party Bound Model"). The general contractor is not bound unless the subcontractor bid is actually accepted. This freedom allows the general contractor to speculate on seeking a better and lower bid through opportunistic post-general bid behavior. See Comment, "Bid Shopping and Peddling in the Subcontract Construction Industry," 18 U.C.L.A. L. Rev. 389 (1970). Other possible solutions, however, do not present such an opportunity. The parties could make a firm contract at the time of bid submission by the general contractor subject to the condition that the general contractor bid is accepted ("Both Parties Bound Model"). Alternatively, the parties could be free to negotiate a contract after the general contractor bid is accepted ("No Party Bound Model").

Early empirical studies of the construction industry bid process conducted after the *Baird* case determined that general contractors attached little importance to subcontractor "firm" offers and thus argued that making the subcontractor bid irrevocable to protect the general contractor was both unnecessary and added to existing structural power imbalances. Franklin Schultz, "The Firm Offer Puzzle: A Study of Business Practice in the Construction Industry," 19 U. Chi. L. Rev. 237 (1952). A later study determined that a firm contract at the time of the general contractor used the bid, subject to a condition of acceptance of the general bid, was a preferable solution. Note, "Another Look at Construction Bidding and Contracts at Formation," 53 Va. L. Rev. 1720 (1967). Still other studies preferred a rule in which neither party was bound until a contract was negotiated after the general contractor bid was accepted. Note, "Construction Contracts—The Problem of Offer and Acceptance in the General Contractor-Subcontractor Relationship," 37 U. Cin. L. Rev. 798 (1968). Still later studies continue the debate on the most appropriate rule. Thomas J. Stipanowich, "Reconstructing Construction Law: Reality and Reform in a Transactional System," 1998 Wis. L. Rev. 463 (1998). As you read the construction cases below, try to decide whether you favor a One Party Bound Model, a Both Parties Bound Model, or a Neither Party Bound Model.

Construction contracts are also subject to a confusing mixture of applicable law. Common law applies to cases involving only services. The UCC applies to transactions involving only the sale of goods. UCC § 2–102. Problematically, most subcontract bids are "hybrid" contracts involving a mixture of goods and services. While the UCC does not exclude application to hybrid contracts, courts traditionally adopt an "all-or-nothing" common law approach and select either the UCC or the common law based on whether services or goods are dominant. See, e.g., *Princess Cruises, Inc. v. General Electric Co.*, 143 F.3d 828 (4th Cir. 1998) (applied common law as contract predominately for services). Some argue that an expanded application of the UCC would resolve many construction contract issues. Note, "Construction Contracting: Building Better Law With the Uniform Commercial Code," 52 Case W. L. Rev. 1067 (2002).

JAMES BAIRD CO. v. GIMBEL BROS., INC.

United States Court of Appeals, Second Circuit
64 F.2d 344 (1933)

L. HAND, Circuit Judge.

The plaintiff sued the defendant for breach of a contract to deliver linoleum under a contract of sale; the defendant denied the making of the contract; the parties tried the case to the judge under a written stipulation and he directed judgment for the defendant. The facts as found, bearing on the making of the contract, the only issue necessary to discuss, were as follows: The defendant, a New York merchant, knew that the Department of Highways in Pennsylvania had asked for bids for the construction of a public building. It sent an employee to the office of a contractor in Philadelphia, who had possession of the specifications, and the employee there computed the amount of the linoleum which would be required on the job, underestimating the total yardage by about one-half the proper amount. In ignorance of this mistake, on December twenty-fourth the defendant sent to some twenty or thirty contractors, likely to bid on the job, an offer to supply all the linoleum required by the specifications at two different lump sums, depending upon the quality used. These offers concluded as follows: "If successful in being awarded this contract, it will be absolutely guaranteed, . . . and . . . we are offering these prices for reasonable" (sic), "prompt acceptance after the general contract has been awarded." The plaintiff, a contractor in Washington, got one of these on the twenty-eighth, and on the same day the defendant learned its mistake and telegraphed all the contractors to whom it had sent the offer, that it withdrew it and would substitute a new one at about double the amount of the old. This withdrawal reached the plaintiff at Washington on the afternoon of the same day, but not until after it had put in a bid at Harrisburg at a lump sum, based as to linoleum upon the prices quoted by the defendant. The public authorities accepted the plaintiff's bid on

December thirtieth, the defendant having meanwhile written a letter of confirmation of its withdrawal, received on the thirty-first. The plaintiff formally accepted the offer on January second, and, as the defendant persisted in declining to recognize the existence of a contract, sued it for damages on a breach.

Unless there are circumstances to take it out of the ordinary doctrine, since the offer was withdrawn before it was accepted, the acceptance was too late. Restatement of Contracts, § 35. To meet this the plaintiff argues as follows: It was a reasonable implication from the defendant's offer that it should be irrevocable in case the plaintiff acted upon it, that is to say, used the prices quoted in making its bid, thus putting itself in a position from which it could not withdraw without great loss. While it might have withdrawn its bid after receiving the revocation, the time had passed to submit another, and as the item of linoleum was a very trifling part of the cost of the whole building, it would have been an unreasonable hardship to expect it to lose the contract on that account, and probably forfeit its deposit. While it is true that the plaintiff might in advance have secured a contract conditional upon the success of its bid, this was not what the defendant suggested. It understood that the contractors would use its offer in their bids, and would thus in fact commit themselves to supplying the linoleum at the proposed prices. The inevitable implication from all this was that when the contractors acted upon it, they accepted the offer and promised to pay for the linoleum, in case their bid were accepted.

It was of course possible for the parties to make such a contract, and the question is merely as to what they meant; that is, what is to be imputed to the words they used. Whatever plausibility there is in the argument, is in the fact that the defendant must have known the predicament in which the contractors would be put if it withdrew its offer after the bids went in. However, it seems entirely clear that the contractors did not suppose that they accepted the offer merely by putting in their bids. If, for example, the successful one had repudiated the contract with the public authorities after it had been awarded to him, certainly the defendant could not have sued him for a breach. If he had become bankrupt, the defendant could not prove against his estate. It seems plain therefore that there was no contract between them. And if there be any doubt as to this, the language of the offer sets it at rest. The phrase, "if successful in being awarded this contract," is scarcely met by the mere use of the prices in the bids. Surely such a use was not an "award" of the contract to the defendant. Again, the phrase, "we are offering these prices for . . . prompt acceptance after the general contract has been awarded," looks to the usual communication of an acceptance, and precludes the idea that the use of the offer in the bidding shall be the equivalent. It may indeed be argued that this last language contemplated no more then an early notice that the offer had been accepted, the actual acceptance being the bid, but that would wrench its natural meaning too far, especially in the light of the preceding phrase. The contractors had a ready escape from their difficulty by insisting upon a contract before they used the figures; and in commercial transactions it does not in the end promote justice to seek strained interpretations in aid of those who do not protect themselves.

But the plaintiff says that even though no bilateral contract was made, the defendant should be held under the doctrine of "promissory estoppel." This is to be chiefly found in those cases where persons subscribe to a venture, usually charitable, and are held to their promises after it has been completed. It has been applied much more broadly, however, and has now been generalized in section 90, of the Restatement of Contracts. We may arguendo accept it as it there reads, for it does not apply to the case at bar. Offers are ordinarily made in exchange for a consideration, either a counter-promise or some other act which the promisor wishes to secure. In such cases they propose bargains; they presuppose that each promise or performance is an inducement to the other. Wisconsin, etc., Ry. v. Powers, 191 U. S. 379, 386, 387, 24 S. Ct. 107, 48 L. Ed. 229; Banning Co. v. California, 240 U. S. 142, 152, 153, 36 S. Ct. 338, 60 L. Ed. 569. But a man may make a promise without expecting an equivalent; a donative promise, conditional or absolute. The common law provided for such by sealed instruments, and it is unfortunate that these are no longer generally available. The doctrine of "promissory estoppel" is to avoid the harsh results of allowing the promisor in such a case to repudiate, when the promisee has acted in reliance upon the promise. Siegel v. Spear & Co., 234 N. Y. 479, 138 N. E. 414, 26 A. L. R. 1205. Cf. Allegheny College v. National Bank, 246 N. Y. 369, 159 N. E. 173, 57 L. R. A. 980. But an offer for an exchange is not meant to become a promise until a consideration has been received, either a counter-promise or whatever else is stipulated. To extend it would be to hold the offeror regardless of the stipulated condition of his offer. In the case at bar the defendant offered to deliver the linoleum in exchange for the plaintiff's acceptance, not for its bid, which was a matter of indifference to it. That offer could become a promise to deliver only when the equivalent was received; that is, when the plaintiff promised to take and pay for it. There is no room in such a situation for the doctrine of "promissory estoppel."

Nor can the offer be regarded as of an option, giving the plaintiff the right seasonably to accept the linoleum at the quoted prices if its bid was accepted, but not binding it to take and pay, if it could get a better bargain elsewhere. There is not the least reason to suppose that the defendant meant to subject itself to such one-sided obligation. True, if so construed, the doctrine of "promissory estoppel" might apply, the plaintiff having acted in reliance upon it, though, so far as we have found, the decisions are otherwise. Ganss v. Guffey Petroleum Co., 125 App. Div. 760, 110 N. Y. S.

176; Comstock v. North, 88 Miss. 754, 41 So. 374. As to that, however, we need not declare ourselves.

Judgment affirmed.

NOTES AND QUESTIONS

1.   *No Party Bound Model.* Judge Hand determined that while the subcontractor made an offer on December 28, the terms or conditions of that offer indicated it could not be accepted until after the general contractor was awarded the contract and notified the subcontractor of acceptance. The general contractor bid was accepted on December 30, and it formally "accepted" the subcontract bid on January 2. However, on December 28, the same day it had submitted its original bid, the subcontractor revoked the bid and substituted one for double the amount. Unfortunately, the general contractor had already used the first subcontractor bid to submit its own general bid. Assuming the general contractor acted reasonably and fairly, was it fair for Judge Hand to allocate the risk of subcontractor bid mistake to the general contractor? What policy justified allocating the risk of error away from the party committing the error, especially when another party justifiably relied on the bid? Who is in the best position to prevent the error—the person who made it or another?

2.   *Option contract analysis.* At the time *James Baird Co.* was released in 1933, the 1932 Restatement (First) of Contracts § 45 was released. That section provided that an offer to enter into a unilateral contract stated an implied-in-law subsidiary promise not to revoke the offer after the offeree tendered or began the requested performance. Why did Judge Hand not apply this rule to the case? The citation to Restatement (First) of Contracts § 35 is the parallel to Restatement (Second) of Contracts § 36 on the termination of an offer. It appears that Judge Hand characterized the subcontractor's offer as one to enter a bilateral contract. If Judge Hand thought the subcontractor's offer was an invitation to enter a bilateral contract and not a unilateral contract, does the first restatement provide any additional help? Restatement (First) of Contracts § 24 included an "option" concept in the definition of an offer: "An offer is also a contract, commonly called an option, if the requisites of a formal or an informal contract exist." Under that definition, what is required to make an offer irrevocable as an option? First, a promise of irrevocability must be found, either expressed by the parties or implied by the court. Next, that promise must be made enforceable by some legal doctrine— either bargained-for consideration or expected detrimental reliance in the form of promissory estoppel.

Judge Hand rejects promissory estoppel as found in Restatement (First) of Contracts § 90. Why? Does he think that promissory estoppel simply does not apply to an offer? If so, is this because he thinks an offer is not a promise or because he interprets the offer in this case as demanding consideration? Stated another way, if the offer had not been qualified by specific acceptance language, do you think that Judge Hand would have applied promissory estoppel to make the offer irrevocable once used? Judge Hand acknowledged that if the subcontractor had made an express promise to keep its offer open, the general contractor's reliance "might" have made the promise enforceable under promissory estoppel. Does this suggest that Judge Hand thought no express promise was made and none could be implied? Even if such a promise was implied, do you think Judge Hand would have applied promissory estoppel? What do you think Judge Hand meant by the following language: "The contractors had a ready escape from their difficulty by insisting upon a contract before they used the figures; and in commercial transactions it does not in the end promote justice to seek strained interpretations in aid of those who do not protect themselves"

3.   *Offer not a promise.* It appears that Judge Hand does not think an offer is a promise: "But an offer for an exchange is not meant to become a promise until a consideration has been received, either a counter-promise or whatever else is stipulated. To extend it would be to hold the offeror regardless of the stipulated condition of his offer." Does Judge Hand confuse the definition of a "promise" with a "contract"? He suggests that an offer does not become a promise until the stipulated consideration is received. Has he confused the definition of a promise with a theory of legal obligation making a promise enforceable? Some scholars support this notion. See Robert Samek, "Performance Utterances and the Concept of Contracts," 43 Australian J. Phil. 196, 204–205 (1965) and Peter Meijes Tiersma, "Reassessing Unilateral Contracts: The Role of Offer, Acceptance and Promise," 26 U. C. Davis L. Rev. 1, 20–21 (1992). A better reasoned approach might consider an offer to be a promise subject to a condition. This allows a more reasoned approach to applying promissory estoppel and other promissory notions. See Melvin A. Eisenberg, "The Revocation of Offers," 2004 Wis. L. Rev. 271, 273–276 (2004) ("The position that an offer is not a promise is incorrect.").

4.   *Fear of contract.* Judge Hand's refusal to create contractual obligations in this case may be an example of what Roy Kreitner calls "fear of contract." See Roy Kreitner, "Fear of Contract,"2004 Wis. L. Rev. 429 (2004). Kreitner observes that many formalist and neo-formalist theories of contract law seem to be grounded in the proposition that "classical legal thought advanced an idea of absolute liability within strictly confined boundaries. . . ." See id. at 431. That is, for Kreitner, formalist and neo-formalist contract theories suggest that relationships that are properly within the bounds of contract law—such as a fully negotiated agreement between parties of equal bargaining power involving offer, acceptance, and consideration—create an absolute liability on the part of the parties to perform or, in the event of breach, pay damages. Within that sphere, the parties are free to craft any scheme of reciprocal rights and duties they wish, regardless of the reasonableness of that scheme in the absence of a contract. Thus, for instance, two parties can contract to conduct a boxing match that, in the absence of the contract (and compliance with state regulations), would otherwise violate both tort standards of care and criminal law. Moreover, the remedy for breach of that contract would be based upon the contract standard of attempting to compensate the non-breaching party sufficiently to put that party in the position he would have occupied had

the contract been fully performed, rather than a tort standard of liability based upon the non-breaching party's detrimental change of position.

Because of the extraordinary scope of contractual relations in defining relationships between parties and because of the absolute liability attendant upon parties who enter those relationships, Kreitner characterizes the formalist and neo-formalist positions as rejecting attempts by courts to impose contractual liability in situations where the parties did not intend it. Thus, some formalist scholars, according to Kreitner, oppose creation of contractual liability on the basis of promissory estoppel because that doctrine imposes an unassented-to contract on the basis of an essentially tort-like theory of liability (detrimental reliance). See id. at 433–34, 455 ("Global conceptual formalists fear the expansion of contractual liability beyond the very nature of contract and beyond its inherent justifications within corrective justice. Another way of putting this is that they fear imposition of contractual liability that is not directly tied to consent.").

Kreitner suggests that this fear of contract arises from a singular focus on contract as an "isolated exchange, where the parties make a private law for themselves." See id. at 455. While that focus may be useful in some circumstances, Kreitner also suggests that contract law should be viewed as a public good that facilitates cooperative exchange and increases social welfare: "Contract . . . is best understood as a framework for cooperation among societal agents. It serves as an infrastructure that provides a means to carry out a range of different kinds of collaborative projects. The infrastructure, in turn, provides benefits even to those who are not using it at any given moment, because it structures in productive ways the interactions and potential interactions among past, present, and future participants." Id. Which of these visions is more compelling as an organizing or justifying force for enforcement of contract promises? What is the purpose of contract law for individuals? For society in general? When, if ever, should the interests of the polity justify judicial imposition of terms into ostensibly private contracts to which the parties themselves never agreed?

DRENNAN v. STAR PAVING COMPANY

Supreme Court of California (en banc)
51 Cal.2d 409, 333 P.2d 757 (1958)

TRAYNOR, Justice.*

Defendant appeals from a judgment for plaintiff in an action to recover damages caused by defendant's refusal to perform certain paving work according to a bid it submitted to plaintiff.

---

*   Justice Roger Traynor (1900–1983) was an Associate Justice of the California Supreme Court from 1940–1964 and Chief Justice from 1964–1970. Traynor was generally viewed as one of the finest judges in the United States never to sit on the United States Supreme Court. He is most famous for his opinion in Greenman v. Yuba Power Products, Inc., 59 Cal. 2d 57, 377 P.2d 897, 27 Cal.Rptr. 697 (1963), in which he developed the theory of strict liability in tort. Prior to this 1963 opinion and in response to the plight of seriously injured plaintiffs otherwise required to prove

On July 28, 1955, plaintiff, a licensed general contractor, was preparing a bid on the 'Monte Vista School Job' in the Lancaster school district. Bids had to be submitted before 8:00 p.m. Plaintiff testified that it was customary in that area for general contractors to receive the bids of subcontractors by telephone on the day set for bidding and to rely on them in computing their own bids. Thus on that day plaintiff's secretary, Mrs. Johnson, received by telephone between fifty and seventy-five subcontractors' bids for various parts of the school job. As each bid came in, she wrote it on a special form, which she brought into plaintiff's office. He then posted it on a master cost sheet setting forth the names and bids of all subcontractors. His own bid had to include the names of subcontractors who were to perform one-half of one per cent or more of the construction work, and he had also to provide a bidder's bond of ten per cent of his total bid of $317,385 as a guarantee that he would enter the contract if awarded the work.

Late in the afternoon, Mrs. Johnson had a telephone conversation with Kenneth R. Hoon, an estimator for defendant. He gave his name and telephone number and stated that he was bidding for defendant for the paving work at the Monte Vista School according to plans and specifications and that his bid was $7,131.60. At Mrs. Johnson's request he repeated his bid. Plaintiff listened to the bid over an extension telephone in his office and posted it on the master sheet after receiving the bid form from Mrs. Johnson. Defendant's was the lowest bid for the paving. Plaintiff computed his own bid accordingly and submitted it with the name of defendant as the subcontractor for the paving. When the bids were opened on July 28th, plaintiff's proved to be the lowest, and he was awarded the contract.

On his way to Los Angeles the next morning plaintiff stopped at defendant's office. The first person he met was defendant's construction engineer, Mr. Oppenheimer. Plaintiff testified:

> I introduced myself and he immediately told me that they had made a mistake in their bid to me the night before, they couldn't do it for the price they had bid, and I told him I would expect him to carry through with their original bid because I had used it in compiling my bid and the job was being awarded them. And I would have to go and do the job according to my bid and I would expect them to do the same.

Defendant refused to do the paving work for less than $15,000. Plaintiff testified that he "got figures from other people" and after trying

---

negligence against manufacturers, courts developed various theories of express and implied manufacturer warranties. These legal warranty fictions became strained over time. In Greenman, Justice Traynor discarded those theories to hold manufacturers strictly liable in defective product liability cases regardless of the absence of negligence or a fictional warranty.

for several months to get as low a bid as possible engaged L & H Paving Company, a firm in Lancaster, to do the work for $10,948.60.

The trial court found on substantial evidence that defendant made a definite offer to do the paving on the Monte Vista job according to the plans and specifications for $7,131.60, and that plaintiff relied on defendant's bid in computing his own bid for the school job and naming defendant therein as the subcontractor for the paving work. Accordingly, it entered judgment for plaintiff in the amount of $3,817.00 (the difference between defendant's bid and the cost of the paving to plaintiff) plus costs.

Defendant contends that there was no enforceable contract between the parties on the ground that it made a revocable offer and revoked it before plaintiff communicated his acceptance to defendant.

There is no evidence that defendant offered to make its bid irrevocable in exchange for plaintiff's use of its figures in computing his bid. Nor is there evidence that would warrant interpreting plaintiff's use of defendant's bid as the acceptance thereof, binding plaintiff, on condition he received the main contract, to award the subcontract to defendant. In sum, there was neither an option supported by consideration nor a bilateral contract binding on both parties.

Plaintiff contends, however, that he relied to his detriment on defendant's offer and that defendant must therefore answer in damages for its refusal to perform. Thus the question is squarely presented: Did plaintiff's reliance make defendant's offer irrevocable?

Section 90 of the Restatement of Contracts states:

> A promise which the promisor should reasonably expect to induce action or forbearance of a definite and substantial character on the part of the promisee and which does induce such action or forbearance is binding if injustice can be avoided only by enforcement of the promise.

This rule applies in this state. Edmonds v. County of Los Angeles, 40 Cal. 2d 642, 255 P. 2d 772. . . .

Defendant's offer constituted a promise to perform on such conditions as were stated expressly or by implication therein or annexed thereto by operation of law. (See 1 Williston, Contracts (3rd. ed.), § 24A, p. 56, § 61, p. 196.) Defendant had reason to expect that if its bid proved the lowest, it would be used by plaintiff. It induced "action . . . of a definite and substantial character on the part of the promisee."

Had defendant's bid expressly stated or clearly implied that it was revocable at any time before acceptance we would treat it accordingly. It was silent on revocation, however, and we must therefore determine whether there are conditions to the right of revocation imposed by law or reasonably inferable in fact. In the analogous problem of an offer for a unilateral contract, the theory is now obsolete that the offer is revocable at any time before complete performance. Thus section 45 of the Restatement of Contracts provides:

> If an offer for a unilateral contract is made, and part of the consideration requested in the offer is given or tendered by the offeree in response thereto, the offeror is bound by a contract, the duty of immediate performance of which is conditional on the full consideration being given or tendered within the time stated in the offer, or, if no time is stated therein, within a reasonable time.

In explanation, comment b states that the:

> main offer includes as a subsidiary promise, necessarily implied, that if part of the requested performance is given, the offeror will not revoke his offer, and that if tender is made it will be accepted. Part performance or tender may thus furnish consideration for the subsidiary promise. Moreover, merely acting in justifiable reliance on an offer may in some cases serve as sufficient reason for making a promise binding (see § 90).

Whether implied in fact or law, the subsidiary promise serves to preclude the injustice that would result if the offer could be revoked after the offeree had acted in detrimental reliance thereon. Reasonable reliance resulting in a foreseeable prejudicial change in position affords a compelling basis also for implying a subsidiary promise not to revoke an offer for a bilateral contract.

The absence of consideration is not fatal to the enforcement of such a promise. It is true that in the case of unilateral contracts the Restatement finds consideration for the implied subsidiary promise in the part performance of the bargained-for exchange, but its reference to section 90 makes clear that consideration for such a promise is not always necessary. The very purpose of section 90 is to make a promise binding even though there was no consideration "in the sense of something that is bargained for and given in exchange." (See 1 Corbin, Contracts 634 et seq.) Reasonable reliance serves to hold the offeror in lieu of the consideration ordinarily required to make the offer binding. In a case involving similar facts the Supreme Court of South Dakota stated that:

> [W]e believe that reason and justice demand that the doctrine (of section 90) be applied to the present facts. We cannot believe that by accepting this doctrine as controlling in the state of facts before us we will abolish the requirement of a consideration in contract cases, in any different sense than an ordinary estoppel abolishes some legal requirement in its application. We are of the opinion, therefore, that the defendants in executing the agreement (which was not supported by consideration) made a promise which they

should have reasonably expected would induce the plaintiff to submit a bid based thereon to the Government, that such promise did induce this action, and that injustice can be avoided only by enforcement of the promise.

Northwestern Engineering Co. v. Ellerman, 69 S.D. 397, 408, 10 N.W. 2d 879, 884; . . . . cf. James Baird Co. v. Gimbel Bros., 2 Cir., 64 F. 2d 344.

When plaintiff used defendant's offer in computing his own bid, he bound himself to perform in reliance on defendant's terms. Though defendant did not bargain for this use of its bid neither did defendant make it idly, indifferent to whether it would be used or not. On the contrary it is reasonable to suppose that defendant submitted its bid to obtain the subcontract. It was bound to realize the substantial possibility that its bid would be the lowest, and that it would be included by plaintiff in his bid. It was to its own interest that the contractor be awarded the general contract; the lower the subcontract bid, the lower the general contractor's bid was likely to be and the greater its chance of acceptance and hence the greater defendant's chance of getting the paving subcontract. Defendant had reason not only to expect plaintiff to rely on its bid but to want him to. Clearly defendant had a stake in plaintiff's reliance on its bid. Given this interest and the fact that plaintiff is bound by his own bid, it is only fair that plaintiff should have at least an opportunity to accept defendant's bid after the general contract has been awarded to him.

It bears noting that a general contractor is not free to delay acceptance after he has been awarded the general contract in the hope of getting a better price. Nor can he reopen bargaining with the subcontractor and at the same time claim a continuing right to accept the original offer. See, R. J. Daum Const. Co. v. Child, Utah, 247 P. 2d 817, 823. In the present case plaintiff promptly informed defendant that plaintiff was being awarded the job and that the subcontract was being awarded to defendant.

Defendant contends, however, that its bid was the result of mistake and that it was therefore entitled to revoke it. It relies on the rescission cases of M. F. Kemper Const. Co. v. City of Los Angeles, 37 Cal. 2d 696, 235 P. 2d 7, and Brunzell Const. Co. v. G. J. Weisbrod, Inc., 134 Cal. App. 2d 278, 285 P. 2d 989. . . . In those cases, however, the bidder's mistake was known or should have been known to the offeree, and the offeree could be placed in status quo. Of course, if plaintiff had reason to believe that defendant's bid was in error, he could not justifiably rely on it, and section 90 would afford no basis for enforcing it. Robert Gordon, Inc. v. Ingersoll-Rand, Inc., 7 Cir., 117 F. 2d 654, 660. Plaintiff, however, had no reason to know that defendant had made a mistake in submitting its bid, since there was usually a variance of 160 per cent between the highest and lowest bids for paving in the desert around Lancaster. He committed himself to performing the main contract in reliance on defendant's figures. Under these circumstances defendant's mistake, far from relieving it of its obligation, constitutes an additional reason for enforcing it, for it misled plaintiff as to the cost of doing the paving. Even had it been clearly understood that defendant's offer was revocable until accepted, it would not necessarily follow that defendant had no duty to exercise reasonable care in preparing its bid. It presented its bid with knowledge of the substantial possibility that it would be used by plaintiff; it could foresee the harm that would ensue from an erroneous underestimate of the cost. Moreover, it was motivated by its own business interest. Whether or not these considerations alone would justify recovery for negligence had the case been tried on that theory (see Biakanja v. Irving, 49 Cal.2d 647, 650, 320 P.2d 16), they are persuasive that defendant's mistake should not defeat recovery under the rule of section 90 of the Restatement of Contracts. As between the subcontractor who made the bid and the general contractor who reasonably relied on it, the loss resulting from the mistake should fall on the party who caused it.

Leo F. Piazza Paving Co. v. Bebek & Brkich, 141 Cal. App. 2d 226, 296 P. 2d 368, 371, and Bard v. Kent, 19 Cal. 2d 449, 122 P. 2d 8, 139 A.L.R. 1032, are not to the contrary. In the Piazza case the court sustained a finding that defendants intended, not to make a firm bid, but only to give the plaintiff 'some kind of an idea to use' in making its bid; there was evidence that the defendants had told plaintiff they were unsure of the significance of the specifications. There was thus no offer, promise, or representation on which the defendants should reasonably have expected the plaintiff to rely. The Bard case held that an option not supported by consideration was revoked by the death of the optionor. The issue of recovery under the rule of section 90 was not pleaded at the trial, and it does not appear that the offeree's reliance was "of a definite and substantial character" so that injustice could be avoided "only by the enforcement of the promise."

There is no merit in defendant's contention that plaintiff failed to state a cause of action, on the ground that the complaint failed to allege that plaintiff attempted to mitigate the damages or that they could not have been mitigated. Plaintiff alleged that after defendant's default, "plaintiff had to procure the services of the L & H Co. to perform said asphaltic paving for the sum of $10,948.60." Plaintiff's uncontradicted evidence showed that he spent several months trying to get bids from other subcontractors and that he took the lowest bid. Clearly he acted reasonably to mitigate damages. In any event any uncertainty in plaintiff's allegation as to damages could have been raised by special demurrer. Code Civ. Proc. § 430, subd. 9. It was not so raised and was therefore waived. Code Civ. Proc. § 434.

The judgment is affirmed.

GIBSON C. J., and SHENK, SCHAUER, SPENCE and McCOMB, JJ., concur.

NOTES AND QUESTIONS

1.   *Comparing* Baird *and* Drennan. The *Drennan* case was decided in 1958, after the 1932 release of the first restatement but before the second restatement in 1979. As a result, both *Baird* and *Drennan* arose under the same restatement, although the *Baird* court applied Pennsylvania law and the *Drennan* court applied California law. Do you think state law accounts for the different outcomes? If the two cases apply the same law, do you think the different language or terms of the offer accounts for the different outcomes? Both cases determined that there was no bilateral contract formed under classical contract analysis: no offer and acceptance. However, unlike Judge Hand in *Baird*, Judge Traynor in *Drennan* determined that promissory estoppel applied. Given the *Drennan* case reference to *Baird*, is it possible that Judge Traynor intended to rebuke the earlier approach and set the law on a different course? See Alfred S. Konefsky, "Freedom and Interdependence in Twentieth-Century Contract Law: Traynor and Hand and Promissory Estoppel," 65 U. Cin. L. Rev. 1169 (1997).

2.   *Effect on second Restatement.* Both *Baird* and *Drennan* were decided after the first restatement but well before the second restatement. Restatement (Second) of Contracts § 87(2) is new and has no direct counterpart in the first restatement. Illustration 6 to § 87(2) was explicitly based upon *Drennan*:

> 6.   A submits a written offer for paving work to be used by B as a partial basis for B's bid as general contractor on a large building. As A knows, B is required to name his subcontractors in his general bid. B uses A's offer and B's bid is accepted. A's offer is irrevocable until B had a reasonable opportunity to notify A of the award and B's acceptance of A's offer.

It is thus clear that if *Baird* and *Drennan* represent divergent views of the same problem, Judge Traynor's view prevailed in terms of influencing the second restatement.

3.   *Implied subsidiary promise.* Judge Traynor implies a subcontractor promise to keep its bid open or irrevocable until the general contractor has an opportunity to be awarded the bid contract and notify the subcontractor of acceptance. Is the promise implied-in-law or implied-in-fact? A promise is not enforceable absent a theory of legal obligation. Does Judge Traynor use a theory of consideration or a theory of reliance in the form of promissory estoppel? Does it make a difference? Judge Hand would not imply such a subsidiary promise in *Baird*. If Star Paving had made clear that its bid was revocable, would Justice Traynor respect that intent? What is the meaning of the following statement from *Drennan*: "Had defendant's bid expressly stated or clearly implied that it was revocable at any time before acceptance we would treat it accordingly."? How would you compare the language of Judge Hand: "The contractors had a ready escape from their difficulty by insisting upon a

contract before they used the figures; and in commercial transactions it does not in the end promote justice to seek strained interpretations in aid of those who do not protect themselves."?

If these two quotations agree that both judges would respect the clearly expressed intent of the subcontractor, then *Baird* and *Drennan* can be read to merely express default rules. Which default rule do you favor: A presumption that favors the general contractor unless the subcontractor states otherwise (*Drennan*) or one that favors the subcontractor unless the general contractor specifies otherwise (*Baird*)? As between a general contractor and a subcontractor, who might be better equipped to understand the rules of the bidding game and negate the default rule?

4. *Damages.* The *Drennan* case awarded the general contractor damages in the amount of $3,817, the difference between the Star Paving bid of $7,131 and L & H Paving bid of $10,948. Is this damage award necessary to compensate the general contractor for a reliance loss, an expectancy loss, or both?

5. *Drennan limitations.* Having created an implication of irrevocability, Judge Traynor realizes that a general contractor might act opportunistically between the time it is awarded the bid and the time it accepts the subcontractor bid. Accordingly, he invokes limitations under which the subcontractor bid will not be irrevocable: bid shopping and bid chopping. Under bid shopping, the general contractor tries to find a cheaper bid from another subcontractor using the bound subcontractor bid as the ceiling. Under bid chopping, the general contractor tries to renegotiate the subcontractor's bid to induce it to lower the bid. For a discussion of both, see Michael L. Closen and Donald G. Weiland, "The Construction Industry Bidding Cases: Application of Traditional Contract, Promissory Estoppel, and Other Theories to the Relations Between General Contractors and Subcontractors," 13 J. Marshall L. Rev. 565, 566 (1980).

6. *Irrevocable by statute.* Restatement (Second) of Contracts § 87(1)(b) provides that an offer is binding as an option contract if it is "made irrevocable by statute." State and federal government contract rules often provide that submitted bids are not revocable after the bid-opening date.

BERRYMAN V. KMOCH

Supreme Court of Kansas
221 Kan. 304, 559 P.2d 790 (1977)

FROMME, Justice.

Wade Berryman, a landowner, filed this declaratory judgment action to have an option contract declared null and void. Norbert H. Kmoch, the optionee, answered and counter-claimed seeking damages for Berryman's failure to convey the land. After depositions were taken and discovery proceedings completed both parties filed separate motions for summary judgment. The trial court entered a summary judgment for plaintiff and held the option was granted without consideration, was in effect an offer to sell subject to withdrawal at any time prior to acceptance and was withdrawn in July, 1973, prior to its being exercised by Kmoch. Kmoch has appealed.

The option agreement dated June 19, 1973, was signed by Wade Berryman of Meade, Kansas, and was addressed to Mr. Norbert H. Kmoch, 1155 Ash Street, Denver, Colorado. The granting clause provided:

> For $10.00 and other valuable consideration, I hereby grant unto you or your assigns an option for 120 days after date to purchase the following described real estate: (Then followed the legal description of 960 acres of land located in Stanton County, Kansas.)

The balance of the option agreement sets forth the terms of purchase including the price for the land and the growing crops, the water rights and irrigation equipment included in the sale, the time possession was to be delivered to the purchaser, and other provisions not pertinent to the questions presented here on appeal.

Before examining the questions raised on appeal it will be helpful to set forth a few of the facts admitted and on which there is no dispute. Berryman was the owner of the land. Kmoch was a Colorado real estate broker. A third person, Samuel N. Goertz, was a Nebraska agricultural consultant. Goertz learned that Berryman was interested in selling the land and talked to Berryman about obtaining an option on the land for Kmoch. Goertz talked to Kmoch and Kmoch prepared the option contract dated June 19, 1973. Goertz and Kmoch flew to Johnson, Kansas, where a meeting with Berryman had been arranged. At this meeting the option agreement was signed by Berryman. Although the agreement recited the option was granted "for $10.00 and other valuable consideration," the $10.00 was not paid.

The next conversation between Berryman and Kmoch occurred during the latter part of July, 1973. Berryman called Kmoch by telephone and asked to be released from the option agreement. Nothing definite was worked out between them. Berryman sold the land to another person. In August, Kmoch decided to exercise the option and went to the Federal Land Bank representative in Garden City, Kansas, to make arrangements to purchase the land. He was then informed by the bank representative that the land had been sold by Berryman. Kmoch then recorded the option agreement in Stanton County. After a telephone conversation with Berryman was unproductive, Kmoch sent a letter to Berryman in October, 1973, attempting to exercise his option on the land. Berryman responded by bringing the present action to have the option declared null and void.

Appellant, Kmoch, acknowledges that the $10.00 cash consideration recited in the option agreement was never paid. However, he points out the agreement included a provision for 'other valuable consideration' and that he should have been permitted to introduce evidence to establish time spent and expenses incurred in an effort to interest others in joining him in acquiring the land. He points to the deposition testimony of Goertz and another man by the name of Robert Harris, who had examined the land under option. Their services were sought by Kmoch to obtain a farm report on the land which might interest other investors. In addition appellant argues that promissory estoppel should have been applied by the trial court as a substitute for consideration.

An option contract to purchase land to be binding must be supported by consideration the same as any other contract. If no consideration was given in the present case the trial court correctly found there was no more than a continuing offer to sell. An option contract which is not supported by consideration is a mere offer to sell which may be withdrawn at any time prior to acceptance. . . .

The appellant in arguing his points on appeal makes, what appears to be, a self-defeating contention that the parol evidence rule excludes evidence of non-payment of the consideration expressed in the written instrument. K.S.A. 16–108 provides:

> The want or failure in the whole or in part, of the consideration of a written contract, may be shown as a defense, total or partial, as the case may be, in an action on such contract, brought by one who is not an innocent holder in good faith.

Neither of the parties in this case can be classified as an innocent holder in good faith. They are both subject to the rule that parol evidence to establish a failure to pay a cash payment acknowledged in a written contract does not violate the parol evidence rule. (First Construction Co., Inc. v. Gallup, 204 Kan. 73, Syl. 3, 460 P. 2d 594.)

We turn next to appellant's contention that the option contract should have been enforceable under the doctrine of promissory estoppel. This doctrine has been discussed in Marker v. Preferred Fire Ins. Co., 211 Kan. 427, 506 P.2 d 1163, and in Kirkpatrick v. Seneca National Bank, 213 Kan. 61, 515 P. 2d 781. In Marker it is held:

> In order for the doctrine of promissory estoppel to be invoked the evidence must show that the promise was made under circumstances where the promisor intended and reasonably expected that the promise would be relied upon by the promisee and further that the promisee acted reasonably in relying upon the promise. Furthermore promissory estoppel should be applied only if a refusal to enforce it would be virtually to sanction the perpetration of fraud or would result in other injustice. (211 Kan. 427, Syl. 4, 506 P. 2d 1163.)

In Kirkpatrick it is held:

> Under the doctrine of promissory estoppel a promise is binding
> and will be enforced when it is a promise which the promisor
> should reasonably expect to induce action or forbearance of a
> definite and substantial character on the part of the promisee and
> which does induce such action or forbearance and if injustice can
> be avoided only by enforcement of the promise. (213 Kan. 61, Syl.
> 1, 515 P. 2d 781.)

In order for the doctrine of promissory estoppel to be invoked as a
substitute for consideration the evidence must show (1) the promise was
made under such circumstances that the promisor reasonably expected the
promisee to act in reliance on the promise, (2) the promisee acted as could
reasonably be expected in relying on the promise, and (3) a refusal by the
court to enforce the promise must be virtually to sanction the perpetration
of fraud or must result in other injustice.

The requirements are not met here. This was an option contract
promising to sell the land to appellant. It was not a contract listing the real
estate with Kmoch for sale to others. Kmoch was familiar with real estate
contracts and personally drew up the present option. He knew no
consideration was paid for the same and that it had the effect of a
continuing offer subject to withdrawal at any time before acceptance. The
acts which appellant urges as consideration conferred no special benefit on
the promisor or on his land. The evidence which appellant desires to
introduce in support of promissory estoppel does not relate to acts which
could reasonably be expected as a result of extending the option promise.
It relates to time, effort, and expense incurred in an attempt to interest
other investors in this particular land. The appellant chose the form of the
contract. It was not a contract listing the land for sale with one entrusted
with duties and obligations to produce a buyer. The appellant was not
obligated to do anything and no basis for promissory estoppel could be
shown by the evidence proposed.

An option contract can be made binding and irrevocable by subsequent
action in reliance upon it even though such action is neither requested nor
given in exchange for the option promise. An option promise is no different
from other promises in this respect but cases are rare in which an option
holder will be reasonably induced to change his position in reliance upon
an option promise that is neither under seal nor made binding by a
consideration, or in which the option promisor has reason to expect such
change of position. (1A Corbin on Contracts, § 263, pp. 502–504.)

When an option is conditioned upon a performance of certain acts, the
performance of the acts may constitute a consideration to uphold a contract
for option; but there is no such condition imposed if the acts were not
intended to benefit nor were they incurred on behalf of the optionor.

The appellant argues that to assume Berryman gave the option without expecting something from him in return is to avoid the realities of the business world and that consideration was encompassed by a promise for a promise. The difficulty with that argument is apparent. Appellant did not promise to purchase the land. He was required to do nothing and any assertion that Berryman expected him to raise and pay money for the land as consideration for the option confuses motive with consideration.

In 17 Am. Jur. 2d, Contracts, s 93, pp. 436, 437, it is said:

The motive which prompts one to enter into a contract and the consideration for the contract are distinct and different things. . . . These inducements are not . . . either legal or equitable consideration, and actually compose no part of the contract

In 1 Williston on Contracts, 3rd Ed., s 111, p. 439, it is stated:

Though desire to obtain the consideration for a promise may be, and ordinarily is, the motive inducing the promisor to enter into a contract, yet this is not essential nor, on the other hand, can any motive serve in itself as consideration

Appellant here confuses Berryman's possible motives—to sell the land—with consideration given. The fact Berryman expected appellant to expend time and money to find a buyer is really irrelevant because he was not bound to do so. He made no promise legally enforceable by Berryman to that effect. To be sufficient consideration, a promise must impose a legal obligation on the promisor. (17 Am. Jur. 2d, Contracts, § 105, pp. 450–451.) As stated in 1A Corbin on Contracts, § 263, p. 505:

So, if the only consideration is an illusory promise, there is no contract and no binding option, although there may still be an operative offer and a power of acceptance.

Time and money spent by a party in trying to sell property for which he holds an option cannot be construed as a consideration to the party from whom he has secured the option. . . .

Two cases relied on by appellant to support his position are Talbott v. Nibert, supra, and Steel v. Eagle, 207 Kan. 146, 483 P. 2d 1063. They are not persuasive and are readily distinguishable on the facts.

In Talbott the plaintiff had acquired an option to purchase majority stock interests in an oil drilling company from another stockholder. In reliance on the option plaintiff personally obtained valuable drilling contracts for the company, paid off a $23,000.00 mortgage on a drilling rig and pulled the company out of financial straits. During this time the stock had increased in value from $90.00 per share to $250.00 per share, largely as a result of plaintiff's efforts. It was plaintiff's intention to acquire a controlling interest in the company by exercising the option, this the optionor knew. The court found the option-offer was duly accepted and the purchase price was tendered before revocation. In our present case the option-offer was withdrawn before acceptance. We will discuss the withdrawal of the option later in this opinion.

In Steel the option was for the sale of a milling company. The option agreement stated that the optionee promised to place $5,000.00 with an escrow agent no later than a specified time in the future and that if the option was not exercised according to its terms the $5,000.00 would be forfeited. It was held that the option was adequately supported by consideration, a promise for a promise. The optionor granted the option and promised to transfer title to the company. The optionee promised to pay $5,000.00 as evidence of good faith, said sum to be forfeited in event the option was not exercised. This is not the case here. Our present option recited a completed payment of $10.00, even though it had not been paid. Payment during the option period was not contemplated by either party and the tender of the $10.00 was not made by defendant-appellant in his counter-claim when that pleading was filed.

Now we turn to the question of revocation or withdrawal of the option-promise before acceptance.

Where an offer is for the sale of an interest in land or in other things, if the offeror, after making the offer, sells or contracts to sell the interest to another person, and the offeree acquires reliable information of that fact, before he has exercised his power of creating a contract by acceptance of the offer, the offer is revoked.

In Restatement of the Law, Second, Contracts, § 42, p. 96, it is said:

An offeree's power of acceptance is terminated when the offeror takes definite action inconsistent with an intention to enter into the proposed contract and the offeree acquires reliable information to that effect.

The appellant in his deposition admitted that he was advised in July, 1973, by telephone that Berryman no longer wanted to be obligated by the option. Appellant further admitted that he was advised in August, 1973, by a representative of the Federal Land Bank, which held a substantial mortgage on the land, that Berryman had disposed of this land. The appellant's power of acceptance was terminated thereby and any attempted exercise of the option in October came too late when you consider the appellant's own admissions.

Summary judgment was therefore proper and the judgment is affirmed.

NOTES AND QUESTIONS

1. *Express option contract.* Unlike *Drennan*, the *Berryman* case considers an express option contract. Restatement (Second) of Contracts § 25

defines an option contract as "a promise which meets the requirements for the formation of a contract and limits the promisor's power to revoke." In the June 19th "contract," Berryman appears to clearly grant Kmoch an option for 120 days to purchase the land. Is a promise of irrevocability expressly or impliedly made for the 120-day period? If so, does the option contract meet the "requirements for the formation of a contract"? How is this determined? Did Berryman bargain for $10 or for "other valuable consideration"? What form might that other consideration take? Is it possible that Berryman would grant the option with little monetary consideration for the purpose of encouraging Kmoch to make investigation and complete the purchase?

2.   *Restatement (Second) of Contracts rule for reliance on offer.* As mentioned in the notes following the *Drennan* case, Restatement (Second) of Contracts § 87(2) had no counterpart in the first restatement and adopts the *Drennan* rule. It is reasonably clear that in bid cases, the subcontractor should expect the general contractor to use its bid (indeed that is the hope), and the use is a "substantial action." Should Berryman have expected Kmoch to incur substantial reliance on the option contract? Should Restatement (Second) of Contracts § 87(2) be limited to construction bid cases? See Margaret N. Kniffin, "Innovation or Aberration: Recovery for Reliance on a Contract Offer, As Permitted by the New Restatement (Second) of Contracts," 62 U. Det. L. Rev. 23 (1984).

3.   *False recital of nominal consideration in option contract.* As to option contracts, Restatement (Second) of Contracts § 87(1)(a) provides that an offer is binding as an option contract if it is in writing, signed, proposes an exchange on fair terms, and "recites a purported consideration." *Comment c* provides that the signed writing has vital significance as a formality, while the "ceremonial manual delivery of a dollar or a peppercorn is an inconsequential formality." In order to prevent false oral testimony to overcome the writing, the writing is conclusively preferred. This is in sharp contrast to the false recital of nominal consideration in other contracts. See Restatement (Second) of Contracts § 71, *cmt. b* ("Moreover, a mere pretense of a bargain does not suffice, as where there is a false recital of consideration or where the purported consideration is merely nominal. In such cases there is no consideration and the promise is enforced, if at all, as a promise binding without consideration."). The theory and result in Restatement (Second) of Contracts has not been universally adopted and indeed may constitute a minority rule. See *Lewis v. Fletcher*, 101 Idaho 530, 617 P.2d 834 (1980) (illustrating that second restatement rule is a minority rule, but the case was decided shortly after the new provision was announced in 1979). Does this help explain the result in *Berryman* since the option contract recited the payment of "$10 and other valuable consideration," which Berryman testified was never paid? How should the courts determine whether the signed document is correct and whether the consideration was paid or not paid? How did the court decide in *Berryman*? Did Kmoch acknowledge that the $10 had not been paid? If you represented Kmoch, what meaning would you attach to the language "For . . . and other valuable

consideration?" Do you agree with the approach of the restatement? Should the courts enforce the writing or evaluate testimony as to whether $10 was paid?

4. *Reliance on a purported transfer of an interest in real property for nominal consideration.* In *Segars v. City of Cornelia*, 60 Ga.App. 457, 4 S.E.2d 60, 62 (1939), the city of Cornelia, Georgia, purportedly executed a written contract with Mrs. E.E. Segars for an easement to discharge the contents of the city sewer system into the creek above her land in exchange for a consideration of one dollar. I.T. Sellers, the city councilman responsible for obtaining such easements from affected property owners, testified: "I had the consideration stated in the release, I think, and it was for one dollar, but whether or not I paid her the dollar I don't know." Id. The written contract was allegedly lost—at least no copy was ever found in the city's files—and no easement was recorded. See id. Mrs. Segars's successor in interest, E.E. Segars, later sued the city for damages caused by the deposits of ever increasing flows of raw sewage onto his property. See id. at 61. The court held that the nominal consideration was sufficient to support the contract: "Where a money consideration is stated in writing, the contract is still good although the money may not actually have been paid." Id.

Joseph Siprut, in an insightful student comment, notes that many courts in the nominal consideration context often require some additional indicia of enforceability. See Joseph Siprut, Comment, "The Peppercorn Reconsidered: Why a Promise to Sell Blackacre for Nominal Consideration Is Not Binding, But Should Be," 97 Nw. U. L. Rev. 1809, 1819 (2003). Thus, in *Segars*, while the court ostensibly upheld the contract on the basis of nominal consideration, the final paragraph of the opinion shows the court resting its conclusion on the city's detrimental reliance on the purported contract. See id.

What legitimate business considerations could drive contracting parties to execute an option contract granting an option to purchase real property at a specified price while reciting a mere nominal consideration? Can these cases be explained by the parties' ignorance of the legal effects of their purported nominal considerations? If it is true that many parties are generally unaware of these legal effects, how should courts respond to the possibilities of opportunistic behavior by a party who is aware of the legal rule applicable in her jurisdiction?

5. *Mailbox rule and option contracts.* Recall from the earlier discussion of the mailbox rule and Restatement (Second) of Contracts § 63(a) that acceptance is generally effective upon dispatch. However, under Restatement (Second) of Contracts § 63(b), exercise of an option is effective only upon receipt by the offeror and not dispatch by the offeree. *Comment f* explains the different treatment on the basis that the existence of the option in the first place provides adequate protection for offeree reliance not generally available in the other contexts.

3.   PRE-OFFER RELIANCE ON NEGOTIATIONS

Precontractual "negotiations" and precontractual "agreements" present a rich opportunity to consider and balance the reasonable expectations of the parties. Since the parties are merely negotiating, by definition they have not expressed mutual assent to common terms of a contract. Nonetheless, because of assurances or statements made during the course of negotiations, one or both parties might well expect the negotiations to conclude favorably or, at the very least, to continue in good faith until and unless reasonable disagreement about a specific term requires the negotiations to terminate. Of course, the parties could simply enter an express contract to negotiate, which would obligate the parties to negotiate in good faith. But absent such an express agreement, contract law generally does not favor contractual liability based on negotiations because the terms of the deal are simply too vague and uncertain. In these circumstances, should the law provide a remedy for a person who relies on an indefinite or vague assurance made during the course of negotiations? If so, what theory supports the obligation and what is the nature of the obligation? Theories vary on these important matters with general consensus only upon the single idea that at some point precontractual liability is appropriate. The case below explores the application of promissory estoppel. Is this theory the same as liability based on a contract?

POP'S CONES, INC. V. RESORTS INTERNATIONAL HOTEL, INC.

Superior Court of New Jersey
307 N.J.Super. 461, 704 A.2d 1321 (1998)

KLEINER, J.A.D.

Plaintiff, Pop's Cones, Inc., t/a TCBY Yogurt, ("Pop's"), appeals from an order of the Law Division granting defendant, Resorts International, Inc. ("Resorts"), summary judgment and dismissing its complaint seeking damages predicated on a theory of promissory estoppel. Affording all favorable inferences to plaintiff's contentions, Brill v. Guardian Life Ins. Co. of America, 142 N.J. 520, 536, 666 A.2d 146 (1995), we conclude that Pop's presented a prima facie claim sufficient to withstand summary dismissal of its complaint. See R. 4:46–2; Brill, supra, 142 N.J. at 540, 666 A. 2d 146. In reversing summary judgment, we rely upon principles of promissory estoppel enunciated in Section 90 of the Restatement (Second) of Contracts, and recent cases which, in order to avoid injustice, seemingly relax the strict requirement of "a clear and definite promise" in making a *prima facie* case of promissory estoppel.

I

Pop's is an authorized franchisee of TCBY Systems, Inc. ("TCBY"), a national franchisor of frozen yogurt products. Resorts is a casino hotel in Atlantic City that leases retail space along "prime Boardwalk frontage," among other business ventures.

From June of 1991 to September 1994, Pop's operated a TCBY franchise in Margate, New Jersey. Sometime during the months of May or June 1994, Brenda Taube ("Taube"), President of Pop's, had "a number of discussions" with Marlon Phoenix ("Phoenix"), the Executive Director of Business Development and Sales for Resorts, about the possible relocation of Pop's business to space owned by Resorts. During these discussions, Phoenix showed Taube one location for a TCBY vending cart within Resorts Hotel and "three specific locations for the operation of a full service TCBY store."

According to Taube, she and Phoenix specifically discussed the boardwalk property occupied at that time by a business trading as "The Players Club." These discussions included Taube's concerns with the then-current rental fees and Phoenix's indication that Resorts management and Merv Griffin personally were "very anxious to have Pop's as a tenant" and that "financial issues . . . could easily be resolved, such as through a percentage of gross revenue." In order to allay both Taube's and Phoenix's concerns about whether a TCBY franchise at The Players Club location would be successful, Phoenix offered to permit Pop's to operate a vending cart within Resorts free of charge during the summer of 1994 so as to "test the traffic flow." This offer was considered and approved by Paul Ryan, Vice President for Hotel Operations at Resorts.

These discussions led to further meetings with Phoenix about the Players Club location, and Taube contacted TCBY's corporate headquarters about a possible franchise site change. During the weekend of July 4, 1994, Pop's opened the TCBY cart for business at Resorts pursuant to the above stated offer. On July 6, 1994, TCBY gave Taupe initial approval for Pop's change in franchise site. In late July or early August of 1994, representatives of TCBY personally visited the Players Club location, with Taube and Phoenix present.

Based on Pop's marketing assessment of the Resorts location, Taube drafted a written proposal dated August 18, 1994, addressing the leasing of Resorts' Players Club location and hand-delivered it to Phoenix. Taube's proposal offered Resorts "7% of net monthly sales (gross less sales tax) for the duration of the [Player's Club] lease . . . [and][i]f this proposal is acceptable, I'd need a 6 year lease, and a renewable option for another 6 years."

In mid-September 1994, Taube spoke with Phoenix about the status of Pop's lease proposal and "pressed [him] to advise [her] of Resorts' position. [Taube] specifically advised [Phoenix] that Pop's had an option to renew the lease for its Margate location and then needed to give notice to its landlord of whether it would be staying at that location no later than October 1, 1994." Another conversation about this topic occurred in late September when Taube "asked Phoenix if [Pop's] proposal was in the ballpark of what Resorts was looking for." He responded that it was and that "we are 95% there, we just need Belisle's signature on the deal." Taube admits to having been advised that Belisle had "ultimate responsibility for signing off on the deal" but that Phoenix "assured [her] that Mr. Belisle would follow his recommendation, which was to approve the deal, and that [Phoenix] did not anticipate any difficulties." During this conversation, Taube again mentioned to Phoenix that she had to inform her landlord by October 1, 1994, about whether or not Pop's would renew its lease with them. Taube stated: "Mr. Phoenix assured me that we would have little difficulty in concluding an agreement and advised [Taube] to give notice that [Pop's] would not be extending [its] Margate lease and 'to pack up the Margate store and plan on moving.' "

Relying upon Phoenix's "advice and assurances," Taube notified Pop's landlord in late-September 1994 that it would not be renewing the lease for the Margate location.

In early October, Pop's moved its equipment out of the Margate location and placed it in temporary storage. Taube then commenced a number of new site preparations including: (1) sending designs for the new store to TCBY in October 1994; and (2) retaining an attorney to represent Pop's in finalizing the terms of the lease with Resorts.

By letter dated November 1, 1994, General Counsel for Resorts forwarded a proposed form of lease for The Players Club location to Pop's attorney. The letter provided:

> Per our conversation, enclosed please find the form of lease utilized for retail outlets leasing space in Resorts Hotel. You will note that there are a number of alternative sections depending upon the terms of the deal. As I advised, I will contact you . . . to inform you of our decision regarding TCBY. . . .

By letter dated December 1, 1994, General Counsel for Resorts forwarded to Pop's attorney a written offer of the terms upon which Resorts was proposing to lease the Players Club space to Pop's. The terms provided:

> [Resorts is] willing to offer the space for an initial three (3) year term with a rent calculated at the greater of 7% of gross revenues or: $50,000 in year one; $60,000 in year two; and $70,000 in year three . . . [with] a three (3) year option to renew after the initial term. . . .

The letter also addressed a "boilerplate lease agreement" provision and a proposed addition to the form lease. The letter concluded by stating:

This letter is not intended to be binding upon Resorts. It is intended to set forth the basic terms and conditions upon which Resorts would be willing to negotiate a lease and is subject to those negotiations and the execution of a definitive agreement. . . . [W]e think TCBY will be successful at the Boardwalk location based upon the terms we propose. We look forward to having your client as part of . . . Resorts family of customer service providers and believe TCBY will benefit greatly from some of the dynamic changes we plan. . . . [W]e would be pleased . . . to discuss this proposal in greater detail. (emphasis added).

In early-December 1994, Taube and her attorney met with William Murtha, General Counsel of Resorts, and Paul Ryan to finalize the proposed lease. After a number of discussions about the lease, Murtha and Ryan informed Taube that they desired to reschedule the meeting to finalize the lease until after the first of the year because of a public announcement they intended to make about another unrelated business venture that Resorts was about to commence. Ryan again assured Taube that rent for the Players Club space was not an issue and that the lease terms would be worked out. "He also assured [Taube] that Resorts wanted TCBY . . . on the boardwalk for the following season."

Several attempts were made in January 1995 to contact Resorts' representatives and confirm that matters were proceeding. On January 30, 1995, Taube's attorney received a letter stating:

This letter is to confirm our conversation of this date wherein I advised that Resorts is withdrawing its December 1, 1994 offer to lease space to your client, TCBY.[4]

According to Taube's certification, "As soon as [Pop's] heard that Resorts was withdrawing its offer, we undertook extensive efforts to reopen [the] franchise at a different location. Because the Margate location had been re-let, it was not available." Ultimately, Pop's found a suitable location but did not reopen for business until July 5, 1996.

On July 17, 1995, Pop's filed a complaint against Resorts seeking damages. The complaint alleged that Pop's "reasonably relied to its detriment on the promises and assurances of Resorts that it would be permitted to relocate its operation to [Resorts'] Boardwalk location. . . ."

After substantial pre-trial discovery, defendant moved for summary judgment. After oral argument, the motion judge, citing Malaker Corp. Stockholders Protective Comm. v. First Jersey Nat. Bank, 163 N. J. Super.

---

[4] Apparently, in late January 1995, Resorts spoke with another TCBY franchise, Host Marriott, regarding the Players Club's space. Those discussions eventually led to an agreement to have Host Marriott operate a TCBY franchise at the Players Club location. That lease was executed in late May 1995, and TCBY opened shortly thereafter.

463, 395 A. 2d 222 (App. Div. 1978), certif. denied, 79 N.J. 488, 401 A. 2d 243 (1979), rendered a detailed oral opinion in which he concluded, in part:

> The primary argument of the defendant is that the plaintiff is unable to meet the requirements for a claim of Promissory Estoppel as there was no clear and definite promise ever made to plaintiff; and, therefore, any reliance on the part of plaintiff upon the statements of the Resorts agent were not reasonable. . . .

> I think that even if a jury would find that a lease was promised, there was lack of specificity in its terms so as to not rise to the level of what is necessary to meet the first element for Promissory Estoppel. There was no specificity as to the term of this lease. There was no specificity as to the starting date of this lease. There was no specificity as to the rent, although it was represented that rent would not be a problem. Rent had not been agreed upon, and it is not certified that it had been agreed upon. When they left that meeting, according to . . . plaintiff's own facts, they didn't have a lease; they would still have to work out the terms of the lease. It was not in existence at the time. . . .

> We don't have facts in dispute. Neither side, neither the defendant nor the plaintiff, can attest to the terms of the lease, of the essential terms of the lease or still not agreed upon at the time of that the meeting was over in December of 1994.

Based on Brill, supra, 142 N.J. at 540, 666 A. 2d 146, the judge concluded that the evidence was so one-sided that defendant was entitled to prevail as a matter of law.

It is quite apparent from the motion judge's reasons that he viewed plaintiff's complaint as seeking enforcement of a lease which had not yet been fully negotiated. If that were plaintiff's intended remedy, we would agree with the judge's conclusion. However, plaintiff's complaint, after reciting the facts from the inception of Taube's initial contact with defendant until January 30, 1995, stated:

> 19. As a result of its reasonable reliance on the promises and assurances made to it by Resorts, Pop's has been significantly prejudiced and has suffered significant damages, including the following:

>> a. the loss of its Margate location and its ability to earn profits during the 1995 summer season;

>> b. out-of-pocket expenses, including attorney's fees; and

>> c. out-of-pocket expenses in attempting to locate an alternate location.

Wherefore, Pop's demands judgment against defendant, Resorts International Hotel, Inc., for damages, costs of suit and for other and further legal and equitable relief as the Court may deem just and proper.

It seems quite clear from plaintiff's complaint that plaintiff was not seeking damages relating to a lease of the boardwalk property, but rather was seeking damages flowing from its reliance upon promises made to it prior to October 1, 1994, when it failed to renew its lease for its Margate location. Thus, plaintiff's claim was predicated upon the concept of promissory estoppel and was not a traditional breach of contract claim.

The doctrine of promissory estoppel is well-established in New Jersey. Malaker, supra, 163 N.J. Super. at 479, 395 A. 2d 222 ("Suffice it to say that given an appropriate case, the doctrine [of promissory estoppel] will be enforced."). A promissory estoppel claim will be justified if the plaintiff satisfies its burden of demonstrating the existence of, or for purposes of summary judgment, a dispute as to a material fact with regard to, four separate elements which include:

> (1) a clear and definite promise by the promisor; (2) the promise must be made with the expectation that the promisee will rely thereon; (3) the promisee must in fact reasonably rely on the promise, and (4) detriment of a definite and substantial nature must be incurred in reliance on the promise.

[*Ibid.*]

The essential justification for the promissory estoppel doctrine is to avoid the substantial hardship or injustice which would result if such a promise were not enforced. *Id.* at 484, 395 A.2d 222.

In *Malaker,* the court determined that an implied promise to lend an unspecified amount of money was not "a clear and definite promise" justifying application of the promissory estoppel doctrine. Id. at 478–81, 395 A. 2d 222. Specifically, the court concluded that the promisor-bank's oral promise in October 1970 to lend $150,000 for January, February and March of 1971 was not "clear and definite promise" because it did not describe a promise of "sufficient definition." *Id.* at 479, 395 *A.*2d 222.

It should be noted that the court in *Malaker* seems to have heightened the amount of proof required to establish a "clear and definite promise" by searching for "*an express promise* of a 'clear and definite' nature." Id. at 484, 395 A. 2d 222 (emphasis added). This sort of language might suggest that New Jersey Courts expect proof of most, if not all, of the essential legal elements of a promise before finding it to be "clear and definite."

Although earlier New Jersey decisions discussing promissory estoppel seem to greatly scrutinize a party's proofs regarding an alleged "clear and definite promise by the promisor," *see, e.g., id.* at 479, 484, 395 A. 2d 222, as a prelude to considering the remaining three elements of a promissory estoppel claim, more recent decisions have tended to relax the strict adherence to the *Malaker* formula for determining whether a *prima facie* case of promissory estoppel exists. This is particularly true where, as here, a plaintiff does not seek to enforce a contract not fully negotiated, but instead seeks damages resulting from its detrimental reliance upon promises made during contract negotiations despite the ultimate failure of those negotiations.

In Peck v. Imedia, Inc., 293 N.J. Super. 151, 679 A.2d 745 (App. Div.) certif. denied, 147 N.J. 262, 686 A. 2d 763 (1996), we determined that an at-will employment contract offer was a "clear and definite promise" for purposes of promissory estoppel. See id. at 165–68, 679 A.2d 745. The employment contract offer letter contained the position title, a "detailed position description . . . as well as information on . . . benefits" and an annual salary. Id. at 156, 679 A.2d 745. We recognized that even though an employer can terminate the employment relationship at any time, there may be losses incident to reliance upon the job offer itself. Id. at 167–68, 679 A. 2d 745. See also Mahoney v. Delaware McDonald's Corp., 770 F.2d 123, 127 (8th Cir. 1985) (holding that plaintiff's purchase of property for lease to defendant in reliance upon defendant's representation that "[w]e have a deal" created cause of action for promissory estoppel); Bercoon, Weiner, Glick & Brook v. Manufacturers Hanover Trust Co., 818 F. Supp. 1152, 1161 (N.D. Ill. 1993) (holding that defendant's representation that lease was "done deal" and encouragement of plaintiff to terminate existing lease provided plaintiff with cause of action for promissory estoppel).

Further, the Restatement (Second) of Contracts § 90 (1979), "Promise Reasonably Inducing Action or Forbearance," provides, in pertinent part:

> (1) A promise which the promisor should reasonably expect to induce action or forbearance on the part of the promisee or a third person and which does induce such action or forbearance is binding *if injustice can be avoided only by enforcement of the promise.* The remedy granted for breach may be limited as justice requires. [*Ibid.* (emphasis added).]

The *Restatement* approach is best explained by illustration 10 contained within the comments to Section 90, and based upon Hoffman v. Red Owl Stores, Inc., 26 Wis. 2d 683, 133 N.W.2d 267 (1965):

> 10. A, who owns and operates a bakery, desires to go into the grocery business. He approaches B, a franchisor of supermarkets. B states to A that for $18,000 B will establish A in a store. B also advises A to move to another town and buy a small grocery to gain experience. A does so. Later B advises A to sell the grocery, which A does, taking a capital loss and foregoing expected profits from the summer tourist trade. B also advises A to sell his bakery to

raise capital for the supermarket franchise, saying "Everything is ready to go. Get your money together and we are set." A sells the bakery taking a capital loss on this sale as well. Still later, B tells A that considerably more than an $18,000 investment will be needed, and the negotiations between the parties collapse. At the point of collapse many details of the proposed agreement between the parties are unresolved. The assurances from B to A are promises on which B reasonably should have expected A to rely, and A is entitled to his actual losses on the sales of the bakery and grocery and for his moving and temporary living expenses. Since the proposed agreement was never made, however, A is not entitled to lost profits from the sale of the grocery or to his expectation interest in the proposed franchise from B. [Restatement (Second) of Contracts § 90 cmt. d, illus. 10 (1979).]

We particularly note our recent discussion in Mazza v. Scoleri, 304 N.J. Super. 555, 701 A. 2d 723 (App. Div. 1997). Although Mazza did not focus on the issue of promissory estoppel, it expressly adopted the exception to the Statute of Frauds enunciated in Restatement (Second) of Contracts, § 139(1) (1979). Mazza, supra, 304 N.J. Super. at 560, 701 A. 2d 723. That section provides:

A promise which the promisor should reasonably expect to induce action or forbearance on the part of the promisee or a third person and which does induce the action or forbearance is enforceable notwithstanding the Statute of Frauds if injustice can be avoided only by enforcement of the promise. The remedy granted for breach is limited as justice requires. [Restatement (Second) of Contracts § 139(1) (1979).]

Mazza also instructs, citing Citibank v. Estate of Simpson, 290 N.J. Super. 519, 530, 676 A. 2d 172 (App. Div. 1996), that "New Jersey typically gives considerable weight to Restatement views, and has, on occasion, adopted those views as the law of this State when they speak to an issue our courts have not yet considered." Mazza, 304 N.J. Super. at 560, 701 A. 2d 723 (citations omitted). It is thus quite clear that Section 90 of the Restatement complements the exception to the Statute of Frauds discussed in Section 139(1).

As we read the Restatement, the strict adherence to proof of a "clear and definite promise" as discussed in *Malaker* is being eroded by a more equitable analysis designed to avoid injustice. This is the very approach we adopted in *Peck, supra,* wherein even in the absence of a clear and definite contract of employment, we permitted the plaintiff to proceed with a cause of action for damages flowing from plaintiff's losses based on her detrimental reliance on the promise of employment. 293 N.J. Super. at 168, 679 A. 2d 745.

The facts as presented by plaintiff by way of its pleadings and certifications filed by Taube, which were not refuted or contradicted by defendant before the motion judge or on appeal, clearly show that when Taube informed Phoenix that Pop's option to renew its lease at its Margate location had to be exercised by October 1, 1994, Phoenix instructed Taube to give notice that it would *not* be extending the lease. According to Phoenix, virtually nothing remained to be resolved between the parties. Phoenix indicated that the parties were "95% there" and that all that was required for completion of the deal was the signature of John Belisle. Phoenix assured Taube that he had recommended the deal to Belisle, and that Belisle would follow the recommendation. Phoenix also advised Pop's to "pack up the Margate store and plan on moving."

It is also uncontradicted that based upon those representations that Pop's, in fact, did not renew its lease. It vacated its Margate location, placed its equipment and personalty into temporary storage, retained the services of an attorney to finalize the lease with defendant, and engaged in planning the relocation to defendant's property. Ultimately, it incurred the expense of relocating to its present location. That plaintiff, like the plaintiff in *Peck*, relied to its detriment on defendant's assurances seems unquestionable; the facts clearly at least raise a jury question. Additionally, whether plaintiff's reliance upon defendant's assurances was reasonable is also a question for the jury.

Conversely, following the Section 90 approach, a jury could conclude that Phoenix, as promisor, should reasonably have expected to induce action or forbearance on the part of plaintiff to his precise instruction "*not to renew the lease*" and to "pack up the Margate store and plan on moving." In discussing the "character of reliance protected" under Section 90, comment b states:

> The principle of this Section is flexible. The promisor is affected only by reliance which he does or should foresee, and enforcement must be necessary to avoid injustice. Satisfaction of the latter requirement may depend on the reasonableness of the promisee's reliance, on its definite and substantial character in relation to the remedy sought, on the formality with which the promise is made, on the extent to which evidentiary, cautionary, deterrent and channeling functions of form are met by the commercial setting or otherwise, and on the extent to which such other policies as the enforcement of bargains and the prevention of unjust enrichment are relevant. . . . [Restatement (Second) of Contracts § 90 cmt. b (1979) (citations omitted).]

Plaintiff's complaint neither seeks enforcement of the lease nor speculative lost profits which it might have earned had the lease been fully and successfully negotiated. Plaintiff merely seeks to recoup damages it incurred, including the loss of its Margate leasehold, in reasonably relying to its detriment upon defendant's promise. Affording plaintiff all favorable inferences, its equitable claim raised a jury question. See Brill, supra, 142 N.J. at 540, 666 A. 2d 146. Plaintiff's complaint, therefore, should not have been summarily dismissed.

Reversed and remanded for further appropriate proceedings.

NOTES AND QUESTIONS

1.   *Indefinite promise and* Hoffman v. Red Owl. The court in *Pop's Cones* determined that the promise was adequate for the application of promissory estoppel in the context of failed contract negotiations. Therefore, the promise need not be "clear and definite." *Pop's Cones* raises the question of whether promissory estoppel must be based on a true promise or whether an indefinite or even illusory promise will do. What requirements, if any, does the Restatement (Second) of Contracts § 90 provide with respect to the clarity and definiteness of the promise? If § 90 is interpreted to contain no such requirements, does that imply that an indefinite or illusory promise will suffice? Does the court state or imply that an indefinite or illusory promise is adequate? Promises that are indefinite or illusory create problems for promissory estoppel recovery beyond the context of negotiations. These problems include determining whether the purported promisor actually made such a promise, whether the promisee reasonably relied on that promise, and the extent to which broad application of promissory estoppel doctrine infringes upon the freedom to negotiate. See Michael B. Metzger and Michael J. Phillips, "Promissory Estoppel and Reliance on Illusory Promises," 44 Sw. L. J. 841 (1990) (arguing that in appropriate cases promissory estoppel should be extended to illusory promises).

The court in *Pop's Cones* cites with approval the famous Wisconsin case *Hoffman v. Red Owl Stores*, 26 Wis.2d 683, 133 N.W.2d 267 (1967). A grocery store chain made vague assurances to Hoffman of becoming a franchisee. When the franchise did not mature, Hoffman sued, asserting that he had relied in various ways on those assurances. Red Owl argued the assurances were not enforceable under contract law because they were too indefinite. While agreeing with that proposition, the court enforced the assurances anyway by arguing "this is not a breach of contract action." Rather, Hoffman brought an action under promissory estoppel. Normally, estoppel bars a person from asserting claims and defenses, from seeking remedies, from presenting testimony, or from making certain arguments. Hoffman, on the other hand, used the doctrine offensively as a cause of action in which the defense of indefiniteness was not easily available because of the flexibility of reasonable reliance (versus contractual assent). How would Hohfeld rationalize this conceptualization? Does Restatement (Second) of Contracts § 90 contemplate the use of the doctrine affirmatively in the form of an action to recover damages? See also Gregory E. Maggs, "Estoppel and Textualism," 54 Am. J. Comp. L. 167, 184 (2006).

2.   *Contract and duty to negotiate.* The actionable "promise" in *Pop's Cones* was Phoenix's assurance that the deal was certain (or nearly so) and his advice that Pop's Cones should not extend its other lease. Is there a special quality to such an assurance made in the context of negotiations? Is it clear that negotiations had terminated, and the deal was completed? Was there a contract? If so, was there a contract to complete negotiations or a contract on the specified lease terms? Some have argued that such general assurances that the "deal is done" in the context of negotiations create, at a minimum, an "implied contract to negotiate." The terms of such implied contracts require the parties to continue to negotiate in good faith in an effort to conclude negotiations. Under this characterization, neither party would be free to withdraw or terminate negotiations without reason, but neither would be compelled to perform if good faith efforts failed to establish an agreement. Upon termination without reason, reliance damages would be available. A few cases follow this reasoning to determine that unclear language and lack of contractual assent do not preclude enforcement of a true agreement to negotiate. See *Channel Home Centers v. Grossman*, 795 F.2d 291 (3rd Cir. 1986); Charles L. Knapp, "Enforcing the Contract to Bargain," 44 N.Y.U. L. Rev. 673, 685, 723 (1969); E. Allan Farnsworth, "Precontractual Liability and Preliminary Agreements: Fair Dealing and Failed Negotiations," 87 Colum. L. Rev. 217, 270 (1987); Melvin A. Eisenberg, "The Emergence of Dynamic Contract Law," 88 Cal. L. Rev. 1743, 1796–1797 (2000). An implied agreement to negotiate is similar to an express agreement to negotiate undertaken when the parties do not wish to make a binding agreement with open terms. An express agreement to negotiate imposes upon both parties the duty to continue to negotiate in good faith, thereby negating the normal right to terminate negotiations at-will or without cause. Since there is no larger agreement upon which to base expectancy damages, the remedy of the injured party is most often based on reliance, but not promissory estoppel. See E. Allan Farnsworth, "Precontractual Liability and Preliminary Agreements: Fair Dealing and Failed Negotiations," 87 Colum. L. Rev. 217, 263 (1987). As an alternative, the context of negotiations might be used to imply a promise to inform the other party of a change in willingness to continue to negotiate. The breaching party would be liable for reliance damages incurred by the injured party after the implied promise arose, continuing through the notice of termination. Juliet P. Kostritsky, "Bargaining With Uncertainty, Moral Hazard, and Sunk Costs: A Default Rule for Precontractual Negotiations," 44 Hastings L. J. 621 (1993). Still others argue law and economics scholars have improperly overlooked precontractual opportunism on the theory that little is invested and substitutes are adequately available. Thus, the requisite trust required in such negotiations demands a new theory of obligation designed to proscribe precontractual opportunism. G. Richard Shell, "Opportunism and Trust in the Negotiation of Commercial Contracts: Toward a New Cause of Action," 44 Vand. L. Rev. 221 (1991). Finally, still others argue that even mistake in negotiations that harms the other party should be actionable under tort theory. Randy E. Barnett and Mary E. Becker, "Beyond Reliance: Promissory Estoppel, Contract Formalities, and Misrepresentations," 15 Hofstra L. Rev.

443, 489–491 (1987) and Mark P. Gergen, "Liability for Mistake in Contract Formation," 64 S. Cal. L. Rev. 1, 34 (1990).

3. *Damages.* Pop's Cones did not seek normative "expectancy damages," but rather only "reliance damages," including the loss of income it would have received from the Margate location had it not vacated in reliance on the assurance. It also sought reimbursement of its out-of-pocket expenses incurred in preparation for the new lease with Resorts. But Pop's Cones did not however seek to recover its "expectancy damages" measured by the projected net profits it anticipated from the Resorts lease between its projected opening date at the Player's Club location and the date it actually opened in an alternative location on July 5, 1996. Nor could Pop's Cones have recovered for its lost profits thereafter, as the profit from that location as well as those from the Resorts lease would have constituted a double recovery.

4. *International precontractual liability and CISG.* How does international civil law account for the common law notion of precontractual liability? CISG art. 7(1) requires observance of good faith in international sale transactions. The good faith standard was highly contested in the CISG drafting and thus is unlikely to be extended to create a duty of good faith in precontractual settings. See Nadia E. Nedzel, "A Comparative Study of Good Faith, Fair Dealing, and Precontractual Liability," 12 Tul. Euro. Civ. LF 97, 151 (1997) and John Lein & Carla Bachechi, "Precontractual Liability and the Duty of Good Faith Negotiation in International Transactions," 17 Houston J. Int'l L. 1 (1994).

5. *Contracting without consent.* Omri Ben-Shahar proposes a novel solution to resolving problems created by an aborted negotiation process such as that in *Pop's Cones.* See Omri Ben-Shahar, "Contracts Without Consent: Exploring a New Basis for Contractual Liability," 152 U. Pa. L. Rev. 1829 (2004). Ben-Shahar observes that the bargain theory of contracts requires that parties expend time and resources negotiating with competing offers and counteroffers until, finally, one party indicates mutual assent by accepting the last counteroffer and creating a contract. See id. at 1829–30. At any time during negotiations and before creation of a contract, each party remains free to walk away from the deal without any liability to the other. See id.

As an alternative, Ben-Shahar suggests that negotiations should be governed by a principle of "no-retraction," that is that "[a] party who manifests a willingness to enter into a contract at given terms should not be able to freely retract from her manifestation." Id. at 1830. Instead of being removed from the table by a successive counteroffer, each manifestation of an intent to be bound creates an option in the other party that it may later accept if further negotiations prove unfruitful. See id.

> [U]nder the no-retraction principle, each party should have a right to enforce a contractual obligation according to the meaning intended by the other. Further, even when the parties have not reached a full-blown agreement or an understanding over terms, as in the case where both parties make serious, but nonconforming, precontractual

representations of the proposed terms, the legal consequence should not be mutual rejection accompanied by the freedom to walk away. Rather, the representations of the parties give rise to bilateral options: each party can bind . . . the other to the terms that party proposed. If the proposal is incomplete and gaps need to be filled, they will be filled with terms most favorable (within reason) to the proposing party. Thus, while a party is unable to retract, it is only from a deal that includes terms she proposed, supplemented by terms most favorable to her. I will argue that the enforced-against party has no reasonable grounds to reject a deal containing such terms. Id. at 1831.

How would the outcome of *Pop's Cones* change, if at all, under Ben-Shahar's proposal? What are the benefits or harms of such an approach to negotiation and contract formation? Do current negotiation ethics and standards provide any support for this proposal? Consider a negotiation for a car with a $25,000 sticker price—what would happen if the prospective buyer offered $21,000 and the seller responded with a counteroffer of $27,500?

4. PRECONTRACTUAL AGREEMENTS

The previous section explored the application of promissory estoppel and good faith to "pure negotiations" in order to protect the reasonable precontractual reliance on various forms of assurances made during the course of those negotiations. In contractual terms, the pure negotiations have not matured in an agreement on all material terms, and the parties have not yet expressed the intent to be bound. If the parties do not reach a final agreement, classic contract law does not view such negotiations as creating a contract. Consequently, without a contract, the parties cannot sue for breach and damages.

Nonetheless, parties often find it advantageous to provide assurances of "eventual agreement" in the course of negotiations. In response, one party may justifiably and detrimentally rely on the reasonable expectation of eventual agreement generated by such assurances that the parties will reach agreement. While classic contract law does not provide a remedy for such non-contractual assurances, courts have provided a limited protection in the doctrines of promissory estoppel and good faith negotiations. While traditional contract law does not ordinarily apply promissory estoppel to "qualified promises" and good faith ordinarily applies only to "performance obligations" created under an otherwise valid contract, equity seeks some intermediate protections for reliance based on assurances of eventual agreement. The *Pop's Cones* case is an excellent example where the court imposed liability in part because the assurance of eventual agreement had progressed to the stage of additional encouragement to incur the precise reliance actually incurred.

While significant, cases like *Pop's Cones* are nonetheless rare because sophisticated business parties are reluctant or refuse to incur reliance costs without more than a verbal assurance that a deal is certain to occur. Likewise, failed negotiations, even at the eleventh hour, are a fact of life in the business world. Too many problems and issues not yet contemplated may undo the best intentions to reach eventual agreement. In these cases, courts require something more than a naked assurance of an eventual agreement. In many cases, the "something more" takes the form of a "precontractual agreement." To grant comfort for one or both parties to incur at least preliminary reliance expenses, the parties often reach intermediate agreement on most or all the general terms, which justifies them in executing an intermediate agreement stating the settled terms, while at the same time acknowledging the need for further negotiation to reach final agreement. That precontractual agreement occupies a significantly more important role and function in contract law than pure negotiation liability.

Like the assurance of eventual agreement in the negotiation context, the precontractual agreement ordinarily acknowledges agreement on the principal terms. Many different purposes may be served by the signing of a letter of intent. One of those may be the desire of one or both parties to protect agreement on some points against backsliding renegotiation. Unlike the assurance of eventual agreement, the precontractual agreement is normally in writing, executed by one or both parties, and expressly states further bargaining must occur before a formal or final contractual agreement is reached. The precontractual agreement has many monikers in the commercial world including "letter of intent," "memorandum of understanding," "agreement in principle," "memorandum of intent," and "agreement to agree," to name a few. But the issue in each case remains the same. Does the precontractual agreement evidence an objective intent to form a traditional contract? If so, the failure to complete the bargaining or execute the final formal document breaches the agreement giving rise to a cause of action for breach and damages. If the precontractual agreement does not evidence objective contractual intent, the parties are legally free to withdraw from negotiations and refuse to complete the transaction without contractual consequence.

The answer to this uncertain question inevitably plunges a court into a searching analysis to resolve the traditional contract "all or nothing" approach. Either a contract exists or it does not. The economic consequences can be catastrophic and often turn on quite subtle features of the bargaining relationship. Indeed, the outcome can even depend upon whether the determination rests with a judge or with a jury. Judges tend to give more credence to the reservation caveats in the precontractual agreements, while that subtlety is often lost on a jury engaged in a meaningful search for truthful intent. A relatively recent example serves as an important reminder. In the enormously famous 1986 *Texaco* case discussed in the notes below, a Texas jury awarded Pennzoil a $10.53 billion judgment against Texaco for tortious interference with Pennzoil's contract to merge with Getty Oil. It was the largest civil jury award in the history of the United States and followed a dismissal of Pennzoil's preliminary injunction suit against Getty Oil itself in the Delaware Chancery Court. The Chancery Court reasoned that Pennzoil was unlikely to succeed on the merits of breach of contract suit against Getty Oil because the "agreement in principle" was subject to the execution of a formal merger agreement and approval by the Getty Oil shareholders.

In some important ways, reliance is more likely, predictable, and therefore more reasonable in precontractual agreement cases than in negotiation cases if for no other reason than that these agreements explicitly purpose to encourage the parties to proceed with independent due diligence and incur other deal investigative expenses. On the other hand, the express reservations in the precontractual agreement that it is not a contract and will not become so until either further bargaining is concluded or a more formal and complete contract is later executed surely puts both parties on notice that they incur such costs at their peril. Why would a reasonable businessperson incur such expenses? Perhaps for the simple reason that each party does so knowing the material terms are fixed and the information to be gathered will be judged against that fixed model with the complete freedom to walk away from the deal without further breach costs if that information does not match expectation. See Wendell H. Holmes, "The Freedom Not to Contract," 60 Tul. L. Rev. 751 (1986).

Two restatement provisions are most often relevant. Restatement (Second) of Contracts § 27 provides that manifestations of assent that are in themselves sufficient to conclude a contract will not be prevented from becoming a contract merely because the parties also manifest an intent to prepare and adopt a written memorial thereof. In other words, where the parties have concluded a contract that includes a term requiring them to reduce their agreement to a formal writing, Section 27 permits courts to enforce the parties' agreement and treat the lack of a final written memorial as merely a breach of one of the terms of that agreement.

This rule is subject to an important exception. Where the circumstances show that the agreements are merely preliminary negotiations, a contract will not be formed unless both parties execute a future complete writing. Thus, where the parties' negotiations are not sufficient to create a contract, a court should not use the Section 27 rule to impose an agreement based upon those preliminary negotiations. Rather, the creation of a final written memorandum is a necessary precondition to contractual liability.

The proper referent in these cases is the objective intent of the parties. Typically, if a party plaintiff makes out a prima facie case that the preliminary negotiations constituted an agreement, the defendant must establish that the plaintiff knew or should have known that the defendant regarded the agreement as incomplete and intended no obligation until there was assent to further terms or the agreed terms were reduced to writing. Restatement (Second) of Contracts § 27, *cmt. b.* Restatement (Second) of Contracts § 26 is often relevant as well and provides that a contract is not formed where an actor intends to make a bargain in the future, but only upon the making of some further manifestation of assent.

In a path-breaking article on the topic in 1969, Professor Charles Knapp advocated a rejection of the all or nothing approach and thus limited recognition of "contracts to bargain" independent of the later agreement. Charles L. Knapp, "Enforcing the Contract to Bargain," 44 N.Y.U. L. Rev. 673, 679 (1969). Later, Professor Allan Farnsworth argued that a flexible approach to traditional contract law adequately protected such arrangements and recognized a middle ground approach rather than the all or nothing approach. See E. Allan Farnsworth, "Precontractual Liability and Preliminary Agreements: Fair Dealing and Failed Negotiations," 87 Colum. L. Rev. 217, 218 (1987). Both approaches however rely upon the doctrine of good faith in the negotiating process. See also, Harvey L. Temkin, "When Does the 'Fat Lady' Sing?: An Analysis of 'Agreements in Principle' in Corporate Acquisitions," 55 Fordham L. Rev. 125 (1986).

Finally, it is tempting to state this problem simply as a drafting failure and assess the risk of error against the party who failed to communicate objectively its intent that a contract has not yet been formed. But how is that intent to be communicated? What language will be effective? In very real terms, this is a serious pragmatic and continually occurring problem.

The famous case of *Texaco v. Pennzoil* demonstrates the seriousness of the problems potentially raised by letters of intent. See *Texaco, Inc. v. Pennzoil Co.*, 729 S.W.2d 768 (Tex. Ct. App. 1987). By all accounts, Gordon P. Getty was in a fine mood as he began a champagne celebration in a New York hotel on the evening of January 3, 1984. The next day, a press release was to be issued publicly announcing an "agreement in principle" to merge Getty Oil Company with a new company to be co-owned by Mr. Getty and Pennzoil. The Getty Board had conditionally approved the deal in a 14–1 vote. Under the terms of the proposed merger, Pennzoil would acquire 43% of Getty Oil's shares for approximately $110 per share. Following the merger, Mr. Getty would control 57% of the new company after controlling only 40.2% of Getty Oil. Although most thought the deal was final, it was subject to several significant caveats— the most important including: (i) the transaction was labeled merely an "agreement in principle," (ii) the execution of a later definitive merger agreement was to follow, and (iii) approval by Getty Oil shareholders was still necessary.

The celebration was short lived. On January 5, 1984, Texaco entered into negotiations with Mr. Getty and the J. Paul Getty Museum, which owned 11.8% of Getty Oil. Texaco offered $125 per share, and so both Mr. Getty and the Museum recommended that the Getty Oil Board accept the Texaco offer and reject the lower Pennzoil offer. Naturally, Pennzoil objected and sent a letter to the Getty Board that it had already approved its deal. Nonetheless, on January 8, 1984, the Texaco deal was announced with the signing of another formal merger agreement. At that time, it was relatively settled merger law that a merger agreement in principle with a formal contract contemplated was not an agreement at all until the signing of the formal contract, and either party was free to walk away prior to that time.

Furious, Pennzoil filed a motion in the Delaware Chancery Court seeking a preliminary injunction on the basis of a breach of contract claim against Getty Oil, the other party to the alleged contract. The motion was denied because Pennzoil failed to prove it was likely to succeed on the merits of its breach of contract claim. As a result, Pennzoil decided to sue Texaco, not a party to the Pennzoil and Getty Oil "contract," in the Texas courts for a tortious interference with that contract or contract relation. Texaco completed the Getty Oil acquisition for $128 per share. The presence of a valid contract is not always required for tortious interference that can be based either on a valid contract or the business relation. Indeed, the Restatement (Second) of Torts §§ 766 & 766 separate the two torts. Some scholars argue that separation is difficult while acknowledging that a valid contract is not always necessary and may be a valid alternative to a claim for lack of good faith against one of the parties to the contract. See Mark P. Gergen, "Tortious Interference: How It Is Engulfing Commercial Law, Why This Is Not Entirely Bad, And a Prudential Response," 38 Ariz. L. Rev. 1175 (1996) (Pennzoil's weak bad faith breach of contract claim against Getty Oil transmuted into much better tort claim against Texaco, not a party to the Pennzoil-Getty Oil business relationship).

The Texas jury was more hospitable than the Delaware Chancery court. The Texas court determined that the tort of intentional interference with contract rights requires that (i) Texaco had knowledge of the existence of Pennzoil's contract "rights," and (ii) must have actively induced the breach of those rights. Texaco had sufficient knowledge of the existence of those rights, even though it may not have known for certain that a binding contract had been made between Pennzoil and Getty Oil. The jury shocked the corporate world and awarded Pennzoil nearly $11 billion in damages, including an award of $3 billion in punitive damages. At that time the award was the largest civil verdict in history. The award was upheld by the Texas Court of Appeals, although the punitive damage award was reduced from $3 billion to $1 billion. See *Texaco, Inc. v. Pennzoil Co.*, 729 S.W.2d 768 (Tex. Ct. App. 1987). Texas law required that Texaco post a bond to appeal, but it could not afford to do so. When the U.S. Supreme Court refused to waive the requirement, Texaco filed bankruptcy. The Texas Supreme Court refused to review the case, but eventually Texaco was able to settle the case for a mere $3 billion and emerge from bankruptcy.

The *Texaco* case has been called one of the top ten contract law developments during from 1980 to 1990. E. Allan Farnsworth, "Developments in Contract Law During the 1980s: The Top Ten," 41 Case W. Res. L. Rev. 203 (1990). Professor Farnsworth cites the *Texaco* case as one reason for the rise in efforts to find reasonable liability grounds for precontractual liability. See the earlier discussion of that topic in the notes following the *Pop's Cones* case. For other discussions of the case, see Andrew R. Klein, Comment, "Devil's Advocate: Salvaging the Letter of Intent," 37 Emory L. J. 139 (1988); Christopher M. Goffinet, "The $10.53 Billion Question—When Are the Parties Bound?: Pennzoil and the Use of Agreements in Principle in Mergers and Acquisitions," 40 Vand. L. Rev. 1367 (1987); Timothy S. Feltham, "Tortious Interference with Contractual Relations: The Texaco Inc. v. Pennzoil Co. Litigation," 33 N.Y.L. Sch. L. Rev. 111 (1988); and James B. Sales, "The Tort of Interference with Contract: An Argument for Requiring a 'Valid Existing Contract' to Restrain the Use of Tort Law in Circumventing Contract Law Remedies," 22 Tex. Tech. L. Rev. 123 (1991).

F. CONTRACTING IN THE INFORMATION ERA

The information era exploded into the social, political, cultural, economic, and commercial lives of the general public in the mid-1990s. The most ubiquitous feature of the modern information-based economy, the Internet, has permanently altered the means by which contracting parties identify their needs, potential contracting partners, and negotiate, shop, and contract to purchase required goods and services. Specifically, the Internet potentially lowers the costs of all levels of the contracting process. First, the Internet lowers *search* costs. Before the information age, for example, the process of buying a car often started with a fuzzy list of features the buyer would like to have, along with identification of one or more producers. Automobile-oriented magazines could direct potential buyers to the few specific models covered in their pages every month, some buyers could identify potential vehicles through word-of-mouth reports from friends and associates, and a buyer could always risk a visit to the local dealerships to look at the cars first-hand. Now, a buyer can identify relevant sources of information through Google, Yahoo, AltaVista, Clusty, or other Internet search engines, log onto any number of free decision-engine services, learn about various features offered by different producers, rate the importance of those features, and receive a list of vehicles that satisfy those criteria. Instead of the days or weeks of searching required in the pre-information era context, a dedicated buyer might spend a few hours searching for information about features, costs, available suppliers, and so on.

Second, the Internet lowers *information* costs. Not only is it easier for a buyer to search for products and services that will satisfy its particular needs, but also the cost of that information in terms of time and money is drastically lower than in the pre-information era. As Judge Easterbrook of the Seventh Circuit (and author of the opinions in two of the leading cases below) has noted, the Internet represents a reduction of the costs of information copying and dissemination similar to that caused by Gutenberg's moveable type printing press and the Xerox photocopier. See Frank H. Easterbrook, *Cyberspace and the Law of the Horse*, 1996 U. Chi. Legal F. 207, 208 (1996) (noting that the reduction of copying costs in cyberspace "continues a trend that began when Gutenberg invented movable type and gave rise to political demand for what has become copyright law"). Before the information era, producers who wanted buyers to learn about their products had to buy expensive print, television, or radio advertising or rely on word-of-mouth. Buyers likewise had to incur substantial costs in locating information about products in which they were interested. Now, producers, consumers, third parties interested in selling related products, and others all can—and do—send and receive information about various goods and services on the Internet or send the information by email for a de minimis cost. Importantly, producers no longer have exclusive control over disseminating information about their reputations or their products. As illustrated by the numerous product weblogs, third-party reviews, and consumer complaint websites that proliferate on the Internet, interested consumers can now access a wider range of critical material about both producers and their products than ever before.

Third, producers in the information age have lower *menu* costs. The term "menu costs" refers to the costs that a producer of goods and services must incur to alter its pricing structure or standard contract terms in response to changing marketplace conditions. Amy E. Cortese, *Good-bye to Fixed Pricing?*, Business Week May 4, 1998, at 71. "For a company with a large product line, it could take months for price adjustments to filter down to distributors, retailers, and salespeople." Id. Information technology, however, permits producers to alter their pricing structures nearly instantaneously and costlessly. See id. As a result, producers can change their entire price scheme in response to general changes in the market, or they can tailor their pricing and even their contract terms to the characteristics of the particular consumer to whom they are attempting to make a sale. Such pricing discrimination based upon information about particular consumers is probably widespread in Internet-based contracting. Amazon.com, for example, dropped its pricing discrimination policies after a consumer discovered that the company charged him a high price for a CD when his computer showed him to be a repeat customer and a low price when Amazon.com believed him to be a first-time customer. See Robert A. Hillman & Jeffrey J. Rachlinski, Standard Form Contracting in the Electronic Age, 77 N.Y.U. L. Rev. 429, 471–72 (2002). Price discrimination is a generally inoffensive and common business practice. See id. at 472. But the ease with which producers can change both their prices and their contract terms in response to individual consumer characteristics raises the possibility that producers may offer superior terms and prices to savvy consumers who are known to compare prices and read boilerplate, while offering inferior or even oppressive terms to consumers who do not. See id.

Fourth, information age commercial practices offer increased opportunities for both *customization* and *standardization* of contract terms. Margaret Jane Radin, for example, has proposed that producers could provide consumers with a menu of boilerplate contract terms, allowing individual consumers to choose whether to accept the default arbitration clause or to purchase the right to litigate in federal or state court for an additional charge. See Margaret Jane Radin, *Online Standardization and the Integration of Text and Machine*, 70 Fordham L. Rev. 1125, 1144–45 (2002) ("Instead of the take it or leave it set a fine print terms, a web site could offer a menu of choices for various clauses, and the user could check boxes for which ones were desired. One might choose the warranty disclaimer (free) or the two-year warranty (pay $1 extra); one might choose to accede to the arbitration clause (free) or the clause allowing litigation in one's home state (pay $2 extra)."); see also Omri Ben-Shahar, Boilerplate: The Foundation of Market Contracts (2007); Nancy Kim, Wrap Contracts: Foundations and Ramifications (2013). Many producers already offer a limited menu of choices, including options for consumers to purchase extended warranties, service contracts, or better shipping options. See id. Whether producers provide consumers with the freedom to alter the standardized boilerplate terms, of course, depends upon whether the market demands that flexibility. At the same time, information technology also tends to standardize transactions. Producers can access their competitors' online form contract terms and quickly and easily adopt those terms in their prices and own contracts. Similarly, because there is no human-to-human contact between consumers and producers, there are also no opportunities for individuation of contract terms that could otherwise occur in the real-world contracting context

Consider how each of these factors affects the parties' contracting behavior and expectations, as well as how the court responded to these issues. Do changes in contracting practices in the information age represent merely an extension of the issues addressed by previous cases in this chapter, or do they radically alter the very nature of contract? Is the contract law developed by pre-information era courts still sufficient to regulate the parties' relationships in age of the Internet? Finally, consider whether these questions can even be answered. Judge Easterbrook, author of the lead case below, stated in a 1996 symposium that "I don't know much about cyberspace; what I do know will be outdated in five years (if not five months!); and my predictions about the direction of change are worthless, making any effort to tailor the law to the subject futile." Frank H.

Easterbrook, *Cyberspace and the Law of the Horse*, 1996 U. Chi. Legal F. 207, 208 (1996). Was he right?

CHAPTER 4

THE SCOPE OF CONTRACTUAL OBLIGATIONS

■ ■ ■

The two previous chapters addressed to the enforceability of promises and the mechanics of the agreement process. However, most contractual disputes do not relate to such matters, but rather to the scope and meaning of the contract itself. This chapter assumes that a contract has been formed and endeavors to determine the content of its terms and the meaning of those terms. Controversies tend to cluster around a few central themes including (1) whether the parties intended a writing to preclude prior representations and understandings from adding to or varying the terms of the writing (the "parol evidence rule"); (2) the unprovided case (an omitted term to be supplied by law or implied through intent); (3) the problem of the meaning of ambiguous terms selected by the parties (an interpretation issue resolved by choosing between the two meanings); (4) the problem of bad faith (good faith implied by law to attach to all contractual rights and obligations); and (5) independent obligations implied by law (implied warranties).

The making of a contract is a form of private lawmaking where the parties create new rights and duties for their own self-interest. Naturally, there are limits to this power. A contract may not displace public law to alter the application of governmental rules to the contracting parties, such as by displacing a rule of criminal law. But the power of contract is more extensive in the field of private law that governs the relationship between individuals and their property, at least if the private law at issue concerns only the contracting parties. Contract law, for example, might well alter the normative tort rules that would otherwise apply between the parties to the contract. Obviously, such a contract has no application to tort rules between the contracting parties and other persons who are not a party to the contract. Given this enormous range of contractual influence, it should not be surprising that serious disputes arise between contracting parties, particularly when one the parties attempts to use the contract itself to shield or displace rights created under other private law, such as tort and property law. No contract can expressly consider every conceivable question regarding its performance or nonperformance. Consequently, disagreements regarding the scope and meaning of contracts occupy a large share of contractual disputes. The largest share of these disputes relates to understanding precisely the terms and meaning of the parties' agreement. When that question becomes unclear, a court must resolve the issue by choosing between the opposing views of the parties to the contract. This chapter concerns the rules that guide courts in this process.

It is tempting to suggest that the scope and meaning of a contract involves little more than determining the intent of the parties. Such a model is not entirely satisfactory for several reasons, each relating to the cluster of central interpretive themes discussed above.

First, the mutual intent of the parties to limit the scope of their contractual rights and obligations to the terms contained in a written memorial may not be clear. For example, the parol evidence rule purposes to define and limit the universe of terms and meanings that are the subject of a court's determination of the parties' intentions where the parties have reduced at least some part of their agreement to writing. In applying the parol evidence rule, however, the writing itself might not expressly consider the effect of the writing regarding prior negotiations, understandings, and agreements. It is simple to presume the written terms displace inconsistent oral terms. But it is often not obvious that the parties intended the writing to discharge other collateral oral agreements regarding additional arrangements between the parties that supplement the written contract.

Second, the parties may fail to consider or agree as to which party should bear the risk of certain future contingencies. When the agreement does not consider a particular contingency, should the law supply a reasonable substitute, and if so, what policy supports such an approach? If possible, should a court attempt to infer what the parties would have provided if they had considered the matter (presumed intent)? If so, what policy supports such implication, and on what basis would a court make such an implication?

Third, the parties may not share the same intentions. While the objective theory of assent reduces the risks of unenforceability because of a lack of actual agreement as to the parties' respective intentions, in some cases even an objective assessment of their intent will not produce a single, reasonable meaning. If the parties choose the same ambiguous term for their agreement, but at the time of contract attach different but plausible meanings to the same term, how should the court choose which meaning should prevail?

Fourth, the public in some situations may have a legitimate interest in regulating some aspects of the parties' agreement, even if that agreement expressly considers those matters. This last area of difficulty in determining party intent addresses two separate situations. On the one hand, the public interest in ensuring that the regime of contract itself remains a trustworthy, coherent, and useful tool for the private organization of legal relationships may require courts to impose constraints upon the parties' actions. Thus, it is axiomatic that every contract has the power to shape the contractual relationship between the parties, but what about other private law, such as tort law? Is all or part of tort law subject to contract law? On the other hand, contract law may provide parties with a pre-established set of default terms that the parties may vary by explicit contract. The ancient doctrine of *caveat emptor* provided that the purchaser of real estate, goods, or services was protected only by the contract as to the quality of the contractual subject matter. Does the law now displace *caveat emptor* and imply certain quality features? If so, are such features themselves immutable to contract?

A. IDENTIFYING THE TERMS OF A WRITTEN AGREEMENT: THE PAROL EVIDENCE RULE

When the parties to a contract reduce the terms of their agreement to a writing, intending that writing to be the final expression of their agreement, the terms of the writing may not be contradicted by evidence of any other prior agreement. But this simplistic description serves mostly to create an illusion of certainty. John H. Murray, Jr., "The Parol Evidence Rule: A Clarification," 4 Duq. U. L. Rev. 337, 337–338 (1965). In its simplest form, the "parol evidence rule" precludes proof of terms to add to or vary the terms of subsequent written contract where the writing was intended as the final and complete expression of the agreement. Restatement (Second) of Contracts § 213; UCC § 2–202. From that simple beginning emerges a complex web of convoluted doctrine famously described over a century ago as "[f]ew things in our law are darker than this, or fuller of subtle difficulties." James B. Thayer, "The 'Parol Evidence' Rule," 6 Harv. L. Rev. 325 (1893). John H. Wigmore, a famous authority on evidence, once quipped that "[t]here is no magic in the writing itself." Comment, "The Parol Evidence Rule: A Conservative View," 19 U. Chi. L. Rev. 348 (1951). A court later observed that the rule is a "positive menace to the due administration of justice." Comment, "The Parol Evidence Rule: Is It Necessary?," 44 N.Y.U. L. Rev. 972 (1969). Nonetheless, the rule survives today, albeit in different forms in different states. A lawyer can ill afford to ignore its idiosyncrasies and does so to the peril of the client.

Over time, various theories have been advanced to justify the parol evidence rule. Originally, the rule was said to grant the subsequent writing preferential status in order to make it immune to perjured testimony and slippery memory. Charles T. McCormick, "The Parol Evidence Rule as a Procedural Device for Control of the Jury," 41 Yale L. J. 365, 366–367 (1931). This view comports with the historical development of the rule in England. John H. Wigmore, "A Brief History of the Parol Evidence Rule,"4 Colum. L. Rev. 338, 350 (1904). Another variant, and perhaps the most influential, is the modern view that the parol evidence rule is simply an embodiment of the larger contractual notion allowing parties to mutually "discharge" prior obligations. Restatement (Second) of Contracts § 213 (integrated agreement "discharges" prior inconsistent agreements). If this is true of antecedent contractual agreements, it is certainly true of lower status preliminary negotiations. Arthur L. Corbin, "The Parol Evidence Rule," 53 Yale L. J. 603, 607–608 (1944). Perhaps also the rule fosters wiser drafting by encouraging the parties to include all terms in the later writing in order to avoid the risk of later exclusion by the rule. Comment, "The Parol Evidence Rule: Is It Necessary?," 44 N.Y.U. L. Rev. 972, 982 (1969). Some doubt the rule has ever had such an effect. Justin A. Sweet, "Contract Making and Parol Evidence: Diagnosis and Treatment of a Sick Rule," 53 Cornell L. Rev. 1036 (1967). Worse, perhaps, the rule excludes truthful evidence of earlier agreements on the theory that the later writing was intended to discharge all prior agreements. In practice, the parol evidence rule is less concerned with the truth of the agreement or testimony than with the theoretical higher dignity of a later written contract constituting the final and exclusive statement of all matters previously discussed or promised relating to the same subject matter. Making matters worse yet, the rule is inconsistently applied at various levels in various states.

If the policy of a rule that excludes truth offends notions of justice, the rule itself must also find its roots in a form of justice that respects the bargaining process according to its true "give and take" nature. Through such a process, parties will bargain away some terms in exchange for others on the reasonable belief that the written deal is the final deal. Does it offend that process to permit one of the parties to offer proof of other agreed terms that did not find their way into the writing? John H. Murray, Jr., "The Parol Evidence Rule: A Clarification," 4 Duq. U. L. Rev. 337, 338 (1965). Over time, through cases testing the limits and fairness of the rule, the doctrine has been narrowed through a laundry list of "justice" exceptions, but its roots are firmly planted. The exceptions have not yet swallowed the rule. Consequently, no lawyer can wisely ignore its reach when attempting to offer proof to a jury of a promise once made that failed to make its way into a later written contract embracing the same subject matter.

A few clues to Professor Thayer's "dark imaginings" begin with the name of the rule itself. The term "parol" is French in origin, meaning spoken or oral. Joseph Urquico, "Parol Evidence Rule," 5 Notre Dame L. 303 (1920). But the rule applies with equal force to written evidence. The rule is stated as one of "evidence" and admittedly permits the judge to exclude certain types of evidence from the jury to determine its truth, but this alone does not make it a rule of evidence. Rules of evidence are generally reserved for testing the quality of proof, whereas the parol evidence rule bars any proof of the fact itself, regardless of the quality of the evidence. This aspect led a noted evidence scholar to conclude that the rule is not one of evidence, but rather of substantive law. John H. Wigmore, "A Brief History of the Parol Evidence Rule," 4 Colum. L. Rev. 338 (1904). Indeed, if one adopts Roscoe Pound's definition of a "rule" as a "legal precept attaching a definite detailed legal consequence to a definite detailed state of fact," the parol evidence rule barely even qualifies as a rule. 2 Pound, Jurisprudence 124 (1959) and Lawrence M. Friedman, "Law, Rules, and the Interpretation of Written Documents," 59 Nw. U. L. Rev. 751 (1965). Moreover, while there is substantial agreement as to the core aspects of the rule, the margins are less clear. Notably, most of the controversy concerns whether the parties truly intended the writing to discharge prior and contemporaneous negotiations and agreements. See John D. Calamari & Joseph M. Perillo, "A Plea for a Uniform Parol Evidence Rule and Principles of Contract Interpretation," 42 Ind. L. J. 333, 337 (1967). These difficulties led one noted scholar to conclude the "parol evidence rule" might just as well have been called the "paper and ink rule." Arthur L. Corbin, "The Parol Evidence Rule," 53 Yale L. J. 603, 606 (1944).

The following materials consider the traditional as well as the modern parol evidence rule and the way it has evolved through the first and second restatements. In all cases, understanding will be greatly advanced by separating two related but necessarily independent questions. First, what evidence will a judge consider to determine the parol evidence outcome (admission of the proffered evidence)? Second, what rules shape the parol evidence outcome regardless of what evidence the judge considers?

1.   INTEGRATION TEST AND COLLATERAL AGREEMENT RULE

As with most contract doctrines, the parol evidence rule is derived from the intent of the parties discerned from the written contract. The specific relevant intent is the "discharging intent" of the writing with regard to prior negotiations. Arthur L. Corbin, "The Parol Evidence Rule," 53 Yale L. J. 603, 607–608 (1944). Some level of contract negotiations precedes every contract, and so the written contract will be intended to have some effect on those negotiations. The question is one of degree. Clearly, later written terms would discharge earlier contrary oral and written terms. Accordingly, earlier terms should never be permitted to "vary" the terms in the later writing. But the writing might be silent with regard to the earlier oral or written terms. In these cases, may the earlier oral or written terms "add" to those already expressed in the later writing? If so, together the oral and written terms would then express the entire agreement of the parties. When one of the parties asserts that the later writing discharged the earlier oral or written terms, the parol evidence rule is activated to resolve the matter. It does so by a judge deciding a question of fact. Did the parties intend the later written agreement to become their final, complete, and "integrated" expression, or did they intend the prior oral or written agreements to become part of their total agreement? Importantly, the parol evidence rule does not resolve asserted different intents by the parties. It only provides a legal construct empowering the judge to resolve the disagreement regarding the "legal" intent to be associated with the later writing. John H. Murray, Jr., "The Parol Evidence Rule: A Clarification," 4 Duq. U. L. Rev. 337, 338 (1965).

Early common law refused to admit evidence of an earlier "collateral agreement" when the subject matters were related. To be admitted, an early "distinctness test" required that the earlier parol agreement relate to a distinct subject matter.

THOMPSON V. LIBBEY

Supreme Court of Minnesota
34 Minn. 374, 26 N.W. 1 (1885)

Appeal from an order of the district court, Dakota county, denying motion for new trial.

MITCHELL, J.

The plaintiff being the owner of a quantity of logs marked "H. C. A.," cut in the winters of 1882 and 1883, and lying in the Mississippi river, or on its banks, above Minneapolis, defendant and the plaintiff, through his agent, D. S. Mooers, having fully agreed on the terms of a sale and purchase of the logs referred to, executed the following written agreement:

AGREEMENT

HASTINGS, MINN., June 1, 1883.

I have this day sold to R. C. Libbey, of Hastings, Minn., all my logs marked "H. C. A.," cut in the winters of 1882 and 1883, for ten dollars a thousand feet, boom scale at Minneapolis, Minnesota. Payment, cash, as fast as scale bills are produced.

[Signed]
J. H. Thompson,
Per D. S. Mooers,
R. C. Libbey.

This action having been brought for the purchase money, and defendant having pleaded a warranty of the quality of the logs, alleged to have been made at the time of the sale, and a breach of it, offered on the trial oral testimony to prove the warranty, which was admitted, over the objection of plaintiff that it was incompetent to prove a verbal warranty, the contract of sale being in writing. This raises the only point in the case.

No ground was laid for the reformation of the written contract, and any charge of fraud on part of plaintiff or his agent in making the sale was on the trial expressly disclaimed. No rule is more familiar than that "parol contemporaneous evidence is inadmissible to contradict or vary the terms of a valid written instrument," and yet none has given rise to more misapprehension as to its application. It is a rule founded on the obvious inconvenience and injustice that would result if matters in writing, made with consideration and deliberation, and intended to embody the entire agreement of the parties, were liable to be controlled by what Lord Coke expressively calls "the uncertain testimony of slippery memory." Hence, where the parties have deliberately put their engagements into writing in such terms as to import a legal obligation, without any uncertainty as to the object or extent of such engagement, it is conclusively presumed that the whole engagement of the parties, and the manner and extent of their undertaking, was reduced to writing. 1 Greenl. Ev. § 275. Of course, the rule presupposed that the parties intended to have the terms of their complete agreement embraced in the writing, and hence it does not apply where the writing is incomplete on its face and does not purport to contain the whole agreement; as in the case of mere bills of parcels, and the like.

But in what manner shall it be ascertained whether the parties intended to express the whole of their agreement in the writing? It is sometimes loosely stated that where the whole contract be not reduced to writing, parol evidence may be admitted to prove the part omitted. But to allow a party to lay the foundation for such parol evidence by oral testimony that only part of the agreement was reduced to writing, and then prove by parol the part omitted, would be to work in a circle, and to permit the very evil which the rule was designed to prevent. The only criterion of the completeness of the written contract as a full expression of the agreement of the parties is the writing itself. If it imports on its face to be a complete expression of the whole agreement—that is, contains such language as imports a complete legal obligation—it is to be presumed that the parties here introduced into it every material item and term; and parol evidence cannot be admitted to add another term to the agreement, although the writing contains nothing on the particular one to which the parol evidence is directed. The rule forbids to add by parol when the writing is silent, as well as to vary where it speaks,—2 Phil. Ev. (Cow. & H. Notes,) 669; Naumberg v. Young, 44 N. J. Law, 333; Hei v. Heller, 53 Wis. 415; S. C. 10 N. W. Rep. 620—and the law controlling the operation of a written contract becomes a part of it, and cannot be varied by parol any more than what is written. 2 Phil. Ev. (Cow. & H. Notes,) 668; La Farge v. Rickert, 5 Wend. 187; Creery v. Holly, 14 Wend. 26. . . . The written agreement in the case at bar, as it appears on its face, in connection with the law controlling its construction and operation, purports to be a complete expression of the whole agreement of the parties as to the sale and purchase of these logs, solemnly executed by both parties. There is nothing on its face (and this is a question of law for the court) to indicate that it is a mere informal and incomplete memorandum. Parol evidence of extrinsic facts and circumstances would, if necessary, be admissible, as it always is, to apply the contract to its subject matter, or in order to a more perfect understanding of its language. But in that case such evidence is used, not to contradict or vary the written instrument, but to aid, uphold, and enforce it as it stands. The language of this contract "imports a legal obligation, without any uncertainty as to its object or the extent of the engagement," and therefore "it must be conclusively presumed that the whole engagement of the parties, and the manner and extent of the undertaking, was reduced to writing." No new term, forming a mere incident to or part of the contract of sale, can be added by parol. That in case of a sale of personal property a warranty of its quality is an item and term of the contract of sale, and not a separate and independent collateral contract, and therefore cannot be added to the written agreement by oral testimony, has been distinctly held by this court, in accordance, not only with the great weight of authority, but also, as we believe, with the soundest principles. Jones v. Alley, 17 Minn. 292 (Gil. 269.)

We are referred to Healy v. Young, 21 Minn. 389, as overruling this. This is an entire misapprehension of the point decided in the latter case. In Healy v. Young the claim of defendant was that for a certain consideration plaintiff agreed verbally to release a certain debt, and also to convey certain personal property; and that, in part performance of this prior verbal agreement, he executed a bill of sale of the property. What was decided was that the execution in writing of the bill of sale in part performance of this verbal agreement did not preclude defendant from proving by parol the prior agreement. The parties had not put their original agreement in writing, and the bill of sale executed in part performance in no way superseded it. Moreover, the promise to release the debt was a distinct collateral matter from that covered by the bill of sale, and in that view of the case it was immaterial whether the oral agreement preceded or was contemporaneous with the bill of sale.

In opposition to the doctrine of Jones v. Alley, we are referred to a few cases which seem to hold that parol evidence of a warranty is admissible on the ground that a warranty is collateral to the contract of sale, and that the rule does not exclude parol evidence of matters collateral to the subject of the written agreement. It seems to us that this is based upon a misapprehension as to the sense in which the term "collateral" is used in the rule invoked. There are a great many matters that, in a general sense, may be considered collateral to the contract; for example, in the case of leases, covenants for repairs, improvements, payment of taxes, etc., are, in a sense, collateral to a demise of the premises. But parol evidence of these would not be admissible to add to the terms of a written lease. So, in a sense, a warranty is collateral to a contract of sale, for the title would pass without a warranty. It is also collateral in the sense that its breach is no ground for a rescission of the contract by the vendor, but that he must resort to his action on the warranty for damages. But, when made, a warranty is a part of the contract of sale. The common sense of men would say, and correctly so, that when, on a sale of personal property, a warranty is given, it is one of the terms of the sale, and not a separate and independent contract. To justify the admission of a parol promise by one of the parties to a written contract on the ground that it is collateral, the promise must relate to a subject distinct from that to which the writing relates. . . .

We have carefully examined all the cases cited in the quite exhaustive brief of counsel for defendant, and find but very few that are at all in conflict with the views already expressed, and these few do not commend themselves to our judgment. Our conclusion therefore is that the court erred in admitting parol evidence of a warranty, and therefore the order refusing a new trial must be

Reversed.

NOTES AND QUESTIONS

1.   *Early parol evidence test.* The *Thompson* court takes a very narrow view of the collateral agreement rule. What do you suppose the court means by the following statement: "To justify the admission of a parol promise by one of the parties to a written contract on the ground that it is collateral, the promise must relate to a subject distinct from that to which the writing relates."? How does the court apply the distinctness test? What does the distinctness test presume? Do you agree with that presumption?

2.   *Role of judge and jury.* Notice the *Thompson* court makes the determination of whether the parol evidence is admissible. If not, the evidence does not reach the trier of fact, be that a judge or jury, to determine whether the promise was truthfully made. Thompson, the seller of logs, sued Libbey, the purchaser of the logs, to obtain payment according to the terms of the original written contract. In defense, Libbey asserted that his refusal to pay was justified because of Thompson's breach of an oral promise warranting that the logs were of a specified quality. The trial court judge admitted Libbey's testimony as to the existence of the oral warranty. The jury believed Libbey, or perhaps Thompson did not even contest the fact that he made the warranty. Since the Supreme Court reversed the trial judge's decision to admit the evidence of the oral warranty, what is the point of a new trial? Is it relevant to the parol evidence rule even if Thompson admits he made the warranty so that the truth of the statement is not in doubt?

3.   *Express warranties and contract disclaimers.* The written contract did not state that the logs were sold "as is" or without any warranties, express or otherwise. If the contract had stated a written disclaimer of prior express warranties, how do you think the conflict should be resolved? See UCC § 2–316(1). Stated another way, does the parol evidence in general grant greater dignity to the writing or the prior oral negotiations? If the answer is that the

later writing is more important, why would the written disclaimer not always discharge prior oral warranties?

4.   *Interpretation rules and other exceptions.* The *Thompson* court also mentioned that not all extrinsic evidence is precluded by the parol evidence rule, even if the subject matters of the two agreements are closely related. Notably, such evidence may be admitted in order to have a more perfect understanding of its language. Also, there are numerous fairness exceptions. Both topics are explored in separate sections later in this chapter.

By the early twentieth century and the time of Restatement (First) of Contracts, the collateral agreement rule gradually expanded to relax the distinct subject matter test applied in *Thompson v. Libbey*. Both restatements express the requisite discharging intent of the writing in terms of the stage of "integration" of the writing. Restatement (First) of Contracts § 228; Restatement (Second) of Contracts § 209(1). Specifically, did the parties intend the writing to be an integrated writing, and if so, did they intend the integration to be total (discharge all prior evidence) or only partial (discharge only prior inconsistent evidence)? Arthur L. Corbin, "The Parol Evidence Rule," 53 Yale L. J. 603, 607–608 (1944). Total integration is easily the most important issue considered by the parol evidence rule. John D. Calamari & Joseph M. Perillo, "A Plea for a Uniform Parol Evidence Rule and Principles of Contract Interpretation," 42 Ind. L. J. 333, 337 (1967). The reason is simple. Under both restatements, the parol evidence rule does not bar evidence of prior negotiations to add terms to supplement a "partially integrated" writing provided the additional terms do not vary any terms expressed in the writing. Restatement (First) of Contracts §§ 229, 239; Restatement (Second) of Contracts §§ 210(2), 213(1). However, if the writing is "totally integrated," then the parol evidence rule bars evidence even of consistent additional terms. Restatement (First) of Contracts §§ 228, 237; Restatement (Second) of Contracts §§ 210(1), 213(2). So the rule always bars parol evidence to vary or contradict the written terms of a later agreement, but unless the writing is considered totally integrated, parol evidence can be admitted to add terms to supplement the agreement.

So stated, the integration test searches for the discharging intent of the parties. Ordinarily the subject of "intent" involves a question of fact for a jury. But in the parol evidence rule context, courts have traditionally treated this particular intent issue as a question of law. The reason? The law (judge)/fact (jury) dichotomy is most often resolved by reference to the general (judge)/specific (jury) application doctrine. Since integration "intent" is an objective intent, and not the subjective intent of the particular speaker, most judges decide the integration test. William C. Whitford, "The Role of the Jury (and the Fact/Law Distinction) in the Interpretation of Written Contracts," 2001 Wis. L. Rev. 931, 934 (2001); Ronald

J. Allen & Michael S. Pardo, "The Myth of the Law—Fact Distinction," 97 Nw. U. L. Rev. 1769, 1782 (2003); and Restatement (Second) of Contracts § 209, *comment c* (question of fact ordinarily decided by the judge).

A serious challenge to the application of the parol evidence rule and the integration test occurs when the same parties go beyond mere negotiation of terms and actually make two agreements at approximately the same time. Where one of these contemporaneous agreements is oral and the other is in writing, and the writing is silent as to the oral agreement, the parol evidence rule may bar enforcement of the otherwise valid oral agreement. Is the parol agreement separate and distinct from the later writing, or is it collateral in form? William G. Hale, "The Parol Evidence Rule," 4 Or. L. Rev. 91, 95 (1925). If separate and distinct, the parol evidence rule does not apply.

Under the test applied in *Thompson v. Libbey*, the analysis is simple. The court examines the written record of the agreement and determines whether the writing is a full, final, or complete integration of the parties' contract. If the court determines that it is a complete integration, the analysis ends. If not, the court admits the parol evidence to supplement or explain the writing.

As the parol evidence rule developed in the early twentieth century, courts added additional nuances to this basic analysis. As described in the next case, *Mitchill v. Lath*, courts came to consider not just the "four corners" of the document, but also additional contextual factors that might indicate that the writing was not a complete integration. Thus, in *Thompson*, the terse written record, in the context of what might normally be included in such bargains, might not be a complete integration of the agreement. As this theme developed, courts added additional tests for integration and the collateral agreement rule. The first and easiest test for "distinctness" is normally determined by reference to whether the two agreements share common consideration. Restatement (First) of Contracts § 240(1)(a); Restatement (Second) of Contracts § 216(2)(a). For example, if a buyer agrees in a signed written agreement to purchase a house from a seller for $750,000 and also orally agrees to rent the premises back to the seller for six months for a total $10,000 rent, the two agreements do not share common consideration. Each agreement was supported by separate consideration. As a result, the buyer may not use the parol evidence rule to prevent the seller from introducing evidence of the prior or contemporaneous "collateral" rental agreement, even if the later writing includes a merger clause (a concept discussed later). The parol evidence rule simply does not apply to the independent or ancillary agreement. Restatement (First) of Contracts § 240(1)(a); Restatement (Second) of Contracts § 216(2)(a).

On the other hand, the parties could structure the same transaction so that it would fail the distinctness test and trigger the parol evidence rule. Suppose that the parties orally agreed that instead of paying rent back to the buyer, the seller would reduce the purchase price by $10,000 to $740,000. The two agreements share common consideration ($750,000) and related subject matters (purchase of the home), but the writing is silent (and therefore not inconsistent) with regard to the oral rental agreement. In such circumstances, how is a judge to determine whether the collateral promise in form is also doctrinally collateral such that evidence of it might be admitted? Once again, both restatements commonly resolve this question by reference to whether the first rental agreement might naturally be expected to be included in the second written purchase agreement. Restatement (First) of Contracts § 240(1)(b) ("is such an agreement as might naturally be made as a separate agreement by parties situated as were the parties to the written contract"); Restatement (Second) of Contracts § 216(2)(b) ("such a term as in the circumstances might naturally be omitted from the writing").

A judge, not a jury, decides the common "natural omission" test. The reason relates back to the objective theory of contracts. Since the natural omission test seeks to understand the objective discharging intent of the parties, the judge decides whether these two parties objectively expressed discharging intent in the later writing. If not, evidence of the parol rental agreement is admitted to the trier of fact (normally a jury) to determine whether in fact the disputed rental agreement was actually made. What evidence does the judge consider in making this determination and whose intent matters? Evidence includes: (i) the facial completeness of the later writing itself; (ii) a comparison of the terms of the two alleged agreements; (iii) the circumstances surrounding the making of the two alleged agreements; and (iv) oral and written extrinsic evidence of prior or contemporaneous negotiations regarding what the parties intended. On this score, the two restatements are incredibly different.

The case below, *Mitchill v. Lath*, was decided in 1928. Accordingly, the Restatement (First) of Contracts § 230 reflects the approach utilized by the New York Court:

Restatement (First) of Contracts § 230 (1932) Standard of Interpretation Where There Is Integration

The standard of interpretation of an integration, except where it produces an ambiguous result, or is excluded by a rule of law establishing a definite meaning, is the meaning that would be attached to the integration by a reasonably intelligent person acquainted with all operative usages and knowing all the circumstances prior to and contemporaneous with the making of the integration, other than oral statements by the parties of what they intended it to mean.

Professor Samuel Williston,* the reporter for the Restatement (First) of Contracts, thus understood there were three levels of evidence that a judge might entertain to resolve the "naturalness" test: (i) the completeness of the writing itself (the so-called "four corners rule"); (ii) the circumstances surrounding the execution of the writing; and (iii) the oral and written evidence of the parties as to what they specifically intended. Restatement (First) of Contracts § 230 specifically excludes consideration of the oral and written evidence of the parties but expressly approves an examination of the writing as well as surrounding circumstances. The first restatement thus does not adopt the four corners rule.

The *Mitchill* case is considered the quintessential referent for the Restatement (First) of Contracts "collateral agreement rule." As you study the case, consider the dilemma of Catherine Mitchill as she argues that her promise to purchase the farm was expressly subject to the seller's prior or contemporaneous oral promise to remove an unsightly icehouse across the road. The icehouse was located on a pond used for recreational swimming, making it particularly obnoxious. Also, trucks made deliveries to the icehouse at all hours of the night, making loud noises and disturbing sleep. Therefore, assume for the moment that Catherine Mitchill would not have agreed to purchase the farm unless Charles Lath also promised to remove the icehouse. So if the promise was vitally important, why would her lawyer not include the icehouse promise in the agreement to purchase the farm? If you decide that Lath made the promise and that, at the time the farm purchase agreements were executed, both Catherine Mitchill and Charles Lath subjectively intended that his promise to remove the icehouse was not to be discharged by the written purchase agreement, could the court nonetheless exclude the promise? If so, whose discharging intent is controlling? Finally, assume that Charles Lath merely changed his mind after executing the purchase documents and now does not intend to remove the icehouse because he understands the parol evidence rule might prevent Catherine Mitchill from introducing evidence of his promise. In such cases, what is the role of his lawyer?

---

* Samuel Williston (1861–1963) graduated from Harvard Law School in 1888, clerked with Supreme Court Justice Horace Gray for one year, practiced law in Boston for another year, and in 1890 joined the Harvard law faculty. He remained at Harvard Law until his retirement in 1938. Notably, he was the reporter for four uniform laws, including the Uniform Sales Act (the predecessor to the Uniform Commercial Code), and was the Reporter for the Restatement (First) of Contracts. His treatise on Contracts is a classic and is continually edited and cited as an authority by judges, lawyers, and law professors. For a comprehensive discussion of Williston's career, see Mark L. Movsesian, "Rediscovering Williston," 62 Wash. & Lee L. Rev. 207 (2005).

MITCHILL V. LATH

Court of Appeals of New York
247 N.Y. 377, 160 N.E. 646 (1928)

Action by Catherine C. Mitchill against Charles Lath and another. Judgment of Special Term in plaintiff's favor, directing specific performance of an agreement to remove an icehouse, was affirmed by the Appellate Division (220 App. Div. 776, 221 N. Y. S. 864), and defendants appeal.

ANDREWS, J.

In the fall of 1923 the Laths owned a farm. This they wished to sell. Across the road, on land belonging to Lieutenant Governor Lunn, they had an icehouse which they might remove. Mrs. Mitchill looked over the land with a view to its purchase. She found the icehouse objectionable. Thereupon "the defendants orally promised and agreed, for and in consideration of the purchase of their farm by the plaintiff, to remove the said icehouse in the spring of 1924." Relying upon this promise, she made a written contract to buy the property for $8,400, for cash and mortgage and containing various provisions usual in such papers. Later receiving a deed, she entered into possession, and has spent considerable sums in improving the property for use as a summer residence. The defendants have not fulfilled their promise as to the icehouse, and do not intend to do so. We are not dealing, however, with their moral delinquencies. The question before us is whether their oral agreement may be enforced in a court of equity.

This requires a discussion of the parol evidence rule—a rule of law which defines the limits of the contract to be construed. Glackin v. Bennett, 226 Mass. 316, 115 N. E. 490. It is more than a rule of evidence, and oral testimony, even if admitted, will not control the written contract (O'Malley v. Grady, 222 Mass. 202, 109 N. E. 829), unless admitted without objection (Brady v. Nally, 151 N. Y. 258, 45 N. E. 547). It applies, however, to attempts to modify such a contract by parol. It does not affect a parol collateral contract distinct from and independent of the written agreement. It is, at times, troublesome to draw the line. Williston, in his work on Contracts (section 637) points out the difficulty. "Two entirely distinct contracts," he says,

> [E]ach for a separate consideration, may be made at the same time, and will be distinct legally. Where, however, one agreement is entered into wholly or partly in consideration of the simultaneous agreement to enter into another, the transactions are necessarily bound together. . . . Then if one of the agreements is oral and the other in writing, the problem arises whether the bond is sufficiently close to prevent proof of the oral agreement.

That is the situation here. It is claimed that the defendants are called upon to do more than is required by their written contract in connection with the sale as to which it deals.

The principle may be clear, but it can be given effect by no mechanical rule. As so often happens it is a matter of degree, for, as Prof. Williston also says, where a contract contains several promises on each side it is not difficult to put any one of them in the form of a collateral agreement. If this were enough, written contracts might always be modified by parol. Not form, but substance, is the test.

In applying this test, the policy of our courts is to be considered. We have believed that the purpose behind the rule was a wise one, not easily to be abandoned. Notwithstanding injustice here and there, on the whole it works for good. Old precedents and principles are not to be lightly cast aside, unless it is certain that they are an obstruction under present conditions. New York has been less open to arguments that would modify this particular rule, than some jurisdictions elsewhere. Thus in Eighmie v. Taylor, 98 N. Y. 288, it was held that a parol warranty might not be shown, although no warranties were contained in the writing.

Under our decisions, before such an oral agreement as the present is received to vary the written contract, at least three conditions must exist:

(1) The agreement must in form be a collateral one;

(2) it must not contradict express or implied provisions of the written contract;

(3) it must be one that parties would not ordinarily be expected to embody in the writing, or, put in another way, an inspection of the written contract, read in the light of surrounding circumstances, must not indicate that the writing appears "to contain the engagements of the parties, and to define the object and measure the extent of such engagement." Or, again, it must not be so clearly connected with the principal transaction as to be part and parcel of it.

The respondent does not satisfy the third of these requirements. It may be, not the second. We have a written contract for the purchase and sale of land. The buyer is to pay $8,400 in the way described. She is also to pay her portion of any rents, interest on mortgages, insurance premiums, and water meter charges. She may have a survey made of the premises. On their part, the sellers are to give a full covenant deed of the premises as described, or as they may be described by the surveyor, if the survey is had, executed, and acknowledged at their own expense; they sell the personal property on the farm and represent they own it; they agree that all amounts paid them on the contract and the expense of examining the title shall be a lien on the property; they assume the risk of loss or damage by fire until the deed is delivered; and they agree to pay the broker his commissions. Are they to do more? Or is such a claim inconsistent with these precise provisions? It could not be shown that the plaintiff was to pay $500 additional. Is it also implied that the defendants are not to do anything unexpressed in the writing?

That we need not decide. At least, however, an inspection of this contract shows a full and complete agreement, setting forth in detail the obligations of each party. On reading it, one would conclude that the reciprocal obligations of the parties were fully detailed. Nor would his opinion alter if he knew the surrounding circumstances. The presence of the icehouse, even the knowledge that Mrs. Mitchill thought it objectionable, would not lead to the belief that a separate agreement existed with regard to it. Were such an agreement made it would seem most natural that the inquirer should find it in the contract. Collateral in form it is found to be, but it is closely related to the subject dealt with in the written agreement—so closely that we hold it may not be proved.

Where the line between the competent and the incompetent is narrow the citation of authorities is of slight use. Each represents the judgment of the court on the precise facts before it. How closely bound to the contract is the supposed collateral agreement is the decisive factor in each case. But reference may be made to Johnson v. Oppenheim, 55 N. Y. 280, 292; Thomas v. Scutt, 127 N. Y. 133, 27 N. E. 961. . . . Of these citations, Johnson v. Oppenheim and the two in the Appellate Division relate to collateral contracts said to have been the inducing cause of the main contract. They refer to leases. A similar case is Wilson v. Deen, 74 N. Y. 531. All hold that an oral stipulation, said to have been the inducing cause for the subsequent execution of the lease itself, concerning some act to be done by the landlord, or some condition as to the leased premises, might not be shown. In principal they are not unlike the case before us. Attention should be called also to Taylor v. Hopper, 62 N. Y. 649, where it is assumed that evidence of a parol agreement to remove a barn, which was an inducement to the sale of lots, was improper.

We do not ignore the fact that authorities may be found that would seem to support the contention of the appellant. Such are Erskine v. Adeane (1873) L. R. 8 Ch. App. 756, and Morgan v. Griffith (1871) L. R. 6 Exch. 70, where, although there was a written lease a collateral agreement of the landlord to reduce the game was admitted. In this state, Wilson v. Deen might lead to the contrary result. Neither are they approved in New Jersey. Naumberg v. Young, 44 N. J. Law, 331, 43 Am. Rep. 380. Nor in view of later cases in this court can Batterman v. Pierce, 3 Hill, 171, be considered an authority. A line of cases in Massachusetts, of which Durkin v. Cobleigh, 156 Mass. 108, 30 N. E. 474, 17 L. R. A. 270, 32 Am. St. Rep. 436, is an example, have to do with collateral contracts made before a deed is given. But the fixed form of a deed makes it inappropriate to insert collateral agreements, however closely connected with the sale. This may be cause for an exception. Here we deal with the contract on the basis of which the deed to Mrs. Mitchill was given subsequently, and we confine ourselves to the question whether its terms may be modified.

Finally there is the case of Chapin v. Dobson, 78 N. Y. 74, 76, 34 Am. Rep. 512. This is acknowledged to be on the borderline and is rarely cited except to be distinguished. Assuming the premises, however, the court was clearly right. There was nothing on the face of the written contract, it said, to show that it intended to express the entire agreement. And there was a finding, sustained by evidence, that there was an entire contract, only part of which was reduced to writing. This being so, the contract as made might be proved.

It is argued that what we have said is not applicable to the case as presented. The collateral agreement was made with the plaintiff. The contract of sale was with her husband, and no assignment of it from him appears. Yet the deed was given to her. It is evident that here was a transaction in which she was the principal from beginning to end. We must treat the contract as if in form, as it was in fact, made by her.

Our conclusion is that the judgment of the Appellate Division and that of the Special Term should be reversed and the complaint dismissed, with costs in all courts.

LEHMAN, J. (dissenting).

I accept the general rule as formulated by Judge ANDREWS. I differ with him only as to its application to the facts shown in the record. The plaintiff contracted to purchase land from the defendants for an agreed price. A formal written agreement was made between the sellers and the plaintiff's husband. It is on its face a complete contract for the conveyance of the land. It describes the property to be conveyed. It sets forth the purchase price to be paid. All the conditions and terms of the conveyance to be made are clearly stated. I concede at the outset that parol evidence to show additional conditions and terms of the conveyance would be inadmissible. There is a conclusive presumption that the parties intended to integrate in that written contract every agreement relating to the nature or extent of the property to be conveyed, the contents of the deed to be delivered, the consideration to be paid as a condition precedent to the delivery of the deeds, and indeed all the rights of the parties in connection with the land. The conveyance of that land was the subject matter of the written contract, and the contract completely covers that subject.

The parol agreement which the court below found the parties had made was collateral to, yet connected with, the agreement of purchase and sale. It has been found that the defendants induced the plaintiff to agree to purchase the land by a promise to remove an icehouse from land not covered by the agreement of purchase and sale. No independent consideration passed to the defendants for the parol promise. To that extent the written contract and the alleged oral contract are bound together. The same bond usually exists wherever attempt is made to prove a parol agreement which is collateral to a written agreement. Hence "the problem arises whether the bond is sufficiently close to prevent proof of the oral agreement." See Judge Andrews' citation from Williston on Contracts, § 637.

Judge Andrews has formulated a standard to measure the closeness of the bond. Three conditions, at least, must exist before an oral agreement may be proven to increase the obligation imposed by the written agreement. I think we agree that the first condition that the agreement "must in form be a collateral one" is met by the evidence. I concede that this condition is met in most cases where the courts have nevertheless excluded evidence of the collateral oral agreement. The difficulty here, as in most cases, arises in connection with the two other conditions.

The second condition is that the "parol agreement must not contradict express or implied provisions of the written contract." Judge Andrews voices doubt whether this condition is satisfied. The written contract has been carried out. The purchase price has been paid; conveyance has been made; title has passed in accordance with the terms of the written contract. The mutual obligations expressed in the written contract are left unchanged by the alleged oral contract. When performance was required of the written contract, the obligations of the parties were measured solely by its terms. By the oral agreement the plaintiff seeks to hold the defendants to other obligations to be performed by them thereafter upon land which was not conveyed to the plaintiff. The assertion of such further obligation is not inconsistent with the written contract, unless the written contract contains a provision, express or implied, that the defendants are not to do anything not expressed in the writing. Concededly there is no such express provision in the contract, and such a provision may be implied, if at all, only if the asserted additional obligation is "so clearly connected with the principal transaction as to be part and parcel of it," and is not "one that the parties would not ordinarily be expected to embody in the writing." The hypothesis so formulated for a conclusion that the asserted additional obligation is inconsistent with an implied term of the contract is that the alleged oral agreement does not comply with the third condition as formulated by Judge ANDREWS. In this case, therefore, the problem reduces itself to the one question whether or not the oral agreement meets the third condition.

I have conceded that upon inspection the contract is complete. "It appears to contain the engagements of the parties, and to define the object and measure the extent of such engagement;" it constitutes the contract between them, and is presumed to contain the whole of that contract. Eighmie v. Taylor, 98 N. Y. 288. That engagement was on the one side to convey land; on the other to pay the price. The plaintiff asserts further agreement based on the same consideration to be performed by the defendants after the conveyance was complete, and directly affecting only other land. It is true, as Judge ANDREWS points out, that "the presence of the icehouse, even the knowledge that Mrs. Mitchill though it objectionable, would not lead to the belief that a separate agreement existed with regard to it;" but the question we must decide is whether or not, *assuming* an agreement was made for the removal of an unsightly icehouse from one parcel of land as an inducement for the purchase of another parcel, the parties would ordinarily or naturally be expected to embody the agreement for the removal of the icehouse from one parcel in the written agreement to convey the other parcel. Exclusion of proof of the oral agreement on the ground that it varies the contract embodied in the writing may be based only upon a finding or presumption that the written contract was intended to cover the oral negotiations for the removal of the icehouse which lead up to the contract of purchase and sale. To determine what the writing was intended to cover, "the document alone will not suffice. What it was intended to cover cannot be known till we know what there was to cover. The question being whether certain subjects of negotiation were intended to be covered, we must compare the writing and the negotiations before we can determine whether they were in fact covered." Wigmore on Evidence (2d Ed.) § 2430.

The subject matter of the written contract was the conveyance of land. The contract was so complete on its face that the conclusion is inevitable that the parties intended to embody in the writing all the negotiations covering at least the conveyance. The promise by the defendants to remove the icehouse from other land was not connected with their obligation to convey except that one agreement would not have been made unless the other was also made. The plaintiff's assertion of a parol agreement by the defendants to remove the icehouse was completely established by the great weight of evidence. It must prevail unless that agreement was part of the agreement to convey and the entire agreement was embodied in the writing.

The fact that in this case the parol agreement is established by the overwhelming weight of evidence is, of course, not a factor which may be considered in determining the competency or legal effect of the evidence. Hardship in the particular case would not justify the court in disregarding or emasculating the general rule. It merely accentuates the outlines of our problem. The assumption that the parol agreement was made is no longer obscured by any doubts. The problem, then, is clearly whether the parties are presumed to have intended to render that parol agreement legally ineffective and nonexistent by failure to embody it in the writing. Though we are driven to say that nothing in the written contract which fixed the terms and conditions of the stipulated conveyance suggests the existence of any further parol agreement, an inspection of the contract, though it is complete on its face in regard to the subject of the conveyance, does not, I think, show that it was intended to embody negotiations or agreements, if any, in regard to a matter so loosely bound to the conveyance as the removal of an icehouse from land not conveyed.

The rule of integration undoubtedly frequently prevents the assertion of fraudulent claims. Parties who take the precaution of embodying their oral agreements in a writing should be protected against the assertion that other terms of the same agreement were not integrated in the writing. The limits of the integration are determined by the writing, read in the light of the surrounding circumstances. A written contract, however complete, yet covers only a limited field. I do not think that in the written contract for the conveyance of land here under consideration we can find an intention to cover a field so broad as to include prior agreements, if any such were made, to do other acts on other property after the stipulated conveyance was made.

In each case where such a problem is presented, varying factors enter into its solution. Citation of authority in this or other jurisdictions is useless, at least without minute analysis of the facts. The analysis I have made of the decisions in this state leads me to the view that the decision of the courts below is in accordance with our own authorities and should be affirmed.

CARDOZO, C. J., and POUND, KELLOGG and O'BRIEN, JJ., concur with ANDREWS, J.

LEHMAN, J., dissents in opinion in which CRANE, J., concurs.

Judgment accordingly.

NOTES AND QUESTIONS

1.   *Natural omission test.* Is it possible to make a determination whether the farm purchase documents were completely integrated and intended to discharge the icehouse promise by examining the purchase documents alone? How can the natural omission test be applied without at least assuming the icehouse promise existed and then comparing the subject matter of the two agreements? Since both the majority and dissent apply the same natural omission tests, why do they reach opposite outcomes? Is it the evidence the two sides are willing to consider, or is it simply what each side makes of the same evidence?

2.   *"Parol" evidence defined.* The use of the term "parol," meaning oral or verbal, is a misnomer. Since it applies with equal force to exclude written evidence in the form of letters, telegrams, memoranda, and even preliminary written drafts, the rule might be better referred to as the "extrinsic evidence rule." See Arthur L. Corbin, "The Parol Evidence Rule," 53 Yale L. J. 603, 611 (1944); Joseph Urquico, "Parol Evidence Rule," 5 Notre Dame L. 303 (1920);

Williston on Contracts § 33.7 (4th Ed. 2006); E. Allan Farnsworth, Contracts § 7.2 (Aspen, 4th Ed. 2004); and Joseph M. Perillo, Calamari and Perillo on Contracts § 3.2 (West, 5th Ed. 2003).

3. *Prior, contemporaneous, and subsequent parol evidence.* Two of the leading contracts scholars around the time of the Restatement (First) of Contracts agreed that the rule (i) does not apply to subsequent agreements, and (ii) does apply to prior agreements. They disagreed about whether it applied to "contemporaneous" evidence. Professor Samuel Williston, the reporter for the Restatement (First) of Contracts, took the position that contemporaneous evidence should be treated the same as "prior" evidence. To no surprise, the restatement reflects his view. See Restatement (First) of Contracts § 237 (title mentions both prior and contemporaneous, but text of section refers only to contemporaneous). See also Restatement (First) of Contracts § 237, *cmt. a.* Professor Arthur L. Corbin* thought otherwise. According to Corbin, terms are either prior or subsequent, and the additional contemporaneous category simply confused the matter. See Arthur L. Corbin, "The Parol Evidence Rule," 53 Yale L. J. 603, 617 (1944) (assent at the same moment to two agreements predetermines the writing is not completely integrated). Corbin's view eventually was adopted in the Restatement (Second) of Contracts § 213(1) ("A binding integrated agreement discharges 'prior' agreements to the extent it is inconsistent with them.").

4. *Rule of evidence or substantive law.* Early on, Professor James B. Thayer, a professor of law at Harvard Law School and a highly regarded expert on evidence, regarded the parol evidence rule not as a rule of evidence at all, but rather a rule of substantive law. James B. Thayer, "The 'Parol Evidence' Rule," 6 Harv. L. Rev. 325, 326–329 (1893). However, since the integration question has become a question of law for the judge, the parol evidence rule inherits a procedural function that permits the judge to exclude the evidence from the consideration of the jury. Charles T. McCormick, "The Parol Evidence Rule as a Procedural Device for Control of the Jury,"41 Yale L. J. 365, 371 (1931). In any event, adherents of the substantive law view have won the debate. Restatement (First) of Contracts § 237, *cmt. a* ("The rule, however, is not one of evidence but of substantive law."); Restatement (Second) of Contracts § 213, *cmt. a* ("It is not a rule of evidence but a rule of substantive law.").

The primary consequence of the distinction is whether the doctrine of waiver applies. Typically, rules of evidence require timely objection to

---

* Arthur Linton Corbin (1874–1967) was born in Colorado but left to study and receive his undergraduate degree from the University of Kansas in 1894. He then graduated magna cum laude from Yale Law School in 1899. He returned to Colorado to practice law and teach high school until he was offered a position on the Yale Law School faculty in 1903 to teach contracts where he taught until he retired in 1943. Corbin on Contracts is a classic treatise and judges and legal scholars frequently cite his work. He contributed as Special Advisor and Reporter for the chapter on Remedies of the Restatement (First) of Contracts. He also influenced the Restatement (Second) of Contracts. See Joseph M. Perillo, "Twelve Letters from Arthur L. Corbin to Robert Braucher," 50 Wash. & Lee L. Rev. 755 (1993). Robert Braucher was the initial reporter for the Restatement (Second) of Contracts before resigning to become a judge on the Massachusetts Supreme Judicial Court. E. Allen Farnsworth then completed the work.

evidentiary matters. The failure to do so means the evidence so admitted becomes part of the permanent record of the case and is not reviewable for the first time on appeal. Most cases determine that the parol evidence rule is substantive and therefore can be raised for the first time on appeal and used as a basis in law to reverse a lower court ruling. See Williston on Contracts § 33:3 (4th Ed. 2006).

5. *Four corners rule and the collateral agreement rule.* Of course, the narrower the evidence considered by the judge to determine stage of integration, the more likely the parol evidence rule will have a more expansive and exclusionary effect regarding prior extrinsic evidence. Stated another way, parol evidence is self-serving to a degree because it tends to prove the writing was not intended to be complete. According to Williston, extrinsic evidence is not admissible to determine the issue of integration for purposes of applying the parol evidence rule. Rather, that issue must be determined from the subject writing itself by the trial court as matter of law. If the writing purports or appears on its face to be a complete expression of the whole agreement, the court should presume that the parties introduced into it every material item, and parol evidence cannot be admitted to add another term to the agreement. Williston on Contracts § 33:16.

But this rule cannot literally apply to determine the "natural" omission test. In applying that test, the judge must consider at least the subject matter of the parol agreement to determine its relationship to the subject matter of the writing. Without the comparison, the test simply cannot be applied. In addition to examining the subject matter of the parol and written agreements, the judge must next determine whether the parties intended the latter to discharge the former. Charles T. McCormick, "The Parol Evidence Rule as a Procedural Device for Control of the Jury," 41 Yale L. J. 365, 377 (1931).

While the four corners approach is perhaps no longer the majority rule, it has a lingering presence in many states. See, e.g., Ethyl Corporation v. Forcum-Lannom Associates, Inc., 433 N.E.2d 1214 (Ind.App. 1982); Independent Energy v. Trigen Energy, 944 F.Supp. 1184 (S.D.N.Y. 1996); and Air Safety, Inc. v. Teachers Realty, 185 Ill.2d 457, 236 Ill. Dec. 8, 706 N.E.2d 882 (1999).

6. *Unique objective versus subjective integration intent.* The determination of whether the parties might "naturally" include or exclude the evidence requires a search for the intent of those parties. The note above discusses the evidence that may be considered. But is the judge searching for the intent of one of these parties or the intent of both? Of course, in *Mitchill v. Lath* the court was faced with conflicting intent perspectives. For this reason, the Restatement (First) of Contracts § 230 did not search for the actual subjective intent of either. To do so would engage the court in a search for the presumed subjective intent, at least unless the court was willing to consider the testimony of the parties. As a consequence, Restatement (First) of Contracts § 230 engaged in a search for an objective "mythical intent" of a "reasonably intelligent person." The mythical intent was that of a reasonably

intelligent person acquainted with all operative usages and knowing all the circumstances prior to and contemporaneous with the making of the integration. Oral statements of the parties as to what they actually intended would not be considered. Did the majority in *Mitchill v. Lath* employ this test?

One interpretation is that the Restatement (First) of Contracts normally leaves the court in a position of having to resolve integration stage and consequent discharge intent solely from the face of the second document (and surrounding circumstances). Nicholas R. Weiskopf, "Supplementing Written Agreements: Restating the Parol Evidence Rule in Terms of Credibility and Relative Fault," 34 Emory L. J. 93, 101 (1985). Carefully examine again the majority opinion in *Mitchill*. What is suggested by the language of the opinion set forth below?

> At least, however, an inspection of this contract shows a full and complete agreement, setting forth in detail the obligations of each party. On reading it, one would conclude that the reciprocal obligations of the parties were fully detailed. Nor would this opinion alter if he knew the surrounding circumstances. The presence of the icehouse, even the knowledge that Mrs. Mitchill thought it objectionable, would not lead to the belief that a separate agreement existed with regard to it. Were such an agreement made it would seem most natural that the inquirer should find it in the contract. Collateral in form it is found to be, but it is closely related to the subject dealt with in the written agreement so closely that we hold it may not be proved.

Did the court consider extrinsic evidence of integration or only the face of the document? Was the decision in accord with the parol evidence rule stated in Restatement (First) of Contracts? In the final analysis, how does the court determine that the promise to remove the icehouse was not an agreement that "might naturally be made as a separate agreement"? By reference to the parties actual intent or by reference to what a mythical person (like the judge) might think in similar circumstances? Exactly whose intent is Restatement (First) of Contracts § 230 seeking?

7. *Famous and poetic.* The *Mitchill v. Lath* case is quite famous and generated the following poem. Douglass G. Boshkoff, "Selected Poems on the Law of Contracts," 66 N.Y.U. L. Rev. 1533, 1544 (1991).

8. *No jury involved.* Was the majority concerned with the possibility that the admission of parol evidence might mislead the jury? This was an action in equity seeking specific enforcement, so a jury was not involved. If the doctrine developed out of a concern over the reliability of a jury, why would it have any application to this case and action?

9. *Truth or consequences?* The court in *Mitchill v. Lath* obviously considered evidence that Charles Lath did, in fact, make the promise and even assumed that he made such a promise. If it is true that he made the promise and that Catherine Mitchill relied on that promise in purchasing and

renovating the farm, why is his promise not enforceable as envisioned in Chapters 2 and 3? What justifiable feature of the parol evidence rule operates to defeat an otherwise legitimate theory of obligation?

10. *Second restatement integration and collateral agreement rule.* Restatement (Second) of Contracts § 216(2)(b) adopts and employs a similar judge determined natural omission test for the collateral agreement rule and, when applicable, regards the written instrument as only partially integrated. The partial integration determination then allows the parol evidence to add its terms to the overall contract of the parties so as to include the terms of both the parol and written agreements. The *Masterson v. Stine* case below considers a difference between the first and second restatements—the admission of testimonial evidence of negotiations to prove the integration or natural omission.

11. *Consistency test.* The majority in *Mitchill v. Lath* stated that in order for the parol agreement to vary the terms of the writing, three conditions must exist: (i) the parol agreement must be collateral in form; (ii) it must not contradict express or implied terms of the writing; and (iii) it must be an agreement the parties would not ordinarily be expected to put into the agreement. Since the majority ultimately determined that the parol agreement, if made, would normally be included in the agreement by the parties, the majority did not decide the "contradiction" issue. The majority nonetheless suggested that the parol agreement would require the seller to do more than what was required in the writing and thus might violate the contradiction test because the writing at least "implied" the seller was to do no more. Would this not always be the case? If this standard is adopted, no parol agreement could ever be admitted because it would always require more than the writing. Do you agree with this standard? The dissent devoted more time to this question than the majority. What was the dissenting view on consistency?

––––––––––

Like the Restatement (First) of Contracts, the Restatement (Second) of Contracts regards the collateral agreement rule and its natural omission test as an ultimate test of integration. If the parol agreement would not naturally be included in the writing, the writing is only partially integrated. Restatement (Second) of Contracts § 216(2)(b). The consequence of partial integration is that consistent additional terms of the parol agreement are admissible to supplement the writing. Restatement (Second) of Contracts § 216(1). Regardless of whether the writing is partially or completely integrated, the terms of the parol agreement may not contradict or vary the writing. Restatement (Second) of Contracts § 213(1).

The Restatement (Second) approach to the integration question was foreshadowed and reflected in the 1968 case of *Masterson v. Sine*, 28 Cal.2d 222, 65 Cal. Rptr. 545, 436 P.2d 561 (1968) and its majority opinion by

Chief Justice Traynor. There, Dallas and Rebecca Masterson owned a ranch that they conveyed to Medora and Lu Sine. The conveyance contained a reservation "unto Grantors [the Mastersons] herein an option to purchase [the ranch] on or before February 25, 1968 [for] the same consideration as being paid heretofore. . . ." Medora Sine was Dallas' sister and wife of Lu Sine. After the conveyance, Dallas was adjudicated bankrupt, and his trustee in bankruptcy and Rebecca sought to exercise the option.

At trial, the Sines attempted to introduce parol evidence to prove that at the time of the conveyance of the ranch the parties intended that the ranch would be kept in the Masterson family and that the option to repurchase was personal to the grantors. If this restriction were imposed on the option, the trustee in bankruptcy would have no right to exercise the option. In reversing the trial court and permitting introduction of parol evidence to prove the personal nature of the option, Justice Traynor opined:

> In formulating the rule governing parol evidence, several policies must be accommodated. One policy is based on the assumption that written evidence is more accurate than human memory. This policy, however, can be adequately served by excluding parol evidence of agreements that directly contradict the writing. Another policy is based on the fear that fraud or unintentional invention by witnesses interested in the outcome of the litigation will mislead the finder of facts. McCormick has suggested that the party urging the spoken as against the written word is most often the economic underdog, threatened by severe hardship if the writing is enforced. In his view the parol evidence rule arose to allow the court to control the tendency of the jury to find through sympathy and without a dispassionate assessment of the probability of fraud or faulty memory that the parties made an oral agreement collateral to the written contract, or that preliminary tentative agreements were not abandoned when omitted from the writing. (See McCormick, Evidence (1954) § 210.) He recognizes, however, that if this theory were adopted in disregard of all other considerations, it would lead to the exclusion of testimony concerning oral agreements whenever there is a writing and often defeat the true intent of the parties.

> Evidence of oral collateral agreements should be excluded only when the fact finder is likely to be misled. The rule must therefore be based on the credibility of the evidence. One such standard, adopted by section 240(1)(b) of the Restatement of Contracts, permits proof of a collateral agreement if it "is such an agreement as might naturally be made as a separate agreement by the parties situated as were the parties to the written contract." The draftsmen of the Uniform Commercial Code would exclude the

evidence in still fewer instances: "If the additional terms are such that, if agreed upon, they would certainly have been included in the document in the view of the court, then evidence of their alleged making must be kept from the trier of fact."

The option clause in the deed in the present case does not explicitly provide that it contains the complete agreement, and the deed is silent on the question of assignability. Moreover, the difficulty of accommodating the formalized structure of a deed to the insertion of collateral agreements makes it less likely that all of the terms of such an agreement were included. The statement of the reservation of the option might well have been placed in the recorded deed solely to preserve the grantors' rights against any possible future purchasers and this function could well be served without any mention of the parties' agreement that the option was personal. There is nothing in the record to indicate that the parties to this family transaction, through experience in land transactions or otherwise, had any warning of the disadvantages of failing to put the whole agreement in the deed. This case is one, therefore, in which it can be said that a collateral agreement such as that alleged "might naturally be made in a separate agreement." A fortiori, the case is not one in which the parties "would certainly" have included the collateral agreement in the deed. . . .

In the present case defendants offered evidence that the parties agreed that the option was not assignable in order to keep the property in the Masterson family. The trial court erred in excluding that evidence.

Id. (citations omitted). The *Masterson* holding and reasoning parallel the expansive approach taken by the Restatement (Second) of Contracts regarding determinations of integration. Writings do not prove themselves. Under both formulations, a writing may be *evidence* that it is fully or partially integrated, but other factors may suggest that the parties actually had a contrary intent. Just as a writing containing a declaration that "the parties represent and warrant that neither party executes this contract under duress" cannot exclude evidence that one party signed with a gun to her head, even an apparently (to the court) complete and integrated writing is not necessarily so.

Part of the shift in emphasis from the first to the second restatement is owed to the different views of the scholars of the day. The Restatement (First) of Contracts, reflecting the view of Professor Samuel Williston, largely required the judge to determine integration from the face of the contract itself: "It is generally held that the contract must appear on its face to be incomplete in order to permit parol evidence of additional terms."

Williston on Contracts § 33:16 (4th Ed. 2006). Under this view, if the written instrument appeared completely integrated solely from the "plain meaning" deciphered only from the "four corners of the document," it could not be modified. Professor Arthur Corbin thought otherwise. Arthur L. Corbin, "The Parol Evidence Rule," 53 Yale L. J. 603, 610–612 (1944) and Arthur L. Corbin, "The Interpretation of Words and the Parol Evidence Rule," 50 Cornell L. Q. 161, 162 (1965). Moreover, Corbin argued that the search should be for the precise intent of the parties. In this he disagreed with Williston who argued the intent of a reasonable person was more appropriate.

The UCC version of the parol evidence rule, cited and discussed above in the majority opinion in *Masterson*, states that "[t]he draftsmen of the Uniform Commercial Code would exclude the evidence in still fewer instances." UCC § 2–202(b) provides that the terms of a writing "intended by the parties as a final expression of their agreement with respect to the terms included therein" may not be contradicted by evidence of any prior agreement or contemporaneous oral agreement. But the writing may be supplemented by evidence of consistent additional terms "unless the court finds the writing to have been intended also as a complete and exclusive statement of the terms of the agreement." UCC § 2–202(b). As stated, this view allows consistent terms to supplement the writing, provided a court determines the writing is only partially integrated and not completely integrated.

The UCC version of the collateral agreement rule is reflected in UCC § 2–202(b), *cmt. 3:* "If the additional terms are such that, if agreed upon, they would certainly have been included in the document in the view of the court, then evidence of their alleged making must be kept from the trier of fact." Do you agree with the majority that this collateral agreement rule would exclude less evidence? Certainly it may be reasonable to assume that, in the absence of a rule that presumes the writing is a final expression, the four corners rule would not be applied and greater evidence would be considered by the judge. See Keith A. Rowley, "Contract Construction and Interpretation: From the 'Four Corners' to Parol Evidence (And Everything In Between)," 69 Miss. L. J. 73, 336–337 (1999).

UCC § 2–202 should be read in connection with UCC § 1–303(d) (2001) (former UCC § 1–205), which generally provides that a course of dealing between the parties and usage of trade in the trade or industry in which they are engaged "supplement" the terms of an agreement. UCC § 1–303(b) (2001) provides that a "course of dealing" includes a sequence of conduct between the parties to a particular transaction that is fairly regarded as establishing a common basis of understanding (and thus part of their agreement). Usage of trade is defined in UCC § 1–303(c) (2001) to include a regular practice of dealing with a matter so as to justify an expectation that it will be observed in this contract. Since trade usage is an *implied-in-*

law term, it is not based upon the agreement of the parties. Evidence of such trade usage—even though it is technically extrinsic to the written agreement—is therefore admissible in all cases and not prohibited by the parol evidence rule. See Joseph H. Levie, "Trade Usage and Custom Under the Common Law and the Uniform Commercial Code," 40 N.Y.U. L. Rev. 1101, 1111 (1965). Under the predecessor Uniform Sales Act, such usage was treated as extrinsic to the agreement and therefore subject to the parol evidence rule. See Edwin W. Patterson, "The Interpretation and Construction of Contracts," 64 Colum. L. Rev. 833, 847–852 (1964). The UCC however treats such matters as part of the agreement. Amy H. Kastely, "Stock Equipment for the Bargains in Fact: Trade Usage, 'Express Terms,' and Consistency Under Section 1–205 of the Uniform Commercial Code," 64 N. C. L. Rev. 777, 779 (1985).

Finally, some empirical studies of the types of cases in which courts apply or refuse to apply the parol evidence rule indicate that the rule depends more upon the perceived status and relative bargaining power of the parties than upon the elements of the restatement tests. See Robert Childres & Stephen J. Spitz, "Status in the Law of Contract,"47 N.Y.U. L. Rev. 1, 7, 24 (1972) (analyzing relevance of party status to availability of certain contract rights, such as application of the parol evidence rule, and noting rule usually does not apply to party alleging inferior bargaining position) and Michael A. Lawrence, Comment, "The Parol Evidence Rule in Wisconsin: Status in the Law of Contract, Revisited," 1991 Wis. L. Rev. 1071, 1095 (1991) (further developing earlier Childres & Spitz empirical study and confirming importance of status in application of parol evidence rule). As Professors Childres and Spitz observe, "[a]ny person who alleges inferior bargaining position or an abuse of bargaining power should and usually does get his evidence to the trier of fact." Robert Childres & Stephen J. Spitz, "Status in the Law of Contract," 47 N.Y.U. L. Rev. 1, 24 (1972).

2. EFFECT OF A MERGER OR INTEGRATION CLAUSE

Lack of confidence in the parol evidence rule to protect the written agreement from parol supplementation should hardly be surprising. Where the parties share a common interest in making certain their written agreement is completely integrated and therefore cannot be supplemented by prior or contemporaneous extrinsic terms, it may be wise to include a "merger clause" in the agreement stating just such a mutual intent. The term "merger" clause attaches from the view that the effect of the clause is to "merge" prior negotiations into the final integrated writing. This merger makes the integrated writing both the final expression of the terms stated therein and parties' the entire agreement. Accordingly, a merger clause expressly states that there are no other terms, express or implied, and the entire agreement of the parties is limited to the terms expressed in the document. Wise counsel often includes such a clause at the end of a document to take account of and avoid various problems with the parol evidence rule. Karl N. Llewellyn, "The Modern Approach to Counseling and Advocacy—Especially in Commercial Transactions," 46 Colum. L. Rev. 167, 171–173 (1946). Even the CISG, which does not state a parol evidence rule, would not prevent the parties agreeing to such a clause as a matter of shared intent.

The Restatement (First) of Contracts did not state a rule discussing a "private" parol evidence rule or merger clause. The Restatement (Second) of Contracts § 216 likewise does not refer to the doctrine in its black letter rule but the commentary is more helpful:

> *Comment e. Written term excluding oral terms ("merger" clause).* Written agreements often contain clauses stating that there are no representations, promises or agreements between the parties except those found in the writing. Such a clause may negate the apparent authority of an agent to vary orally the written terms, and if agreed to is likely to conclude the issue whether the agreement is completely integrated. Consistent additional terms may then be excluded even though their omission would have been natural in the absence of such a clause. But such a clause does not control the question whether the writing was assented to as an integrated agreement, the scope of the writing if completely integrated, or the interpretation of the written terms.

The comment suggests that a merger clause could negate the collateral agreement rule in appropriate cases—such as where the omission would have been natural in the absence of such a clause. But, the same comment cautions that the merger clause does not establish complete integration as a matter of law. Nonetheless, the presence of a merger clause is powerful evidence of complete integration. Professor Williston designated the merger clause as the most important factor to determine whether a writing is completely integrated. See Williston on Contracts § 33.21 (4th Ed. 2006). However, as the comment suggests, while some courts treat the merger clause as conclusive, some do not.

Notably, Restatement (Second) of Contracts § 214 specifically provides that a merger or integration clause cannot bar parol evidence "to establish (a) that the writing is or is not an integrated agreement; [or] (b) that the integrated agreement, if any, is completely or partially integrated . . . ." The comments further provide, "Whether a writing has been adopted as an integrated agreement and, if so, whether the agreement is completely or partially integrated are questions determined by the court preliminary to determination of a question of interpretation or to application of the parol evidence rule. . . . Writings do not prove themselves; ordinarily, if there is a dispute, there must be testimony that there was a signature or other manifestation of assent." Restatement (Second) of Contracts § 214, cmt. a.

The next case, Lee v. Joseph E. Seagram & Sons, Inc., addresses another issue relating to integration and merger clauses.

LEE v. JOSEPH E. SEAGRAM & SONS, INC.

United States Court of Appeals, Second Circuit
552 F.2d 447 (1977)

GURFEIN, Circuit Judge:

This is an appeal by defendant Joseph E. Seagram & Sons, Inc. ("Seagram") from a judgment entered by the District Court, Hon. Charles H. Tenney, upon the verdict of a jury in the amount of $407,850 in favor of the plaintiffs on a claim asserting common law breach of an oral contract. The court also denied Seagram's motion under Rule 50(b), Fed. R. Civ. P., for judgment notwithstanding the verdict. Harold S. Lee, et al. v. Joseph E. Seagram and Sons, 413 F. Supp. 693 (S. D. N. Y. 1976). It had earlier denied Seagram's motion for summary judgment. The plaintiffs are Harold S. Lee (now deceased) and his two sons, Lester and Eric ("the Lees"). Jurisdiction is based on diversity of citizenship. We affirm.

The jury could have found the following. The Lees owned a 50% interest in Capitol City Liquor Company, Inc. ("Capitol City"), a wholesale liquor distributorship located in Washington, D.C. The other 50% was owned by Harold's brother, Henry D. Lee, and his nephew, Arthur Lee. Seagram is a distiller of alcoholic beverages. Capitol City carried numerous Seagram brands and a large portion of its sales were generated by Seagram lines.

The Lees and the other owners of Capitol City wanted to sell their respective interests in the business and, in May 1970, Harold Lee, the father, discussed the possible sale of Capitol City with Jack Yogman ("Yogman"), then Executive Vice President of Seagram (and now President), whom he had known for many years. Lee offered to sell Capitol City to Seagram but conditioned the offer on Seagram's agreement to relocate Harold and his sons, the 50% owners of Capitol City, in a new distributorship of their own in a different city.

About a month later, another officer of Seagram, John Barth, an assistant to Yogman, visited the Lees and their co-owners in Washington and began negotiations for the purchase of the assets of Capitol City by Seagram on behalf of a new distributor, one Carter, who would take it over after the purchase. The purchase of the assets of Capitol City was consummated on September 30, 1970 pursuant to a written agreement. The promise to relocate the father and sons thereafter was not reduced to writing.

Harold Lee had served the Seagram organization for thirty-six years in positions of responsibility before he acquired the half interest in the Capitol City distributorship. From 1958 to 1962, he was chief executive officer of Calvert Distillers Company, a wholly-owned subsidiary. During this long period he enjoyed the friendship and confidence of the principals of Seagram.

In 1958, Harold Lee had purchased from Seagram its holdings of Capitol City stock in order to introduce his sons into the liquor distribution business, and also to satisfy Seagram's desire to have a strong and friendly distributor for Seagram products in Washington, D.C. Harold Lee and Yogman had known each other for 13 years.

The plaintiffs claimed a breach of the oral agreement to relocate Harold Lee's sons, alleging that Seagram had had opportunities to procure another distributorship for the Lees but had refused to do so. The Lees brought this action on January 18, 1972, fifteen months after the sale of the Capitol City distributorship to Seagram. They contended that they had performed their obligation by agreeing to the sale by Capitol City of its assets to Seagram, but that Seagram had failed to perform its obligation under the separate oral contract between the Lees and Seagram. The agreement which the trial court permitted the jury to find was "an oral agreement with defendant which provided that if they agreed to sell their interest in Capitol City, defendant in return, within a reasonable time, would provide the plaintiffs a Seagram distributorship whose price would require roughly an amount equal to the capital obtained by the plaintiffs for the sale of their interest in Capitol City, and which distributorship would be in a location acceptable to plaintiffs." No specific exception was taken to this portion of the charge. By its verdict for the plaintiffs, we must assume as Seagram notes in its brief that this is the agreement which the jury found was made before the sale of Capitol City was agreed upon.[2]

Appellant urges several grounds for reversal. It contends that, as a matter of law, (1) plaintiffs' proof of the alleged oral agreement is barred by the parol evidence rule; and (2) the oral agreement is too vague and indefinite to be enforceable. Appellant also contends that plaintiffs' proof of damages is speculative and incompetent.

---

[2]   The complaint alleged that Seagram agreed to "obtain" or "secure" or "provide" a "similar" distributorship within a reasonable time, and plaintiffs introduced some testimony to that effect. Although other testimony suggested that Seagram agreed merely to provide an opportunity for the Lees to negotiate with third parties, and Judge Tenney indicated in his denial of judgment n. o. v. that Seagram merely agreed "to notify plaintiffs as they learned of distributors who were considering the sale of their businesses," 413 F. Supp. at 698–99, the jury was permitted to find that the agreement was in the nature of a commitment to provide a distributorship. There was evidence to support such a finding, and the jury so found.

I

Judge Tenney, in a careful analysis of the application of the parol evidence rule, decided that the rule did not bar proof of the oral agreement. We agree.

The District Court, in its denial of the defendant's motion for summary judgment, treated the issue as whether the written agreement for the sale of assets was an "integrated" agreement not only of all the mutual agreements concerning the sale of Capitol City assets, but also of all the mutual agreements of the parties. Finding the language of the sales agreement "somewhat ambiguous," the court decided that the determination of whether the parol evidence rule applies must await the taking of evidence on the issue of whether the sales agreement was intended to be a complete and accurate integration of all of the mutual promises of the parties.

Seagram did not avail itself of this invitation. It failed to call as witnesses any of the three persons who negotiated the sales agreement on behalf of Seagram regarding the intention of the parties to integrate all mutual promises or regarding the failure of the written agreement to contain an integration clause.

Appellant contends that, as a matter of law, the oral agreement was "part and parcel" of the subject-matter of the sales contract and that failure to include it in the written contract barred proof of its existence. Mitchill v. Lath, 247 N.Y. 377, 380, 160 N.E. 646 (1928). The position of appellant, fairly stated, is that the oral agreement was either an inducing cause for the sale or was a part of the consideration for the sale, and in either case, should have been contained in the written contract. In either case, it argues that the parol evidence rule bars its admission.

Appellees maintain, on the other hand, that the oral agreement was a collateral agreement and that, since it is not contradictory of any of the terms of the sales agreement, proof of it is not barred by the parol evidence rule. Because the case comes to us after a jury verdict we must assume that there actually was an oral contract, such as the court instructed the jury it could find. The question is whether the strong policy for avoiding fraudulent claims through application of the parol evidence rule nevertheless mandates reversal on the ground that the jury should not have been permitted to hear the evidence. See Fogelson v. Rackfay Constr. Co., 300 N.Y. 334 at 337–38, 90 N.E. 2d 881 (1950).

The District Court stated the cardinal issue to be whether the parties "intended" the written agreement for the sale of assets to be the complete and accurate integration of all the mutual promises of the parties. If the written contract was not a complete integration, the court held, then the parol evidence rule has no application.[3] We assume that the District Court determined intention by objective standards. See 3 Corbin on Contracts §§ 573–574. The parol evidence rule is a rule of substantive law. Fogelson v. Rackfay Constr. Co., supra. . . .

The law of New York is not rigid or categorical, but is in harmony with this approach. As Judge Fuld said in Fogelson:

> Decision in each case must, of course, turn upon the type of transaction involved, the scope of the written contract and the content of the oral agreement asserted.

300 N.Y. at 338, 90 N.E.2d at 883. And the Court of Appeals wrote in Ball v. Grady, 267 N.Y. 470, 472, 196 N.E. 402, 403 (1935):

> In the end, the court must find the limits of the integration as best it may by reading the writing in the light of surrounding circumstances.

Accord, Fogelson, supra, 300 N.Y. at 338, 90 N.E.2d 881. Thus, certain oral collateral agreements, even though made contemporaneously, are not within the prohibition of the parol evidence rule "because (if) they are separate, independent, and complete contracts, although relating to the same subject. . . . (t)hey are allowed to be proved by parol, because they were made by parol, and no part thereof committed to writing." Thomas v. Scutt, 127 N.Y. 133, 140–41, 27 N.E. 961, 963 (1891).

Although there is New York authority which in general terms supports defendant's thesis that an oral contract inducing a written one or varying the consideration may be barred, See e.g., Fogelson v. Rackfay Constr. Co., supra, 300 N.Y. at 340, 90 N.E. 2d 881, the overarching question is whether, in the context of the particular setting, the oral agreement was one which the parties would ordinarily be expected to embody in the writing. Ball v. Grady, supra, 267 N.Y. at 470, 196 N.E. 402; . . . . See Restatement on Contracts § 240. For example, integration is most easily inferred in the case of real estate contracts for the sale of land, e.g., Mitchill v. Lath, supra, 247 N.Y. 377, 160 N.E. 646, or leases, Fogelson, supra; . . . . In more complex situations, in which customary business practice may be more varied, an oral agreement can be treated as separate and independent of the written agreement even though the written contract contains a strong integration clause. See Gem Corrugated Box Corp. v. National Kraft Container Corp., 427 F.2d 499, 503 (2d Cir. 1970).

Thus, as we see it, the issue is whether the oral promise to the plaintiffs, as individuals, would be an expectable term of the contract for

---

[3]   Though the parties have not urged the particular choice of law applicable, both parties appear to assume that New York law governs. We note that in cases of this type, which depend so much on their particular facts and for which direct precedent is therefore so sparse, virtually all jurisdictions would be expected to follow general common law principles.

the sale of assets by a corporation in which plaintiffs have only a 50% interest, considering as well the history of their relationship to Seagram.

Here, there are several reasons why it would not be expected that the oral agreement to give Harold Lee's sons another distributorship would be integrated into the sales contract. In the usual case, there is an identity of parties in both the claimed integrated instrument and in the oral agreement asserted. Here, although it would have been physically possible to insert a provision dealing with only the shareholders of a 50% interest, the transaction itself was a corporate sale of assets. Collateral agreements which survive the closing of a corporate deal, such as employment agreements for particular shareholders of the seller or consulting agreements, are often set forth in separate agreements. See Gem Corrugated Box Corp. v. National Kraft Container Corp., supra, 427 F.2d at 503 ("it is . . . plain that the parties ordinarily would not embody the stock purchase agreement in a writing concerned only with box materials purchase terms"). It was expectable that such an agreement as one to obtain a new distributorship for certain persons, some of whom were not even parties to the contract, would not necessarily be integrated into an instrument for the sale of corporate assets. As with an oral condition precedent to the legal effectiveness of an otherwise integrated written contract, which is not barred by the parol evidence rule if it is not directly contradictory of its terms, Hicks v. Bush, 10 N.Y. 2d 488, 225 N.Y.S. 2d 34, 180 N.E.2d 425 (1962); cf. 3 Corbin on Contracts § 589, "it is certainly not improbable that parties contracting in these circumstances would make the asserted oral agreement. . . ." 10 N.Y. 2d at 493, 225 N.Y.S. 2d at 39, 180 N.E.2d at 428.

Similarly, it is significant that there was a close relationship of confidence and friendship over many years between two old men, Harold Lee and Yogman, whose authority to bind Seagram has not been questioned. It would not be surprising that a handshake for the benefit of Harold's sons would have been thought sufficient. In point, as well, is the circumstance that the negotiations concerning the provisions of the sales agreement were not conducted by Yogman but by three other Seagram representatives, headed by John Barth. The two transactions may not have been integrated in their minds when the contract was drafted.[4]

Finally, the written agreement does not contain the customary integration clause, even though a good part of it (relating to warranties and negative covenants) is boilerplate. The omission may, of course, have been caused by mutual trust and confidence, but in any event, there is no such

---

[4] Barth in a confidential memorandum dated June 12, 1970 to Yogman and Edgar Bronfman stated that "he (Harold Lee) would very much like to have another distributorship in another area for his two sons." Apparently Barth, who was not present at Harold Lee's meeting with Yogman, assumed that this was a desire on the part of Lee rather than a promise made by Yogman for Seagram.

strong presumption of exclusion because of the existence of a detailed integration clause, as was relied upon by the Court of Appeals in Fogelson, supra, 300 N.Y. at 340, 90 N.E. 881.

Nor do we see any contradiction of the terms of the sales agreement. Mitchill v. Lath, supra, 247 N.Y. at 381, 160 N.E. 646; 3 Corbin on Contracts § 573, at 357. The written agreement dealt with the sale of corporate assets, the oral agreement with the relocation of the Lees. Thus, the oral agreement does not vary or contradict the money consideration recited in the contract as flowing to the selling corporation. That is the only consideration recited, and it is still the only consideration to the corporation.[5]

We affirm Judge Tenney's reception in evidence of the oral agreement and his denial of the motion under Rule 50(b) with respect to the parol evidence rule.

II

Appellant contends, however, that the jury verdict cannot stand because the oral agreement was so vague and indefinite as to be unenforceable. First, appellant argues that the failure to specify purchase price, profitability or sales volume of the distributorship to be provided, is fatal to the contract's validity. The contention is that, because the oral agreement lacks essential terms, the courts cannot determine the rights and obligations of the parties. See 1 Corbin on Contracts § 95, at 394. Second, appellant contends that the agreement is unenforceable because there were no specific limits to plaintiffs' discretion in deciding whether to accept or reject a particular distributorship; and hence the agreement was illusory.[6]

The alleged agreement, as the jury was permitted to find, was to provide the Lees with a liquor distributorship of approximately half the value and profit potential of Capitol City, within a reasonable time. The distributorship would be "in a location acceptable to plaintiffs," and the price would require roughly an amount equal to the plaintiffs' previous investment in Capitol City. The performance by plaintiffs in agreeing to

---

[5] Cf. Mitchill v. Lath, 247 N.Y. 377, 380–81, 160 N.E. 646, 647 (1928) (to escape the parol evidence rule, the oral agreement "must not contradict express or implied provisions of the written contract."). The parties do not contend, and we would be unwilling to hold, that the oral agreement was not "in form a collateral one." Id.

[6] Appellant makes two other contentions in this regard, which may be disposed of summarily. It argues that the evidence introduced by plaintiffs was so contradictory and confusing that the jury could not ascertain Seagram's obligations with any definiteness. Although plaintiffs apparently did not try their case on a single coherent theory, see note 2 supra, the short answer is that, by its verdict, the jury gave credence to some of the evidence, discounted the remainder, and drew its inferences accordingly. Id. Second, appellant suggests that the evidence demonstrates at best Seagram's friendly willingness to help the Lees in their efforts to relocate, but no commitment to undertake any legal obligation. The short answer again is that there was contrary testimony which the jury chose to believe.

the sale of Capitol City caused the counter-performance of the oral promise to mature.

Once the nature of the agreement found by the jury is recognized, it becomes clear that appellant's contentions are without merit. As for the alleged lack of essential terms, there was evidence credited by the jury, which did establish the purchase price, profitability and sales volume of the distributorship with reasonable specificity. In addition to the direct testimony of the Lees, there was evidence that distributorships were valued, as a rule of thumb, at book value plus three times the previous year's net profit after taxes. Between this industry standard and the reference to the Capitol City transaction, there was extrinsic evidence to render the parties' obligations reasonably definite. Professor Corbin has observed that a court should be slow to deny enforcement "if it is convinced that the parties themselves meant to make a 'contract' and to bind themselves to render a future performance. Many a gap in terms can be filled, and should be, with a result that is consistent with what the parties said and that is more just to both of them than would be a refusal of enforcement." Corbin on Contracts § 97, at 425–26. New York courts are in accord in hesitating to find that a contract is too indefinite for enforcement. . . . The requirement that the alleged oral agreement be performed within a reasonable time is particularly unobjectionable, see Valley Nat'l Bank, supra, especially in light of the fact, which Seagram knew, that plaintiffs would have to reinvest the proceeds from the sale of Capitol City within one year or suffer adverse tax consequences.[7]

As for the alleged unbridled discretion which the oral agreement conferred on the plaintiffs, we similarly conclude that there is no fatal defect. We note at the outset that the requirement that the new distributorship be "acceptable" to the Lees did not render the agreement illusory in the sense that it is not supported by consideration; the Lee's part of the bargain was to join in the sale of Capitol City's assets and assignment of its franchise, which they had already performed. More importantly, we do not agree that the Lees had "unbridled" discretion. New York courts would in all events impose an obligation of good faith on the Lees' exercise of discretion, see, e.g., Wood v. Lucy, Lady Duff-Gordon, 222 N.Y. 88, 118 N.E. 214 (1917), and there was also extrinsic evidence of what would constitute an "acceptable distributorship," and hence constitute reasonable performance by Seagram. Seagram appears to contend that if it had tendered reasonable performance, by offering an acceptable distributorship

---

[7] Seagram also appears to contend that a promise to "relocate" is insufficiently specific. We disagree. Aside from the ordinary meaning of the word, the jury could rely on evidence, which was introduced, of other efforts by Seagram to "provide" a distributorship for other distributors including Seagram's successful effort to provide Chet Carter with the Capitol City distributorship by purchasing it on his behalf, cf. Borden v. Chesterfield Farms, Inc., 27 A.D.2d 165, 277 N.Y.S. 2d 494 (1st Dep't 1967), and Harold Lee's own experience in his original purchase of the 50% interest in Capitol City directly from Seagram.

to the Lees, that the Lees nevertheless could have found it not "acceptable." This is not correct. It is true that Seagram could not have forced the Lees to take a distributorship, because they had not promised to do so. But Seagram's tender of reasonable performance would discharge its obligations under the oral agreement, whether or not the Lees "accepted." See 15 Williston on Contracts §§ 1808–10 (3d ed. 1972). The Lees could not prevent Seagram from fulfilling its obligations by unreasonably refusing an acceptable distributorship. Since the obligations of the parties under the contract therefore were ascertainable, it was not void for indefiniteness.

Affirmed.

NOTES AND QUESTIONS

1.   *Promissory estoppel to avoid parol evidence rule.* Because the parol evidence rule did not bar admission of the parol promise, promissory estoppel was not argued in this case. Would the seller be able to use promissory estoppel to make the promise enforceable even if the parol evidence would bar admission? Certainly if the parol agreement is truly collateral, promissory estoppel could be used as a theory of obligation even if the parol promise is not supported by independent consideration. But using promissory estoppel to trump the parol evidence rule is somewhat more problematic and doctrinally inconsistent. In every case such a promissory estoppel "exception" would surely swallow the general rule, totally emasculating the general rule itself. For a discussion of these issues, see Michael B. Metzger, "The Parol Evidence: Promissory Estoppel's Next Conquest?" 36 Vand. L. Rev. 1383 (1983) (arguing the benefits of allowing promissory estoppel to engulf the parol evidence rule).

2.   *Absence of merger clause.* The *Lee* case did not involve a merger or integration clause. What inference did the court draw from the failure to include such a customary clause? Have such clauses become so customary that an omission of the clause creates a presumption the writing is not integrated? What effect would this court have accorded the writing if a merger clause had been included? For a discussion of the general effect of merger clauses (sometimes conclusive but mostly not) see Karl N. Llewellyn, "The Modern Approach to Counseling and Advocacy—Especially in Commercial Transactions," 46 Colum. L. Rev. 167, 171–173 (1946); and Comment, "The 'Merger Clause' and The Parol Evidence Rule," 27 Tex. L. Rev. 361 (1949).

3.   *Subject matter relationship.* How does the court view the subject matter relationship between the parol agreement and the written agreement? Was the case decided under the first or second restatement?

3.   PAROL EVIDENCE RULE & VALID CONTRACT REQUIREMENT

The parol evidence rule has never applied when the evidence is not offered simply to prove an additional term but rather to prove some defect in the formation of the agreement itself. Stated another way, the integration standard is not applicable to a written contract not otherwise validly created. As a consequence, characterizing evidence as parol evidence is unfortunate when intended to establish defective formation and has created confusion. See John E. Murray, Jr., "The Parol Evidence Rule: A Clarification," 4 Duq. U. L. Rev. 337, 343–344 (1965); and Justin Sweet, "Promissory Fraud and the Parol Evidence Rule," 49 Cal. L. Rev. 877 (1961).

The first restatement addressed the problem of application of the parol evidence rule to an unenforceable or invalid written contract in three separate provisions. Restatement (First) of Contracts § 241 expressly permitted proof that the parties had orally agreed that their written agreement would not become an enforceable contract until the occurrence of some contingent, future event, even if the writing was completely integrated. Such oral agreements, however, still could not be offered if they were inconsistent with the writing. Also, Restatement (First) of Contracts § 242 provided that parol evidence could be admitted to prove the agreement had a reasonably susceptible meaning. The same outcome sanctioned evidence offered to prove any term in the agreement was untrue. Restatement (First) of Contracts § 244.

The Restatement (Second) of Contracts collects these themes and provides that the level of integration is irrelevant to the admission of the evidence for any such purpose. Restatement (Second) of Contracts § 214 states five major categories of "exceptions" where an objection based on the parol evidence rule is simply made irrelevant by the purpose of the admission of the evidence to establish: (i) that the writing is or is not an integrated agreement; (ii) that the integrated agreement, if any, is completely or partially integrated; (iii) the meaning of the writing, whether or not integrated; (iv) illegality, fraud, duress, mistake, lack of consideration, or other invalidating cause; or (v) ground for granting or denying rescission, reformation, specific performance, or other remedy.

The first two exceptions relate to whether the writing is integrated, and, if so, whether the integration is partial or complete. These are not mere reiterations of the "collateral agreement rule," if for no other reason than Restatement (Second) of Contracts § 216(2) affirmatively states in a separate section that the writing is not completely integrated if the collateral agreement might naturally be omitted from the writing. Thus, while the collateral agreement rule states an objective feature of integration, Restatement (Second) of Contracts § 214 refers to the specific integration intent of the party asserting the writing was not intended to be completely integrated. As such, the "integration" tests referred to in Restatement (Second) of Contracts § 214(a)–(b) (specific integration intent) and Restatement (Second) of Contracts § 216(2)(b) (collateral agreement integration test) stand on different footings, use different standards, but are directed to the same ends.

The third clause permits introduction of agreement and negotiation prior to and contemporaneous with the adoption of a writing to establish the meaning of the writing. The clause expressly states that such extrinsic evidence is admissible regardless of whether the writing is integrated. This clause is so important that it is the subject of the entire next section discussing "interpretation."

The fourth clause considers several matters relating to the evidence of defects in contract formation that prevent enforcement of the purported agreement. Fraud, in particular, requires special comment and further consideration because of an awkward tension with merger clauses (and thus the parol evidence rule) purporting to negate any reliance on misrepresentations made during negotiations. In almost all cases, the misrepresentation will contradict or make conditional some written obligation specified in the contract itself. Introduction of evidence of the misrepresentation must overcome the parol evidence rule, often made even more problematic by a specific merger clause purporting to negate reliance on any such misrepresentation.

For most purposes, fraud may be divided into two broad categories. The first type is generally referred to as fraud in the execution and is relatively rare. Execution fraud relates to a misrepresentation concerning what the defrauded party is signing (e.g., representation that the document is an application for a loan when in fact it is a promissory note). The second type, and far more common, is referred to as fraud in the inducement. Such fraud does not relate to the document signed, but to some character of the subject matter of the contract (e.g., "this house does not have termites," when the maker of the statement knows otherwise). As discussed in Chapter 6, execution fraud generally means the assent normally represented by the signature is not meaningful and no contract at all is formed (a so-called "void" contract). Restatement (Second) of Contracts § 163. Inducement fraud does not negate the formation of a contract, but the deception utilized by the maker does allow the victim to assert the fraud in order to rescind the contract (so-called "voidable" contract under Restatement (Second) of Contracts § 7). See Restatement (Second) of Contracts § 164.

So, to which type of fraud does Restatement (Second) of Contracts § 214(d) refer, and does it make a difference? Unfortunately the answer is murky. While evidence of execution fraud should not be subject to the parol evidence rule at all because there is no valid written contract to assert supremacy, inducement fraud is more common, and different states treat its relationship with the parol evidence rule differently. This is especially so if the written agreement contains a merger clause purporting to negate reliance on such fraud. Some courts will admit proof of the fraud regardless of the presence of a merger clause, and some courts use the parol evidence rule to bar admission even in the absence of a merger clause. See Justin

Sweet, "Promissory Fraud and the Parol Evidence Rule," 49 Cal. L. Rev. 877 (1961). Many cases address alleged misrepresentations in connection with the purchase of real estate under agreements including a merger clause. Another group of cases considers promissory notes stating an unconditional obligation to pay alleged to have been executed on the basis that the note would only be enforced upon the occurrence of some condition. In each case, the parol evidence rule determines whether the jury will be afforded the opportunity to consider the evidence of the fraud.

DANANN REALTY CORP. v. HARRIS
Court of Appeals of New York
5 N.Y. 2d 317, 157 N.E. 2d 597, 184 N.Y.S. 2d 599 (1959)

BURKE, Judge.

The plaintiff in its complaint alleges, insofar as its first cause of action is concerned, that it was induced to enter into a contract of sale of a lease of a building held by defendants because of oral representations, falsely made by the defendants, as to the operating expenses of the building and as to the profits to be derived from the investment. Plaintiff, affirming the contract, seeks damages for fraud.

At Special Term, the Supreme Court sustained a motion to dismiss the complaint. On appeal, the Appellate Division unanimously reversed the order granting the dismissal of the complaint. Thereafter the Appellate Division granted leave to appeal, certifying the following question: 'Does the first cause of action in the complaint state facts sufficient to constitute a cause of action?'

The basic problem presented is whether the plaintiff can possibly establish from the facts alleged in the complaint (together with the contract which was annexed to the complaint) reliance upon the misrepresentations (Cohen v. Cohen, 1 A.D.2d 586, 151 N.Y.S. 2d 949, affirmed 3 N.Y. 2d 813, 166 N.Y.S. 2d 10).

We must, of course, accept as true plaintiff's statements that during the course of negotiations defendants misrepresented the operating expenses and profits. Such misrepresentations are undoubtedly material. However, the provisions of the written contract which directly contradict the allegations of oral representations are of equal importance in our task of reaching a decisive answer to the question posed in these cases.

The contract, annexed to and made a part of the complaint, contains the following language pertaining to the particular facts of representations:

> The Purchaser has examined the premises agreed to be sold and is familiar with the physical condition thereof. The Seller has not made and does not make any representations as to the physical condition, rents, leases, expenses, operation or any other matter

or thing affecting or related to the aforesaid premises, except as herein specifically set forth, and the Purchaser hereby expressly acknowledges that no such representations have been made, and the Purchaser further acknowledges that it has inspected the premises and agrees to take the premises "as is" . . . It is understood and agreed that all understandings and agreements heretofore had between the parties hereto are merged in this contract, which alone fully and completely expresses their agreement, and that the same is entered into after full investigation, neither party relying upon any statement or representation, not embodied in this contract, made by the other. The Purchaser has inspected the buildings standing on said premises and is thoroughly acquainted with their condition. (Emphasis supplied.)

Were we dealing solely with a general and vague merger clause, our task would be simple. A reiteration of the fundamental principle that a general merger clause is ineffective to exclude parol evidence to show fraud in inducing the contract would then be dispositive of the issue (Sabo v. Delman, 3 N.Y. 2d 155, 164 N.Y.S. 2d 714). To put it another way, where the complaint states a cause of action for fraud, the parol evidence rule is not a bar to showing the fraud either in the inducement or in the execution despite an omnibus statement that the written instrument embodies the whole agreement, or that no representations have been made.

Here, however, plaintiff has in the plainest language announced and stipulated that it is not relying on any representations as to the very matter as to which it now claims it was defrauded. Such a specific disclaimer destroys the allegations in plaintiff's complaint that the agreement was executed in reliance upon these contrary oral representations (Cohen v. Cohen, supra). The Sabo case, supra, dealt with the usual merger clause. The present case, as the Cohen case, additionally, includes a disclaimer as to specific representations.

This specific disclaimer is one of the material distinctions between this case and Bridger v. Goldsmith, supra, and Crowell-Collier Pub. Co. v. Josefowitz, 5 N.Y. 2d 998, 184 N.Y.S. 2d 859. In the Bridger case, the court considered the effect of a general disclaimer as to representations in a contract of sale, concluding that the insertion of such a clause at the insistence of the seller cannot be used as a shield to protect him from his fraud. Another material distinction is that nowhere in the contract in the Bridger case is there a denial of reliance on representations, as there is here. Similarly, in Crowell-Collier Pub. Co. v. Josefowitz, supra, only a general merger clause was incorporated into the contract of sale. Moreover, the complaint there additionally alleged that further misrepresentations were made after the agreement had been signed, but while the contract was held in escrow and before it had been finally approved.

Consequently, this clause, which declares that the parties to the agreement do not rely on specific representations not embodied in the contract, excludes this case from the scope of the Jackson, Angerosa, Bridger and Crowell-Collier cases, supra.

The complaint here contains no allegations that the contract was not read by the purchaser. We can fairly conclude that plaintiff's officers read and understood the contract, and that they were aware of the provision by which they aver that plaintiff did not rely on such extra-contractual representations. It is not alleged that this provision was not understood, or that the provision itself was procured by fraud. It would be unrealistic to ascribe to plaintiff's officers such incompetence that they did not understand what they read and signed. Although this court in the Ernst case discounted the merger clause as ineffective to preclude proof of fraud, it gave effect to the specific disclaimer of representation clause, holding that such a clause limited the authority of the agent, and hence, plaintiff had notice of his lack of authority. But the larger implication of the Ernst case is that, where a person has read and understood the disclaimer of representation clause, he is bound by it. The court rejected, as a matter of law, the allegation of plaintiffs "that they relied upon an oral statement made to them in direct contradiction of this provision of the contract." The presence of such a disclaimer clause "is inconsistent with the contention that plaintiff relied upon the misrepresentation, and was led thereby to make the contract." Kreshover v. Berger, 135 App. Div. 27, 28, 119 N.Y.S. 737, 738.

It is not necessary to distinguish seriatim the cases in other jurisdictions as they are not, in the main, in point or in, a few instances, clash with the rule followed in the State of New York. The marshaling of phrases plucked from various opinions and references to generalizations, with which no one disagrees, cannot subvert the fundamental precept that the asserted reliance must be found to be justifiable under all the circumstances before a complaint can be found to state a cause of action in fraud. We must keep in mind that "opinions must be read in the setting of the particular cases and as the product of preoccupation with their special facts" (Freeman v. Hewit, 329 U.S. 249, 252, 67 S.Ct. 274, 276, 91 L.Ed. 265). When the citations are read in the light of this caveat, we find that they are generally concerned with factual situations wherein the facts represented were matters peculiarly within the defendant's knowledge, as in the cases of Sabo v. Delman, supra, and Jackson v. State of New York, supra.

The general rule was enunciated by this court over a half a century ago in Schumaker v. Mather, 133 N.Y. 590, 596, 30 N.E. 755, 757, that "if the facts represented are not matters peculiarly within the party's knowledge, and the other party has the means available to him of knowing, by the exercise of ordinary intelligence, the truth, or the real quality of the subject of the representation, he must make use of those means, or he will not be heard to complain that he was induced to enter into the transaction by misrepresentations. . . .

Very recently this rule was approved as settled law by this court in the case of Sylvester v. Bernstein, 283 App. Div. 333, 127 N.Y.S. 2d 746, affirmed 307 N.Y. 778, 121 N.E. 2d 616.

In this case, of course, the plaintiff made a representation in the contract that it was not relying on specific representations not embodied in the contract, while, it now asserts, it was in fact relying on such oral representations. Plaintiff admits then that it is guilty of deliberately misrepresenting to the seller its true intention. To condone this fraud would place the purchaser in a favored position. This is particularly so, where, as here, the purchaser confirms the contract, but seeks damages. If the plaintiff has made a bad bargain he cannot avoid it in this manner.

If the language here used is not sufficient to estop a party from claiming that he entered the contract because of fraudulent representations, then no language can accomplish that purpose. To hold otherwise would be to say that it is impossible for two businessmen dealing at arm's length to agree that the buyer is not buying in reliance on any representations of the seller as to a particular fact.

Accordingly, the order of the Appellate Division should be reversed and that of Special Term reinstated, without costs. The question certified should be answered in the negative.

FULD, Judge (dissenting).

If a party has actually induced another to enter into a contract by means of fraud and so the complaint before us alleges I conceive that language may not be devised to shield him from the consequences of such fraud. The law does not temporize with trickery or duplicity, and this court, after having weighed the advantages of certainty in contractual relations against the harm and injustice which result from fraud, long ago unequivocally declared that:

> a party who has perpetrated a fraud upon his neighbor may (not) contract with him, in the very instrument by means of which it was perpetrated, for immunity against its consequences, close his mouth from complaining of it, and bind him never to seek redress. Public policy and morality are both ignored if such an agreement can be given effect in a court of justice. The maxim that fraud vitiates every transaction would no longer be the rule, but the exception. Bridger v. Goldsmith, 143 N.Y. 424, 428, 38 N.E. 458, 459.

It was a concern for similar considerations of policy which persuaded Massachusetts to repudiate the contrary rule which it had initially espoused. "The same public policy that in general sanctions the avoidance of a promise obtained by deceit," wrote that state's Supreme Judicial Court in Bates v. Southgate, 308 Mass. 170, 182, 31 N.E. 2d 551, 558, 133 A.L.R. 1349:

> strikes down all attempts to circumvent that policy by means of contractual devices. In the realm of fact it is entirely possible for a party knowingly to agree that no representations have been made to him, while at the same time believing and relying upon representations which in fact have been made and in fact are false but for which he would not have made the agreement. To deny this possibility is to ignore the frequent instances in everyday experience where parties accept . . . and act upon agreements containing . . . exculpatory clauses in one from or another, but where they do so, nevertheless, in reliance upon the honesty of supposed friends, the plausible and disarming statements of salesmen, or the customary course of business. To refuse relief would result in opening the door to a multitude of frauds and in thwarting the general policy of the law.

It is impossible, on either principle or reasoning, to distinguish the present case from the many others which this court has decided. See e.g., Bridger v. Goldsmith, 143 N.Y. 424, 428, 38 N.E. 458, 459, supra; . . . As far back as 1894, we decided, in the Bridger case, 143 N.Y. 424, 38 N.E. 458, 459, supra, that the plaintiff was not prevented from bringing an action for fraud, based on oral misrepresentations, even though the written contract provided that it was "understood and agreed" that the defendant seller had not made,

> for the purpose of inducing the sale . . . or the making of this agreement, any statements or representations . . . other than

the single one therein set forth (143 N.Y. at pages 426–427, 38 N.E. at page 459). And, just today, we are holding, in the Crowell-Collier Publishing case, that the plaintiffs were not barred from suing the defendants for fraud in inducing them to make the contract, despite its recital that:

> This Agreement constitutes the entire understanding between the parties, (and) was not induced by any representations . . . not herein contained.

In addition, in Jackson v. State of New York, 210 App. Div. 115, 205 N.Y.S. 658, affirmed 241 N.Y. 563, 150 N.E. 556, supra, the contract provided that:

> the contract (plaintiff's predecessor in interest) agreed that he had satisfied himself by his own investigation regarding all the conditions of the work to be done and that his conclusion to enter

into the contract was based solely upon such investigation and not upon any information or data imparted by the State.

It was held that even this explicit disavowal of reliance did not bar the plaintiff from recovery. In answering the argument that the provision prevented proof either of misrepresentation by the defendant or reliance on the part of the plaintiff, the Appellate Division, in an opinion approved by this court, wrote: 'a party to a contract cannot, by misrepresentation of a material fact, induce the other party to the contract to enter into it to his damage, and then protect himself from the legal effect of such misrepresentation by inserting in the contract a clause to the effect that he is not to be held liable for the misrepresentation which induced the other party to enter into the contract. The effect of misrepresentation and fraud cannot be thus easily avoided' (210 App. Div. at pages 119–120, 205 N.Y.S. at page 661).

Although the clause in the contract before us may be differently worded from those in the agreements involved in the other cases decided by this court, it undoubtedly reflects the same thought and meaning, and the reasoning and the principles which the court deemed controlling in those cases are likewise controlling in this one. Their application, it seems plain to me, compels the conclusion that the complaint herein should be sustained and the plaintiff accorded a trial of its allegations.

It is said, however, that the provision in this contract differs from those heretofore considered in that it embodies a specific and deliberate exclusion of a particular subject. The quick answer is that the clause now before us is not of such a sort. On the contrary, instead of being limited, it is all-embracing, encompassing every representation that a seller could possibly make about the property being sold and, instead of representing a special term of a bargain, is essentially "boiler plate." See Contract of Sale, Standard N.Y.B.T.U. Form 8041; Bicks, Contracts for the Sale of Realty (1956 ed.), pp. 79–80, 94–95. The more elaborate verbiage in the present contract cannot disguise the fact that the language which is said to immunize the defendants from their own fraud is no more specific than the general merger clause in Sabo v. Delman, 3 N.Y.2d 155, 164 N.Y.S.2d 714, supra, and far less specific than the provision dealt with in the Jackson case, 210 App.Div. 115, 205 N.Y.S. 58, affirmed 241 N.Y. 563, 150 N.E. 556, supra, or in Crowell-Collier.

In any event, though, I cannot believe that the outcome of a case such as this, in which the defendant is charged with fraud, should turn on the particular language employed in the contract. As Judge Augustus Hand, writing for the Federal Court of Appeals, observed, "the ingenuity of draftsmen is sure to keep pace with the demands of wrongdoers, and if a deliberate fraud may be shielded by a clause in a contract that the writing contains every representation made by way of inducement, or that utterances shown to be untrue were not an inducement to the agreement," a fraudulent seller would have a simple method of obtaining immunity for his misconduct. Arnold v. National Aniline & Chem. Co., 2 Cir., 20 F.2d 364, 369.

The guiding rule that fraud vitiates every agreement which it touches has been well expressed not only by the courts of this state, but by courts throughout the country and by the House of Lords in England. And, in recognizing that the plaintiff may assert a cause of action in fraud, the courts have not differentiated between the type or form of exculpatory provision inserted in the contract. It matters not, the cases demonstrate, whether the clause simply recites that no representations have been made or more fully stipulates that the seller has not made any representations concerning certain enumerated subjects and that the purchaser has made his own investigation and has not relied upon any representation by the seller, not embodied in the writing. See e.g., Sabo v. Delman, 3 N.Y. 2d 155, 161–162, 164 N.Y.S. 2d 714, 717–718, supra; Ernst Iron Works v. Duralith Corp., 270 N.Y. 165, 169, 200 N.E. 683, 684, supra. . . .

In England, in the Pearson case (1907) A.C. 351, supra, the contract to perform certain construction work provided that:

> the contractor 'should satisfy himself' as to various specified items connected with the job and that the defendant corporation . . . did not hold itself responsible for the accuracy of (such) information (p. 351).

After performing the contract, the plaintiffs brought a deceit action, claiming damages for false representations as to the very items concerning which they had agreed they would satisfy themselves. The House of Lords reversed the judgment directed for the defendants and held that the action could be maintained; the Lord Chancellor, after noting that "[t]he contract contained clauses . . . to the effect that the contractors must not rely on any representation . . . but must ascertain and judge of the facts for themselves" (p. 353), went on to say (pp. 353–354):

> Now it seems clear that no one can escape liability for his own fraudulent statements by inserting in a contract a clause that the other party shall not rely upon them.

Lord Ashbourne, concurring with the Lord Chancellor, pointed out that the clause relied upon "might in some cases be part of a fraud, and might advance and disguise a fraud" (p. 360) and Lord Hereford, also concurring, declared (p. 362) that, if the "protecting clause" be inserted fraudulently,

> When the fraud succeeds, surely those who designed the fraudulent protection cannot take advantage of it. Such a clause

would be good protection against any mistake or miscalculation, but fraud vitiates every contract and every clause in it.

In the Dieterich case, 115 Wash. 365, 197 P. 1, supra, the contract contained the provision that

> This land is sold to (the plaintiff buyer) . . . with the understanding that he has personally and carefully inspected said premises, and is purchasing the same by said inspection, and not from any other sayings or inducements by (the seller) . . . and there has been no other inducements other than recited herein.

Despite this explicit disclaimer of reliance and inducement, the Washington Supreme Court decided that the recital did not bar the plaintiff from showing "the fraudulent nature of the contract" (115 Wash. at page 373, 197 P. at page 3), and, in the course of its opinion, observed (115 Wash. at page 368, 197 P. at page 2) that the contention of the defendants to the contrary was "effectually answered by the Court of Appeals of New York, in the case of Bridger v. Goldsmith, 143 N.Y. 424, 38 N.E. 458."

In Martin v. Harris, 121 Neb. 372, 236 N.W. 914, 915, supra, the agreement recited:

> There have been no representations of the reasonable value of any of the properties herein described made by or to either party to this contract. Each party is relying upon his own judgment of such values after a personal inspection of the properties.

The plaintiff, alleging that the defendant fraudulently misrepresented the value of the property, sought damages. Again, despite the explicit statement that such a pre-presentation had not been made and the specific disavowal of reliance thereon, the court upheld the plaintiff's right to bring the action (121 Neb. at page 376, 236 N.W. 914).

In the Ganley case, 170 Minn. 373, 212 N.W. 602, supra, too, the disclaimer was quite specific, reading in this way:

> The (plaintiff) contractor has examined the said contracts . . . and the specifications and plans forming a part thereof, and is familiar with the location of said work and the conditions under which the same must be performed . . . and is not relying upon any statement made by the company in respect thereto.

In deciding that a defendant could not protect himself against liability for fraud by such a provision or, indeed, by any language, the court wrote in no uncertain terms (170 Minn. at page 377, 212 N.W. at page 603):

> The law should not, and does not, permit a covenant of immunity to be drawn that will protect a person against him own fraud. Such is not enforceable because of public policy. Industrial &

General Trust, Ltd. v. Tod, 180 N.Y. 215, 73 N.E. 7. Language is not strong enough to write such a contract. Fraud destroys all consent. It is the purpose of the law to shield only those whose armor embraces good faith. Theoretically, if there is no fraud, the rule we announce is harmless. If there is fraud, the rule we announce is wholesome. Whether the rule is effective depends upon the facts. Public interest supports our conclusion.

And, said the court, while the argument that a party should have the right "to let his work to a certain person because the other will therein agree that he relies and acts only upon his own knowledge and not upon the representations of his adversary," might on first thought seem plausible, it does not stand analysis.

> It may be desirable in dealing with unscrupulous persons to have this clause as a shield against wrongful charges of fraud. But if there is no fraud that fact will be established on the trial. The merits of defendant's claim reach only the expense and annoyance of litigation. But every party should have his day in court. . . . We are unable to formulate a rule of law sustaining defendant's contention which would not at the same time give opportunities for the commission of fraud for which the wronged party would have no redress. (170 Minn. at page 376, 212 N.W. at page 603).

And in the Lutfy case, 57 Ariz. 495, 115 P. 2d 161, 160, supra, the contract of sale contained as specific a disavowal of reliance upon a particular representation as could be written:

> It is understood and agreed that there is no representation or warranty that the "year model" of said property, as hereinbefore stated, correctly states the year in which said property was manufactured, but is merely used by the parties hereto for convenience in describing it. . . . Purchaser agrees that he has made an independent investigation of the property and has relied solely upon his own investigation with reference thereto in entering into this contract, and has placed no reliance and acted upon no representations or warranties upon the part of the Seller.

The plaintiff, suing for damages, alleged that the defendant had falsely represented the year model of the automobile which he purchased, and the high court of Arizona held that he could prove that such a representation had been made and that he had relied upon it, notwithstanding the contract's most explicit recital to the contrary (57 Ariz. at page 506, 115 P. 2d at page 166):

> If binding upon (plaintiff) appellant, it would protect appellee from the consequences of any fraudulent misrepresentations it might have made to appellant to induce him to sign the contract and, as we see it, any provision in a contract making it possible

for a party thereto to free himself from the consequences of his own fraud in procuring its execution is invalid and necessarily constitutes no defense.

The cases cited all upholding the sufficiency of a complaint based on fraud no matter how the exculpatory language in the contract is phrased show how firmly established the rule is, and the passages quoted show how compelling are the reasons for the rule. Nor is their force or value weakened or impaired by the decisions upon which the court now appears to rely. Except for Cohen v. Cohen, 3 N.Y. 2d 813, 166 N.Y.S. 2d 10, no one of them has anything to do with the adequacy of the complaint as a pleading; two are concerned with the proof adduced at the trial (Schumaker v. Mather, 133 N.Y. 590, 30 N.E. 755; Ernst Iron Works v. Duralith Corp., 270 N.Y. 165, 200 N.E. 683, supra), while the third deals with the subject of res judicata (Sylvester v. Bernstein, 283 App. Div. 333, 127 N.Y.S. 2d 746, affirmed 307 N.Y. 778, 121 N.E. 2d 616).

In the Ernst Iron Works case, the appeal was, as I have noted, taken after trial and was concerned with the proof and not, as is the present appeal, with the sufficiency of the complaint. The contract contained both a blanket merger clause and a recital that the defendant "makes no representation regarding previous sales" (270 N.Y. 165, 200 N.E. 683) in Buffalo, where the plaintiff did business. Notwithstanding that provision, the plaintiff claimed that he had relied upon a representation by the defendant's salesman that the product had not been sold in that city, and testimony to that effect was received at the trial. The court did reverse the judgment for the plaintiff, but not on any theory that the specific disclaimer clause barred suit or that the evidence was inadmissible because of it. It was the court's conclusion, based on the evidence adduced at the trial, first, that the false representation attributed to the defendant had not been made (270 N.Y. at pages 169–170, 200 N.E. 683, 684); second, that, in any event, the defendant's salesman did not have authority to make such a representation and the plaintiff knew this (270 N.Y. at pages 170–171, 200 N.E. 684–685); and, finally, that "it (was) clear (from the proof at the trial) that the plaintiff did not rely upon the statement" (270 N.Y. at pages 171–172, 200 N.E. at page 685). And most significantly, the court did not question the general principle but affirmed it, stating that "[a] rogue cannot protect himself from liability for his fraud by inserting a printed clause in his contract" (270 N.Y. at page 169, 200 N.E. at page 684.)

As to Cohen v. Cohen (3 N.Y. 2d 813, 166 N.Y.S. 2d 11) I dissented from the decision there made and still consider it to have been wrongly decided. Constrained to accept it, I do so, but I cannot subscribe to extending its application beyond its own peculiar fact setting. A husband and wife had separated; there were bitter mutual recriminations followed by three separate lawsuits. The parties were ultimately reconciled and their lawyers drew a settlement agreement, which they executed, reciting that the husband had not made any representations "as to the continuation of the marital status." The wife sometime later brought another action, alleging that her husband had falsely represented that he "would effect a reconciliation with (her), return to live with her . . . permanently, and permanently resume their marital relationship." As is quite evident, the Cohen case is a most unusual one not only because it involved an agreement designed to settle pending marital litigation, but because of the extraordinary and promissory nature of the misrepresentation alleged. Indeed, the only resemblance claimed for the cases that is, for Cohen and the present one is that in both there is a specific disclaimer by the plaintiff of the very representations charged against the defendant. However, as noted above (5 N.Y. 2d at pages 325–326, 184 N.Y.S. 2d 606), since the provision in the contract before us encompasses every representation which a seller of real estate could possibly have made, including those alleged, even the asserted similarity does not in fact exist.

Contrary to the intimation in the court's opinion (5 N.Y. 2d at page 323, 184 N.Y.S. 2d 604), the non-reliance clause cannot possibly operate as an estoppel against the plaintiff. Essentially equitable in nature, the principle of estoppel is to be invoked to prevent fraud and injustice, not to further them. The statement that the representations in question were not made was, according to the complaint, false to the defendant's knowledge. Surely, the perpetrator of a fraud cannot close the lips of his victim and deny him the right to state the facts as they actually exist. Indeed, the contention that a person, such as the defendant herein, could urge an estoppel was considered and emphatically disposed of in Bridger v. Goldsmith with this statement:

> The question now is whether (the no-representation non-inducement clause) can be given the effect claimed for it by the learned counsel for the defendant, to preclude the plaintiff from alleging fraud in the sale, and pursuing in the courts the remedies which the law gives in such cases. It cannot operate by way of estoppel, for the obvious reason that the statements were false to the defendant's knowledge. He may, indeed, have relied upon its force and efficacy to protect him from the consequences of his own fraud, but he certainly could not have relied upon the truth of any statement in it. A mere device of the guilty party to a contract, intended to shield himself from the results of his own fraud practiced upon the other party, cannot well be elevated to the dignity and importance of an equitable estoppel (143 N.Y. 424, 427–428, 38 N.E. 458, 459, emphasis supplied; See also, Angerosa v. White Co., 248 App. Div. 425, 433–434, 290 N.Y.S. 204, 215–216, affirmed 275 N.Y. 524, 11 N.E.2d 325, supra).

The rule heretofore applied by this court presents no obstacle to honest business dealings, and dishonest transactions ought not to receive judicial protection. The clause in the contract before us may lend support to the defense and render the plaintiff's task of establishing its claim more difficult, but it should not be held to bar institution of an action for fraud. Whether the defendants made the statements attributed to them and, if they did, whether the plaintiff relied upon them, whether, in other words, the defendants were guilty of fraud, are questions of fact not capable of determination on the pleadings alone. The plaintiff in entitled to its day in court.

CONWAY, C. J., and DESMOND, DYE, FROESSEL and VAN VOORHIS, JJ., concur with BURKE, J.

FULD, J., dissents in a separate opinion.

Order reversed, etc.

NOTES AND QUESTIONS

1.   *Character of fraud.* Was the alleged fraud characterized as execution fraud or inducement fraud? Should it make any difference? Do you suspect that if the alleged fraud had been characterized as execution fraud, the merger clause would have any effect regardless of specificity? What do you make of the majority opinion statement: "To put it another way, where the complaint states a cause of action for fraud, the parol evidence rule is not a bar to showing the fraud either in the inducement or in the execution despite an omnibus statement that the written instrument embodies the whole agreement, or that no representations have been made." Is the court conflating execution and inducement fraud? If so, do you think this is appropriate?

2.   *Problematic "specific" merger clause.* The majority opinion is careful in referencing that a "general and vague merger clause" would be regarded differently than one that purports to specifically identify the misrepresentation to be disclaimed. Indeed, in *Sabo v. Delman*, 3 N.Y.2d 155, 164 N.Y.S. 2d 714, 143 N.E.2d 906, 909 (1957), decided just two years before *Danann*, the New York Court of Appeals affirmed its adherence to the general notion that "fraud vitiates every transaction." What is the policy supporting a distinction between a general and specific disclaimer distinction? Regardless of the specificity of the disclaimer, fraud remains fraud. Restatement (Second) of Contracts § 164(1) provides one answer by making inducement fraud actionable only if the defrauded party is "justified" in relying on the fraud. Does the restatement shift the reference from the existence of the fraud to the reasonableness of the reliance on the fraud?

Not surprisingly, and based on the strength of the dissent, other states follow the dissenting opinion approach. See e.g., Snyder v. Lovercheck, 992 P.2d 1079, 1084 (Wyo. 1999) ("The effect of merger and disclaimer clauses on pre-contractual misrepresentations poses significant questions of public policy. There are two prevailing views on the subject. One school of thought focuses on the sanctity of the right to contract, and holds that a party is bound by a specific disclaimer even if the contract was fraudulently obtained. The other school of thought latches on to the age-old proposition that fraud vitiates all contracts, and holds that a party to a contract is not bound by a disclaimer if it was fraudulently obtained. Wyoming subscribes to the latter view.").

3.   *Standard form contracts.* Do you think the effect of a merger clause should depend upon specific assent to that particular clause? Recall that Karl N. Llewellyn argued that form contracts actually created two contracts: a contract on negotiated terms and a separate contract on boilerplate. The latter terms were significantly more suspect and only presumptively enforceable (from signature and "duty to read") unless the clause (i) impaired the meaning of the negotiated terms; or (ii) was unfair. Under this now famous "circle of assent" analysis, should a general merger clause or even a specific merger clause be enforced if part of the boilerplate terms? See Karl N. Llewellyn, The Common Law Tradition 370–371 (1960); John E. Murray, Jr., "The Parol Evidence Process and Standardized Agreements Under the Restatement (Second) of Contracts," 123 U. Pa. L. Rev. 1342, 1360–1362 (1974); and Robert M. Lloyd, "The 'Circle of Assent' Doctrine: An Important Innovation in Contract Law," 7 Transactions: Tenn. J. Bus. L. 237 (2006).

B. INTERPRETING THE TERMS OF THE AGREEMENT

Once the parol evidence rule is applied to determine if any additional terms become part of the agreement, the "expanded" agreement becomes a conceptual whole. What further role lurks for parol evidence that its own rule has not yet quantified? Understanding this critical "interpretation" component is very important and understandably has evolved over time. At a basic level, "interpretation" simply refers to the process by which courts determine the "legal meaning" of contract language chosen by the parties. See Restatement (Second) of Contracts § 200. ("Interpretation of a promise or agreement or a term thereof is the ascertainment of its meaning.").

Obviously, language is not always clear, nor does it mean the same thing to the parties to the contract. Oliver Wendell Holmes, "The Theory of Legal Interpretation," 12 Harv. L. Rev. 417 (1899) ("A word generally has several meanings, even in a dictionary."). Therefore, contract language can be either vague or ambiguous. A term is vague if it has an unclear contextual meaning (a range of meanings on both sides of a core objective meaning) and ambiguous if it is subject to a double meaning (not with a range, but two separate meanings). E. Allan Farnsworth, " 'Meaning' in the Law of Contracts," 76 Yale L. J. 939, 953 (1967). Nonetheless, both vagueness and ambiguity result in a "misunderstanding" between the parties at the time the contract is made.

What is the effect of the misunderstanding? Where the misunderstanding relates to a core or essential term, either vagueness or ambiguity might prevent the formation of a contract itself. Restatement

(Second) of Contracts §§ 20(1) and 201(3). The *Raffles v. Wichelhaus* case presented in an earlier chapter is a good example. The reference to the ship "Peerless" was ambiguous because two meanings were plausible, and neither party knew or had reason to know the meaning attached by the other. The Restatement (Second) of Contracts confines the failure of contract formation to cases involving "material" differences. Some argue contract failure should be confined to cases of true ambiguity and not those involving mere vagueness. William F. Young, Jr., "Equivocation in the Making of Agreements," 64 Colum. L. Rev. 619, 646 (1964). Nonetheless, Restatement (Second) of Contracts §§ 20(1) and 201(3) arguably embrace a broader materiality standard. Notwithstanding apparent assent, if the vagueness or ambiguity masks hidden dissent or material misunderstanding, a contract simply may not exist.

But, in all other cases, the contract survives. Therefore some legal doctrine must determine which or whose meaning prevails. This secondary level of interpreting the agreement—which comes into play only after determining that the parties have formed an enforceable contract—focuses on resolution of these "lesser" interpretative problems, involving vagueness or ambiguity. The purpose of interpretation is to ascertain the meaning of a term. Restatement (Second) of Contracts § 200. In all cases, the effort is to ascertain the principal purpose of the parties. Restatement (Second) of Contracts § 202(1). Even integrated agreements may be interpreted, notwithstanding the parol evidence rule. Restatement (Second) of Contracts §§ 212(1) and 214(c). In general, matters of interpretation are questions of law, meaning that resolution of the meaning of a contract or term is determined by the court, not the jury. Restatement (Second) of Contracts § 212(2). But it is often the case that the parties raise disputes of fact regarding the terms of the agreement itself or the factual context surrounding the making of the agreement. In that case, the jury (or the judge in a bench trial) must first receive evidence from the parties and render a finding of fact that resolves the dispute. With the findings of fact in hand, the court may then proceed with the process of interpretation.

As with the parol evidence rule, and under the modern view, evidence of meaning may be presented for the purpose of proving a consistent meaning (reasonably susceptible) with the term, but not to contradict the term itself (although often the plain meaning may be contradicted). Arthur L. Corbin, "The Interpretation of Words and the Parol Evidence Rule," 50 Cornell L. Q. 161 (1965). To begin analysis, it is worth noting the comment of a distinguished jurist:

> Under the prevailing will theory of contract, parties, like Humpty Dumpty, may use words as they please. If they wish the symbols "one Caterpillar D9G tractor" to mean "500 railroad cars full of watermelons," that's fine—provided parties share this weird meaning. A meaning held by one party only may not be invoked

to change the ordinary denotation of a word, however. E.g., Skycom Corp. v. Telstar Corp., 813 F.2d 810, 814–16 (7th Cir.1987). Intent must be mutual to be effective; unilateral intent does not count. Still less may the parties announce that they "share" an unusual meaning to the detriment of strangers, who have no way of finding out what was in the contracting parties' heads. TKO Equipment Co. v. C & G Coal Co., Inc., 863 F.2d 541 (7th Cir. 1988) (Easterbrook, J.).

To a considerable degree, the current Restatement (Second) of Contracts § 201(2) reflects this view. Doctrinally, one simply cannot impose his or her meaning upon the other party absent some standard permitting the imposition. Restatement (Second) of Contracts § 201(2) considers two such imposition or supremacy doctrines where both parties have attached a different meaning to an agreement or term. Under § 201(2)(a), if one of the parties actually knew that the other party attached a different meaning to the term, and the "innocent" party did not know of the difference, the court should adopt the meaning understood by the innocent party. Thus, in *Raffles v. Wichelhaus*, if the cotton buyer had known at the time of contracting that there were two ships Peerless—October and December—bound for Liverpool and that the seller (1) intended the December Peerless and (2) did not know of the October Peerless, § 201(2)(a) requires the court to adopt the seller's meaning. Restatement (Second) of Contracts § 201(2)(b) provides a similar test where the innocent party had no reason to know of the ambiguity and the other party had reason to know of the innocent party's meaning. In the *Raffles* counterfactual above, the court should prefer the seller's meaning where the buyer had only days previously entered another cotton futures contract to arrive on the December Peerless. Since the buyer in *Raffles* claimed he had intended the October Peerless, the recently prior contract for the December Peerless could potentially give the seller reason to know of the existence of both ships. Both doctrines are relative fault-based doctrines preferring the meaning attached by the "only innocent party." So if a culpable party knew or should have known the meaning attached by the other innocent party, the legal meaning will be that of the only innocent party. Of course, to be truly innocent, the "only innocent party" must similarly not know or have reason to know of the meaning attached by the culpable party.

While the "only innocent party" rule appears superficially fair and reasonable, a hidden problem exists. The party asserting a particular meaning will be the plaintiff who must carry the burden of proving its meaning prevails. Many reasonable interpretation cases will fail solely because the plaintiff cannot carry its burden. This is particularly likely in a vagueness case where the subject term embraces both meanings and the plaintiff seeks a narrower meaning than the objective meaning implies. In such cases, the other party will almost always be able to rely on a broader objective meaning unless in the unlikely event the plaintiff can prove the defendant knew or should have known the plaintiff's narrower subjective meaning. Even cases involving ambiguity display a similar characteristic. While a subject term might be reasonably susceptible of both meanings, the plaintiff will have the burden to prove the defendant knew or should have known the meaning attached by the plaintiff.

At a policy level, interpretative squabbles are both common and troubling because resolution implicates the ancient tension between the objective and subjective theories of resolving contractual controversies. Objective solutions are often more predictable and involve fewer proof problems, but often ignore the specific and reasonable subjective intent of the parties. Since contract law remains the dominant form of private law making where the parties design and create their own desirable set of duties and correlative rights based upon the economic assumptions by each, why and when should the objective theory interfere with this process?

The early part of the nineteenth century was dominated by "mechanical jurisprudence" and objectification of contract law by early classical theorists like Christopher Langdell, Oliver Wendell Holmes, and Samuel Williston. See Roscoe Pound, "Mechanical Jurisprudence," 8 Colum. L. Rev. 605 (1908). By the first part of the twentieth century, classic contract theory began to exhibit growing pains under the strain of Legal Realists like Roscoe Pound, Arthur Corbin, and Karl Llewellyn who turned the path of the law toward sociological jurisprudence through a reasoned search for the subjective intent of each party. Richard E. Speidel, "Restatement Second: Omitted Terms and Contract Method," 67 Cornell L. Rev. 785, 788 (1982) (arguing that the second restatement moved from rules to standards submitting to attacks by Realists that there was a set of universal rules that could solve all questions fairly). Perhaps no doctrinal area exhibits this tension more completely than the process of legal interpretation. While Corbin was not a proponent of the objective theory, he nonetheless provided a quintessential description:

> Contracting parties must be made to know that it is their written words that constitute their contract, not their intentions that they try to express in the words. They, not the court, have chosen the words; and they, not the court, have made the contract. Its legal operation must be in accordance with the meaning that the words convey to the court, not the meaning that they intend to convey. Arthur L. Corbin, "The Interpretation of Words and the Parol Evidence Rule," 50 Cornell L. Q. 161 (1965).

Strict adherence to the objective theory inevitably leads to an application of the "plain meaning rule." That rule generally provides that where a writing appears to be complete and "not ambiguous on its surface," the court must interpret the words with their ordinary meaning and must not resort to any extrinsic evidence for ascertaining the intent of one or both parties. Sanford Shane, "Ambiguity and Misunderstanding in the Law,"25 T. Jefferson L. Rev. 167, 180 (2002). While the plain meaning rule has been repeatedly attacked by scholars, it nonetheless remains the dominant theory of contract interpretation in the United States. Margaret N. Kniffin, "A New Trend in Contract Interpretation: The Search for Reality as Opposed to Virtual Reality," 74 Or. L. Rev. 643 (1995) (revised the Corbin treatise on Contracts section on Interpretation). Finally, while the discussion below endeavors to separate the parol evidence rule from interpretation, the truth is that the separation is more difficult than might otherwise be imagined. See Eric A. Posner, "The Parol Evidence Rule, The Plain Meaning Rule, and the Principles of Contractual Interpretation," 146 U. Pa. L. Rev. 533, 534 (1997) and Peter Linzer, "The Comfort of Certainty: Plain Meaning and the Parol Evidence Rule," 71 Fordham L. Rev. 799 (2002).

Under the objective theory, a term is ambiguous only if a court cannot ascertain a reasonably objective meaning within the "four corners" of the document itself. On the other hand, the subjective theory requires the court to consider all evidence to determine the actual intent of the parties and then to determine whose meaning should control or whether the misunderstanding constitutes a serious failure of assent blocking the formation of the contract itself. Far from involving a simple choice between two rules (objective versus subjective), this choice implicates judicial philosophy and legal reasoning. Peter M. Tiersma, "A Message in a Bottle: Text, Autonomy, and Statutory Interpretation," 76 Tulane L. Rev. 431 (2001).

Of course, the Restatement (Second) of Contracts states a particular position in this warfare. If an agreement is "completely integrated," parol evidence of prior or contemporaneous agreements may not be introduced for the purpose of contradicting a term in the writing or even for the purpose of supplementing the agreement with a consistent additional term. Restatement (Second) of Contracts §§ 215 and 216(1). Nevertheless, it is generally recognized that this addition and variation prohibition does not necessarily preclude resort to the same parol evidence offered for the very different purpose of the interpretation of the terms stated in the contract. There are two views on this matter.

The older and more restrictive view is that of Professor Samuel Williston articulated in the Restatement (First) of Contracts. That view holds that, except where it produces an "ambiguous" result, the standard of interpretation is the meaning that would be attached by a reasonably intelligent person acquainted with all operative usages and knowing all the circumstances other than oral statements by the parties of what they intended it to mean. Restatement (First) of Contracts § 230.

The newer and more liberal view is that of Professor Arthur Corbin articulated in the Restatement (Second) Contracts. That view holds that the parol evidence rule is inapplicable to all matters of interpretation without regard to whether the agreement is partially or completely integrated and without reference to a first determination of ambiguity. Arthur L. Corbin, "The Interpretation of Words and the Parol Evidence Rule," 50 Cornell L. Q. 161, 189 (1965) (since a promise supported by consideration depends upon both parties, the court must take into account the understanding of each party unless one of the parties is estopped from asserting their own interpretation by conduct); Restatement (Second) of Contracts § 214(c).

This view also has been adopted by the Uniform Commercial Code, which does not require a threshold determination that a term is ambiguous in order to authorize interpretation, at least if in a record. Otherwise, the statute takes no position on the ambiguity test. UCC § 2–202(2), *cmt. 5* ("In interpreting terms in a record, subsection (2) permits either party to introduce evidence drawn from a course of performance, a course of dealing, or a usage of trade without any preliminary determination by the court that the term at issue is ambiguous. This article takes no position on whether a preliminary determination of ambiguity is a condition to the admissibility of evidence drawn from any other source or on whether a contract clause can exclude an otherwise applicable implied-in-fact source.").

The principal difference between the two views will occur where the parties state a term in writing and then orally agree the term means something subjectively peculiar. To borrow an example from *Raffles v. Wichelhaus*, assume that A and B make a contract for the sale of Bombay cotton to be delivered by the ship "Peerless." There are two ships of the same name sailing at materially different times, October and December. Assume a reasonable person knowing all the facts and circumstances would conclude the term referred to October Peerless. Nonetheless, A and B orally agree that the term refers to December Peerless. Since the term Peerless in this context has an objective meaning (October Peerless), it is not ambiguous and a jurisdiction requiring threshold ambiguity would determine the term meant October Peerless. Any evidence that the parties intended otherwise would be excluded. In a jurisdiction that does not require ambiguity, the evidence of specific intent would be admissible. By way of clarification, under the older ambiguity rule, the parties are not free to attach special meanings to ordinary words. Nicholas R. Weiskopf, "Supplementing Written Agreements: Restating The Parol Evidence Rule In Terms of Credibility and Relative Fault," 34 Emory L. J. 93, 101 (1985). Stated another way, words are accorded their "plain meaning." Oliver W. Holmes, "The Theory of Legal Interpretation," 12 Harv. L. Rev. 417, 420

(1899). The newer view seeks the subjective meaning of each term without regard to the ordinary meaning of the words used.

Of course, even under the newer view, a litigant party who wishes to establish a subjective meaning must prove that its meaning does not violate the parol evidence rule itself. Thus, when does simple "interpretation" morph into "addition" or "variation" of the agreement and thus invoke the parol evidence rule? The most satisfactory answer is probably that the evidence may only be offered for the limited purpose of resolving an ambiguity or vagueness. While this appears superficially the same as the older version ambiguity rule, application is truly different. First, the newer version does not require a threshold determination of ambiguity. Only the purpose of the introduction need be established. If the party offers the evidence to interpret a term rather than addition or variation of the agreement, it is admissible. E. Allan Farnsworth, "'Meaning' In The Law of Contracts," 76 Yale L. J. 939 (1967).

The newer version has made progress in eliminating the possibility that the parties will be bound by an objective meaning contrary to a special meaning, but only in limited circumstances. Where a special meaning is shared by both parties, it will become the legal meaning. Restatement (Second) of Contracts § 201(1). Of course, litigation in such cases is rare because the parties agree on the shared meaning. However, where the parties do not share a special meaning, the party seeking the advantage of a special meaning contradicting an objective meaning will face difficult proof obstacles. The party seeking the special meaning must prove the other party knew or should have known of this special meaning, and it did not know and did not have reason to know of the other party's objective meaning. This is quite burdensome. Proving the other party knew or should have known of the special meaning is difficult. Also, it will always be difficult to prove that the party seeking the special meaning either did not know or did not have reason to know the other party was relying on an objective meaning of the same term. Eyal Zamir, "The Inverted Hierarchy of Contract Interpretation and Supplementation," 97 Colum. L. Rev. 1710, 1728 (1997) (arguing that contract law should be viewed as public law rather than private law because it invokes the power of the state and federal courts to enforce the contracts).

In the cases below, determine three things. First, does the court apply the older or newer interpretation version? Second, is there a reasonable and broader objective meaning of the term in question? Third, if the term is susceptible to a reasonable and broader objective meaning, is the plaintiff attempting to prove a narrower subjective meaning?

PACIFIC GAS AND ELECTRIC CO. v. G. W. THOMAS DRAYAGE & RIGGING CO.

Supreme Court of California
69 Cal.2d 33, 442 P.2d 641, 69 Cal.Rptr. 561 (1968)

TRAYNOR, Chief Justice.

Defendant appeals from a judgment for plaintiff in an action for damages for injury to property under an indemnity clause of a contract.

In 1960 defendant entered into a contract with plaintiff to furnish the labor and equipment necessary to remove and replace the upper metal cover of plaintiff's steam turbine. Defendant agreed to perform the work "at (its) own risk and expense" and to "indemnify" plaintiff "against all loss, damage, expense and liability resulting from . . . injury to property, arising out of or in any way connected with the performance of this contract." Defendant also agreed to procure not less than $50,000 insurance to cover liability for injury to property. Plaintiff was to be an additional named insured, but the policy was to contain a cross-liability clause extending the coverage to plaintiff's property.

During the work the cover fell and injured the exposed rotor of the turbine. Plaintiff brought this action to recover $25,144.51, the amount it subsequently spent on repairs. During the trial it dismissed a count based on negligence and thereafter secured judgment on the theory that the indemnity provision covered injury to all property regardless of ownership.

Defendant offered to prove by admissions of plaintiff's agents, by defendant's conduct under similar contracts entered into with plaintiff, and by other proof that in the indemnity clause the parties meant to cover injury to property of third parties only and not to plaintiff's property.[1] Although the trial court observed that the language used was "the classic language for a third party indemnity provision" and that "one could very easily conclude that . . . its whole intendment is to indemnify third parties," it nevertheless held that the "plain language" of the agreement also required defendant to indemnify plaintiff for injuries to plaintiff's property. Having determined that the contract had a plain meaning, the court refused to admit any extrinsic evidence that would contradict its interpretation.

When a court interprets a contract on this basis, it determines the meaning of the instrument in accordance with the " . . . extrinsic evidence

---

[1] Although this offer of proof might ordinarily be regarded as too general to provide a ground for appeal (Evid. Code, § 354, subd. (a); Beneficial, etc., Ins. Co. v. Kurt Hitke & Co. (1956) 46 Cal. 2d 517, 522, 297 P. 2d 428; Stickel v. San Diego Elec. Ry. Co. (1948) 32 Cal. 2d 157, 162–164, 195 P. 2d 416; Douillard v. Woodd (1942) 20 Cal. 2d 665, 670, 128 P.2 d 6), since the court repeatedly ruled that it would not admit extrinsic evidence to interpret the contract and sustained objections to all questions seeking to elicit such evidence, no formal offer of proof was required. (Evid. Code, § 354, subd. (b); Beneficial, etc., Ins. Co. v. Kurt Hitke & Co., supra, 46 Cal. 2d 517, 522, 297 P. 2d 428; Estate of Kearns (1950) 36 Cal. 2d 531, 537, 225 P. 2d 218.)

of the judge's own linguistic education and experience." (3 Corbin on Contracts (1960 ed.) (1964 Supp. § 579, p. 225, fn. 56).) The exclusion of testimony that might contradict the linguistic background of the judge reflects a judicial belief in the possibility of perfect verbal expression. (9 Wigmore on Evidence (3d ed. 1940) § 2461, p. 187.) This belief is a remnant of a primitive faith in the inherent potency[2] and inherent meaning of words.[3]

The test of admissibility of extrinsic evidence to explain the meaning of a written instrument is not whether it appears to the court to be plain and unambiguous on its face, but whether the offered evidence is relevant to prove a meaning to which the language of the instrument is reasonably susceptible. (Continental Baking Co. v. Katz (1968) 68 A.C. 527, 536–537, 67 Cal. Rptr. 761, 439 P. 2d 889; Parsons v. Bristol Development Co. (1965) 62 Cal. 2d 861, 865, 44 Cal. Rptr. 767, 402 P. 2d 839. . . .)

A rule that would limit the determination of the meaning of a written instrument to its four-corners merely because it seems to the court to be clear and unambiguous, would either deny the relevance of the intention of the parties or presuppose a degree of verbal precision and stability our language has not attained.

Some courts have expressed the opinion that contractual obligations are created by the mere use of certain words, whether or not there was any intention to incur such obligations.[4] Under this view, contractual obligations flow, not from the intention of the parties but from the fact that they used certain magic words. Evidence of the parties' intention therefore becomes irrelevant.

In this state, however, the intention of the parties as expressed in the contract is the source of contractual rights and duties.[5] A court must

---

[2] E.g., "The elaborate system of taboo and verbal prohibitions in primitive groups; the ancient Egyptian myth of Khern, the apotheosis of the word, and of Thoth, the Scribe of Truth, the Giver of Words and Script, the Master of Incantations; the avoidance of the name of God in Brahmanism, Judaism and Islam; totemistic and protective names in mediaeval Turkish and Finno-Ugrian languages; the misplaced verbal scruples of the 'Precieuses;' the Swedish peasant custom of curing sick cattle smitten by witchcraft, by making them swallow a page torn out of the psalter and put in dough. . . ." from Ullman, The Principles of Semantics (1963 ed.) 43. (See also Ogden and Richards, The Meaning of Meaning (rev. ed. 1956) pp. 24–47.)

[3] "Rerum enim vocabula immutabilia sunt, homines mutabilia," (Words are unchangeable, men changeable) from Dig. XXXIII, 10, 7, s 2, de sup. leg. as quoted in 9 Wigmore on Evidence, op. cit. supra, § 2461, p. 187.

[4] "A contract has, strictly speaking, nothing to do with the personal, or individual, intent of the parties. A contract is an obligation attached by the mere force of law to certain acts of the parties, usually words, which ordinarily accompany and represent a known intent." (Hotchkiss v. National City Bank of New York (S.D.N.Y. 1911) 200 F. 287, 293. See also C. H. Pope & Co. v. Bibb Mfg. Co. (2d Cir. 1923) 290 F. 586, 587; see 4 Williston on Contracts (3d ed. 1961) § 612, pp. 577–578, § 613, p. 583.)

[5] "A contract must be so interpreted as to give effect to the mutual intention of the parties as it existed at the time of contracting, so far as the same is ascertainable and lawful." (Civ. Code, § 1636; see also Code Civ. Proc. § 1859; Universal Sales Corp. v. Cal. Press Mfg. Co. (1942) 20 Cal.

ascertain and give effect to this intention by determining what the parties meant by the words they used. Accordingly, the exclusion of relevant, extrinsic evidence to explain the meaning of a written instrument could be justified only if it were feasible to determine the meaning the parties gave to the words from the instrument alone.

If words had absolute and constant referents, it might be possible to discover contractual intention in the words themselves and in the manner in which they were arranged. Words, however, do not have absolute and constant referents. "A word is a symbol of thought but has no arbitrary and fixed meaning like a symbol of algebra or chemistry, ..." (Pearson v. State Social Welfare Board (1960) 54 Cal. 2d 184, 195, 5 Cal. Rptr. 553, 559, 353 P. 2d 33, 39.) The meaning of particular words or groups of words varies with the " . . . verbal context and surrounding circumstances and purposes in view of the linguistic education and experience of their users and their hearers or readers (not excluding judges). . . . A word has no meaning apart from these factors; much less does it have an objective meaning, one true meaning." (Corbin, The Interpretation of Words and the Parol Evidence Rule (1965) 50 Cornell L. Q. 161, 187.) Accordingly, the meaning of a writing " . . . can only be found by interpretation in the light of all the circumstances that reveal the sense in which the writer used the words. The exclusion of parol evidence regarding such circumstances merely because the words do not appear ambiguous to the reader can easily lead to the attribution to a written instrument of a meaning that was never intended. (Citations omitted.)" (Universal Sales Corp. v. Cal. Press Mfg. Co., supra, 20 Cal. 2d 751, 776, 128 P. 2d 665, 679 (concurring opinion); see also, e.g., . . .

Although extrinsic evidence is not admissible to add to, detract from, or vary the terms of a written contract, these terms must first be determined before it can be decided whether or not extrinsic evidence is being offered for a prohibited purpose. The fact that the terms of an instrument appear clear to a judge does not preclude the possibility that the parties chose the language of the instrument to express different terms. That possibility is not limited to contracts whose terms have acquired a particular meaning by trade usage,[6] but exists whenever the parties'

2d 751, 760, 128 P. 2d 665; Lemm v. Stillwater Land & Cattle Co. (1933) 217 Cal. 474, 480, 19 P. 2d 785.)

[6] Extrinsic evidence of trade usage or custom has been admitted to show that the term "United Kingdom" in a motion picture distribution contract included Ireland (Ermolieff v. R.K.O. Radio Pictures (1942) 19 Cal. 2d 543, 549–552, 122 P. 2d 3); that the word "ton" in a lease meant a long ton or 2,240 pounds and not the statutory ton of 2,000 pounds (Higgins v. Cal. Petroleum, etc., Co. (1898) 120 Cal. 629, 630–632, 52 P. 1080); that the word "stubble" in a lease included not only stumps left in the ground but everything "left on the ground after the harvest time" (Callahan v. Stanley (1881) 57 Cal. 476, 477–479); that the term "north" in a contract dividing mining claims indicated a boundary line running along the "magnetic and not the true meridian" (Jenny Lind Co. v. Bower & Co. (1858) 11 Cal. 194, 197–199) and that a form contract for purchase and sale was actually an agency contract (Body-Steffner Co. v. Flotill Products (1944) 63 Cal. App. 2d 555, 558–

understanding of the words used may have differed from the judge's understanding.

Accordingly, rational interpretation requires at least a preliminary consideration of all credible evidence offered to prove the intention of the parties. 7 Civ. Code, § 1647; Code Civ. Proc. § 1860; see also 9 Wigmore on Evidence, op. cit. supra, § 2470, fn. 11, p. 227. Such evidence includes testimony as to the "circumstances surrounding the making of the agreement . . . including the object, nature and subject matter of the writing . . ." so that the court can "place itself in the same situation in which the parties found themselves at the time of contracting." (Universal Sales Corp. v. Cal. Press Mfg. Co., supra, 20 Cal. 2d 751, 761, 128 P. 2d 665, 671; Lemm v. Stillwater Land & Cattle Co., supra, 217 Cal. 474, 480–481, 19 P. 2d 785.) If the court decides, after considering this evidence, that the language of a contract, in the light of all the circumstances, is "fairly susceptible of either one of the two interpretations contended for. . . ." (Balfour v. Fresno C. & I. Co. (1895) 109 Cal. 221, 225, 44 P. 876, 877; . . . extrinsic evidence relevant to prove either of such meanings is admissible.[8]

In the present case the court erroneously refused to consider extrinsic evidence offered to show that the indemnity clause in the contract was not intended to cover injuries to plaintiff's property. Although that evidence was not necessary to show that the indemnity clause was reasonably susceptible of the meaning contended for by defendant, it was nevertheless relevant and admissible on that issue. Moreover, since that clause was reasonably susceptible of that meaning, the offered evidence was also admissible to prove that the clause had that meaning and did not cover injuries to plaintiff's property.[9] Accordingly, the judgment must be reversed. . . .

562, 147 P. 2d 84). See also Code Civ. Proc. § 1861; Annot., 89 A.L.R. 1228; Note (1942) 30 Cal. L. Rev. 679.

   [8]   Extrinsic evidence has often been admitted in such cases on the stated ground that the contract was ambiguous (e.g., Universal Sales Corp. v. Cal. Press Mfg. Co., supra, 20 Cal. 2d 751, 761, 128 P. 2d 665). This statement of the rule is harmless if it is kept in mind that the ambiguity may be exposed by extrinsic evidence that reveals more than one possible meaning.

   [9]   The court's exclusion of extrinsic evidence in this case would be error even under a rule that excluded such evidence when the instrument appeared to the court to be clear and unambiguous on its face. The controversy centers on the meaning of the word "indemnify" and the phrase "all loss, damage, expense and liability." The trial court's recognition of the language as typical of a third party indemnity clause and the double sense in which the word "indemnify" is used in statutes and defined in dictionaries demonstrate the existence of an ambiguity. (Compare Civ. Code, § 2772, "Indemnity is a contract by which one engages to save another from a legal consequence of the conduct of one of the parties, or of some other person," with Civ. Code, § 2527, "Insurance is a contract whereby by one undertakes to indemnify another against loss, damage, or liability, arising from an unknown or contingent event." Black's Law Dictionary (4th ed. 1951) defines "indemnity" as "A collateral contract or assurance, by which one person engages to secure another against an anticipated loss or to prevent him from being damaged by the legal consequences of an act or forbearance on the part of one of the parties or of some third person." Stroud's Judicial Dictionary (2d ed. 1903) defines it as a "Contract . . . to indemnify against a liability. . . ." One of the definitions given to "indemnify" by Webster's Third New Internat. Dict. (1961 ed.) is "to exempt from incurred penalties or liabilities.")

The judgment is reversed.

PETERS, MOSK, BURKE, SULLIVAN, and PEEK, JJ., concur.

McCOMB, J., dissents.

NOTES AND QUESTIONS

1. *Plain meaning rule.* Does Justice Traynor suppose that words have a "plain meaning"? What is the intent of his claim that "[a] word is a symbol of thought but has no arbitrary and fixed meaning like a symbol of algebra or chemistry"? Justice Holmes once remarked that "[a] word is not a crystal, transparent and unchanged; it is the skin of a living thought and may vary greatly in color and content according to the circumstances and the time in which it is used." Towne v. Eisner, 245 U.S. 418, 425 (1918). Do you think Traynor and Holmes philosophically agree? David G. Garner, "A Failed Coup on the Judicial Monarchy," 1999 B.Y.U. L. Rev. 887. Indeed, if a reasonable argument exists that a term requires interpretation, is the term already being interpreted? Stanley E. Fisch, "Normal Circumstances, Literal Language, Direct Speech Acts, The Ordinary, The Obvious, What Goes Without Saying, and Other Special Cases," 4 Critical Inquiry 625, 637 (1978).

2. *"Knew or had reason to know" analysis.* Has the Restatement (Second) of Contracts embraced or abandoned the "plain meaning rule"? What is the focus of language that in cases of misunderstanding, there must be an inquiry into the meaning attached to the words by each party and into what each party knew or had reason to know? Melvin A. Eisenberg, "The Emergence of Dynamic Contract Law," 88 Cal. L. Rev. 1743, 1769 (2000).

3. *Who decides what?* Is it reasonably clear that the judge decides whether a term is ambiguous and therefore that decision is reviewable *de novo* by an appellate court as in *Pacific Gas and Electric Co.*? The second restatement suggests that, historically, placing primary responsibility for determining ambiguity in the hands of the judge, rather than the jury, arose because of low literacy rates among lay juries at the time the rule developed.

Plaintiff's assertion that the use of the word "all" to modify "loss, damage, expense and liability" dictates an all inclusive interpretation is not persuasive. If the word "indemnify" encompasses only third-party claims, the word "all" simply refers to all such claims. The use of the words "loss," "damage," and "expense" in addition to the word "liability" is likewise inconclusive. These words do not imply an agreement to reimburse for injury to an indemnitee's property since they are commonly inserted in third-party indemnity clauses, to enable an indemnitee who settles a claim to recover from his indemnitor without proving his liability. (Carpenter Paper Co. v. Kellogg (1952) 114 Cal. App. 2d 640, 651, 251 P. 2d 40. Civ. Code, § 2778, provides: "1. Upon an indemnity against liability . . . the person indemnified is entitled to recover upon becoming liable; 2. Upon an indemnity against claims, or demands, or damages, or costs . . . the person indemnified is not entitled to recover without payment thereof; . . . .")

The provision that defendant perform the work "at his own risk and expense" and the provisions relating to insurance are equally inconclusive. By agreeing to work at its own risk defendant may have released plaintiff from liability for any injuries to defendant's property arising out of the contract's performance, but this provision did not necessarily make defendant an insurer against injuries to plaintiff's property. Defendant's agreement to procure liability insurance to cover damages to plaintiff's property does not indicate whether the insurance was to cover all injuries or only injuries caused by defendant's negligence.

Analytically, what meaning is attached to a word or other symbol by one or more people is a question of fact. But general usage as to the meaning of words in the English language is commonly a proper subject for judicial notice without the aid of evidence extrinsic to the writing. Historically, moreover, partly perhaps because of the fact that jurors were often illiterate, questions of interpretation of written documents have been treated as questions of law in the sense that they are decided by the trial judge rather than by the jury. Likewise, since an appellate court is commonly in as good a position to decide such questions as the trial judge, they have been treated as questions of law for purposes of appellate review. Restatement (Second) of Contracts § 212 *cmt. d.*

But in many cases, interpretation depends not on an understanding of "general usage as to the meaning of words in the English language," but rather on disputed questions of fact relating to the context of the agreement or to the credibility of antagonistic parties each asserting their own self-interested version of contractual intent. Where the meaning of the document turns on such disputes of fact or questions of credibility, the jury's fact-finding expertise resolves the disputed facts, determines party and witness credibility, and—in the case of an ambiguity that persists after such findings—decides which of the offered reasonable interpretations the parties intended. See Restatement (Second) of Contracts § 212(2); see also Keith A. Rowley, "Contract Construction and Interpretation: From the 'Four Corners' to Parol Evidence (And Everything In Between)," 69 Miss. L. J. 73, 94–96 (1999). For a general discussion of the role of the jury in American contract law, see Mark P. Gergen, "The Jury's Role in Deciding Normative Issues in American Common Law," 68 Fordham L. Rev. 407, 440–461 (1999).

4.   *Old rules die hard.* The plain meaning rule was completely eviscerated in California in a 1968 trilogy of famous cases beginning with *Masterson v. Sine*, 68 Cal.2d 222, 65 Cal.Rptr. 545, 436 P.2d 561 (1968); *Pacific Gas and Electric Co. v. G. W. Thomas Drayage Co.*, 69 Cal.2d 33, 69 Cal.Rptr. 561, 442 P.2d 641 (1968); and *Delta Dynamics, Inc. v. Arioto*, 69 Cal.2d 525, 72 Cal.Rptr. 785, 446 P.2d 785 (1968). In the third case, three of seven judges dissented. Still later, the Ninth Circuit criticized *Pacific Gas & Electric* as casting "a long shadow of uncertainty over all transactions negotiated and executed under the law of California." *Trident Center v. Connecticut General Life Insurance Co.*, 847 F.2d 564 (9th Cir. 1988) (Kozinski. J.). In *Trident Center*, the loan contract at issue unambiguously—according to the 9th Circuit's opinion—prohibited prepayment of a loan within the first twelve years. See id. at 566 ("It is difficult to imagine language that more clearly or unambiguously expresses the idea that Trident may not unilaterally prepay the loan during its first 12 years."). The court further rejected Trident Center's argument that the default provisions of the loan agreement would permit it to prepay the loan with a 10% penalty, reasoning that "the clause on which Trident relies is not on its face reasonably susceptible to Trident's proffered interpretation." Id. at 567. Nonetheless, the 9th Circuit concluded that the

Pacific Gas standard required a remand to permit Trident Center to submit parol evidence in support of its preferred interpretation. See id. at 569–70. Given that the 9th Circuit concluded as a matter of law that the loan agreement was not reasonably susceptible to Trident Center's proffered meaning, did it correctly apply the *Pacific Gas* standard? These cases and likely effects are discussed extensively in Harry G. Prince, "Contract Interpretation in California: Plain Meaning, Parol Evidence and Use of the 'Just Result' Principle," 31 Loy. L. A. L. Rev. 557, 577 (1998).

6. *Two stages remain.* Even Justice Traynor's rejection of the plain meaning rule is not without limits. The liberal view thus more accurately relaxes the plain meaning rule rather than eliminating it. The difference is what evidence is considered under the first step. Under the plain meaning rule, the judge would determine from the four corners of the document and without the aid of extrinsic evidence whether the term had a plain meaning. If so, introduction of further evidence to explain another meaning is excluded. Under Justice Traynor's position, the first stage is relaxed, and the judge will consider extrinsic evidence to determine whether the term is "reasonably susceptible" to more than one plain meaning. This first stage only considers the evidence provisionally—not for determining what the terms mean but rather whether the language used in the integration *could* reasonably mean what each of the parties asserts was their intent. If so, evidence is admitted so that the fact finder can determine which meaning controls—the process of interpretation. In the second, or interpretation, stage, the fact finder determines the choice between two meanings to which the writing is reasonably susceptible. Restatement (Second) of Contracts § 212(2).

7. *UCC does not require ambiguity.* The UCC trumps common law because it is statutory. UCC § 2–202(a) states that a writing intended to be a final expression of an agreement may not be contradicted by prior or contemporaneous oral agreement, but may nonetheless be "explained" or supplemented by course of performance, course of dealing, or usage of trade. Comment 1 makes clear that the "explanation" rule does not require threshold ambiguity.

8. *CISG approach.* The CISG Art. 8(3) essentially rejects the American parol evidence rule, but CISG Art. 8(1) contains familiar rules of interpretation—all relevant circumstances are considered to determine the intent of the parties. However, CISG Art. 8(2) makes reasonably clear that the "intent" referent is to the understanding a reasonable person would have had under the circumstances and thus adopts an objective standard. See John E. Murray, Jr., "An Essay on the Formation of Contracts and Related Matters Under The United Nations Convention on Contracts for the International Sale of Goods," 8 J. L. & Comm. 11, 46 (1988); Michael P. Van Alstine, "Consensus, Dissensus, and Contractual Obligation Through the Prism of Uniform International Sales Law," 37 Va. J. Int'l L. 1, 42 (1996).

The *Pacific Gas & Electric Case* considers the admissibility of parol evidence in the form of prior negotiations. What about other types of interpretative evidence? In general, courts rely upon a body of interpretive tools, beginning with the text itself. As shown in the *Frigaliment Importing Co.* case below, courts may examine the parties' text through a number of lenses that, although technically extrinsic to the contract, are nonetheless permissible means of interpreting a document. First and foremost, courts often rely upon meanings supplied by dictionaries. If the text refers to another document, such as a statute, regulation, a trade publication, and so on, the court may deem the additional document "incorporated by reference" into the parties' agreement. Likewise, common trade usages may supply meaning to otherwise ambiguous terms. Finally, courts may employ commonly accepted common law rules of interpretation. These rules of interpretation include the obvious analysis of grammar and punctuation, but also extend to more abstract postulates such as *ejusdem generis* (a list of specific terms followed by a general term will limit the meaning of the general term to the same class of things as those specifically identified), *noscitur a sociis* (the meaning of an ambiguous term within a list of specific terms will be limited by the meaning of the specific terms), *expressio unius exclusio alterius est* (the expression of one thing is the exclusion of others), and *contra proferentem* (ambiguities should be construed against the drafter). Where analysis and interpretation of the text fails to resolve the ambiguity, the court must turn to less certain sources of meaning, such as the parties' course of performance under their contract, their negotiations, and their prior dealings. The following famous case explores the use of various forms of evidence to determine the legal meaning of a term in the contract.

FRIGALIMENT IMPORTING CO. V. B.N.S. INTERNATIONAL SALES CORP.

United States District Court Southern District New York
190 F. Supp. 116 (1960)

FRIENDLY, Circuit Judge.

The issue is, what is chicken? Plaintiff says "chicken" means a young chicken, suitable for broiling and frying. Defendant says "chicken" means any bird of that genus that meets contract specifications on weight and quality, including what it calls "stewing chicken" and plaintiff pejoratively terms "fowl." Dictionaries give both meanings, as well as some others not relevant here. To support its meaning, plaintiff sends a number of volleys over the net; defendant essays to return them and adds a few serves of its own. Assuming that both parties were acting in good faith, the case nicely illustrates Holmes' remark "that the making of a contract depends not on the agreement of two minds in one intention, but on the agreement of two sets of external signs—not on the parties' having meant the same thing but on their having said the same thing." The Path of the Law, in Collected Legal Papers, p. 178. I have concluded that plaintiff has not sustained its burden of persuasion that the contract used "chicken" in the narrower sense.

The action is for breach of the warranty that goods sold shall correspond to the description, New York Personal Property Law, McKinney's Consol. Laws, c. 41, § 95. Two contracts are in suit. In the first, dated May 2, 1957, defendant, a New York sales corporation, confirmed the sale to plaintiff, a Swiss corporation, of:

US Fresh Frozen Chicken, Grade A, Government Inspected, Eviscerated

2½–3 lbs. and 1½–2 lbs. each

all chicken individually wrapped in cryovac, packed in secured fiber cartons or wooden boxes, suitable for export

75,000 lbs. 2½–3 lbs @$33.00

25,000 lbs. 1½–2 lbs @$36.50

per 100 lbs. FAS New York

scheduled May 10, 1957 pursuant to instructions from Penson & Co., New York.

The second contract, also dated May 2, 1957, was identical save that only 50,000 lbs. of the heavier "chicken" were called for, the price of the smaller birds was $37 per 100 lbs., and shipment was scheduled for May 30. The initial shipment under the first contract was short but the balance was shipped on May 17. When the initial shipment arrived in Switzerland, plaintiff found, on May 28, that the 2½–3 lbs. birds were not young chicken suitable for broiling and frying but stewing chicken or "fowl;" indeed, many of the cartons and bags plainly so indicated. Protests ensued. Nevertheless, shipment under the second contract was made on May 29, the 2½–3 lbs. birds again being stewing chicken. Defendant stopped the transportation of these at Rotterdam.

This action followed. Plaintiff says that, notwithstanding that its acceptance was in Switzerland, New York law controls under the principle of Rubin v. Irving Trust Co., 1953, 305 N.Y. 288, 305, 113 N.E. 2d 424, 431; defendant does not dispute this, and relies on New York decisions. I shall follow the apparent agreement of the parties as to the applicable law.

Since the word 'chicken' standing alone is ambiguous, I turn first to see whether the contract itself offers any aid to its interpretation. Plaintiff says the 1½–2 lbs. birds necessarily had to be young chicken since the older birds do not come in that size, hence the 2½–3 lbs. birds must likewise be young. This is unpersuasive—a contract for 'apples' of two different sizes could be filled with different kinds of apples even though only one species came in both sizes. Defendant notes that the contract called not simply for chicken but for "US Fresh Frozen Chicken, Grade A, Government Inspected." It says the contract thereby incorporated by reference the Department of Agriculture's regulations, which favor its interpretation; I shall return to this after reviewing plaintiff's other contentions.

The first hinges on an exchange of cablegrams which preceded execution of the formal contracts. The negotiations leading up to the contracts were conducted in New York between defendant's secretary, Ernest R. Bauer, and a Mr. Stovicek, who was in New York for the Czechoslovak government at the World Trade Fair. A few days after meeting Bauer at the fair, Stovicek telephoned and inquired whether defendant would be interested in exporting poultry to Switzerland. Bauer then met with Stovicek, who showed him a cable from plaintiff dated April 26, 1957, announcing that they "are buyer" of 25,000 lbs. of chicken 2½–3 lbs. weight, Cryovac packed, grade A Government inspected, at a price up to 33› per pound, for shipment on May 10, to be confirmed by the following morning, and were interested in further offerings. After testing the market for price, Bauer accepted, and Stovicek sent a confirmation that evening. Plaintiff stresses that, although these and subsequent cables between plaintiff and defendant, which laid the basis for the additional quantities under the first and for all of the second contract, were predominantly in German, they used the English word "chicken;" it claims this was done because it understood "chicken" meant young chicken whereas the German word, "Huhn," included both "Brathuhn" (broilers) and "Suppenhuhn" (stewing chicken), and that defendant, whose officers were thoroughly conversant with German, should have realized this. Whatever force this argument might otherwise have is largely drained away by Bauer's testimony that he asked Stovicek what kind of chickens were wanted, received the answer "any kind of chickens," and then, in German, asked whether the cable meant "Huhn" and received an affirmative response. Plaintiff attacks this as contrary to what Bauer testified on his deposition in March, 1959, and also on the ground that Stovicek had no authority to interpret the meaning of the cable. The first contention would be persuasive if sustained by the record, since Bauer was free at the trial from the threat of contradiction by Stovicek as he was not at the time of the deposition; however, review of the deposition does not convince me of the claimed inconsistency. As to the second contention, it may well be that Stovicek lacked authority to commit plaintiff for prices or delivery dates other than those specified in the cable; but plaintiff cannot at the same time rely on its cable to Stovicek as its dictionary to the meaning of the contract and repudiate the interpretation given the dictionary by the man in whose hands it was put. See Restatement of the Law of Agency, 2d, § 145; 2 Mecham, Agency § 1781 (2d ed. 1914); Park v. Moorman Mfg. Co., 1952, 121 Utah 339, 241 P. 2d 914, 919, 40 A.L.R. 2d 273; . . . . Plaintiff's reliance on the fact that the contract forms contain the words "through the intermediary of: _____," with the blank not filled, as negating agency, is wholly unpersuasive; the purpose of this clause was to permit filling in the name of an intermediary to whom a commission would be payable, not to blot out what had been the fact.

Plaintiff's next contention is that there was a definite trade usage that "chicken" meant "young chicken." Defendant showed that it was only beginning in the poultry trade in 1957, thereby bringing itself within the principle that "when one of the parties is not a member of the trade or other circle, his acceptance of the standard must be made to appear" by proving either that he had actual knowledge of the usage or that the usage is "so generally known in the community that his actual individual knowledge of it may be inferred." 9 Wigmore, Evidence (3d ed. § 1940) 2464. Here there was no proof of actual knowledge of the alleged usage; indeed, it is quite plain that defendant's belief was to the contrary. In order to meet the alternative requirement, the law of New York demands a showing that "the usage is of so long continuance, so well established, so notorious, so universal and so reasonable in itself, as that the presumption is violent that the parties contracted with reference to it, and made it a part of their agreement." Walls v. Bailey, 1872, 49 N.Y. 464, 472–473.

Plaintiff endeavored to establish such a usage by the testimony of three witnesses and certain other evidence. Strasser, resident buyer in New York for a large chain of Swiss cooperatives, testified that "on chicken I would definitely understand a broiler." However, the force of this testimony was considerably weakened by the fact that in his own transactions the witness, a careful businessman, protected himself by using 'broiler' when that was what he wanted and 'fowl' when he wished older birds. Indeed, there are some indications, dating back to a remark of Lord Mansfield, Edie v. East India Co., 2 Burr. 1216, 1222 (1761), that no credit should be given "witnesses to usage, who could not adduce instances in verification." 7 Wigmore, Evidence (3d ed. 1940), § 1954; . . . . While Wigmore thinks this goes too far, a witness' consistent failure to rely on the alleged usage deprives his opinion testimony of much of its effect. Niesielowski, an officer of one of the companies that had furnished the stewing chicken to defendant, testified that "chicken" meant "the male species of the poultry industry. That could be a broiler, a fryer or a roaster," but not a stewing chicken; however, he also testified that upon receiving defendant's inquiry for "chickens," he asked whether the desire was for "fowl or frying chickens" and, in fact, supplied fowl, although taking the precaution of asking defendant, a day or two after plaintiff's acceptance of the contracts in suit, to change its confirmation of its order from "chickens," as defendant had originally prepared it, to "stewing chickens." Dates, an employee of Urner-Barry Company, which publishes a daily market report on the poultry trade, gave it as his view that the trade meaning of "chicken" was "broilers and fryers." In addition to this opinion testimony, plaintiff relied on the fact that the Urner-Barry service, the Journal of Commerce, and Weinberg Bros. & Co. of Chicago, a large supplier of poultry, published quotations in a manner which, in one way or another, distinguish between "chicken," comprising broilers, fryers and certain other categories, and "fowl," which, Bauer acknowledged, included stewing chickens. This material would be impressive if there were nothing to the contrary. However, there was, as will now be seen.

Defendant's witness Weininger, who operates a chicken eviscerating plant in New Jersey, testified "Chicken is everything except a goose, a duck, and a turkey. Everything is a chicken, but then you have to say, you have to specify which category you want or that you are talking about." Its witness Fox said that in the trade 'chicken' would encompass all the various classifications. Sadina, who conducts a food inspection service, testified that he would consider any bird coming within the classes of "chicken" in the Department of Agriculture's regulations to be a chicken. The specifications approved by the General Services Administration include fowl as well as broilers and fryers under the classification "chickens." Statistics of the Institute of American Poultry Industries use the phrases "Young chickens" and "Mature chickens," under the general heading "Total chickens." and the Department of Agriculture's daily and weekly price reports avoid use of the word "chicken" without specification.

Defendant advances several other points which it claims affirmatively support its construction. Primary among these is the regulation of the Department of Agriculture, 7 C.F.R. §§ 70.300–70.370, entitled, "Grading and Inspection of Poultry and Edible Products Thereof." and in particular § 70.301 which recited:

Chickens. The following are the various classes of chickens:

(a) Broiler or fryer . . .
(b) Roaster . . .
(c) Capon . . .
(d) Stag . . .
(e) Hen or stewing chicken or fowl . . .
(f) Cock or old rooster . . .

Defendant argues, as previously noted, that the contract incorporated these regulations by reference. Plaintiff answers that the contract provision related simply to grade and Government inspection and did not incorporate the Government definition of "chicken," and also that the definition in the Regulations is ignored in the trade. However, the latter contention was contradicted by Weininger and Sadina; and there is force in defendant's argument that the contract made the regulations a dictionary, particularly since the reference to Government grading was already in plaintiff's initial cable to Stovicek.

Defendant makes a further argument based on the impossibility of its obtaining broilers and fryers at the 33› price offered by plaintiff for the 2½–3 lbs. birds. There is no substantial dispute that, in late April, 1957, the price for 2½–3 lbs. broilers was between 35› and 37› per pound, and that when defendant entered into the contracts, it was well aware of this and intended to fill them by supplying fowl in these weights. It claims that plaintiff must likewise have known the market since plaintiff had reserved shipping space on April 23, three days before plaintiff's cable to Stovicek, or, at least, that Stovicek was chargeable with such knowledge. It is scarcely an answer to say, as plaintiff does in its brief, that the 33› price offered by the 2½–3 lbs. "chickens" was closer to the prevailing 35› price for broilers than to the 30› at which defendant procured fowl. Plaintiff must have expected defendant to make some profit—certainly it could not have expected defendant deliberately to incur a loss.

Finally, defendant relies on conduct by the plaintiff after the first shipment had been received. On May 28 plaintiff sent two cables complaining that the larger birds in the first shipment constituted "fowl." Defendant answered with a cable refusing to recognize plaintiff's objection and announcing "We have today ready for shipment 50,000 lbs. chicken 2½–3 lbs. 25,000 lbs. broilers 1½–2 lbs.," these being the goods procured for shipment under the second contract, and asked immediate answer "whether we are to ship this merchandise to you and whether you will accept the merchandise." After several other cable exchanges, plaintiff replied on May 29 "Confirm again that merchandise is to be shipped since resold by us if not enough pursuant to contract chickens are shipped the missing quantity is to be shipped within ten days stop we resold to our customers pursuant to your contract chickens grade A you have to deliver us said merchandise we again state that we shall make you fully responsible for all resulting costs."[2] Defendant argues that if plaintiff was sincere in thinking it was entitled to young chickens, plaintiff would not have allowed the shipment under the second contract to go forward, since the distinction between broilers and chickens drawn in defendant's cablegram must have made it clear that the larger birds would not be broilers. However, plaintiff answers that the cables show plaintiff was insisting on delivery of young chickens and that defendant shipped old ones at its peril. Defendant's point would be highly relevant on another disputed issue—whether if liability were established, the measure of damages should be the difference in market value of broilers and stewing chicken in New York or the larger difference in Europe, but I cannot give it weight on the issue of interpretation. Defendant points out also that plaintiff proceeded to deliver some of the larger birds in Europe, describing them as "poulets;" defendant argues that it was only when plaintiff's customers

---

[2] These cables were in German; "chicken," "broilers" and, on some occasions, "fowl," were in English.

complained about this that plaintiff developed the idea that "chicken" meant "young chicken." There is little force in this in view of plaintiff's immediate and consistent protests.

When all the evidence is reviewed, it is clear that defendant believed it could comply with the contracts by delivering stewing chicken in the 2½– 3 lbs. size. Defendant's subjective intent would not be significant if this did not coincide with an objective meaning of "chicken." Here it did coincide with one of the dictionary meanings, with the definition in the Department of Agriculture Regulations to which the contract made at least oblique reference, with at least some usage in the trade, with the realities of the market, and with what plaintiff's spokesman had said. Plaintiff asserts it to be equally plain that plaintiff's own subjective intent was to obtain broilers and fryers; the only evidence against this is the material as to market prices and this may not have been sufficiently brought home. In any event it is unnecessary to determine that issue. For plaintiff has the burden of showing that "chicken" was used in the narrower rather than in the broader sense, and this it has not sustained.

This opinion constitutes the Court's findings of fact and conclusions of law. Judgment shall be entered dismissing the complaint with costs.

NOTES AND QUESTIONS

1.   *The term "chicken."* Judge Friendly states that "the word 'chicken' standing alone is ambiguous." Do you agree? The term "chicken" does not appear ambiguous in the sense of having a double meaning. For example, while a chicken is part of a broader species including birds, not all birds are chickens. At the same time, as evidenced by the case, there are several species of chickens as a food product. As a result, when the seller assumed and shipped "stewing chicken," and the buyer accepted but argued the term meant "broiler or frying chicken," a problem of vagueness developed. The parties intended two different types of chickens, so whose meaning controls? Restatement (Second) of Contracts § 201(2) appears to treat vagueness and ambiguity the same, resolving the matter against the party most at fault for the misunderstanding upon proper proof and upon the lack of proof against the plaintiff, who carries the burden of proof to win its case.

2.   *Mere matter of failed proof.* In the actual case, the buyer accepted the chickens and sued alleging breach of contract. Given the state of the record, how would the case have been determined if the buyer rejected the chickens and the seller sued alleging breach of contract? Do you think the seller would have been better able to prove its meaning than the buyer? If not, what does this tell about cases of misunderstanding in equipoise (where both parties offer a rational meaning of a vague term, but neither was at fault in not knowing the other party's understanding)?

3.   *Preliminary determination of vagueness or ambiguity.* If New York is a plain meaning rule jurisdiction, the court must first find the term ambiguous

before it can admit evidence to interpret. Even in California, the court must first find the term is "reasonably susceptible" to two meanings before it can admit evidence to interpret. Why do you think the plain meaning rule and its threshold "ambiguity" determination from the four corners of the document itself remains the dominant rule in the United States? Do you think the California rule substantially expands the plain meaning rule?

4. *Types of evidence considered to resolve the interpretation question.* Once a term is determined either ambiguous or reasonably susceptible to two separate meanings, the interpretation process begins in earnest. Even the early objectivist argued a word almost never had but one meaning. Oliver Wendell Holmes, "The Theory of Legal Interpretation," 12 Harv. L. Rev. 417 (1899) ("A word generally has several meanings, even in a dictionary."). Restatement (Second) of Contracts clearly rejects the approach of a required ambiguity, at least with respect to usage of trade. Other types of evidence are more suspect.

Restatement (Second) of Contracts § 202 provides several rules or "guides" to determine (i) what meanings are reasonably possible and (ii) how to choose among those meanings. First, the meaning of words and terms is highly contextual, and therefore the court should seek to understand the entire situation as it appeared to the parties at the time the contract was made. Restatement (Second) of Contracts § 202(2), *cmt. d.* Second, when possible, a word or term is interpreted in accordance with its generally prevailing meaning. Restatement (Second) of Contracts § 202(3)(a), *cmt. e.* Third, technical terms are construed in accordance with their common technical meaning. Restatement (Second) of Contracts § 202(3)(b), *cmt. f.* Fourth, course of performance without objection is accorded great significance. Restatement (Second) of Contracts § 202(4), *cmt. g.* Finally, words are interpreted consistently with their context as opposed to an interpretation that contradicts the context. Restatement (Second) of Contracts § 202(5), *cmt. h.* For a discussion of these and other rules of interpretation, see Edwin W. Patterson, "The Interpretation and Construction of Contracts," 64 Colum. L. Rev. 833 (1964).

5. *Interpretation versus construction.* Although not universally accepted, the process of interpretation and construction can be distinguished. The process of interpretation searches for a reasonable meaning attached by each party. Construction, on the other hand, attaches legal consequences to the interpretative process. See Edwin W. Patterson, "The Interpretation and Construction of Contracts," 64 Colum. L. Rev. 833, 835 (1964).

6. *Law as literature.* In the 1970s, scholars began an interdisciplinary movement that came to be known as Law and Literature.

> The Law and Literature movement embraces two distinct forms of scholarship. What is often called Law *in* Literature scholarship is a species of conventional literary criticism and history that treats works of imaginative literature that contain legal themes or depict legal practice. . . . Dickens's *Bleak House*, in its searing portrayal of

the British legal system, might be described as a "literary criticism of law." . . . [T]he second category of Law and Literature [is] often called Law *as* Literature. This scholarship employs the techniques and principles of literary criticism, theory, and interpretation to better understand the writing, thought, and social practice that constitute legal systems and offers these techniques and principles as tools for reforming those legal systems. Guyora Binder & Robert Weisberg, Literary Criticisms of Law 3 (2000).

In many ways, Law and Literature techniques operate on a meta-level of legal interpretation and analysis. As you may have already discovered in your legal studies, judicial opinions depend not only upon the applicable law, but also— if not more so—upon the literary narrative or story that underlies that opinion. Similarly, as both *Pacific Gas* and *Frigaliment* indicate, a contract is not merely a set of dry words upon a page—it is part of the narrative of the parties' relationship that started with their initial meeting and ended, perhaps tragically, perhaps comedically, with the judicial opinion rendering judgment upon them.

————————

C. SUPPLEMENTING THE AGREEMENT WITH IMPLIED TERMS

The process of interpretation involves the search for the meaning of the words and terms chosen by the parties in making their contract. Restatement (Second) of Contracts § 200. Stated another way, the process of interpretation involves determining the correlative rights and obligations of the parties under the contract with the chosen words and terms. The process of construction is different and begins only after interpretation comes to an end. Construction is the process whereby a court extends legal effect to a contract for a situation in which the parties have not provided a relevant term to interpret. Restatement (Second) of Contracts § 204. See John Dickinson, "The Problem of the Unprovided Case," 81 U. Penn. L. Rev. 115 (1932); E. Allan Farnsworth, "Disputes over Omission in Contracts," 68 Colum. L. Rev. 860 (1968).

And while interpretation searches for the meaning attached by the parties to terms provided in their agreement, construction supplies terms where the parties omitted them. In such cases, the search for the intent of the parties is meaningless because the agreement is silent on the matter. Because of this aspect, the search does not seek to supply a term the parties would have provided had they considered the matter. The so-called "hypothetical bargaining" process only provides insights as to what is otherwise "reasonable" under the circumstances. Rather, a court must apply a term that "comports with community standards of fairness and policy rather than analyze a hypothetical model of the bargaining process." Restatement (Second) of Contracts § 204, *cmt. d.*

In very real terms, this view of the construction process represents a movement from a "rules based" approach in the Restatement (First) to a "standards based" approach in the Restatement (Second). See E. Allan Farnsworth, "Ingredients in the Redaction of the Restatement (Second) of Contracts," 81 Colum. L. Rev. 1 (1981) and Richard F. Speidel, "Restatement Second: Omitted Terms and Contract Method," 67 Cornell L. Rev. 785, 786 (1982). Notably, influencing the movement was the adoption of the Uniform Commercial Code whose reporter, Karl Llewellyn, was a noted Legal Realist. Not surprisingly, the Restatement (Second) of Contracts opts into the Realist approach under the influence of Arthur Corbin who was an advisor to both restatements. Samuel Williston was the reporter for the Restatement (First) of Contracts and a proponent of the rules-based approach advocated earlier by Langdell and Holmes. Robert Braucher, "Offer and Acceptance in the Second Restatement," 74 Yale L. J. 302, 303 (1964) (Professor Williston, the reporter, "provided a bridge between the contrasting dogmatisms of O. W. Holmes and C. C. Langdell, on the one hand, and the focus of mid-twentieth-century thought on purpose and function, on the other."). But according to Roscoe Pound, this view of the law in transition was simply a form of "mechanical jurisprudence" inflexible by nature to account for the change in society. Roscoe Pound, "Mechanical Jurisprudence," 8 Colum. L. Rev. 605 (1908). Nonetheless, Pound saw the Legal Realist movement less as a school of thought and more as a perspective on how the law should react to a changing society. Roscoe Pound, "Fifty Years of Jurisprudence," 51 Harv. L. Rev. 777, 790–798 (1938). See also, G. Edward White, "From Sociological Jurisprudence to Realism: Jurisprudence and Social Change in Early Twentieth-Century America," 58 Va. L. Rev. 999 (1972).

As a consequence of this debate, there is a rather remarkable transition from the Restatement (First) of Contracts where the failure to provide for an essential term, such as an "agreement to agree," usually resulted in no contract at all. In contrast, the Restatement (Second) of Contracts § 204, with no corollary in the Restatement (First) of Contracts, might well supply a term, much like the Uniform Commercial Code. See E. Allan Farnsworth, Disputes over Omission in Contracts," 68 Colum. L. Rev. 860 (1968); Robert Braucher, "Interpretation and Legal Effect in the Second Restatement of Contracts," 81 Colum. L. Rev. 13, 14–15 (1981) (Braucher was the first reporter for the Restatement (Second) but resigned to accept an appointment on the Massachusetts Supreme Judicial Court and therefore attributes the innovation of Section 204 to Farnsworth, the reporter who concluded the restatement work).

Restatement (Second) of Contracts § 204 requires first that the parties to a bargain, sufficiently defined as a contract, must "fail to provide" some essential term. That being the case, the court is to supply a term that is "reasonable under the circumstances." The first question is objectively determined. The second question is slightly more elusive. What exactly is a term that is "reasonable under the circumstances"?

The Restatement (Second) of Contracts § 204 commentary provides some useful insights and guidelines. As noted in the comments, § 204 does not direct the court to determine the presumed intent of the parties had they actually considered the matter, although such evidence provided by an examination of the other terms of the contract may well provide insights to what might be "reasonable" under the circumstances. Restatement (Second) of Contracts § 204, *cmt. d.* The court must supply a term that "comports with community standards of fairness and policy" rather than a hypothetical model of the bargaining process. Restatement (Second) of Contracts § 204, *cmt. d.* While heralded as a movement in the right direction, the lack of standards is troubling. See Richard F. Speidel, "Restatement Second: Omitted Terms and Contract Method,"67 Cornell L. Rev. 785, 803–805 (1982).

In the case to follow, try to determine what community standards of fairness apply and how that determination relates to a similar endeavor under UCC § 2–204(3). As you do so, try to determine the relationship between such a determination and standards of good faith articulated in Restatement (Second) of Contracts § 205. See Harold Dubroff, "The Implied Covenant of Good Faith in Contract Interpretation and Gap-Filling: Reviling a Revered Relic," 80 St. John's L. Rev. 559 (2006).

1.   COMMON LAW IMPLICATIONS

WOOD V. LUCY, LADY DUFF-GORDON

Court of Appeals of New York
222 N.Y. 88, 118 N.E. 214 (1917)

CARDOZO, J.

The defendant styles herself "a creator of fashions." Her favor helps a sale. Manufacturers of dresses, millinery, and like articles are glad to pay for a certificate of her approval. The things which she designs, fabrics, parasols, and what not, have a new value in the public mind when issued in her name. She employed the plaintiff to help her to turn this vogue into money. He was to have the exclusive right, subject always to her approval, to place her indorsements on the designs of others. He was also to have the exclusive right to place her own designs on sale, or to license others to market them. In return she was to have one-half of 'all profits and revenues' derived from any contracts he might make. The exclusive right was to last at least one year from April 1, 1915, and thereafter from year to year unless terminated by notice of 90 days. The plaintiff says that he kept the contract on his part, and that the defendant broke it. She placed her indorsement on fabrics, dresses, and millinery without his knowledge, and withheld the profits. He sues her for the damages, and the case comes here on demurrer.

The agreement of employment is signed by both parties. It has a wealth of recitals. The defendant insists, however, that it lacks the elements of a contract. She says that the plaintiff does not bind himself to anything. It is true that he does not promise in so many words that he will use reasonable efforts to place the defendant's indorsements and market her designs. We think, however, that such a promise is fairly to be implied. The law has outgrown its primitive stage of formalism when the precise word was the sovereign talisman, and every slip was fatal. It takes a broader view today. A promise may be lacking, and yet the whole writing may be "instinct with an obligation," imperfectly expressed. . . . If that is so, there is a contract.

The implication of a promise here finds support in many circumstances. The defendant gave an exclusive privilege. She was to have no right for at least a year to place her own indorsements or market her own designs except through the agency of the plaintiff. The acceptance of the exclusive agency was an assumption of its duties. Phoenix Hermetic Co. v. Filtrine Mfg. Co., 164 App. Div. 424, 150 N. Y. Supp. 193; . . . . We are not to suppose that one party was to be placed at the mercy of the other. Hearn v. Stevens & Bro., 111 App. Div. 101, 106, 97 N. Y. Supp. 566; . . . . Many other terms of the agreement point the same way. We are told at the outset by way of recital that:

> The said Otis F. Wood possesses a business organization adapted to the placing of such indorsements as the said Lucy, Lady Duff-Gordon, has approved.

The implication is that the plaintiff's business organization will be used for the purpose for which it is adapted. But the terms of the defendant's compensation are even more significant. Her sole compensation for the grant of an exclusive agency is to be one-half of all the profits resulting from the plaintiff's efforts. Unless he gave his efforts, she could never get anything. Without an implied promise, the transaction cannot have such business "efficacy, as both parties must have intended that at all events it should have." Bowen, L. J., in the Moorcock, 14 P. D. 64, 68. But the contract does not stop there. The plaintiff goes on to promise that he will account monthly for all moneys received by him, and that he will take out all such patents and copyrights and trade-marks as may in his judgment be necessary to protect the rights and articles affected by the agreement. It is true, of course, as the Appellate Division has said, that if he was under no duty to try to market designs or to place certificates of indorsement, his promise to account for profits or take out copyrights would be valueless. But in determining the intention of the parties the promise has a value. It helps to enforce the conclusion that the plaintiff had some duties. His promise to pay the defendant one-half of the profits and revenues resulting from the exclusive agency and to render accounts monthly was a promise to use reasonable efforts to bring profits and revenues into existence. For this conclusion the authorities are ample. Wilson v. Mechanical Orguinette Co., 170 N. Y. 542, 63 N. E. 550; Phoenix Hermetic Co. v. Filtrine Mfg. Co., supra. . . .

The judgment of the Appellate Division should be reversed, and the order of the Special Term affirmed, with costs in the Appellate Division and in this court.

CUDDEBACK, McLAUGHLIN, and ANDREWS, JJ., concur. HISCOCK, C. J., and CHASE and CRANE, JJ., dissent.

Order reversed, etc.

NOTES AND QUESTIONS

1. *The role of interpretation.* In order to justify supplying a term to *fill-the-gap* to resolve an omitted case, the court must first utilize rules of interpretation to determine that the contract does not consider the question and that the parties did not express intent against supplication. In order to resolve the interpretative question, courts engage in a process similar to that used to resolve vagueness and ambiguity problems.

2. *Implied-in-fact and implied-in-law compared.* Once the court decides to "create" or "imply" a term to fill the gap created by the parties who failed to provide for an omitted case, that term is "implied-in-law." In contrast, "implied-in-fact" terms are derived from the contractual language used and conduct by the parties, and are the same as express terms. In contrast, implied-in-law terms usually do not depend upon the intent of the parties, which is indeterminable in the particulars. Specifically, courts turn to implied-in-law terms in two situations. First, as illustrated by *Wood*, courts may adopt implied-in-law terms to fill gaps in the parties' contracts. Second, the common law and the UCC both impose mandatory default terms, even where the parties attempt to contract explicitly on a particular issue. Therefore, fairness and public policy most often provide the justification for implied-in-law terms. See Restatement (Second) of Contracts § 204, *cmt. d.* Did Justice Cardozo imply an obligation to use "reasonable efforts" from the other terms of the agreement or law in general? What do you think he meant when he stated: "We think, however, that such a promise is fairly to be implied. The law has outgrown its primitive stage of formalism when the precise word was the sovereign talisman, and every slip was fatal"? For an excellent historical discussion of the *Wood* case, see Walter F. Pratt, Jr., "American Contract Law at the Turn of the Century," 39 S. C. L. Rev. 415 (1988).

3. *Default and immutable terms.* If the parties had considered a potential gap in their respective rights and duties, but elected not to address

the issue in their contract, there would be no need for a court to supply an implied-in-law term. In such cases, it may be quite inefficient for the parties to specify all terms, especially those not likely to occur. David Charny, "Hypothetical Bargains: The Normative Structure of Contract Interpretation," 89 Mich. L. Rev. 1815 (1991). Equally important, the court will not supply a term for an omitted case if the parties expressed an intent to the contrary. For this reason, implication is a *default rule* rather than an *immutable* or *mandatory rule*. See Randy E. Barnett, "The Sound of Silence: Default Rules and Contractual Consent," 78 Va. L. Rev. 821 (1992). For an economic theory analyzing immutable gap-filler terms, see Ian Ayres & Robert Gertner, "Filling Gaps in Incomplete Contracts: An Economic Theory of Default Rules,"99 Yale L. J. 87 (1989) (arguing most rules are default rules and immutable rules are most often justified to protect (i) parties outside the contract and (ii) even more rarely, parties to the contract). See also Arthur Lenhoff, "Optional Terms (*Jus Dispositivum*) and Required Terms (*Jus Cogens*) in the Law of Contracts," 45 Mich. L. Rev. 39 (1946).

Immutable rules—rules that are determined by the state and implied by law into every contract regardless of party intent—paternalistically replace freedom of contract rules. Immutable rules normally are justifiable only when, as a result of systemic bargaining power disparities, market failures, or other potential inefficiencies in the bargaining process, the parties cannot protect themselves. For example, UCC § 2–309(3) states an immutable rule that an agreement dispensing with notification is invalid if its operation would be unconscionable. See, e.g., Leibel v. Raynor Manufacturing Co., 571 S.W. 2d 640 (Ky.App. 1978) (distributorship agreements of indefinite duration and involving the sale of goods may be terminated at-will and without cause, but not without "adequate" advance notice of the termination). In a dispute over a "without notice" clause in a sale of goods contract, a court would consider the unconscionability of that clause and its effects, despite that the parties had apparently expressly agreed that notice was not necessary. In contrast, UCC § 2–314 provides a default rule that attaches an implied warranty of merchantability to every contract, *unless* the parties agree to opt out of that implied warranty. For an example of such an opt-out provision, examine the warranty terms on your last any significant consumer goods purchase. You will likely find "[seller] makes no other warranty, either express or implied, EITHER OF FITNESS FOR A PARTICULAR PURPOSE OR OF MERCHANTABILITY, except as stated above" or similar words to that effect. In interpreting such a contract, a court would not consider UCC § 2–314, implied warranty of merchantability, because the parties had expressly agreed that default term would not be part of their contract.

Many, if not most, implied-in-law terms are merely "default rules" and may be varied by the parties under several theories. First, courts may imply terms based upon a hypothetical bargain the parties would have made had they actually bargained over the issue based upon relational aspects of the parties. See Lisa Bernstein, "Social Norms and Default Rules Analysis," 3 S. Cal. Interdisc. L. J. 59 (1993); Jay M. Feinman, "Relational Contract and

Default Rules," 3 S. Cal. Interdisc. L. J. 43 (1993). Randy Barnett has suggested application of a consent theory that examines the agreement for probable assent to the implied-in-law terms. See Randy E. Barnett, "The Sound of Silence: Default Rules and Contractual Consent," 78 Va. L. Rev. 821 (1992). Finally, some suggest that courts should adopt penalty default rules to penalize strategic gaming by a party. Ian Ayres & Robert Gertner, Filling Gaps in Incomplete Contracts: An Economic Theory of Default Rules, 99 Yale L. J. 87 (1989). Others argue it is all nonsense, and judges simply make rules they think appropriate. See W. David Slawson, "The Futile Search for Principles for Default Rules," 3 S. Cal. Interdisc. L. J. 29 (1993).

4.   *UCC sources of default and immutable gap-filler rules.* A contract for the sale of goods is governed by the Uniform Commercial Code that states a number of "reasonable" default rule gap fillers including where the mentioned term is omitted from the contract: UCC § 2–305 (price), UCC § 2–306 (quantity), UCC § 2–308 (place of delivery), UCC § 2–309 (time of delivery), and UCC § 2–310 (time and place for payment), to name a few. Under UCC § 1–302(a), (c) (2001) (formerly UCC §1–102(3)), rules stated in the UCC are default rules, and the parties may modify those "off-the-rack" terms by agreement unless the UCC provides otherwise.

The Uniform Commercial Code also states immutable rules including good faith. UCC §§ 1–201(20) (2001); 1–304 (2001); 2–103; and 1–302(a) (2001) (good faith may not be eliminated). In exclusive dealing contracts, the UCC implies an obligation to use "best efforts." UCC § 2–306(2). What is the difference between reasonable efforts and best efforts? Is best efforts a higher standard of obligation? See Daniel J. Coplan, "When Is 'Best Efforts' Really 'Best Efforts': An Analysis of the Obligation to Exploit in Entertainment Licensing Agreements," 31 Sw. U. L. Rev. 725 (2002) and E. Allan Farnsworth, "On Trying to Keep One's Promises: The Duty of Best Efforts in Contract Law," 46 U. Pitt. L. Rev. 1 (1984).

5.   *CISG gap-filler provisions.* For a discussion of similar cases governed by the CISG, see Alejandro M. Garro, "The Gap-Filling Role of the UNIDROIT Principles in International Sales Law: Some Comments on the Interplay Between the Principles and the CISG," 69 Tul. L. Rev. 1150 (1994).

After applying interpretation rules, courts do not always supply a term for an omitted case, even if such a term would have been reasonable under the circumstances. As you read the next case, try to determine why the court refused to supply a reasonable term.

CITY OF YONKERS v. OTIS ELEVATOR COMPANY

United States Court of Appeals, Second Circuit
844 F.2d 42 (1988)

MAHONEY, Circuit Judge:

This diversity case, acknowledged by all parties to be governed by New York law, arises out of the City of Yonkers' ("Yonkers") attempt to prevent a major employer within its borders, Otis Elevator Company ("Otis"), from moving out of the city. After Yonkers and the Yonkers Community Development Agency (the "Agency") granted Otis various benefits, Otis stayed in the city for a number of years. However, the Otis facility was rendered uneconomical due to technological changes in the manufacture of elevators, Otis' main product. Otis then left the city, ultimately selling the facility to the Port Authority of New York and New Jersey. Yonkers and the Agency then brought suit in the United States District Court for the Southern District of New York seeking damages from Otis and United Technologies Corporation ("United"), Otis' parent. After discovery, the district court, John E. Sprizzo, Judge, granted defendants' motion for summary judgment, and imposed a sanction of five thousand dollars upon plaintiffs and their counsel, Vito J. Cassan, for filing an unjustified fraud claim.

We affirm.

Background

Otis was founded in Yonkers in 1853, and continued in business there until 1976. In 1968, Otis' Yonkers plant required modernization and expansion to remain commercially viable. However, expansion appeared impossible due to limited land space, and Otis therefore considered alternatives, some of which involved closing the Yonkers plant.

The president of Otis, Ralph Weller, authorized Otis representatives to meet with Yonkers officials to try to solve Otis' space problems. A plan drafted by the Charles T. Main Company was rejected by Otis, but negotiations continued. Otis then formulated its own plan internally, tailored to meet Otis' land and space requirements in Yonkers. This plan recommended the use of urban renewal (with its accompanying provision for condemnation) to allow Otis to expand to the east of the plant. Accordingly, Otis notified Yonkers that if an adjoining parcel of land could be made available, Otis would be willing to expand and modernize its plant. After further negotiation, Otis, Yonkers and the Yonkers Urban Renewal Agency entered into a letter of intent dated June 5, 1972 which provided in relevant part:

(1) The purpose of this letter and of the commitments set forth herein is the realization of the following goals:

(a) the retention by Otis of its existing usable manufacturing facilities in Yonkers;

(b) the improvement and expansion of those facilities with the cooperation and assistance of federal, state and local agencies;

(c) the improvement in the aesthetic appearance of the older section of Yonkers in which these facilities are located; and

(d) the continuation of existing opportunities for employment and training of the unemployed and the underemployed, such as are now provided by Otis.

The Yonkers City Council adopted an urban renewal plan on September 26, 1972 which included the land in question and set forth a number of goals and conditions, including obligations of Otis. At this point, Yonkers and the Agency began purchasing and clearing the property adjacent to the Otis factory, using funding received from the federal and state government as well as Yonkers' own resources. Otis also invested substantial funds renovating its Yonkers physical plant.

On September 13, 1974, the Agency and Otis entered into a land disposition agreement, and the Agency executed an indenture conveying the property adjacent to the Otis factory, which Yonkers had acquired, to Otis. Because most of the obligations between the parties relating to the details of the land transfer and renovation had been completed, on December 29, 1976, the parties entered into a termination agreement, which released the parties from further liability with respect to these obligations. Moreover, the actual redevelopment and construction were substantially completed; on November 3, 1976, the Agency accordingly issued a certificate of completion.

By 1982, however, the technology of elevator manufacture had undergone substantial change. The Yonkers plant was used to manufacture three mechanical components. In the early 1980's, two of those three were replaced by electronic components. Accordingly, operation of the Yonkers plant became economically unfeasible, and Otis closed it down in 1982.

Yonkers then commenced this action in the United States District Court for the Southern District of New York. None of the agreements or other documents pertaining to this situation includes any specific commitment by Otis to continue production at its Yonkers facility, and obviously there was therefore no specific commitment to do so for any designated period of time. Yonkers contends, however, that under various theories,[2] Otis was obliged to continue in operation in Yonkers "for a reasonable time to be set by law, . . . alleged to be at least sixty years." Otis denies any such obligation, and further contends that the New York statute of frauds, N. Y. Gen. Oblig. Law § 5–701 subd. (a)(1) (McKinney 1978), precludes any relief for Yonkers because the asserted contract between the parties was not to be performed within one year from its making, and the

---

[2] Yonkers' complaint stated claims of implied contract, quasi contract, breach of contract, "bad faith acceptance" by Otis, "fraudulent retention" by Otis and United, and estoppel.

crucial asserted term as to duration was not memorialized in a writing subscribed by Otis.

After discovery, the district court issued an opinion, 649 F. Supp. 716 (S. D. N. Y. 1986), which determined that the New York statute of frauds applied to the contract alleged in Yonkers' complaint, there was no writing sufficient to satisfy the statute of frauds, and even assuming arguendo that the statute of frauds did not bar plaintiffs' claim, defendants had demonstrated that no rational finder of fact could find for plaintiffs on the facts of this case on either a theory of contract (express or implied), equitable estoppel or unjust enrichment. See id. at 726. Defendants' motion for summary judgment was accordingly granted.[3]

The district court also imposed a Rule 11 sanction of five thousand dollars upon plaintiffs and their attorney, Vito J. Cassan, for filing fraud claims that "lacked any colorable factual basis," id. at 735, reaffirming an earlier opinion, 106 F.R.D. 524 (S. D. N. Y. 1985), which imposed the sanction upon finding "that the plaintiffs' allegations of fraud had no basis in fact, . . . that . . . plaintiffs were afforded an ample opportunity to withdraw those allegations and unjustifiably refused to do so," and that "[i]t was only after defendants' motion [for summary judgment] was brought that plaintiffs finally consented to withdraw the fraud claim." Id. at 525. The amount of the sanction was apparently premised upon the cost to defendants of moving to dismiss plaintiffs' fraud claims.

This appeal followed.

Discussion

A. *Summary Judgment*

Our role in reviewing the district court's grant of summary judgment is to determine whether a material issue of fact exists and whether the law was applied correctly below. 10 C. Wright, A. Miller & M. Kane, Federal Practice and Procedure § 2716, at 654 (2d ed. 1983). . . .

Plaintiffs contend that Otis was obligated to remain in the city for "a reasonable time," that in 1982 a reasonable time had not yet passed, and therefore that Otis' withdrawal in that year constituted a breach of contract. Yonkers argues in the alternative that if no contractual liability is found to exist, relief should be provided on the basis of quasi-contract or equitable estoppel.

Plaintiffs concede that no express promise to remain for a reasonable time was made by Otis.[4] They argue instead for a promise implied either in fact or in law.

---

[3] An earlier motion for summary judgment was also granted, but with leave to replead. See 607 F. Supp. 1416 (S. D. N. Y. 1985).

[4] We do not rely upon the New York statute of frauds as a ground for our affirmance. Defendants never pleaded the statute of frauds, even by amendment, despite the requirement of

Implied terms have been divided into three categories: (1) terms that the parties intended, (2) terms that the parties would have intended had they thought about it and (3) terms that are fair. The first involves a search for the parties' intention, the second involves a search for the parties' hypothetical intention, the third has nothing to do with the parties' intention, except that the court will generally not imply a term in the face of the parties' expressed intent to the contrary. . . . "Implied in law" or "constructive" terms . . . include the second and third categories.

Helen Hadjiyannakis, The Parol Evidence Rule and Implied Terms: The Sounds of Silence, 54 Fordham L. Rev. 35, 38 n. 22 (1985) (citations omitted); see . . . Wood v. Lucy, Lady Duff-Gordon, 222 N.Y. 88, 91, 118 N.E. 214, 214 (1917); Restatement (Second) of Contracts § 204 comment d (1981).

We next apply these criteria to the question presented for our decision. The record shows that the parties bargained to retain Otis' presence, but that the only limit on its subsequent right to leave was economic reality. The deposition testimony of several of the witnesses establishes that Otis would not have agreed to a term requiring Otis to operate its Yonkers facility for a period of time or even for a reasonable time. As Eugene Hull, a vice president of Otis, testified at his deposition:

Q: (by the defense) If in the course of negotiations with respect to the letter of intent Yonkers or the Community Development Agency ever requested the inclusion of a provision of a letter of intent which would have provided that Otis could not close or relocate its Yonkers production facilities for more than ten years from the date of the letter of intent, would you have agreed to such a provision?

* * *

A: No, I would have been reluctant to commit ourselves to any specific period, you know. Whatever it might be, without, you know, a lot of serious consideration.

Q: Why is that?

A: Well, simply because, you know, there are and would be alternatives to providing production facilities with our other plants in the country, whether to make or buy the equipment that

---

Fed.R.Civ.P. 8(c) that a responsive pleading "shall set forth" the defense. Even if the district court correctly concluded that the defense was not thereby waived, see 649 F. Supp. at 726 n. 14; but see 5 C. Wright & A. Miller, Federal Practice and Procedure § 1278, at 341 n. 38 (1969 & Supp. 1987), and cases there cited, it is not clear that the New York statute of frauds bars recovery here. See e.g., Morris Cohon & Co. v. Russell, 23 N.Y.2d 569, 575–76, 297 N.Y.S. 2d 947, 953, 245 N.E. 2d 712, 715 (1969) (implied term as to rate of compensation need not be memorialized in writing); Blye v. Colonial Corp. of America, 102 A.D. 2d 297, 298–301, 476 N.Y.S. 2d 874, 875–76 (1st Dep't 1984) (same). Accordingly, since there is an adequate alternative ground for affirmance, we do not reach the issue. See Alfaro Motors, Inc. v. Ward, 814 F.2d 883, 887 (2d Cir. 1987).

we manufactured there [sic] could have been provided by General Dynamics or General Electric, and we're continually making studies whether we should manufacture or buy.

So with the changes in technology going on at the time in the industry, it would be pretty hard to commit yourself.

Ralph Weller, Otis' president, and William Granville, an Otis vice president, testified to the same effect.

In any event, as stated earlier, there is no contention that the parties specifically agreed that Otis would remain in Yonkers, much less remain for a fixed period of time. Both sides believed, however, that the size of Otis' reinvestment in its Yonkers facility would guarantee the long term presence of Otis in Yonkers. Mr. Weller so testified, as did Alphons Yost, executive director of the Agency, and Alfred DelBello, then Mayor of Yonkers. Yost nonetheless testified that this was a "hope," and "that the length of time that Otis would operate in Yonkers could have been unilaterally determined by Otis."

The letter of intent, quoted above, similarly supports this view. That letter contains a clear distinction between "goals" and "commitments." Otis' continuing presence was only a goal, not a commitment. Yonkers argues that this is mere semanticism, and if only one or the other term had appeared, that argument might have some merit. Both were employed, however, and there is a clear difference between them.

This distinction and its implications were noted by Brett Auerbahn, the project director of the Agency, who noted in a memorandum analyzing the letter of intent:

Has Otis gone any further than stating that it is their goal to remain in Yonkers? There appear to be a great number of sanctions against the City should it fail to meet up to its part of the obligation but no similar sanctions against the Otis Elevator Company.

We further note that although Otis drafted the letter of intent, Seymour Scher, then city manager of Yonkers, wrote a letter to Granville in anticipation of the letter of intent which also referred to the retention of Otis as a goal of the project. Moreover, the legal counsel of the Yonkers Department of Development wrote Yost a memorandum analyzing the letter of intent with respect to Otis' obligation to provide employment, which stated that "[f]ailure to meet these goals does not give a legal right to the other parties."

Whether one views the resulting situation as negating any limit on Otis' mobility or as creating an implied promise to stay only as long as the plant remained economically feasible, the result is the same. Yonkers does not dispute Otis' professed reason for closing the plant: technological changes in the product and a corresponding change in the manufacturing capability needed to produce that product. In its Rule 3(g) statement of material facts as to which it contended there was no genuine issue to be tried, Otis asserted that two of the three components manufactured at its Yonkers facility were replaced by electronic components and rendered obsolete, Otis was able to satisfy its requirements for the third component from its other plants, and Yonkers production was accordingly terminated because there was no business justification for its continuance. In its responding Rule 3(g) statement, Yonkers stated that Otis' Yonkers facility operated at a profit until it was closed, and that Yonkers "never assumed the risk of Otis's making a poor business judgment with reference to its need or use of its expanded and modernized Yonkers facility," effectively conceding the factual premise for closure of the Yonkers plant asserted by Otis.

We conclude that this is not an appropriate case for the imposition of the implied promise for which plaintiffs contend, and that no genuine issue of material fact concerning that question is presented by this record. We refer again to the implied promise which Yonkers must establish to prevail in this litigation: that Otis promised to continue operation of its Yonkers facility for a period which exceeded the duration of its actual continuance; i.e., for a period which extended beyond the time when Otis made an unchallenged determination that there was no business justification, in the light of subsequent technological developments, for continued use of the Yonkers facility.

No rational trier of fact could conclude that this was the intention of the parties, which they inadvertently failed to express; or that the parties never considered the duration of Otis' commitment to Yonkers, but would have agreed upon the promise for which Yonkers contends had they done so. Cf. Barco Urban Renewal Corp. v. Housing Authority, 674 F.2d 1001, 1007 (3d Cir. 1982) (right of first refusal deemed to continue for a commercially reasonable time where no time explicitly set by contract). Nor can we conclude that this promise must be implied as a matter of fairness, akin to the implication of a covenant of fair dealing. See e.g., Roli-Blue, Inc. v. 69/70th St. Assoc., 119 A.D. 2d 173, 176–78, 506 N.Y.S. 2d 159, 161–62 (1st Dep't 1986.) The implied promise for which Yonkers contends is not only outside the contemplation of the parties, but indeed extraordinary.[7] The fair reading of this situation, it seems to us, is that Yonkers was relying upon, and Otis was deterred from departing by, the very considerable investment Otis made in renovating its Yonkers plant. When compelling business developments overcame that incentive to stay, Yonkers was left with a modernized manufacturing facility which was sold by Otis to another entity and continues to produce at least some jobs and income for

---

[7] Yonkers highlights the implausibility of its position by asserting in its complaint that Otis was obliged to remain in Yonkers "for a reasonable time to be set by law, . . . alleged to be at least sixty years."

Yonkers. However understandable Yonkers' disappointment at Otis' departure may be, it would be an imposition by the court to add an obligation to the contract between the parties which appears manifestly unreasonable on the record before us, rather than an obvious requirement of justice and fair dealing.

Our disposition of the contract claim also disposes of the quasi-contractual cause of action, because such relief is unavailable where an express contract covers the subject matter. Stissi v. Interstate & Ocean Transport Co., 814 F.2d 848, 851 (2d Cir. 1987); . . . Restatement of Restitution § 107(1) (1937). Because we believe that Otis performed its obligations under the contract, see Restatement of Restitution § 107(1) (1937), no quasi-contractual relief is appropriate.

Yonkers' final argument on the merits is that relief based upon equitable estoppel should be provided. It asserts that such relief is available where there is a misrepresentation of fact, reasonable reliance upon that misrepresentation, and injury caused by the reliance. See . . . J. Calamari & J. Perillo, Contracts § 11–29(b) (3d ed. 1987). Otis argues that Rothschild and the theory of equitable estoppel have been overruled *sub silentio* by Huggins v. Castle Estates, Inc., 36 N.Y. 2d 427, 369 N.Y.S. 2d 80, 330 N.E.2d 48 (1975), and that Yonkers must proceed under a theory of promissory estoppel. That theory requires "a clear and unambiguous promise; a reasonable and foreseeable reliance by the party to whom the promise is made; and an injury sustained by the party asserting the estoppel by reason of his reliance." Ripple's of Clearview, Inc. v. Le Havre Associates, 88 A.D. 2d 120, 121–23, 452 N.Y.S. 2d 447, 449 (2d Dep't 1982) (citation omitted); see R.G. Group, Inc. v. Horn & Hardart Co., 751 F.2d 69, 78 (2d Cir. 1984) (quoting Ripple's of Clearview as stating the New York rule).

We need not decide that question, however, because here there was neither a misrepresentation nor a clear promise, so neither theory is satisfied. Moreover, Yonkers officials were aware of the weakness of their position at the time they contracted, rendering reliance unreasonable. Insofar as Yonkers seeks to imply a restriction on the use of property through equitable estoppel, furthermore, the New York Court of Appeals has admonished courts to apply that doctrine to realty with great caution. Huggins v. Castle Estates, Inc., 36 N.Y. 2d 427, 433, 369 N.Y.S. 2d 80, 87, 330 N.E.2d 48, 53 (1975).

* * * *

Conclusion

The judgment of the district court is affirmed.

NOTES AND QUESTIONS

1.   *How does the case differ from Wood v. Lucy, Lady Duff-Gordon?* What does the court determine through interpretation that avoids a *Wood*-like outcome? Is the result based on the intent of the parties or public policy?

2.   *Statements of contractual purpose.* Note the explicit emphasis of the June 5, 1975 letter of intent on the purpose of the parties to the contract. From a drafting perspective, what function do such statements of purpose serve? Based in part upon your reading of *Otis Elevator Co.*, how can such contractual statements of purpose affect a court's interpretation of an ambiguity or a gap in the parties' contract?

3.   *Alternatives to contract recovery.* Judicially crafted gap fillers and implied-in-law terms make sense only in connection with a contractual skeleton or framework in which to fit the additional terms. Note that the court refuses to even consider implying a promise in the promissory estoppel context; rather, promissory estoppel requires a clear and unambiguous promise by the promisor. Why should a court be more reluctant to imply a promise in the promissory estoppel context than in the case of an express contract?

4.   *"Integration" of promissory estoppel and quasi-contractual relief.* After determining that it would not fill the "gap" in the contract alleged by Yonkers, the court further stated, "Our disposition of the contract claim also disposes of the quasi-contractual cause of action, because such relief is unavailable where an express contract covers the subject matter." Why should the fact that the parties have defined their relationship through an express contract prohibit the City of Yonkers from pursuing non-contractual relief through a restitution theory? Would that same reasoning also apply to a promissory estoppel claim similarly made in the face of an express contract?

5.   *Equitable estoppel and misrepresentation.* The court is arguably incorrect in its description of the elements of equitable estoppel when it asserts that equitable estoppel requires a misrepresentation. As discussed in Chapter 2, equitable estoppel may be asserted upon any representation of present-existing fact upon which the maker has reason to know the recipient will rely and upon which the recipient reasonably does rely. An equitably estopped party is said to be estopped from asserting a legal position that is inconsistent with its prior statement of fact, regardless of whether the inconsistency arises because of misrepresentation, changed circumstances, newly discovered facts, or any other reason.

2.   CAVEAT EMPTOR & WARRANTIES

Legal history often develops concise expressions or maxims covering supposed traditional legal principles. One such case involves the maxim *caveat emptor*, meaning literally "let the buyer beware." In essence, *caveat emptor* meant that the *buyer* implicitly agreed to bear all risks of poor quality, bad workmanship, or other defects in the property being sold. *Caveat emptor* shifted these risks from the seller—who would bear those risks before the sale in the form of her investment in the property (and thus would lose that investment if the property was of such poor quality that it could not be sold)—to the buyer at the moment of sale. Only if the seller committed fraud in making the sale could the buyer recover for patent or latent defects. In part, the maxim may be attributable to the notion that the buyer has full right of inspection before purchase. Theoretically, such a loss shifting principle should be limited to reasonably discoverable patent defects. However, the doctrine also applied to latent defects. What commercial policy supports such a doctrine? Early research suggested that the common law development of *caveat emptor* was based upon repetition of erroneous interpretation in early cases. See "Caveat Emptor—The Rule of the Common Law—Not of the Civil Law," 12 Am. Jurist & L. Mag. 94, 95–98 (1834). Moreover, the English common law version was contrary to the Roman civil law doctrine.

It should not be surprising that ecclesiastical law and Roman civil law took a dim view of a market sale of a product not as described or promised. See Harold J. Berman, "The Religious Sources of General Contract Law: An Historical Perspective," 4 J. L. & Relig. 103, 106 (1986) (Canon law was foundational to development of contract and was based on idea that breach of promise is a sin and therefore actionable as opposed to actionable as a breach of the bargain and a moral wrong done to the other party). St. Thomas Aquinas views are illustrative.

As described by Walter Hamilton, Aquinas addresses three fundamental issues arising from a sale and purchase of defective goods. See Walton H. Hamilton, "The Ancient Maxim Caveat Emptor," 40 Yale L.J. 1133, 1138 (1931). First, Aquinas deals with the general question, "[i]s a sale rendered unlawful by a defect in the thing sold?" Id. (quoting Summa Theologica, Ethinus II). If the seller knows of a defect in the goods but does not reveal the defect to the buyer, the seller's action is sinful, and the sale is void. *See id.* If the seller does not know of the defect, then the sale was not sinful, and the seller need merely account to the buyer for the loss. See id. Second, Aquinas asks whether a seller must disclose of laws in the goods and concludes the seller must disclose secret flaws, but has no duty to reveal "manifest" flaws (although to do so anyway would be virtuous). Id. Although the origin of the *caveat emptor* maxim relates to the early sixteenth century, the seventeenth century case of *Chandler v. Lopus,* 79 Eng. Rep. 3 (1603), is generally credited with entrenching the notion in English common law. See Walton H. Hamilton, "The Ancient Maxim Caveat Emptor," 40 Yale L. J. 1133, 1166 (1931); A. W. Brian Simpson, A History of the Common Law of Contract 536 (Oxford University Press 1975). In *Chandler*, the buyer of a stone sued the jeweler who "affirmed" the stone was a "bezoar stone" (sought for its apparent medicinal qualities), although the stone was not. The seller prevailed on the theory that no "warranty" had been given. Still later, a disappointed buyer could maintain a tort action in deceit if the buyer could prove *scienter*—a knowing intent to deceive. An action on assumpsit also developed merely on the basis of the express warranty, *scienter* being irrelevant. See A. W. Brian Simpson, A History of the Common Law of Contract 537 (1975). The original action was for deceit and required the purchaser to prove that the seller made an express warranty known to be false at the time of the sale. Still later, a tort action in deceit could be obtained if the buyer could prove *scienter*, but an action on assumpsit also developed merely on the basis of the express warranty with *scienter* being irrelevant. Walton H. Hamilton, "The Ancient Maxim Caveat Emptor," 40 Yale L. J. 1133, 1169 (1931). Absent an express warranty, innocently or intentionally made regarding some aspect of the thing sold, the buyer thus owned the risk of latent defects. Patent defects were discoverable absent disguise, and any such disguise was a form of fraud. Because of the more easily satisfied burden of proof in the assumpsit action, the law of warranty moved from tort to contract early in the twentieth century. See James J. White, "Freeing the Tortious Soul of Express Warranty Law," 72 Tul. L. Rev. 2089 (1998).

With suspicious English common law roots, and civil and canon law disdain, the maxim *caveat emptor* nevertheless developed higher status in American jurisprudence. An early notable case—*Seixas and Seixas v. Woods*, 2 Caine R. 48 (N.Y. 1804)—involved an innocent sale of nearly worthless peachum wood advertised as a more valuable braziletto wood. Both the buyer and seller had inspected the wood without discovery of the error, as the two woods were difficult to distinguish. Absent an express warranty that the wood was braziletto, the buyer's case was dismissed under the *caveat emptor* doctrine. Walton H. Hamilton, "The Ancient Maxim Caveat Emptor," 40 Yale L. J. 1133, 1179 (1931). Despite later American jurisprudential disdain for the maxim, it was declared to be of such "universal acceptance" as to impose upon the buyer the risk of purchase and to relieve the seller from liability for latent defects in the absence of an express warranty or legal assurance to the contrary. *Barnard v. Kellogg*, 77 U.S. 383, 388 (1870). As Professor Jan Narveson observes, *caveat emptor* still has persuasive force in a market economy because of a presumption that both the consumer and the producer in market transactions are pursuing the transaction not out of any interest in the welfare of the other party, but rather solely for their own respective benefits. See Jan Narveson, "Consumers' Rights in the Laissez-Faire Economy: How Much Caveat for the Emptor?" 7 Chap. L. Rev. 181, 187 (2004). Under this libertarian presumption, consumers have certain rights to receive truthful information regarding the transaction, but also have responsibilities with respect to guarding their own interests. See id. at 187–199.

Not surprisingly, Karl Llewellyn, the father of the Uniform Commercial Code, took the early view that with respect to the sale of goods, the doctrine of caveat emptor ran contrary to the ordinary understanding of the buyer and seller. Llewellyn thus argued for a broadened implied warranty of quality against latent defects. Karl N. Llewellyn, "On Warranty, Quality and Society (Part I)," 36 Colum. L. Rev. 699, 722 (1936).

Nonetheless, the doctrine of *caveat emptor* had its adherents, at least when the product error was innocent. See James M. Buchanan, "In Defense of *Caveat Emptor*," 38 U. Chi. L. Rev. 64 (1970). Perhaps because of early common law misgivings, the National Conference of Commissioners adopted the Uniform Sales Act ("USA") in 1906. The USA was patterned after the English Sale of Goods Act of 1893. K. C. T. Sutton, "Warranties Under the Sales of Goods Act and the Uniform Commercial Code," 6 Melb. U. L. Rev. 150 (1967). About 32 states adopted the Act in thirty years. Karl N. Llewellyn, "On Warranty, Quality and Society (Part II)," 37 Colum. L. Rev. 341, 381 (1937). USA § 15 set forth a statutory section with regard to an "implied warranty of quality." The section provided that the only implied warranties of quality or fitness for a particular purpose were those set forth in the section's six paragraphs. USA § 15(2)–(3) provided that, absent a defect obvious upon inspection, an item purchased by description from a merchant in those goods was subject to an implied warranty that the goods are of merchantable quality. See William L. Prosser, "The Implied Warranty of Merchantable Quality," 27 Minn. L. Rev. 118 (1943). The warranty required the seller to deliver goods of sound quality without regard to the particular needs of the buyer. USA § 15(1) implied a warranty that goods purchased in reliance on the seller's recommendation for a particular purpose must be reasonably fit for that purpose. See generally Gordon J. Gose, "Implied Warranty of Quality Under the Uniform Sales Act," 4 Wash. L. Rev. 15 (1929).

a. Warranty Liability

In 1951, the Uniform Commercial Code was adopted and also continued the implied warranties of quality (merchantability) and fitness for a particular purpose. As discussed above, the UCC implied warranties contrast sharply with the common law, which, outside of narrowly defined contexts such as the implied warranty of habitability in real estate transactions, generally does not provide any comparable implied warranties. UCC § 2–314 states the modern implied warranty of merchantability. UCC § 2–314(2)(c) elaborates on the quality requirements of goods to be merchantable and notably includes the requirement that such goods must be "fit for the ordinary purposes for which such goods are used." UCC § 2–315 states the modern implied warranty of fitness for a particular purpose. UCC § 2–315 provides that where the seller has reason to know of a buyer's particular purpose for the purchase, and that the buyer is relying upon the seller's skill or judgment to select suitable goods, an implied warranty exists that the goods are fit for that particular purpose.

While the text of § 2–315 suggests that the test for establishing the implied warranty of fitness for a particular purpose depends solely on the seller's understanding of the buyer's purpose and the seller's perception of the buyer's reliance, Comment 1 clarifies that "[t]he buyer, of course, must actually be relying on the seller." UCC § 2–315 *cmt. 1*.

Both implied warranties are only default rules, and thus the parties may contract out of those warranties altogether (exclusion) or alter or limit any implied warranties to meet their particular needs (modification). UCC § 2–316(2) imposes slightly different requirements for exclusions or modifications of these implied warranties. To exclude or modify the warranty of merchantability, the language of the exclusion or modification need not be written, but must specifically mention "merchantability." See id. If the merchantability exclusion or modification is in writing, the language of the exclusion or modification must be conspicuous. See id. To exclude or modify the warranty of fitness for a particular purpose, the language of the exclusion or modification must be in writing and conspicuous. See id. Notwithstanding the requirement that the exclusion or modification of the warranty of merchantability specifically mention merchantability, UCC § 2–316(2) further provides that language such as "[t]here are no warranties which extend beyond the description on the face hereof" is sufficient to exclude all implied warranties. Likewise, UCC § 2–316(3) provides that words such as goods are sold "as is" or "with all faults" are adequate to eliminate both implied warranties. UCC § 2–316(3)(a).

As the foregoing discussion suggests, an express warranty as to the quality of goods was enforceable as a promise and was never truly subject to the *caveat emptor* doctrine. UCC § 2–313 defines an express warranty to include an affirmation, promise, description, or sample relating to the goods that become part of the "basis of the bargain" for which such goods were purchased. The "basis of the bargain" language creates serious questions regarding the nature of the buyer's reliance on the express warranty to induce the purchase decision. Unlike implied warranties, which are easily disclaimed, express warranties—once incorporated into the parties' contract—cannot be disclaimed. UCC § 2–316(1). UCC § 2–316(1) states the general rule of interpretation that warranties and warranty exclusions or modifications contained within the same contract should be read as consistent with one another where such an interpretation is reasonable. But where no reasonable reconciliation between contract warranties and warranty exclusions or modifications is possible, "negation or limitation is inoperative to the extent that such construction is unreasonable." UCC § 2–316(1). Importantly, warranty exclusions contained in a written contract that contradict parol express warranties frequently raise parol evidence rule problems for the party to whom the warranty was made. See Richard F. Broude, "The Consumer and the Parol

Evidence Rule: Section 2–202 of the Uniform Commercial Code," 19 Duke L. J. 881, 882–83 (1970).

USA § 12 required the buyer to prove actual reliance on the express warranty. UCC § 2–313 does not state a requirement of explicit reliance, although it does state the express warranty, however made, must become a part of the "basis of the bargain." UCC § 2–313, *cmt. 3* (emphasis added) provides:

> In actual practice affirmations of fact made by the seller about the goods during a bargain are regarded as part of the description of those goods, hence *no particular reliance on such statements need be shown in order to weave them into the fabric of the agreement.* Rather, any fact which is to take such affirmations, once made, out of the agreement requires clear affirmative proof. The issue normally is one of fact.

Accordingly, the "basis of the bargain" test differs somewhat from the USA, which required specific reliance. See K. C. T. Sutton, "Warranties Under the Sales of Goods Act and the Uniform Commercial Code," 6 Melb. U. L. Rev. 150, 153 (1967). However, since Comment 3 states the issue is one of fact, is proof of reliance no longer necessary? Has reliance been eliminated? If not, what factual determinations underlie the "basis of the bargain" test?

KEITH V. BUCHANAN

Court of Appeal California
173 Cal.App.3d 13, 220 Cal.Rptr. 392 (1985)

OCHOA, Associate Justice.

This breach of warranty case is before this court after the trial court granted defendants' motion for judgment at the close of plaintiff's case during the trial proceedings. We hold that an express warranty under section 2–313 of the California Uniform Commercial Code was created in this matter, and that actual reliance on the seller's factual representation need not be shown by the buyer. The representation is presumed to be part of the basis of the bargain, and the burden is on the seller to prove that the representation was not a consideration inducing the bargain. We affirm all other aspects of the trial court's judgment but reverse in regard to its finding that no express warranty was created and remand for further proceedings consistent with this opinion.

STATEMENT OF FACTS

Plaintiff, Brian Keith, purchased a sailboat from defendants in November 1978 for a total purchase price of $75,610. Even though plaintiff belonged to the Waikiki Yacht Club, had attended a sailing school, had joined the Coast Guard Auxiliary, and had sailed on many yachts in order to ascertain his preferences, he had not previously owned a yacht. He attended a boat show in Long Beach during October 1978 and looked at a number of boats, speaking to sales representatives and obtaining advertising literature. In the literature, the sailboat which is the subject of this action, called an "Island Trader 41," was described as a seaworthy vessel. In one sales brochure, this vessel is described as "a picture of sure-footed seaworthiness." In another, it is called "a carefully well-equipped, and very seaworthy live-aboard vessel." Plaintiff testified he relied on representations in the sales brochures in regard to the purchase. Plaintiff and a sales representative also discussed plaintiff's desire for a boat which was ocean-going and would cruise long distances.

Plaintiff asked his friend, Buddy Ebsen, who was involved in a boat building enterprise, to inspect the boat. Mr. Ebsen and one of his associates, both of whom had extensive experience with sailboats, observed the boat and advised plaintiff that the vessel would suit his stated needs. A deposit was paid on the boat, a purchase contract was entered into, and optional accessories for the boat were ordered. After delivery of the vessel, a dispute arose in regard to its seaworthiness.

Plaintiff filed the instant lawsuit alleging causes of action in breach of express warranty and breach of implied warranty. The trial court granted defendants' Code of Civil Procedure section 631.8 motion for judgment at the close of plaintiff's case. The court found that no express warranty was established by the evidence because none of the defendants had undertaken in writing to preserve or maintain the utility or performance of the vessel, nor to provide compensation for any failure in utility or performance. It found that the written statements produced at trial were opinions or commendations of the vessel. The court further found that no implied warranty of fitness was created because the plaintiff did not rely on the skill and judgment of defendants to select and furnish a suitable vessel, but had rather relied on his own experts in selecting the vessel.

DISCUSSION

I.   EXPRESS WARRANTY

California Uniform Commercial Code section 2–313[1] provides, inter alia, that express warranties are created by (1) any affirmation of fact or

---

[1]   Section 2–313: Express Warranties by Affirmation, Promise, Description, Sample.

   (1) Express warranties by the seller are created as follows:

      (a) Any affirmation of fact or promise made by the seller to the buyer which relates to the goods and becomes part of the basis of the bargain creates an express warranty that the goods shall conform to the affirmation or promise.

      (b) Any description of the goods which is made part of the basis of the bargain creates an express warranty that the goods shall conform to the description.

      (c) Any sample or model which is made part of the basis of the bargain creates an express warranty that the whole of the goods shall conform to the sample or model.

promise made by the seller to the buyer which relates to the goods and becomes part of the basis of the bargain, and (2) any description of the goods which is made part of the basis of the bargain. Formal words such as "warranty" or "guarantee" are not required to make a warranty, but the seller's affirmation of the value of the goods or an expression of opinion or commendation of the goods does not create an express warranty.

In addition, the Song-Beverly Consumer Warranty Act (Civ. Code, § 1790 et seq.) establishes broad statutory control over warranties in consumer sales where consumer goods are used or bought for use primarily for personal, family, or household purposes. Provisions of the Civil Code relating to warranties do not affect the rights and obligations of parties under the Commercial Code, except that where conflicts exist between the code provisions, the rights guaranteed to buyers of consumer goods under the provisions of the Consumer Warranty Act prevail. (Civ. Code, § 1790.3.)

The Act defines an express warranty, in pertinent part, as "[a] written statement arising out of a sale to the consumer of a consumer good pursuant to which the manufacturer, distributor, or retailer undertakes to preserve or maintain the utility or performance of the consumer good or provide compensation if there is a failure in utility or performance. . . . " (Civ. Code, § 1791.2, subd. (a)(1).) Again, formal words are not required in order to create an express warranty, but statements of value, opinion, or commendation do not create a warranty.

The trial court appropriately found that there was no written undertaking to preserve or maintain the utility or performance of a consumer good or to provide compensation if there was a failure in utility or performance at the time the purchase contract for the sailboat was made. No claim, therefore, is cognizable that an express warranty existed in this action pursuant to the provisions of the Song-Beverly Consumer Warranty Act. However, at the time of argument on the motion for judgment, plaintiff's counsel had argued claims based on express warranty under the provisions of both the Civil Code and the Commercial Code, and no analysis was undertaken in regard to express warranty under the provisions of the California Uniform Commercial Code.

California Uniform Commercial Code section 2–313, regarding express warranties, was enacted in 1963 and consists of the official text of Uniform Commercial Code section 2–313 without change. In deciding whether a statement made by a seller constitutes an express warranty under this provision, the court must deal with three fundamental issues. First, the court must determine whether the seller's statement constitutes an

_____

(2) It is not necessary to the creation of an express warranty that the seller use formal words such as 'warrant' or 'guarantee' or that he have a specific intention to make a warranty, but an affirmation merely of the value of the goods or a statement purporting to be merely the seller's opinion or commendation of the goods does not create a warranty.

"affirmation of fact or promise" or "description of the goods" under California Uniform Commercial Code section 2–313, subdivision (1)(a) or (b) or whether it is rather "merely the seller's opinion or commendation of the goods" under section 2–313, subdivision (2). Second, assuming the court finds the language used susceptible to creation of a warranty, it must then be determined whether the statement was "part of the basis of the bargain." Third, the court must determine whether the warranty was breached. (See Sessa v. Riegle (E. D. Pa. 1977) 427 F. Supp. 760, 765.)

A warranty relates to the title, character, quality, identity, or condition of the goods. The purpose of the law of warranty is to determine what it is that the seller has in essence agreed to sell. (A. A. Baxter Corp. v. Colt Industries, Inc. (1970) 10 Cal. App. 3d 144, 153, 88 Cal. Rptr. 842.):

> Express warranties are chisels in the hands of buyers and sellers. With these tools, the parties to a sale sculpt a monument representing the goods. Having selected a stone, the buyer and seller may leave it almost bare, allowing considerable play in the qualities that fit its contours. Or the parties may chisel away inexactitudes until a well-defined shape emerges. The seller is bound to deliver, and the buyer to accept, goods that match the sculpted form. Special Project: Article Two Warranties in Commercial Transactions, Express Warranties—Section 2–313 (1978–79) 64 Cornell L. Rev. 30 (hereafter cited as Warranties in Commercial Transactions) at pp. 43–44.

A. AFFIRMATION OF FACT, PROMISE OR DESCRIPTION VERSUS STATEMENT OF OPINION, COMMENDATION OR VALUE.

"The determination as to whether a particular statement is an expression of opinion or an affirmation of fact is often difficult, and frequently is dependent upon the facts and circumstances existing at the time the statement is made." (Willson v. Municipal Bond Co. (1936) 7 Cal. 2d 144, 150, 59 P. 2d 974.) Recent decisions have evidenced a trend toward narrowing the scope of representations which are considered opinion, sometimes referred to as "puffing" or "sales talk," resulting in an expansion of the liability that flows from broad statements of manufacturers or retailers as to the quality of their products. Courts have liberally construed affirmations of quality made by sellers in favor of injured consumers. (Hauter v. Zogarts (1975) 14 Cal. 3d 104, 112, 120 Cal. Rptr. 681, 534 P. 2d 377; see also 55 Cal.Jur.3d, Sales, § 74, p. 580.) It has even been suggested "that in an age of consumerism all seller's statements, except the most blatant sales pitch, may give rise to an express warranty." (1 Alderman and Dole, A Transactional Guide to the Uniform Commercial Code (2d ed. 1983) p. 89.)

Courts in other states have struggled in efforts to create a formula for distinguishing between affirmations of fact, promises, or descriptions of goods on the one hand, and value, opinion, or commendation statements on the other. The code comment indicates that the basic question is:

"What statements of the seller have in the circumstances and in objective judgment become part of the basis of the bargain?" The commentators indicated that the language of subsection (2) of the code section was included because "common experience discloses that some statements or predictions cannot fairly be viewed as entering into the bargain." (See U. Com. Code com. 8 to Cal. U. Com. Code, § 2–313, West's Ann. Com. Code (1964) p. 250.)

Statements made by a seller during the course of negotiation over a contract are presumptively affirmations of fact unless it can be demonstrated that the buyer could only have reasonably considered the statement as a statement of the seller's opinion. Commentators have noted several factors which tend to indicate an opinion statement. These are (1) a lack of specificity in the statement made, (2) a statement that is made in an equivocal manner, or (3) a statement which reveals that the goods are experimental in nature. (See Warranties in Commercial Transactions, supra, at pp. 60–64.)

It is clear that statements made by a manufacturer or retailer in an advertising brochure which is disseminated to the consuming public in order to induce sales can create express warranties. (Fundin v. Chicago Pneumatic Tool Co. (1984) 152 Cal. App. 3d 951, 957, 199 Cal. Rptr. 789. . . . In the instant case, the vessel purchased was described in sales brochures as "a picture of sure-footed seaworthiness" and "a carefully well-equipped and very seaworthy vessel." The seller's representative was aware that appellant was looking for a vessel sufficient for long distance ocean-going cruises. The statements in the brochure are specific and unequivocal in asserting that the vessel is seaworthy. Nothing in the negotiation indicates that the vessel is experimental in nature. In fact, one sales brochure assures prospective buyers that production of the vessel was commenced "after years of careful testing." The representations regarding seaworthiness made in sales brochures regarding the Island Trader 41 were affirmations of fact relating to the quality or condition of the vessel.

B. "PART OF THE BASIS OF THE BARGAIN" TEST.

Under former provisions of law, a purchaser was required to prove that he or she acted in reliance upon representations made by the seller. (Grinnell v. Charles Pfizer & Co. (1969) 274 Cal. App. 2d 424, 440, 79 Cal. Rptr. 369.) California Uniform Commercial Code section 2–313 indicates only that the seller's statements must become "part of the basis of the bargain." According to official comment 3 to this Uniform Commercial Code provision, "no particular reliance . . . need be shown in order to weave [the seller's affirmations of fact] into the fabric of the agreement. Rather, any fact which is to take such affirmations, once made, out of the agreement requires clear affirmative proof." (See U. Com. Code com. 3 to Cal. U. Com. Code, § 2–313, West's Ann. Com. Code (1964) p. 249.)

The California Supreme Court, in discussing the continued viability of the reliance factor, noted that commentators have disagreed in regard to the impact of this development. Some have indicated that it shifts the burden of proving non-reliance to the seller, and others have indicated that the code eliminates the concept of reliance altogether. (Hauter v. Zogarts, supra, 14 Cal. 3d at pp. 115–116, 120 Cal. Rptr. 681, 534 P. 2d 377.) The court did not resolve this issue, but noted that decisions of other states prior to that time had "ignored the significance of the new standard and have held that consumer reliance still is a vital ingredient for recovery based on express warranty." (Id., at p. 116, fn. 13. . . .)

The shift in language clearly changes the degree to which it must be shown that the seller's representation affected the buyer's decision to enter into the agreement. A buyer need not show that he would not have entered into the agreement absent the warranty or even that it was a dominant factor inducing the agreement. A warranty statement is deemed to be part of the basis of the bargain and to have been relied upon as one of the inducements for the purchase of the product. In other words, the buyer's demonstration of reliance on an express warranty is "not a prerequisite for breach of warranty, as long as the express warranty involved became part of the bargain. See White & Summers, Uniform Commercial Code (2d ed. 1980) § 9–4. If, however, the resulting bargain does not rest at all on the representations of the seller, those representations cannot be considered as becoming any part of the 'basis of the bargain.' " . . . (Allied Fidelity Ins. Co. v. Pico (Nev. S. Ct. 1983) 656 P. 2d 849, 850.)

The official Uniform Commercial Code comment in regard to section 2–313 "indicates that in actual practice affirmations of fact made by the seller about the goods during a bargain are regarded as part of the description of those goods; hence no particular reliance on such statements need be shown in order to weave them into the fabric of the agreement." (Young & Cooper, Inc. v. Vestring (1974) 214 Kan. 311, 521 P. 2d 281, 291. . . .) It is clear from the new language of this code section that the concept of reliance has been purposefully abandoned. (Interco Inc. v. Randustrial Corp. (Mo. App. 1976) 533 S. W. 2d 257, 261. . . .)

The change of the language in section 2–313 of the California Uniform Commercial Code modifies both the degree of reliance and the burden of proof in express warranties under the code. The representation need only be part of the basis of the bargain, or merely a factor or consideration inducing the buyer to enter into the bargain. A warranty statement made by a seller is presumptively part of the basis of the bargain, and the burden is on the seller to prove that the resulting bargain does not rest at all on the representation.

The buyer's actual knowledge of the true condition of the goods prior to the making of the contract may make it plain that the seller's statement was not relied upon as one of the inducements for the purchase, but the burden is on the seller to demonstrate such knowledge on the part of the buyer. Where the buyer inspects the goods before purchase, he may be deemed to have waived the seller's express warranties. But, an examination or inspection by the buyer of the goods does not necessarily discharge the seller from an express warranty if the defect was not actually discovered and waived. (Doak Gas Engine Co. v. Fraser (1914) 168 Cal. 624, 627, 143 P. 1024. . . .)

Appellant's inspection of the boat by his own experts does not constitute a waiver of the express warranty of seaworthiness. Prior to the making of the contract, appellant had experienced boat builders observe the boat, but there was no testing of the vessel in the water.[3] Such a warranty (seaworthiness) necessarily relates to the time when the vessel has been put to sea (Werner v. Montana (1977) 117 N.H. 721, 378 A.2d 1130, 1134–35) and has been shown to be reasonably fit and adequate in materials, construction, and equipment for its intended purposes (Daly v. General Motors Corp. (1978) 20 Cal. 3d 725, 739, 144 Cal. Rptr. 380, 575 P. 2d 1162 . . .).

In this case, appellant was aware of the representations regarding seaworthiness by the seller prior to contracting. He also had expressed to the seller's representative his desire for a long distance ocean-going vessel. Although he had other experts inspect the vessel, the inspection was limited and would not have indicated whether or not the vessel was seaworthy. It is clear that the seller has not overcome the presumption that the representations regarding seaworthiness were part of the basis of this bargain.

II.   IMPLIED WARRANTY

Appellant also claimed breach of the implied warranty of fitness for a particular purpose[4] in regard to the sale of the subject vessel. An implied warranty of fitness for a particular purpose arises when a "seller at the time of contracting has reason to know any particular purpose for which

---

[3]   Evidence was presented of examination or inspection of the boat after the making of the contract of sale and prior to delivery and acceptance of the vessel. Such an inspection would be irrelevant to any issue of express warranty. Although it deals with implied warranties as opposed to express warranties, the Uniform Commercial Code comment 8 to section 2–316 (Cal. U. Com. Code, § 2–316) is instructive: "Under paragraph (b) of subdivision (3) warranties may be excluded or modified by the circumstances where the buyer examines the goods or a sample or model of them before entering into the contract. 'Examination' as used in this paragraph is not synonymous with inspection before acceptance or at any other time after the contract has been made. It goes rather to the nature of the responsibility assumed by the seller at the time of the making of the contract." (See U. Com. Code com. 8 to Cal. U. Com. Code, § 2–316, West's Ann. Com. Code (1964) p. 308, emphasis added.)

[4]   No claim of breach of implied warranty of merchantability has been presented in this action.

the goods are required and that the buyer is relying on the seller's skill or judgment to select or furnish suitable goods," which are fit for such purpose. (Cal. U. Com. Code, § 2–315.) The Consumer Warranty Act makes such an implied warranty applicable to retailers, distributors, and manufacturers. (Civ. Code, §§ 1791.1, 1792.1, 1792.2, subd. (a).) An implied warranty of fitness for a particular purpose arises only where (1) the purchaser at the time of contracting intends to use the goods for a particular purpose, (2) the seller at the time of contracting has reason to know of this particular purpose, (3) the buyer relies on the seller's skill or judgment to select or furnish goods suitable for the particular purpose, and (4) the seller at the time of contracting has reason to know that the buyer is relying on such skill and judgment. (Metowski v. Traid Corp. (1972) 28 Cal. App. 3d 332, 341, 104 Cal. Rptr. 599.)

The reliance elements are important to the consideration of whether an implied warranty of fitness for a particular purpose exists.

> If the seller had no reason to know that he was being relied upon, his conduct in providing goods cannot fairly be deemed a tacit representation of their suitability for a particular purpose. And if the buyer did not in fact rely, then the principal justification for imposing a fitness warranty disappears. (See Warranties in Commercial Transactions, supra, at p. 89.)

The major question in determining the existence of an implied warranty of fitness for a particular purpose is the reliance by the buyer upon the skill and judgment of the seller to select an article suitable for his needs. . . .

The trial court found that the plaintiff did not rely on the skill and judgment of the defendants to select a suitable vessel, but that he rather relied on his own experts.

> Our sole task is to determine whether the evidence, viewed in the light most favorable to [respondent], sustains [these] findings. . . . Moreover, in examining the sufficiency of the evidence to support a questioned finding an appellate court must accept as true all evidence tending to establish the correctness of the finding as made, taking into account, as well, all inferences which might reasonably have been thought by the trial court to lead to the same conclusion. . . . If appellate scrutiny reveals that substantial evidence supports the trial court's findings and conclusions, the judgment must be affirmed. (Board of Education v. Jack M. (1977) 19 Cal. 3d 691, 697, 139 Cal. Rptr. 700, 566 P. 2d 602.)

A review of the record reveals ample evidence to support the trial court's finding. Appellant had extensive experience with sailboats at the time of the subject purchase, even though he had not previously owned such a vessel. He had developed precise specifications in regard to the type of boat he wanted to purchase. He looked at a number of different vessels, reviewed their advertising literature, and focused on the Island Trader 41 as the object of his intended purchase. He also had friends look at the boat before making the final decision to purchase. The trial court's finding that the buyer did not rely on the skill or judgment of the seller in the selection of the vessel in question is supported by substantial evidence.

The trial court's judgment that no express warranty existed in this matter is reversed. The trial court's judgment is affirmed in all other respects. Since considerable contradictory evidence was elicited at trial relating to the asserted breach of warranty of seaworthiness of the subject vessel, and since the trial court made no finding in regard to that issue, the matter is remanded to the trial court for further proceedings consistent with this opinion. Each party is to bear his own costs on appeal.

STONE, P.J., and GILBERT, J., concur.

NOTES AND QUESTIONS

1.   *Statements of opinion, value, commendation, or "puff." Keith* noted that while formal words are not required in order to create an express warranty, statements of value, opinion, or commendation do not create a warranty. Why not? What is the definition of the term "warranty"? UCC § 2–313(2) states that "an affirmation merely of the value of the goods or a statement purporting to be merely the seller's opinion or commendation of the goods does not create a warranty." Comment 8 to UCC § 2–313 further provides that "some statements or predictions cannot fairly be viewed as entering into the bargain." Does the comment suggest that justified reliance is relevant to determining whether statements enter into the bargain or are deemed to be puffery? Are such statements puffery because the buyer's reliance on them is unjustified? Do you think the statements should be evaluated according to the intent of the maker of the statement or the objective understanding of the purchaser? See generally Penny LaDean Dykas, Comment, "Opinion v. Express Warranty: How Much Puff Can a Salesman Use?" 28 Idaho L. Rev. 167 (1992). Moreover, scholarly discussion suggests a higher standard for sales talk to rise to the level of a warranty than case law actually demonstrates. See Charles Pierson, Comment, "Does 'Puff' Create an Express Warranty of Merchantability? Where the Hornbooks Go Wrong," 36 Duq. L. Rev. 887 (1998).

For comparative purposes, common law requires that a statement constitutes a "misrepresentation" only if it is a false assertion of "fact" (which can include state of mind). Restatement (Second) of Contracts § 159, *cmt. a.* While a statement of opinion is therefore also a statement of fact because it reflects the state of mind of the maker, the nature of the statement also implies that the maker does not possess definitive information on the matter to make it a fact. Therefore, statements of personal judgment of quality, value, authenticity, or similar matter are not a "fact." Restatement (Second) of Contracts § 168(a), *cmt. a.* Ordinarily, a person is "not justified in relying upon" a mere statement of opinion unless the maker is in a position of trust and confidence with the recipient or other special circumstances exist to justify high respect for the opinion. Restatement (Second) of Contracts § 169. How would *Keith* be analyzed under the common law regarding the existence and reliance on an express warranty? Stated another way, do statements of value or quality hold any more or less value under common law than under the UCC? To answer this question, you might review the materials in Chapter 2 regarding the nature of a "promise."

2.   *"Seaworthiness" test to distinguish puffery and warranty. Keith* adopts a "presumptive test" that statements made by a seller during the course of negotiation regarding a contract to purchase are "presumptively affirmations of fact" unless it can be demonstrated that the buyer could only have reasonably considered the statement the seller's "opinion." Under this approach, what must the purchaser prove? How can a seller defend? The *Keith* dispute related to the "seaworthiness" of the vessel. What exactly would a reasonable person expect from a 41-foot seaworthy vessel? Transpacific travel? West coast port-to-port travel? Overnight cruising capability on the open seas?

3.   *Basis of the bargain test.* Under UCC §§ 2–313(1)(a)–(c), no form of express warranty is actionable unless the warranty becomes part of the "basis of the bargain" concerning the purchase of the goods. UCC § 2–313, Comment 3 makes clear that the seller need not "intend" to make a warranty and thus the test depends on the objective understanding of the purchaser. Further, once a warranty statement is made, it becomes presumptively part of the basis of the bargain. Indeed, under Comment 3, once a warranty is made, the seller can only remove that warranty from the presumptive basis of the bargain by "clear affirmative proof." How does *Keith* implement this test involving relative buyer–seller proof of reliance? Does the Court require the buyer to prove that the purchase would not have occurred absent the warranty (specific reliance test) or that the warranty was a dominant factor in purchase decision (presumed reliance by significance of the warranty)? If the warranty was irrelevant to the purchase decision, can it still become part of the basis of the bargain (reliance irrelevant test)? Or is there some middle ground? See John E. Murray, Jr., "'Basis of Bargain': Transcending Traditional Concepts," 66 Minn. L. Rev. 283 (1982); Sidney Kwestel, "Express Warranty as Contractual— The Need for a Clear Approach," 53 Mercer L. Rev. 557 (2002). *Keith* adopts a two-prong middle ground approach requiring: (i) that a warranty is a factor or consideration inducing the buyer to enter into the bargain; and (ii) since once made the warranty is presumptively part of the basis of the bargain, the seller has the burden of proof to establish that the resulting bargain does not rest at all on the representation. What then is left for the plaintiff's proof and thus the major obstacle to recovery? If the plaintiff need only prove a warranty was made and the seller must then prove the warranty was not a factor at all in the decision to make the purchase, how successful do you think the seller will be? Even if a warranty exists, is the buyer's knowledge of that warranty at least an element of the case? See Mathew A. Victor, "Express Warranties Under the UCC—Reliance Revisited," 25 New Eng. L. Rev. 477 (1990); Thomas J. Holdych & Bruce D. Mann, "The Basis of the Bargain Requirement: A Market and Economic Based Analysis of Express Warranties—Getting What You Pay for and Paying for What You Get," 45 DePaul L. Rev. 781 (1996).

Given the unlikely proof that the warranty was not part of the buyer's decision to make the purchase, what element of the case takes on a more important dimension? Given the uncertainty associated with the distinction between warranty and puffery, might this test assume more importance? If so, how do the notes above resolve this question in cases of doubt? If again the buyer presumptively wins, how can a buyer ever lose an express warranty case when the product fails to comply with the terms of a marginal express warranty? Does the confluence of all these factors create strict liability against the seller for even marginal expressions considered an express warranty? See Wayne K. Lewis, "Toward a Theory of Strict 'Claim' Liability: Warranty Relief for Advertising Representations," 47 Ohio St. L. J. 671 (1986). Given the difficulties with the "basis of the bargain" test, how does Revised UCC § 2–313 treat the requirement?

4. *Waiver by inspection.* The *Keith* court mentions that a buyer's actual knowledge of the true condition of the goods prior to purchase may make it plain that the seller's express warranty was not relied upon as an inducement for the purchase. When effective, it appears the *Keith* Court views physical inspection as a primary method for the seller to prove that the express warranty, even if made, did not become a "basis of the bargain." For example, if in this case, the buyer inspected the boat and knew it was not "seaworthy," the buyer would be precluded from suing for a breach of the admitted express warranty. Even though expert boat builders physically inspected the boat, why was that inspection ineffective as to the express warranty that the yacht was seaworthy?

The court also mentions that in such cases, the express warranty may be deemed "waived" by the purchaser. The term "waiver" is most often defined as a "voluntary and intentional relinquishment of a known right." Calamari and Perillo on Contracts § 11.29(c) (Fifth Edition 2003). Do you think the use of the term "waiver" is accurate in this context? Do you think that a buyer truly intends to relinquish the right to insist on strict compliance with an express warranty merely because the buyer inspects the goods? If the inspection occurs "after" the contract is made but before delivery, would the inspection still be relevant to express warranties? Read footnote 3 in the case. UCC § 2–316(3)(b) provides that the "implied" warranties of merchantability and fitness for a particular purpose are eliminated if the buyer examines or refuses to examine the goods and the defects would have been discoverable. The section does not mention express warranties. Indeed, under UCC § 2–316(1), express warranties incorporated in the parties contract may not be eliminated by the seller. What is the difference between the seller eliminating an express warranty and a buyer waiving an express warranty? Does the distinction make sense?

Inspection plays a role in various aspects of the common law as well. For example, Restatement (Second) of Contracts § 154 will not permit a contract to be avoided on the basis of a mutual mistake where one party bears the "risk" of the mistake. What role should an actual inspection, or a failure to inspect when given the opportunity, play in this outcome? Also, under Restatement

(Second) of Contracts § 164, misrepresentation is only actionable provided the misled party was justified in relying on the misrepresentation. What role should an actual inspection or a failure to inspect when given the opportunity play in this outcome? See the discussion in *Hill.*

5.   *Privity requirement.* At common law, a warranty was a contractual matter and therefore confined to the parties to the contract. Therefore, while the manufacturer and dealer are liable for warranty breaches to the original purchaser because they are all parties to the contract of sale, a second buyer from the first purchaser was barred from suing for the same warranty breach because that person was never a party to the original sales contract. In cases like *Keith* where only economic loss occurs, the same "privity to contract" rule applies, and the common law rule continues unless a particular state law modifies the rule. Some argue that the warranty privity requirement should be eliminated and be available to all remote purchasers. See Richard E. Speidel, "Warranty Theory, Economic Loss, and the Privity Requirement: Once More into the Void," 67 B. U. L. Rev. 9 (1987). Revised UCC § 2–313(1) creates the term "immediate buyer" to identify the original purchaser. But unlike the original version, Revised UCC § 2–313A(1)(b) identifies the term "remote purchaser" as a person who purchases or leases from the immediate buyer. While Revised UCC § 2–313A(5) permits the seller to limit remedies to a remote purchaser, if such a limitation is absent, the seller remains liable to the remote purchaser to the same extent as to the immediate buyer except that lost profits are excluded. Revised UCC § 2–313A(5)(b).

A few states (Texas and Alabama) do not extend the warranty of merchantability to "used" goods even though UCC § 2–314 makes no distinction between new and used goods. Although it is likely that the sale of used goods may occur more frequently by non-merchants and therefore not be covered by the warranty, the distinction between new and used goods is rejected in all other states. See Kendall M. Gray, "Merchantability and Used Goods: Do You Really Get What You Pay For,?" 45 Baylor L. Rev. 665 (1993). Because of abuses in connection with the sale of used cars, in 1982 the Federal Trade Commission adopted the "Used Car Rule," requiring a car window disclosure label on used cars disclosing (i) whether the car is sold "as is" or with an express warranty; (ii) service contract liability; (iii) a suggestion that the consumer ask the dealer whether the car may be inspected on or off the lot; and (iv) a warning that spoken promises are difficult to enforce and that buyers should therefore obtain all promises in writing. Compliance failures are considered deceptive trade practices. See 16 C.F.R. § 455 (1986) and Janet Resetar, "Implied Warranty and the Used Car Rule," 46 La. L. Rev. 1239 (1986) (Congress vetoed the rule but this veto was later declared unconstitutional in *Process Gas Consumer Group v. Consumer Energy Council,* 463 U.S. 1216 (1983)).

6.   *Implied warranty of fitness for a particular purpose.* UCC § 2–315 creates an implied warranty of fitness for a particular purpose. In order for the warranty to be implied-in-law, the seller must know buyer's "particular purpose" for the goods, recommend a particular product to suit that purpose,

and the buyer must rely on the seller's skill and judgment in the selection and recommendation. As a result, reliance on the seller's recommendation is critical. For this reason, UCC § 2–316(3)(b) negates the reliance requirement when the buyer actually inspected the goods prior to purchase, or refused to do so, and in either event the inspection would have made clear the goods were not appropriate. The *Keith* court determined that inspection by the buyer and his experts *after* the yacht was purchased was adequate to determine that the yacht was indeed not seaworthy (as defined by the buyer's needs). Ignoring for the moment that the inspection occurred after purchase, why would such an inspection eliminate an implied warranty of seaworthiness but not an express warranty of seaworthiness? Does the distinction make sense to you?

What do you suppose that a purchaser's "particular purpose" might include? In order to invoke this particular implied warranty, must the particular purpose be any purpose other than an ordinary purpose? See Crane v. Bagge & Son, Inc., 2005 WL 1576544 (Cal. App. 2d Dist.). If so, why do you suppose this requirement exists? If the requirement were otherwise, how would the implied fitness warranty overlap with the implied merchantability warranty?

7. *CISG and express warranties.* The CISG does not state seller obligations specifically in terms of a "warranty"; however CISG Art. 35(1) requires the seller to deliver goods that "are of the quantity, quality and description required by the contract." However, CISG Art. 35(2) provides that goods are not conforming unless they (i) are fit for the purposes of similar goods; (ii) are fit for the buyer's particular purpose known to the seller where the buyer relies on the seller's skill and judgment; and (iii) possess the qualities of any sample or model. See Richard E. Speidel, "The Revision of Article 2, Sales in Light of the United Nations Convention on Contracts for the International Sale of Goods," 16 Nw. J. Int'l L. & Bus. 165 (1995). However, all CISG conformity rules are subject to elimination by agreement because CISG Art 35(2) includes the phrase "except where the parties have otherwise agreed." John E. Murray, Jr., "An Essay on the Formation of Contracts and Related Matters Under The United Nations Convention on Contracts for the International Sale of Goods," 8 J. L. & Com. 11, 12 (1988).

8. *Implied warranty of merchantability.* UCC § 2–314(1) provides that a warranty that goods are merchantable is implied in a sale of goods by a merchant of those types of goods. UCC § 2–314(2)(c) generally states that goods are merchantable if they are "fit for the ordinary purposes for which such goods are used." *Keith* stated in note 4 that no claim was made for breach of the warranty of merchantability. Why do you think the buyer and counsel decided not to pursue this implied-in-law warranty? While lack of merchantability clearly implies that the goods are defective for their generally intended use, does an express warranty or a warranty for a particular purpose require that the goods be defective? Stated another way, could goods be perfectly merchantable and yet breach either an express warranty or the warranty of fitness for a particular purpose?

10. *Non-UCC implied warranty of quality.* The materials above are concerned with UCC statutory overrides of the common law doctrine of *caveat emptor* that apply only with respect to the sale of goods. Where does that leave the common law doctrine of *caveat emptor* with respect to transactions not involving the sale of goods? Stated another way, does the Restatement (Second) of Contracts include any provisions regarding implied promises similar to merchantability and fitness for a particular purpose? Certainly, as with an express warranty, an express promise of quality would be enforceable just as any other promise. But absent such a promise, does the law imply a promise or warranty of quality? There has been considerable erosion involving the construction and sale of new homes, and many states now imply a warranty of fitness for a particular purpose in the form of an implied-in-law "warranty of habitability." The concept first evolved around 1930 in England where it was held that a purchaser of a house under construction was entitled to an implied warranty of habitability, but not if the house had been completed. Until around 1960, the United States followed the same rules. Jeff Sovern, "Toward a Theory of Warranties in the Sale of New Homes: Housing the Implied Warranty Advocates, Law and Economics Mavens, and Consumer Psychologists," 1993 Wis. L. Rev. 13, 20. After that period, a number of courts extended the implied warranty of habitability to completed homes. Howard Belser, "Caveat Emptor—Purchase From Builder-Vendor Implied Warranty of Fitness and Habitability," 3 Cum.-Samford L. Rev. 216 (1972). The warranty does not have a consistent title and is often referred to as involving skillful construction that may extend the warranty in some cases beyond mere habitability, although much depends upon the scope of the meaning of the term "habitability." See Timothy Davis, "The Illusive Warranty of Workmanlike Performance: Constructing a Conceptual Framework," 72 Neb. L. Rev. 981 (1993). With the explosion of cases in the 1970s and variable nature of the scope of the warranty, in 1975 the National Conference of Commissioners on Uniform State Laws adopted the Uniform Land Transactions Act. Section 2–309 of that Act basically stated an implied warranty of habitability and skillful construction that could not be entirely eliminated by agreement. See Barbara J. Britzke, "Residential Real Estate Transactions: A Comparison of the Uniform Land Transactions Act and Maryland Law," 13 U. Balt. L. Rev. 43 (1983). Many states have adopted versions of the Act. Lenders involved in the construction process may also incur liability under the warranty. See "Banks: Implied Warranty of Liability," 36–SEP Real Est. L. Rep. 6 (2006).

In response to the growing accountability trend for construction defects, the warranty of "habitability" began to stretch, perhaps illogically. In *Reed v. King*, 145 Cal.App. 3d 261, 193 Cal.Rptr. 130 (1983), a California court determined that the failure to disclose a bloody past of a residence (e.g., site of a heinous murder) could be a misrepresentation sustaining an equitable action for rescission. Later, in *Stambovsky v. Ackley*, 169 A.D.2d 254, 572 N.Y.S.2d 672 (1991), a New York court determined that the failure to disclose that a house was "haunted" was grounds for rescission. As a result of such decisions, a number of states have adopted legislation codifying the doctrine of *caveat emptor* involving the sale of real estate, severing buyer remedies based on allegations that the house was the site of a murder, felony, or suicide, or in some cases, that it was the abode of a person who had or died from AIDS. See Daniel M. Warner, "Caveat Spiritus: A Jurisprudential Reflection Upon the Law of Haunted Houses and Ghosts," 28 Val. L. Rev. 207 (1993). While nationally, real estate brokers generally have a positive fiduciary duty to disclose material defects that impact the value of property, the required disclosure of the health of the previous owner or occupant is understandably more suspect. See Ross R. Hartog, Note, "The Psychological Impact of AIDS on Real Property and a Real Estate Broker's Duty to Disclose," 36 Ariz. L. Rev. 757 (1994).

b. Warranty Disclaimers

Sellers exercise advance contractual control over ultimate liability for potential later breaches of warranties in two important but essentially distinct fashions. The seller can attempt to eliminate the warranty promise itself in the contract of sale, the subject of this section. Sellers can also use the contract of sale to limit the extent of liability arising from a warranty not effectively eliminated in the contract. The subject of contractual limitation on liability is covered in the damages chapter, while this section considers the requirements and limitations associated with contractual waivers, disclaimers, and eliminations of warranties. See Russel J. Weintraub, "Disclaimer of Warranties and Limitation of Damages Under the UCC," 53 Tex. L. Rev. 60 (1974).

Importantly, warranty disclaimers are mostly a matter of state law, and, therefore, the particular provisions of the common law and UCC usually control. But federal law also plays a modest role in limiting or qualifying the role of contractual elimination of warranties. For example, the Magnuson-Moss provisions of the Federal Trade Commission Improvement Act place limits on the types of disclaimers a seller may use to disclaim implied warranties. Mostly, Magnuson-Moss requires specific disclosure requirements that apply to written express warranties supplemented by various consumer remedies triggered by the failure to properly disclose. In many instances, Magnuson-Moss also provides for the recovery of attorney fees as is common under most consumer protection and deceptive trade practices statutes. See Barkley Clark & Michael J. Davis, "Beefing Up Product Warranties: A New Dimension in Consumer Protection," 23 Kan. L. Rev. 567 (1975); Kurt A. Strasser, "Magnuson-Moss Warranty Act: An Overview and Comparison with UCC Coverage, Disclaimer, and Remedies in Consumer Warranties," 27 Mercer L. Rev. 1111 (1976); and Donald F. Clifford, Jr., "Non-UCC Statutory Provisions Affecting Warranty Disclaimers and Remedies in Sales of Goods," 71 N.C.L. Rev. 1011 (1993).

UCC warranty disclaimer provisions are arranged according to the type of warranty. There are separate rules and requirements for the disclaimers to be effective for express warranties (UCC § 2–316(1)) and for implied warranties of merchantability and fitness for a particular purpose (UCC § 2–316(2)). Somewhat confusingly, UCC § 2–316(3) provides special words such as "as is" that have the same effect even where the details of the prior subsections are not otherwise satisfied. Importantly, and as discussed in more detail in the previous section regarding good faith, UCC § 1–302(a) (2001) provides that the provisions of the UCC may be varied by agreement unless otherwise provided in the UCC itself. Consequently, express and implied warranties created by the UCC may be eliminated subject only to express limitations stated on such contractual disclaimers.

There are two similar but different problems considered below. First, what result obtains when an express warranty is made verbally or in the sale contract, but the contract also disclaims any express warranty? The verbal express warranty raises questions regarding the parol evidence rule, whereas the written warranty disclaimed in the same document raises an issue of internal documentary inconsistency. In such cases, which prevails—the warranty or the disclaimer? This issue is normally controlled by the application of UCC § 2–316. The second problem is broader and involves internal inconsistencies among the various warranties. This issue normally occurs where the seller makes an express warranty, but does not properly disclaim the implied warranties of merchantability and fitness for a particular purpose. This issue is normally controlled by the application of UCC § 2–317.

Where the express warranty and implied warranties cannot be read consistently and cumulatively, the court must determine which warranty prevails. To solve this conundrum, UCC § 2–317 establishes a three-tier approach. First, UCC § 2–317(c) provides that the express warranty displaces an inconsistent implied warranty of merchantability, but not the implied warranty of fitness for a particular purpose. Accordingly, the inconsistent implied warranty of merchantability is preempted by the express warranty, even when the express warranty is far more narrow than that the goods are fit for the ordinary purposes for which such goods are used. This result normally occurs when the express warranty provides a specific warranty in lieu of all "other warranties," but fails properly to disclaim merchantability under the rules of UCC § 2–316(2) that require the disclaimer to be conspicuous, if in writing, and to mention the term merchantability, or alternatively, under UCC § 2–316(3)(a) to state the product is essentially sold "as is" (which it is not because of the express warranty).

The implied warranty of fitness for a particular purpose is not disclaimed by an inconsistent express warranty. See UCC § 2–317(c). In these cases, the warranty that usually survives is the one that is more explicit, under the assumption that that warranty more properly reflects the objective reliance of the buyer. As a result, exact or technical specifications generally overrule inconsistent samples or models. See UCC §§ 2–317(a)–(b).

Implied Warranties. Contractual disclaimer of the implied warranties of merchantability and fitness for a particular purpose is permissible but must follow one of two alternative pathways under UCC §§ 2–316(2)–(3). The easiest alternative is for the contract simply to state that the goods are sold "as is," "with all faults," or other similar language that makes plain to a consumer that there are no implied warranties. UCC § 2–316(3)(a). Such terms make clear to the consumer that the buyer takes the entire risk with regard to the quality of the goods. UCC § 2–316, *cmt. 7.* Both implied warranties may also be eliminated or "modified" by course of dealing, course of performance, and trade usage. UCC § 2–316(3)(c).

The other alternative involves more specificity. In order to exclude or modify the implied warranty of merchantability under this test, the language of the disclaimer must mention the term "merchantability" and, in the case of a written disclaimer, must be conspicuous. UCC § 2–316(3)(a). Like merchantability, a disclaimer of the warranty of fitness for a particular purpose must be conspicuous, but unlike merchantability, this implied warranty can only be disclaimed in a written document.

Finally, even though the contract itself does not specifically disclaim any implied warranty, both will be eliminated as to defects that have been or could have been revealed from the buyer's inspection of the goods or a sample. UCC § 2–316(3)(b). The examination or refusal to examine must occur before, not after, the goods are purchased. Moreover, in order to invoke the refusal to examine consequence, the seller must specifically demand that the buyer inspect the goods. Simply making the goods available for inspection will not suffice. UCC § 2–316, *cmt. 8.* However, the limits of inspection are not infinite as explained by the following comment:

> Application of the doctrine of "caveat emptor" in all cases where the buyer examines the goods regardless of statements made by the seller is, however, rejected by this Article. Thus, if the offer of examination is accompanied by words as to their merchantability or specific attributes and the buyer indicates clearly that he is relying on those words rather than on his examination, they give rise to an "express" warranty.

Express Warranties. The disclaimer of express warranties is understandably infinitely more difficult than the disclaimer of implied warranties because, logically speaking, the disclaimer contradicts the making of the warranty in the first instance. Of course, when the disclaimer and the warranty can be viewed consistently, that will be the case. UCC § 2–316(1). When that is not the case, the express warranty prevails over the disclaimer.

An important exception exists to this basic and fundamental rule. A parenthetical within the statutory provision provides that the invalid disclaimer rule is subject to the parol evidence rule stated in UCC § 2–202. UCC § 2–316(1). Consequently, if an express oral warranty precedes or is contemporaneous with the execution a written sales contract that contains a disclaimer of all warranties express or implied, admissibility of evidence to prove the making of the express warranty will depend upon the operation of the parol evidence rule. If the sales contract is completely integrated, the evidence will not be admitted. UCC § 2–202. The evidence could be admitted if the contract is only partially integrated, but not to contradict any term of the contract. UCC § 2–202(b). Since the oral warranty would contradict the later written disclaimer, absent some other parol evidence exception, the admissibility of evidence of the oral warranty is problematic. The situation is even more problematic when the contract reflects a well-drafted merger clause declaring the sale contract a final expression of all terms. Thus, unless some exception exists, such as admitting the evidence of the oral warranty to prove fraud on the part of the seller, the parol evidence rule will grant greater dignity to the written disclaimer than the oral warranty. See UCC § 1–103(b) (2001) (incorporating common law parol evidence exceptions such as fraud).

The following case presents an analysis of the situation where both the warranty and the disclaimer are stated in the same written contract. The parol evidence rule is ordinarily not implicated in such cases.

CONSOLIDATED DATA TERMINALS V. APPLIED DIGITAL DATA SYSTEMS, INC.

United States Court of Appeals, Ninth Circuit
708 F.2d 385 (1983)

Fletcher, Circuit Judge:

Applied Digital Data Systems, Inc. (ADDS), a manufacturer, appeals from a district court judgment for $585,489.61 entered against it and in favor of Consolidated Data Terminals (CDT), a distributor, for damages arising from transactions involving computer terminals . . . . We affirm the district court's conclusion that ADDS was liable to CDT for compensatory damages based on breach of contractual warranty. . . .

BACKGROUND

ADDS is a manufacturer of computer equipment, including cathode-ray computer terminals (CRT's). CDT distributes such terminals in California. In December, 1976, ADDS and CDT entered into a written distributorship agreement that made CDT a non-exclusive sales outlet for ADDS terminals. Under the agreement, ADDS promised to accept CDT purchase orders according to a fixed schedule of prices, while CDT promised to use "best efforts" to promote the lease and sale of ADDS products. CDT further promised to refrain from selling any other terminals deemed "competitive" by ADDS. Paragraph 2 of the contract provided that it was subject to cancellation by either party at any time upon 90-day notice. Paragraph 22 contained a merger clause stating in effect that no agreements between the parties existed outside of the written agreement, and specified that New York law would govern the agreement. The terms of this distributorship agreement were incorporated by reference into the sales contracts covering every item of equipment sold by ADDS to CDT.

For a time, relations between ADDS and CDT were satisfactory. But in late 1977, CDT ordered for the first time some of ADDS's newest and supposedly most advanced terminals, the Regent 100's. In written specifications, ADDS stated that these rather inexpensive CRT's would operate at the relatively high speed of 19,200 baud (1920 characters per second). In promotional literature, ADDS also claimed that the Regents would be "inherently reliable." In fact, as it turned out, none of the Regent 100 terminals was capable of attaining the 19,200 baud performance rate. Also, the Regent 100's were plagued by design errors and production problems that caused many of them to malfunction seriously. The district court found that "as many as 25%" were totally inoperative upon delivery. "When introduced, the terminals did not operate properly at any level above 4,800 baud and occasionally did not operate properly at 1,200 baud." CDT received a steady stream of complaints and returns from the customers to whom it distributed Regent 100's.

When informed of the problems with the Regent 100 terminals, ADDS attempted to perform its warranty obligations. ADDS distributed "releases" with proposed solutions for specific problems encountered with the terminals, established a repair depot where CDT customers could ship the defective equipment for service, and on one occasion, sent a special team of engineers to customer sites to work on the malfunctioning terminals. As a result of these efforts, all or most of the Regent 100's became functional within a year after the first terminal deliveries, but these terminals never operated at rates approaching 19,200 baud. According to testimony by a former ADDS salesman, the specifications on the Regent 100 model were eventually lowered to 1,900 baud.

Due in part to the continuing problems with Regent terminals, CDT discontinued efforts to sell Regent 100 terminals to its customers. For several months, CDT placed no additional orders for Regents. But in June, 1978, Intel Co., a large user of computer terminals, asked for bids to supply 127 Regent terminals and other computer equipment. ADDS, which had previously sold Regents directly to Intel, submitted a bid to supply terminals for the order. CDT submitted a bid to fill the entire order, including other equipment in addition to the Regent terminals. Upon receiving the initial bids, Intel informed CDT that its bid was successful because it was lowest, and notified ADDS that its bid was too high. Afterwards, ADDS learned the amount of CDT's bid on the terminals, lowered its asking price, and was awarded the final contract to supply the terminals. CDT was awarded the contract to supply the remainder of the equipment specified in the bid. When it learned of the ADDS-Intel terminal contract, CDT ceased dealing with ADDS. It entered into a new agreement to distribute terminals made by Hazeltine, another manufacturer whose products CDT could not previously sell under the ADDS distributorship agreement, since ADDS deemed Hazeltine terminals to be "competitive" with its models. Later, in 1979, CDT entered into another such agreement with Televideo, another "competitive" concern. CDT enjoyed considerable success selling these terminals, and also increased its sales of Lear-Siegler CRT products, which it had been permitted to sell under the ADDS distributorship agreement.

In December, 1978, CDT filed this diversity action against ADDS, alleging several breaches of contract, breach of an implied covenant of good faith and fair dealing, unlawful interference with prospective business advantage, and fraud in the inducement to enter the distributorship agreement. ADDS answered and counterclaimed against CDT for $68,117.17, the unpaid balance owed by CDT to ADDS upon terminals delivered to CDT. Upon ADDS's motion before trial, District Judge Spencer Williams dismissed the breach of covenant of good faith and fair dealing cause of action. CDT's other claims were tried before District Judge Daniel H. Thomas. On the third day of the four-day bench trial, CDT was permitted to amend its complaint to add new claims for fraud and negligence by ADDS in its design, manufacture, and sale of Regent 100 terminals.[2]

At the close of trial, the district court concluded that ADDS had breached its warranties contained in the sales contracts governing the Regent 100 terminals that it sold to CDT. The court ruled that the purported limitation on remedies contained in the distributorship agreement did not absolve ADDS from either direct or consequential damages stemming from this breach. The court also found that ADDS had negligently designed and sold the Regent 100 line of terminals, fraudulently representing that they were "inherently reliable" while knowing that the Regent terminals it had already sold were experiencing operational problems. Finally, the court ruled that ADDS, by submitting its second, lower bid to Intel, tortiously interfered with CDT's economic

---

[2]   CDT's original complaint alleged that ADDS had fraudulently induced CDT to enter the distributorship agreement by promising to provide CDT with sales leads, a promise that it never intended to perform and did not perform. Although considerable evidence concerning this issue was introduced at trial, the district court denied recovery on this claim.

The new fraud claim introduced by CDT during trial was distinct, since it related not to alleged misrepresentations concerning the distributorship agreement, but to misrepresentations concerning specific CRT's sold by ADDS to CDT.

relationship with Intel. Consolidated Data Terminals v. Applied Digital Data Systems, Inc., 512 F. Supp. 581, 586–87 (N. D. Cal. 1981).

By way of damages, the court found that CDT had incurred $15,000.00 in expenses and lost sales time because of the services it had provided customers who had bought defective Regent terminals. The court also concluded that ADDS's breaches of warranty caused the termination of the ADDS-CDT distributorship agreement. Absent the Regent controversy, the court reasoned, CDT would have continued to realize profits through 1980 on sales of ADDS products. Therefore, the court awarded the projected profits on these sales as consequential damages in the amount of $11,842.50. Further, the court refused to deduct profits earned by CDT on sales of Hazeltine and Televideo equipment between 1978 and 1980 in mitigation of these damages, since it found that this equipment was not "in actuality" competitive with ADDS terminals. Next, the court found that CDT would have realized a profit of $266 on each of the 127 terminals it should have sold to Intel, and awarded $28,702.00 in compensatory tort damages. Finally, the court found that ADDS's "fraudulent conduct and wrongful interference with CDT's advantageous economic relationship with Intel was in knowing and conscious disregard of CDT's rights and interests," and awarded CDT punitive damages of $500,000.00. Id. at 587–88.

From the total liability of $655,544.50 imposed upon ADDS, the court subtracted $70,054.89 to satisfy ADDS's counterclaim. The district court accordingly entered judgment for CDT in the amount of $585,489.61.

Pursuant to Federal Rule of Civil Procedure 59(a), ADDS filed a motion requesting the district court to amend its judgment. ADDS specifically objected to the finding of liability for tortious interference, arguing that a business is always free to "interfere" with negotiations of a competitor by lowering its bid. The district court responded by entering an amended finding that an actual contract had been formed between CDT and Intel before ADDS lowered its bid on the 127 Regent terminals. It ruled that since "competition" for the bid had already ended when ADDS submitted its revised bid, the submission constituted an unlawful interference with contract.

ADDS appeals from this ruling and from the original judgment of the district court. CDT cross-appeals from the dismissal of its claim for breach of covenant of good faith and fair dealing.

DISCUSSION

A. BREACH OF WARRANTY.

The evidence adduced at trial revealed no substantial dispute concerning the quality of the Regent 100 terminals sold by ADDS to CDT.

The terminals were poorly designed, and failed to perform according to specifications. The specifications represented that the Regent 100's would operate at a speed of 19,200 baud; because CDT relied on the specifications when ordering the terminals, this statement constituted an express warranty.[4] In fact, none of the terminals ever operated at 19,200 baud, and the specification on the terminal was ultimately reduced to 1,900 baud, less than one-tenth the speed originally promised. This by itself supports the district court's conclusion that ADDS breached a warranty covering the Regent 100 terminals it sold. We affirm that ruling.

ADDS contends that even if the Regent 100's failed to perform as promised, the warranty disclaimer clause incorporated into each Regent 100 contract negatives any other ADDS promise contained in oral or written descriptions of the goods or in promotional literature. Paragraph 6 of the "Terms and Conditions" incorporated into each terminal sale states that "ADDS makes no warranty, express or implied,"[5] other than a ninety-day guarantee covering materials and workmanship. We do not need to consider whether the Regent problems constituted defects in "materials" or "workmanship" because we conclude that the disclaimer cannot be permitted to override the highly particularized warranty created by the specifications.

Where a contract includes both specific warranty language and a general disclaimer of warranty liability, the former prevails over the latter where the two cannot be reasonably reconciled. N.Y. U.C.C. § 2–316(1) (McKinney's 1964). According to the New York Court of Appeals:

> An attempt to both warrant and refuse to warrant goods creates an ambiguity which can only be resolved by making one term yield to the other. . . . Section 2–316 (subd. [1]) of the Uniform Commercial Code provides that warranty language prevails over

---

[4]　N.Y. U.C.C. § 2–313(1)(a) (McKinney's 1964) defines an express warranty to include "[a]ny affirmation of fact or promise made by the seller to the buyer which relates to the goods and becomes part of the basis of the bargain."

[5]　The provision stated in full that:

6.　　WARRANTY

ADDS warrants each new communications and terminal product manufactured by it to be free from defects in material and workmanship under normal use and service for a period of 90 days from the date of shipment. ADDS' sole obligation under this warranty is limited to making good, at its factory, any product or any part or parts thereof found to be defective, provided the buyer bears the cost of shipping charges in connection with the repair or replacement of the defective equipment.

ADDS MAKES NO WARRANTY, EXPRESS OR IMPLIED; AND ANY IMPLIED WARRANTY OF MERCHANTABILITY OR OF FITNESS FOR A PARTICULAR PURPOSE WHICH EXCEEDS THE FOREGOING WARRANTY IS HEREBY DISCLAIMED BY ADDS AND EXCLUDED FROM ANY AGREEMENT MADE BY ACCEPTANCE OF ANY ORDER PURSUANT TO THIS AGREEMENT. ADDS will not be liable for any consequential damages, loss or expense arising in connection with the use of or the inability to use its products or goods for any purpose whatsoever. ADDS' maximum liability shall not in any case exceed the contract price for the products.

the disclaimer, if the two cannot be reasonably reconciled. Wilson Trading Corp. v. David Ferguson, Ltd., 23 N.Y. 2d 398, 405, 244 N.E.2d 685, 689, 297 N.Y.S. 2d 108, 113 (1968) (citation omitted).

Thus, we conclude that the express statements warranting that the Regent 100's would perform at a 19,200 baud rate prevail over the general warranty disclaimer, and properly formed the basis for CDT's breach of warranty action.

* * *

AFFIRMED in part, REVERSED in part, and REMANDED in part.

NOTES AND QUESTIONS

1.   *Express warranty and disclaimer.* The ADDS written specifications regarding the Regent 100 CRT terminals stated that the baud rate was 19.2 kbps, and separate promotional literature stated that the terminals were "inherently reliable." In fact, neither expression was in accord with the facts. Do either or both the expressions constitute an "express" warranty under UCC § 2–313? If so, why? Each contract of sale for terminals stated, "ADDS makes no warranty, express or implied" with regard to the terminals. Were both the warranties and disclaimer contained in the same document? Notice that the terms of the distributorship agreement were incorporated by reference into every sales contract. If so, why was the warranty disclaimer ineffective under UCC § 2–316(1)? If not in the same document (expanded to include those incorporated by reference), should the court have considered whether evidence of the warranties was admissible under the parol evidence rule? If so, would CDT have likely prevailed under its breach of warranty claim? Did this contract reflect a merger clause? What should be the effect of such a clause under the parol evidence rules as applied to written disclaimers preceded by prior express oral warranties?

2.   *Combined effect of warranty and disclaimer in same contract.* UCC § 2–316(1) stating rules regarding the disclaimer of warranties obviously applies only when there is an express warranty. Should it be possible to read a contract as a whole, combine the effect of the warranty and disclaimer together, and conclude that no warranty was made? Did the court consider this approach? The purpose of allowing the warranty to prevail over the disclaimer, assuming a warranty exists, is to protect a buyer from "unexpected and unbargained" language of an inconsistent disclaimer. UCC § 2–316, *cmt. 1.* If the buyer is aware of both the warranty and the disclaimer, would a reasonable buyer conclude that a warranty had been made? If not, is the purpose of the invalid disclaimer well served by eliminating the disclaimer? Would a reasonable person simply conclude no warranty at all was made? See U.S. Fibres, Inc. v. Proctor & Schwartz, Inc., 509 F.2d 1043 (6th Cir. 1975) (court read the warranty and disclaimer together to conclude no warranty was actually made).

D. INSURANCE CONTRACTS

Insurance contracts present special problems for contract law. The insurer always drafts such contracts as standard forms, and these standard form insurance contracts are presented to the consumer on a take-it-or-leave-it basis without opportunity for negotiation. This makes the insurance contract a paradigmatic example of a *contract of adhesion*. These two features invoke related but yet doctrinally separate matters. First, the doctrine of *contra proferentem,* construes any "ambiguity" against the drafter, as described in Restatement (Second) of Contracts § 206 (continuing the rule in Restatement (First) of Contracts § 236(d)):

§ 206. Interpretation Against The Draftsman

In choosing among the reasonable meanings of a promise or agreement or a term thereof, that meaning is generally preferred which operates against the party who supplies the words or from whom a writing otherwise proceeds.

This doctrine has its most common application in insurance contracts. See Restatement (Second) of Contracts § 206 *cmt. b* (noting "insurers are more likely than the insured party to participate in drafting prescribed forms and to review them carefully before putting them into use").

Of course, the doctrine is not limited to insurance contracts and reaches other standardized or boilerplate language. Michelle E. Boardman, "*Contra Proferentem*: The Allure of Ambiguous Boilerplate," 104 Mich. L. Rev. 1105 (2006). But in contrast to general contracts—where courts do not universally or strictly apply *contra proferentem*, especially in cases involving relatively equal bargaining power—courts commonly apply the doctrine strictly in insurance contracts. See James M. Fischer, "Why Are Insurance Contracts Subject to Special Rules of Interpretation?: Text Versus Context," 24 Ariz. St. L. J. 995, 1002 (1992); Eugene R. Anderson & James J. Fournier, "Why Courts Enforce Insurance Policyholders' Objectively Reasonable Expectations of Insurance Coverage," 5 Conn. Ins. L. J. 335 (1998). In any case of ambiguity in an insurance contract, courts nearly universally resolve the ambiguity against the insurance company regardless of the equality of the bargaining power of the insured.

Like many doctrines, this one also has its critics. See Michael B. Rappaport, "The Ambiguity Rule and Insurance Law: Why Insurance Contracts Should Not Be Construed Against The Drafter," 30 Ga. L. Rev. 171 (1995) and David S. Miller, Note, "Insurance as Contract: The Argument for Abandoning the Ambiguity Doctrine," 88 Colum. L. Rev. 1849 (1988).

Second, even in the absence of an ambiguity, the Restatement (Second) of Contracts § 201(2)(b) provides, in essence, that an insured's meaning will control over the insurance company meaning where (1) the insured had no reason to know of the insurance company's meaning; and (2) the insurance company did have reason to know of the insured's reasonable objective understanding. An early pioneering article on the interpretation of insurance contracts contended that disparate bargaining power and the adhesive (non-negotiable) nature of such contracts justified judicial imposition of the doctrine now normatively regarded as the "doctrine of reasonable expectations:" "The objectively reasonable expectations of applicants and intended beneficiaries regarding the terms of insurance contracts will be honored even though painstaking study of the policy provisions would have negated those expectation." Robert E. Keeton, "Insurance Law Rights at Variance with Policy Provisions," 83 Harv. L. Rev. 961, 967 (1970).

The doctrine was adopted by Restatement (Second) of Contracts § 211(2) considering the proper interpretation of standardized agreements, like insurance contracts: "Such a writing [a standardized agreement] is interpreted wherever reasonable as treating alike all those similarly situated, without regard to their knowledge or understanding of the standard terms of the writing." Comment e provides in relevant part:

> One who assents to standard contract terms normally assumes that others are doing likewise and that all who do so are on an equal footing. . . . Apart from governmental regulation, courts in construing and applying a standardized contract seek to effectuate the *reasonable expectations* of the average member of the public who accepts it. The result may be to give the advantage of a restrictive reading to some sophisticated customers who contracted with knowledge of an ambiguity or dispute. [Emphasis Added].

Likewise, Restatement (Second) of Contracts § 211(3) excludes terms from an agreement if the insurance company has reason to know that the insured would not accept the contract if the insured was aware of the provision. Some consider the restatement view of the doctrine of reasonable expectations as more narrow than originally envisioned by Professor Keeton. Roger C. Henderson, "The Doctrine of Reasonable Expectations in Insurance Law After Two Decades," 51 Ohio St. L. J. 823, 846–847 (1990) (doctrine only triggered where the insurance company has reason to believe the insured would not accept the term) and Roger C. Henderson, "The Formulation of the Doctrine of Reasonable Expectations and the Influence of Forces Outside Insurance Law," 5 Conn. Ins. L. J. 69, 76 (1998).

As to be expected, the reasonable expectations doctrine has been controversial collecting considerable support and less dissent. Compare William A. Mayhew, "Reasonable Expectations: Seeking a Principled Application," 13 Pepp. L. Rev. 267 (1986) and Mark C. Rahdert, "Reasonable Expectations Reconsidered," 18 Conn. L. Rev. 323 (1986); with

Stephen J. Ware, Comment, "A Critique of the Reasonable Expectations Doctrine," 56 U. Chi. L. Rev. 1461 (1989). Because of the importance of the doctrine and the volume of scholarly commentary, an important empirical study was undertaken to determine whether the doctrine was widely adopted and concluded that nearly half the states had adopted it, and, at that time, only Idaho had rejected it. Roger C. Henderson, "The Doctrine of Reasonable Expectations in Insurance Law After Two Decades,"51 Ohio St. L. J. 823 (1990).

ATWATER CREAMERY CO. v. WESTERN NAT'L MUTUAL INS. CO.

Supreme Court of Minnesota
366 N.W.2D 271 (Minn. 1985)

WAHL, Justice.

Atwater Creamery Company (Atwater) sought a declaratory judgment against its insurer, Western National Mutual Insurance Company (Western), seeking coverage for losses sustained during a burglary of the creamery's storage building. Atwater joined Strehlow Insurance Agency and Charles Strehlow (Strehlow), its agent, as defendants, seeking damages in the alternative due to Strehlow's alleged negligence and misrepresentation. The Kandiyohi County District Court granted a directed verdict for Strehlow because Atwater failed to establish an insurance agent's standard of care by expert testimony. The trial court then dismissed the jury for lack of disputed issues of fact and ordered judgment in favor of the insurer, concluding that the burglary insurance policy in effect defined burglary so as to exclude coverage of this burglary. We affirm the directed verdict for Strehlow but reverse as to the policy coverage.

Atwater does business as a creamery and as a supplier of farm chemicals in Atwater, Minnesota. It was insured during the time in question against burglary, up to a ceiling of $20,000, by Western under Merchantile Open Stock Burglary Policy SC10–1010–12, which contained an "evidence of forcible entry" requirement in its definition of burglary. The creamery had recovered small amounts under this policy for two separate burglaries prior to the events in this case.

Atwater built a separate facility, called the Soil Center, a few blocks away from its main plant in 1975 for the purpose of storing and selling chemicals. The Soil Center is a large rectangular building with two regular doors along the north side and two large, sliding doors, one each on the east and west sides. There are no other entrances or exits to or from the building itself. One of the doors on the north side leads into the office in the northwest corner of the building. It is secured by a regular dead bolt lock, opened with a key. There is no access into the main portion of the building from the office. Persons entering the main area must use the other door on the north side which is secured by a padlock after hours. The large sliding doors on the east and west are secured by large hasps on each side of each door which are held tight by turnbuckles that must be loosened before the doors can be opened.

Inside the main area of the building, along the north wall, is a large storage bin with three separate doors, each of which is secured by a padlock. Between the storage bin and the office is an "alleyway," entered through the large sliding doors, which runs east and west the length of the building. Trucks are stored in the alleyway when not in use.

Sometime between 9:30 p.m., Saturday, April 9, and 6 a.m., Monday, April 11, 1977, one or more persons made unauthorized entry into the building, took chemicals worth $15,587.40, apparently loading them on the truck that had been parked inside and driving away after loosening the turnbuckles on the east door and closing it. The truck was later found parked near the town dump, with the key still in the ignition.

Larry Poe, the plant manager at the Soil Center, had left at 9:30 p.m. on Saturday, after making sure everything was properly secured. On Monday morning, the north side doors were locked securely, but two of the three doors to the storage bin were ajar. Their padlocks were gone and never found. The turnbuckles had been loosened on the east sliding door so that it could be easily opened or closed.

An investigation by the local police, the Kandiyohi County Sheriff's Department, and the Minnesota Bureau of Criminal Investigation determined that no Atwater Creamery employees, past or present, were involved in the burglary. Suspicion settled on persons wholly unconnected with the creamery or even with the local area, but no one has been apprehended or charged with the crime.

Atwater filed a claim with Western under the burglary policy. Western denied coverage because there were no visible marks of physical damage to the exterior at the point of entrance or to the interior at the point of exit, as required by the definition of burglary in the policy. The creamery then brought suit against Western for the $15,587.40 loss, $7,500 in other directly related business losses and costs, disbursements and reasonable attorney fees.

Charles H. Strehlow, the owner of the Strehlow Insurance Agency in Willmar, Minnesota, and Western's agent, testified that he is certain he mentioned the evidence-of-forcible-entry requirement to Poe and members of the Atwater Board of Directors but was unable to say when the discussion occurred. Poe and the board members examined do not remember any such discussion. None of the board members had read the policy, which is kept in the safe at the main plant, and Poe had not read it in its entirety. He stated that he started to read it but gave up because he could not understand it.

The issues on appeal are:

1. whether the conformity clause in the policy operates to substitute the statutory definition of the crime of burglary for the definition of burglary in the policy; [and]

2. whether the reasonable expectations of the insured as to coverage govern to defeat the literal language of the policy. . . .

1. CONFORMITY CLAUSE.

Atwater argues that the conformity clause in the burglary insurance policy operates to substitute the statutory definition of burglary for the policy definition. The conformity clause reads:

14. Terms of Policy Conformed to Statute. Terms of this policy which are in conflict with the statutes of the State wherein this policy is issued are hereby amended to conform to such statutes.

The burglary definition in the policy reads:

[T]he felonious abstraction of insured property (1) from within the premises by a person making felonious entry therein by actual force and violence, of which force and violence there are visible marks made by tools, explosives, electricity or chemicals upon, or physical damage to, the exterior of the premises at the place of such entry, or * * * (3) from within the premises by a person making felonious exit therefrom by actual force and violence as evidenced by visible marks made by tools, explosives, electricity or chemicals upon, or physical damage to, the interior of the premises at the place of such exit.

Minnesota Statutes § 609.58, subd. 2 (1982), reads:

Whoever enters a building without the consent of the person in lawful possession, * * * with intent to commit a crime in it, or whoever remains within a building without the consent of the person in lawful authority, with intent to commit a crime in it, commits burglary.

The question is whether the two definitions actually conflict with each other. We conclude that they do not.

The statutory definition of burglary operates to impose criminal sanctions on those whose acts fall within its purview. The purpose of the policy definition, however, is to limit the risk the insurer is willing to underwrite. There is no reason an insurer must necessarily define terms in its contracts in the same manner as a statute that exists for an entirely different purpose. We do not agree, however, with the insurer's argument that a conformity clause operates to substitute statutory provisions for policy provisions only where the statute is one that directly regulates insurance. *Maryland Casualty Co. v. American Lumber & Wrecking Co.,* 204 Minn. 43, 282 N.W. 806 (1938), cited by Western to support its argument, merely stands for the proposition that where there is a statute regulating the insurance industry, the industry must conform to that statute. We hold that an insurance policy provision must be in direct conflict with a statute before a conformity clause operates to substitute the statutory provisions for the policy provision. It makes no difference whether the statute is one regulating insurance.

An insurer may limit the risks against which it is willing to indemnify the insured. The policy definition of burglary is different and more limited than the criminal statute definition, but there is no conflict between the two given their disparate functions. The difference between the two, however, has a bearing on the insured's reasonable expectations in purchasing burglary insurance.

2. APPLICATION OF THE POLICY DEFINITION OF BURGLARY.

The definition of burglary in this policy is one used generally in burglary insurance. Courts have construed it in different ways. It has been held ambiguous and construed in favor of coverage in the absence of visible marks of forceable entry or exit. . . . We reject this analysis because we view the definition in the policy as clear and precise. It is not ambiguous.

In determining the intent of the parties to the insurance contract, courts have looked to the purpose of the visible-marks-of-forcible-entry requirement. These purposes are two: to protect insurance companies from fraud by way of "inside jobs" and to encourage insureds to reasonably secure the premises. *See* 5 Appleman § 3176 at 517. As long as the theft involved clearly neither an inside job nor the result of a lack of secured premises, some courts have simply held that the definition does not apply. . . .

In the instant case, there is no dispute as to whether Atwater is attempting to defraud Western or whether the Soil Center was properly secured. The trial court found that the premises were secured before the robbery and that the law enforcement investigators had determined that it was not an "inside job." To enforce the burglary definition literally against the creamery will in no way effectuate either purpose behind the restrictive definition. We are uncomfortable, however, with this analysis given the right of an insurer to limit the risk against which it will indemnify insureds.

At least three state courts have held that the definition merely provides for one form of evidence which may be used to prove a burglary and that, consequently, other evidence of a burglary will suffice to provide coverage. *Ferguson v. Phoenix Assurance Co. of New York,* 189 Kan. 459, 370 P.2d 379 (1962); *National Surety Co. v. Silberberg Bros.,* 176 S.W. 97 (Tex.Civ.App.1915); *Rosenthal v. American Bonding Co. of Baltimore,* 124 N.Y.S. 905 (N.Y.Sup.Ct.1910). The Nebraska Supreme Court recently rejected this argument in *Cochran v. MFA Mutual Insurance Co.,* 201 Neb. 631, 271 N.W.2d 331 (1978). The *Cochran* court held that the definition is not a rule of evidence but is a limit on liability, is unambiguous and is applied literally to the facts of the case at hand. We, too, reject this view of the definition as merely a form of evidence. The policy attempts to comprehensively define burglaries that are covered by it. In essence, this approach ignores the policy definition altogether and substitutes the court's or the statute's definition of burglary. This we decline to do, either via the conformity clause or by calling the policy definition merely one form of evidence of a burglary.

Some courts and commentators have recognized that the burglary definition at issue in this case constitutes a rather hidden exclusion from coverage. Exclusions in insurance contracts are read narrowly against the insurer. Running through the many court opinions refusing to literally enforce this burglary definition is the concept that the definition is surprisingly restrictive, that no one purchasing something called burglary insurance would expect coverage to exclude skilled burglaries that leave no visible marks of forcible entry or exit. Professor Robert E. Keeton, in analyzing these and other insurance cases where the results often do not follow from the rules stated, found there to be two general principles underlying many decisions. These principles are the reasonable expectations of the insured and the unconscionability of the clause itself or as applied to the facts of a specific case. *Keeton, Insurance Law Rights at Variance with Policy Provisions,* 83 Harv. L. Rev. 961 (1970). Keeton's article and subsequent book, *Basic Text on Insurance Law (*1971), have had significant impact on the construction of insurance contracts.

The doctrine of protecting the reasonable expectations of the insured is closely related to the doctrine of contracts of adhesion. Where there is unequal bargaining power between the parties so that one party controls all of the terms and offers the contract on a take-it-or-leave-it basis, the contract will be strictly construed against the party who drafted it. Most courts recognize the great disparity in bargaining power between insurance companies and those who seek insurance. Further, they recognize that, in the majority of cases, a lay person lacks the necessary skills to read and understand insurance policies, which are typically long, set out in very small type and written from a legalistic or insurance expert's perspective. Finally, courts recognize that people purchase insurance relying on others, the agent or company, to provide a policy that meets their needs. The result of the lack of insurance expertise on the part of insureds and the recognized marketing techniques of insurance companies is that "[t]he objectively reasonable expectations of applicants and intended beneficiaries regarding the terms of insurance contracts will be honored even though painstaking study of the policy provisions would have negated those expectations." Keeton, 83 Harv.L.Rev. at 967.

The traditional approach to construction of insurance contracts is to require some kind of ambiguity in the policy before applying the doctrine of reasonable expectations. Several courts, however, have adopted Keeton's view that ambiguity ought not be a condition precedent to the application of the reasonable-expectations doctrine.

As of 1980, approximately ten states had adopted the newer rule of reasonable expectations regardless of ambiguity. *Davenport Peters Co. v. Royal Globe Insurance Co.,* 490 F.Supp. 286, 291 (D.Mass.1980). Other states, such as Missouri and North Dakota, have joined the ten since then. Most courts recognize that insureds seldom see the policy until the premium is paid, and even if they try to read it, they do not comprehend it. Few courts require insureds to have minutely examined the policy before relying on the terms they expect it to have and for which they have paid.

The burglary definition is a classic example of a policy provision that should be, and has been, interpreted according to the reasonable expectations of the insured. *C & J Fertilizer, Inc. v. Allied Mutual Insurance Co.,* 227 N.W.2d 169 (Iowa 1975). *C & J Fertilizer* involved a burglary definition almost exactly like the one in the instant case as well as a burglary very similar to the Atwater burglary. The court applied the reasonable-expectations-regardless-of-ambiguity doctrine, noting that "[t]he most plaintiff might have reasonably anticipated was a policy requirement of visual evidence (abundant here) indicating the burglary was an 'outside' not an 'inside' job. The exclusion in issue, masking as a definition, makes insurer's obligation to pay turn on the skill of the burglar, not on the event the parties bargained for: a bona fide third party burglary resulting in loss of plaintiff's chemicals and equipment." *Id.* at 177. The burglary in *C & J Fertilizer* left no visible marks on the exterior of the building, but an interior door was damaged. In the instant case, the facts are very similar except that there was no damage to the interior doors; their padlocks were simply gone. In *C & J Fertilizer,* the police concluded that an "outside" burglary had occurred. The same is true here.

Atwater had a burglary policy with Western for more than 30 years. The creamery relied on Charles Strehlow to procure for it insurance suitable for its needs. There is some factual dispute as to whether Strehlow ever told Poe about the "exclusion," as Strehlow called it. Even if he had said that there was a visible-marks-of-forcible-entry requirement, Poe could reasonably have thought that it meant that there must be clear evidence of a burglary. There are, of course, fidelity bonds which cover employee theft. The creamery had such a policy covering director and manager theft. The fidelity company, however, does not undertake to insure against the risk of third-party burglaries. A business that requests and purchases burglary insurance reasonably is seeking coverage for loss from third-party burglaries whether a break-in is accomplished by an inept burglar or by a highly skilled burglar. Two other burglaries had occurred at the Soil Center, for which Atwater had received insurance proceeds under the policy. Poe and the board of the creamery could reasonably have expected the burglary policy to cover this burglary where the police, as well as the trial court, found that it was an "outside job."

The reasonable-expectations doctrine gives the court a standard by which to construe insurance contracts without having to rely on arbitrary rules which do not reflect real-life situations and without having to bend and stretch those rules to do justice in individual cases. As Professor Keeton points out, ambiguity in the language of the contract is not irrelevant under this standard but becomes a factor in determining the reasonable expectations of the insured, along with such factors as whether the insured was told of important, but obscure, conditions or exclusions and whether the particular provision in the contract at issue is an item known by the public generally. The doctrine does not automatically remove from the insured a responsibility to read the policy. It does, however, recognize that in certain instances, such as where major exclusions are hidden in the definitions section, the insured should be held only to reasonable knowledge of the literal terms and conditions. The insured may show what actual expectations he or she had, but the factfinder should determine whether those expectations were reasonable under the circumstances.

We have used the reasonable-expectations-of-the-insured analysis to provide coverage where the actual language interpreted as the insurance company intended would have proscribed coverage. *Canadian Universal Insurance Co. v. Fire Watch, Inc.,* 258 N.W.2d 570 (Minn.1977). Western correctly points out that the issue there concerned a special endorsement issued subsequent to the policy which reduced coverage without notice to the insured. While the issue is somewhat different in the instant case, it is not so different that the general concept is made inapplicable.

In our view, the reasonable-expectations doctrine does not automatically mandate either pro-insurer or pro-insured results. It does place a burden on insurance companies to communicate coverage and exclusions of policies accurately and clearly. It does require that expectations of coverage by the insured be reasonable under the circumstances. Neither of those requirements seems overly burdensome. Properly used, the doctrine will result in coverage in some cases and in no coverage in others.

We hold that where the technical definition of burglary in a burglary insurance policy is, in effect, an exclusion from coverage, it will not be interpreted so as to defeat the reasonable expectations of the purchaser of the policy. Under the facts and circumstances of this case, Atwater reasonably expected that its burglary insurance policy with Western would cover the burglary that occurred. Our holding requires reversal as to policy coverage. . . .

NOTES AND QUESTIONS

1. *Inequality of bargaining power.* The doctrine of reasonable expectations was founded upon the power imbalance created by an adhesion contract and the inequality of bargaining power between the insurance company and the insured. Should the education or sophistication of the insured play a significant role in this analysis? Does *Atwater Creamery* support in any way an ideal of freedom of contract between equals? See Daniel D. Barnhizer, "Inequality of Bargaining Power," 76 U. Colo. L. Rev. 139 (2005).

2. *The resurgence of formalism?* For several years beginning in 2003, the Michigan Supreme Court issued a series of opinions in which it has emphasized freedom of contract, certainty, and a general restriction on the discretion of judges to overturn or rewrite contracts deemed unreasonable. See, e.g., *Wilkie v. Auto-Owners Ins. Co.*, 469 Mich. 41, 664 N.W.2d 776 (2003). For example, in *Rory v. Continental Ins. Co.*, 703 N.W.2d 23 (Mich. 2005), the Michigan Supreme Court drastically curtailed the ability of judges to review contracts for unconscionability (discussed in detail in Chapter 6) on the grounds of freedom of contract:

> A fundamental tenet of our jurisprudence is that unambiguous contracts are not open to judicial construction and must be *enforced as written.* Courts enforce contracts according to their unambiguous terms because doing so respects the freedom of individuals freely to arrange their affairs via contract. . . .
>
> This approach, where judges . . . rewrite the contract . . . is contrary to the bedrock principle of American contract law that parties are free to contract as they see fit, and the courts are to enforce the agreement as written absent some highly unusual circumstance such as a contract in violation of law or public policy. . . . The notion, that free men and women may reach agreements regarding their affairs without government interference and that courts will enforce those agreements, is ancient and irrefutable. It draws strength from common-law roots and can be seen in our fundamental charter, the United States Constitution, where government is forbidden from impairing the contracts of citizens, art. I, § 10, cl. 1. Our own state constitutions over the years of statehood have similarly echoed this limitation on government power. It is, in short, an unmistakable and ineradicable part of the legal fabric of our society.

See also James F. Hogg, "Consumer Beware: The Varied Application of Unconscionability Doctrine to Exculpation and Indemnification Clauses in Michigan, Minnesota, and Washington," 2006 Mich. St. L. Rev. 1011 (analyzing *Rory*). Given this clear return to a formalist jurisprudence, what changes in contracting behavior would you expect to see between Michigan parties compared to parties contracting in a jurisdiction that had adopted the reasonable expectations doctrine? How would your presentation of a contract case change if you were arguing before a Michigan court, as opposed to a California or Iowa court? Are there any benefits to the Michigan approach?

3.   *Private autonomy and reasonable expectations.* Is the doctrine of reasonable expectations more threatening to the intent of the parties than the doctrine of *contra proferentem*? Can you see why some courts might continue to insist on some ambiguity to construe language against the insurance company? Deni Associates of Florida, Inc. v. State Farm Fire & Casualty Insurance Co., 711 So.2d 1135 (Fla. 1998).

4.   *Sources of the insured's expectations.* What determines the "reasonable expectations" of the insured? Would the insured's knowledge (or lack thereof) in any of these situations have affected the outcome of the case? If, at the time of the sale of the insurance policy in *Atwater Creamery*, the insurance agent had explained the meaning of the policy asserted by the insurance company, would that explanation have been sufficient to obviate the insured's reasonable expectations to the contrary? What if the issue of coverage limits had never been discussed by the parties in any way at the time of contracting—could the insureds still assert that reasonable expectations formed after contract formation should control?

E. THE IMPLIED OBLIGATION OF GOOD FAITH

Beyond any peradventure, contract law implies by law an obligation of good faith and fair dealing upon each party in performance and enforcement of rights and duties under a contract. Restatement (Second) of Contracts § 205. That section had no counterpart in Restatement (First) of Contracts, and yet the obligation has been a part of the law for ages. Of course, between the Restatement (First) and Restatement (Second), the Uniform Commercial Code was adopted in 1951. Not surprisingly, it reflected a remarkably similar statement: "[E]very contract or duty within [the Uniform Commercial Code] imposes an obligation of good faith in its performance or enforcement." UCC § 1–304 (2001). That same first version of the Uniform Commercial Code defined "good faith" to mean "honesty in fact and the observance of reasonable commercial standards of fair dealing." UCC § 1–201(20) (2001). Perhaps precisely because of its remarkable malleability, the phrase and doctrine has long been the "darling of draftsmen." E. Allan Farnsworth, "Good Faith Performance and Commercial Reasonableness Under the Uniform Commercial Code," 30 U. Chi. L. Rev. 666, 667 (1963). Unfortunately, malleable does not always translate to certainty, causing one famous author to muse that "good faith and the like are words to conjure with, whenever we feel like conjuring." Grant Gilmore, "The Good Faith Purchase Idea and the Uniform Commercial Code: Confessions of a Repentant Draftsman," 15 Ga. L. Rev. 605, 629 (1981). Years later, another author observed that while the doctrine was firmly implanted in law, "neither courts nor commentators have articulated an operational standard that distinguishes good faith performance from bad faith performance." Steven J. Burton, "Breach of Contract and the Common Law Duty to Perform in Good Faith," 94 Harv. L. Rev. 369 (1980). And yet, a few wrinkles have been solved.

Importantly, there is remarkable agreement that good faith is not an actionable independent duty. Instead, "good faith" operates to define the breach of a duty expressly stated in the contract:

> Having concluded that no contract exists, there can be no derivative implied covenant of good faith and fair dealing applicable to these parties. Under Massachusetts law, "[t]he covenant of good faith and fair dealing is implied in every contract." UNO Rests., Inc. v. Boston Kenmore Realty Corp., 441 Mass. 376, 805 N.E.2d 957, 964 (2004). "The covenant may not, however, create rights and duties not otherwise provided for in the existing contractual relationship, as the purpose of the covenant is to guarantee that the parties remain faithful to the intended and agreed expectations of the parties in their performance." Id. In other words, the implied covenant of good faith and fair dealing governs conduct of parties after they have entered into a contract; without a contract, there is no covenant to be breached. Where, as here, the parties have not yet reached a binding agreement, there is no duty to negotiate in good faith. See Levenson v. L.M.I. Realty Corp., 31 Mass.App.Ct. 127, 575 N.E.2d 370, 372 (1991) (rejecting the argument that where defendant stopped short of binding himself to a contract he nevertheless had a duty to negotiate the terms in good faith). Massachusetts Eye and Ear Infirmary v. QLT Phototherapeutics, Inc., 412 F.3d 215, 230 (1st Cir. 2005).

And yet over one hundred years earlier, Oliver Wendell Holmes famously remarked:

> Nowhere is the confusion between legal and moral ideas more manifest than in the law of contract. Among other things, here again the so called primary rights and duties are invested with a mystic significance beyond what can be assigned and explained. The duty to keep a contract at common law means a prediction that you must pay damages if you do not keep it,—and nothing else. Oliver Wendell Holmes, "The Path of the Law," 10 Harv. L. Rev. 457, 462 (1897).

Is contractual "good faith" a moral concept designed to punish the reason for the breach? Alternatively, does "good faith" provide a lens for determining whether a party has breached its contract duties in the first place? If the latter, and the term is implied in law, does it not serve to expand the edges of the duty and, if so, by what measurable dimension?

In an early pioneering article that influenced the inclusion of Restatement (Second) of Contracts § 205, Professor Robert S. Summers argued that there was a "growing interest in devising legal standards of contractual morality," generated in part by the early inclusion in the UCC an express obligation of good faith. Robert S. Summers, "'Good Faith' in General Contract Law and the Sales Provisions of the Uniform Commercial Code," 54 Va. L. Rev. 195 (1968). In the article, Professor Summers presents his famous argument that "good faith" is best understood as an excluder—that is, the term "good faith" has no meaning of its own, but nonetheless serves to exclude many types of commonly understood forms of "bad faith" conduct.

Arguably the standard doctrinal formulation of the good faith performance duty was articulated in a 1933 New York Court of Appeals decision as:

> In every contract there is an implied covenant that neither party shall do anything which will have the effect of destroying or injuring the right of the other party to receive the "fruits of the contract," which means that in every contract there is an implied obligation of good faith and fair dealing. Kirke La Shelle Co. v. Paul Armstrong Co., 263 N.Y. 79, 188 N.E. 163, 167 (1933).

Notice that the "fruits of the contract" analysis focuses upon the reasonable expectation of the benefit of the promise and duty to be received by proper good faith performance by the other party. This is particularly noteworthy and applicable in cases where the contract allocates discretionary decision-making authority to be exercised by one party after the contract has been formed. Without some reasonable expectation parameter, the decision maker would be free to exercise the discretion in their own favor and self-interest without regard to the expectations of the other party when the contract was formed.

Some scholars have pursued this analysis to suggest that bad faith embraces breaching behavior designed to recapture "foregone opportunities" that the breaching party reasonably understood were precluded by the contract at issue and thus allocated to the other non-breaching party. Steven J. Burton, "Breach of Contract and the Common Law Duty to Perform in Good Faith," 94 Harv. L. Rev. 369, 378 (1980). See also Steven J. Burton, "Good Faith Performance of a Contract Within Article 2 of the Uniform Commercial Code," 67 Iowa L. Rev. 1, 3 (1981) (drawing corollaries between the common law application of good faith in the multiple applications of the doctrine in UCC Article 2). Other scholars have emphasized the "opportunistic behavior" aspect of foregone opportunities. Timothy J. Muris, "Opportunistic Behavior and the Law of Contracts," 65 Minn. L. Rev. 521 (1981). Still others return to the reasonable expectations analysis of the non-breaching party based upon the express and implied terms and their context. Michael P. Van Alstine, "Of Textualism, Party Autonomy, and Good Faith," 40 Wm. & Mary L. Rev. 1223 (1999).

In the case to follow, determine if the contract allocated to the alleged breaching party a measure of discretion to be later exercised. If so, was that discretion exercised so as to recapture foregone opportunities in an opportunistic way (bad faith) or in a manner to satisfy the reasonable expectations of the non-breaching party (good faith)? If you determine that bad faith existed, determine what contractual duty was breached and a reasonable way to approach damages. For a general discussion of what every law student should know about "good faith," see generally Richard E. Speidel, "The 'Duty' of Good Faith in Contract Performance and Enforcement," 46 J. Legal Educ. 537 (1996) (top ten list for students to understand).

LOCKE V. WARNER BROS., INC.

Court of Appeals, California
57 Cal.App.4th 354, 66 Cal.Rptr.2d 921 (1997)

KLEIN, Presiding Justice.

Plaintiffs and appellants Sondra Locke (Locke) and Caritas Films, a California corporation (Caritas) (sometimes collectively referred to as Locke) appeal a judgment following a grant of summary judgment in favor of defendant and respondent Warner Bros. (Warner).

The essential issue presented is whether triable issues of material fact are present which would preclude summary judgment.

We conclude triable issues are present with respect to whether Warner breached its development deal with Locke by categorically refusing to work with her, and whether Warner fraudulently entered into said agreement without the intention to work with Locke. The judgment therefore is reversed as to the second and fourth causes of action and otherwise is affirmed.

FACTUAL AND PROCEDURAL BACKGROUND

1. *Locke's dispute with Eastwood.*

In 1975, Locke came to Warner to appear with Clint Eastwood in *The Outlaw Josey Wales*. During the filming of the movie, Locke and Eastwood began a personal and romantic relationship. For the next dozen years, they lived in Eastwood's Los Angeles and Northern California homes. Locke also appeared in a number of Eastwood's films. In 1986, Locke made her directorial debut in *Ratboy*.

In 1988, the relationship deteriorated, and in 1989 Eastwood terminated it. Locke then brought suit against Eastwood, alleging numerous causes of action. That action was resolved by a November 21, 1990 settlement agreement and mutual general release. Under said agreement, Eastwood agreed to pay Locke additional compensation in the sum of $450,000 "on account of past employment and Locke's contentions" and to convey certain real property to her.

2.   *Locke's development deal with Warner.*

According to Locke, Eastwood secured a development deal for Locke with Warner in exchange for Locke's dropping her case against him. Contemporaneously with the Locke/Eastwood settlement agreement, Locke entered into a written agreement with Warner, dated November 27, 1990. It is the Locke/Warner agreement which is the subject of the instant controversy.

The Locke/Warner agreement had two basic components. The first element states Locke would receive $250,000 per year for three years for a "non-exclusive first look deal." It required Locke to submit to Warner any picture she was interested in developing before submitting it to any other studio. Warner then had 30 days either to approve or reject a submission.

The second element of the contract was a $750,000 "pay or play" directing deal. The provision is called "pay or play" because it gives the studio a choice: it can either "play" the director by using the director's services, or pay the director his or her fee.

Unbeknownst to Locke at the time, Eastwood had agreed to reimburse Warner for the cost of her contract if she did not succeed in getting projects produced and developed. Early in the second year of the three-year contract, Warner charged $975,000 to an Eastwood film, "*Unforgiven.*"

Warner paid Locke the guaranteed compensation of $1.5 million under the agreement. In accordance with the agreement, Warner also provided Locke with an office on the studio lot and an administrative assistant. However, Warner did not develop any of Locke's proposed projects or hire her to direct any films. Locke contends the development deal was a sham, that Warner never intended to make any films with her, and that Warner's sole motivation in entering into the agreement was to assist Eastwood in settling his litigation with Locke.

3.   *Locke's action against Warner.*

On March 10, 1994, Locke filed suit against Warner, alleging four causes of action.

The first cause of action alleged sex discrimination in violation of public policy. Locke alleged Warner denied her the benefit of the bargain of the development deal on account of her gender.

The third cause of action, captioned "Tortious Breach of the Implied Covenant of Good Faith and Fair Dealing in Violation of Public Policy," alleged a similar claim. Locke pled that in denying her the benefits of the

Warner/Locke agreement, Warner was "motivated by [its] discriminatory bias against women in violation of . . . public policy."[1]

The second cause of action alleged that Warner breached the contract by refusing to consider Locke's proposed projects and thereby deprived her of the benefit of the bargain of the Warner/Locke agreement.

Lastly, the fourth cause of action alleged fraud. Locke pled that at the time Warner entered into the agreement with her, it concealed and failed to disclose it had no intention of honoring the agreement.

Warner answered, denied each and every allegation and asserted various affirmative defenses.

4.   *Warner's motion for summary judgment and opposition thereto.*

On January 6, 1995, Warner filed a motion for summary judgment. Warner contended it did not breach its contract with Locke because it did consider all the projects she presented, and the studio's decision not to put any of those projects into active development or "hand" Locke a script which it already owned was not a breach of any express or implied contractual duty. Warner asserted the odds are slim a producer can get a project into development and even slimmer a director will be hired to direct a film. During the term of Locke's deal, Warner had similar deals with numerous other producers and directors, who fared no better than Locke.

As for Locke's sex discrimination claims, Warner averred there was no evidence it ignored Locke's projects or otherwise discriminated against her on account of her gender. Finally, Warner urged the fraud claim was meritless because Locke had no evidence that when Warner signed the contract, it did not intend to honor the deal, and moreover, Warner had fulfilled its contractual obligations to Locke.

In opposing summary judgment, Locke contended Warner breached the agreement in that it had no intention of accepting any project regardless of its merits. Locke also asserted Warner committed fraud by entering into the agreement without any intention of approving any project with Locke or allowing Locke to direct another film.

Locke's opposition papers cited the deposition testimony of Joseph Terry, who recounted a conversation he had with Bob Brassel, a Warner executive, regarding Locke's projects. Terry had stated to Brassel:

> Well, Bob, this woman has a deal on the lot. She's a director that you want to work with. You have a deal with her. . . . I've got five here that she's interested in. And then I would get nothing. . . . I was told [by Brassel], Joe, we're not going to work with her, and

---

[1]   We construe both the first and third causes of action as purporting to allege a claim for tortious wrongful discharge in violation of the public policy against sex discrimination. (Foley v. Interactive Data Corp. (1988) 47 Cal. 3d 654, 665–671, 254 Cal. Rptr. 211, 765 P. 2d 373; Rojo v. Kliger (1990) 52 Cal. 3d 65, 88–91, 276 Cal. Rptr. 130, 801 P. 2d 373.)

then, 'That's Clint's deal.' And that's something I just completely did not understand.

Similarly, the declaration of Mary Wellnitz stated:

> She worked with Locke to set up projects at Warner, without success. Shortly after she began her association with Locke, Wellnitz submitted a script to Lance Young, who at the time was a senior vice president of production at Warner. After discussing the script, Young told Wellnitz, "Mary, I want you to know that I think Sondra is a wonderful woman and very talented, but, if you think I can go down the hall and tell Bob Daly that I have a movie I want to make with her he would tell me to forget it. They are not going to make a movie with her here."

5.   *Trial court's ruling.*

On February 17, 1995, the trial court granted summary judgment in favor of Warner. Thereafter, the trial court signed an extensive order granting summary judgment. The order stated:

> Under the contract, Warner had no obligation either to put into development any of the projects submitted to the studio for its consideration, or to 'hand off' to Locke any scripts for her to direct that it previously had acquired from someone else. The implied covenant of good faith and fair dealing cannot be imposed to create a contract different from the one the parties negotiated for themselves. Warner had the option to pass on each project Locke submitted. Warner was not required to have a good faith or 'fair' basis for declining to exercise its right to develop her material. Such a requirement would be improper and unworkable. A judge or jury cannot and should not substitute its judgment for a film studio's when the studio is making the creative decision of whether to develop or produce a proposed motion picture. Such highly subjective artistic and business decisions are not proper subjects for judicial review. Moreover, Warner had legitimate commercial and artistic reasons for declining to develop the projects Locke submitted.

With respect to Locke's claim she was defrauded by Warner when it entered into the agreement with the undisclosed intention not to honor its contractual obligations, the trial court ruled that because Warner did not breach its contractual obligations to Locke, the fraud claim was meritless. Also, it could not be inferred from the statements by Young and Brassel that two years earlier, when Warner entered into agreement, it had no intention of working with Locke.

As for the two causes of action alleging sex discrimination, the trial court found no evidence Warner declined to develop the projects Locke submitted, and declined to use her directing services, on account of her gender.

Locke filed a timely notice of appeal from the judgment.

CONTENTIONS

Locke contends: the trial court erred by granting Warner's motion for summary judgment based on its conclusion there were no disputed issues of material fact; the trial court erred in weighing the evidence, resolving doubts against Locke, the non-moving party, and adopting only those inferences favorable to Warner where the evidence supported contrary inferences; and the trial court committed reversible error first by failing to make any findings or evidentiary rulings and then by adopting Warner's defective ruling.

DISCUSSION

1. *Standard of appellate review.*

As we recently stated in PMC, Inc. v. Saban Entertainment, Inc. (1996) 45 Cal. App. 4th 579, 590, 52 Cal. Rptr. 2d 877, summary judgment "motions are to expedite litigation and eliminate needless trials." They are granted "if all the papers submitted show that there is no triable issue as to any material fact and that the moving party is entitled to a judgment as a matter of law."

* * * *

Our review is guided by the foregoing principles.

2. *A triable issue exists as to whether Warner breached its contract with Locke by failing to evaluate Locke's proposals on their merits.*

As indicated, the second cause of action alleged Warner breached the contract by "refusing to consider the projects prepared by [Locke] and depriving [Locke] of the benefit of the bargain of the Warner-Locke agreement."[3]

In granting summary judgment on this claim, the trial court ruled "[a] judge or jury cannot and should not substitute its own judgment for a film studio's when the studio is making the creative decision of whether to develop or produce a proposed motion picture. Such highly-subjective artistic and business decisions are not proper subjects for judicial review."

---

[3]   Contrary to Warner's contention Locke is raising an unpled claim for breach of the implied covenant of good faith and fair dealing, the second cause of action for breach of contract adequately alleges Warner deprived Locke of the benefit of the bargain of the development deal by refusing to consider her projects. Such conduct by Warner, if proven, would amount to a breach of the covenant, implied "in every contract that neither party will do anything which will injure the right of the other to receive the benefits of the agreement." (Comunale v. Traders & General Ins. Co. (1958) 50 Cal.2d 654, 658, 328 P.2d 198; accord Waller v. Truck Ins. Exchange, Inc. (1995) 11 Cal. 4th 1, 36, 44 Cal. Rptr. 2d 370, 900 P. 2d 619.)

The trial court's ruling missed the mark by failing to distinguish between Warner's right to make a subjective creative decision, which is not reviewable for reasonableness, and the requirement the dissatisfaction be bona fide or genuine.

a.   *General principles.*

"[W]here a contract confers on one party a discretionary power affecting the rights of the other, a duty is imposed to exercise that discretion in good faith and in accordance with fair dealing." (Perdue v. Crocker National Bank (1985) 38 Cal. 3d 913, 923, 216 Cal. Rptr. 345, 702 P. 2d 503; accord Kendall v. Ernest Pestana, Inc. (1985) 40 Cal. 3d 488, 500, 220 Cal. Rptr. 818, 709 P. 2d 837.) It is settled that in " 'every contract there is an implied covenant that neither party shall do anything which will have the effect of destroying or injuring the right of the other party to receive the fruits of the contract. . . .' " (Kendall, supra, at p. 500, 220 Cal.Rptr. 818, 709 P. 2d 837. . . .)

Therefore, when it is a condition of an obligor's duty that he or she be subjectively satisfied with respect to the obligee's performance, the subjective standard of honest satisfaction is applicable. (1 Witkin, Summary of Cal. Law (9th ed. 1987) Contracts, § 729, p. 659; Rest. 2d, Contracts, § 228, coms. a, b.)

> Where the contract involves matters of fancy, taste or judgment, the promisor is the sole judge of his satisfaction. If he asserts in good faith that he is not satisfied, there can be no inquiry into the reasonableness of his attitude. Traditional examples are employment contracts . . . and agreements to paint a portrait, write a literary or scientific article, or produce a play or vaudeville act." (1 Witkin, Summary of Cal. Law, supra, § 730, p. 660; accord Schuyler v. Pantages (1921) 54 Cal. App. 83, 85–87, 201 P. 137.) In such cases, "the promisor's determination that he is not satisfied, when made in good faith, has been held to be a defense to an action on the contract. [citations]" (Mattei v. Hopper (1958) 51 Cal. 2d 119, 123, 330 P. 2d 625, italics added.)

Therefore, the trial court erred in deferring entirely to what it characterized as Warner's "creative decision" in the handling of the development deal. If Warner acted in bad faith by categorically rejecting Locke's work and refusing to work with her, irrespective of the merits of her proposals, such conduct is not beyond the reach of the law.

b.   *Locke presented evidence from which a trier of fact reasonably could infer Warner breached the agreement by refusing to consider her proposals in good faith.*

Merely because Warner paid Locke the guaranteed compensation under the agreement does not establish Warner fulfilled its contractual obligation. As pointed out by Locke, the value in the subject development deal was not merely the guaranteed payments under the agreement, but also the opportunity to direct and produce films and earn additional sums, and most importantly, the opportunity to promote and enhance a career.

Unquestionably, Warner was entitled to reject Locke's work based on its subjective judgment, and its creative decision in that regard is not subject to being second-guessed by a court. However, bearing in mind the requirement that subjective dissatisfaction must be an honestly held dissatisfaction, the evidence raises a triable issue as to whether Warner breached its agreement with Locke by not considering her proposals on their merits.

As indicated, the deposition testimony of Joseph Terry recounted a conversation he had with Bob Brassel, a Warner executive, regarding Locke's projects. In that conversation, Brassel stated "Joe, we're not going to work with her, and then, That's Clint's deal."

Similarly, the declaration of Mary Wellnitz recalled a conversation she had with Lance Young, a senior vice president of production at Warner. After discussing the script with Wellnitz, Young told her:

> Mary, I want you to know that I think Sondra is a wonderful woman and very talented, but, if you think I can go down the hall and tell Bob Daly that I have a movie I want to make with her he would tell me to forget it. They are not going to make a movie with her here.

The above evidence raises a triable issue of material fact as to whether Warner breached its contract with Locke by categorically refusing to work with her, irrespective of the merits of her proposals. While Warner was entitled to reject Locke's proposals based on its subjective dissatisfaction, the evidence calls into question whether Warner had an honest or good faith dissatisfaction with Locke's proposals, or whether it merely went through the motions of purporting to "consider" her projects.

c.   *No merit to Warner's contention Locke seeks to rewrite the instant agreement to limit Warner's discretionary power.*

Warner argues that while the implied covenant of good faith and fair dealing is implied in all contracts, it is limited to assuring compliance with the express terms of the contract and cannot be extended to create obligations not contemplated in the contract. (Racine & Laramie, Ltd. v. Department of Parks & Recreation (1992) 11 Cal. App. 4th 1026, 1032, 14 Cal. Rptr. 2d 335.)

This principle is illustrated in Carma Developers (Cal.), Inc. v. Marathon Development California, Inc. (1992) 2 Cal.4th 342, 351–352, 6 Cal.Rptr.2d 467, 826 P.2d 710, wherein the parties entered into a lease agreement which stated that if the tenant procured a potential sublessee and asked the landlord for consent to sublease, the landlord had the right to terminate the lease, enter into negotiations with the prospective sublessee, and appropriate for itself all profits from the new arrangement. Carma recognized "[t]he covenant of good faith finds particular application in situations where one party is invested with a discretionary power affecting the rights of another." (Id., at p. 372, 6 Cal. Rptr. 2d 467, 826 P. 2d 710.) The court expressed the view that "[s]uch power must be exercised in good faith." At the same time, Carma upheld the right of the landlord under the express terms of the lease to freely exercise its discretion to terminate the lease in order to claim for itself—and deprive the tenant of—the appreciated rental value of the premises. (Id., at p. 376, 6 Cal. Rptr. 2d 467, 826 P. 2d 710.)

In this regard, Carma stated:

We are aware of no reported case in which a court has held the covenant of good faith may be read to prohibit a party from doing that which is expressly permitted by an agreement. On the contrary, as a general matter, implied terms should never be read to vary express terms. The general rule [regarding the covenant of good faith] is plainly subject to the exception that the parties may, by express provisions of the contract, grant the right to engage in the very acts and conduct which would otherwise have been forbidden by an implied covenant of good faith and fair dealing. . . . This is in accord with the general principle that, in interpreting a contract "an implication . . . should not be made when the contrary is indicated in clear and express words." 3 Corbin, Contracts, § 564, p. 298 (1960). . . . As to acts and conduct authorized by the express provisions of the contract, no covenant of good faith and fair dealing can be implied which forbids such acts and conduct. And if defendants were given the right to do what they did by the express provisions of the contract there can be no breach." (Carma Developers (Cal.), Inc., supra, 2 Cal.4th at p. 374, 6 Cal. Rptr. 2d 467, 826 P. 2d 710, italics added.)

In Third Story Music, Inc. v. Waits (1995) 41 Cal.App.4th 798, 801, 48 Cal. Rptr. 2d 747, the issue presented was "whether a promise to market music, or to refrain from doing so, at the election of the promisor is subject to the implied covenant of good faith and fair dealing where substantial consideration has been paid by the promisor."

In that case, Warner Communications obtained from TSM the worldwide right to manufacture, sell, distribute and advertise the musical output of singer/songwriter Tom Waits. (Third Story Music, Inc., supra, 41 Cal. App. 4th at pp. 800–801, 48 Cal. Rptr. 2d 747.) The agreement also specifically stated that Warner Communications "may at our election refrain from any or all of the foregoing." (Id., at p. 801, 48 Cal. Rptr. 2d

747.) TSM sued Warner Communications for contract damages based on breach of the implied covenant of good faith and fair dealing, claiming Warner Communications had impeded TSM's receiving the benefit of the agreement. (Id., at p. 802, 48 Cal. Rptr. 2d 747.) Warner Communications demurred to the complaint, alleging the clause in the agreement permitting it to "at [its] election refrain from doing anything to profitably exploit the music is controlling and precludes application of any implied covenant." (Ibid.) The demurrer was sustained on those grounds. (Ibid.)

The reviewing court affirmed, holding the implied covenant was unavailing to the plaintiff. (Third Story Music, Inc., supra, 41 Cal. App. 4th at pp. 808–809, 48 Cal. Rptr. 2d 747.) Because the agreement expressly provided Warner Communications had the right to refrain from marketing the Waits recordings, the implied covenant of good faith and fair dealing did not limit the discretion given to Warner Communications in that regard. Ibid.; Carma Developers Cal., Inc., supra, 2 Cal.4th at p. 374, 6 Cal. Rptr. 2d 467, 826 P. 2d 710.)

Warner's reliance herein on Third Story Music, Inc. is misplaced. The Locke/Warner agreement did not give Warner the express right to refrain from working with Locke. Rather, the agreement gave Warner discretion with respect to developing Locke's projects. The implied covenant of good faith and fair dealing obligated Warner to exercise that discretion honestly and in good faith.

In sum, the Warner/Locke agreement contained an implied covenant of good faith and fair dealing, that neither party would frustrate the other party's right to receive the benefits of the contract. (Comunale, supra, 50 Cal. 2d at p. 658, 328 P. 2d 198; Waller, supra, 11 Cal.4th at p. 36, 44 Cal. Rptr. 2d 370, 900 P. 2d 619.) Whether Warner violated the implied covenant and breached the contract by categorically refusing to work with Locke is a question for the trier of fact.

3.   *A triable issue exists as to whether Warner made a fraudulent promise.*

In the fourth cause of action, Locke pled at the time Warner entered into the agreement with her, it concealed and failed to disclose it had no intention of honoring the agreement.[4]

The trial court held that because Warner did not breach any express or implied obligations owed to Locke, she could not prevail on the fraud claim However, as explained above, a triable issue exists as to whether Warner breached the agreement with Locke. Therefore, the trial court's rationale for disposing of the fraud claim is undermined.

---

[4]   Although Warner contends Locke has an unalleged claim for fraudulent concealment, the fourth cause of action adequately pled a cause of action for fraud. In addition to pleading a promise was made and was not fulfilled, Locke alleged Warner did not intend to perform when it made the promise. (Civ. Code § 1710, subd. (4); Tenzer v. Superscope, Inc. (1985) 39 Cal. 3d 18, 30, 216 Cal. Rptr. 130, 702 P. 2d 212, 5 Witkin, Summary of Cal. Law (9th ed. 1988) Torts, § 685, pp. 786–787.)

The trial court also ruled Locke could not prevail on the fraud claim because there was no evidence Warner had a fraudulent intent at the time the parties entered into the contract. The trial court acknowledged Locke "filed a declaration of her development assistant, Mary Wellnitz, in which Ms. Wellnitz states that a Warner Bros. executive, Lance Young, remarked in late 1992 that Warner Bros. was 'not going to make a movie' with Ms. Locke also offered the deposition testimony of a third party, Joe Terry, in which he recalled a 1993 conversation with another Warner Bros. production executive, Bob Brassel, in which Mr. Brassel said that the studio was not going to work with Ms. Locke. However, the Court does not believe that these statements would permit a jury to infer that two years earlier, when plaintiffs and the defendant entered into their contract, Warner Bros. intended to breach its obligations."

We disagree. Fraudulent intent must often be established by circumstantial evidence, and may be "inferred from such circumstances as defendant's . . . failure even to attempt performance, . . . " (Tenzer v. Superscope, Inc., supra, 39 Cal. 3d at p. 30, 216 Cal. Rptr. 130, 702 P. 2d 212.) Based on the above evidence that Warner had expressed an absolute unwillingness to work with Locke, a trier of fact reasonably could infer Warner never intended to give Locke's proposals a good faith evaluation and that Warner entered into the agreement with Locke solely as an accommodation to Eastwood, who had promised to reimburse Warner for any losses under the agreement. The trial court erred in concluding such an inference could not be drawn from the evidence. We conclude the issue of fraudulent intent is one for the trier of fact.

4.   *Locke waived any error in the trial court's ruling with respect to her causes of action alleging gender bias.*

Locke's opening brief does not assert any error in the trial court's disposition of her two causes of action alleging sex discrimination. Accordingly, this court may treat the claims as having been waived.

* * *

DISPOSITION

The judgment is reversed with respect to the second and fourth causes of action and is otherwise affirmed. Locke to recover costs on appeal.

KITCHING and ALDRICH, JJ., concur.

NOTES AND QUESTIONS

1.   *Subjective dissatisfaction or something more?* Assuming that Warner Brothers Studios truly subjectively believed that Ms. Locke's proposals were not meritorious, would it be contractually entitled to reject them? Was there evidence questioning whether that was the case? If so, was the evidence

credible? See Gerard Mantese and Marc L. Newman, "Still Keeping the Faith: The Duty of Good Faith Revisited," 76 Mich. B. J. 1190, 1192 (1997).

2.   *Derivative or independent duty.* The contract gave Warner Brothers the right to exercise its own discretion, but the obligation of good faith read into the contract an "honest dissatisfaction" duty. Do you think that was the reasonable expectation of Ms. Locke? Do you think Warner Brothers thought it was required to be dissatisfied with the proposals before rejecting them? If Warner Brothers truly thought the proposals meritorious and would make money, why would the Studio reject the proposals? See discussion, Teri J. Dobbins, "Losing Faith: Extracting the Implied Covenant of Good Faith from (Some) Contracts," 84 Or. L. Rev. 227, 248 (2005).

3.   *UCC good faith.* UCC § 1–302(b) (2001) (formerly UCC § 1–102(3)) identifies the duty of good faith performance as a mandatory default term that may not be disclaimed by the contracting parties. The parties to a sale of goods transaction may, however, "determine the standards by which the performance of such obligations is to be measured if such standards are not manifestly unreasonable." UCC § 1–302(b) (2001) (formerly UCC § 1–102(3)). Article 2 then explicitly imposes duties of good faith performance upon one or both parties depending upon the transactional context. See UCC §§ 2–305(2) (requiring party entitled to fix price in contract with open price term to do so in good faith), 2–306 (establishing quantity term in output or requirements contracts according to actual output or requirements "as may occur in good faith"), and 2–311 (good faith in specifying performances due under contract).

4.   *CISG and good faith.* The CISG does not directly impose a good faith obligation, but Article 7 does provide that good faith in international trade is to be regarded. See Emily M. S. Houh, "The Doctrine of Good Faith in Contract Law: A (Nearly) Empty Vessel?" 2005 Utah L. Rev. 1 (2005) and Joseph M. Perillo, "UNIDROIT Principles of International Commercial Contracts: The Black Letter Text and a Review," 63 Fordham L. Rev. 281 (1994).

5.   *The tort of "bad faith" ambiguous drafting.* If an insurance company deliberately chooses an ambiguous term in order to argue later claim denial, should such behavior constitute an actionable tort? See generally Richard A. Posner, "The Law and Economics of Contract Interpretation," 83 Tex. L. Rev. 1581 (2005).

6.   *Settlement and aftermath.* Following the decision in *Locke*, the litigation dragged on for two more years before the parties settled. Locke's attorney reportedly stated that "the agreement reaches beyond money considerations to create writing and directing opportunities for Locke, who had been all but blacklisted by the major studios for a decade." Ann W. O'Neill, "Actress' Settlement Ends Long Legal Saga," LOS ANGELES TIMES, May 25, 1999. As of this writing, the entry for Sondra Locke at IMDb.com does not list any director credits after 1997 or actor credits after 2000.

F. COURSE OF DEALING, USAGE & COURSE OF PERFORMANCE

"Usage" evidence encompasses business habit and practice in a particular community or business as well as the practice between the parties to this and prior contracts. Restatement (Second) of Contracts § 219. Both the common law and the Uniform Commercial Code regard "usage" evidence as relevant to the interpretation and meaning of an agreement, and "ambiguity" is not required as a condition of admissibility. See Restatement (Second) of Contracts §§ 220 & 221 and UCC § 1–303(d) (2001) (formerly UCC § 1–205(1)). See Joseph H. Levie, "Trade Usage and Custom Under the Common Law and the Uniform Commercial Code," 40 N.Y.U. L. Rev. 1101 (1965). There are three common categories of "usage," each enjoying a particular niche in the evidentiary hierarchy: "trade usage" (UCC § 1–303(c) (2001) (formerly UCC § 1–205(2)) and Restatement (Second) of Contracts § 222; "course of dealing" (UCC § 1–303(b) (2001) (formerly UCC § 1–205(3)) and Restatement (Second) of Contracts § 223; and "course of performance" (UCC § 2–208 and revised UCC § 1–303(a) (2001)) and Restatement (Second) of Contracts § 202(4)). See Linda J. Rusch, "Is the Saga of the Uniform Commercial Code Article 2 Revisions Over? A Brief Look at What NCCUSL Finally Approved," 6 Del. L. Rev. 41 (2003).

The next case discusses the relationship among the various types of evidence, but it should be noted that express terms "generally" control all usages. See UCC §§ 2–208(2) & 1–303(e) (2001) and Restatement (Second) of Contracts § 203(b). Absent controlling relevant express terms, "course of performance" is the most important of the evidentiary trilogy because it involves the repeated actual performance of the parties to the contract in dispute with an opportunity for the other to object to nonconforming performance. UCC §§ 2–208(1)–(2) and Restatement (Second) of Contracts §§ 202(4) & 203(b). In a similar manner, "course of dealing" is the next in importance because, although not involving actual performance of the contract in dispute, it does involve performance by the same parties to other previous contracts. UCC § 1–303(d)–(e) (2001); Restatement (Second) of Contracts §§ 223 & 203(b). Finally, while "trade usage" is relevant to interpret the contract, it is the least accurate assessment of contractual meaning because it is evidence inferring intent from general trade standards and understandings by others generally rather than the dealings between the two parties to a contract and then only when it is reasonably clear that the party to be bound is reasonably aware of the existence and scope of the trade usage. UCC §§ 1–303(c), (d), (e) & (g) (2001); Restatement (Second) of Contracts § 222 & 203(b).

Of the trilogy, "trade usage" is the most problematic, particularly where the party to be bound does not regularly conduct extensive business in the locality where the trade usage is determined. Only the trade usage from the location where the performance is to occur is utilized. UCC § 1–303(c) (2001). Because of this feature, and to prevent the element of unfair surprise, the party seeking the advantage of the trade usage must provide the other party notice in order to prevent unfair surprise. UCC § 1–303(g) (2001). Other limitations require that the trade usage be so regularly observed that there is a reasonable expectation that it will be observed with respect to the transaction in question. UCC § 1–303(c) (2001) and Restatement (Second) of Contracts § 222(1).

This discussion illustrates that the trade usage must actually exist. It need not be ancient or even universal, but it must be commercially accepted by "regular observance." UCC § 1–303(c) (2001). But once usage is established, evidence of that usage is not conditioned upon the determination of an ambiguity or even that the usage evidence is otherwise "consistent" with the language of the agreement. Restatement (Second) of Contracts § 222, *cmt. b*. Accordingly, the threshold key to the admission of trade usage is proving regular observance, a matter of proof normally reserved for expert witnesses. Even if the trade usage exists, when will it be binding upon a party? Normally, parties are bound by usages of the trade if they are a member of that trade and, even if not, should have been aware of the usage. UCC § 1–303(d) (2001). See Elizabeth Warren, "Trade Usage and Parties in the Trade: An Economic Rationale for an Inflexible Rule," 42 U. Pitt. L. Rev. 515 (1981) (arguing for a single standard that a party who ought to know about a usage should be bound regardless of whether a member of a particular trade or not).

As explored earlier in this chapter, "parol evidence" may not be introduced to "contradict" an express term in a writing, regardless of whether the writing is partially or totally integrated. See Restatement (Second) of Contracts § 215. Therefore evidence of prior or contemporaneous agreements or negotiations is simply not admissible to contradict a term of the writing. The Uniform Commercial Code states a similar rule prohibiting contradiction. UCC § 2–202. Nonetheless, even a completely integrated agreement may be supplemented or explained by course of performance, course of dealing, and trade usage. UCC § 2–202(a) and Restatement (Second) of Contracts § 214(c). Inevitably, the tension between the explanatory value of usages will conflict with the contradiction value of the parol evidence rule. Who rules supreme?

The common law grants "greater weight" to express terms than usages. Restatement (Second) of Contracts § 203(b). Similarly, and perhaps more strongly, in a contract involving the sale of goods, express terms "control" usages. UCC § 2–208(2) & UCC § 1–303(e) (2001). On the other hand, usages may "qualify" written terms of an agreement. UCC § 1–303(d) (2001). This language creates difficult questions regarding the balance between trade usage and express terms of the agreement. Prior to the adoption of the Uniform Commercial Code, trade usage was a mere "gap-filler," but is now actually part of the agreement with the rest of the written terms. See Amy Kastely, "Stock Equipment for the Bargain in Fact: Trade Usage, 'Express Terms,' and Consistency Under Section 1–205 of the Uniform Commercial Code," 64 N.C. L. Rev. 777 (1986).

In a way, this understanding forces courts to resolve tensions between terms of an agreement that are themselves somewhat inconsistent. In a famous case, the court determined that trade usage should be excluded whenever it cannot be reasonably construed as consistent with the terms of the contract. Columbia Nitrogen Corp. v. Royster Co., 451 F.2d 3, 6–7 (4th Cir. 1971). This view excludes trade usage unless consistent with written terms. Another approach recognizes that UCC § 1–303(e) (2001) (formerly UCC § 1–205(4)) is not a form of a parol evidence rule and therefore admits trade usage unless it is totally negated by the written term. Which approach is followed by the *Swanson* case below?

SWANSON V. BECO CONST. CO., INC.

145 Idaho 59, 175 P.3d 748 (Idaho 2007)

EISMANN, Chief Justice.

This is an appeal from the grant of summary judgment holding that an equipment lease agreement was not ambiguous and that an alleged usage of trade was not applicable. We affirm the judgment of the district court, as modified, and award attorney fees on appeal.

I. FACTS AND PROCEDURAL HISTORY

In the summer of 2004, BECO Construction Co., Inc., (BECO) was working on a government construction contract in downtown Pocatello, and Ted A. Swanson, d/b/a Swanson Construction (Swanson) had been hired to perform some of the work on that project. Swanson had been in the construction business for ten or eleven years, doing mostly excavation and hauling. He owned various items of construction equipment, including a Bobcat skid steer loader (Bobcat).

BECO had been using a rented skid steer loader, but had repeated mechanical problems with that loader. It approached Swanson to see whether he would rent his Bobcat to BECO. Swanson was not in the business of leasing his equipment, but agreed to do so. He understood that BECO would be using the Bobcat for a week or so until the other skid steer it was renting was repaired. To determine an appropriate charge, Swanson contacted an equipment rental company to find out what that company charged per day for a skid steer loader. He was told $300 plus tax, and so decided to charge BECO $300 per day. On August 27, 2004, the parties entered into a hand-written lease for the Bobcat. The lease provided that its term would be from "8-27-04 until finished" and that BECO was to pay rent of $300 "per working day." The lease also required Swanson to deliver the Bobcat "clean, serviced + full of fuel in need of no repairs," and it required BECO to return it "in same condition."

BECO had the Bobcat in its possession from August 27 through October 18, 2004. Swanson had twice contacted BECO wanting to have his Bobcat returned, and each time he was told that BECO was still using it. On October 18, 2004, at 8:00 p.m., he went to the jobsite and retook possession of his Bobcat.

Swanson billed BECO $13,200 for the use of his Bobcat. BECO refused to pay, and on December 20, 2004, Swanson filed this action seeking to recover from BECO the sum of $13,200 in unpaid rent, damages for failure to return the Bobcat in the condition required by the lease, and prejudgment interest. On February 3, 2005, BECO paid $6,219 as the maximum amount it believed it should owe under the lease.

On August 25, 2005, Swanson moved for summary judgment. He supported the motion with his affidavit in which he listed the forty-four days for which he contended he was entitled to rental payments and asserted that it would cost $590 in service and new tires to put the Bobcat in the same condition it had been when leased. In his supporting brief, Swanson argued that "working day" meant every day that BECO was working on the job site.

BECO responded by arguing that the term "working day" was ambiguous. It submitted the affidavit of its president in which he stated that the Idaho Transportation Department uses a different definition of "working day" in its contracts. BECO's president also asserted that Swanson was entitled to only $219 for BECO's failure to return the Bobcat in the same condition it had been when leased.

After oral argument on the motion, the district court on October 6, 2005, granted Swanson partial summary judgment regarding the meaning of the term "working day." The district court stated that it was unambiguous and meant the days BECO was working on the jobsite. It also ordered Swanson to submit an affidavit showing how many days BECO was working on the jobsite during the lease term. The court denied summary judgment on the claim seeking damages for the failure to return the Bobcat in the condition required by the lease.

On October 12, 2005, Swanson filed his second affidavit, stating in essence that BECO was working on the job site on each of the forty-four days listed in his prior affidavit. On November 1, 2005, the district court granted Swanson partial summary judgment on the issue of unpaid rent. It held that Swanson was entitled to $13,200 in rent (44 days x $300 per day), less the $6,219 paid by BECO after the lawsuit was filed, for a net judgment of $6,981 in unpaid rent. It held that the damages claimed regarding the condition of the Bobcat would have to be tried.

On November 18, 2005, Swanson moved to dismiss its claim for the remaining damages. The district court granted the motion and entered judgment for Swanson in the sum of $6,981 plus costs and attorney fees in the sum of $4,207, for a total judgment of $11,188.

BECO filed three successive motions for reconsideration, which the district court denied. The court also awarded Swanson additional costs and attorney fees for responding to those motions. The final judgment entered in favor of Swanson totaled $13,358.65. BECO then timely appealed.

II. ISSUES ON APPEAL

1. Did the district court err in holding that the phrase "per working day" is unambiguous?

2. Was there a genuine issue of material fact as to the number of working days that BECO had the Bobcat during the term of the lease?

3. Did the district court err in refusing to construe the parties' lease as including a practice among commercial equipment lessors of discounting the daily rental charge when the equipment is kept by the lessee for a period longer than one week?

4. Is either party entitled to an award of attorney fees on appeal?

III. ANALYSIS

A. Did the District Court Err in Holding that the Phrase "Per Working Day" Is Unambiguous?

Ken Wright, the project supervisor for BECO, asked Swanson if he would lease BECO the Bobcat. Swanson wrote out a lease on a work order form he used in his business. The handwritten portion of the lease agreement stated as follows:

> Rent 1 Bobcat 773 SkidSteer to start 8-27-04 until finished. Machine to be delivered clean serviced + full of fuel in need of no repairs and to be returned in same condition Becco [sic] responsible for all repairs while rented. Original hours as of 8-27-04 (1052). Tires + 60% or 7/8. Renter to keep machined [sic] serviced.

> (per day $300.^{00})

> Rent to be per working day.

Swanson testified in his deposition that he inserted the words "per working day" because those words were in lease contracts he signed when he leased equipment. The record does not indicate that Swanson and Wright ever discussed the meaning of the term "working day." Swanson simply wrote the lease agreement and Wright signed it on behalf of BECO, agreeing that BECO would pay Swanson $300 per working day for the lease of the Bobcat. BECO contends that the term "working day" is ambiguous.

"Whether a contract is ambiguous is a question of law over which we exercise free review." *Howard v. Perry,* 141 Idaho 139, 142, 106 P.3d 465, 468 (2005). Ambiguities can be either patent or latent. "Idaho courts look solely to the face of a written agreement to determine whether it is [patently] ambiguous." *Ward v. Puregro Co.,* 128 Idaho 366, 369, 913 P.2d 582, 585 (1996). . . . "A latent ambiguity is not evident on the face of the instrument alone, but becomes apparent when applying the instrument to the facts as they exist." *In re Estate of Kirk,* 127 Idaho 817, 824, 907 P.2d 794, 801 (1995). BECO does not contend that there is any latent ambiguity regarding the parties' equipment lease. It contends that the term "working day" is patently ambiguous.

To determine whether a contract is patently ambiguous, a court looks at the face of the document and gives the words or phrases used their established definitions in common use or settled legal meanings. *Pinehaven Planning Bd. v. Brooks,* 138 Idaho 826, 70 P.3d 664 (2003). For a contract term to be ambiguous, there must be at least two different reasonable interpretations of the term, *Armstrong v. Farmers Ins. Co. of Idaho,* 143 Idaho 135, 139 P.3d 737 (2006), or it must be nonsensical, *Purdy v. Farmers Ins. Co. of Idaho,* 138 Idaho 443, 65 P.3d 184 (2003).

The term "working day" has an established definition. It means "a day when work is normally done as distinguished from Sundays and legal holidays." *Webster's Third New Int'l Dictionary of the English Language,* 2635 (Philip Babcock Gove et al. eds., G. & C. Merriam Co.1971). There is nothing on the face of the parties' agreement indicating that they intended some other meaning. Giving the words "working day" their normal meaning would not conflict with any other provisions of the written lease or create any uncertainty as to its meaning. There is nothing in the context of the lease that would indicate that the term should be given a different meaning.

BECO argued to the district court that the term "working day" was patently ambiguous for two reasons. First, BECO submitted an excerpt from the Idaho Transportation Department's "Standard Specifications for Highway Construction" that gave a different definition of "working day." The excerpt from the Transportation Department's standard specifications stated as follows:

> **Working Day** Any day except Saturdays, Sundays, and State recognized legal holidays on which weather or other conditions not under control of the Contractor will permit activities on the critical path to proceed for at least 5 hours of the day. Activities shall include, but are not limited to: engineering, surveying, permitting, submittals, approvals, procurement, fabrication, and construction.

Parties are certainly free to include in their contracts definitions of words used therein, even if those definitions vary from the normal meanings of the words. In its contracts, the Transportation Department can define the term "working day" any way it desires. However, that definition has no relevance here. There is nothing on the face of the parties' written lease indicating that they intended to incorporate the Transportation Department's definition into their agreement. The Transportation Department's definition is irrelevant to this case. Even though irrelevant, the Transportation Department's definition supports the dictionary definition of the term "working day." Under the Transportation Department's definition, a "working day" is not a day upon which work is actually done.

Second, BECO argued that Swanson's counsel gave two different meanings to the term during his oral argument on Swanson's motion for summary judgment. During that argument, Swanson's counsel stated, "Every day that they were out on the site is a working day. Whether they use the piece of equipment or not is irrelevant." Later in his argument, Swanson's counsel discussed three exhibits that were attached to Swanson's affidavit filed on August 25, 2005. Those exhibits were invoices listing the days for which Swanson was demanding payment. When asked by the district court where his client got the dates listed on the invoices, Swanson's counsel stated that the dates were "the dates that the piece of equipment was being used at this site." Based upon these statements, BECO argued to the district court that the term "working day" could mean either every day that BECO was working on the job site or every day that it was actually using the Bobcat on the job site. Swanson's counsel responded that his answer to the district court's question should not be construed as an assertion that BECO had to actually use the Bobcat for it to be a "working day." He was just informing the court that Swanson was on the job site every day and saw BECO using the Bobcat on those days.

After the district court granted partial summary judgment on the ground that the term "working day" was not ambiguous, BECO deposed Swanson. In his deposition, Swanson initially stated that "per day" and "per working day" meant the same thing. In response to questioning, he clarified that "per day" and "per working day" were intended to distinguish between a daily charge and a charge based upon the number of hours the equipment was actually used, as shown by its hour meter. He testified that in his experience, commercial lessors of equipment charge per day rather than per hour of actual use because a customer could keep the equipment for days without actually using it. When asked what a "working day" was, Swanson responded that it was a day during which work was done on the job, whether or not the leased equipment was actually used that day. He added it would not include Sundays unless arrangements had been made to work on Sunday.

Swanson's understanding of the meaning of the term "working day" is not relevant if the lease agreement is unambiguous. The determination of whether a contract is ambiguous on its face must be decided by giving the words or phrases used their ordinary meanings. *Shawver v. Huckleberry Estates, L.L.C.,* 140 Idaho 354, 93 P.3d 685 (2004). A party's subjective, undisclosed interpretation of a word or phrase cannot make the contract ambiguous. If it could, then all contracts would be rendered ambiguous merely by a party asserting a misunderstanding of the meaning of one or more of the words used. The voluntary failure to read a contract does not excuse a party's performance. *Belk v. Martin,* 136 Idaho 652, 39 P.3d 592 (2001). Similarly, a party's failure to determine the ordinary meaning of the words used in a contract does not make it ambiguous.

"The intent of the parties is determined from the plain meaning of the words." *Clear Lakes Trout Co., Inc. v. Clear Springs Foods, Inc.,* 141 Idaho 117, 120, 106 P.3d 443, 446 (2005). A contract is not rendered ambiguous on its face because one of the parties thought that the words used had some meaning that differed from the ordinary meaning of those words. As explained in 17A Am.Jur.2d, Contracts, § 348 (2004):

> If the language used by the parties is plain, complete, and unambiguous, the intention of the parties must be gathered from that language, and from that language alone, no matter what the actual or secret intentions of the parties may have been. Presumptively, the intent of the parties to a contract is expressed by the natural and ordinary meaning of their language referable to it, and such meaning cannot be perverted or destroyed by the courts through construction, for the parties are presumed to have intended what the terms clearly state. Only when the language of the contract is ambiguous may a court turn to extrinsic evidence of the contracting parties' intent.

BECO did not contend that the term "working day" was a term of art within the construction industry. *See, J.R. Simplot Co. v. Rycair, Inc.,* 138 Idaho 557, 67 P.3d 36 (2003) (Parol evidence may be received to interpret a term of art in a contract). In fact, BECO did not present any relevant evidence as to an alternative definition of the term. When the term "working day" is given its ordinary meaning, the lease agreement is not ambiguous. Swanson is entitled to rent for every day of the lease term except Sundays and holidays.

B. Was There a Genuine Issue of Material Fact as to the Number of Working Days that BECO Had the Bobcat During the Term of the Lease?

[Eds.—The court considered BECO's argument that BECO should not be liable for rent on days for which it retained but did not use the skidsteer loader. The court concluded that it was irrelevant whether BECO used the skidsteer loader or not because the contract required payment for any working day for which BECO had possession of the loader.]

C. Did the District Court Err in Refusing to Construe the Parties' Lease as Including a Practice Among Commercial Equipment Lessors of Discounting the Daily Rental Charge When the Equipment Is Kept by the Lessee for a Period Longer than One Week?

In its first motion for reconsideration, BECO raised the issue that there was a usage of trade that would require Swanson to reduce the rental charge for his Bobcat. BECO contends that there is a usage of trade among commercial lessors of construction equipment to charge weekly and monthly rates that result in a per day rent that is less than the daily rental rate. In support of that contention, it provided the affidavit of a man who has managed an equipment rental business for six years. He stated that there is a custom and practice among commercial lessors of construction equipment to reduce the amount charged per day if the customer keeps the equipment for one week or longer. According to him, commercial lessors charge a daily rate, a weekly rate that results in a lesser charge per day than the daily rate, and a monthly rate that results in a lesser charge per day than the weekly rate. He also stated that commercial lessors charge rent based upon the length of time the equipment is actually kept by the customer even if the customer originally agreed to pay a daily rate upon the assumption that the equipment would be returned in less than one week. There is no contention that there is a usage of trade among commercial lessors regarding the percentage of reduction in the per day rental charge when the customer keeps the equipment one week or longer.

Idaho Code § 28–1–303(e) provides that "the express terms of an agreement and any applicable . . . usage of trade shall be construed wherever reasonable as consistent with each other." A "usage of trade" is defined as "any practice or method of dealing having such regularity of observance in a place, vocation, or trade as to justify an expectation that it will be observed with respect to the transaction in question." I.C. § 28–1–303(c). A usage of trade "is relevant in ascertaining the meaning of the parties' agreement, may give particular meaning to specific terms of the agreement, and may supplement or qualify the terms of the agreement," I.C. § 28–1–303(d), but it cannot conflict with the express terms of the agreement, I.C. § 28–1–303(e)(1).

BECO argues that the usage of trade among commercial lessors of construction equipment to give a discount in the rental charged per day when the customer keeps the equipment for one week or longer supplements the rental agreement between Swanson and BECO in this case. Assuming that the usage of trade among commercial lessors of construction equipment would apply to someone like Swanson who leased his equipment one time,[3] the district court did not err in holding that the

---

[3] A commercial lessor of equipment has an economic incentive to provide discounts for longer-term rentals in order to create a repeat-customer base among those who would routinely be

claimed usage of trade did not apply in this case. Usage of trade cannot supplant the express terms of a contract. I.C. § 28–1–303(e)(1). The contract in this case provided, "Rent 1 Bobcat 773 SkidSteer to start 8-27-04 until finished . . . rent [of $300] to be per working day." The express terms of the contract provide that the rent is $300 per working day during the term of the lease. The alleged usage of trade would conflict with, not supplement, the express terms of the parties' contract. Therefore, the district court did not err in holding that it does not apply in this case.

* * *

IV. CONCLUSION

The judgment of the district court must be modified by reducing it to $13,058.65. We affirm the judgment as modified and award Swanson costs, including a reasonable attorney fee, on appeal.

Justices BURDICK, J. JONES, W. JONES and HORTON concur.

NOTES AND QUESTIONS

1. *Trade usage and regular observance.* Swanson was able to elude evidence of the trade usage of equipment leasing industry pricing practices. Since a practice must be "regularly observed" in order to be admissible, how did BECO attempt to establish such a practice and its regular observance?

2. *Members and nonmembers of a trade.* Members of a trade are normally bound by their own trade usage even if not aware of the trade usage, while nonmembers are normally bound by trade usage only if they should have been aware of the trade usage. How did the court define the "trade" in question? Was Swanson a member of the trade so defined? What was the trade usage in question? Was this usage "regularly observed" in the defined trade? Was Swanson specifically aware of the trade and the trade usage, and if not, should it have been so aware?

3. *CISG treatment.* Like the UCC and the common law, CISG Art. 9 defines and uses the trilogy of usages for purposes of interpretation. However, the CISG does not rank the trilogy in a hierarchical form. See Henry D. Gabriel, "Primer on the United Nations Convention on the International Sale of Goods From the Perspective of the Uniform Commercial Code," 7 Ind. Int'l & Comp. L. Rev. 279, 283 (1997).

4. *Express exclusion of trade usage.* Given that Swanson was the target of undesirable trade usage (e.g., that commercial equipment lessors typically provided discounted rates for long-term rentals), should a contract be able to expressly exclude trade usage? Such a provision would be designed to elevate the control of the specific language of the contract over local customs. See Roger

---

renting equipment. No similar financial incentive exists for someone who is not in the business of leasing equipment and is not seeking repeat customers.

W. Kirst, "Usage of Trade and Course of Dealing: Subversion of UCC Theory," 1977 U. Ill. L. F. 811.

5.   *Consistency rule.* How does the court resolve the question of the "consistency" between the "volume discount" price reduction for longer rental periods trade usage and the express written term stating only a $300.00 "per working day" lease price? Is it possible that the contract could have included both written formulations? What does this suggest about whether trade usage is an actual part of the agreement with equal dignity of other written terms?

G. EMPLOYMENT CONTRACTS

When employment contracts do not state a specific duration, what are the legitimate expectations of the employer and the employee with regard to the duration of employment? A reasonable employment period could be inferred and implied-in-fact from the particular and unique facts of each case depending on the nature of employee reliance and other relevant factors. However, and perhaps uniquely, American jurisprudence has followed the "employment at will" doctrine that generally provides that an employee may be discharged without cause and at any time. Of course, the opposite side of the doctrine is that an at-will employee may also resign without giving any reason and at any time.

Notwithstanding the equal abilities of both parties to an employment contract of indefinite term to terminate that contract at will, many courts and commentators accept that the balance of power clearly tilts toward the employer as the employee expends a finite human resource developing the employer's business. Once expended, that human resource cannot be replaced or reused, and so untimely employment termination while arguably promoting the changing needs of business often leaves an unemployed employee with few options.

Under 19th century English law, employment created without specific expectation regarding duration was generally presumed to exist for one year. Employment beyond a year created a presumption of another year, and so on. However, in the latter part of the nineteenth century American common law adopted the presumption of at-will employment. See J. Peter Shapiro & James F. Tune, Note, "Implied Contract Rights to Job Security," 26 Stan. L. Rev. 335, 349 (1974).

The harsh doctrine is clearly a feature of contractual freedom and *laissez-faire* judicial attitude, and given its pre-eminence in American jurisprudence, one would expect the doctrine has long roots in English common law. Unfortunately, that is far from the truth because the doctrine is uniquely of American vintage, and the basis of the doctrine's roots have been challenged as suspect and even wrong. Rather than rejecting the doctrine outright, twentieth century American jurisprudence, coupled with state and federal protective legislation, have gradually engrafted "exceptions" to the doctrine necessary to protect legitimate policy interests of American workers. What is left for study is both unsavory and incomprehensible.

As might be expected, the doctrine has come under serious attack from many fronts, and thus the notes following the next case chronicle numerous exceptions. Notwithstanding these assaults on the citadel, the doctrine remains a mainstay of American employment jurisprudence. Deborah A. Ballam, "Exploding the Original Myth Regarding Employment At-Will: The True Origins of the Doctrine," 17 Berkeley J. Empl. & Labor L. 91 (1996).

As with all controversies, there are other views. Some use Law & Economics theory to argue that erosion of the doctrine would make employers more reluctant to hire. See Richard A. Epstein, "In Defense of the Contract At-Will," 51 U. Chi. L. Rev. 947 (1984); Andrew P. Morris, "Bad Data, Bad Economics, and Bad Policy: Time to Fire the Wrongful Discharge Law," 74 Tex. L. Rev. 1901 (1996). Others disagree. See Peter Linzer, "The Decline of Assent: At-Will Employment as a Case Study of the Breakdown of Private Law Theory," 20 Ga. L. Rev. 323 (1986). As Richard Epstein argues, the balance of bargaining power in the at-will employment relationship is actually substantially more nuanced than its critics credit. Employers, for example, have incentives not to abuse their right to terminate at will because such abuse negatively affects their remaining workforce morale and increases labor costs. See Richard A. Epstein, "In Defense of the Contract At-Will," 51 U. Chi. L. Rev. 947, 973–76 (1984); cf. Daniel D. Barnhizer, "Mentoring as Duty and Privilege," Mich. Bar J., Jan. 2003, at 47 (noting that law firms must pay as much as $200,000 to $500,000 to replace a departing associate, including lost revenues, lost training expenses, lost institutional knowledge, and replacement costs). In many cases, employees may also have access to better information and greater incentives to bargain for more of the contractual surplus than does the employer or the employer's agents. See id. In the market for law firm associates, for example, web sites such as "Greedy Associates"— http://www.greedyassociates.com—provide a clearinghouse for information on law firm pay structures, quality of life, quality of work, likelihood of advancement, and other elements of law firm reputation critical to bargaining over the terms of employment. Likewise, prospective employees often bargain for new employment from a superior position—their current employment. See Daniel D. Barnhizer, "Inequality of Bargaining Power," 76 U. Colo. L. Rev. 139, 205 n.274 (2005) ("[E]mployees routinely seek to improve their bargaining power with current and prospective employers by seeking other employment while they are still employed.").

As noted above, modern courts have grafted several exceptions on the default presumption that an employment contract is at-will. First, the parties may opt out of the default rule simply by providing for a definite term of employment. University employment contracts for untenured professors, for instance, will typically specify that the employment period shall cover the semester, academic year, or multi-year period for which the professor is supposed to teach. Thus, Professor Barnhizer's initial contract at Michigan State provided for a three-year employment term as an assistant professor. That definite three-year term removed the contract from the at-will presumption, and termination of his employment during that term (at least without cause) would have been a breach of contract.

Second, the parties may rebut the at-will presumption by providing that the employee may be terminated only for "cause." This may be left in a general sense of termination for "good" or "just" cause only, or the parties may actually specify the events or actions that will justify termination of the contract. Good drafting practices suggest a mixed approach, such as: "*Employment Term and Termination of Employment*: The term of this Employment Agreement shall be one year, renewable for one year terms. Employee may be terminated upon two weeks notice during the original or any successive one year term only for good cause, including but not limited to substantial failure to perform one or more duties listed in Employee's job description, insubordination, criminal indictment. . . ."

Notably, many terminated employees attempt to build a breach of contract or promissory estoppel claim from statements in the employee handbook. Consider, for example, an employee handbook that lists actions for which the employer will terminate the employee, such as being drunk on the job, use of illicit substances, or misuse of company funds. A savvy employee may argue, perhaps under the interpretive principle of *expressio unius exclusio alterius est*, that by listing terminable offenses, the handbook impliedly promised not to terminate an employee for offenses or conduct not contained in the list. Courts are generally unfriendly toward such claims absent some indication that the employer intended the employee handbook to be incorporated in the employment contract. See, e.g., Mudd v. Hoffman Homes for Youth, Inc., 374 Pa. Super. 522, 529, 543 A.2d 1092, 1096 (1988) ("[I]n order for a handbook to be construed as a contract, it 'must contain unequivocal provisions that the employer intended to be bound by it, and, in fact denunciated the principle of at-will employment.'").

Employees commonly assert that the terms of an employee handbook create an implied-in-fact contract of employment rebutting the at-will employment presumption. This is particularly common where the employee handbook states that an employee will only be discharged for cause. However, most well-drafted employee handbooks also contain written disclaimers such as "the policies and procedures set forth by the Company provide guidelines for management and employees during employment but do not create contractual rights regarding termination or otherwise." See *Donahue v. Federal Express Corp.*, 753 A.2d 238 (Pa.Super.

2000) (cited by *Dufner*). The effectiveness of the disclaimers often depends upon whether the employee is or should have been aware of and understood the disclaimer. See Julia Barnhart, Comment, "The Implied-In-Fact Contract Exception to At-Will Employment: A Call for Reform," 45 UCLA L. Rev. 817 (1998) and Amy M. Carlson, Comment, "States Are Eroding At-Will Employment Doctrines: Will Pennsylvania Join the Crowd?" 42 Duq. L. Rev. 511, 530 (2004) (suggesting broader acceptance of an implied-in-fact term requiring discharge only for cause). Also, employees generally are not bound by an employer's unilateral modifications to the handbook after the employer began work. To do so would require the employee to quit. However, the employee will be bound too if steps are taken to achieve specific assent beyond continued work, such as a new signature agreeing to the new terms. Compare *Asmus v. Pacific Bell*, 23 Cal.4th 1, 96 Cal.Rptr.2d 179, 999 P.2d 71 (2000) (continued performance acceptance of new modified terms) and *Demasse v. ITT Corp.*, 194 Ariz. 500, 984 P.2d 1138 (1999) (employee not bound by continued performance).

Third, the employee may rebut the presumption by a showing that the employee provided "additional consideration" over and above what the contract required. This may be performing substantial additional duties or incurring substantial hardship on behalf of the employer, or it may arise from detrimental reliance on some promise of the employer for a definite term of employment. Indeed, promissory estoppel remains the most common employee allegation to overcome the presumption of at-will employment. Indeed, in a 1997 article, one scholar noted that over half of all promissory estoppel allegations are asserted to support an employee's wrongful discharge claim in an at-will employment context. See Sidney W. DeLong, "The New Requirement of Promissory Estoppel: Section 90 As Catch-22," 1997 Wis. L. Rev. 943, 1003–07 . To secure employee loyalty, employers often make assurances regarding employment longevity that in other promissory estoppel contexts might be adequate to render the promise enforceable. But in the employment context, the "strength" of the at-will "presumption" often outweighs such estoppel considerations. These include statements like, "you will be here until you retire," "your position will never be taken away and you can have it as long as you want it," and "you will be the first person to work here for fifty years." Id. See also Robert J. Conner, Comment, "A Study of the Interplay Between Promissory Estoppel and At-Will Employment in Texas," 53 SMU L. Rev. 579 (2000).

Notably, the additional consideration must still have some promise of definite employment attached to it. Consider an employee like Barker in *Barker v. CTC Sales Corp.*, 199 Ga. App. 742, 406 S.E.2d 88 (Ga. Ct. App. 1991), discussed in Chapter 2. Barker, working for a failing company, refused a job offer from a third party and relocated his family in reliance on CTC Sales' promise that Barker would remain employed until CTC Sales was insolvent. The court first held that the employer's promise was only for an indefinite term. Barker nonetheless claimed that "even if the terms of his hiring were indefinite, his detrimental reliance on Mahaffey's promise constitutes *consideration in addition to normal employment services*, and is thus sufficient to except this situation from the general rule of terminability at the will of either party and prohibits termination until after a 'reasonable time.'" Id. (emphasis added). The court rejected this argument as well, holding that the additional consideration could not change the indefinite term of employment to a definite term.

Fourth, the presumption may be defeated where the termination would violate public policy. The public policy exception is narrow, however. As discussed in Chapter 6, the "public policy" usually must be specifically enunciated in a statute, regulation, or judicial decision. Alison Dufner made such a claim. Why was it rejected? See Clark W. Sabey, Note, "Scalpels and Meat Cleavers: Carving a Public Policy Exception to the At-Will Employment Doctrine," 1993 Utah L. Rev. 597.

Finally, discharged at-will employees often claim that the termination was in bad faith. Building upon your understanding that good faith is not an independent duty, but rather attaches to other obligations created by the contractual relationship between the parties or by statute, does this statement make sense? Is it consistent with your understanding of good faith after reviewing the *Locke* case? See J. Wilson Parker, "At-Will Employment and the Common Law: A Modest Proposal to De-Marginalize Employment Law," 81 Iowa L. Rev. 347 (1995).

CHAPTER 5

WHEN AN ENFORCEABLE PROMISE BECOMES DUE: BREACH OF PROMISE & NON-SATISFACTION OF CONDITIONS

■ ■ ■

Earlier chapters focused on contract formation and interpretation. Later chapters will discuss various legal excuses why an otherwise valid contract may be unenforceable against one or both parties. These doctrines, such as public policy, the Statute of Frauds, unconscionability, fraud, duress, impracticability, and so on, excuse one or both parties from the legal consequences of breach. Where these doctrines apply, a failure to perform does not cause a "breach." In contrast, this chapter considers the general concept of breach of contract, while Chapter 9 considers various remedies available to the parties once a valid contract is breached. In this sense, "breach" of a contract is linked to "any non-performance" of a duty under that contract when that duty becomes due. Restatement (Second) of Contracts § 235(2). As a corollary, full or perfect performance of a contractual duty discharges that duty. Restatement (Second) of Contracts § 235(1). Therefore, a contract serves two distinct functions—defining both the scope and the timing of the contractual duties of both parties.

One or both (or all) of the parties may breach one or more contractual duties, before, during, or after full performance by the other party. Thus, in a requirements contract for the sale of automotive components in multiple lots to a manufacturer on thirty-days credit payment terms, the seller may breach by failing to deliver any components, making only partial deliveries, or delivering nonconforming components. Alternatively, the buyer may breach by failing to pay for some or all of the deliveries. The analysis of breach, therefore, requires both a determination of the terms and meaning of the parties' contract and an analysis of the effect of a breach by one party on the other party's obligation to perform at a later time. In the example above, for instance, if the buyer fails to pay for the first shipment, at what point does that failure discharge the seller's duties to provide components in future deliveries? Likewise, if the seller consistently delivers non-conforming components or makes late or incomplete deliveries, what is the buyer's obligation to continue paying for goods already received? This chapter organizes its exploration of this timing analysis by subject matters controlling the timing of when a performance is due. By definition, the failure to perform a duty before that

417

duty is due is not a breach. Consequently, the other party is not entitled to any contractual remedy at that point in the contractual relationship.

This chapter addresses these issues in two contexts—anticipatory repudiation and conditions on party performance. First, in some circumstances, a party may declare that it intends not to perform at some time well before the duty to perform actually becomes due. Alternatively, supervening events may raise significant doubts that a party will render performance when due. In the components requirements contract described above, for instance, the seller may suffer extraordinary price increases that make the production of components less profitable (although not impracticable) and may threaten to slow or withhold deliveries until it receives a price increase. Alternatively, labor unrest or systemic disruptions in raw materials may cause the buyer to be concerned regarding whether the seller will actually be able to complete performance when due. In both cases, technically, the seller has not breached the contract because its performance is not yet due at the time of the declaration or events giving rise to the buyer's concern regarding future performance. In such cases, must the other party wait until the time the performance is due to declare a breach and seek alternative sources of performance, along with pursuing a remedy for the resulting breach? This topic is considered first under the doctrine of "anticipatory repudiation."

Second, every promise of a performance is subject to some type of "condition." The only question is whether the condition arises by operation of law ("constructive conditions") or by the express language and implied conduct of the parties ("express conditions"). Since a condition is defined as an event that must occur before performance becomes due, conditions are extremely powerful contractual tools for regulating the timing of the parties' performances. Restatement (Second) of Contracts § 224. Specifically, performance of a promise subject to a condition cannot become due unless the condition either occurs or is excused. Restatement (Second) of Contracts § 225(1). Thus, the nonoccurrence of a condition either discharges an instant or existing promise of performance or prevents that promise of performance from creating a duty in the promisor in the first place. For example, in the context of an automobile insurance contract, the insurer promises to pay a certain sum to the insured. The insurer's promise is conditioned upon the occurrence of an insured event—an automobile accident. If the accident does not occur, the insurer's duty to perform according to the terms of its promise never becomes instant, that is, it never imposes a duty of payment upon the insurer. The insurer's "failure" to pay any money to the insured before an accident occurs is not a breach, because absent the satisfaction of the condition—an accident—the insurer never has a duty to pay. See also Restatement (Second) of Contracts § 225(2).

Although powerful tools for the timing of contractual duties and performances, conditions may also impose harsh results upon a party to the contract. In the automobile insurance contract example above, the contract may further condition the insurer's duty to pay upon the insured making the damaged car available for inspection by an insurance adjuster within a reasonable time following the accident. If the insured unknowingly permits the car to be destroyed or sold before such an inspection, the nonoccurrence of the condition may discharge the insurer's duty to pay. Because the nonoccurrence of a condition precludes the other party from seeking any remedy for breach of the contract, the common law imposes several mitigating doctrines upon conditions for fairness and equity, including waiver, estoppel (reliance), and excuse to prevent forfeiture.

A. ANTICIPATORY REPUDIATION

The classic definition of a contract "breach" contemplates nonperformance of a duty when that duty is due. Restatement (Second) of Contracts § 235(2). But it is also possible to "breach" a duty before it is due by repudiating that duty—i.e., declaring an intent not to perform before performance is due. Such a declaration of intent constitutes an "anticipatory repudiation." Generally, a clear repudiation of a duty before it is due discharges the injured party's duty to perform (like a condition discussed in the next section) and creates an immediate claim for total breach and damages at the time of the repudiation. Restatement (Second) of Contracts § 253(2) (discharge injured party's duties) and § 253(1) (repudiation gives rise to a claim for damages and total breach).

The development of the modern anticipatory repudiation rule struggles to reconcile competing policies. Consider the example of a contract for the sale of wheat, with payment due thirty days after delivery. If, before the delivery date, the buyer declares that it will not pay for the wheat, that declaration creates certain rights and privileges in the seller. Clearly, an anticipatory repudiation of the obligation to pay for the wheat would discharge the seller's duty to deliver the wheat upon the delivery date and creates a privilege in the seller against the buyer's claims for breach of contract for non-delivery. But such contracts often involve deliveries several months in the future—does the seller have to wait until the delivery date has passed before suing the buyer for breach of contract? It is one thing to suggest that an anticipatory repudiation discharges the injured party's duties. Such a discharge promotes policies of economic efficiency and mitigation of damages by permitting the injured party immediately to obtain a substitute performance. Likewise, from an economic analysis perspective, the power to repudiate and terminate a bad deal limits risks and reduces overall transaction costs, thereby arguably encouraging the making of contracts. Arthur Rosett, "Partial, Qualified, and Equivocal Repudiation of Contract," 81 Colum. L. Rev. 93 (1981). But it is quite another thing to create a right in the injured party to sue immediately for damages for total breach at the time of the repudiation. Modern anticipatory repudiation doctrine partly resolves this tension by requiring a clear and unequivocal declaration of anticipatory repudiation before the buyer may sue for breach. Equivocal statements, such as "I am unsure whether I will be able to perform," "I would like to explore cancelling this contract," and so on, may create sufficient uncertainty in the other party to justify suspending performance until that uncertainty is resolved, but do not give the injured party a right to sue immediately for breach. While this rule is superficially clear, there will always be marginal cases. Both parties may understand a declaration of intent not to perform as absolute and unequivocal, even though a reasonable observer might interpret the declaration as equivocal. Likewise, even where repudiation is clearly unequivocal, it could be based on the repudiating party's mistaken but good faith belief that its performance is no longer due. Who should assume the risk of an unclear, marginal, and equivocal repudiation?

Early English common law determined breach could occur before performance was due, but the outcome was heavily criticized. In the famous case of *Hochster v. De La Tour*, 118 Eng. Rep. 922 (Q.B. 1853), on April 12, Hochster agreed to serve De La Tour as his courier on his three-month European tour beginning on June 1. On May 11, De La Tour wrote Hochster that he had changed his mind, would not require his services, and refused to pay any compensation. Hochster brought suit on May 22. De La Tour argued that the May 22 suit was premature and improper because no breach could occur prior to June 1 when the time for performance was to begin. The court determined that when De La Tour discharged Hochster on May 11, this also discharged Hochster's duty to perform on June 1. In addition to discharging Hochster's duty to perform (and duty to hold himself ready to perform), the court also created a right in Hochster to sue De La Tour immediately, on the date of the anticipatory repudiation, for breach:

> If the plaintiff has no remedy for breach of the contract unless he treats the contract in force, and acts upon it down to the 1st of June 1852, it follows that, till then, he must enter into no employment which will interfere with his promise "to start with the defendant on such travels on the day and the year," and that he must then be properly equipped in all respects as a courier for a three months' tour on the continent of Europe. . . . The man who wrongfully renounces a contract into which he has deliberately entered cannot justly complain if he is immediately sued for compensation in damages by the man whom he has injured. *Hochster v. De La Tour*, 118 Eng. Rep. 922, 926–927 (Q.B. 1853).

Thus, according to the court, two legal consequences attached from De la Tour's repudiation: (i) Hochster's duties were immediately discharged and he was free to mitigate and find other employment; and (ii) Hochster had a right to sue immediately for damages (even though other employment might mitigate the damage claim and would be unknown until after the date performance was due). Indeed, having repudiated the contract, the repudiating party is hardly in a position to complain if the injured party does not mitigate damages before the time for performance is regularly due on the contract. See Joseph H. Beale, Jr., "Damages Upon Repudiation of a Contract," 17 Yale L. J. 443 (1907). As a policy matter, as a condition to sue for breach of the repudiated contract, any other outcome on the first holding would force an employee to decline other employment and stand ready to perform on the repudiated contract until after the repudiated performance is due. Clearly, the employee should have the choice (but not the obligation) to accept other gainful employment without sacrificing the right to sue for a breach on the repudiated contract. See Lawrence J. Meyer, Comment, "Anticipatory Breach of Contract—Effects of Repudiation," 8 Miami L. Q. 68, 69 (1953).

Nonetheless, the court's holding granting the injured party the right to sue immediately upon repudiation was the subject of substantial criticism. Such an immediate right to sue does not necessarily follow from a discharge of the injured party's duty to perform. Moreover, the right to sue immediately for "breach" of the contract upon an anticipatory repudiation increases the uncertainty attached to an over-inclusive damage award. See Samuel Williston, "Repudiation of Contracts," 14 Harv. L. Rev. 317 (Part I) and 421 (Part 2), 432 (1901). Others were more sympathetic to the dual approach. Henry Winthrop Ballantine, "Anticipatory Breach and the Enforcement of Contractual Duties," 22 Mich. L. Rev. 329 (1924) and Herbert R. Limburg, "Anticipatory Repudiation of Contracts," 10 Cornell L. Q. 135 (1924) (articulating that the injured party's "obligations" are discharged while the injured party merely has the "right" to pursue an immediate suit for damages). Nonetheless, early supporters generally agreed that an effective repudiation discharged the injured party's duty to perform, as well as created an immediate right to sue for a breach of contract:

> Its basis in principle is that a promise to perform in the future by implication includes an engagement not deliberately to compromise the probability of performance. A promise is a verbal act designed as a reliance to the promisee, and so as a means to the forecast of his own conduct. Abstention from any deliberate act before the time of performance which makes impossible that reliance and that forecast ought surely to be included by implication. Such intermediate uncertainties as arise from the vicissitudes of the promisor's affairs are, of course, a part of the risk, but it is hard to see how, except by mere verbalism, it can be supposed that the promisor may within the terms of his undertaking gratuitously add to those uncertainties by

announcing his purpose to default. Even the opponents of the doctrine concede that, if there be such an implied promise, its breach may drag in the damages upon the main promise. Equitable Trust Co. v. Western Pac. Ry., 244 F. 485, 502 (S.D.N.Y. 1917) (Hand, J.).

This conclusion by Judge Learned Hand that a repudiating promisor "gratuitously" adds to the uncertainties of the contract by announcing the repudiation essentially equates an anticipatory repudiation with a current and immediate breach of the implied contractual duty of good faith and fair dealing. See E. Allan Farnsworth, Contracts § 8.20 at 583, n.8 (4th ed. 2004). By permitting the injured party to sue for damages at any time following the repudiation as if the contract had been breached, the *Hochster* rule on anticipatory repudiation creates substantial complexities for the measurement of damages under both the common law and the UCC. See Thomas H. Jackson, "'Anticipatory Repudiation' and the Temporal Element of Contract Law: An Economic Inquiry Into Contract Damages in Cases of Prospective Nonperformance," 31 Stan. L. Rev. 69 (1978); Dena DeNooyer, Comment, "Remedying Anticipatory Repudiation—Past, Present and Future?" 52 SMU L. Rev. 1787 (1999); and John A. Sebert, Jr., "Remedies Under Article Two of the Uniform Commercial Code: An Agenda for Review," 130 U. Pa. L. Rev. 360 (1981).

Following general acceptance of the doctrine, courts and commentators attempted to identify situations constituting a true anticipatory repudiation (versus a simple equivocation) and whether an otherwise valid repudiation could be withdrawn. On the latter score, since an anticipatory repudiation is in fact "not a breach," it can be withdrawn unless the injured party detrimentally relies upon that anticipatory repudiation. In this sense, unlike a breach—which cannot be withdrawn— a repudiation is like a waiver of performance by the repudiating party that can be retracted unless and until the injured party incurs detrimental reliance. See Lauriz Void, "Withdrawal of Repudiation After Anticipatory Breach of Contract," 5 Tex. L. Rev. 9 (1926); Note, "Withdrawal of Anticipatory Repudiation of Contractual Obligations," 28 Colum. L. Rev. 1062 (1928); John T. Whealen, Note, "Contracts—Acts Constituting Renunciation and Liabilities Therefor," 2 Kan. L. Rev. 408 (1954); and Alphonse M. Squillante, "Anticipatory Repudiation and Retraction," 7 Val. U. L. Rev. 373 (1973).

The doctrine was firmly embedded in Restatement (First) of Contracts § 318, as amended in 1948, which provided that an anticipatory repudiation was equivalent to a total breach. Restatement (First) of Contracts § 318 provided that repudiation included both (i) a positive statement indicating that the promisor will not or cannot substantially perform the contractual duties; as well as (ii) any voluntary affirmative act rendering substantial performance of the contractual duties actually or apparently impossible. In explaining its adoption of the term "repudiation" rather than anticipatory "breach" and the reasoning behind permitting the repudiating party to withdraw its repudiation, the Restatement (First) of Contracts § 318, *cmt. d* clarified that an anticipatory repudiation does not cause any real injury until the non-repudiating party has either relied or filed suit. The distinction between breach and repudiation lies in the fact that "[a]n ordinary breach of contract that has once arisen cannot be utterly nullified or destroyed by any conduct of a defaulting party. . . . In case of an anticipatory repudiation, however, withdrawal of it before either an action has been brought, or other change of position made by the other party to the contract nullifies all effects of the breach." Id.

Accordingly, Restatement (First) of Contracts § 319 provided that the repudiating party could "nullify" the repudiation by notifying the non-repudiating party of the retraction before the party detrimentally relied or instituted a cause of action for breach. But the injured party may still elect to treat a repudiation as a breach, even while urging the repudiating party to perform. Restatement (First) of Contracts § 320. Thus, the injured party does not "waive" the right to rely on the repudiation, even when urging the repudiating party to perform. Restatement (Second) of Contracts is consistent on all these points. See Restatement (Second) of Contracts §§ 253 (effect of repudiation), 256 (nullification), and 257 (injured party urging performance). The UCC adopts the same treatment. See UCC §§ 2–610 (repudiation) and 2–611 (retraction). Even international law is similar. CISG § 72(1) and UNIDROIT Principles 7.3.3. See also Arthur Rosett, "Critical Reflections on the United Nations Convention on Contracts for the International Sale of Goods," 45 Ohio St. L. J. 265 (1984).

The potential severity of the anticipatory repudiation doctrine raises two significant issues. First, since repudiation constitutes a total breach before the actual time of performance, what is the appropriate measure of damages? See Restatement (Second) of Contracts § 253(1). The concept of partial and total breach is the subject explored in Chapter 9, as well as below under the doctrine of substantial performance involving constructive conditions.

Second, what words or conduct are sufficient to trigger an anticipatory repudiation? See Restatement (Second) of Contracts § 250 (repudiation includes statement by obligor indicating intent to commit breach that would constitute a total breach at the time of performance or voluntary conduct rendering obligor actually or apparently unable to perform). Of course, an obligor may make statements or engage in conduct that makes the obligee insecure regarding the ability or intent of the obligor to perform in the future. In such circumstances, the insecure obligee may have a right to seek or demand adequate assurance that the obligor will perform when performance comes due. See Restatement (Second) of Contracts § 251. Likewise, UCC § 2–609 provides a similar right to seek assurance that the obligor's performance will be forthcoming when due. See generally Thomas M. Campbell, Note, "The Right to Assurance of Performance Under UCC § 2–609 and Restatement (Second) of Contracts § 251: Toward a Uniform Rule of Contract Law," 50 Fordham L. Rev. 1292 (1982) and Deanna Wise, Comment, "Proposed Amendments to Article 2 of the Uniform Commercial Code: The Tangled Web of Anticipatory Repudiation and the Right to Demand Assurances," 40 U. Kan. L. Rev. 287 (1991).

A statement or an act constitutes a legal "repudiation" when it communicates that the obligor will commit a breach (Restatement (Second) of Contracts § 250(1)) or involves some voluntary act rendering the obligor actually or apparently unable to perform without a breach (Restatement (Second) of Contracts § 250(2)). UCC § 2–610 and common law are similar on these points, although the UCC requires that the repudiation "substantially impair the value of the contract." Restatement (Second) of Contracts § 250, *cmt. b* provides in relevant part:

> b.   *Nature of statement.* In order to constitute a repudiation, a party's language must be sufficiently positive to be reasonably interpreted to mean that the party will not or cannot perform. Mere expression of doubt as to his willingness or ability to perform is not enough to constitute a repudiation, although such an expression may give an obligee reasonable grounds to believe that the obligor will commit a serious breach and may ultimately result in a repudiation under the rule stated in § 251. However, language that under a fair reading "amounts to a statement of intention not to perform except on conditions which go beyond the contract" constitutes a repudiation.

Restatement (Second) of Contracts § 250 *cmt. d* extends this analysis to note that the "threatened breach must be of sufficient gravity that, if the breach actually occurred, it would of itself give the obligee a claim for damages for total breach under § 243(1)." In some cases, an obligor may mistakenly believe that its performance under the contract is excused and will mistakenly, but in good faith, declare that it will not continue to perform. If a reasonable person in the injured party's position would objectively consider such a statement to be a repudiation (regardless of the good faith of the obligor), that statement will constitute an anticipatory repudiation. See generally Keith A. Rowley, "A Brief History of Anticipatory Repudiation in American Contract Law," 69 U. Cin. L. Rev. 565, 569 (2001). Consequently, both parties bear significant risks in connection with the anticipatory repudiation doctrine. A wrong guess, even as to reasonable grounds for assurance, can have disastrous consequences particularly where a court later determines that the statement or conduct neither constituted a repudiation nor created reasonable grounds for demanding assurance of future performance. On the other hand, ignoring the conduct may threaten or reduce later recovery for failure to properly mitigate damages. The horns of this dilemma caused one commentator to observe that the law is surprisingly forgiving to promise breakers and quite harsh to the nonbreaching victim. E. Allan Farnsworth, "Legal Remedies for Breach of Contract," 70 Colum. L. Rev. 1145 (1970).

TRUMAN L. FLATT & SONS CO., INC. V. SCHUPF
Appellate Court of Illinois
271 Ill.App.3d 983, 649 N.E.2d 990 (1995)

Presiding Justice KNECHT delivered the opinion of the court.

Plaintiff Truman L. Flatt & Sons Co., Inc., filed a complaint seeking specific performance of a real estate contract made with defendants Sara Lee Schupf, Ray H. Neiswander, Jr., and American National Bank and Trust Company of Chicago (American), as trustee under trust No. 23257. Defendants filed a motion for summary judgment, which the trial court granted. Plaintiff now appeals from the trial court's grant of the motion for summary judgment. We reverse and remand.

In March 1993, plaintiff and defendants entered a contract in which defendants agreed to sell plaintiff a parcel of land located in Springfield, Illinois. The contract stated the purchase price was to be $160,000. The contract also contained the following provisions:

1.   This transaction shall be closed on or before June 30, 1993, or upon approval of the relief requested from the Zoning Code of the City of Springfield, Illinois, whichever first occurs ("Closing Date"). The closing is subject to contingency set forth in paragraph 14.

* * *

14.   This Contract to Purchase Real Estate is contingent upon the Buyer obtaining, within one hundred twenty (120) days after the date hereof, amendment of, or other sufficient relief of, the Zoning Code of the City of Springfield to permit the construction and operation of an asphalt plant. In the event the City Council of the City of Springfield denies the request for such use of the property, then this contract shall be voidable at Buyer's option and if Buyer elects to void this contract Buyer shall receive a refund of the earnest money paid.

On May 21, plaintiff's attorney sent a letter to defendants' attorney informing him of substantial public opposition plaintiff encountered at a public meeting concerning its request for rezoning. The letter concluded:

The day after the meeting all of the same representatives of the buyer assembled and discussed our chances for successfully pursuing the re-zoning request. Everyone who was there was in agreement that our chances were zero to none for success. As a result, we decided to withdraw the request for rezoning, rather than face almost certain defeat.

The bottom line is that we are still interested in the property, but the property is not worth as much to us a 35-acre parcel zoned I–1, as it would be if it were zoned I–2. At this juncture, I think it is virtually impossible for anyone to get that property re-zoned I–2, especially to accommodate the operation of an asphalt plant. In an effort to keep this thing moving, my clients have authorized me to offer your clients the sum of $142,500.00 for the property, which they believe fairly represents its value with its present zoning classification. Please check with your clients and advise whether or not that revision in the contract is acceptable. If it is, I believe we can accelerate the closing and bring this matter to a speedy conclusion. Your prompt attention will be appreciated. Thanks.

Defendants' attorney responded in a letter dated June 9, the body of which stated, in its entirety:

In reply to your May 21 letter, be advised that the owners of the property in question are not interested in selling the property for $142,500 and, accordingly, the offer is not accepted.

I regret that the zoning reclassification was not approved.

Plaintiff's attorney replied back in a letter dated June 14, the body of which stated, in its entirety:

My clients received your letter of June 9, 1993, with some regret, however upon some consideration they have elected to proceed with the purchase of the property as provided in the contract. At your convenience please give me a call so that we can set up a closing date.

After this correspondence, plaintiff's attorney sent two more brief letters to defendants' attorney, dated June 23 and July 6, each requesting information concerning the status of defendants' preparation for fulfillment of the contract. Defendants' attorney replied in a letter dated July 8. The letter declared it was the defendants' position plaintiff's failure to waive the rezoning requirement and elect to proceed under the contract at the time the rezoning was denied, coupled with the new offer to buy the property at less than the contract price, effectively voided the contract. Plaintiff apparently sent one more letter in an attempt to convince defendants to honor the contract, but defendants declined. Defendants then arranged to have plaintiff's earnest money returned.

Plaintiff filed a complaint for specific performance and other relief against defendants and American, asking the court to direct defendants to comply with the terms of the contract. Defendants responded by filing a "motion to strike, motion to dismiss or, in the alternative, motion for summary judgment." The motion for summary judgment sought summary judgment on the basis plaintiff repudiated the contract.

Prior to the hearing on the motions, plaintiff filed interrogatories requesting, among other things, information concerning the current status of the property. Defendants' answers to the interrogatories stated defendants had no knowledge of any third party's involvement in a potential sale of the property, defendants had not made any offer to sell the property to anyone, no one had made an offer to purchase the property or discussed the possibility of purchasing the property, and defendants had not sold the property to, received any offer from, or discussed a sale of the property with, any other trust member.

After a hearing on the motions, the trial court granted the defendants' motion for summary judgment without explaining the basis for its ruling. Plaintiff filed a post-trial motion to vacate the judgment. The trial court denied the post-trial motion, declaring defendants' motion for summary judgment was granted because plaintiff had repudiated the contract. Plaintiff now appeals the trial court's grant of summary judgment, arguing the trial court erred because (1) it did not repudiate the contract, and (2) even if it did repudiate the contract, it timely retracted that repudiation.

Plaintiff contends the trial court erred in granting summary judgment. Summary judgment is proper when the resolution of a case hinges on a question of law and the moving party's right to judgment is clear and free from doubt. . . . Here, there are no facts in dispute. Thus, the question is whether the trial court erred in declaring defendant was entitled to judgment as a matter of law based on those facts.

Plaintiff first argues summary judgment was improper because the trial court erred in finding plaintiff had repudiated the contract.

> The doctrine of anticipatory repudiation requires a clear manifestation of an intent not to perform the contract on the date of performance. . . . That intention must be a definite and unequivocal manifestation that he will not render the promised performance when the time fixed for it in the contract arrives. [Citation.] Doubtful and indefinite statements that performance may or may not take place are not enough to constitute anticipatory repudiation. (In re Marriage of Olsen (1988), 124 Ill. 2d 19, 24, 123 Ill. Dec. 980, 982, 528 N.E.2d 684, 686.)

These requirements exist because "[a]nticipatory breach is not a remedy to be taken lightly." (Olsen, 124 Ill. 2d at 25, 123 Ill. Dec. at 983, 528 N.E.2d at 687.) The Restatement (Second) of Contracts adopts the view of the Uniform Commercial Code (UCC) and states "language that under a fair reading 'amounts to a statement of intention not to perform except on conditions which go beyond the contract' constitutes a repudiation. Comment 2 to Uniform Commercial Code § 2–610." (Restatement (Second) of Contracts § 250, Comment b, at 273 (1981).) Whether an anticipatory repudiation occurred is a question of fact and the judgment of the trial court thereon will not be disturbed unless it is against the manifest weight of evidence. Leazzo v. Dunham (1981), 95 Ill. App. 3d 847, 850, 51 Ill. Dec. 437, 440, 420 N.E. 2d 851, 854.

As can be seen, whether a repudiation occurred is determined on a case-by-case basis, depending on the particular language used. Both plaintiff and defendants, although they cite Illinois cases discussing repudiation, admit the cited Illinois cases are all factually distinguishable from the case at hand because none of those cases involved a request to change a term in the contract. According to the commentators, a suggestion for modification of the contract does not amount to a repudiation. (J. Calamari & J. Perillo, Contracts § 12–4, at 524–25 n. 74 (3d ed. 1987) (hereinafter Calamari), citing Unique Systems Inc. v. Zotos International, Inc. (8th Cir. 1980), 622 F. 2d 373.) Plaintiff also cites cases in other jurisdictions holding a request for a change in the price term of a contract does not constitute a repudiation. (Wooten v. DeMean (Mo. Ct. App. 1990), 788 S.W. 2d 522; Stolper Steel Products Corp. v. Behrens Manufacturing Co. (1960), 10 Wis. 2d 478, 103 N.W.2d 683.) Defendants attempt to distinguish these cases by arguing here, under the totality of the language in the letter and the circumstances surrounding the letter, the request by plaintiff for a decrease in price clearly implied a threat of nonperformance if the price term was not modified. We disagree.

The language in the May 21 letter did not constitute a clearly implied threat of nonperformance. First, although the language in the May 21 letter perhaps could be read as implying plaintiff would refuse to perform under the contract unless the price was modified, given the totality of the language in the letter, such an inference is weak. More important, even if such an inference were possible, Illinois law requires a repudiation be manifested clearly and unequivocally. Plaintiff's May 21 letter at most created an ambiguous implication whether performance would occur. Indeed, during oral argument defense counsel conceded the May 21 letter was "ambiguous" on whether a repudiation had occurred. This is insufficient to constitute a repudiation under well-settled Illinois law. Therefore, the trial court erred in declaring the May 21 letter anticipatorily repudiated the real estate contract as a matter of law.

Moreover, even if plaintiff had repudiated the contract, the trial court erred in granting summary judgment on this basis because plaintiff timely retracted its repudiation. Only one published decision has discussed and applied Illinois law regarding retraction of an anticipatory repudiation, Refrigeradora Del Noroeste, S.A. v. Appelbaum (1956), 138 F. Supp. 354 (holding the repudiating party has the power of retraction unless the injured party has brought suit or otherwise materially changed position), aff'd in part & rev'd in part on other grounds (1957), 248 F. 2d 858. The Restatement (Second) of Contracts states:

> The effect of a statement as constituting a repudiation under § 250 or the basis for a repudiation under § 251 is nullified by a retraction of the statement if notification of the retraction comes to the attention of the injured party before he materially changes his position in reliance on the repudiation or indicates to the other party that he considers the repudiation to be final. (Emphasis added.) (Restatement (Second) of Contracts § 256(1), at 293 (1981).)

The UCC adopts the same position:

> Retraction of Anticipatory Repudiation. (1) Until the repudiating party's next performance is due he can retract his repudiation unless the aggrieved party has since the repudiation cancelled or materially changed his position or otherwise indicated that he considers the repudiation final. (Emphasis added.) (810 ILCS 5/2–611(1) (West 1992).)

Professors Calamari and Perillo declare section 2–611 of the UCC:

> [I]s in general accord with the common law rule that an anticipatory repudiation may be retracted until the other party has commenced an action thereon or has otherwise changed his position. The Code is explicit that no other act of reliance is necessary where the aggrieved party indicates "that he considers the repudiation final." (Emphasis added.) (Calamari § 12.7, at 528.)

"The majority of the common law cases appear to be in accord with this position." (Calamari § 12.7, at 528 n. 93.) Other commentators are universally in accord. Professor Farnsworth states: "The repudiating party can prevent the injured party from treating the contract as terminated by retracting before the injured party has acted in response to it." (Emphasis added.) (2 E. Farnsworth, Contracts § 8.22, at 482 (1990).) Professor Corbin declares one who has anticipatorily repudiated his contract has the power of retraction until the aggrieved party has materially changed his position in reliance on the repudiation. (4 A. Corbin, Corbin on Contracts § 980, at 930–31 (1951) (hereinafter Corbin).) Corbin goes on to say the assent of the aggrieved party is necessary for retraction only when the repudiation is no longer merely anticipatory, but has become an actual breach at the time performance is due. (4 Corbin § 980, at 935.) Williston states an anticipatory repudiation can be retracted by the repudiating party "unless the other party has, before the withdrawal, manifested an election to rescind the contract, or changed his position in reliance on the repudiation." (Emphasis added.) 11 W. Jaeger, Williston on Contracts § 1335, at 180 (3d ed. 1968) (hereinafter Williston).

Defendants completely avoid discussion of the common-law right to retract a repudiation other than to say Illinois is silent on the issue. Defendants then cite Stonecipher v. Pillatsch (1975), 30 Ill. App. 3d 140, 332 N.E. 2d 151, Builder's Concrete Co. v. Fred Faubel & Sons Inc. (1978), 58 Ill. App. 3d 100, 15 Ill. Dec. 517, 373 N.E.2d 863, and Leazzo v. Dunham (1981), 95 Ill. App. 3d 847, 51 Ill. Dec. 437, 420 N.E.2d 851, as well as Williston § 1337, at 185–86. These authorities stand for the proposition that after an anticipatory repudiation, the aggrieved party is entitled to choose to treat the contract as rescinded or terminated, to treat the anticipatory repudiation as a breach by bringing suit or otherwise changing its position, or to await the time for performance. The UCC adopts substantially the same position. (810 ILCS 5/2–610 (West 1992).) Defendants here assert they chose to treat the contract as rescinded, as they had a right to do under well-settled principles of law.

Plaintiff admits the law stated by defendants is well settled, and admits if the May 21 letter was an anticipatory breach, then defendants had the right to treat the contract as being terminated or rescinded. However, plaintiff points out defendants' assertions ignore the great weight of authority, discussed earlier, which provides a right of the repudiating party to retract the repudiation before the aggrieved party has chosen one of its options allowed under the common law and listed in Stonecipher, Builder's Concrete, and Leazzo. Plaintiff argues defendants' letter of June 9 failed to treat the contract as rescinded, and absent notice or other manifestation defendants were pursuing one of their options, plaintiff was free to retract its repudiation. Plaintiff is correct.

Defendants' precise theory that plaintiff should not be allowed to retract any repudiation in this instance is ambiguous and may be given two interpretations. The first is Illinois should not follow the common-law rule allowing retraction of an anticipatory repudiation before the aggrieved party elects a response to the repudiation. This theory warrants little discussion, because the rule is well settled. Further, defendants have offered no public policy reason to disallow retraction of repudiation other than the public interest in upholding the "sanctity of the contract."

The second possible interpretation of defendants' precise theory is an aggrieved party may treat the contract as terminated or rescinded without notice or other indication being given to the repudiating party, and once such a decision is made by the aggrieved party, the repudiating party no longer has the right of retraction. It is true no notice is required to be given to the repudiating party if the aggrieved party materially changes its position as a result of the repudiation. (See, e.g., Calamari § 12–7, at 528 n. 92, citing Bu-Vi-Bar Petroleum Corp. v. Krow (10th Cir. 1930), 40 F. 2d 488, 493.) Here, however, the defendants admitted in their answers to plaintiff's interrogatories they had not entered another agreement to sell the property, nor even discussed or considered the matter with another party. Defendants had not changed their position at all, nor do defendants make any attempt to so argue. As can be seen from the language of the Restatement, the UCC, and the commentators, shown earlier, they are in accord that where the aggrieved party has not otherwise undergone a material change in position, the aggrieved party must indicate to the other party it is electing to treat the contract as rescinded. This can be accomplished either by bringing suit, by notifying the repudiating party, or by in some other way manifesting an election to treat the contract as rescinded. Prior to such indication, the repudiating party is free to retract its repudiation. The Restatement (Second) of Contracts provides the following illustrations:

> 2. On February 1, A contracts to supply B with natural gas for one year beginning on May 1, payment to be made each month. On March 1, A repudiates. On April 1, before B has taken any action in response to the repudiation, A notifies B that he retracts his repudiation. B's duties under the contract are not discharged, and B has no claim against A.

* * *

> The facts being otherwise as stated in Illustration 2, on March 15, B notifies A that he cancels the contract. B's duties under the contract are discharged and B has a claim against A for damages for total breach. . . . (Emphasis added.) Restatement (Second) of Contracts § 256, Comments a, c (1981).

This rule makes sense as well. If an aggrieved party could treat the contract as rescinded or terminated without notice or other indication to the repudiating party, the rule allowing retraction of an anticipatory repudiation would be eviscerated. No repudiating party ever would be able to retract a repudiation, because after receiving a retraction, the aggrieved party could, if it wished, simply declare it had already decided to treat the repudiation as a rescission or termination of the contract. Defendants' theory would effectively rewrite the common-law rule regarding retraction of anticipatory repudiation so that the repudiating party may retract an anticipatory repudiation only upon assent from the aggrieved party. This is not the common-law rule, and we decline to adopt defendants' proposed revision of it.

Applying the actual common-law rule to the facts here, plaintiff sent defendants a letter dated June 14, which clearly and unambiguously indicated plaintiff intended to perform under the contract. However, defendants did not notify plaintiff, either expressly or impliedly, of an intent to treat the contract as rescinded until July 8. Nor is there anything in the record demonstrating any indication to plaintiff, prior to July 8, of an intent by defendants to treat the contract as rescinded or terminated. Thus, assuming plaintiff's May 21 request for a lower purchase price constituted an anticipatory repudiation of the contract, plaintiff successfully retracted that repudiation in the letter dated June 14 because defendants had not yet materially changed their position or indicated to plaintiff an intent to treat the contract as rescinded. Therefore, because plaintiff had timely retracted any alleged repudiation of the contract, the trial court erred in granting summary judgment for defendants on the basis plaintiff repudiated the contract. Defendants were not entitled to judgment as a matter of law.

The trial court's grant of summary judgment for defendants is reversed, and the cause is remanded.

Reversed and remanded.

NOTES AND QUESTIONS

1. *Paragraph 14 zoning condition.* Paragraph 14 of the contract stated an express condition that the purchase was contingent upon buyer's ability to obtain a zoning change to build an asphalt plant. Whose contractual obligation was the condition designed to protect, the buyer or the seller? If the term was intended to protect the buyer, and the buyer had made no attempt to seek a zoning variance, would the buyer be entitled to invoke the condition to discharge its purchase obligation? Assuming that the buyer made reasonable but unsuccessful efforts to obtain the zoning change, may the seller refuse to sell since the condition (zoning change) did not occur? If not, does this suggest that the buyer cannot rely on a condition in its favor without some effort, and that the seller cannot invoke a condition designed to protect the other party? Is this result consistent with the intent of the parties? Does the Chapter 8 discussion of "waiver" of a NOM clause apply with equal force to an express condition? As discussed in the last section of this chapter, an obligor whose duty is subject to an express condition may "waive" the condition, thereby promising to perform notwithstanding the nonoccurrence of the condition. Did the buyer's May 21st letter waive the rezoning condition or repudiate the contract? Should the seller be able to waive a condition favoring the buyer?

2. *Buyer's alleged repudiation.* The seller and trial court argued that the buyer's May 21st letter repudiated the contract (rather than simply waiving the condition). If so, the seller was privileged to terminate the contract, discharge its duty to sell, and sue for any damages (arguably none, unless determined by a resale at a lower price, and a resale was not in play). The May 21st letter contained at least five statements relevant to repudiation: (i) the request for zoning change was withdrawn in the face of near certain defeat (condition waiver or repudiation of contract?); (ii) we are still interested in the property, but it is not worth as much as currently zoned (negotiation or repudiation?); (iii) in an effort to keep things moving, we are offering $142,500 (negotiation or repudiation?); (iv) please check with your clients and advise whether the price adjustment is acceptable (negotiation or repudiation?); and (v) if acceptable, we can accelerate the closing and bring the matter to a speedy conclusion (negotiation or repudiation?).

Restatement (Second) of Contracts § 250, *cmt. b* makes clear that the statements must be "sufficiently positive to be reasonably interpreted to mean the party will not or cannot perform." Whose interpretation matters under this standard, the buyer's actual, subjective intent or the seller's objective understanding? Do you think this was a question to be decided as a matter of law by the court on summary judgment or as a question of fact by a jury at trial?

Under repudiation doctrine, what is the legal effect of proposing a modification to the contract? Does the mere proposal of a modification repudiate the contract as a *per se* declaration that the proposing party will not perform under the original terms if the proposal is not accepted? On this account, UCC § 2–610, *cmt. 2* states:

> Under the language of this section, a demand by one or both parties for more than the contract calls for in the way of counter-performance is not itself a repudiation nor does it invalidate a plain expression of desire for future performance. However, when under a fair reading it amounts to a statement of intention not to perform except on conditions which go beyond the contract, it becomes a repudiation.

Did the May 21st letter objectively indicate that the buyer would not proceed unless the seller agreed to a price reduction? The seller concluded that the buyer's price reduction offer implicitly threatened not to perform unless the seller agreed to the proposed modification. In light of the buyer's request that the seller let the buyer know whether the proposal was satisfactory, was the seller's subjective understanding reasonable? Shouldn't the parties generally have the freedom to propose modifications without committing a repudiation? Does that result promote the ability of the parties to adjust voluntarily to changes? Do other doctrines adequately police coerced modifications?

3. *Seller's response to alleged repudiation.* The closing was not scheduled until June 30. In response to the buyer's May 21st letter suggesting a lower price, the seller responded in a June 9th letter that it was not interested in lowering the price. Insisting on performance under the terms of the contract is certainly not a repudiation. Assuming that the May 21st letter was not a sufficiently clear repudiation, what appears to be the status of the contract after the June 9th letter? Following the seller's June 9th letter, the buyer immediately responded on June 14th that it was nonetheless prepared to close on June 30th pursuant to the terms of the original contract. Absent a response, the buyer wrote two more letters on June 23rd and July 6th inquiring about the status of the closing. What is the status of the contract on June 30th, assuming that the buyer did not repudiate the contract?

4. *Retraction before reliance.* Even if the buyer repudiated the contract in its May 21st letter, the closing was not scheduled until June 30th. What is the significance of the buyer's June 14th letter stating that the buyer was prepared to proceed to a closing on June 30th under the terms of the contract? Clearly, the buyer waived the zoning change condition at that point. Restatement (Second) of Contracts § 256(1) provides that a repudiation may be

retracted provided the retraction occurs before the injured party either: (i) materially changes position in reliance on repudiation; or (ii) indicates to the repudiating party that the repudiation is considered final. See also UCC § 2–611. The seller agreed that it had not materially changed its position in reliance on the repudiation. Therefore, the buyer could still retract the repudiation, provided the seller did not notify the buyer that it considered the repudiation to be final. Given the uncertainty of whether a statement constitutes a repudiation, do you expect that an injured party will communicate in all but the clearest cases that it is treating the repudiation as final? What is the purpose in doing so? The seller is always privileged to rely on the repudiation until it is retracted and notice is not necessary. Of course, relying on a weak repudiation carries the same risk as communicating that the repudiation is final: if the statement was not a repudiation, the injured party will have breached the contract. Does the court make clear that the injured party must communicate that it is treating the repudiation as final?

5.   *Reasonable grounds for assurance.* If an injured party mistakenly treats a statement or conduct as a repudiation, and a court later determines that no repudiation occurred, then the injured party will breach by failing to perform when its performance comes due. Accordingly, a weak but ineffective repudiation does not discharge the duty of performance of the other party. Restatement (Second) of Contracts § 253(2). Because of the uncertainty surrounding whether a particular statement constitutes an unequivocal repudiation, it may be wise to adopt an intermediate position. First, the injured party could seek clarification whether the other party is repudiating the contract. This gives the other party a chance to clarify or retract. Alternatively, without giving up rights under the putative repudiation, the injured party could urge the party to perform notwithstanding the repudiation. See Restatement (Second) of Contracts § 257.

Importantly, under Restatement (Second) of Contracts § 251(1), when an injured party has "reasonable grounds" to believe that the obligor will commit a breach, the injured party may "demand adequate assurance" of due performance and suspend performance until such assurance is forthcoming. See Gregory S. Crespi, "The Adequate Assurances Doctrine After U.C.C. § 2–609: A Test of the Efficiency of the Common Law," 38 Vill. L. Rev. 179 (1993). See also UCC § 2–609(1). However, an obligee may not demand assurance from the obligor until and unless "reasonable grounds" exist to trigger that right to seek assurance. Restatement (Second) of Contracts § 251, *cmts. a, c.* Restatement (Second) of Contracts § 251, *cmt. c* provides that the reasonable grounds inquiry must examine all the circumstances of the particular case, and must rest on facts that arose only after contract formation. "Conduct by a party that indicates his doubt as to his willingness or ability to perform but that is *not sufficiently positive to amount to a repudiation* . . . may give reasonable grounds for such a belief." Id. (emphasis added). In this light and in the right circumstances, even minor breaches may foreshadow material breaches and events extrinsic to the parties' contract may also give rise to the reasonable grounds necessary to justify a demand for assurance. See id.

Assume that you are seller's counsel and that your client—after receiving the May 21st letter—has decided to cancel the contract. Realizing that the language of the May 21st letter does not unequivocally repudiate the contract, what correspondence would you recommend to your client? Does the May 21st letter at least represent "reasonable grounds" to "demand adequate assurance" and suspend performance until it was received? As a policy matter, do you think reasonable grounds to demand assurance should be more flexibly applied than repudiation? Restatement (Second) of Contracts § 251, *cmt. d* provides that a written demand is preferable, but not required. See UCC § 2–609(1) (demand must be in writing). In all cases, the demand must be made in good faith. For a discussion of these issues, see James J. White, "Eight Cases and Section 251," 67 Cornell L. Rev. 841 (1982). Indeed, some argue demand for assurance should be required under the UCC as a means for reducing controversy, risk, and litigation. See Robert A. Hillman, "Keeping the Deal Together After Material Breach—Common Law Mitigation Rules, the UCC and the Restatement (Second) of Contracts," 47 U. Colo. L. Rev. 553 (1976).

Once reasonable grounds for assurance exist, what may the aggrieved party demand in the form of assurance? If the reasonable grounds for insecurity arise from the obligor's insolvency, timely actual performance may be the only means of providing adequate assurance. See Restatement (Second) of Contracts § 252(1). Aside from insolvency, the nature of the assurance must fit the circumstances. The demanding party may require only those assurances necessary to eliminate the particular reasonable grounds for insecurity. Restatement (Second) of Contracts § 251, *cmt. e*. Unless appropriate assurance is received within a "reasonable time," the injured party may treat the failure to provide timely assurance as a firm repudiation. Restatement (Second) of Contracts § 251(2).

One further point complicates the assurance provision. Adequate assurance may only be requested under common law when the reasonable grounds exist that the obligor's non-performance would constitute a total breach. Restatement (Second) of Contracts § 251(1). A repudiation constitutes a total breach. Restatement (Second) of Contracts §§ 243(2) and 253(1). However, total breach in the context of reasonable grounds for insecurity is a more complicated factual question. Where only the payment of money remains, ordinarily a total breach will not occur. Restatement (Second) of Contracts § 243(3). Where the obligor must perform in other ways, the remaining performance must "substantially impair the value of the contract" to the injured party. Restatement (Second) of Contracts § 243(4). For further clarity on partial versus total breach factors and substantial impairment of contract value, see UCC § 2–610 and Restatement (Second) of Contracts § 243, *cmt. e*.

B. CONDITIONAL PROMISES

Mutual promises may be classified as either "dependent" or "independent" of each other, notwithstanding that consideration doctrine dictates each promise is binding precisely because each was sought in exchange for the other. Early English common law generally viewed promises as "independent" from each other. E. Allan Farnsworth, Contracts § 8.9 (4th ed. 2004). "Independent" promises are legally enforceable regardless of when and whether the other party has performed the return promise. Therefore, one party's failure to perform an independent promise does not discharge the other party's obligation to perform its return promise. Rather, the promisee must answer in defense and then bring a separate suit to enforce a breach on the return promise. For example, in *Nichols v. Raynbred*, 80 Eng. Rep. 238 (K.B. 1615), a seller sued a buyer for the purchase price of a cow. The seller was not required to prove delivery of the cow and, more importantly, the buyer was prevented from using that fact as a defense. Rather, the buyer was required to bring a separate action for the failure to deliver. While some question the extent of this "independent" promise view, it no doubt existed to some measure. See William H. McGovern, Jr., "Dependent Promises in the History of Leases and Other Contracts," 52 Tul. L. Rev. 659 (1978) and A.W. Brian Simpson, A History of the Common Law of Contract—The Rise and Fall of The Action of Assumpsit 465–466 (1996 Reprint) (explaining the doctrine referred to as a "promise against a promise"). In contrast, the performances of "dependent" promises are linked to each other. A promisor may assert a promisee's failure to perform a dependent promise as a defense against a suit brought to enforce the promisor's promise.

By the eighteenth century, Lord Mansfield largely dispelled the notion that mutual promises are truly independent. In *Kingston v. Preston*, 99 Eng. Rep. 437 (K.B. 1773), Lord Mansfield suggested that while independent promises are possible if the parties expressly declare that intent, in most cases mutual promises are dependent on each other. Therefore, not only is the nonperformance of a return promise actionable as a breach, the same nonperformance is also a legal excuse for the nonperformance of the first promise. E. Allan Farnsworth, Contracts § 8.9 (4th ed. 2004). The English common law dependent promise view in *Kingston* ultimately displaced the independent promise rule as a default rule. The parties remained free to declare in the contract that promises were truly independent.

The development of the dependent promise view eventually expanded well beyond the use of the nonperformance of the dependent promise as a defense to the enforcement of the return promise. The doctrine also embraced the nonoccurrence of any other fact specified by the parties as necessary for performance, and this development broadened the dependent promise view into the doctrine of conditions. See Clarence Ashley, "Conditions in Contract," 14 Yale L.J. 424, 428–429 (1905). Under the law of conditions, the nonoccurrence of any specified fact (including performance of the return promise) could operate as a defense or legal excuse for the failure to perform the return promise. The linkage between the dependent promise and conditions doctrines is explored later in *Jacob & Youngs*. By the early twentieth century, Professor Corbin summarized the following state of affairs:

> A certain fact may operate as a condition, because the parties intended that it should and said so in words. It is then an express condition. It may operate as a condition because the parties intended that it should, such intention being reasonably inferable from conduct other than words. It is then a condition implied in fact. Lastly, it may operate as a condition because the court believes that the parties would have intended it to operate as such if they had thought about it at all, or because the court believes that by reason of the *mores* of the time justice requires that it should so operate. It may then be described as a condition implied by law, or better as a *constructive condition*. Arthur L. Corbin, "Conditions in the Law of Contracts," 28 Yale L.J. 739, 743–44 (1919).

The use of the term "conditions" to replace "dependent promises" remained. A condition is generally a fact that must occur before a promise become due. See Restatement (First) of Contracts § 250 and Restatement (Second) of Contracts § 224.

The doctrine of conditions remains complex, mostly because the nonoccurrence of a fact or return promise provides a legal excuse for nonperformance of a return promise. This creates complex policy issues, especially when returning the doctrine of conditions to the doctrine of dependent promises. Will only a slight or immaterial failure of performance trigger the legal excuse, or must the promissory failure be somewhat significant or substantial? If so, how should the court assess the materiality of the nonoccurrence of the condition? These questions are explored in the *Jacob & Youngs* case later in this text.

Modern law subjects every promise to some condition, either implied by law or created expressly by the parties. See generally Clarence Ashley, "Conditions in Contract," 14 Yale L.J. 424 (1904); Arthur L. Corbin, "Conditions in the Law of Contract," 28 Yale L.J. 739 (1918). Nonsatisfaction of a condition means that performance of the promise subject to that condition never becomes due. If performance never becomes due, it is impossible to breach that promise, absent anticipatory repudiation. Since every promise is conditional, the remaining question is how and why the attached condition arises. Most commonly, conditions arise by implication in law to protect parties from becoming obligated to perform in frustration of their reasonable but unexpressed expectations. Implied by law, or "constructive conditions," are introduced in Chapter 8 (see discussion of *Taylor v. Caldwell*) and give legal effect to an excusing supervening event (music hall destruction by fire) that prevents the required performance from becoming due (rental of music hall). As a corollary matter, since the performance will never become due, it is also discharged. This chapter considers (1) express conditions created by the parties; and (2) a different basis for judicial implication of conditions based on the timing of the performances according to the nature and quality of the agreed exchanges.

Whether expressly created by the parties or arising by legal implication (Restatement (Second) of Contracts § 226), a condition is an event that must occur before performance of the promise becomes due. Restatement (Second) of Contracts § 224. Regardless of the nature of the condition, the effect is always the same. The failure of the condition means the other party's performance does not become due, making breach legally impossible. Restatement (Second) of Contracts § 225(1). Consequently, that duty is also discharged by the nonoccurrence of the condition. Restatement (Second) of Contracts § 225(2). Moreover, the nonsatisfaction of the condition itself rarely constitutes a breach of contract unless the party also promised to satisfy the condition. Restatement (Second) of Contracts § 225(3).

1. EXPRESS CONDITIONS

Express conditions are created by the agreement of the parties, not implied in law by a court. Restatement (Second) of Contracts § 226. Of course, in cases of doubt, vague language purporting to create an express condition may require a court to interpret the language to determine if a condition exists. But such conditions remain express conditions even though they may also be implied in fact from the vague expressions of the parties. See Restatement (Second) of Contracts § 226, *cmt. c.*

As a drafting matter, express conditions provide the parties with tools to provide that one or both parties need not perform contract promises unless a specified event occurs. Restatement (Second) of Contracts § 225. For example, a buyer may be unwilling to purchase a home unless satisfactory financing can be obtained. The discharging importance of a condition means that the parties must choose reasonably clear language to create the condition. Specific language is not required, but the language should convey to the other party that the failure of the condition means that the transaction or performance will not occur. Language such as "provided that," "contingent upon," "on condition that," and "if" are common, but good drafting practices generally also specify what will happen if the condition does not occur. Restatement (Second) of Contracts § 226, *cmt. a.* As with all contract terms, courts must use the principles of judicial interpretation discussed in Chapter 4 to determine the meaning of the conditional language or even if the parties intended an express condition at all. However, because of the potential for forfeiture created by conditions, special rules guide the interpretative process.

In cases of doubt, language and circumstances are interpreted to *not create* a condition in order to reduce the obligee's risk of forfeiture, at least if the event is within the obligee's control or the obligee has otherwise assumed the risk. Restatement (Second) of Contracts § 227(1). Also, if the event is within the control of the obligee, in cases of doubt, language and circumstances are interpreted to create a promise by the obligee that the event will occur, rather than to condition the obligor's duty to perform. Restatement (Second) of Contracts § 227(2). The following case reviews the serious impact and effect of an express condition.

OPPENHEIMER & CO., INC. V. OPPENHEIM, APPEL, DIXON & CO.

Court of Appeals of New York
86 N.Y.2d 685, 660 N.E.2d 415, 636 N.Y.S.2d 734 (1995)

CIPARICK, Justice.

The parties entered into a letter agreement setting forth certain conditions precedent to the formation and existence of a sublease between them. The agreement provided that there would be no sublease between the parties "unless and until" plaintiff delivered to defendant the prime landlord's written consent to certain "tenant work" on or before a specified deadline. If this condition did not occur, the sublease was to be deemed "null and void." Plaintiff provided only oral notice on the specified date. The issue presented is whether the doctrine of substantial performance applies to the facts of this case. We conclude it does not for the reasons that follow.

I.

In 1986, plaintiff Oppenheimer & Co. moved to the World Financial Center in Manhattan, a building constructed by Olympia & York Company (O & Y). At the time of its move, plaintiff had three years remaining on its existing lease for the 33rd floor of the building known as One New York Plaza. As an incentive to induce plaintiff's move, O & Y agreed to make the rental payments due under plaintiff's rental agreement in the event plaintiff was unable to sublease its prior space in One New York Plaza.

In December 1986, the parties to this action entered into a conditional letter agreement to sublease the 33rd floor. Defendant already leased space on the 29th floor of One New York Plaza and was seeking to expand its operations. The proposed sublease between the parties was attached to the letter agreement. The letter agreement provided that the proposed sublease would be executed only upon the satisfaction of certain conditions. Pursuant to paragraph 1(a) of the agreement, plaintiff was required to obtain:

the Prime Landlord's written notice of confirmation, substantially to the effect that [defendant] is a subtenant of the Premises reasonably acceptable to Prime Landlord.

If such written notice of confirmation were not obtained:

on or before December 30, 1986, then this letter agreement and the Sublease . . . shall be deemed null and void and of no further force and effect and neither party shall have any rights against nor obligations to the other.

Assuming satisfaction of the condition set forth in paragraph 1(a), defendant was required to submit to plaintiff, on or before January 2, 1987, its plans for "tenant work" involving construction of a telephone communication linkage system between the 29th and 33rd floors. Paragraph 4(c) of the letter agreement then obligated plaintiff to obtain the prime landlord's "written consent" to the proposed "tenant work" and deliver such consent to defendant on or before January 30, 1987. Furthermore, if defendant had not received the prime landlord's written consent by the agreed date, both the agreement and the sublease were to be deemed "null and void and of no further force and effect," and neither party was to have "any rights against nor obligations to the other." Paragraph 4(d) additionally provided that, notwithstanding satisfaction of the condition set forth in paragraph 1(a), the parties "agree not to execute and exchange the Sublease unless and until . . . the conditions set forth in paragraph (c) above are timely satisfied."

The parties extended the letter agreement's deadlines in writing and plaintiff timely satisfied the first condition set forth in paragraph 1(a) pursuant to the modified deadline. However, plaintiff never delivered the prime landlord's written consent to the proposed tenant work on or before the modified final deadline of February 25, 1987. Rather, plaintiff's attorney telephoned defendant's attorney on February 25 and informed defendant that the prime landlord's consent had been secured. On February 26, defendant, through its attorney, informed plaintiff's attorney that the letter agreement and sublease were invalid for failure to timely deliver the prime landlord's written consent and that it would not agree to an extension of the deadline. The document embodying the prime landlord's written consent was eventually received by plaintiff on March 20, 1987, 23 days after expiration of paragraph 4(c)'s modified final deadline.

Plaintiff commenced this action for breach of contract, asserting that defendant waived and/or was estopped by virtue of its conduct[1] from

---

[1]   Plaintiff argued that it could have met the deadline, but failed to do so only because defendant, acting in bad faith, induced plaintiff into delaying delivery of the landlord's consent. Plaintiff asserted that the parties had previously extended the agreement's deadlines as a matter of course.

insisting on physical delivery of the prime landlord's written consent by the February 25 deadline. Plaintiff further alleged in its complaint that it had substantially performed the conditions set forth in the letter agreement.

At the outset of trial, the court issued an order in limine barring any reference to substantial performance of the terms of the letter agreement. Nonetheless, during the course of trial, the court permitted the jury to consider the theory of substantial performance, and additionally charged the jury concerning substantial performance. Special interrogatories were submitted. The jury found that defendant had properly complied with the terms of the letter agreement, and answered in the negative the questions whether defendant failed to perform its obligations under the letter agreement concerning submission of plans for tenant work, whether defendant by its conduct waived the February 25 deadline for delivery by plaintiff of the landlord's written consent to tenant work, and whether defendant by its conduct was equitably estopped from requiring plaintiff's strict adherence to the February 25 deadline. Nonetheless, the jury answered in the affirmative the question, "Did plaintiff substantially perform the conditions set forth in the Letter Agreement?," and awarded plaintiff damages of $1.2 million.

Defendant moved for judgment notwithstanding the verdict. The Supreme Court granted the motion, ruling as a matter of law that "the doctrine of substantial performance has no application to this dispute, where the Letter Agreement is free of all ambiguity in setting the deadline that plaintiff concededly did not honor." The Appellate Division reversed the judgment on the law and facts, and reinstated the jury verdict. The Court concluded that the question of substantial compliance was properly submitted to the jury and that the verdict should be reinstated because plaintiff's failure to deliver the prime landlord's written consent was inconsequential.

This Court granted defendant's motion for leave to appeal and we now reverse.

II.

Defendant argues that no sublease or contractual relationship ever arose here because plaintiff failed to satisfy the condition set forth in paragraph 4(c) of the letter agreement. Defendant contends that the doctrine of substantial performance is not applicable to excuse plaintiff's failure to deliver the prime landlord's written consent to defendant on or before the date specified in the letter agreement and that the Appellate Division erred in holding to the contrary. Before addressing defendant's arguments and the decision of the court below, an understanding of certain relevant principles is helpful.

A condition precedent is "an act or event, other than a lapse of time, which, unless the condition is excused, must occur before a duty to perform a promise in the agreement arises" (Calamari and Perillo, Contracts § 11–2, at 438 [3d ed.]; see, Restatement [Second] of Contracts § 224. . . .). Most conditions precedent describe acts or events which must occur before a party is obliged to perform a promise made pursuant to an existing contract, a situation to be distinguished conceptually from a condition precedent to the formation or existence of the contract itself. . . . In the latter situation, no contract arises "unless and until the condition occurs" (Calamari and Perillo, Contracts § 11–5, at 440 [3d ed]).

Conditions can be express or implied. Express conditions are those agreed to and imposed by the parties themselves. Implied or constructive conditions are those "imposed by law to do justice" (Calamari and Perillo, Contracts § 11–8, at 444 [3d ed]). Express conditions must be literally performed, whereas constructive conditions, which ordinarily arise from language of promise, are subject to the precept that substantial compliance is sufficient. The importance of the distinction has been explained by Professor Williston:

> Since an express condition . . . depends for its validity on the manifested intention of the parties, it has the same sanctity as the promise itself. Though the court may regret the harshness of such a condition, as it may regret the harshness of a promise, it must, nevertheless, generally enforce the will of the parties unless to do so will violate public policy. Where, however, the law itself has imposed the condition, in absence of or irrespective of the manifested intention of the parties, it can deal with its creation as it pleases, shaping the boundaries of the constructive condition in such a way as to do justice and avoid hardship. (5 Williston, Contracts § 669, at 154 [3d ed].)

In determining whether a particular agreement makes an event a condition courts will interpret doubtful language as embodying a promise or constructive condition rather than an express condition. This interpretive preference is especially strong when a finding of express condition would increase the risk of forfeiture by the obligee (see, Restatement [Second] of Contracts § 227[1]).

Interpretation as a means of reducing the risk of forfeiture cannot be employed if "the occurrence of the event as a condition is expressed in unmistakable language" (Restatement [Second] of Contracts § 229, comment a, at 185; see, § 227, comment b [where language is clear, "(t)he policy favoring freedom of contract requires that, within broad limits, the agreement of the parties should be honored even though forfeiture results"]). Nonetheless, the nonoccurrence of the condition may yet be excused by waiver, breach or forfeiture. The Restatement posits that "[t]o the extent that the non-occurrence of a condition would cause disproportionate forfeiture, a court may excuse the non-occurrence of that condition unless its occurrence was a material part of the agreed exchange" (Restatement [Second] of Contracts § 229).

Turning to the case at bar, it is undisputed that the critical language of paragraph 4(c) of the letter agreement unambiguously establishes an express condition precedent rather than a promise, as the parties employed the unmistakable language of condition ("if," "unless and until"). There is no doubt of the parties' intent and no occasion for interpreting the terms of the letter agreement other than as written.

Furthermore, plaintiff has never argued, and does not now contend, that the nonoccurrence of the condition set forth in paragraph 4(c) should be excused on the ground of forfeiture.[2] Rather, plaintiff's primary argument from the inception of this litigation has been that defendant waived or was equitably estopped from invoking paragraph 4(c). Plaintiff argued secondarily that it substantially complied with the express condition of delivery of written notice on or before February 25th in that it gave defendant oral notice of consent on the 25th.

Contrary to the decision of the Court below, we perceive no justifiable basis for applying the doctrine of substantial performance to the facts of this case. The flexible concept of substantial compliance "stands in sharp contrast to the requirement of strict compliance that protects a party that has taken the precaution of making its duty expressly conditional" (2 Farnsworth, Contracts § 8.12, at 415 [2d ed 1990]). If the parties "have made an event a condition of their agreement, there is no mitigating standard of materiality or substantiality applicable to the non-occurrence of that event" (Restatement [Second] of Contracts § 237, comment d, at 220). Substantial performance in this context is not sufficient, "and if relief is to be had under the contract, it must be through excuse of the non-occurrence of the condition to avoid forfeiture" (id. . . .).

Here, it is undisputed that plaintiff has not suffered a forfeiture or conferred a benefit upon defendant. Plaintiff alludes to a $1 million licensing fee it allegedly paid to the prime landlord for the purpose of securing the latter's consent to the subleasing of the premises. At no point, however, does plaintiff claim that this sum was forfeited or that it was expended for the purpose of accomplishing the sublease with defendant. It is further undisputed that O & Y, as an inducement to effect plaintiff's move to the World Financial Center, promised to indemnify plaintiff for damages resulting from failure to sublease the 33rd floor of One New York Plaza. Consequently, because the critical concern of forfeiture or unjust enrichment is simply not present in this case, we are not presented with an occasion to consider whether the doctrine of substantial performance is

---

[2]   The Restatement defines the term "forfeiture" as "the denial of compensation that results when the obligee loses [its] right to the agreed exchange after [it] has relied substantially, as by preparation or performance on the expectation of that exchange" (§ 229, comment b).

applicable, that is, whether the courts should intervene to excuse the nonoccurrence of a condition precedent to the formation of a contract.

The essence of the Appellate Division's holding is that the substantial performance doctrine is universally applicable to all categories of breach of contract, including the nonoccurrence of an express condition precedent. However, as discussed, substantial performance is ordinarily not applicable to excuse the nonoccurrence of an express condition precedent.

Our precedents are consistent with this general principle. In Maxton Bldrs. v. Lo Galbo, 68 N.Y. 2d 373, 509 N.Y.S. 2d 507, 502 N.E.2d 184, the defendants contracted on August 3 to buy a house, but included in the contract the condition that if real estate taxes were found to be above $3,500 they would have the right to cancel the contract upon written notice to the seller within three days. On August 4 the defendants learned that real estate taxes would indeed exceed $3,500. The buyers' attorney called the seller's attorney and notified him that the defendants were exercising their option to cancel. A certified letter was sent notifying the seller's attorney of that decision on August 5 but was not received by the seller's attorney until August 9. We held the cancellation ineffective and rejected defendants' argument that reasonable notice was all that was required, stating: "It is settled . . . that when a contract requires that written notice be given within a specified time, the notice is ineffective unless the writing is actually received within the time prescribed" (id., at 378, 509 N.Y.S. 2d 507, 502 N.E.2d 184). We so held despite the fact that timely oral notice was given and the contract did not provide that time was of the essence.

In Jungmann & Co. v. Atterbury Bros., 249 N.Y. 119, 163 N.E. 123, the parties entered into a written contract for the sale of 30 tons of casein. The contract contained the following clause:

> Shipment: May–June from Europe. Advice of shipment to be made
> by cable immediately goods are dispatched (Id.).

Plaintiff shipped the first 15 tons but gave no notice to the defendant, who rejected the shipment. Plaintiff thereafter shipped the remaining 15 tons to defendant, but again failed to provide notice by cable and instead sent two letters. Defendant rejected the remaining 15 tons. This Court was not persuaded by the argument that the defendant had received notice of shipment by other means and thus suffered no harm. "Even if that be true," we stated, "the fact remains that the plaintiff was obligated under its contract to see that defendant obtained advice of shipment by cable" (Id., at 121, 163 N.E. 123). Plaintiff's failure to "perform all conditions precedent required of it," and "to give notice according to the terms of the contract" barred it from recovery (Id., at 122, 163 N.E. 123).

Plaintiff's reliance on the well-known case of Jacob & Youngs v. Kent, 230 N.Y. 239, 129 N.E. 889, is misplaced. There, a contractor built a summer residence and the buyer refused to pay the remaining balance of the contract price on the ground that the contractor used a different type of pipe than was specified in the contract. The buyer sought to enforce the contract as written. This would have involved the demolition of large parts of the structure at great expense and loss to the seller. This Court, in an opinion by then-Judge Cardozo, ruled for the contractor on the ground that "an omission, both trivial and innocent, will sometimes be atoned for by allowance of the resulting damage, and will not always be the breach of a condition to be followed by a forfeiture" (230 N.Y., at 241, 129 N.E. 889). But Judge Cardozo was careful to note that the situation would be different in the case of an express condition:

> This is not to say that the parties are not free by apt and certain words to effectuate a purpose that performance of every term shall be a condition of recovery. That question is not here. This is merely to say that the law will be slow to impute the purpose, in the silence of the parties, where the significance of the default is grievously out of proportion to the oppression of the forfeiture (Id., at 243–244, 129 N.E. 889).

The quoted language contradicts the Appellate Division's proposition that the substantial performance doctrine applies universally, including when the language of the agreement leaves no doubt that an express condition precedent was intended (see, 205 A.D. 2d, at 414, 613 N.Y.S. 2d 622). More importantly, Jacob & Youngs lacks determinative significance here on the additional ground that plaintiff conferred no benefit upon defendant. The avoidance-of-forfeiture rationale that engendered the rule of Jacob & Youngs is simply not present here, and the case therefore "should not be extended by analogy where the reason for the rule fails" (Van Iderstine Co. v. Barnet Leather Co., 242 N.Y. 425, 434, 152 N.E. 250).

The lease renewal and insurance cases relied upon by plaintiff are clearly distinguishable and explicable on the basis of the risk of forfeiture existing therein. For example, in Sy Jack Realty Co. v. Pergament Syosset Corp., 27 N.Y. 2d 449, 452, 318 N.Y.S. 2d 720, 267 N.E.2d 462, this Court gave effect to a late notice of lease renewal. Importantly, while we reaffirmed the general rule "that notice, when required to be 'given' by a certain date, is insufficient and ineffectual if not received within the time specified," we held that the prior courts properly invoked the rule that equity "relieves against . . . forfeitures of valuable lease terms when default in notice has not prejudiced the landlord" (Id., quoting Jones v. Gianferante, 305 N.Y. 135, 138, 111 N.E. 2d 419; see also J.N.A. Realty Corp. v. Cross Bay Chelsea, 42 N.Y. 2d 392, 397, 397 N.Y.S. 2d 958, 366 N.E.2d 1313 ["when a tenant in possession under an existing lease has neglected to . . . renew, he might suffer a forfeiture if he has made valuable improvements on the property"]). We stated: "Since a long-standing location for a retail business is an important part of the good will of that enterprise, the tenant stands to lose a substantial and valuable asset" (Id., 27 N.Y. 2d, at 453, 318 N.Y.S. 2d 720, 267 N.E.2d 462).

III.

In sum, the letter agreement provides in the clearest language that the parties did not intend to form a contract "unless and until" defendant received written notice of the prime landlord's consent on or before February 25, 1987. Defendant would lease the 33rd floor from plaintiff only on the condition that the landlord consent in writing to a telephone communication linkage system between the 29th and 33rd floors and to defendant's plans for construction effectuating that linkage. This matter was sufficiently important to defendant that it would not enter into the sublease "unless and until" the condition was satisfied. Inasmuch as we are not dealing here with a situation where plaintiff stands to suffer some forfeiture or undue hardship, we perceive no justification for engaging in a "materiality-of-the-nonoccurrence" analysis. To do so would simply frustrate the clearly expressed intention of the parties. Freedom of contract prevails in an arm's length transaction between sophisticated parties such as these, and in the absence of countervailing public policy concerns there is no reason to relieve them of the consequences of their bargain. If they are dissatisfied with the consequences of their agreement, "the time to say so [was] at the bargaining table" (Maxton, supra, at 382, 509 N.Y.S. 2d 507, 502 N.E.2d 184).

Finally, the issue of substantial performance was not for the jury to resolve in this case. A determination whether there has been substantial performance is to be answered, "if the inferences are certain, by the judges of the law" (Jacob & Youngs v. Kent, 230 N.Y. 239, 243, 129 N.E. 889 supra).

Accordingly, the order of the Appellate Division should be reversed, with costs, and the complaint dismissed. . . .

Order reversed, etc.

NOTES AND QUESTIONS

1.   *Condition to contract formation or performance of promise under existing contract.* The operative effect of the condition in the *Oppenheimer* case is unusual. By the terms of the letter agreement, the attached sublease was to be "executed" only upon the satisfaction of certain specified conditions. Restatement (Second) of Contracts § 224 defines a condition as an event that must occur before performance "under a contract" becomes due. Do the various letter agreement terms referred to as "conditions" upon which a sublease will be executed fall within this definition? Restatement (First) of Contracts § 250 refers to conditions precedent and subsequent. A condition precedent is defined as a fact that must occur before a duty arises. Restatement (First) of Contracts § 250(1). A condition subsequent is defined as a fact that extinguished a duty

to make compensation for a breach of a contractual promise. Do the various letter agreement terms referred to as "conditions" upon which a sublease will be executed fall within this definition?

Restatement (First) of Contracts § 24 defines an offer as a promise "conditional" upon an act, forbearance, or return promise being given in exchange. However, Restatement (Second) of Contracts § 24 defines an offer as a manifestation of willingness to enter into a bargain. Comparing the two, it is quite obvious that Restatement (First) of Contracts used the term "condition" more broadly and that the Restatement (Second) of Contracts confined the use of the term "condition" to those events that prevent a duty under an "existing contract" from becoming due. This distinguishing characteristic helps to explain the elimination of the distinction between conditions precedent and subsequent, as well as the use of facts or events that prevent the formation of a contract. Formation requirements are now confined to offer and acceptance. See Restatement (Second) of Contracts § 224, *cmt. c*. Viewed in this light, are the letter agreement terms that must be satisfied before the sublease will be executed true conditions? One difference might be that events that must occur before a contract is formed leave both parties free to retreat from the transaction until the events occur and a contract is formed. If a contract does not yet exist, does either party have a duty of good faith and fair dealing with respect to the occurrence of a condition within its control?

For example, paragraph 1(a) required Oppenheimer to obtain the landlord's written consent by December 30, 1986 that Oppenheim was an acceptable tenant. Paragraph 4(c) further required Oppenheimer to obtain and deliver the landlord's written consent by January 30, 1987 that Oppenheim's proposed tenant communication improvements were acceptable. Importantly, paragraph 4(d) provided that the sublease would not be executed unless the paragraph 1(a) and 4(c) conditions were "timely satisfied." Did Oppenheimer have a contractual duty to exercise good faith and fair dealing to obtain the landlord's written consents, even though these "conditions" were for the most part within Oppenheimer's control? Could Oppenheim maintain an action for the failure of Oppenheimer to do so? Do you see the difference between events that might be fairly attached to the formation of a contract versus those that are attached to promises to become due under an existing contract? However, in this case, although the sublease was never executed, the letter agreement appears to be a valid contract.

2. *Conditioning language.* Forgetting for the moment the somewhat artificial distinction between conditions to contract formation and to performance of promises, examine carefully the express language chosen to create the conditions. Restatement (Second) of Contracts § 226, *cmt. a* provides that an express condition may be created by the parties by any language, but it is customary to use words such as "provided that" or "if." Notice that the conditioning language in paragraph 1(a) of the letter agreement used the words "if such written notice of conformation were not obtained" and then coupled that language with a specific consequence of failure that the proposed sublease "shall be deemed null and void and of no further force and effect and neither

party shall have any rights against nor obligations to the other." Paragraph 4(c) stated similar language.

What is the theoretical value of including words making clear both the express condition itself, as well as the effect of the failure of the condition? Given that the effect of the condition forfeits the affected party's rights to pursue a breach remedy under the contract, courts take a dim view of doubtful conditional language as a form of private ordering "surprise" forfeiture. This accounts for the interpretation preferences construing doubtful language as not creating a condition—to protect a party from a surprise forfeiture of rights for breach of contract. See Restatement (Second) of Contracts § 227, *cmt. b.* Where is the surprise forfeiture when the contract language specifically identifies the consequences of a condition failure? Does this create any clues regarding drafting techniques used in connection with the creation of express conditions?

3. *Time of essence clauses.* Paragraph 4(d) provided that the sublease would not be executed unless the paragraph 1(a) and 4(c) conditions were "timely satisfied." Such "time-is-of-the-essence" clauses are important to the determination of whether duties are discharged following the failure of a condition. See Restatement (Second) of Contracts § 242(c). But courts seldom strictly enforce time-is-of-the-essence clauses as express conditions. Rather, courts construe such clauses as promises, and thus the doctrine of substantial performance (discussed later) applies. Restatement (Second) of Contracts § 227(2)(a). However, if the language is very clear that delayed performance results in forfeiture, the court will strictly enforce the clause absent excuse. Moreover, agreements including time-is-of-the-essence clauses do not automatically mean that the failure to comply with the time constraint itself materially breached the contract. This means that in some cases, even if the time clause is breached, substantial performance may still be adequate to satisfy the condition precedent to the other party's performance. "Only if the circumstances, viewed as of the time of the breach, indicate that performance or tender on that day is of genuine importance are the injured party's remaining duties discharged immediately, with no period of time during which they are merely suspended." Restatement (Second) of Contracts § 242, *cmt. d;* see also Johnny W. Mims, Note, "Time Is of the Essence: Condition or Covenant," 27 Baylor L. Rev. 817 (1975).

4. *Strict enforcement of written notice requirements.* Somewhat like the Statute of Frauds, a written notice requirement protects an innocent party from false allegations of oral notice. However, Chapter 8 distinguishes the effect of technical writing requirements imposed by public law (Statute of Frauds) and those imposed purely by private ordering (NOM clauses). As discussed, NOM clauses are usually not enforced under common law, but are typically enforceable by statute under UCC § 2–209(2). If a NOM clause generally is not enforceable under common law, do you see any principled reason why a clause requiring "written notification" of the satisfaction of a condition should be strictly enforced? One reason might include mutual agreement. A NOM clause purports to preclude the parties from mutually

agreeing to rescind or modify their agreement. A party benefiting from the written notice requirement could waive that requirement, but absent such a waiver, should the other party be free unilaterally to disregard the written notice requirement?

Restatement (Second) of Contracts § 84 specifically addresses waivers of conditions and is discussed in more detail in the last section of this chapter. Generally, Restatement (Second) of Contracts § 84(1)(a) provides that the benefited party (Oppenheim) may "waive" a condition in any form, including a writing requirement, unless the condition is a material part of the agreed exchange. Restatement (Second) of Contracts § 84, *cmt. d* discusses the materiality requirement:

> d. *Conditions which may be waived.* The rule of subsection (1) applies primarily to conditions which may be thought of as procedural or technical, or to instances in which the non-occurrence of condition is comparatively minor. Examples are conditions which merely relate to the time or manner of the return performance or provide for the giving of notice or the supplying of proofs. . . .

It is reasonably clear that the landlord's approval of the communication system was a material part of the agreed exchange. But it is also reasonably clear that the written notice requirement was more "procedural or technical," particularly when coupled with the actual oral notification. Thus it is reasonably clear that Oppenheim could waive the written notification requirement, but perhaps not the landlord consent (the later requiring a theory of obligation such as consideration or estoppel). Although the court cites with approval a law review article suggesting that express conditions should be strictly enforced, the article actually argues that all conditions should be subject to substantial performance to avoid inequitable and harsh results in all but the most extreme cases. See Robert Childres, "Conditions in the Law of Contracts," 45 N.Y.U. L. Rev. 33 (1970).

Was there any evidence in this case that Oppenheim's counsel did not receive timely oral notification of the satisfaction of the landlord's consent? If not, why does the court adopt a strict formalist approach requiring written notice rather than oral notice? What was important and material to effectuate the reasonable intent of the parties—the landlord's timely approval and oral notification, or timely approval and written notification? Separating the form of notification (oral versus written) from the actual nonoccurrence of the conditional event (landlord timely consent) tends to shift the analysis to the materiality of the notice provision versus the condition itself.

Does the opinion suggest that Oppenheim's counsel intentionally "waived" the written notice requirement when Oppenheimer's counsel telephoned on February 25th to communicate the landlord had orally approved the telecommunication system? In fact, following client instructions, Oppenheim's counsel wrote a letter the next day, on February 26th stating the written notice condition had not occurred, and therefore, the condition failed.

5. *Conditions of satisfaction.* Contracts often condition one party's performance on that party's satisfaction with the other party's performance. Express conditions of satisfaction raise several issues. Most important is testing the legal effect of the satisfaction standard. Does the satisfaction relate to subjective but honest dissatisfaction of one party, or does it relate to the objective satisfaction of that party? The contract may also require satisfaction of a third-party expert. Restatement (Second) of Contracts § 228 permits the parties to use clear language to create honest but subjective dissatisfaction conditions. However, given the clear opportunity for obligee forfeiture by virtue of an honest but unreasonable dissatisfaction, the common law requires very clear language to that effect to make certain the obligee understood and accepted that risk at the time of contract formation. Otherwise, an objective standard is preferred. Early common law nearly always applied an honest but subjective standard. See James Brook, "Conditions of Personal Satisfaction in the Law of Contracts," 27 N.Y.L. Sch. L. Rev. 103 (1981). See also UCC § 2–326 (conditions of satisfaction regarding goods) and Steven Petrikis, Note, "Conditions of Personal Satisfaction Under the Uniform Commercial Code: Is There Room for Unreasonableness?," 42 U. Pitt. L. Rev. 375 (1980).

Where the satisfaction of a third-party professional, such as an architect, is invoked, Restatement (Second) of Contracts § 228, *cmt. b* extends greater deference, presumably on the theory that independent professionals are less likely to exhibit dishonest personal subjective dissatisfaction:

> *b.   Preference for objective standard.* . . . The situation differs from that where the satisfaction of a third party such as an architect, surveyor or engineer is concerned. . . . These professionals, even though employed by the obligor, are assumed to be capable of independent judgment, free from the selfish interests of the obligor. . . .

Of course, regardless of whether the parties employ a subjective or objective standard, the party benefiting from the satisfaction term must exercise that term in good faith under common law and the UCC.

Cases involving personal services and particularly contracts for artistic personal services are also given more preference for an honest but purely subjective standard. Restatement (Second) of Contracts § 228, *cmt. b* provides:

> *b.   Preference for objective standard.* . . . If, however, the circumstance with respect to which a party is to be satisfied is such that the application of the objective test is impracticable, the rule of this section is not applicable. A court will then, for practical reasons, apply a subjective test of honest satisfaction, even if the agreement admits of doubt on the point and even if the result will be to increase the obligee's risk of forfeiture. . . . [Illustration 2 applies this standard to a portrait where the buyer must be "entirely satisfied."].

2. ORDERING OF PERFORMANCES

Conditions provide a critical drafting tool for the ordering of party performances under the contract and determining whether the parties must perform simultaneously or whether one party must perform first before the other incurs an obligation to perform. Contracts for the purchase and sale of readily available goods illustrate the use of conditions to require simultaneous performance—a convenience store owner has no contractual duty to hand over the candy bar unless the purchaser simultaneously offers payment. In contrast, contracts for performance of personal services over time often require greater sophistication regarding when the service provider must perform and the service recipient must pay. The owner of a house will rarely be willing to pay the full cost of painting services in advance of seeing the final product. At the same time, the provider of time and resources—who may not recover those lost inputs if the contract later falls apart—will often require installment payments to help finance the progress of the work, rather than waiting until the end of the contract to be compensated. Thus, a painting services provider will generally require some form of payment up front to cover materials, as well as periodic progress payments. The parties are always free to expressly order their performances. Contracts involving a significant expenditure of time and resources commonly include express conditions ordering the performances of the parties. But absent the use of express conditions to determine the order and sequence of performance, the common law provides two primary constructive conditions default rules that are implied by law. Constructive ordering conditions are the primary subject of this section.

Constructive Conditions for Simultaneous Exchanges. Where performances can be exchanged simultaneously, they are due simultaneously. Restatement (Second) of Contracts § 234(1). In a simultaneous performance exchange, each party's duty to perform is subject to an "implied condition" that the other party actually performs or offers to perform ("tender"). Restatement (Second) of Contracts § 238. This protects each party from a breach unless the other party at least minimally offers to perform. If one party fails to tender performance, the other party does not breach the contract by refusing to perform its own promises. Many, if not most, consumer transactions in goods are simultaneous transactions because the goods are available for immediate purchase.

Constructive Condition for Nonsimultaneous Exchanges. Where performances cannot be exchanged simultaneously because one party's performance takes time, the performance requiring time is due first. Restatement (Second) of Contracts § 234(2). In a non-simultaneous exchange, the party's performance due second is subject to an "implied condition" that the first party's performance will not be materially defective. Restatement (Second) of Contracts § 237. In other words, the first party must substantially perform before the other party's performance becomes due. Many, if not most, service and construction contracts, as well as manufactured goods contracts, are non-simultaneous exchanges. This protects the second party from having to pay for an uncured materially defective performance. Of course, the condition does not require perfect performance and contemplates an opportunity to cure. Several factors are considered to determine whether a performance is materially defective. Restatement (Second) of Contracts § 241. Where a party renders a materially defective performance, the defective performance does not discharge the other party's duty to perform. Rather, the duty is "suspended." See Restatement (Second) of Contracts § 225(1). This gives the party whose performance was materially defective an opportunity to cure. Restatement (Second) of Contracts § 242. But when cure is no longer legally permissible, the suspended duty is discharged because the implied condition did not occur. Restatement (Second) of Contracts § 225(2). The concept of "material failure" was created from early judicial doctrine requiring that a party need only "substantially perform" in order to require the other party to perform. Accordingly, while substantial performance is not perfect performance and thus constitutes a breach of contract entitling the other party to damages, the other party receiving substantial performance must still perform as if there is no condition of perfect performance.

EL DORADO HOTEL PROPERTIES, LTD. V. MORTENSEN

Arizona Court of Appeals
136 Ariz. 292, 665 P.2d 1014 (1983)

BIRDSALL, Judge.

This appeal is from a summary judgment in favor of El Dorado Hotel Properties, Ltd., a limited partnership, and United Bank of Arizona in the amount of $1,900,000 principal and $56,219 interest found to be due on a promissory note plus $20,000 attorney fees, and foreclosing a deed of trust given as security for the payment of the note. The appellee El Dorado was the payee and beneficiary of the note and deed of trust while appellee United Bank had only a security interest. Our references hereafter to the appellee are to El Dorado. The appellants were the trustors obligated on the note and their assignees and successors in interest. We refer to them hereafter collectively as the appellants.

The note and deed of trust arose out of the sale of the El Dorado Country Club property by the appellee to the appellants. The sale, which closed January 25, 1982, was for $2,200,000. The appellants paid a total of $300,000 earnest money and payment at closing, and gave the note for the balance of $1,900,000. The next payment of $400,000 was due on March 1, 1982. It is that payment which concerns us in this appeal.

As a part of the sale agreement the parties provided in the deed of trust for the release of portions of the property. We are also concerned here with this release provision.

The appellants' contentions on appeal include a claim that the trial court erred, as a matter of law, in holding that the release provision did not contemplate simultaneous performance by the parties. We agree and set aside the judgment.

The promissory note provided that it was to be paid "in installments" as follows:

"$400,000 on March 1, 1982. . . . "

The note also contained a standard acceleration provision that "should default be made in payment of any installment of principal or interest when due the whole sum of principal and interest shall become immediately due at the option of the holder. . . . " The note also contained a statement that it was secured by the deed of trust.

The release provision in the deed of trust was relatively short and concise and since it is the interpretation of that provision with which we are most concerned we set it forth in its entirety:

Upon payment of the $400,000.00 plus interest payment due on March 1, 1982, the trustors shall be entitled to have released free and clear of the purchase money Deed of Trust given to secure the unpaid balance herein 70,000 square feet of the subject real estate and any easement reasonably necessary for development of the first released parcel and any subsequent releases provided that:

(a) Trustors shall have submitted to Beneficiary a plat of the subject property showing the location of the original release and the location, proposed use, size and order of future parcels to be released. This plat shall be approved by Beneficiary to be consonant with the requirements set forth in this paragraph. Such approval shall not be unreasonably withheld.

(b) The parcel to be released shall be a compact parcel, one side of which shall be entirely contiguous to a property boundary of the subject parcel.

(c) The parcel selected shall not unduly harm or be to the detriment of the utilization of the balance of the property.

(d) No portion of any release shall include the golf course, clubhouse or the parking area reasonably necessary for the operation of the clubhouse and golf course.

(e) The parcel shall not interfere with access to the balance of the property.

(f) Purchaser shall pay the cost of all documentation and surveys necessary for the release.

In addition to the above release, trustors shall be entitled to future releases at the rate of $7.00 per square foot for all payments toward the reduction of principal of the unpaid purchase price and provided that the releases meet the following criteria:

(a) That they meet all criteria set forth for the original release above, except that the future releases must be contiguous on one boundary to the previously released land. In lieu of being contiguous to a previously released parcel, it must be contiguous to a boundary of the property although it may be contiguous to both.

(b) Releases may only be granted when purchaser is not in default under the terms of the Deed of Trust.

(c) Beneficiary shall cooperate in any rezoning sought by Trustors.

In addition the following facts were before the trial court by way of the pleadings, affidavits and depositions at the time the motion for summary judgment was submitted. Although we must view the facts in their most favorable light to the appellants, Elerick v. Rocklin, 102 Ariz. 78, 425 P .2d 103 (1967), these facts were actually undisputed. The appellants did not secure a loan commitment for funds with which to make the March 1 payment until late February, when they contacted the appellee and secured an agreement that if the payment was made by noon on March 5 there would be no default. On March 3 counsel for the appellants, Mr. John F. Battaile, III, notified counsel for the appellees, Mr. S. Leonard Scheff, by phone, that he would be delivering the "release plat" and "deed of release" for the first released parcel. Scheff advised him that his client would not consider reviewing the plat; there was not sufficient time to review it; the deed would not be placed in escrow; and insisted that the payment must be made first. By letter dated March 4 Scheff not only confirmed the conversation but advised that if unconditional payment was not made by noon March 5 he would file the foreclosure action. Battaile's written response, also March 4, contained further information concerning the provisions of the release agreement, that is, for example, advising that the use to which the released parcel would be put was "to hold for investment."[1] Battaile also wrote: " . . . our client intends to make the payment tomorrow . . . we are entitled to the release upon payment . . . " This letter contains some self-serving statements concerning prior discussions about what parcel would be released, etc. We do not concern ourselves with these assertions since they are material only to the

---

[1]   The appellee contends such a use did not satisfy the requirement to advise to what use the property would be put. We need not consider that contention here since the resolution of this issue involves disputed fact questions.

determination of fact issues. Neither the trial court nor this court can weigh the evidence or make findings of disputed fact in a summary judgment proceeding.

On March 5, before noon, the appellants delivered a cashier's check for $400,000 to the title company trustee with a letter authorizing the funds to be disbursed when the deed of release, etc. was recorded.[3] Scheff directed the title company to refuse the payment and the foreclosure complaint was filed on March 5.

The trial court's explanation for its ruling was contained in a minute entry:

> THE COURT FINDS that there are no genuine issues of material fact to be litigated. The note in question states: "We promise to pay . . . $400,000.00 on March 1, 1982 . . . " The note indicates on its face that it is secured by a deed of trust, and the deed of trust contains the phrase, "see release provisions on attached Exhibit B."

> Exhibit B states: "Upon payment of the $400,000.00 plus interest, payment due on March 1, 1982, the Trustors shall be entitled to have released . . . "

> Defendants did not make that payment pursuant to the terms of the note; they deposited the funds and directed that they be held hostage for performance of an obligation to which the defendants "shall be entitled" after payment.

> Where the performance of one party requires a period of time, (e.g. examination and verification of the release provision) and the performance of the other party does not, (the $400,000.00 payment) their performances cannot be simultaneous. Since one of the parties must perform first, he must forego the security that a requirement of simultaneous performance affords against disappointment of his expectation of an exchange of performances, and he must bear the burden of financing the other party before the latter has performed (See Comment E, Section 234, Restatement of Contracts 2d.)

> IT IS ORDERED that plaintiff's Motion for Summary Judgment is hereby GRANTED. (all emphasis in the original)

This reliance on the Restatement was misplaced. Section 234 actually provides:

---

[3]   The general partner of the appellee, Jerome Shull, the only person authorized to approve the release and the person who authorized the extension to March 5 for the payment, left the country on March 4 and did not return until after the foreclosure action had been commenced.

(1) Where all or part of the performances to be exchanged under an exchange of promises can be rendered simultaneously, they are to that extent due simultaneously, unless the language or the circumstances indicate the contrary.

(2) Except to the extent stated in Subsection (1), where the performance of only one party under such an exchange requires a period of time, his performance is due at an earlier time than that of the other party, unless the language or the circumstances indicate the contrary.

Comment (e) to Sec. 234 is concerned principally with employment or construction contracts where the work must be done before payment is made. The comment is not only inapplicable to the instant dispute but if utilized might even lead to a requirement that the "examination and verification of the release provision" be accomplished first.

The fact situation which is most applicable here is found in comment (b) which states, in part, that where a time is fixed for the performance of one of the parties (the payment of $400,000.00 on March 1) and no time is fixed for the other (the approval and delivery of the release) simultaneous performance is possible and will be required unless the language or the circumstances indicate the contrary. The illustration given in the Restatement is:

(2) A promises to sell land to B, the deed to be delivered on July 1. B promises to pay A $50,000, no provision being made for the time of payment. Delivery of the deed and payment of the price are due simultaneously.

Other authorities agree with the Restatement. See S. Williston, A Treatise on the Law of Contracts Sec. 835 (3rd ed. 1962); 17A C.J.S. Contracts Sec. 344 (1963).

The appellants presented the trial court with an affidavit of Bruce Mortensen in which he avers, upon his own personal knowledge from conversations and other negotiations with Mr. Shull, that the parcel, release of which was requested with the $400,000 tender, was the very parcel Mr. Shull expected to release first. The description of this parcel, and at least arguably the other information required under the release provision, was furnished by March 4. Whether this was in time to permit simultaneous exchange of the release deed and the payment is a material disputed fact question and summary judgment is not permissible. Sellers v. Allstate Insurance Company, 113 Ariz. 419, 555 P. 2d 1113 (1976).

Not only did the trial court err in its utilization of the Restatement, it also erred in holding, as a matter of law, that the provision "upon payment" meant "after payment." Although one meaning for upon is after, the word also has other meanings, such as "as soon as," "at the time of," or "in case of," all depending on the context in which it is used. Sanford v. Luce, 245 Iowa 74, 60 N.W. 2d 885 (1953). It may also mean "before, after or simultaneously with," People v. Williams, 24 Cal. 2d 848, 151 P. 2d 244 (1944). In Hays v. Arizona Corporation Commission, 99 Ariz. 358, 409 P. 2d 282 (1965), the court held use of the word "upon" as it appeared in a statute did not necessarily imply immediacy, but within a reasonable time after. The statute, A.R.S. § 40–609, provided for the renewal of a certificate of convenience and necessity. The statute read:

> A certificate or permit shall not be granted for a term exceeding ten years, but upon the expiration thereof it shall, at the request of the holder, be renewed for a period of time equal to that of the original certificate or permit, unless good cause is shown for refusal thereof. (emphasis supplied)

We do not believe that opinion is authority for the proposition advanced here by the appellee that the word "upon" in the deed of trust meant "after" in view of the context and subject matter of the statute.

The payment and release could be exchanged simultaneously if the release information was provided in sufficient time. According to the Restatement of Contracts 2d, section 234, supra, if the performances can be rendered simultaneously they are due simultaneously unless the language or the circumstances indicate the contrary. We find neither language nor circumstances indicating the contrary. We realize that the resolution of disputed facts may establish circumstances that will prove controlling, but the appellees were not entitled to summary judgment on the record before the trial court.

The judgment is reversed and the cause remanded for further proceedings.

NOTES AND QUESTIONS

1. *Failure of language.* It is clear from the brief facts that the seller expected that the buyer would first make payment, and then the seller would release the deed after receiving the payment or, at the earliest, simultaneously, if the buyer release request was submitted well in advance for review and approval. Assuming this to be the case, how would you rewrite the contract to achieve that result? Do you think language governing the submission and review time would be helpful?

2. *Trial court rule and holding.* The trial court opinion is confusing. First, the court correctly states that the payment of money (buyer) does not require time. Second, the court correctly states that examination and verification of the release (seller) does require time. The court then quotes the Restatement (Second) of Contracts § 234(2) nonsimultaneous exchange default rule. That rule requires the party whose performance requires time to perform first (seller). But the court determined the seller should prevail as a matter of

law, even though it did not perform at all, much less perform first. How do you reconcile the facts, rule, and decision? Notwithstanding the reference to the default rule regarding nonsimultaneous exchanges, does the trial court decide in favor of the seller because the express "upon payment" language of the contract required the buyer to perform first?

3. *Appellate court rule and holding.* The appellate court opinion correctly notes that Restatement (Second) of Contracts § 234 prefers a simultaneous exchange default rule in order to avoid the problem referred to by the trial court. If the party whose performance takes time is required to perform first, that party must proceed without a guarantee of trailing performance by the other party. To avoid that risk, Restatement (Second) of Contracts § 234 prefers that all exchanges be simultaneous if possible. Restatement (Second) of Contracts § 234, *cmt. b* notes four categories of cases in which simultaneous performance is possible *and therefore required*: (1) the contract requires both performances at the same fixed time; (2) the contract fixes the time of performance by one party but is silent as to the other party; (3) the contract is silent regarding time for performance; (4) the contract fixes the same period in which both parties must perform. In a fifth category—where the contract fixes different times for performance by each party—simultaneous performance may be possible *but is not required*. See id.

Thus, where an agreement specifies matters each party must accomplish to perform, the only time the nonsimultaneous rule applies is when the parties specify a different time for each performance. In this case, the parties did not specify a different time for each performance, and therefore, the fifth rule does not apply. Accordingly, this is a case governed by the simultaneous exchange rule. As a result, the tender of payment of money will trigger the corresponding obligation to tender the deed release (provided there was adequate time for review, and the record implied adequate time was given). If so, tender of the money would trigger a breach for failure to tender the deed release. See Restatement (Second) of Contracts § 238. According to the appellate court, since the parties discussed timing, the nonsimultaneous default rule did not apply and is not preferred. Do you agree? At least the appellate court disagrees with the trial court's conclusion that the words "upon payment" meant that the default rules did not apply and that the buyer was required to perform first by express language.

3.   CONSTRUCTIVE CONDITIONS

To understand the *raison d'être* for constructive conditions of exchange, imagine contract law without them. A party's breach would provide the injured party a cause of action for breach, but would not itself excuse the injured party's obligation to perform. Even if the breaching party failed to perform at all, the injured party would be required to perform in order to avoid a later claim for reciprocating breach in a cause of action based on the first breach. On the other hand, if any breach discharged the duty of the second party to perform, substantial injustice would be inflicted on a party who had substantially, but not perfectly, performed. Accordingly, "[r]ules of substantial performance were developed to protect plaintiffs who had almost but not quite, completed performance." Grant Gilmore, The Death of Contract 74 (1974).

Parties create express conditions in their agreements, and by necessary implication often express those conditions (or putative conditions) in ambiguous terms. Such ambiguities in creating conditions raise difficult issues for courts that generally enforce express conditions strictly. See Restatement (Second) of Contracts § 226. In contrast, courts—not the parties—imply constructive conditions to fulfill the reasonable but unexpressed intent of the parties and to promote fairness in the enforcement of otherwise unconditional promises. See Restatement (Second) of Contracts § 226. While courts imply constructive conditions in many circumstances, such as to discharge a duty by reason of a supervening event (see *Taylor v. Caldwell* in Chapter 8) and to determine the sequence of related contractual performance obligations (see Restatement (Second) of Contracts § 234), this section discusses the most common and ancient of all constructive conditions—the doctrine of substantial performance.

The doctrine of substantial performance regulates the effect of less-than-perfect performance by the first party required to perform on the second party's return obligation to perform. As a default rule, the party required to perform first is the party whose performance requires the most time (nonsimultaneous exchanges). Restatement (Second) of Contracts § 234(2). The first party materially breaches the contract if it does not substantially perform. See Restatement (Second) of Contracts § 241. If the breach is material, and the breaching party fails to cure that breach, the injured party has two options. The injured party may cancel the contract and sue for total breach because substantial performance is a condition of the second party's performance obligation. See Restatement (Second) of Contracts §§ 236 and 237. Alternatively, the injured party may continue with the contract and sue for partial breach. See Restatement (Second) of Contracts § 236. Where the breach is not material, the injured party must continue the contract and may not cancel. Nonetheless, substantial performance is not perfect performance. Any failure to perform as promised under the contract, even if that performance was substantial, constitutes a breach of contract giving the injured party a right to sue for that partial breach. Restatement (Second) of Contracts § 236 (partial breach), §§ 243 and 241, *cmt. a.* See also UCC § 2–106(4) and Eric G. Andersen, "A New Look at Material Breach in the Law of Contracts," 21 U. C. Davis L. Rev. 1073 (1988).

Accordingly, the materiality of the first party's performance controls whether the second party's performance is discharged (uncured material breach) or not (substantial performance). While some have criticized the substantial performance rule because it requires the injured party to continue the contract and its own performance while retaining the right for damages for partial breach, it has nonetheless become a mainstay of the domestic and international common law. Compare, William H. Lawrence, "Cure After Breach of Contract Under the Restatement (Second) of Contracts: An Analytical Comparison with the Uniform Commercial Code," 70 Minn. L. Rev. 713 (1986), with Joseph M. Perillo, "UNIDROIT Principles of International Commercial Contracts: The Black Letter Text and a Review," 63 Fordham L. Rev. 281 (1994).

Since Chapter 9 carefully explores contract damages for both partial and total breach, this section focuses on the triggering event throttling between the two—the materiality of the breach itself. Importantly, even when a breach is material, the other party's performance duty is not discharged; it is merely suspended. See Restatement (Second) of Contracts § 225(1). Only the breaching party's failure to cure the material breach discharges the non-breaching party's duty to perform. See Restatement (Second) of Contracts § 225(2). Suspension, as opposed to immediate discharge, gives the breaching party an opportunity to cure the defective performance. Thus, this two-step process—involving (1) a period for suspension-cure and (2) discharge—promotes a policy of preserving contracts notwithstanding a breach. See Arthur Rosett, "Contract Performance: Promises, Conditions and the Obligation to Communicate," 22 U.C.L.A. L. Rev. 1083 (1974) and Robert A. Hillman, "Keeping the Deal Together After Material Breach—Common Law Mitigation Rules, the UCC, and the Restatement (Second) of Contracts," 47 U. Colo. L. Rev. 553 (1976).

Both the concepts of the materiality of the breach (Restatement (Second) of Contracts § 241) and the proper duration of the cure period justifying cancellation and discharge (Restatement (Second) of Contracts § 242) are imbued with uncertainty. That uncertainty can be viewed in two ways. On the one hand, since both are uncertain, the common law may encourage the parties to work through the breach cooperatively, rather than rushing to combative litigation. Alternatively, the uncertainty may force parties to take unnecessary risks in responding to breaches and allocate too much power to the breaching party. A party that improvidently terminates a contract for a non-material breach or without providing sufficient opportunity for cure risks a court judgment that the terminating party itself materially breached the contract.

Under the restatement standard, courts assess the materiality of breach by balancing various factors relating to the impact upon each of the parties. The first two factors relate to the effect of the breach on the injured party and include the extent to which the injured party (i) will be deprived of the benefit reasonably expected; and (ii) can be adequately compensated for the deprived benefit. Restatement (Second) of Contracts §§ 241(a)–(b).

The remaining three factors consider the effect on the breaching party of granting the injured party the right to cancel the contract and include (i) the extent of forfeiture, (ii) likelihood cure will occur; and (iii) whether the breach occurred notwithstanding the exercise of good faith and fair dealing. Restatement (Second) of Contracts §§ 241(c)–(e).

Where a material breach occurs, the injured party's duty to perform is suspended until the breaching party's right to cure expires. As with the materiality determination, the determination of whether the breaching party's right to cure a material breach has expired is also determined through a consideration of various factors. The factors include (i) all the factors important in the materiality determination; (ii) the extent to which the injured party reasonably believes further delay will prevent or hinder making substitute arrangements; and (iii) whether the agreement makes performance on the date specified truly important or material. Restatement (Second) of Contracts §§ 242(a)–(c).

JACOB & YOUNGS V. KENT

Court of Appeals of New York
230 N.Y. 239, 129 N.E. 889 (1921)

CARDOZO, J.

The plaintiff built a country residence for the defendant at a cost of upwards of $77,000, and now sues to recover a balance of $3,483.46, remaining unpaid. The work of construction ceased in June 1914, and the defendant then began to occupy the dwelling. There was no complaint of defective performance until March 1915. One of the specifications for the plumbing work provides that:

All wrought-iron pipe must be well galvanized, lap welded pipe of the grade known as "standard pipe" of Reading manufacture.

The defendant learned in March 1915, that some of the pipe, instead of being made in Reading, was the product of other factories. The plaintiff was accordingly directed by the architect to do the work anew. The plumbing was then encased within the walls except in a few places where it had to be exposed. Obedience to the order meant more than the substitution of other pipe. It meant the demolition at great expense of substantial parts of the completed structure. The plaintiff left the work untouched, and asked for a certificate that the final payment was due. Refusal of the certificate was followed by this suit.

The evidence sustains a finding that the omission of the prescribed brand of pipe was neither fraudulent nor willful. It was the result of the oversight and inattention of the plaintiff's subcontractor. Reading pipe is distinguished from Cohoes pipe and other brands only by the name of the manufacturer stamped upon it at intervals of between six and seven feet.

Even the defendant's architect, though he inspected the pipe upon arrival, failed to notice the discrepancy. The plaintiff tried to show that the brands installed, though made by other manufacturers, were the same in quality, in appearance, in market value, and in cost as the brand stated in the contract—that they were, indeed, the same thing, though manufactured in another place. The evidence was excluded, and a verdict directed for the defendant. The Appellate Division reversed, and granted a new trial.

We think the evidence, if admitted, would have supplied some basis for the inference that the defect was insignificant in its relation to the project. The courts never say that one who makes a contract fills the measure of his duty by less than full performance. They do say, however, that an omission, both trivial and innocent, will sometimes be atoned for by allowance of the resulting damage, and will not always be the breach of a condition to be followed by a forfeiture. Spence v. Ham, 163 N. Y. 220, 57 N. E. 412, 51 L. R. A. 238. . . . The distinction is akin to that between dependent and independent promises, or between promises and conditions. Anson on Contracts (Corbin's Ed.) § 367; 2 Williston on Contracts, § 842. Some promises are so plainly independent that they can never by fair construction be conditions of one another. Rosenthal Paper Co. v. Nat. Folding Box & Paper Co., 226 N. Y. 313, 123 N. E. 766. . . . Others are so plainly dependent that they must always be conditions. Others, though dependent and thus conditions when there is departure in point of substance, will be viewed as independent and collateral when the departure is insignificant. 2 Williston on Contracts, §§ 841, 842; Eastern Forge Co. v. Corbin, 182 Mass. 590, 592, 66 N. E. 419. . . . Considerations partly of justice and partly of presumable intention are to tell us whether this or that promise shall be placed in one class or in another. The simple and the uniform will call for different remedies from the multifarious and the intricate. The margin of departure within the range of normal expectation upon a sale of common chattels will vary from the margin to be expected upon a contract for the construction of a mansion or a "skyscraper." There will be harshness sometimes and oppression in the implication of a condition when the thing upon which labor has been expended is incapable of surrender because united to the land, and equity and reason in the implication of a like condition when the subject-matter, if defective, is in shape to be returned. From the conclusion that promises may not be treated as dependent to the extent of their uttermost minutiae without a sacrifice of justice, the progress is a short one to the conclusion that they may not be so treated without a perversion of intention. Intention not otherwise revealed may be presumed to hold in contemplation the reasonable and probable. If something else is in view, it must not be left to implication. There will be no assumption of a purpose to visit venial faults with oppressive retribution.

Those who think more of symmetry and logic in the development of legal rules than of practical adaptation to the attainment of a just result will be troubled by a classification where the lines of division are so wavering and blurred. Something, doubtless, may be said on the score of consistency and certainty in favor of a stricter standard. The courts have balanced such considerations against those of equity and fairness, and found the latter to be the weightier. The decisions in this state commit us to the liberal view, which is making its way, nowadays, in jurisdictions slow to welcome it. Dakin & Co. v. Lee, 1916, 1 K. B. 566, 579. Where the line is to be drawn between the important and the trivial cannot be settled by a formula. "In the nature of the case precise boundaries are impossible." 2 Williston on Contracts, § 841. The same omission may take on one aspect or another according to its setting. Substitution of equivalents may not have the same significance in fields of art on the one side and in those of mere utility on the other. Nowhere will change be tolerated, however, if it is so dominant or pervasive as in any real or substantial measure to frustrate the purpose of the contract. . . . There is no general license to install whatever, in the builder's judgment, may be regarded as "just as good." Easthampton L. & C. Co., Ltd. v. Worthington, 186 N. Y. 407, 412, 79 N. E. 323. The question is one of degree, to be answered, if there is doubt, by the triers of the facts (Crouch v. Gutmann; Woodward v. Fuller, supra), and, if the inferences are certain, by the judges of the law (Easthampton L. & C. Co., Ltd. v. Worthington, supra). We must weigh the purpose to be served, the desire to be gratified, the excuse for deviation from the letter, the cruelty of enforced adherence. Then only can we tell whether literal fulfillment is to be implied by law as a condition. This is not to say that the parties are not free by apt and certain words to effectuate a purpose that performance of every term shall be a condition of recovery. That question is not here. This is merely to say that the law will be slow to impute the purpose, in the silence of the parties, where the significance of the default is grievously out of proportion to the oppression of the forfeiture. The willful transgressor must accept the penalty of his transgression. . . . For him there is no occasion to mitigate the rigor of implied conditions. The transgressor whose default is unintentional and trivial may hope for mercy if he will offer atonement for his wrong. Spence v. Ham, supra.

In the circumstances of this case, we think the measure of the allowance is not the cost of replacement, which would be great, but the difference in value, which would be either nominal or nothing. Some of the exposed sections might perhaps have been replaced at moderate expense. The defendant did not limit his demand to them, but treated the plumbing as a unit to be corrected from cellar to roof. In point of fact, the plaintiff never reached the stage at which evidence of the extent of the allowance became necessary. The trial court had excluded evidence that the defect was unsubstantial, and in view of that ruling there was no occasion for the plaintiff to go farther with an offer of proof. We think, however, that the offer, if it had been made, would not of necessity have been defective because directed to difference in value. It is true that in most cases the cost of replacement is the measure. Spence v. Ham, supra. The owner is entitled to the money which will permit him to complete, unless the cost of completion is grossly and unfairly out of proportion to the good to be attained. When that is true, the measure is the difference in value. Specifications call, let us say, for a foundation built of granite quarried in Vermont. On the completion of the building, the owner learns that through the blunder of a subcontractor part of the foundation has been built of granite of the same quality quarried in New Hampshire. The measure of allowance is not the cost of reconstruction.

> There may be omissions of that which could not afterwards be supplied exactly as called for by the contract without taking down the building to its foundations, and at the same time the omission may not affect the value of the building for use or otherwise, except so slightly as to be hardly appreciable. Handy v. Bliss, 204 Mass. 513, 519, 90 N. E. 864, 134 Am. St. Rep. 673. Cf. . . . 2 Williston on Contracts, § 805, p. 1541.

The rule that gives a remedy in cases of substantial performance with compensation for defects of trivial or inappreciable importance has been developed by the courts as an instrument of justice. The measure of the allowance must be shaped to the same end.

The order should be affirmed, and judgment absolute directed in favor of the plaintiff upon the stipulation, with costs in all courts.

McLAUGHLIN, J.

I dissent. The plaintiff did not perform its contract. Its failure to do so was either intentional or due to gross neglect which, under the uncontradicted facts, amounted to the same thing, nor did it make any proof of the cost of compliance, where compliance was possible.

Under its contract it obligated itself to use in the plumbing only pipe (between 2,000 and 2,500 feet) made by the Reading Manufacturing Company. The first pipe delivered was about 1,000 feet and the plaintiff's superintendent then called the attention of the foreman of the subcontractor, who was doing the plumbing, to the fact that the specifications annexed to the contract required all pipe used in the plumbing to be of the Reading Manufacturing Company. They then examined it for the purpose of ascertaining whether this delivery was of that manufacture and found it was. Thereafter, as pipe was required in the progress of the work, the foreman of the subcontractor would leave word at its shop that he wanted a specified number of feet of pipe, without in any way indicating of what manufacture. Pipe would thereafter be delivered and installed in the building, without any examination whatever. Indeed, no examination, so far as appears, was made by the plaintiff, the subcontractor, defendant's architect, or any one else, of any of the pipe except the first delivery, until after the building had been completed. Plaintiff's architect then refused to give the certificate of completion, upon which the final payment depended, because all of the pipe used in the plumbing was not of the kind called for by the contract. After such refusal, the subcontractor removed the covering or insulation from about 900 feet of pipe which was exposed in the basement, cellar, and attic, and all but 70 feet was found to have been manufactured, not by the Reading Company, but by other manufacturers, some by the Cohoes Rolling Mill Company, some by the National Steel Works, some by the South Chester Tubing Company, and some which bore no manufacturer's mark at all. The balance of the pipe had been so installed in the building that an inspection of it could not be had without demolishing, in part at least, the building itself.

I am of the opinion the trial court was right in directing a verdict for the defendant. The plaintiff agreed that all the pipe used should be of the Reading Manufacturing Company. Only about two-fifths of it, so far as appears, was of that kind. If more were used, then the burden of proving that fact was upon the plaintiff, which it could easily have done, since it knew where the pipe was obtained. The question of substantial performance of a contract of the character of the one under consideration depends in no small degree upon the good faith of the contractor. If the plaintiff had intended to, and had, complied with the terms of the contract except as to minor omissions, due to inadvertence, then he might be allowed to recover the contract price, less the amount necessary to fully compensate the defendant for damages caused by such omissions. Woodward v. Fuller, 80 N. Y. 312. . . . But that is not this case. It installed between 2,000 and 2,500 feet of pipe, of which only 1,000 feet at most complied with the contract. No explanation was given why pipe called for by the contract was not used, nor that any effort made to show what it would cost to remove the pipe of other manufacturers and install that of the Reading Manufacturing Company. The defendant had a right to contract for what he wanted. He had a right before making payment to get what the contract called for. It is no answer to this suggestion to say that the pipe put in was just as good as that made by the Reading Manufacturing Company, or that the difference in value between such pipe and the pipe made by the Reading Manufacturing Company would be either "nominal or nothing." Defendant contracted for pipe made by the Reading Manufacturing Company. What his reason was for requiring this kind of pipe is of no importance. He wanted that and was entitled to it. It may have been a mere whim on his part, but even so, he had a right to this kind of pipe, regardless of whether some other kind, according to the opinion of the contractor or experts, would have been "just as good, better, or done just as well." He agreed to pay only upon condition that the pipe installed were made by that company and he ought not to be compelled to pay unless that condition be performed. Schultze v. Goodstein, 180 N. Y.

248, 73 N. E. 21; Spence v. Ham, supra; . . . . The rule, therefore, of substantial performance, with damages for unsubstantial omissions, has no application. . . .

What was said by this court in Smith v. Brady, supra, is quite applicable here:

> I suppose it will be conceded that every one has a right to build his house, his cottage or his store after such a model and in such style as shall best accord with his notions of utility or be most agreeable to his fancy. The specifications of the contract become the law between the parties until voluntarily changed. If the owner prefers a plain and simple Doric column, and has so provided in the agreement, the contractor has no right to put in its place the more costly and elegant Corinthian. If the owner, having regard to strength and durability, has contracted for walls of specified materials to be laid in a particular manner, or for a given number of joists and beams, the builder has no right to substitute his own judgment or that of others. Having departed from the agreement, if performance has not been waived by the other party, the law will not allow him to allege that he has made as good a building as the one he engaged to erect. He can demand payment only upon and according to the terms of his contract, and if the conditions on which payment is due have not been performed, then the right to demand it does not exist. To hold a different doctrine would be simply to make another contract, and would be giving to parties an encouragement to violate their engagements, which the just policy of the law does not permit. (17 N. Y. 186, 72 Am. Dec. 422).

I am of the opinion the trial court did not err in ruling on the admission of evidence or in directing a verdict for the defendant.

For the foregoing reasons I think the judgment of the Appellate Division should be reversed and the judgment of the Trial Term affirmed. . . .

Order affirmed, etc.

NOTES AND QUESTIONS

1. *Fastidious adherence to idiosyncratic preference?* Why would Kent insist on Reading pipe? Would not any pipe suffice? As Judge Cardozo observed in *Jacob & Youngs* ". . . the brands installed, though made by other manufacturers, were the same in quality, in appearance, in market value, and in cost as the brand stated in the contract—that they were, indeed, the same thing, though manufactured in another place." Assuming the pipe to be of equal quality, why would Kent insist on replacement at great and significant cost? As it turns out, the story is more complicated than Cardozo declared. In

an excellent historical analysis, Richard Dansig notes that the Reading Manufacturing Co. was one of four wrought iron pipe manufacturers—Reading, Cohoes, Byers, and Southchester. See Richard Dansig, The Capacity Problem in Contract Law 120–123 (1978). All four brands were identical in quality and price, and Dansig reports an interview with a pipe wholesaler who opined, "[t]he manufacturer's name would make absolutely no difference in pipe or in price." Id. The *Jacob Youngs* contract may have named Reading pipe simply in response to trade bulletins that warned, "When wrought iron pipe is desired, the specifications often read 'genuine wrought iron pipe' but as this does not always exclude wrought iron containing steel scrap, it is safer to mention the name of a manufacturer known not to use scrap." Id.

This sort of contextualism in the modern form of legal archeology enhances the intuitive understanding of the motivations for many famous cases. See Judith L. Maute, "Response: The Values of Legal Archaeology," 2000 Utah L. Rev. 223, 227. While fascinating, some find legal archaeology atheoretical and useful primarily as an explanatory tool. Patricia D. White, "Afterword and Response: What Digging Does and Does Not Do,"2000 Utah L. Rev. 301.

2. *Express or constructive condition?* The construction contract in question specifically provided that "[a]ll wrought-iron pipe must be well galvanized, lap welded pipe of the grade known as 'standard pipe' of Reading manufacture." Judge Cardozo did not interpret this language as creating an express condition: "This is not to say that the parties are not free by apt and certain words to effectuate a purpose that performance of every term shall be a condition of recovery. That question is not here." What prevented Cardozo from interpreting that language as an express condition? If the language regarding the use of Reading pipe was not an express condition, then it amounted to no more than doubtful conditional language construed as a "promise" to use such pipe. Restatement (Second) of Contracts § 227(2)(a). The distinction is important. As noted in the *Oppenheimer* case and trailing notes, express conditions require strict performance, whereas parties may satisfy constructive conditions by substantial performance. Substantial but imperfect performance remains a breach subjecting the breaching party to damages, but substantial performance does not discharge the injured party's return obligation to perform. Accordingly, the injured party must still perform, but may recover damages for the less-than-perfect performance.

3. *Damage measure.* Judge Cardozo determined that the proper measure of damages was "not the cost of replacement, which would be great, but the difference in value, which would be either nominal or nothing." Chapter 9 addresses various mechanisms for measuring damages caused by breach in detail. Briefly, however, Restatement (Second) of Contracts § 347 generally provides the injured party a right to "loss in value" monetary damages based on an "expectancy interest." The expectancy interest is the difference between the value of what was promised minus the value of what was actually received. Under this standard, what is the difference in value between the promised house (with Reading pipe) and the house as is (with Cohoes pipe)? Restatement

(Second) of Contracts § 348(2) provides a special alternative rule specifically applicable to cases involving a breach "in defective or unfinished construction." Where the injured party cannot prove the loss in value with reasonable certainty, the injured party may instead recover monetary damages based on the (i) diminution in the market price of the property caused by the defect; (ii) the reasonable cost of completing performance; or (iii) the reasonable cost of remedying the defects. However, the cost to remedy measure is only available where the "cost is not clearly disproportionate to the probable loss in value."

Where performance is defective (as in *Jacob & Youngs*) rather than incomplete, proof of loss in value with reasonable certainty is usually not feasible. As a result, the injured party normally may recover the cost to "remedy the defect." The remedial recovery will usually exceed the loss in value, but the small resulting windfall is usually preferred to the more serious risk of undercompensation from loss in value. Restatement (Second) of Contracts § 348, *cmt. c.* But in many cases, a large portion of the cost to remedy will involve a significant cost to undo what was improperly done. In those cases, the cost to remedy the defects will be disproportionately large compared to the minute loss in value measure and will impose a forfeiture on the breaching party. In such cases, the injured party is not likely to actually make the improvements because the great cost will result in such a small value increase in value. Accordingly, in such cases, the loss in value measure will be preferred.

Do you think this case involved just such a situation? If the loss in value is nominal and it costs $50,000 to tear up the walls and the home to substitute the Reading pipe, do you think the homeowner would pocket the $50,000 or spend the money fixing the home, even though the repairs do not increase the value of the home? Restatement (Second) of Contracts § 348(2) was based on Restatement (First) of Contracts § 346(1)(a)(i), which provided that the cost to remedy did not involve "unreasonable economic waste." Restatement (Second) of Contracts § 348(2) rejected the economic waste doctrine because injured parties presumptively will not make such expenditures and will thus receive a windfall. Does this question depend in part upon whether the property involved is the injured party's personal residence? This issue is explored in more detail in Chapter 9 in connection with the *Peevyhouse* case. For another legal archaeological exploration on that case, see Judith L. Maute, "*Peevyhouse v. Garland Coal & Mining Co.* Revisited: The Ballad of Willie and Lucille," 89 Nw. U. L. Rev. 1341 (1995).

4. *Substantial performance versus material breach.* An uncured material breach discharges the other party's duty to perform. Restatement (Second) of Contracts § 225(2). The restatement does not utilize the phrase "substantial performance" developed by Judge Cardozo in *Jacob & Youngs*. However, material breach is the antithesis of substantial performance. While Restatement (Second) of Contracts § 241 lists various competing factors to make this determination, these factors are indeterminate. In reality, legal actors have little ex ante guidance regarding exactly when and how performance crosses the line to fall short of substantial performance and thus

becomes a material breach. One suggestion advocates applying these factors to promote the ability of injured parties to avail themselves of the cancellation remedy that accompanies a finding of material breach "only when, given the particular facts of the case at hand, the victim needs that ability." Eric G. Andersen, "A New Look at Material Breach in the Law of Contracts," 21 U. C. Davis L. Rev. 1073, 1077 (1988). Those situations occur where the victim needs "to secure and enhance the likelihood that *future* duties will be properly performed," either by the original party or by the victim of the breach securing alternative performance or the money value of alternative performance. Id.

Utilizing this standard, is there any value in *Jacob & Youngs* in awarding Kent the right to cancel the contract, in addition to an award of monetary damages? Would this ever occur once performance is completed? If not, then is *Jacob & Youngs* truly about the right to cancel the contract or the proper measure of damages? Why the discussion of substantial performance at all? See Amy B. Cohen, "Reviving *Jacob & Youngs, Inc. v. Kent*: Material Breach Doctrine Reconsidered," 42 Vill. L. Rev. 65 (1997).

5. *UCC perfect tender rule.* The UCC rejects the substantial performance doctrine. Rather, it requires that tender of goods must perfectly conform to the requirements of the contract. UCC § 2–601(a) provides that "if the goods or the tender of delivery fail in any respect to conform to the contract, the buyer may reject the whole." The doctrine is often criticized as too harsh. See John Honnold, "Buyer's Right of Rejection," 97 U. Pa. L. Rev. 457 (1949). Several exceptions mitigate the harshness of this rule. See George L. Priest, "Breach and Remedy for the Tender of Nonconforming Goods Under the Uniform Commercial Code: An Economic Approach," 91 Harv. L. Rev. 960 (1978). Most importantly, the UCC provides the nonconforming seller a liberal right to cure the defective performance. UCC § 2–508(1) allows cure upon rejection so long as the time for original performance has not expired. UCC § 2–508(2) allows the seller to cure even after the time for performance has passed, but only under two limited circumstances. The right to cure and damage measurement are the subject of further discussion in Chapter 9.

6. *CISG approach.* CISG Art. 25 adopts a standard of fundamental breach rather than perfect tender. UNIDROIT Art. 7.3.1. follows with a standard of fundamental non-performance. Thus, the CISG standard more resembles common law than the UCC.

7. *Willful transgressor.* Judge Cardozo opines that the doctrine of substantial performance will not protect a willful transgressor: "The willful transgressor must accept the penalty of his transgression." What do you think he means? Does willfulness increase the damage measure or simply allow cancellation as a material breach? Restatement (Second) of Contracts § 241(e) also suggests a similar point in its multi-factor analysis to determine whether a breach is material by referencing "the extent to which the behavior of the party failing to perform or to offer to perform comports with standards of good faith and fair dealing." Restatement (Second) of Contracts § 241, *cmt. f* explains that courts often and imprecisely equate "willfulness" of the breach with a

failure to conform with the standards of "good faith and fair dealing." Notably, compliance or non-compliance with this factor is, standing alone, not conclusive on the question of whether the breach is material. To some degree, the requirement of good faith imports the moral requirement of subjective honesty and belief in conduct. Does such an appeal to morality and subjective honesty make sense, or should courts restrict analysis of a party's good faith only to purely economic and analytical reasoning of business risks? See Eric G. Andersen, "Three Degrees of Promising," 2003 B.Y.U. L. Rev. 829 and Caroline N. Brown, "Teaching Good Faith," 44 St. Louis U. L. J. 1377 (2000).

8.   *Dependent and independent promises.* Judge Cardozo refers to minor deviations of contractual duties as constructive conditions and as similar to dependent promises: "The distinction is akin to that between dependent and independent promises, or between promises and conditions. . . . Some promises are so plainly independent that they can never by fair construction be conditions of one another. . . . Others are so plainly dependent that they must always be conditions. Others, though dependent and thus conditions when there is departure in point of substance, will be viewed as independent and collateral when the departure is insignificant." Clearly, conditions are far broader than mere promises and include any fact specified by the parties that must occur before performance is due. On what basis did Judge Cardozo create the constructive condition of substantial performance? Was it the presumed intent of the parties, justice, or both? What do you think he means by the following reference: "Considerations partly of justice and partly of presumable intention are to tell us whether this or that promise shall be placed in one class or in another."?

9.   *Total and partial breach.* The primary function of the material breach doctrine is to determine when the other party's performance may be suspended. Unless timely cured, the uncured material breach results in total breach. A total breach gives the injured party the option to terminate the contract by discharging the injured party's own obligation of performance and suing for damages for total breach, or to continue to perform and sue for partial breach. Compare Restatement (Second) of Contracts §§ 242 (determining duration of cure period for a material breach), with 243(1) (total breach discharges performance obligation of injured party). In addition to a discharge of duties, the injured party's claim for damages in a total breach takes the place of all remaining rights under the contract. Restatement (Second) of Contracts § 236(1). As a consequence, damages are measured on the assumption that neither party will render further performance. See Restatement (Second) of Contracts § 347 for the general measure of damages for total breach as discussed in Chapter 9 (generally loss in value + other incidental and consequential losses – cost avoided – losses avoided). However, a partial breach generally entitles the injured party to only actual damages to the date of the breach. See Restatement (Second) of Contracts §§ 236(2) and 243(4).

Stated another way, a total breach is an uncured material breach that the injured party elects to treat as total in order to terminate the future performance of both parties. However, if an uncured material breach qualifies to be treated as a total breach, it will nonetheless be only a partial breach unless the injured party elects to treat it as a total breach. Normally, this election is manifested by the willingness of the injured party to continue the performance of the contract, notwithstanding the uncured material breach.

4. EXCUSE, WAIVER, AND OTHER RELIEF FROM EFFECT OF CONDITIONS

Several doctrines mitigate the potentially harsh effects—often forfeiture by one party of the expected benefits of the contract—of express and constructive conditions. The doctrine of substantial performance, discussed above, actually provides one example of a mitigating doctrine, although it is often analyzed separately from and is not subject to the effect of the mitigating principles discussed in this section. In each of these mitigating doctrines, some behavior or equitable principle overrides the nonoccurrence of the condition and its normal consequence of discharging the other party's obligation to perform. In each case, excuse of the nonoccurrence of the condition causes the correlative duty to become due. Stated another way, the excuse of the condition converts the conditional duty into an unconditional duty.

Doctrine of Good Faith. The parties must exercise good faith and fair dealing: (i) to refrain from preventing or hindering the occurrence of the condition (doctrine of prevention); and (ii) to take affirmative steps to cause its occurrence, at least when the occurrence is within that party's control. See Restatement (Second) of Contracts § 245. For example, if a buyer's obligation to purchase a home is subject to a condition that the buyer obtains financing, the buyer must exercise a good faith effort to apply for and obtain financing. The buyer's failure to make such a good faith effort excuses the condition, the obligation to purchase becomes unconditional, and the failure to purchase—even without financing— breaches the contract. Similarly, the seller must exercise good faith in refraining from any conduct that would prevent the buyer from obtaining financing. The seller's interference in the buyer's attempts to satisfy the financing condition excuses that condition and discharges the buyer's obligation to purchase the home.

Doctrine of Waiver. The party who benefits from the nonoccurrence of the condition may waive the effect of the condition in most cases. "Waiver" is commonly but inexactly referred to as a "voluntary relinquishment of a known right." Restatement (Second) of Contracts § 84, *cmt. b.* However, contractual waiver of conditions at common law does not require that the waiving party actually "know" their legal rights. A lesser standard involving a mere "reason to know" is adequate. Restatement (Second) of Contracts § 93.

The application of waiver rules to conditions varies depending on the nature of the conditions. Generally it is easier to waive constructive conditions, since waiver of material express conditions is not binding in some cases. Restatement (Second) of Contracts § 84(1)(a). However, all constructive conditions may be waived regardless of materiality. Restatement (Second) of Contracts § 246.

Normally, waiver occurs when a party makes an express or implied promise to perform notwithstanding the nonsatisfaction of an express or constructive condition. Obviously, if the waiver promise was given in exchange for negotiated consideration, the promise is permanently enforceable. Similarly, if the other party relies on the waiver, promissory estoppel may also make the waiver promise permanently enforceable. However, in all other cases, a waiver can be retracted with reasonable notice given before the time for the condition to occur has expired. Restatement (Second) of Contracts § 84(2)(a) and Restatement (Second) of Contracts § 84, *cmt. f.* Most often, the "promise" to waive is not express, but rather is implied from the waiving party's acceptance of performance notwithstanding the nonsatisfaction of the condition. Restatement (Second) of Contracts § 247.

Specifically, a waiver of an express condition is not effective if the condition was a material part of the exchange "and the promisee was under no duty that it occur." Restatement (Second) of Contracts § 84(1)(a). The materiality limitation prevents the concept of waiver from eviscerating the legal principle requiring strict compliance with express conditions. However, like the concept of material breach, the concept of material express condition is potentially illusive. Restatement (Second) of Contracts § 84, *cmt. d* suggests that the materiality limitation substantially restricts the waiver doctrine to conditions that are procedural, technical, or comparatively minor in nature. See Bryan Gibson, Comment, "Contract-Specific Performance—Conditions Precedent and Contractual Benefits—Waiver of Condition Precedent: *O'Reilly v. Marketers Diversified* Inc.," 6 U. Brit. Colum. L. Rev. 431 (1971) and David V. Snyder, "The Law of Contract and the Concept of Change: Public and Private Attempts to Regulate Modification, Waiver, and Estoppel," 1999 Wisc. L. Rev. 607. Perhaps the importance of and caution attendant to waiver is best expressed in *Bank v. Truck Ins. Exchange*, 51 F.3d 736, 737–739 (7th Cir. 1995) (Posner, J.):

> We are asked, in this diversity breach of contract case, to decide whether one of the parties waived one of its rights under the contract. Waiver is one of a multitude of contract doctrines that allow oral testimony to modify the terms of an apparently clear written contract. There is no more vexing question in contract law than when a written contract can be rewritten by oral testimony. "Always" is an unsatisfactory answer because it defeats one of the main purposes of written contracts, which is to protect a

contracting party against the vagaries of juries. . . . "Never" is equally unsatisfactory, because of the acute danger of misinterpretation by a reader ignorant of the contract's commercial setting. [Earlier] we concluded that the law draws the line between "objective" and "subjective" testimony. The former, illustrated by evidence of trade usage, is evidence that is capable of being given by disinterested witnesses. The latter is the self-serving testimony of one of the parties to the contract. Objective testimony can be used to help interpret a written contract even if the contract seems unambiguous; subjective testimony is admissible (if the parties do not agree to its use) only if the contract seems ambiguous . . . . . The potential inconsistency of the doctrine of waiver so understood with the principle that parties should not be allowed to get out of their written contracts by self-serving testimony is manifest. You can always say that the other party to your contract had orally waived the enforcement of a provision favorable to him. Yet all that waiver means, when it is carefully defined, is the intentional relinquishment of a right. . . . "Waiver" is often used as a synonym for "forfeiture," as when the failure to present a ground to the district court is deemed to "waive" the ground in the court of appeals. But we mean to use it here in its strict sense of a voluntary relinquishment. Any mentally competent person is allowed to relinquish most of his constitutional rights without any formalities; it might seem all the clearer that he should be able to relinquish his contractual rights without formalities.

Doctrine of Excuse to Avoid Forfeiture. Courts may also excuse conditions that would cause an unconscionable forfeiture. See Restatement (Second) of Contracts § 229. Even though both unconscionability and the excuse to avoid forfeiture doctrine limit the freedom of the parties to contract, they are applied at different moments in time. Unconscionability is determined at the time the contract is formed, whereas courts analyze whether to excuse conditions to avoid a forfeiture at the time of the occurrence of the condition. Compare Restatement (Second) of Contracts § 208 (unconscionability), with Restatement (Second) of Contracts § 229 (forfeiture excuse). Forfeiture in this sense implies a "denial of compensation that results when the obligee loses his right to the agreed exchange after he has relied substantially, as by preparation or performance, on the expectation of that exchange." Disproportionality is applied by balancing the obligee's described forfeiture with the importance of the condition to the other party. Restatement (Second) of Contracts § 229, *cmt. b.*

As with other penalties, the law will not enforce an unjust penalty, even one devised by the parties. A similar notion exists in the context of the common law refusal to enforce a liquidated damages provision that constitutes a disproportionate penalty. See Restatement (Second) of Contracts § 356(1). Curiously, as with waiver of express conditions, the condition excuse by reason of disproportionate forfeiture can only occur where the condition was not a material part of the exchange. Compare Restatement (Second) of Contracts § 229, with Restatement (Second) of Contracts § 84(1)(a). Materiality in this context is much the same as with waiver. Of course, the occurrence of every condition results in a forfeiture of that party's remaining rights under the contract. Nonetheless, such a party may always seek restitution for excess benefits unjustly conferred upon the other party. Thus, disproportionate forfeiture must mean something more than the loss of a restitution interest and, more particularly, rests with the loss of the reliance and expectancy interests. The importance of that loss must be compared with the importance of the condition to the other party. Forfeiture excuse cases are inextricably tied to equitable balancing of the reasonable expectations of the parties.

HOLIDAY INNS OF AMERICA, INC. V. KNIGHT

Supreme Court of California
70 Cal.2d 327, 74 Cal.Rptr. 722, 450 P.2d 42 (1969)

TRAYNOR, Chief Justice.

Plaintiffs appeal from a judgment for defendants in an action seeking a declaration that a contract was still effective. The judgment was entered after plaintiffs' motion for summary judgment was denied and defendants' motion for summary judgment was granted.

The pleadings and affidavits of the parties establish the following undisputed facts.

Plaintiffs are the successors in interest to the optionee under a written option contract between the optionee and the owners of the option property, defendant D. Manley Knight and his mother, Mary Knight. Mary Knight is now deceased and D. Manley Knight is the sole owner of the property. Although his wife is also named a defendant herein, she has no interest in the contract or the option property. We will therefore refer to D. Manley Knight as defendant.

The contract, executed on September 30, 1963, granted an option to purchase real property in Orange County for $198,633, the price to be subject, however, to prescribed adjustments for changes in the cost of living. Unless cancelled as provided in the agreement, the option could be exercised by giving written notice thereof no later than April 1, 1968. The contract provided for an initial payment of $10,000 and for four additional payments of $10,000 to be made directly to the optionors on July 1 of each year, commencing in 1964, unless the option was exercised or cancelled before the next such payment became due. These payments were not to be applied to the purchase price. The cancellation provision provided that:

> [I]t is mutually understood that failure to make payment on or before the prescribed date will automatically cancel this option without further notice.

On December 9, 1963, the parties amended the contract by executing escrow instructions that provided that the annual payments were to be deposited in escrow with the Security Title Insurance Company, and that, in:

> [T]he event you (Security Title) do not receive the $10,000 annual payments (by July 1) and upon receiving notice from Optionors to cancel the option, without further instructions from Optionee you are to terminate the escrow.

The initial payment of $10,000 and the annual installments for 1964 and 1965 were paid. After the execution of the contract, plaintiffs expended "great amounts of money" to develop a major residential and commercial center on the land adjacent to the option property. These expenditures have caused the option property to increase substantially in value since the contract was executed. Plaintiffs' purpose in entering into the contract was to put themselves in a position to secure the advantage of this increase in value resulting from their development efforts.

In 1966 plaintiffs mailed a check for $10,000 to defendant. It was made out to D. Manley Knight and his wife, Lavinia Knight, and dated June 30, 1966. Defendant received the check on July 2, 1966 and returned it to plaintiffs on July 8, stating that the option contract was cancelled. On July 8 plaintiffs tendered another check directly to defendant, and he again refused it. On July 15 plaintiffs deposited a $10,000 check with Security Title payable to defendant. Security Title tendered the check to defendant, but his attorney returned it to plaintiffs on July 27 and advised them that the agreement was terminated pursuant to the cancellation provision.

Plaintiffs contend that payment of the annual installment was timely on the ground that the check became the property of defendant when mailed; that even if the payment was late, the trial court should have relieved them from forfeiture and declared the option in force under section 3275 of the Civil Code; and that, in any event, the trial court erred in excluding extrinsic evidence offered to prove that the escrow instructions modified the contract to permit payment at any time before defendant notified the title company that the option was cancelled. Since the undisputed facts establish that plaintiffs are entitled to relief from forfeiture pursuant to section 3275, it is unnecessary to consider plaintiffs' other contentions.

Section 3275 provides:

> Whenever, by the terms of an obligation, a party thereto incurs a forfeiture, or a loss in the nature of a forfeiture, by reason of his failure to comply with its provisions, he may be relieved therefrom, upon making full compensation to the other party, except in case of a grossly negligent, willful, or fraudulent breach of duty.

The tumultuous history of this section has been recorded in a lengthy series of major decisions in the area of property and contract law.

Although most of the cases considering section 3275 have involved land sale contracts, its proscriptions against forfeiture apply in any case in which the party seeking relief from default has brought himself within the terms of the section by pleading and proving facts that justify its application. (Barkis v. Scott, supra, 34 Cal. 2d at pp. 118, 120, 208 P. 2d 367.) In determining whether a given case falls within section 3275, however, it is necessary to consider the nature of the contract and the specific clause in question. Although the contract in the instant case is an option contract, the question is not whether the exercise of the option was timely, but whether the right to exercise the option in the future was forfeited by a failure to pay the consideration for that right precisely on time. Defendant's reliance on Cummings v. Bullock (9th Cir. 1966) 367 F.2d 182, and Wilson v. Ward (1957) 155 Cal. App. 2d 390, 317 P. 2d 1018, is therefore misplaced. Both those cases dealt with the time within which an option must be exercised and correctly held that such time cannot be extended beyond that provided in the contract. To hold otherwise would give the optionee, not the option he bargained for, but a longer and therefore more extensive option. In the present case, however, plaintiffs are not seeking to extend the period during which the option can be exercised but only to secure relief from the provision making time of the essence in tendering the annual payments. . . . In a proper case, relief will be granted under section 3275 from such a provision. . . .

The sole issue in this case is whether the plaintiffs have brought themselves within section 3275; whether there would be a loss in the nature of a forfeiture suffered by plaintiffs if the option contract were terminated. Essentially, the position of defendant is that there is no forfeiture since plaintiffs got precisely what they bargained for, namely, the exclusive right to buy the property for the three years during which they made payments. Cancellation because of the late 1966 payment amounts to nothing more than terminating a contract providing for that exclusive right during 1966. As viewed by defendant, this contract is in effect wholly executory and therefore its termination would not result in a forfeiture to either party. . . .

To sustain defendant's argument, the contract would have to be viewed as a series of independent contracts, each for a one-year option. Only if this were true, could it be said that plaintiffs received their bargained for equivalent of the $30,000 payments. . . . The economic realities of the transaction, however, do not support this analysis. First, the language of the agreement states that the "Optioners hereby grant to Optionee the exclusive right and option for a five year period. . . ." The parties agreed to bind themselves to a period of five years with the price payable in five installments. On the basis of risk allocation, it is clear that each payment of the $10,000 installment was partially for an option to buy the land during that year and partially for a renewal of the option for another year up to a total of five years. With the passage of time, plaintiffs have paid more and more for the right to renew, and it is this right that would be forfeited by requiring payment strictly on time. At the time the forfeiture was declared, plaintiffs had paid a substantial part of the $30,000 for the right to exercise the option during the last two years. Thus, they have not received what they bargained for and they have lost more than the benefit of their bargain. In short, they will suffer a forfeiture of that part of the $30,000 attributable to the right to exercise the option during the last two years.[3]

Plaintiffs have at all times remained willing and able to continue with the performance of the contract and have acted in good faith to accomplish this end. Defendant has not suffered any injury justifying termination of the contract, and none of his reasonable expectations have been defeated. Moreover, he will receive the benefit of his bargain, namely, the full price of the option granted plaintiffs. As we stated in Barkis, "when the default has not been serious and the vendee is willing and able to continue with his performance of the contract, the vendor suffers no damage by allowing the vendee to do so." (Barkis v. Scott, supra, 34 Cal. 2d at p. 122, 208 P. 2d at p. 371.)

The judgment is reversed and the trial court is directed to enter a summary judgment for plaintiffs in accord with the views herein expressed.

NOTES AND QUESTIONS

1. *Mailbox rule.* Apparently the 1966 payment due on July 1, 1966 was dated on June 30, 1966 and mailed on that day. It was not received, however, until July 2, 1966, one day late. Restatement (Second) of Contracts § 63(a) states that generally, acceptance is valid when mailed. However, Restatement (Second) of Contracts § 63(b) provides that acceptance under an option contract

---

[3] Plaintiffs also allege forfeiture of "great amounts of money" expended for the development of surrounding land. Evidently none of the investment was made in the option property. Since there is nothing to indicate that the development was not highly profitable in its own right or that inclusion of defendant's property was necessary to make the development a success, it would not seem that any part of these expenditures can be considered forfeited by a termination of the contract. (Cf. Scarbery v. Bill Patch Land & Water Co., supra, where the plaintiff offered evidence justifying the allocation of collateral development expenditures to the amounts forfeited by cancellation.)

is not valid until actually received by the offeror. As a consequence, the exercise of the option for an additional year was invalid in this case. Accordingly, the Holiday Inn argument that the payment was valid when mailed is incorrect.

2. *Holiday Inn forfeiture.* What did Judge Traynor decide that Holiday Inn forfeited? Did the refusal of the seller to accept the late payment cause any forfeiture of the land already developed by Holiday Inn? Did the failure of the seller cause Holiday Inn to lose the undisputed value of the adjacent land caused by its adjacent development? Or did Judge Traynor simply determine that Holiday Inn would forfeit the $30,000 expended in 1963, 1964, and 1965?

3. *Disproportionate forfeiture.* Assuming Holiday Inn would forfeit the $30,000, how material to the seller was the condition that payment must be received by July 1 of each year? Did Holiday Inn seek to extend the deadline for exercising the option to purchase the land for approximately $200,000 beyond April 1, 1968? Given that the only purpose of the option was to allocate the increase in value of the land caused by the adjacent development, do you see why the seller would argue the July 1 deadline was a valid time-is-of-the-essence clause? Had Holiday Inn attempted to extend the April 1, 1968 deadline in a similar manner, do you think it would have been successful?

4. *Purpose of option.* The purpose of the option and the $10,000 annual payment was to allow Holiday Inn to retain the right to speculate on the value of the adjacent property. Given the great increase in value of that land, do you think Holiday Inn would intentionally risk loss of that value by making a payment one day late? Since the payment was only one day late and the eventual option exercise date of April 1, 1968 was not extended, how would you compare and evaluate the respective forfeitures of the two parties?

5. *California statutory law.* The case relies on a California statute similar to that in Restatement (Second) of Contracts § 229. If the common law applied, would you expect a different outcome?

CHAPTER 6

CONTRACTS UNENFORCEABLE BY OPERATION OF LAW

■ ■ ■

This chapter addresses situations in which the state will refuse to lend its enforcement powers to private agreements and contracts by operation of law, or because of a defect in contract formation, even where the parties have apparently satisfied all of the requirements for formation (i.e., mutual assent) and enforceability (i.e., consideration).

The category of contracts deemed "void," "voidable," or "unenforceable" comprises several distinct subcategories that address different fundamental flaws concerning the bargaining process, the substantive terms of the parties' agreement, and subsequent or supervening events occurring after execution. These include:

- Illegal contracts or contracts that contravene public policy (contract is void).

- Contracts required to be evidenced by a written memorandum pursuant to the Statute of Frauds (contract is unenforceable).

- Contracts so grossly one-sided and unfair as to shock the conscience of the court (contract is unenforceable).

- Contracts executed through fraud, duress, or undue influence (contract is voidable).

- Contracts executed where one or both parties are mistaken (contract is voidable).

- Contracts where a party's executory obligations have become impracticable or a party's principle purpose has been frustrated because of supervening events after execution (executory obligations are discharged and contract is unenforceable with respect to nonperformance of those obligations).

In each situation, the parties appear to have complied with all the formalities necessary to conclude an enforceable contract. At the same time, the defects are so severe that courts may refuse to enforce the agreement or specific terms thereof.

The next three chapters address these distinct types of "defenses" to contract. This chapter deals with the doctrines of illegality, public policy, the Statute of Frauds, and unconscionability, all of which render contracts either void or unenforceable. Chapter 7 analyzes defenses based upon defects in the bargaining process that, with minor exceptions for physical duress and fraud in the execution, render the contract voidable at the option of the innocent party (fraud, duress, undue influence, and mistake). Finally, Chapter 8 explores the doctrines of impossibility, impracticability, frustration of purpose, and modification, all of which discharge remaining executory obligations of one or both parties, thereby rendering the remaining executory obligations unenforceable.

A. THE DISTINCTION BETWEEN VOID AND VOIDABLE CONTRACTS

At the outset, it is important to distinguish between contracts that are void—i.e., that cannot be enforced at either party's election—and those that are merely voidable—i.e., contracts that the promisee may choose to enforce or avoid at the promisee's election. Examples of the former include contracts that are contrary to public policy, contracts that violate the Statute of Frauds, unconscionable contracts, and contracts formed where one party obtains the other party's apparent consent through fraud in the execution of the agreement or through physical coercion. See James M. Kerr, "Void Contracts," 17 W. Jurist 488 (1883) (surveying categories of void contracts, including contracts that contravene the Statute of Frauds or public policy, contracts without "adequate consideration," contracts to avoid public duties, contracts to promote a crime or aid in evasion of the law, contracts in restraint of trade, and contracts that violate "precepts of morality"). Voidable contracts, such as agreements induced by fraudulent misrepresentations, contracts by infants, and other similar defenses, are the subject of Chapter 7.

The distinction between "void" contracts and "voidable" contracts often appears merely semantic. In a sense, even if a contract is illegal or contrary to public policy (as with an agreement for prostitution or the sale of illegal drugs), violates the Statute of Frauds, is facially unconscionable, or was procured by fraud in the execution or physical duress, the victim must undertake some affirmative legal action to avoid enforcement of the agreement. Thus, for example, if A forces B to execute a contract by placing a gun to B's head and threatening, "Sign, or I'll shoot," the resulting contract bears all the external indicia of an enforceable agreement. B can choose to follow through with the agreement or can attempt to avoid the agreement by seeking a declaratory judgment or refusing to perform and asserting any appropriate defenses, demurrers, or denials in response to a suit by A. Thus, in a practical sense, all flawed agreements can be viewed as voidable contracts, regardless of whether they are *void ab initio*—void from the beginning. Indeed, some commentators have observed that the distinction is too vague to be useful, preferring instead a more general term, such as "unenforceable" contracts. See, e.g., Juliet P. Kostrisky, "Illegal Contracts and Efficient Deterrence: A Study in Modern Contract Theory," 74 Iowa L. Rev. 115, 118–21 & n.7 (1988) ("The use of the word 'void' to describe the consequences of an illegal contract is commonplace but not particularly useful.") (citing E. Allan Farnsworth, Contracts § 5.1 at 397 (1982)).

On the other hand, the distinction still has important legal consequences. Arthur Corbin explained the difference in terms of three categories—unenforceable contracts, void contracts, and voidable contracts. The category of unenforceable contracts comprises both void and voidable contracts. See Arthur L. Corbin, "Offer and Acceptance, And Some of the Resulting Legal Relations," 26 Yale L. J. 169, 180 (1917). Within that category, the distinction between void and voidable contracts lies in the legal relations between the parties resulting from that categorization. According to Corbin, *void* contracts involve the parties acting in a way that would ordinarily create a contract—manifestations of mutual assent and consideration, for example. But the attempted contract is so flawed that while "[r]ights and other relations will exist after such a transaction, . . . *they will not be contract rights and relations.*" Id. (emphasis added). Thus, two parties may mutually agree to exchange a kilogram of cocaine (perhaps with additional warranties that the coke will be "pure," "uncut," or "organically grown and sustainably harvested") for $15,000. This transaction has all of the external indicia of a contract, but because of the illegality of the transaction, it never creates *in personam* rights in either party to enforce the contract. In the case of voidable contracts, however, Corbin observes that the transaction between the parties may be said to create a contract subject to the power of one of the parties to avoid the contract at a later time (and presumably a correlative liability in the other party). See id.

Although courts and commentators appear to be relaxing the distinction between void and voidable in some situations—as, for example, in contracts that fail to comply with the Statute of Frauds (discussed below)—the distinction still produces important legal consequences. The Restatement (Second) of Contracts, for example, observes that the injured party may later ratify a contract that is merely "voidable", while a void contract may not be ratified. See Restatement (Second) of Contracts §§ 163 *cmt. c* & 174 *cmt. b*. A third-party good faith purchaser for value may acquire valid property rights in property sold pursuant to a voidable contract, but not one that is void ab initio. See Curtis Nyquist, "A Spectrum Theory of Negotiability," 78 Marq. L. Rev. 897, 919 (1995) ("Does the duress make the contract voidable or is it of such severity that the contract is entirely void? If the buyer holds a voidable title, the seller can recover the property from the buyer but not from a subsequent good faith purchaser. However, if the buyer's title is void, a subsequent purchaser takes a title that is also void."). Similarly, a party to a void contract may not maintain a cause of action for tortious interference with contract. See James B. Sales, "The Tort of Interference with Contract: An Argument for Requiring a 'Valid Existing Contract' to Restrain the Use of Tort Law in Circumventing Contract Law Remedies," 22 Tex. Tech. L. Rev. 123, 133–34 (1991). A void contract, in other words, never exists as an enforceable obligation of either party.

B. THE PUBLIC POLICY DOCTRINE

The rule that the state should not apply its enforcement powers to contracts that contravene public policy seems obvious. Ultimately, legal obligations arising under private contracts are enforceable by resort to state sanction, up to and including the use of state-legitimized force against a breaching party. While contract law permits private parties to take advantage of a flexible tool for creating this "private law" to define their respective rights and duties, the state cannot permit the parties to usurp its enforcement powers to achieve ends contrary to the continued existence or legitimacy of the state or to the interests of the public that forms that state.

In general, contracts that contravene public policy are void. As stated in the Restatement (Second) of Contracts § 178, a promise or agreement is unenforceable on grounds of public policy in situations (1) where the legislature has directly declared certain agreements or promises illegal; or (2) where judicial precedent has recognized the existence of a public policy against enforcement of such promises.

This general rule is subject to a plethora of exceptions and qualifications. Many exceptions have been developed in response to the widely varying situations in which the illegality or violation of public policy arises. As one commentator notes, the illegality doctrine is confusing and unsettled. See George A. Strong, "The Enforceability of Illegal Contracts," 12 Hastings L.J. 347 (1960). These contracts arise where the contract injures the public interest (whether declared by the legislature or the courts), the contract contains an illegal promise (even if the promised performance itself is not illegal), or where a lawful promise "has been or will be performed in an illegal manner." Id.

Professor Strong's complaint echoes that of an earlier treatise writer, Elisha Greenwood, whose 770-page compendium on the doctrine of public policy begins by noting "[t]he comparatively unsettled condition in which the writer found a good portion of the law upon the subject [of the doctrine of public policy], and . . . that no attempt has ever been made, on this side of the Atlantic, to elaborate the law upon the live and practical topic which the writer has undertaken in the following pages to present. . . . " Elisha Greenwood, The Doctrine of Public Policy in the Law of Contract (1883). Nor does the doctrine seem now any more settled than in Strong's and Greenwood's days.

Beyond the varied situations that may make a contract or promise illegal, the degree of fault, intent, or wrongfulness of the parties may differ greatly depending on context. While agreements that contravene public policy have historically been described as void, courts and legislatures have softened this rule somewhat in situations where non-enforcement of the contract would itself violate other public policies or where the degree of fault for the illegality is not evenly distributed between the parties. Thus, a party who enters an illegal contract through gullibility, dependence upon the other party's expertise, or lack of sophistication regarding the legal requirements of the transaction may be entitled to recovery even though the underlying contract is illegal or contrary to public policy. For an excellent survey and analysis of the situations in which courts have permitted enforcement of otherwise illegal contracts, see Juliet P. Kostrisky, "Illegal Contracts and Efficient Deterrence: A Study in Modern Contract Theory," 74 Iowa L. Rev. 115 (1988) (arguing that exceptions to general rule that illegal contracts are void can be justified as promoting efficient deterrence).

1. ILLEGAL CONTRACTS

The Restatement (Second) of Contracts avoids distinguishing between contracts that violate some provision of law (illegal contracts) and contracts that contravene the more amorphous requirements of public policy. See Restatement (Second) of Contracts § 178(1) ("A promise or other term of an agreement is unenforceable on grounds of public policy if legislation provides that it is unenforceable or the interest in its enforcement is clearly outweighed in the circumstances by a public policy against the enforcement of such terms."). The distinction is still useful, however, in terms of identifying the source of the public policy upon which a court may refuse to enforce a contract. A statute, regulation, constitutional provision, or other specific, legislative declaration of law that declares certain types of contracts to be void or unenforceable appears to provide the clearest possible statement regarding the content of a policy of the body public. But just as the Restatement (Second) of Contracts §§ 178(b) & 178(c) permit courts substantial leeway in balancing the interests of society and the public in determining whether to enforce an otherwise illegal contract, the dividing line between whether a contract actually violates or contributes to a violation of a statute, regulation, or other rule is likewise blurred. As you read the following case, consider the reasons for avoiding a bright-line rule that would bar enforcement of all contracts that violate a provision of the law in themselves or that contribute to such a violation.

ANHEUSER-BUSCH BREWING ASS'N V. MASON

Supreme Court of Minnesota
44 Minn. 318, 46 N.W. 558 (1890)

COLLINS, J.

This action was brought to recover a balance claimed to be due plaintiff (a corporation) for and on account of bottled beer sold to the defendant. The answer alleged that at the time of the sale defendant, as plaintiff well knew, was the keeper of a house of prostitution; that plaintiff sold the beer expressly for use and dispensation in and for carrying on and maintaining said house; and that when sold and delivered it was agreed between plaintiff and defendant that the beer was to be paid for out of the profits accruing to the latter from her unlawful occupation. On the trial, defendant made no attempt to establish the defense as pleaded, but relied wholly upon admissions made by plaintiff's agent, when testifying, that he did not know just what was done with the beer, but that, when selling it to defendant, he supposed she would sell or use it in her brothel. On this admission, as we understand the record, the case was dismissed by the trial court.

While it would seem quite unnecessary so to do, it may be well to call attention at the outset to the fact that this case should not be confounded with one wherein the vendor in selling his goods has violated a statute requiring him to first procure a license, as was that of Solomon v. Dreschler, 4 Minn. 278 (Gil. 197). Nor is it one in which the vendor has sold a proper article of merchandise in a legitimate way, but with the knowledge that it is to be disposed of by the vendee in direct violation of the law; for illustration, a sale of spirituous liquors by a qualified wholesale dealer, with full knowledge that the purchaser intended to retail the same in defiance of a prohibitory law, or without first obtaining the required license to sell, or a sale of poison by a druggist, knowing that it was intended for use in committing murder. The illegality of the transaction now under discussion occurs, if at all, in a matter collateral to the sale, incidentally implicated with it, and out of considerations of public policy solely. It has been well said that the consideration essential to a valid contract must not only be valuable, but it must be lawful, not repugnant to law or sound policy or good morals. Ex turpi contractu actio non oritur.[1] The reports, both English and American, are replete with cases in which contracts of all descriptions have been held invalid on account of an illegality of consideration, illustrations of the acknowledged rule that contracts are unlawful and non-enforceable when founded on a consideration contra bonos mores, or against the principles of sound policy, or founded in fraud, or in contravention of positive provisions of a statute. The utmost difficulty

[1] Authors' Note: "From an immoral or iniquitous contract an action does not arise." Black's Law Dictionary (6th ed. 1990).

has been experienced by the courts in applying the general rule, however, and an examination of the authorities wherein an application has been necessary will convince the reader that the conclusions reached and announced in the English tribunals are beyond reasonable reconciliation. This want of harmony, and that more uniform and consistent results have obtained in this country, is thoroughly demonstrated in two cases with us, (Tracy v. Talmage—first opinion by Judge SELDEN, and the second, on motion for rehearing, by Judge COMSTOCK—14 N. Y. 162, and Hill v. Spear, 50 N. H. 253) in each of which the principal cases in both countries are ably and carefully reviewed, and the law applicable to the question involved in this action stated in accordance with the great weight of authority in the United States as well as in England. These cases, now regarded as leading on this side of the Atlantic, announce the rule to be that mere knowledge by a vendor of the unlawful intent of a vendee will not bar a recovery upon a contract of sale, yet, if, in any way, the former aids the latter in his unlawful design to violate a law, such participation will prevent him from maintaining an action to recover. The participation must be active to some extent. The vendor must do something in furtherance of the purchaser's design to transgress, but positive acts in aid of the unlawful purpose are sufficient, though slight. While it is certain that a contract is void when it is illegal or immoral, it is equally as certain that it is not void simply because there is something immoral or illegal in its surroundings or connections. It cannot be declared void merely because it tends to promote illegal or immoral purposes. The American text-writers generally admit this to be the prevailing rule of law in the states upon this point. 1 Whart. Cont. § 343; Hil. Sales, 490, 492; 1 Pars. Cont. 456; Story, Cont. (5th Ed.) § 671; Story, Confl. Law, § 253; Greenh. Pub. Pol. 589. However, it has been suggested that this statement is subject to the modification that the unlawful use, of which the vendor is advised, must not be a felony or crime involving great moral turpitude. See Hanauer v. Doane, 12 Wall. 342; Tatum v. Kelley, 25 Ark. 209. . . .

Without expressly indorsing the result in some of the cases, or all that has been said by the courts in their opinions when making an application to the facts then in hand, of the rule so exhaustively examined and approved in Tracy v. Talmage, and Hill v. Spear, supra, we cite, in support of the propositions therein contended for, and upon which we rest a reversal of the order of dismissal made by the court below. . . .

The agent who made the sales, upon whose testimony the defendant saw fit to rest her case, knew that she was engaged in the unlawful business of keeping a house of ill fame, and admits also that he supposed the beer would be used or sold in her place of business. Nothing further was shown which connected the plaintiff or its agent with any violation of the law. The burden was upon the defendant to show that an enforcement of the contract would be in violation of the settled policy of the state, or injurious to the morals of its people, and no court should declare a contract illegal on doubtful or uncertain grounds. And it may be difficult to distinguish between the cases in which the vendor, with knowledge of the vendee's unlawful purpose, does not become a confederate, and those wherein he aids and assists to an extent sufficient to vitiate the sale; but this difficulty is not apparent in the case at bar. Order reversed.

NOTES AND QUESTIONS

1. *Source of the illegality.* On what basis did Mason argue that the contract with Anheuser-Busch was illegal? What statute or public policy did the agreement allegedly violate or contravene? How would the court's analysis have differed, if at all, if the events of this case had occurred twenty years later, after passage of the Eighteenth Amendment to the United States Constitution?

2. *A confederation of thieves.* Note that Mason appears to be attempting to avoid enforcement of a contract by claiming she has engaged in illegal activity, of which Anheuser-Busch knew and in which the company allegedly participated. The case appears to turn on the issue of whether Anheuser-Busch's agent, who admitted knowing that the beer would be sold in Mason's house of prostitution, was a confederate of Mason and participated in the criminal activity. Is there a meaningful distinction between (i) contracts for an illegal activity versus contracts that take place in illegal or immoral circumstances or (ii) those that are merely collateral with illegal activity? What actions by Anheuser-Busch would have been sufficient to make the company a confederate of Mason's and thereby render this contract unenforceable under the illegal contracts doctrine?

3. *Efficient deterrence and the superior risk bearer.* Professor Juliet Kostrisky has proposed that the responses of courts to the problem of illegal contracts can best be understood in terms of efficient deterrence. Professor Kostrisky notes that while courts often state the rule that illegal contracts are void and of no legal effect in apparently absolute terms, the actual treatment of such contracts is quite varied. In addition to holding illegal contracts void ab initio, courts also give one of the parties a right to avoid or affirm the contract, give only one party a right to enforce the contract, give a partially performing party a right of rescission and restitution, or give both parties a right to rescind but not to enforce. See Juliet P. Kostrisky, "Illegal Contracts and Efficient Deterrence: A Study in Modern Contract Theory," 74 Iowa L. Rev. 115, 120–21 (1988).

An absolute rule that illegal contracts are void ab initio would mean that the parties' losses would always lie where they were when one or both parties ceased performance. For example, if Mason had succeeded in having his contract with Anheuser-Busch declared void, Mason would have received a substantial shipment of alcohol for which Anheuser-Busch could not enforce Mason's return promise of future payment. Anheuser-Busch would, in that case, be left bearing all the costs associated with non-enforcement of the illegal contract.

In contrast, Professor Kostrisky argues that the graduated relief structure actually applied by courts—as opposed to an all-or-nothing void contract approach—places the risk of nonenforcement of a contract for illegality on the cheapest risk avoider. See id. at 121. Thus, a court should permit some recovery by a plaintiff seeking to enforce an otherwise illegal contract where the plaintiff was (i) in a significantly weaker bargaining position, (ii) was not a repeat player with respect to the subject matter of the contract, (iii) lacked knowledge of the illegality, (iv) did not participate significantly in the wrongdoing, or (v) other contexts in which it would be more beneficial to societal welfare to permit the plaintiff to enforce the contract, or to obtain rescission and restitution. See id. at 126–27. For example, an illegal loan contract between a bank and a consumer should be enforceable to some extent by the consumer because the bank is in a better position to know of, and prevent, the illegality. In contrast, the same contract between the bank and a sophisticated borrower should not be enforceable by either party because both are presumably equally efficient at assessing and bearing the risk of nonenforcement. See id. at 136–40. How well does the holding in *Anheuser-Busch* fit with Professor Kostrisky's efficient deterrence argument?

2. CONTRACTS IN CONTRAVENTION OF PUBLIC POLICY

Situations in which the legislature has explicitly declared a particular class of contracts to be illegal, or in which the parties attempt to avail themselves of public mechanisms for enforcement of an illegal contract, are relatively rare. The more common—and potentially more insidious—use of the public policy doctrine involves cases in which a court makes its own determination of the existence and content of a public policy that would be contravened by enforcement of an otherwise valid contract. In reading the cases below, it is important to recognize the potential dangers inherent in a legal rule that affords an unelected judiciary broad authority to intervene in private contracts to effect vague standards such as "public policy."

First, the public policy doctrine appears to contravene directly principles of freedom of contract and private autonomy. The illegality or public policy that justify courts' refusal to enforce illegal contracts comes from two sources—legislative declarations that certain conduct or transactions are prohibited (statutes) or judicial determinations of public policy. Although the doctrine is relatively easy to apply in cases where the legislature has declared certain types of promises and agreements to be illegal or unenforceable, it poses unsettling questions of vagueness, bias, and paternalism where the only source of public policy is the court's own determination. The court in *Printing and Numerical Registering Co. v. Sampson*, [1874–75] L.R. 19 Eq. 462 (Ct.Ch.1875), expressed, and partly resolved, this tension by recognizing that freedom of contract and private autonomy themselves are "public policies" worthy of protection:

It must not be forgotten that you are not to extend arbitrarily those rules which say that a given contract is void as being against public policy, because if there is one thing which more than another public policy requires it is that men of full age and competent understanding shall have the utmost liberty of contracting, and that their contracts when entered into freely and voluntarily shall be held sacred and shall be enforced by Courts of justice.

Although eloquent, the *Printing and Numerical Registering Co.* court's admonition provides little protection against courts determined to impose their own versions of public policy upon private contracts.

Second, the value of the illegal contracts or public policy doctrine lies in the quality of the statutes and public policies it seeks to promote. For example, in a 1937 article comparing legal remedies for usury and unfair economic exchanges under the French and German civil codes, John P. Dawson observed that a rule prohibiting contracts contrary to good morals ("contra bonos mores") could create disastrous results if the regime charged with enforcing public morality (and the judiciary representing that regime) itself suffered from moral failings. John P. Dawson "Economic Duress and the Fair Exchange in French and German Law," 12 Tul. L. Rev. 42, 49, 69–70 (1937–38). Specifically, Dawson reviewed judicial treatments of Article 138 § 1 of the German Civil Code of 1900, which provided that "a transaction that is contra bonos mores" is void. See id. at 49. Notably, in itself this provision virtually codifies the common law standard that agreements in contravention of public policy are void. But as interpreted and applied by the Nazi regime, "good public morals" became merely another tool for the oppressive actions of the state. See id. On a broader level, once courts are vested with the power to rewrite private contracts according to a judge's conception of public policy, how can that power meaningfully be restrained?

Third, the source of such judicially created public policies itself challenges principles essential to the rule of law. As you read the following case, consider how the courts determine the content and application of the public policies purportedly at issue and whether judges are competent to make such determinations.

HEWITT V. HEWITT

Supreme Court of Illinois
77 Ill.2d 49, 31 Ill.Dec. 827, 394 N.E.2d 1204 (1979)

UNDERWOOD, Justice:

The issue in this case is whether plaintiff Victoria Hewitt, whose complaint alleges she lived with defendant Robert Hewitt from 1960 to 1975 in an unmarried, family-like relationship to which three children have been born, may recover from him "an equal share of the profits and properties accumulated by the parties" during that period.

Plaintiff initially filed a complaint for divorce, but at a hearing on defendant's motion to dismiss, admitted that no marriage ceremony had taken place and that the parties have never obtained a marriage license. In dismissing that complaint the trial court found that neither a ceremonial nor a common law marriage existed; that since defendant admitted the paternity of the minor children, plaintiff need not bring a separate action under the Paternity Act (Ill.Rev.Stat. 1975, ch. 1063/4, par. 51 Et seq.) to have the question of child support determined; and directed plaintiff to make her complaint more definite as to the nature of the property of which she was seeking division.

Plaintiff thereafter filed an amended complaint alleging the following bases for her claim: (1) that because defendant promised he would "share his life, his future, his earnings and his property" with her and all of defendant's property resulted from the parties' joint endeavors, plaintiff is entitled in equity to a one-half share; (2) that the conduct of the parties evinced an implied contract entitling plaintiff to one-half the property accumulated during their "family relationship"; (3) that because defendant fraudulently assured plaintiff she was his wife in order to secure her services, although he knew they were not legally married, defendant's property should be impressed with a trust for plaintiff's benefit; (4) that because plaintiff has relied to her detriment on defendant's promises and devoted her entire life to him, defendant has been unjustly enriched.

The factual background alleged or testified to is that in June 1960, when she and defendant were students at Grinnell College in Iowa, plaintiff became pregnant; that defendant thereafter told her that they were husband and wife and would live as such, no formal ceremony being necessary, and that he would "share his life, his future, his earnings and his property" with her; that the parties immediately announced to their respective parents that they were married and thereafter held themselves out as husband and wife; that in reliance on defendant's promises she devoted her efforts to his professional education and his establishment in the practice of pedodontia, obtaining financial assistance from her parents for this purpose; that she assisted defendant in his career with her own special skills and although she was given payroll checks for these services she placed them in a common fund; that defendant, who was without funds at the time of the marriage, as a result of her efforts now earns over $80,000 a year and has accumulated large amounts of property, owned either jointly with her or separately; that she has given him every assistance a wife and mother could give, including social activities designed to enhance his social and professional reputation.

The amended complaint was also dismissed, the trial court finding that Illinois law and public policy require such claims to be based on a valid marriage. The appellate court reversed, stating that because the parties had outwardly lived a conventional married life, plaintiff's conduct had not "so affronted public policy that she should be denied any and all relief" (62 Ill.App.3d 861, 869, 20 Ill.Dec. 476, 482, 380 N.E.2d 454, 460), and that plaintiff's complaint stated a cause of action on an express oral contract. We granted leave to appeal. Defendant apparently does not contest his obligation to support the children, and that question is not before us.

The appellate court, in reversing, gave considerable weight to the fact that the parties had held themselves out as husband and wife for over 15 years. The court noted that they lived "a most conventional, respectable and ordinary family life" (62 Ill.App.3d 861, 863, 20 Ill.Dec. 476, 478, 380 N.E.2d 454, 457) that did not openly flout accepted standards, the "single flaw" being the lack of a valid marriage. Indeed the appellate court went so far as to say that the parties had "lived within the legitimate boundaries of a marriage and family relationship of a most conventional sort" (62 Ill.App.3d 861, 864, 20 Ill.Dec. 476, 479, 380 N.E.2d 454, 457), an assertion which that court cannot have intended to be taken literally. Noting that the Illinois Marriage and Dissolution of Marriage Act (Ill.Rev.Stat.1977, ch. 40, par. 101 Et seq.) does not prohibit nonmarital cohabitation and that the Criminal Code of 1961 (Ill.Rev.Stat.1977, ch. 38, par. 11–8(a)) makes fornication an offense only if the behavior is open and notorious, the appellate court concluded that plaintiff should not be denied relief on public policy grounds.

In finding that plaintiff's complaint stated a cause of action on an express oral contract, the appellate court adopted the reasoning of the California Supreme Court in the widely publicized case of Marvin v. Marvin (1976), 18 Cal.3d 660, 134 Cal.Rptr. 815, 557 P.2d 106, quoting extensively therefrom. In Marvin, Michelle Triola and defendant Lee Marvin lived together for 7 years pursuant to an alleged oral agreement that while "the parties lived together they would combine their efforts and earnings and would share equally any and all property accumulated as a result of their efforts whether individual or combined." . . . In her complaint she alleged that, in reliance on this agreement, she gave up her career as a singer to devote herself full time to defendant as "companion, homemaker, housekeeper and cook." . . . In resolving her claim for one-half the property accumulated in defendant's name during that period the California court held that "The courts should enforce express contracts between nonmarital partners except to the extent that the contract is explicitly founded on the consideration of meretricious sexual services" and that "In the absence of an express contract, the courts should inquire into the conduct of the parties to determine whether that conduct demonstrates an implied contract, agreement of partnership or joint venture, or some other tacit understanding between the parties. The courts may also employ the doctrine of quantum meruit, or equitable remedies such as constructive or resulting trusts, when warranted by the facts of the case." . . . The court reached its conclusions because:

> In summary, we believe that the prevalence of nonmarital relationships in modern society and the social acceptance of them, marks this as a time when our courts should by no means apply the doctrine of the unlawfulness of the so-called meretricious relationship to the instant case. . . .

> The mores of the society have indeed changed so radically in regard to cohabitation that we cannot impose a standard based on alleged moral considerations that have apparently been so widely abandoned by so many. . . .

It is apparent that the Marvin court adopted a pure contract theory, under which, if the intent of the parties and the terms of their agreement are proved, the pseudo-conventional family relationship which impressed the appellate court here is irrelevant; recovery may be had unless the implicit sexual relationship is made the explicit consideration for the agreement. In contrast, the appellate court here, as we understand its opinion, would apply contract principles only in a setting where the relationship of the parties outwardly resembled that of a traditional family. It seems apparent that the plaintiff in Marvin would not have been entitled to recover in our appellate court because of the absence of that outwardly appearing conventional family relationship.

The issue of whether property rights accrue to unmarried cohabitants can not, however, be regarded realistically as merely a problem in the law of express contracts. Plaintiff argues that because her action is founded on an express contract, her recovery would in no way imply that unmarried cohabitants acquire property rights merely by cohabitation and subsequent separation. However, the Marvin court expressly recognized and the appellate court here seems to agree that if common law principles of express contract govern express agreements between unmarried cohabitants, common law principles of implied contract, equitable relief and constructive trust must govern the parties' relations in the absence of such an agreement. (18 Cal.3d 660, 678, 134 Cal.Rptr. 815, 827, 557 P.2d 106, 118; 62 Ill.App.3d 861, 867–68, 20 Ill.Dec. 476, 380 N.E.2d 454.) In all probability the latter case will be much the more common, since it is unlikely that most couples who live together will enter into express agreements regulating their property rights. (Bruch, Property Rights of De Facto Spouses, Including Thoughts on the Value of Homemakers' Services, 10 Fam.L.Q. 101, 102 (1976).) The increasing incidence of nonmarital cohabitation referred to in Marvin and the variety of legal remedies therein sanctioned seem certain to result in substantial amounts of litigation, in which, whatever the allegations regarding an oral contract, the proof will necessarily involve details of the parties' living arrangements.

Apart, however, from the appellate court's reliance upon Marvin to reach what appears to us to be a significantly different result, we believe there is a more fundamental problem. We are aware, of course, of the increasing judicial attention given the individual claims of unmarried cohabitants to jointly accumulated property, and the fact that the majority of courts considering the question have recognized an equitable or contractual basis for implementing the reasonable expectations of the parties unless sexual services were the explicit consideration. (See cases collected in Annot., 31 A.L.R.2d 1255 (1953) and A.L.R.2d Later Case Service supplementing vols. 25 to 31.) The issue of unmarried cohabitants' mutual property rights, however, as we earlier noted, cannot appropriately be characterized solely in terms of contract law, nor is it limited to considerations of equity or fairness as between the parties to such relationships. There are major public policy questions involved in determining whether, under what circumstances, and to what extent it is desirable to accord some type of legal status to claims arising from such relationships. Of substantially greater importance than the rights of the immediate parties is the impact of such recognition upon our society and the institution of marriage. Will the fact that legal rights closely resembling those arising from conventional marriages can be acquired by those who deliberately choose to enter into what have heretofore been commonly referred to as "illicit" or "meretricious" relationships encourage formation of such relationships and weaken marriage as the foundation of our family-based society? In the event of death shall the survivor have the status of a surviving spouse for purposes of inheritance, wrongful death actions, workmen's compensation, etc.? And still more importantly: what of the children born of such relationships? What are their support and inheritance rights and by what standards are custody questions resolved? What of the sociological and psychological effects upon them of that type of environment? Does not the recognition of legally enforceable property and custody rights emanating from nonmarital cohabitation in practical effect equate with the legalization of common law marriage at least in the circumstances of this case? And, in summary, have the increasing numbers of unmarried cohabitants and changing mores of our society (Bruch, Property Rights of De Facto Spouses Including Thoughts on the Value of Homemakers' Services, 10 Fam.L.Q. 101, 102–03 (1976); Nielson, In re Cary: A Judicial Recognition of Illicit Cohabitation, 25 Hastings L.J. 1226 (1974)) reached the point at which the general welfare of the citizens of this State is best served by a return to something resembling the judicially created common law marriage our legislature outlawed in 1905?

Illinois' public policy regarding agreements such as the one alleged here was implemented long ago in Wallace v. Rappleye (1882), 103 Ill. 229,

249, where this court said: "An agreement in consideration of future illicit cohabitation between the plaintiffs is void." This is the traditional rule, in force until recent years in all jurisdictions. (See, e.g., Gauthier v. Laing (1950), 96 N.H. 80, 70 A.2d 207; Grant v. Butt (1941), 198 S.C. 298, 17 S.E.2d 689.) Section 589 of the Restatement of Contracts (1932) states, "A bargain in whole or in part for or in consideration of illicit sexual intercourse or of a promise thereof is illegal." See also 6A Corbin, Contracts sec. 1476 (1962), and cases cited therein.

It is true, of course, that cohabitation by the parties may not prevent them from forming valid contracts about independent matters, for which it is said the sexual relations do not form part of the consideration. (Restatement of Contracts secs. 589, 597 (1932); 6A Corbin, Contracts sec. 1476 (1962).) Those courts which allow recovery generally have relied on this principle to reduce the scope of the rule of illegality. Thus, California courts long prior to Marvin held that an express agreement to pool earnings is supported by independent consideration and is not invalidated by cohabitation of the parties, the agreements being regarded as simultaneous but separate. (See, e.g., Trutalli v. Meraviglia (1932), 215 Cal. 698, 12 P.2d 430; see also Annot., 31 A.L.R.2d 1255 (1953), and cases cited therein.) More recently, several courts have reasoned that the rendition of housekeeping and homemaking services such as plaintiff alleges here could be regarded as the consideration for a separate contract between the parties, severable from the illegal contract founded on sexual relations. (Kozlowski v. Kozlowski (1979), 80 N.J. 378, 403 A.2d 902; Marvin v. Marvin (1976), 18 Cal.3d 660, 670 n.5, 134 Cal.Rptr. 815, 822 n.5, 557 P.2d 106, 113 n.5. . . . In Latham v. Latham (1976), 274 Or. 421, 547 P.2d 144, and Carlson v. Olson (Minn.1977), 256 N.W.2d 249, on allegations similar to those in this case, the Minnesota Supreme Court adopted Marvin and the Oregon court expressly held that agreements in consideration of cohabitation were not void, stating:

> "We are not validating an agreement in which the only or primary consideration is sexual intercourse. The agreement here contemplated all the burdens and amenities of married life." 274 Or. 421, 427, 547 P.2d 144, 147.

The real thrust of plaintiff's argument here is that we should abandon the rule of illegality because of certain changes in societal norms and attitudes. It is urged that social mores have changed radically in recent years, rendering this principle of law archaic. It is said that because there are so many unmarried cohabitants today the courts must confer a legal status on such relationships. This, of course, is the rationale underlying some of the decisions and commentaries. (See, e.g., Marvin v. Marvin (1976), 18 Cal.3d 660, 683, 134 Cal.Rptr. 815, 831, 557 P.2d 106, 122; Beal v. Beal (1978), 282 Or. 115, 577 P.2d 507; Kay & Amyx, Marvin v. Marvin: Preserving the Options, 65 Cal.L.Rev. 937 (1977).) If this is to be the result, however, it would seem more candid to acknowledge the return of varying forms of common law marriage than to continue displaying the naiveté we believe involved in the assertion that there are involved in these relationships contracts separate and independent from the sexual activity, and the assumption that those contracts would have been entered into or would continue without that activity.

Even if we were to assume some modification of the rule of illegality is appropriate, we return to the fundamental question earlier alluded to: If resolution of this issue rests ultimately on grounds of public policy, by what body should that policy be determined? Marvin, viewing the issue as governed solely by contract law, found judicial policy-making appropriate. Its decision was facilitated by California precedent and that State's no-fault divorce law. In our view, however, the situation alleged here was not the kind of arm's length bargain envisioned by traditional contract principles, but an intimate arrangement of a fundamentally different kind. The issue, realistically, is whether it is appropriate for this court to grant a legal status to a private arrangement substituting for the institution of marriage sanctioned by the State. The question whether change is needed in the law governing the rights of parties in this delicate area of marriage-like relationships involves evaluations of sociological data and alternatives we believe best suited to the superior investigative and fact-finding facilities of the legislative branch in the exercise of its traditional authority to declare public policy in the domestic relations field. (Strukoff v. Strukoff (1979), 76 Ill.2d 53, 27 Ill.Dec. 762, 389 N.E.2d 1170; Siegall v. Solomon (1960), 19 Ill.2d 145, 166 N.E.2d 5.) That belief is reinforced by the fact that judicial recognition of mutual property rights between unmarried cohabitants would, in our opinion, clearly violate the policy of our recently enacted Illinois Marriage and Dissolution of Marriage Act. Although the Act does not specifically address the subject of nonmarital cohabitation, we think the legislative policy quite evident from the statutory scheme.

The Act provides:

This Act shall be liberally construed and applied to promote its underlying purposes, which are to:

(1) provide adequate procedures for the solemnization and registration of marriage;

(2) strengthen and preserve the integrity of marriage and safeguard family relationships. (Ill.Rev.Stat.1977, ch. 40, par. 102.)

We cannot confidently say that judicial recognition of property rights between unmarried cohabitants will not make that alternative to marriage more attractive by allowing the parties to engage in such relationships with greater security. As one commentator has noted, it may make this alternative especially attractive to persons who seek a property arrangement that the law does not permit to marital partners. (Comment, 90 Harv.L.Rev. 1708, 1713 (1977).) This court, for example, has held void agreements releasing husbands from their obligation to support their wives. (Vock v. Vock (1937), 365 Ill. 432, 6 N.E.2d 843; . . . .) In thus potentially enhancing the attractiveness of a private arrangement over marriage, we believe that the appellate court decision in this case contravenes the Act's policy of strengthening and preserving the integrity of marriage.

The Act also provides: "Common law marriages contracted in this State after June 30, 1905 are invalid." (Ill.Rev.Stat.1977, ch. 40, par. 214.) The doctrine of common law marriage was a judicially sanctioned alternative to formal marriage designed to apply to cases like the one before us. In Port v. Port (1873), 70 Ill. 484, this court reasoned that because the statute governing marriage did not "prohibit or declare void a marriage not solemnized in accordance with its provisions, a marriage without observing the statutory regulations, if made according to the common law, will still be a valid marriage." (70 Ill. 484, 486.) This court held that if the parties declared their present intent to take each other as husband and wife and thereafter did so a valid common law marriage existed. (Cartwright v. McGown (1887), 121 Ill. 388, 398, 12 N.E. 737.) Such marriages were legislatively abolished in 1905, presumably because of the problems earlier noted, and the above-quoted language expressly reaffirms that policy.

While the appellate court denied that its decision here served to rehabilitate the doctrine of common law marriage, we are not persuaded. Plaintiff's allegations disclose a relationship that clearly would have constituted a valid common law marriage in this State prior to 1905. The parties expressly manifested their present intent to be husband and wife; immediately thereafter they assumed the marital status; and for many years they consistently held themselves out to their relatives and the public at large as husband and wife. Revealingly, the appellate court relied on the fact that the parties were, to the public, husband and wife in determining that the parties living arrangement did not flout Illinois public policy. It is of course true, as plaintiff argues, that unlike a common law spouse she would not have full marital rights in that she could not, for example, claim her statutory one-third share of defendant's property on his death. The distinction appears unimpressive, however, if she can claim one-half of his property on a theory of express or implied contract.

Further, in enacting the Illinois Marriage and Dissolution of Marriage Act, our legislature considered and rejected the "no-fault" divorce concept that has been adopted in many other jurisdictions, including California. (See Uniform Marriage and Divorce Act secs. 302, 305.) Illinois appears to be one of three States retaining fault grounds for dissolution of marriage. (Ill.Rev.Stat.1977, ch. 40, par. 401; Comment, Hewitt v. Hewitt, Contract Cohabitation and Equitable Expectations Relief for Meretricious Spouses,

12 J. Mar. J. Prac. & Proc. 435, 452–53 (1979).) Certainly a significantly stronger promarriage policy is manifest in that action, which appears to us to reaffirm the traditional doctrine that marriage is a civil contract between three parties the husband, the wife and the State. (Johnson v. Johnson (1942), 381 Ill. 362, 45 N.E.2d 625; VanKoten v. VanKoten (1926), 323 Ill. 323, 154 N.E. 146.) The policy of the Act gives the State a strong continuing interest in the institution of marriage and prevents the marriage relation from becoming in effect a private contract terminable at will. This seems to us another indication that public policy disfavors private contractual alternatives to marriage.

Lastly, in enacting the Illinois Marriage and Dissolution of Marriage Act, the legislature adopted for the first time the civil law concept of the putative spouse. The Act provides that an unmarried person may acquire the rights of a legal spouse only if he goes through a marriage ceremony and cohabits with another in the good-faith belief that he is validly married. When he learns that the marriage is not valid his status as a putative spouse terminates; common law marriages are expressly excluded. (Ill.Rev.Stat.1977, ch. 40, par. 305.) The legislature thus extended legal recognition to a class of nonmarital relationships, but only to the extent of a party's good-faith belief in the existence of a valid marriage. Moreover, during the legislature's deliberations on the Act Marvin was decided and received wide publicity. (See Note, 12 J. Mar. J. Prac. & Proc. 435, 450 (1979).) These circumstances in our opinion constitute a recent and unmistakable legislative judgment disfavoring the grant of mutual property rights to knowingly unmarried cohabitants. We have found no case in which recovery has been allowed in the face of a legislative declaration as recently and clearly enacted as ours. Even if we disagreed with the wisdom of that judgment, it is not for us to overturn or erode it. Davis v. Commonwealth Edison Co. (1975), 61 Ill.2d 494, 496–97, 336 N.E.2d 881.

Actually, however, the legislature judgment is in accord with the history of common law marriage in this country. "Despite its judicial acceptance in many states, the doctrine of common-law marriage is generally frowned on in this country, even in some of the states that have accepted it." (52 Am.Jur.2d 902 Marriage sec. 46 (1970).) Its origins, early history and problems are detailed in In re Estate of Soeder (1966), 7 Ohio App.2d 271, 220 N.E.2d 547, where that court noted that some 30 States did not authorize common law marriage. Judicial criticism has been widespread even in States recognizing the relationship. (See, e.g., Baker v. Mitchell (1941), 143 Pa.Super. 50, 54, 17 A.2d 738, 741, "a fruitful source of perjury and fraud * * *"; Sorensen v. Sorensen (1904), 68 Neb. 483, 500, 100 N.W. 930.) "It tends to weaken the public estimate of the sanctity of the marriage relation. It puts in doubt the certainty of the rights of inheritance. It opens the door to false pretenses of marriage and the imposition on estates of suppositious heirs." 7 Ohio App.2d 271, 290, 220 N.E.2d 547, 561.

In our judgment the fault in the appellate court holding in this case is that its practical effect is the reinstatement of common law marriage, as we earlier indicated, for there is no doubt that the alleged facts would, if proved, establish such a marriage under our pre-1905 law. (Cartwright v. McGown (1887), 121 Ill. 388, 12 N.E. 737.) The concern of both the Marvin court and the appellate court on this score is manifest from the circumstance that both courts found it necessary to emphasize marital values "the structure of society itself largely depends upon the institution of marriage," Marvin v. Marvin (1976), 18 Cal.3d 660, 684, 134 Cal.Rptr. 815, 831, 557 P.2d 106, 122) and to deny any intent to "derogate from" (18 Cal.3d 660, 684, 134 Cal.Rptr. 815, 831, 557 P.2d 106, 122) or "denigrate" (Hewitt v. Hewitt (1978), 62 Ill.App.3d 861, 868, 20 Ill.Dec. 476, 380 N.E.2d 454) that institution. Commentators have expressed greater concern: "(T)he effect of these cases is to reinstitute common-law marriage in California after it has been abolished by the legislature." (Clark, The New Marriage, Williamette L.J. 441, 449 (1976). "(Hewitt) is, if not a direct resurrection of common-law marriage contract principles, at least a large step in that direction." Reiland, Hewitt v. Hewitt: Middle America, Marvin and Common-Law Marriage, 60 Chi.B.Rec. 84, 88–90 (1978).

We do not intend to suggest that plaintiff's claims are totally devoid of merit. Rather, we believe that our statement in Mogged v. Mogged (1973), 55 Ill.2d 221, 225, 302 N.E.2d 293, 295, made in deciding whether to abolish a judicially created defense to divorce, is appropriate here:

> Whether or not the defense of recrimination should be abolished or modified in Illinois is a question involving complex public-policy considerations as to which compelling arguments may be made on both sides. For the reasons stated hereafter, we believe that these questions are appropriately within the province of the legislature, and that, if there is to be a change in the law of this State on this matter, it is for the legislature and not the courts to bring about that change.

We accordingly hold that plaintiff's claims are unenforceable for the reason that they contravene the public policy, implicit in the statutory scheme of the Illinois Marriage and Dissolution of Marriage Act, disfavoring the grant of mutually enforceable property rights to knowingly unmarried cohabitants. The judgment of the appellate court is reversed and the judgment of the circuit court of Champaign County is affirmed.

NOTES AND QUESTIONS

1.   *Sources of public policy.* Note the different sources of public policy analyzed by the *Hewitt* court to determine whether to enforce the contracts at

issue. How did the court use statutes relating to family law, marriage (both statutory and common law), and probate law to develop a statement of public policy on an issue not explicitly addressed by the statutory law? How does this treatment compare to the analysis by the *Anheuser-Busch* court? What other sources did the court address in determining the content of their respective jurisdictions' public policy on the enforcement of contracts between cohabiting parties?

2.   *Hierarchy of sources of public policy.* Of all the sources of public policy examined by the *Hewitt* court, are any more determinative of public policy than others? Clearly, a legislative declaration that a particular class of contracts is contrary to public policy and unenforceable should be presumptively not rebuttable. But in *Hewitt*, for example, the court bases its determination that public policy barred enforcement of the contract for support partly on separate determinations that enforcement would be inconsistent with legislative pronouncements in other areas of the law and that the legislature had explicitly stated the elements necessary for recovery by putative spouses. Is this latter source of public policy as determinative as an unambiguous legislative statement of policy? What about a court's reliance upon extrinsic reports of changing social mores and practices, or the impact of a new judicial determination of public policy on existing social and legal institutions?

3.   *Contract in the family sphere.* Many of the cases in this casebook address contracting problems arising out of complex intrafamilial relationships. See, e.g., *Dougherty v. Salt* (gift of promissory note by Aunt Tillie to nephew Charlie unsupported by consideration even though promissory note recited that consideration had been given); *Hamer v. Sidway* (promise by uncle to nephew of $5,000 if nephew refrained from drinking, smoking, and certain forms of gambling until age of 21 supported by consideration); *Kirksey v. Kirksey* (promise by landowner to provide living arrangements for poor relative held to be unenforceable promise of a gift); and *Wright v. Newman* (implied promise by defendant to support unrelated child held enforceable on grounds of promissory estoppel). Do these cases, as well as *Hewitt*, indicate that contract is particularly unsuited as a mechanism for resolving disputes between individuals engaged in family, conjugal, or similar relationships? What potential alternatives are there for managing the promissory relationships between family members?

4.   *Judicial competence and public policy.* The *Hewitt* court opined that the judiciary may be unsuited to make some determinations of public policy:

> In our view, however, the situation alleged here was not the kind of arm's length bargain envisioned by traditional contract principles, but an intimate arrangement of a fundamentally different kind. The issue, realistically, is whether it is appropriate for this court to grant a legal status to a private arrangement substituting for the institution of marriage sanctioned by the State. The question whether change is needed in the law governing the rights of parties in this delicate area of marriage-like relationships involves

evaluations of sociological data and alternatives we believe best suited to the superior investigative and fact-finding facilities of the legislative branch in the exercise of its traditional authority to declare public policy in the domestic relations field.

Given that judicial declarations of public policy often occur in the context of an adversarial proceeding between two parties, or in some cases between one party and a representative of a class of individuals comprising the opposing party, are there any situations in which the *Hewitt* court would deem a court competent to make or change public policy in the absence of express legislation?

5. *Bargaining power, marriage, and the enforceability of contracts for marital services.* Note that *Hewitt* involved substantial power imbalances between the parties. Does this case illustrate potential bargaining power disparities that might exist between the parties in "negotiating" or "performing" a contract for marital services? Does gender play a role in the way either court addresses the potential for inequality of bargaining power between the parties? What about bargaining power disparities based upon informational advantages? In *Hewitt*, it appears that the male defendant was responsible for convincing the female plaintiff that a formal marriage was unnecessary, suggesting that he may have known (or at least should bear the responsibility for the parties' mistake) that the law required otherwise to make his purported promise enforceable. How should courts address this apparent gross disparity of bargaining power, if at all?

6. *Remedies outside of contract law.* As discussed in Chapters 2 and 3, the doctrines of promissory estoppel and quantum meruit provide for the enforcement of promises "outside" of contract law. Specifically, in *Hewitt*, the promisee provided substantial benefits to the promisor during the course of their relationship. If the public policy doctrine prevents enforcement of the defendant's promises under contract law, why should the parties be denied recovery under non-contract principles and doctrines? Indeed, some courts have occasionally permitted quantum meruit recovery in such situations. See John W. Wade, "Benefits Obtained Under Illegal Transactions—Reasons For and Against Allowing Restitution," 25 Tex. L. Rev. 31, 31–33 (1946) (surveying judicial treatments of claims for restitution under contracts deemed void as contrary to public policy). What arguments can you make in favor of permitting the promisee to recover in restitution? Why might restitution not provide a particularly favorable recovery for the promisee?

3. COVENANTS NOT TO COMPETE IN EMPLOYMENT CONTRACTS

"Covenant not to compete" clauses are widely used in business in contracts of employment and in contracts for the sale and purchase of a business. Under such a covenant relating to an employment contract, an employee may covenant that, should the employee terminate the employment or be terminated, the employee will not go to work for a competitor of the employer engaged in the same or similar business, within a proscribed geographic area, for a limited period of time following the termination. Such covenants are carefully scrutinized by the courts and are subject to a host of special restrictions tailored to the particular problems raised by noncompetition clauses. In general, courts will invalidate or rewrite ("blue pencil") such clauses unless they are reasonably required to protect a significant interest, are reasonably narrow in geographic scope, and are for a reasonably short period of time. Covenants in the context of a sale of a business, where the seller covenants not to compete with the purchaser of the business, are given broader latitude than those in the context of employment.

Despite this careful scrutiny of noncompetition agreements by the courts on behalf of the employee, covenants not to compete continue to threaten the ability of employees to change employers. As Professor Rachel Arnow-Richman has observed, there is anecdotal evidence that employers are increasingly requiring their employees to agree to restrictive—perhaps overly restrictive—noncompetition clauses as a means of prophylactically protecting the employer's trade secrets. See Rachel Arnow-Richman, "Cubewrap Contracts and Worker Mobility: The Dilution of Employee Bargaining Power via Standard Form Noncompetes," 2006 Mich. St. L. Rev. 963. Even more troubling, Arnow-Richman further notes that at least some employers appear to be purposefully delaying presenting noncompete agreements until the employee's bargaining power is at its weakest, such as by including the agreement in the human resources packet that new employees typically find waiting for them on their first day of work at a new job. Such "cubewrap" contracts, although often unenforceable, are rarely litigated due to their widespread use in some industries and their *in terrorem* effects within the employees' corporate culture.

As you read the following case, consider the differences between the parties and the negotiated noncompetition clause at issue in *ABC, Inc. v. Wolf* and those of the parties and boilerplate clauses at issue in more typical employment cases. For example, would this case have turned out differently (or even been brought) if the employee were a famous football player, a mid-level manager, a veterinarian, or a hairdresser? What public policy implications are raised by the fact that many employees do not understand the noncompetition clauses, cannot afford to litigate the clauses, or are afraid of harming their reputations with their employers or in their industries if they do try to have covenants not to compete in their employment contracts declared invalid?

AMERICAN BROADCASTING COMPANIES, INC. v. WOLF

Court of Appeals of New York
52 N.Y.2d 394, 438 N.Y.S.2d 482, 420 N.E.2d 363 (1981)

OPINION OF THE COURT

COOKE, Chief Judge.

This case provides an interesting insight into the fierce competition in the television industry for popular performers and favorable ratings. It requires legal resolution of a rather novel employment imbroglio.

The issue is whether plaintiff American Broadcasting Companies, Incorporated (ABC), is entitled to equitable relief against defendant Warner Wolf, a New York City sportscaster, because of Wolf's breach of a good faith negotiation provision of a now expired broadcasting contract with ABC. In the present circumstances, it is concluded that the equitable relief sought by plaintiff—which would have the effect of forcing Wolf off the air—may not be granted.

I.

Warner Wolf, a sportscaster who has developed a rather colorful and unique on-the-air personality, had been employed by ABC since 1976. In February, 1978, ABC and Wolf entered into an employment agreement which, following exercise of renewal option, was to terminate on March 5, 1980. The contract contained a clause, known as a good-faith negotiation and first-refusal provision, that is at the crux of this litigation: "You agree, if we so elect, during the last ninety (90) days prior to the expiration of the extended term of this agreement, to enter into good faith negotiations with us for the extension of this agreement on mutually agreeable terms. You further agree that for the first forty-five (45) days of this renegotiation period, you will not negotiate for your services with any other person or company other than WABC-TV or ABC. In the event we are unable to reach an agreement for an extension by the expiration of the extended term hereof, you agree that you will not accept, in any market for a period of three (3) months following expiration of the extended term of this agreement, any offer of employment as a sportscaster, sports news reporter, commentator, program host, or analyst in broadcasting (including television, cable television, pay television and radio) without first giving us, in writing, an opportunity to employ you on substantially similar terms and you agree to enter into an agreement with us on such terms." Under this provision, Wolf was bound to negotiate in good faith with ABC for the 90-day period from December 6, 1979 through March 4, 1980. For the first 45 days, December 6 through January 19, the negotiation with ABC was to be exclusive. Following expiration of the 90-day negotiating period and the contract on March 5, 1980, Wolf was required, before *accepting* any other offer, to afford ABC a right of first refusal; he could comply with this provision either by refraining from accepting another offer or by first tendering the offer to ABC. The first-refusal period expired on June 3, 1980 and on June 4 Wolf was free to accept any job opportunity, without obligation to ABC.

Wolf first met with ABC executives in September, 1979 to discuss the terms of a renewal contract. Counterproposals were exchanged, and the parties agreed to finalize the matter by October 15. Meanwhile, unbeknownst to ABC, Wolf met with representatives of CBS in early October. Wolf related his employment requirements and also discussed the first refusal-good faith negotiation clause of his ABC contract. Wolf furnished CBS a copy of that portion of the ABC agreement. On October 12, ABC officials and Wolf met, but were unable to reach agreement on a renewal contract. A few days later, on October 16 Wolf again discussed employment possibilities with CBS.

Not until January 2, 1980 did ABC again contact Wolf. At that time, ABC expressed its willingness to meet substantially all of his demands. Wolf rejected the offer, however, citing ABC's delay in communicating with him and his desire to explore his options in light of the impending expiration of the 45-day exclusive negotiation period.

On February 1, 1980, after termination of that exclusive period, Wolf and CBS orally agreed on the terms of Wolf's employment as sportscaster for WCBS-TV, a CBS-owned affiliate in New York. During the next two days, CBS informed Wolf that it had prepared two agreements and divided his annual compensation between the two: one covered his services as an on-the-air sportscaster, and the other was an off-the-air production agreement for sports specials Wolf was to produce. The production agreement contained an exclusivity clause which barred Wolf from performing "services of any nature for" or permitting the use of his "name, likeness, voice or endorsement by, any person, firm or corporation" during the term of the agreement, unless CBS consented. The contract had an effective date of March 6, 1980.

Wolf signed the CBS production agreement on February 4, 1980. At the same time, CBS agreed in writing, in consideration of $100 received from Wolf, to hold open an offer of employment to Wolf as sportscaster until June 4, 1980, the date on which Wolf became free from ABC's right of first refusal. The next day, February 5, Wolf submitted a letter of resignation to ABC.

Representatives of ABC met with Wolf on February 6 and made various offers and promises that Wolf rejected. Wolf informed ABC that they had delayed negotiations with him and downgraded his worth. He stated he had no future with the company. He told the officials he had made a "gentlemen's agreement" and would leave ABC on March 5. Later in

February, Wolf and ABC agreed that Wolf would continue to appear on the air during a portion of the first-refusal period, from March 6 until May 28.

ABC commenced this action on May 6, 1980, by which time Wolf's move to CBS had become public knowledge. The complaint alleged that Wolf, induced by CBS breached both the good-faith negotiation and first-refusal provisions of his contract with ABC. ABC sought specific enforcement of its right of first refusal and an injunction against Wolf's employment as a sportscaster with CBS.

After a trial, Supreme Court found no breach of the contract, and went on to note that, in any event, equitable relief would be inappropriate. A divided Appellate Division, while concluding that Wolf had breached both the good-faith negotiation and first-refusal provisions, nonetheless affirmed on the ground that equitable intervention was unwarranted. There should be an affirmance.

II.

Initially, we agree with the Appellate Division that defendant Wolf breached his obligation to negotiate in good faith with ABC from December, 1979 through March, 1980. When Wolf signed the production agreement with CBS on February 4, 1980, he obligated himself not to render services "of any nature" to any person, firm or corporation on and after March 6, 1980. Quite simply, then, beginning on February 4 Wolf was unable to extend his contract with ABC; his contract with CBS precluded him from legally serving ABC in any capacity after March 5. Given Wolf's existing obligation to CBS, any negotiations he engaged in with ABC, without the consent of CBS, after February 4 were meaningless and could not have been in good faith.

At the same time, there is no basis in the record for the Appellate Division's conclusion that Wolf violated the first-refusal provision by entering into an oral sportscasting contract with CBS on February 4. The first-refusal provision required Wolf, for a period of 90 days after termination of the ABC agreement, either to refrain from accepting an offer of employment or to first submit the offer to ABC for its consideration. By its own terms, the right of first refusal did not apply to offers accepted by Wolf prior to the March 5 termination of the ABC employment contract. It is apparent, therefore, that Wolf could not have breached the right of first refusal by accepting an offer during the term of his employment with ABC. Rather, his conduct violates only the good-faith negotiation clause of the contract. The question is whether this breach entitled ABC to injunctive relief that would bar Wolf from continued employment at CBS. To resolve this issue, it is necessary to trace the principles of specific performance applicable to personal service contracts.

III. A

Courts of equity historically have refused to order an individual to perform a contract for personal services (e.g., 4 Pomeroy, Equity Jurisprudence [5th ed.], § 1343, at pp. 943–944; 5A Corbin, Contracts, § 1204; see *Haight v. Badgeley*, 15 Barb. 499; Willard, Equity Jurisprudence, at pp. 276–279). Originally this rule evolved because of the inherent difficulties courts would encounter in supervising the performance of uniquely personal efforts[4] (e.g., 4 Pomeroy, Equity Jurisprudence, § 1343; 5A Corbin, Contracts, § 1204; see, also, *De Rivafinoli v. Corsetti*, 4 Paige Ch. 264, 270). During the Civil War era, there emerged a more compelling reason for not directing the performance of personal services: the Thirteenth Amendment's prohibition of involuntary servitude. It has been strongly suggested that judicial compulsion of services would violate the express command of that amendment[5] (*Arthur v. Oakes*, 63 F. 310, 317; Stevens, Involuntary Servitude by Injunction, 6 Corn. L. Q. 235; Calamari & Perillo, The Law of Contracts [2d ed.], § 16–5). For practical, policy and constitutional reasons, therefore, courts continue to decline to affirmatively enforce employment contracts.

Over the years, however, in certain narrowly tailored situations, the law fashioned other remedies for failure to perform an employment agreement. Thus, where an employee refuses to render services to an employer in violation of an existing contract, and the services are unique or extraordinary, an injunction may issue to prevent the employee from furnishing those services to another person for the duration of the contract (see, e.g., *Shubert Theatrical Co. v. Gallagher*, 206 App.Div. 514, 201 N.Y.S. 577). Such "negative enforcement" was initially available only when the employee had expressly stipulated not to compete with the employer for the term of the engagement (see, e.g., *Lumley v. Wagner*, 1 De G.M. & G. 604, 42 Eng.Rep. 687; *Shubert Theatrical Co. v. Rath*, 271 F. 827, 830–833; 4 Pomeroy, Equity Jurisprudence [5th ed.], § 1343, at p. 944). Later cases permitted injunctive relief where the circumstances justified implication of a negative covenant (see, e.g., *Montague v. Flockton*, L.R. 16 Eq. 189 [1873],

---

[4] The New York Court of Chancery in De Rivafinoli v. Corsetti (4 Paige Chs. 264, 270) eloquently articulated the traditional rationale for refusing affirmative enforcement of personal service contracts: "I am not aware that any officer of this court has that perfect knowledge of the Italian language, or possesses that exquisite sensibility in the auricular nerve which is necessary to understand, and to enjoy with a proper zest, the peculiar beauties of the Italian opera, so fascinating to the fashionable world. There might be some difficulty, therefore, even if the defendant was compelled to sing under the direction and in the presence of a master in chancery, in ascertaining whether he performed his engagement according to its spirit and intent. It would also be very difficult for the master to determine what effect coercion might produce upon the defendant's singing, especially in the livelier airs; although the fear of imprisonment would unquestionably deepen his seriousness in the graver parts of the drama. But one thing at least is certain; his songs will be neither comic, or even semi-serious, while he remains confined in that dismal cage, the debtor's prison of New York."

[5] It is well established that legislative enactments may not coerce performance of services by penalizing nonperformance (e.g., People v. Lavender, 48 N.Y.2d 334, 338–339, 422 N.Y.S.2d 924, 398 N.E.2d 530).

4 Pomeroy, Equity Jurisprudence [5th ed.], § 1343; 5A Corbin, Contracts, § 1205). In these situations, an injunction is warranted because the employee either expressly or by clear implication agreed not to work elsewhere for the period of his contract. And, since the services must be unique before negative enforcement will be granted, irreparable harm will befall the employer should the employee be permitted to labor for a competitor (see 5A Corbin, Contracts, § 1206, at p. 412).

III. B

After a personal service contract terminates, the availability of equitable relief against the former employee diminishes appreciably. Since the period of service has expired, it is impossible to decree affirmative or negative specific performance. Only if the employee has expressly agreed not to compete with the employer following the term of the contract, or is threatening to disclose trade secrets or commit another tortious act, is injunctive relief generally available at the behest of the employer (see, e.g., *Reed, Roberts Assoc. v. Strauman*, 40 N.Y.2d 303, 386 N.Y.S.2d 677, 353 N.E.2d 590; *Purchasing Assoc. v. Weitz*, 13 N.Y.2d 267, 246 N.Y.S.2d 600, 196 N.E.2d 245 . . .). Even where there is an express anticompetitive covenant, however, it will be rigorously examined and specifically enforced only if it satisfies certain established requirements (see, e.g., *Reed, Roberts Assoc. v. Strauman, supra*, 40 N.Y.2d at pp. 307–308, 386 N.Y.S.2d 677, 353 N.E.2d 590; *Purchasing Assoc. v. Weitz, supra*, at pp. 266–267; see, generally, Calamari & Perillo, The Law of Contracts [2d ed.], §§ 16–19, at pp. 601–602). Indeed, a court normally will not decree specific enforcement of an employee's anticompetitive covenant unless necessary to protect the trade secrets, customer lists or good will of the employer's business, or perhaps when the employer is exposed to special harm because of the unique nature of the employee's services[6] (see, e.g., *Reed, Roberts Assoc. v. Strauman, supra*, 40 N.Y.2d at p. 308, 386 N.Y.S.2d 677, 353 N.E.2d 590; *Purchasing Assoc. v. Weitz, supra*, 13 N.Y.2d at pp. 272–273, 246 N.Y.S.2d 600, 196 N.E.2d 245; . . . 6A Corbin, Contracts, § 1394). And, an otherwise valid covenant will not be enforced if it is unreasonable in time, space or scope or would operate in a harsh or oppressive manner (e.g., *Reed, Roberts Assoc. v. Strauman*, 40 N.Y.2d, at p. 307, 386 N.Y.S.2d 677, 353 N.E.2d 590 *supra; Clark Paper & Mfg. Co. v. Stenacher*, 236 N.Y. 312, 140 N.E. 708; 6A Corbin, Contracts, § 1394). There is, in short, general judicial disfavor of anticompetitive covenants contained in employment contracts (e.g., *Reed, Roberts Assoc. v. Strauman, supra*, 40 N.Y.2d at p. 307, 386 N.Y.S.2d 677, 353 N.E.2d 590).

---

[6]   Although an employee's anticompetitive covenant may be enforceable where the employee's services were special or unique (Reed, Roberts Assoc. v. Strauman, 40 N.Y.2d 303, 308, 386 N.Y.S.2d 677, 353 N.E.2d 590, supra; Purchasing Assoc. v. Weitz, 13 N.Y.2d 267, 272–273, 246 N.Y.S.2d 600, 196 N.E.2d 245, supra), no New York case has been found where enforcement has been granted, following termination of the employment contract, solely on the basis of the uniqueness of the services.

Underlying the strict approach to enforcement of these covenants is the notion that, once the term of an employment agreement has expired, the general public policy favoring robust and uninhibited competition should not give way merely because a particular employer wishes to insulate himself from competition (e.g., *Clark Paper & Mfg. Co. v. Stenacher*, 236 N.Y. 312, 319–320, 140 N.E. 708, supra; 6A Corbin, Contracts, § 1394, at p. 100). Important, too, are the "powerful considerations of public policy which militate against sanctioning the loss of a man's livelihood" (*Purchasing Assoc. v. Weitz*, 13 N.Y.2d at p. 272, 246 N.Y.S.2d 600, 196 N.E.2d 245, *supra*). At the same time, the employer is entitled to protection from unfair or illegal conduct that causes economic injury. The rules governing enforcement of anticompetitive covenants and the availability of equitable relief after termination of employment are designed to foster these interests of the employer without impairing the employee's ability to earn a living or the general competitive mold of society.

III. C

Specific enforcement of personal service contracts thus turns initially upon whether the term of employment has expired. If the employee refuses to perform during the period of employment, was furnishing unique services, has expressly or by clear implication agreed not to compete for the duration of the contract and the employer is exposed to irreparable injury, it may be appropriate to restrain the employee from competing until the agreement expires. Once the employment contract has terminated, by contrast, equitable relief is potentially available only to prevent injury from unfair competition or similar tortious behavior or to enforce an express and valid anticompetitive covenant. In the absence of such circumstances, the general policy of unfettered competition should prevail.

IV.

Applying these principles, it is apparent that ABC's request for injunctive relief must fail. There is no existing employment agreement between the parties; the original contract terminated in March, 1980. Thus, the negative enforcement that might be appropriate during the term of employment is unwarranted here. Nor is there an express anticompetitive covenant that defendant Wolf is violating, or any claim of special injury from tortious conduct such as exploitation of trade secrets. In short, ABC seeks to premise equitable relief after termination of the employment upon a simple, albeit serious, breach of a general contract negotiation clause. To grant an injunction in that situation would be to unduly interfere with an individual's livelihood and to inhibit free competition where there is no corresponding injury to the employer other than the loss of a competitive edge. Indeed, if relief were granted here, any breach of an employment contract provision relating to renewal negotiations logically would serve as the basis for an open-ended restraint upon the employee's ability to earn a living should he ultimately choose not to extend his employment. Our public policy, which favors the free exchange of goods and services through established market mechanisms, dictates otherwise.

Equally unavailing is ABC's request that the court create a noncompetitive covenant by implication. Although in a proper case an implied-in-fact covenant not to compete for the term of employment may be found to exist, anticompetitive covenants covering the postemployment period will not be implied. Indeed, even an express covenant will be scrutinized and enforced only in accordance with established principles.

This is not to say that ABC has not been damaged in some fashion or that Wolf should escape responsibility for the breach of his good-faith negotiation obligation. Rather, we merely conclude that ABC is not entitled to equitable relief. Because of the unique circumstances presented, however, this decision is without prejudice to ABC's right to pursue relief in the form of monetary damages, if it be so advised.

Accordingly, the order of the Appellate Division should be affirmed.

FUCHSBERG, Judge (dissenting).

I agree with all the members of this court, as had all the Justices at the Appellate Division, that the defendant Wolf breached his undisputed obligation to negotiate in good faith for renewal of his contract with ABC. Where we part company is in the majority's unwillingness to mold an equitable decree, even one more limited than the harsh one the plaintiff proposed, to right the wrong.

Central to the disposition of this case is the first-refusal provision. Its terms are worth recounting. They plainly provide that, in the 90-day period immediately succeeding the termination of his ABC contract, before Wolf could accept a position as sportscaster with another company, he first had to afford ABC the opportunity to engage him on like terms. True, he was not required to entertain offers, whether from ABC or anyone else, during that period. In that event he, of course, would be off the air for that 90 days, during which ABC could attempt to orient its listeners from Wolf to his successor. On the other hand, if Wolf wished to continue to broadcast actively during the 90 days, ABC's right of first refusal put it in a position to make sure that Wolf was not doing so for a competitor. One way or the other, however labeled, the total effect of the first refusal agreement was that of an express conditional covenant under which Wolf could be restricted from appearing on the air other than for ABC for the 90-day posttermination period.

One need not be in the broadcasting business to understand that the restriction ABC bargained for, and Wolf granted, when they entered into the original employment contract was not inconsequential. The earnings of broadcasting companies are directly related to the "ratings" they receive. This, in turn, is at least in part dependent on the popularity of personalities like Wolf. It therefore was to ABC's advantage, once Wolf came into its employ, especially since he was new to the New York market, that it enhance his popularity by featuring, advertising and otherwise promoting him. This meant that the loyalty of at least part of the station's listening audience would become identified with Wolf, thus enhancing his potential value to competitors, as witness the fact that, in place of the $250,000 he was receiving during his last year with ABC, he was able to command $400,000 to $450,000 per annum in his CBS "deal." A reasonable opportunity during which ABC could cope with such an assault on its good will had to be behind the clause in question.

Moreover, it is undisputed that, when in late February Wolf executed the contract for an extension of employment during the 90-day hiatus for which the parties had bargained, ABC had every right to expect that Wolf had not already committed himself to an exclusivity provision in a producer's contract with CBS in violation of the good-faith negotiation clause (see majority opn. at pp. 397–398, at p. 483 of 438 N.Y.S.2d, at p. 364 of 420 N.E.2d). Surely, had ABC been aware of this gross breach, had it not been duped into giving an uninformed consent, it would not have agreed to serve as a self-destructive vehicle for the further enhancement of Wolf's potential for taking his ABC-earned following with him.

In the face of these considerations, the majority rationalizes its position of powerlessness to grant equitable relief by choosing to interpret the contract as though there were no restrictive covenant, express or implied. However, as demonstrated, there is, in fact, an express three-month negative covenant which, because of Wolf's misconduct, ABC was effectively denied the opportunity to exercise. Enforcement of this covenant, by enjoining Wolf from broadcasting for a three-month period, would depart from no entrenched legal precedent. Rather, it would accord with equity's boasted flexibility (see 11 Williston, Contracts [3d ed.], § 1450, at pp. 1043–1044; 6A Corbin, Contracts, § 1394, at p. 100; see, generally, 20 N.Y.Jur. [rev.], Equity, §§ 79, 83, 84).

That said, a few words are in order regarding the majority's insistence that Wolf did not breach the first-refusal clause. It is remarkable that, to this end, it has to ignore its own crediting of the Appellate Division's express finding that, as far back as February 1, 1980, fully a month before the ABC contract was to terminate, "Wolf and CBS orally agreed on the terms of Wolf's employment as sportscaster for WCBS-TV" (majority opn., at p. 399, at p. 484 of 438 N.Y.S.2d, at p. 365 of 420 N.E.2d; see *American Broadcasting Cos. v. Wolf*, 76 A.D.2d 162, 166, 170–171, 430 N.Y.S.2d 275). It follows that the overt written CBS-Wolf option contract, which permitted

Wolf to formally accept the CBS sportscasting offer at the end of the first-refusal period, was nothing but a charade.

Further, on this score, the majority's premise that Wolf could not have breached the first-refusal clause when he accepted the producer's agreement, exclusivity provision and all, *during* the term of his ABC contract, does not withstand analysis. So precious a reading of the arrangement with ABC frustrates the very purpose for which it had to have been made. Such a classical exaltation of form over substance is hardly to be countenanced by equity (see *Washer v. Seager*, 272 App.Div. 297, 71 N.Y.S.2d 46, affd. 297 N.Y. 918, 79 N.E.2d 745).

For all these reasons, in my view, literal as well as proverbial justice should have brought a modification of the order of the Appellate Division to include a 90-day injunction—no more and no less than the relatively short and certainly not unreasonable transitional period for which ABC and Wolf struck their bargain.

NOTES AND QUESTIONS

1. *Purposes of noncompete clauses.* Why did ABC include the noncompete clause in Wolf's 1978 employment agreement? Do those business justifications extend to more mundane employment agreements, such as sales staff or mid-level executives? To what extent do those justifications mirror the concerns surrounding injunctive relief for employment contracts discussed in Chapter 6?

2. *Incentives to litigate noncompete clauses.* In *ABC v. Wolf*, which party had the greatest incentive and ability to challenge the validity of the noncompete clause—Wolf or CBS? Why? What benefits might a competitor achieve by hiring a famous personality from ABC? What if Wolf, instead of being an on-air sportscaster with a distinct and marketable persona, had been a highly skilled cameraman or engineer at ABC? Would CBS have had the same incentives to litigate? What if similarly skilled employees could be hired from non-competing sources?

3. *Assessing the reasonableness of the noncompete clause.* Timing can be critical for determining the reasonableness of noncompetition clauses. In *King v. Head Start*, 886 So.2d 769 (Ala.2004), the court rewrote a noncompete agreement between a hairdresser and her employer that prohibited her from working for any competing hair salon within a two-mile radius of any of her employer's locations for one year following termination. The court based its decision on factors such as the plaintiff's age, the difficulty of developing new skills, the hardships enforcement of the clause would pose to the plaintiff's family, and the fact that the employer's thirty locations effectively prevented plaintiff from any employment as a hairdresser. As Professor Rachel Arnow-Richman notes in an insightful analysis of the *King* decision, however, all of the factors relied upon by the court arose at the time of termination, or the "back end" of the contract. See Rachel Arnow-Richman, "Cubewrap Contracts

and Worker Mobility: The Dilution of Employee Bargaining Power via Standard Form Noncompetes," 2006 Mich. St. L. Rev. 963. In contrast, if the court had examined the reasonableness of the noncompete clause at the "front end" of the parties' contractual relationship, when the plaintiff was just beginning her working career, had no family, and many options, the clause might have been reasonable for both parties. To what extent, if any, did such timing issues play a role in *ABC, Inc. v. Wolf*?

C. UNCONSCIONABILITY—CONTRACTS VOID FOR UNFAIRNESS

The doctrine of unconscionability—under which courts may refuse to enforce part or all of a purported agreement that is so unfair, inequitable, one-sided, or unjust that it "shocks the conscience"—has ancient roots. The Roman law, for example, provided in the Twelve Tables—one of the constitutional bodies of law of the Roman Republic—for relief from contracts for the sale of land for less than half of its actual value under the doctrine of *laesio enormis*. Modern Civil Codes similarly provide protections against enforcement of grossly unfair bargains. James Gordley, "Equality in Exchange," 69 Cal. L. Rev. 1587, 1587, 1592–99 (1981) (noting similarity between German doctrine of *wucher*, French doctrine of *lésion*, and common law doctrine of unconscionability in regulating unjust or unfair bargains).

The origins of unconscionability doctrine in the common law are murky. Both law and equity courts had long refused enforcement to contracts considered too shocking, unfair, absurd, or fraught with indicia of fraud and duress, without developing a unitary doctrine justifying that refusal. See John A. Spanogle, Jr., "Analyzing Unconscionability Problems," 117 U. Pa. L. Rev. 931, 938 (1969). In James v. Morgan, 83 Eng. Rep. 323 (1663), for example, the court refused to enforce an agreement for the sale and purchase of a horse, the price of which was to be determined according to the number of nails in the horse's shoes. The buyer was to pay a barley corn for the first nail, two for the second, and so on, doubling the price (and presumably adding to the preceding sum) with each additional nail, up to a total of 32 nails. The final "price" of the horse under this formula would have been 4,000 bushels. See William B. Davenport, Unconscionability and the Uniform Commercial Code, 22 U. Miami L. Rev. 121, 124–25 (1967) (describing *James v. Morgan* and relating additional case of *Thornborough v. Whiteacre* in which the purported consideration for a £4 payment was two grains of rye, to be doubled each Monday for a year, resulting in a contract for a greater amount of rye than existed in the world).

The common law recognized an explicit doctrine of, and standard for, unconscionability in *Earl of Chesterfield v. Janssen*, 28 Eng. Rep. 82, 100 (Ch. 1751), in which the court famously stated, "[Unconscionability] may be apparent from the intrinsic nature and subject of the bargain itself; such as no man in his senses and not under delusion would make on the one hand, and as no honest and fair man would accept on the other; which are unequitable and unconscientious bargains: and of such even the common law has taken notice . . . ," a formulation of the doctrine still used by modern courts. See, e.g., Williams v. Walker-Thomas Furniture Co., 350 F.2d 445, 450 n.12 ("The traditional test as stated in Greer v. Tweed . . . is 'such as no man in his senses and not under delusion would make on the one hand, and as no honest or fair man would accept, on the other.'"). U.S. courts acknowledged the doctrine of unconscionability over a century later in a dictum in *Scott v. United States*, 79 U.S. (12 Wall.) 443 (1870), but the doctrine continued unsettled for another 70 years.

1. HISTORY & PURPOSE OF THE DOCTRINE OF UNCONSCIONABILITY

Unconscionability remained at the periphery of contract law until promulgation of Official Drafts of § 2–302 of the UCC and adoption of the UCC in numerous jurisdictions throughout the 1960s. Prior to the direct treatment of unconscionability in the UCC, some courts did overturn contracts as shocking to the conscience, but many others arguably manipulated facts and legal doctrines such as consideration, public policy, and other contract rules to achieve apparently just results in hard cases. Observing this judicial tendency to manipulate facts and doctrine to avoid enforcement of unfair contracts, Llewellyn famously noted that "covert tools are never reliable tools." See Karl Llewellyn, Book Review, "O. Prausnitz, The Standardization of Commercial Contracts in English and Continental Law (1937)," 52 Harv. L. Rev. 700, 702–03 (1939); see also Karl Llewellyn, The Common Law Tradition 364–65 (1960) (arguing in favor of explicit application of unconscionability standard). As the primary drafter of the UCC, Llewellyn's Realist jurisprudence and distaste for covert rules may be perceived in § 2–302's explicit permission to courts to refuse to enforce unconscionable terms and contracts. As the Official Comment to § 2–302 observes, that provision purposed to permit courts to regulate the unconscionability of a contract or term without having to engage in such judicial subterfuges:

> This section is intended to make it possible for the courts to police explicitly against the contracts or clauses which they find to be unconscionable. In the past such policing has been accomplished by adverse construction of language, by manipulation of the rules of offer and acceptance or by determinations that the clause is contrary to public policy or to the dominant purpose of the contract. This section is intended to allow the court to pass directly on the unconscionability of the contract or particular

clause therein and to make a conclusion of law as to its unconscionability.

UCC § 2–302 *cmt. 1.* Section 2–302 itself provided courts with broad discretion to determine the unconscionability of contracts within their commercial contexts:

> § 2–302. Unconscionable Contract or Clause.
>
> (1) If the court as a matter of law finds the contract or any clause of the contract to have been unconscionable at the time it was made the court may refuse to enforce the contract, or it may enforce the remainder of the contract without the unconscionable clause, or it may so limit the application of any unconscionable clause as to avoid any unconscionable result.
>
> (2) When it is claimed or appears to the court that the contract or any clause thereof may be unconscionable the parties shall be afforded a reasonable opportunity to present evidence as to its commercial setting, purpose and effect to aid the court in making the determination.

Problematically, however, the UCC is remarkably silent regarding the standards for determining whether a contract or term is, in fact, unconscionable. The comments to § 2–302 are little help in this endeavor:

> The basic test is whether, in the light of the general commercial background and the commercial needs of the particular trade or case, the clauses involved are so one-sided as to be unconscionable under the circumstances existing at the time of the making of the contract. Subsection (2) makes it clear that it is proper for the court to hear evidence upon these questions. The principle is one of the prevention of oppression and unfair surprise (cf. Campbell Soup Co. v. Wentz, 172 F.2d 80 (3d Cir. 1948)) and not of disturbance of allocation of risks because of superior bargaining power.

UCC § 2–302 *cmt. 1.* Additional cases and explanations cited in the commentary did not resolve this ambiguity. It thus fell to the courts to determine the standards under which courts could deny enforcement to contracts on the basis of unconscionability. As you read the next case, consider whether UCC § 2–302 provides any meaningful guidance to courts attempting to police against unconscionable contracts.

WILLIAMS V. WALKER-THOMAS FURNITURE CO.

United States Court of Appeals District of Columbia Circuit
350 F.2d 445 (D.C. Ct. App. 1965)

J. SKELLY WRIGHT, Circuit Judge:

Appellee, Walker-Thomas Furniture Company, operates a retail furniture store in the District of Columbia. During the period from 1957 to 1962 each appellant in these cases purchased a number of household items from Walker-Thomas, for which payment was to be made in installments. The terms of each purchase were contained in a printed form contract which set forth the value of the purchased item and purported to lease the item to appellant for a stipulated monthly rent payment. The contract then provided, in substance, that title would remain in Walker-Thomas until the total of all the monthly payments made equaled the stated value of the item, at which time appellants could take title. In the event of a default in the payment of any monthly installment, Walker-Thomas could repossess the item.

The contract further provided that 'the amount of each periodical installment payment to be made by (purchaser) to the Company under this present lease shall be inclusive of and not in addition to the amount of each installment payment to be made by (purchaser) under such prior leases, bills or accounts; and all payments now and hereafter made by (purchaser) shall be credited pro rata on all outstanding leases, bills and accounts due the Company by (purchaser) at the time each such payment is made.' The effect of this rather obscure provision was to keep a balance due on every item purchased until the balance due on all items, whenever purchased, was liquidated. As a result, the debt incurred at the time of purchase of each item was secured by the right to repossess all the items previously purchased by the same purchaser, and each new item purchased automatically became subject to a security interest arising out of the previous dealings.

On May 12, 1962, appellant Thorne purchased an item described as a Daveno, three tables, and two lamps, having total stated value of $391.10. Shortly thereafter, he defaulted on his monthly payments and appellee sought to replevy all the items purchased since the first transaction in 1958. Similarly, on April 17, 1962, appellant Williams bought a stereo set of stated value of $514.95.[1] She too defaulted shortly thereafter, and appellee sought to replevy all the items purchased since December, 1957. The Court of General Sessions granted judgment for appellee. The District of Columbia Court of Appeals affirmed, and we granted appellants' motion for leave to appeal to this court.

---

[1] At the time of this purchase her account showed a balance of $164 still owing from her prior purchases. The total of all the purchases made over the years in question came to $1,800. The total payments amounted to $1,400.

Appellants' principal contention, rejected by both the trial and the appellate courts below, is that these contracts, or at least some of them, are unconscionable and, hence, not enforceable. In its opinion in Williams v. Walker-Thomas Furniture Company, 198 A.2d 914, 916 (1964), the District of Columbia Court of Appeals explained its rejection of this contention as follows:

Appellant's second argument presents a more serious question. The record reveals that prior to the last purchase appellant had reduced the balance in her account to $164. The last purchase, a stereo set, raised the balance due to $678. Significantly, at the time of this and the preceding purchases, appellee was aware of appellant's financial position. The reverse side of the stereo contract listed the name of appellant's social worker and her $218 monthly stipend from the government. Nevertheless, with full knowledge that appellant had to feed, clothe and support both herself and seven children on this amount, appellee sold her a $514 stereo set.

'We cannot condemn too strongly appellee's conduct. It raises serious questions of sharp practice and irresponsible business dealings. A review of the legislation in the District of Columbia affecting retail sales and the pertinent decisions of the highest court in this jurisdiction disclose, however, no ground upon which this court can declare the contracts in question contrary to public policy. We note that were the Maryland Retail Installment Sales Act, Art. 83 §§ 128–153, or its equivalent, in force in the District of Columbia, we could grant appellant appropriate relief. We think Congress should consider corrective legislation to protect the public from such exploitive contracts as were utilized in the case at bar.'

We do not agree that the court lacked the power to refuse enforcement to contracts found to be unconscionable. In other jurisdictions, it has been held as a matter of common law that unconscionable contracts are not enforceable. While no decision of this court so holding has been found, the notion that an unconscionable bargain should not be given full enforcement is by no means novel. In Scott v. United States, 79 U.S. (12 Wall.) 443, 445, 20 L.Ed. 438 (1870), the Supreme Court stated:

* * * If a contract be unreasonable and unconscionable, but not void for fraud, a court of law will give to the party who sues for its breach damages, not according to its letter, but only such as he is equitably entitled to. * * *

Since we have never adopted or rejected such a rule, the question here presented is actually one of first impression.

Congress has recently enacted the Uniform Commercial Code, which specifically provides that the court may refuse to enforce a contract which it finds to be unconscionable at the time it was made. 28 D.C.CODE § 2–302 (Supp. IV 1965). The enactment of this section, which occurred subsequent to the contracts here in suit, does not mean that the common law of the District of Columbia was otherwise at the time of enactment, nor does it preclude the court from adopting a similar rule in the exercise of its powers to develop the common law for the District of Columbia. In fact, in view of the absence of prior authority on the point, we consider the congressional adoption of § 2–302 persuasive authority for following the rationale of the cases from which the section is explicitly derived. Accordingly, we hold that where the element of unconscionability is present at the time a contract is made, the contract should not be enforced.

Unconscionability has generally been recognized to include an absence of meaningful choice on the part of one of the parties together with contract terms which are unreasonably favorable to the other party. Whether a meaningful choice is present in a particular case can only be determined by consideration of all the circumstances surrounding the transaction. In many cases the meaningfulness of the choice is negated by a gross inequality of bargaining power.[7] The manner in which the contract was entered is also relevant to this consideration. Did each party to the contract, considering his obvious education or lack of it, have a reasonable opportunity to understand the terms of the contract, or were the important terms hidden in a maze of fine print and minimized by deceptive sales practices? Ordinarily, one who signs an agreement without full knowledge of its terms might be held to assume the risk that he has entered a one-sided bargain.[8] But when a party of little bargaining power, and hence little real choice, signs a commercially unreasonable contract with little or no knowledge of its terms, it is hardly likely that his consent, or even an objective manifestation of his consent, was ever given to all the terms. In such a case the usual rule that the terms of the agreement are not to be

---

[7] See Henningsen v. Bloomfield Motors, Inc., supra Note 2, 161 A.2d at 86, and authorities there cited. Inquiry into the relative bargaining power of the two parties is not an inquiry wholly divorced from the general question of unconscionability, since a one-sided bargain is itself evidence of the inequality of the bargaining parties. This fact was vaguely recognized in the common law doctrine of intrinsic fraud, that is, fraud which can be presumed from the grossly unfair nature of the terms of the contract. See the oft-quoted statement of Lord Hardwicke in Earl of Chesterfield v. Janssen, 28 Eng. Rep. 82, 100 (1751):

'* * * (Fraud) may be apparent from the intrinsic nature and subject of the bargain itself; such as no man in his senses and not under delusion would make * * *.'

And cf. Hume v. United States, supra Note 3, 132 U.S. at 413, 10 S.Ct. at 137, where the Court characterized the English cases as 'cases in which one party took advantage of the other's ignorance of arithmetic to impose upon him, and the fraud was apparent from the face of the contracts.' See also Greer v. Tweed, supra Note 3.

[8] See RESTATEMENT, CONTRACTS § 70 (1932), Note, 63 HARV. L. REV. 494 (1950). See also Daley v. People's Building, Loan & Savings Ass'n, 178 Mass. 13, 59 N.E. 452, 453 (1901), in which Mr. Justice Holmes, while sitting on the Supreme Judicial Court of Massachusetts, made this observation:

* * * Courts are less and less disposed to interfere with parties making such contracts as they choose, so long as they interfere with no one's welfare but their own. * * * It will be understood that we are speaking of parties standing in an equal position where neither has any oppressive advantage or power * * *.

questioned should be abandoned and the court should consider whether the terms of the contract are so unfair that enforcement should be withheld.

In determining reasonableness or fairness, the primary concern must be with the terms of the contract considered in light of the circumstances existing when the contract was made. The test is not simple, nor can it be mechanically applied. The terms are to be considered 'in the light of the general commercial background and the commercial needs of the particular trade or case.' Corbin suggests the test as being whether the terms are 'so extreme as to appear unconscionable according to the mores and business practices of the time and place.' 1 CORBIN, op. cit. supra Note 2.[12] We think this formulation correctly states the test to be applied in those cases where no meaningful choice was exercised upon entering the contract.

Because the trial court and the appellate court did not feel that enforcement could be refused, no findings were made on the possible unconscionability of the contracts in these cases. Since the record is not sufficient for our deciding the issue as a matter of law, the cases must be remanded to the trial court for further proceedings.

So ordered.

DANAHER, Circuit Judge (dissenting):

The District of Columbia Court of Appeals obviously was as unhappy about the situation here presented as any of us can possibly be. Its opinion in the Williams case, quoted in the majority text, concludes: 'We think Congress should consider corrective legislation to protect the public from such exploitive contracts as were utilized in the case at bar.'

My view is thus summed up by an able court which made no finding that there had actually been sharp practice. Rather the appellant seems to have known precisely where she stood.

There are many aspects of public policy here involved. What is a luxury to some may seem an outright necessity to others. Is public oversight to be required of the expenditures of relief funds? A washing machine, e.g., in the hands of a relief client might become a fruitful source of income. Many relief clients may well need credit, and certain business establishments will take long chances on the sale of items, expecting their pricing policies will afford a degree of protection commensurate with the risk. Perhaps a remedy when necessary will be found within the provisions of the 'Loan Shark' law, D.C.CODE §§ 26–601 et seq. (1961).

* * * *

---

[12] See Henningsen v. Bloomfield Motors, Inc., supra Note 2; Mandel v. Liebman, 303 N.Y. 88, 100 N.E.2d 149 (1951). The traditional test as stated in Greer v. Tweed, supra Note 3, 13 Abb.Pr.,N.S., at 429, is 'such as no man in his senses and not under delusion would make on the one hand, and as no honest or fair man would accept, on the other.'

I join the District of Columbia Court of Appeals in its disposition of the issues.

NOTES AND QUESTIONS

1. *Add-on security clauses.* At the time of the *Williams* decision, thirty-six other jurisdictions—including Maryland, which borders the District of Columbia—explicitly regulated (and therefore implicitly permitted) by statute the use of add-on security clauses of substantially the same form as employed by the Walker-Thomas Furniture Co. See Arthur Allen Leff, "Unconscionability and the Code—The Emperor's New Clause," 115 U. Pa. L. Rev. 485, 554–55 (1967). Assuming that the company was driven solely by commercial concerns (and there is no evidence to the contrary), what is the business purpose of such clauses? Why would a business that sold household goods on credit desire such an apparently stringent and onerous security provision in its credit installment sale contracts? If the lower court on remand concluded that the Walker-Thomas Furniture Co. add-on clause was in fact unconscionable, what alternatives would the company have for retaining a comparable degree of security in its credit sales contracts?

2. *Expansion of UCC § 2–302 to the general law of contract.* Was *Williams* decided under the common law or under UCC § 2–302? Technically, Judge Wright merely confirmed that the common law of the District of Columbia mirrored the unconscionability provisions of the UCC.

3. *Aftermath of Williams.* Assume that you represent Walker-Thomas Furniture Co. Following *Williams*, what advice would you give to your client regarding how the company should respond to that decision? What would have been the appropriate response by the Walker-Thomas Furniture Co. following the *Williams* decision? Note that Judge Wright does <u>not</u> hold that the add-on security clause was unconscionable, but rather remands for further findings as to whether the company's clause was unconscionable. In an insightful and well-researched student comment, Eben Colby analyzed the impact of the *Williams* case upon the business practices of the Walker-Thomas Furniture Co. See Eben Colby, Comment, "What Did the Doctrine of Unconscionability Do to the Walker-Thomas Furniture Company?," 34 Conn. L. Rev. 625 (2002). First, contrary to Judge Skelly Wright's implications that consumers like Williams could not understand the add-on security clauses at issue, Colby concluded that it is likely that Williams and consumers like her had "street" knowledge of the effects of such clauses. See id. at 652 & 625 n.1 (noting that Walker-Thomas Furniture was well known in Williams' neighborhood and filed approximately 100 writs of replevin each year, and relating report that rioters outside the company following the death of Dr. Martin Luther King, Jr. were heard to shout, "Get the books! Get the books!"). Second, later cases involving the company indicate that, following *Williams*, it made only incremental, obfuscatory changes to its form contracts that nonetheless maintained substantially the same security provisions. See id. at 653–54. Third, following the decision, the company stopped using writs of replevin to seize property

from delinquent borrowers, but continued to pursue vigorously their rights in default. See id. at 656–57. Finally, the company substantially tightened credit following the *Williams* decision and other actions under consumer protection legislation, such as the Truth in Lending Act, leaving poor residents of the city less able to obtain credit on any terms than before the decision. See id. at 658 ("[T]o the detriment of its customers, the furniture company 'certainly tightened up' the amount of credit that it made available to customers after the Williams decision, further reducing the credit available to Washington's poor.").

4.   *The "accidental" inclusion of unconscionability in UCC § 2–302.* Professor Allen R. Kamp provides a fascinating history of the UCC drafting process in "Uptown Act: A History of the Uniform Commercial Code: 1940–49," 51 SMU L. Rev. 275 (1998). Section 1–C of Llewellyn's original drafts of the Revised Uniform Sales Act of 1941—the immediate predecessor to UCC § 2–302—dealt with the problem of oppressive standard form contracts. As originally drafted, § 1–C directed courts to regulate the terms of standard form contracts in accord with principles of fairness, equity, and trade practices, and the section did not address unconscionability. See id. at 306. Hiram Thomas, spokesperson and attorney for the New York Merchants Association during the initial UCC drafting process, was "notorious for speaking without thinking" and this quality may have led to the inclusion of "unconscionability" within later drafts of § 2–302. Id. at 306.

2.   ELEMENTS OF UNCONSCIONABILITY

Judge Skelly Wright's decision in *Williams* opened the door for later courts to police the fairness of bargains directly through unconscionability. Additionally, the growing judicial willingness to entertain explicit unconscionability claims in both common law and sale of goods cases attracted the attention of scholars attempting to come to grips with the relationship between a regime of contract ostensibly based upon private autonomy and freedom of contract, and a doctrine that explicitly permits courts to engage in a post hoc review of contract terms considered unfair. See E. Allan Farnsworth, Contracts § 4.28 at 298 (4th ed. 2004) ("As scholars lavished more ink on this section than on any comparable passage in the Code, the doctrine of unconscionability rapidly gained wide acceptance."). Supporters of the UCC's direct approach to unconscionability argued that the doctrine provided a much-needed and flexible tool by which courts could regulate bargains tainted by fraud, duress, and undue influence without engaging in judicial subterfuge. Critiques of modern unconscionability doctrine focused upon, among other things, (1) the lack of any meaningful restrictions on judicial discretion; (2) the inability of unconscionability to remedy later incrementally unfair behavior by the offending party; and (3) the likelihood that, while the doctrine might help out the party in front of the court in the short term, it was likely to injure the class to which that party belongs in the long term. See Arthur Allen

Leff, "Unconscionability and the Code—The Emperor's New Clause," 115 U. Pa. L. Rev. 485, 556–57 (1967):

> [N]ot all old ladies or farmers are without defenses. Put briefly, the typical has a tendency to become stereotypical, with what may be unpleasant results even for the beneficiaries of the judicial benevolence. One can see it enshrined in the old English equity courts' jolly treatment of English seamen as members of a happy, fun-loving race (with, one supposes, a fine sense of rhythm), but certainly not to be trusted to take care of themselves. What effect, if any, this had upon the sailors is hidden behind the judicial chuckles as they protected their loyal sailor boys, but one cannot help wondering how many sailors managed to get credit at any reasonable price. In other words, the benevolent have a tendency to colonize, whether geographically or legally.

Ironically, Arthur Allen Leff's important and thoroughly enjoyable article, "Unconscionability and the Code—The Emperor's New Clause," 115 U. Pa. L. Rev. 485 (1967), not only made a scathing critique of unconscionability under UCC § 2–302, but also provided later courts with the framework most commonly used to describe and analyze unconscionability claims. For Leff, unconscionability easily divided into two separate inquiries. First, a bargain may be said to be unconscionable because of flaws in the bargaining process such as fraud, duress, hard bargaining tactics, and use of adhesive standard form contracts or burying important terms in fine print and legalese. Leff described such "'bargaining naughtiness' as 'procedural unconscionability.'" See id. at 487.

Alternatively, the terms of the contract themselves may be oppressive or unfairly surprising. Leff described these "evils in the resulting contract as 'substantive unconscionability.'" See id. Many, if not most, courts require a showing of both procedural and substantive elements to support a finding of unconscionability, often analyzing these elements on a sliding scale in which great procedural unconscionability will require only a minimal showing of substantive unconscionability, and vice versa. The court in *Stirlen v. Supercuts, Inc.*, 51 Cal. App. 4th 1519, 60 Cal. Rptr. 2d 138 (Cal. App. 1997), summarized the inquiry and balancing typical of this majority test for unconscionability:

> The procedural element focuses on two factors: 'oppression' and 'surprise.' . . . . 'Oppression' arises from an inequality of bargaining power which results in no real negotiation and 'an absence of meaningful choice.' . . . . 'Surprise' involves the extent to which the supposedly agreed-upon terms of the bargain are hidden in the prolix printed form drafted by the party seeking to enforce the disputed terms. . . ."

Substantive unconscionability is less easily explained. "Cases have talked in terms of 'overly harsh' or 'one-sided' results. . . . One commentator has pointed out, however, that ' . . . unconscionability turns not only on a "one-sided" result, but also on an absence of justification for it.' . . . , which is only to say that substantive unconscionability must be evaluated as of the time the contract was made. . . . The most detailed and specific commentaries observe that a contract is largely an allocation of risks between the parties, and therefore that a contractual term is substantively suspect if it reallocates the risks of the bargain in an objectively or unreasonable or unexpected manner. . . . But not all unreasonable risk allocations are unconscionable; rather enforceability of the clause is tied to the procedural aspects of unconscionability . . . such that the greater the unfair surprise or inequality of bargaining power, the less unreasonable the risk allocation which will be tolerated. . . ." (A & M Produce Co. v. FMC Corp., *supra* 135 Cal.App.3d at p. 487, 186 Cal.Rptr. 114.) In *California Grocers Assn. v. Bank of America, supra,* 22 Cal.App.4th 205, 27 Cal.Rptr.2d 396, this court rejected the "reasonableness" standard applied in *A & M Produce Co. v. FMC Corp., supra,* 135 Cal.App.3d at pp. 486–487, 186 Cal.Rptr. 114, as being inherently subjective. (California Grocers Assn. v. Bank of America, *supra,* 22 Cal.App.4th at p. 214, 27 Cal.Rptr.2d 396.) We instead reverted to the traditional standard of unconscionability—contract terms so one-sided as to "shock the conscience." (Id.)

One commentator sums up the matter as follows: "'[p]rocedural unconscionability' has to do with matters relating to freedom of assent. 'Substantive unconscionability' involves the imposition of harsh or oppressive terms on one who has assented freely to them." Hawkland UCC Series § 302:02 (Art. 2), p. 246. The prevailing view is that these two elements must *both* be present in order for a court to exercise its discretion to refuse to enforce a contract or clause under the doctrine of unconscionability. *Id.,* § 3–302:03 (Art. 2), p. 249, and cases cited at fn. 4, § 302:05 (Art. 2), p. 266. (internal citations omitted).

Other courts, however, permit a finding of unconscionability on the basis of substantive failings alone. See, e.g., Maxwell v. Fidelity Fin. Serv., Inc., 184 Ariz. 82, 907 P.2d 51 (1995) ("[A] claim of unconscionability can be established with a showing of substantive unconscionability alone, especially in cases involving either price-cost disparity or limitation of remedies."); Kugler v. Romain, 58 N.J. 522, 279 A.2d 640 (1971) (sale of educational books at 2.5 times market value held to be excessive price-value disparity that would support a finding of unconscionability).

A third approach appears to reject the procedural–substantive dichotomy in favor of a balancing test involving analysis of multiple variables. See, e.g., Wille v. Southwestern Bell Tel. *Co.*, 219 Kan. 755, 549 P.2d 903, 906–07 (1976); C & J Fertilizer, Inc. v. Allied Mut. Ins. Co., 227 N.W.2d 169, 181 (Iowa 1975) ("[A] court considering a claim of unconscionability should examine the factors of assent, unfair surprise, notice, disparity of bargaining power, and substantive unfairness."). In *Wille*, for instance, the court identified ten separate factors indicative of an unconscionable contract, including use of preprinted forms, excessive price, denial of basic remedies to buyers of consumer goods, penalty clauses, the circumstances surrounding execution of the contract, use of fine print, use of incomprehensible language, imbalance in the rights and obligations of the parties, exploitation of certain classes of disadvantaged bargainers, and inequality of bargaining power. 549 P.2d at 907.

3. UNCONSCIONABILITY AND ARBITRATION

Courts routinely use unconscionability doctrine to police arbitration clauses in consumer, employment, franchise, and similar types of contracts. See Daniel D Barnhizer, *Context as Power: Defining the Field of Battle for Advantage in Contractual Interactions*, 45 WAKE FOREST L. REV. 607, 619–26 (2010) (surveying California cases involving arbitration clauses and unconscionability). But state law may not effectively create a blanket prohibition against arbitration clauses.

For example, in *AT&T Mobility LLC. v. Concepcion*, 563 U.S. 321, 131 S.Ct. 1740 (2011), the U.S. Supreme Court examined a California common law rule that made all class action waivers in arbitration clauses per se unconscionable. Reasoning that "[a]rbitration is poorly suited to the higher stakes of class arbitration" and that an across-the-board prohibition against arbitration agreements that do not provide for class actions would vitiate Congress's purpose in enacting the Federal Arbitration Act, the Court held that the California rule was invalid under that Act. Following this decision, it remains to be seen how producers will react to this strong federal policy in favor of enforcing arbitration agreements.

Similarly, two years later in *Marmet Health Care Center, Inc. v. Brown*, __ U.S. ___, 132 S.Ct. 1201 (2012), the Court considered a similar West Virginia rule that prohibited enforcement of arbitration terms for injury or wrongful death in nursing home contracts as contrary to public policy. The Court remanded for further review of the lower court's alternative determination that the arbitration clauses were unconscionable, noting that it could not determine "to what degree the state court's alternative holding was influenced by the invalid, categorical rule . . . against predispute arbitration agreements."

D.   THE STATUTE OF FRAUDS—
CONTRACTS UNENFORCEABLE FOR
WANT OF A SIGNED WRITING

Generally, oral contracts are enforceable, and neither the common law nor the UCC require any particular form to make a contract enforceable. For a remarkable illustration of this general rule, see Texaco, Inc. v. Pennzoil, Co., 729 S.W.2d 768 (Tex. App. 1987) where the Texas court of appeals sustained a judgment of more than $8 billion (including punitive damages) for tortious interference with an oral contract to sell interests in the Getty Oil Company.

The Statute of Frauds, however, identifies specific contexts in which an otherwise valid oral contract must be evidenced by a written memorial of the transaction and signed by the party against whom enforcement of the contract is sought. The original Statute of Frauds, passed by the English parliament as the 1677 Act for Prevention of Fraud and Perjuries, was deemed necessary because of evidentiary problems unique to English law at the time relating to the difficulty of proving the existence and terms of oral agreements. The seventeenth century English evidentiary issues that made the original statute necessary are now an anachronism; indeed, the English parliament repealed most of the 1677 Act in 1954, leaving only contracts for the sale of land and promises to answer for the debt, default, or miscarriage of another. See 68 Harv. L. Rev. 383 (1954). See also Hugh Evander Willis, "The Statute of Frauds—A Legal Anachronism," 3 Ind. L. J. 427, 429–432 (1928) ("[T]he original reasons for the Statute of Frauds no longer exist, and . . . no new reasons have arisen for a Statute of Frauds in the case of contracts."). Nonetheless, despite frequent criticism and calls for repeal or reform, some version of the Statute of Frauds exists in every state in the U.S. Moreover, certain aspects of the Statute of Frauds, such as the requirement of a writing and signature, have been incorporated into numerous other state and federal statutes.

Karl Llewellyn, principal drafter of the UCC, remains probably the most famous proponent of the Statute of Frauds, arguing that the statute provides important benefits in terms of certainty and preserving records of transactions. For Llewellyn, the Statute of Frauds imposed a requirement of additional physical evidence in order to increase the security and predictability of the limited class of transactions without the Statute. Karl N. Llewellyn, "What Price Contract?" 40 Yale L. J. 704, 746–47 (1931).

Llewellyn considered the Statute "an amazing product," particularly well-suited to perform these functions in a modern, industrial economy in which numerous large firms depended extensively upon low-cost internal recordkeeping to coordinate their activities. See id. at 747 ("Meantime the modern developments of business—large units, requiring internal written records if files are to be kept straight, and officers informed, and departments coordinated, and the work of shifting personnel kept track of; the practice of confirming oral deals in writing, the use of typewriters, of forms—all these confirm the policy of the statute; all these reduce the price in disappointments exacted for its benefits.").

Llewellyn incorporated a version of the Statute of Frauds in UCC § 2–201, though softening the formal requirements and providing mechanisms by which an otherwise valid contract might fail under the Statute but nonetheless remain enforceable. Section 2–201 applies the Statute of Frauds' requirement of a written memorial signed by the party to be charged to all transactions for the sale of goods for a price of $500 or more. But § 2–201 also makes explicit that the writing only needs to evidence that the party to be charged assented to a transaction between the parties for a specific quantity of goods. The writing does not need to include any material terms other than the quantity of goods sold.

Moreover, the UCC Statute of Frauds provision also contains several savings clauses that permit enforcement of a contract even if it would otherwise fail under the general rule. First, § 2–201(2) creates a "merchant's exception" to the U.C.C. Statute of Frauds. This exception deems the Statute of Frauds satisfied in some cases where a merchant sends a written confirmation of the transaction that would satisfy the Statute as against the sender. If the recipient has reason to know of the writing's contents and fails to object in writing within 10 days, the recipient may not raise the Statute as a defense. See Section 4 of this chapter below. Additionally, § 2–201(3) provides three exceptions to the general rule of nonenforceability of oral contracts: (a) the seller begins production of goods specially manufactured for the buyer that are unsuitable for sale to others (the specially manufactured goods exception); (b) the party to be charged admits the existence of the contract in court (the judicial admission exception); and (c) acceptance of payment (in whole or in part) by the seller or acceptance of delivery (in whole or in part) by the buyer (the partial performance exception). As the Official Comment to UCC § 2–201 makes clear, these exceptions are intended to enforce unmemorialized oral agreements where there are other sufficient evidences of the parties' bargain. See UCC § 2–201 *cmt. 1 & 2* ("Receipt and acceptance either of goods or of the price constitutes an unambiguous overt admission by both parties that a contract actually exists.").

Notably, however, while a contract may be fully evidenced under the specially manufactured goods exception by a substantial beginning of the seller's performance, the contract formed under the judicial admission or partial performance exception is enforceable only to the extent of the contract actually admitted or partially performed. Thus, if a manufacturer substantially begins manufacturing 1,000 widgets imprinted with the buyer's logo, that is sufficient under UCC § 2–201(3)(a) to prove a contract for the entire 1,000 widget contract. In contrast, if the widgets are not specially manufactured for a single buyer, and the seller manufactures and delivers the first lot of 100 widgets before the buyer repudiates the parties' oral agreement, the seller may enforce the oral agreement only to the extent of the part performance—that is, for the 100 widgets actually delivered. See UCC § 2–201 *cmt. 2* ("'Partial performance' as a substitute for the required memorandum can validate the contract only for the goods which have been accepted or for which payment has been made and accepted.").

Other commentators have strongly criticized the Statute of Frauds as an historical anachronism that fails to serve a useful purpose and may indeed promote, rather than restrict, injustice. See Michael Braunstein, "Remedy, Reason and the Statute of Frauds: A Critical Economic Analysis," 1989 Utah L. Rev. 383, 391–97 (noting that strict enforcement of the Statute of Frauds would produce inequitable results and economic inefficiency, but also observing that "[t]he present situation, which involves numerous exceptions to the statute that often are based on inconsistent rationales, is not only unpredictable but is largely unknowable."); see also Francis M. Burdick, "A Statute for Promoting Fraud," 16 Colum. L. Rev. 273, 273–74 (1916) (suggesting that in many cases the Statute of Frauds is contrary to actual business practices and may in fact promote, instead of prevent, fraud). In one influential article, Professor Joseph M. Perillo, for example, reviewed the many different functions served by legal formalities. See Joseph M. Perillo, "The Statute of Frauds in Light of the Functions and Dysfunctions of Form,"43 Fordham L. Rev. 39, 43–69 (1974). Specifically, a legal formality such as the bargained-for exchange requirement of consideration doctrine can potentially serve a wide range of functions, including psychological, classifying, cautionary, clarifying, managerial, publicity, educational, regulatory, and evidentiary functions. See id. The Statute of Frauds, however, arguably serves only two of these identified functions of form well—the psychological function that refers to contracting parties' need to mark the formation of their legal relationship with some magical, sacramental, or psychologically significant act, and the evidentiary function that refers to the tendency of a formal requirement to produce evidence of the parties' transaction. See id. at 69. In exchange, the formalistic requirements of the Statute of Frauds may also create injustice by "sacrific[ing] equity in the individual instance." Id. at 70. See also Eric A. Posner, "Norms, Formalities, and the Statute of Frauds: A Comment," 144 U. Pa. L. Rev. 1971, 1977–78, 1980–86 (1996) (noting importance of assessing value of Statute of Frauds in terms of relative costs and benefits).

Outside of the debate on the usefulness of the Statute, any Statute of Frauds issue can be broken down into the following three-part analysis. First, is the contract "within" the Statute of Frauds? That is, does the subject matter fall within one of the enumerated transaction types, such as a sale of an interest in real property or a contract not capable of performance within a year of the making thereof, that are identified by the Statute of Frauds as falling within its scope? If not, no Statute of Frauds writing requirement applies. Many states, as well as the Congress, however, have adopted legislation making particular types of contracts enforceable only when evidenced by a signed written document.

Second, if the contract is within the Statute of Frauds, is it evidenced by a written memorial and signed by the party to be charged? As discussed herein, the written memorial's purpose is merely to provide evidence of the transaction and need not be a complete integration of the parties' agreement. The signature of the party to be charged element requires some mark affixed to the writing by the party against whom enforcement is sought that authenticates the document and indicates that the signer has somehow adopted or assented to the terms contained therein. If these requirements are met, the court may enforce the contract. As pointed out in the materials accompanying *Lucy v. Zehmer* in Chapter 2, the Statute produces something of an anomaly—subject to the UCC's "merchant's exception," the contract can be enforced against the party to be charged, but not against the other party who did not sign a "note or memorandum."

Third, if a contract within the scope of the Statute of Frauds is not evidenced by a writing or signed by the party to be charged, is compliance with the statute excused? In most American jurisdictions, a failure to satisfy the Statute renders the parties' oral contract unenforceable, not void. As discussed in detail below, the distinction is important. Because the oral contract actually exists, a defendant's failure to plead non-compliance with the Statute of Frauds as an affirmative defense waives that issue and renders the oral contract enforceable. Similarly, an admission in pleadings or in open court that an oral contract exists, part performance, or detrimental reliance can render the oral contract wholly or partially enforceable. This result would be impossible if the Statute of Frauds rendered a noncomplying oral contract void ab initio, since a void contract cannot, by definition, become enforceable. Alternatively, some jurisdictions permit a non-breaching party to an unenforceable oral contract to recover outside of contract through restitution or promissory estoppel.

The remainder of this section addresses each of these elements of the Statute of Frauds analysis in detail.

1. IS THE CONTRACT WITHIN THE STATUTE OF FRAUDS

Determining whether the parties' transaction is within the scope of the Statute of Frauds can be complicated. The "Statute of Frauds" actually comprises numerous individual statutory provisions contained in often widely separated sections of the state codes in which they appear. The traditional scope of the Statute of Frauds was established by Section 4 of the original 1677 Act, which was largely followed by individual state jurisdictions. Section 4 identified five transaction types covered by the statute:

(1) contracts by an executor or administrator to pay damages out of his own estate

(2) contracts to act as a surety for the debts or defaults of another person;

(3) contracts made in consideration of marriage;

(4) contracts for the sale of an interest in real property; and

(5) contracts not to be performed within one year of the making thereof.

Additionally, the UCC adds a sixth category—roughly analogous to § 17 of the 1677 Act—covering contracts for the sale of goods at a price of $500 or more. See UCC § 2–201(1). If a particular contract falls within the scope of any of these six situations, it must be evidenced by a writing and signed by the party against whom enforcement is sought—the "party to be charged"—or the contract is unenforceable unless the writing requirement is otherwise excused. Moreover, many federal and state statutes require written memorializations of agreements in other transactional contexts, such as an agreement to arbitrate under the Federal Arbitration Act or an agreement to transfer a copyright. See 9 U.S.C. § 2 ("A written provision in . . . a contract . . . to settle by arbitration a controversy thereafter arising out of such contract . . . or an agreement in writing to submit to arbitration an existing controversy arising out of such a contract . . . shall be valid, irrevocable, and enforceable, save upon such grounds as exist at law or in equity for the revocation of any contract."); 17 U.S.C. § 204(a) ("A transfer of copyright ownership, other than by operation of law, is not valid unless an instrument of conveyance, or a note or memorandum of the transfer, is in writing and signed by the owner of the rights conveyed or such owner's duly authorized agent.").

A full discussion of the first three types of contracts within the Statute of Frauds—a promise by an executor to pay damages out of his own estate, suretyship contracts, and contracts made in consideration of marriage—is beyond the scope of this text. The latter three, in contrast, provide examples of issues commonly litigated concerning the scope of the Statute of Frauds. The UCC Statute of Frauds—UCC § 2–201—straightforwardly provides that any contract for the sale of goods at a price of $500 or more is within the statute. Contracts for the sale of an interest in real property comprise not just the sale of a fee interest, but also long-term leaseholds, rents, easements, equitable interests in realty, and option contracts for the purchase or sale of realty or an interest therein.

The Statute of Frauds requirements of a signed memorial evidencing contracts not to be performed within one year of the making thereof may be one of the least defensible provisions in the original Statute of Frauds. As indicated in the case below, the determination of whether a particular contract is capable of performance within a year of its making is potentially complex, particularly because judicial hostility to this provision has led courts to apply artificially narrow and literal interpretations of the statute. As you read the following case, consider whether there exist any other potential justifications for this provision and whether the other contract types covered by the statute may suffer similar failures of justification.

COAN V. ORSINGER

United States Court of Appeals District of Columbia Circuit
265 F.2d 575, 105 U.S.App.D.C. 201 (1959)

BASTIAN, Circuit Judge.

Appellant (plaintiff) filed this action for breach of contract for personal services and damages resulting therefrom. The complaint alleges that on September 30, 1956, appellant discussed with appellee Orsinger, in the presence of witnesses, the terms of the contract. Appellant was to assume the duties of resident manager of an apartment development operated by Tyler Gardens Incorporated, of which corporation Orsinger is president, for which services appellant was to receive $75.00 per week in addition to a rent-free apartment for the duration of the contract. This proposed agreement was to continue 'until the plaintiff (appellant) completed his law studies as a student duly matriculated in Georgetown University Law Center, Washington, D.C. or was obliged to discontinue these studies.' This agreement was confirmed orally the following day in the offices of appellees. On October 12, 1956, appellant assumed his duties as resident manager. On November 17, 1956, he received a letter[1] terminating the

---

[1]   That letter read:

November 16, 1956
Mr. Carl Coan
Tyler Gardens Corporation
399 West Broad Street
Falls Church, Virginia

Dear Carl:

   I have given further thought and reflection to our conversation of today and I feel that our seven weeks experiment, though noble, would not be fair to either you or the people I represent. In my opinion this job, like Parkwood, is too big to be handled on a basis where you can give it only part time attention. To try to do justice to your education and to my confidence in you may result in your education suffering and our friendship deteriorating.

   Consequently, I am relieving you and Pat of any further duties at Tyler Gardens effective this date. However, I am sure my owners would not object if you wish to remain in the apartment, rent-free, until January 15, 1957, which is two months from today.

contract, and this termination was confirmed by Orsinger in an oral conference on December 1, 1956.

Orsinger, in his answer to the complaint, denied having entered into any contract on his own behalf but admitted that there was an oral contract with Tyler Gardens, whose agent he claimed to be in the making of the contract. He denied, however, that the contract was to last for any definite period alleging that it was terminable at the will of either party. Tyler Gardens admitted entering into a contract of employment with appellant but denied that it was to last for any stated period of time, claiming that it was terminable at the will of either party. Among other defenses, including the charge that appellant was properly discharged, appellees urged the defense of the statute of frauds. After the taking of appellant's deposition, appellees filed a motion for summary judgment (Fed.R.Civ.P. 56, 28 U.S.C.A.), which the court granted. This appeal followed.

Appellant's complaint and his deposition, construed most favorably for appellant (as they must be in this posture of the case), present no genuine issue of fact to be tried by a jury. Assuming, as we must, the truth of all his allegations, the suit is barred by the statute of frauds. The pertinent parts of the statute read as follows:

> Title 12, D.C.Code, § 302 (1951): No action shall be brought whereby to charge * * * any person upon any agreement * * * that is not to be performed within the space of one year from the making thereof, unless the agreement upon which such action shall be brought, or some memorandum or note thereof, shall be in writing, which need not state the consideration, and signed by the party to be charged therewith or some other person thereunto by him lawfully authorized.

Appellant contends that the statute of frauds is not applicable to his alleged contract of employment with appellees since it could be performed within a year. This would result, it is contended, if appellant were obliged to discontinue his law studies because of 'deficient scholarship or for some similar reason,'[2] a contingency which could occur within a year.

That contingency contemplates an annulment of the terms of the contract and would operate as a defeasance, thereby terminating and discharging the contract. Further performance under the contract would be impossible by either party. This annulment or defeasance provision does

Kindest regards.

Sincerely yours,

ORSINGER AND DOOLEY Victor J. Orsinger

VJO/ac

[2] Quoting from affidavits of appellant's father and appellant himself.

not contemplate the performance of the contract but only its termination and cancellation. Although it could be annulled within a year, it was none the less a personal service contract to last for more than a year, e.g., until appellant completed his studies at Georgetown University Law School. Although this annulment or defeasance provision relieves the parties from further performance of the contract, it is not the type of performance that is necessary to take the case out of the operation of the statute.

The court, in Blue Valley Creamery Co. v. Consolidated Products Co., 8 Cir., 1936, 81 F.2d 182, 185, spoke very clearly on this issue:

> * * * The statute looks to the performance and not the defeat of the contract, and a defeasance within a year would not constitute a performance according to the express intent of the parties, that performance should continue longer than a year.

> It is generally held that a contract for a definite period extending over a year is not taken out of the statute by an option allowing either party to terminate it within a year. The performance contemplated by the statute is a full and complete performance, and a cancellation is not such a performance. (Citing cases)

> Much of the confusion in considering the applicability of the statute apparently arises from failing to keep in mind the distinction between a contingency of such a nature as fulfills the obligation and one that defeats or prevents it from being performed. The one that depends upon the defeasance or matter of avoidance is within the statute, while the other is not.

In Union Car Advertising Co. v. Boston Elevated Ry. Co., 1 Cir., 1928, 26 F.2d 755, 58 A.L.R. 1007, the court held that the fact that a contract may be terminated, or further performance rendered impossible, within the period of one year, does not take it out of the statute where the obligation is one which cannot be performed within the year; that discharge from liability under a contract is not performance thereof. Citing, among other, Street v. Maddux, Marshall, Moss & Mallory, infra, and Williston on Contracts, §§ 495, 496, 497, 498, 499, 500.

Street v. Maddux, Marshall, Moss & Mallory, 1928, 58 App.D.C. 42, 24 F.2d 617, is authority for the proposition that a parol contract requiring three years for its performance is none the less a contract within the statute of frauds because it provides for annulment within a year, since annulment of a contract and its performance are distinctly different conceptions. There the owner of an apartment house in the District of Columbia sued on a verbal contract whereby he assigned the rents of that apartment to the defendant and authorized the defendant to pay itself a commission on the rents, in exchange for financial assistance required to prevent foreclosure. The agreement was to run for a period of three years unless the plaintiff sold the property during that period, in which event the agreement was to cease. Plaintiff sued because it was claimed that defendant failed to prevent the foreclosure. The defense was the statute of frauds.

On appeal, this court affirmed a judgment for the defendant, holding that the statute barred recovery. We held that it was apparent from the parol contract that the parties did not contemplate its performance within a year after it was made, and that the fact that it should immediately cease and be of no effect if the plaintiff sold the property prior to the expiration of the year period contemplated annulment and not the performance of the contract.

We therefore held that the annulment of a contract and its performance are distinctly different conceptions and that, although the parol contract in issue might be annulled within a year, it was none the less a contract the performance of which required three years. The court stated:

> In Warner v. Texas & Pacific Railway, 164 U.S. 418, 434, 17 S.Ct. 147, 153 (41 L.Ed. 495), upon which appellant relies, the correct rule was laid down for determining whether or not a parol contract was within the statute of frauds when the court said: 'The question is not what the probable, or expected, or actual performance of the contract was; but whether the contract, according to the reasonable interpretation of its terms, required that it should not be performed within the year.' (Emphasis by this court) 58 App.D.C. at page 44, 24 F.2d at page 619.

The courts thus recognize a distinct difference between a contingency which fulfills the terms of a contract and one which prevents fulfillment. If the contingency which fulfills and completes the terms of the contract happens or could possibly happen within a year, the contract is not within the statute. On the other hand, if the contingency prevents or discharges the parties from performing their obligations under the contract within a year, then the contract is within the statute.

Here, on the present state of the record, there is an oral contract for personal services for a period exceeding one year but subject to annulment which might occur within a year. This in no way helps to further the performance of the contract but rather serves to defeat it, rendering performance impossible, and thus bringing the contract within the statute.

It seems clear, taking appellant's version of the contract, that it would be impossible to perform the terms of the contract within the space of one year, since appellant had just started law school that fall (September 1956) and would not complete his studies before some time in 1959 at the earliest.

We see no force in the argument that defeasance should be restricted to an act of one of the parties, and this argument is not borne out by the authorities. But even if it were so, the defeasance here would be the result of appellant's act—voluntary or otherwise. The defeasance would occur if he should be obliged to discontinue his law studies because of poor or deficient scholarship, or for some similar reason.

We find it unnecessary to pass on other objections urged by appellees against the contract, although they seem to have merit. The contract certainly seems so vague and uncertain as to be unenforceable; and, from the deposition of appellant himself, it seems that the contract may be unilateral and not bilateral.[4]

We have examined appellant's other contentions and find no error.

Affirmed.

DANAHER, Circuit Judge (dissenting).

This case involves an oral personal service contract, admittedly entered into. Appellees insist they are free, with complete impunity, to breach their own agreement, the plan of which originated with appellee Orsinger and the promises of which were undertaken by the appellee corporation.

Appellee Orsinger was president of the corporate appellee which in 1956 became the owner of Tyler Gardens, a 482-unit apartment development in Falls Church, Virginia. Orsinger's affidavit in support of the appellees' motion for summary judgment discloses that he knew that

---

[4]   See the following extract from the deposition of appellant:

Q. Did he (Orsinger) tell you that you could not quit the Tyler Gardens job as long as you were in law school?

A. No.

Q. He never told you that you could not quit the job at Tyler Gardens and find another one while you were still in law school, did he?

A. No. But we had an understanding that I would hold the job while I was in law school.

Q. Let me ask the reporter to read that question to you because the answer is not responsive.

(Question read by the reporter)

A. I said no, but also said the agreement was that I would hold the job while I was in law school.

Q. That you had told me before, but the basic answer to this question, which has just been read to you by the reporter was 'no,' was it not?

A. That is correct.

Q. In other words, there were no strings attached to this thing; you could leave the Tyler Gardens job any time you wanted, could you not?

A. That was not my understanding of it.

Q. You mean Mr. Orsinger told you that you could not quit Tyler Gardens at any time while you were in law school.

A. No. He did not tell me that, but my understanding was that I would not quit on him and he would not quit on me.

Q. But he did not attach any strings to you, did he?

A. What do you mean by 'strings'?

Q. He did not tell you that you could not quit the job at Tyler Gardens any time you wanted, did he?

A. No. I have already said that. No.

'one of the development's needs was a resident manager preferably a husband-wife team.' He, for some years, had been a summertime neighbor of appellant's parents. From appellant's mother he learned, on September 30, 1956, that appellant had recently returned from Army service and had already secured a position as a real estate salesman. Upon his further ascertaining that appellant had registered as a student at the Georgetown Law Center, Orsinger suggested that he 'might be able to offer a less precarious position but with compensation which would enable the plaintiff to take care of himself and his family and finance his education.' Orsinger's interest in appellant stemmed not only from his friendship with appellant's parents, his neighbors, but from the fact, as he said, that he once had had the 'double burden of financing my law school education and taking care of my family.' Orsinger's proposition to the appellant was discussed in the presence of the latter's family, and appellant was asked to meet Orsinger the following day at the latter's Washington law office. 'I told him that the position was available at a salary of $75.00 a week, plus a two bedroom apartment worth $93.00 per month.' He was getting a college graduate and the assistance of the latter's wife for about $95 per week, all tax deductible to his company, a bargain, he might have thought.

Appellant accepted Orsinger's offer. In his reliance thereupon, he gave up his prospective employment with the real estate company. Upon payment of two months' rent, he obtained a release from the owners of the apartment he already had where he sacrificed his redecoration costs of $85. He undertook the expense of moving to Tyler Gardens, and about October 12, 1956, entered upon his duties as resident manager of Tyler Gardens. Some weeks later, without prior notice, appellant received from Orsinger a letter dated November 16, 1956, purporting to terminate appellant's service as resident manager and further advising 'I am relieving you and Pat (appellant's wife) of any further duties at Tyler Gardens effective this date.'

Against this factual background, appellant's complaint alleged that the contract was to continue in full force and effect 'until the plaintiff completed his law studies as a student duly matriculated in Georgetown University Law Center, Washington, D.C., or was obliged to discontinue these studies.' (Emphasis added.)

Appellees rely here solely upon the Statute of Frauds, so I discuss no other point. They insist they may not be charged with liability for damages flowing from the breach since the contract was not to be performed within a year. Clearly, they argue, the oral contract was to run for nearly three years.

The agreement as alleged could have been performed in two ways. Under the first clause, the appellees could have continued to employ the appellant throughout his entire three year law school course. They could have continued the promised payments, and appellant with his wife could have rendered the managerial services as originally contemplated by all parties. Surely my colleagues must concede that as so outlined, the first clause could have been fully performed. Any contract must be tested by its terms, and complete performance as demonstrated, could so have been had in accordance with the terms stated here.

But it was not a case simply of a three year commitment by the respective parties. This agreement could have been fully performed in another manner. It was stated in the alternative. My colleagues fail to distinguish between a discharge from liability because of a refusal to perform the first clause, and the possibly complete and timely performance of the second. These parties agreed that appellees would engage the appellant's services until he 'was obliged to discontinue' his law school studies. That eventuality might have depended upon many accounts, scholastic failure, financial strictures, prolonged incapacity because of Army service disability or what not. But it clearly could have occurred within the year. Had it so developed, the contract would have been fully performed on both sides, exactly in accordance with its provision, precisely as the parties had agreed. Thus, if performance follows the terms, if it accomplishes what the parties specified, and if that result could have occurred within the year, the requirements of the statute are met. The contract called for performance until appellant 'was obliged to discontinue' his studies. This contingency did not defeat the contract; it simply advanced a basis upon which it could be carried out. Obviously the statute applies only where performance of the contract in accordance with its terms can not occur within the year.

In other words we should examine the contract not in terms of nonliability for its breach but with respect to what was required for its performance. Thus viewed, we see that the parties agreed upon an alternative clause which admitted of performance within the year. Hence the contract was not within the statute.

Clearly distinguishable are cases where the parties have agreed upon a basis—not for performance—but for defeasance of the contract. Our case of Street v. Maddux, Marshall, Moss & Mallory, 1928, 58 App.D.C. 42, 24 F.2d 617 is illustrative. There the plaintiff in exchange for financial assistance assigned to the defendant the rents from his apartment house and authorized the defendant to pay itself a certain commission out of the rents. The contract was to run for three years unless, within that time, the plaintiff decided to sell the property. Accordingly the right of the plaintiff to sell the subject matter of the contract was not contemplated to be a performance of it, but rather provided a basis for its defeasance. The owner's reserved right to terminate brought the contract within the statute.

I think the governing principle here to be applied is to be discerned from the Supreme Court's discussion in the Warner case, supra note 1. There the Court criticized its earlier decision in Packet Co. v. Sickles (5 Wall. 580, 18 L.Ed. 550) which it noted was against the weight of authority and not in accord with the terms of the contract itself. Concluding that the clauses considered were true alternatives and that the one did not state a basis for defeasance of the performance called for by the other, the Court said (164 U.S. at page 431, 17 S.Ct. at page 152):

> The terms 'during the continuance of' and 'last so long' would seem to be precisely equivalent, and the full performance of the contract to be limited alike by the life of the patent and by the life of the boat. It is difficult to understand how the duration of the patent and the duration of the boat differed from one another in their relation to the performance or the determination of the contract; or how a contract to use an aid to navigation upon a boat, so long as she shall last can be distinguished in principle from a contract to support a man, so long as he shall live, which has often been decided, and is generally admitted, not to be within the statute of frauds.

So here. Suppose the questioned allegation had read that the contract was to continue in full force and effect 'until the plaintiff might be obliged to discontinue his studies, or until he shall have completed his law studies at Georgetown University Law Center.' Can it be doubted that the parties thus would be seen to have agreed that performance would be deemed complete if continued until the appellant should have been obliged to discontinue his studies? Or can it be doubted that such an eventuality might occur within the year? As the Supreme Court said, such a contract clearly is 'generally admitted not to be within the statute of frauds.' The performance being thus complete, we see the parties achieving precisely what they themselves said would constitute performance. There is no element of defeasance in it, I submit.

Myriad cases support the distinction for which I contend and which, if applied, would take this case out of the statute. It is not to be supposed that certiorari would be granted here and more extended discussion will serve no special purpose. I think summary judgment should not have been granted.

NOTES AND QUESTIONS

1. *Did the Statute of Frauds one-year provision produce a just result in this case?* Do you think the "one year" clause served a useful social purpose in this case? Coan alleged that the contract was to continue "until the plaintiff (appellant) completed his law studies as a student duly matriculated in Georgetown University Law Center . . . or was obliged to discontinue these studies." Apparently, Coan's complaint was dismissed on summary judgment.

Hence, his assertion of the facts was to be taken as accepted. Orsinger and Tyler Gardens both alleged that the contract was terminable at will (at the will of either party). If their claim was correct, was the contract capable of full performance within the space of one year? The majority opinion proceeds upon the assumption that the contract was for a three-year period, consistent with Coan's complaint. That opinion turns on the distinction between "full performance" and "performance cut short by reason of a condition or contingency." Does the majority's distinction between full performance, on the one hand, and performance (complete upon its face) cut down by the falling in of a condition make sense to you? See Restatement (Second) of Contracts § 130 *cmt. b.* Is this a distinction that individuals not trained in the law would be likely to be aware of and understand?

2.   *Judge Danaher's dissent.* Do you find his analysis persuasive? Were there two distinct ways in which the contract could have been performed, one of those ways possibly happening within the space of one year? He provided a hypothetical: Suppose the contract had provided that it would continue until Coan might be obliged to discontinue his studies. He suggested that if that had been the contract, all would agree that it would not be within the reach of the Statute. Do you agree with this assertion? If so, does the decision of the majority applying the Statute make any sense?

3.   *Judicial inclination to restrict the reach of the Statute to the narrowest possible basis.* As pointed out in the introductory materials to this section, many authors have urged that the Statute be repealed either by legislatures and/or by courts giving it the narrowest possible interpretation. Many courts have followed this suggestion. A common case law ruling is that, if the contract could possibly be performed within the space of one year, it is not caught by the Statute. Thus Restatement (Second) of Contracts § 130 Comment *a* states:

> Under the prevailing interpretation, the enforceability of a contract under the one-year provision does not turn on the actual course of subsequent events, nor on the expectations of the parties as to the probabilities. Contracts of uncertain duration are simply excluded; the provision covers only those contracts whose performance cannot possibly be completed within a year.

In C.R. Klewin, Inc. v. Flagship Properties, Inc., 220 Conn. 569, 600 A.2d 772 (1991), the Connecticut Supreme Court held that a contract expected to last for three to ten years was not caught by the Statute since it might have been fully performed within the space of one year. The court so held despite a district court conclusion that the contract as a matter of law could not have been performed within one year. The plaintiff, in his deposition, had said that the entire project was intended to be constructed in three to ten years. The Supreme Court referred to the fact that the one-year provision had been repealed in England and that the concept had been much criticized in the literature. As a provision designed to address the likelihood of witnesses recalling with accuracy beyond a period of one year, the court pointed to the six-year statute of limitations normally applicable to a claim for breach of contract. The court also pointed out that the calculation of the time involved is measured from the date of the contract to full performance and not from the start of performance. Thus it does not effectively distinguish between contracts covering a long versus a short period of performance. The court held that for a contract to be caught, its performance beyond the space of one year must be found in the express language of the contract. Contracts of "indefinite duration" were not caught.

4.   *Creating a "patchwork" of exceptions.* Many courts have held that a contract of employment for life is not caught by the statute since the employee might die within the first year and thus fully perform within that time period. In contrast, an employment contract for two years is clearly caught by the statute. Do you think that such a distinction makes sense? Do you think that a statutory provision giving rise to such distinctions should be preserved? See Matthew R. Chapman, "Who Can Afford Common Sense? The Illinois Supreme Court Rejects Time-Honored Exception to Statute of Frauds One Year Rule in *McInerney v. Charter Golf, Inc.*," 43 St. Louis U. L.J. 137, 137–38 (1999) (describing death exception and noting possible trend in some jurisdictions—notably Illinois—toward reversing the exception). But while this patchwork of narrow interpretations and judicially created exceptions may permit enforcement of contracts in individual cases, is that approach a proper function of the court given the Statute of Fraud's relatively explicit mandate? Would courts be more likely to achieve justice in individual cases by a broad reading of the Statute that creates sufficient numbers of unenforceable contracts that legislatures are forced to reform or repeal the Statute?

5.   *Contracts where one side has fully performed.* Restatement (Second) of Contracts § 130(2) provides:

> When one party to a contract has completed his performance, the one-year provision of the Statute does not prevent enforcement of the promises of other parties.

6.   *In order to be protected under the Statute of Frauds, must the defendant swear under oath that he did not enter into the oral contract alleged by the plaintiff?* Notice that the defendant in this case admitted that the parties had reached an oral agreement but asserted that this contract was not for a period of three years, but at will. Thus no problem of false swearing arose in this case and others of a similar fact pattern. The same was true in the *McIntosh* case included later in this chapter. The plaintiff there alleged a one-year contract and the defendant, while admitting that an oral agreement had been reached, asserted that it was for employment at will and not for one year. But suppose that you represent the defendant who tells you that he did enter into the oral contract as alleged by the plaintiff. Can you as counsel then assert the Statute as a defense?

Sometimes this difficult problem can be avoided by filing a motion to dismiss based on the plaintiff's pleading of a multi-year contract and yet failure to plead the requisite signed note or memorandum. Once the case goes into discovery, can counsel deny the making of the contract (knowing this to be untrue) or continue to represent the defendant if the defendant answers falsely to the pertinent question during a deposition? Counsel's role as an officer of the court, reinforced by the professional responsibility rules, says no. Note that the UCC § 2–201 provides a "judicial admission" exception to the requirement of a signed note or memorandum. For a discussion of these ethical problems and applicable professional conduct rules, see Carl A. Pierce, "Client Misconduct in the 21st Century," 35 UMPSLR 731 (2005) and Daniel J. Pope, "Client Perjury: Should a Lawyer Defend the System or the Client?," 64 Def. Couns. J. 447 (1997).

2. SATISFYING THE WRITING REQUIREMENT

The Statute of Frauds generally requires only that, to be enforceable, the parties' agreement be evidenced by a written memorialization and signed by the party to be charged. This requirement is most obviously satisfied by a typical written, integrated contract, containing all of the terms of the parties' bargain. Indeed, the obvious relationship between the written memorialization requirement of the Statute of Frauds and the parol evidence rule's general prohibition on the admission of parol evidence to supplement, explain, vary, or contradict the terms of an integrated and unambiguous written agreement often leads law students to a confusing conflation of the two rules. But, while both rules may deal with the legal implications of a written memorialization of the parties' bargain, it is critical to recognize that the Statute of Frauds and the parol evidence rule address very different concerns. The parol evidence rule defines the scope of the terms that a court may consider as comprising the parties' agreement. The issue facing the court in a parol evidence rule situation is not the enforceability of the parties' agreement, but rather whether the written memorial before the court represents a complete and unambiguous statement of the parties' bargain.

In contrast, if a contract is within the Statute of Frauds, the court's analysis must shift to the sufficiency of the written memorialization of that contract, not its meaning. The memorandum may, but need not, be a fully integrated and written contract. Where the parol evidence rule inquiry addresses the completeness and meaning of the writing, the Statute of Frauds inquiry focuses on whether the writing evidences that the parties actually did make an enforceable oral agreement. Consequently, a writing that will satisfy the statute may differ significantly in both content and form from the written agreement typically at issue in a parol evidence rule situation:

- The memorandum may be made contemporaneously with the parties' oral agreement, following that agreement (including even during court proceedings) or, in some cases, before the agreement.

- The memorandum need only show the assent of one party to the contract, in the form of a signature by the party to be charged.

- The memorandum may comprise multiple writings, prepared at different times.

- The memorandum may be prepared by its maker for purely internal purposes, and it does not need to be transmitted to the other party to the transaction.

- The memorandum must have existed at some point in time, but a later loss or destruction of the memorandum will not prevent it from satisfying the Statute of Frauds.

The requirements for satisfying the memorandum requirement differ depending on whether the contract arises under the common law or is governed by Article 2 of the UCC. With respect to common law contracts, the memorandum must identify the parties to the contract, the subject matter of the contract, and the essential terms of the contract. The most troubling of these requirements is that the applicable writing or memorandum state with "reasonable certainty" the "essential terms" of the contract. See Restatement (Second) of Contracts § 131(c). Generally, the essential terms are those necessary to enable a court to calculate the expectancy remedy of a non-breaching party. Ordinarily, these terms may include identification of the parties and of the contract subject matter, quantity, price, and time for performance. However, for purposes of the Statute of Frauds, courts have been more lenient because the restatement requires only reasonable certainty with regard to these terms.

UCC § 2–201 relaxes these standards somewhat for sale of goods contracts. A memorandum sufficient to satisfy § 2–201 must (1) be "sufficient to indicate that a contract for sale has been made between the parties and signed by the party against whom enforcement is sought . . . "; and (2) indicate the quantity of goods sold. See UCC § 2–201(1). Importantly, while § 2–201 specifically notes that non-quantity terms that are omitted or incorrectly stated will not render a contract unenforceable, "the contract is not enforceable . . . beyond the quantity of goods shown in such writing."

In addition to these substantive requirements, in both cases the memorandum must be signed by the party against whom enforcement is sought—the "party to be charged." See Restatement (Second) of Contracts § 131 ("[A] contract within the Statute of Frauds is enforceable if it is evidenced by any writing, signed by or on behalf of the party to be charged. . . ."); UCC § 2–201(1) ("[A] contract for the sale of goods for the price of $500 or more is not enforceable by way of action or defense unless there is some writing sufficient to indicate that a contract for sale has been made between the parties and signed by the party against whom enforcement is sought or by his authorized agent or broker."). The signature requirement may be satisfied by any mark that may be reasonably understood by the other party to the contract as indicating the signer's intent to authenticate the written document and to adopt or assent to that document. Thus, a handwritten signature subscribed on the signature line of a written contract will clearly satisfy the requirement, but so will a typewritten signature or mark on firm letterhead, so long as the mark indicates to a reasonable observer the signer's intent to authenticate and adopt the writing. Restatement (Second) of Contracts § 134 ("The signature to a memorandum may be any symbol made or adopted with an intention, actual or apparent, to authenticate the writing as that of the signer."). The UCC adopts an explicitly expansive definition of a "signed" writing to "include[ ] any symbol executed or adopted with present intention to adopt or accept a writing." UCC § 1–201(37) (2001) (formerly UCC § 1–201(39) ("includes any symbol executed or adopted by a party with present intention to authenticate a writing."). As the official comments indicate:

> a complete signature is not necessary. Authentication may be printed, stamped or written; it may be by initials or by thumbprint. It may be on any part of the document and in appropriate cases may be found in a billhead or letterhead. No catalog of possible authentications can be complete and the court must use common sense and commercial experience in passing upon these matters. The question always is whether the symbol was executed or adopted by the party with present intention to authenticate the writing. UCC § 1–201(39) *cmt. 39.*

See also Restatement (Second) of Contracts § 134 *cmt. a:*

> The traditional form of signature is of course the name of the signer, handwritten in ink. But initials, thumbprint or an arbitrary code sign may also be used; and the signature may be written in pencil, typed, printed, made with a rubber stamp, or impressed into the paper.

With the rapid development of electronic contracting mechanisms in the 1990s, some courts and commentators questioned whether the Statute of Frauds could be satisfied by an electronic "writing" and "signature," such as a click on a virtual "I accept" button or an electronically transmitted name. See, e.g., In re RealNetworks, Inc., Privacy Litigation, 2000 WL 631341 (N.D.Ill. 2000) (analyzing whether electronic clickwrap agreement constituted writing). To a large extent, these concerns have been resolved by case law or by statute. See id. (holding that electronic agreement is a written agreement sufficient to satisfy writing requirement of Federal Arbitration Act § 2). The now-withdrawn 2003 Revisions to the UCC, for example, attempted to define the record necessary to satisfy the § 2–201

Statute of Frauds as "information that is inscribed on a tangible medium or that is stored in an electronic or other medium and is retrievable in perceivable form." UCC § 2–201(m) (2003) (withdrawn). In 2000, Congress enacted the Electronic Signatures in Global and National Commerce Act ("E-Sign"), which provided that electronic records shall be deemed equivalent to a physical writing where such writing is required by law. 15 U.S.C. § 7001 ("Notwithstanding any statute, regulation, or other rule of law . . . a contract relating to such transaction may not be denied legal effect, validity, or enforceability solely because an electronic signature or electronic record was used in its formation."). E-Sign specifically permitted state legislatures to preempt its requirements by enacting the Uniform Electronic Transactions Act ("UETA") into state law, 15 U.S.C. § 7002, and a majority of states have made such enactments.

The vagueness of the Statute's sufficiency requirements for contracts arising under the common law creates substantial opportunities for litigation. As you read the following case, consider whether the Statute of Frauds memorandum requirement serves any useful function or whether the Statute causes the parties and the court to focus unnecessarily on the sufficiency of the memorandum, rather than the existence and terms of the contract.

CRABTREE V. ELIZABETH ARDEN SALES CORP.

Court of Appeals of New York
305 N.Y. 48, 110 N.E.2d 551 (1953)

FULD, Judge.

In September of 1947, Nate Crabtree entered into preliminary negotiations with Elizabeth Arden Sales Corporation, manufacturers and sellers of cosmetics, looking toward his employment as sales manager. Interviewed on September 26th, by Robert P. Johns, executive vice-president and general manager of the corporation, who had apprised him of the possible opening, Crabtree requested a three-year contract at $25,000 a year. Explaining that he would be giving up a secure well-paying job to take a position in an entirely new field of endeavor which he believed would take him some years to master he insisted upon an agreement for a definite term. And he repeated his desire for a contract for three years to Miss Elizabeth Arden, the corporation's president. When Miss Arden finally indicated that she was prepared to offer a two-year contract, based on an annual salary of $20,000 for the first six months, $25,000 for the second six months and $30,000 for the second year, plus expenses of $5,000 a year for each of those years, Crabtree replied that that offer was "interesting." Miss Arden thereupon had her personal secretary make this memorandum on a telephone order blank that happened to be at hand:

EMPLOYMENT AGREEMENT WITH NATE CRABTREE

Date Sept. 26-1947 6: PM

At 681-5th Ave * * *

Begin 20000.

6 months 25000.

6 months 30000.

5000.   per year Expense money

(2 years to make good)

Arrangement with Mr. Crabtree By Miss Arden Present Miss Arden Mr. John Crabtree Miss O'Leary

A few days later, Crabtree phoned Mr. Johns and telegraphed Miss Arden; he accepted the "invitation to join the Arden organization," and Miss Arden wired back her "welcome." When he reported for work, a "pay-roll change" card was made up and initialed by Mr. Johns, and then forwarded to the payroll department. Reciting that it was prepared on September 30, 1947, and was to be effective as of October 22d, it specified the names of the parties, Crabtree's "Job Classification" and, in addition, contained the notation that "This employee is to be paid as follows:

First six months of employment

$20,000. per annum

Next six months of employment

25,000. per annum

After one year of employment

30,000. per annum

Approved by RPJ (initialed)

After six months of employment, Crabtree received the scheduled increase from $20,000 to $25,000, but the further specified increase at the end of the year was not paid. Both Mr. Johns and the comptroller of the corporation, Mr. Carstens, told Crabtree that they would attempt to straighten out the matter with Miss Arden, and, with that in mind, the comptroller prepared another 'pay-roll change' card, to which his signature is appended, noting that there was to be a "Salary increase" from $25,000 to $30,000 a year, "per contractual arrangements with Miss Arden." The latter, however, refused to approve the increase and, after further fruitless discussion, plaintiff left defendant's employ and commenced this action for breach of contract.

At the ensuing trial, defendant denied the existence of any agreement to employ plaintiff for two years, and further contended that, even if one had been made, the statute of frauds barred its enforcement. The trial court found against defendant on both issues and awarded plaintiff damages of about $14,000, and the Appellate Division, two justices dissenting, affirmed. Since the contract relied upon was not to be performed within a year, the primary question for decision is whether there was a memorandum of its terms, subscribed by defendant, to satisfy the statute of frauds, Personal Property Law, § 31.

Each of the two payroll cards the one initialed by defendant's general manager, the other signed by its comptroller unquestionably constitutes a memorandum under the statute. That they were not prepared or signed with the intention of evidencing the contract, or that they came into existence subsequent to its execution, is of no consequence, see Marks v. Cowdin, 226 N.Y. 138, 145, 123 N.E. 139, 141; Spiegel v. Lowenstein, 162 App.Div. 443, 448–449, 147 N.Y.S. 655, 658; see, also, Restatement, Contracts, ss 209, 210, 214; it is enough, to meet the statute's demands, that they were signed with intent to authenticate the information contained therein and that such information does evidence the terms of the contract. See Marks v. Cowdin, supra, 226 N.Y. 138, 123 N.E. 139. . . . Those two writings contain all of the essential terms of the contract the parties to it, the position that plaintiff was to assume, the salary that he was to receive except that relating to the duration of plaintiff's employment. Accordingly, we must consider whether that item, the length of the contract, may be supplied by reference to the earlier unsigned office memorandum, and, if so, whether its notation, '2 years to make good,' sufficiently designates a period of employment.

The statute of frauds does not require the memorandum * * * to be in one document. It may be pieced together out of separate writings, connected with one another either expressly or by the internal evidence of subject-matter and occasion. Marks v. Cowdin, supra, 226 N.Y. 138, 145, 123 N.E. 139, 141, see, also, 2 Williston, op cit., p. 1671; Restatement, Contracts, s 208, subd. (a). Where each of the separate writings has been subscribed by the party to be charged, little if any difficulty is encountered. See, e.g., Marks v. Cowdin, supra, 226 N.Y. 138, 144–145, 123 N.E. 139, 141. Where, however, some writings have been signed, and others have not as in the case before us there is basic disagreement as to what constitutes a sufficient connection permitting the unsigned papers to be considered as part of the statutory memorandum. The courts of some jurisdictions insist that there be a reference, of varying degrees of specificity, in the signed writing to that unsigned, and, if there is no such reference, they refuse to permit consideration of the latter in determining whether the memorandum satisfies the statute. See, e.g., Osborn v. Phelps, 19 Conn. 63; Hewett Grain & Provision Co. v. Spear, 222 Mich. 608, 193 N.W. 291. That conclusion is based upon a construction of the statute which requires that the connection between the writings and defendant's acknowledgment of the one not subscribed, appear from examination of the papers alone, without the aid of parol evidence. The other position which has gained increasing support over the years is that a sufficient connection between the papers is established simply by a reference in them to the same subject matter or transaction. See, e.g., Frost v. Alward, 176 Cal. 691, 169 P. 379; Lerned v. Wannemacher, 9 Allen, 412, 91 Mass. 412. The statute is not pressed 'to the extreme of a literal and rigid logic,' Marks v. Cowdin, supra, 226 N.Y. 138, 144, 123 N.E. 139, 141, and oral testimony is admitted to show the connection between the documents and to establish the acquiescence, of the party to be charged, to the contents of the one unsigned. See Beckwith v. Talbot, 95 U.S. 289, 24 L.Ed. 496. . . .

The view last expressed impresses us as the more sound, and, indeed although several of our cases appear to have gone the other way, see, e.g., Newbery v. Wall, 65 N.Y. 484 . . . this court has on a number of occasions approved the rule, and we now definitively adopt it, permitting the signed and unsigned writings to be read together, provided that they clearly refer to the same subject matter or transaction. See, e.g., Peabody v. Speyers, 56 N.Y. 230. . . .

The language of the statute "Every agreement * * * is void, unless * * * some note or memorandum thereof be in writing, and subscribed by the party to be charged," Personal Property Law, § 31—does not impose the requirement that the signed acknowledgment of the contract must appear from the writings alone, unaided by oral testimony. The danger of fraud and perjury, generally attendant upon the admission of parol evidence, is at a minimum in a case such as this. None of the terms of the contract are supplied by parol. All of them must be set out in the various writings presented to the court, and at least one writing, the one establishing a contractual relationship between the parties, must bear the signature of the party to be charged, while the unsigned document must on its face refer to the same transaction as that set forth in the one that was signed. Parol evidence to portray the circumstances surrounding the making of the memorandum serves only to connect the separate documents and to show that there was assent, by the party to be charged, to the contents of the one unsigned. If that testimony does not convincingly connect the papers, or does not show assent to the unsigned paper, it is within the province of the judge to conclude, as a matter of law, that the statute has not been satisfied. True, the possibility still remains that, by fraud or perjury, an agreement never in fact made may occasionally be enforced under the subject matter or transaction test. It is better to run that risk, though, than to deny enforcement to all agreements, merely because the signed document made no specific mention of the unsigned writing. As the United States Supreme Court declared, in sanctioning the admission of parol evidence to establish the connection between the signed and unsigned writings. "There may be cases in which it would be a violation of reason and common sense to ignore a reference which derives its significance from such (parol) proof. If there is ground for any doubt in the matter, the general rule should be enforced. But where there is no ground for doubt, its enforcement would aid, instead of discouraging, fraud." Beckwith v. Talbot, supra, 95 U.S. 289, 292, 24 L.Ed. 496. . . . Turning to the writings in the case before us the unsigned office memo, the payroll change form initialed by the general manager Johns, and the paper signed by the comptroller Carstens it is apparent, and most patently, that all three refer on their face to the same transaction. The parties, the position to be filled by plaintiff, the salary to be paid him, are all identically set forth; it is hardly possible that such detailed information could refer to another or a different agreement. Even more, the card signed by Carstens notes that it was prepared for the purpose of a 'Salary increase per contractual arrangements with Miss Arden.' That certainly constitutes a reference of sorts to a more comprehensive 'arrangement,' and parol is permissible to furnish the explanation.

The corroborative evidence of defendant's assent to the contents of the unsigned office memorandum is also convincing. Prepared by defendant's agent, Miss Arden's personal secretary, there is little likelihood that that paper was fraudulently manufactured or that defendant had not assented to its contents. Furthermore, the evidence as to the conduct of the parties at the time it was prepared persuasively demonstrates defendant's assent to its terms. Under such circumstances, the courts below were fully justified in finding that the three papers constituted the 'memorandum' of their agreement within the meaning of the statute.

Nor can there be any doubt that the memorandum contains all of the essential terms of the contract. . . . Only one term, the length of the employment, is in dispute. The September 26th office memorandum contains the notation, '2 years to make good.' What purpose, other than to denote the length of the contract term, such a notation could have, is hard to imagine. Without it, the employment would be at will, see Martin v. New York Life Ins. Co., 148 N.Y. 117, 121, 42 N.E. 416, 417, and its inclusion may not be treated as meaningless or purposeless. Quite obviously, as the courts below decided, the phrase signifies that the parties agreed to a term, a certain and definite term, of two years, after which, if plaintiff did not 'make good,' he would be subject to discharge. And examination of other parts of the memorandum supports that construction. Throughout the writings, a scale of wages, increasing plaintiff's salary periodically, is set out; that type of arrangement is hardly consistent with the hypothesis that the employment was meant to be at will. The most that may be argued from defendant's standpoint is that '2 years to make good,' is a cryptic and ambiguous statement. But, in such a case, parol evidence is admissible to explain its meaning. See Martocci v. Greater New York Brewery, 301 N.Y. 57, 63, 92 N.E.2d 887, 889. . . . Having in mind the relations of the parties, the course of the negotiations and plaintiff's insistence upon security of employment, the purpose of the phrase or so the trier of the facts was warranted in finding was to grant plaintiff the tenure he desired.

The judgment should be affirmed, with costs.

LOUGHRAN, C. J., and LEWIS, CONWAY, DESMOND, DYE AND FROESSEL, JJ., concur.

NOTES AND QUESTIONS

1.   *Essential terms and the written memorandum.* To satisfy the Statute of Frauds, the memorandum must contain the essential terms of the parties' agreement. What makes a term essential? Was the term regarding the length of Crabtree's contract a "promissory" term? Courts have said that any "promissory" term is essential and must be found in the writing. See e.g. Justice Cardozo writing for the court in *Marks v. Cowdin*, 226 N.Y. 138, 123 N.E. 139 (1919). What evidence would a court use to determine whether there was an "essential" term that had been omitted from the writing?

2.   *The Statute of Frauds and parol evidence.* Justice Cardozo observed in *Marks* that it is always necessary to relate the words of a contract or memorandum to their corresponding reality through parol evidence. "We are turning signs and symbols into their equivalent realities. This must always be done to some extent, no matter how many are the identifying tokens. 'In every case, the words must be translated into things and facts by parol evidence.' . . . " Compare that statement to Justice Traynor's reasoning in *Pacific Gas and Electric Co.* regarding the relationship between words and their contexts:

> If words had absolute and constant referents, it might be possible to discover contractual intention in the words themselves and in the manner in which they were arranged. Words, however, do not have absolute and constant referents. "A word is a symbol of thought but has no arbitrary and fixed meaning like a symbol of algebra or chemistry, ... " The meaning of particular words or groups of words varies with the ". . . verbal context and surrounding circumstances and purposes in view of the linguistic education and experience of their users and their hearers or readers (not excluding judges). . . . A word has no meaning apart from these factors; much less does it have an objective meaning, one true meaning.

What do these two quotes suggest about the relationship between the parol evidence rule, the Statute of Frauds, and a court's search for the meaning of a written agreement?

3.   *Incorporation by reference and acts of independent significance.* Consider an employment contract that provides:

> The terms and conditions of employment found in the current "Employees' Manual" are incorporated in this agreement as if set out fully in the text. In the event of any conflict between the express

terms of this agreement and the terms in the "Employees' Manual," these express terms shall prevail.

Is there a problem of "he said, she said" slippery testimony involved when evidence of the content of the Employees' Manual is introduced at trial? Said Judge Fuld in *Crabtree*:

> The courts of some jurisdictions insist that there be a reference, of varying degrees of specificity, in the signed writing to that unsigned, and, if there is no such reference, they refuse to permit consideration of the latter in determining whether the memorandum satisfies the statute. . . . That conclusion is based upon a construction of the statute which requires that the connection between the writings and defendant's acknowledgment of the one not subscribed, appear from examination of the papers alone, without the aid of parol evidence. The other position which has gained increasing support over the years is that a sufficient connection between the papers is established simply by a reference in them to the same subject matter or transaction.

Clearly, the unsigned writing to be incorporated must have been in existence at the time of the signing of the note or memorandum. Do you see any potential opportunity for fraud if Judge Fuld's "other position" is implemented? How did this court "stitch" the secretary's note to the pay records?

Consider a contract for the sale and purchase of a house and associated property. Suppose that the note or memorandum signed by the seller says, "I agree to sell my house in Edina to John Jones . . . [with other necessary and appropriate terms]." Do the words "my house in Edina" constitute an adequate description of the property to be sold to permit enforcement of the contract? Remember *Lucy v. Zehmer* and the words "Ferguson farm." Is there a risk of slippery testimony being used to establish the identity of "my house in Edina?" The problem addressed by the Statute of Frauds is at its most acute when the issue is to be resolved on the basis of oral testimony of the parties or their "affiliates." Giving meaning to the words "my house in Edina" does not depend upon any such slippery testimony. A city official can testify, based on review of the city records (real estate tax rolls), that the seller owned only one house in Edina and that it was situated at 440 Browndale Avenue. The apparently ambiguous description of the property to be sold can be resolved and made clear and specific through the testimony of a third party who has records to substantiate and who has no interest in the lawsuit. We sometimes refer to such testimony as proof of "facts of independent significance." There is a great deal of difference between giving effect to the words "my house in Edina" and accepting oral testimony of one of the parties or other "bystanders" of a promissory term of the contract not found in the note or memorandum.

4. *Did Elizabeth Arden deny making the two-year employment agreement?* The court notes that she both denied agreeing to a two-year term and, in addition, pleaded the Statute as an affirmative defense. Does the

verdict of the jury suggest that she may have committed perjury? How do you suppose the secretary testified?

3. EXCUSING COMPLIANCE FAILURE

If an oral contract is within the Statute of Frauds, and the parties fail to satisfy the memorandum requirement, the contract is unenforceable. In that event, a party may breach the contract without fear of contract liability, and the non-breaching party generally has no right to an action for damages under that contract. Such an opportunistic breach creates economic waste.

> Only by enforcing contracts, at least to the extent of awarding damages, can wasteful breach be avoided. For this purpose, breach is wasteful when nonperformance costs the nondefaulting party more than it benefits the defaulting party. When the statute of frauds applies, contract remedies are not available and wasteful breach results. This is the reason for the many exceptions to the statute of frauds.

Michael Braunstein, "Remedy, Reason and the Statute of Frauds: A Critical Economic Analysis," 1989 Utah L. Rev. 383, 385. In the face of the potential for waste and injustice created by the Statute of Frauds, courts and legislatures have three basic options. See id. at 390–91 (noting that "[i]n resolving statute of frauds issues, lawmakers have three alternatives"—strict enforcement of the Statute, repeal the Statute, or "ameliorate its impact by finding exceptions to it so that many oral contracts are enforced."). First, if the waste and injustice created by the Statute (i.e., its costs) are lower than the benefits provided by the Statute in terms of reduced fraud, then the Statute should be strongly enforced according to its terms and without exceptions, provided there are no superior alternatives. The English repeal of the original Statute of Frauds, the judicial hostility to application of the statute in the United States, and the scores of commentators who have argued vigorously for the Statute's reform or repeal suggest that this is not the case.

The second option—repeal of the Statute—was adopted by the English parliament in 1954 with respect to the "one year" provision. Given that the Statute of Frauds is a creature of the law of 49 separate state codes in the United States, it seems at least possible that an incomplete repeal of the Statute in even a large majority of jurisdictions could work substantial hardships on the uninformed party in interstate transactions.

The third option represents the approach of U.S. courts: judicially restrict the scope of application and operation of the Statute by adopting narrow interpretations of its provisions and creating numerous exceptions that soften its effects and impacts when the parties fail to satisfy its requirements. Such exceptions generally fall into two categories. On the one hand, if the parties' contract is unenforceable, the parties may still proceed on non-contractual or quasi-contractual theories of enforceability and recovery, such as restitution. On the other hand, principles of promissory estoppel, equitable estoppel, and the doctrine of part performance may provide a basis for enforcing the contract terms themselves by barring the breaching party from raising the Statute of Frauds as a defense.

The Restatement (First) of Contracts § 90 provided for promissory estoppel as a general doctrine. The Restatement (Second) of Contracts reworded that section and added the new subsection (2). But in addition, it added a new § 139 dealing specifically with the availability of a promissory estoppel theory in the face of a Statute of Frauds affirmative defense. As you read the following case, consider whether this third approach to ameliorating the potential injustice and economic inefficiency created by the Statute of Frauds yields superior results compared to either complete repeal or outright enforcement of the Statute.

MCINTOSH V. MURPHY

Supreme Court of Hawaii
52 Haw. 29, 469 P.2d 177 (1970)

LEVINSON, Justice.

This case involves an oral employment contract which allegedly violates the provision of the Statute of Frauds requiring 'any agreement that is not to be performed within one year from the making thereof' to be in writing in order to be enforceable. HRS s 656–1(5). In this action the plaintiff-employee Dick McIntosh seeks to recover damages from his employer, George Murphy and Murphy Motors, Ltd., for the breach of an alleged one-year oral employment contract.

While the facts are in sharp conflict, it appears that defendant George Murphy was in southern California during March, 1964 interviewing prospective management personnel for his Chevrolet-Oldsmobile dealerships in Hawaii. He interviewed the plaintiff twice during that time. The position of sales manager for one of the dealerships was fully discussed but no contract was entered into. In April, 1964 the plaintiff received a call from the general manager of Murphy Motors informing him of possible employment within thirty days if he was still available. The plaintiff indicated his continued interest and informed the manager that he would be available. Later in April, the plaintiff sent Murphy a telegram to the effect that he would arrive in Honolulu on Sunday, April 26, 1964. Murphy then telephoned McIntosh on Saturday, April 25, 1964 to notify him that the job of assistant sales manager was open and work would begin on the following Monday, April 27, 1964. At that time McIntosh expressed surprise at the change in job title from sales manager to assistant sales manager but reconfirmed the fact that he was arriving in Honolulu the next day, Sunday. McIntosh arrived on Sunday, April 26, 1964 and began work on the following day, Monday, April 27, 1964.

As a consequence of his decision to work for Murphy, McIntosh moved some of his belongings from the mainland to Hawaii, sold other possessions, leased an apartment in Honolulu and obviously forwent any other employment opportunities. In short, the plaintiff did all those things which were incidental to changing one's residence permanently from Los Angeles to Honolulu, a distance of approximately 2200 miles. McIntosh continued working for Murphy until July 16, 1964, approximately two and one-half months, at which time he was discharged on the grounds that he was unable to close deals with prospective customers and could not train the salesmen.

At the conclusion of the trial, the defense moved for a directed verdict arguing that the oral employment agreement was in violation of the Statute of Frauds, there being no written memorandum or note thereof. The trial court ruled that as a matter of law the contract did not come within the Statute, reasoning that Murphy bargained for acceptance by the actual commencement of performance by McIntosh, so that McIntosh was not bound by a contract until he came to work on Monday, April 27, 1964. Therefore, assuming that the contract was for a year's employment, it was performable within a year exactly to the day and no writing was required for it to be enforceable. Alternatively, the court ruled that if the agreement was made final by the telephone call between the parties on Saturday, April 25, 1964, then that part of the weekend which remained would not be counted in calculating the year, thus taking the contract out of the Statute of Frauds. With commendable candor the trial judge gave as the motivating force for the decision his desire to avoid a mechanical and unjust application of the Statute.

The case went to the jury on the following questions: (1) whether the contract was for a year's duration or was performable on a trial basis, thus making it terminable at the will of either party; (2) whether the plaintiff was discharged for just cause; and (3) if he was not discharged for just cause, what damages were due the plaintiff. The jury returned a verdict for the plaintiff in the sum of $12,103.40. The defendants appeal to this court on four principal grounds, three of which we find to be without merit. The remaining ground of appeal is whether the plaintiff can maintain an action on the alleged oral employment contract in light of the prohibition of the Statute of Frauds making unenforceable an oral contract that is not to be performed within one year.

I.   TIME OF ACCEPTANCE OF THE EMPLOYMENT AGREEMENT

The defendants contend that the trial court erred in refusing to give an instruction to the jury that if the employment agreement was made more than one day before the plaintiff began performance, there could be no recovery by the plaintiff. The reason given was that a contract not to be performed within one year from its making is unenforceable if not in writing.

The defendants are correct in their argument that the time of acceptance of an offer is a question of fact for the jury to decide. But the trial court alternatively decided that even if the offer was accepted on the Saturday prior to the commencement of performance, the intervening Sunday and part of Saturday would not be counted in computing the year for the purposes of the Statute of Frauds. The judge stated that Sunday was a non-working day and only a fraction of Saturday was left which he would not count. In any event, there is no need to discuss the relative merits of either ruling since we base our decision in this case on the doctrine of equitable estoppel which was properly briefed and argued by both parties before this court, although not presented to the trial court.

II.   ENFORCEMENT BY VIRTUE OF ACTION IN RELIANCE ON THE ORAL CONTRACT

In determining whether a rule of law can be fashioned and applied to a situation where an oral contract admittedly violates a strict interpretation of the Statute of Frauds, it is necessary to review the Statute itself together with its historical and modern functions. The Statute of Frauds, which requires that certain contracts be in writing in order to be legally enforceable, had its inception in the days of Charles II of England. Hawaii's version of the Statute is found in HRS § 656–1 and is substantially the same as the original English Statute of Frauds.

The first English Statute was enacted almost 300 years ago to prevent 'many fraudulent practices, which are commonly endeavored to be upheld by perjury and subornation of perjury.' 29 Car. 2, c. 3 (1677). Certainly, there were compelling reasons in those days for such a law. At the time of enactment in England, the jury system was quite unreliable, rules of evidence were few, and the complaining party was disqualified as a witness so he could neither testify on direct-examination nor, more importantly, be cross-examined. Summers, The Doctrine of Estoppel and the Statute of Frauds, 79 U. Pa. L. Rev. 440, 441 (1931). The aforementioned structural and evidentiary limitations on our system of justice no longer exist.

Retention of the Statute today has nevertheless been justified on at least three grounds: (1) the Statute still serves an evidentiary function thereby lessening the danger of perjured testimony (the original rationale); (2) the requirement of a writing has a cautionary effect which causes reflection by the parties on the importance of the agreement; and (3) the writing is an easy way to distinguish enforceable contracts from those which are not, thus channeling certain transactions into written form.

In spite of whatever utility the Statute of Frauds may still have, its applicability has been drastically limited by judicial construction over the years in order to mitigate the harshness of a mechanical application.[3] Furthermore, learned writers continue to disparage the Statute regarding it as 'a statute for promoting fraud' and a 'legal anachronism.'

Another method of judicial circumvention of the Statute of Frauds has grown out of the exercise of the equity powers of the courts. Such judicially imposed limitations or exceptions involved the traditional dispensing power of the equity courts to mitigate the 'harsh' rule of law. When courts have enforced an oral contract in spite of the Statute, they have utilized the legal labels of 'part performance' or 'equitable estoppel' in granting relief. Both doctrines are said to be based on the concept of estoppel, which operates to avoid unconscionable injury. 3 Williston, Contracts § 533A at 791 (Jaeger ed. 1960), Summers, supra at 443–49; Monarco v. Lo Greco, 35 Cal.2d 621, 220 P.2d 737 (1950) (Traynor, J.).

Part performance has long been recognized in Hawaii as an equitable doctrine justifying the enforcement of an oral agreement for the conveyance of an interest in land where there has been substantial reliance by the party seeking to enforce the contract. Perreira v. Perreira, 50 Haw. 641, 447 P.2d 667 (1968) (agreement to grant life estate). . . . Other courts have enforced oral contracts (including employment contracts) which failed to satisfy the section of the Statute making unenforceable an agreement not to be performed within a year of its making. This has occurred where the conduct of the parties gave rise to an estoppel to assert the Statute. . . .

It is appropriate for modern courts to cast aside the raiments of conceptualism which cloak the true policies underlying the reasoning behind the many decisions enforcing contracts that violate the Statute of Frauds. There is certainly no need to resort to legal rubrics or meticulous legal formulas when better explanations are available. The policy behind enforcing an oral agreement which violated the Statute of Frauds, as a policy of avoiding unconscionable injury, was well set out by the California Supreme Court. In Monarco v. Lo Greco, 35 Cal.2d 621, 623, 220 P.2d 737, 739 (1950), a case which involved an action to enforce an oral contract for

---

[3]   Thus a promise to pay the debt of another has been construed to encompass only promises made to a creditor which do not benefit the promisor (Restatement of Contracts § 184 (1932); 3 Williston, Contracts § 452 (Jaeger ed. 1960)); a promise in consideration of marriage has been interpreted to exclude mutual promises to marry (Restatement, supra § 192; 3 Williston, supra § 485); a promise not to be performed within one year means a promise not performable within one year (Restatement, supra § 198; 3 Williston, supra, § 495); a promise not to be performed within one year may be removed from the Statute of Frauds if one party has fully performed (Restatement, supra § 198; 3 Williston, supra § 504); and the Statute will not be applied where all promises involved are fully performed (Restatement, supra § 219; 3 Williston, supra § 528).

the conveyance of land on the grounds of 20 years performance by the promisee, the court said:

The doctrine of estoppel to assert the statute of frauds has been consistently applied by the courts of this state to prevent fraud that would result from refusal to enforce oral contracts in certain circumstances. Such fraud may inhere in the unconscionable injury that would result from denying enforcement of the contract after one party has been induced by the other seriously to change his position in reliance on the contract * * *.

See also Seymour v. Oelrichs, 156 Cal. 782, 106 P. 88 (1909) (an employment contract enforced).

In seeking to frame a workable test which is flexible enough to cover diverse factual situations and also provide some reviewable standards, we find very persuasive section 217A of the Second Restatement of Contracts.[5] That section specifically covers those situations where there has been reliance on an oral contract which falls within the Statute of Frauds. Section 217A states:

(1) A promise which the promisor should reasonably expect to induce action or forbearance on the part of the promisee or a third person and which does induce the action or forbearance is enforceable notwithstanding the Statute of Frauds if injustice can be avoided only by enforcement of the promise. The remedy granted for breach is to be limited as justice requires.

(2) In determining whether injustice can be avoided only by enforcement of the promise, the following circumstances are significant: (a) the availability and adequacy of other remedies, particularly cancellation and restitution; (b) the definite and substantial character of the action or forbearance in relation to the remedy sought; (c) the extent to which the action or forbearance corroborates evidence of the making and terms of the promise, or the making and terms are otherwise established by clear and convincing evidence; (d) the reasonableness of the action or forbearance; (e) the extent to which the action or forbearance was foreseeable by the promisor. [Compare: Restatement (Second) § 139.]

We think that the approach taken in the Restatement is the proper method of giving the trial court the necessary latitude to relieve a party of the hardships of the Statute of Frauds. Other courts have used similar approaches in dealing with oral employment contracts upon which an employee had seriously relied. See Alaska Airlines, Inc. v. Stephenson, 217 F.2d 295 (9th Cir. 1954); Seymour v. Oelrichs, 156 Cal. 782, 106 P. 88

---

[5] Restatement (Second) of Contracts § 217A (Supp. Tentative Draft No. 4, 1969)[Eds. Now Restatement (Second) of Contracts § 139.].

(1909). This is to be preferred over having the trial court bend over backwards to take the contract out of the Statute of Frauds. In the present case the trial court admitted just this inclination and forthrightly followed it.

There is no dispute that the action of the plaintiff in moving 2200 miles from Los Angeles to Hawaii was foreseeable by the defendant. In fact, it was required to perform his duties. Injustice can only be avoided by the enforcement of the contract and the granting of money damages. No other remedy is adequate. The plaintiff found himself residing in Hawaii without a job.

It is also clear that a contract of some kind did exist. The plaintiff performed the contract for two and one-half months receiving $3,484.60 for his services. The exact length of the contract, whether terminable at will as urged by the defendant, or for a year from the time when the plaintiff started working, was up to the jury to decide.

In sum, the trial court might have found that enforcement of the contract was warranted by virtue of the plaintiff's reliance on the defendant's promise. Naturally, each case turns on its own facts. Certainly there is considerable discretion for a court to implement the true policy behind the Statute of Frauds, which is to prevent fraud or any other type of unconscionable injury. We therefore affirm the judgment of the trial court on the ground that the plaintiff's reliance was such that injustice could only be avoided by enforcement of the contract.

Affirmed.

ABE, Justice (dissenting).

The majority of the court has affirmed the judgment of the trial court; however, I respectfully dissent.

I.

Whether alleged contract of employment came within the Statute of Frauds: As acknowledged by this court, the trial judge erred when as a matter of law he ruled that the alleged employment contract did not come within the Statute of Frauds; however, I cannot agree that this error was not prejudicial as this court intimates.

On this issue, the date that the alleged contract was entered into was all important and the date of acceptance of an offer by the plaintiff was a question of fact for the jury to decide. In other words, it was for the jury to determine when the alleged one-year employment contract was entered into and if the jury had found that the plaintiff had accepted the offer[1] more than one day before plaintiff was to report to work, the contract would have come within the Statute of Frauds and would have been unenforceable.

---

[1]   Plaintiff testified that he accepted the offer in California over the telephone.

Sinclair v. Sullivan Chevrolet Co., 31 Ill.2d 507, 202 N.E.2d 516 (1964); Chase v. Hinkley, 126 Wis. 75, 105 N.W. 230 (1905).

II.

This court holds that though the alleged one-year employment contract came within the Statute of Frauds, nevertheless the judgment of the trial court is affirmed 'on the ground that the plaintiff's reliance was such that injustice could only be avoided by enforcement of the contract.'

I believe this court is begging the issue by its holding because to reach that conclusion, this court is ruling that the defendant agreed to hire the plaintiff under a one-year employment contract. The defendant has denied that the plaintiff was hired for a period of one year and has introduced into evidence testimony of witnesses that all hiring by the defendant in the past has been on a trial basis. The defendant also testified that he had hired the plaintiff on a trial basis.

Here on one hand the plaintiff claimed that he had a one-year employment contract; on the other hand, the defendant claimed that the plaintiff had not been hired for one year but on a trial basis for so long as his services were satisfactory. I believe the Statute of Frauds was enacted to avoid the consequences this court is forcing upon the defendant. In my opinion, the legislature enacted the Statute of Frauds to negate claims such as has been made by the plaintiff in this case. But this court holds that because the plaintiff in reliance of the one-year employment contract (alleged to have been entered into by the plaintiff, but denied by the defendant) has changed his position, "injustice could only be avoided by enforcement of the contract." Where is the sense of justice?

Now assuming that the defendant had agreed to hire the plaintiff under a one-year employment contract and the contract came within the Statute of Frauds, I cannot agree, as intimated by this court, that we should circumvent the Statute of Frauds by the exercise of the equity powers of courts. As to statutory law, the sole function of the judiciary is to interpret the statute and the judiciary should not usurp legislative power and enter into the legislative field. A. C. Chock, Ltd. v. Kaneshiro, 51 Haw. 87, 93, 451 P.2d 809 (1969); Miller v. Miller, 41 Ohio Op. 233, 83 N.E.2d 254 (Ct.C.P.1948). Thus, if the Statute of Frauds is too harsh as intimated by this court, and it brings about undue hardship, it is for the legislature to amend or repeal the statute and not for this court to legislate.

KOBAYASHI, J., joins in this dissent.

NOTES AND QUESTIONS

1. *Did the use of promissory estoppel in this case produce a superior result?* The answer turns on whether we believe McIntosh's testimony as to the contents of the phone call including a one-year term contract or Murphy's

testimony that the employment was to be at will. Apparently, the jury believed McIntosh and not Murphy, but the risk of a jury resolving such "he said, she said" conflicting testimony was the basic justification for the original Statute of Frauds. This is precisely the point of Justice Abe's dissent. Do you think that the majority's use of promissory estoppel produced a superior result?

2.   *The Restatement (Second) of Contracts § 139 rationale.* Can you explain and justify the inclusion of this section in the Restatement? Would not § 90 alone be sufficient? Are there differences between the application of § 90 and § 139?

3.   *The timing issue.* Do you agree with the court's counting of time here with respect to the "one year" rule?

4.   *Part performance.* Said the majority:

> It is also clear that a contract of some kind did exist. The plaintiff performed the contract for two and one-half months receiving $3,484.60 for his services. The exact length of the contract, whether terminable at will as urged by the defendant, or for a year from the time when the plaintiff started working, was up to the jury to decide.

Is the majority seeking to invoke a "part performance" explanation of their decision? Do you think that McIntosh's traveling to Hawaii and working for some two-and-one-half months was necessarily referable to a one-year contract?

5.   *Restitution-based theories of recovery under the Statute of Frauds.* Besides reliance-based justifications for contractual enforcement, restitution may also provide a basis for recovery by the non-breaching party in the face of a contract rendered unenforceable by the Statute of Frauds. As with the reliance-based theories, how can restitution justify an exception to the Statute of Frauds' clear command that oral contracts within the Statute are unenforceable?

6.   *Outright fraud.* Many courts allow a remedy based on the tort of fraud where the elements of that tort can be proved. One of the most common situations where courts allow a fraud-based recovery is where the defendant promised the plaintiff that an appropriate note or memorandum had been signed—"I put it in the mail last night." Some courts extend this remedy to situations where the defendant promised that she would sign an appropriate note or memorandum. The first such example can be explained on the basis of a classic estoppel in pais—not promissory estoppel. The second may raise an insurmountable burden of proof for the plaintiff—proof of an intent not to execute the promise at the time the promise was made. Promissory estoppel, on the other hand, can solve the second situation.

7.   *Exceptions to the writing requirement under UCC § 2–201.* The UCC provides four mechanisms by which a contract that would otherwise be unenforceable under the Statute of Frauds can be enforced. First, in contracts between merchants under UCC § 2–201(2), a merchant may be held liable under a written confirmation signed by the party seeking to enforce the

contract if the recipient fails to send a timely objection—see Section 4 below. Second, under UCC § 2–201(3)(a), a seller who makes a substantial beginning on the manufacture of specially manufactured goods for the buyer that cannot be sold elsewhere in the ordinary course of business may enforce the contract against the buyer despite the absence of a signed memorandum. Third, UCC § 2–201(3)(b) provides for the enforceability of a contract if the party to be charged admits in a pleading, testimony, or other statement before a court that a contract exists, although such a contract will only be enforceable to the extent of the quantity of goods admitted. Fourth, under UCC § 2–201(3)(c), a contract for the sale of goods is enforceable to the extent of any goods delivered and accepted or payment received and accepted. Although some courts have held that the list of exceptions under UCC § 2–201(2) and (3) is exclusive—thus prohibiting any recovery under theories of estoppel—the UCC does specifically provide in § 1–103 (2001) that the UCC should be supplemented by principles of equity, including estoppel. See Joseph M. Perillo, Calamari and Perillo on Contracts § 19.48 at 801 (5th ed. 2003).

4. MERCHANT'S EXCEPTION

Karl Llewellyn, as a principal author of the UCC, was of the view that the Statute of Frauds law was, to some extent, out of step with business practice. One of the results of this thinking was the addition of subsection (2) to the UCC Statute of Frauds § 2–201:

> Between merchants if within a reasonable time a writing in confirmation of the contract and sufficient against the sender is received and the party receiving it has reason to know its contents, it satisfies the requirements of subsection (1) against such party unless written notice of objection to its contents is given within ten days after it is received.

Prior to the enactment of this subsection, the party sending the "confirmation" would be bound (since this would be a sufficient "note or memorandum"), but the receiver would not. The new subsection changed this result by providing that, among merchants, the transmission of a written "confirmation" of the oral contract, which is in a form binding on the sender, becomes binding on the receiver if not objected to within ten days of receipt. In other words, the memorandum from the sender becomes binding as the receiver's memorandum in the absence of timely objection.

Case law, including the case that follows, has made it plain that an oral agreement must have been reached in fact prior to the sending of such a "confirmation" for that confirmation to become binding on the receiver. Were this not the case, a merchant could initiate contact with a "confirmation" and then claim that a contract was entered into if there was no timely objection. Such a result would violate the basic contract law assumption that commitment results from the acceptance of an offer. As a general rule, an offeror cannot force the addressee to take action in order to avoid being found to have entered into a binding contract. Thus, fundamental to the application of the merchant's exception is a finding that an oral agreement preceded the issuance by one of the parties of a "confirmation" notice. See UCC § 2–201, *cmt.* 3. Needless to say, this "merchant's exception" is not found in the common law. Since the CISG lacks any Statute of Frauds provision, there is no express "merchant's exception" to be found there. See William S. Dodge, "Teaching the CISG in Contracts," 50 J. Legal Educ. 72–73 (2000).

Determining when and under what circumstances a writing constitutes such a "confirmation" has challenged a number of courts. See Dodge, *supra,* at 74 and the cases cited in footnote 10 to that article. See also Gregory Scott Crespi, "Is a Signed Offer Sufficient to Satisfy the Statute of Frauds?," 80 N.D. L. Rev. 1 (2004). As you read the following case, consider the substantial risks of unfairness and surprise created by some readings of the merchant's exception of UCC § 2–201(2). Is the type of writing envisioned by UCC § 2–201(1) sufficiently specific to justify depriving a party when she fails to recognize a "confirmation" and make a timely objection? Of the statute of fraud defense? Or, should the confirmation provide the receiving merchant with a more explicit notice or warning regarding its nature and the opportunity of the recipient to reject? See Janet L. Raimondo, "U.C.C. § 2–201(2)—A Search for a Just Interpretation: *Bazak International Corp. v. Mast Industries,*" 64 St. John's L. Rev. 181, 183, 193 (1989).

HARVEST RICE, INC. V. FRITZ AND MERTICE LEHMAN ELEVATOR AND DRYER, INC.

Supreme Court of Arkansas
365 Ark. 573, 231 S.W.3d 720 (2006)

JIM GUNTER, Justice.

Appellant, Harvest Rice, Inc., appeals an order from the Desha County Circuit Court granting summary judgment in favor of appellee, Fritz and Mertice Lehman Elevator and Dryer, Inc. d/b/a Lehman Elevator. The circuit court dismissed appellant's breach-of-contract action on the basis that its buyer report did not satisfy the merchant's exception to the Arkansas Statute of Frauds, pursuant to Ark.Code Ann. § 4–2–201(2) (Repl.2001). We reverse and remand the circuit court's ruling.

Prior to April 1, 2003, Harvest, who is in the business of buying, selling, and milling rice, orally negotiated to purchase 67,500 hundredweights of rough rice from Lehman, a grain elevator in Gillett, at $5.10 per hundredweight plus shipping costs for delivery to Harvest's place of business in McGehee by May 31, 2003. Gerald Loyd, a principal Harvest employee, negotiated with Park Eldridge, a co-owner of Lehman. On April 1, 2003, following the negotiations, Loyd faxed a buyer report to Eldridge containing the quantity, price, date of delivery, and other terms. According to Mr. Eldridge's deposition testimony, he did not see the faxed copy of the buyer report until several days later because his fax machine was out of paper. On April 15, 2003, Mr. Eldridge faxed a letter to Harvest, objecting to the terms of the buyer report and informing Harvest that he would be unable to make the sale of rice at the desired levels. Harvest made a demand upon Lehman to perform, but Lehman did not do so. There is no signed, written contract between Harvest and Lehman.

On May 5, 2003, Harvest filed a complaint, alleging breach of contract, and prayed for damages in the amount of cost, or, in the alternative, the difference in market price at the time appellant learned of the breach. Lehman filed an answer and counterclaim on May 22, 2003, pleading the affirmative defenses of the Statute of Frauds, waiver, estoppel, set off, and a failure to mitigate damages. On January 26, 2004, Lehman filed a motion for partial summary judgment, arguing that there was never an oral contract, and if there were, it violated the Arkansas Statute of Frauds and was unenforceable as a matter of law. On February 24, 2004, Harvest filed a response and cross-motion for summary judgment, arguing that a failure to deliver the agreed-upon quantities constituted a breach rather than a repudiation of the contract. Harvest sought damages in the amount of $91,125.00 as a result of the alleged breach.

On March 6, 2005, the circuit court entered an order, granting Lehman's motion for summary judgment and dismissing Harvest's complaint with prejudice, ruling that the buyer report did not have clear, confirmatory language that is required to sustain the merchants' exception under Ark.Code Ann. § 4–2–201(2). From this order, Harvest now brings its appeal.

For its sole point on appeal, Harvest argues that the circuit court erred as a matter of law in finding that the buyer report did not constitute a writing in confirmation of a contract because it lacked emblematic contractual language. Specifically, Harvest makes three allegations of error. First, there is no requirement that a writing in confirmation of a contract contain clear, confirmatory language. Second, the buyer report in this case contains language that confirms an oral contract. Finally, the seller signature line on the buyer report does not affect the document's status as a writing in confirmation of a contract.

In response, Lehman argues that the circuit court correctly found that the buyer report was not a writing in confirmation of a contract under the merchant's exception of Ark.Code Ann. § 4–2–201(2). Specifically, Lehman contends that the buyer's report lacked clear, confirmatory language referencing a previous oral agreement with Harvest.

Our standard of review for summary judgment cases is well established. . . . Summary judgment should only be granted when it is clear that there are no genuine issues of material fact to be litigated, and the moving party is entitled to judgment as a matter of law. . . . The purpose of summary judgment is not to try the issues, but to determine whether there are any issues to be tried. . . .

With this standard of review in mind, we turn to the present case. Under Arkansas's Statute of Frauds, a "contract for the sale of goods for the price of five hundred dollars ($500) or more is not enforceable by way of action or defense unless there is some writing sufficient to indicate that a contract for sale has been made between the parties and signed by the party against whom enforcement is sought . . . [.]"Ark.Code Ann. § 4–2–201(1) (Repl.2001). The merchants' exception, found at Ark.Code Ann. § 4–2–201, provides in pertinent part:

> (2) Between merchants if within a reasonable time a writing in confirmation of the contract and sufficient against the sender is received and the party receiving it has reason to know its contents, it satisfies the requirements of subsection (1) against such party unless written notice of objection to its contents is given within ten (10) days after it is received.

Id.

The question of whether a writing constitutes a confirmation of an oral agreement sufficient to satisfy the Statute of Frauds is a question of law for the court. *General Trading International, Inc. v. Wal-Mart Stores, Inc.,* 320 F.3d 831, 835–36. . . . In *Wal-Mart,* the Eighth Circuit said that the confirmatory writing still must satisfy the dictates of section 4–2–201(2) in that it must be "sufficient to indicate . . . the consummation of a contract, not mere negotiations." *Id.* at 836. The Eighth Circuit in *Wal-Mart* held that an e-mail from a seasonal buyer at Wal-Mart failed "sufficiently to indicate the formation or existence of any agreement between the parties" and was devoid of "any language concerning an agreement on the issue of $200,000 for markdowns [on seasonal vine reindeer]." *Id.* The circuit court concluded that "the language in the email does not constitute a sufficient writing for purposes of the statute of frauds because it does not evince any agreement between the parties on price markdowns." *Id.* at 836–37 (quoting *R.S. Bennett & Co. v. Econ. Mech. Indus.,* 606 F.2d 182, 186 (7th Cir.1979)) (a section 2–201(2) writing must "indicate [ ] that the parties have already made a deal or reached an agreement" (applying Illinois U.C.C.)). The circuit court further noted that both parties agreed that courts require an unequivocal objection to a confirmatory writing alleging an oral agreement. *Id.* at 837 . . .). The *Wal-Mart* court held that reply e-mails from the reindeer vendor constituted an unequivocal objection because they contained different terms and demands for payment. *Id.*

Harvest contends that the prior negotiations via cell phone between Mr. Loyd and Mr. Eldridge constituted an agreement and that the buyer report faxed on April 1 was a confirmatory writing contemplated by the merchants' exception. However, Lehman asserts that Harvest's buyer report is merely an offer that Lehman did not accept.

We agree with Harvest's position. Here, unlike the e-mail messages in *Wal-Mart, supra,* Harvest's buyer report is "sufficient to indicate . . . the consummation of a contract, not mere negotiations." *Id.* at 836. The buyer report contains the following terms: (1) the seller, Lehman, (2) the buyer, Gerald Loyd for Harvest, (3) the variety and grade of rice, (4) the quantity of rice, (5) the price of $5.33 per hundredweight, including costs, (6) the ship date of May 31, 2003, (6) [sic] the term of weekly payments, (7) the number of loads as 122 loads, (8) the date at which the overdue storage charges commence, (9) additional terms in the "Additional Comments" section, and (10) a handwritten note by Mr. Loyd, which reads, "Thank You Park." Thus, the specificity of Harvest's buyer report is distinguishable from the e-mail in *Wal-Mart, supra,* that merely stated, "I'm going to change the reserve on the account to $600,000 [up from $400,000] and will release the rest of the payment." *Wal-Mart,* 320 F.3d at 836. Harvest's buyer report on its face appears to evince a prior oral agreement between Harvest and Lehman. Therefore, we hold that, as a matter of law, the buyer report satisfies the merchants' exception as a "writing in confirmation of the contract," pursuant to Ark.Code Ann. § 4–2–201(2), for purposes of removing the alleged contract from the Arkansas Statute of Frauds.

We consistently have stated that the purpose of summary judgment is not to try the issue but to determine if there are issues to be tried. . . . If fair-minded persons differ about the conclusion to be drawn or if inconsistent hypotheses might reasonably have been drawn from the supporting testimony, a summary judgment should have been denied. . . . Here, we conclude that the issue of whether an agreement had, in fact, been reached would be for the jury to decide upon remand. *See* Ark.Code Ann. § 4–2–201. Based upon the foregoing conclusions, as well as our standard of review in summary-judgment cases, we hold the circuit court erred in granting summary judgment. Accordingly, we reverse and remand for trial.

Reversed and remanded.

NOTES AND QUESTIONS

1.   *Was the existence of a concluded oral agreement prior to the issuance of the "confirmation" established?* Why did the court remand for further findings regarding the existence of a contract after concluding that the merchant exception applied? In other words, what is the proper relationship between a court's analysis under § 2–201(2) and the question of whether the parties entered an oral contract for the sale of goods?

2.   *Does proof of the preexisting oral agreement solve the issue of fair notice to the receiver?* The seller in this case claimed that it did not receive the

April 1 fax of the buyer report because the seller's fax machine ran out of paper. If true, does this lack of notice—and therefore a lack of any ability to object to the supposed "written confirmation"—create problems of injustice? What arguments can you raise that might alleviate such justice concerns?

3.   *Should fair notice to the receiver of the fact that the writing constitutes a "confirmation" be required?* The *Harvest Rice* court and the Eighth Circuit in the *General Trading International, Inc. v. Wal-Mart Stores, Inc.* case discussed therein both held that the written confirmation need only be "sufficient to indicate the consummation of a contract, not mere negotiations." See also Bazak Intern. Corp. v. Mast Indus., 535 N.E.2d 633 (1989) ("in determining whether writings are confirmatory documents within UCC 2–201(2), neither explicit words of confirmation nor express references to the prior agreement are required, and the writings are sufficient so long as they afford a basis for believing that they reflect a real transaction between the parties."). In contrast, several courts have held that the writing must clearly indicate that it is a "confirmation" of the oral agreement. Which position better represents the likely understandings of persons engaged in commercial transactions?

4.   *Was the "confirmation" ambiguous?* Given the consequence of the receipt of such a notice without timely objection, some courts have held that the nature of the writing as a "confirmation" should be clear and not ambiguous. Was the "confirmation" in the above case "ambiguous"?

CHAPTER 7

CONTRACTS UNENFORCEABLE BY ELECTION: REGULATING THE AGREEMENT PROCESS

■ ■ ■

A. INTRODUCTION

Even when the parties have formed a contract through expression of apparent assent supported by a theory of legal obligation such as consideration, one or more parties may be able to avoid the legal relations created by the contract. Unlike "void" or "unenforceable" contracts discussed in the previous chapter, such contracts are referred to as "voidable" contracts and are enforceable unless a party with the power of avoidance elects to exercise that power. See Restatement (Second) of Contracts § 7 ("A voidable contract is one where one or more parties have the power, by a manifestation of election to do so, to avoid the legal relations created by the contract, or by ratification of the contract to extinguish the power of avoidance."). While one of the parties holds the power to avoid the contract, the other party is subject to a correlative liability in that the power holder has the ability to alter the existing legal relations between the parties, and the liability holder has no legal capacity to resist that change in relations. See Wesley Newcomb Hohfeld, "Some Fundamental Legal Conceptions as Applied in Judicial Reasoning," 23 Yale L.J. 16, 44–54 (1913) (describing powers as the ability to alter legal relations between two parties and liabilities as being subject to having one's legal relations altered by the exercise of a power).

For example, as discussed later in this chapter, the infancy doctrine provides that an infant may incur only voidable contracts. If a car dealer contracts to sell a car on credit to a 15-year-old "infant," the contract terms create a set of rights, duties, privileges, and immunities in the parties— convey the car, pay for the car, freely use the car, do not dispossess the buyer of the car, etc.—for as long as the contract remains in force. But, during the term of the contract and the parties' performances, the infancy doctrine also creates in the infant a power to avoid the contract at any time before the infant's 18th birthday (or a reasonable time thereafter). This power of avoidance means that the infant power holder has the ability to alter the legal relations between the parties at any time by avoiding the contract. Correlatively, the car dealer remains under a liability to have the contract's rights, duties, privileges, and no-rights stripped away if the infant chooses to exercise the power of avoidance.

The power of ratification or affirmance necessarily accompanies the power of avoidance in most situations. Since a voidable contract is an enforceable contract, it continues in force unless the power to avoid is properly exercised. In contrast, the power of ratification extinguishes any future power to avoid. See Restatement (Second) of Contracts § 8. In Hohfeldian terms, the power to ratify implies a correlative liability on the other party, since affirmance of the contract extinguishes the other party's liability for potential avoidance of the contract. Thus, in the infancy example above, the infant has a power to affirm or ratify the contract by failing to exercise the power of avoidance within a reasonable time after reaching the age of majority. Exercise of this power is a one-time event— the infant cannot later change its mind and attempt to avoid the contract.

The power of avoidance implicates the final set of Hohfeldian correlatives: immunity and disability. See Wesley Newcomb Hohfeld, "Some Fundamental Legal Conceptions as Applied in Judicial Reasoning," 23 Yale L. J. 13, 55 (1913). As Hohfeld described in summarizing the relationship between rights, powers, privileges, and immunities:

> [A] power bears the same general contrast to an immunity that a right does to a privilege. A right is one's affirmative claim against another, and a privilege is one's freedom from the right or claim of another. Similarly, a power is one's affirmative "control" over a given legal relation as against another; whereas immunity is one's freedom from the legal power or "control" of another as regards some legal relation. Id.

With respect to many defenses creating a power of avoidance, the power holder also possesses immunity against attempts by the subject party to control or alter the legal relations between the parties. Thus, in the infancy situation discussed above, the infant possesses the dual powers of avoidance and ratification that subject the car dealer to the liability that the infant will alter the legal relations between the parties by exercising one of its powers. On the other hand, the infant is immune to similar attempts by the dealer to alter the parties' legal relations. In other situations, such as with the defense of mutual mistake, both parties may possess a power of avoidance without a corresponding immunity/disability jural relationship.

With that background, the central concerns of this chapter are the factors that create the power of avoidance and the consequences associated with a proper exercise of that power. These grounds serve an important policy function in contract law because the power of avoidance may be, and most often is, exercised in the absence of a breach of the contract by the other party. If for any reason the power to avoid is not properly exercised, it will be extinguished. The contract will be ratified and fully enforceable. The party holding the power to avoid will be required to perform, and a failure to do so will constitute a breach. Accordingly, perhaps the most important reason to carefully consider the grounds for proper exercise of the power of avoidance is to establish a method to eliminate the other party's right to otherwise enforce the contract by way of breach and a breach remedy against the party holding the power of avoidance.

Equally compelling, absent ratification of the contract, the power of avoidance may be exercised either before or after performance by either or both parties. When exercised before performance, avoidance is normally asserted as a defense or "shield" against enforcement of the contract and especially to immunize the power holder from the other party's pursuit of a remedy for breach. Since the power holder may either avoid or ratify the contract, a conscious choice must be made to determine whether the power holder values the performance of the other party more than avoiding its own performance. If the former, the power holder elects to ratify. If the latter, the power holder elects to avoid.

For example, suppose B, a real estate developer, and A, a prospective buyer, enter into a contract for the sale of a five-acre parcel of land ideally suited to A's requirements. To induce A to enter the contract, B falsely warrants A that the common road for the development has been plotted and is being constructed along the western border of the parcel. In fact, the common road has been plotted and is being constructed through the middle of A's parcel. Upon discovery of the misrepresentation, A may choose to exercise the power of avoidance if the severance of the parcel substantially diminishes its value to A. If A is successful in exercising the power, the contract would be rescinded, and A would receive restitution damages. On the other hand, if the placement of the road does not substantially affect A's enjoyment of the land, A may choose instead to affirm the contract and sue for damages for the breach of warranty, claiming expectancy damages likely measured by the difference between the value promised and the value received.

Where the power of avoidance is exercised after partial or full performance by either of the parties, the decision to avoid or ratify necessarily implicates further consequences to the parties. As discussed below, the exercise of the power to avoid has the normative effect of canceling or rescinding the contract, thus requiring each party to restore the other party to the *status quo ante* existing before the contract was formed. Generally, each party must return to the other the exact consideration received or the monetary equivalent. Since, once cancelled, the contract no longer exists, the legal form of the bilateral obligation to return consideration is cast in terms of the law of restitution. Since each ground for rescission and trailing restitution has developed under a unique history, the relative restitution obligations remain in flux in many states.

As mentioned, the power holder often has no breach remedy against the other party, particularly where the other party has fully and perfectly performed. So, the proper exercise of the power to avoid may be the power holder's exclusive defense to a breach of contract action by the other party where the power holder does not intend to perform. In these cases, the power is exercised as a "shield" in defense to the other party's breach of contract action.

In other cases where the power holder has partially or fully performed, the exercise of the power may nonetheless be exercised to avoid or rescind the contract again requiring *status quo ante* restitution. In these cases, the power is exercised as a "sword" in the form of a specific action to rescind the contract in order to trigger trailing *status quo ante* restitution. Because the relative restitution rights of the parties depends on balancing the equities of each particular case, using rescission as a sword rather than a shield might decrease the equitable position of the power holder. For example, since equity generally requires the party seeking an equitable action to begin the action with clean hands—i.e., without having engaged in his or her own wrongdoing—will this aspect be important if the power holder is not in a position to return the consideration in its original form or equivalent value?

Of course, if only one party holds the power of avoidance, that party may also choose to ratify the contract. If so, the failure to perform by the other party is a breach of the contract. Interestingly, and as further explored in Chapter 9, the material uncured breach of the other party also creates an independent ground for rescinding the contract. A material and uncured breach (usually referred to as a "total breach") presents the injured party with a choice quite similar to the one existing in favor of the holder of a power of avoidance. The total breach entitles the injured party to bring either (i) an equitable action to terminate or cancel the contract (Restatement (Second) of Contracts § 373) and seek the quasi-contractual restitution remedy for any benefit conferred on the other party; or (ii) a legal action to enforce the contract itself either through an action for damages on the contract (Restatement (Second) of Contracts § 346) or specific performance of the contract where money damages are inadequate (Restatement (Second) of Contracts § 357). The second alternative actions on the contract are explored in Chapter 9, whereas the first alternative actions to rescind the contract are discussed in this chapter. Mostly, because monetary damages for breach of the contract normally exceed the restitutionary benefit conferred on the breaching party, damages on the contract are preferred. In the rare cases discussed in Chapter 9, the alternative rescission and restitution action is preferred where the benefit conferred is greater than damages on the contract.

In both cases, the presence of the power of avoidance and the other party's total breach present the holder with an elective choice or "election of remedies." Historically, remedies to "enforce the contract" by seeking monetary damages have been regarded as inconsistent with, and an alternative to, remedies to "rescind the contract" by seeking restitution as if the contract did not exist. The choice of one of the remedies might, therefore, preclude the other on the ground that only one of the remedies was elected. Likewise, a party holding the power of avoidance might be precluded from exercising that power by some action or inaction constituting ratification or affirmance. Accordingly, before exploring the grounds creating the power of avoidance, this chapter begins with a consideration of preclusion by election and affirmance. Importantly, however, the law continues to evolve in this area largely because of the consequences resulting from the merger of law and equity.

B. PRECLUSION BY AFFIRMATION OR ELECTION OF REMEDIES

While affirmation and election of remedies are doctrinally distinct, they remain consequentially linked. Thus, while the "election" to pursue a particular remedy "on the contract" may constitute affirmation of a voidable contract, that same conduct may also constitute an election to preclude pursuit of an inconsistent remedy relating to a contract that is not voidable. Accordingly, affirmation and election of remedies are related by preclusive effects, but each applies in different contexts. For example, affirmation has no relevance for determining the expectancy, reliance, and restitution damages interests discussed in Chapter 9 as remedies for breach of contract. In situations involving mere breach of contract, the nonbreaching party generally only has a choice of which damages interest to pursue as a remedy for the breach. At that point, and without additional facts and circumstances giving rise to a power of avoidance, the nonbreaching party's remedies arise solely within the contract. Consequently, the breached contracts addressed in Chapter 9 do not give rise to any power of affirmation, only an election regarding which of several remedies the injured party will pursue.

1. PRECLUSION BY AFFIRMATION OF A VOIDABLE CONTRACT

A contract is voidable only if one or more of the parties have the power to avoid the legal relations created by the contract by manifesting an election to do so. The power may be extinguished by ratification of the contract. Restatement (Second) of Contracts § 7. Since the exercise of the power to avoid or ratify is not based on the intent of the power holder or the detrimental reliance of the other party, unintended and often unjust consequences may occur in connection with the power.

Modern law provides that a voidable contract generally may not be avoided in part. Restatement (Second) of Contracts § 383. The entire contract must be avoided, including any part already performed. This rule prevents the power holder from avoiding any disadvantageous aspects of the contract while ratifying any advantageous parts. While modern contract law applies the no partial avoidance rule to all voidable contracts, earlier law generally applied the prohibition only to contracts voidable by reason of fraud or misrepresentation. Restatement (First) of Contracts § 487. The only exception relates to divisible contracts where a single contract can be divided into separate parts where the parties' exchange agreed equivalents as to the same part. Restatement (Second) of Contracts § 240. Where both parties have fully performed with regard to a "divisible portion," the power holder may avoid either the entire contract or the remaining divisible portions. Restatement (Second) of Contracts § 383 & Restatement (Second) of Contracts § 240 (divisible performance pairing). Of course, in some situations the parties may have a relationship that involves a series of separate agreements. The rule does not preclude avoiding only one of two entirely separate contracts. Restatement (Second) of Contracts § 383 *cmt. a.*

Most commonly, a party holding the power of avoidance may extinguish that power (thus creating an Hohfeldian immunity in the other party and a correlative disability in the power holder) by manifesting an intention to the other party to continue with the contract. Restatement (Second) of Contracts § 380(1). Such a manifestation constitutes an "affirmance" and has the effect of ratifying the contract. Accordingly, a promise to affirm an otherwise voidable duty is binding. Restatement (Second) of Contracts § 85.

Even absent an express promise, a party holding a power of avoidance may affirm a voidable contract by undertaking any act with respect to anything received from the other party that is inconsistent with disaffirmance. Restatement (Second) of Contracts § 380(1). This generally occurs when the power holder exercises dominion and control over what has been received from the other party, as if the power holder were the owner of that property. Restatement (Second) of Contracts § 380 *cmt. b.* A similar rule exists in the context of the sale of goods where acceptance may be deemed to occur when the buyer commits any act inconsistent with seller's ownership. See UCC § 2–606(1)(c). Because the power of avoidance is triggered by the other party's conduct in connection with the bargaining process, the power is not extinguished while that conduct continues. Restatement (Second) of Contracts § 380 *cmt. b.* For example, a minor has the power to avoid a contract, and that power cannot be extinguished, even by affirmative ratification of the contract, until the minor becomes of legal age to contract. For similar reasons, if the bargaining defect is not known, the power to avoid cannot be extinguished until the party with the power learns of the defect. For example, in the case of a mistake, the power holder cannot extinguish the power until after the mistake is discovered. Restatement (Second) of Contracts § 380(2).

The power holder may also trigger affirmance through the inconsistent dominion rule by failing to tender a return of the consideration received in the exchange in connection with a declaration of disaffirmance. If the other party rejects the return, the power holder has a lien on the consideration received to extent that the other party refuses to return the power holder's consideration. After a reasonable time, the power holder can dispose of the other party's consideration and credit the proceeds against the consideration furnished but not yet returned by the other party. Restatement (Second) of Contracts § 380(3).

In addition to affirmative acts, including a promise to affirm and exercising dominion and control over the consideration received, the power to avoid can be extinguished by mere delay. See Restatement (Second) of Contracts § 381; John M. Friedman, "Delay as a Bar to Rescission," 26 Cornell L. Q. 426 (1941); and Sol Goodell, Need Rescission Be Sought Within a Reasonable Time?, Tex. L. Rev. 342 (1929). Accordingly, the party holding the power to avoid must exercise that power within a reasonable time of when the power is created and known to exist. Restatement (Second) of Contracts §§ 381(1)–(2). Since the power to avoid is equitable in nature, it may also be lost where the parties have substantially performed and damages would adequately compensate the power holder. Restatement (Second) of Contracts § 381(2). Several factors are relevant in determining what period of time is reasonable: (i) whether the delay has entitled the power holder to speculate on the profitability of avoidance at the other party's expense; (ii) the extent that delay results in justified detrimental reliance by the other party or a third person; (iii) whether the ground for avoidance was created through the fault of the other party; and (iv) the extent to which the other party's conduct contributes to the delay. Restatement (Second) of Contracts § 381(3).

Once the power holder effectively exercises the power of avoidance, the election is normally irrevocable, and the power holder cannot thereafter affirm, unless of course the other party consents to the new affirmance. Restatement (Second) of Contracts § 382(1). In this respect, the rules relating to exercise of the powers of avoidance and of ratification in many ways resemble the rules governing the powers of acceptance, rejection, and revocation in the context of offer and acceptance. But in the case of the power to avoid or to ratify, if the other party refuses to recognize the election to avoid by refusing to accept a tender of the return of consideration, such refusal will be deemed consent to the later affirmance. Restatement (Second) of Contracts § 382(1). For purposes of this irrevocability rule, the power holder is not "deemed" to exercise the power to avoid (regardless of whether actual avoidance has been otherwise manifested) until the power holder (i) receives a return of consideration; (ii) obtains a final judgment on the exercise of the power to avoid; or (iii) the other party materially relied on the prior disaffirmance. Restatement (Second) of Contracts § 382(3). Thus, while a rejection is said to remove an offer from any possible future acceptance, an exercise of the power of avoidance may not be fully effective until the completion of some additional act by the other party or by a court.

2. PRECLUSION BY ELECTION OF REMEDIES

Generally, a party with the power of avoidance has no duty to perform while the power to avoid remains active. Restatement (Second) of Contracts § 385(1) ("Unless an offer to restore performance received is a condition of avoidance, a party has no duty of performance while his power of avoidance exists."). As the restatement suggests, in some cases proper exercise of the power of avoidance requires that the power holder tender or attempt to return the consideration received from the other party. See id. If such a tender of the original consideration is required, then the power holder may have to pay damages for nonperformance, unless that party tenders return of the consideration before the power of avoidance is terminated. Restatement (Second) of Contracts § 385(2) ("If an offer to restore performance received is a condition of avoidance, a duty to pay damages is terminated by such an offer made before the power of avoidance is lost."). In this way, modern law attempts to override the ancient differences discussed below between law and equity where law required a tender as a condition of an action for rescission (avoidance), while equity did not. D. Leslie Smith, "*Restitutio In Integrum* In Equitable Rescission," 17 U. N. B. L. J. 66, 69 (1967) (the court must do what is practically just). With the merger of law and equity, the tender condition is no longer important, at least in states that no longer follow the old common law rule. However, while this section concentrates on election of remedies—and thus differences between law and equity where the two have not merged—an important linkage to the avoidance section above remains. Even where a tender of consideration may no longer remain important as a condition to the exercise of a power of avoidance, recall that the mere retention of the consideration, coupled with the exercise of the dominion and control resembling that of an owner, may itself preclude avoidance. See Restatement (Second) of Contracts § 380(1).

However, beyond retention of consideration potentially constituting an affirmance of a voidable contract, the question remains whether, without more, the retention further constitutes some form of an implicit election to "waive" the right to sue for rescission to set aside the contract, thereby confining the party to an action to enforce the contract rather than set it aside. The remedies following each approach are quite different. Ordinarily, an action for rescission to set aside the contract is followed by restitution of consideration by each party to restore each to *status quo* before the contract was formed. Such *ex ante* remedies are dramatically different than actions to enforce a contract, normally by way of money damages designed to compensate the injured party for the other party's failure to perfectly perform (breach). In rare cases, where money damages are inadequate to compensate the injured party, equity might require specific performance by the breaching party of that party's contract obligations. The remedial concept triggered by the other party's breach is the subject of Chapter 9.

Modern contract law provides that if a party has more than one remedy (e.g., rescission and restitution or monetary damages), the choice to pursue one by suit or otherwise ordinarily does not bar a prayer in the alternative for the other relief. Restatement (Second) of Contracts § 378. But where the remedies are "inconsistent," and the other party materially changes its position in reliance upon the power holder's choice of remedy, such pleadings in the alternative are not permitted. Restatement (Second) of Contracts § 378. Generally, since restitution remedies are awarded when the contract is set aside, that remedy is considered "inconsistent" with remedies sought as if the contract was otherwise enforceable (money damages or specific performance). Restatement (Second) of Contracts § 378 *cmt. a.* Importantly, the mere election of remedies is not binding, even under modern law, unless and until the other party has materially changed position in reliance on the remedy pursued. For example, a breaching purchaser of real property might well conclude that an action for damages by the injured party will not require the return of the consideration itself (the real estate). If, after an action for money damages is filed by the injured seller, the breaching purchaser relies by making substantial improvements to the real estate, the modern rule would preclude the injured seller from pursuing other remedies, even if otherwise available. In such circumstances, the injured seller would be precluded from amending the complaint to add an alternative but inconsistent remedy of rescission (e.g., based on a voidable contract) and restitution. See Restatement (Second) of Contracts § 378 *cmt. a.* Otherwise, modern pleading rules generally allow inconsistent claims to be pled in alternative counts, at least provided recovery of one is uncertain. See Fed. Rule Civ. Proc. § 8(e)(2). Of course, duplicate recovery is not allowed. See Dan B. Dobbs, "Pressing Problems for the Plaintiff's Lawyer in Rescission: Election of Remedies and Restoration of Consideration," 26 Ark. L. Rev. 322, 324 (1972).

Assuming for the moment that an action to rescind is chosen, the restitution remedy to follow generally seeks to place the parties in their respective *status quo* before the contract was formed. A party seeking rescission of the contract by exercising the power of avoidance will not be granted restitution unless either that party returns or offers to return, conditional on reciprocal restitution, any consideration received or the court can assure such a balanced return when granting relief. Restatement (Second) of Contracts § 384(1). Logical exceptions exist when (i) the property was worthless when received or has been lost or stolen as a result of its own defects; or (ii) the property has been used or disposed of without knowledge of grounds for restitution provided justice requires compensation in its place. Restatement (Second) of Contracts § 384(2).

The older common law rule, however, lingers in many states and severely restricts the ability of a plaintiff to plead inconsistent relief. So a discussion of those rules remains instructive. Historically, and particularly before the merger of law and equity, a suit for damages was deemed an action to enforce the contract. In contrast, courts deemed a suit for restitution an election to terminate or cancel the contract. However communicated, the notice of termination or cancellation was traditionally referred to as "rescission" (a party's unilateral avoidance or unmaking of a contract for a legally sufficient reason). This reinforced an "election" of remedies of sorts, requiring the plaintiff to seek either contract damages for breach of the contract or quasi-contractual relief for restitution, but not both.

Also before the merger of law and equity, a rescission-related action could be brought either in law or equity. See W. A. Gardner, "The Difference Between an Action for Rescission and One Upon Rescission," 60 Cent. L. J. 384 (1905) and Charles C. Rodriguez, "Return of Benefits as a Prerequisite to Contracts Rescission," 15 Wash. & Lee L. Rev. 113 (1958). In order to maintain a proper law action "on rescission" ("legal rescission"), the plaintiff was required to give notice to the defendant that the contract was being terminated, tender the consideration received from the defendant, and demand a return of the consideration transferred to the defendant. Restatement (Second) of Contracts § 384 *cmt. b.* If the defendant voluntarily complied, the parties were essentially returned to the *status quo ante*—the relative situations of the parties before their contract. If the defendant refused, the plaintiff's law action was "not for rescission of the contract," but simply to obtain restitution in the form of a return of the consideration transferred to the defendant. Since restitution is equitable in nature, the plaintiff had to make a prior tender to avoid the defendant's equitable argument that it was unjust to force disgorgement when the defendant had no assurance of a return of consideration furnished by the defendant.

In contrast, a plaintiff seeking rescission in equity—"equitable rescission"—did not attempt such a prior unilateral rescission and tender. Rather, the equitable rescission action requested a court to decree a rescission. Such a judicial rescission normally required a return of considerations by both parties to bring each to a position of *status quo ante*. Usually, a court would refuse to make a decree of equitable rescission unless the plaintiff could demonstrate that the plaintiff could also restore the defendant's consideration. Because a successful equitable rescission action subjected both sides to simultaneous duties to return the other party's consideration, the legal rescission "tender requirement" did not apply. See Dan B. Dobbs, "Pressing Problems for the Plaintiff's Lawyer in Rescission: Election of Remedies and Restoration of Consideration," 26 Ark. L. Rev. 322, 341–344 (1972).

With the merger of law and equity, modern law has largely eliminated these formalistic distinctions and adopted the non-tender rule of equitable rescission. Nonetheless, as discussed in this chapter and in Chapter 5 in the materials on total or material breach, the grounds for seeking rescission are many and varied. The Uniform Commercial Code, in fact, dispensed with the term "rescission" entirely because it had too many meanings. Thus, UCC §§ 2–106(3)–(4) use the term "cancellation" to refer to bringing an end to the contract because of the breach by the other party, whereas "termination" refers to bringing an end to the contract for grounds other than breach. See Henry Gabriel, "The Seller's Election of Remedies Under the Uniform Commercial Code: An Expectation Theory," 23 Wake Forest L. Rev. 429 (1988).

In part, the simplification of the common law—relating to rescission and restitution and the UCC's rejection of "rescission" in favor of the cancellation and termination terminology—resulted from scholarly criticism of the unfairness of the ancient election rule that could create unjust consequences without regard to the specific intent of the party making a deemed election. See Charles P. Hine, "Election of Remedies, A Criticism," 26 Harv. L. Rev. 707 (1913); Amos S. Deinhard & Benedict S. Deinhard, "Election of Remedies," 6 Minn. L. Rev. 341 (1921) (Part I) & 6 Minn. L. Rev. 480 (1922) (Part II); George B. Fraser, "Election of Remedies: An Anachronism," 29 Ok. L. Rev. 1 (1976); and Les Mendelsohn, "Election of Remedies and Settlement—New Lyrics to an Outworn Tune," 12 St. Mary's L. J. 367 (1980).

As you read and study these materials, you will learn that the approach of the Restatement (Second) of Contracts, and the common law, generally "restricts" the void category to relatively few categories, such as fraud in the execution and physical duress. But is this "all or nothing approach" appealing? If not, what criteria might you suggest to replace the existing paradigm? If a facts and circumstances test, what critical factors would you select to morph a voidable contract into a void contract?

C. LACK OF LEGAL CAPACITY OF ONE OF THE PARTIES

Common law has consistently provided that it is not possible for a person to make a contract with herself. See Restatement (First) Contracts § 15 *cmt. a.* There must be at least two parties to a contract, and the same party cannot even act in a representative capacity on one side and personally on the other. Restatement (Second) of Contracts § 9. For example, a trustee might make a promise on behalf of the trust to herself in her individual capacity, but such a contract would be considered "void." See Restatement (First) Contracts § 15, illus. 2.

Modern law adopts a different view. Where the contract involves multiple parties in a special relationship such as a fiduciary relationship, modern law tends to characterize the resulting contract as "voidable" rather than "void." Accordingly, the contract is enforceable unless the transaction is not on fair terms and each party did not know all the material facts. Thus, a contract between a fiduciary and a beneficiary is voidable unless on fair terms and the beneficiary was aware of all relevant facts. See Restatement (Second) of Contracts § 173.

Persons are presumed to have the capacity to enter a contract. Restatement (Second) of Contracts § 12(2). In this sense, the term "capacity" means the legal capacity to incur at least voidable contractual duties. Restatement (Second) of Contracts § 12(1). Perhaps not surprisingly, the shifting boundaries of legal capacity to contract demonstrate a continually evolving political dynamic as various status groups within society were first denied the ability to contract, but later acquired that legal capacity in conjunction with the development of greater political rights overall. This development became particularly pronounced beginning with the American Industrial Revolution and later periods of development of the industrial economy in the late-nineteenth and early-twentieth centuries. The connection between greater contract rights and greater political power follows naturally from the fact that the ability to contract is critically linked to the power to acquire, own, and dispose of property.

Under the common law as it existed for much of the nineteenth century, a married woman generally could not legally contract with her husband or with third parties, could not convey real or personal property to or from her husband, and could not acquire or dispose of property to or from third parties without her husband's consent. See W. A. Coutts, "The Rule That a Married Woman Can Only Make Such Contracts as Relate to Her Separate Estates: Surveyed and Analyzed," 47 Cent. L. J. 363 (1898). Without the capacity to enter legally binding contracts, married women could not engage in business or sue or be sued without joinder of their husbands. As a result, common law regarded the husband and wife as one person, and the marriage resulted in the "civil death" of the married woman. Also, a married woman was required to render obedience, domestic service, and submission to her husband, much like a vassal to a lord. While equity often allowed a married woman a separate equitable estate, true reform relied upon nineteenth-century adoption of state Married Women's Property Acts. See Peggy A. Rabkin, "The Origins of Law Reform: The

Social Significance of the Nineteenth-Century Codification Movement and Its Contribution to the Passage of the Early Married Women's Property Acts," 24 Buff. L. Rev. 683 (1975). Although Arkansas is generally credited with the passage of the first such statute in 1835, the year 1848 is commonly thought of as a watershed year for women's rights, as that year saw both the Seneca Falls Convention (declaring that all men and women are created equal) and New York state's adoption of its Married Women's Property Act. Richard H. Chused, "Married Women's Property Law: 1800–1850," 71 Geo. L. J. 1359 (1983). For important insight into similar coverture rules applicable to foreign women married to American men, see Janet M. Calvo, "Spouse-Based Immigration Laws: The Legacies of Coverture,"28 San Diego L. Rev. 593 (1991).

While common law restricted the rights of married women to contract, many state statutory schemes actually restricted the rights of members of other disfavored status groups to make contracts. For example, before 1865 and the enactment of the Thirteenth Amendment when slavery was largely legalized, the Supreme Court determined in *Scott v. Sandford*, 60 U.S. (19 How.) 393 (1856), that the Constitution had not intended to include black slaves and their decedents as citizens or people. Accordingly, Dred Scott was neither a citizen nor a person. Whether emancipated or not, slaves owned only those rights specifically granted to them. As a result, slaves had no right to maintain or defend a lawsuit, or to own property. Slaves could contract only with the consent of their master, and various state "slave codes" rendered slave contracts executed without such consent void.

> XXXIII. . . . . *Be it enacted*, that no owner, master or mistress of any slave . . . shall permit or suffer any of his, her or their slaves to go and work . . . without a ticket in writing . . .

> XXXIV. And whereas several owners of slaves have permitted them to keep canoes, and to breed and raise horses, neat cattle and hogs, and to traffic and barter in several parts of this Province, for the particular and peculiar benefits of such slaves, by which means they have not only an opportunity of receiving and concealing stolen good, but to plot and confederate together, and form conspiracies dangerous to the peace and safety of the whole Province; *Be it therefore enacted* that it shall not be lawful for any slave so to buy, sell, trade, traffic, deal or barter for any goods or commodities, . . . nor shall any slave be permitted to keep any boat, pettiauger or canoe, or to raise and breed for the use and benefit of such slave, any horses, mares, neat cattle, sheep or hogs, under pain of forfeiting all the goods and commodities which shall be so bought, sold, traded, trafficked, dealt or bartered for, by any slave, . . . and it shall and may be lawful for any person . . . to seize and take away from any slave all such goods, commodities, boats, pettiaugers, canoes, horses, mares, neat cattle, sheep or

hogs . . . . An Act for the Better Ordering and Governing Negroes and other Slaves in this Province, 1740 S.C. Acts §§ 33, 34 at 163, 171 (reprinted in The First Laws of the State of South Carolina Part I (John. D. Cushing comp.)) (1981).

As with infants and the mentally infirm, such state laws were intended to "protect" slaves who were deemed incapable of exercising independent judgment. For an excellent description of this sordid period of history, see Anthony R. Chase, "Race, Culture, and Contract Law: From the Cottonfield to the Courtroom," 28 Conn. L. Rev. 1, 7–25 (1995). See also Blake D. Morant, "Law, Literature, and Contract: An Essay in Realism," 4 Mich. J. Race & L. 1 (1998) and Blake D. Morant, "The Relevance of Race and Disparity in Discussions of Contract Law," 31 New Eng. L. Rev. 669 (1997). Even fully emancipated African-Americans were often denied the capacity to contract. See Stephen A. Siegel, "The Federal Government's Power to Enact Color-Conscious Laws: An Originalist Inquiry," 92 Nw. U. L. Rev. 477 (1998). Even further, various state law "black codes" denied African-Americans the right to contract during the reconstruction period and Jim Crow era. See Donald H. Ziegler, "A Reassessment of the Younger Doctrine in Light of the Legislative History of Reconstruction," 1983 Duke L. J. 987; Peter W. Scroth, "Corruption and Accountability of the Civil Service in the United States," 54 Am. J. Comp. L. 553, 558 (2006). Other forms remained for some time. For example, closed-shop labor contracts under the original Wagner Act did not include anti-discrimination provisions, thereby effectively banning many African-Americans from obtaining union jobs. See Cheryl I. Harris, "Whitewashing Race: Scapegoating Culture," 94 Cal. L. Rev. 907 (2006).

Other immigrant classes also suffered broad discrimination against their legal capacity. For example, President Arthur signed the Chinese Exclusion Act of 1882, for the first time barring immigrants from entry to the United States based on nationality. Kitty Calavita, "Collisions at the Intersection of Gender, Race, and Class: Enforcing the Chinese Exclusion Laws," 40 Law & Soc'y Rev. 249 (2006); Thomas Wuil Joo, "New 'Conspiracy Theory' of the Fourteenth Amendment: Nineteenth Century Chinese Civil Rights Cases and the Development of Substantive Due Process Jurisprudence," 29 U.S.F. L. Rev. 353 (1995). American Indians suffered a different form of contractual discrimination because of sovereign immunity granted to tribes. See, e.g., Ryan T. Koczera, "American Indian Law—Sovereign Immunity—Indian Tribes Enjoy Sovereign Immunity from Suits on Contracts, Whether Those Contracts Involve Governmental or Commercial Activities and Whether They Were Made On or Off a Reservation," 76 U. Det. Mercy L. Rev. 927 (1999); Katherine J. Florey, "Choosing Tribal Law: Why State Choice-of-Law Principles Should Apply to Disputes with Tribal Contacts," 55 Am. U. L. Rev. 1627 (2006).

The enactment of the Fourteenth Amendment in 1865 and similar state laws were the beginning of the end to many of these contractual discriminations that were in large part simply part of a broader pattern of discrimination. Nonetheless, notwithstanding the force of law for over 100 years, some argue that law alone will not cure discrimination without attitudinal, cultural, and moral adjustments. See Michael Selmi, "Was the Disparate Impact Theory a Mistake?," 53 UCLA L. Rev. 701 (2006).

What is clear from much of this dark history is that the power to acquire and dispose of property by contract was an inseparable right to full citizenship, if not basic constitutional liberty. The literature and scholarship in these areas are for too expansive to be explored here. Nonetheless, the connection between power, property, and contract ought to be apparent.

1. CONTRACTS WITH MINORS

Minors have long been limited in their capacity to enter binding contracts. Both Roman law and medieval law, for example, recognized that contracts made by minors were voidable at the option of the infant either when made or upon reaching the age of majority, albeit with some interspersed periods of uncertainty. See A. W. Brian Simpson, Common Law of Contract 540–542 (1975).

Under modern law, a natural person has full legal capacity to incur contractual duties unless that person is an "infant." Restatement (Second) of Contracts § 12(2)(b). Unless state law provides otherwise, an infant has the capacity to incur only voidable contractual duties until the beginning of the day before the person's eighteenth birthday, although in many states both men and women have full capacity upon marriage. Restatement (Second) of Contracts § 14 *cmt. a.* The justification for the age restriction is that unsophisticated infants might enter into foolish contracts with unscrupulous adults. Larry A. DiMatteo, "Deconstructing the Myth of the 'Infancy Law Doctrine': From Incapacity to Accountability,"21 Ohio N.U. L. Rev. 481 (1994). But the law has not always been static in this regard.

Importantly, infant contracts were not always voidable, but began life as void under nineteenth century American judicial history. But the harshness of the rule gradually changed at the turn of the twentieth century to allow honest minors to retain the benefits of the contract and forfeit voidability. See Larry A. DiMatteo, "Deconstructing the Myth of the 'Infancy Law Doctrine': From Incapacity to Accountability," 21 Ohio N.U. L. Rev. 481, 486 (1994). Under common law, the age of majority to contract was twenty-one, but states generally have lowered the age of majority for contract and for other purposes by statute. See Richard A. Lord, Williston on Contracts § 9:3 (1993). Roman law categorized infants as those under the age of seven with no right to contract independently, those in puberty with limited contractual rights, and those above puberty with full contract rights. See Melvin John Dugas, Comment, "The Contractual Capacity of Minors: A Survey of the Prior Law and the New Articles," 62 Tul. L. Rev. 745, 746 (1988). See also Simon Goodfellow, Note, "Who Gets the Better Deal?: A Comparison of the U.S. and English Infancy Doctrines," 29 Hastings Int'l & Comp. L. Rev. 135 (2005). Especially with the growth of the Internet and electronic commerce, both the ability of infants to contract and the age at which persons attain their majority for purposes of contracting have become increasingly important. Couple this growing importance with statutes making different age presumptions for different purposes, and a true quandary appears as a series of never ending unconnected dots of social struggle. See Rhonda Gay Hartman, "Adolescent Autonomy: Clarifying an Ageless Conundrum," 51 Hastings L. J. 1265 (2000). Many examples are listed and discussed in Larry Cunningham, "A Question of Capacity: Towards A Comprehensive and Consistent Vision of Children and Their Status Under Law," 10 U. C. Davis J. Juv. L. & Pol'y 275 (2006). For example, before the ratification of the Twenty-sixth Amendment in 1971 (lowering voting age to 18), minors below 21 were not able to vote in all states. The legal military draft age is 18. Federal law mandates as a condition of disbursement of federal highway funds to individual states that state legislatures adopt a minimum state drinking age of 21. Federal Firearms Licensees may not sell a handgun to anyone under 21, although in many states persons as young as 18 may legally purchase one in a sale by a private individual. *Roper v. Simmons*, 543 U.S. 551 (2005), held "juvenile death penalty" laws unconstitutional to the extent that they permit the death penalty for those committing crimes when under the age of 18 (the law in many states was previously 16). Minors are incapable of giving informed consent with respect to many activities of daily life without parental consent. See Vt. Stat. Ann. tit. 18 § 5142 (permitting marriage by 14-year-old minors with parental consent). On the other hand, a minor's right to obtain an abortion cannot be done conditioned on a parent's consent. Most children under the age of 18 may not make a will regardless of the extent of their wealth. While a parent has a duty to support a minor, most states have enacted emancipation exceptions where the child is capable of self-support.

While young adults have achieved many advances toward fully enfranchisement of political, social, and economic rights, many injustices remain. In most states, the actual capacity of the minor is irrelevant, as is the fairness of the bargain or even misrepresentation of age. Some states recognize that intentional misrepresentation of age constitutes a tort or a form of estoppel that may vitiate the minor's power to disaffirm. See Restatement (Second) of Contracts § 14 *cmt. f*; see also Larry A. DiMatteo, "Deconstructing the Myth of the 'Infancy Law Doctrine': From Incapacity to Accountability," 21 Ohio N.U. L. Rev. 481 (1994). Also, minors are often liable on contracts for necessaries, such as food, shelter, and clothing, although sellers and lessors may only sue for restitution of the value of such necessaries, not the contract price. Restatement (Second) of Contracts § 12 *cmt. f.*

Perhaps most controversial is the general rule that when infancy is asserted as a shield in a suit by the other party to enforce the contract, the infant's disaffirmance revests title to the property in the other party so long as the property still exists. But if the infant has dissipated the property, the other party has no further remedy. The risk of loss falls upon the other party. Restatement (Second) of Contracts § 14 *cmt. c.* A few states have restricted this rule by statute or case law requiring the minor to restore the consideration. Moreover, since a minor may exercise a power of avoidance, the minor may also exercise a power to affirm. A contract with a minor is affirmed when the minor either expressly affirms or fails to disaffirm the contract within a reasonable time after reaching the age of majority.

As might be expected, the dissipation rule is the most controversial. Upon proper disaffirmance, the majority rule—represented by the *Halbman* case below—places the risk of the dissipation upon the other party, regardless of whether the minor uses the infancy doctrine as a sword or a shield. Some jurisdictions, as discussed in the notes following *Halbman*, mitigate the harsh results of strict application of the dissipation rule when the minor brings suit using the infancy doctrine as a sword. This minority rule allocates risk depending upon whether the transaction itself was for credit or cash. In cash transactions, the minor would not be able to sue, retrieve the cash, and return damaged or depreciated purchased assets. But in a credit transaction, the minor could return damaged goods and simply refuse to pay for the property or the damage. Of course, services can never be returned. In reading the cases, try to decide which view you prefer from a matter of fairness and if your decision has anything to do with your independent views as to whether the infancy rule itself is sensible.

HALBMAN V. LEMKE

Supreme Court of Wisconsin
99 Wis.2d 241, 298 N.W.2d 562 (1980)

CALLOW, Justice.

On this review we must decide whether a minor who disaffirms a contract for the purchase of a vehicle which is not a necessity must make restitution to the vendor for damage sustained by the vehicle prior to the time the contract was disaffirmed. The court of appeals, 91 Wis. 2d 847, 282 N. W. 2d 638, affirmed the judgment in part, reversed in part, and remanded the cause to the circuit court for Milwaukee County, the Honorable Robert J. Miech presiding.

I.

[Eds.—James Halbman, a minor, contracted to purchase a 1968 Oldsmobile from Michael Lemke for $1250. At the time of purchase, Halbman paid $1,000 in cash, took possession of the car, and promised to pay $25 per week until the balance was paid. Five weeks later, after Halbman had paid a total of $1,100, the car suffered severe mechanical problems. Halbman took the car to a garage where it was repaired for $637.40, but Halbman refused to pay the garage. Halbman tendered the car title back to Lemke and disaffirmed the contract. The garage removed the engine and transmission and towed to car to Halbman's father's house, where it was vandalized and rendered unsalvageable. Halbman sued Lemke to demand return of the $1,100 he had paid toward the car. The trial court held for Halbman, and Lemke appealed that judgment.]

II.

The sole issue before us is whether a minor, having disaffirmed a contract for the purchase of an item which is not a necessity and having tendered the property back to the vendor, must make restitution to the vendor for damage to the property prior to the disaffirmance. Lemke argues that he should be entitled to recover for the damage to the vehicle up to the time of disaffirmance, which he claims equals the amount of the repair bill.

Neither party challenges the absolute right of a minor to disaffirm a contract for the purchase of items which are not necessities. That right, variously known as the doctrine of incapacity or the "infancy doctrine," is one of the oldest and most venerable of our common law traditions. See: Grauman, Marx & Cline Co. v. Krienitz, 142 Wis. 556, 560, 126 N. W. 50 (1910). . . . Although the origins of the doctrine are somewhat obscure, it is generally recognized that its purpose is the protection of minors from foolishly squandering their wealth through improvident contracts with crafty adults who would take advantage of them in the marketplace. . . . Thus it is settled law in this state that a contract of a minor for items which are not necessities is void or voidable at the minor's option. Id. at 23, 158 N. W. 2d 288. . . .

Once there has been a disaffirmance, however, as in this case between a minor vendee and an adult vendor, unresolved problems arise regarding the rights and responsibilities of the parties relative to the disposition of the consideration exchanged on the contract. As a general rule a minor who disaffirms a contract is entitled to recover all consideration he has conferred incident to the transaction. Schoenung v. Gallet, supra. In return the minor is expected to restore as much of the consideration as, at the time of disaffirmance, remains in the minor's possession. Thormaehlen v. Kaeppel, supra, 86 Wis. at 380, 56 N. W. 1089. . . . The minor's right to disaffirm is not contingent upon the return of the property, however, as disaffirmance is permitted even where such return cannot be made. Olson v. Veum, 197 Wis. 342, 345, 222 N. W. 233 (1928). . . .

The return of property remaining in the hands of the minor is not the issue presented here. In this case we have a situation where the property cannot be returned to the vendor in its entirety because it has been damaged and therefore diminished in value, and the vendor seeks to recover the depreciation. Although this court has been cognizant of this issue on previous occasions, we have not heretofore resolved it. See: Schoenung v. Gallet, supra, 206 Wis. at 57–58, 238 N. W. 852. . . .

The law regarding the rights and responsibilities of the parties relative to the consideration exchanged on a disaffirmed contract is characterized by confusion, inconsistency, and a general lack of uniformity as jurisdictions attempt to reach a fair application of the infancy doctrine in today's marketplace. See: Robert G. Edge, Voidability of Minors' Contracts: A Feudal Doctrine in a Modern Economy, 1 Ga. L. Rev. 205 (1967). . . . That both parties rely on this court's decision in Olson v. Veum, supra, is symptomatic of the problem.

In Olson a minor, with his brother, an adult, purchased farm implements and materials, paying by signing notes payable at a future date. Prior to the maturity of the first note, the brothers ceased their joint farming business, and the minor abandoned his interest in the material purchased by leaving it with his brother. The vendor initiated an action against the minor to recover on the note, and the minor (who had by then reached majority) disaffirmed. The trial court ordered judgment for the plaintiff on the note, finding there had been insufficient disaffirmance to sustain the plea of infancy. This court reversed, holding that the contract of a minor for the purchase of items which are not necessities may be disaffirmed even when the minor cannot make restitution. Lemke calls our attention to the following language in that decision:

> To sustain the judgment below is to overlook the substantial distinction between a mere denial by an infant of contract liability where the other party is seeking to enforce it and those cases where he who was the minor not only disaffirms such contract but seeks the aid of the court to restore to him that with which he has parted at the making of the contract. In the one case he is using his infancy merely as a shield, in the other also as a sword. 197 Wis. at 344, 222 N. W. 233.

From this Lemke infers that when a minor, as a plaintiff, seeks to disaffirm a contract and recover his consideration, different rules should apply than if the minor is defending against an action on the contract by the other party. This theory is not without some support among scholars. See Calamari and Perillo, The Law of Contracts, sec. 126, 207–09 (Hornbook Series 1970), treating separately the obligations of the infant as a plaintiff and the infant as a defendant.

Additionally, Lemke advances the thesis in the dissenting opinion by court of appeals Judge Cannon, arguing that a disaffirming minor's obligation to make restitution turns upon his ability to do so. For this proposition, the following language in Olson v. Veum, supra, 197 Wis. at 345, 222 N. W. 233, is cited:

> The authorities are clear that when it is shown, as it is here, that the infant cannot make restitution, then his absolute right to disaffirm is not to be questioned.

In this case Lemke argues that the Olson language excuses the minor only when restitution is not possible. Here Lemke holds Halbman's $1,100, and accordingly there is no question as to Halbman's ability to make restitution.

Halbman argues in response that, while the "sword-shield" dichotomy may apply where the minor has misrepresented his age to induce the contract, that did not occur here and he may avoid the contract without making restitution notwithstanding his ability to do so.

The principal problem is the use of the word "restitution" in Olson. A minor, as we have stated, is under an enforceable duty to return to the vendor, upon disaffirmance, as much of the consideration as remains in his possession. When the contract is disaffirmed, title to that part of the purchased property which is retained by the minor revests in the vendor; it no longer belongs to the minor. See Restatement (Second) of Contracts, sec. 18B, comment c, (Tent. Draft No. 1, 1964). The rationale for the rule is plain: a minor who disaffirms a purchase and recovers his purchase price should not also be permitted to profit by retaining the property purchased. The infancy doctrine is designed to protect the minor, sometimes at the expense of an innocent vendor, but it is not to be used to bilk merchants out of property as well as proceeds of the sale. Consequently, it is clear that, when the minor no longer possesses the property which was the subject matter of the contract, the rule requiring the return of property does not apply.[1] The minor will not be required to give up what he does not have.

---

[1] Although we are not presented with the question here, we recognize there is considerable disagreement among the authorities on whether a minor who disposes of the property should be made to restore the vendor with something in its stead. The general rule appears to limit the minor's responsibility for restoration to specie only. Terrace Company v. Calhoun, 37 Ill. App. 3d 757, 347 N. E. 2d 315, 320 (1976); Adamowski v. Curtiss-Wright Flying Service, 300 Mass. 281, 15 N. E. 2d 467 (1938); Quality Motors v. Hays, 216 Ark. 264, 225 S. W. 2d 326, 328 (1949). But see: Boyce v. Doyle, 113 N. J. Super. 240, 273 A. 2d 408 (1971), adopting a "status quo" theory which requires the minor to restore the pre-contract status quo, even if it means returning proceeds or other value; Fisher v. Taylor Motor Co., 249 N. C. 617, 107 S. E. 2d 94 (1959), requiring the minor to restore only the property remaining in the hands of the minor, " 'or account for so much of its value as may have been invested in other property which he has in hand or owns and controls.' " Id. at 97. Finally, some attention is given to the "New Hampshire Rule" or benefits theory which requires the disaffirming minor to pay for the contract to the extent he benefited from it. Hall v. Butterfield, 59 N. H. 354 (1879); Porter v. Wilson, 106 N. H. 270, 209 A. 2d 730 (1965). See also : 19 Hastings L. J. 1199, 1205–08 (1968); 52 Marq. L. Rev. 437 (1969); Calamari and Perillo, The Law of Contracts, secs. 129, 215–16 (Hornbook Series 1970).

We conclude that Olson does no more than set forth the foregoing rationale and that the word "restitution" as it is used in that opinion is limited to the return of the property to the vendor. We do not agree with Lemke and the court of appeals' dissent that Olson requires a minor to make restitution for loss or damage to the property if he is capable of doing so.

Here Lemke seeks restitution of the value of the depreciation by virtue of the damage to the vehicle prior to disaffirmance. Such a recovery would require Halbman to return more than that remaining in his possession. It seeks compensatory value for that which he cannot return. Where there is misrepresentation by a minor or willful destruction of property, the vendor may be able to recover damages in tort. See, e.g., Kiefer v. Fred Howe Motors, Inc., supra. . . . But absent these factors, as in the present case, we believe that to require a disaffirming minor to make restitution for diminished value is, in effect, to bind the minor to a part of the obligation which by law he is privileged to avoid. See: Nelson v. Browning, supra at 875–76. . . .

The cases upon which the petitioner relies for the proposition that a disaffirming minor must make restitution for loss and depreciation serve to illustrate some of the ways other jurisdictions have approached this problem of balancing the needs of minors against the rights of innocent merchants. In Barber v. Gross, 74 S. D. 254, 51 N. W. 2d 696 (1952), the South Dakota Supreme Court held that a minor could disaffirm a contract as a defense to an action by the merchant to enforce the contract but that the minor was obligated by a South Dakota statute, upon sufficient proof of loss by the plaintiff, to make restitution for depreciation. Cain v. Coleman, 396 S. W. 2d 251 (Tex. Civ. App. 1965), involved a minor seeking to disaffirm a contract for the purchase of a used car where the dealer claimed the minor had misrepresented his age. In reversing summary judgment granted in favor of the minor, the court recognized the minor's obligation to make restitution for the depreciation of the vehicle. The Texas court has also ruled, in a case where there was no issue of misrepresentation, that upon disaffirmance and tender by a minor the vendor is obligated to take the property "as is." Rutherford v. Hughes, 228 S. W. 2d 909, 912 (Tex. Civ. App. 1950). Scalone v. Talley Motors, Inc., 158 N. Y. S. 2d 615, 3 App. Div. 2d 674 (1957), and Rose v. Sheehan Buick, Inc., 204 So. 2d. 903 (Fla. App. 1967), represent the proposition that a disaffirming minor must do equity in the form of restitution for loss or depreciation of the property returned. Because these cases would at some point force the minor to bear the cost of the very improvidence from which the infancy doctrine is supposed to protect him, we cannot follow them.

As we noted in Kiefer, modifications of the rules governing the capacity of infants to contract are best left to the legislature. Until such changes are forthcoming, however, we hold that, absent misrepresentation or tortious damage to the property, a minor who disaffirms a contract for the purchase of an item which is not a necessity may recover his purchase price without liability for use, depreciation, damage, or other diminution in value.

Recently the Illinois Court of Appeals came to the same conclusion. In Weisbrook v. Clyde C. Netzley, Inc., 58 Ill. App. 3d 862, 374 N. E. 2d 1102 (1978), a minor sought to disaffirm a contract for the purchase of a vehicle which developed engine trouble after its purchase. In the minor's action the dealer counterclaimed for restitution for use and depreciation. The court affirmed judgment for the minor and, with respect to the dealer's claim for restitution, stated:

> In the present case, of course, the minor plaintiff never misrepresented his age and, in fact, informed defendant that he was 17 years old. Nor did plaintiff represent to defendant that his father was to be the owner or have any interest in the automobile. There is no evidence in the present case that plaintiff at the time of entering the contract with defendant intended anything more than to enjoy his new automobile. He borrowed the total purchase price and paid it to defendant carrying out the transaction fully at the time of taking delivery of the vehicle. Plaintiff sought to disaffirm the contract and the return of the purchase price only when defendant declined to make repairs to it. In these circumstances we believe the weight of authority would permit the minor plaintiff to disaffirm the voidable contract and that defendant-vendor would not be entitled to recoup any damages which he believes he suffered as a result thereof.

Id. at 1107. . . . We believe this result is consistent with the purpose of the infancy doctrine.

The decision of the court of appeals is affirmed.

NOTES AND QUESTIONS

1. *Restoration of consideration.* *Halbman* appears to represent the majority view. However, the minority view is equally well reasoned, concluding that when the minor asserts infancy as a defensive shield, the minor is not liable for dissipation of the seller's consideration. But when the minor uses the infancy doctrine to disaffirm and sues for the return of consideration, the minor is responsible for depreciation in the assets tendered back to the seller. See Dodson v. Shrader, 824 S.W.2d 545 (Tenn. 1992). Which view do you prefer and why? Does the offensive use of the infancy doctrine as a sword to permit the infant to retain any benefits dissipated during the performance of the contract make any sense? If so, under what rationale?

2. *Recreational waivers involving negligent personal injury.* Should an infant be entitled to execute a legally binding waiver of liability for negligent infliction of personal injuries? If not, should a parent's signature bind the infant so that the infant's disaffirmance before reaching majority and after

injury is ineffective? See Sharon v. City of Newton, 437 Mass. 99, 769 N.E.2d 738 (2002) (high school cheerleader's signature held not binding by itself, but father's additional signature was binding on the child). Consider the case of minors contracting with providers of organized sports activities such as fencing, horseback riding, archery, riflery, swimming, gymnastics, and the multitude of other childhood activities that involve some theoretical or real element of risk of injury. What would happen to the market for organized provision of such activities if there were no mechanism for waiver of liability for negligence? Are there any alternative mechanisms by which organizers could protect themselves against such liability? Do you think a parent should have the right to waive a third-party liability to their child for negligent infliction of physical injury? When injury results from gross negligence, the waiver is generally invalid on grounds of public policy.

3. *Why switch from void to merely voidable?* As the introductory materials explained, early legal history treated infancy contracts as void, not voidable. Can you articulate the policy justifications for and against the switch? What other related doctrines are implicated by a switch from void to voidable contracts by infants? What policy questions relate to the possible solutions of those questions?

4. *Application of UCC. Halbman* involved the sale of goods (a car). Why does the court cite common law contract rules? Could it be that the UCC itself assumes that most commercial transactions will not involve minors and in any event incorporates all common law not otherwise specifically displaced by a rule in the UCC? Specifically, what does UCC § 1–103 (2001) ("Unless displaced by the particular provisions of [the Uniform Commercial Code], the principles of law and equity, including the . . . law relative to capacity to contract . . . supplement its provisions.") suggest about the capacity to contract? See generally, Robert A. Hillman, "Construction of the Uniform Commercial Code: UCC Section 1–103 and 'Code' Methodology," 18 B. C. L. Rev. 655, 659 (1977).

5. *The "necessaries" exception.* The court begins with the statement that the car was not "a necessity." Should courts assess whether a given item is or is not a necessity from a subjective or objective perspective? In other words, should "necessities" be limited in scope to the bare minimum necessary for sustenance in contemporary society, such as food, shelter, and clothing? Or should the determination of whether a particular good is a necessity depend upon the individual needs, desires, and circumstances of the minor? Can you conceive of some circumstances where a car might be necessary to some minors but not to others? What about questions of degree? If transportation is deemed a necessity for a 16-year-old working minor, does that include a contracts for bus fare, a bicycle, a motorcycle, a 1978 Oldsmobile Cutlass Salon that "runs good," a new Dodge Neon, or a Cadillac? If the court determines that the parties have contracted for a necessity, how should the court measure the minor's liability? The two most obvious measures are expectancy damages measured by the contract itself or restitution damages measured by the value of the

benefit conferred upon the minor. Given the capacity issues in question, is a market or restitution valuation more appropriate?

6.   *Ratification after reaching the age of majority.* An infant need not take any action to disaffirm a contract until the age of majority. Restatement (Second) of Contracts § 14 *cmt. c.* Does this suggest that a minor's ratification of a contract before reaching the age of majority is not effective? If the contract itself is voidable because of infancy, should not also the ratification be voidable if made while a minor? The rules are clear that if the minor takes no action to disaffirm the contract within a "reasonable time" after reaching majority, the delay will constitute ratification by failure to exercise objection while retaining the fruits of the contract. A "reasonable time" will simply vary from case-to-case, depending in part on the sophistication of the minor.

2.   MENTAL CAPACITY

Like infancy contracts, contracts with the mentally infirm were historically considered void rather than voidable. See Dexter v. Hall, 82 U. S. (15 Wall.) 9, 20 (1872) (contracts with lunatics are void rather than merely voidable because the lunatic has nothing the law recognizes as a mind as a prerequisite for the then required "meeting of the minds"); Milton D. Green, "Public Policies Underlying the Law of Mental Incompetency," 38 Mich. L. Rev. 1189, 1193 (1940). Both Restatement (First) of Contracts § 13 and Restatement (Second) of Contracts § 7, however, suggested that an incompetent person could enter only voidable contracts. Moreover, Restatement (First) of Contracts § 18 and Restatement (Second) of Contracts § 12(1) state virtually identical versions of required mental capacity. However, unlike Restatement (First) of Contracts, Restatement (Second) of Contracts § 12(2) lists separately identifiable categories of incapacity including guardianship, infancy, mental illness or defect, and intoxication. Each form of listed incapacity is then supported by a separate provision: Restatement (Second) of Contracts § 13 (guardianship), § 14 (infancy), § 15 (mental illness or defect), and § 16 (intoxication).

The traditional common law test for mental incapacity sufficient to avoid a contract considered only whether a person could understand the nature and consequences of the transaction—the so-called "cognitive test." Restatement (Second) of Contracts § 15 was particularly important because it purported to "expand" the voidable contract category to include a new category of voidable contracts where the incompetent party could understand the transaction, but could not control their behavior with respect to the transaction. As the case below argues, this expanded "volitional test" encompassed those transactions where the person understood the nature and consequences of the transaction, but nonetheless could not exercise personal control over their behavior, including entering a particular contract.

The volitional test, however, raises problems of notice and fairness to the other party to the transaction. While a party lacking an understanding of the nature and consequences of a particular transaction might exhibit bizarre behavior providing notice to a third party, the volitional test encompasses situations in which the incompetent person appears wholly rational to the other party to the contract. Consequently, in an otherwise fair transaction, the third party would arguably have no reason to suspect the mental illness of the other party. Restatement (Second) of Contracts § 15 thus permits avoidance under the volitional test only where "the other party has reason to know of [the incompetent party's] condition."

Because of this difficulty in detection and lack of notice to contracting parties, the common law imposes stricter rules regarding restitution of consideration. As discussed in the preceding section, the traditional majority rule on infancy only requires the minor to return what remains of the consideration and only in its current form, even if depreciated or otherwise damaged. But a mental incompetent (or guardian) must normally make full restitution as a condition of disaffirmance. This notion is reflected in Restatement (Second) of Contracts § 15(2) that subjects disaffirmance in fair transactions to transactions where disaffirmance would not be "unjust." Comment f clarifies that a fair contract is not voidable if the other party had no reason to know of the incompetency, and the mentally incompetent party cannot fully restore the consideration in the transaction.

Arguably, no person affected more change in the view and definition of "insanity" than Professor Milton D. Green, who wrote a series of four related articles referred to in the Reporter's Notes to Restatement (Second) of Contracts § 15. See Milton D. Green, "Public Policies Underlying the Law of Mental Incompetency," 38 Mich. L. Rev. 1189 (1940); Milton D. Green, "Judicial Tests of Mental Incompetency," 6 Mo. L. Rev. 141 (1941); Milton D. Green, "The Operative Effect of Mental Incompetency on Agreements and Wills," 21 Tex. L. Rev. 554 (1943); Milton D. Green, "Fraud, Undue Influence and Mental Incompetency," 43 Colum. L. Rev. 176 (1943); and Milton D, Green, "Proof of Mental Incompetency and the Unexpressed Major Premise," 53 Yale L. J. 271 (1944). The articles were prepared as a series of five articles on mental incompetency and in satisfaction of Professor Green's attainment of his Doctor of the Science of Law at Columbia University. The articles remain today profoundly important and enlightening by raising the level of mental capacity understanding. For a contemporary analysis of the cognitive test, see Elyn R. Saks, "Competency to Refuse Psychotropic Medication: Three Alternatives to the Law's Cognitive Standard," 47 U. Miami L. Rev. 689 (1993).

ORTELERE V. TEACHERS' RETIREMENT BOARD

Court of Appeals of New York
25 N.Y.2d 196, 250 N.E.2d 460, 303 N.Y.S.2d 362 (1969)

BREITEL, Judge.

This appeal involves the revocability of an election of benefits under a public employees' retirement system and suggests the need for a renewed examination of the kinds of mental incompetency which may render voidable the exercise of contractual rights. The particular issue arises on the evidently unwise and foolhardy selection of benefits by a 60-year-old teacher, on leave for mental illness and suffering from cerebral arteriosclerosis, after service as a public schoolteacher and participation in a public retirement system for over 40 years. The teacher died a little less than two months after making her election of maximum benefits, payable to her during her life, thus causing the entire reserve to fall in. She left surviving her husband of 38 years of marriage and two grown children.

There is no doubt that any retirement system depends for its soundness on an actuarial experience based on the purely prospective selections of benefits and mortality rates among the covered group, and that retrospective or adverse selection after the fact would be destructive of a sound system. It is also true that members of retirement systems are free to make choices that to others may seem unwise or foolhardy. The issue here is narrower than any suggested by these basic principles. It is whether an otherwise irrevocable election may be avoided for incapacity because of known mental illness which resulted in the election when, except in the barest actuarial sense, the system would sustain no unfavorable consequences.

The husband and executor of Grace W. Ortelere, the deceased New York City schoolteacher, sued to set aside her application for retirement without option, in the event of her death. It is alleged that Mrs. Ortelere, on February 11, 1965, two months before her death from natural causes, was not mentally competent to execute a retirement application. By this application, effective the next day, she elected the maximum retirement allowance (Administrative Code of City of New York, § B20—46. 0). She thus revoked her earlier election of benefits under which she named her husband a beneficiary of the unexhausted reserve upon her death. Selection of the maximum allowance extinguished all interests upon her death.

Following a non-jury trial in Supreme Court, it was held that Grace Ortelere had been mentally incompetent at the time of her February 11 application, thus rendering it "null and void and of no legal effect." The Appellate Division, by a divided court, reversed the judgment of the Supreme Court and held that, as a matter of law, there was insufficient proof of mental incompetency as to this transaction (31 A. D. 2d 139, 295 N. Y. S. 2d 506).

Mrs. Ortelere's mental illness, indeed, psychosis, is undisputed. It is not seriously disputable, however, that she had complete cognitive judgment or awareness when she made her selection. A modern understanding of mental illness, however, suggests that incapacity to contract or exercise contractual rights may exist, because of volitional and affective impediments or disruptions in the personality, despite the intellectual or cognitive ability to understand. It will be recognized as the civil law parallel to the question of criminal responsibility which has been the recent concern of so many and has resulted in statutory and decisional changes in the criminal law (e.g., A. L. I. Model Penal Code, § 4. 01; Penal Law, § 30. 05; Durham v. United States, 214 F. 2d 862).

Mrs. Ortelere, an elementary schoolteacher since 1924, suffered a "nervous breakdown" in March, 1964 and went on a leave of absence expiring February 5, 1965. She was then 60 years old and had been happily married for 38 years. On July 1, 1964 she came under the care of Dr. D'Angelo, a psychiatrist, who diagnosed her breakdown as involutional psychosis, melancholia type. Dr. D'Angelo prescribed, and for about six weeks decedent underwent, tranquilizer and shock therapy. Although moderately successful, the therapy was not continued since it was suspected that she also suffered from cerebral arteriosclerosis, an ailment later confirmed. However, the psychiatrist continued to see her at monthly intervals until March 1965. On March 28, 1965 she was hospitalized after collapsing at home from an aneurysm. She died two days later; the cause of death was "Cerebral thrombosis due to Hypertensive Heart Disease."

As a teacher she had been a member of the Teachers' Retirement System of the City of New York (Administrative Code, § B20–3.0). This entitled her to certain annuity and pension rights, pre-retirement death benefits, and empowered her to exercise various options concerning the payment of her retirement allowance.

Some years before, on June 28, 1958, she had executed a "Selection of Benefits under Option One" naming her husband as beneficiary of the unexhausted reserve. Under this option upon retirement her allowance would be less by way of periodic retirement allowances, but if she died before receipt of her full reserve the balance of the reserve would be payable to her husband. On June 16, 1960, two years later, she had designated her husband as beneficiary of her service death benefits in the event of her death prior to retirement.

Then on February 11, 1965, when her leave of absence had just expired and she was still under treatment, she executed a retirement application, the one here involved, selecting the maximum retirement allowance payable during her lifetime with nothing payable on or after death. She also, at this time, borrowed from the system the maximum cash withdrawal permitted, namely, $8,760. Three days earlier she had written the board, stating that she intended to retire on February 12 or 15 or as soon as she received "the information I need in order to decide whether to take an option or maximum allowance." She then listed eight specific questions, reflecting great understanding of the retirement system, concerning the various alternatives available. An extremely detailed reply was sent, by letter of February 15, 1965, although by that date it was technically impossible for her to change her selection. However, the board's chief clerk, before whom Mrs. Ortelere executed the application, testified that the questions were "answered verbally by me on February 11th." Her retirement reserve totaled $62,165 (after deducting the $8,760 withdrawal), and the difference between electing the maximum retirement allowance (no option) and the allowance under "option one" was $901 per year or $75 per month. That is, had the teacher selected "option one" she would have received an annual allowance of $4,494 or $375 per month, while if no option had been selected she would have received an annual allowance of $5,395 or $450 per month. Had she not withdrawn the cash the annual figures would be $5,247 and $6,148 respectively.

Following her taking a leave of absence for her condition, Mrs. Ortelere had become very depressed and was unable to care for herself. As a result her husband gave up his electrician's job, in which he earned $222 per week, to stay home and take care of her on a full-time basis. She left their home only when he accompanied her. Although he took her to the Retirement Board on February 11, 1965, he did not know why she went, and did not question her for fear "she'd start crying hysterically that I was scolding her. That's the way she was. And I wouldn't upset her."

The Orteleres were in quite modest circumstances. They owned their own home, valued at $20,000, and had $8,000 in a savings account. They also owned some farmland worth about $5,000. Under these circumstances, as revealed in this record, retirement for both of the Orteleres or the survivor of them had to be provided, as a practical matter, largely out of Mrs. Ortelere's retirement benefits.

According to Dr. D'Angelo, the psychiatrist who treated her, Mrs. Ortelere never improved enough to "warrant my sending her back (to teaching)." A physician for the Board of Education examined her on February 2, 1965 to determine her fitness to return to teaching. Although not a psychiatrist but rather a specialist in internal medicine, this physician 'judged that she had apparently recovered from the depression' and that she appeared rational. However, before allowing her to return to teaching, a report was requested from Dr. D'Angelo concerning her condition. It is notable that the Medical Division of the Board of Education on February 24, 1965 requested that Mrs. Ortelere report to the board's "panel psychiatrist" on March 11, 1965.

Dr. D'Angelo stated "(a)t no time since she was under my care was she ever mentally competent" that "mentally she couldn't make a decision of any kind, actually, of any kind, small or large." He also described how involutional melancholia affects the judgment process: "They can't think rationally, no matter what the situation is. They will even tell you, 'I used to be able to think of anything and make any decision.' 'Now,' they say, 'even getting up, I don't know whether I should get up or whether I should stay in bed.' Or, 'I don't even know how to make a slice of toast any more.' Everything is impossible to decide, and everything is too great an effort to even think of doing. They just don't have the effort, actually, because their nervous breakdown drains them of all their physical energies."

While the psychiatrist used terms referring to "rationality," it is quite evident that Mrs. Ortelere's psychopathology did not lend itself to a classification under the legal test of irrationality. It is undoubtedly, for this reason, that the Appellate Division was unable to accept his testimony and the trial court's finding of irrationality in the light of the prevailing rules as they have been formulated.

The well-established rule is that contracts of a mentally incompetent person who has not been adjudicated insane are voidable. Even where the contract has been partly or fully performed it will still be avoided upon restoration of the status quo. . . .

Traditionally, in this State and elsewhere, contractual mental capacity has been measured by what is largely a cognitive test. . . . Under this standard the "inquiry" is whether the mind was "so affected as to render him wholly and absolutely incompetent to comprehend and understand the nature of the transaction" (Aldrich v. Bailey, Supra, at p. 89, 30 N. E. at p. 265). A requirement that the party also be able to make a rational judgment concerning the particular transaction qualified the cognitive test. . . . Conversely, it is also well recognized that contractual ability would be affected by insane delusions intimately related to the particular transaction. . . .

These traditional standards governing competency to contract were formulated when psychiatric knowledge was quite primitive. They fail to account for one who by reason of mental illness is unable to control his conduct even though his cognitive ability seems unimpaired. When these standards were evolving it was thought that all the mental faculties were simultaneously affected by mental illness. (Green, Mental Incompetency, 38 Mich. L. Rev. 1189, 1197–1202.) This is no longer the prevailing view (Note, Mental Illness and the Law of Contracts, 57 Mich. L. Rev. 1020, 1033–1036).

Of course, the greatest movement in revamping legal notions of mental responsibility has occurred in the criminal law. The nineteenth century cognitive test embraced in the M'Naghten rules has long been criticized and changed by statute and decision in many jurisdictions (see M'Naghten's Case, 10 Clark & Fin. 200; 8 Eng. Rep. 718 (House of Lords, 1843). . . .

While the policy considerations for the criminal law and the civil law are different, both share in common the premise that policy considerations must be based on a sound understanding of the human mind and, therefore, its illnesses. Hence, because the cognitive rules are, for the most part, too restrictive and rest on a false factual basis they must be re-examined. Once it is understood that, accepting plaintiff's proof, Mrs. Ortelere was psychotic and because of that psychosis could have been incapable of making a voluntary selection of her retirement system benefits, there is an issue that a modern jurisprudence should not exclude, merely because her mind could pass a "cognition" test based on nineteenth century psychology.

There has also been some movement on the civil law side to achieve a modern posture. For the most part, the movement has been glacial and has been disguised under traditional formulations. Various devices have been used to avoid unacceptable results under the old rules by finding unfairness or overreaching in order to avoid transactions. . . .

In this State there has been at least one candid approach. In Faber v. Sweet Style Mfg. Corp., 40 Misc. 2d 212, at p. 216, 242 N. Y. S. 2d 763, at p. 768, Mr. Justice MEYER wrote: "incompetence to contract also exists when a contract is entered into under the compulsion of a mental disease or disorder but for which the contract would not have been made" (noted in 39 N. Y. U. L. Rev. 356). This is the first known time a court has recognized that the traditional standards of incompetency for contractual capacity are inadequate in light of contemporary psychiatric learning and applied modern standards. Prior to this, courts applied the cognitive standard giving great weight to objective evidence of rationality. . . .

It is quite significant that Restatement (Second) of Contracts, states the modern rule on competency to contract. This is in evident recognition, and the Reporter's Notes support this inference, that, regardless of how the cases formulated their reasoning, the old cognitive test no longer explains the results. Thus, the new Restatement section reads:

> (1) A person incurs only voidable contractual duties by entering into a transaction if by reason of mental illness or defect * * * (b) he is unable to act in a reasonable manner in relation to the transaction and the other party has reason to know of his condition. Restatement (Second) of Contracts (T. D. No. 1, April 13, 1964), § 18C.

See also, Allen, Ferster, Weihofen, Mental Impairment and Legal Incompetency, p. 253 (Recommendation b) and pp. 260–282; and Note, 57 Mich. L. Rev. 1020, Supra, where it is recommended "that a complete test for contractual incapacity should provide protection to those persons whose contracts are merely uncontrolled reactions to their mental illness, as well as for those who could not understand the nature and consequences of their actions" (at p. 1036).

The avoidance of duties under an agreement entered into by those who have done so by reason of mental illness, but who have understanding, depends on balancing competing policy considerations. There must be stability in contractual relations and protection of the expectations of parties who bargain in good faith. On the other hand, it is also desirable to protect persons who may understand the nature of the transaction but who, due to mental illness, cannot control their conduct. Hence, there should be relief only if the other party knew or was put on notice as to the contractor's mental illness. Thus, the Restatement provision for avoidance contemplates that "the other party has reason to know" of the mental illness (Id.).

When, however, the other party is without knowledge of the contractor's mental illness and the agreement is made on fair terms, the proposed Restatement rule is:

> The power of avoidance under subsection (1) terminates to the
> extent that the contract has been so performed in whole or in part
> or the circumstances have so changed that avoidance would be
> inequitable. In such a case a court may grant relief on such
> equitable terms as the situation requires. (Restatement (Second)
> of Contracts, Supra, § 18C, subd. (2).)

The system was, or should have been, fully aware of Mrs. Ortelere's condition. They, or the Board of Education, knew of her leave of absence for medical reasons and the resort to staff psychiatrists by the Board of Education. Hence, the other of the conditions for avoidance is satisfied.

Lastly, there are no significant changes of position by the system other than those that flow from the barest actuarial consequences of benefit selection.

Nor should one ignore that in the relationship between retirement system and member, and especially in a public system, there is not involved a commercial, let alone an ordinary commercial, transaction. Instead the nature of the system and its announced goal is the protection of its members and those in whom its members have an interest. It is not a sound scheme which would permit 40 years of contribution and participation in the system to be nullified by a one-instant act committed by one known to be mentally ill. This is especially true if there would be no substantial harm to the system if the act were avoided. On the record none may gainsay that her selection of a "no option" retirement while under psychiatric care, ill with cerebral arteriosclerosis, aged 60, and with a family in which she had always manifested concern, was so unwise and foolhardy that a factfinder might conclude that it was explainable only as a product of psychosis.

On this analysis it is not difficult to see that plaintiff's evidence was sufficient to sustain a finding that, when she acted as she did on February 11, 1965, she did so solely as a result of serious mental illness, namely, psychosis. Of course, nothing less serious than medically classified psychosis should suffice or else few contracts would be invulnerable to some kind of psychological attack. Mrs. Ortelere's psychiatrist testified quite flatly that as an involutional melancholiac in depression she was incapable of making a voluntary "rational" decision. Of course, as noted earlier, the trial court's finding and perhaps some of the testimony attempted to fit into the rubrics of the traditional rules. For that reason rather than reinstatement of the judgment at Trial Term there should be a new trial under the proper standards frankly considered and applied.

Accordingly, the order of the Appellate Division should be reversed, without costs, and the action remanded to Special Term for a new trial.

JASEN, Judge (dissenting).

Where there has been no previous adjudication of incompetency, the burden of proving mental incompetence is upon the party alleging it. I agree with the majority at the Appellate Division that the plaintiff, the husband of the decedent, failed to sustain the burden incumbent upon him of proving deceased's incompetence.

The evidence conclusively establishes that the decedent, at the time she made her application to retire, understood not only that she was retiring, but also that she had selected the maximum payment during her lifetime.

Indeed, the letter written by the deceased to the Teachers' Retirement System prior to her retirement demonstrates her full mental capacity to understand and to decide whether to take on option or the maximum allowance. The full text of the letter reads as follows:

February 8, 1965

Gentlemen:

I would like to retire on Feb. 12 or Feb. 15. In other words, just as soon as possible after I receive the information I need in order to decide whether to take an option or maximum allowance. Following are the questions I would like to have answered:

1. What is my "average" five-year salary?

2. What is my maximum allowance?

3. I am 60 years old. If I select option four-a with a beneficiary (female) 27 years younger, what is my allowance?

4. If I select four-a on the pension part only, and take the maximum annuity, what is my allowance?

5. If I take a loan of 89% of my year's salary before retirement, what would my maximum allowance be?

6. If I take a loan of $5,000 before retiring, and select option four-a on both the pension and annuity, what would my allowance be?

7. What is my total service credit? I have been on a leave without pay since Oct. 26, 1964.

8. What is the "factor" used for calculating option four-a with the above beneficiary?

Thank you for your promptness in making the necessary calculations. I will come to your office on Thursday afternoon of this week.

It seems clear that this detailed, explicit and extremely pertinent list of queries reveals a mind fully in command of the salient features of the Teachers' Retirement System. Certainly, it cannot be said that the decedent could possess sufficient capacity to compose a letter indicating such a comprehensive understanding of the retirement system, and yet lack the capacity to understand the answers.

As I read the record, the evidence establishes that the decedent's election to receive maximum payments was predicated on the need for a higher income to support two retired persons—her husband and herself. Since the only source of income available to decedent and her husband was decedent's retirement pay, the additional payment of $75 per month that she would receive by electing the maximum payment was a necessity. Indeed, the additional payments represented an increase of 20% over the benefits payable under option 1. Under these circumstances, an election of maximal income during decedent's lifetime was not only a rational, but a necessary decision.

Further indication of decedent's knowledge of the financial needs of her family is evidenced by the fact that she took a loan for the maximum amount ($8,760) permitted by the retirement system at the time she made application for retirement.

Moreover, there is nothing in the record to indicate that the decedent had any warning, premonition, knowledge or indication at the time of retirement that her life expectancy was, in any way, reduced by her condition.

Decedent's election of the maximum retirement benefits, therefore, was not so contrary to her best interests so as to create an inference of her mental incompetence.

Indeed, concerning election of options under a retirement system, it has been held:

> Even where no previous election has been made, the court must make the election for an incompetent which would be in accordance with what would have been his manifest and reasonable choice if he were sane, and, in the absence of convincing evidence that the incompetent would have made a different selection, it is presumed that he would have chosen the option yielding the largest returns in his lifetime. (Schwartzberg v. Teachers' Retirement Bd., 273 App. Div. 240, 242–243, 76 N. Y. S. 2d 488, affd. 298 N. Y. 741, 83 N. E. 2d 146; emphasis supplied.)

Nor can I agree with the majority's view that the traditional rules governing competency to contract "are, for the most part, too restrictive and rest on a false factual basis."

The issue confronting the courts concerning mental capacity to contract is under what circumstances and conditions should a party be relieved of contractual obligations freely entered. This is peculiarly a legal decision, although, of course, available medical knowledge forms a datum which influences the legal choice. It is common knowledge that the present state of psychiatric knowledge is inadequate to provide a fixed rule for each and every type of mental disorder. Thus, the generally accepted rules which have evolved to determine mental responsibility are general enough in application to encompass all types of mental disorders, and phrased in a manner which can be understood and practically applied by juries composed of laymen.

The generally accepted test of mental competency to contract which has thus evolved is whether the party attempting to avoid the contract was capable of understanding and appreciating the nature and consequences of the particular act or transaction which he challenges. . . . This rule represents a balance struck between policies to protect the security of transactions between individuals and freedom of contract on the one hand, and protection of those mentally handicapped on the other hand.

In my opinion, this rule has proven workable in practice and fair in result. A broad range of evidence including psychiatric testimony is admissible under the existing rules to establish a party's condition. . . . In the final analysis, the lay jury will infer the state of the party's mind from his observed behavior as indicated by the evidence presented at trial. Each juror instinctively judges what is normal and what is abnormal conduct from his own experience, and the generally accepted test harmonizes the competing policy considerations with human experience to achieve the fairest result in the greatest number of cases.

As in every situation where the law must draw a line between liability and non-liability, between responsibility and non-responsibility, there will be borderline cases, and injustices may occur by deciding erroneously that an individual belongs on one side of the line or the other. To minimize the chances of such injustices occurring, the line should be drawn as clearly as possible.

The Appellate Division correctly found that the deceased was capable of understanding the nature and effect of her retirement benefits, and exercised rational judgment in electing to receive the maximum allowance during her lifetime. I fear that the majority's refinement of the generally accepted rules will prove unworkable in practice, and make many contracts vulnerable to psychological attack. Any benefit to those who understand what they are doing, but are unable to exercise self-discipline, will be outweighed by frivolous claims which will burden our courts and undermine the security of contracts. The reasonable expectations of those who innocently deal with persons who appear rational and who understand what they are doing should be protected.

Accordingly, I would affirm the order appealed from.

Order reversed, without costs, and a new trial granted.

NOTES AND QUESTIONS

1.   *Who may assert the contract is avoidable?* The prior section revealed that modern law permits only the minor to avoid the contract on the basis of lack of capacity. Is the same true with regard to mental illness or defect? The language of the Restatement (Second) of Contracts makes clear that the self-help avoidance remedy is only available to the incompetent party. Restatement (Second) of Contracts § 15(1). And like contracts with minors, contracts with a mentally incompetent party historically were void and not merely voidable. See Dexter v. Hall, 82 U. S. (15 Wall) 9, 20 (1872) (a lunatic is *non compos mentis* or has nothing the law recognizes as a mind to engage a "meeting of the minds"). Thus, historically neither party could use the courts to enforce the contract in any fashion. With the erosion of the meeting of the minds requirement, such contracts became merely voidable by the incompetent. As with contracts with minors, the modern rule allows the incompetent person to decide (normally through a representative) whether to retain the benefits of a beneficial contract or to avoid the consequences of an unfavorable contract.

2.   *Proving incompetency.* Adjudication of incompetency is conclusive regarding incapacity at the time of the adjudication, although many jurisdictions treat adjudication as creating only a presumption of incompetency as to later transactions. See Henry Weihofen, "Mental Incompetency to Contract or Convey," 39 S. Cal. L. Rev. 211, 211–213 (1966). While adjudication is not a prerequisite under the Restatement (Second) of Contracts, mere mental weakness is also inadequate. Indeed, in the absence of an incompetency adjudication, the party—or their representative or estate—may establish incompetency under either the "cognitive test" or the "volitional test." Compare Restatement (Second) of Contracts § 15(1)(a) (cognitive test), with Restatement

(Second) of Contracts § 15(1)(b) (volitional test). Since the avoidance remedy is only available to the incompetent party, that party retains the burden to prove legal incapacity. Restatement (Second) of Contracts § 15 *cmt. c.* Under the cognitive test, the party must prove he or she was unable reasonably to understand the nature and consequences of the transaction. While the test has been criticized as vague and ambiguous, it remains accepted in most jurisdictions. See Milton D. Green, "Judicial Tests of Mental Incompetency," 6 Mo. L. Rev. 141 (1941). When established, the cognitive test does not require that the innocent party had been aware of the mental defect, but even a person otherwise failing the cognitive test might enter a valid contract if the contract was executed at a particularly lucid moment. Does the *Ortelere* majority determine that Grace Ortelere satisfied the cognitive test? If so, why?

Alternatively, as the *Ortelere* majority notes, some jurisdictions also embrace a broader volitional test. Unlike the cognitive test, the volitional test does not require that the party prove that he or she was unable to understand the nature and consequences of the transaction. Under the volitional test, a mentally infirm person might actually understand the nature and consequences of the transaction, but nonetheless be unable to control their behavior. Accordingly, the volitional test only requires that the party be unable to act in a reasonable manner. But unlike the cognitive test, the volitional test requires that the other party must have reason to know of the condition. See Restatement (Second) of Contracts § 15(1)(b). In *Farber,* a famous pre-Restatement (Second) of Contracts New York case cited by the *Ortelere* majority, a previously conservative businessman went on a spending spree after he passed from depression to manic depression. In one transaction, he contracted to purchase land, but two weeks later he was committed to a mental institution and later sued to avoid the contract. Even though the court concluded that manic depression affected motivation rather than ability to understand, the contract was rescinded since this particular party would not have entered the transaction but for the manic depression. See Farber v. Sweet Style *Mfg.* Corp., 40 Misc.2d 212, 242 N.Y.S.2d 763 (Sup. Ct. 1963). The Restatement (Second) of Contracts § 15(1)(b) does not entirely adopt the *Farber* position because it requires that the innocent party be aware of the condition. Does the *Ortelere* majority follow the more conservative Restatement (Second) of Contracts version or the broader *Farber* version? In other words, was the Teacher's Retirement Board aware or should they have been aware of Grace Ortelere's mental defect? If so, did the court reject the broader view expressed in *Farber* (not requiring awareness by the other party)?

3.   *Legal effect of performance.* Because the objective theory of contracts bases the determination of whether the contract is voidable on whether the competent party knew of the incompetency, the power of avoidance terminates when the transaction is fully or partially performed such that avoidance would create injustice to either party. Accordingly, the clear majority rule is that the incompetent party may not avoid a contract in good faith, for fair consideration, and without notice of the incompetence by the competent party, at least unless the competent party can be restored to pre-contractual status quo.

Restatement (Second) of Contracts § 15(2) and Restatement (Second) of Contracts § 15 *cmt. f*. Because of the lack of knowledge requirement, this section applies mostly to cognitive test incompetency transactions. What then should be the effect of legal performance and consideration restoration under the volitional test?

4.   *Supervening incompetence.* A competent person may of course enter into a contract requiring further documents to be executed according to the terms of the contract. For example, a person may enter into a contract to sell real estate that requires a later execution of a deed in favor of the purchaser. If the seller is competent at the time of the execution of the contract but becomes incompetent before the deed is executed, and the purchaser learns of the incompetence, the performance rule discussed above would not protect the purchaser because of knowledge of the incompetency. Accordingly, the incompetent person (or representative) could avoid the deed and contract. What options are available to the purchaser? As discussed above, normally only the incompetent party may avoid a contract. While the self-help avoidance remedy is not available to the competent party, that party may apply to a court requesting that the contract to be performed be cancelled unless a guardian is appointed to finalize the documentation with assurance the transaction will be final. See Restatement (Second) of Contracts § 15 *cmt. c, illus. 2.*

5.   *Restoration of consideration.* Since the cognitive test may be asserted to avoid a contract even if the other party did not know of the mental infirmity, and application of the cognitive test involves considerable uncertainty, the restoration of consideration rules are considerably more stringent than those involving minors. While a minor is ordinarily only required to restore what remains of the consideration, the mentally infirm must normally make full restoration even if the original consideration has dissipated. See, e.g., *Hauer v. Union State Bank*, 192 Wis.2d 576, 532 N.W.2d 456 (App. 1995). Equitable exceptions normally exist where the competent party acted with knowledge of the other party's incompetency or where the incompetent received little actual benefit from the transaction. See Restatement (Second) of Contracts § 15(2) (terminating power of avoidance entirely where the consideration was fair and the other party acted without knowledge of the infirmity). Given the nature of the volitional test, will the competent party be entitled to restoration?

6.   *Ratification and avoidability.* Absent an untimely death, all minors ultimately reach the age of majority at age 18 with full capacity to contract. This necessarily dictates that all minors must positively disaffirm their infancy contracts within a reasonable time of reaching the age of majority. The failure to do so constitutes a ratification by failing to object to the contract's status while retaining the benefits of the contract. Should the same ratification rules apply to mental incompetents? Indeed, how does a mental incompetent disaffirm a contract in the first place? At least under the cognitive test, does not the fact of mental incompetency presume the person was generally not fully aware of the contract? Of course, unlike infancy, modern medicine can help cure or certainly mitigate the effects of mental illness. Upon reaching such competency status, do you think the same positive ratification rules should

apply to the formerly mentally ill as to minors? How would such a person recall a contract had been made when they were mentally ill? Alternatively, given that individuals can control and treat many mental illnesses through medication, should those individuals be able to avoid contracts undertaken when they voluntarily stop taking those medications and thus render themselves incompetent?

7. *Intoxication, drug addiction, and capacity to contract.* Early common law did not recognize drunkenness as a defense to avoid the consequences of a contract. As stated by Lord Coke, although an intoxicated person is treated as *non compos mentis* or without the mind to contract, drunkenness cannot be used to avoid a contract made while in such a state. The early theory was that a person was not privileged to disable him or herself. See Sidney J. Dudley, "Intoxication as a Defense to an Express Contract," 62 U. Pa. L. Rev. 34, 35–36 (1913); Ronald Splitt, "Contracts—Specific Performance—Intoxication," 33 N. D. L. Rev. 113 (1957). But under modern law, courts may regard compulsive alcoholism or other forms of drug addiction as a form of mental illness. This theory of mental illness based upon alcoholism or drug addiction is not generally successful as a defense, perhaps because such addictions typically involve an initial voluntary ingestion that later causes incompetent or involuntary conduct. Restatement (First) of Contracts did not specifically consider intoxication. Restatement (Second) of Contracts § 16, on the other hand, departs from the mental illness standard so that intoxication only creates a power of avoidance where the other party has reason to know of the impairment at the time of contract execution. As with mental illness, a party intoxicated or inebriated at the time of contracting may establish such intoxication under either a cognitive or volitional test. Because the visual effects of alcohol intoxication are normally more obvious, the reason to know standard presents less difficulty. Moreover, in cases like *Lucy v. Zehmer* discussed in Chapter 2, in which the parties drank heavily enough for Zehmer to describe himself as "high as a Georgia pine," courts occasionally seem to require an extraordinary degree of intoxication before they will permit a party to avoid a contract. Presumably, the alcohol standard will apply to other drug abuse forms.

Like other forms of voidable contracts, a contract voidable by reason of intoxication or drug abuse will be deemed ratified unless the power of avoidance is exercised promptly. In the case of temporary intoxication, on becoming sober, a person must promptly exercise the power of avoidance and also restore the other party to *status quo*, unless the consideration was dissipated while the person was intoxicated. See Restatement (Second) of Contracts § 16 *cmt. c.*

8. *Application of UCC.* As with contracts with minors, the UCC appears to assume that most commercial transactions will not involve inebriated parties and incorporates the common law standards for dealing with such issues. See UCC § 1–103 (2001). See generally Robert A. Hillman, "Construction of the Uniform Commercial Code: UCC Section 1–103 and 'Code' Methodology," 18 B. C. L. Rev. 655, 659 (1977).

9. *Application of CISG.* Like the UCC, the CISG is silent regarding the capacity of the parties to contract. Accordingly, this matter is left to domestic law. William S. Dodge, "Teaching the CISG in Contracts," 50 J. Legal Educ., 72, 78 (2000). Since incompetent parties are less likely to engage in international transactions, this approach is understandable. Further, unlike the UCC, the CISG does not apply to transactions in consumer goods, further justifying the absence of a specific rule on mental incapacity. Helen Elizabeth Hartnell, "Rousing the Sleeping Dog: The Validity Exception to the Convention on Contracts for the International Sale of Goods," 18 Yale J. Int'l L. 1, 62–87 (1993).

3. CONTRACTS AFFECTED BY A RELATIONSHIP OF TRUST AND CONFIDENCE

Modern contract law, with its focus on the objective manifestations of assent by the parties, functions best in regulating bargains between two parties dealing at arms' length. But in some situations, the parties interact on a deeper level that may not be objectively apparent to an outside observer. For example, contracts and promises arising in the family context, such as *Dougherty v. Salt, Hamer v. Sidway, Kirksey v. Kirksey*, and *Wright v. Newman*, create problems for the objective theory of contract law. In those situations, the family relationship makes it obvious that the parties share a subjective understanding at the time of promise that they owe and are relying upon familial standards of behavior and obligation, not the standards that exist between strangers. Similarly, the parties may have created between themselves some other type of relationship in which one or both parties are justified in believing that the other will not act contrary to their interests. Contract law is thus understandably suspicious of contracts between different parties when there is a pre-existing relationship between those parties that creates an expectation in one of the parties that the party with superior information will disclose all relevant facts known to that party. Accordingly, in such relationships of "trust and confidence," a person's non-disclosure of a known fact is equivalent to an affirmative assertion that the fact does not exist when the other person is entitled to know the fact. Restatement (Second) of Contracts § 161(d). Similarly, a person is ordinarily not justified in relying on a statement of "opinion" rather than a statement of fact unless the recipient is in a relationship of trust and confidence with the maker of the opinion and the reliance on the opinion is reasonable. Restatement (Second) of Contracts § 169(a). In either event, the non-disclosure or the statement of opinion might have the effect of making the contract voidable. Restatement (Second) of Contracts § 164(a).

Undue influence depends in part on unfair persuasion of a party who, by virtue of the "relation between them," is justified in assuming that the other party will not act inconsistent with their welfare. Restatement (Second) of Contracts § 177(1). Such a "relationship" includes one of trust and confidence. See Restatement (Second) of Contracts § 177 *cmt. a*. Also, a contract between a fiduciary and a beneficiary is voidable by the beneficiary unless the contract is on fair terms and the beneficiary had a full understanding of all legal rights and all relevant facts that the fiduciary knew or should have known. Restatement (Second) of Contracts § 173. Finally, a promise by a fiduciary to violate a fiduciary duty is void as contrary to public policy. Restatement (Second) of Contracts § 193.

Those voidable consequences depend in part on understanding the difference between a relationship of "trust and confidence" and a "fiduciary relationship." Neither relationship is specifically defined in the Restatement (Second) of Contracts, but the commentary is helpful. A "fiduciary" is a person who undertakes to act in the interests of another person. See Austin W. Scott, "The Fiduciary Principle," 37 Cal. L. Rev. 539, 540 (1949). For example, a trustee is a fiduciary because a trustee must act in the interests of the trust beneficiaries. Restatement (Second) of Trusts § 2. Similarly, agency is a form of "fiduciary relationship" resulting when one person (agent) consents to act on behalf of another (principal) and subject to that person's control. Restatement (Second) of Agency § 1 & Restatement (Third) of Agency § 1.01. Law students should particularly note that lawyers are agents of their clients and as such owe their clients fiduciary duties. As a matter of the common law of agency, the term "fiduciary" is used as a signal indicating that the agent owes fiduciary obligations to the principal, notably including the duty to act loyally in the principal's interest. Restatement (Third) of Agency § 1.01 *cmt. e*.

The actual duties owed by any particular class of fiduciaries to the beneficiary of that fiduciary relationship differ substantially depending on the nature and context of the relationship. For example, although both trustees and agents are fiduciaries, a trustee is not an agent because the trustee does not act subject to the control of any beneficiary. Restatement (Second) of Trusts § 8. Thus, the broader category of fiduciary relationships comprises the trustee/beneficiary, agent/principal, and a number of other specialized relationships.

In a similar fashion, the fiduciary concept arose in equity as a specific subcategory of a relationship of "trust and confidence." See L. S. Sealy, "Fiduciary Relationships," 1962 Cambridge L.J. 69, 71–72; Deborah A. DeMott, "Beyond Metaphor: An Analysis of Fiduciary Obligation," 1988 Duke L. J. 879, 880. For example, a relationship of trust and confidence normally exists between members of the same family and may arise in other contexts where one party may be reasonably expected to trust and rely upon the judgment and advice of another. Thus, the relationship between physician and patient, while ordinarily not a fiduciary or agency relationship, is normally one of trust and confidence. See Restatement (Second) of Contracts § 161 *cmt. f*. The various relationships mentioned create a cascading of sorts from the broad to the narrow with trust and confidence the broadest because it encompasses both the trust and agency relationships. Likewise, the trust fiduciary relationship is broader than the agency relationship because while both inclusively require the presence of a person acting on behalf of another, the agency relationship adds the further requirement that the agent act subject to the control of the principal.

The point here is simple. In analyzing various consequences of contract law, it is often important to also examine the relationship between the parties to the contract. The relationship might be created by the contract itself or might exist prior to the creation of the contract.

D. ABUSE OF THE BARGAINING PROCESS BY ONE OF THE PARTIES

Assuming competent parties execute a contract, courts generally attempt to police the distinction between enforceable and voidable contracts through analysis of the bargaining process, rather than assessing the fairness of the bargain or exchange of considerations. In this regard, recall the Chapter 2 discussion of the peppercorn theory of consideration and the doctrine of fair exchange. That discussion revealed that courts avoid assessing the fairness of the bargain from the perspective of the fairness of the exchanged considerations. In other words, as long as the parties abide by the accepted process for creation of enforceable bargains, courts will rarely overturn the resulting bargain even if it appears to be unfair to one of the parties. Of course, as suggested in the two-pronged procedural and substantive standard for unconscionability, deep flaws in the bargaining process often signal similar flaws in the substance of the bargain and vice versa.

Historically, the two most common categories of bargaining abuse involved deception and coercion by one of the parties in the formation of the contract. At a minimum, when applicable, these doctrines regulating misrepresentations and duress recognize a formative defect and therefore create a power of avoidance in the innocent party. Stated another way, deception and coercion violate accepted bargaining conventions by impairing in some way the free and rational exercise of the victim's volitional choice to enter or refuse the contract. Even if the resulting agreement between the parties bears all the outward indicia of a valid and properly formed contract—such as offer, acceptance, and consideration— the procedural flaws nonetheless threaten the entire existence of the contract and create a presumption that the exchange was unfair. Accordingly, the bargaining process flaws, such as deception and coercion, provide the victim with both a shield or privilege against enforcement of the contract and a power to avoid the contract altogether. Abuse of the bargaining process, like contracting with parties lacking the capacity to contract, implicates the very existence of the contract.

Moreover, while both deceit and coercive conduct may create a power to avoid the contract, deceit in particular began as a tort doctrine. For that historical reason, ancient deceit and modern fraud actions most often implicate a choice between an action on the contract and an action to rescind the contract. The modern rules of election and preclusion are discussed at the beginning of this chapter. However, unlike most other avoidance grounds, fraud uniquely implicates both remedies because it operates both as an independent cause of action in tort (for which the plaintiff may recover both compensatory and punitive damages) and a defense to contract (giving rise to a power of avoidance in the victim). While most avoidance grounds do not create a monetary remedy for breach of contract, the victim of tort fraud may recover monetary damages in appropriate cases.

This unique nature of fraud creates a broader range of strategic choices in the injured party. First, tort fraud requires the plaintiff to plead and prove six elements: (1) misrepresentation, (2) of material fact, (3) made with scienter, (4) upon which the plaintiff reasonably and detrimentally relied, (5) causing, (6) damages. See Restatement (Second) Torts § 525 ("One who fraudulently makes a misrepresentation of fact, opinion, intention or law for the purpose of inducing another to act or to refrain from action in reliance upon it, is subject to liability to the other in deceit for pecuniary loss caused to him by his justifiable reliance upon the misrepresentation."). But a successful tort fraud plaintiff may recover compensatory damages measured by the contract expectancy (discussed in Chapter 9) and any other species of tort damages, including punitives.

Second, contract fraud provides a basis for avoidance of the contract and does not require proof of all the elements of a tort fraud cause of action. In essence, contract fraud is easier to prove in part because the "remedy" is merely avoidance of a contract obtained through misrepresentation, rather than an affirmative damages claim against a tortfeasor. This is because contract law views fraud only from the perspective of avoidance and not as a breach of contract. While fraud in tort requires *scienter* (knowing intent to deceive), contractual avoidance does not. Thus, contract avoidance is more broadly available than damages for fraud in tort. Finally, provided the loss is purely economic, the measure of losses will be different under tort fraud in connection with a contract and tort fraud between strangers. Between strangers, tort fraud produces a recovery under the out-of-pocket rule to place the plaintiff in the status quo that existed before the tort. However, a majority of courts measure damages for tort fraud in connection with a contractual party by the contract benefit-of-bargain rule to place the plaintiff in the same position the plaintiff would have been in if the promise had been true.

The materials below relate the story of a doctrine in constant development. Early English common law did not permit the use of fraud in the inducement as a defense to an action for the price. Thus, if the seller induced the buyer to overvalue the subject matter of the contract through misrepresentations, the seller could nonetheless recover under a contract action. The defrauded purchaser's remedy lay solely in later pursuing an independent action known as the tort of deceit. A. W. Brian Simpson, A History of the Common Law of Contract 244–245 (Oxford Press 1975). This early distinction in part explains the odd way and manner of choosing to sue on the contract or to rescind the contract. See Michelle Oberman, "Sex, Lies and the Duty to Disclose," 47 Ariz. L. Rev. 871 (2005).

1. INTENTIONAL AND NEGLIGENT MISREPRESENTATION

The term "fraud" is broadly used in contracts as well as torts. Fraud with respect to the nature of documents signed (fraud in execution) prevents the formation of a contract. See Restatement (Second) of Contracts § 163 and discussion of "void" contracts in Chapter 6. As used in this section, fraud relative to the nature of the consideration itself (fraud in inducement) does not prevent the formation of the contract and thus creates an election of remedies in favor of the injured party.

Fraud in the inducement creates only a voidable contract. Restatement (Second) of Contracts § 164(1). As such, the defrauded or injured party has a power to avoid the contract and obtain rescission and restitution for any consideration transferred to the fraudulent party. Alternatively, the injured party can affirm the contract and seek damages on the affirmed contract. While an action for damages on the contract alone might constitute an election to affirm or ratify the contract that extinguishes the power of rescission, the claims may be pleaded in the alternative with an ultimate election by the end of the trial to avoid double recovery. See Martha Stewart Yerkes, "Election of Remedies in the Case of Fraudulent Misrepresentation," 26 S. Cal. L. Rev. 159 (1953).

While the fraud ordinarily also constitutes the tort of misrepresentation, since the tort was committed in connection with a contract, in most cases monetary damages are calculated according to the normative contract measure (benefit-of-bargain rule) rather than the normative tort measure (out-of-pocket rule). A majority of state courts have rejected the tort out-of-pocket rule and adopted the contract benefit-of-bargain rule measure. See, e.g., Syester v. Banta, 257 Iowa 613, 133 N.W.2d 666 (1965) ("Although the court's instructions on measure of damage were closer to the 'out of pocket' rule than to the 'benefit of bargain' rule to which we are committed . . . defendants make no complaint."). Moreover, other tort damage limitation rules also favor the contract measure. For example, absent personal injury, the injured party's loss is purely economic and the "economic loss rule" discussed in Chapter 9 normally utilizes the contract damage measure. In the case of the sale of goods, remedies for material misrepresentation or fraud are likewise measured under a breach of contract benefit-of-the-bargain rule approach, thus repealing the tort out-of-pocket rule. See UCC § 2–721 ("Remedies for material misrepresentation or fraud include all remedies available under this Article for non-fraudulent breach."); Gary L. Monserud, "Measuring Damages After Buyer's Affirmation of an Article 2 Sales Contract Induced by Fraud: A Study of Code Jurisprudence in Light of Section 2–721 and Pre-Code Conflicts in Remedial Theory," 1996 Colum. Bus. L. Rev. 423.

Several factors influence an injured party's decision to pursue one or both remedies (rescission and restitution versus damages on the contract). First, contract law itself does not impose a damage remedy for misrepresentation. Rather, the injured party may recover damages only by pleading and proving the comparatively more stringent elements of a tort fraud cause of action, even though such damages are measured by the normative contract benefit-of-bargain rule. Of course, a tortious misrepresentation not made in connection with the formation of a contract would be based entirely in tort law, and if successful, damages would be measured in accordance with the normative tort out-of-pocket rule. But regardless of the measurement standard, damages on the contract for the tort of misrepresentation will *only exist* if the "tort requirements" for misrepresentation are first satisfied. Accordingly, to sue on the contract for damages related to a misrepresentation, the elements of the tort of misrepresentation must be proven.

In all cases, and as discussed above, the law of tort misrepresentation generally requires (1) a misrepresentation, (2) of material fact, (3) made with scienter—that is, with a knowing intent to deceive, (4) upon which the plaintiff reasonably and detrimentally relies, (5) causing, (6) damages. See Fleming James, Jr. & Oscar S. Gray, "Misrepresentation," 37 Md. L. Rev. 286, 289–297 (1977) (Part I) & 37 Md. L. Rev. 488 (1977) (Part II). However, the contractual conceptualization of misrepresentation is considerably broader than tort conceptualization and often does not even require *scienter*. While the tort damage claim (while measured in contractual terms) requires knowledge that the assertion was false, contract law may permit avoidance even where the deceitful party made a material but merely innocent misrepresentation. The tort damage claim would generally not be available in such cases. Accordingly, the provable state of mind of the maker of the assertion often plays a role in determining whether the injured party pursues the tort fraud action for benefit-of-the-bargain damages rather than the contractual action for rescission and restitution.

For contract purposes, inducement of assent by either a fraudulent or material misrepresentation upon which the recipient is justified in relying renders a contract voidable. Restatement (Second) of Contracts § 164(1). A "misrepresentation" is an assertion not in accord with the facts. Restatement (Second) of Contracts § 159. For this purpose, "facts" include assertions regarding past events as well as current circumstances, but do not include future events. Restatement (Second) of Contracts § 159 *cmt. c.* Two separate sections describe when conduct is equivalent to an "assertion." First, "concealment" intended to keep another from learning true facts of which the party would otherwise have learned is equivalent to an assertion of a fact and is therefore a misrepresentation. Restatement (Second) of Contracts § 160. Second, "non-disclosure" is also equivalent to an assertion and therefore a misrepresentation, but only where (i) the person knows disclosure is necessary to prevent a previous assertion from being fraudulent or material ("duty to correct"); (ii) the person knows disclosure would correct a material mistake of the other party, but only if non-disclosure amounts to a failure to act in good faith; (iii) the person knows that disclosure would correct a mistake regarding the contents of a writing evidencing the agreement; or (iv) when the other person is entitled to know the fact by reason of a relationship of trust and confidence between them. See id.

The remainder of the restatement misrepresentation sections describe when a misrepresentation is either fraudulent or material and the voidable consequences thereof. A misrepresentation is fraudulent when the maker (i) knows or believes the assertion is not in accord with the facts; (ii) does not have the confidence that he states or implies in the truth of the statement; or (iii) knows that he does not have the basis that he states or implies for the assertion. Restatement (Second) of Contracts § 162(1). Since both the first and third definitions state a *scienter* requirement, they are common to both torts and contracts. The second definition is not generally common to tort law, however, because *scienter* is less evident. For tort law, such assertions might not be adequate to maintain an independent tort action for damages, but may nonetheless be adequate to invoke the power of avoidance and are therefore significant. See Derry v. Peek, 14 App. Cas. 337 (House of Lords, Eng., 1889) and Fleming James, Jr. & Oscar S. Gray, "Misrepresentation," 37 Md. L. Rev. 286, 297 (1977) (Part I). Under tort law, the failure of belief is not a misrepresentation itself, but rather an inference of fraud to be presented to the trier of fact.

A misrepresentation is material if it is likely to induce a reasonable person to manifest assent. Restatement (Second) of Contracts § 162(2). Again, unlike tort law, this form of misrepresentation does not state a *scienter* requirement and therefore is generally not actionable in tort damages. Nonetheless, it may be the basis of rescission.

In each case, rescission for either fraudulent or material misrepresentation will only occur if the other party to the contract is justified in relying on the misrepresentation. Restatement (Second) of

Contracts § 164(1). Justified reliance is slightly different conceptually than "reasonable" reliance discussed in Chapter 2 regarding promissory estoppel. While promissory estoppel reasonable reliance requires an element of foreseeability and substantiality, the same is not necessarily required for justified reliance, which focuses more on the nature of the reliance based on the subjective nature of the injured party. However, justified reliance becomes particularly problematic as assertions move from fact through opinion (Restatement (Second) of Contracts §§ 168–169), statements of law (Restatement (Second) of Contracts § 170), assertions of intention (Restatement (Second) of Contracts § 171), and statements of fault (Restatement (Second) of Contracts § 172). Nonetheless, the justification requirement eliminates misrepresentations regarding peripheral and unimportant facts, as well as matters that are not objectively serious. See Restatement (Second) of Contracts § 164 *cmt. d.*

HILL V. JONES

Court of Appeals of Arizona
151 Ariz. 81, 725 P.2d 1115 (1986)

MEYERSON, Judge.

Must the seller of a residence disclose to the buyer facts pertaining to past termite infestation? This is the primary question presented in this appeal. Plaintiffs Warren G. Hill and Gloria R. Hill (buyers) filed suit to rescind an agreement to purchase a residence. Buyers alleged that Ora G. Jones and Barbara R. Jones (sellers) had made misrepresentations concerning termite damage in the residence and had failed to disclose to them the existence of the damage and history of termite infestation in the residence. The trial court dismissed the claim for misrepresentation based upon a so-called integration clause in the parties' agreement.

Sellers then sought summary judgment on the "concealment" claim arguing that they had no duty to disclose information pertaining to termite infestation and that even if they did, the record failed to show all of the elements necessary for fraudulent concealment. The trial court granted summary judgment, finding that there was "no genuinely disputed issue of material fact and that the law favors the . . . defendants." The trial court awarded sellers $1,000.00 in attorney's fees. Buyers have appealed from the judgment and sellers have cross-appealed from the trial court's ruling on attorney's fees.

I.   FACTS

In 1982, buyers entered into an agreement to purchase sellers' residence for $72,000. The agreement was entered after buyers made several visits to the home. The purchase agreement provided that sellers were to pay for and place in escrow a termite inspection report stating that the property was free from evidence of termite infestation. Escrow was scheduled to close two months later.

One of the central features of the house is a parquet teak floor covering the sunken living room, the dining room, the entryway and portions of the halls. On a subsequent visit to the house, and when sellers were present, buyers noticed a small "ripple" in the wood floor on the step leading up to the dining room from the sunken living room. Mr. Hill asked if the ripple could be termite damage. Mrs. Jones answered that it was water damage. A few years previously, a broken water heater in the house had in fact caused water damage in the area of the dining room and steps which necessitated that some repairs be made to the floor. No further discussion on the subject, however, took place between the parties at that time or afterwards.

Mr. Hill, through his job as maintenance supervisor at a school district, had seen similar "ripples" in wood which had turned out to be termite damage. Mr. Hill was not totally satisfied with Mrs. Jones's explanation, but he felt that the termite inspection report would reveal whether the ripple was due to termites or some other cause.

The termite inspection report stated that there was no visible evidence of infestation. The report failed to note the existence of physical damage or evidence of previous treatment. The realtor notified the parties that the property had passed the termite inspection. Apparently, neither party actually saw the report prior to close of escrow.

After moving into the house, buyers found a pamphlet left in one of the drawers entitled "Termites, the Silent Saboteurs." They learned from a neighbor that the house had some termite infestation in the past. Shortly after the close of escrow, Mrs. Hill noticed that the wood on the steps leading down to the sunken living room was crumbling. She called an exterminator who confirmed the existence of termite damage to the floor and steps and to wood columns in the house. The estimated cost of repairing the wood floor alone was approximately $5,000.

Through discovery after their lawsuit was filed, buyers learned the following. When sellers purchased the residence in 1974, they received two termite guarantees that had been given to the previous owner by Truly Nolen, as well as a diagram showing termite treatment at the residence that had taken place in 1963. The guarantees provided for semi-annual inspections and annual termite booster treatments. The accompanying diagram stated that the existing damage had not been repaired. The second guarantee, dated 1965, reinstated the earlier contract for inspection and treatment. Mr. Jones admitted that he read the guarantees when he received them. Sellers renewed the guarantees when they purchased the residence in 1974. They also paid the annual fee each year until they sold the home.

On two occasions during sellers' ownership of the house but while they were at their other residence in Minnesota, a neighbor noticed "streamers" evidencing live termites in the wood tile floor near the entryway. On both occasions, Truly Nolen gave a booster treatment for termites. On the second incident, Truly Nolen drilled through one of the wood tiles to treat for termites. The neighbor showed Mr. Jones the area where the damage and treatment had occurred. Sellers had also seen termites on the back fence and had replaced and treated portions of the fence.

Sellers did not mention any of this information to buyers prior to close of escrow. They did not mention the past termite infestation and treatment to the realtor or to the termite inspector. There was evidence of holes on the patio that had been drilled years previously to treat for termites. The inspector returned to the residence to determine why he had not found evidence of prior treatment and termite damage. He indicated that he had not seen the holes in the patio because of boxes stacked there. It is unclear whether the boxes had been placed there by buyers or sellers. He had not found the damage inside the house because a large plant, which buyers had purchased from sellers, covered the area. After investigating the second time, the inspector found the damage and evidence of past treatment. He acknowledged that this information should have appeared in the report. He complained, however, that he should have been told of any history of termite infestation and treatment before he performed his inspection and that it was customary for the inspector to be given such information.

Other evidence presented to the trial court was that during their numerous visits to the residence before close of escrow, buyers had unrestricted access to view and inspect the entire house. Both Mr. and Mrs. Hill had seen termite damage and were therefore familiar with what it might look like. Mr. Hill had seen termite damage on the fence at this property. Mrs. Hill had noticed the holes on the patio but claimed not to realize at the time what they were for. Buyers asked no questions about termites except when they asked if the "ripple" on the stairs was termite damage. Mrs. Hill admitted she was not "trying" to find problems with the house because she really wanted it.

II.   CONTRACT INTEGRATION CLAUSE

We first turn to the trial court's ruling that the agreement of the parties did not give buyers the right to rely on the statement made by Mrs. Jones that the "ripple" in the floor was water damage. We find this ruling to be in error. The contract provision upon which the trial court based its ruling reads as follows:

> That the Purchaser has investigated the said premises, and the Broker and the Seller are hereby released from all responsibility regarding the valuation thereof, and neither Purchaser, Seller, nor Broker shall be bound by any understanding, agreement,

promise, representation or stipulation expressed or implied, not specified herein.

In Lutfy v. R. D. Roper & Sons Motor Co., 57 Ariz. 495, 506, 115 P. 2d 161, 166 (1941), the Arizona Supreme Court considered a similar clause in an agreement and concluded that "any provision in a contract making it possible for a party thereto to free himself from the consequences of his own fraud in procuring its execution is invalid and necessarily constitutes no defense." The court went on to hold that "parol evidence is always admissible to show fraud, and this is true, even though it has the effect of varying the terms of a writing between the parties." 57 Ariz. at 506–507, 115 P. 2d at 166; Barnes v. Lopez, 25 Ariz. App. 477, 480, 544 P. 2d 694, 697 (1976). In this case, the claimed misrepresentation occurred after the parties executed the contract.[1] Assuming, for the purposes of this decision, that the integration clause would extend to statements made subsequent to the execution of the contract, the clause could not shield sellers from liability should buyers be able to prove fraud.

III. DUTY TO DISCLOSE

The principal legal question presented in this appeal is whether a seller has a duty to disclose to the buyer the existence of termite damage in a residential dwelling known to the seller, but not to the buyer, which materially affects the value of the property. For the reasons stated herein, we hold that such a duty exists.

This is not the place to trace the history of the doctrine of caveat emptor. Suffice it to say that its vitality has waned during the latter half of the 20th century. E.g., Richards v. Powercraft Homes, Inc., 139 Ariz. 242, 678 P. 2d 427 (1984) (implied warranty of workmanship and habitability extends to subsequent buyers of homes). . . . The modern view is that a vendor has an affirmative duty to disclose material facts where:

1. Disclosure is necessary to prevent a previous assertion from being a misrepresentation or from being fraudulent or material;

2. Disclosure would correct a mistake of the other party as to a basic assumption on which that party is making the contract and if nondisclosure amounts to a failure to act in good faith and in accordance with reasonable standards of fair dealing;

3. Disclosure would correct a mistake of the other party as to the contents or effect of a writing, evidencing or embodying an agreement in whole or in part;

---

[1] Buyers' fraud theory is apparently based on the premise that they were not bound under the contract until a satisfactory termite inspection report was submitted.

4. The other person is entitled to know the fact because of a relationship of trust and confidence between them. Restatement (Second) of Contracts § 161 (1981) (Restatement); see Restatement (Second) of Torts § 551 (1977).

Arizona courts have long recognized that under certain circumstances there may be a "duty to speak." Van Buren v. Pima Community College Dist. Bd., 113 Ariz. 85, 87, 546 P. 2d 821, 823 (1976). . . . As the supreme court noted in the context of a confidential relationship, "[s]uppression of a material fact which a party is bound in good faith to disclose is equivalent to a false representation." Leigh v. Loyd, 74 Ariz. 84, 87, 244 P. 2d 356, 358 (1952). . . .

Thus, the important question we must answer is whether under the facts of this case, buyers should have been permitted to present to the jury their claim that sellers were under a duty to disclose their (sellers') knowledge of termite infestation in the residence. This broader question involves two inquiries. First, must a seller of residential property advise the buyer of material facts within his knowledge pertaining to the value of the property? Second, may termite damage and the existence of past infestation constitute such material facts?

The doctrine imposing a duty to disclose is akin to the well-established contractual rules pertaining to relief from contracts based upon mistake. Although the law of contracts supports the finality of transactions, over the years courts have recognized that under certain limited circumstances it is unjust to strictly enforce the policy favoring finality. Thus, for example, even a unilateral mistake of one party to a transaction may justify rescission. Restatement § 153.

There is also a judicial policy promoting honesty and fair dealing in business relationships. This policy is expressed in the law of fraudulent and negligent misrepresentations. Where a misrepresentation is fraudulent or where a negligent misrepresentation is one of material fact, the policy of finality rightly gives way to the policy of promoting honest dealings between the parties. See Restatement § 164(1).

Under certain circumstances nondisclosure of a fact known to one party may be equivalent to the assertion that the fact does not exist. For example "[w]hen one conveys a false impression by the disclosure of some facts and the concealment of others, such concealment is in effect a false representation that what is disclosed is the whole truth." State v. Coddington, 135 Ariz. 480, 481, 662 P. 2d 155, 156 (App. 1983). Thus, nondisclosure may be equated with and given the same legal effect as fraud and misrepresentation. One category of cases where this has been done involves the area of nondisclosure of material facts affecting the value of property, known to the seller but not reasonably capable of being known to the buyer.

Courts have formulated this "duty to disclose" in slightly different ways. For example, the Florida Supreme Court recently declared that "where the seller of a home knows of facts materially affecting the value of the property which are not readily observable and are not known to the buyer, the seller is under a duty to disclose them to the buyer." Johnson v. Davis, 480 So. 2d 625, 629 (Fla. 1985) (defective roof in three-year old home). In California, the rule has been stated this way:

> [W]here the seller knows of facts materially affecting the value or desirability of the property which are known or accessible only to him and also knows that such facts are not known to, or within the reach of the diligent attention and observation of the buyer, the seller is under a duty to disclose them to the buyer. Lingsch v. Savage, 213 Cal. App. 2d 729, 735, 29 Cal. Rptr. 201, 204 (1963); contra Ray v. Montgomery, 399 So. 2d 230 (Ala. 1980); see generally W. Prosser & W. Keeton, The Law of Torts § 106 (5th ed. 1984).[2]

We find that the Florida formulation of the disclosure rule properly balances the legitimate interests of the parties in a transaction for the sale of a private residence and accordingly adopt it for such cases.

As can be seen, the rule requiring disclosure is invoked in the case of material facts.[3] Thus, we are led to the second inquiry—whether the existence of termite damage in a residential dwelling is the type of material fact which gives rise to the duty to disclose. The existence of termite damage and past termite infestation has been considered by other courts to be sufficiently material to warrant disclosure. See generally Annot., 22 A. L. R. 3d 972 (1968).

In Lynn v. Taylor, 7 Kan. App. 2d 369, 642 P. 2d 131 (1982), the purchaser of a termite-damaged residence brought suit against the seller and realtor for fraud and against the termite inspector for negligence. An initial termite report found evidence of prior termite infestation and recommended treatment. A second report indicated that the house was termite free. The first report was not given to the buyer. The seller contended that because treatment would not have repaired the existing damage, the first report was not material. The buyer testified that he would not have purchased the house had he known of the first report. Under these circumstances, the court concluded that the facts contained in the first report were material. See Hunt v. Walker, 483 S. W. 2d 732 (Tenn. App.

---

[2] There are variations on this same theme. For example, Pennsylvania has limited the obligation of disclosure to cases of dangerous defects. Glanski v. Ervine, 269 Pa. Super. 182, 191, 409 A. 2d 425, 430 (1979).

[3] Arizona has recognized that a duty to disclose may arise where the buyer makes an inquiry of the seller, regardless of whether or not the fact is material. Universal Inv. Co. v. Sahara Motor Inn, Inc., 127 Ariz. 213, 215, 619 P. 2d 485, 487 (1980). The inquiry by buyers whether the ripple was termite damage imposed a duty upon sellers to disclose what information they knew concerning the existence of termite infestation in the residence.

1971) (severe damage to the residence by past termite infestation); Mercer v. Woodard, 166 Ga. App. 119, 123, 303 S. E. 2d 475, 481–82 (1983) (duty of disclosure extends to fact of past termite damage).

Although sellers have attempted to draw a distinction between live termites[4] and past infestation, the concept of materiality is an elastic one which is not limited by the termites' health. "A matter is material if it is one to which a reasonable person would attach importance in determining his choice of action in the transaction in question." Lynn v. Taylor, 7 Kan. App. 2d at 371, 642 P. 2d at 134–35. For example, termite damage substantially affecting the structural soundness of the residence may be material even if there is no evidence of present infestation. Unless reasonable minds could not differ, materiality is a factual matter which must be determined by the trier of fact. The termite damage in this case may or may not be material. Accordingly, we conclude that buyers should be allowed to present their case to a jury.

Sellers argue that even assuming the existence of a duty to disclose, summary judgment was proper because the record shows that their "silence . . . did not induce or influence" the buyers. This is so, sellers contend, because Mr. Hill stated in his deposition that he intended to rely on the termite inspection report. But this argument begs the question. If sellers were fully aware of the extent of termite damage and if such information had been disclosed to buyers, a jury could accept Mr. Hill's testimony that had he known of the termite damage he would not have purchased the house.

Sellers further contend that buyers were put on notice of the possible existence of termite infestation and were therefore "chargeable with the knowledge which [an] inquiry, if made, would have revealed." Godfrey v. Navratil, 3 Ariz. App. 47, 51, 411 P. 2d 470 (1966) (quoting Luke v. Smith, 13 Ariz. 155, 162, 108 P. 494, 496 (1910)). It is also true that "a party may . . . reasonably expect the other to take normal steps to inform himself and to draw his own conclusions." Restatement § 161 comment d. Under the facts of this case, the question of buyers' knowledge of the termite problem (or their diligence in attempting to inform themselves about the termite problem) should be left to the jury.[5]

By virtue of our holding, sellers' cross-appeal is moot.

Reversed and remanded.

CONTRERAS, P. J., and YALE MCFATE, J. (Retired), concur.

---

[4]   Sellers acknowledge that a duty of disclosure would exist if live termites were present. Obde v. Schlemeyer, 56 Wash. 2d 449, 353 P. 2d 672 (1960).

[5]   Sellers also contend that they had no knowledge of any existing termite damage in the house. An extended discussion of the facts on this point is unnecessary. Simply stated, the facts are in conflict on this issue.

NOTES AND QUESTIONS

1. *Avoidance or damages?* Buyers sought rescission of the purchase agreement rather than damages on the contract to purchase. Why? If the buyers had sought monetary damages, how would those damages have been measured? The trial court denied rescission and granted sellers' attorney fees. What explains the radically different outcome at the appellate level? The buyers asserted that the sellers made misrepresentations concerning termite damage in the home (but not the non-existence of termites) and failed to disclose the termite damage and termite history. Are these the same form of misrepresentation? If not, what is the difference? What was the basis of the misrepresentation claim? Did the sellers voluntarily assert the home was termite free or in response to a direct question regarding the same? If not, can concealment alone be the basis of an assertion of a fact constituting a form of misrepresentation? If so, what is the legal basis for doing so?

2. *Attorney fees.* The American Rule on attorney fees provides that, absent contractual agreement to the contrary or other exceptional circumstances or statute, each side must bear its own legal expenses. Why do you suppose the trial court awarded the sellers $1,000 for attorney fees? Why did the sellers appeal that aspect of the trial court decision?

3. *Effect of integration clause.* The trial court dismissed the misrepresentation claim, however framed, on the basis of the integration clause. Did the trial court dismiss the concealment claim on the same basis? Is concealment a form of misrepresentation? If so, and the integration clause effectively cured the misrepresentation claim, why was the clause not effective as to the concealment claim? Did the trial court utilize the integration clause to block admission of parol evidence to show misrepresentation? Since the alleged misrepresentation occurred after the contract was executed, is evidence thereof subject to the parol evidence rule? If not, is the reason because of the timing of the misrepresentation or the fact that even parol evidence is admissible to prove fraud? Assuming that even parol evidence is admissible to show fraud in the absence of an integration clause, what does the presence of the integration clause add to the sellers' misrepresentation defense? Does it seek to destroy "justified" reliance on a misrepresentation even if made? If so, do you think such a purpose should be sanctioned by the court? If not, and you represented the sellers' in this case and prior to purchase, would you continue to recommend the inclusion of such a clause? If so, why? Does the clause have a broader purpose than eliminating responsibility for misrepresentations?

4. *Duty to disclose.* The duty to disclose identified in *Hill* is in tension with the general principle of contract law that parties dealing at arms' length typically do not have an affirmative duty to protect the other party's interests. Restatement (Second) of Contracts § 161 Comment d illustrates and clarifies this tension:

> In many situations, if one party knows that the other is mistaken as to a basic assumption, he is expected to disclose the fact that would correct the mistake. A seller of real or personal property is, for

example, ordinarily expected to disclose a known latent defect of quality or title that is of such a character as would probably prevent the buyer from buying at the contract price. . . . Nevertheless, a party need not correct all mistakes of the other and is expected only to act in good faith and in accordance with reasonable standards of fair dealing, as reflected in prevailing business ethics. A party may, therefore, reasonably expect the other to take normal steps to inform himself and to draw his own conclusions. If the other is indolent, inexperienced or ignorant, or if his judgment is bad or he lacks access to adequate information, his adversary is not generally expected to compensate for these deficiencies.

Which of these paradigms best reflects your actual expectations in dealing with others in your business affairs, including your contracts for housing, financial aid, real property, transportation, and with your law school? Does the subject matter and context of the transaction alter your expectations regarding the other party's duty to disclose? It is worth noting that the scope of this duty to disclose has an ancient pedigree. Consider St. Thomas Aquinas's discussion of whether a seller is bound to state defects in the thing sold:

> Article 3. Whether the seller is bound to state the defects of the thing sold?
>
> * * *
>
> I answer that, It is always unlawful to give anyone an occasion of danger or loss, although a man need not always give another the help or counsel which would be for his advantage in any way; but only in certain fixed cases, for instance when someone is subject to him, or when he is the only one who can assist him. Now the seller who offers goods for sale, gives the buyer an occasion of loss or danger, by the very fact that he offers him defective goods, if such defect may occasion loss or danger to the buyer—loss, if, by reason of this defect, the goods are of less value, and he takes nothing off the price on that account—danger, if this defect either hinder the use of the goods or render it hurtful, for instance, if a man sells a lame for a fleet horse, a tottering house for a safe one, rotten or poisonous food for wholesome. Wherefore if such like defects be hidden, and the seller does not make them known, the sale will be illicit and fraudulent, and the seller will be bound to compensation for the loss incurred.
>
> On the other hand, if the defect be manifest, for instance if a horse have but one eye, or if the goods though useless to the buyer, be useful to someone else, provided the seller take as much as he ought from the price, he is not bound to state the defect of the goods, since perhaps on account of that defect the buyer might want him to allow a greater rebate than he need. Wherefore the seller may look to his own indemnity, by withholding the defect of the goods. The Summa Theologica of St. Thomas Aquinas II–II, Q.77 (Fathers of the English

Dominican Province trans. 1920) (Kevin Knight ed. 2006), available at http://www.newadvent.org/summa.

To what extent does this thirteenth century ethical analysis mirror modern ethical expectations and duties?

Importantly, the restatement frames the duty to disclose in terms of the failure of a basic assumption. This mistake as to a basic assumption of the parties provides the basis for the unilateral mistake doctrine discussed later in this chapter. In general, a contract is voidable where one party at the time of contracting is mistaken as to a basic assumption and that mistake has a material effect on the agreed exchange of performances, provided that enforcement would be unconscionable or that the other party had reason to know of, or caused, the mistake. See Restatement (Second) of Contracts § 153. In the circumstances at issue in *Hill*, would the doctrine of unilateral mistake adequately protect the buyer? If so, what is the necessity of a separate duty to disclose a material fact if the lack of knowledge of that fact by the buyer provides an identical rescission remedy? Doctrinally, what are the differences between these two concepts?

When a party seeks monetary damages for fraud on the contract and not rescission, the case is somewhat less broad than a rescission action, since the contractual grounds for rescission are broader than the tort elements of fraud. However, the presence of the tort fraud further presents the rare possibility of an award of punitive damages. Restatement (Second) of Contracts § 355 states that "[p]unitive damages are not recoverable for a breach of contract unless the conduct constituting the breach is also a tort for which punitive damages are recoverable." This rule follows naturally from the proposition that a mere breach of contract is not a wrong, but rather just obligates the breaching party to compensate the non-breaching party for damages caused by the breach. See Restatement (Second) of Contracts § 355 *cmt. a* (noting that the purpose of awarding contract damages is to compensate, rather than to punish). In contrast, tort law seeks to redress a morally wrong injury caused by the involuntary "transaction" forced upon the victim. Thus, in addition to compensating the victim for out-of-pocket damages, tort law also permits recovery of punitive damages to punish the tortfeasor "for his outrageous conduct and to deter him and others like him from similar conduct in the future." Restatement (Second) Torts § 908(1).

The student is bound to ask the question, "Why are punitive damages recoverable in tort for willful or wanton conduct but not in contract for willful or wanton breach?" The best, but least satisfying, answer is that the Courts of King's and Queen's Bench in the eighteenth and nineteenth centuries said so, and American courts followed suit. But, the student will say, "Is that any reason to deny punitive damages for willful breach of contract today?" After all, the injury caused to a non-breaching party by a particularly egregious and willful bad faith breach or by fraudulent, coercive, or unconscionable conduct will often be indistinguishable from the moral and economic injuries caused by an involuntary tort. Indeed, it is arguable that a particularly willful or wanton breach of contract may be more deserving of punishment because such conduct opportunistically exploits the other party's voluntarily induced contract vulnerabilities and is thus not only morally culpable, but also threatens the integrity of the institution of contract.

The purpose of tort law is to punish and deter, as well as to compensate the victim for harm done. Tort law began as a subset of criminal law, and it continues today to have some of the same characteristics as the criminal law, namely to protect and vindicate the public interest in a safe and peaceful environment. An award of damages for the tort of negligence is intended as much as a vindication of the public interest in providing an incentive not to be negligent as it is to compensate the victim for the harm caused. But surely, the award of damages for breach of contract is intended to serve at least two distinct purposes: first, to compensate the victim, and second to encourage others by example not to commit breaches of contract. While the award of damages for breach of contract may be compensation when viewed from the position of the plaintiff, it is likely to be viewed as punishment for committing the breach from the point of view of the defendant. The public versus private interests distinction thus does not justify the exclusion of punitive damages from contract remedies.

Several writers have researched and described the evolution of the common law from the twelfth century onwards with respect to the issue of punitive damages and how and when the rules of contract and tort separated. See, for instance, George T. Washington, "Damages in Contract at Common Law," 47 Law Q. Rev. 345 (1931) and Timothy J. Sullivan, "Punitive Damages in the Law of Contract: The Reality and the Illusion of Legal Change," 61 Minn. L. Rev. 207 (1977). Until well into the nineteenth century, the determination and assessment of damages was left to the jury with little if any guidance from the judge. But starting in the seventeenth century, judges began to establish limited controls over the jury's previously unfettered discretion as to remedies. Courts first reacted to absurd jury awards by adopting rules permitting new trials based on runaway jury behavior. English judges, however, were much more reticent to exercise such control over jury verdicts involving torts than over verdicts involving contracts. "It was against this background of judicial disinclination to meddle with jury verdicts in tort cases that the doctrine of punitive damages emerged." Timothy J. Sullivan, "Punitive Damages in the Law of Contract: The Reality and the Illusion of Legal Change," 61 Minn. L. Rev. 207, 213 (1977). Judges were more likely to interfere with verdicts based on breach of contract since the measure of damage was often clearer.

Other policy-based reasons further justify the contract rule against punitive damages. First, permitting punitive damages for pure breach of contract actions would inject undesirable uncertainty into commercial transactions, undermining risk allocations under the contract. Indeed, punitive damages in tort are often considered as a necessary tool for preventing tortfeasors from reducing their degree of care in light of the uncertainty of future tort liability. If a primary purpose of contract law is to provide contracting parties—particularly in commercial transactions— with mechanisms for increasing the predictability and certainty of their voluntary transactions, punitive damages would threaten the usefulness of contract to such parties. See, e.g., Leslie E. John, "Formulating Standards for Awards of Punitive Damages in the Borderland of Contract and Tort," 74 Cal. L. Rev. 2033 (1986) (suggesting that punitive damages cannot be recovered for breach of contract because they are never foreseeable).

Second, because the non-breaching party to a commercial contract may often purchase a substitute performance in the event of breach, compensatory damages will usually be sufficient. In the unusual case where the injured party has no adequate remedy at law—that is, where the injury is of a type that cannot be compensated by damages—courts may force the breaching party to fulfill its duties under the contract through an order of specific performance. Third, unlike a tort, a contract is the outcome of mutual intent. Presumptively, contracting parties do not intend to accept the risk of punitive damages. This third explanation harks back to the "will" theory of contract discussed in Chapter 2. See Laurence P. Simpson, "Punitive Damages for Breach of Contract," 20 Ohio St. L. J. 284 (1959). Alternatively, Judge Richard Posner has argued persuasively that contract law should promote "efficient" breaches by the parties. See, e.g., Richard Posner, Economic Analysis of Law 118–126 (6th ed. 2003) If the purpose of contract is to promote the transfer of goods and services to those who can put those goods and services to their highest, best, and most valuable use, then it follows that contracting parties should be permitted—or even encouraged—to breach their contracts where the breach and compensation would either make at least one party better off and no party worse off, or increase the total wealth of the parties (even if one party is made worse off by the breach) overall. See id.; cf. Oliver Wendell Holmes, "The Path of the Law," 10 Harv. L. Rev. 457, 462 (1897) ("The duty to keep a contract at common law means a prediction that you must pay damages if you do not keep it,—and nothing else."). By way of contrast, William S. Dodge, in "The Case for Punitive Damages in Contracts," 48 Duke L. J. 629 (1999), argued that punitive damages should be available for all willful breaches of contract, including both opportunistic and efficient breaches. He suggested that Posner's theory of "efficient breach" has now become the standard explanation of why punitive damages are not awarded for breach of contract.

ENHANCE-IT, LLC v. AMERICAN ACCESS TECHNOLOGIES, INC.

United States District Court for South Carolina
413 F. Supp. 2d 626 (2006)

DUFFY, District Judge.

This matter is before the court on Plaintiff Enhance-It, L.L.C.'s ("Enhance-It" or "Plaintiff") Motion to Amend its Complaint. Defendant American Access Technologies, Inc. ("AAT" or "Defendant") opposes this Motion.

BACKGROUND

Plaintiff Enhance-It is a South Carolina limited liability company that purchased ultraviolet lighting products from AAT and AAT's predecessor in interest. In its Second Amended Complaint, Plaintiff alleged that AAT shipped it defective goods, and asserted causes of action for (1) breach of contract, (2) negligence, (3) fraud and misrepresentation, (4) breach of warranty of merchantability, (5) breach of warranty of fitness for particular use, (6) breach of express warranty, and (7) breach of contract accompanied by a fraudulent act. In an order dated October 5, 2005, the court dismissed Plaintiff's Second (negligence), Third (fraud and misrepresentation), and Seventh (breach of contract accompanied by fraudulent act) causes of action. The court dismissed the Third and Seventh causes of action because the Second Amended Complaint did not include specific factual allegations sufficient to meet the heightened pleading requirements of Rule 9(b).[1]

On October 19, 2005, based upon the parties' agreement and consent, the court entered an Amended Scheduling Order. Under this Order, the parties had until December 1, 2005 to file motions to amend their pleadings. Accordingly, on December 1, 2005, Plaintiff filed a Motion to Amend the Second Amended Complaint and attached a proposed Third Amended Complaint. This Third Amended Complaint attempts to correct those deficiencies of the Second Amended Complaint that prompted this court to dismiss Plaintiff's fraud and breach of contract accompanied by a fraudulent act causes of action.[2]

* * *

---

[1] Federal Rule 9(b) requires that "[i]n all averments of fraud or mistake, the circumstances constituting fraud or mistake shall be stated with particularity."

[2] In the Third Amended Complaint, Fraud and Misrepresentation is the second cause of action and Breach of Contract Accompanied by Fraudulent Act is the sixth cause of action.

ANALYSIS

In this case, because Plaintiff filed the Motion to Amend the complaint within the time prescribed by the scheduling order, Defendant cannot claim that the proposed amendment was untimely. Nonetheless, Defendant argues that Plaintiff's motion should be denied because it is futile. Defendant contends that the proposed additional causes of action— fraud and breach of contract accompanied by fraudulent act—would not survive a motion to dismiss for failure to state a claim (1) because the allegedly false statement made by Defendant was an expression of opinion and cannot be considered fraudulent; and (2) because these causes of action are barred by South Carolina law.

(1) False Statement

Under South Carolina law, in order to prove fraud, the following elements must be shown: (1) a representation; (2) its falsity; (3) its materiality; (4) either knowledge of its falsity or a reckless disregard of its truth or falsity; (5) intent that the representation be acted upon; (6) the hearer's ignorance of its falsity; (7) the hearer's reliance on its truth; (8) the hearer's right to rely thereon; and (9) the hearer's consequent and proximate injury. Regions Bank v. Schmauch, 354 S.C. 648, 582 S.E. 2d 432, 444 (2003). Defendant claims that the facts as alleged in the proposed Third Amended Complaint do not support a fraud cause of action and that the motion to amend should therefore be denied as futile. Specifically, Defendant argues that Plaintiff's proposed Complaint fails to describe a representation by Defendant that can be considered false.[3]

As the Supreme Court of South Carolina has held:

Deceit or fraudulent representation, in order to be actionable, must relate to existing or past facts, and the fact that a promise made in the course of negotiations is never performed does not in and of itself constitute nor evidence fraud. A mere breach of a contract does not constitute fraud. . . . [a] future promise is not fraudulent unless such a future promise was part of a general design or plan existing at the time, made as part of a general scheme to induce the signing of a paper or to make one act, as he otherwise would not have acted, to his injury.

Coleman v. Stevens, 124 S.C. 8, 117 S.E. 305, 307 (1923); see also Bishop Logging Co. v. John Deere Indus. Equipment Co., 455 S.E.2d 183, 187–188 (1995) (holding that, where a fully mechanized swamp logging system was an unprecedented and untried concept and the defendant informed plaintiff that the system had never been attempted, the defendant's statements about the future performance of the system were

---

[3] Defendant does not contest that Plaintiff has properly alleged all other necessary elements of fraud.

statements of opinion or promises of future performance as opposed to false statements of present or pre-existing fact; therefore, the defendant's representation cannot be the basis for a finding of fraud).

In this case, the representation Plaintiff claims to be false is as follows:

> John Presley, a representative of AAT, allegedly told Plaintiff that AAT "had tested a new ballast to be utilized in the UV lighting it was selling to Plaintiff . . . and that it had tested the ballast for a year with good results, and that the new ballast would be better than the part it replaced." (Third Amended Complaint at 4.)

Plaintiff further alleges that John Presley:

> knew the ballast had not been tested for a year, and further knew that rather than obtaining "good results" from the testing, the results demonstrated that the ballasts were defective. (Third Amended Complaint at 4.)

Defendant argues that these alleged statements are merely statements of opinion and expressions of intention and are not a proper basis for an action in fraud.

Defendant is correct that any representations or guarantees as to the future performance of the ballasts are not actionable. Nonetheless, the representation that the ballasts had been tested, regardless of the results of these tests, is a representation of fact, not opinion. Accordingly, if the ballasts had, in fact, not been tested, representing that they had been tested is a false representation of a pre-existing fact that can serve as the basis for a fraud cause of action. The court therefore finds that the Third Amended Complaint alleges the necessary elements of fraud such that the proposed amendment is not obviously futile.

(2) South Carolina Law Regarding the Economic Loss Rule and Election of Remedies

Defendant alleges that Plaintiff is requesting a remedy in tort for what is a purely breach of contract claim. Defendant therefore argues that South Carolina's economic loss rule bars these tort claims. Defendant correctly notes that under South Carolina law, "if the cause of action is predicated on the alleged breach, or even negligent breach, of a contract between the parties, an action in tort will not lie." Meddin v. Southern Ry.-Carolina Division, 218 S.C. 155, 62 S.E. 2d 109, 112 (1950); see Tadlock Painting Co. v. Maryland Cas. Co., 322 S.C. 498, 473 S.E.2d 52, 55 (1996) (stating that the South Carolina Court of Appeals upheld the trial court's dismissal of the negligence action because the basis of it was breach of the contract, and the law is well-settled that breach of contractual duties does not give rise to an action in tort for negligence); Foxfire Village, Inc. v. Black & Veatch, Inc., 304 S.C. 366, 404 S.E.2d 912, 917–918 (1991) ("As a matter of law, if the duty to advise another arises merely from agreement of the parties, breach of the duty does not create a cause of action for negligent conduct."). However, where the contract creates a certain relationship between the parties, and certain duties arise by operation of law, irrespective of the contract, because of this relationship, the breach of such duties will warrant an action in tort. See Kennedy v. Columbia Lumber and Mfg. Co., Inc., 299 S.C. 335, 384 S.E.2d 730, 737 (1989) (holding that a cause of action in tort will be available where a builder has violated a legal duty, no matter the type of resulting damage; the economic loss rule will still apply where duties are created solely by contract). As was said in one South Carolina case, St. Charles Merc. Co. v. Armour & Co., 156 S.C. 397, 153 S.E. 473, 477 (1930), "[a]ctions in tort often have their beginning in contractual matters."

Here, Plaintiff does not allege mere failure to fulfill contractual obligations. Instead, it alleges that Defendant knew, at the time it promised that the ballast had been "tested for a year with good results," that such ballasts had never been tested. (Third Amended Complaint at 4.) Plaintiff relied upon this allegedly untrue statement in continuing contractual relations with Defendant. Thus, contrary to Defendant's assertion, it is not the case that "Plaintiff is attempting to take a simple contract and warranty claim and blow it out of proportion by alleging that the shipment of defective goods was somehow fraudulent." (Def. Opposition to Motion to Amend at 1.) "The case at bar does not involve any such attempt to dress up a contract claim in a fraud suit of clothes." Triangle Underwriters, Inc. v. Honeywell, Inc., 604 F.2d 737, 747 (2d Cir. 1979) (examining allegation to determine whether to apply the statute of limitations for fraud or contract). In this case, Plaintiff has alleged that Defendant violated a duty imposed by tort law, i.e., the duty not to commit fraud. Accordingly, Defendant is not entitled to the protection of the economic loss rule, which protects only those defendants who have breached only contractual duties. City of Richmond, Va. v. Madison Management Group, Inc., 918 F.2d 438, 447 (4th Cir. 1990).

Defendant next argues that "Plaintiff's fraud claims fail to state any facts which are separate and apart from a contractual bargain for the sale and purchase of goods." As such, Defendant argues that Plaintiff's only remedy is under the contract. The court does not agree. As a general rule, a party induced to enter a contract by fraud has a choice among causes of action and remedies. If the fraud gives rise to a breach of promise or warranty, he may elect to sue in contract or in tort. . . . Under South Carolina law, "[w]hen an identical set of facts entitle the plaintiff to alternative remedies, he may plead and prove his entitlement to either or both; however, the plaintiff may not recover both." Minyard Enterprises, Inc. v. Southeastern Chemical & Solvent Co., 184 F.3d 373, 381 (4th Cir. 1999). . . . "This rule rests on the principle that the plaintiff should have a full opportunity to prove his claim to some form of relief, but he should not receive a double recovery." Baeza, 309 S.E.2d at 766 (S.C. Ct. App. 1983). Generally, a party is not required to make an election of remedies until after the verdict is entered and prior to the entry of judgment. Minyard Enterprises, Inc., 184 F.3d at 381.

In this case, Plaintiff's fraud and breach of contract claims are based upon the same facts. Plaintiff, therefore, may not recover under both causes of action, but is not required to make an election of remedies at this time. Should this matter proceed to trial, Plaintiff may plead and prove both fraud and breach of contract causes of action although Plaintiff will ultimately be limited to one recovery. Save Charleston Found., 333 S.E.2d at 64. . . .

The court finds that Plaintiff's Third Amended Complaint alleges facts sufficient to support the proposed additional causes of action and such causes of action are not obviously barred by the laws of South Carolina. As such, the proposed amendment is not clearly insufficient or frivolous on its face. Accordingly, as required by Rule 15(a), the court grants Plaintiff leave to amend the pleading.

CONCLUSION

It is therefore ORDERED, for the foregoing reasons, that Plaintiff's Motion to Amend the Complaint is hereby GRANTED.

NOTES AND QUESTIONS

1.   *Election of remedies.* The plaintiff does not need to make its election of remedies at any particular time in the action. Rather, the modern rule on election simply precludes a double recovery. Do you think this is a positive development in the law?

2.   *Tortious breach or separate tort.* The court analyzes and separates a separate tort claim from a separate contract claim and allows that a tort of fraud can arise from the contractual relationship when in the form of fraud in the inducement.

3.   *Punitive damages under the UCC and the CISG.* Both the UCC and the CISG bar awards of punitive damages. UCC § 1–305 (2001) (formerly UCC § 1–106), for example, follows the common law in limiting "penal" damages:

> The remedies provided by this Act shall be liberally administered to the end that the aggrieved party may be put in as good a position as if the other party had fully performed but neither consequential or special nor penal damages may be had except as specifically provided in this Act or by other rule of law.

Likewise, the CISG limits damages to compensatory awards and precludes punitive damages. See Amy A. Kirby, "Punitive Damages in Contract Actions: The Tension Between the United Nations Convention on Contracts for the International Sale of Goods and U.S. Law," 16 J.L. & Com. 215 (1997).

4. *Promises as misrepresentations.* Many fraud claims involve situations in which the only statement at issue is a promise of future performance. Recall the definition of a promise from Chapter 2. Under what situations can a promise be equivalent to an affirmative misrepresentation?

2. DURESS

Duress law has changed radically throughout history, but some things remain common. Most importantly, duress has been consistently confined to behavior that overcomes the "free will" of a party to the contract. However, the effects of duress have varied with time. In the late eighteenth century, duress was actionable only if the resulting agreement was coerced by actual, not threatened, imprisonment, fear of loss of life, or serious physical injury. Joseph M. Perillo, "The Origins of the Objective Theory of Contract Formation and Interpretation," 69 Fordham L. Rev. 427, 467–468 (2000). By the time of the Restatement (First) of Contracts, attitudes had changed, and courts began to recognize that a party's ability to exercise volition freely could be overcome by pressures short of physical coercion or threats of physical harm. As a consequence, the duress doctrine expanded the ability of parties to avoid contracts coerced by a greater range of improper threats, including threats of physical harm (which still generally render a contract void), emotional or psychological harm, or economic injury. Importantly, and in sharp contrast to the push for an objective theory of contract in other contexts such as offer and acceptance and interpretation, the common law doctrine of duress actually shifted over time from an objective standard to a more subjective standard. Under modern duress doctrine, the improper threat must overcome the free will of the actual victim of the duress. Whether that threat would have overcome the free exercise of volition of a reasonable person or a person of "ordinary" bravery has become largely irrelevant under the modern test. See Restatement (Second) of Contracts § 175 *cmt. b*:

> It is sometimes said that the threat must arouse such fear as precludes a party from exercising free will and judgment or that it must be such as would induce assent on the part of a brave man or a man of ordinary firmness. The rule stated in this Section omits any such requirement because of its vagueness and impracticability.

For example, in *Silsbee v. Webber*, 171 Mass. 378, 50 N.E. 555 (1898) (Holmes, J.), the duress consisted of a threat to inform the victim's husband that the victim's son had embezzled funds from the threat maker, with awareness in both parties that the victim subjectively believed that this information would drive the husband insane. The *Silsbee* court rejected the traditional objective assessment of the victim's bravery in favor of a standard that focused upon whether the threat was sufficient to overcome the will of the party claiming duress. "If a party obtains a contract by creating a motive from which the other party ought to be free, and which . . . is, and is known to be, sufficient to produce the result, it does not matter that the motive would not have prevailed with a differently constituted person, whether the motive be a fraudulently created belief or an unlawfully created person." Id. at 556. The same subjectivity applies to the inducement requirement. In all cases, the duress must induce the making of the contract. See Restatement (Second) of Contracts § 174 *cmt. c*:

> A party's manifestation of assent is induced by duress if the duress substantially contributes to his decision to manifest his assent. The test is subjective and the question is, did the threat actually induce assent on the part of the person claiming to be the victim of duress. Threats that would suffice to induce assent by one person may not suffice to induce assent by another.

Of course, the ready availability of one or more reasonable alternatives to the coerced manifestation of assent, such as access to prompt judicial proceedings or opportunities to "cover" the threatened injuries through the open market, negate the defense of duress. Restatement (Second) of Contracts § 175(1). In such situations, the mere presence of a threat, however wrongful, cannot overcome the recipient's free will. See John Dalzell, "Duress by Economic Pressure," 20 N. C. L. Rev. 237 (Part I) and 341 (Part II) (1942).

Modern duress law normally renders a transaction voidable rather than void. Compare Restatement (Second) of Contracts § 174 (physical coercion renders contract void because such coercion prevents formation of the contract) and Restatement (Second) of Contracts § 175 (duress resulting from a source other than physical coercion renders contract voidable). The distinction normally involves absence of consent (void) versus coerced consent (voidable). Duress makes the contract void when the party does not intend to enter the contract, but is nonetheless physically compelled to do so. Restatement (Second) of Contracts § 174. Thus, for example, a party who enters a hospital room and causes a conscious but extraordinarily weak stroke victim to "sign" a contract by placing a pen in the victim's hand and physically manipulating the hand to produce a signature has only accomplished a mechanical act insufficient to create a contract. The resulting "mechanical assent" is not assent at all. Restatement (Second) of Contracts § 174 *cmt. a*. Consequently, no contract ever comes into being, and the ordinary rules relating to void contracts— discussed in Chapter 6—apply, including a bar against tortious interference with contract claims and the unenforceability of reliance-based claims by innocent third parties on the contract. Restatement (Second) of Contracts § 174 *cmt. b*.

The more common form of voidable duress occurs when a party's assent is induced by an improper threat that leaves the victim with no reasonable alternative. Restatement (Second) of Contracts § 175(1). Importantly, not all threats are improper; indeed every negotiation carries an implicit threat by both parties that, unless their respective needs and reservation prices are met, they will not consent to the bargain. The second restatement identifies two classes of improper threats. First, some threats are per se improper, regardless of their effect upon the exchange. These include a threat involving (1) commission of a crime or tort, (2) criminal prosecution, (3) bad faith use of civil process, and (4) "a breach of the duty of good faith and fair dealing under a contract with the recipient." Restatement (Second) of Contracts § 176(1). Second, outside of these four classes of threats that are improper in and of themselves, a threat may also be improper based upon its impact on the resulting exchange between the parties. If the threat induces an exchange that is not on fair terms, the threat is improper if (i) the act would harm the recipient without significantly benefiting the maker; (ii) the effectiveness of the threat is significantly increased by prior threats or unfair dealing; or (iii) the threat involves the use of power for illegitimate ends. Restatement (Second) of Contracts § 176(2).

In the mid-twentieth century, courts moved again to expand the contours of the duress doctrine by acknowledging that a party's economic circumstances may in some circumstances wrongfully or improperly overcome that party's will and eliminate reasonable alternatives. Traditional common law approaches to claims of economic duress generally barred claims of duress relating to mere business losses that could be compensated in the courts, regardless of whether the legal process could provide timely relief. See John Dalzell, "Duress by Economic Pressure," 20 N.C. L. Rev. 237 (1942). Over time, however, courts gradually expanded the situations in which dire economic circumstances caused in some part by one of the parties could supply the basis for duress. For example, in *McGregor v. The Erie Railway Co.*, 35 N.J.L. 89, 1871 WL 6760 (N.J. Sup. 1871), the court recognized that in cases involving a gross disparity of bargaining power—such as between a shipper that must get its goods to market as soon as possible and a common carrier that refuses to comply with its duty to carry goods unless the shipper pays in excess of published rates—then a form of duress could permit the shipper to avoid an agreement to pay the higher, extorted rates:

> In ordinary cases between individuals, where a person has no power to enforce an unjust claim but by legal remedies, and another pays it, even under protest, he cannot recover it. Both parties are on an equal footing. But where they are not on an equal footing, and money is paid, not by compulsion of law, but by compulsion of the circumstances, as where it is paid to relieve goods from an illegal restraint which could not otherwise be reasonably obtained, or to compel the performance of a duty by

others in order to enjoy or obtain a right, there it may be recovered back. Of this latter kind may be moneys paid under color of tolls, or charges on turnpikes or railroads.

Nonetheless, whether you view the expansion of economic duress as positive or negative to the development of the relationship between social contract and private ordering through individual contracts, its uncertain parameters encourage unsettling interference in the bargaining process. "[T]he unproven assumption of the doctrine is that the amount of corrective intervention needed to keep a contractual regime from becoming a power order will not be so great that it destroys the vitality of decentralized decision making through contract." Roberto Mangabeira Unger, The Critical Legal Studies Movement, 96 Harv. L. Rev. 561, 629 (1983).

Study carefully the contractual intervention below under the rubric of economic duress and determine whether you think this proper under a larger theory of social contract. Alternatively, are such interventions unwarranted intrusion on the private bargaining between two capable commercial parties. See also Comment, "Economic Duress After The Demise of the Free Will Theory: A Proposed Tort Analysis," 53 Iowa L. Rev. 892 (1968) (duress doctrine developed through judicial decisions, only a few states have codified the doctrine, and UCC leaves the matter to common law development per UCC § 1–103 incorporation by reference).

TOTEM MARINE TUG & BARGE, INC. v. ALYESKA PIPELINE SERVICE CO.

Supreme Court of Alaska
584 P.2d 15 (1978)

BURKE, Justice.

This appeal arises from the superior court's granting of summary judgment in favor of defendants-appellees Alyeska Pipeline Services, et al., in a contract action brought by plaintiffs-appellants Totem Marine Tug & Barge, Inc., Pacific, Inc., and Richard Stair.

The following summary of events is derived from the materials submitted in the summary judgment proceedings below.

Totem is a closely held Alaska corporation which began operations in March of 1975. Richard Stair, at all times relevant to this case, was vice-president of Totem. In June of 1975, Totem entered into a contract with Alyeska under which Totem was to transport pipeline construction materials from Houston, Texas, to a designated port in southern Alaska, with the possibility of one or two cargo stops along the way. In order to carry out this contract, which was Totem's first, Totem chartered a barge (The "Marine Flasher") and an ocean-going tug (the "Kirt Chouest"). These charters and other initial operations costs were made possible by loans to

Totem from Richard Stair individually and Pacific, Inc., a corporation of which Stair was principal stockholder and officer, as well as by guarantees by Stair and Pacific.

By the terms of the contract, Totem was to have completed performance by approximately August 15, 1975. From the start, however, there were numerous problems which impeded Totem's performance of the contract. For example, according to Totem, Alyeska represented that approximately 1,800 to 2,100 tons of regular uncoated pipe were to be loaded in Houston, and that perhaps another 6,000 or 7,000 tons of materials would be put on the barge at later stops along the west coast. Upon the arrival of the tug and barge in Houston, however, Totem found that about 6,700 to 7,200 tons of coated pipe, steel beams and valves, haphazardly and improperly piled, were in the yard to be loaded. This situation called for remodeling of the barge and extra cranes and stevedores, and resulted in the loading taking thirty days rather than the three days which Totem had anticipated it would take to load 2,000 tons. The lengthy loading period was also caused in part by Alyeska's delay in assuring Totem that it would pay for the additional expenses, bad weather and other administrative problems.

The difficulties continued after the tug and barge left Houston. It soon became apparent that the vessels were traveling more slowly than anticipated because of the extra load. In response to Alyeska's complaints and with its verbal consent, on August 13, 1975, Totem chartered a second tug, the "N. Joseph Guidry." When the "Guidry" reached the Panama Canal, however, Alyeska had not yet furnished the written amendment to the parties' contract. Afraid that Alyeska would not agree to cover the cost of the second tug, Stair notified the "Guidry" not to go through the Canal. After some discussions in which Alyeska complained of the delays and accused Totem of lying about the horsepower of the first tug, Alyeska executed the amendment on August 21, 1975.

By this time the "Guidry" had lost its preferred passage through the Canal and had to wait two or three additional days before it could go through. Upon finally meeting, the three vessels encountered the tail of a hurricane that lasted for about eight or nine days and which substantially impeded their progress.

The three vessels finally arrived in the vicinity of San Pedro, California, where Totem planned to change crews and refuel. On Alyeska's orders, however, the vessels instead pulled into port at Long Beach, California. At this point, Alyeska's agents commenced off-loading the barge, without Totem's consent, without the necessary load survey, and without a marine survey, the absence of which voided Totem's insurance. After much wrangling and some concessions by Alyeska, the freight was off-loaded. Thereafter, on or about September 14, 1975, Alyeska terminated the contract. Although there was talk by an Alyeska official of reinstating the contract, the termination was affirmed a few days later at a meeting at which Alyeska officials refused to give a reason for the termination.

Following termination of the contract, Totem submitted termination invoices to Alyeska and began pressing the latter for payment. The invoices came to something between $260,000 and $300,000. An official from Alyeska told Totem that they would look over the invoices but that they were not sure when payment would be made perhaps in a day or perhaps in six to eight months. Totem was in urgent need of cash as the invoices represented debts which the company had incurred on 10–30 day payment schedules. Totem's creditors were demanding payment and according to Stair, without immediate cash, Totem would go bankrupt. Totem then turned over the collection to its attorney, Roy Bell, directing him to advise Alyeska of Totem's financial straits. Thereafter, Bell met with Alyeska officials in Seattle, and after some negotiations, Totem received a settlement offer from Alyeska for $97,500. On November 6, 1975, Totem, through its president Stair, signed an agreement releasing Alyeska from all claims by Totem in exchange for $97,500.

On March 26, 1976, Totem, Richard Stair, and Pacific filed a complaint against Alyeska, which was subsequently amended. In the amended complaint, the plaintiffs sought to rescind the settlement and release on the ground of economic duress and to recover the balance allegedly due on the original contract. In addition, they alleged that Alyeska had wrongfully terminated the contract and sought miscellaneous other compensatory and punitive damages.

Before filing an answer, Alyeska moved for summary judgment against the plaintiffs on the ground that Totem had executed a binding release of all claims against Alyeska and that as a matter of law, Totem could not prevail on its claim of economic duress. In opposition, plaintiffs contended that the purported release was executed under duress in that Alyeska wrongfully terminated the contract; that Alyeska knew that Totem was faced with large debts and impending bankruptcy; that Alyeska withheld funds admittedly owed knowing the effect this would have on plaintiffs and that plaintiffs had no alternative but to involuntarily accept the $97,500 in order to avoid bankruptcy. Plaintiffs maintained that they had thus raised genuine issues of material fact such that trial was necessary, and that Alyeska was not entitled to judgment as a matter of law. Alyeska disputed the plaintiffs' assertions.

On November 30, 1976, the superior court granted the defendant's motion for summary judgment. This appeal followed.

I

* * *

II

As was noted above, a court's initial task in deciding motions for summary judgment is to determine whether there exist genuine issues of material fact. In order to decide whether such issues exist in this case, we must examine the doctrine allowing avoidance of a release on grounds of economic duress.

This court has not yet decided a case involving a claim of economic duress or what is also called business compulsion. At early common law, a contract could be avoided on the ground of duress only if a party could show that the agreement was entered into for fear of loss of life or limb, mayhem or imprisonment. 13 Williston on Contracts, § 1601 at 649 (3d ed. Jaeger 1970). The threat had to be such as to overcome the will of a person of ordinary firmness and courage. Id., s 1602 at 656. Subsequently, however, the concept has been broadened to include myriad forms of economic coercion which force a person to involuntarily enter into a particular transaction. The test has come to be whether the will of the person induced by the threat was overcome rather than that of a reasonably firm person. Id., s 1602 at 657.

At the outset it is helpful to acknowledge the various policy considerations which are involved in cases involving economic duress. Typically, those claiming such coercion are attempting to avoid the consequences of a modification of an original contract or of a settlement and release agreement. On the one hand, courts are reluctant to set aside agreements because of the notion of freedom of contract and because of the desirability of having private dispute resolutions be final. On the other hand, there is an increasing recognition of the law's role in correcting inequitable or unequal exchanges between parties of disproportionate bargaining power and a greater willingness to not enforce agreements which were entered into under coercive circumstances.

There are various statements of what constitutes economic duress, but as noted by one commentator, "The history of generalization in this field offers no great encouragement for those who seek to summarize results in any single formula." Dawson, Economic Duress: An Essay in Perspective, 45 Mich. L. Rev. 253, 289 (1947). Section 492(b) of the Restatement of Contracts defines duress as:

> any wrongful threat of one person by words or other conduct that induces another to enter into a transaction under the influence of such fear as precludes him from exercising free will and judgment,

if the threat was intended or should reasonably have been expected to operate as an inducement.

Professor Williston states the basic elements of economic duress in the following manner:

1. The party alleging economic duress must show that he has been the victim of a wrongful or unlawful act or threat, and

2. Such act or threat must be one which deprives the victim of his unfettered will. 13 Williston on Contracts, § 1617 at 704 (footnotes omitted).

Many courts state the test somewhat differently, eliminating use of the vague term "free will," but retaining the same basic idea. Under this standard, duress exists where: (1) one party involuntarily accepted the terms of another, (2) circumstances permitted no other alternative, and (3) such circumstances were the result of coercive acts of the other party. Undersea Engineering & Construction Co. v. International Telephone & Telegraph Corp., 429 F. 2d 543, 550 (9th Cir. 1970. . . . The third element is further explained as follows:

> In order to substantiate the allegation of economic duress or business compulsion, the plaintiff must go beyond the mere showing of reluctance to accept and of financial embarrassment. There must be a showing of acts on the part of the defendant which produced these two factors. The assertion of duress must be proven by evidence that the duress resulted from defendant's wrongful and oppressive conduct and not by the plaintiff's necessities. W. R. Grimshaw Co., supra, 111 F. Supp. at 904.

As the above indicates, one essential element of economic duress is that the plaintiff show that the other party by wrongful acts or threats, intentionally caused him to involuntarily enter into a particular transaction. Courts have not attempted to define exactly what constitutes a wrongful or coercive act, as wrongfulness depends on the particular facts in each case. This requirement may be satisfied where the alleged wrongdoer's conduct is criminal or tortious but an act or threat may also be considered wrongful if it is wrongful in the moral sense. Restatement of Contracts, § 492, comment g. . . .

In many cases, a threat to breach a contract or to withhold payment of an admitted debt has constituted a wrongful act. Hartsville Oil Mill v. United States, 271 U. S. 43, 49, 46 S. Ct. 389, 391, 70 L. Ed. 822, 827 (1926); Austin Instrument, Inc. v. Loral Corp., 29 N. Y. 2d 124, 324 N. Y. S. 2d 22, 25, 272 N. E. 2d 533, 535 (1971). . . . Implicit in such cases is the additional requirement that the threat to breach the contract or withhold payment be done in bad faith. See Louisville Title Insurance Co. v. Surety Title &

Guaranty Co., 60 Cal. App. 3d 781, 132 Cal. Rptr. 63, 76, 79 (1976); Restatement (Second) of Contracts, § 318 comment (e).

Economic duress does not exist, however, merely because a person has been the victim of a wrongful act; in addition, the victim must have no choice but to agree to the other party's terms or face serious financial hardship. Thus, in order to avoid a contract, a party must also show that he had no reasonable alternative to agreeing to the other party's terms, or, as it is often stated, that he had no adequate remedy if the threat were to be carried out. First National Bank of Cincinnati v. Pepper, 454 F. 2d 626, 632–33 (2d Cir. 1972); Austin Instrument, supra, 324 N. Y. S. 2d at 25, 272 N. E. 2d at 535. . . . What constitutes a reasonable alternative is a question of fact, depending on the circumstances of each case. An available legal remedy, such as an action for breach of contract, may provide such an alternative. First National Bank of Cincinnati, supra; Austin Instrument, supra; Tri-State Roofing, supra. Where one party wrongfully threatens to withhold goods, services or money from another unless certain demands are met, the availability on the market of similar goods and services or of other sources of funds may also provide an alternative to succumbing to the coercing party's demands. Austin Instrument, supra; Tri-State Roofing, supra. Generally, it has been said that "(t)he adequacy of the remedy is to be tested by a practical standard which takes into consideration the exigencies of the situation in which the alleged victim finds himself." Ross Systems, 173 A. 2d at 262. See also First National Bank of Cincinnati, supra at 634; Dalzell, Duress By Economic Pressure I, 20 N. Carolina L. Rev. 237, 240 (1942).

An available alternative or remedy may not be adequate where the delay involved in pursuing that remedy would cause immediate and irreparable loss to one's economic or business interest. For example, in Austin Instrument, supra, and Gallagher Switchboard Corp. v. Heckler Electric Co., 36 Misc. 2d 225, 232 N. Y. S. 2d 590 (N. Y. Sup. Ct. 1962), duress was found in the following circumstances: A subcontractor threatened to refuse further delivery under a contract unless the contractor agreed to modify the existing contract between the parties. The contractor was unable to obtain the necessary materials elsewhere without delay, and if it did not have the materials promptly, it would have been in default on its main contract with the government. In each case such default would have had grave economic consequences for the contractor and hence it agreed to the modifications. In both, the courts found that the alternatives to agreeing to the modification were inadequate (i. e., suing for breach of contract or obtaining the materials elsewhere) and that modifications therefore were signed under duress and voidable.

Professor Dalzell, in Duress By Economic Pressure II, 20 N. Carolina L. Rev. 340, 370 (1942), notes the following with regard to the adequacy of legal remedies where one party refuses to pay a contract claim:

Nowadays, a wait of even a few weeks in collecting on a contract claim is sometimes serious or fatal for an enterprise at a crisis in its history. The business of a creditor in financial straits is at the mercy of an unscrupulous debtor, who need only suggest that if the creditor does not care to settle on the debtor's own hard terms, he can sue. This situation, in which promptness in payment is vastly more important than even approximate justice in the settlement terms, is too common in modern business relations to be ignored by society and the courts.

This view finds support in Capps v. Georgia Pacific Corporation, 253 Or. 248, 453 P. 2d 935 (1969). There, the plaintiff was owed $157,000 as a commission for finding a lessee for defendant's property but in exchange for $5,000, the plaintiff signed a release of his claim against defendant. The plaintiff sued for the balance of the commission, alleging that the release had been executed under duress. His complaint, however, was dismissed. On appeal, the court held that the plaintiff had stated a claim where he alleged that he had accepted the grossly inadequate sum because he was in danger of immediately losing his home by mortgage foreclosure and other property by foreclosure and repossession if he did not obtain immediate funds from the defendant. One basis for its holding was found in the following quote by a leading commentator in the area of economic duress:

> The most that can be claimed (regarding the law of economic duress) is that change has been broadly toward acceptance of a general conclusion that in the absence of specific countervailing factors of policy or administrative feasibility, restitution is required of any excessive gain that results, in a bargain transaction, from impaired bargaining power, whether the impairment consists of economic necessity, mental or physical disability, or a wide disparity in knowledge or experience. Dawson, Economic—Duress An Essay In Perspective, 45 Mich. L. Rev. 253, 289 (1947).

III

Turning to the instant case, we believe that Totem's allegations, if proved, would support a finding that it executed a release of its contract claims against Alyeska under economic duress. Totem has alleged that Alyeska deliberately withheld payment of an acknowledged debt, knowing that Totem had no choice but to accept an inadequate sum in settlement of that debt; that Totem was faced with impending bankruptcy; that Totem was unable to meet its pressing debts other than by accepting the immediate cash payment offered by Alyeska; and that through necessity, Totem thus involuntarily accepted an inadequate settlement offer from Alyeska and executed a release of all claims under the contract. If the release was in fact executed under these circumstances,[5] we think that under the legal principles discussed above that this would constitute the type of wrongful conduct and lack of alternatives that would render the release voidable by Totem on the ground of economic duress. We would add that although Totem need not necessarily prove its allegation that Alyeska's termination of the contract was wrongful in order to sustain a claim of economic duress, the events leading to the termination would be probative as to whether Alyeska exerted any wrongful pressure on Totem and whether Alyeska wrongfully withheld payment from Totem.

One purpose of summary judgment, however, is to pierce the allegations in the pleadings in an effort to determine whether genuine issues of fact exist. As the moving party, Alyeska had the burden of showing that there were no such genuine issues and that it was entitled to judgment as a matter of law. E.g., Brock v. Rogers and Babler, Inc., 536 P. 2d 778, 782 (Alaska 1975). Alyeska showed that Totem had executed the release, that Totem had been represented by counsel at the negotiating session leading to the settlement and release and that appellant Stair, who actually signed the release on behalf of Totem, was fully aware of the consequences of such a release. Such evidence, by itself, would have entitled Alyeska to summary judgment in its favor. As a matter of law, there is no doubt that a valid release of all claims arising under a contract will bar any subsequent claims based on that contract.

To avoid summary judgment once the moving party meets its burden, the non-moving party must produce competent evidence showing that there are issues of material fact to be tried. Id. The respondent must set forth specific facts showing that it could produce admissible evidence reasonably tending to dispute the movants evidence or establish an affirmative defense. Id. The court then must draw all reasonable inferences in favor of the non-moving party and against the movant. E.g., Clabaugh v. Bottcher, 545 P. 2d 172, 175 n. 5 (Alaska 1976).

In entering summary judgment against Totem, the court below reasoned as follows:

> The plaintiffs, specifically Mr. Stair, assert the release and settlement should be held for naught because of duress and coercion exerted upon him and his corporation by the defendants' action.

> Mr. Stair fails to show that the release and settlement negotiated by his attorneys was involuntary on his part. Mr. Stair did not personally participate in the negotiations which resulted in the

---

[5] By way of clarification, we would note that Totem would not have to prove that Alyeska admitted to owing the precise sum Totem claimed it was owed upon termination of the contract but only that Alyeska acknowledged that it owed Totem approximately that amount which Totem sought.

release and settlement. No affidavit or other suggestion of evidence has been submitted to demonstrate that upon trial the plaintiffs could sustain their burden of proof required to set aside the release and settlement.

As thus stated, the superior court's decision clearly misstated the standard applicable on motions for summary judgment. A party opposing summary judgment need not establish that he will ultimately prevail at trial. Gablick v. Wolfe, 469 P. 2d 391, 395 (Alaska 1970). Although we may affirm a trial court's grant of summary judgment if alternative grounds exist for upholding its judgment, Moore v. State, 553 P. 2d 8, 21 (Alaska 1976), we do not believe that summary judgment was properly granted in this case.

Our examination of the materials presented by Totem in opposition to Alyeska's motion for summary judgment leads us to conclude that Totem has made a sufficient factual showing as to each of the elements of economic duress to withstand that motion. There is no doubt that Alyeska disputes many of the factual allegations made by Totem[7] and drawing all inferences in favor of Totem, we believe that genuine issues of material fact exist in this case such that trial is necessary. Admittedly, Totem's showing was somewhat weak in that, for example, it did not produce the testimony of Roy Bell, the attorney who represented Totem in the negotiations leading to the settlement and release. At trial, it will probably be necessary for Totem to produce this evidence if it is to prevail on its claim of duress. However, a party opposing a motion for summary judgment need not produce all of the evidence it may have at its disposal but need only show that issues of material fact exist. 10 C. Wright and A. Miller, Federal Practice and Procedure: Civil, § 2727 at 546 (1973). Therefore, we hold that the superior court erred in granting summary judgment for appellees and remand the case to the superior court for trial in accordance with the legal principles set forth above.

IV

One final issue remains in this appeal. Appellants Richard Stair and Pacific, Inc. contend that even if Totem is ultimately found to be bound by the release it executed, Stair and Pacific are not similarly bound because they did not sign the release. This contention is without merit. Neither Stair individually nor Pacific were parties to the original contract between Totem and Alyeska, nor were they parties to the amendment. No contention has been made that they were even third party beneficiaries to that contract. As they were not parties to the original contract, it follows

---

[7]   For example, Alyeska has denied that it ever admitted to owing any particular sum to Totem and has disputed the truthfulness of Totem's assertions of impending bankruptcy. Other factual issues which remain unresolved include whether or not Alyeska knew of Totem's financial situation after termination of the contract and whether Alyeska did in fact threaten by words or conduct to withhold payment unless Totem agreed to settle.

that Stair and Pacific had no contractual claims against Alyeska which they could have released and thus it is irrelevant whether or not they executed the release. Stair and Pacific's fate in this lawsuit, therefore, depends entirely on Totem's success or failure in pursuing its contractual claims against Alyeska.

REVERSED and REMANDED.

NOTES AND QUESTIONS

1. *Nature of wrongful threat.* What was the nature of the "wrongful" threat in the terms of Restatement (Second) of Contracts § 176? Notice there are two standards. One applies to exchanges not on fair terms, while the other applies regardless of the fairness. Was the exchange in this case "fair"? Do you have adequate information to properly evaluate the economic extent of Alyeska's damage claim? If not, then at this stage of the trial, which threat element is most likely involved?

2. *Cause of hardship.* While it is clear that duress is available when an improper threat induces a person with no reasonable alternative to form a contract, does this mean that duress embraces striking a hard bargain with someone in dire economic hardship? Most courts also require that the party exerting duress must cause the hardship itself. See Selmer Co. v. Blakeslee-Midwest Co., 704 F.2d 924 (7th Cir. 1983). Thus, driving a hard bargain with a person already in difficulty is not economic duress. Note that Totem's urgent need for cash arguably arose from the fact that the company overextended itself with its creditors and investors in order to get the Alyeska contract. Did Alyeska cause Totem's hardship or simply try to take advantage of Totem's hardship? Do you think this is a policy line worth drawing? If so, are there any other contractual protections for those in desperate economic circumstances?

3. *Settlement policy.* Parties are clearly encouraged to settle their own disputed obligations. In *Totem,* both parties had good faith, disputed claims, although Alyeska admittedly owed some amount. Does the application of the duress doctrine undermine the policy in favor of legitimate settlements? Parties often negotiate settlement agreements in situations where one of them suffers from a gross disparity of bargaining power arising from unequal financial resources. How do you suggest drawing a line between a settlement voidable for duress and a hard fought but legitimate settlement of a good faith, disputed claim?

4. *UCC approach.* In the next chapter, parties to a contract often agree to settle disputes, and then one party may later fail to comply with the terms of the settlement. A breach of the settlement agreement will require that the settlement promise is enforceable under some theory of legal obligation. When a party owes a fixed sum of money but refuses to pay unless the other party accepts less, what is the consideration for the promise to accept less? Does the UCC require consideration for modifications of existing agreements? See UCC § 2–209(1). See also Robert A. Hillman, "Policing Contract Modifications Under

the UCC: Good Faith and the Doctrine of Economic Duress," 64 Iowa L. Rev. 849 (1979) (arguing that the absence of specific statutory language on economic duress has led to ineffective applications and results).

5.   *The blackmailer's fallacy.* To what extent is the proposition that duress denies the victim any reasonable alternatives merely a legal fiction? Alternatively, does the victim of duress really lack any bargaining power? Consider the problem of the blackmailer's fallacy. A blackmailer who has information that will cause $x damages to the victim should theoretically be able to extract almost that entire amount—$x – $1—as payment for nondisclosure. See John C. Harsanyi, "Measurement of Social Power, Opportunity Costs, and the Theory of Two-person Bargaining Games," in Roderick Bell, et al., Political Power: A Reader in Theory and Research at 226, 232–33 (1969). But by approaching the victim, the blackmailer also gives the victim power to impose costs on the blackmailer by either refusing to pay or exposing the blackmailer to criminal charges. Id. In this situation, then, both sides have power and incentive to bargain to some result between $0 and $x. Id.

Thus, although we would expect the dominant party in a duress or extortion situation to extract every available benefit from the weaker party, such an absolute disparity of bargaining power is unlikely. In reality, the victim of duress (or blackmail) still possesses substantial bargaining power, at least in the form of the ability to impose additional costs upon the stronger party:

> Even the most intuitively obvious case of an apparently "absolute" disparity of bargaining power—the hoary "your money or your life" demand by the highwayman or tax collector—never really removes all power from the victim of the duress. A victim of the most extreme coercion still possesses some power to choose between unpleasant alternatives. . . .

> The victim of the most egregious forms of duress still retains considerable power over the situation. He may comply, or he may resist. The power of confronting unjust opponents as a choice was made obvious by Gandhi's and Martin Luther King, Jr.'s use of passive disobedience as a tool to achieve their social aims. If the victim resists and fails—and thus concludes the encounter as a martyred corpse, an unconscious body or a part of the penal system such as Nobel Peace Prize winners Nelson Mandela of South Africa and Aung San Suu Kyi of Burma—the victim still retains the power to affect the outcome of the interaction with the stronger party. Unconscious victims require disposal or their evidence can increase the likelihood of apprehension; corpses create their own problems of concealment and disposal, and convicts impose substantial costs upon the penal system. All of these outcomes, however, have a real impact upon the ability of the criminal or tax collector to engage in their livelihood and thus demonstrate the power of the victim to affect the

outcome of his or her interaction with the criminal or tax collector. Daniel D. Barnhizer, "Inequality of Bargaining Power," 76 U. Colo. L. Rev. 139, 163–64 (2005).

Given that the victim of duress likely always has the power to resist to some extent, should the standards for duress be changed to require the victim to attempt to resist before courts will permit avoidance on the basis of duress? Why or why not?

6. *The nature of consent under duress.* It is often said that the victim of duress does not truly consent to the proposed contract. But as John Dalzell notes, even—or perhaps particularly—in cases of physical duress there is little question that the victim desperately desires and in a sense truly consents to the contract rather than the threatened alternative:

> We have talked of contracts signed under duress as lacking "real consent." When I feel that I must choose between having a bullet lodged in my head and signing a contract, my desire to escape the bullet would hardly be described as unreal or merely apparent; and the signing of the contract is simply the expression of that fear of death. * * * Faced with the choice that was offered, the victim of duress gives a genuine consent rather than suffer the alternative consequences. John Dalzell, "Duress by Economic Pressure," 20 N.C. L. Rev. 237, 238–39 (1942).

If Dalzell is correct, what exactly is the problem in the process of contract formation that the duress doctrine is supposed to police? In contrast, consider misrepresentation doctrine which, among other things, addresses a failure of consideration in that the deceived party does not receive the consideration for which she bargained. In the case of duress, both parties must be aware of the threat, and it is likely that both parties give genuine consent, even if one of the parties must choose between unpleasant alternatives. The problem of duress, then, appears only tangentially related to the process of contract formation. Is there any satisfactory way to explain duress doctrine as an abuse of the contracting process, or should it be conceived as a more tort-like response, similar to assault or wrongful imprisonment?

3. UNDUE INFLUENCE

Virtually no case exists for a tort of undue influence, and consequently relief, if any, may be found only in rescission of the contract. When considering undue influence, it is important to consider its historical relationship with duress and its subsequent evolution considering the expansion of duress. See Lonnie Chunn, Note, "Duress and Undue Influence—A Comparative Analysis," 22 Baylor L. Rev. 572 (1970). As with the duress, undue influence has largely escaped the influence of the objective theory of contracts. See Joseph M. Perillo, "The Origins of the Objective Theory of Contract Formation and Interpretation," 69 Fordham L. Rev. 427, 467–468 (2000). Accordingly, the principal inquiry in undue influence is "unfair persuasion" rather than the coercion focus of duress. Indeed, undue influence continues a design to protect where duress cannot be shown. See Restatement (Second) of Contracts § 177 *cmt. b.*

While early undue influence law focused on contracts induced by a dominant party against a subservient party, the doctrine eventually expanded to buttress or cover early "near miss" duress law cases then focused on overcoming the free will of another short of physical compulsion. See John P. Dawson, "Economic Duress—An Essay in Perspective," 45 Mich. L. Rev. 253, 262 (1947). Still later, undue influence evolved to require domination of one party over another. See Restatement (First) of Contracts § 497.

While maintaining its dominance roots, modern undue influence law has considerably expanded to cover additional circumstances. While the focus remains on unfair persuasion and not coercion by duress, the relationships where undue influence can be expected to occur has considerably expanded. Today, undue influence can occur in two contexts: (i) unfair persuasion of a subservient party under the domination of another person; or (ii) unfair persuasion of a person by another using a relationship of trust and confidence to deceive the other party. See Restatement (Second) of Contracts § 177(1). Neither relationship requires coercive threats, only "unfair persuasion." See Ray D. Madoff, "Unmasking Undue Influence," 81 Minn. L. Rev. 571 (1997) (noting the particular modern application in will contests by disinherited natural heirs). In the first situation, one party utilizes a dominant psychological position in an unfair manner to induce assent that the subservient party would not otherwise freely give. In the second situation, one party uses a relationship of trust and confidence to unfairly persuade a person to give assent that would otherwise not be freely given. Accordingly, the first question often requires a determination or analysis of the relationship between the parties. This part of the equation is more objective. However, the second step requires an analysis of whether "unfair persuasion" was utilized in a manner that "seriously impaired the free and competent exercise of judgment" by the other party. See Restatement (Second) of Contracts § 177 *cmt. b.* If so, the transaction is voidable by the victim. Restatement (Second) of Contracts § 177(2). Particularly vulnerable to undue influence are business transactions between an attorney and client, where undue influence may be presumed from the fiduciary relationship and the contract set aside unless the contract is on fair terms and the client manifested assent with free will absent from the influence of the attorney. See Restatement (Second) of Contracts § 173 and Harry S. Raleigh, Jr., "Attorney Beware—The Presumption of Undue Influence and the Attorney-Beneficiary," 47 Notre Dame Law, 330 (1971).

Despite these contours, the essence of undue influence cases is the unfair persuasion by one of another, seriously compromising the weaker party's exercise of free and sound judgment to induce that person to enter a contract that otherwise would not have occurred. In the following case, determine whether you think there was either a dominant–subservient or a confidential relationship. If not, has the doctrine expanded to other relationships that seriously impair free will?

ODORIZZI V. BLOOMFIELD SCHOOL DISTRICT

District Court of Appeal of California
246 Cal. App. 2d 123, 54 Cal. Rptr. 533 (1966)

FLEMING, Justice.

Appeal from a judgment dismissing plaintiff's amended complaint on demurrer.

Plaintiff Donald Odorizzi was employed during 1964 as an elementary school teacher by defendant Bloomfield School District and was under contract with the District to continue to teach school the following year as a permanent employee. On June 10 he was arrested on criminal charges of homosexual activity, and on June 11 he signed and delivered to his superiors his written resignation as a teacher, a resignation which the District accepted on June 13. In July the criminal charges against Odorizzi were dismissed under Penal Code, section 995, and in September he sought to resume his employment with the District. On the District's refusal to reinstate him he filed suit for declaratory and other relief.

Odorizzi's amended complaint asserts his resignation was invalid because obtained through duress, fraud, mistake, and undue influence and given at a time when he lacked capacity to make a valid contract. Specifically, Odorizzi declares he was under such severe mental and emotional strain at the time he signed his resignation, having just completed the process of arrest, questioning by the police, booking, and release on bail, and having gone for forty hours without sleep, that he was incapable of rational thought or action. While he was in this condition and unable to think clearly, the superintendent of the District and the principal of his school came to his apartment. They said they were trying to help him and had his best interests at heart, that he should take their advice and immediately resign his position with the District, that there was no time to consult an attorney, that if he did not resign immediately the District would suspend and dismiss him from his position and publicize the proceedings, his "afore described arrest" and cause him "to suffer extreme embarrassment and humiliation"; but that if he resigned at once the incident would not be publicized and would not jeopardize his chances of securing employment as a teacher elsewhere. Odorizzi pleads that because of his faith and confidence in their representations they were able to substitute their will and judgment in place of his own and thus obtain his signature to his purported resignation. A demurrer to his amended complaint was sustained without leave to amend.

By his complaint plaintiff in effect seeks to rescind his resignation pursuant to Civil Code, section 1689, on the ground that his consent had not been real or free within the meaning of Civil Code, section 1567, but had been obtained through duress, menace, fraud, undue influence, or mistake. A pleading under these sections is sufficient if, stripped of its conclusions, it sets forth sufficient facts to justify legal relief. . . . In our view the facts in the amended complaint are insufficient to state a cause of action for duress, menace, fraud, or mistake, but they do set out sufficient elements to justify rescission of a consent because of undue influence. We summarize our conclusions on each of these points.

No duress or menace has been pleaded. Duress consists in unlawful confinement of another's person, or relatives, or property, which causes him to consent to a transaction through fear. (Civ. Code, § 1569.) Duress is often used interchangeably with menace . . . , but in California menace is technically a threat of duress or a threat of injury to the person, property, or character of another. (Civ. Code, § 1570; Restatement, Contracts, §§ 492, 493) We agree with respondent's contention that neither duress nor menace was involved in this case, because the action or threat in duress or menace must be unlawful, and a threat to take legal action is not unlawful unless the party making the threat knows the falsity of his claim. . . . The amended complaint shows in substance that the school representatives announced their intention to initiate suspension and dismissal proceedings under Education Code, section 13403, 13408 et seq. at a time when the filing of such proceedings was not only their legal right but their positive duty as school officials. (Ed. Code, § 13409; Board of Education, etc. v. Weiland, 179 Cal. App. 2d 808, 4 Cal. Rptr. 286) Although the filing of such proceedings might be extremely damaging to plaintiff's reputation, the injury would remain incidental so long as the school officials acted in good faith in the performance of their duties. . . . Neither duress nor menace was present as a ground for rescission.

Nor do we find a cause of action for fraud, either actual or constructive. (Civ. Code, §§ 1571 to 1574.) Actual fraud involves conscious misrepresentation, or concealment, or non-disclosure of a material fact that induces the innocent party to enter the contract. (Civ. Code, § 1572; Pearson v. Norton, 230 Cal. App. 2d 1, 7, 40 Cal. Rptr. 634; Restatement, Contracts, § 471) A complaint for fraud must plead misrepresentation, knowledge of falsity, intent to induce reliance, justifiable reliance, and resulting damage. . . . While the amended complaint charged misrepresentation, it failed to assert the elements of knowledge of falsity, intent to induce reliance, and justifiable reliance. A cause of action for actual fraud was therefore not stated. . . .

Constructive fraud arises on a breach of duty by one in a confidential or fiduciary relationship to another which induces justifiable reliance by the latter to his prejudice. (Civ. Code, § 1573) Plaintiff has attempted to bring himself within this category, for the amended complaint asserts the existence of a confidential relationship between the school superintendent and principal as agents of the defendant, and the plaintiff. Such a confidential relationship may exist whenever a person with justification places trust and confidence in the integrity and fidelity of another. . . . Plaintiff, however, sets forth no facts to support his conclusion of a confidential relationship between the representatives of the school district and himself, other than that the parties bore the relationship of employer and employee to each other. Under prevailing judicial opinion no presumption of a confidential relationship arises from the bare fact that parties to a contract are employer and employee; rather, additional ties must be brought out in order to create the presumption of a confidential relationship between the two. (Anno., 100 A. L. R. 875) The absence of a confidential relationship between employer and employee is especially apparent where, as here, the parties were negotiating to bring about a termination of their relationship. In such a situation each party is expected to look after his own interests, and a lack of confidentiality is implicit in the subject matter of their dealings. We think the allegations of constructive fraud were inadequate.

As to mistake, the amended complaint fails to disclose any facts that would suggest that consent had been obtained through a mistake of fact or of law. The material facts of the transaction were known to both parties. Neither party was laboring under any misapprehension of law of which the other took advantage. The discussion between plaintiff and the school district representatives principally attempted to evaluate the probable consequences of plaintiff's predicament and to predict the future course of events. The fact that their speculations did not forecast the exact pattern which events subsequently took does not provide the basis for a claim that they were acting under some sort of mistake. The doctrine of mistake customarily involves such errors as the nature of the transaction, the identity of the parties, the identity of the things to which the contract relates, or the occurrence of collateral happenings. (Restatement, Contracts, § 502, comment e) Errors of this nature were not present in the case at bench.

However, the pleading does set out a claim that plaintiff's consent to the transaction had been obtained through the use of undue influence.

Undue influence, in the sense we are concerned with here, is a shorthand legal phrase used to describe persuasion that tends to be coercive in nature, persuasion that overcomes the will without convincing the judgment. . . . The hallmark of such persuasion is high pressure, a pressure which works on mental, moral, or emotional weakness to such an extent that it approaches the boundaries of coercion. In this sense, undue influence has been called overpersuasion. . . . Misrepresentations of law or fact are not essential to the charge, for a person's will may be overborne without misrepresentation. By statutory definition undue influence includes "taking an unfair advantage of another's weakness of mind; or . . . taking a grossly oppressive and unfair advantage of another's necessities or distress." (Civ. Code, § 1575) While most reported cases of undue influence involve persons who bear a confidential relationship to one another, a confidential or authoritative relationship between the parties need not be present when the undue influence involves unfair advantage taken of another's weakness or distress. . . .

We paraphrase the summary of undue influence given the jury by Sir James P. Wilde in Hall v. Hall, L. R. 1, P & D 481, 482 (1868):

> To make a good contract a man must be a free agent. Pressure of whatever sort which overpowers the will without convincing the judgment is a species of restraint under which no valid contract can be made. Importunity or threats, if carried to the degree in which the free play of a man's will is overborne, constitute undue influence, although no force is used or threatened. A party may be led but not driven, and his acts must be the offspring of his own volition and not the record of someone else's.

In essence undue influence involves the use of excessive pressure to persuade one vulnerable to such pressure, pressure applied by a dominant subject to a servient object. In combination, the elements of undue susceptibility in the servient person and excessive pressure by the dominating person make the latter's influence undue, for it results in the apparent will of the servient person being in fact the will of the dominant person.

Undue susceptibility may consist of total weakness of mind which leaves a person entirely without understanding (Civ. Code, § 38); or, a lesser weakness which destroys the capacity of a person to make a contract even though he is not totally incapacitated (Civ. Code, § 39 . . .); or, the first element in our equation, a still lesser weakness which provides sufficient grounds to rescind a contract for undue influence (Civ. Code, § 1575 . . .). Such lesser weakness need not be long-lasting nor wholly incapacitating, but may be merely a lack of full vigor due to age . . . , physical condition . . . , emotional anguish . . . , or a combination of such factors. The reported cases have usually involved elderly, sick, senile persons alleged to have executed wills or deeds under pressure. (Malone v. Malone, 155 Cal. App. 2d 161, 317 P. 2d 65 (constant importuning of a senile husband); Stewart v. Marvin, 139 Cal. App. 2d 769, 294 P. 2d 114 (persistent nagging of elderly spouse)). In some of its aspects this lesser weakness could perhaps be called weakness of spirit. But whatever name we give it, this first element of undue influence resolves itself into a lessened capacity of the object to make a free contract.

In the present case plaintiff has pleaded that such weakness at the time he signed his resignation prevented him from freely and competently applying his judgment to the problem before him. Plaintiff declares he was under severe mental and emotional strain at the time because he had just completed the process of arrest, questioning, booking, and release on bail and had been without sleep for forty hours. It is possible that exhaustion and emotional turmoil may wholly incapacitate a person from exercising his judgment. As an abstract question of pleading, plaintiff has pleaded that possibility and sufficient allegations to state a case for rescission.

Undue influence in its second aspect involves an application of excessive strength by a dominant subject against a servient object. Judicial consideration of this second element in undue influence has been relatively rare, for there are few cases denying persons who persuade but do not misrepresent the benefit of their bargain. Yet logically, the same legal consequences should apply to the results of excessive strength as to the results of undue weakness. Whether from weakness on one side, or strength on the other, or a combination of the two, undue influence occurs whenever there results "that kind of influence or supremacy of one mind over another by which that other is prevented from acting according to his own wish or judgment, and whereby the will of the person is over-borne and he is induced to do or forbear to do an act which he would not do, or would do, if left to act freely." (Webb v. Saunders, 79 Cal. App. 2d 863, 871, 181 P. 2d 43, 47) Undue influence involves a type of mismatch that our statute calls unfair advantage. (Civ. Code, § 1575) Whether a person of subnormal capacities has been subjected to ordinary force or a person of normal capacities subjected to extraordinary force, the match is equally out of balance. If will has been overcome against judgment, consent may be rescinded.

The difficulty, of course, lies in determining when the forces of persuasion have overflowed their normal banks and become oppressive flood waters. There are second thoughts to every bargain, and hindsight is still better than foresight. Undue influence cannot be used as a pretext to avoid bad bargains or escape from bargains which refuse to come up to expectations. A woman who buys a dress on impulse, which on critical inspection by her best friend turns out to be less fashionable than she had thought, is not legally entitled to set aside the sale on the ground that the saleswoman used all her wiles to close the sale. A man who buys a tract of desert land in the expectation that it is in the immediate path of the city's growth and will become another Palm Springs, an expectation cultivated in glowing terms by the seller, cannot rescind his bargain when things turn out differently. If we are temporarily persuaded against our better judgment to do something about which we later have second thoughts, we must abide the consequences of the risks inherent in managing our own affairs. (Estate of Anderson, 185 Cal. 700, 706–707 (198 P. 407)).

However, overpersuasion is generally accompanied by certain characteristics that tend to create a pattern. The pattern usually involves several of the following elements:

(1) discussion of the transaction at an unusual or inappropriate time,

(2) consummation of the transaction in an unusual place,

(3) insistent demand that the business be finished at once,

(4) extreme emphasis on untoward consequences of delay,

(5) the use of multiple persuaders by the dominant side against a single servient party,

(6) absence of third-party advisers to the servient party, and

(7) statements that there is no time to consult financial advisers or attorneys.

If a number of these elements are simultaneously present, the persuasion may be characterized as excessive. The cases are illustrative:

Moore v. Moore, 56 Cal. 89, 93, and 81 Cal. 195, 22 P. 589, 874. The pregnant wife of a man who had been shot to death on October 30 and buried on November 1 was approached by four members of her husband's family on November 2 or 3 and persuaded to deed her entire interest in her husband's estate to his children by a prior marriage. In finding the use of undue influence on Mrs. Moore, the court commented:

> It was the second day after her late husband's funeral. It was at a time when she would naturally feel averse to transacting any business, and she might reasonably presume that her late husband's brothers would not apply to her at such a time to transact any important business, unless it was of a nature that would admit of no delay. And as it would admit of delay, the only reason which we can discover for their unseemly haste is, that they thought that she would be more likely to comply with their wishes then than at some future time, after she had recovered from the shock which she had then so recently experienced. If for that reason they selected that time for the accomplishment of their purpose, it seems to us that they not only took, but that they designed to take, an unfair advantage of her weakness of mind. If they did not, they probably can explain why they selected that inappropriate time for the transaction of business which might have been delayed for weeks without injury to any one. In the absence of any explanation, it appears to us that the time was selected with reference to just that condition of mind that she

alleges that she was then in. Taking an unfair advantage of another's weakness of mind is undue influence, and the law will not permit the retention of an advantage thus obtained. (Civ. Code, § 1575)

Weger v. Rocha, 138 Cal. App. 109, 32 P. 2d 417. Plaintiff, while confined in a cast in a hospital, gave a release of claims for personal injuries for a relatively small sum to an agent who spent two hours persuading her to sign. At the time of signing plaintiff was in a highly nervous and hysterical condition and suffering much pain, and she signed the release in order to terminate the interview. The court held that the release had been secured by the use of undue influence.

Fyan v. McNutt, 266 Mich. 406, 254 N. W. 146 (1934). At issue was the validity of an agreement by Mrs. McNutt to pay Fyan, a real estate broker, a five-percent commission on all moneys received from the condemnation of Mrs. McNutt's land. Earlier, Fyan had secured an option from Mrs. McNutt to purchase her land for his own account and offer it for sale as part of a larger parcel to Wayne County for an airport site. On July 25 Fyan learned from the newspapers that the county would probably start condemnation proceedings rather than obtain an airport site by purchase. Fyan, with four others, arrived at Mrs. McNutt's house at 1 a. m. on July 26 with the commission agreement he wanted her to sign. Mrs. McNutt protested being awakened at that hour and was reluctant to sign, but Fyan told her he had to have the paper in Detroit by morning, that the whole airport proposition would fall through if she did not sign then and there, that there wasn't time to wait until morning to get outside advice. In holding the agreement invalid the Michigan Supreme Court said:

> The late hour of the night at which her signature was secured over her protest and plea that she be given until the next day to consider her action, the urge of the moment, the cooperation of the others present in their desire to obtain a good price for their farm lands, the plaintiff's anxiety over the seeming weakness of his original option, all combined to produce a situation in which, to say the least, it is doubtful that the defendant had an opportunity to exercise her own free will. * * * A valid contract can be entered into only when there is a meeting of the minds of the parties under circumstances conducive to a free and voluntary execution of the agreement contemplated. It must be conceived in good faith and come into existence under circumstances that do not deprive the parties of the exercise of their own free will.

The difference between legitimate persuasion and excessive pressure, like the difference between seduction and rape, rests to a considerable extent in the manner in which the parties go about their business. For example, if a day or two after Odorizzi's release on bail the superintendent of the school district had called him into his office during business hours and directed his attention to those provisions of the Education Code compelling his leave of absence and authorizing his suspension on the filing of written charges, had told him that the District contemplated filing written charges against him, had pointed out the alternative of resignation available to him, had informed him he was free to consult counsel or any adviser he wished and to consider the matter overnight and return with his decision the next day, it is extremely unlikely that any complaint about the use of excessive pressure could ever have been made against the school district.

But, according to the allegations of the complaint, this is not the way it happened, and if it had happened that way, plaintiff would never have resigned. Rather, the representatives of the school board undertook to achieve their objective by overpersuasion and imposition to secure plaintiff's signature but not his consent to his resignation through a high-pressure carrot-and-stick technique—under which they assured plaintiff they were trying to assist him, he should rely on their advice, there wasn't time to consult an attorney, if he didn't resign at once the school district would suspend and dismiss him from his position and publicize the proceedings, but if he did resign the incident wouldn't jeopardize his chances of securing a teaching post elsewhere.

Plaintiff has thus pleaded both subjective and objective elements entering the undue influence equation and stated sufficient facts to put in issue the question whether his free will had been overborne by defendant's agents at a time when he was unable to function in a normal manner. It was sufficient to pose " * * * the ultimate question * * * whether a free and competent judgment was merely influenced, or whether a mind was so dominated as to prevent the exercise of an independent judgment." (Williston on Contracts, § 1625 (rev. ed.); Restatement, Contracts, § 497, comment c) The question cannot be resolved by an analysis of pleading but requires a finding of fact.

We express no opinion on the merits of plaintiff's case, or the propriety of his continuing to teach school (Ed. Code, § 13403), or the timeliness of his rescission (Civ. Code, § 1691). We do hold that his pleading, liberally construed, states a cause of action for rescission of a transaction to which his apparent consent had been obtained through the use of undue influence.

The judgment is reversed.

ROTH, P. J., and HERNDON, J., concur.

NOTES AND QUESTIONS

1. *Factors of implicating "unfair persuasion."* The *Odorizzi* court identified seven factors useful to determine whether a particular contract is

the product of undue influence, which include: (1) discussion of the transaction at an unusual or inappropriate time; (2) consummation of the transaction in an unusual place; (3) insistent demand that the business be finished at once; (4) extreme emphasis on untoward consequences of delay; (5) the use of multiple persuaders by the dominant side against a single servient party; (6) absence of third-party advisers to the servient party; and (7) statements that there is no time to consult financial advisers or attorneys. Does the court require all factors to find undue influence? Were all factors satisfied in this case?

2. *Relationship between contract and rape law.* The court states that the "difference between legitimate persuasion and excessive pressure, like the difference between seduction and rape, rests to a considerable extent in the manner in which the parties go about their business." While insensitive in comparing rape to sex, the statement does invoke contract parallels in rape law that used to require physical force. Modern rape law recognizes non-physical force, but some have criticized the non-physical force standards as over-inclusive. For an article suggesting workable parallelism between rape notions of non-physical force in contract undue influence law, see Ann T. Spence, Note, "A Contract Reading of Rape Law: Redefining Force to Include Coercion," 37 Colum. J.L. & Soc. Probs. 57 (2003).

3. *Sexual orientation consequences.* The case notes that Odorizzi was arrested for criminal homosexual activity. Given the subjective nature of "unfair persuasion," is it possible to properly analyze this case absent some contextual understanding of the personalized effects of sexual orientation in California in 1964? See Curtis Nyquist, Patrick Ruiz & Frank Smith, "Using Students as Discussion Leaders on Sexual Orientation and Gender Identity Issues in First-Year Courses," 49 J. Legal Educ. 535 (1999) (citing and discussing *Odorizzi*).

4. *Premarital agreements.* Do you think courts should attempt to police undue influence in contracts negotiated in the context of personal relationships? See Brian Bix, "Bargaining in the Shadow of Love: The Enforcement of Premarital Agreements and How We Think About Marriage," 40 Wm. & Mary L. Rev. 145 (1998). How likely is it that a court will be able to unwind and accurately assess the complex interpersonal relationships and commitments that lead to such contracts? Should the court be more or less willing to find such contracts tainted by undue influence?

5. *Gender and undue influence.* Like the defenses of unconscionability, and to a lesser extent, duress, and in contrast to misrepresentation, undue influence depends upon personal characteristics of the party asserting the defense in addition to external factors. Specifically, the party claiming the defense must convince a court or jury that the party was particularly weak and susceptible to influence or pressure. Some commentators have observed the tendency of courts to adopt—unconsciously or otherwise—biased stereotypes of weakness in members of certain status groups, including women, the poor, minorities, and the uneducated. See, e.g., Arthur Allen Leff,

"Unconscionability and the Code—The Emperor's New Clause," 115 U. Pa. L. Rev. 485, 556–57 (1967) ("[I]t is arguable that sometimes [judicial stereotypes of weakness] were wrong; not all old ladies . . . are without defenses. Put briefly, the typical has a tendency to become stereotypical, with what may be unpleasant results even for the beneficiaries of the judicial benevolence."); Brian Alan Ross, "Undue Influence and Gender Inequity," 19 Women's Rts. L. Rep. 97, 97–98 (1997) (noting in the context of will disputes that "it seems that the [undue influence] doctrine is largely a judicial vehicle for implementing social policy case by case through the use of such concepts as fairness, justice, and morality. Undue influence decisions often appear to be driven by oppressive, stereotypical assumptions about women and their 'proper' role in society, especially in a 'meretricious' relationship"). Moreover, as Richard Delgado suggests, enshrined judicial stereotypes may perpetuate negative self-images in the target status group. See Richard Delgado, "Storytelling for Oppositionists and Others: A Plea for Narrative," 87 Mich. L. Rev. 2411, 2412–13 (1988). Delgado observes that both the dominant "ingroup" and subordinated "outgroups" create and share stories and narratives about themselves and their relations with other groups. See id. In the civil rights context, for instance, Delgado opines that the principle instrument of subordination in the minds of many minority individuals "is the prevailing mindset by means of which members of the dominant group justify the world as it is, that is, with whites on top, and browns and blacks at the bottom." Id.

To what extent is it realistic to assume that members of a particular status group define their self-identities by judicial stereotypes in contract defenses? If such stereotypes exist, who is more to blame for their perpetuation—the judge who relies upon them or the attorney who, in fulfilling her duty of zealous advocacy on behalf of her client, diligently exploits existing stereotypes to craft a compelling narrative for the court?

E. FAILURE OF THE BARGAINING PROCESS

The ancient Roman law maxim *pacta sunt servanda* expresses the formalist notion that agreements are to be strictly observed. Accordingly, when the parties have negotiated a contract and voluntarily accepted correlative legal obligations in a fair exchange supported by a theory of legal obligation such as consideration, the resulting contract and duties created are absolute. The failure to perform in accordance with the strict terms of contractual duties creates a breach with resulting remedies discussed in Chapter 9. See Hoffman F. Fuller, "Mistake and Error in the Law of Contracts," 33 Emory L. J. 41 (1984).

However, appearances can be deceiving. Each party will make several assumptions regarding the nature of the bargain at the time the contract is formed. Those assumptions may be erroneous "mistakes" or "misunderstandings" in common parlance. What is the effect of the erroneous assumptions on the status of the contract? Chapter 5 considered how contract law treats erroneous assumptions made at the time of the contract about the course of future events. This chapter considers how contract law treats erroneous assumptions made at the time of the contract about facts thought to exist at the time the contract is made. Understandably, the maxim *pacta sunt servanda* suggests courts should allocate the risk of erroneous assumptions to the party making the error. Thus, a buyer who pays $1,000,000 for a painting she erroneously believes to be an original Picasso normally bears the risk that the painting is actually a cheap copy or that the market for Picasso paintings will collapse in the future. Likewise, a seller who sells a painting at a garage sale for a dollar, erroneously believing it to be a crude and inelegant scrawl by an untalented 10-year-old child, bears the risk that the painting is actually a Picasso or that the untalented 10-year-old child will later become a famous artist. In either case, if the erroneous buyer refuses to pay or the erroneous seller refuses to convey title, that party breaches the parties' contract.

In a few extreme cases, the nature and context of the error may permit the erroneous party to avoid the contract, or it may excuse that party's future obligations under the contract. The appropriate remedy—a power of avoidance giving rise to a rescission and restitution on the one hand or merely an excuse for non-performance of future obligations under the contract—depends upon whether the erroneous assumption relates to predictions regarding future events or instead relates to facts in existence at the time the contract is formed. Although courts and commentators commonly conflate these arguments, the majority approach is to separate them because of the differences in remedies. See E. Allan Farnsworth, Julia L. Brickell & Stephen P. Chawaga, "Relief for Mutual Mistake and Impracticability," 1 J.L. & Com. 1 (1981).

In the first instance, an error regarding future events rarely, if ever, justifies the creation of a power of avoidance in the erroneous party. If the error is material, and if the contract language itself does not allocate the risk of the erroneous assumption to party negatively affected by the assumption, contract law might provide that party a remedy in the form of discharging future duties while leaving past performance in *status quo*. These matters are discussed further in Chapter 5 on breach and conditions. But not all scholars agree that doctrinal separation is either accurate or justified. See Andrew Kull, "Mistake, Frustration and the Windfall Principle of Contract Remedies," 43 Hastings L. J. 1, 2–3 (1991) and Robert A. Hillman, "An Analysis of the Cessation of Contractual Relations," 68 Cornell L. Rev. 617 (1983).

Where the error relates to facts in existence at the time of contract formation, simply discharging forward duties may not be appropriate or fair, especially where both parties have substantially performed. In these cases, since the defect relates to the formation of the contract itself, serious errors create a power of avoidance in one or both parties. The power of avoidance is exercised in the form of rescission and followed by restitution by both parties to the *status quo ante* existing before the contract was made.

The principal forms of actionable errors relating to facts in existence at the time the contract is formed involve mutual mistake and unilateral mistake. Understandably, one might expect contract law to be more sympathetic to commonly shared mutual mistakes than simply an error by one of the parties. Accordingly, the discussion below concerning unilateral mistake attaches more conditions to create the power of avoidance in favor of the erroneous party. After all, the innocent party made no error and will lose the benefit of the contract if the power of rescission is granted.

Finally, parties may occasionally make a "mistake in integration," as distinguished from the defenses of mutual and unilateral mistake. A mistake in integration occurs where the parties' written memorialization of their actual contract fails to reflect accurately their actual contract. For example, assume that A and B orally agree to buy and sell 100 widgets at $54 apiece. To memorialize their bargain (as required by the UCC § 2–201 Statute of Frauds), A sends B a form contract that mistakenly shows the quantity as 1,000 widgets. In that case, the writing fails to reflect the true mutual understanding of the parties—the writing is in error and not the parties assumptions.

Given that the parties actually did enter a binding contract, rescission and restitution is inappropriate as a remedy for such drafting errors. The correct remedy in such cases is to simply reform the document. If the other party refuses to do so, the aggrieved party may petition the court to equitably "reform" the writing in accordance with the true understanding and agreement of the parties. See Restatement (Second) of Contracts § 155 ("Where a writing . . . fails to express the agreement because of a mistake of both parties as to the contents or effect of the writing, the court may at the request of a party reform the writing to express the agreement . . ."). Of course, the party seeking reformation will have the burden to prove, generally by clear and convincing evidence, that the writing is not in accord with the agreed facts. See Restatement (Second) of Contracts § 155 *cmt. c* (burden of proof for mistake in integration "is commonly summarized in a standard that requires the trier of the facts to be satisfied by 'clear and convincing evidence' before reformation is granted"). In such cases, the parol evidence rule is not a bar to the presentation of the evidence of prior agreements and negotiations because the evidence is not admitted to enlarge the agreement but to simply reform and correct an error. See Restatement (Second) of Contracts § 214(e). However, the most common reason for denying reformation is the failure of the party seeking reformation to prove the "true" agreement, thus rendering the action one for merely unilateral mistake or error. See Wex S. Malone, "The Reformation of Writings for Mutual Mistake of Fact," 24 Geo. L. J. 613, 616 (1936). Equitable reformation is based on the maxim that equity seeks to effectuate substance of the transaction when contrary to the form. See Howard W. Brill, "Reformation in Arkansas," 1998 Ark. L. Notes 1.

1. MUTUAL MISTAKE

The modern mitigating doctrine of mistake or error is only about a century old in the United States. Under earlier law, the doctrine of consideration made such a concept irrelevant by treating the erroneous promise as an irrational promise not supported by consideration. The independent correlative doctrine of mistake or error did not develop until the nineteenth century with the "meeting of the minds" requirement. As with consideration failures, early mistake law prevented the formation of a contract. A. W. Brian Simpson, Common Law of Contract 535 (1975). However, with the Holmesian objectification of contract law, mistake doctrine assumed a different and narrower posture and contracts made upon a common mutual mistake as to an existing fact become voidable at the election of either party. See Oliver Wendell Holmes, The Common Law 242 (1881) and Robert L. Birmingham, "Holmes on 'Peerless': Raffles v. Wichelhaus and the Objective Theory of Contract," 47 U. Pitt. L. Rev. 183 (1985). Compare, Restatement (First) of Contracts § 502, with Restatement (Second) of Contracts § 156. The objectification of contract law thus considerably narrowed the reach of the early nineteenth century mistake consequence that prevented the formation of a contract in the absence of a subjective meeting of the minds. Now the mutual mistake must be objectively confirmed in both parties and proven by the party asserting mutual mistake. Grant Gilmore, The Death of Contract 44 (1974).

The traditional introduction in many contracts classes to the doctrine of mutual mistake analyzes *Sherwood v. Walker*, 66 Mich. 568, 33 N.W. 919 (1887). Here, *Sherwood* is discussed as a squib in *Lenawee County Board of Health v. Messerly*, 417 Mich. 17, 331 N.W.2d 203 (1982) (abrogating *Sherwood* in favor of the modern standard for mutual mistake), below. In *Sherwood*, Walker—a cattle importer and breeder—sold to Sherwood—a banker—a cow named "Rose 2d of Aberlone." During Sherwood's cattle shopping, Walker showed Rose to Sherwood at Walker's Greenfield farm "upon which were some blooded cattle supposed to be barren as breeders." Walker further stated to Sherwood, "that they [the cattle on the Greenfield farm] were probably barren, and would not breed." After inspecting the cattle and agreeing on a price of $0.055/pound, live weight, Sherwood purchased Rose. Walker confirmed the terms of the purchase by letter.

Six days later, Sherwood attempted to take delivery of Rose, and Walker refused to deliver, arguing that the contract should be avoidable by reason of the parties' mutual mistake. The court majority opinion agreed, reasoning that because the mistake went to the "substance of the thing bargained for," rather than to the value of the thing, the mistake was sufficient to avoid the contract.

It appears from the record that both parties supposed this cow was barren and would not breed, and she was sold by the pound for an insignificant sum as compared with her real value if a breeder. She was evidently sold and purchased on the relation of her value for beef, unless the [buyer] had learned of her true condition, and concealed such knowledge from the [sellers]. Before the [buyer] secured the possession of the animal, the [sellers] learned that she was with calf, and therefore of great value, and undertook to rescind the sale by refusing to deliver her. The question arises whether they had a right to do so. The circuit judge ruled that this fact did not avoid the sale and it made no difference whether she was barren or not. I am of the opinion that the court erred in this holding. I know that this is a close question, and the dividing line between the adjudicated cases is not easily discerned. But it must be considered as well settled that a party who has given an apparent consent to a contract of sale may refuse to execute it, or he may avoid it after it has been completed, if the assent was founded, or the contract made, upon the mistake of a material fact,—such as the subject-matter of the sale, the price, or some collateral fact materially inducing the agreement; and this can be done when the mistake is mutual. . . .

If there is a difference or misapprehension as to the substance of the thing bargained for; if the thing actually delivered or received is different in substance from the thing bargained for, and intended to be sold, then there is no contract; but if it be only a difference in some quality or accident, even though the mistake may have been the actuating motive to the purchaser or seller, or both of them, yet the contract remains binding. "The difficulty in every case is to determine whether the mistake or misapprehension is as to the substance of the whole contract, going, as it were, to the root of the matter, or only to some point, even though a material point, an error as to which does not affect the substance of the whole consideration." [citation omitted] It has been held, in accordance with the principles above stated, that where a horse is bought under the belief that he is sound, and both vendor and vendee honestly believe him to be sound, the purchaser must stand by his bargain, and pay the full price, unless there was a warranty.

It seems to me, however, in the case made by this record, that the mistake or misapprehension of the parties went to the whole substance of the agreement. If the cow was a breeder, she was worth at least $750; if barren, she was worth not over $80. The parties would not have made the contract of sale except upon the understanding and belief that she was incapable of breeding, and of no use as a cow. It is true she is now the identical animal that they thought her to be when the contract was made; there is no mistake as to the identity of the creature. Yet the mistake was not of the mere quality of the animal, but went to the very nature of the thing. A barren cow is substantially a different creature than a breeding one. There is as much difference between them for all purposes of use as there is between an ox and a cow that is capable of breeding and giving milk. If the mutual mistake had simply related to the fact whether she was with calf or not for one season, then it might have been a good sale, but the mistake affected the character of the animal for all time, and for its present and ultimate use. She was not in fact the animal, or the kind of animal, the defendants intended to sell or the plaintiff to buy. She was not a barren cow, and, if this fact had been known, there would have been no contract. The mistake affected the substance of the whole consideration, and it must be considered that there was no contract to sell or sale of the cow as she actually was. The thing sold and bought had in fact no existence. She was sold as a beef creature would be sold; she is in fact a breeding cow, and a valuable one. The court should have instructed the jury that if they found that the cow was sold, or contracted to be sold, upon the understanding of both parties that she was barren, and useless for the purpose of breeding, and that in fact she was not barren, but capable of breeding, then the defendants had a right to rescind, and to refuse to deliver, and the verdict should be in their favor.

The majority concluded that the mutual mistake justified avoidance because the mistake went to the "substance" of the thing sold rather than its value. In contrast, the dissent focused upon different facts suggesting that the parties were in fact consciously ignorant of the fertility or lack thereof of Rose 2d of Aberlone.

In this case neither party knew the actual quality and condition of this cow at the time of the sale. The [sellers] say, or rather said, to the [buyer], "they had a few head left on their farm in Greenfield, and asked [the buyer] to go and see them, stating to [the buyer] that in all probability they were sterile and would not breed." [The buyer] did go as requested, and found there these cows, including the one purchased, with a bull. The cow had been exposed, but neither knew she was with calf or whether she would breed. The [sellers] sold the cow for what they believed her to be, and the [buyer] bought her as he believed she was, after the statements made by the [sellers]. No conditions whatever were attached to the terms of sale by either party. It was in fact as absolute as it could well be made, and I know of no precedent as authority by which this court can alter the contract thus made by these parties in writing,—interpolate in it a condition by which, if the [sellers] should be mistaken in their belief that the cow was barren, she could be returned to them and their contract should be annulled. It is not the duty of courts to destroy contracts when called upon to enforce them, after they have been legally made. There was no mistake of any material fact by either of the parties in the case as would license the vendors to rescind. There was no difference between the parties, nor misapprehension, as to the substance of the thing bargained for, which was a cow supposed to be barren by one party, and believed not to be by the other. As to the quality of the animal, subsequently developed, both parties were equally ignorant, and as to this each party took his chances. If this were not the law, there would be no safety in purchasing this kind of stock.

As discussed in *Lenawee County Board of Health v. Messerly*, below, the substance/value distinction explored in *Sherwood* proved difficult to apply, and courts have continued searching for a workable standard. Given the historical vacillation in the role of mistake in contract law, it is not surprising that various theories have been advanced to justify or attack its appropriateness. Compare Kenneth L. Schneyer, "The Culture of Risk: Deconstructing Mutual Mistake," 34 Am. Bus. L.J. 429 (1997); Janet K. Smith & Richard L. Smith, "Contract Law, Mutual Mistake, and Incentives to Produce and Disclose Information," 19 J. Legal Stud. 467 (1990); and Anthony T. Kronman, "Mistake, Disclosure, Information, and the Law of Contracts," 7 J. Legal Stud. 1 (1978). Fairness alone is normatively inadequate to the task, if for no other reason than that one party's gain is the other party's loss. In other words, gains and losses tend to balance each other. Another approach might suggest that mistake indicates a lack of mutual assent, but of course such a justification would render the contract void, not voidable.

Modern mistake theory focuses upon the seriousness and consequences of the mistake. The mistake must relate to a basic assumption having a "material effect" on the agreed exchange of performances of the parties. Restatement (Second) of Contracts § 152(1). The material effect requirement is not universally applied, but all courts require some substantial impact. See Val D. Ricks, "American Mutual Mistake: Half-Civilian Mongrel, Consideration Reincarnate," 58 La. L. Rev. 663, 666 (1998). Nonetheless, the materiality requirement is often difficult to apply and therefore highly unpredictable. See Eric Rasmussen & Ian Ayres, "Mutual and Unilateral Mistake in Contract Law," 22 J. Legal Stud. 309, 322 (1993). Restatement (Second) of Contracts § 152, *cmt. c* provides as follows:

A party cannot avoid a contract merely because both parties were mistaken as to a basic assumption on which it was made. . . . It is not enough for him to prove that he would not have made the contract had it not been for the mistake. He must show that the resulting imbalance in the agreed exchange is so severe that he can not fairly be required to carry it out. Ordinarily, he will be able to do this by showing that the exchange is not only less desirable to him but is also more advantageous to the other party.

Early law of mistake defined the term as an unintentional act, omission, or error arising from ignorance, surprise, imposition, or misplaced confidence. See Roland R. Foulke, "Mistake in Contract," 11 Colum. L. Rev. 197, 198 (1911). Modern law of mistake defines the term "mistake" more narrowly. In this context, a mistake is an erroneous belief that is not in accord with the facts existing at the time of the making of the contract. Restatement (Second) of Contracts § 151. Thus, the term excludes common mistake elements, such as an improvident act or an erroneous prediction or judgment regarding future events. Restatement (Second) of Contracts § 151, *cmt. a.* However, the term "facts" does include the law. Accordingly, an erroneous belief with regard to the law as found in statutes, regulations, or case law is included within the term "mistake." Restatement (Second) of Contracts § 151, *cmt. b.*

Because of these definitions, care must be taken to distinguish mistakes and misunderstandings. Technically, a misunderstanding is a different meaning attached to an existing fact, whereas a mistake is a belief that is not in accord with the facts. This subtle difference produces one significant consequence—a misunderstanding, especially as to a material term, often prevents contract formation because the parties have not expressed mutual assent regarding that term. In contrast, mutually mistaken parties do mutually assent to the material terms of their contracts—permitting formation of the contract—but are mistaken as to basic assumptions underlying those agreements, which may render the contract voidable. Compare, Restatement (Second) of Contracts § 20(1), with Restatement (Second) of Contracts § 152(1).

For example, in *Raffles v. Wichelhaus*, discussed in Chapter 3, each party attached a different meaning to the term "to arrive ex *Peerless*" with one party understanding that term to mean "to arrive ex [October] *Peerless*" and the other understanding it as "to arrive ex [December] *Peerless*." Although they apparently used the same words for their agreement, their fundamentally different understandings of those words meant that they never assented to the actual terms of the contract, and no contract was formed. In contrast, in *Sherwood v. Walker, supra,* both parties clearly understood the contract to concern the same cow, one "Rose 2d of Aberlone." But they were apparently mistaken regarding a basic assumption relating to that cow, namely whether Rose could get pregnant. To be fair, this distinction between mistake and misunderstanding, drawn from the second restatement, may be mere legal smoke and mirrors. As with the quasi-Aristotelian logic in *Sherwood*, where the court attempts to distinguish mistakes going to the "substance" or "nature" of the cow from mistakes going to the value of the cow, the distinction between mistake and misunderstanding is not without criticism. See Keith A. Rowley, "To Err Is Human," 104 Mich. L. Rev. 1407 (2006) (book review of E. Allan Farnsworth book on Alleviating Mistakes: Reversal and Forgiveness for Flawed Perceptions (Oxford Press 2004)). Professor Farnsworth was the reporter for the final portion of the Restatement (Second) of Contracts and the author of the mistake doctrine.

The doctrine of risk allocation is an explicit part of modern mutual mistake law. Indeed, Restatement (Second) of Contracts § 152(1) states an exception to its application when the affected party bears the "risk of the mistake." Restatement (Second) of Contracts § 154 states three situations when the risk of a mistake is allocated to a party:

(a) the agreement allocates the risk to that party;

(b) that party is aware he has only limited knowledge of the mistaken fact and yet treats that knowledge as sufficient; or

(c) the court allocates the risk to that party because it is reasonable to do so.

However, apart from insurance contracts, which are risk contracts by nature, contracts do not ordinarily specifically allocate the risk of mistake. Moreover, judicial allocation essentially results in an implied term allocating risk to the affected party. See Hoffman F. Fuller, "Mistake and Error in the Law of Contracts," 33 Emory L. J. 41, 59 (1984). Of course, distinctions between terminology and risk analysis depend critically upon an assumed level of consciousness regarding the factual matter. Melvin Eisenberg provides an excellent description of level of consciousness in the contracting process involves the concept of "tacit assumption" rather than express assumption. See Melvin A. Eisenberg, "Mistake in Contract Law," 91 Cal. L. Rev. 1573, 1622–23 (2003). As Eisenberg notes, "[a] more colloquial expression that captures the concept of tacit assumptions is the phrase 'taken for granted.' . . . Tacit assumptions are not made explicit, even where they are the basis of a contract, just because they are taken for granted and therefore don't need to be expressed. They are so deeply embedded that it simply doesn't occur to the parties to make them explicit. . . ." Id.

Finally, cases involving the sale of goods are governed by the UCC. However, the UCC does not have a separate "mistake doctrine" statute. As with other matters not directly addressed by a statute, the UCC adopts the common law in such cases, and where state common law varies, applies the common law of the state whose law governs the transaction. See UCC § 1–

103(b) (2001) and Robert A. Hillman, "Construction of the Uniform Commercial Code: UCC Section 1–103 and 'Code' Methodology," 18 B. C. L. Rev. 655, 659 (1977).

LENAWEE COUNTY BOARD OF HEALTH V. MESSERLY

Supreme Court of Michigan
417 Mich. 17, 331 N.W.2d 203 (1982)

RYAN, Justice.

In March of 1977, Carl and Nancy Pickles, appellees, purchased from appellants, William and Martha Messerly, a 600-square-foot tract of land upon which is located a three-unit apartment building. Shortly after the transaction was closed, the Lenawee County Board of Health condemned the property and obtained a permanent injunction that prohibits human habitation on the premises until the defective sewage system is brought into conformance with the Lenawee County sanitation code.

We are required to determine whether appellees should prevail in their attempt to avoid this land contract on the basis of mutual mistake and failure of consideration. We conclude that the parties did entertain a mutual misapprehension of fact, but that the circumstances of this case do not warrant rescission.

I

The facts of the case are not seriously in dispute. In 1971, the Messerlys acquired approximately one acre plus 600 square feet of land. A three-unit apartment building was situated upon the 600-square-foot portion. The trial court found that, prior to this transfer, the Messerlys' predecessor in title, Mr. Bloom, had installed a septic tank on the property without a permit and in violation of the applicable health code. The Messerlys used the building as an income investment property until 1973 when they sold it, upon land contract, to James Barnes who likewise used it primarily as an income-producing investment.[1]

Mr. and Mrs. Barnes, with the permission of the Messerlys, sold approximately one acre of the property in 1976, and the remaining 600 square feet and building were offered for sale soon thereafter when Mr. and Mrs. Barnes defaulted on their land contract. Mr. and Mrs. Pickles evidenced an interest in the property, but were dissatisfied with the terms of the Barnes-Messerly land contract. Consequently, to accommodate the Pickleses' preference to enter into a land contract directly with the Messerlys, Mr. and Mrs. Barnes executed a quitclaim deed which conveyed their interest in the property back to the Messerlys. After inspecting the

---

[1]   James Barnes was married shortly after he purchased the property. Mr. and Mrs. Barnes lived in one of the apartments on the property for three months and, after they moved, Mrs. Barnes continued to aid in the management of the property.

property, Mr. and Mrs. Pickles executed a new land contract with the Messerlys on March 21, 1977. It provided for a purchase price of $25,500. A clause was added to the end of the land contract form which provides:

17. Purchaser has examined this property and agrees to accept same in its present condition. There are no other or additional written or oral understandings.

Five or six days later, when the Pickleses went to introduce themselves to the tenants, they discovered raw sewage seeping out of the ground. Tests conducted by a sanitation expert indicated the inadequacy of the sewage system. The Lenawee County Board of Health subsequently condemned the property and initiated this lawsuit in the Lenawee Circuit Court against the Messerlys as land contract vendors, and the Pickleses, as vendees, to obtain a permanent injunction proscribing human habitation of the premises until the property was brought into conformance with the Lenawee County sanitation code. The injunction was granted, and the Lenawee County Board of Health was permitted to withdraw from the lawsuit by stipulation of the parties.

When no payments were made on the land contract, the Messerlys filed a cross-complaint against the Pickleses seeking foreclosure, sale of the property, and a deficiency judgment. Mr. and Mrs. Pickles then counterclaimed for rescission against the Messerlys, and filed a third-party complaint against the Barneses, which incorporated, by reference, the allegations of the counterclaim against the Messerlys. In count one, Mr. and Mrs. Pickles alleged failure of consideration. Count two charged Mr. and Mrs. Barnes with willful concealment and misrepresentation as a result of their failure to disclose the condition of the sanitation system. Additionally, Mr. and Mrs. Pickles sought to hold the Messerlys liable in equity for the Barneses' alleged misrepresentation. The Pickleses prayed that the land contract be rescinded.

After a bench trial, the court concluded that the Pickleses had no cause of action against either the Messerlys or the Barneses as there was no fraud or misrepresentation. This ruling was predicated on the trial judge's conclusion that none of the parties knew of Mr. Bloom's earlier transgression or of the resultant problem with the septic system until it was discovered by the Pickleses, and that the sanitation problem was not caused by any of the parties. The trial court held that the property was purchased "as is," after inspection and, accordingly, its "negative * * * value cannot be blamed upon an innocent seller." Foreclosure was ordered against the Pickleses, together with a judgment against them in the amount of $25,943.09.[3]

---

[3]   The parties stipulated that this amount was due on the land contract, assuming that the contract was valid and enforceable.

Mr. and Mrs. Pickles appealed from the adverse judgment. The Court of Appeals unanimously affirmed the trial court's ruling with respect to Mr. and Mrs. Barnes but, in a two-to-one decision, reversed the finding of no cause of action on the Pickleses' claims against the Messerlys. Lenawee County Board of Health v. Messerly, 98 Mich. App. 478, 295 N. W. 2d 903 (1980).[4] It concluded that the mutual mistake[5] between the Messerlys and the Pickleses went to a basic, as opposed to a collateral, element of the contract,[6] and that the parties intended to transfer income-producing rental property but, in actuality, the vendees paid $25,500 for an asset without value.[7]

Since the mutual mistake issue was dispositive in the Court of Appeals, we find its consideration necessary to a proper determination of this case.

We granted the Messerlys' application for leave to appeal. 411 Mich. 900 (1981).[8]

---

[4] Judge MacKenzie dissented from this part of the opinion. She would have held that the trial court's refusal to grant rescission to Mr. and Mrs. Pickles was not an abuse of discretion: "I would find that the trial court correctly denied rescission to Mr. and Mrs. Pickles, who received essentially the same property they bargained for and failed to prove that any mistake or failure of consideration existed at the time the parties entered into the contract."98 Mich. App 494.

[5] Mr. and Mrs. Pickles did not allege mutual mistake as a ground for rescission in their pleadings. However, the trial court characterized their failure of consideration argument as mutual mistake resulting in failure of consideration. Recognizing a potential difficulty in reversing the trial court on an issue not raised by the pleadings, the Court of Appeals devoted a footnote to an explanation of its decision to consider the mutual mistake argument.

"4. The pleadings below set forth the Pickleses' theory as failure of consideration. However, it appears that the trial judge considered the failure of consideration issue to be essentially rooted in an allegation of mutual mistake. While issues not pleaded or otherwise presented to the trial court are not available for use on appeal, Long Mfg Co Inc., v Wright-Way Farm Service, Inc., 39 Mich. App. 546 197 NW 2d 862 (1972), rev'd on other grounds, [391 Mich 82, 214 N. W. 2d 816] (1974), we address the issue of mutual mistake as one 'otherwise presented to the trial court.'

We further note that an exception to the general rule that an issue not raised before the trial court cannot be raised on appeal exists where the issue has been fully briefed, and this Court in the interest of justice chooses to consider it. Turner v. Ford Motor Co, 81 Mich App 521, 525, fn 2; 265 NW 2d 400 (1978)." 98 Mich App 485, fn 4, 295 N. W. 2d 903.

[6] Mr. and Mrs. Pickles did not appeal the trial court's finding that there was no fraud or misrepresentation by the Messerlys or Mr. and Mrs. Barnes. Likewise, the propriety of that ruling is not before this Court today.

[7] The trial court found that the only way that the property could be put to residential use would be to pump and haul the sewage, a method which is economically unfeasible, as the cost of such a disposal system amounts to double the income generated by the property. There was speculation by the trial court that the adjoining land might be utilized to make the property suitable for residential use, but, in the absence of testimony directed at that point, the court refused to draw any conclusions. The trial court and the Court of Appeals both found that the property was valueless, or had a negative value.

[8] The Court of Appeals decision to affirm the trial court's finding of no cause of action against Mr. and Mrs. Barnes has not been appealed to this Court and, accordingly, the propriety of that ruling is not before us today.

II

We must decide initially whether there was a mistaken belief entertained by one or both parties to the contract in dispute and, if so, the resultant legal significance.[9]

A contractual mistake "is a belief that is not in accord with the facts." 1 Restatement Contracts, 2d, § 151, p 383. The erroneous belief of one or both of the parties must relate to a fact in existence at the time the contract is executed. Richardson Lumber Co. v. Hoey, 219 Mich. 643, 189 N. W. 923 (1922); Sherwood v. Walker, 66 Mich. 568, 580, 33 N. W. 919 (1887) (Sherwood, J., dissenting). That is to say, the belief which is found to be in error may not be, in substance, a prediction as to a future occurrence or non-occurrence. Henry v. Thomas, 241 Ga. 360, 245 S. E. 2d 646 (1978); Hailpern v. Dryden, 154 Colo. 231, 389 P. 2d 590 (1964). But see Denton v. Utley, 350 Mich. 332, 86 N. W. 2d 537 (1957).

The Court of Appeals concluded, after a de novo review of the record, that the parties were mistaken as to the income-producing capacity of the property in question. 98 Mich. App. 487–488, 295 N. W. 2d 903. We agree. The vendors and the vendees each believed that the property transferred could be utilized as income-generating rental property. All of the parties subsequently learned that, in fact, the property was unsuitable for any residential use.

Appellants assert that there was no mistake in the contractual sense because the defect in the sewage system did not arise until after the contract was executed. The appellees respond that the Messerlys are confusing the date of the inception of the defect with the date upon which the defect was discovered.

This is essentially a factual dispute which the trial court failed to resolve directly. Nevertheless, we are empowered to draw factual inferences from the facts found by the trial court. GCR 1963, 865. 1(6).

An examination of the record reveals that the septic system was defective prior to the date on which the land contract was executed. The Messerlys' grantor installed a nonconforming septic system without a permit prior to the transfer of the property to the Messerlys in 1971. Moreover, virtually undisputed testimony indicates that, assuming ideal soil conditions, 2,500 square feet of property is necessary to support a sewage system adequate to serve a three-family dwelling. Likewise, 750 square feet is mandated for a one-family home. Thus, the division of the parcel and sale of one acre of the property by Mr. and Mrs. Barnes in 1976

---

[9]   We emphasize that this is a bifurcated inquiry. Legal or equitable remedial measures are not mandated in every case in which a mutual mistake has been established.

made it impossible to remedy the already illegal septic system within the confines of the 600-square-foot parcel.[10]

Appellants do not dispute these underlying facts which give rise to an inference contrary to their contentions.

Having determined that when these parties entered into the land contract they were laboring under a mutual mistake of fact, we now direct our attention to a determination of the legal significance of that finding.

A contract may be rescinded because of a mutual misapprehension of the parties, but this remedy is granted only in the sound discretion of the court. Harris v. Axline, 323 Mich. 585, 36 N. W. 2d 154 (1949). Appellants argue that the parties' mistake relates only to the quality or value of the real estate transferred, and that such mistakes are collateral to the agreement and do not justify rescission, citing A & M Land Development Co. v. Miller, 354 Mich. 681, 94 N. W. 2d 197 (1959).

In that case, the plaintiff was the purchaser of 91 lots of real property. It sought partial rescission of the land contract when it was frustrated in its attempts to develop 42 of the lots because it could not obtain permits from the county health department to install septic tanks on these lots. This Court refused to allow rescission because the mistake, whether mutual or unilateral, related only to the value of the property.

> There was here no mistake as to the form or substance of the contract between the parties, or the description of the property constituting the subject matter. The situation involved is not at all analogous to that presented in Scott v Grow, 301 Mich 226;. 3 NW 2d 254; 141 ALR 819 (1942). There the plaintiff sought relief by way of reformation of a deed on the ground that the instrument of conveyance had not been drawn in accordance with the intention and agreement of the parties. It was held that the bill of complaint stated a case for the granting of equitable relief by way of reformation. In the case at bar plaintiff received the property for which it contracted. The fact that it may be of less value than the purchaser expected at the time of the transaction is not a sufficient basis for the granting of equitable relief, neither fraud nor reliance on misrepresentation of material facts having been established. 354 Mich. 693–694, 94 N. W. 2d 197.

Appellees contend, on the other hand, that in this case the parties were mistaken as to the very nature of the character of the consideration and

---

[10] It is crucial to distinguish between the date on which a belief relating to a particular fact or set of facts becomes erroneous due to a change in the fact, and the date on which the mistaken nature of the belief is discovered. By definition, a mistake cannot be discovered until after the contract is executed. If the parties were aware, prior to the execution of a contract, that they were in error concerning a particular fact, there would be no misapprehension in signing the contract. Thus stated, it becomes obvious that the date on which a mistaken fact manifests itself is irrelevant to the determination whether or not there was a mistake.

claim that the pervasive and essential quality of this mistake renders rescission appropriate. They cite in support of that view Sherwood v. Walker, 66 Mich. 568, 33 N. W. 919 (1887), the famous "barren cow" case. In that case, the parties agreed to the sale and purchase of a cow which was thought to be barren, but which was, in reality, with calf. When the seller discovered the fertile condition of his cow, he refused to deliver her. In permitting rescission, the Court stated:

> It seems to me, however, in the case made by this record, that the mistake or misapprehension of the parties went to the whole substance of the agreement. If the cow was a breeder, she was worth at least $750; if barren, she was worth not over $80. The parties would not have made the contract of sale except upon the understanding and belief that she was incapable of breeding, and of no use as a cow. It is true she is now the identical animal that they thought her to be when the contract was made; there is no mistake as to the identity of the creature. Yet the mistake was not of the mere quality of the animal, but went to the very nature of the thing. A barren cow is substantially a different creature than a breeding one. There is as much difference between them for all purposes of use as there is between an ox and a cow that is capable of breeding and giving milk. If the mutual mistake had simply related to the fact whether she was with calf or not for one season, then it might have been a good sale; but the mistake affected the character of the animal for all time, and for her present and ultimate use. She was not in fact the animal, or the kind of animal, the defendants intended to sell or the plaintiff to buy. She was not a barren cow, and, if this fact had been known, there would have been no contract. The mistake affected the substance of the whole consideration, and it must be considered that there was no contract to sell or sale of the cow as she actually was. The thing sold and bought had in fact no existence. She was sold as a beef creature would be sold; she is in fact a breeding cow, and a valuable one.

> The court should have instructed the jury that if they found that the cow was sold, or contracted to be sold, upon the understanding of both parties that she was barren, and useless for the purpose of breeding, and that in fact she was not barren, but capable of breeding, then the defendants had a right to rescind, and to refuse to deliver, and the verdict should be in their favor. 66 Mich. 577–578, 33 N. W. 919.

As the parties suggest, the foregoing precedent arguably distinguishes mistakes affecting the essence of the consideration from those which go to its quality or value, affording relief on a per se basis for the former but not the latter. See e.g., Lenawee County Board of Health v. Messerly, 98 Mich. App. 478, 492, 295 N. W. 2d 903 (1980) (Mackenzie, J., concurring in part).

However, the distinctions which may be drawn from Sherwood and A & M Land Development Co. do not provide a satisfactory analysis of the nature of a mistake sufficient to invalidate a contract. Often, a mistake relates to an underlying factual assumption which, when discovered, directly affects value, but simultaneously and materially affects the essence of the contractual consideration. It is disingenuous to label such a mistake collateral. McKay v. Coleman, 85 Mich. 60, 48 N. W. 203 (1891). Corbin, Contracts (One Vol. ed.), § 605, p. 551.

Appellant and appellee both mistakenly believed that the property that was the subject of their land contract would generate income as rental property. The fact that it could not be used for human habitation deprived the property of its income-earning potential and rendered it less valuable. However, this mistake, while directly and dramatically affecting the property's value, cannot accurately be characterized as collateral because it also affects the very essence of the consideration. "The thing sold and bought [income generating rental property] had in fact no existence." Sherwood v. Walker, 66 Mich. 578, 33 N. W. 919.

We find that the inexact and confusing distinction between contractual mistakes running to value and those touching the substance of the consideration serves only as an impediment to a clear and helpful analysis for the equitable resolution of cases in which mistake is alleged and proven. Accordingly, the holdings of A & M Land Development Co. and Sherwood with respect to the material or collateral nature of a mistake are limited to the facts of those cases.

Instead, we think the better-reasoned approach is a case-by-case analysis whereby rescission is indicated when the mistaken belief relates to a basic assumption of the parties upon which the contract is made, and which materially affects the agreed performances of the parties. . . . Rescission is not available, however, to relieve a party who has assumed the risk of loss in connection with the mistake. . . .

All of the parties to this contract erroneously assumed that the property transferred by the vendors to the vendees was suitable for human habitation and could be utilized to generate rental income. The fundamental nature of these assumptions is indicated by the fact that their invalidity changed the character of the property transferred, thereby frustrating, indeed precluding, Mr. and Mrs. Pickles' intended use of the real estate. Although the Pickleses are disadvantaged by enforcement of the contract, performance is advantageous to the Messerlys, as the property at issue is less valuable absent its income-earning potential. Nothing short of rescission can remedy the mistake. Thus, the parties' mistake as to a basic assumption materially affects the agreed performances of the parties.

Despite the significance of the mistake made by the parties, we reverse the Court of Appeals because we conclude that equity does not justify the remedy sought by Mr. and Mrs. Pickles.

Rescission is an equitable remedy that is granted only in the sound discretion of the court. . . . A court need not grant rescission in every case in which the mutual mistake relates to a basic assumption and materially affects the agreed performance of the parties.

In cases of mistake by two equally innocent parties, we are required, in the exercise of our equitable powers, to determine which blameless party should assume the loss resulting from the misapprehension they shared.[13] Normally that can only be done by drawing upon our "own notions of what is reasonable and just under all the surrounding circumstances."

Equity suggests that, in this case, the risk should be allocated to the purchasers. We are guided to that conclusion, in part, by the standards announced in § 154 of the Restatement of Contracts 2d, for determining when a party bears the risk of mistake. Section 154(a) suggests that the court should look first to whether the parties have agreed to the allocation of the risk between themselves. While there is no express assumption in the contract by either party of the risk of the property becoming uninhabitable, there was indeed some agreed allocation of the risk to the vendees by the incorporation of an "as is" clause into the contract which, we repeat, provided:

> Purchaser has examined this property and agrees to accept same
> in its present condition. There are no other or additional written
> or oral understandings.

That is a persuasive indication that the parties considered that, as between them, such risk as related to the "present condition" of the property should lie with the purchaser. If the "as is" clause is to have any meaning at all, it must be interpreted to refer to those defects which were

---

[13] This risk-of-loss analysis is absent in both A & M Land Development Co. and Sherwood, and this omission helps to explain, in part, the disparate treatment in the two cases. Had such an inquiry been undertaken in Sherwood, we believe that the result might have been different. Moreover, a determination as to which party assumed the risk in A & M Land Development Co. would have alleviated the need to characterize the mistake as collateral so as to justify the result denying rescission. Despite the absence of any inquiry as to the assumption of risk in those two leading cases, we find that there exists sufficient precedent to warrant such an analysis in future cases of mistake.

unknown at the time that the contract was executed.[15] Thus, the parties themselves assigned the risk of loss to Mr. and Mrs. Pickles.[16]

We conclude that Mr. and Mrs. Pickles are not entitled to the equitable remedy of rescission and, accordingly, reverse the decision the Court of Appeals.

WILLIAMS, C. J., and COLEMAN, FITZGERALD, KAVANAGH and LEVIN, JJ., concur.

RILEY, J., not participating.

NOTES AND QUESTIONS

1.   *Nature of the mutual mistake?* The *Lenawee County* accepted the trial court's determination that the parties had been mutually mistaken regarding the income producing nature of the property. Specifically, both parties had assumed that the property was income producing, but that "fact" turned out to be untrue. For actionable mutual mistake to exist, the mutual mistake must relate to a fact in existence at the time the contract was formed. Restatement (Second) of Contracts § 152(1). Was the property income producing at the time of the contract? At the time the contract was formed, the septic system was out of code, but the problem was not yet discoverable. This led the seller to argue this was not a fact in existence at the time the contract was formed, but a subsequent supervening event. As discussed in the next chapter, such supervening events usually do not excuse performance except in extraordinary circumstances. Moreover, even if a supervening event does excuse the future performance of one or both parties, the event will not justify rescission of the contract. If court had agreed with the seller's argument, do you think it likely the buyers would have obtained a return of the purchase price? Is mutual mistake the only arguable ground for rescission?

2.   *Shift from essence or quality to risk allocation.* Unlike the cited *Sherwood* case, *Lenawee County* addresses mistake doctrine as a question of which party should bear the risk of loss. For this purpose, the court focuses on Restatement (Second) of Contracts § 154. There was no counterpart to that section in Restatement (First) of Contracts, and hence the common law struggled with fine line distinctions between mere value or quality (which did not provide a basis for rescission) and those affecting (or destroying) the essence or nature of the consideration to one of the parties (which did provide a basis for rescission). The drafters of Restatement (Second) of Contracts § 154 attempted to eliminate such distinctions as artificial. See Restatement

---

[15] An "as is" clause waives those implied warranties which accompany the sale of a new home, Tibbitts v. Openshaw, 18 Utah 2d 442, 425 P. 2d 160 (1967), or the sale of goods. M. C. L. § 440. 2–316(3)(a); M. S. A. § 19. 2–316(3)(a). Since implied warranties protect against latent defects, an "as is" clause will impose upon the purchaser the assumption of the risk of latent defects, such as an inadequate sanitation system, even when there are no implied warranties.

[16] An "as is" clause does not preclude a purchaser from alleging fraud or misrepresentation as a basis for rescission. See 97 A. L. R. 2d 849. However, Mr. and Mrs. Pickles did not appeal the trial court's finding that there was no fraud or misrepresentation, so we are bound thereby.

(Second) of Contracts § 154 *cmt. a* ("Stating these rules in terms of the allocation of risk avoids such artificial and specious distinctions as are sometimes drawn between 'intrinsic' and 'extrinsic' mistakes or between mistakes that go to the 'identity' or 'existence' of the subject matter and those that go merely to its 'attributes,' 'quality' or 'value.'"). Do you agree that such distinctions are artificial? While technically the modern risk allocation test shifts analysis from the existence of a mistake to whether the party seeking rescission assumed the risk of the mistake, is there really any dramatic difference in outcome absent an express allocation of risk clause in the contract? Absent one party bearing the risk of a mutual mistake, what is the effect of mutual mistake to the adversely affected party? See Restatement (Second) of Contracts § 152(a).

3. *Breach of promise?* If mutual mistake did not give rise to a power of avoidance (and hence a remedy of rescission and restitution), would the mistaken party have any basis for recovery of losses caused by the mistake? Is it possible for a mutual mistake to create a cause of action for breach of contract (and thus money damages)? If the UCC governed this matter and the court could not determine any breach of an express promise, could the court imply any promises that the property was fit for its ordinary rental purposes? See UCC § 2–314(2)(c). What about the duty of good faith performance under both the common law and UCC § 1–304 (2001) (formerly UCC § 1–102(3))? Since this case does not involve the sale of goods, and absent the discussed "as is" clause, would the buyer be foreclosed from arguing a warranty of habitability discussed in the last chapter, or would the doctrine of *caveat emptor* apply?

4. *Effect of "as is" clause.* In the context of a sale of goods, an "as is" clause effectively negates all implied warranties, including the implied warranty that the goods are fit for their ordinary purposes. However, the "as is" language must make clear "in common understanding" that there is no implied warranty. See UCC § 2–316(3)(a). When the "as is" clause is effective, it simply removes a promise and any trailing remedy that might otherwise accrue from a breach of that promise.

While the "as is" clause clearly negates implied warranties, does it necessarily follow that such a clause also positively allocates risk of loss to a party caused by a mistaken assumption by both parties to the contract? In fact, in footnote 15 of *Lenawee County*, the court cites to the effect of an "as is" clause to negate implied warranties under the UCC. Impliedly, the court also regarded the simple "as is" clause as a specific allocation of all unknown facts in existence at the time of the contract. Accordingly, the court treated the "as is" clause as an allocation of risk by the agreement of the parties. See Restatement (Second) of Contracts § 154(a). Do you agree? In analyzing whether a particular contract clause allocates or assigns the risk of unknown facts at the time of contract, what should be the touchstone? Would you expect the court to utilize the rules of interpretation to try to understand the meaning each party attached to such a clause? In this case, the court stated that to have "any meaning at all, it must be interpreted to refer to those defects which were unknown at the time that the contract was executed." Do you agree? Is this an application of the plain meaning rule? Since the trial court did not rule on the meaning of the clause relative to the allocation of risk formulation, should the case have been remanded to determine the meaning of the "as is" clause in this case, or does the court infer that such clauses will always serve a similar risk allocation function as a matter of law? In other jurisdictions where more sympathy might exist for alternative meanings, can you suggest a reason that the clause in this case was ambiguous and thereafter reasonably susceptible to an alternative meaning?

5.   *Effect of inspection.* The "as is" clause in this case stated that the property had been "examined" by the buyer prior to purchase, and therefore the buyer "agrees to accept the same in its present condition." Given the court's enthusiasm for the effect of "as is" clauses under the UCC, is it surprising that the court did not also reference the effect of inspection of goods prior to purchase? See UCC § 2–316(3)(b). How does the UCC treat the effect of an inspection and why does the UCC have two separate sections referring to the effect of an "as is" clause and the effect of inspection? The inspection clause eliminates liability and thus allocates the risk to the party for discoverable defects or those "defects which an examination ought in the circumstances to have revealed." Is this nearly as broad as the effect of an "as is" clause? If not, does this raise a legitimate interpretative issue as to whether the parties intended Clause 17 as an "as is" clause or an inspection clause? If so, who decides such a question, and does it require a remand of the case?

6.   *Effect of failure to discover on rescission.* Restatement (Second) of Contracts § 157 states that a mistaken party's failure to know or discover the facts before making the contract is not a bar to avoidance unless the failure amounts to a lack of good faith. Is there a difference between this provision and its application to avoidance and the UCC inspection clause that applies to negate an implied warranty? If so, does UCC § 1–103 adopt the view of Restatement (Second) of Contracts § 157? Quite obviously, the effect of failure to inspect and discover a fact is treated quite differently when involving a damage remedy for breach of an implied warranty rather than an action for equitable rescission based upon mistake. Does the same issue apply to rescission based on misrepresentation? Stated another way, is a misrepresentation rescission case subject to the assumption of risk doctrine stated in Restatement (Second) of Contracts § 154? While cases differ on the rescission effect of a negligent failure to discover a mistake, both Restatement (First) of Contracts § 508 and Restatement (Second) of Contracts § 157 are similar. Thus, the mere fact that party "could have" avoided the mistake by the exercise of reasonable care does not preclude avoidance. However, "gross negligence" in the failure to discover a mistake normally defeats rescission. See Restatement (Second) of Contracts § 157 *cmt. a.* Generally, the transition from the first to the second restatement involves adding a good faith standard. While "good faith" as stated in Restatement (Second) of Contracts § 205 extends only to contractual obligations and not contractual negotiations, the rule in Restatement (Second) of Contracts § 157 extends that doctrine to negotiations. Thus, while the failure to act in good faith during contractual

negotiations might not constitute a contract breach, it may nevertheless bar a mistaken party from rescission relief. Restatement (Second) of Contracts § 157 *cmt. a.*

7. *Allocation of risk by reason of "conscious ignorance."* In addition to the allocation of risk by agreement discussed above, Restatement (Second) of Contracts § 154(b) also allocates the risk of mistake to a party who treats his limited knowledge as sufficient regarding a fact that turns out to be otherwise. The commentary thus provides that a party may be allocated the risk of a mistake even when that party did not agree to bear the risk. Restatement (Second) of Contracts § 154 *cmt. c.* Given that the party who bears the risk is not truly mistaken but simply treats his knowledge regarding an untrue fact as sufficient, this allocation is often referred to as allocation on the basis of conscious ignorance rather than mistake of fact. For example, an illustration provides that where one party proposes a provision to allow an adversely affected party to rescind the contract in the event of a material error in a third-party inspection report and the other party refuses, the initial party proposing the insertion bears the risk of a mistake in the report. Restatement (Second) of Contracts § 154 *cmt. c.* (illustration).

8. *Allocation of risk by court on other reasonable grounds.* Restatement (Second) of Contracts § 154(c) also provides that absent allocation of risk by agreement or conscious ignorance, the court might nonetheless allocate the risk to a party on other grounds when it is reasonable to do so. The commentary suggests that the court in such cases should consider the purpose of the agreement and the parties as well as normative human behavior. Restatement (Second) of Contracts § 154 *cmt. d.* Accordingly, this process resembles the one discussed in Chapter 4 regarding the court supplying an omitted term under Restatement (Second) of Contracts § 204. For example, a builder contracts with a landowner to build a house on the land. Both parties believe that subsoil conditions are normal, but in fact some water must be drained at an expense that leaves the builder with no profit. The court will allocate this risk to the builder such that the contract is not voidable for the mutual mistake. See Restatement (Second) of Contracts § 154 *cmt. d, illus. 5.*

9. *Distinguishing allocation of risks from other interpretive problems.* Every party, upon entering a contract, knows (or should know) that one or both parties lack complete information regarding the subject matter of the contract and that the contract may not be as good a deal as it first appeared. To a certain extent, then, a failure of the parties to allocate the risk of mistake expressly in their contract terms is equivalent to any other ambiguity that the parties fail to resolve through express terms. See Eric A. Posner, "Economic Analysis of Contract Law After Three Decades: Success or Failure?," 112 Yale L.J. 829–46 (2003). In other words, a mere mutual mistake presents the court with a rational decision by the parties submit to a judicial determination of where to place the losses, rather than bear the additional negotiation and transaction costs necessary to identify risks of mistake and agree upon an express allocation in the event those risks materialize. Do you agree or disagree with

Professor Posner's analysis? Are there any good reasons for maintaining rescission and restitution as a remedy for mistake?

10. *Mutual mistake and ante-nuptial contracts.* Consider the mistake and allocation of risk problems raised by prenuptial contracts. Many parties enter such contracts sharing a mutually mistaken belief as to the suitability of the other party as a marriage or spousal partner. See Ann Laquer Estin, "Economics and the Problem of Divorce," 2 U. Chi. L. Sch. Roundtable 517, 578–582 (1995). Should courts provide such parties a grounds for avoiding the ante-nuptial contract (and obtaining rescission and restitution) in the face of such mutual mistakes? To what extent do other equitable and public policy factors weigh against such relief? Alternatively, should courts merely assume that ante-nuptial contracts by definition allocate the risks of such mistakes between the parties?

2. UNILATERAL MISTAKE

Given the difficulties surrounding mutual mistake, it would be quite easy to simply dismiss the possibility of remedial action where only one party was mistaken regarding the facts existing at the time the contract was formed. It is arguable that most contracts involve a unilateral mistake by one party, especially in cases involving buyer's remorse. Moreover, enforcing contracts involving only unilateral mistake rewards the diligence of the nonmistaken party. Consequently, one early view was that contract law failed to recognize unilateral mistake as a defense at all. See Restatement (First) of Contracts § 503 (a mistake of only one party that forms the basis on which he enters into a transaction does not of itself render the transaction voidable). However, at least where the mistake is clear and palpable to one party but not the other, the party recognizing the mistake may not unilaterally "snap-up" the bargain at the expense of the other. See Benedict I. Lubell, "Unilateral Palpable and Impalpable Mistake in Construction Contracts," 16 Minn. L. Rev. 137 (1932). Thus, the early doctrine was clearly too severe, at least when the non-mistaken party was aware of the other party's mistake at the time of the contract. Enforcing the contract under such circumstances simply encouraged cannibalistic behavior and the failure to disclose or correct the error before the contract was formed. See Roland R. Foulke, "Mistake in Contract," 11 Colum. L. Rev. 197, 299 (1911).

While modern contract law has come to recognize the equitable remedy of rescission on behalf of the unilaterally mistaken party, the remedy is narrowly tailored to protect the respective informational rights of the parties. Restatement (Second) of Contracts § 153 allows rescission for unilateral mistake, but only for situations involving material mistakes, provided that the mistaken party does not bear the risk of the mistake. See Restatement (Second) of Contracts § 154. Importantly, the contract is voidable only if one of two other conditions are present. Either enforcement of the contract must be unconscionable, or the other party had reason to know of the mistake (or caused the mistake). The unconscionability limitation protects the reasonable expectations of the non-mistaken party. This will most often require the mistaken party to prove a radical economic difference between mistaken outcome and the outcome had the mistake been known. See Restatement (Second) of Contracts § 153 *cmt. c.* However, if the mistaken party can prove that the other party had reason to know of the mistake, the contract is voidable even if it is not an unconscionable result. Restatement (Second) of Contracts § 153 *cmt. e.*

In this sense, unilateral mistake resembles misrepresentation doctrine. Recall that non-disclosure is equivalent to an affirmative misrepresentation where a party knows disclosure would correct a mistake of the other party and the failure to disclose fails to comply with standards of good faith. Restatement (Second) of Contracts § 161(b). Such non-disclosure creates a voidable contract. Restatement (Second) of Contracts § 164. However, the duty to disclose is broader than unilateral mistake because it does not require a showing of a material effect on the agreed exchange and applies regardless of whether the mistaken party bears the risk of the mistake. Consequently, the law of unilateral mistake is sparingly applied and universally confusing. See Andrew Kull, "Unilateral Mistake: The Baseball Card Case," 70 Wash. U. L. Q. 57 (1992). Law and economic scholars argue that requiring disclosure in such snap-up transactions induces more efficient behavior of the parties. See Anthony T. Kronman, "Mistake, Disclosure, Information and the Law of Contracts," 7 J. Leg. Studies 1 (1978) (the law should protect information obtained from conscious search but not accidental discovery); Robert L. Birmingham, "The Duty to Disclose and the Prisoner's Dilemma: *Laidlaw v. Organ*," 29 Wm. & Mary L. Rev. 249 (1988) (inefficient to over invest in information search since it must be disclosed without cost to the other party).

Unilateral mistake presents the unique opportunity to compare with non-disclosure analysis and the competing policies. Importantly, the cases explore the situations in which unilateral mistake might apply and non-disclosure does not. For a broad overview of disclosure and mistake law, see Melvin A. Eisenberg, "Disclosure in Contract Law," 91 Cal. L. Rev. 1645 (2003).

CUMMINGS V. DUSENBURY

Appellate Court of Illinois
129 Ill.App.3d 338, 472 N.E.2d 575 (1984)

HOPF, Justice:

Defendants, Liph and Patricia Dusenbury, sold a house to Michael and Lori Cummings, plaintiffs. Soon after moving into the home, the Cummings sued for rescission of the contract for the sale. After a bench trial, the circuit court of Carroll County found that because of a unilateral mistake, the Cummings were entitled to rescission of the real estate contract and damages, less an amount for rent for the period of time they occupied the premises.

On appeal, the Dusenburys contend that the trial court erred in finding that a unilateral mistake existed so as to allow rescission of the contract and a return to the status quo as existed before the contract was made. The Dusenburys argue that a unilateral mistake does not allow rescission. Rather, they urge, the mistake must be mutual. The mistake in the present case concerned whether the home purchased by the Cummings was suitable for year round living. The trial court found that, by the standards in the industry, it was not, and it held that it would be unconscionable to enforce the contract for sale of the home. The Dusenburys also argue that the Cummings did not exercise reasonable care in determining whether or not the home was a "year round home." They further urge that they have not been placed in status quo and that there was a variance between the pleadings and the proof, i. e., the complaint did not plead unilateral mistake.

The Cummings raise a number of issues by way of cross-appeal. They urge, inter alia, that the trial court erred in denying their request for punitive damages and in not determining whether an implied warranty of habitability had been breached.

The house in issue was built by the Dusenburys during the winter of 1973–74. It was a kit home, made of logs, and had a log interior. The Dusenburys lived in it on weekends for several years while selling lots and building other homes at Lake Carroll. In 1977 they lived in the subject house for a year. Some leakage occurred after this so the windows were removed and set in foam rubber with adhesive. After this, the windows stopped leaking. The roof, Liph Dusenbury testified, only leaked when there was an extremely cold winter with quite a bit of snow. He had no condensation or leakages during the year he lived in the house. He then put the house on the market and leased it to a number of different people, none of whom complained about leaks.

The Cummings first looked at the house in July of 1982. After viewing the property with realtors they made arrangements to have a realtor contact the sellers and ask specific questions about the home. Realtor Patricia Barrett testified that she called the Dusenburys from her office on July 23, 1982. Barrett testified it was a Saturday, that the Cummings were present in her office and that she probably talked to Mrs. Dusenbury. She asked questions from a list that was introduced into evidence. Barrett asked the questions that had been given to her by the Cummings and wrote down some notes as given by Mrs. Dusenbury. The first question on the list concerned the heating costs and the notation indicated that the electric bill was $120 a month in 1980. Barrett testified that Mrs. Dusenbury said the windows were thermopane, they didn't sweat, and that "it was a year round house." She indicated that the Cummings were concerned about being able to remain warm in the house during the winter.

The Cummings moved into the house in mid-August 1982. Michael Cummings testified that soon after moving in they found that the roof leaked when it rained. They found that the windows leaked and they had a problem with flies coming into the house. He indicated the fly problem got worse in the winter and in the wintertime the walls would drip from condensation and were wet to the touch. In the fall when it rained the roof would leak in three or four places but when winter started the roof leaked all over the place. Photographs of the leaks from the windows and roof were admitted into evidence. Cummings testified that his 19-month-old child was affected by the condensation on the walls because the furniture had to be moved away from the walls to keep it dry. He also stated that one of the realtors who showed him the house may have suggested that insulation and walls be added to the interior surface.

Duane Hanson testified as an expert for the plaintiffs. He had built many log homes in the area and had inspected the subject house. He saw stains on the wall and signs of moisture on the windowsills. He testified that the homes he built had no moisture problems and that the roof on the subject house needed repairs in the amount of $3,000 to $20,000 depending on how much was done. He noted that some of the sills may have had dry rot forming and that re-caulking could eliminate the fly problem. Hanson testified that the minimum property standards for HUD or FHA, as they exist today, would not be met by the house in issue. Hanson testified that while the log home industry began upgrading the thickness of woods in the early 1970s the subject house was still meant to be a second or vacation home and was not really classified as a year round house, even at the time it was built.

Arnold Prowant, another building contractor, also testified for plaintiffs. He indicated the roof leaked because it expanded and contracted and recommended that a new roof be placed over the old roof. Because the walls of the house were only about two and one-half inches thick, he suggested studding the outside walls with 2 x 4s, putting on a layer of visqueen and fiberglass insulation, and then siding the outside.

Defendant Liph Dusenbury testified that he built the house in the winter of 1973 and spring of 1974. He indicated that the water marks on the interior walls got there during construction and that he replaced the single pane windows with thermopane windows in 1974. He sold the house on contract to an individual who moved in it for a few months and then defaulted and disappeared. He denied having had a phone call with Pat Barrett on July 23, 1982.

The trial court took judicial notice of the fact that July 23, 1982, was a Friday. The Cummings had testified that realtor Barrett had made the phone call to Mrs. Dusenbury on a Saturday. Liph Dusenbury stated that he did not talk to realtor Barrett until the closing and he never indicated verbally or in writing that the house was a year round home.

Patricia Dusenbury testified that during the winter in 1978 during a heavy snow period she and Liph lived in the house and there had been no problems, although she did indicate there was a roof leak around the fireplace. Some of the defective thermopane windows were replaced. Mrs. Dusenbury also testified that to the best of her knowledge she never spoke with realtor Barrett on the telephone.

The first issue raised by the Dusenburys is the contention that the doctrine of unilateral mistake was improperly applied so as to allow rescission of the contract. They contend that only mutual mistake, not unilateral mistake, can justify rescission. They rely on the case of Diedrich v. Northern Illinois Publishing (1976), 39 Ill. App. 3d 851, 350 N. E. 2d 857. However, Diedrich included the following pertinent language: "If by reason of a mistake of fact by one of the parties to a contract not due to his negligence, the contract is different with respect to the subject matter or terms from what was intended, equity will rescind the contract where the parties can be placed in status quo. (Steinmeyer v. Schroeppel (1907), 226 Ill. 9, 80 N. E. 564.)" (Diedrich v. Northern Illinois Publishing (1976), 39 Ill. App. 3d 851, 857, 350 N. E. 2d 857.) In light of this language it is apparent that Diedrich does not require that a mistake be mutual.

The unilateral mistake principle was also set forth in the following manner:

> If there is apparently a valid contract in writing, but by reason of a mistake of fact by one of the parties, not due to his negligence, the contract is different with respect to the subject matter or terms from what was intended, equity will give to such party a remedy by cancellation where the parties can be placed in status quo. The ground for relief is, that by reason of the mistake there was no mutual assent to the terms of the contract. (Steinmeyer v. Schroeppel (1907), 226 Ill. 9, 13, 80 N. E. 564, 565.)

Steinmeyer involved an erroneous calculation made on a bill for lumber. The court found that the contract should not be rescinded on account of this error, for if equity would grant relief on account of such a mistake, there would be no stability in contracts.

In a case that held to the contrary, Wil-Fred's, Inc. v. Metropolitan Sanitary District of Chicago (1978), 57 Ill. App. 3d 16, 14 Ill. Dec. 667, 372 N. E. 2d 946, rescission was allowed where a mistake in bidding by a contract was viewed as (1) a material feature of the contract; (2) so grave that the consequences would work a hardship and be unconscionable; (3)

due care was exercised; and (4) the other party could be placed in status quo. The court also noted that relief is generally refused for errors in judgment and allowed for errors which are clerical or mathematical. . . . However, the court looked to the facts surrounding the error rather than the labels of "judgment" or "mathematical" in deciding that rescission of the contract should be allowed.

The doctrine of unilateral mistake was also applied in the case of National Supermarkets, Inc. v. The First National Bank of Springfield (1979), 72 Ill. App. 3d 221, 28 Ill. Dec. 435, 390 N. E. 2d 602, where a purchaser under a purchase option of a real estate contract sought specific performance. A misunderstanding arose concerning the vendors' failure to strike a 30-day notice of termination provision. Because the purchaser had no reason to know of this misunderstanding, the court held that it should not "be made to suffer the burden of any unilateral mistake resulting from the vendors' failure to strike the notice language from the agreement." (72 Ill. App. 3d 221, 28 Ill. Dec. 435, 438, 390 N. E. 2d 602, 605.) Although this case is factually distinguishable from the case at bar, it does indicate that unilateral mistake principles have recently been applied to allow rescission of real estate contracts. See also Bucciero v. Drinkwater (1982), 13 Mass. App. 551, 434 N. E. 2d 1315; Pearl v. Merchants-Warren National Bank of Salem (1980), 9 Mass. App. 853, 400 N. E. 2d 1314.

Generally, the rule is that the unilateral mistake of one party to a contract may not be relied upon to relieve that party from its obligations under the contract where the party's own negligence and lack of prudence resulted in the mistake. Harney-Morgan Chevrolet Olds Co. v. Rabin (1983), 118 Ill. App. 3d 602, 74 Ill. Dec. 100, 104, 455 N. E. 2d 130, 134.

John J. Calnan Co. v. Talsma Builders, Inc. (1977), 67 Ill. 2d 213, 10 Ill. Dec. 242, 367 N. E. 2d 695, involved a situation where a clerical error was made in a contract. The court set forth the requirements for showing a mistake much as set forth in the case of Wil-Freds, Inc. v. Metropolitan Sanitary District of Chicago (1978), 57 Ill. App. 3d 16, 14 Ill. Dec. 667, 372 N. E. 2d 946, quoted above. Although the clerical error was viewed as a "material feature" of the contract, the court determined that the plaintiff had failed to exercise reasonable care, and defendant could not be placed in status quo. Thus, the Calnan court found that the evidence supporting rescission was against the manifest weight of the evidence.

In the case at bar the Dusenburys argue that the mistake concerned the question of whether the home was a "year round house." They contend that this is a case of judgment or opinion as opposed to a factual representation. They equate "year round house" with "good house," "nice location" or "you'll be happy with it." Thus, the Dusenburys equate the phrase with the "puffing" that occurs every day in the marketplace. We disagree. We believe the mistake was a material part of the contract.

In the instant case, the trial court found that the home purchased by the Cummings was not suitable for year round living. It determined that the mistake made in this regard was material to the contract, such that if it were enforced it would be unconscionable. The court found that plaintiffs had made inquiry on July 23, 1982, in Barrett's office, as to whether the home was a year round home. Implicit in this finding is the fact that plaintiffs must have been told it was a "year round" home by defendants.

In its memorandum opinion, the trial court discussed the warranty of habitability doctrine and quoted at length from Redarowicz v. Ohlendorf (1982), 92 Ill. 2d 171, 65 Ill. Dec. 411, 441 N. E. 2d 324, although the court found that the subject house was not "new" and thus could not be covered by an implied warranty of habitability as set forth by Redarowicz. Despite this, it is apparent that the policy of Redarowicz was implicitly supportive of the trial court's ruling that the unilateral mistake doctrine operated to allow the rescission here. In any event, we agree that no implied warranty existed in the present case.

Applying the principles of unilateral mistake to the case at bar, we believe the Cummings met the basic requirements of that doctrine. The requirements as set forth in John J. Calnan Co. v. Talsma Builders, Inc. (1977), 67 Ill. 2d 213, 10 Ill. Dec. 242, 367 N. E. 2d 695, are, first, that the mistake relate to a material feature of the contract. Here, the house in issue is located in an area with severe winters, and was purchased for year round use. Although the question of what constitutes a "year round" home is somewhat a question of personal taste, there was evidence in the record that this home was built as a vacation house, and was not suitable for winter use by a young family. Although one could argue that the Cummings could have determined for themselves that the house lacked the features necessary for being comfortable in the winter, this argument is somewhat negated by the fact that the record shows they made diligent inquiry into whether it was suitable for winter use. The trial court found that the defendants were aware of plaintiffs' concern in this regard, and that although defendants indicated they had no problems when they inhabited the house, the fact remains that the house, as sold, was not what plaintiffs had bargained for when they purchased the home. When one buys a house as a primary residence, its suitability for year round living is a material feature of the bargain.

We believe the plaintiffs exercised reasonable care in ascertaining the suitability of the home for winter living. Although plaintiffs could have called in independent parties for an analysis of the insulation, windows and heating system, the fact that they were advised by the sellers, who had lived in it, that it was suitable for year round living may have prevented them from looking into the question any further. Although the sellers deny having spoken to the Cummings on July 23, 1982, the trial court specifically found that a call took place on that date. There was ample evidence to support the trial court's determination that reasonable care was used.

The next question is whether the rescission could be made and still place the Dusenburys in status quo. Some guidance on this issue was set forth when the equitable doctrine of rescission was described as follows:

> As in other cases of rescission, the vendee is ordinarily required to restore the status quo, insofar as he has received any benefit, as a condition of his right to rescind; but he is not required to put the other party in the same situation in which he was before the contract, where the latter has rendered it impossible by the nature of his fraud or other act, or where from the nature of the land and the purpose for which it was purchased, it is impossible to restore the status quo, as where the purchase was of timberland and the purchaser had cut timber thereon; in such a case all that the purchaser can be required to do is to reimburse the vendor for the value of the timber removed. Hakala v. Illinois Dodge City Corp. (1978), 64 Ill. App. 3d 114 [21 Ill. Dec. 1, 5], 380 N. E. 2d 1177, 1181, quoting from 77 Am. Jur. 2d Vendor & Purchaser sec. 565 (1975).

The Dusenburys argue they cannot be put back in the same situation because they made certain changes in the thermostats; because a realtors/brokers commission was paid; and because they lost possession rights for a year. However, under the terms of the judgment, the Dusenburys were paid $275 monthly rent for the time period they were out of possession. Because of this, and because they had rented the property out in the past, we believe they have been returned to their former position. With regard to the thermostats, there is no indication from the record that the value of the house was affected by that change.

Regarding the brokers commission, we refer to the quote from Hakala, above. As that case indicates, one must be returned to status quo "insofar as [the other] received any benefit." In the case at bar, it does not appear that the Cummings received any benefit from that provision of the contract, or from the fact that the Dusenburys paid their realtors commission. Thus, we believe that the parties' positions were substantially returned to the status quo.

In sum, the facts and evidence adduced at trial support the trial court's determination that the doctrine of unilateral mistake should allow rescission of the contract.

The Dusenburys' final contention is that the Cummings' complaint does not contain the allegations necessary to plead unilateral mistake. They argue that they were not advised that the Cummings would proceed on the unilateral mistake theory. The inference which is to be drawn from this contention is that the Dusenburys were somehow prejudiced by

Cummings' failure to include this point in the pleadings. However, assuming the Dusenburys were prejudiced, they do not say how or in what manner this occurred.

It is generally held that a variance between the allegations and the proof will not be deemed material unless it misleads the adverse party to his prejudice. (Stowell v. Satorius (1953), 413 Ill. 482, 109 N. E. 2d 734, 739.) Here the Dusenburys make no showing of prejudice, and none will be presumed to have occurred.

Moving on to the issues raised by the Cummings by way of cross-appeal, their first contention is that the trial court erred in not finding fraud on the part of defendants. They urge that the Dusenburys knew of the problems with the roof, windows and condensation, but never revealed existence of these problems to plaintiffs. If fraud had been found, then the Cummings would have been entitled to punitive or exemplary damages.

Generally, in Illinois fraud consists of a concealment of an existing fact accompanied by scienter, deception and injury. (Central States Joint Board v. Continental Assurance Co. (1983), 117 Ill. App. 3d 600, 73 Ill. Dec. 107, 453 N. E. 2d 932; see cases collected 73 Ill. Dec. at 110, 453 N. E. 2d at 935.) To establish fraud, the Central States court held, there must be concealment with an intention to deceive and under circumstances creating a duty to speak. Although there was some evidence that defendants told plaintiffs that the home was a year round home, there was no clear showing that this was done intentionally. In fact, the trial court's finding of mistake is blatantly inconsistent with a finding that the Dusenburys intended to deceive the Cummings. In any event we see no indication in the record of an intentional misrepresentation. Additionally, this issue was presented to the trier of fact and rejected. Because it is a factual question, it is best resolved by the trial court.

The Cummings also contend in their cross-appeal that the implied warranty of habitability should be applicable here. They urge that because they were the first purchasers of the home and because they purchased it from the builder, the doctrine of implied warranty of habitability, as set forth in Petersen v. Hubschman Construction Co., Inc. (1979), 76 Ill. 2d 31, 27 Ill. Dec. 746, 389 N. E. 2d 1154, and its progeny, should be applicable. However, we believe this would be too great an expansion of that doctrine for, although it has been expanded to include a change in hands of ownership of a home, it is limited to latent defects which manifest themselves "within a reasonable time after the purchase of the house." (Redarowicz v. Ohlendorf (1982), 92 Ill. 2d 171, 185, 65 Ill. Dec. 411, 441 N. E. 2d 324.) In the instant case the house was built in 1973–74 and plaintiffs sought to rescind the contract in 1983. Thus the house was at least nine years old. It also had had a number of tenants. Given this situation it would not be appropriate to find an implied warranty of habitability in this case. See Schoenrock v. Anden Corp. (1984), 125 Ill. App. 3d 118, 80 Ill. Dec. 355, 465 N. E. 2d 146.

We recognize that countervailing policies such as caveat emptor and finality of contract are frequently employed in contract cases. However, in the case at bar evidence shows that the Cummings sought to purchase a year round home, and the sellers knew of their intended use. The house would apparently need substantial work to the walls and roof in order to solve the problems it currently has. The record shows that the Cummings used reasonable care in inquiring about the suitability of the home. Additionally, the parties were returned to the status quo. Therefore, we believe the equitable relief of rescission was properly allowed in the case at bar.

The judgment of the circuit court of Carroll County is affirmed.

AFFIRMED.

NOTES AND QUESTIONS

1. *Duty to disclose.* Did the sellers fail to disclose that the house was not a year-round house in a manner that creates a voidable contract under Restatement (Second) of Contracts §§ 161(b) and 164? It was disputed whether Mrs. Dusenbury misrepresented that fact to the realtor. Assuming there was no misrepresentation, was this a non-disclosure that qualifies under Restatement (Second) of Contracts § 162(b)?

2. *Status quo restoration.* Restatement (Second) of Contracts § 376 states that a party avoiding a contract on grounds including mistake is entitled to restitution for any benefit conferred upon the other party. Restatement (Second) of Contracts § 153 does not mention restitution as a condition of avoidance, but the court states such a requirement in cases involving unilateral mistake. Do you see why? Is the other party entitled to restitution as well under all avoidance cases? See Restatement (Second) of Contracts § 384.

3. *Cognitive biases and unilateral mistakes.* Consider situations involving sophisticated repeat players, such as retail merchants offering extended warranties on consumer electronics, and unsophisticated one-shot players, such as consumers purchasing a computer or stereo system. The producer, by virtue of its nearly exclusive access to information about its production processes, materials and components, warranty claims, and failure rates, knows more or less exactly the probability that any given product will fail within a given warranty period. The producer is also aware that consumers lack such information and, because of cognitive biases and bounded rationality, will be unable to determine the value of an extended warranty on the offered goods. See W. David Slawson, Binding Promises 26–34 (1996) (analyzing producers' superior access to information about their products as arguably insurmountable edge in bargaining power). In many contexts, producers make a profit margin of several hundred percent on extended warranties. Given this

massive disparity in information and that the producer knows or should know that the consumer is mistaken as to the likelihood of product failure within the warranty or extended warranty period, should the consumer be entitled to rescind such extended warranty agreements on the basis of unilateral mistake?

CHAPTER 8

CONTRACTS UNENFORCEABLE BY LATER EVENTS: DISCHARGE OF FUTURE DUTIES ABSENT A BREACH

■ ■ ■

Previous chapters considered grounds for asserting that a validly formed and otherwise enforceable contract is void and unenforceable by operation of law (Chapter 6) or voidable and unenforceable by election of one or both of the parties (Chapter 7). Whether void and invalid by law or voidable and invalid from the beginning by election, the effect of both doctrines meant the contract was unenforceable *ab initio*. In the face of the doctrines that void or voidable contracts never came into being, the typical remedial response involved restitution designed to restore the parties to their respective positions before the contract was formed. Limited restitution adjustments were explored to balance the equities involved, such as minors returning damaged property.

The void and voidable doctrines developed in response to problematic defects associated with contract formation and performance. In many cases, the parties to the contract had engaged in various degrees of performance of their obligations under that contract before the contract was declared void or voidable. In such situations, the fact that the parties had apparently consented to a contract and had begun made it difficult to simply assert that the contract was never formed. In response, courts simply adopted various mechanisms designed to unwind the defective contractual relationship. Judicial intrusion into the otherwise private contractual relationship purportedly was justified because the defects existing at the time of contract formation barred judicial enforcement of contractual obligations.

Instead of defects existing at the time of formation, this chapter considers the problems raised by unexpected contractual catastrophes after formation. In this situation, there is nothing wrong with the contract itself, at least in terms of whether the parties created a valid agreement between themselves. Rather, post-formation, an event occurred without the fault of either party but making full performance by one party literally impossible, highly impracticable, or at the very least more expensive or drastically less beneficial than originally anticipated. In the face of such supervening events, the disadvantaged party likely will refuse to or simply cannot perform otherwise valid contractual obligations.

Judicial indifference to such "supervening events" leaves the affected party without a legal excuse for the resulting nonperformance. In turn, nonperformance constitutes a breach entitling the other party to monetary damages explored in the next chapter. At one extreme, it may seem harsh to simply enforce the literal terms of the contract. But at the other extreme, strict enforcement represents a form of judicial indifference to the failure of the parties specifically to consider the effect of potential supervening events on the contract itself. Should a court superimpose its Solomonic wisdom on the parties? See Sheldon W. Halpern, "Application of the Doctrine of Commercial Impracticability: Searching for 'The Wisdom of Solomon,'" 135 U. Pa. L. Rev. 1123 (1987). Certainly such intervention is unwarranted when the contract specifically allocates the risk of the occurrence of the supervening event to one of the parties. Insurance contracts for example are explicitly designed to allocate such risks. Most contracts, however, are not insurance contracts, but rather involve an exchange of other services or goods. In some cases, non-insurance contracts do expressly provide for the effects of supervening events. Such clauses are referred to as *force majeure* clauses. See generally Gerhard Wagner, "In Defense of the Impossibility Defense," 27 Loy. U. Chi. L. J. 55 (1995) and Mark P. Gergen, "A Defense of Judicial Reconstruction of Contracts," 71 Ind. L. J. 45 (1995).

When such contracts are silent regarding the effect of supervening events, a court must determine whether the event merits judicial excuse and, if so, the appropriate remedy. In essence, the parties are fighting after the formation of the contractual relationship and after an unexpected supervening event alters at least one of the parties' purpose or ability to perform under that contract. Making the contract invalid *ab initio* would deny both parties the value of their intended exchange at least up to the time the event occurred. Consequently, a discharge of future obligations might make more sense, with some restitution adjustments if past exchanged performances are unequal. But what justifies the legal excuse if one is to be found?

One justification for judicial excuse might be the supposed intent of the parties. A search for the supposed intent of the parties allocates the risk of the occurrence of such an event to the unaffected party. What is the basis for an implied intent analysis, especially in the unique domain of contractual private ordering? In other words, are courts justified in presuming they can identify the parties' implied intent? Would empirical studies of contracting parties' intent in similar contracts help justify implying that same intention where the parties are silent? Does that make the implication normative in a world of private ordering? Does the implication simply reward the affected party for failing to address specifically the unanticipated supervening issue in the contract? If the parties want to change the normative assumption of enforceability, shouldn't they do so in the contract instead of imposing the costs of their failure to contract upon the courts and public justice system?

Another justification might be fairness. But such an implication simply mirrors social mores. Is such an implication justified in private ordering or is it better served in the public law domain? See Mary Joe Frug, "Rescuing Impossibility Doctrine: A Postmodern Feminist Analysis of Contract Law," 140 U. Pa. L. Rev. 1021 (1992) and Patrick S. Shin, "Vive la Difference? A Critical Analysis of the Justification of Sex-Dependent Workplace Restrictions on Dress and Grooming," 14 Duke J. Gender L. & Pol'y 491 (2007) (discussing whether normative legal standards are meaningful analytical tools as discrimination determinants reflecting societal mores). See also Jeffrey M. Lipshaw, "The Bewitchment of Intelligence: Language and Ex Post Illusions of Intention," 78 Temp. L. Rev. 99, 99 (2005) (suggesting that "[t]he proper focus of courts . . . is a pragmatic resolution of disputes, and not a search for mutual intention" in the face of parties' failure to contract explicitly to resolve potential ambiguity or allocate risks for future events).

Not surprisingly, contract law begins with the assumption that a contract should be enforced as written by the parties. However, a careful reading of history clarifies that contract law has always embraced some form of legal excuse to accommodate supervening events, at least where the contract itself was silent. It is equally true that with the growing sophistication of commercial parties and transactions, the basic contours of supervening event excuse law have evolved. Would you expect the doctrine to narrow or expand from medieval to modern times? Intent-based implications tend to be subjectively oriented and arise from an interpretation of the actual agreement in accordance with the rules discussed in Chapter 4. Fairness and justice-based implications tend to be objectively determined and often take the form of implied-in-law "constructive conditions" discussed in Chapter 5.

A. HISTORICAL DEVELOPMENT OF THE IMPOSSIBILITY DOCTRINE

Civil law generally followed the Latin phrase *pacta sunt servanda* meaning that "agreements must be kept." The maxim represents a serious civil law commitment to enforce strictly voluntarily made promises and to some degree signifies a departure from common law. Indeed, the doctrine is generally attributed to Roman law because of its Latin phraseology but may in fact have stronger roots in canon law. Richard Hyland, "Pacta Sunt Servanda: A Meditation," 34 Va. J. Int'l L. 405 (1994). The civil law version reflects a basic legal norm as well as an ethical rule based on a self-evident and moral value. Civil law provides a state sanction for moral norms and thus it is generally true that legal contracts are more strictly enforced—although with greater attention to common sense and good faith in interpreting the parties' agreement—with less legal excuse than under common law.

Unlike civil and canon law, common law has always embraced a more flexible excuse doctrine. Medieval law embraced grounds upon which a court would not enforce promises as a matter of law, even though supported by consideration. The reasons were simple enough. The law distrusted the jury, and the doctrine of consideration, by its nature, excluded legal excuse. In the early sixteenth century, a promise had to be "honest, lawful and possible" to be enforceable. By the seventeenth century, the doctrine of assumpsit required a promise to be (i) lawful, (ii) possible to perform, (iii) clear and certain, (iv) supported by consideration, and (v) serious and substantial. A.W. Brian Simpson, A History of the Common Law of Contract—The Rise and Fall of The Action of Assumpsit 506–507 (1996 Reprint). Early cases were sparse, but the rationale for the "possible to perform" requirement was that it was absurd for the law to purport to "enforce" a promise literally impossible to perform. See James Gordley, "Impossibility and Changed and Unforeseen Circumstances," 52 Am. J. Comp. L. 513 (2004).

Nonetheless, the common law distinguished cases involving promises impossible to perform when made from those rendered impossible to perform by subsequent events. The latter category received less favorable treatment. Generally, promises involving supervening impossibility were void only if the impossibility developed through an act of God or a later change in law. See William Herbert Page, "The Development of the Doctrine of Impossibility of Performance," 18 Mich. L. Rev. 589 (1920). Early cases refused to recognize supervening impossibility when a stranger caused the impossibility, even though the impossibility occurred without fault of the party asserting the excuse. As a result, contract doctrine eventually developed a gloss of enforceability notwithstanding lack of fault. A.W. Brian Simpson, A History of the Common Law of Contract—The Rise and Fall of The Action of Assumpsit 525–526 (1996 Reprint). The general rule of enforceability regardless of fault for the breach also later influenced the measure of damage recovery where the reason for the breach became equally unimportant. Public law developed quite differently where the "fault" of the person was very important (e.g., criminal law and even some aspects of private law such as tort). Quite later, Oliver Wendell Holmes would comment on this distinctive lack of fault in contract law:

> The only universal consequence of a legally binding promise is, that the law makes the promisor pay damages if the promised event does not come to pass. In every case it leaves him free from interference until the time for fulfillment has gone by, and

therefore free to break his contract if he chooses. Oliver Wendell Holmes, Jr., The Common Law 236 (1881).

Commenting on this statement, Professor Gilmore attributed the development of the formalist approach in contracts to Holmes, and not Langdell, who did little more than organize the notion of a "general theory" of contract law. "Damages in contract, [Holmes] pointed out, were one thing and damages in tort another; the contract-breaker was not to be held responsible, as the tortfeasor was, for all the consequences of his actions." Grant Gilmore, The Death of Contract 14-15 (1974).

As discussed in the next chapter, modern scholarly literature generally recognizes the inadequacy of monetary damages to compensate fully the nonbreaching party for the loss of the value of full performance. Proposed solutions range from making specific performance the normative remedy, eliminating the concept of efficient breach to allow the nonbreaching party to recover any profit the breaching party receives as a result of the breach, and cover or virtual specific performance. See Melvin A. Eisenberg, "Actual and Virtual Specific Performance, the Theory of Efficient Breach, and the Indifference Principle In Contract Law," 93 Cal. L. Rev. 975 (2005) (exploring the difference between contractual remedial philosophy designed to make the breaching party indifferent to breach versus making the nonbreaching party whole as if performance occurred).

The medieval doctrine that contracts are enforceable regardless of the fault of the breaching party traces its roots to *Paradine v. Jane*, 82 Eng. Rep. 897 (K.B 1647). During the English Civil War (1642–1651), Jane leased land from Paradine for a period of years. An enemy German prince and his army took possession of the land and held it for nearly three years. When Jane failed to pay the rent for that period, Paradine brought suit. Jane defended arguing that he was forcibly prevented from occupying the land according to the terms of the lease through no fault of his own. The court determined that lack of fault does not excuse or discharge a duty voluntarily assumed or created by a party to a contract. In such cases, the party seeking excuse must provide for the excuse in the contract itself and failure to do so means the promise is enforceable:

> [B]ut when the party by his own contract creates a duty or charge upon himself, he is bound to make it good, if he may, notwithstanding any accident by inevitable necessity, because he might have provided against it by his contract. And therefore if the lease covenant to repair a house, though it be burnt by lightening, or thrown down by enemies, yet he ought to repair it. Id.

The fact that the supervening event occurred through no fault of the party unable to perform is legally irrelevant. Excuse must be found in the contract itself for a duty voluntarily assumed. Since Jane could still pay the rent, he was obligated to do so even though the lease was of no value to him since he could not occupy the land. In effect, Jane and not Paradine had assumed the risk of such a failure absent excuse in the contract or a Paradine promise guaranteeing possession. An interesting historical footnote reveals that the "enemy German prince" was actually the King's nephew who commanded Royalists troops during the English Civil War. Jane's counsel may have pleaded that the prince was nonetheless an alien enemy to rely on precedent excusing performance made impossible by such enemies. See John D. Wladis, "Contract and Uncommon Events: The Development of the Doctrine of Impossibility of Performance in English Contract Law," 75 Geo. L. J. 1575, 1579 (1987).

Notwithstanding the manifest enforceability doctrine expressed in *Paradine,* earlier cases had already embraced the "impossible to perform" doctrine in three important situations. See Frederick C. Woodward, "Impossibility of Performance, as an Excuse for Breach of Contract," 1 Colum. L. Rev. 529 (1901). First, "supervening illegality" was embraced in *Abbot of Westminster v. Clerke*, 73 Eng. Rep. 59 (K.B. 1536) (seller's contractual duty to sell wheat discharged by adoption of a later statute making the sale illegal). The supervening illegality need not be statutory in nature. Second, "supervening death or disability" was acknowledged as a basis for excusing contractual performance under a contract to provide personal services. See *Hyde v. Dean of Windsor*, 78 Eng. Rep. 798 (Q.B. 1597) (death of contract party discharges duty to perform personal service contract). Whether a contract involves rendition of personal services by a particular promisor is a question of fact. Of course, many contracts do not involve personal service, and hence the death of the promisor is not a legal excuse. For example, a debtor's death does not discharge the debt that remains enforceable against the decedent's estate, whereas the death of a portrait painter would normally discharge the duty to paint a portrait. Third, courts excused contract performance for "supervening destruction" of the subject matter of the contract. See *Williams v. Lloyd*, 82 Eng. Rep. 95 (K.B. 1629) (death of horse by an act of God discharged the bailee's duty to return the horse). The destruction of the contract subject matter discharges the duty to perform when the existence of the subject matter is necessary for the performance. See generally E. Allan Farnsworth, Contracts § 9.5 (Aspen, 4th Ed. 2004) and Note, "The Fetish of Impossibility in the Law of Contracts," 53 Colum. L. Rev. 94 (1953).

B. MODERN IMPOSSIBILITY, IMPRACTICABILITY, & FRUSTRATION

Modern common law impossibility doctrine generally evolved from the English common law rule that private agreements are strictly enforced (*Paradine* (1647)). This traditional rule was subject to three not "possible to perform" exceptions including (i) supervening illegality (*Abbot* (1536)),

(ii) supervening death (*Hyde* (1597)), and (iii) supervening destruction (*Williams* (1629)). All three exceptions shared a common theme—literal impossibility of the promisor to provide a service or convey property. The general rule involved the obligation of a promisor to pay money but not convey property or services. Viewed this way, the general rule and the exceptions represent the perspective of the party whose performance involves the payment of money (general rule) and the party whose performance requires the transfer of property or services (the exceptions). Understandably, it is more difficult to excuse the mere payment of money than to excuse the transfer of services or property made literally and objectively impossible by an unexpected supervening event. Modern common law adopted these themes but altered them in two ways. First, with respect to excuse of performance concerning services and property, modern law requires a lesser showing of impossibility to justify excusing performance under the contract. Instead of traditional notions of objective impossibility, modern doctrine excuses performance based upon a more flexible and subjective impracticability standard. Second, with respect to the payment of money, modern law narrows the *Paradine* general rule by adopting a legal excuse doctrine that excuses such performance where the supervening event has frustrated the purpose of the contract.

Modern Objective Impossibility Doctrine. Two centuries after *Paradine*, the celebrated English common law case of *Taylor v. Caldwell*, 122 Eng. Rep. 309 (K.B. 1863), reiterated the general doctrine and the exceptions in a case involving supervening destruction of the subject matter of the contract. Caldwell rented the Surry Gardens and Music Hall to Taylor for a four-day period so that he could conduct a series of grand concerts. Before the scheduled concerts, but after Taylor expended sums preparing for the concerts and in reliance on the contract, the music hall was badly damaged by an accidental fire. Caldwell could not deliver occupancy. Taylor sued for various reliance costs, and Caldwell defended on the grounds that the music hall was destroyed by fire, thereby rendering his performance impossible. Taylor won a trial court verdict on the basis that *Paradine* required strict performance of a contractual duty unless the contract itself absolved Caldwell. Since the contract was silent, Caldwell was liable for the reliance damages. Caldwell appealed and the court reversed, affirming the "supervening destruction" exception to the *Paradine* general rule of strict liability. Specifically, the court noted that a positive contractual duty is nonetheless subject to an "implied condition" that the subject matter required for performance must continue to exist at the time of performance. Where the subject matter is destroyed through no fault of either party, the failure to perform is not a breach because the implied condition legally excused performance. The court based the "implied condition" on the supposed intent of the parties to contract only for objectively possible performances. Thus, legal excuse is implied-in-law by way of an "implied condition" unless the contract provides otherwise.

The law of "implied conditions," otherwise referred to as "constructive conditions," is fully explored in Chapter 5. Generally, a condition is a future event whose occurrence discharges the future duty of performance before it becomes due. Accordingly, a failure to perform that duty is not a breach since the duty fails to become due.

The 19th-century *Taylor* "supervening impossibility" doctrine developed further in modern 20th century contract law. In 1932, the Restatement (First) of Contracts § 457 provided that the duty of a promisor was discharged when, after formation of the contract, a duty became "impossible" by reason of a supervening event not reasonably anticipated and occurring without the fault of that party. The historical models of impossibility were embraced, including "supervening illegality" in Restatement (First) of Contracts § 458, "supervening death or incapacity" in Restatement (First) of Contracts § 459, and "supervening destruction" in Restatement (First) of Contracts § 460. These themes were also carried into the Restatement (Second) of Contracts § 264 ("supervening illegality"), Restatement (Second) of Contracts § 262 ("supervening death or incapacity"), and Restatement (Second) of Contracts § 263 ("supervening destruction"). The same impossibility doctrine is also adopted by UCC § 2–615(a), which implies a constructive condition that a seller's performance requirement to deliver goods is legally excused if a supervening event makes the delivery impossible.

The Restatement (First) of Contracts, Restatement (Second) of Contracts, and the UCC do not make any significant changes to common law with regard to strict impossibility. However, slight language changes make clear the specific elements associated with the doctrine: (i) performance of a duty to render services or transfer goods or property must be literally impossible; (ii) the excused party must not bear the risk of the occurrence of the supervening event as a "basic assumption" of the contract, (iii) the event must have occurred without the fault of the excused party, and (iv) the contract must not have assigned the risk of the event to the excused party. See Restatement (Second) of Contracts § 261. Moreover, the question of constructive conditions is not a fact question for the jury. Generally, analysis of constructive conditions is a law matter for the court.

The impossibility and fault issues require little explanation. The risk analysis is more intricate and implicates risk assigned by a court as well as that assigned by the contract itself. Contracts, among other things, are mechanisms for assigning and sharing risk of loss between the parties. A contract for the sale of 50,000 bushels of wheat in 90 days implicitly allocates the risk that the price of wheat will rise before the delivery date to the seller and the risk that the price will fall to the buyer. That same contract may or may not allocate other risks, such as the risk of loss of the seller's wheat before the delivery date. In the absence of specific language to the contrary, a court's "shared risk analysis" presumes the risk is objectively shared by both parties. Obvious risks, such as fluctuations in the price of wheat over the period of the contract, are governed by the contract terms because the parties presumably anticipated those risks in negotiating their agreement. But in other cases, the "supervening event" is of the type most parties assume will not occur even though the contract is silent on the matter. Thus, while the parties might implicitly anticipate risks such as poor local growing conditions, a quarantine prohibiting any shipment of wheat to the buyer would clearly be an unanticipated event. Clearly, the supervening illegality, death, and destruction of the subject matter exceptions to the general rule of enforceability fit this pattern. This helps explain why such events are nearly automatic legal excuse cases, at least unless the party specifically assumed the risk in the contract.

The risk assignment question is more intuitive and simply expresses the notion that the parties may specifically negate the default rule regarding legal excuse for supervening events that make performance impossible. This device allows the private ordering rules of contract law to trump the implicit assumption, provided the parties specifically contract around the general default rule of impossibility. See, e.g., Subha Narasimhan, "Of Expectations, Incomplete Contracting, and the Bargain Principle," 74 Cal. L. Rev. 1123 (1986). Where the parties expressly contracted to allocate the risk of a future supervening event, the risk allocation if that event occurs is a non-issue because the contract language controls. Thus, a wheat contract that provides that the seller's duty to deliver is excused if the crop is destroyed by blight, wind, or fire expressly places the risk of non-delivery on the buyer for those three risks. The risk assignment question becomes more difficult when the contract assigns some risks to one of the parties, but the contract becomes impossible to perform because of an entirely unanticipated event. In the wheat contract above, if the crop is destroyed by flooding, the buyer will argue for a strict interpretation of the contract terms to impose the risk of loss on the seller, while the seller will argue that the listed risks should be interpreted to include other, similar risks. This requires a court to interpret the contract and infer a broader general intent to assume from the specific narrower assumption. The rules discussed in Chapter 4 regarding interpretation control this question.

Modern "Subjective" Impracticability Doctrine. The 1932 Restatement (First) of Contracts and the 1981 Restatement (Second) of Contracts ushered in a broader view of the term "impossibility." The *Taylor* "supervening impossibility" doctrine involved literal and objective impossibility by supervening destruction (as was the case with supervening illegality or supervening death). The Restatements expanded the impossibility doctrine to embrace performance that was rendered merely "impracticable," in addition to actually impossible performance. This expansion did not permit a party to escape contractual obligations simply because performance became more subjectively difficult or expensive. See Restatement (First) of Contracts § 457 (mere unanticipated expense or difficulty not impracticable). Rather, a successful impracticability defense under the restatement rules requires an extreme and unreasonable expense and difficulty that cannot be surmounted by reasonable efforts. Compare Restatement (First) of Contracts §§ 454 (impossibility defined to include impracticability) and 455 (mere subjective impossibility by a particular promisor does not discharge a duty unless also objectively impossible or at least objectively impracticable), with Restatement (Second) of Contracts § 261 (discharge by supervening impracticability rather than mere impossibility). Similarly, UCC § 2–615 is couched in terms of supervening impracticability rather than supervening impossibility. In accordance with this expansion, the older version of common law impossibility remained in effect while at the same time a broader case not involving true impossibility might result in discharge under the impracticability doctrine. The resolution of impossibility cases remains largely unchanged from the common law and thus requires little explanation. The expanded impracticability doctrine adds a considerable degree of flexibility and hence complexity. A "near miss" impossibility excuse might now qualify for an impracticability excuse in appropriate cases.

The great difficulty lies in appropriate differentiation between performance that becomes "merely" more difficult or expensive and that which becomes "extreme and unreasonable." The first major issue is whether the supervening event must render the performance impossible or impracticable for any party to perform. In many cases, the supposed impracticability is merely a "subjective" impracticability in which some hypothetical party could perform, but performance by the actual party to the contract is impossible or impracticable. It is tempting, therefore, to divide impracticability into objective and subjective elements. Objective impracticability theoretically could apply where the performance cannot be rendered by anyone. Subjective impracticability would cover situations where, although performance is possible by some promisors, it is not possible by the particular promisor. *Resist this temptation.* This view is rejected as misleading because promisors assume the risk of their own inability to perform. See Restatement (Second) of Contracts § 261, *cmt. e.* Rather the impracticability doctrine requires more difficulty than the term "subjective impracticability" implies.

The second major issue with respect to the more flexible impracticability doctrine addresses the boundaries between truly impossible performance (which is clearly excused) and performance that, while more difficult or expensive, does not rise to the level of impracticability. Difficult and borderline cases must be left to flexible judicial equitable jurisprudence, but the bookends can be identified. See

Richard A. Posner & Andrew M. Rosenfield, "Impossibility and Related Doctrines in Contract Law: An Economic Analysis," 6 J. Legal Stud. 83 (1977); Robert A. Hillman, "Court Adjustment of Long-Term Contracts: An Analysis Under Modern Contract Law," 1987 Duke L. J. 1; Aaron J. Wright, Note, "Rendered Impracticable: Behavioral Economics and the Impracticability Doctrine," 26 Cardozo L. Rev. 2183 (2005); and John Elofson, "The Dilemma of Changed Circumstances in Contract Law: An Economic Analysis of the Foreseeability and Superior Risk Bearer Tests," 30 Colum. J. L. & Soc. Probs. 1 (1996). First, traditional or historically true impossibility cases continue to qualify as also impracticable. That makes true impossibility cases "near automatic discharge," cases but also means that impracticability does not "require" impossibility in that sense. Second, all contracts contemplate simple market changes. Thus market downturn cannot by itself make performance impracticable. After all, impracticability must mean more than merely that performance has become more expensive or less profitable. Restatement (Second) of Contracts § 261, *cmt. d* provides:

> d. *Impracticability.* Events that come within the rule stated in this Section are generally due either to "acts of God" or to acts of third parties. . . . Performance may be impracticable because extreme and unreasonable difficulty, expense, injury, or loss to one of the parties will be involved. . . . However, "impracticability" means more than "impracticality." A mere change in the degree of difficulty or expense . . . unless well beyond the normal range, does not amount to impracticability since it is this sort of risk that a fixed-price contract is intended to cover.

Close cases involve intensive fact-based examinations to balance the fairness of implicating a constructive condition as legal excuse. Indeed, each contract party presumably accepts the risks of increased costs or decreased revenue occurring through a normal range of deviation in the marketplace. Cases involving the sale of goods might be slightly less rigid in this regard. On the other hand, an increase in costs associated with radical changes in the marketplace precipitated by abnormal market events that renders performance extremely or unreasonably difficulty or costly will support an impracticability defense. See UCC § 2–615, *cmt. 4.* This difficulty must be extreme, but need not be so extreme that performance would threaten the disadvantaged party with bankruptcy. Indeed, a federal bankruptcy remedy already exists for performance made impossible by bankruptcy. Thus, "extreme and unreasonable" must contemplate a financial calamity caused by an unanticipated event creating serious, but less than absolute, financial ruin. See Georgette Chapman Poindexter, "Impossible, Impracticable, or Just Expensive? Allocation of Expense of Ancillary Risk in the CMBS Market," 36 J. Marshall L. Rev. 653 (2003). Nonetheless, the application remains flexible and uncertain. See also Stephen G. Davidson, Note, "Contracts—Doctrine of Impossibility," 41 Tul. L. Rev. 709 (1967) and Paul E. Holtzmuller, Comment, "Contracts—Impossibility—Inaccessibility of Usual and Customary Route," 8 Wm. & Mary L. Rev. 679 (1967).

Modern Frustration of Purpose Doctrine. In June 1902, C.S. Henry responded to an advertisement by Paul Krell to lease rooms in an apartment on June 26 and 27 that were represented as ideal for viewing the coronation processions of King Edward VII. Henry paid a deposit of £25 on the £75 lease. When King Edward's coronation procession was cancelled, Henry refused to pay the rent despite that the rooms were presumably available. In response, Krell sued for payment of the balance, and Henry counterclaimed for return of the deposit. As discussed in greater detail below, this case gave rise to the doctrine of frustration of purpose. Like the impossibility/impracticability doctrine, the doctrine of frustration of purpose addresses situations in which a supervening event after contract formation interferes with the parties' expectations under that contract. But unlike the former doctrine, frustration of purpose involves situations in which performance of the contract remains feasible, but the purpose for which one or both parties entered the contract has been defeated. What purpose or function does frustration serve that impracticability does not? One explanation is that impracticability does not excuse performance requiring only the payment of money. The primary function of impracticability is to excuse performance where a supervening event makes the performance of services or the transfer of property either impossible or at least impracticable. In contrast, frustration excuses performance requiring only the payment of money when the payment is feasible and possible but nonetheless pointless to the promisor. In such cases, the consideration to be furnished either cannot be tendered or there is no point to doing so because the promisor's reason for entering into the contract can no longer be fulfilled.

While a twentieth century doctrinal innovation, frustration is firmly rooted in American contract law. Frustration doctrine originated in the celebrated English common law case of *Krell v. Henry*, 2 Eng. Rep. 740 (K.B. 1903), which extended the *Taylor* impossibility doctrine to frustration cases not involving destruction of the subject matter of the contract.

Referencing *Taylor* (and indirectly *Paradine*), Krell argued that the rent was due unless the language of the contract specifically excused payment if the coronation failed to occur. Moreover, in any event, *Taylor* did not apply because there was no destruction of premises. The apartment was not destroyed and was still available, Henry had the means to pay, and the contract did not expressly excuse payment if the coronation did not occur. The court rejected each argument, reasoning that destruction of the premises was not necessary to imply a constructive condition. Rather, the court may imply such a condition where it is reasonable to assume from the silence of the contract and the surrounding circumstances that the entire basis and essential purpose of the contract was for the purpose of viewing the coronation. In this case, the essential and indeed only reason for the contract was to rent a room to view the coronation. Both parties must have contemplated that if the coronation did not occur, the obligation to pay rent would be discharged. Because the occurrence of the coronation was an implied condition of the payment of rent, the failure to pay rent did not breach the contract because the obligation never came due. Although modern law would normally allow a return of the deposit made under restitution theory, Henry abandoned that claim. See Restatement (First) of Contracts § 468(1); Restatement (Second) of Contracts § 377.

In 1932, prompted by *Krell*, Restatement (First) of Contracts § 288 provided that where an assumed purpose forms the basis on which both parties enter into a contract, and supervening events frustrate this object or effect without fault of a promisor, that party's performance duty is discharged unless the parties agreed otherwise. In 1981, the Restatement (Second) of Contracts § 265 included a similar frustration doctrine providing that a party's performance duty is discharged when that party's principal purpose for entering the contract is substantially frustrated without fault of that party. The non-occurrence of the event causing the frustration must be a basic assumption of the contract, and the contract must not allocate the risk to the party seeking discharge. Under both Restatements, restitution is available to both parties if the considerations exchanged at the time of discharge are not equal. See Restatement (First) of Contracts § 468(1); Restatement (Second) of Contracts § 377. See Nicholas R. Weiskopf, "Frustration of Contractual Purpose—Doctrine or Myth?" 70 St. John's L. Rev. 239 (1996).

While UCC § 2–615(a) specifically embraces impracticability, it fails to mention frustration. Since the section refers to legal excuse for a seller, it is tempting to conclude UCC § 2–615 offers no help to a frustrated buyer. However, UCC § 2–615, *cmt. 9* specifically mentions that a buyer may utilize the doctrine of impracticability as well. Also, UCC § 1–103 (2001) adopts common law by reference unless a UCC section specifically displaces common law. See Robert A. Hillman, "Construction of the Uniform Commercial Code: UCC Section 1–103 and 'Code' Methodology," 18 B. C. L. Rev. 655, 659 (1977). This doctrine should sweep into the UCC all the common law frustration doctrine available to buyers of goods in situations where supervening events have frustrated the buyer's purpose for entering a sale of goods contract. See also Steven Walt, "Expectations, Loss Distribution and Commercial Impracticability," 24 Ind. L. Rev. 65 (1990) and John D. Waldis, "Impracticability as Risk Allocation: The Effect of Changed Circumstances Upon Contract Obligations for the Sale of Goods," 22 Ga. L. Rev. 503 (1988).

Modern Impracticability and Frustration Risk Analysis.
Restatement (Second) of Contracts §§ 261 (supervening impracticability) and 265 (supervening frustration) provide two related but independent risk analysis paradigms. Both ask a court to determine whether the party seeking an excuse for non-performance bears the risk of the supervening event. If the party seeking excuse bears the risk, neither doctrine will provide legal excuse and discharge of contractual duties. In that situation, the non-performing party breaches the contract.

Technically impracticability and frustration can apply to both parties. But in non-barter exchange transactions where one party's performance involves a transfer of property or services and the other party's performance involves the payment of money, it is preferable to apply impracticability doctrine to the party whose performance involves the provision of property or services. On the other hand, courts should apply frustration doctrine to the party whose performance involves the payment of money.

In either case, Restatement (Second) of Contracts §§ 261 and 265 state the same risk analysis. First, a party bears the risk of a supervening event unless the non-occurrence of the event was a "basic assumption of the contract." Second, a party bears the risk of a supervening event if the contract "language or circumstances" indicate that party bears the risk. These are two quite different concepts. The first proposition implicates a judicial allocation of the loss to the party seeking excuse because the purpose or performance of the contract does not depend upon the occurrence or non-occurrence of the supervening event. The second proposition analyzes whether the parties themselves allocated the risk to the party seeking excuse. Accordingly, the first provides for a policy and fairness analysis, whereas the second searches for the intent of the parties.

Before analyzing these two concepts, note the similarity between the supervening event and mistake of fact risk analysis. Restatement (Second) of Contracts § 154 describes the mistake risk analysis in similar, but slightly different terms. This leads to a common but somewhat misleading observation that the frustration and impossibility doctrines cover "latent mistakes," meaning that the problem could have been avoided by agreement and that the excuse would not be necessary if the parties did not share a common mistake in failing to consider the effect of the event when the contract was formed. But the remedies associated with the mistake and impracticability/frustration doctrines belie the latent mistake hypothesis. In cases of mistake, courts order rescission of the contract *ab initio*. In contrast, a party successfully asserting a supervening event defense receives a discharge of further contractual duties from the date of the occurrence of the event.

While mistake and supervening event defenses provide for different remedies, both doctrines permit parties to contract explicitly for the allocation of risk. Allocation by agreement is the same in mistake and supervening event cases. Contracting parties have complete liberty to allocate the risk of a mistake or supervening event by their agreement. See Restatement (Second) of Contracts § 154, *cmt. b*; Restatement (Second) of Contracts § 261, *cmt. c*; and Restatement (Second) of Contracts § 265, *cmt. b*. In the face of such an express allocation of risk, a court may not provide for rescission or excuse. The mistake and supervening event rules therefore operate as default rules, and the parties may contract around those rules.

Allocation by agreement can of course occur where the language is expressly and clearly stated in a written contract. But in some cases, the contract may not expressly allocate the risk of a specific factual mistake or supervening event. Nonetheless, other contract language and/or parol evidence surrounding the making of the agreement may support the inference that the parties intended to allocate the risk to the party seeking rescission or excuse:

> Even absent an express agreement, a court may decide, after considering all the circumstances, that a party impliedly assumed such a greater obligation. . . . Circumstances relevant in deciding whether a party has assumed a greater obligation include his ability to have inserted a provision in the contract expressly shifting the risk of impracticability to the other party. . . . If the supervening event was not reasonably foreseeable when the contract was made, the party claiming discharge can hardly be expected to have provided against its occurrence. However, if it was reasonably foreseeable, or even foreseen, the opposite conclusion does not necessarily follow. Factors such as the practical difficulty of reaching agreement on the myriad of conceivable terms of a complex agreement may excuse a failure to deal with improbable contingencies. Restatement (Second) of Contracts § 261, *cmt. c*.

Generally, if the supervening event was reasonably foreseeable, the promisor will forfeit the excuse where the agreement itself does not allocate the risk of the foreseeable event to the other party. From one perspective, since nearly every act of God, war, or other event has already occurred in history, is it not possible to foresee nearly everything? If so, is the foreseeability test meaningful as an exception, or does it swallow the general rule of excuse? To avoid these concerns, some have argued that the test for the foreseeability of an event ought to be limited to events "so unlikely to occur that reasonable parties see no need explicitly to allocate the risk of its occurrence." See Pietro Trimarchi, "Commercial Impracticability in Contract Law: An Economic Analysis," 11 Int'l Rev. L. & Econ. 63, 65 (1991).

In an important article, Professor Farnsworth, the author of the Restatement (Second) of Contracts, developed a two-tier analysis of the effect of foreseeability. See E. Allan Farnsworth, "Disputes over Omission in Contracts," 68 Colum. L. Rev. 860 (1968). Professor Farnsworth suggested problems concerning impracticability and frustration resulted only because the parties failed to provide for the contingency in their contract. Two explanations exist. The parties either did not foresee the contingency, or they did foresee the contingency but failed to provide for it. The court should first determine if the parties did foresee the contingency and, if so, next determine the intentions with regard to the risk of the contingencies from their negotiations. If the parties did not foresee the contingency, then a judicial search for intent is irrelevant. In such a case, the court should simply imply a just and fair result. The judicial decision making process normatively should involve a search for what is the parties should reasonably expect given the other terms of the agreement.

How does the doctrine of conscious ignorance under mistake law differ, if at all, from the doctrine of implied assumptions under supervening event law? Restatement (Second) of Contracts § 154, *cmt. c* provides as follows with regard to conscious ignorance:

> Even though the mistaken party did not agree to bear the risk of the mistake, he may have been aware when he made the contract that his knowledge with respect to the facts was limited. If he was not only so aware that his knowledge was limited but undertook to perform in the face of that awareness, he bears the risk of the mistake.

Accordingly, the consciously ignorant party "impliedly" assumes the risk of the mistake. In most cases, with minimal costs, the mistaken party could have eliminated the mistake by a reasonable search for the truth. Natural limitations should apply to this doctrine. In many cases based on the economics of the particular transaction, the search will be too time consuming and expensive to fairly and reasonably justify that the mistaken party impliedly assumed the risk by failing to conduct the search or investigation. See Melvin A. Eisenberg, "Mistake in Contract Law," 91 Cal. L. Rev. 1573, 1632 (2003). Does the same doctrine apply to foreseeable contingencies?

TRANSATLANTIC FINANCING CORP. V. UNITED STATES

United States Court of Appeals for the District of Columbia
363 F.2d 312 (1966)

J. SKELLY WRIGHT, Circuit Judge

This appeal involves a voyage charter between Transatlantic Financing Corporation, operator of the SS CHRISTOS, and the United States covering carriage of a full cargo of wheat from a United States Gulf port to a safe port in Iran. The District Court dismissed a libel filed by Transatlantic against the United States for costs attributable to the ship's diversion from the normal sea route caused by the closing of the Suez Canal. We affirm.

On July 26, 1956, the Government of Egypt nationalized the Suez Canal Company and took over operation of the Canal. On October 2, 1956, during the international crisis that resulted from the seizure, the voyage charter in suit was executed between representatives of Transatlantic and the United States. The charter indicated the termini of the voyage but not the route. On October 27, 1956, the SS CHRISTOS sailed from Galveston for Bandar Shapur, Iran, on a course that would have taken her through Gibraltar and the Suez Canal. On October 29, 1956, Israel invaded Egypt. On October 31, 1956, Great Britain and France invaded the Suez Canal Zone. On November 2, 1956, the Egyptian Government obstructed the Suez Canal with sunken vessels and closed it to traffic.

On or about November 7, 1956, Beckmann, representing Transatlantic, contacted Potosky, an employee of the United States Department of Agriculture, who appellant concedes was unauthorized to bind the Government, requesting instructions concerning disposition of the cargo and seeking an agreement for payment of additional compensation for a voyage around the Cape of Good Hope. Potosky advised Beckmann that Transatlantic was expected to perform the charter according to its terms, that he did not believe Transatlantic was entitled to additional compensation for a voyage around the Cape, but that Transatlantic was free to file such a claim. Following this discussion, the CHRISTOS changed course for the Cape of Good Hope and eventually arrived in Bandar Shapur on December 30, 1956.

Transatlantic's claim is based on the following train of argument. The charter was a contract for a voyage from a Gulf port to Iran. Admiralty principles and practices, especially stemming from the doctrine of deviation, require us to imply into the contract the term that the voyage was to be performed by the "usual and customary" route. The usual and customary route from Texas to Iran was, at the time of contract, via Suez, so the contract was for a voyage from Texas to Iran via Suez. When Suez was closed this contract became impossible to perform. Consequently, appellant's argument continues, when Transatlantic delivered the cargo by going around the Cape of Good Hope, in compliance with the Government's demand under claim of right, it conferred a benefit upon the United States for which it should be paid in quantum meruit.

The doctrine of impossibility of performance has gradually been freed from the earlier fictional and unrealistic strictures of such tests as the "implied term" and the parties' "contemplation." Page, The Development of the Doctrine of Impossibility of Performance, 18 Mich. L. Rev. 589, 596

(1920). It is now recognized that "A thing is impossible in legal contemplation when it is not practicable; and a thing is impracticable when it can only be done at an excessive and unreasonable cost." Mineral Park Land Co. v. Howard, 172 Cal. 289, 293, 156 P. 458, 460, L. R. A. 1916F, 1 (1916). Accord, . . . Restatement, Contracts § 454 (1932); UCC (U. L. A.) § 2–615, comment 3. The doctrine ultimately represents the ever-shifting line, drawn by courts hopefully responsive to commercial practices and mores, at which the community's interest in having contracts enforced according to their terms is outweighed by the commercial senselessness of requiring performance.[1] When the issue is raised, the court is asked to construct a condition of performance based on the changed circumstances, a process which involves at least three reasonably definable steps. First, a contingency—something unexpected—must have occurred. Second, the risk of the unexpected occurrence must not have been allocated either by agreement or by custom. Finally, occurrence of the contingency must have rendered performance commercially impracticable.[3] Unless the court finds these three requirements satisfied, the plea of impossibility must fail.

The first requirement was met here. It seems reasonable, where no route is mentioned in a contract, to assume the parties expected performance by the usual and customary route at the time of contract.[4] Since the usual and customary route from Texas to Iran at the time of contract[5] was through Suez, closure of the Canal made impossible the

---

[1]   While the impossibility issue rarely arises, as it has here, in a suit to recover the cost of an alternative method of performance, compare Annot., 84 A. L. R. 2d 12, 19 (1962), there is nothing necessarily inconsistent in claiming commercial impracticability for the method of performance actually adopted; the concept of impracticability assumes performance was physically possible. Moreover, a rule making nonperformance a condition precedent to recovery would unjustifiably encourage disappointment of expectations.

[3]   Compare UCC § 2–615(a), which provides that, in the absence of an assumption of greater liability, delay or non-delivery by a seller is not a breach if performance as agreed is made "impracticable" by the occurrence of a "contingency" the non-occurrence of which was a "basic assumption on which the contract was made." To the extent this limits relief to "unforeseen" circumstances, comment 1, see the discussion below, and compare UCC § 2–614(1). There may be a point beyond which agreement cannot go, UCC § 2–615, comment 8, presumably the point at which the obligation would be "manifestly unreasonable," § 1–102(3), in bad faith, § 1–203, or unconscionable, § 2–302. For an application of these provisions see Judge Friendly's opinion in United States v. Wegematic Corporation, 2 Cir., 360 F.2d 674 (1966).

[4]   UCC § 2–614, comment 1, states: "Under this Article, in the absence of specific agreement, the normal or usual facilities enter into the agreement either through the circumstances, usage of trade or prior course of dealing." So long as this sort of assumption does not necessarily result in construction of a condition of performance, it is idle to argue over whether the usual and customary route is an "implied term." The issue of impracticability must eventually be met. One court refused to imply the Suez route as a contract term, but went on to rule the contract had been "frustrated." Carapanayoti & Co. Ltd. v. E. T. Green Ltd. (1959) 1 Q. B. 131. The holding was later rejected by the House of Lords. Tsakiroglou & Co. Ltd. v. Noblee Thorl G.m.b.H. (1960) 2 Q.B. 348.

[5]   The parties have spent considerable energy in disputing whether the "usual and customary" route by which performance was anticipated is defined as of the time of contract or of performance. If we were automatically to treat the expected route as a condition of performance, this matter would be crucial, and we would be compelled to choose between unacceptable alternatives. If we assume as a constructive condition the usual and customary course always to mean the one in use at the time of contract, any substantial diversion (we assume the diversion would have to be substantial) would nullify the contract even though its effect upon the rights and

expected method of performance. But this unexpected development raises rather than resolves the impossibility issue, which turns additionally on whether the risk of the contingency's occurrence had been allocated and, if not, whether performance by alternative routes was rendered impracticable.[6]

Proof that the risk of a contingency's occurrence has been allocated may be expressed in or implied from the agreement. Such proof may also be found in the surrounding circumstances, including custom and usages of the trade. . . . The contract in this case does not expressly condition performance upon availability of the Suez route. Nor does it specify "via Suez" or, on the other hand, "via Suez or Cape of Good Hope."[7] Nor are there provisions in the contract from which we may properly imply that the continued availability of Suez was a condition of performance.[8] Nor is there

---

obligations of the parties is insignificant. Nor would it be desirable, on the other hand, to assume performance is conditioned on the availability of any usual and customary route at the time of performance. It may be that very often the availability of a customary route at the time of performance other than the route expected to be used at the time of contract should result in denial of relief under the impossibility theory; certainly if no customary route is available at the time of performance the contract is rendered impossible. But the same customarily used alternative route may be practicable in one set of circumstances and impracticable in another, as where the goods are unable to survive the extra journey. Moreover, the "time of performance" is no special point in time; it is every moment in a performance. Thus the alternative route, in our case around the Cape, may be practicable at some time during performance, for example while the vessel is still in the Atlantic Ocean, and impracticable at another time during performance, for example after the vessel has traversed most of the Mediterranean Sea. Both alternatives, therefore, have their shortcomings, and we avoid choosing between them by refusing automatically to treat the usual and customary route as of any time as a condition of performance.

[6] In criticizing the "contemplation" test for impossibility Professor Patterson pointed out: "Contemplation" is appropriate to describe the mental state of philosophers but is scarcely descriptive of the mental state of business men making a bargain. It seems preferable to say that the promisee expects performance by (the) means . . . the promisor expects to (or which on the facts known to the promisee it is probable that he will) use. It does not follow as an inference of fact that the promisee expects performance by only that means. . . . Patterson, supra Note 2, at 947.

[7] In Glidden Company v. Hellenic Lines, Limited, 2 Cir., 275 F.2d 253 (1960), the charter was for transportation of materials from India to America "via Suez Canal or Cape of Good Hope, or Panama Canal," and the court held performance was not "frustrated." In his discussion of this case, Professor Corbin states: "Except for the provision for an alternative route, the defendant would have been discharged, for the reason that the parties contemplated an open Suez Canal as a specific condition or means of performance." 6 CORBIN, supra, § 1339, at 399 n. 57. Appellant claims this supports its argument, since the Suez route was contemplated as usual and customary. But there is obviously a difference, in deciding whether a contract allocates the risk of a contingency's occurrence, between a contract specifying no route and a contract specifying Suez. We think that when Professor Corbin said, "Except for the provision for an alternative route," he was referring, not to the entire provision—"via Suez Canal or Cape of Good Hope" etc.—but to the fact that an alternative route had been provided for. Moreover, in determining what Corbin meant when he said "the parties contemplated an open Suez Canal as a specific condition or means or performance," consideration must be given to the fact, recited by Corbin, that in Glidden the parties were specifically aware when the contract was made the Canal might be closed, and the promisee had refused to include a clause excusing performance in the event of closure. Corbin's statement, therefore, is most accurately read as referring to cases in which a route is specified after negotiations reflecting the parties' awareness that the usual and customary route might become unavailable. Compare Held v. Goldsmith, 153 La. 598, 96 So. 272 (1919).

[8] The charter provides that the vessel is "in every way fitted for the voyage," and the "P. & I. Bunker Deviation Clause" refers to "the contract voyage" and the "direct and/or customary route." Appellant argues that these provisions require implication of a voyage by the direct and

anything in custom or trade usage, or in the surrounding circumstances generally, which would support our constructing a condition of performance. The numerous cases requiring performance around the Cape when Suez was closed, see e.g., Ocean Tramp Tankers Corp. v. V/O Sovfracht (The Eugenia) (1964) 2 Q. B. 226, and cases cited therein, indicate that the Cape route is generally regarded as an alternative means of performance. So the implied expectation that the route would be via Suez is hardly adequate proof of an allocation to the promisee of the risk of closure. In some cases, even an express expectation may not amount to a condition of performance.[9] The doctrine of deviation supports our assumption that parties normally expect performance by the usual and customary route, but it adds nothing beyond this that is probative of an allocation of the risk.[10]

---

customary route. Actually they prove only what we are willing to accept—that the parties expected the usual and customary route would be used. The provisions in no way condition performance upon nonoccurrence of this contingency.

There are two clauses which allegedly demonstrate that time is of importance in this contract. One clause computes the remuneration "in steaming time" for diversions to other countries ordered by the charterer in emergencies. This proves only that the United States wished to reserve power to send the goods to another country. It does not imply in any way that there was a rush about the matter. The other clause concerns demurrage and dispatch. The charterer agreed to pay Transatlantic demurrage of $1,200 per day for all time in excess of the period agreed upon for loading and unloading, and Transatlantic was to pay dispatch of $600 per day for any saving in time. Of course this provision shows the parties were concerned about time, see Gilmore & Black, The Law of Admiralty § 4–8 (1957), but the fact that they arranged so minutely the consequences of any delay or speedup of loading and unloading operates against the argument that they were similarly allocating the risk of delay or speed-up of the voyage.

[9] UCC § 2–614(1) provides: "Where without fault of either party . . . the agreed manner of delivery . . . becomes commercially impracticable but a commercially reasonable substitute is available, such substitute performance must be tendered and accepted." Compare Mr. Justice Holmes' observation: "You can give any conclusion a logical form. You always can imply a condition in a contract. But why do you imply it? It is because of some belief as to the practice of the community or of a class, or because of some opinion as to policy. . . ." Holmes, The Path of the Law, 10 Harv. L. Rev. 457, 466 (1897).

[10] The deviation doctrine, drawn principally from admiralty insurance practice, implies into all relevant commercial instruments naming the termini of voyages the usual and customary route between those points. 1 Arnould, Marine Insurance and Average § 376, at 522 (10th ed. 1921). Insurance is cancelled when a ship unreasonably "deviates" from this course, for example by extending a voyage or by putting in at an irregular port, and the shipowner forfeits the protection of clauses of exception which might otherwise have protected him from his common law insurer's liability to cargo. See Gilmore & Black, supra Note 8, § 2–6, at 59–60. This practice, properly qualified, see id. § 3–41, makes good sense, since insurance rates are computed on the basis of the implied course, and deviations in the course increasing the anticipated risk make the insurer's calculations meaningless. Arnould, supra, § 14, at 26. Thus the route, so far as insurance contracts are concerned, is crucial, whether express or implied. But even here, the implied term is not inflexible. Reasonable deviations do not result in loss of insurance, at least so long as established practice is followed. See Carriage of Goods by Sea Act § 4(4), 49 Stat. 1210, 46 U.S.C. § 1304(4); and discussion of "held covered" clauses in Gilmore & Black, supra, § 3–41, at 161. Some "deviations" are required. E.g., Hirsch Lumber Co. v. Weyerhaeuser Steamship Co., 2 Cir., 233 F.2d 791, cert. denied, 352 U.S. 880. 77 S. Ct. 102, 1 L. Ed. 2d 80 (1956). The doctrine's only relevance, therefore, is that it provides additional support for the assumption we willingly make that merchants agreeing to a voyage between two points expect that the usual and customary route between those points will be used. The doctrine provides no evidence of an allocation of the risk of the route's unavailability.

If anything, the circumstances surrounding this contract indicate that the risk of the Canal's closure may be deemed to have been allocated to Transatlantic. We know or may safely assume that the parties were aware, as were most commercial men with interests affected by the Suez situation, see The Eugenia, supra, that the Canal might become a dangerous area. No doubt the tension affected freight rates, and it is arguable that the risk of closure became part of the dickered terms. UCC § 2–615, comment 8. We do not deem the risk of closure so allocated, however. Foreseeability or even recognition of a risk does not necessarily prove its allocation. Compare UCC § 2–615, Comment 1; Restatement, Contracts § 457 (1932). Parties to a contract are not always able to provide for all the possibilities of which they are aware, sometimes because they cannot agree, often simply because they are too busy. Moreover, that some abnormal risk was contemplated is probative but does not necessarily establish an allocation of the risk of the contingency that actually occurs. In this case, for example, nationalization by Egypt of the Canal Corporation and formation of the Suez Users Group did not necessarily indicate that the Canal would be blocked even if a confrontation resulted.[12] The surrounding circumstances do indicate, however, a willingness by Transatlantic to assume abnormal risks, and this fact should legitimately cause us to judge the impracticability of performance by an alternative route in stricter terms than we would were the contingency unforeseen.

We turn then to the question whether occurrence of the contingency rendered performance commercially impracticable under the circumstances of this case. The goods shipped were not subject to harm from the longer, less temperate Southern route. The vessel and crew were fit to proceed around the Cape.[13] Transatlantic was no less able than the United States to purchase insurance to cover the contingency's occurrence. If anything, it is more reasonable to expect owner-operators of vessels to insure against the hazards of war. They are in the best position to calculate the cost of performance by alternative routes (and therefore to estimate the amount of insurance required), and are undoubtedly sensitive to international troubles which uniquely affect the demand for and cost of their services. The only factor operating here in appellant's favor is the

---

[12] Sources cited in the briefs indicate formation of the Suez Canal Users Association on October 1, 1956, was viewed in some quarters as an implied threat of force. See N.Y. Times, Oct. 2, 1956, p. 1, col. 1, noting, on the day the charter in this case was executed, that "Britain has declared her freedom to use force as a last resort if peaceful methods fail to achieve a satisfactory settlement." Secretary of State Dulles was able, however, to view the statement as evidence of the canal users' "dedication to a just and peaceful solution." The Suez Problem 369–370 (Department of State Pub. 1956).

[13] The issue of impracticability should no doubt be "an objective determination of whether the promise can reasonably be performed rather than a subjective inquiry into the promisor's capability of performing as agreed.", Symposium, The Uniform Commercial Code and Contract Law: Some Selected Problems, 105 U. Pa. L. Rev. 836, 880, 887 (1957). Dealers should not be excused because of less than normal capabilities. But if both parties are aware of a dealer's limited capabilities, no objective determination would be complete without taking into account this fact.

added expense, allegedly $43,972.00 above and beyond the contract price of $305,842.92, of extending a 10,000-mile voyage by approximately 3,000 miles. While it may be an overstatement to say that increased cost and difficulty of performance never constitute impracticability, to justify relief there must be more of a variation between expected cost and the cost of performing by an available alternative than is present in this case,[14] where the promisor can legitimately be presumed to have accepted some degree of abnormal risk, and where impracticability is urged on the basis of added expense alone.[15]

We conclude, therefore, as have most other courts considering related issues arising out of the Suez closure,[16] that performance of this contract was not rendered legally impossible. Even if we agreed with appellant, its theory of relief seems untenable. When performance of a contract is deemed impossible it is a nullity. In the case of a charter party involving carriage of goods, the carrier may return to an appropriate port and unload its cargo, The Malcolm Baxter, Jr., 277 U.S. 323, 48 S. Ct. 516, 72 L. Ed. 901 (1928),

---

[14] Two leading English cases support this conclusion. The Eugenia, supra, involved a time charter for a trip from Genoa to India via the Black Sea. The charterers were held in breach of the charter's war clause by entering the Suez Canal after the outbreak of hostilities, but sought to avoid paying for the time the vessel was trapped in the Canal by arguing that, even if they had not entered the Canal, it would have been blocked and the vessel would have had to go around the Cape to India, a trip which "frustrated" the contract because it constituted an entirely different venture from the one originally contemplated. The lower court agreed, but the House of Lords (see Lord Denning's admirable treatment. (1964) 2 Q. B. at 233), "swallowing" the difficulty of applying the frustration doctrine to hypothetical facts, reversed, holding that the contract had to be performed. Especially relevant is the fact that the case expressly overruled Sociate Franco Tunisienne D'Armement v. Sidermar S.P.A. (The Massalia) (1961) 2 Q. B. 278, where a voyage charter was deemed frustrated because the Cape route was "highly circuitous" and cost 195s. per long ton to ship iron ore, rather than 134s. via Suez, a difference well in excess of the difference in this case. In Tsakiroglou & Co. Ltd. v. Noblee Thorl G.m.b.H., supra Note 4, the difference to the seller under a C.I.F. contract in freight costs caused by the Canal's closure was per ton instead of per ton-precisely twice the cost. The House of Lords found no frustration.

[15] See UCC § 2–615, comment 4: "Increased cost alone does not excuse performance unless the rise in cost is due to some unforeseen contingency which alters the essential nature of the performance."

[16] Appellant seeks to distinguish the English cases supporting our view. The Eugenia, supra, appellant argues, involved a time charter. True, but it overruled The Massalia, supra Note 14, which involved a voyage charter. Indeed, when the time charter is for a voyage the difference is only verbal. See Carver, Carriage of Goods By Sea 256–257 (10th ed. 1957). More convincing is the argument that Tsakiroglou & Co. Ltd., supra Note 4, involved a contract for the sale of goods, where the seller agreed to a C.I.R. clause requiring him to ship the goods to the buyer. There is a significant difference between a C.I.F. contract and voyage or time charters. The effect of delay in the former due to longer sea voyages is minimized, since the seller can raise money on the goods he has shipped almost at once, and the buyer, once he takes up the documents, can deal with the goods by transferring the documents before the goods arrive. See Tsakiroglou & Co. Ltd., supra Note 4 (1960) 2 Q. B. at 361. But this difference is not so material that impossibility in C.I.F. contracts is unrelated to impossibility in charter parties. It would raise serious questions for a court to require sellers under C.I.F. contracts to perform in circumstances under which the sellers could be refused performance by carriers with whom they have entered into charter parties for affreightment. See The Eugenia, supra (1964) 2 Q. B. at 241. Where the time of the voyage is unimportant, a charter party should be treated the same as a C.I.F. contract in determining impossibility of performance. These cases certainly are not distinguishable, as appellant suggests, on the ground that they refer to "frustration" rather than to "impossibility." The English regard "frustration" as substantially identical with "impossibility."

subject of course to required steps to minimize damages. If the performance rendered has value, recovery in quantum meruit for the entire performance is proper. But here Transatlantic has collected its contract price, and now seeks quantum meruit relief for the additional expense of the trip around the Cape. If the contract is a nullity, Transatlantic's theory of relief should have been quantum meruit for the entire trip, rather than only for the extra expense. Transatlantic attempts to take its profit on the contract, and then force the Government to absorb the cost of the additional voyage.[17] When impracticability without fault occurs, the law seeks an equitable solution, . . . and quantum meruit is one of its potent devices to achieve this end. There is no interest in casting the entire burden of commercial disaster on one party in order to preserve the other's profit. Apparently the contract price in this case was advantageous enough to deter appellant from taking a stance on damages consistent with its theory of liability. In any event, there is no basis for relief.

Affirmed.

NOTES AND QUESTIONS

1. *CISG impracticability.* CISG Art. 79(1) provides that a party is not liable for failure to perform any obligation if the failure was due to an impediment beyond that party's control that could not reasonably be expected to have been taken into account at the time of the contract or to have later avoided. Would this provision have protected Transatlantic against the increased costs caused by the canal closure?

2. *UCC analysis.* The court references UCC § 2–615. Is the UCC applicable? If not, why would the court reference the UCC rather than the common law and the Restatement (First) of Contracts? Does the UCC apply a different standard or reach a different outcome than the test for common law impracticability?

3. *Three-factor test.* The court adopts a three-factor test for impracticability: (i) a supervening event, (ii) neither the agreement nor the surrounding circumstances expressly or implicitly allocate the risk to the party seeking excuse for non-performance, and (iii) the supervening event renders performance impracticable. The closing of the Suez Canal after the contract was made is obviously a supervening event. But that occurrence simply triggers the second and third analysis. The carriage contract simply stated the final destination for the goods, but not the route. Transatlantic argued that since the "normal route" from the US to Iran was through the Suez Canal, that route should be an implied term of the contract. How did the court address this

---

[17] The argument that the UCC requires the buyer to pay the additional cost of performance by a commercially reasonable substitute was advanced and rejected in Symposium, supra Note 13, 105 U. Pa. L. Rev. at 884 n. 205. In Dillon v. United States, 156 F. Supp. 719, 140 Ct. Cl. 508 (1957), relief was afforded for some of the cost of delivering hay from a commercially unreasonable distance, but the suit was one in which the plaintiff had suffered losses far in excess of the relief given.

argument? The court determined that the closing of the Suez Canal was reasonably foreseeable. Does that fact alone allocate the risk to the party seeking legal excuse since Transatlantic failed to include the route in the contract? What is the effect of supervening events that are foreseeable at the time the contract is formed? Must all such events be accounted for in the contract? Finally, the alternate route was obviously not impossible as Transatlantic took that route. Does the existence of a possible or practicable alternative performance bar a successful impracticability defense? How did the court analyze this factor?

4. *Force majeure clause.* Would the presence of a traditional *force majeure* clause have protected Transatlantic in this case? Does a *force majeure* clause simply grant legal excuse, or does it also grant a positive remedy for an alternative but more expensive performance? If only the former, what language would you have provided in the contract to protect Transatlantic? Why do you suppose Transatlantic failed to include such a clause in the contract? Do you think the United States would have agreed? If not, does that failure alone and the resulting silence preclude legal excuse? Does it preclude recovery for additional compensations?

MEL FRANK TOOL & SUPPLY, INC. V. DI-CHEM CO.

Supreme Court of Iowa
580 N.W.2d 802 (1998)

LAVORATO, Justice.

City authorities informed a lessee, a chemical distributor, that it could no longer use its leased premises to store its hazardous chemicals because of a recently enacted ordinance. The lessee vacated the premises, and the lessor sued for breach of the lease and for damages to the premises. The district court awarded the lessor judgment for unpaid rent and for damages to the premises. The lessee appeals, contending that the district court should have found that the city's actions constituted extraordinary circumstances rendering the performance of the lease impossible. The lessee also contends that language in the lease releases it from liability. In addition, the lessee challenges a district court finding that a real estate agent represented the lessee and prepared the lease on its behalf. We affirm.

I. FACTS

Di-Chem Company is a chemical distributor. In May 1994, Di-Chem began negotiating with Mel Frank Tool & Supply, Inc. to lease a storage and distribution facility in Council Bluffs, Iowa. Mel Frank's real estate agent handled the negotiations so there were no actual face-to-face negotiations between the parties. However, a day before the lease was executed, Mel Frank's owner, Dennis Frank, talked with Di-Chem representatives who were touring the premises. Frank asked them what

Di-Chem was going to be selling and was told chemicals. The agent brought the lease to Frank for his signature.

The lease appears to be an Iowa State Bar Association form. See Iowa State Bar Association Official Form No. 164. The lease was to start June 1, 1994 and end May 31, 1997. The lease limited Di-Chem's use of the premises to "storage and distribution."

Some of the chemicals Di-Chem distributes are considered "hazardous material." There was no testimony that Dennis Frank was aware of this at the time the lease was executed. A Di-Chem representative, who was present during the earlier-mentioned conversation with Dennis Frank, testified that hazardous materials did not come up in the conversation.

The lease contained several provisions that bear on the issues in this appeal. One requires Di-Chem to "make no unlawful use of the premises and . . . to comply with all . . . City Ordinances." There is also a destruction-of-premises provision that allows either party to terminate the lease under certain circumstances.

On July 21, 1995, the city's fire chief and several other city authorities inspected the premises. Following the inspection, the city's fire marshal wrote Di-Chem, stating:

> At the time of the inspection the building was occupied as Hazardous Materials Storage. I have given you a copy of 1994 Uniform Fire Code, which the City has adopted, covering Hazardous Material Storage. As you can see the building does not comply with the Code requirements that creates Health and Life Safety Hazards. The Hazardous Materials must be removed within seven (7) days to eliminate the hazard.

The letter also informed Di-Chem of the following code deficiencies: complete fire sprinkler system, mechanical exhaust system, spill control, and drainage control. Both Frank and Di-Chem representatives testified they understood the letter to mean that if these deficiencies were eliminated, Di-Chem could continue to store hazardous material. There was testimony that the changes in the code occurred after Di-Chem took occupancy of the premises.

On August 2 Di-Chem informed Mel Frank by letter of the city's action and enclosed a copy of the city's July 25 letter to Di-Chem. In its August 2 letter Di-Chem informed Mel Frank of its intention to re-locate "as soon as possible to avoid civil and criminal proceedings at the hands of the city." Di-Chem also stated:

> [W]e believe the city has overreacted and probably has no authority to order us to remove our materials from the property. . . . Nevertheless, we are not willing to contest the city's

position, and we feel compelled to remove our operation beyond the city limits.

Di-Chem also stated it intended to pay the rental for the month of August and vacate the premises by September 1.

Thereafter Dennis Frank and Di-Chem representatives met with city officials about what it would take to correct the various code deficiencies to allow Di-Chem to continue storing hazardous materials. Di-Chem representatives and Dennis Frank briefly considered bringing the building up to code. There was talk about the possibility of Di-Chem splitting the costs with Mel Frank, but Dennis Frank felt the cost was prohibitive.

On October 23 Di-Chem notified Mel Frank by letter of its intention to vacate the premises by the end of October. The letter in part stated: "The city's position that we cannot legally store all of our inventory at this site prior to extensive alteration of the building makes the structure useless to us as a chemical warehouse." True to its word, Di-Chem vacated the premises.

II. PROCEEDINGS

Later, Mel Frank sued for breach of the lease and for damages to the property. Di-Chem asserted several affirmative defenses: mutual mistake, illegal contract, failure to mitigate damages, fraud in the inducement, and impossibility.

The parties tried the case to the court. In its ruling the court stated the issue this way:

> The principal issue to be determined is whether the defendant may voluntarily terminate the lease agreement based upon defendant's position that the warehouse could not be used for storing hazardous materials [resulting from] the inspection of various departments of the City of Council Bluffs. The conclusion of this issue must be based upon the intention of the litigating parties as well as the terms and conditions of the written lease agreement.

The court found for Mel Frank. The court found that Mel Frank had "no reason to believe or [know] that chemicals classified as hazardous would be stored in the warehouse." The court relied on the testimony of Norm Wirtala, an officer of Di-Chem:

> Mr. Wirtala testified he would be in a "superior position of knowledge" concerning the items to be stored in the building and that he had a general understanding of fire code requirements for the storage of hazardous materials due to his experience in the business although [neither] he nor his agents claimed to have examined the Council Bluffs' fire codes as they

may have related to hazardous materials and building specifications for storage of hazardous materials.

With this the court concluded that there was clear and conclusive [evidence] that the plaintiff made no representations to the defendant that the warehouse was suitable for any specific purpose, nor were any discussions or representations made concerning the character of the products to be stored by the defendant. Consequently, this Court concludes the lease was breached by the defendants for vacating the premises and failing to pay the balance of the lease term as required by its terms and conditions and the defendants owe the sum of $55,913.77 for rent [and $2,357.00 for damage to the property].

III. SCOPE OF REVIEW

The action here was one at law. Our review is therefore for correction of errors. Iowa R. App. P. 4. The district court's findings of fact have the force of a special jury verdict and are binding if supported by substantial evidence. See Iowa R. App. P. 14(f)(1). Evidence is substantial if a reasonable mind could find it adequate to reach the same finding. Pierce v. Farm Bureau Mut. Ins. Co., 548 N.W. 2d 551, 553 (Iowa 1996). We are not, however, bound by the district court's application of legal principles or the court's conclusions of law. Hagan v. Val-Hi, Inc., 484 N.W. 2d 173, 175 (Iowa 1992).

IV. IMPOSSIBILITY OF PERFORMANCE

A. The Law

The introduction to the Restatement (Second) of Contracts covers impossibility of performance but with a different title: impracticability of performance and frustration of purpose. See Restatement (Second) of Contracts ch. 11, at 309 (1981) [hereinafter Restatement]. According to the Restatement:

> [C]ontract liability is strict liability. . . . The obligor is therefore liable in damages for breach of contract even if he is without fault and even if circumstances have made the contract more burdensome or less desirable than he had anticipated. . . . The obligor who does not wish to undertake so extensive an obligation may contract for a lesser one by using one of a variety of common clauses: . . . he may reserve a right to cancel the contract. . . . The extent of his obligation then depends on the application of the rules of interpretation. . . . Id.

Even though the obligor has not restricted his or her obligation by agreement, a court may still grant relief: "An extraordinary circumstance may make performance so vitally different from what was reasonably to be expected as to alter the essential nature of that performance." Id. In these circumstances, "the court must determine whether justice requires a departure from the general rule that the obligor bear the risk that the contract may become more burdensome or less desirable." Id. at 310. Whether extraordinary circumstances exist justifying discharge is a question of law for the court. Id.

The Restatement recognizes three distinct grounds for the discharge of the obligor's contractual duty:

> First, the obligor may claim that some circumstance has made his own performance impracticable. . . . Second, the obligor may claim that some circumstance has so destroyed the value to him of the other party's performance as to frustrate his own purpose in making the contract. . . . Third, the obligor may claim that he will not receive the agreed exchange for the obligee's duty to render that agreed exchange, on the ground of either impracticability or frustration. Id.

The rationale behind the doctrines of impracticability and frustration is whether the nonoccurrence of the circumstance was a basic assumption on which the contract was made. Id. at 310–11. The parties need not have been conscious of alternatives for them to have had a "basic assumption." Id. at 311. The Restatement gives an example:

> Where an artist contracts to paint a painting and dies, the artist's death is an "event the nonoccurrence of which was a basic assumption on which the contract was made, even though the parties never consciously addressed themselves to that possibility." Id.

Under the Restatement's rationale:

> [T]he obligor is relieved of his duty because the contract, having been made on a different "basic assumption," is regarded as not covering the case that has arisen. It is an omitted case, falling within a "gap" in the contract. Ordinarily, the just way to deal with the omitted case is to hold that the obligor's duty is discharged, in the case of changed circumstances, or has never arisen, in the case of existing circumstances, and to shift the risk to the obligee. Id.

B.   Discharge by Supervening Frustration

For reasons that follow, we think the facts of this case fall within the parameters of section 265 of the Restatement. Section 265 provides:

> Where, after a contract is made, a party's principal purpose is substantially frustrated without his fault by the occurrence of an event the nonoccurrence of which was a basic assumption on which the contract was made, his remaining duties to render

performance are discharged, *unless the language or the circumstances indicate the contrary.*

(Emphasis added.) As mentioned, this is one of the three grounds the Restatement recognizes for discharging the obligor's contractual duty. See id. ch. 11, at 310.

The rule deals with the problem that arises when a change in circumstances makes one party's performance virtually worthless to the other, frustrating the purpose in making the contract. Id. § 265 cmt. a, at 335. The obligor's contractual obligation is discharged only if three conditions are met:

> First, the purpose that is frustrated must have been a principal purpose of that party in making the contract. It is not enough that he had in mind some specific object without which he would not have made the contract. The object must be so completely the basis of the contract that, as both parties understand, without it the transaction would make little sense. *Second, the frustration must be substantial. It is not enough that the transaction has become less profitable for the affected party or even that he will sustain a loss. The frustration must be so severe that it is not fairly to be regarded as within the risks that he assumed under the contract.* Third, the non-occurrence of the frustrating event must have been a basic assumption on which the contract was made. . . . The foreseeability of the event is . . . a factor in that determination, but the mere fact that the event was foreseeable does not compel the conclusion that its non-occurrence was not such a basic assumption.

Id. (emphasis added).

Under this Restatement section, the following pertinent illustration appears:

> A leases a gasoline station to B. A change in traffic regulations so reduces B's business that he is unable to operate the station except at a substantial loss. B refuses to make further payments of rent. If B can still operate the station, even though at such a loss, his principal purpose of operating a gasoline station is not substantially frustrated. B's duty to pay rent is not discharged, and B is liable to A for breach of contract. The result would be the same if substantial loss were caused instead by a government regulation rationing gasoline or a termination of the franchise under which B obtained gasoline. Id. § 265 cmt. a, illus. 6, at 336.

Iowa case law is in accord with Restatement section 265. See Conklin v. Silver, 187 Iowa 819, 822–23, 174 N.W. 573, 574 (1919). The facts in Conklin parallel those in illustration 6 set out above.

In Conklin, the lease provided that the lessees were to only use the premises for iron, metal, and rag business. Id. at 820, 174 N.W. at 573. The lease also prohibited the lessees from "engag[ing] in or permit[ting] any unlawful business on the premises, nor to permit the premises to be occupied for any business deemed extra hazardous on account of fire." Id.

About a month into the lease, the Iowa legislature passed a statute declaring as a nuisance the storage of rags "within the fire limits of any city, unless it be in a building of fireproof construction." Id. at 821, 174 N.W. at 573. The statute applied to the lessees because the premises were within the fire limits of the city and were not of fireproof construction. Id. For this reason, the lessees claimed the statute made its business unlawful, exposed them to criminal prosecution, and deprived them of any substantial or beneficial use of the property thereby releasing them from further obligation to pay rent. Id.

This court rejected the lessees' contention and affirmed a directed verdict in favor of the plaintiff-lessor for the unpaid rent. There was evidence that the lessee also dealt in junk metal. For this reason the court concluded:

> Altogether, we are satisfied that, while the operation of the statute mentioned served to narrow or restrict, to some extent, the scope of the business of the lessees, we think the evidence is insufficient to sustain a finding that it deprives them of the beneficial use of the leased property; and, as the defense is an affirmative one, the burden of establishing which is upon the party pleading it, the trial court did not err in refusing to submit it to the verdict of the jury. Id. at 822, 174 N.W. at 574.

The court continued:

> [T]he right to buy, sell, store, and ship junk metals of all kinds, not only in the building but upon the entire lot, is not, in any sense, a mere incident of the rag business, and that a loss of the privilege of using the building for the handling of rags does not deprive the lessees of the beneficial enjoyment of the property for the other specified uses. It may possibly render the use less valuable or less profitable, but there is no rule or principle of law that makes that fact a matter of defense or of counterclaim in an action upon the lease. Id. at 822–23, 174 N.W. at 574.

The Restatement and Conklin represent the prevailing view:

> The parties to a lease may lawfully agree or stipulate that if by reason of a subsequent prohibitory or restrictive statute, ordinance, or administrative ruling, the tenant is prevented from legally using the premises for the purpose for which it was contemplated, the tenant may surrender or terminate the lease

for which it was contemplated and be relieved from further liability for rent. In the absence of such a provision for termination, however, there is some uncertainty as to the effect of subsequent legal prohibition or restriction on the use of the premises. *It may generally be said that in the absence of any such stipulation, a valid police regulation which forbids the use of rented property for certain purposes, but leaves the tenant free to devote the property to other legal uses not forbidden or restricted by the terms of the lease, does not invalidate the lease or affect the rights and liabilities of the parties to the lease. And, even though the lease by its terms restricts the tenant's use of the premises to certain specified purposes, but not to a single purpose, the prevailing view is that the subsequent enactment of the legislation prohibiting the use of the premises for one, or less than all, of the several purposes specified does not invalidate the lease or justify the tenant in abandoning the property, even though the legislation may render its use less valuable. If there is a serviceable use for which the property is still available consistent with the limitations of the demise, the tenant is not in a position to assert that it is totally deprived of the benefit of the tenancy.*

49 Am. Jur. 2d Landlord & Tenant § 531, at 442–43 (1995) (emphasis added).

Based on the foregoing authorities, we reach the following conclusions. A subsequent governmental regulation like a statute or ordinance may prohibit a tenant from legally using the premises for its originally intended purpose. In these circumstances, the tenant's purpose is substantially frustrated thereby relieving the tenant from any further obligation to pay rent. The tenant is not relieved from the obligation to pay rent if there is a serviceable use still available consistent with the use provision in the lease. The fact that the use is less valuable or less profitable or even unprofitable does not mean the tenant's use has been substantially frustrated.

C.   The Merits

It is clear from the pleadings and testimony that Di-Chem was asserting a defense of frustration of purpose. Di-Chem had the burden of persuasion to prove that defense. See Conklin, 187 Iowa at 822, 174 N.W. at 574. The district court's decision in favor of Mel Frank is a determination that Di-Chem did not carry its burden on this defense.

Di-Chem produced no evidence that all of its inventory of chemicals consisted of hazardous material. In fact, its own correspondence to Mel Frank indicates otherwise. For example, Di-Chem's October 23 letter to Mel Frank stated: "The city's position that we cannot legally store *all* of our inventory at this site prior to extensive alteration of the building makes the structure useless to us as a chemical warehouse." (Emphasis added.) A reasonable inference from this statement is that not all Di-Chem's inventory consisted of hazardous material.

Testimony from one of Di-Chem's representatives corroborates this inference:

Q. Were you involved at all in the discussions with the City of Council Bluffs relative to the various code deficiencies that existed at the building?

A. My involvement was that the city had pointed out that there was some deficiencies with the building and asked us to remove *what* chemicals they found objective.

(Emphasis added.)

Another Di-Chem representative testified that Di-Chem's product line included industrial chemicals and food additives. Presumably, food additives are not hazardous materials.

Given the posture of this appeal, Di-Chem has to establish as a matter of law that its principal purpose for leasing the facility—storing and distributing chemicals—was substantially frustrated by the city's actions. Di-Chem presented no evidence as to the nature of its inventory and what percentage of the inventory consisted of hazardous chemicals. The company also failed to show what its lost profits, if any, would be without the hazardous chemicals. Thus, there is no evidence from which the district court could have found the city's actions substantially frustrated Di-Chem's principal purpose of storing and distributing chemicals. Put another way, there is insufficient evidence that the city's action deprived Di-Chem of the beneficial enjoyment of the property for other uses, i.e., storing and distributing non-hazardous chemicals.

Simply put, Di-Chem failed to establish its affirmative defense of what it has termed impossibility. We must therefore affirm the district court's decision as to this issue.

V. LEASE LANGUAGE

Di-Chem also relies on language in the lease which it claims releases it from further obligation to pay rent. The language is found in clause 13 of the lease, which is entitled "Fire and Casualty, Partial Destruction of Premises," and provides:

(a) In the event of a partial destruction or damage of the leased premises, which is a business interference, that is, which prevents the conducting of a normal business operation and which damage is reasonably repairable within sixty (60) days after its occurrence, this lease shall not terminate but the rent for the leased premises shall abate during the time of such business interference. In the event of partial destruction, Landlord shall repair such damages within 60 days of its occurrence unless prevented from so doing by acts of God, the elements . . . or other causes beyond Landlord's reasonable control.

(b) Zoning. Should the zoning ordinance of the city . . . make it impossible for Landlord, using diligent and timely effort to obtain necessary permits and to repair and/or rebuild so that Tenant is not able to conduct its business on these premises, then such partial destruction shall be treated as a total destruction as in the next paragraph provided.

(c) Total Destruction of Business Use. In the event of a destruction or damage of the leased premises . . . so that Tenant is not able to conduct its business on the premises or the then current legal use for which the premises are being used and which damages cannot be repaired within sixty (60) days this lease may be terminated at the option of either the Landlord or Tenant. Such termination in such event shall be effected by written notice of one party to the other, within twenty (20) days after such destruction. Tenant shall surrender possession within ten (10) days after such notice issues, and each party shall be released from all future obligations hereunder. . . .

Di-Chem contends that because it was not able to store and distribute the hazardous chemicals, it was "not able to conduct its business on the premises," as specified in clause 13(b). Di-Chem concludes, therefore, that a "total destruction of business use" occurred in accordance with clause 13(c) and for that reason each party was released from all future obligations under the lease.

There is not even a hint of recognition of clause 13 in the district court's ruling. The reason is obvious: clause 13 simply does not apply to the facts of this case. Clause 13 must be read in its entirety and construed in context.

As the title in clause 13 suggests, the clause's language covers the situation where there has been a temporary interruption of the tenant's business because of a partial destruction of the premises. In these circumstances, the lease gives the landlord a period of time to repair or rebuild. During this period the tenant's rent abates but the lease continues in force.

Clause 13 also covers the situation where the landlord cannot rebuild or repair the premises because of some zoning prohibition. A common example involves a nonconforming use. Typically, zoning ordinances prohibit an owner from rebuilding if, for example, fifty percent of the building has been destroyed. In these circumstances, the tenant cannot legally continue in business on the premises and for this reason the lease considers the tenant's business use has been totally destroyed. In this situation, both the landlord and the tenant have the option to terminate the lease with no further obligation on either's part.

One cannot reasonably interpret clause 13 to cover the situation where a subsequent governmental regulation prohibits the use of the premises for one of several purposes specified in the lease. The district court was correct in ignoring clause 13. . . .

VII. DISPOSITION.

In sum, we conclude Di-Chem has failed to establish—as a matter of law—that it is entitled to relief via its impossibility defense or the terms of the lease. The district court's erroneous finding that the real estate agent represented Di-Chem was harmless. We affirm.

AFFIRMED.

NOTES AND QUESTIONS

1.   *Supervening   impracticability   by   governmental   regulation.* Restatement (Second) of Contracts § 261 provides that a party's duty to perform is discharged when made "impracticable" by a supervening event occurring without fault of the discharged party and the non-occurrence of which was a basic assumption of the contract. Restatement (Second) of Contracts § 264 states a specific instance in which the non-occurrence of a supervening event was a basic assumption of the contract, namely the assumption that applicable law will not change to prevent the promised performances. Restatement (Second) of Contracts § 264, *cmt. a* provides: "It is a 'basic assumption on which the contract was made' that the law will not intervene to make performance impracticable when it is due." The fact that it is "possible" for a party to perform if that party breaks the law is irrelevant.

Restatement (Second) of Contracts § 261 clearly provides that a supervening event will not discharge performance if the "language or circumstances" indicate that performance is not to be discharged notwithstanding the occurrence of an otherwise qualifying supervening change in governmental regulations or orders. In such a case, the affected party essentially agrees or assumes the risk of foregoing the legal excuse and paying damages for the resulting unexcused breach by failure to perform. Restatement (Second) of Contracts § 264, *cmt. b* makes clear that the governmental regulation may emanate from any level of government and disregards distinctions between "law," "regulation," and "order."

It was clear that the city amended its Fire Code after execution of the lease. The lease prohibited any unlawful use of the premises, but at the time of the lease the Fire Code apparently did not prohibit storage of hazardous materials. Indeed, if Mel Frank made certain changes to the building (sprinkler, exhaust, spill, and drainage), the hazardous materials could continue to be stored on the premises. But it is equally clear that the hazardous materials could not be stored after the Fire Code amendments without improvements and repairs to the building. Arguably, then, the issue in this case boils down to whether the lease required Mel Frank to make the alterations and, if not, was Di-Chem excused from the lease because it could not continue to store hazardous materials. The parties discussed but failed to agree on the necessary alterations, and Di-Chem vacated the premises believing further performance was excused on the basis of impracticability from supervening change in governmental regulations.

Does the court accept the impracticability doctrine as stated in Restatement (Second) of Contracts §§ 261 and 264? If so, why did Di-Chem lose? Was it clear that a basic assumption of the contract at the time of formation included the notion that supervening governmental regulation would not prohibit Di-Chem from using the building for its intended purpose of "storage and distribution"? Is the storage of hazardous materials "storage" within the meaning of the lease language? Is it relevant that Mel Frank did not know exactly what type of materials were to be stored on the premises, provided such storage was legal at the time the lease was executed? Was the case decided on the basis of Restatement (Second) of Contracts §§ 261 and 264? Did the change in the Fire Code prevent the property from being used for "storage and distribution"?

2. *Supervening frustration.* Assuming for the moment that the change in the Fire Code did not prevent the premises from being used for "storage and distribution," then the Restatement (Second) of Contracts §§ 261 and 264 impracticability legal excuse is not available to Di-Chem. Stated another way, the premises remain available for use in accordance with the terms of the lease. If so, why do the court and Di-Chem shift analysis to Restatement (Second) of Contracts § 265 and discharge by frustration of purpose? Di-Chem now argues its purpose in leasing the premises (to store hazardous materials) has been frustrated by a supervening event (change in the Fire Code). This appears to be quite true and yet Di-Chem once again loses. Why?

Recall the early roots of the frustration doctrine in *Krell v. Henry.* The landlord leased the premises to the tenant for the specific known purpose of viewing the coronation. In this case, was Mel Frank aware that Di-Chem leased the premises primarily to legally store hazardous chemicals? Assuming that was Di-Chem's principal or primary purpose, would frustration depend upon Mel Frank's knowledge of the same?

3. *Lease language.* Di-Chem also argued particular lease language allocated the risk of the supervening change to Mel Frank. The lease clause referenced was set forth under a section titled "Fire and Casualty, Partial Destruction of Premises." Were any portion of the premises affected by fire, casualty, or partially destroyed?

4. *UCC frustration.* Does UCC § 2–615 cover frustration of purpose or only impracticability? If the latter, is it possible to make a frustration argument in a case governed by the UCC? If so, how would you do so?

C. DISCHARGE OF DUTY BY ASSENT OR MODIFICATION

At some point in their relationship, the parties to a contract may mutually agree to discharge or alter their respective duties under the contract. This section deals with several mechanisms by which the parties may alter or rearrange their contractual relationships after contract formation, including:

- Rescission;
- Executory bilateral accords (also known as accord and satisfaction); and
- Substituted contracts.

Rescission addresses situations in which the parties simply wish to terminate all future contractual relationships. If so, the parties could simply mutually agree to rescind, terminate, or cancel their initial agreement and discharge all contractual duties created. See Restatement (Second) of Contracts § 283(2) ("An agreement of rescission discharges all remaining duties of performance of both parties."). Mutual rescission agreements typically create little conceptual or legal difficulty, even when an oral agreement purports to rescind a prior written agreement within the Statute of Frauds. Restatement (Second) of Contracts § 149(1) (transfer of real property). But see Restatement (Second) of Contracts § 283(2) ("It is a question of interpretation whether the parties also agree to make restitution with respect to performance that has been rendered."). Other situations, such as where a supervening event has changed the relative benefits and obligations of the parties, the parties may wish to preserve the contractual relationship itself but modify some or all of the terms of that relationship. In many such supervening event situations, the unforeseen event might have legally excused the party from its obligation to continue to perform under the materials discussed above. But often the parties react to changed circumstances by modifying the original contract after formation to preserve the contractual relationship—particularly where the increased burdens are shared and modest. Typically such agreements contemplate that one of the parties will voluntarily assume an increased duty as compensation to the other party for agreeing to continue to perform notwithstanding the unforeseen event. In that case, the parties may agree to a new contract that simultaneously discharges any prior agreements and creates a new set of contractual rights and duties different from the prior agreement. Where both parties consent to discharge and new terms, their new agreement fully satisfies all the requirements of contract formation, including manifestations of mutual assent and a bargained-for exchange of considerations. As with rescission agreements, such bilateral modifications typically present few analytical difficulties. But agreements purporting to modify the duties of only one of the parties because of some unforeseen supervening event create significant enforceability problems. See Subha Narasimhan, "Modification: The Self-Help Specific Performance Remedy," 97 Yale L. J. 61 (1987).

If enforceable, in legal terms the bilateral modification causes two connected events. First, the parties have mutually rescinded the original contract. Accordingly, the duties created by the initial contract are discharged. However, with modification, a second event occurs in the form of a new contract with its modified duties substituted for the initial contract duties. This section considers the enforceability of the modified contract. If the parties fail to modify properly, the initial contract may remain enforceable because the parties never legally discharged their duties under that contract.

Thus, the legal enforceability of a modification is critical in determining which set of rights and duties govern the parties' relationship—the original contract or the modification. Chapter 7 considered whether a promisor of a modified contract could rescind the modified contract (normally a release) because of economic duress and enforce the terms of the original contract. See Restatement (Second) of Contracts §§ 175 (duress by threat makes a contract voidable) and 176 (improper threat includes threat of crime, tort, criminal prosecution, bad faith abuse of civil process, and breach of good faith and fair dealing). An action for rescission based on economic duress assumes the modified contract is enforceable absent the action for rescission.

This section considers the initial enforceability of the purportedly modified contract in two contexts. The first—an "executory bilateral accord"—considers the duty discharged in the future, but only upon completion of "satisfaction" of an accord agreement. Restatement (Second) of Contracts § 281(1) ("An accord is a contract under which an obligee promises to accept a stated performance in satisfaction of the obligor's existing duty."). The accord agreement thus does not discharge an obligor's duty, but rather merely suspends that duty until the obligor fulfills the terms of the satisfaction. The obligor's breach of the satisfaction terms entitles the obligee to elect to sue for breach of either the original contract or the executory accord agreement. Restatement (Second) of Contracts § 281(2). This has enormous consequences with regard to the settlement of lawsuits and is amplified in the *Clark* case below.

The second context deals with "substituted contracts" under which an obligee accepts the substituted contract in satisfaction of the obligor's duty under the original contract. Restatement (Second) of Contracts § 279(1). If the substituted contract involves the substitution of another party to release the original obligor, the substituted contract results in a "novation." Restatement (Second) of Contracts § 280. A "substituted contract" immediately discharges the original duty, and, if the obligor breaches the substituted contract, the obligee may sue only to enforce the substituted contract duty. Restatement (Second) of Contracts § 279(2). The critical difference between an executory bilateral accord and a substituted contract concerns when the obligor's duty under the original contract is discharged. An executory bilateral accord discharges an obligor's duty under the original agreement only upon a later satisfaction of the terms of the accord. A substituted contract discharges the obligor's duties under the original contract immediately upon execution.

The difference in timing of the discharge of the obligor's duty raises significant issues for the obligee. Under an executory bilateral accord, if the obligor fails to satisfy—i.e., breaches—the terms of the accord, the obligee may elect to enforce either the original agreement or the executory bilateral accord upon failure of later satisfaction. However, under a substituted contract, the obligee may never enforce the original contract and must exclusively enforce the substituted contract. Because of this stark difference, classification difficulties result where the parties fail to clearly specify the modified contract is an executory bilateral accord or a substituted contract. In these cases, a court must interpret the language of the modified contract to determine its intended character in accordance with the rules of interpretation and construction discussed in Chapter 4. However, many courts presume that a modified contract is an executory bilateral accord, rather than a substituted contract. This presumption preserves the interests of the obligee that never received either the promised original or modified satisfaction. Restatement (Second) of Contracts § 281, *cmt. e.* ("In resolving doubts in this regard, a court is less likely to conclude that an obligee was willing to accept a mere promise in satisfaction of an original duty that was clear than in satisfaction of one that was doubtful.").

Regardless of whether a court classifies the modified contract as an executory bilateral accord or a substituted contract, the modified contract must be supported by consideration to be enforceable. See Restatement (Second) of Contracts § 279, *cmt. b* and Restatement (Second) of Contracts § 281, *cmt. d.* Like many aspects of consideration doctrine discussed at length in Chapter 2, the evolution of consideration doctrine in the context of modified contracts has a tortured history. In broad general terms, the common law "preexisting legal duty rule," together with myriad exceptions, prohibits any modification without consideration. Given that the requirement that every modification be supported by some additional consideration likely flies in the face of most contracting parties' reasonable expectations, this rule appears tailor-made for permitting parties to escape otherwise valid obligations. Indeed, some regard the preexisting legal duty rule as the primary villain giving the consideration doctrine its poor reputation in modern contract law. Edwin W. Patterson, "An Apology for Consideration," 58 Colum. L. Rev. 929, 936 (1958). UCC Article 2 eliminates the preexisting legal duty rule and requires only that modifications be made in good faith. See UCC § 2–209(1) ("An agreement modifying a contract within this Article needs no consideration to be binding.") and *cmt. 2* ("[M]odifications . . . must meet the test of good faith imposed by this Act.").

The preexisting legal duty rule essentially provides that an obligee receives absolutely no legal consideration (not even a peppercorn) for an obligor's promise to render "exactly the same" performance required by the original contract. After all, why would an obligee voluntarily agree to pay more for exactly the same performance required by the original contract? One explanation of course is economic coercion. The sequence of performances under a contract—such as where a builder receives the bulk of payment in advance, completes half of the project, and then threatens to abandon the project if the owner does not agree to increased compensation—may create opportunities for opportunistic exploitation in the form of a mid-performance threat not to complete performance without a promise of additional compensation. Even if the substituted performance is somewhat different, such "hold-up" contracts are not voluntarily formed, and often are subject to rescission on grounds of "economic duress" discussed in Chapter 7. But that the threats and opportunistic behavior do not give rise to an economic duress claim, is the modified agreement nonetheless enforceable? Does the mere making of a modification imply enforceability, or does the modified agreement require independent consideration?

The answer depends upon whether the matter is governed by common law or the UCC. As noted above, the UCC has abandoned the preexisting legal duty rule and merely requires modifications to be made in good faith. The common law still clutches to the remnants of the ancient preexisting legal duty rule and thus requires "fresh" consideration for the modified contract. The new consideration, if it exists, will be found in the bargain for the obligor's promise of new or modified performance. An obligor's promise to render exactly the same performance as required under the old contract in "exchange" for greater payment from the obligee is merely gratuitous and will not supply the necessary consideration. Common law therefore continues to examine the comparative nature of the obligor's original and modified performance obligations in a search for a peppercorn. As discussed in Chapter 2, the modern bargain theory of consideration generally does not examine the fairness or equivalency of the exchanged considerations. It is enough that the obligee truly sought the modified promise of performance. Compare Restatement (Second) of Contracts §§ 71 (bargain and sought), with 79 (adequacy of consideration).

According to this analysis, if the obligor's modified promise of performance does not differ from that originally promised, the obligor may not enforce the obligee's return modified promise. Restatement (Second) of

Contracts § 73. Moreover, while a different performance may arise from the ashes of a doubtful original promised performance now subject to an honest dispute regarding its nature and extent, a mere pretense of a bargain will not do. Restatement (Second) of Contracts § 73. This "doctrine of difference" is similarly reflected in the modified contract context. Restatement (Second) of Contracts § 278 (a duty is discharged if the obligee accepts the obligor's offer of a performance that "differs from what is due" and is therefore referred to as qualifying "substituted performance").

Outside the context of economic duress situations, subsequent events may create hardship and unfairness on the obligor. Near miss and failed impracticability and frustration cases illustrate this situation nicely. Although changed circumstances may not support a supervening event defense, the required performance may change so radically that the obligor may refuse to continue without some compensatory change in the contract. In the face of such a refusal, the obligee may sue for breach of contract or anticipatory repudiation and/or seek a substitute performance from a third party. But lawsuits and substituted performance—i.e., mitigation—are expensive, cause delays, and interfere with long-term business relationships and reputation. Consequently, the obligee may—begrudgingly—agree to modify the original contract to secure performance at less cost than seeking substitute performance from a third party and a suit for money damages from the original obligor. Again assuming that the obligor's demand for a modification does not constitute economic duress, these situations represent the best test cases for strict application of the formalist preexisting legal duty rule or a more flexible rule respecting the parties' private ordering.

Fortunately, while common law retains the preexisting legal duty rule, it has also developed mitigating doctrines. The most important specifically addresses situations under which the common law will enforce a modification of an executory contract notwithstanding the absence of consideration (because of the preexisting legal duty rule). In cases not involving unfair pressure, Restatement (Second) of Contracts § 89(a) provides that a promise modifying an executory duty (not fully performed) is binding notwithstanding the absence of consideration provided the modification is "fair and equitable" in view of circumstances "not anticipated" when the contract was formed.

1. DOCTRINAL DEVELOPMENT

Modern applications of the "fresh" consideration necessary to make modification promises enforceable have narrowed the historic pre-existing legal duty rule. While UCC § 2–209(1) rejects the necessity of fresh consideration and the pre-existing legal duty rule entirely, common law fragments remain. See Restatement (Second) of Contracts § 73. Mostly, common law searches for any meaningful difference from the duty to be performed under the original contract as the bargained-for consideration supporting the modified promise. See Restatement (Second) of Contracts § 73 ("[A] similar performance is consideration if it differs from what was required by the duty in a way which reflects more than the pretense of a bargain."). Other theories of obligation also narrow the effect of the pre-existing legal duty rule, including unanticipated circumstances and material change in position in reliance on the promise. See Restatement (Second) of Contracts § 89.

The next three cases consider the modern pre-existing legal duty rule in different contexts. The next section assumes the existence of a valid theory of obligation, but it explores whether some remnant of the Statute of Frauds precludes enforcement.

a.   Preexisting Legal Duty Rule

The preexisting legal duty rule has caused considerable tension in contract law. As the original guardian of unjustified "hold up" cases where one party refused to complete performance unless the other party paid more for originally contracted services, the doctrine soon expanded to cover cases where an honest dispute existed regarding the nature of the original services. Modern contract law considers "hold up" cases under the economic duress doctrine discussed in Chapter 7. But what remains of the common law preexisting legal duty rule in other cases? Some have argued that the common law consideration requirement for modifications should be abandoned (like UCC § 2–209(1)) and to use the economic duress doctrine to police abusive behavior involving an unwarranted threat to breach a contract. Kevin M. Teevan, "Consensual Path to Abolition of Preexisting Duty Rule," 34 Val. U. L. Rev. 43 (1999). Others argue that economic analysis supports the use of economic duress doctrine to police empty threats. Daniel A. Graham and Ellen R. Peirce, "Contract Modification: An Economic Analysis of the Hold-Up Game," 52 Law & Contemp. Probs. 9 (1989). Do you agree?

ANGEL V. MURRAY

Supreme Court of Rhode Island
113 R.I. 482, 322 A.2d 630 (1974)

ROBERTS, Chief Justice.

This is a civil action brought by Alfred L. Angel and others against John E. Murray, Jr., Director of Finance of the City of Newport, the city of Newport, and James L. Maher, alleging that Maher had illegally been paid the sum of $20,000 by the Director of Finance and praying that the defendant Maher be ordered to repay the city such sum. The case was heard by a justice of the Superior Court, sitting without a jury, who entered a judgment ordering Maher to repay the sum of $20,000 to the city of Newport. Maher is now before this court prosecuting an appeal.

The record discloses that Maher has provided the city of Newport with a refuse-collection service under a series of five-year contracts beginning in 1946. On March 12, 1964, Maher and the city entered into another such contract for a period of five years commencing on July 1, 1964, and terminating on June 30, 1969. The contract provided, among other things, that Maher would receive $137,000 per year in return for collecting and removing all combustible and noncombustible waste materials generated within the city.

In June of 1967 Maher requested an additional $10,000 per year from the city council because there had been a substantial increase in the cost of collection due to an unexpected and unanticipated increase of 400 new dwelling units. Maher's testimony, which is uncontradicted, indicates the 1964 contract had been predicated on the fact that since 1946 there had been an average increase of 20 to 25 new dwelling units per year. After a public meeting of the city council where Maher explained in detail the reasons for his request and was questioned by members of the city council, the city council agreed to pay him an additional $10,000 for the year ending on June 30, 1968. Maher made a similar request again in June of 1968 for the same reasons, and the city council again agreed to pay an additional $10,000 for the year ending on June 30, 1969.

The trial justice found that each such $10,000 payment was made in violation of law. His decision, as we understand it, is premised on two independent grounds. First, he found that the additional payments were unlawful because they had not been recommended in writing to the city council by the city manager. Second, he found that Maher was not entitled to extra compensation because the original contract already required him to collect all refuse generated within the city and, therefore, included the 400 additional units. The trial justice further found that these 400 additional units were within the contemplation of the parties when they entered into the contract. It appears that he based this portion of the decision upon the rule that Maher had a preexisting duty to collect the refuse generated by the 400 additional units, and thus there was no consideration for the two additional payments.

I.

[Eds.—The Court determined the city council had the power to modify the contract.]

II.

Having found that the city council had the power to modify the 1964 contract without the written recommendation of the city manager, we are still confronted with the question of whether the additional payments were illegal because they were not supported by consideration.

A.

As previously stated, the city council made two $10,000 payments. The first was made in June of 1967 for the year beginning on July 1, 1967, and ending on June 30, 1968. Thus, by the time this action was commenced in October of 1968, the modification was completely executed. That is, the money had been paid by the city council, and Maher had collected all of the refuse. Since consideration is only a test of the enforceability of executory promises, the presence or absence of consideration for the first payment is unimportant because the city council's agreement to make the first payment was fully executed at the time of the commencement of this action. See Salvas v. Jussaume, 50 R.I. 75, 145 A. 97 (1929). . . . However, since both payments were made under similar circumstances, our decision regarding the second payment (Part B, infra) is fully applicable to the first payment.

B.

It is generally held that a modification of a contract is itself a contract, which is unenforceable unless supported by consideration. See Simpson, supra, § 93. In Rose v. Daniels, 8 R.I. 381 (1866), this court held that an agreement by a debtor with a creditor to discharge a debt for a sum of money less than the amount due is unenforceable because it was not supported by consideration.

Rose is a perfect example of the preexisting duty rule. Under this rule an agreement modifying a contract is not supported by consideration if one of the parties to the agreement does or promises to do something that he is legally obligated to do or refrains or promises to refrain from doing something he is not legally privileged to do. . . . In Rose there was no consideration for the new agreement because the debtor was already legally obligated to repay the full amount of the debt.

Although the preexisting duty rule is followed by most jurisdictions, a small minority of jurisdictions, Massachusetts, for example, find that there is consideration for a promise to perform what one is already legally obligated to do because the new promise is given in place of an action for damages to secure performance. See Swartz v. Lieberman, 323 Mass. 109, 80 N.E.2d 5 (1948). . . . Swartz is premised on the theory that a promisor's forbearance of the power to breach his original agreement and be sued in an action for damages is consideration for a subsequent agreement by the promisee to pay extra compensation. This rule, however, has been widely criticized as an anomaly. . . .

The primary purpose of the preexisting duty rule is to prevent what has been referred to as the "hold-up game." See 1A Corbin, supra, § 171. A classic example of the "hold-up game" is found in Alaska Packers' Ass'n v. Domenico, 117 F. 99 (9th Cir. 1902). There 21 seamen entered into a written contract with Domenico to sail from San Francisco to Pyramid Harbor, Alaska. They were to work as sailors and fishermen out of Pyramid Harbor during the fishing season of 1900. The contract specified that each man would be paid $50 plus two cents for each red salmon he caught. Subsequent to their arrival at Pyramid Harbor, the men stopped work and demanded an additional $50. They threatened to return to San Francisco if Domenico did not agree to their demand. Since it was impossible for Domenico to find other men, he agreed to pay the men an additional $50. After they returned to San Francisco, Domenico refused to pay the men an additional $50. The court found that the subsequent agreement to pay the men an additional $50 was not supported by consideration because the men had a preexisting duty to work on the ship under the original contract, and thus the subsequent agreement was unenforceable.

Another example of the "hold-up game" is found in the area of construction contracts. Frequently, a contractor will refuse to complete work under an unprofitable contract unless he is awarded additional compensation. The courts have generally held that a subsequent agreement to award additional compensation is unenforceable if the contractor is only performing work that would have been required of him under the original contract. See, e.g., Lingenfelder v. Wainwright Brewing Co., 103 Mo. 578, 15 S.W. 844 (1891), which is a leading case in this area. . . .

These examples clearly illustrate that the courts will not enforce an agreement that has been procured by coercion or duress and will hold the parties to their original contract regardless of whether it is profitable or unprofitable. However, the courts have been reluctant to apply the preexisting duty rule when a party to a contract encounters unanticipated difficulties and the other party, not influenced by coercion or duress, voluntarily agrees to pay additional compensation for work already required to be performed under the contract. For example, the courts have found that the original contract was rescinded . . . ; abandoned, . . . or waived.

Although the preexisting duty rule has served a useful purpose insofar as it deters parties from using coercion and duress to obtain additional compensation, it has been widely criticized as a general rule of law. With regard to the preexisting duty rule, one legal scholar has stated:

> There has been a growing doubt as to the soundness of this doctrine as a matter of social policy. . . . In certain classes of cases, this doubt has influenced courts to refuse to apply the rule, or to ignore it, in their actual decisions. Like other legal rules, this rule is in process of growth and change, the process being more active

here than in most instances. The result of this is that a court should no longer accept this rule as fully established. It should never use it as the major premise of a decision, at least without giving careful thought to the circumstances of the particular case, to the moral deserts of the parties, and to the social feelings and interests that are involved. It is certain that the rule, stated in general and all-inclusive terms, is no longer so well settled that a court must apply it though the heavens fall. 1A Corbin, supra, § 171; see also Calamari & Perillo, supra, § 61.

The modern trend appears to recognize the necessity that courts should enforce agreements modifying contracts when unexpected or unanticipated difficulties arise during the course of the performance of a contract, even though there is no consideration for the modification, as long as the parties agree voluntarily.

Under the Uniform Commercial Code, § 2–209(1), which has been adopted by 49 states, "(a)n agreement modifying a contract (for the sale of goods) needs no consideration to be binding." See G. L. 1956 (1969 Reenactment) § 6A–2–209(1). Although at first blush this section appears to validate modifications obtained by coercion and duress, the comments to this section indicate that a modification under this section must meet the test of good faith imposed by the Code, and a modification obtained by extortion without a legitimate commercial reason is unenforceable.

The modern trend away from a rigid application of the preexisting duty rule is reflected by s 89D(a) of the American Law Institute's Restatement Second of the Law of Contracts,[1] which provides: "A promise modifying a duty under a contract not fully performed on either side is binding (a) if the modification is fair and equitable in view of circumstances not anticipated by the parties when the contract was made. . . ."

We believe that § 89D(a) is the proper rule of law and find it applicable to the facts of this case. It not only prohibits modifications obtained by coercion, duress, or extortion but also fulfills society's expectation that agreements entered into voluntarily will be enforced by the courts.[3] See

---

[1] The first nine chapters of the Restatement Second of the Law of Contracts were given tentative approval by the American Law Institute at successive meetings from 1964 to 1972. These chapters, that include §§ 1–255, were published by the Institute in 1973 in a hard-cover edition. Herbert Wechsler, Director of the Institute, in a foreword to this edition indicates that although these sections are still tentative and await final approval, it is unlikely that any further changes will be made.

[3] The drafters of s 89D(a) of the Restatement Second of the Law of Contracts use the following illustrations in comment (b) as examples of how this rule is applied to certain transactions:

> 1. By a written contract A agrees to excavate a cellar for B for a stated price. Solid rock is unexpectedly encountered and A so notifies B. A and B then orally agree that A will remove the rock at a unit price which is reasonable but nine times that used in computing the original price, and A completes the job. B is bound to pay the increased amount.

generally Horwitz, The Historical Foundations of Modern Contract Law, 87 Harv. L. Rev. 917 (1974). Section 89D(a), of course, does not compel a modification of an unprofitable or unfair contract; it only enforces a modification if the parties voluntarily agree and if (1) the promise modifying the original contract was made before the contract was fully performed on either side, (2) the underlying circumstances which prompted the modification were unanticipated by the parties, and (3) the modification is fair and equitable.

The evidence, which is uncontradicted, reveals that in June of 1968 Maher requested the city council to pay him an additional $10,000 for the year beginning on July 1, 1968, and ending on June 30, 1969. This request was made at a public meeting of the city council, where Maher explained in detail his reasons for making the request. Thereafter, the city council voted to authorize the Mayor to sign an amendment to the 1964 contract which provided that Maher would receive an additional $10,000 per year for the duration of the contract. Under such circumstances we have no doubt that the city voluntarily agreed to modify the 1964 contract.

Having determined the voluntariness of this agreement, we turn our attention to the three criteria delineated above. First, the modification was made in June of 1968 at a time when the five-year contract which was made in 1964 had not been fully performed by either party. Second, although the 1964 contract provided that Maher collect all refuse generated within the city, it appears this contract was premised on Maher's past experience that the number of refuse-generating units would increase at a rate of 20 to 25 per year. Furthermore, the evidence is uncontradicted that the 1967–1968 increase of 400 units "went beyond any previous expectation." Clearly, the circumstances that prompted the city council to modify the 1964 contract

---

2. A contracts with B to supply for $300 a laundry chute for a building B has contracted to build for the Government for $150,000. Later A discovers that he made an error as to the type of material to be used and should have bid $1,200. A offers to supply the chute for $1,000, eliminating overhead and profit. After ascertaining that other suppliers would charge more, B agrees. The new agreement is binding.

3. A is employed by B as a designer of coats at $90 a week for a year beginning November 1 under a written contract executed September 1. A is offered $115 a week by another employer and so informs B. A and B then agree that A will be paid $100 a week and in October execute a new written contract to that effect, simultaneously tearing up the prior contract. The new contract is binding.

4. A contracts to manufacture and sell to B 2,000 steel roofs for corn cribs at $60. Before A begins manufacture a threat of a nationwide steel strike raises the cost of steel about $10 per roof, and A and B agree orally to increase the price to $70 per roof. A thereafter manufactures and delivers 1,700 of the roofs, and B pays for 1,500 of them at the increased price without protest, increasing the selling price of the corn cribs by $10. The new agreement is binding.

5. A contracts to manufacture and sell to B 100,000 castings for lawn mowers at 50 cents each. After partial delivery and after B has contracted to sell a substantial number of lawn mowers at a fixed price, A notifies B that increased metal costs require that the price be increased to 75 cents. Substitute castings are available at 55 cents, but only after several months delay. B protests but is forced to agree to the new price to keep its plant in operation. The modification is not binding.

were unanticipated.[4] Third, although the evidence does not indicate what proportion of the total this increase comprised, the evidence does indicate that it was a "substantial" increase. In light of this, we cannot say that the council's agreement to pay Maher the $10,000 increase was not fair and equitable in the circumstances.

It is clearly a contractual provision requiring the contractor to hold the city harmless and to defend it in any litigation arising out of the performance of his obligations under the contract, whether a result of affirmative action or some omission or neglect on the part of Maher or his agents or employees. We are persuaded that the portion of sec. 2(a) specifically referred to by the court refers to losses resulting to Maher from some action or omission on the part of his own agents or employees. It cannot be disputed, however, that any losses that resulted from an increase in the cost of collecting from the increased number of units generating refuse in no way resulted from any action on the part of either Maher or his employees. Rather, whatever losses he did entail by reason of the requirement of such extra collection resulted from actions completely beyond his control and thus unanticipated.

The judgment appealed from is reversed, and the cause is remanded to the Superior Court for entry of judgment for the defendants.

NOTES AND QUESTIONS

1. *Effect of full performance.* Before exploring the enforceability of an executory contract, the court notes that the city had performed its first promise to pay an additional $10,000 in June 1967. A fully performed promise is no longer "executory." The Court noted that " . . . consideration is only a test of the enforceability of executory promises, [and] the presence or absence of consideration for the first payment is unimportant because the city council's agreement to make the first payment was fully executed at the time of the commencement of this action." Chapter 2 explored consideration cases involving payments in a continuing executory contract. In those cases (e.g., *Webb v. McGowin*), the promisor attempted to use consideration doctrine as a shield to terminate future payments, not to seek a return of past payments. Characteristically, full performance of a promise unsupported by consideration

---

[4] The trial justice found that sec. 2(a) of the 1964 contract precluded Maher from recovering extra compensation for the 400 additional units. Section 2(a) provided:

> The Contractor, haring made his proposal after his own examinations and estimates, shall take all responsibility for, and bear, any losses resulting to him in carrying out the contract; and shall assume the defense of, and hold the City, its agents and employees harmless from all suits and claims arising from the use of any invention, patent, or patent rights, material, labor or implement, by or from any act, omission or neglect of, the Contractor, his agents or employees, in carrying out the contract. (Emphasis added).

The trial justice, quoting the italicized portion of sec. 2(a), found that this section required that any losses incurred in the performance of the contract were Maher's responsibility. In our opinion, however, the trial justice overlooked the thrust of sec. 2(a) when read in its entirety.

is merely a completed "gift" that is generally enforceable upon delivery or performance. Waiver and estoppel provide another equally compelling theory. Once the promise is fully performed, the maker waives or is estopped from using the consideration doctrine as a sword to retrieve past payments. These actions are far more rare than attempts to use the lack of consideration as a shield. See Williston on Contracts § 7.37 (4th Ed. 2006). Do you see why lack of consideration is more effective as a shield against a suit to enforce the promise than as a sword to recover payments already made?

2.   *Modified contract status.* The court notes that a modified contract is a contract itself. If so, what happened to the original contract? Does this analogy suggest that the modification involves a simultaneous two-step process: (1) rescission of the original contract and (2) substitution of a new modified contract? What is the significance of the "substituted contract" concept? Is the importance related to the discharge of duties under the original contract by way of a substitution of the new duty? See Restatement (Second) of Contracts § 279.

3.   *Partial payment of a debt.* As the court notes, the quintessential modern pre-existing legal duty rule concerns enforceability of a creditor's promise to accept less than the full amount of the debt owed to induce a lump-sum payment of less than the full amount owed. Is the creditor then precluded from seeking the remaining unpaid balance from the debtor? If the creditor's promise was not supported by consideration, the promise to accept less than the full amount of the debt is not enforceable. Unless the parties contested or disputed the precise amount of the debt, the preexisting legal duty rule negates consideration, thereby permitting the creditor to accept the partial payment and sue for the balance. Indeed, the preexisting legal duty rule owes its origins to the partial debt payment context. In *Pinnel's Case*, 77 Eng. Rep. 237 (1602), Lord Coke declared in dictum that ". . . payment of a less sum on the [due] day in satisfaction of a greater, cannot be any satisfaction of the whole, because it appears to the judges that by no possibility, a lesser sum can be a satisfaction to the plaintiff for a greater sum . . . [but] . . . the gift of a horse, hawk, or robe . . ." in satisfaction is good. See William S. Hemingway, "The Rule in *Pinnel's Case*," 13 Va. L. Rev. 380 (1927); Joseph Gold, "Present Status of the Rule in *Pinnel's Case*," 30 Ky. L. J. 187 (1942); and James S. Curtin, "The Rule in *Pinnel's Case*: An Historical Analysis of a Legal Anachronism," 22 Loy. L. Rev. 691 (1976). *Pinnel's Case* was memorialized in *Foakes v. Beer*, 9 App. Cas. 605 (1884) when the House of Lords determined that a creditor could recover interest on a judgment even though the full amount of the judgment had been paid in reliance on a promise of complete discharge of the entire debt. See Merton L. Ferson, "Rule in *Foakes v. Beer*," 31 Yale L. J. 15 (1921); William G. Stinson, Jr., Comment, Pre Existing Duty Rule of Foakes v. Beer—A Victory by Default for Stare Decisis, 11 Ariz. L. Rev. 344 (1969); and Janet O'Sullivan, "In Defence of *Foakes v. Beer*," 55 Cambridge L.J. 219 (1996).

Despite the criticism of the rule in debt payment cases, it has remained the generally accepted rule. However, dissatisfaction with the outcome has created exceptions that can nearly eclipse the general rule. For example, nearly any bargained-for consideration in the form of a variation of the debtor's obligation to pay a fixed sum of money on a fixed date will do. Following the "horse, hawk, or robe" limitation of *Pinnel's Case*, courts will enforce the creditor's promise when the debtor's payment obligation is modified in seemingly insignificant ways—substitution of payment forms other than money or acceleration of the payment date.

Importantly, the *Foakes v. Beer* rule only applies to "liquidated claims" where there is no dispute as to the amount due. Where a legitimate dispute exists, the parties have considerable flexibility to resolve and "settle" their dispute under the accord and satisfaction rules discussed in connection with the *Clark* case.

4.   *The seamen hold-up case.* The court refers to *Alaska Packers' Ass'n v. Domenico*, 117 F. 99 (9th Cir. 1902), as a classic example of the "hold-up game." The seamen agreed to serve on a fishing vessel sailing from San Francisco to Alaska. But while in transit they refused to work unless paid additional wages. The captain promised to pay the additional wages upon return to port but then later refused payment after the voyage ended. In a later comment on the case, Judge Posner wrote:

> *Alaska Packers' Ass'n* shows that because the legal remedies for breach of contract are not always adequate, a refusal to honor a contract may force the other party to the contract to surrender his rights—in *Alaska Packers' Ass'n*, the appellant's right to the libelants' labor at the agreed wage. It undermines the institution of contract to allow a contract party to use the threat of breach to get the contract modified in his favor not because anything has happened to require modification in the mutual interest of the parties but simply because the other party, unless he knuckles under to the threat, will incur costs for which he will have no adequate legal remedy. If contractual protections are illusory, people will be reluctant to make contracts. Allowing contract modifications to be voided in circumstances such as those in *Alaska Packers' Ass'n* assures prospective contract parties that signing a contract is not stepping into a trap, and by thus encouraging people to make contracts promotes the efficient allocation of resources. *Selmer Co. v. Blakeslee-Midwest Co.*, 704 F.2d 924, 927 (7th Cir. 1983).

Later, a revealing historical analysis of the records involved in *Alaska Packers' Ass'n*. disclosed that far from a hold-up, the seamen involved in the demand asserted valid claims. It seems that the seamen were mostly native tribes who received lower wages than those of competitors. To make matters worse, the Association nets were less effective, thereby reducing the size of the catch and the resulting wages. See Debora L. Threedy, "A Fish Story: *Alaska Packers' Association v. Domenico*," 2000 Utah L. Rev. 185.

5.   *The absence of coercion and consideration.* The court describes a trend in favor of enforcing contract modifications voluntarily made, even when traditional consideration is absent. Given that the preexisting legal duty rule

renders modifications unenforceable because of a lack of consideration, is the absence of coercion all that is necessary? The court adopts the rationale of Restatement (Second) of Contracts § 89 to enforce the city's promise. However, the preexisting legal duty rule is reflected in Restatement (Second) of Contracts § 73. Could the court have just as easily decided the case under Restatement (Second) of Contracts § 73 by finding a "peppercorn" of consideration in the similar, yet different, refuse collection performance obligation? Why did the court determine that the modification was "fair and equitable in view of circumstances not anticipated by the parties when the contract was made" within the meaning of Restatement (Second) of Contracts § 89? Did the court reverse the trial court because of an error of law or an error of fact? Note that the trial court explicitly determined as a factual matter that "these 400 additional units were within the contemplation of the parties when they entered into the contract." If so, why the reversal?

b.   Agreed Resolution of Disputes—Accord and Satisfaction

The preexisting legal duty rule discussion above relates mostly to the common law assumption that a purported modification under which an obligor assumes no greater or different burden than imposed under the original contract lacks consideration. Consequently, the common law remnants of the preexisting legal duty rule lurk mostly in the modification of liquidated and undisputed claims. However, new issues arise when a valid dispute (versus improper threat of breach) is introduced into the equation.

The existence of a valid dispute involves some uncertainty. The common law is clear that surrendering or forbearing an "invalid claim" is not consideration for the promise received in exchange. This proposition may be expressed in terms of consideration comprising a bargained-for exchange of *legal* detriments. A promise to surrender a claim that has no legal merit—i.e., a frivolous or bad faith claim—clearly cannot supply consideration for an agreement because the purported claimant has no real claim to begin with.

Generally, a claim is invalid if there is a valid defense to enforceability. Of course, this test involves a good deal of hindsight and might not be determinable until the claimant has unsuccessfully litigated the claim. Clearly, if the asserted claim is litigated and turns out to be invalid, consideration to settle it would be lacking. But litigation to test the merits of a particular claim generally moots the need for pre-trial settlement of that claim. Consequently, both restatements attempted to develop tests to distinguish between settlement of invalid claims (which would not provide a consideration) and settlement of at least arguably valid claims (which would provide consideration for a settlement) without compromising the preexisting legal duty rule.

Early courts usually focused on a "doubtful test" providing that a claim is valid if at least doubtful under the law or facts that the claim would be sustained if litigated. Clarke B. Whittier, "The Restatement of Contracts and Consideration," 18 Cal. L. Rev. 611, 619 (1930). Restatement (First) of Contracts § 76(b) provided that the surrender or forbearance of an "invalid claim" by a person who does not have an "honest and reasonable belief" in the claim's possible validity does not provide consideration for a promise of settlement. This test represents the majority view that requires the claimant honestly to believe the claim may fairly be determined to be valid if litigated. The objective unreasonableness of a claim does provide some evidence of bad faith and thus lack of a true subjective "honest belief." But the honesty test proved as unpredictable as the doubtful test. Clarke B. Whittier, "The Restatement of Contracts and Consideration," 18 Cal. L. Rev. 611, 619 (1930).

Accordingly, Restatement (Second) of Contracts § 74 replaced the "honesty and reasonable belief" test with an even more objective and predictable formulation. Under this standard, forbearance or surrender of a claim constitutes bona fide consideration for a promise made in settlement of that claim, even if the claim later turns out to be invalid. Such a settlement constitutes consideration provided: (i) the claim is doubtful at the time of settlement by reason of uncertainty as to the facts or law, or (ii) the party with the claim "believes" it may fairly determined to be valid.

> b. *Requirement of good faith.* The policy favoring compromise of disputed claims is clearest, perhaps, where a claim is surrendered at a time when it is uncertain whether it is valid or not. Even though the invalidity later becomes clear, the bargain is to be judged as it appeared to the parties at the time; if the claim was then doubtful, no inquiry is necessary as to their good faith. Even though the invalidity should have been clear at the time, the settlement of an honest dispute is upheld. But a mere assertion or denial of liability does not make a claim doubtful, and the fact that invalidity is obvious may indicate that it was known. In such cases Subsection (1)(b) requires a showing of good faith. Restatement (second) of Contracts § 74, *cmt. b.*

This reconciliation purports to introduce an objective "doubtful" test as well as a subjective "belief" test. However, where the claim clearly is not objectively doubtful, an irrational subjective belief in the validity of the claim will not alone suffice. Where a claim is clearly not objectively doubtful, the subjective standard will suffice only where the person asserting the subjective belief can also show that belief honestly existed, thus the requirement that the party prove good faith belief. While it is certainly easier to prove a belief is honest when any objectively reasonable person would also entertain the belief (unlikely since the claim was not objectively doubtful), the subjective good faith standard at least provides the party asserting the belief an opportunity to prove that belief to a jury.

Assuming that the claim satisfies the doubtful or belief test, does the settlement agreement discharge the claim? The answer depends upon whether the parties intend the settlement arrangement as an "accord and satisfaction" or rather a "substituted contract." Compare Restatement (Second) of Contracts § 281 (accord and satisfaction) and Restatement (Second) of Contracts § 279 (substituted contract).

CLARK V. ELZA

Court of Appeals of Maryland
286 Md. 208, 406 A.2d 922 (1979)

ELDRIDGE, Judge.

This case presents the question of whether an executory oral agreement to settle a pending lawsuit may be raised as a defense to prevent a plaintiff from pursuing his original cause of action. It also presents the threshold issue of whether a trial court's refusal to enforce such a settlement agreement, where enforcement was sought in the underlying legal action, may be immediately appealed. We answer these questions in the affirmative.

As a result of injuries sustained in an automobile accident, the plaintiffs, Floyd L. Elza and his wife Myrtle E. Elza, filed suit in the Circuit Court for Baltimore County. They alleged that the defendants, Swannie B. Clark and Linda Sue Woodward, were legally responsible for their injuries. After the case was scheduled for trial, settlement negotiations ensued between the parties. A figure of $9,500.00 was verbally agreed upon; the trial judge was notified; and the case was removed from the trial calendar. The defendants forwarded a release and an order of satisfaction to the plaintiffs' attorney, and later sent a settlement draft to the plaintiffs' attorney. Thereafter, these papers were returned unexecuted with the statement that the $9,500.00 settlement was no longer adequate. The reason given for this change of mind was that on the day after the oral agreement, Mr. Elza had visited a new physician who informed him that his injuries were more extensive than he originally believed.

The plaintiffs then advised the court that they were no longer willing to go through with the settlement. In response, the defendants filed in the tort action a "Motion to Enforce Settlement." At a hearing on the motion the plaintiffs argued that the settlement agreement was not binding on them because it was merely an executory accord, and could only be enforced upon satisfaction. The court observed that if the agreement were a substituted contract, as opposed to an executory accord, then it would be binding. Finding that the intention of the parties was to create an executory accord, the trial judge denied the motion of the defendants to enforce the settlement. The effect of this ruling was that trial upon the original tort action could proceed, notwithstanding the supposed settlement.

The defendants then took an appeal to the Court of Special Appeals, and the plaintiffs moved to dismiss the appeal. The Court of Special Appeals, in an unreported opinion, dismissed the appeal as premature because the trial court had not yet rendered a final judgment in the tort case. The court reasoned:

> Here, the order . . . denying appellants' motion to enforce settlement did not deny appellees the means of further prosecuting their claims nor did it deny appellants the right to defend against those claims. In short, it did not settle and conclude the rights of the parties involved in the action and, thus, constituted an interlocutory order which is not appealable at this time.

The defendants petitioned this Court for a writ of certiorari, challenging the ruling that the case was not appealable and arguing that the purported settlement was effective. We granted the petition with respect to both issues. . . . [Eds.—The Court determined the case was properly appealed.]

As previously mentioned, the trial court refused to enforce the settlement agreement on the ground that it was an "executory accord" and not a "substitute contract." An executory accord is defined in 6 Corbin on Contracts § 1268, p. 71 (1962) as follows:

> The term "accord executory" is and always has been used to mean an agreement for the *future discharge* of an existing claim by a substituted performance. In order for an agreement to fall within this definition, it is the promised performance that is to discharge the existing claim, and not the promise to render such performance. Conversely, all agreements for a future discharge by a substituted performance are accords executory. It makes no difference whether or not the existing claim is liquidated or unliquidated, undisputed or disputed, except as these facts bear upon the sufficiency of the consideration for some promise in the new agreement. It makes no difference whether or not a suit has already been brought to enforce the original claim; or whether that claim arises out of an alleged tort or contract or quasi-contract. . . . (Emphasis Added).

. . . On the other hand, where the parties intend the new agreement itself to constitute a substitute for the prior claim, then this substituted contract immediately discharges the original claim. Under this latter type of arrangement, since the original claim is fully extinguished at the time the agreement is made, recovery may only be had upon the substituted contract. . . .

It is often extremely difficult to determine the factual question of whether the parties to a compromise agreement intended to create an executory accord or a substitute contract. However, unless the evidence demonstrates that the new agreement was designed to be a substitute for the original cause of action, it is presumed that the parties each intended to surrender their old rights and liabilities only upon performance of the new agreement. In other words, unless there is clear evidence to the contrary, an agreement to discharge a pre-existing claim will be regarded as an executory accord. . . .

In light of the above-discussed principles, we agree with the trial court that the settlement agreement in this case was an executory accord and not a substitute contract. This conclusion is supported by the fact that a "release" was to be executed upon performance of the settlement contract. If a substitute contract were intended, the underlying tort cause of action would have been released when the agreement was made, notwithstanding the fact that performance had not yet been rendered. Holding in abeyance the release of the tort claim until the settlement agreement was performed would be inconsistent with the principle that a substitute contract serves to replace the initial claim. . . . Furthermore, to the extent that there is any doubt, under this Court's decision in Porter v. Berwyn Fuel & Feed, supra, 244 Md. at 639, 224 A. 2d 662, such doubt is resolved in favor of finding an executory accord.

After concluding that the oral settlement agreement was an executory accord, the circuit court permitted the plaintiffs to proceed to trial on their original cause of action. In so ruling, we believe that the circuit court erred as to the effect of an unexecuted accord.

It is true that several cases set forth the principle, adopted by the court below, that an executory accord is unenforceable and is no defense against a suit on the prior claim. . . . Nevertheless the modern view, and in our judgment the better view, is summarized by 6 Corbin, supra, § 1274, p. 104, as follows:

> An accord executory does not in itself operate as a discharge of the previous claim, for the reason that it is not so intended or agreed. In nearly every case, however, the parties intend that the duty created by the previous transaction shall be suspended during the period fixed for performance of the accord. As long as the debtor has committed no breach of the accord, therefore, the creditor should be allowed to maintain no action for the enforcement of the prior claim. His right of action should be held to be suspended as the parties intended.

This is also the position adopted by the Restatement of Contracts, Vol. II, § 417 (1932):

Section 417. An Accord; Its Effect When Performed and When Broken.

Except as stated in §§ 142, 143 with reference to contracts for the benefit of third persons and as stated in § 418, the following rules are applicable to a contract to accept in the future a stated performance in satisfaction of an existing contractual duty, or a duty to make compensation:

(a) Such a contract does not discharge the duty, but suspends the right to enforce it as long as there has been neither a breach of the contract nor a justification for the creditor in changing his position because of its prospective non-performance.

(b) If such a contract is performed, the previously existing duty is discharged.

(c) If the debtor breaks such a contract the creditor has alternative rights. He can enforce either the original duty or the subsequent contract.

(d) If the creditor breaks such a contract, the debtor's original duty is not discharged. The debtor acquires a right of action for damages for the breach, and if specific enforcement of that contract is practicable, he acquires an alternative right to the specific enforcement thereof. If the contract is enforced specifically, his original duty is discharged.

Comment: B. The rules governing the validity and effect of accord and satisfaction are applicable as well where the pre-existing duty arises from a tort as where it is based on contract.

Thus, an executory accord does not discharge the underlying claim until it is performed. Until there is a breach of the accord or a justifiable change of position based upon prospective non-performance, the original cause of action is suspended. As long as the "debtor" (i.e., the defendant in a tort case) neither breaches the accord nor provides a reasonable basis for concluding that he will not perform, the "creditor" (i.e., the plaintiff) has no right to enforce the underlying cause of action.

These principles have been applied to enforce executory accords under circumstances similar to those in the instant case. In Warner v. Rossignol, supra, 513 F. 2d 678, a tort plaintiff in a bifurcated trial obtained a finding that the defendant was liable for the plaintiff's injuries. Prior to the jury trial on the issue of damages, the parties arrived at an oral settlement agreement; the court was notified; and the case removed from the trial calendar. After an initial delay in payment, the defendant tendered his check, which was refused by the plaintiff. The plaintiff then moved for a jury trial on the damages question, and, in response, the defendant filed a "motion to enforce the settlement." The trial court denied the plaintiff's motion, and granted that of the defendant. On appeal the plaintiff argued that the settlement was unenforceable because it was an unconsummated accord. The United States Court of Appeals rejected this contention, characterizing it as "plainly wrong." Similarly, the court refused to accept the defendant's argument that the agreement was a "substitute contract" and not an executory accord. However, it went on to uphold the enforceability of the accord, declaring (513 F.2d at 683):

> We hold, therefore, that while the agreement to compromise was binding and enforceable against a defaulting party barring plaintiff from proceeding with his original action in breach of the agreement plaintiff did not entirely relinquish his original cause upon entering into the agreement of compromise. The tort action would only be conclusively terminated when the $6,000 was paid against delivery of the releases and dismissal stipulation; until then it remained in abeyance and if defendant repudiated the settlement or committed a material breach of its terms, plaintiff could elect either to sue for $6,000 or to rescind and press forward upon the original cause. . . .

Although the precise question here presented does not appear to have been discussed by this Court in any prior opinion, nevertheless our decisions seem to reflect the position of the above-cited cases, the Restatement, and Corbin. See, e.g., Chicora Fer. Co. v. Dunan, 91 Md. 144, 46 A. 347 (1900). Moreover, it is logical to hold that executory accords are enforceable. An executory accord is simply a type of bilateral contract. As long as the basic requirements to form a contract are present, there is no reason to treat such a settlement agreement differently than other contracts that are binding. This is consistent with the public policy dictating that courts should "look with favor upon the compromise or settlement of law suits in the interest of efficient and economical administration of justice and the lessening of friction and acrimony." Chertkof v. Harry C. Weiskittel Co., 251 Md. 544, 550, 248 A. 2d 373, 377 (1968), cert. denied, 394 U.S. 974, 89 S. Ct. 1467, 22 L. Ed. 2d 754 (1969).

In sum, the circuit court should not have permitted the plaintiffs to proceed with the underlying tort action in violation of their settlement agreement.[4]

---

[4] The plaintiffs in their brief in this Court also argue that there was a mutual mistake concerning the extent of Mr. Elza's injuries, and that this justifies their avoidance of the settlement agreement. However, this issue was not encompassed in the petition for a writ of certiorari, was not raised by the plaintiffs in a cross-petition for a writ of certiorari, and therefore cannot be raised for the first time in their brief in this Court. Maryland Rule 813a. Furthermore, even if it were properly before us, there would be no basis in this record for finding a mutual mistake of fact.

Judgment of the Court of Special Appeals reversed and case remanded to that Court with directions to reverse the judgment of the Circuit Court for Baltimore County and remand the case for further proceedings not inconsistent with this opinion. Respondents to pay costs.

NOTES AND QUESTIONS

1. *Accord versus substituted performance or substituted contract.* The Elzas filed a tort suit seeking damages from Clark for negligent physical injury. Thereafter, the parties reached an "oral agreement" to settle the tort lawsuit under which Clark promised to pay $9,500 in exchange for the Elzas releasing. Later the Elzas refused to sign various release and settlement documents, arguing that a subsequent discovery disclosed the injuries were more serious than thought. That explains the Elzas' motive, but is that adequate to breach an oral promise to settle? What was the consideration for the Elzas' promise to settle? Assuming consideration existed, why did the Elzas argue the settlement was an accord and not a substituted contract?

According to Restatement (Second) of Contracts § 281(1), an "accord" is an enforceable bilateral contract itself under which an obligee (the Elzas) promises to accept a stated performance ($9,500) in satisfaction of the obligor's (Clark) existing tort liability duty. The court refers to a bilateral accord as an "executory accord." Performance of the accord is the satisfaction of the bilateral promise and discharges the original duty. But until satisfaction of the bilateral executory accord, the accord merely suspends the obligor's (Clark) duty. Only actual satisfaction (payment) according to the terms of the bilateral accord agreement "discharges" the obligor's (Clark) duty under the tort suit. Restatement (Second) of Contracts § 281(2). As with any bilateral contract, either party can breach the executory accord. A breach by the obligor (Clark) in the form of a failure to fully satisfy the accord, gives the obligee (the Elzas) a choice: (i) pursue the original tort suit; or (ii) pursue the breach of the accord contract. Compare Restatement (Second) of Contracts § 281(2) (obligor breach with obligee right to pursue either claim), with § 281(3) (obligee breach entitles obligor to seek specific performance of the accord—in this case in the form of a "Motion to Enforce Settlement").

The most natural corollary to "accord and satisfaction" is the concept of a "substituted contract." Restatement (Second) of Contracts § 279(1) defines a "substituted contract" as one that is itself accepted by the obligee (the Elzas) in satisfaction of the obligor's (Clark) existing duty. Unlike with accord and satisfaction, the Elzas can only sue for breach of the substituted contract and may no longer pursue the tort claim as it was discharged upon acceptance of the substituted contract.

However, a third alternative exists that was not well articulated by the court and perhaps not by the Elzas' counsel. Restatement (Second) of Contracts § 278(1) considers the effect of an offer of a "unilateral accord." Like any unilateral offer, the offer may be revoked by the offeror at any time before acceptance (satisfaction). In this case, a unilateral offer requires acceptance by performance, and thus a contract can only be created by the acceptance. Revocation prior to performance is not a breach of contract. Restatement (Second) of Contracts §§ 50(2) and 53(3).

With these three alternatives in mind, how would you analyze Elza's intent? Do you think Elza intended to create a (i) unilateral accord offer, (ii) bilateral executory accord, or (iii) substituted contract? Does it make any sense for Elza to argue bilateral executory accord versus substituted contract when the outcome under either is the same if Elza breaches?

If you represented Elza, which type of settlement arrangement would you suggest? What factors would lead you to seek a substituted contract over a bilateral executory accord? Given that a breach of a bilateral executory accord gives your client more options, why would you seek a substituted contract? Which would you prefer as defense counsel and why? Assuming the Elzas prefer an accord rather than a substituted contract, what factors would cause you to advise a unilateral accord instead of a bilateral accord? Once you determine which arrangement is preferred, how can you assure your client obtains the desired result?

2.   *Mistake and personal injury settlements.* As footnote 4 acknowledges, the Elzas' counsel also argued that even if the parties did create a valid bilateral executory accord, the contract was voidable for mutual mistake. Injured parties commonly seek to avoid an earlier settlement agreement, sometimes even after accepting the settlement proceeds. The defendant's insurance counsel may often seek a quick settlement immediately after the injured party files a claim. In exchange for an immediate settlement payment, the injured party in such cases always releases the defendant (and therefore the insurer) for any future claims arising out of the insured accident. Although quick settlements avoid the delay and expense of investigation, discovery, and litigation, such settlements generally occur before the parties have determined the full extent and costs of the injury. When the plaintiff later discovers that the injury is far more serious than anticipated, should the release be enforceable to preclude the injured plaintiff from seeking greater and more fair compensation?

This topic was discussed in Chapter 7 with the mistake doctrine. Early cases tended to deny relief to the injured party seeking to avoid settlement agreements on the basis of mistake as courts strictly enforced broad release language. But modern courts scrutinize releases more carefully to determine the fairness of the objective assumptions of the parties regarding the extent of injuries. See generally Dan B. Dobbs, "Conclusiveness of Personal Injury Settlement: Basic Problems," 41 N. C. L. Rev. 665 (1963). Notwithstanding the older history, some courts are broadening mutual mistake applications notwithstanding the specificity of the release language itself, at least with respect to injuries unknown to either party at the time they execute the release. See *Williams v. Glash*, 789 S.W.2d 261 (Tex. 1990)," Michael A. Plotz, Comment, "Personal Injury Releases May Be Set Aside Under the Doctrine of Mutual Mistake When the Injury Later Sued For Was Unknown At the Time of Signing, 32 S. Tex. L. Rev. 311 (1991) and Val D. Ricks, "American Mutual Mistake: Half-Civilian Mongrel, Consideration Reincarnate," 58 La. L. Rev. 663, 671–672 (1998).

3. *Novation.* The *Clark* analysis of the "substituted contract" doctrine involved only two parties. A substituted contract can also involve a third party. A "novation" is a substituted contract that includes a party that was not an obligee or obligor in the original contract. Restatement (Second) of Contracts § 280. Thus novation adds a new party to the original contract. Mostly, the new party is added in substitution for an original party in a manner that discharges the former party's duties while substituting the new party. In the corporate law context, for example, a corporate promoter often enters contracts such as office leases in her own capacity on behalf of a corporation that will be formed at some later date. Upon formation, the corporation usually seeks to substitute itself in place of the promoter in such contracts. If the corporation is well-capitalized and has good credit, a lessor may permit a novation that substitutes the corporation as lessee and discharges the promoter. But if the corporation is thinly capitalized or has poor credit, a lessor may wish to permit the corporation to become a party to the contract but refuse to discharge the promoter. If the original contract does not prohibit such an action (such as by specifying that the lessor must accept a novation substituting the corporation as lessee upon formation and discharge the promoter's liability), the lessor will be able to enforce the lease against both the corporation and the original promoter.

Chapter 10 explores the most common novation mechanism, assignment and delegation. In a delegation, an original obligor delegates all duties to a designated third-party delegatee. If the obligee consents to accept the performance of the third party delegatee in substitution of the duties of the delegator, the delegator's duties under the contract are assumed by the third party and discharged as to the delegator.

4. *UCC accord and satisfaction.* It is quite common to offer a check in "full satisfaction" of less than the amount claimed by a UCC creditor. At the very least, the offer of such a check represents an offer of a unilateral accord. If the creditor simply cashes the check, does that act constitute acceptance of the accord offer and thus extinguish the remainder of the claim? Under the discussion above, this would be the normative common law rule, provided at least a valid disputed claim existed and economic duress was not involved. Does the UCC adopt the same notion? Depending on the size of the creditor, routine checks are cashed without examining the face for qualifying language. Thus, the common law rule might work substantial surprise under the UCC.

UCC § 1–308 (2001) (formerly UCC § 1–207) specifically addresses the matter. While UCC § 1–308(a) (2001) permits the creditor to reserve all rights by so indicating on the check, a 1990 amendment adding UCC § 1–308(b) (2001) makes clear that the section does not apply to accord and satisfaction. To clarify matters, UCC § 1–308, *cmt. 3* (2001) provides:

3.   Subsection (b) states that this section does not apply to an accord and satisfaction. Section 3–311 governs if an accord and satisfaction is attempted by tender of a negotiable instrument as stated in that section. If Section 3–311 does not apply, the issue of whether an accord and satisfaction has been effected is determined by the law of contract. Whether or not Section 3–311 applies, this section has no application to an accord and satisfaction.

Before the 1990 amendment, creditors could accept and cash a full satisfaction check without compromising the remainder of their claim by simply making proper notation that, notwithstanding the full satisfaction notation, the creditor was cashing the check with a full reservation of rights. Thus, before 1990, the creditor generally prevailed in the "battle of check notations" because UCC § 1–308 (2001) trumped the traditional contrary common law rule of accord and satisfaction.

The effect of the 1990 amendment, clarified by the quoted Comment 3, is clear. First, UCC § 1–308 (2001) does not apply to accord and satisfaction matters. As a result, the common law rule concerning accord and satisfaction once again is controlling in all UCC cases (at least those not involving a negotiable instrument). Importantly, UCC § 3–311 is referenced as controlling the law of negotiable instruments such as checks. Thus, UCC § 1–308 (2001) in essence forces resolution of the common law accord and satisfaction rules as applicable to full satisfaction checks to be resolved by UCC § 3–311. That section sets out specific statutory rules for accord and satisfaction cases involving negotiable instruments such as checks. Michael D. Floyd, "How Much Satisfaction Should You Expect From An Accord?" 26 Loy. U. Chi. L.J. 1 (1994) and Jay Winston, "The Evolution of Accord and Satisfaction: Common Law; UCC Section 1–207; UCC Section 3–311," 28 New Eng. L. Rev. 189 (1993).

UCC § 3–311(1) provides that the section applies to a person against whom a claim is asserted if that person proves (i) a good faith tender of an instrument to the claimant as full satisfaction of the claim, (ii) the amount of the claim was unliquidated or subject to a bona fide dispute, and (iii) the claimant obtained payment of the instrument. For this purpose, UCC § 3–103(a)(4) defines good faith as "honesty in fact and the observance of reasonable commercial standards of fair dealing." Accordingly, good faith includes both subjective and objective components regarding honesty. In such circumstances, the claim is normally discharged when the check is cashed, provided that the check notation in full satisfaction was conspicuous. UCC § 3–311(b). An important exception provides discharge does not occur where prior to cashing such a check, an organization claimant sent the debtor a conspicuous statement directing any such checks to be directed to a specific individual and the check was not sent to the designated person. UCC § 3–311(c)(1). Actual knowledge of authorized persons that the check was submitted in full satisfaction may also permit discharge. UCC § 3–311(d).

How do the UCC § 3–311 accord and satisfaction rules compare to the common law accord and satisfaction rules? Are there major differences? If so, what is the point of the differences?

2. EFFECT OF WRITING RESTRICTING ORAL MODIFICATION

Even assuming a modification or amendment is supported by consideration, reliance, or another theory of obligation discussed in the previous section, the written contract itself may specify the requirements for modification. In particular, this section considers enforceability of oral modifications to written contracts. In large part, the effectiveness of contract terms purportedly restricting oral modifications depends upon whether or not the Statute of Frauds requires the original agreement to be in writing. If so, the otherwise enforceable oral modification must also generally be in writing (unless an applicable Statute of Frauds exception applies). The trouble concerns original contracts that are in writing even though the Statute of Frauds did not require the writing.

If public law (i.e., the Statute of Frauds or some other statutory requirement) does not require the original contract to be in writing, what private law would require an oral amendment or modification to be in written form? The parties themselves might seek assurance that the terms of their written contract will prevail over later purported oral modifications. The parties may prefer to prohibit oral modifications, possibly because they fear false allegations of oral modifications, they wish to ensure that modifications are not approved haphazardly, or they prefer the relative precision and more permanent nature of a written record of modifications, especially in complex contractual relationships. The issue is whether and to what extent courts should allow the terms of the written agreement to trump later oral agreements. Particularly where the oral modification was not coerced through some form of economic duress or bad faith, such private "statute of frauds" contract terms purport to protect the parties from false oral allegations of amendment. On the other hand, like the actual Statute of Frauds, when enforceable the terms of the writing could negate the freedom of the parties to voluntarily mutually agree to modify the terms of their written agreement. This particular tension has caused more than its share of difficulty.

These clauses generally adopt one of two forms. Both purport to restrict the right of the parties to orally modify the terms of the original written contract, even if they mutually assent to such a modification. The first, a "no oral modification" ("NOM") clause, purports to prevent the parties from amending the written agreement orally. The second, a "no oral waiver" clause ("NOW"), purports to restrict the power of the parties to relinquish the right to insist on strict compliance with a NOM clause. The NOW clause attempts to prevent a party from temporarily "waiving" the writing requirement of the NOM clause in order to permit oral amendment in a particular case. Notably, the parol evidence rule discussed in Chapter 4 does not preclude parol evidence of either oral modification or oral waiver because the parol modification or waiver occurs after formation of the original contract. As discussed in Chapter 4, the parol evidence rule applies only to parol evidence of prior or contemporaneous agreements or negotiations between the parties, not subsequent events.

The common law and the UCC differ somewhat on this subject. The common law is antagonistic to such clauses, while the UCC generally embraces them. However, the apparent difference is not as significant as the discussion to follow suggests. The UCC Statute of Frauds sweeps all contracts for the sale of goods for at least $500 within its reach, meaning that (absent a class action or similar device) the distinct UCC rule on NOM clauses applies only to low-value cases. Since the UCC and the common law agree that modifications must be in writing when the Statute of Frauds requires the original contract to be in writing, the difficult issues generally arise in common law cases not covered by the Statute of Frauds. Nonetheless, as the *Wisconsin Knife* case set forth below suggests, the UCC language on this point is less than a model of clarity. As such, matters of statutory interpretation assume significant importance.

Contracts "Subject to" the Statute of Frauds. Chapter 6 considered the public law Statute of Frauds requirement that certain contracts must be in writing and signed by the party to be charged to be enforceable. See Restatement (Second) of Contracts § 110 (listing specified subject matters of contracts within the Statute of Frauds) and UCC § 2–201(1) (contracts for the sale of $500 or more in goods are within the Statute of Frauds). Modifications to a contract within the Statute of Frauds must also be in writing and signed by the party to be charged to be enforceable. See Restatement (Second) of Contracts § 149(1); UCC § 2–209(3); and Jeanette K. Brooks, "Parol Modification and the Statute of Frauds: Fitting the Pieces Together Under the Uniform Commercial Code," 21 Campbell L. Rev. 307, 308 (1999). Moreover, except for contracts involving the sale of goods, even a written and signed modification requires an independent basis for enforcement, such as consideration or reliance. See UCC § 2–209(1) (eliminating the consideration requirement to modify contracts for the sale of goods) and John E. Murray, Jr., "The Modification Mystery: Section 2–209 of the Uniform Commercial Code," 32 Vill. L. Rev. 1 (1987). Thus, absent an applicable exception, an *oral modification* to an original written contract within the Statute of Frauds is generally not enforceable even if supported by a theory of obligation. The original written contract alone remains enforceable. As with normative Statute of Frauds cases, parties seeking relief are relegated to arguing exceptions normally based on reliance. Compare Restatement (Second) of Contracts § 139 (reliance exception to Statute of Frauds on original oral agreements), with

Restatement (Second) of Contracts § 150 (Statute of Frauds does not prevent enforcement of an oral modification where necessary to protect a material change in position in reliance on the oral modification). Where the oral modification is not enforceable, restitution "off the contract" remains available to prevent unjust enrichment. Restatement (Second) of Contracts § 375.

Contracts "Not Subject to" the Statute of Frauds. Many, if not most, significant contracts are in written form and signed by the parties, even though the Statute of Frauds does not require such a record. Since the UCC Statute of Frauds embraces nearly all sales of goods, most contracts not required to be in writing are governed by the common law. In the absence of a NOM or NOW clause, the parties to such contracts are free to make oral modifications, regardless of whether the original contract was in writing.

But where the original written contract includes a NOM clause (and perhaps a NOW clause as well), the common law and UCC differ on whether a NOM clause is enforceable. As noted, common law generally determined that a NOM clause does not prevent the parties from later orally modifying their agreement. See Restatement (Second) of Contracts § 283, *cmt. b*:

> Even a provision of the earlier contract to the effect that it can be rescinded only in writing does not impair the effectiveness of an oral agreement of rescission. In the absence of statute, such a self-imposed limitation does not limit the power of the parties subsequently to contract. A different rule is laid down in Uniform Commercial Code § 2–209(2) for contracts for the sale of goods.

In other words, at common law, the parties may always mutually agree to rescind their old agreement and substitute a new one, no matter what the original contract itself provided. The rule is widely accepted and contradicted by only a few jurisdictions. See J. Calamari and J. Perillo, The Law of Contracts § 5–14(b) (2d ed. 1977). However, most courts followed the theory that the parties simply could not prohibit themselves from later mutually rescinding or canceling their prior agreement:

> The most ironclad written contract can always be cut into by the acetylene torch of parol modification supported by adequate proof. The hand that pens a writing may not gag the mouths of the assenting parties. *Wagner v. Graziano*, 136 A.2d 82, 83–84 (Pa. 1957).

> The clause which forbids change, may be changed like any other. *Beatty v. Guggenheim Exploration Co.*, 122 N.E. 378 (N.Y. 1919) (Cardozo, J.).

Therefore the subsequent oral modification simply operated as a rescission of the prior agreement followed by a substitution of the new agreement. Williston on Contracts § 73.22 (4th Ed. 2006); Beth Eisler, "Modification of Sales Contracts Under the Uniform Commercial Code: Section 2–209 Reconsidered," 57 Tenn. L. Rev. 401, 412 (1990); and Martin H. Brinkley, "The Regulation of Contractual Change: A Guide To No Oral Modification Clauses for North Carolina Lawyers," 81 N.C.L. Rev. 2239 (2003). Since the NOM clause itself was unenforceable, the enforceability of a NOW clause is largely irrelevant, except as applied to other contractual matters not involving permanent amendment of the contract. Both the UCC and the common law are silent regarding the enforceability of NOW clauses, but that topic is generally subsumed within the general concept of "waiver" of promises and conditions. Therefore, the NOW clause does not resolve the fundamental issue—whether the NOM clause itself is enforceable. If not, the NOW clause and waiver doctrine generally is unnecessary. However, both NOW and waiver may become important when the NOM clause is otherwise enforceable. Since the base NOM clause is generally not enforceable under common law but generally is enforceable under the UCC, waiver and the NOW clause becomes more important. Unfortunately, NOW clauses in general have received very little attention from the courts or scholars. See generally David V. Snyder, "The Law of Contract and the Concept of Change: Public and Private Attempts To Regulate Modification, Waiver, and Estoppel," 1999 Wisc. L. Rev. 607.

The UCC specifically changes the common law and purports to approve NOM clauses by the following language: "[a] signed agreement which excludes modification or rescission except by a signed writing cannot be otherwise modified or rescinded." UCC § 2–209(2). Unfortunately, because of other UCC § 2–209 provisions, the NOM language is neither absolute nor clear. The general language respecting NOM clauses is subject to the following proviso: "but except as between merchants such a requirement on a form supplied by a merchant must be separately signed by the other party." Accordingly, a NOM clause in an original contract between a merchant and consumer is only binding if the original contract is actually signed by the consumer. Otherwise, a consumer may avoid the operation of the clause. However, as between merchants, the clause is effective if it is included in a controlling form agreement, even if that form agreement was not signed by either party, which may occur in a battle of the forms situation under UCC § 2–207. Of course the NOM clause must be a binding part of the agreement between the merchants exchanging forms. See Chapter 3 and discussion of UCC § 2–207.

More importantly, UCC § 2–209(3)–(4) directly affect the right of a UCC party to insist on strict compliance with an otherwise enforceable UCC § 2–209(2) NOM clause. First, UCC § 2–209(4) provides that a subsequent oral rescission or modification may "operate as a waiver" even though the attempt is otherwise precluded by the NOM clause under UCC § 2–209(2) or the Statute of Frauds requirement in UCC § 2–209(3). Thus, even if a written contract contains a § 2–209(2) NOM clause, a purported oral rescission or modification can still be a waiver of the parties' continuing obligations under the written agreement. Similarly, for a modification that places the contract within the Statute of Frauds (e.g., raises the contract price to $500 or more (see UCC § 2–201(1)), the modification is unenforceable as a contract, but may still be construed as a waiver under § 2–209(4). In either event, the broad UCC § 2–209(4) exemption provides that the attempt to orally modify the written agreement "can operate as a waiver."

This particular language has caused significant difficulty, as illustrated by the *Wisconsin Knife* case below. Does the language "can operate as a waiver" mean that the oral modification is only valid if it constitutes a simple waiver or is more required? Given the minimalist requirements of a "waiver," this exemption would superficially appear to swallow the general rule. Nearly any oral modification would waive the NOM clause.

Technically, a party who relies on an oral promise modifying an original contract can invoke promissory estoppel to avoid the Statute of Frauds. Restatement (Second) of Contracts § 139 (incorporated in sale of goods cases by UCC § 1–103(b) (2001). But promissory estoppel's poorer "waiver" cousin generally does not require reliance and is not commonly thought to avoid the effect of the public law Statute of Frauds. Williston on Contracts § 39.14 (4th ed. 2006). Unlike promissory estoppel, waiver is a temporary concept normally applicable to private law terms created by the parties, rather than public law. Once made, a waiver of a right to strict performance of a promise continues until retracted. If the waiver is later retracted, the duty is reinstated as of the time of the retraction. Williston on Contracts § 39.20 (4th Ed. 2006) and UCC § 2–209(5). Thus, unless a "waiver" is coupled with consideration (rare) or promissory estoppel reliance (more common) to make it permanent, the waiving party may reinstate strict compliance with contractual terms for future and continuing performance with reasonable notice to the other party. UCC § 2–209(5). While "waiver" is generally considered in connection with the excuse of conditions (discussed in Chapter 5), it also applies to promises of future performance. Williston on Contracts § 39.14 (4th ed. 2006). Compare Restatement (Second) of Contracts § 84, *cmt. b* (waiver of a condition), with Restatement (Second) of Contracts § 246, *cmt. b* (waiver of promised performance). Nonetheless, these formalistic rules seriously impair the flexibility of the parties to alter informally their course of performance to account for later contractual developments. See David V. Snyder, "The Law of Contract and the Concept of Change: Public and Private Attempts To Regulate Modification, Waiver, and Estoppel," 1999 Wisc. L. Rev. 607; Beth

A. Eisler, "Modification of Sales Contracts Under the Uniform Commercial Code: Section 2–209 Reconsidered," 57 Tenn. L. Rev. 401 (1990).

The *Cloud Corp.* case below explores the effectiveness of a NOM clause and waiver of that clause under the UCC. In particular, Judge Posner's opinion addresses the various doctrines that may be raised in NOM clause cases, including the statute of frauds, battle of the forms, and waiver under § 2–209(4).

CLOUD CORP. v. HASBRO, INC.
United States Court of Appeals, Seventh Circuit
314 F.3d 289 (2002)

POSNER, CIRCUIT JUDGE.

"Wonder World Aquarium" is a toy that Hasbro, Inc., the well-known designer and marketer of toys, sold for a brief period in the mid-1990s. The toy comes as a package that contains (we simplify slightly) the aquarium itself, some plastic fish, and, depending on the size of the aquarium (for this varies), large or small packets of a powder that when dissolved in distilled water forms a transparent gelatinous filling for the aquarium. The gel simulates water, and the plastic fish can be inserted into it with tweezers to create the illusion of a real fish tank with living, though curiously inert, fish. "Pretend blood," included in some of the packages, can be added for even greater verisimilitude. The consumer can choose among versions of Wonder World Aquarium that range from "My Pretty Mermaid" to "Piranha Attack"-the latter a scenario in which the pretend blood is doubtless a mandatory rather than optional ingredient.

Hasbro contracted out the manufacture of this remarkable product. Southern Clay Products Company was to sell and ship Laponite HB, a patented synthetic clay, to Cloud Corporation, which was to mix the Laponite with a preservative according to a formula supplied by Hasbro, pack the mixture in the packets that we mentioned, and ship them to affiliates of Hasbro in East Asia. The affiliates would prepare and package the final product-that is the aquarium, the packet of gel, and the plastic fish (and "pretend blood")—and ship it back to Hasbro in the United States for distribution to retailers.

Beginning in mid-1995, Hasbro would from time to time issue purchase orders for a specified number of large and small packets to Cloud, which would in turn order the quantity of Laponite from Southern Clay Products that it needed in order to manufacture the specified number of packets. The required quantity of Laponite depended not only on the number of large and small packets ordered by Hasbro but also on the formula that Hasbro supplied to Cloud specifying the proportion of Laponite in each packet. The formula was changed frequently. The less

Laponite per packet specified in the formula, the more packets could be manufactured for a given quantity of the ingredient.

Early in 1997 Hasbro discovered that its East Asian affiliates, the assemblers of the final package, had more than enough powder on hand to supply Hasbro's needs, which were diminishing, no doubt because Wonder World Aquarium was losing market appeal. Mistakenly believing that Hasbro's market was expanding rather than contracting, Cloud had manufactured a great many packets of powder in advance of receiving formal purchase orders for them from Hasbro. Hasbro refused to accept delivery of these packets or to pay for them. Contending that this refusal was a breach of contract, Cloud sued Hasbro in federal district court in Chicago, basing jurisdiction on diversity of citizenship and seeking more than $600,000 in damages based mainly on the price of the packets that it had manufactured and not delivered to Hasbro and now was stuck with-for the packets, being usable only in Wonder World Aquaria, had no resale value. After a bench trial, the district judge ruled in favor of Hasbro.

Cloud does not quarrel with the district judge's findings of fact, but only with her legal conclusions. The governing law is the Uniform Commercial Code as interpreted in Illinois.

The original understanding between Hasbro and Cloud regarding Cloud's role in the Wonder World Aquarium project either was not a contract or was not broken-probably the former, as the parties had not agreed on the price, quantity, delivery dates, or composition of the packets. These essential terms were set forth in the purchase orders that Hasbro sent Cloud, confirming discussions between employees of Cloud and Kathy Esposito, Hasbro's employee in charge of purchasing inputs for the company's foreign affiliates. Upon receipt of a purchase order, Cloud would send Hasbro an order acknowledgment and would order from Southern Clay Products the quantity of Laponite required to fill the purchase order.

In October 1995, which is to say a few months after the launch of Wonder World Aquarium, Hasbro sent a letter to all its suppliers, including Cloud, that contained a "terms and conditions" form to govern future purchase orders. One of the terms was that a supplier could not deviate from a purchase order without Hasbro's written consent. As requested, Cloud signed the form and returned it to Hasbro. Nevertheless, to make assurance doubly sure, every time Hasbro sent a purchase order to Cloud it would include an acknowledgment form for Cloud to sign that contained the same terms and conditions that were in the October letter. Cloud did not sign any of these acknowledgment forms. The order acknowledgments that it sent Hasbro in response to Hasbro's purchase orders contained on the back of each acknowledgment Cloud's own set of terms and conditions-and the provision in Hasbro's letter and forms requiring Hasbro's written consent to any modification of the purchase order was not among them.

There was a space for Hasbro to sign Cloud's acknowledgment form but it never did so. Neither party complained about the other's failure to sign the tendered forms.

Hasbro placed its last purchase orders with Cloud in February and April 1996. The orders for February specified 2.3 million small packets and 3.2 million large ones. For April the numbers were 1.5 and 1.4 million. Hasbro notified Cloud of the formula that it was to use in making the packets and Cloud ordered Laponite from Southern Clay Products accordingly.

Now as it happened Southern Clay Products was having trouble delivering the Laponite in time to enable Cloud to meet its own delivery schedule. In June 1996, amidst complaints from Hasbro's East Asian affiliates that they were running out of powder, and concerned about the lag in Laponite deliveries, Hasbro notified Cloud that it was to use a new formula in manufacturing the powder, a formula that required so much less Laponite that the same quantity would enable Cloud to produce a third again as many packets. Cloud determined that by using the new formula it could produce from the quantity of Laponite that it had on hand 4.5 million small and 5 million large packets, compared to the 3.8 and 3.9 million called for by the February and April orders but not yet delivered. Cloud had delivered 700,000 of the large packets ordered in February and April; that is why it had 7.7 million packets still to deliver under those orders rather than 8.4 million, the total number of packets ordered (2.3 + 3.2 + 1.5 + 1.4 = 8.4).

Although it had received no additional purchase orders, Cloud sent Hasbro an order acknowledgment for 4.5 million small and 5 million large packets with a delivery date similar to that for the April order, but at a lower price per packet, reflecting the smaller quantity of Laponite, the expensive ingredient in the powder, in each packet.

Cloud's acknowledgment was sent in June. Hasbro did not respond to it-at least not explicitly. It did receive it, however. And Kathy Esposito continued having e-mail exchanges and phone conversations with Cloud. These focused on delivery dates and, importantly, on the quantities to be delivered on those dates. Importantly because some very large numbers-much larger than the February and April numbers, numbers consistent however with Cloud's order acknowledgment sent to Hasbro in June-appear in these and other e-mails written by her. In two of the e-mails the quantity Cloud is to ship is described as "more or less depending on the formula," consistent with Cloud's understanding that if the formula reduced the amount of Laponite per packet Cloud should increase the number of packets it made rather than return unused Laponite to Southern Clay Products. A notation made in August by another member of Hasbro's purchasing department, Maryann Ricci-"Cloud O/S; 4,000,000 sm; 3.5

million lg.".-indicates her belief that Cloud had outstanding ("O/S") purchase orders for 4 million small and 3.5 million large packets. These numbers were far in excess of the undelivered portions of the February and April orders; and since all the earlier orders had, so far as we can determine, already been filled and so were no longer outstanding, she must have been referring to the numbers in Cloud's June order acknowledgment.

The district judge, despite ruling for Hasbro, found that indeed "Hasbro intended to exceed the quantities of . . . packages it had ordered from Cloud in February and April of 1996," that "Hasbro was more concerned with prompt product than with the specific terms of its order[s]," and, most important, that "given Hasbro's repeated message that it could not get enough Laponite HB to fill its needs in a timely fashion, Cloud's decision to produce as many packets as possible appeared to be a safe course of action. Cloud was trying to keep pace with Hasbro's Laponite HB needs, a task made virtually impossible by the length of time it took Southern Clay to fill Cloud's Laponite HB orders." The judge even suggested that given Hasbro's desperation, Cloud could have persuaded Hasbro to execute additional purchase orders at prices equal to those in the February and April orders. Instead, rather than trying to take advantage of Hasbro's fix, Cloud reduced its price to reflect its lower cost. A curious consequence of the reduction, unremarked by the parties, is that even if Cloud has no contract remedy, it has (unless time barred) a remedy in quantum meruit for the benefit it conferred on Hasbro by voluntarily reducing the price specified in the February and April purchase orders.

When some months later Hasbro pulled the plug on Wonder World Aquarium, Cloud had not begun delivering any of the additional quantity that it had manufactured over and above the quantities called for in the February and April purchase orders.

Was Cloud commercially unreasonable in producing the additional quantity without a purchase order? If not, should the Uniform Commercial Code, which was intended to conform sales law to the customs and usages of business people, UCC §§ 1–102(2)(b), 1–105 comment 3; In re Merritt Dredging Co., 839 F.2d 203, 206 (4th Cir.1988); Kerry Lynn Macintosh, "Liberty, Trade, and the Uniform Commercial Code: When Should Default Rules Be Based on Business Practices?" 38 Wm. & Mary L. Rev. 1465, 1488–91 (1997), nevertheless condemn Cloud, as the district judge believed, for failing to request written purchase orders for the additional quantity that the change in formula enabled it to manufacture? Or was Hasbro contractually obligated to pay for that additional quantity?

The answers to these questions depend on whether there was a valid modification of the quantity specifications in the February and April purchase orders (obviously Hasbro cannot complain about the price modification!). The October letter provided that purchase orders could not be modified without Hasbro's written consent. Cloud signed the letter and so became bound by it, consideration being furnished by Hasbro's continuing to do business with Cloud. Hasbro's order acknowledgments accompanying its February and April purchase orders also provided that the orders could not be modified without Hasbro's written consent.

Cloud did not sign Hasbro's acknowledgments and its own acknowledgments omitted the provision requiring that any modification have Hasbro's written consent. But these facts have no significance. In the case of discrepant order and acceptance forms, if the acceptance merely adds a term, that term binds the offeror, UCC § 2–207(1); this modification of the common law's "mirror image" rule minimizes transaction costs by eliminating a negotiation over the additional term unless the offeror is unwilling to accede to the offeree's desire for it. But what if the term added by the acceptance contradicts a term in the offer? Then it doesn't become a part of the contract-that much is clear. § 2–207(2)(b). But is there a contract, and if so what are its terms? The UCC doesn't say, but the majority rule, and the rule in Illinois, is that the inconsistent terms cancel each other out and the court fills the resulting void with a term of its own devising. William B. Davenport, Daniel R. Murray & Donald R. Cassling, Uniform Commercial Code with Illinois Code Comments § 5/2–207, Illinois Code Comment 11, pp. 126–27 (Illinois Practice Series, vol. 2a, 1997).

In this case, however, there was neither a supplemental nor an inconsistent term in the acceptance; there was no term concerning modification, and in such a situation Hasbro's term is enforceable. Earl M. Jorgensen Co. v. Mark Construction, Inc., 56 Haw. 466, 540 P.2d 978, 982–83 (1975); 1 James J. White & Robert S. Summers, Uniform Commercial Code 15–16 (4th ed.1995). It is a case of different but not inconsistent terms, in which event the acceptance is effective to make a contract. UCC § 2–207(1). The offeree's silence is not interpreted as rejection in this situation because transaction costs would again be higher if the offeror had to quiz the offeree on whether every term in the offer not mentioned in the acceptance was acceptable to the offeree. Cloud, the offeree, knew that Hasbro wanted the modification provision and if this was unacceptable it should have said so.

For unexpressed reasons the district judge did not focus on the contractual provisions requiring that any modification of a purchase order be in writing. She considered only whether the UCC's statute of frauds required this, and ruled that it did. The quantity term in a contract for the sale of goods for more than $500 must be memorialized in a writing signed by the party sought to be held to that term, UCC § 2–201(1), and so, therefore, must a modification of that term. UCC § 2–209(3). However-and here we part company with the district judge-Kathy Esposito's e-mails, plus the notation that we quoted earlier signed by Maryann Ricci, another member of Hasbro's purchasing department, satisfy the statutory requirement. The UCC does not require that the contract itself be in writing, only that there be adequate documentary evidence of its existence and essential terms, which there was here. Architectural Metal Systems, Inc. v. Consolidated Systems, Inc., 58 F.3d 1227, 1229–31 (7th Cir.1995).

But what shall we make of the fact that Kathy Esposito's e-mails contained no signature? The Electronic Signatures in Global and National Commerce Act, 15 U.S.C. § 7001, provides that in all transactions in or affecting interstate or foreign commerce (the transactions between Cloud and Hasbro were in interstate commerce and affected both interstate and foreign commerce), a contract or other record relating to the transaction shall not be denied legal effect merely because it is in electronic form. That would be conclusive in this case-had the e-mails been sent after the Act took effect in 2000. But they were sent in 1996. The Act does not purport to be applicable to transactions that occurred before its effective date, and, not being procedural, it is presumed not to apply retroactively. But like the court in Shattuck v. Klotzbach, No. 011109A, 2001 WL 1839720, at *2–3 (Mass.Super.Dec.11, 2001), we conclude without having to rely on the federal Act that the sender's name on an e-mail satisfies the signature requirement of the statute of frauds. Toghiyany v. AmeriGas Propane, Inc., 309 F.3d 1088, 1091 (8th Cir.2002), another e-mail case that does not cite the electronic signatures act (maybe because, as in this case, the contract predated the Act), tugs the other way. But it is unclear whether the court thought the absence of a signature fatal or thought that it was that absence combined with the absence of an essential term-the duration of the contract-that triggered the statute of frauds.

Neither the common law nor the UCC requires a handwritten signature, Just Pants v. Wagner, 247 Ill.App.3d 166, 187 Ill.Dec. 38, 617 N.E.2d 246, 251 (1993); . . . cf. Restatement (Second) of Contracts § 134, comment a (1981), even though such a signature is better evidence of identity than a typed one. It is not customary, though it is possible, to include an electronic copy of a handwritten signature in an e-mail, and therefore its absence does not create a suspicion of forgery or other fraud-and anyway an electronic copy of a signature could be a forgery.

The purpose of the statute of frauds is to prevent a contracting party from creating a triable issue concerning the terms of the contract-or for that matter concerning whether a contract even exists-on the basis of his say-so alone. That purpose does not require a handwritten signature, especially in a case such as this in which there is other evidence, and not merely say-so evidence, of the existence of the contract (more precisely, the contract modification) besides the writings. The fact that Cloud produced the additional quantity is pretty powerful evidence of a contract, ..., as it would have been taking a terrible risk in doing so had it thought it would have no right to be paid if Hasbro refused to accept delivery but would instead be stuck with a huge quantity of a product that had no salvage value. Actually, in the case of a contract for goods specially manufactured by the buyer, partial performance by the seller takes the contract outside the statute of frauds, without more. UCC § 2–201(3)(a). This may well be such a case; but we need not decide.

The background to the modification-the fact that the parties had dealt informally with each other (as shown by their disregard of the form contracts), and above all that Hasbro plainly wanted more product and wanted it fast-is further evidence that had Cloud asked for a written purchase order in June 1996 for the additional quantity, Hasbro would have given it, especially since Cloud was offering a lower price.

There is more: "between merchants [a term that embraces 'any transaction with respect to which both parties are chargeable with the knowledge or skill of merchants,' UCC § 2–104(3)] if within a reasonable time a writing in confirmation of the contract and sufficient against the sender is received and the party receiving it has reason to know its contents, it satisfies the requirements of subsection 1 [the statute of frauds] . . . unless written notice of objection to its contents is given within 10 days after it is received." UCC § 2–201(2). Cloud sent an order acknowledgment, reciting the increased quantity, shortly after the oral modification, and Hasbro did not object within ten days. Campbell v. Yokel, 20 Ill.App.3d 702, 313 N.E.2d 628, 628–31 (1974); Klockner, Inc. v. Federal Wire Mill Corp., 663 F.2d 1370, 1374, 1376 (7th Cir.1981); Apex Oil Co. v. Vanguard Oil & Service Co., 760 F.2d 417, 423 (2d Cir.1985).

So Hasbro's statute of frauds defense fails on a number of independent grounds. But what of the contractual requirement of the buyer's consent in writing to any modification? Could that stiffen the requirements of the UCC's statute of frauds? Parties are free to incorporate stronger conditions for contractual modification than the UCC provides: "A signed agreement which excludes modification or rescission except by a signed writing cannot be otherwise modified or rescinded, but except as between merchants such a requirement on a form supplied by the merchant must be separately signed by the other party." UCC § 2–209(2); see Martinsville Nylon Employees Council Corp. v. NLRB, 969 F.2d 1263, 1267 (D.C.Cir.1992); Wisconsin Knife Works v. National Metal Crafters, 781 F.2d 1280, 1292 (7th Cir.1986) (dissenting opinion); Frank A. Rothermel, Comment, "Role of Course of Performance and Confirmatory Memoranda in Determining the Scope, Operation and Effect of 'No Oral Modification' Clauses," 48 U. Pitt. L.Rev. 1239, 1251–52 (1987). The UCC's statute of frauds requires only quantity terms to be in writing. The contractual requirement that the buyer's consent be in writing was not limited to quantity terms, but this makes no difference, since those are the terms in dispute.

Could the contractual statute of frauds (to speak oxymoronically) be broader in a different sense? Specifically, could "consent in writing" require an explicit written statement of consent, missing here, rather than merely an inference of consent from a writing or series of writings? Maybe, but Hasbro does not argue that the contractual statute of frauds in this case has any different scope from the statutory, though it seems highly unlikely that a no-oral-modification clause would be subject to the exception in section 2–201(2) (quoted earlier) to the statute of frauds. Such a clause is added to a contract when the parties want to draft their own statute of frauds, as they are permitted to do; and there is no reason to suppose that they would want to adopt wholesale the limitations that the UCC imposes on its own statute of frauds. If they wanted those limitations they wouldn't need their own, customized clause.

So we may set section 2–201(2) to one side. That leaves intact, however, Cloud's argument, which we have accepted, that there was adequate evidence of written consent to the modification. And it leaves intact still another alternative argument by Cloud: "an attempt at modification" that does not satisfy the statute of frauds nevertheless "can operate as a waiver." § 2–209(4). The word "can" is key. To prevent the "attempt" provision from eviscerating the statute of frauds, the courts require that the attempting modifier, Cloud in this case, must show either that it reasonably relied on the other party's having waived the requirement of a writing, Wisconsin Knife Works v. National Metal Crafters, supra, 781 F.2d at 1286–87 (7th Cir.1986) . . . , or that the waiver was clear and unequivocal. This exception to the statute of frauds applies equally to the "buyer's written consent" provision of the parties' contracts, UCC § 2–209(4); Wisconsin Knife Works v. National Metal Crafters, supra, 781 F.2d at 1284–87, because waiver is a general doctrine of contract law rather than an appendage to the statute of frauds.

The district judge erred by requiring that Cloud show both reasonable reliance and that the waiver was clear and unequivocal. There was no clear and unequivocal waiver, but there was reliance. The judge found reliance. She found that Cloud had been acting in good faith in producing the additional quantity of packets because it reasonably believed that Hasbro wanted the additional quantity. But she concluded that Cloud had been unreasonable in relying on its reasonable belief because it could so easily have insisted on a written purchase order modifying the quantity terms in the February and April orders. Reasonableness, however, is relative to commercial practices and understandings rather than to the desire of judges and lawyers, reflecting their training and professional culture, to see a deal memorialized in a form that leaves no room for misunderstanding the legal consequences. The employees of Hasbro and Cloud who were responsible for the administration of the parties' contractual undertaking were not lawyers. Doubtless because of this, the parties had, as we have noted, been casual about documentation. Cloud had treated the purchase orders as sources of information on how much

Hasbro wanted when and according to what formula, but had paid no attention to them as contracts containing terms and conditions that might bind it. Hasbro had treated Cloud's purchase-order acknowledgments with similar insouciance. The parties had a smooth working relationship the details of which were worked out in informal communications. With time of the essence and the parties on good terms and therefore careless or impatient with formalities, Cloud was reasonable in believing that if Hasbro didn't want to be committed to buying the additional quantity that it plainly wanted in the summer and autumn of 1996, it would so advise Cloud rather than leading Cloud down the primrose path. A practice, under the rubric of "course of dealing," can be evidence of what a contract requires, see, e.g., UCC § 1–205; Restatement (Second) of Contracts § 223 (1981); Frank Novak & Sons, Inc. v. Sommer & Maca Industries, Inc., 182 Ill.App.3d 781, 131 Ill.Dec. 325, 538 N.E.2d 700, 703–05 (1989)-can even, under the rubric of "contract implied in fact," give rise to binding contractual obligations though no words are spoken. Brines v. XTRA Corp., 304 F.3d 699, 703 (7th Cir.2002).

Cloud could have been more careful. But a failure to insist that every i be dotted and t crossed is not the same thing as being unreasonable. In any event, to repeat an earlier point, Hasbro did give its written consent to the modification.

We conclude that the June modification was enforceable and we therefore reverse the judgment and remand the case for a determination of Cloud's damages.

REVERSED AND REMANDED.

NOTES AND QUESTIONS

1.   *Contract formation and terms.* The court observes that the original understanding between the parties "either was not a contract or was not broken—probably the former...." If it was not a contract, how else could that original understanding be properly characterized?

2.   *UCC Statute of Frauds.* Assuming the parties formed a contract by the purchase orders and the exchange of acknowledgment forms, did those writings satisfy UCC § 2–201(1)? Were the purchase orders or acknowledgment forms required to be signed? Were the letters required to be signed? Who was the party "against whom enforcement is sought?" If UCC § 2–201(1) was not satisfied, would UCC § 2–201(2) (merchant's exception) apply? If not, would UCC § 2–201(3)(b) apply?

3.   *Oral modification and the source of the writing requirement.* Why is the NOM clause relevant in this case? Why would UCC § 2–209(3) simply require the modification to be in writing? Does the "waiver" provision of UCC § 2–209(4) apply with equal force to modifications required to be in writing under UCC § 2–209(3) (Statute of Frauds) as well as UCC § 2–209(2) (NOM

clauses)? If so, is the central issue "waiver" within the meaning of UCC § 2–209(4) and not whether the oral modification was required to be in writing by the Statute of Frauds section or the NOM clause section? Do you think the outcome and policies are the same? Does the UCC statutory treatment of a NOM clause "elevate" it to the public law stature of the Statute of Frauds? Of course, NOM clauses do not enjoy such elevated status under the common law.

4. *Actual waiver versus "can operate as a waiver."* It appears that Judge Posner distinguishes a true "waiver" from oral modification conduct that "can operate as a waiver." Why does he consider this necessary? How does he then characterize the parties' oral modification behavior? What is the relevance of distinguishing reliance on a waiver from the making of a clear and unequivocal waiver in this case?

5. *Merchants' proviso exception.* The UCC § 2–209(2) opening clause provides that a signed agreement expressly excluding oral modification or rescission by way of a NOM clause cannot be modified or rescinded except in writing. Do you find this odd? The parties that made the contract appear to have legally prohibited themselves even from orally rescinding the entire written agreement. What advice would you offer a client that had signed such an agreement, but who orally agreed with the other party to simply forget about the contract? The proviso clause provides that a NOM clause will only be enforceable against a consumer if the consumer signs the original agreement containing the NOM clause. Why is this clause necessary when the introductory clause requires a signed agreement in the first instance?

CHAPTER 9

REMEDIES FOR BREACH OF CONTRACT

■ ■ ■

A. INTRODUCTION

Historically, breach of contract has normatively been remedied by assessment of monetary damages against the breaching party (with occasional restitution remedies for the breaching party when appropriate to protect against over-compensation of the injured party). Secondarily, and only when monetary damages were inadequate to compensate the injured party for the consequences of the breach, an equitable remedy may be available by a court order compelling the breaching party to perform according to the contractual terms (specific performance) or not to breach the terms of the contract (injunction). Restatement (Second) of Contracts § 359(1). Failure to comply with the court order threatens contempt of court coupled with civil fines and, although less frequently, potential incarceration.

The ancient roots of this normative relationship between monetary damages at law and equitable injunctive relief can be traced to English common law writs and pleading forms discussed in Chapter 1. An injured party was only permitted to seek equitable injunctive relief when the nature of the alleged law breach did not conform to one of the formal and limited common law writ pleading situations. Most of this chapter therefore considers the calculation, measure, and limitations on monetary damages and, when available, the constraints applicable to injunctive relief.

For the most part, this chapter considers three forms of monetary damage recovery—(1) the restitution interest, (2) the reliance interest, and (3) the expectancy interest. Early common law scholars articulated the function and purpose of these three forms of measuring the compensation due to the nonbreaching party.

The restitution interest is potentially the simplest compensation measurement, requiring the party against whom restitution is sought to disgorge the value of any benefits received from the other party. For example, assume that A owns a diamond with a market value of $5000 but contracts to sell that diamond to B for $3000. Also assume that B pays a third-party jeweler $100 to appraise the diamond before delivery for insurance purposes. If B pays A the promised $3000, but A refuses to tender the diamond, B's restitution damages are the value of the benefit conferred on A—$3000. B may not recover as restitution damages the $100 paid for the appraisal because that was not a benefit received by A.

The difficulty with restitution analysis interest arises from the fact that "restitution" refers to a number of different but related concepts. Restitution (1) may provide an independent cause of action for unjust enrichment, quasi-contract, or quantum meruit in the absence of a promise; (2) may provide a basis for enforcing an otherwise unenforceable promise under Restatement (Second) of Contracts § 86 (promissory restitution in the context of a promise for benefit received); and finally (3) may serve merely as one of several mechanisms to measure damages under Restatement (Second) of Contracts §§ 370–377. The two former inquiries permit a court to deny quantum meruit relief or refuse to enforce the promise if that is what justice requires. See, e.g., Restatement (Second) of Contracts § 86(1) ("A promise made in recognition of a benefit previously received by the promisor from the promisee is binding *to the extent necessary to prevent injustice*.") (emphasis added). In contrast, this chapter focuses solely upon the last context, restitution as a measure of damages for breach of contract. In this latter sense, any equitable balancing or justice of enforcement analysis is overwhelmed by the fact that the parties already have an enforceable contract that itself provides the equitable basis for compensation. While justice considerations may inform the choice of damages measurement rules, courts analyzing restitution as a damages measure have no discretion to deny damages altogether. See Restatement (Second) of Contracts § 371 (award of restitution "may as justice requires be measured *by either*" cost of obtaining benefits received from another source or extent to which property of party against whom restitution is sought has been increased in value).

The reliance interest attempts to compensate the nonbreaching party for expenditures made in performing or preparing to perform that party's obligations under the contract. See Restatement (Second) of Contracts § 349. As opposed to restitution damages, which examine the benefits received by the breaching party, reliance damages focus on the injuries suffered by the nonbreaching party in detrimentally relying upon the enforceability of the contract. In the diamond sale contract described above, for example, B's reliance damages include both the $3000 paid to A and the additional $100 paid to the jeweler to appraise the diamond.

The expectancy interest, in many senses, defines contract law and differentiates that area of law from other compensatory schemes like tort or property law. Expectancy damages attempt to compensate the nonbreaching party for the benefits lost by reason of nonperformance of the contract. In other words, expectancy damages attempt to give the nonbreaching party the value of full performance of the contract and place the nonbreaching party in the position she would have been in if the contract had been fully performed as promised. See Restatement (Second) of Contracts § 347, *cmt. a.* For this reason, expectancy damages are often referred to as "benefit of the bargain" damages. See id. Importantly, expectancy damages are based upon the benefits the nonbreaching party *actually* would have received from full performance, not on what that party hoped to receive. In the diamond example above, assuming B has paid the $3000 to A, she is now entitled to either full performance—tender of the diamond—or the value of that full performance—$5000.

Although this division of the three damages interests available in a breach of contract action is universally recognized, courts and scholars have struggled to provide justifications for the availability of expectancy damages in addition to reliance and restitution damages for breach of contract. As Professors Lon Fuller and William Perdue observed in their influential article, "The Reliance Interest in Contract Damages," expectancy damages do more than merely return the parties to their relative positions existing before the contract and therefore go beyond classical notions of commutative justice. Fuller and Perdue first observe that the three damages interests are not equally justifiable on a normative basis. See Lon L. Fuller and William R. Perdue, "The Reliance Interest in Contract Damages," 46 Yale L. J. 52, 53–57 (Part I) and 373 (Part II) (1936). In Aristotelian terms, the restitution interest protects the injured party's strongest claims for relief because, in that instance, the injured party has been unjustly deprived of something of value, and the benefited party has unjustly received and retained that value. See id. Such a claim represents Aristotle's arithmetic notion of corrective or commutative justice that considers justice in terms of maintaining or restoring the balance of goods and wealth between members of a society. See id. Similarly, the reliance interest also presents a claim for corrective justice since the promisor's improvidently made promise has caused the promise to suffer injury in the form of out-of-pocket losses. See id.

In contrast, the expectancy interest abandons the arithmetical eye for an eye notion of corrective or commutative justice in favor of Aristotle's distributive justice—justice that seeks to create the best or most proper distribution of wealth, honor, and benefits in society as a whole. In expectancy, "the justification for legal relief loses its self-evident quality. It is . . . no easy thing to explain why the normal rule of contract recovery should be that which measures damages by the value of the promised performance." Id.

Modern law has embraced these three monetary damage terms and objectives. Restatement (Second) of Contracts § 344(a) ("expectation interest" in having the benefit of the bargain by being put in as good a position had the contract been performed); Restatement (Second) of Contracts § 344(b) ("reliance interest" in being reimbursed for loss caused by reliance on the contract by being put in as good a position as occurred had the contract not been made); and Restatement (Second) of Contracts § 344(c) ("restitution interest" in having restored any benefit conferred on the other party). Several scholars have found fault with the Fuller and Perdue thesis that while expectancy is the contractual damage norm, its justification is theoretically or empirically weak. See, e.g., W. David Slawson, "Why Expectation Damages for Breach of Contract Must Be the Norm: A Refutation of the Fuller and Perdue 'Three Interests' Thesis," 81 Neb. L. Rev. 839 (2003); Christopher T. Wonnell, "Expectation, Reliance, and the Two Contractual Wrongs," 38 San Diego L. Rev. 53 (2001); Richard Craswell, "Against Fuller and Perdue," 67 U. Chi. L. Rev. 99 (2000); Christopher W. Frost, "Reconsidering the Reliance Interest," 44 St. Louis U. L. J. 1361 (2000); David W. Barnes, "The Net Expectation Interest in Contract Damages," 48 Emory L. J. 1137 (1999). But for whatever reason, the expectancy norm is deeply rooted in our common law.

Each of the three monetary damage measures (expectancy, reliance, and restitution) and particular limitations to each are explored below. Normally, the injured party has a right to damages for any breach. Restatement (Second) of Contracts § 346(1). Even when a specific monetary loss cannot be proven or does not exist, a breach will give rise to a claim for nominal damages. Restatement (Second) of Contracts § 346(2). "Nominal damages" usually refers to a small sum fixed by judicial practice and may be coupled with an award of attorney fees and other court costs, unless the action was frivolous or brought in bad faith. Restatement (Second) of Contracts § 346, *cmt. b.*

Also considered are the alternative equitable injunctive relief remedies, including specific performance (court order to perform) and injunctions (court order compelling not to breach). Restatement (Second) of Contracts § 345(b) (judicial remedies available for the protection of the interests include requiring specific performance of a contract or enjoining its non-performance). Compare Restatement (Second) of Contracts § 357(1) (specific performance), with Restatement (Second) of Contracts § 357(2) (injunction). Importantly, specific performance or an injunction will usually not be ordered where monetary damages would be adequate to protect the expectation interest of the injured party. Restatement (Second) of Contracts § 359(1).

When considering these materials, it is worth remembering that American jurisprudence does not award attorney fees to the victor. Considering the risks and costs and litigation, do you suspect that any measure of contract damages will place the injured party in the same position as if the contract had been fully performed? Do you imagine that contract litigation damages always fail to restore the injured party to status quo? See Melvin A. Eisenberg, "Actual and Virtual Specific Performance, the Theory of Efficient Breach, and the Indifference Principle in Contract Law," 93 Cal. L. Rev. 975, 977 (2005). Given this inadequacy principle, how do you view a court order of specific performance to compel performance in accordance with the terms of the contract?

B. ELECTION OF CONTRACT BREACH REMEDIES

Chapter 7 carefully explored the concept of election of remedies in connection with the assertion of a legal excuse for nonperformance associated with the formation of the contract. Mostly, the excused party was required to decide whether to pursue remedies "on the contract" or to rescind the contract and seek restitution. Most of Chapter 7 focused on the more normative rescission and restitution route. This was simply because most grounds for legal excuse for nonperformance do not also make tidy cases for monetary damages. However, actions for fraud represent a major exception where a party might well choose to keep the contract and sue for damages to make the contract conform as represented. Nonetheless, election rules occupied more than modest exposure to determine when a suit on the contract for damages waived the right to seek rescission and restitution. In theory, election rules prevent a party from pursuing theoretically inconsistent remedies and certainly prevent double recovery or overcompensation. As discussed, modern procedural rules have mitigated many of the negative pleading effects by permitting the parties to plead inconsistent remedies in the alternative, but some remain.

In the context of this chapter, the topic once again assumes some importance because of the multiple potential remedies available. Breach, not legal excuse, is the focus of this chapter, but breach can produce multiple remedy opportunities. First, a choice or election between equitable remedies and monetary damage remedies must be recognized. Is the injured party precluded from seeking injunctive relief only to later discover the remedy is not available, but a properly pled monetary remedy would have been available? If so, is the injured party free to once again plead in the alternative to mitigate the harsh results associated with a poor election? Even if the injured party does not seek injunctive relief, this chapter explores several bases for measuring the proper damage award: the expectancy interest, the reliance interest, and the restitution interest. Again, must the injured party choose one interest at the peril of losing one of the other remedies that may be available? Or may the injured party plead these recovery measures in the alternative, such that a loss on one count does not automatically eliminate a loss on the other two?

These and other matters are explored below. Unfortunately, the common law evolution in the states is not a uniform process. Thus, expect extreme variances among state approaches to these important problems.

C. ELECTION TO SEEK RESCISSION AND RESTITUTION DAMAGES OFF THE CONTRACT

Depending on the timing of the breach and the exchange of considerations, breach will often result in the breaching party having received far too much consideration from the injured party. Chapter 2 explored two concepts of restitution theory, one based on restitution on the contract (promissory restitution) and one involving pure equity. This section explores the election consequences to pursue the restitution interest remedy triggered by the breaching party's conduct. Other chapters have considered the restitution interest in different contexts: (i) Chapter 2 where a contract did not exist, (ii) Chapter 6 where the Statute of Frauds prevented the enforcement of the contract, (iii) Chapter 7 where some defect in the formation of the contract created a legal excuse in favor of one or both of the parties; and (iv) Chapter 8 where a qualifying supervening event occurring after the contract was formed created a legal excuse for nonperformance in favor of one or both of the parties, but an imbalance in exchanged considerations to the date of the supervening event resulted in a restitution claim.

This chapter therefore focuses only on the remaining restitution topic connected to breach, rather than one of the other precipitating events mentioned above. Specifically, Chapter 5 explored the concept of a material uncured breach resulting in an election in favor of the injured party. In such circumstances, the injured party is privileged to elect to continue with the contract by treating the breach as partial and suing for monetary damages resulting from the partial breach. The discussion below assumes that the injured party elects to treat the uncured material breach as a total breach and thus cancels or otherwise terminates the contractual relationship. The injured party may seek monetary damages for the total breach, including the restitution interest of the injured party.

As was explored in greater detail in Chapter 5, rescission, cancellation, or termination is a remedy available at the election of the injured party in the case of total breach by the defendant. Confronted with a total breach by the breaching party, the injured party may seek a forward-looking remedy involving expectancy damages. In this case, the continuing existence and validity of the contract is a necessary predicate of any award of damages. In the alternative, the plaintiff may elect to pursue the retrospective remedy based on the plaintiff's election to rescind the contract and recover restitutionary damages. Restatement (Second) of Contracts § 373(1).

The Losing Contract and Effect of Contract Price. As explored more fully below, the goal of expectancy damages is to place the injured party in as good a position as if the contract had been performed. Restatement (Second) of Contracts § 344(1)(a). A necessary corollary is that the award may not place the injured party in a better position than would have occurred had there been no breach.

Several legitimate conclusions would appear to flow naturally from the "as good as but no better than" syllogism. An important idea to consider is the effect of the contract price. Intuitively, the contract price seemingly places a ceiling (but not a floor) on damage recovery. See Restatement (Second) of Contracts § 344, *cmt. b.* However, because of other losses, such as consequential losses that may escalate the expectancy losses far beyond the actual contract price, the contract itself is seldom a serious limitation on expectancy recovery. See Restatement (Second) of Contracts § 347(b) (any other losses including incidental and consequential losses).

In some cases, a party makes an improvident contract or even deliberately enters into a losing contract in order to purchase market share or for some other business justification. When losing contracts are breached, should the contract price remain a ceiling on the injured party's damage recovery? Two situations might exist.

First, actual reliance costs might exceed expected costs, meaning that had the breaching party fully performed, the other party would have lost money. Should the act of a breach itself justify the injured party in recovering reliance costs that exceed the actual contract price? The other situation involves an uncured material breach resulting in total breach. Generally, the contract operates as a practical upper limit on damages recovery, except where the breaching party commits an uncured material breach before the injured party has fully performed and the injured party seeks restitution off the contract. In such cases, the injured party will argue the value of its services exceeds the contract price, and having committed a serious breach, the breaching party is not in a position to reject a restitution damage recovery. See Restatement (Second) of Contracts § 373(2) (contract price limitation where full performance by injured party and breaching party has only to pay money) and Restatement (Second) of Contracts § 349 (contract price limitation in reliance damages because it is always easy to prove the injured party would have suffered a loss when reliance costs sought exceed the contract price).

This leaves the situation where the injured party has not fully performed, and the breaching party has committed an uncured material breach constituting a total breach. In these situations, an award of damages based on the value of the services provided by the injured party to the breaching party may well be proven with certainty by reference to the costs of the breaching party's substitute performance. Scholars are divided on the justice of this approach. George E. Palmer, "The Contract Price as a Limit on Restitution for Defendant's Breach," 20 Ohio State L.J. 264 (1959). See also Henry Mather, "Restitution as a Remedy for Breach of Contract: The Case of the Partially Performing Seller," 92 Yale L. J. 14

(1982); Bernard E. Gegan, "In Defense of Restitution: A Comment on Mather, Restitution as a Remedy for Breach of Contract: The Case of the Partially Performing Seller," 57 S. Cal. L. Rev. 723 (1984); E. Allan Farnsworth, "Your Loss or My Gain? The Dilemma of the Disgorgement Principle in Breach of Contract," 94 Yale L. J. 1339 (1985); Robert Childres and Jack Garamella, "The Law of Restitution and the Reliance Interest in Contract," 64 Nw. U. L. Rev. 433 (1969); Joseph M. Perillo, "Restitution in a Contractual Context," 73 Colum. L. Rev. 1208 (1973); and Andrew Kull, "Restitution as a Remedy for Breach of Contract," 67 S. Cal. L. Rev. 1465 (1994).

Nonetheless, Restatement (Second) of Contracts § 373, *cmt. d* states the traditional rule and permits restitution recovery in excess of the contract price.As you study the next case, determine how the case facts fit the patterns just described. Should the injured party be entitled to recovery in excess of the contract price?

UNITED STATES V. ALGERNON BLAIR, INC.

United States Circuit Court of Appeals for the Fourth Circuit
479 F.2d 638 (1973)

CRAVEN, Circuit Judge:

May a subcontractor, who justifiably ceases work under a contract because of the prime contractor's breach, recover in quantum meruit the value of labor and equipment already furnished pursuant to the contract irrespective of whether he would have been entitled to recover in a suit on the contract? We think so, and, for reasons to be stated, the decision of the district court will be reversed.

The subcontractor, Coastal Steel Erectors, Inc., brought this action under the provisions of the Miller Act, 40 U.S.C.A. § 270a et seq., in the name of the United States against Algernon Blair, Inc., and its surety, United States Fidelity and Guaranty Company. Blair had entered a contract with the United States for the construction of a naval hospital in Charleston County, South Carolina. Blair had then contracted with Coastal to perform certain steel erection and supply certain equipment in conjunction with Blair's contract with the United States. Coastal commenced performance of its obligations, supplying its own cranes for handling and placing steel. Blair refused to pay for crane rental, maintaining that it was not obligated to do so under the subcontract. Because of Blair's failure to make payments for crane rental, and after completion of approximately 28 percent of the subcontract, Coastal terminated its performance. Blair then proceeded to complete the job with a new subcontractor. Coastal brought this action to recover for labor and equipment furnished.

The district court found that the subcontract required Blair to pay for crane use and that Blair's refusal to do so was such a material breach as to justify Coastal's terminating performance. This finding is not questioned on appeal. The court then found that under the contract the amount due Coastal, less what had already been paid, totaled approximately $37,000. Additionally, the court found Coastal would have lost more than $37,000 if it had completed performance. Holding that any amount due Coastal must be reduced by any loss it would have incurred by complete performance of the contract, the court denied recovery to Coastal. While the district court correctly stated the "normal rule of contract damages," we think Coastal is entitled to recover in quantum meruit.

In United States for Use of Susi Contracting Co. v. Zara Contracting Co., 146 F.2d 606 (2d Cir. 1944), a Miller Act action, the court was faced with a situation similar to that involved here—the prime contractor had unjustifiably breached a subcontract after partial performance by the subcontractor. The court stated:

> For it is an accepted principle of contract law, often applied in the case of construction contracts, that the promisee upon breach has the option to forego any suit on the contract and claim only the reasonable value of his performance. 146 F.2d at 610.

The Tenth Circuit has also stated that the right to seek recovery under quantum meruit in a Miller Act case is clear. Quantum meruit recovery is not limited to an action against the prime contractor but may also be brought against the Miller Act surety, as in this case. Further, that the complaint is not clear in regard to the theory of a plaintiff's recovery does not preclude recovery under quantum meruit. Narragansett Improvement Co. v. United States, 290 F.2d 577 (1st Cir. 1961). A plaintiff may join a claim for quantum meruit with a claim for damages from breach of contract.

In the present case, Coastal has, at its own expense, provided Blair with labor and the use of equipment. Blair, who breached the subcontract, has retained these benefits without having fully paid for them. On these facts, Coastal is entitled to restitution in quantum meruit.

The "restitution interest," involving a combination of unjust impoverishment with unjust gain, presents the strongest case for relief. If, following Aristotle, we regard the purpose of justice as the maintenance of an equilibrium of goods among members of society, the restitution interest presents twice as strong a claim to judicial intervention as the reliance interest, since if A not only causes B to lose one unit but appropriates that unit to himself, the resulting discrepancy between A and B is not one unit but two. Fuller & Perdue, "The Reliance Interest in Contract Damages," 46 Yale L. J. 52, 56 (1936).

The impact of quantum meruit is to allow a promisee to recover the value of services he gave to the defendant irrespective of whether he would have lost money on the contract and been unable to recover in a suit on the contract. Scaduto v. Orlando, 381 F.2d 587, 595 (2d Cir. 1967). The measure of recovery for quantum meruit is the reasonable value of the performance, Restatement of Contracts § 347 (1932); and recovery is undiminished by any loss which would have been incurred by complete performance. 12 Williston on Contracts § 1485, at 312 (3d ed. 1970). While the contract price may be evidence of reasonable value of the services, it does not measure the value of the performance or limit recovery.[7] Rather, the standard for measuring the reasonable value of the services rendered is the amount for which such services could have been purchased from one in the plaintiff's position at the time and place the services were rendered.

It should be noted, however, that in suits for restitution there are many cases permitting the plaintiff to recover the value of benefits conferred on the defendant, even though this value exceeds that of the return performance promised by the defendant. In these cases it is no doubt felt that the defendant's breach should work a forfeiture of his right to retain the benefits of an advantageous bargain.

Since the district court has not yet accurately determined the reasonable value of the labor and equipment use furnished by Coastal to Blair, the case must be remanded for those findings. When the amount has been determined, judgment will be entered in favor of Coastal, less payments already made under the contract. Accordingly, for the reasons stated above, the decision of the district court is reversed and remanded with instructions.

NOTES AND QUESTIONS

1. *Availability of the losing contract restitution remedy.* The general contractor Algernon Blair argued that the construction contract with the subcontractor Coastal Steel required Coastal to pay for its own crane. After completing approximately 28% of the contract with no Algernon crane reimbursement, Coastal decided to stop work and sue Algernon, who in turn hired another subcontractor to complete the project. Why did Coastal not breach the contract when it stopped work after completing only 28%? What legal rule permitted this behavior while foreclosing a suit by Algernon against Coastal?

Once Algernon committed an uncured material breach, Coastal had an option to elect to continue to complete its own performance and then sue

---

[7]   It should be noted, however, that in suits for restitution there are many cases permitting the plaintiff to recover the value of benefits conferred on the defendant, even though this value exceeds that of the return performance promised by the defendant. In these cases it is no doubt felt that the defendant's breach should work a forfeiture of his right to retain the benefits of an advantageous bargain. Fuller & Perdue, supra at 77.

Algernon for partial breach of contract. If Coastal had fully performed the contract, what would it have been entitled to recover? See Restatement (Second) of Contracts § 373(2). The alternative option was to terminate or cancel the contract with Algernon. At that point, Coastal once again had two options. First, it could sue on the contract for total breach damages. Alternatively, since the contract was terminated, it could sue for restitution. Obviously, it elected to sue for restitution. Why do you think it did so? Are any of these three "elections" (terminate or not; sue on the contract; sue off the contract) precluded by the election of remedies provisions? See Restatement (Second) of Contracts § 378.

Algernon alleged the $37,000 restitution recovery was excessive because Coastal had made a poor contract by grossly underestimating its true expenses. Assuming that to be true, is the contract price a limitation on Coastal's recovery? See Restatement (Second) of Contracts § 373(1).

2. *Restitution measure.* Once Coastal determined to sue for restitution, how is that to be measured and what is the function and role of the contract itself in that determination? The trial court determined that even though Algernon owed $37,000 on the contract breach, Algernon was entitled to reduce that amount by any amount it could prove Coastal would lose by completing performance. This is certainly the rule in an expectancy recovery. See Restatement (Second) of Contracts § 347(c) (recovery reduced by any loss avoided by not having to perform). That topic is explored further under expectancy recovery. The appellate court reversed, noting that "recovery is undiminished by any loss which would have been incurred by complete performance."

The court cites Restatement (First) of Contracts § 347(1) (for the total breach of a contract, the injured party can get judgment for the reasonable value of a performance rendered by him, measured as of the time it was rendered) to allow Coastal to recover the market value of the services to Algernon Blair, rather than the contractual price. Restatement (Second) of Contracts § 373(1) also provides that the injured party is entitled to restitution for any benefit conferred on the other party.

However, the measurement of the restitution interest is now contained in Restatement (Second) of Contracts § 371, which provides the restitution interest may be measured, as required by justice, either by (a) the reasonable value received by the breaching party determined by reference to the actual or hypothetical cost to obtain replacement services from another person in the position of the injured party, or (b) the value of the increase in the breaching party's interest. Would the outcome in this case be any different using Restatement (Second) of Contracts § 371(a)? Did Algernon complete the project using another subcontractor? Would the cost to complete not be the measurement standard? Does Algernon have to pay twice? First, Algernon must pay the replacement subcontractor. Must it also pay Coastal, the party injured by the breach? Is that fair, and if so, what justifies this result? Had Coastal breached the contract, Algernon would have hired another subcontractor to complete the project, but unless the cost to complete was greater than the remaining unpaid cost in the original contract, Algernon would simply have paid the full contract price, split between two different parties. How and why is this situation so radically different? How would you decide the "justice" limitation specifically stated in Restatement (Second) of Contracts § 371? Do you think a restatement section must state a "justice" requirement in order for a court to reach a just result? If not, why do some restatement sections specifically mention justice while others are silent? As noted by the scholarly debate earlier, scholars are divided on whether Coastal should be able to recover the market value of its services or whether Coastal's recovery should be limited by the contract price.

3. *Breaching plaintiff and restitution.* Although not addressed by *Algernon Blair*, restitution is available to a breaching party as well as the injured party. See Restatement (Second) of Contracts § 374. Typically, this will occur in situations where a buyer makes a deposit on a purchase contract but is unable to complete the purchase. The injured seller is of course entitled to damages, but if the deposit exceeds those damages, the breaching purchaser is entitled to a return of the excess and may bring a suit to enforce this right. The same rule existed under Restatement (First) § 357(1). Importantly, Restatement (First) of Contracts § 357(1)(a) required that the breach not be deliberate or willful. However, Restatement (Second) of Contracts § 374 blackletter omits the willful breach limitation, as does the intervening UCC § 2–718(2), enacted after the Restatement (First) of Contracts but before the Restatement (Second) of Contracts. However, the commentary somewhat retains the concept:

> b. *Measurement of benefit.* If the party in breach seeks restitution of money that he has paid, no problem arises in measuring the benefit to the other party. See Illustration 1. If, however, he seeks to recover a sum of money that represents the benefit of services rendered to the other party, measurement of the benefit is more difficult. Since the party seeking restitution is responsible for posing the problem of measurement of benefit, doubts will be resolved against him and his recovery will not exceed the less generous of the two measures stated in § 370, that of the other party's increase in wealth. See Illustration 3. If no value can be put on this, he cannot recover. See Illustration 5. Although the contract price is evidence of the benefit, it is not conclusive. However, in no case will the party in breach be allowed to recover more than a ratable portion of the total contract price where such a portion can be determined.
>
> A party who intentionally furnishes services or builds a building that is materially different from what he promised is properly regarded as having acted officiously and not in part performance of his promise and will be denied recovery on that ground even if his performance was of some benefit to the other party. This is not the case, however, if the other party has accepted or agreed to accept the substitute performance. See §§ 278, 279.

The elimination of the willful breach limitation represents a deliberate policy shift. The two competing policies include comparing the overcompensation to the injured party in one case (favored by Restatement (First) of Contracts) with rewarding deliberate breaching behavior (favored by Restatement (Second) of Contracts). The inclusion of a recovery measure in both cases was precipitated by an early important article recognizing that most cases refused to penalize the breaching party by rewarding the injured party with overcompensation. See Arthur L. Corbin, "The Right of a Defaulting Vendee to the Restitution of Installments Paid," 40 Yale L. J. 1013 (1931). See also Comment, "Defaulting Vendee Relieved from Forfeiture," 2 Stan. L. Rev. 235 (1949). Such a shift may reflect a more general acceptance among scholars, lawyers, and judges that breachers of contract are not necessarily wrongdoers. "Rules of contract law are not rules of punishment; the contract breacher is not an outlaw. His restitution interest deserves protection to the extent that it does not subvert the legitimate interests of the party aggrieved by the breach." Joseph M. Perillo, "Restitution in the Second Restatement of Contracts,"81 Colum. L. Rev. 37, 50 (1981).

Accepting the doctrine for the moment as the rule, should the parties be able to expressly alter the rule in the contract itself? Is the rule a default rule or a mandatory rule that in all cases disfavors overcompensation of the injured party to discouraging deliberate and willful breaching behavior? Can overcompensation in such cases be related to punitive damages? See Restatement (Second) of Contracts § 355. Should an intentional and deliberate breach of a contract constitute a tort?

4. *Willful breach doctrines as a quasi-punitive remedy*. As noted above, American contract law is generally unconcerned with the fault of the breaching party. Nonetheless, courts react in many cases to the willfulness of a breach by either conscious or unconscious bias against the breaching party or by application of several doctrines expressly dealing with willfulness. Judge Cardozo's discussion in dicta in *Jacob & Youngs v. Kent*—analyzed in Chapter 5—suggests that the decision whether to apply a cost-of-completion or a difference-in-value measure of damages depends upon the willfulness of the breach. Courts also relax the degree of certainty required to prove the amount of damages in cases of willful breach. See William S. Dodge, "The Case for Punitive Damages in Contracts," 48 Duke L. J. 629, 689 & n.328 (1999). Do you think that such exceptions to the general rule that courts will not inquire into the wrongfulness or fault involved in a breach reflect a hidden agenda by courts to punish "wrongful" breaches of contract?

D. ELECTION TO SEEK DAMAGES ON THE CONTRACT

This section explores the "three measures" of monetary damages for suit to recover those damages on the contract. Modern law has embraced three primary monetary damage terms and objectives. Restatement (Second) of Contracts § 344(a) (*"expectation interest"* in having the benefit of the bargain by being put in as good a position had the contract been performed); Restatement (Second) of Contracts § 344(b) (*"reliance interest"* in being reimbursed for loss caused by reliance on the contract by being put in as good a position as occurred had the contract not been made); and Restatement (Second) of Contracts § 344(c) (*"restitution interest"* in having restored any benefit conferred on the other party).

The expectancy remedy has become the clear norm for modern contract damage purposes. While early scholars questioned the legitimacy of the expectancy norm, the norm was nonetheless acknowledged. See Lon L. Fuller and William R. Perdue, "The Reliance Interest in Contract Damages," 46 Yale L. J. 52, 53–57 (Part I) and 373 (Part II), 53–56 (1936). Later scholars have challenged the early thesis that questioned the expectancy norm and have vigorously defended that norm. See W. David Slawson, "Why Expectation Damages for Breach of Contract Must Be the Norm: A Refutation of the Fuller and Perdue 'Three Interests' Thesis," 81 Neb. L. Rev. 839 (2003); Christopher T. Wonnell, "Expectation, Reliance, and the Two Contractual Wrongs," 38 San Diego L. Rev. 53 (2001); Richard Craswell, "Against Fuller and Perdue," 67 U. Chi. L. Rev. 99 (2000); Christopher W. Frost, "Reconsidering the Reliance Interest," 44 St. Louis U. L. J. 1361 (2000); David W. Barnes, "The Net Expectation Interest in Contract Damages," 48 Emory L. J. 1137 (1999).

Also, as explored earlier in this chapter, injunctive relief may also be available when monetary damages are inadequate. Restatement (Second) of Contracts §§ 357(1)–(2) & 359(1). Each form of breach relief has its own unique characteristics and limitations. Importantly, fault is largely irrelevant to all forms of common law relief. In civil law jurisdictions, fault is often the eye of the storm. John Y. Gotanda, "Damages in Lieu of Performance Because of Breach of Contract," Villanova University School of Law, Public Law and Legal Theory Working Paper N. 2006–8. For an attack on this country's strict liability approach and an argument that a contract damages regime should be "fault-based," see George M. Cohen, "The Fault Lines in Contract Damages," 80 Va. L. Rev. 1225 (1994) and William S. Dodge, "The Case for Punitive Damages in Contracts,"48 Duke L. J. 629 (1999).

1. THE EXPECTANCY INTEREST

The object of the expectancy interest is to protect the injured party's interest in having the "benefit of the bargain" to place that party in "as good a position" (but no better) than would have occurred had the contract been fully performed as promised by the breaching party. Restatement (Second) of Contracts § 344(a). The law normally protects the expectancy interest by entering a judgment or order awarding the injured party a sum of money due under the contract or as monetary damages. Restatement (Second) of Contracts § 345(a). Where the injured party has fully performed and the breaching party has simply failed to pay the required contractual sum, a judgment for that amount ordinarily suffices. Unfortunately, most contractual entanglements are not that simple. In many (if not most) cases a breaching party's failure to perform or defective performance will trigger nonperformance by the injured party—particularly in cases of uncured material or total breach. Calculating the expectancy interest of the injured party in these cases can be quite complex.

To simplify and systematize the computational process, if not the calculation, the proper measure of the expectancy interest is fragmented into several components. Restatement (Second) of Contracts § 347. Which of these measures applies depends upon whether the claim involves a partial breach (injured party continues the contract but sues for losses incurred as a result of the breach) or a total breach (injured party terminates the contractual relationship and, in addition to suing for its losses, must further account for the savings in not completing its own performance). Pursuant to this calculus, and subject to limitations to be later explored, the injured party's measure of the expectancy interest for total breach involves the following four factors:

- "Loss in value" caused by the breaching party's failure or deficiency [**Element 1**];
- Plus any "other loss" caused by the breach, including incidental and consequential losses [**Element 2**];
- Less any "cost avoided" by not having to perform [**Element 3**]; and
- Less any "loss avoided" by not having to perform [**Element 4**].

Because the first two measures consider losses caused by the breach, they apply to partial as well as total breaches. The remaining two measures are normally only associated with a total breach because they involve savings from the injured party's terminating performance by virtue of the uncured material total breach of the breaching party. The Restatement (Second) of Contracts § 347 factor tests can be expressed in convenient equation form:

Expectancy Interest = Loss in value + Other Losses − Costs Avoided − Losses Avoided

The following discussion explores the basics of each element. However, an expanded discussion of each element appears later in the various limitations on the expectancy interest recovery.

Element 1(A). *Loss in Value Component.* The "loss in value" measure covers two distinct situations. First, the breach may occur before the breaching party has rendered any performance at all. In such situations, the loss in value is measured by the value that performance would have had to the nonbreaching party. Second, the breach may occur only after defective or partial performance. In this latter case, the measure of damages is the value full performance would have had to the nonbreaching party minus the value of defective or partial performance actually rendered to the nonbreaching party. See Restatement (Second) of Contracts § 344, *cmt. b.* Since most cases involve defective or partial performance, the "difference in value" measure is the norm. This requires a comparison of the value of what was promised to be received less the value of what was actually received.

For example, assume Sam sold his home to Barbara for its current fair market value of $100,000 with an express promise that the home was termite free. Later, termites were discovered, and the value of a home at the time of sale with such termite infestation would have been $85,000. Barbara's "loss in value" expectancy interest is the difference between the value of the home as promised ($100,000) and the home actually received ($85,000).

Importantly, the loss in value formulation in all cases requires proof of the "market value" of the promise to compare that value to the value established by the contract. Market value is an imprecise if not illusive concept. However, the concept of "market" implies an objective determination rather than a subjective one to determine the intrinsic value to the particular injured party. Where a substitute transaction or actual market repair has occurred and is a reasonable substitute in terms of time and quality, the price of the correction or substitute will be the best proof. But where the transaction cannot be corrected or the injured party decides not do so, market value recovery remains available but simply becomes more difficult to prove. Expert testimony is often the best resource where an actual substitute purchase or repair is either not available or not chosen. However, the fact that the expectancy interest seeks to place the injured party in the "same but no better position" than had the contract been performed as promised inevitably leads to difficult problems of proof of market value. See, e.g., Omri Ben-Shahar, "The Secrecy Interest in Contract Law," 109 Yale L. J. 1885, 1885 (2000) and Ian Ayres and Kristin Madison, "Threatening Inefficient Performance of Injunctions and Contracts," 148 U. Pa. L. Rev. 45, 46–47 (1999).

Element 1(B). *Alternative to Loss in Value Component—Cost of Completion or Repair.* As the above discussion suggests, the market value of the promise may be difficult to prove with a reasonable degree of certainty, especially where the defect is neither repaired nor replaced. At least in limited cases involving defective or unfinished construction, often the best market value measure of the promised performance is the actual cost to repair or complete the construction by another party.

Cases involving an uncured material total breach permit the injured party to make an election to terminate the contractual relationship with the breaching party. That termination allows the project to be completed or corrected by a third party. In those cases, the cost to complete or repair can be added to amounts already paid to the breaching party to determine the true and actual market value of the perfectly performed promise. When that cost exceeds the original contract price, the difference between the total amount paid by the injured party to the breaching party and the correcting party less the actual contract price becomes a nearly irrefutable proof of the market element of the loss in value.

For that reason, Restatement (Second) of Contracts § 348(2) permits and generally prefers that the measure of damages be based on the "reasonable cost of completing performance or of remedying defects." The diminution or loss in value is still permitted, making clear the injured party retains the option to seek the normative market loss in value measure regardless of whether the repair or completion occurred. Restatement (Second) of Contracts § 348(2)(a). However, because of the problems of proving the market value of the promised performance actually received, most defective or incomplete construction projects are simply repaired or completed by another party. Therefore, as discussed in Chapter 5, in most cases, this issue reduces itself to whether the breaching party has committed an uncured material breach allowing the injured party to terminate the contract and hire a replacement contractor.

One important limitation exists and was the subsidiary question raised in the *Jacob & Youngs* case in Chapter 5. Especially where the construction is defective rather than merely incomplete, correction will nearly always involve some significant degree of deconstruction of the portion already completed. In the *Jacob & Youngs* case, the failure to use Reading pipe would have required the destruction of nearly the entire home in order to remove and replace the equal quality Cohoes pipe. Judge Cardozo seized on this aspect of the case to justify implying by law a constructive condition of "substantial performance." Where substantial performance exists, it is the antithesis of material breach and the injured party may not terminate the contract. Where substantial performance occurs, the injured party's only choice (absent a breach itself) is to allow the construction to be completed and then seek correction. In essence, since the discovery of the pipe substitution occurred after the completion of the home, that was the result in *Jacob & Youngs* in any event.

Regardless of whether the breaching party commits a material breach (allowing termination) or an immaterial breach (not allowing termination), the injured party is entitled to an award of monetary damages to compensate for the loss in expectancy. The general measure is the "loss in value." Since that is an objective market measure rather than a subjective idiosyncratic measure known only to the injured party, most cases will create a loss in value monetary award only where the market places the same or similar value on the defective performance as the injured party. In

Jacob & Youngs, Judge Cardozo determined that was not the case, summarizing:

> In the circumstances of this case, we think the measure of the allowance is not the cost of replacement, which would be great, but the difference in value, which would be either nominal or nothing. Jacob & Youngs, Inc. v. Kent, 129 N.E. 889, 891 (1921).

That limitation is expressed in Restatement (Second) of Contracts § 348(2)(b), which allows the injured party in a breach resulting in defective or unfinished construction the following alternative damages to diminution in value:

> The reasonable cost of completing performance or of remedying the defects if that cost is not clearly disproportionate to the probable loss in value to him.

Accordingly, while the doctrine of substantial performance takes into consideration the equitable disproportionality of loss or forfeiture between the breaching and injured parties, so does the ultimate measure of recovery, regardless of whether the breach was material or not. However, material breach cases are much more likely to include incomplete construction projects, rather than complete but defective projects. In those common completed but defective construction cases, the same or similar concept that denies the material breach option will generally also deny the cost to repair. Why? Because the cost to repair includes a significant destruction in value without a commensurate significant increase in market value. Moreover, as will be seen later, the avoidable loss doctrine inherent in Restatement (Second) of Contracts § 347(c) will normally require the injured party to use the cost to complete, rather than the loss in value. As a consequence, this alternative rule has its primary importance in complete or nearly complete construction cases where the deconstruction costs do not add value to the property.

Element 2. *Plus Other Loss Recovery.* Restatement (Second) of Contracts § 347(b) allows the injured party to recover "any other loss" caused by the breach, including incidental and consequential losses. Normally, incidental and consequential losses are characterized by reference to the fact that such losses do not directly arise from the loss in value of the breaching party's performance. Rather, other factors occur as a result of the breaching party's performance causing loss. Incidental losses typically occur after the breach and include additional costs incurred by the injured party to avoid further losses. Thus, incidental losses are generally in the form of monetary outflows by the injured party to deal with the consequences of the breach. Restatement (Second) of Contracts § 347, *cmt. c.* For example, UCC § 2–715(1) provides that incidental damages include expenses incurred by the injured party to take custody and care of rightfully rejected goods. Consequential losses represent losses to the injured party's property or to persons. Restatement (Second) of Contracts § 347, *cmt. c.* Similarly, UCC § 2–715(2) provides a buyer can recover consequential damages for injury to person or property proximately relating to the breach.

While incidental damages are conceptually simple (e.g., custody and care of the breaching party's property), the concept of consequential damages is considerably less tidy. Damages conceptually adopt one of two primary forms generally thought to originate in *Hadley v. Baxendale*, the subject of the foreseeability limitation discussed in the next section. First, "general" or "direct" damages flow from the "ordinary course of events" normatively expected to result from a breach. See, e.g., UCC 2–714(1) (damages for any nonconformity of tender represent the loss resulting in the "ordinary course of events" from the seller's breach). Second, "consequential" or "special" damages do not flow from the ordinary course of events but rather, result from the general or particular needs and requirements of the injured party that the breaching party had reason to know. See, e.g., UCC § 2–715(2)(a). The "had reason to know" language implies a generally accepted objective standard and rejects a more restrictive "tacit agreement" standard that would require the breaching party to specifically contemplate the damage and thus specifically assume the risk.

Characterization of the damages in these groupings is quite important because the contract may limit or exclude consequential damages, thus requiring precise calculation of general damages. Additionally, consequential damages are subject to a more rigid foreseeability test discussed below. The single most important class of consequential damages include profits lost by the injured party on other or collateral contracts as a result of the breach of the contract between the breaching and injured party. Lost profits on the primary contract between the breaching and injured party are general or direct damages because they are always expected and foreseeable as an ordinary course of a breach.

Element 3. *Less Costs Avoided.* In cases involving total breach where the injured party terminates the contract, the injured party will save the cost of any further performance. Restatement (Second) of Contracts § 347(c). Given that the avoidance limitation discussed below most often requires the injured party to terminate its performance, further costs will normally be avoided. Restatement (Second) of Contracts § 347, *cmt. d.* The costs so avoided are subtracted from the "loss in value" determined by the earlier discussion.

Element 4. *Less Losses Avoided.* Also in cases involving total breach where the injured party terminates the contract, the injured party might avoid some losses by salvaging and redirecting some of the resources otherwise to be devoted to completing performance on the terminated contract. Restatement (Second) of Contracts § 347(c). For example, a wrongfully discharged employee will normally seek other employment using the services free by the employer's breach. Restatement (Second) of Contracts § 347, *cmt. d.*

In the next case, consider the expectancy interest and its market formulation in the context of the Court's jury instruction. Did it adequately convey to the jury the required elements of proof? How was market value of the promise to be determined?

HAWKINS V. MCGEE

Supreme Court of New Hampshire
84 N.H. 114, 146 A. 641 (1929)

Defendant's motions for a nonsuit and for a directed verdict on the count in assumpsit were denied, and the defendant excepted. During the argument of plaintiff's counsel to the jury, the defendant claimed certain exceptions, and also excepted to the denial of his requests for instructions and to the charge of the court upon the question of damages, as more fully appears in the opinion. The defendant seasonably moved to set aside the verdict upon the grounds that it was (1) contrary to the evidence; (2) against the weight of the evidence; (3) against the weight of the law and evidence; and (4) because the damages awarded by the jury were excessive. The court denied the motion upon the first three grounds, but found that the damages were excessive, and made an order that the verdict be set aside, unless the plaintiff elected to remit all in excess of $500. The plaintiff having refused to remit, the verdict was set aside "as excessive and against the weight of the evidence," and the plaintiff excepted.

BRANCH, J.

The operation in question consisted in the removal of a considerable quantity of scar tissue from the palm of the plaintiff's right hand and the grafting of skin taken from the plaintiff's chest in place thereof. The scar tissue was the result of a severe burn caused by contact with an electric wire, which the plaintiff received about nine years before the time of the transactions here involved. There was evidence to the effect that before the operation was performed the plaintiff and his father went to the defendant's office, and that the defendant, in answer to the question, "How long will the boy be in the hospital?" replied,

> Three or four days, not over four; then the boy can go home and it will be just a few days when he will go back to work with a good hand.

Clearly this and other testimony to the same effect would not justify a finding that the doctor contracted to complete the hospital treatment in three or four days or that the plaintiff would be able to go back to work within a few days thereafter. The above statements could only be construed as expressions of opinion or predictions as to the probable duration of the treatment and plaintiff's resulting disability, and the fact that these estimates were exceeded would impose no contractual liability upon the defendant. The only substantial basis for the plaintiff's claim is the testimony that the defendant also said before the operation was decided upon,

> I will guarantee to make the hand a hundred per cent perfect hand
> or a hundred per cent good hand.

The plaintiff was present when these words were alleged to have been spoken, and, if they are to be taken at their face value, it seems obvious that proof of their utterance would establish the giving of a warranty in accordance with his contention.

The defendant argues, however, that, even if these words were uttered by him, no reasonable man would understand that they were used with the intention of entering "into any contractual relation whatever," and that they could reasonably be understood only "as his expression in strong language that he believed and expected that as a result of the operation he would give the plaintiff a very good hand." It may be conceded, as the defendant contends, that, before the question of the making of a contract should be submitted to a jury, there is a preliminary question of law for the trial court to pass upon, i.e. "whether the words could possibly have the meaning imputed to them by the party who founds his case upon a certain interpretation," but it cannot be held that the trial court decided this question erroneously in the present case. It is unnecessary to determine at this time whether the argument of the defendant, based upon "common knowledge of the uncertainty which attends all surgical operations," and the improbability that a surgeon would ever contract to make a damaged part of the human body "one hundred per cent perfect," would, in the absence of countervailing considerations, be regarded as conclusive, for there were other factors in the present case which tended to support the contention of the plaintiff. There was evidence that the defendant repeatedly solicited from the plaintiff's father the opportunity to perform this operation, and the theory was advanced by plaintiff's counsel in cross-examination of defendant that he sought an opportunity to "experiment on skin grafting," in which he had had little previous experience. If the jury accepted this part of plaintiff's contention, there would be a reasonable basis for the further conclusion that, if defendant spoke the words attributed to him, he did so with the intention that they should be accepted at their face value, as an inducement for the granting of consent to the operation by the plaintiff and his father, and there was ample evidence that they were so accepted by them. The question of the making of the alleged contract was properly submitted to the jury.

The substance of the charge to the jury on the question of damages appears in the following quotation:

> If you find the plaintiff entitled to anything, he is entitled to recover for what pain and suffering he has been made to endure and for what injury he has sustained over and above what injury he had before.

To this instruction the defendant seasonably excepted. By it, the jury was permitted to consider two elements of damage:

> (1) Pain and suffering due to the operation; and

> (2) positive ill effects of the operation upon the plaintiff's hand. Authority for any specific rule of damages in cases of this kind seems to be lacking, but, when tested by general principle and by analogy, it appears that the foregoing instruction was erroneous.

"By 'damages,' as that term is used in the law of contracts, is intended compensation for a breach, measured in the terms of the contract." Davis v. New England Cotton Yarn Co., 77 N. H. 403, 404, 92 A. 732, 733. The purpose of the law is "to put the plaintiff in as good a position as he would have been in had the defendant kept his contract." 3 Williston Cont. § 1338. . . . The measure of recovery "is based upon what the defendant should have given the plaintiff, not what the plaintiff has given the defendant or otherwise expended." 3 Williston Cont. § 1341. "The only losses that can be said fairly to come within the terms of a contract are such as the parties must have had in mind when the contract was made, or such as they either knew or ought to have known would probably result from a failure to comply with its terms." Davis v. New England Cotton Yarn Co., 77 N. H. 403, 404, 92 A. 732, 733. . . .

The present case is closely analogous to one in which a machine is built for a certain purpose and warranted to do certain work. In such cases, the usual rule of damages for breach of warranty in the sale of chattels is applied, and it is held that the measure of damages is the difference between the value of the machine, if it had corresponded with the warranty and its actual value, together with such incidental losses as the parties knew, or ought to have known, would probably result from a failure to comply with its terms. . . .

The rule thus applied is well settled in this state.

> As a general rule, the measure of the vendee's damages is the difference between the value of the goods as they would have been if the warranty as to quality had been true, and the actual value at the time of the sale, including gains prevented and losses sustained, and such other damages as could be reasonably anticipated by the parties as likely to be caused by the vendor's

failure to keep his agreement, and could not by reasonable care on the part of the vendee have been avoided. Union Bank v. Blanchard, 65 N. H. 21, 23, 18 A. 90, 91; Hurd v. Dunsmore, supra; Noyes v. Blodgett, 58 N. H. 502; P. L. ch. 166, § 69, subd. 7.

We therefore conclude that the true measure of the plaintiff's damage in the present case is the difference between the value to him of a perfect hand or a good hand, such as the jury found the defendant promised him, and the value of his hand in its present condition, including any incidental consequences fairly within the contemplation of the parties when they made their contract. 1 Sutherland, Damages (4th Ed.) § 92. Damages not thus limited, although naturally resulting, are not to be given.

The extent of the plaintiff's suffering does not measure this difference in value. The pain necessarily incident to a serious surgical operation was a part of the contribution which the plaintiff was willing to make to his joint undertaking with the defendant to produce a good hand. It was a legal detriment suffered by him which constituted a part of the consideration given by him for the contract. It represented a part of the price which he was willing to pay for a good hand, but it furnished no test of the value of a good hand or the difference between the value of the hand which the defendant promised and the one which resulted from the operation.

It was also erroneous and misleading to submit to the jury as a separate element of damage any change for the worse in the condition of the plaintiff's hand resulting from the operation, although this error was probably more prejudicial to the plaintiff than to the defendant. Any such ill effect of the operation would be included under the true rule of damages set forth above, but damages might properly be assessed for the defendant's failure to improve the condition of the hand, even if there were no evidence that its condition was made worse as a result of the operation.

It must be assumed that the trial court, in setting aside the verdict, undertook to apply the same rule of damages which he had previously given to the jury, and, since this rule was erroneous, it is unnecessary for us to consider whether there was any evidence to justify his finding that all damages awarded by the jury above $500 were excessive.

Defendant's requests for instructions were loosely drawn, and were properly denied. A considerable number of issues of fact were raised by the evidence, and it would have been extremely misleading to instruct the jury in accordance with defendant's request No. 2, that "the only issue on which you have to pass is whether or not there was a special contract between the plaintiff and the defendant to produce a perfect hand." Equally inaccurate was defendant's request No. 5, which reads as follows: "You would have to find, in order to hold the defendant liable in this case, that Dr. McGee and the plaintiff both understood that the doctor was guaranteeing a perfect result from this operation." If the defendant said that he would guarantee a perfect result, and the plaintiff relied upon that promise, any mental reservations which he may have had are immaterial. The standard by which his conduct is to be judged is not internal, but external. . . . Defendant's request No. 7 was as follows: "If you should get so far as to find that there was a special contract guaranteeing a perfect result, you would still have to find for the defendant unless you also found that a further operation would not correct the disability claimed by the plaintiff." In view of the testimony that the defendant had refused to perform a further operation, it would clearly have been erroneous to give this instruction. The evidence would have justified a verdict for an amount sufficient to cover the cost of such an operation, even if the theory underlying this request were correct.

It is unlikely that the questions now presented in regard to the argument of plaintiff's counsel will arise at another trial, and therefore they have not been considered.

New trial.

NOTES AND QUESTIONS

1. *Promissory language.* Dr. McGee told Hawkins and his father that Hawkins would be in the hospital for "three or four days, not over four." The court said that this statement was not language of promise, but rather a statement of an opinion. On the other hand, the words, "I will guarantee to make the hand a hundred per cent perfect hand or a hundred per cent good hand" did create a promise, giving rise to an action for damages when the promise was not fulfilled. Dr. McGee's lawyer argued that these words should be interpreted in the light of the rule of objective interpretation. No reasonable person would understand these words as anything more than a strong statement of opinion and not promise. Are you persuaded that the difference the court saw between these two statements was "clear"? If so, why?

The question whether the guarantee was a promise or not was judged first as a matter of law by the court. Thus, before the jury could be involved, the court had to rule that it was possible that a reasonable person could understand the words as a promise. Once the court resolved this preliminary issue of law, it was the function of the jury to determine whether, in fact, the words could reasonably be understood by Hawkins to be a promise. As discussed in Chapter 2, courts often distinguish between expressions of intent to make a prediction or express an opinion, neither of which constitutes a promise, and an assurance as to a future event. Do you think the distinction is helpful to properly exclude some language from becoming promissory? Is the distinction between commitment and prediction clear? See Restatement (Second) of Contracts § 2, *cmt. f.*

2. *Total breach versus partial breach.* Assuming that a contract existed and it was breached, do you consider the breach partial or total? How do you make this determination, and what is the relevance? Are there future losses or

costs to be avoided by Hawkins as a result of the breach and Hawkins' not having to perform his side of the contract? What were Hawkins' obligations under the contract? Did he fully perform? If so, does the partial and total breach distinction have any meaning to this particular case?

3. *Expectancy interest loss in value measure.* Having determined the case was contractual and not tort based, the primary measure of damages was designed to protect the expectancy interest. The first component of the expectancy interest is the loss in value measure that requires comparing the market value of the promise to the market value of what was actually received. These two market values are then compared to determine the difference or loss in value. What were the relative market values of the promised perfect hand and the hand following the surgery? Did the jury instructions properly prepare the jury to determine this difficult matter? What proofs of market value were provided by the parties? What proof would you present?

The court also determined it was improper for the trial court to instruct the jury to consider any worsening of the hand as a result of the surgery. Do you understand this instruction? Was the instruction consistent with the expectancy interest formulation in Restatement (Second) of Contracts § 347? Did Hawkins expect any pain and suffering or the severity of pain and suffering actually incurred? If not, is this calculus appropriate under the "loss in value" determination, or is it "any other loss" caused by the breach? See Restatement (Second) of Contracts § 347(c).

4. *The machine analogy.* The court stated that "[a]uthority for any specific rule of damages in cases of this kind seems to be lacking, but, when tested by general principle and by analogy, it appears that the foregoing instruction was erroneous." The opinion then referred by analogy to the measure of damages available for breach of a warranty as to the performance of a machine. Do you find this analogy helpful? If not, why not? Is the analogy cited simply to illustrate that the measure of loss in value is the difference in value between what was promised and what was received? Or is the analogy meant to suggest something more, such as equating personal injury cases with damage to physical equipment? If the latter, is the analogy helpful?

5. *Adequacy of proper expectancy interest.* Assuming that the expectancy interest and its loss in value measure can be properly applied, will the expectancy monetary recovery place Hawkins in the same position as if the contract had been properly performed? The unequivocal answer is almost always "never," and it has less to do with the measurement of the recovery than the risk and costs of litigation. Unless the contract specifies otherwise, American common law requires that each party bear its own litigation expense, win or lose. If an injured party is insured, the insurance company will normally be required to sue or defend, but only with regard to the insurable elements. Normally, this includes medical bills, but seldom is a plaintiff insured against personal injury. Moreover, once medical bills are paid, the insurance company is subrogated (by contract or equity) to the insured's claim, and thus its expenses normally are subtracted first from any recovery. This means that the

legal risk and litigation cost of even a victorious plaintiff must be paid by the plaintiff. As a consequence, given the enormous costs of litigation, regardless of whether the attorney is retained on a fixed fee or contingent fee basis, the plaintiff will simply never be made whole. This aspect of American jurisprudence has led some commentators to suggest specific performance ought to be the normative remedy, even though the legal expense of achieving that order will also not compensate the plaintiff. See Melvin A. Eisenberg, "Actual and Virtual Specific Performance, the Theory of Efficient Breach, and the Indifference Principle in Contract Law," 93 Cal. L. Rev. 975, 977 (2005) and Stewart Macaulay, "The Reliance Interest and the World Outside the Law Schools' Doors," 1991 Wisc. L. Rev. 247.

In contrast, in most foreign common law and civil law jurisdictions, the losing party bears the expense of the prevailing party's litigation costs. See John Gotanda, "Awarding Costs and Attorneys' Fees in International Commercial Transactions," 21 Mich. J. Int'l Law 1 (1999). These costs must be reasonably foreseeable, but this condition is normally satisfied, even in American and foreign contracts. See CISG Art. 74 and UNIDROIT Art. 7.4.4; see, e.g., Zapata Hermanos Sucesores, S.A. v. Hearthside Baking Co., 2001 WL 1000927 (N.D. Ill. 2001).

Which rule do you prefer? Which rule do you think most clearly and fairly advances the interests of the injured party? Does the American rule discourage or encourage litigation? Settlement? If it discourages litigation, why is America so comparatively litigious? Does the attorney fee role work in some magical tandem with contingent fees? Do you think contingent fee cases dominate the landscape in foreign jurisdictions?

6.   *Expectancy interest versus reliance interest.* Reconsider the three damages interests, especially comparing the expectancy and reliance interests. Do you think plaintiffs prefer the reliance interest to the expectancy interest in a contract case involving personal injury? If so, how would you measure the reliance damages? How would the reliance interest measure differ from the expectancy interest measure? Do you think either measure deterred McGee from fulfilling his promise? See Melvin A. Eisenberg, "Actual and Virtual Specific Performance, the Theory of Efficient Breach, and the Indifference Principle in Contract Law," 93 Cal. L. Rev. 975 (2005), preferring expectancy interest:

> If a promisor was only liable for the promisee's costs—that is, if a promisor faced a remedial regime that only implemented the cost principle—the full value of a contract to the promisee would not enter into a purely self-interested calculation by the promisor, and promisors might therefore take too few precautions and breach too often. Id. at 980.

Was the trial court jury instruction more suited to a reliance measure or an expectancy measure? Outline the elements of a proper jury charge in both cases and determine how the trial court and appellate court instruction language fit both paradigms.

7. *Emotional disturbance damages*. The trial judge instructed the jury to determine the value of the pain and suffering Hawkins was made to endure and the injury he sustained "over and above what injury he had before." The court refused to allow the recovery of damages for pain and suffering. Restatement (Second) § 353 states the general rule that recovery for emotional disturbance are ordinarily not permitted in contract law. The rationale is that such damages are "often particularly difficult to establish and to measure." Restatement (Second) § 353, *cmt. a*. However, emotional disturbance or mental distress, including pain and suffering, may be awarded when either the contract or the breach is of such a kind that a serious emotional disturbance is particularly likely. Restatement (Second) § 353. One example involves emotional disturbance involving bodily injury because in such cases the nature of wrong is difficult to separate between tort and contract. Restatement (Second) § 353, *cmt. a*.

8. *Foreseeability limitation on damages*. As discussed later in this chapter, a plaintiff's recovery of contract damages is limited by three factors: foreseeability, certainty, and avoidability. Does the quotation by the court from the *Davis* case, "The only losses that can be said fairly to come within the terms of a contract are such as the parties must have had in mind when the contract was made, or such as they either knew or ought to have known would probably result from a failure to comply with its terms," relate to the foreseeability of damages or to the expectancy of the parties? Does this quotation suggest that the justification for an award of damages is to be found by interpreting what the parties would or might have provided by way of damages had they thought about it? Is this a throwback to the "will theory" of contracts?

9. *Certainty limitation on damages*. Can a jury determine the value to Hawkins of a perfect hand with certainty? Then do you think the jury could fairly determine the value to Hawkins of his hand in its condition as of the date of the trial? It is worth noting that, while in some senses it is both impossible and distasteful to attempt to value the loss suffered by Hawkins, there exist numerous actuarial sources from which it is possible to approximate the dollar value of a lost limb or body part, physical injury, or loss of life. Indeed, tort law routinely engages in such a personal calculus.

10. *Case aftermath*. The complaint included two counts, the first for negligence and the second for breach of contract. At the trial court, Hawkins was awarded a $3,000 jury verdict but, the trial court determined the damages were excessive beyond $500. The appellate opinion then reversed that finding and ordered a new trial. McGee ultimately settled the case for $1,400 and then brought suit against his malpractice insurance company seeking reimbursement for the settlement plus attorney fees and other costs. In *McGee v. United States Fidelity & Guaranty Co.*, 53 F.2d 953 (1st Cir. 1931), the court noted that McGee's insurance policy provided: "The assured shall not voluntarily assume any liability . . . " Both the federal district court and the First Circuit found that Dr. McGee's malpractice insurance policy did not cover contractual liability, the basis of the settlement. Does the fact that the court

found no prima facie case of negligence proven change your view with respect to contractual liability?

AMERICAN STANDARD, INC. V. SCHECTMAN

Supreme Court of Illinois
80 A.D.2d 318, 439 N.Y.S.2d 529 (1981)

HANCOCK, Justice.

Plaintiffs have recovered a judgment on a jury verdict of $90,000 against defendant for his failure to complete grading and to take down certain foundations and other subsurface structures to one foot below the grade line as promised. Whether the court should have charged the jury, as defendant Schectman requested, that the difference in value of plaintiffs' property with and without the promised performance was the measure of the damage is the main point in his appeal. We hold that the request was properly denied and that the cost of completion—not the difference in value—was the proper measure. Finding no other basis for reversal, we affirm.

Until 1972, plaintiffs operated a pig iron manufacturing plant on land abutting the Niagara River in Tonawanda. On the 26-acre parcel were, in addition to various industrial and office buildings, a 60-ton blast furnace, large lifts, hoists and other equipment for transporting and storing ore, railroad tracks, cranes, diesel locomotives and sundry implements and devices used in the business. Since the 1870's plaintiffs' property, under several different owners, had been the site of various industrial operations. Having decided to close the plant, plaintiffs on August 3, 1973 made a contract in which they agreed to convey the buildings and other structures and most of the equipment to defendant, a demolition and excavating contractor, in return for defendant's payment of $275,000 and his promise to remove the equipment, demolish the structures and grade the property as specified.

We agree with Trial Term's interpretation of the contract as requiring defendant to remove all foundations, piers, headwalls, and other structures, including those under the surface and not visible and whether or not shown on the map attached to the contract, to a depth of approximately one foot below the specified grade lines.[2] The proof from

---

[2]   Paragraph 7 of the Agreement states in pertinent part:

7. After the Closing Date, Purchaser shall demolish all of the Improvements on the North Tonawanda Property included in the sale to Purchaser, cap the water intake at the pumphouse end, and grade and level the property, all in accordance with the provisions of Exhibit "C" and "C1" attached hereto.

Exhibit "C" (Notes on demolition and grading) contains specifications for the grade levels for four separate areas shown on Map "C1" and the following instruction:

Except as otherwise excepted all structures and equipment including foundations, piers, headwalls, etc. shall be removed to a depth approximately one foot below grade lines as set forth above. Area common to more than one area will be faired to provide

plaintiffs' witnesses and the exhibits, showing a substantial deviation from the required grade lines and the existence above grade of walls, foundations and other structures, support the finding, implicit in the jury's verdict, that defendant failed to perform as agreed. Indeed, the testimony of defendant's witnesses and the position he has taken during his performance of the contract and throughout this litigation (which the trial court properly rejected), viz., that the contract did not require him to remove all subsurface foundations, allow no other conclusion.

We turn to defendant's argument that the court erred in rejecting his proof that plaintiffs suffered no loss by reason of the breach because it makes no difference in the value of the property whether the old foundations are at grade or one foot below grade and in denying his offer to show that plaintiffs succeeded in selling the property for $183,000—only $3,000 less than its full fair market value. By refusing this testimony and charging the jury that the cost of completion (estimated at $110,500 by plaintiffs' expert), not diminution in value of the property, was the measure of damage the court, defendant contends, has unjustly permitted plaintiffs to reap a windfall at his expense. Citing the definitive opinion of Chief Judge Cardozo in Jacob & Youngs, Inc. v. Kent, 230 N.Y. 239, 129 N.E. 889, he maintains that the facts present a case "of substantial performance" of the contract with omissions of "trivial or inappreciable importance" (p. 245, 129 N.E. 889), and that because the cost of completion was "grossly and unfairly out of proportion to the good to be attained," (p. 244, 129 N.E. 889), the proper measure of damage is diminution in value.

The general rule of damages for breach of a construction contract is that the injured party may recover those damages which are the direct, natural and immediate consequence of the breach and which can reasonably be said to have been in the contemplation of the parties when the contract was made (see Hadley v. Baxendale, 9 Exch. 341, 156 Eng. Reprint 145; Restatement, Contracts, § 346). In the usual case where the contractor's performance has been defective or incomplete, the reasonable cost of replacement or completion is the measure (see, Bellizzi v. Huntley Estates, 3 N.Y. 2d 112, 164 N.Y.S. 2d 395, 143 N.E.2d 802. . . . Restatement, Contracts, § 346). When, however, there has been a substantial performance of the contract made in good faith but defects exist, the correction of which would result in economic waste, courts have measured the damages as the difference between the value of the property as constructed and the value if performance had been properly completed (see Jacob & Youngs, Inc. v. Kent, supra. . . . Restatement, Contracts, § 346, subd. [1], par. [a], cl. [ii], p. 573; Comment b, p. 574. . . .). Jacob & Youngs is illustrative. There, plaintiff, a contractor, had constructed a house for the defendant which was satisfactory in all respects save one: the wrought

---

reasonable transitions, it being intended to provide a reasonably attractive vacant plot for resale.

iron pipe installed for the plumbing was not of Reading manufacture, as specified in the contract, but of other brands of the same quality. Noting that the breach was unintentional and the consequences of the omission trivial, and that the cost of replacing the pipe would be "grievously out of proportion" (Jacob & Youngs, Inc. v. Kent, supra, 230 N.Y. p. 244, 129 N.E. 889) to the significance of the default, the court held the breach to be immaterial and the proper measure of damage to the owner to be not the cost of replacing the pipe but the nominal difference in value of the house with and without the Reading pipe.

Not in all cases of claimed "economic waste" where the cost of completing performance of the contract would be large and out of proportion to the resultant benefit to the property have the courts adopted diminution in value as the measure of damage. Under the Restatement rule, the completion of the contract must involve "unreasonable economic waste" and the illustrative example given is that of a house built with pipe different in name from but equal in quality to the brand stipulated in the contract as in Jacob & Youngs, Inc. v. Kent (supra) (Restatement, Contracts, § 346, subd. [1], par. [a], cl. [ii], p. 573; Illustration 2, p. 576). In Groves v. John Wunder Co., 205 Minn. 163, 286 N.W. 235, plaintiff had leased property and conveyed a gravel plant to defendant in exchange for a sum of money and for defendant's commitment to return the property to plaintiff at the end of the term at a specified grade—a promise defendant failed to perform. Although the cost of the fill to complete the grading was $60,000 and the total value of the property, graded as specified in the contract, only $12,160 the court rejected the "diminution in value" rule, stating:

> The owner's right to improve his property is not trammeled by its small value. It is his right to erect thereon structures which will reduce its value. If that be the result, it can be of no aid to any contractor who declines performance. As said long ago in Chamberlain v. Parker, 45 N.Y. 569, 572: "A man may do what he will with his own, . . . and if he chooses to erect a monument to his caprice or folly on his premises, and employs and pays another to do it, it does not lie with a defendant who has been so employed and paid for building it, to say that his own performance would not be beneficial to the plaintiff." (Groves v. John Wunder Co., supra, 205 Minn., p. 168, 286 N.W. 235).

The "economic waste" of the type which calls for application of the "diminution in value" rule generally entails defects in construction which are irremediable or which may not be repaired without a substantial tearing down of the structure as in Jacob & Youngs (see . . . Groves v. John Wunder Co., supra; . . . Restatement, Contracts, § 346, Illustrations 2, 4, pp. 576–577. . . .).

Where, however, the breach is of a covenant which is only incidental to the main purpose of the contract and completion would be disproportionately costly, courts have applied the diminution in value measure even where no destruction of the work is entailed (see, e.g., Peevyhouse v. Garland Coal & Min. Co., 382 P. 2d 109 [Okla.], cert. den. 375 U.S. 906, 84 S. Ct. 196, 11 L. Ed. 2d 145, holding [contrary to Groves v. John Wunder Co., supra] that diminution in value is the proper measure where defendant, the lessee of plaintiff's lands under a coal mining lease, failed to perform costly remedial and restorative work on the land at the termination of the lease. The court distinguished the "building and construction" cases and noted that the breach was of a covenant incidental to the main purpose of the contract which was the recovery of coal from the premises to the benefit of both parties; and see Avery v. Fredericksen & Westbrook, 67 Cal. App. 2d 334, 154 P. 2d 41).

It is also a general rule in building and construction cases, at least under Jacob & Youngs in New York (see Groves v. John Wunder Co., supra; Ann. 76 A.L.R. 2d 805, § 6, pp. 823–826), that a contractor who would ask the court to apply the diminution of value measure "as an instrument of justice" must not have breached the contract intentionally and must show substantial performance made in good faith (Jacob & Youngs, Inc. v. Kent, supra, 230 N.Y. pp. 244, 245, 129 N.E. 889).

In the case before us, plaintiffs chose to accept as part of the consideration for the promised conveyance of their valuable plant and machines to defendant his agreement to grade the property as specified and to remove the foundations, piers and other structures to a depth of one foot below grade to prepare the property for sale. It cannot be said that the grading and the removal of the structures were incidental to plaintiffs' purpose of "achieving a reasonably attractive vacant plot for resale" (compare Peevyhouse v. Garland Coal & Min. Co., supra). Nor can defendant maintain that the damages which would naturally flow from his failure to do the grading and removal work and which could reasonably be said to have been in the contemplation of the parties when the contract was made would not be the reasonable cost of completion (see 13 N.Y. Jur., Damages, §§ 46, 56; Hadley v. Baxendale, supra). That the fulfillment of defendant's promise would (contrary to plaintiffs' apparent expectations) add little or nothing to the sale value of the property does not excuse the default. As in the hypothetical case posed in Chamberlain v. Parker, 45 N.Y. 569, supra (cited in Groves v. John Wunder Co., supra), of the man who "chooses to erect a monument to his caprice or folly on his premises, and employs and pays another to do it," it does not lie with defendant here who has received consideration for his promise to do the work "to say that his own performance would not be beneficial to the plaintiff[s]" (Chamberlain v. Parker, supra, p. 558).

Defendant's completed performance would not have involved undoing what in good faith was done improperly but only doing what was promised and left undone (compare Jacob & Youngs, Inc. v. Kent, supra; Restatement, Contracts, § 346, Illustration 2, p. 576). That the burdens of performance were heavier than anticipated and the cost of completion disproportionate to the end to be obtained does not, without more, alter the rule that the measure of plaintiffs' damage is the cost of completion. Disparity in relative economic benefits is not the equivalent of "economic waste" which will invoke the rule in Jacob & Youngs, Inc. v. Kent (supra) (see Groves v. John Wunder Co., supra). Moreover, faced with the jury's finding that the reasonable cost of removing the large concrete and stone walls and other structures extending above grade was $90,000, defendant can hardly assert that he has rendered substantial performance of the contract or that what he left unfinished was "of trivial or inappreciable importance" (Jacob & Youngs, Inc. v. Kent, supra, 230 N.Y. p. 245, 129 N.E. 889). Finally, defendant, instead of attempting in good faith to complete the removal of the underground structures, contended that he was not obliged by the contract to do so and, thus, cannot claim to be a "transgressor whose default is unintentional and trivial [and who] may hope for mercy if he will offer atonement for his wrong" (Jacob & Youngs, Inc. v. Kent, supra, p. 244, 129 N.E. 889). We conclude, then, that the proof pertaining to the value of plaintiffs' property was properly rejected and the jury correctly charged on damages.

The judgment and order should be affirmed.

Judgment and Order unanimously affirmed with costs.

SIMONS, J. P., and DOERR, DENMAN and SCHNEPP, JJ., concur.

NOTES AND QUESTIONS

1. *Economic waste standard.* The case references the "economic waste" doctrine as a policy directive for judicial selection of diminution in value or cost to repair. Restatement (First) of Contracts § 346 was titled "Damages For Breach Of A Construction Contract." In essence, Restatement (First) of Contracts § 346(1)(a)(i)–(ii) articulated that the injured party in a case of total breach was entitled to the reasonable cost to correct or complete unless that cost involved "unreasonable economic waste." If so, the diminution (loss) in value rule applied. Restatement (First) of Contracts § 346, *cmt. b* provided:

> b.   The purpose of money damages is to put the injured party in as good a position as that in which full performance would have put him; but this does not mean that he is to be put in the same specific physical position. Satisfaction for his harm is made either by giving him a sum of money sufficient to produce the physical product contracted for or by giving him the exchange value that that product would have had if it had been constructed. In very many cases it makes little difference whether the measure of recovery is based upon

the value of the promised product as a whole or upon the cost of producing and constructing it piecemeal. There are numerous cases, however, in which the value of the finished product is much less than the cost of producing it after the breach has occurred. Sometimes defects in a completed structure cannot be physically remedied without tearing down and rebuilding, at a cost that would be imprudent and unreasonable. The law does not require damages to be measured by a method requiring such economic waste. If no such waste is involved, the cost of remedying the defect is the amount awarded as compensation for failure to render the promised performance.

Restatement (Second) of Contracts § 348(2)(b) governs defective or unfinished construction cases but does not adopt the "economic waste" language standard noted above. Rather, it provides that the reasonable cost to complete or repair is to be utilized unless that cost is "clearly disproportionate" to the probable loss (diminution) in value to him. Restatement (Second) of Contracts § 348, *cmt. c* provides:

> *c.   Incomplete or defective performance.* If the contract is one for construction, including repair or similar performance affecting the condition of property, and the work is not finished, the injured party will usually find it easier to prove what it would cost to have the work completed by another contractor than to prove the difference between the values to him of the finished and the unfinished performance. Since the cost to complete is usually less than the loss in value to him, he is limited by the rule on avoidability to damages based on cost to complete. See § 350(1). If he has actually had the work completed, damages will be based on his expenditures if he comes within the rule stated in § 350(2).

> Sometimes, especially if the performance is defective as distinguished from incomplete, it may not be possible to prove the loss in value to the injured party with reasonable certainty. In that case he can usually recover damages based on the cost to remedy the defects. Even if this gives him a recovery somewhat in excess of the loss in value to him, it is better that he receive a small windfall than that he be under-compensated by being limited to the resulting diminution in the market price of his property.

> Sometimes, however, such a large part of the cost to remedy the defects consists of the cost to undo what has been improperly done that the cost to remedy the defects will be clearly disproportionate to the probable loss in value to the injured party. Damages based on the cost to remedy the defects would then give the injured party a recovery greatly in excess of the loss in value to him and result in a substantial windfall. *Such an award will not be made. It is sometimes said that the award would involve "economic waste," but this is a misleading expression since an injured party will not, even if awarded*

an excessive amount of damages, usually pay to have the defects remedied if to do so will cost him more than the resulting increase in value to him. If an award based on the cost to remedy the defects would clearly be excessive and the injured party does not prove the actual loss in value to him, damages will be based instead on the difference between the market price that the property would have had without the defects and the market price of the property with the defects. This diminution in market price is the least possible loss in value to the injured party, since he could always sell the property on the market even if it had no special value to him. [emphasis added].

In other contexts, the phrase "disproportionate" usually implies a comparison of the benefit to one party versus the cost to the other, but it is not limited to situations involving what may be thought of as "economic waste." The latter phrase implies no value to anyone. However, particularly where the defective construction involves an item of intrinsic value to the injured party, such as a personal residence, is completion or repair without economic value to the homeowner? Even Judge Cardozo suggested in *Jacob & Youngs* that he would have decided otherwise if either (i) the conditional language requiring the use of Reading pipe had been expressed as a condition rather than merely as a promise; or (ii) the breach (using Cohoes rather than Reading pipe) was willful or intentional. In the latter case, justice does not favor saving the breaching party the money, even if the repair expenditure does not proportionately increase the value of the project.

In the context of this case, is "economic waste" the same analysis as "clearly disproportionate?" Since the language of Restatement (Second) of Contracts § 348(2)(b) focuses on the probable loss to "him" (the injured party), does that focus introduce a measure of subjectivity?

2. *The* Peevyhouse *case.* The case references and distinguishes the *Peevyhouse* case. That case involved a mineral rights lease by an Oklahoma farmer to a mining company where the homeowner made it very clear that the strip mining holes must be filled after mineral removal. In fact, during the lease negotiations, they reduced the contract price by $3,000 precisely so that the land would be restored. Nonetheless, the court in *Peevyhouse* did not require the restoration of the land to its original condition, notwithstanding the promise, the intrinsic importance of the homestead, and the $3,000 price reduction. See Judith L. Maute, "*Peevyhouse v. Garland Coal & Mining Co.* Revisited: The Ballad of Willie and Lucille," 89 Nw. U. L. Rev. 1341 (1995) for a legal archaeology account of the lease negotiations and ultimate charges of bribery sustained against some of the judges on the Oklahoma Supreme Court that decided the case. See also R. Darcy, "Conflict and Reform—Oklahoma Judicial Elections 1907–1998," 26 Okla. City U. L. Rev. 519 (2001).

The Peevyhouse family ultimately obtained a 1962 judgment for a mere $300, far less than the cost to repair and far less than the $3,000 lease price reduction. According to Professor Maute, they still lived on the farm in 1995. Injunctive relief is covered later in this chapter and is normatively available when monetary damages are not adequate. See Restatement (Second) of Contracts § 359(1). However, this issue was not raised at the first trial, but rather it was first raised, and rejected, on appeal. Later, a new federal district court suit sought specific performance, but the earlier trial precluded that action on *res judicata* grounds.

3. *The* Groves *case.* Groves owned sizeable sand and gravel deposits. He entered into a seven-year lease granting the right to process and remove sand and gravel. Like the *Peevyhouse* lease, the *Groves* lease required the lessee to restore the land to its original condition at the end of the lease. As matters developed, the restoration required the lessee to remove and store nearly 300,000 cubic yards of "overburden" at the beginning of the lease and then use this material as top cover to restore the property. The lessee willfully refused to comply with the restoration term. The lessee argued that the approximate $60,0000 restoration cost only increased value of the land by approximately $12,160 and therefore was excused under the "economic waste" standard. The trial court agreed and awarded the owner only the lesser diminution in value. On appeal, the Minnesota Supreme Court reversed and awarded the cost to repair and replace. The court argued the "economic waste" limitation on the repair cost only applied to destruction of physical structures. Rather, the 1939 opinion relied more heavily on the "willful" behavior of the lessee following the earlier *Jacob & Youngs* standard announced in 1921 by Judge Cardozo as one of the exceptions to the doctrine of substantial performance. See Richard Posner, Economic Analysis of Law § 4.8 (5th ed. 1998). Do you think that the lessee's behavior in *Peevyhouse* was willful? What is the difference between willful noncompliance and bad faith, an implied term discussed in Chapter 4?

4. *Bad faith and the doctrine of efficient breach.* The concept of "efficient breach" has roots in early 20th century common law and Oliver Wendell Holmes, Jr.'s observation that monetary damage of contract breach are to be compensatory, not punitive, and thus "every person has a legal right to break his contract if he chooses," thereby electing to pay damages rather than perform. See Oliver Wendell Holmes, Jr., The Common Law 236 (1881) and Grant Gilmore, The Death of Contract 16 (1974). In general, the "efficient breach" theory is supported by economic theory in redirecting resources to a superior use. But not every scholar is a huge fan:

> [The "efficient breach" theory] holds that if a promisor would gain more from breaching the contract, even after payment of expectation damages, than the promise would lose, breach is efficient and for that reason should be encouraged. . . . In its most significant application, the theory of efficient breach does nothing to promote efficiency. On the contrary, if widely adopted the theory would promote inefficiency. Melvin A. Eisenberg, "Actual and Virtual Specific Performance, the Theory of Efficient Breach, and the Indifference Principle in Contract Law," 93 Cal. L. Rev. 975, 977–78 (2005).

See also David W. Barnes, "The Anatomy of Contract Damages and Efficient Breach Theory," 6 S. Cal. Interdisc. L. J. 397 (1998); Richard Craswell,

"Contract Remedies, Renegotiation, and the Theory of Efficient Breach," 61 So. Cal. L. Rev. 629 (1988); and Joseph M. Perillo, "Misreading Oliver Wendell Holmes on Efficient Breach and Tortious Interference," 68 Fordham L. Rev. 1085 (2000).

Chapter 4 explores in more detail the implied covenant of good faith. But bad faith is the antithesis of good faith and involves a deliberate intent to frustrate the purposes of the contract. Do you think a theory of efficient breach is conceptually consistent with good faith, or do you think an intentional breach of a contract is *per se* proof of bad faith? If the latter, what damages should the court award? Finally, courts are frequently sensitive to the degree of certainty of proof required for recovery of lost profits based on the wrongfulness of the breaching party's behavior. See, e.g., Christopher W. Frost, "Reconsidering the Reliance Interest," 44 St. Louis U. L. J. 1361, 1372 (2000).

5.   *Efficient breach controversy.* As discussed above, the "efficient breach" concept is controversial. Holmes's early observation that the motive of the contract breaker is irrelevant has been controversial. Under efficient breach theory, a contract breaker intentionally breaches the contract because the breaching party can devote its resources more profitably to other contracts. Thus, the contract breaker can make more profit from the redirection of the contract resources than the damages incurred on the breach. The breach is thus said to be "efficient" from the perspective of the breaching party, and the injured party receives expectancy interest damages and is thus placed in the same position as if the contract had been performed. Indeed, both parties are better off for the breach: The injured party receives expectancy interest damages, and the breaching party receives the excess over those damages.

Critical to this question is whether the motive of the contract breaker plays a role in measuring damages. One approach might be to award the contract breaker's breach "profit" to the injured party. Of course, that approach places the injured party in a better position than performance, but it also allocates the windfall to the innocent party rather than awarding an intentional breach. See, e.g., Daniel Friedman, "The Efficient Breach Fallacy," 18 J. Leg. Stud. 1 (1989) and Ian R. Macneil, "Efficient Breach of Contract: Circles in the Sky," 68 Va. L. Rev. 947 (1982). Cases involving efficient breach are rare because the injured party receives adequate compensation and seldom learns of the breaching party's efficiency profit. For an example, see *Handicapped Children's Education Board v. Lukaszewski*, 112 Wis.2d 197, 332 N.W.2d 774 (1983). In *Lukaszewski*, a teacher was hired at $10,760 annual salary, but before the school year began, she repudiated the school contract and accepted a higher paying job closer to home due in part to health concerns. The new position paid $13,000. The school sued and won an award for $1,026, the additional amount necessary to hire her replacement over and above her original $10,760 salary. In sum, the teacher netted $1,214 after the breach and paying breach damages because of the higher pay at the other position. She was therefore better off by the breach; the school was no worse off. Should the school have also been entitled to her $1,214 windfall, or should the breaching teacher be entitled to retain that amount? That issue was not presented or discussed in the case.

Intriguingly, The current draft of Restatement (Third) of Restitution and Unjust Enrichment § 39 adopts a contrary damages rule that specifically requires disgorgement of profits from a breach if that breach is "opportunistic."

The concept is obviously controversial, and the restitution reversal of the efficient breach will no doubt continue to precipitate considerable debate. Indeed, at the 2005 ALI proceedings, the Reporter made the following observation:

> § 39 . . . is something of an innovation. The innovation consists in the attempt to state a general rule; it is not an attempt to dictate outcomes that have never been thought of before. The Illustrations are all based on real cases; they are not recommendations for how we think life ought to be organized. The general rule has not been stated either this way or any other way, to my knowledge. It does not appear in the Second Restatement of Contracts, and it is not easy to decide how to write it. For these reasons and others, § 39 was the most difficult to prepare and is perhaps the most open to criticism of all the material in the draft.

6.   *The ethics of willful breach—an empirical analysis.* While courts and commentators often seem to treat the business world as filled with hard-nosed bargainers and coldhearted, calculating business people, in reality there are serious ethical and reputational consequences for a willful breach. In one empirical survey of the reactions of business people to a willful breach, for example, 105 respondents out of 168 total stated that deliberately breaching a contract because a better deal can be had elsewhere is unethical. See David Baumer & Patricia Marschall, "Willful Breach of Contract for the Sale of Goods: Can the Bane of Business Be an Economic Bonanza?," 65 Temple L. Rev. 159, 165 (1992). Ninety-six of the respondents stated that they would "almost always" or "always" withhold future business from a party who willfully breached a valid contract, although only 68 respondents stated that they would inform associates of such bad faith conduct. See id. at 166. Finally, 88 of the respondents stated that they would more likely file suit in cases of deliberate breach. See id. If this survey accurately reflects the general attitudes of business people toward willful or deliberate breaches, how would this affect a party's determination of whether to willfully breach a contract? Are there some types of businesses that are more sensitive to, or more insulated from, such reactions to willful breach?

2.   THE RELIANCE INTEREST ALTERNATIVE

In the next section, various limitations on the recovery of monetary damages are explored, including the requirements that (i) the breaching party could reasonably foresee the claimed breach damages at the time the contract was formed (Restatement (Second) of Contracts § 351); (ii) the injured party took reasonable efforts to mitigate any post-breach increase in the amount of claimed damages relating to the breach (Restatement (Second) of Contracts § 350); and (iii) the injured party must be able to prove the amount of damages with reasonable certainty (Restatement (Second) of Contracts § 352). As will be seen in the discussion relating to the certainty limitation, "lost profits" damages on the contract are often the most elusive because proof of such damages implicates difficult problems of income and expense forecasts of future events. Lost profits are recoverable under the "loss in value" category discussed in the previous section. Restatement (Second) of Contracts § 347, *cmt. b* provides in relevant part:

> If no performance is rendered, the loss in value cause by the breach is equal to the value that the performance would have had to the injured party.

While the previous focus was on partial or defective performance, the lost profits component is often best illustrated where no performance occurs by the breaching party. For example, assume that Ann contracts with Bob to landscape his garden at a contract price of $100,000. Immediately after making the contract, but before Ann begins any performance, Bob repudiates the contract. His uncured material total breach discharges Ann's obligation to perform the landscaping services and allows her to recover damages. In this case, assume that Ann's calculated cost of materials and employee labor is $80,000. Had the contract been performed according to its terms, and her costs remained as forecasted, she would have made a profit of $20,000. Assuming that Ann had the capacity to perform as many landscaping contracts she could secure, the expectancy "loss in value" of Bob's breach equals $20,000. In order to recover a judgment for that amount, she must prove her $80,000 forecasted expenses with reasonable certainty, as the $100,000 contract price is easily established. When Ann cannot prove those expenses with reasonable certainty, is Ann precluded from any recovery?

This section explores the important question regarding the implications associated with the injured party's inability to prove expectancy interest damages with reasonable certainty but has incurred actual costs in reliance on the contract. These costs are ordinarily far easier to prove simply by showing receipts for the cost. In the above example, assume that Ann purchased $30,000 in plant material before Bob repudiated and she can only resell the plants for $15,000, meaning that she has lost $15,000. In essence, if Ann cannot prove her total expected $80,000 in expenses with reasonable certainty, she cannot recover her lost profit of $20,000 (now coupled with the additional "other loss" equal to $15,000). In essence, in these cases, the reliance interest alternative at least allows Ann to recover the $15,000 lost in reliance on the contract.

The reliance interest alternative provides that as an alternative to the expectancy interest recovery, the injured party is entitled to damages based on the reliance interest, including expenditures made in preparation for performance. Restatement (Second) of Contracts § 349. An important limitation provides that the reliance interest alternative recovery may be reduced by any loss that the breaching party can prove with reasonable certainty the injured party would have suffered had the contract been fully performed. Restatement (Second) of Contracts § 349. So, in the previous example, Ann would be entitled to recover $15,000 as a reliance interest alternative, unless Bob can prove she would have lost money had the contract been fully performed. Since Ann forecasted a $20,000 profit but could not prove her $80,000 with reasonable certainty, it is unlikely Bob will be able to prove with the same reasonable certainty that Ann would have incurred more than $100,000 in expenses and thus actually lost money (losing contract in reliance terms). Of course, where such proof is possible by the breaching party, the net effect is that the reliance remedy is limited to the contract price. See Restatement (Second) of Contracts § 349, *cmt. a.*

For comparative purposes, recall the *Algernon Blair* case where the breaching party was able to prove with reasonable certainty that Coastal Steel would have lost money on the contract. Since Coastal Steel used Algernon Blair's uncured material total breach to terminate the contract and sue off the contract, the losing contract in reliance terms did not apply.

WALSER V. TOYOTA MOTOR SALES, U.S.A., INC.

United States Court of Appeals for the Eighth Circuit
43 F.3d 396 (1994)

HANSEN, Circuit Judge.

The plaintiffs, Paul Martin Walser and Philip Martin McLaughlin, appeal from a jury verdict in this diversity case awarding them $232,131 in damages on their promissory estoppel claim against Toyota Motor Sales. The plaintiffs argue that the district court erred by instructing the jury that the plaintiffs' damages on their promissory estoppel claim were limited to out-of-pocket expenses. The plaintiffs also argue that the district court erred in declining to award specific performance as an alternative remedy on their promissory estoppel claim, in denying their motion for judgment as a matter of law on their contract claim, in instructing the jury on their contract claim, in requiring them to accept payment from Toyota for $.89 less than the amount of damages and interest awarded, in granting summary judgment on their claim under the Minnesota Motor Vehicle Sale and Distribution Regulations, and in precluding them from taxing costs prior to a final determination of this case on appeal. We affirm.

I.

In 1987, Toyota Motor Sales, U.S.A., conducted market surveys throughout the United States to identify the best markets for the new line of "Lexus" automobiles that Toyota planned to introduce in 1989. The market studies identified the Minneapolis/St. Paul, Minnesota, metropolitan area as a two-dealership market and recommended establishing dealerships in two suburban areas—Wayzata and the Bloomington/Richfield area.

In April 1988, Toyota issued letters of intent for the prospective dealerships in the two locations. The recipient of the letter for the Bloomington/Richfield dealership was unwilling or unable to comply with the conditions of the letter of intent and returned it to Toyota in early 1989. Soon after, Toyota began to search anew for a dealer for the Bloomington/Richfield location. Lexus Central Region Area Manager, James Melton, asked Stephen Haag, the Central Region Market Manager, to contact Walser, who was then co-owner with McLaughlin of a BMW dealership and a Lincoln-Mercury dealership both located in Bloomington. Both Walser and McLaughlin met with Haag and indicated that they would be interested in obtaining the Lexus dealership.

Toyota had instituted a three-step process to establish dealerships. First, the prospective dealer would fill out a formal application and propose a dealership plan to Toyota. If acceptable, then Toyota would issue a letter of intent signed by the head of the Lexus division and to be signed by the prospective dealer, which would contain final conditions that had to be satisfied before the agreement was finalized. If all conditions were satisfied, then a formal dealership agreement would be approved by Toyota and signed by the parties to establish the dealership.

Walser and McLaughlin applied for the Lexus dealership by completing and signing the formal application for the dealership. The application specifically provided that a dealership agreement was not effective until a formal dealership agreement was approved and signed by an officer of Toyota. Walser's preliminary proposals, to have the Lexus dealership share space with the BMW dealership or to move the BMW business and to retrofit the BMW facility for Lexus, were both rejected by Toyota, but negotiations continued between the parties. However, unknown to Toyota, Walser and McLaughlin were also negotiating at the same time to buy a Mazda/BMW dealership in St. Paul.

After the retrofit proposal was rejected, Walser and McLaughlin began negotiating to acquire additional property adjacent to the their Bloomington BMW dealership as a site for the Lexus dealership. On October 15, 1989, Walser's father, R.J. Walser, reached a "handshake deal" to purchase that property for the proposed Lexus dealership from its owner. On October 16, 1989, Walser and McLaughlin wrote Haag and informed him of the agreement to purchase the land but did not disclose that R.J. Walser was buying the land.

On October 17, 1989, Walser and McLaughlin traveled to California to meet with Lexus management and to present their new dealership proposal and financing arrangements. The fact that R.J. Walser was buying the land and that McLaughlin and Walser were in the process of purchasing a Mazda/BMW dealership in St. Paul were not disclosed. Lexus management viewed the proposal favorably, and one executive stated that he was with Walser and McLaughlin.

On October 24, 1989, Walser called Haag to ask whether the letter of intent for the dealership was forthcoming. Haag told Walser that while the letter was not yet executed, things looked positive, the deal was done, only one more signature was needed, and finalizing the deal was basically a rubber stamp. Later that day, R.J. Walser entered into a purchase agreement and paid $50,000 in earnest money for the land for the proposed Lexus dealership.

In December 1989, the letter of intent was formally approved by Lexus management. Haag called Walser and congratulated him and told him that "you're our dealer" and the letter would be coming by mail. Later in the day, however, Melton told Haag that based on new information Lexus had received regarding Walser and McLaughlin's financing for the new dealership, the letter of intent would be put on hold. A couple days later, Haag called Walser to tell him that a mistake had been made and that the letter had not been finally approved. Haag requested additional financial information.

On January 3, 1990, R.J. Walser closed on the property he was purchasing for the proposed Lexus dealership. On February 5, 1990, Walser and McLaughlin provided additional financial information and disclosed that R.J. Walser was available, but not necessary, to supply the required financing. On February 23, 1990, Haag informed Walser that Lexus would not be issuing the letter of intent to him and McLaughlin.

On March 7, 1990, Walser and McLaughlin filed a seven-count complaint in Minnesota state court against Toyota. Walser and McLaughlin sought relief under the following theories: breach of the Minnesota motor vehicle franchise statute (count I); breach of contract (count II); promissory estoppel (count III); joint venture (count IV); fraud (count V); intentional interference with contractual relations (count VI); and interference with a prospective business advantage (count VII). Toyota removed this action to the United States District Court for the District of Minnesota.

The district court granted Toyota's motion for partial summary judgment and dismissed the claims for breach of the Minnesota motor vehicle franchise statute and for recovery on a joint venture theory. Prior to trial, the parties filed a joint stipulation to dismiss without prejudice the claims for intentional interference with contractual relations and interference with a prospective business advantage. The case went to trial in February 1992 on the breach of contract, promissory estoppel, and fraud claims. Walser and McLaughlin sought approximately $7,600,000 in damages, which included expected lost profits. The jury returned a verdict in favor of Toyota on the contract and fraud claims but in favor of Walser and McLaughlin on the promissory estoppel claim. The jury awarded Walser and McLaughlin $232,131 in accordance with the district court's instruction to limit damages on the promissory estoppel claim to Walser and McLaughlin's out-of-pocket expenses.

The district court denied Walser and McLaughlin's post trial request for specific performance and their motions for judgment as a matter of law or for a new trial. Walser and McLaughlin filed a notice of appeal. Subsequently, Toyota tendered a check to Walser and McLaughlin for $276,782.82, which Toyota claimed represented the full amount of the judgment, prejudgment interest, and post judgment interest due. Walser and McLaughlin refused to accept the check because it was $44.98 short of the full amount due. The district court initially entered an order directing them to accept the $276,782.82. Toyota subsequently realized that the amount indeed was short, and the district court entered an amended order to increase the amount due by $44.09. Walser again rejected the payment claiming it was still $.89 short of the full amount due and that additional post judgment interest continued to accrue. Walser asked the district court to amend its order again to reflect these additional amounts, but the district court refused to do so. Walser then filed an amended notice of appeal to include this issue.

II.

This is a diversity case governed by Minnesota law. We review the district court's analysis of Minnesota law de novo. Salve Regina College v. Russell, 499 U.S. 225, 231, 111 S. Ct. 1217, 1220–21, 113 L. Ed. 2d 190 (1991). Walser and McLaughlin raise eight issues in this appeal. We will address them in the order presented in the briefs.

A.

Walser and McLaughlin's principal argument in this appeal is that the district court erred in instructing the jury that damages on their promissory estoppel claim were limited to the out-of-pocket expenditures they made in reliance on Toyota's promise. The jury awarded $232,131 in out-of-pocket expenses. Walser and McLaughlin argue that under Minnesota law, the court should have allowed the jury to consider awarding lost profits of up to $7,600,000 allegedly flowing from Toyota's failure to keep its promise.

Minnesota has adopted the statement of the doctrine of promissory estoppel found at Restatement (Second) of Contracts § 90 (1981). Christensen v. Minneapolis Mun. Employees Retirement Bd., 331 N.W. 2d 740, 749 (Minn. 1983). Section 90 provides, in relevant part:

> A promise which the promisor should reasonably expect to induce action or forbearance on the part of the promisee or a third person and which does induce such action or forbearance is binding if injustice can be avoided only by enforcement of the promise. The remedy granted for breach may be limited as justice requires.

Restatement (Second) of Contracts § 90(1) (1981); see also Cohen v. Cowles Media Co., 479 N.W.2d 387, 391–92 (Minn. 1992) (relying on and quoting from portions of section 90). . . . Of particular significance to this case is the meaning of the last phrase of the quoted section: "The remedy granted for breach may be limited as justice requires." The commentary to section 90 elaborates on the nature of the remedy available for breach based on promissory estoppel:

> A promise binding under this section is a contract, and full-scale enforcement by normal remedies is often appropriate. But the same factors which bear on whether any relief should be granted also bear on the character and extent of the remedy. *In particular, relief may sometimes be limited to restitution or to damages or specific relief measured by the extent of the promisee's reliance rather than by the terms of the promise.* Restatement (Second) of Contracts § 90, cmt. d [Emphasis added].

Minnesota courts have incorporated the underlined language stating:

> When a promise is enforced pursuant to section 90 "[t]he remedy granted for breach *may be limited* as justice requires." Relief may be limited to damages measured by the promisee's reliance. Grouse v. Group Health Plan, 306 N.W.2d 114, 116 (Minn. 1981) (alterations in original) [Emphasis added].

The Minnesota Court of Appeals, relying on Grouse, further stated that "relief may be limited to the party's out-of-pocket expenses made in reliance on the promise." Dallum v. Farmers Union Cent. Exch., Inc., 462 N.W.2d 608, 613 (Minn. Ct. App. 1990) (emphasis added).

The critical question in this case is whether the language of section 90 as interpreted by the Minnesota courts authorized the district court to limit damages to Walser and McLaughlin's out-of-pocket expenses. We conclude that it did. This language is permissive—courts *may* limit relief as justice requires. The Minnesota Court of Appeals specifically stated that:

> [R]elief *may be limited* to the party's out-of-pocket expenses made in reliance on the promise. Dallum, 462 N.W.2d at 613 [Emphasis added].

This permissive language and the Minnesota courts' interpretation of it indicate to us that Minnesota courts, like the other courts addressing this issue, treat the damages decision under section 90 as being within the district court's discretion. See, e.g., Chedd-Angier Prod. Co., Inc. v. Omni Publications Int'l, Ltd., 756 F.2d 930, 937 (1st Cir. 1985) (in determining damages under section 90 "whether to charge full contract damages, or something less, is a matter of discretion delegated to district courts"); Green v. Interstate United Management Serv. Corp., 748 F.2d 827, 831 (3d Cir. 1984) (concluding that district court did not abuse its "equitable discretion" under section 90 "in refusing to allow full-scale enforcement of the promise"); Signal Hill Aviation Co. v. Stroppe, 96 Cal. App. 3d 627, 158 Cal. Rptr. 178, 186 (1979) ("California Supreme Court appeared to emphasize . . . the exercise of judicial discretion in promissory estoppel cases to fashion relief to do justice") (citing C & K Eng'g Contractors v. Amber Steel Co., 23 Cal. 3d 1, 151 Cal. Rptr. 323, 587 P. 2d 1136 (1978)); Gerson Elec. Constr. Co. v. Honeywell, Inc., 117 Ill. App. 3d 309, 72 Ill. Dec. 851, 453 N.E.2d 726, 728 (1983) (decision under section 90 whether the damage award prevents injustice is a policy decision and "necessarily embraces an element of discretion").

We are left then to determine only whether the district court abused its discretion in limiting the damages to out-of-pocket expenses. We will not disturb a district court's discretionary decision if that decision remains within "the range of choice" available to the district court, accounts for all relevant factors, does not rely on any irrelevant factors, and does not constitute a "clear error of judgment." Kern v. TXO Prod. Corp., 738 F. 2d 968, 970 (8th Cir. 1984). We cannot find that the district court abused its discretion in limiting the award of damages on the promissory estoppel claim to out-of-pocket expenses.

The district court's limitation of damages was within the "range of choices" approved by Minnesota courts and our court. The Minnesota Supreme Court has provided that "relief may be limited to damages measured by the promisee's reliance." Grouse, 306 N.W. 2d at 116. We noted earlier that the Minnesota Court of Appeals specifically provided that "relief may be limited to the party's out-of-pocket expenses made in reliance on the promise." Dallum, 462 N.W.2d at 613. Similarly, we have observed that comment d to section 90 specifically states that "relief may sometimes be limited to restitution or to damages or specific relief measured by the extent of the promisee's reliance rather than by the terms of the promise." Westside Galvanizing Serv., Inc. v. Georgia-Pacific, Corp., 921 F.2d 735, 739 (8th Cir. 1990) (quoting comment d). We went on to find that the district court "did not err" in limiting damages to the amount of reliance instead of the full unpaid balance. Id. at 740. Hence, we believe that the district court acted within the "range of choice" available under the law in instructing the jury on the remedy available after a finding of promissory estoppel.[3]

Our review of the record also reveals that the district court did not make a "clear error of judgment" in finding that justice required limiting Walser and McLaughlin to out-of-pocket expenses. Toyota presented evidence that the dealership was far from a certainty and that Walser and McLaughlin would have great difficulty in meeting the capitalization requirements. The negotiations were still in a preliminary stage and broke down at that point. The promise on which they relied did not guarantee that they would get the dealership, as there were other conditions in the letter of intent that still would have had to be satisfied. Walser and McLaughlin could have relied on the promise for only a short period of time, as they were informed by Haag only a couple of days later that he had misinformed them about the status of the letter of intent. Moreover, Walser and McLaughlin have not demonstrated any opportunity they lost by virtue of relying on the promise by Toyota. Accordingly, the district court did not make a clear error of judgment in limiting Walser and McLaughlin's damages on their promissory estoppel claim to out-of-pocket expenses.

We agree with Walser and McLaughlin that the district court is not *required* under Minnesota law to limit the remedy in promissory estoppel cases to out-of-pocket expenses. However, such a limitation is firmly within the range of choices available to the district court, and the district court is free to exercise its discretion in selecting the one which it believes best serves the interests of justice. We conclude that the district court did not abuse its discretion in electing to limit Walser and McLaughlin's recovery on their promissory estoppel claim to out-of-pocket expenses.

---

[3] An illustration provided by the Restatement itself provides additional support for the district court's decision:

> A, who owns and operates a bakery, desires to go into the grocery business. He approaches B, a franchisor of supermarkets. B states to A that for $18,000 B will establish A in a store. B also advises A to move to another town and buy a small grocery to gain experience. A does so. Later B advises A to sell the grocery, which A does, taking a capital loss and foregoing expected profits from the summer tourist trade. B also advises A to sell his bakery to raise capital for the supermarket franchise saying "Everything is ready to go. Get your money together and we are set." A sells the bakery taking a capital loss on this sale as well. Still later, B tells A that considerably more than an $18,000 investment will be needed, and the negotiations between the parties collapse. At the point of collapse many details of the proposed agreement between the parties are unresolved. The assurances from B to A are promises on which B reasonably should have expected A to rely, and A is entitled to his actual losses on the sales of the bakery and for his moving and temporary living expenses. Since the proposed agreement was never made, however, A is not entitled to lost profits from the sale of the grocery or to his expectation interest in the proposed franchise from B. Restatement (Second) of Contracts § 90 cmt. d, illus. 10 (emphasis added). This illustration provides a close analogy to our case and further indicates that the district court correctly denied the recovery of lost profits because the "proposed agreement was never made" in this case. Walser and McLaughlin were still in the negotiation stages with Toyota when the deal broke down, and the jury found for Toyota on the breach of contract claim.

B.

Walser and McLaughlin next argue that the district court erred in limiting out-of-pocket expenses to "the difference between the actual value of the property and the price paid for it." (Jury Instr. No. 34.) They argue that they should have been allowed to "recoup" at least the full amount of the "unamortized capital investments" they made in attempting to obtain the dealership. They claim the full value of their investment totals more than $1,000,000 including the $676,864 they paid for the land and the various expenses in maintaining it.

Although not argued by the parties, we point out that the instruction Walser and McLaughlin complain about defines out-of-pocket expenses only in the damage instruction for fraud and misrepresentation. The promissory estoppel damage instruction provides only that damages are limited to out-of-pocket expenses with no further limitation on out-of-pocket expenses. Even if the fraud damage instruction could be read as a further limitation on promissory estoppel damages, the language of that instruction is not as limited as Walser and McLaughlin represent here. That instruction provides that out-of-pocket expenses are "the difference between the actual value of the property received and the price paid for it, together with such other damages as were naturally and directly caused by the fraud or misrepresentation." (Jury Instr. No. 34.) (emphasis added). If that instruction defined promissory estoppel damages, the jury was still free to add any other damages directly caused by reliance on Toyota's promise but simply chose not to do so in this case.

Moreover, we find no error in the district court's instruction to the extent that it defined their out-of-pocket expenses to be only the difference between the actual value and the amount paid for the property. Such an instruction reflects the amount of damage Walser and McLaughlin suffered from relying on Toyota's promise. For example, while the purchase price of the land totaled $676,864 Walser acknowledged in his trial testimony that the land still had significant value, worth at least $550,000. (Tr. Vol. VI at 23–24.) Their damage from relying on Toyota's promise is essentially the difference between the two amounts. Accordingly, the district court committed no error in instructing the jury on how to determine the damage award.

C.

Walser and McLaughlin next argue that the district court erred in declining to order specific performance of the dealership agreement as an alternative to the monetary award on their promissory estoppel claim. "Specific performance is an equitable remedy . . . 'addressed to the sound discretion of the trial court.' " Lilyerd v. Carlson, 499 N.W. 2d 803, 811 (Minn. 1993) (quoting Flynn v. Sawyer, 272 N.W.2d 904, 910 (Minn. 1978)).

The district court declined to order specific performance noting that the monetary damage award was adequate relief given the facts of this case. (Appellants' App. at 815.) For the same reasons outlined above, we cannot find the district court's decision to deny specific performance to be an abuse of discretion.

D.

[Eds.—The court next rejected Walser's and McLaughlin's claim of error based on the $0.89 shortfall in Toyota's payment of the district court judgment because the minor shortfall did not affect the plaintiffs' substantial rights.]

E.

[Eds.—The court rejected Walser's and McLaughlin's claim of error that the district court denied their motion for judgment as a matter of law on their contract claim.]

F.

Walser and McLaughlin next argue that the district court erred by declining to give two requested jury instructions dealing with the effect of the dealership application and its language indicating that no contract would be formed or would take effect until the dealership agreement was signed. They argue that the district court should have instructed the jury that a contract could be modified by oral agreement even if the parties specified in the contract that it could not be modified or, alternatively, that the dealership application itself was not a binding contract.

The district court decided not to give the oral modification instruction because it found that the application was not a written contract and that there was no evidence in the record of an oral agreement to modify. (Tr. Vol. IX at 2.) Walser and McLaughlin made no objection to the ruling and instead asked the court to give the alternative instruction that the dealership application itself was not a binding contract. The district court then denied the request for the alternative instruction, noting that "it is getting awfully close to the court reciting the facts, invading the province of the jury." (*Id.* at 4.)

"We review jury instructions as a whole to determine whether they fairly and adequately instruct the jury as to the substantive law." Brown v. Stites Concrete, Inc., 994 F.2d 553, 559 (8th Cir. 1993). "The district court has wide discretion in the formulation of jury instructions." Id. We find that the district court did not abuse its discretion in formulating the jury instructions in this case.

We first point out that Walser and McLaughlin made no timely objection to the district court's decision not to give the oral modification instruction. Accordingly, review for plain error is appropriate. However, under any standard of review we find the district court committed no error in denying the instruction because there was no evidence of an oral modification in this case. "A party that fails to introduce sufficient evidence to support a jury instruction is not entitled to it." First Dakota Nat'l Bank v. St. Paul Fire & Marine Ins., 2 F.3d 801, 815 (8th Cir. 1993).

Similarly, we conclude the district court committed no error in denying Walser and McLaughlin's request for an instruction that the dealership application was not a binding contract. First, there is no basis in the record for the instruction. Toyota never argued that the dealership application was a contract that Walser and McLaughlin should have legally enforced against them. It argued only that the dealership application was objective evidence that the parties fully understood that the dealership contract would be formed only upon both parties signing onto the dealership agreement. Moreover, we agree with the district court's assessment that Walser and McLaughlin's requested instruction would risk invading the jury's province to determine the effect of the language in the dealership application. See United States v. White Horse, 807 F.2d 1426, 1430–31 (8th Cir. 1986) (reversing because trial court invaded jury's province). Accordingly, we conclude that the district court committed no error in refusing Walser and McLaughlin's requested instructions to support their contract claim.

* * *

III.

For the foregoing reasons, the judgment of the district court is affirmed.

NOTES AND QUESTIONS

1. *Specific performance denied.* The court denied the plaintiff's claim requesting that Toyota be required by court order to award the Lexus dealership. What was the court's reasoning? Would it have made any difference if the relief had been requested before trial, rather than at the end of the trial? See Restatement (Second) of Contracts § 359(a).

2. *Promissory estoppel claim.* The court mentions that the plaintiff filed three original claims: one for breach of contract, one for the tort of fraud, and one for promissory estoppel. Is promissory estoppel an independent cause of action or merely a basis for enforcing a promise not supported by consideration? Is such a claim nonetheless still a breach of contract claim, or does the absence of consideration transform the claim into something else? If not a breach of contract, is it a tort-based claim? Do you think the promissory estoppel "claim" was merely another theory of obligation seeking essentially a breach of contract award for monetary damages? If so, does that explain why

the plaintiff sought expectancy interest damages for the promissory estoppel claim? Does this case help explain why a contract claim should first and foremost be based upon traditional notions of consideration where justice limitations on damages for promissory estoppel do not exist? Identify and articulate the justice elements that the court used to deny expectancy interest damages and rather limit to reliance damages.

3. *Promissory estoppel reliance and contract reliance compared.* Assume that this was a traditional breach of contract claim not based on promissory estoppel. Further assume that the plaintiff could not prove with reasonable certainty the future lost profits on the Lexus dealership (quite likely as a new business). See Restatement (Second) of Contracts § 352. That would mean that the plaintiff could still seek reliance damages on the breach of contract claim. See Restatement (Second) of Contracts § 349. How would those reliance damages be calculated? How were the reliance damages calculated in this case? Is there a difference in the calculation of reliance damages under a breach of contract claim based on promissory estoppel and one based on consideration? Does the "justice limitation" language in Restatement (Second) of Contracts § 90 relate to a limitation on reliance interest damages or expectancy interest damages? Many of the Restatement (Second) of Contracts § 90 illustrations do not provide for expectancy damages, creating the impression that the "justice limitation" is indeed intended as a general intent to relegate promissory estoppel to reliance damages. See Charles L. Knapp, "Reliance in the Revised Restatement: The Proliferation of Promissory Estoppel," 81 Colum. L. Rev. 52, 57–58 (1981) and Comment, "Once More Into the Breach: Promissory Estoppel and Traditional Damages Doctrine," 37 U. Chi. L. Rev. 559 (1970) (arguing expectancy interest is preferable because certain forms of reliance damages are quite difficult to prove with reasonable certainty, including foregone contractual opportunities). A study of this comparison determined that reliance damages are most often awarded in promissory estoppel cases rather than expectancy damages, not because of the "justice limitation," but because the expectancy is not proven with reasonable certainty. Mary E. Becker, "Promissory Estoppel Damages,"16 Hofstra L. Rev. 131 (1987). Nonetheless, the topic remains controversial, with many scholars and empirical studies supporting both theories. See, e.g., Paul T. Wangerin, "Damages for Reliance Across the Spectrum of Law: Of Blind Men and Legal Elephants," 72 Iowa L. Rev. 47 (1986); Edward Yorio & Steve Thel, "The Promissory Basis of Section 90," 101 Yale L. J. 111 (1991); Robert A. Hillman, "Questioning the 'New Consensus' on Promissory Estoppel: An Empirical and Theoretical Study," 98 Colum. L. Rev. 580 (1998); Eric Mills Holmes, "Restatement of Promissory Estoppel," 32 Willamette L. Rev. 263 (1996); Christopher T. Wonnell, "Expectation, Reliance and the Two Contractual Wrongs," 38 San Diego L. Rev. 53 (2001); and Jean Fleming Powers, "Promissory Estoppel and Wagging the Dog," 59 Ark. L. Rev. 841 (2007).

4. *The many weaknesses of reliance damages in remedying breach of contract.* Intuitively, reliance damages in promissory estoppel cases usually will undercompensate a nonbreaching party if only by denying that party a

chance to recover lost profits resulting from the breached promise. But in many cases, the reliance damages measure also arguably suffers from a number of other weaknesses besides inadequate compensation. See W. David Slawson, "The Role of Reliance in Contract Damages," 76 Cornell L. Rev. 197, 222–228 (1990). First, reliance damages fail to compensate for partial breaches in which the promisor ostensibly fulfills the promise, but the promised performance is less valuable than the promisee had been led to believe. See id. at 222. Second, reliance damages fail to punish "overpromising" in which the promisor intentionally promises more than the promisor intends to deliver in order to lead the promisee into relying to such an extent that the promisee will be forced later to accept an inferior bargain or lose all of its reliance expenditures. See id. at 225–226. Thus, an unscrupulous auto manufacturer could promise to award a promisee a franchise worth $1 million, when in reality the franchise would only be worth $750,000. The $1 million promise would be more likely to induce reliance expenditures, but the promisee's reliance damages would be the same regardless of the value of the promise. See id. Finally, a normative reliance damages measure would encourage both inefficient breach and waste. See id. at 226–27.

3. LIMITATIONS ON THE EXPECTANCY AND RELIANCE INTERESTS

Both the expectancy and reliance interests are subject to three important limitations. Each has separate features and different purposes with a focus on a functional limitation of either the breaching or the injured party.

The first, and arguably most important, limitation is the foreseeability standard. Restatement (Second) of Contracts § 351. Most "other losses" in the form of consequential damages are scrutinized heavily under this limitation. Restatement (Second) of Contracts § 347(b) (other losses and consequential damages). This limitation confines recoverable losses to those the breaching party objectively had reason to foresee at the time of the contract. However, because of the significant implications of consequential damages, they are often the subject of contractual elimination or modification. Elimination and modification of these damages is a topic covered later in this chapter.

The second limitation concerns mitigation avoidance of damages. Once breach occurs, and particularly where the breach is total and the injured party terminates the contract, the injured party must adopt reasonable measures to avoid incurring any further loss that would increase the damage claim against the breaching party. Restatement (Second) of Contracts §§ 347(c) and 350. Importantly, the loss only need be avoided when doing so avoids undue risk, burden, or humiliation. Restatement (Second) of Contracts § 350(1). Also, a party's reasonable but unsuccessful attempts to mitigate do not preclude recovery of the loss not avoided.

Restatement (Second) of Contracts § 350(2). This doctrine is based in equity and attempts to make certain that the breaching party is not penalized by its breach. For example, if Barnes signs a thirty-year lease with the Acme Shopping Center with a lease rate of $1,000,000 per year and repudiates the lease before occupying the space, Acme cannot simply collect $30,000,000 in damages. Rather it must make reasonable efforts to avoid much of that loss by seeking to lease the space to another tenant.

Finally, the certainty limitation permits the injured party to recover only for damages that can be proven with reasonable certainty. Restatement (Second) of Contracts § 352. As discussed above, this often has its greatest impact in attempting to prove lost profits where significant expense forecasting is required, especially in cases of total breach. Where lost profits cannot be proven with reasonable certainty, the injured party often seeks to recover reliance interest damages in the alternative. See Restatement (Second) of Contracts § 349.

a. Foreseeability Limitation

The introductory discussion to the expectancy interest outlined the four essential components of that measure of damages. One included the addition to the loss or diminution in value of any "other loss," including consequential loss, caused by the breach. Restatement (Second) of Contracts § 347(b). This simple language makes the breaching party responsible for potentially expensive losses well beyond the reasonable expectations at the time of contracting. Would a person agree to enter a $20 contract to deliver a package containing valuable documents, knowing that a breach might create $10,000,000 in consequential loss? Even a reasonable $2 profit on the contract is not worth such exposure. Fortunately, sensible minds prevailed in much earlier times to place a significant but reasonable constraint on the scope of compensable consequential losses.

That early but vitally important discussion is attributed to the *Hadley* case below (perhaps because, before this case, damage calculation was left to the undirected jury). See Grant Gilmore, The Death of Contract 83 (1974); Richard Danzig, "*Hadley v. Baxendale*: A Study in the Industrialization of the Law," 4 J. of Legal Studies 249 (1975); and Melvin A. Eisenberg, "The Principle of *Hadley v. Baxendale*," 80 Cal. L. Rev. 563 (1992). The case had two important effects. First, it classifies damages resulting from the breach of contract into two discrete categories: general ("*Hadley I* damages") and consequential ("*Hadley II* damages"). Secondly, it then applies different rules as to when the breaching party is responsible for damages attributable to each category. Importantly, the foreseeability limitation applies only to consequential damages. The modern view of the *Hadley* standard is memorialized in Restatement (Second) of Contracts § 351. Damages are not recoverable for loss that the breaching party did not have reason to foresee as a probable result of the breach at the time the contract was formed. Restatement (Second) of Contracts § 351(a).

Several ideas are locked in that simple structure. First, the time to test the foreseeability is at the time the contract was formed, not later when the contract was breached. This is important, because damages from a particular breach will be more foreseeable at the time of breach than at the time the contract was formed. Thus, this is a limitation on damage recovery. Secondly, the "reason to foresee" standard clearly rejects any requirement that the parties will be liable only where they "tacitly agree" to accept liability for particular types of damages. The breaching party need not have known about the damages or assumed the risk of those damages by agreeing to them at the time of the contract. Rather, the *Hadley* rule charges the breaching party with an objective responsibility equal to all contracting parties. Third, and quite subtly, certain damages in the *Hadley I* category are always or *per se* foreseeable because they flow naturally and in the ordinary course of events from a breach. Restatement (Second) of Contracts § 351(2)(a). These damages are most often referred to simply as "general" or "direct" damages. Stated another way, general damages need not be proven foreseeable because they are deemed foreseeable. The foreseeability test simply does not apply. The task is to get the characterization right in the first instance. However, certain damages in the *Hadley II* category may only be recovered provided they are foreseeable because they do not flow from the ordinary course of events. Restatement (Second) of Contracts § 351(2)(b). These damages are most often referred to as "special" or "consequential" damages. Importantly, the only way to have reason to know of such damages is because of knowledge acquired from some source (usually communicated by the injured party at the time of contracting).

Finally, the foreseeability standard states a specific justice limitation quite similar to that found in Restatement (Second) of Contracts § 90, except that justice in this case is specifically tethered to "disproportionate forfeiture." Restatement (Second) of Contracts § 351(3). The breaching party should be able to avoid unwittingly accepting responsibility for damages far beyond the range dictated by the profit and price of the product or service transaction itself.

HADLEY V. BAXENDALE
Court of Exchequer of England
9 Ex. 341, 156 Eng. Rep. 145 (1854)

[Ed. Note: the complaint in this case consisted of two counts. The first was a count in assumpsit, that the defendants, who were common carriers, had agreed for a fee to transport a broken mill shaft from the plaintiff's mill in Gloucester to a foundry in Greenwich. The defendants had promised to deliver the shaft on the second day after receiving it, but failed for a period of seven days to do so. The second count, also in assumpsit, alleged the same contract to transport the mill shaft, and lack of due care or diligence in the transportation. It further alleged that by reason of this carelessness, the making of a new replacement shaft at the foundry was delayed for five days, during which period the plaintiffs were prevented from working their mill. As a result, the count continued, the plaintiffs were unable to supply many of their customers with flour, were obliged to buy flour on the market to supply those customers, lost profits which otherwise would have accrued to them, and were compelled to pay wages to employees during the five day period even though the mill was idle because of the lack of a mill shaft. The plaintiffs claimed damages of £300.

The first count was dismissed. The defendants paid £25 into court in satisfaction of the plaintiffs' claim under the second count. The jury found the damages under the second count to be £50 and the defendants moved for a new trial on the ground that the jury had received incorrect instructions. Some of the notes of the reporter, and the opinion of the Court of Exchequer, deciding that motion, follow.]

At the trial before Crompton, J., at the last Gloucester Assizes, it appeared that the plaintiffs carried on an extensive business as millers at Gloucester; and that, on the 11th of May, their mill was stopped by a breakage of the crank shaft by which the mill was worked. The steam-engine was manufactured by Messrs, Joyce & Co., the engineers, at Greenwich, and it became necessary to send the shaft as a pattern for the new one to Greenwich. The facture was discovered on the 12th, and on the 13th the plaintiffs sent one of their servants to the office of the defendants, who are the well known carriers trading under the name of Pickford & Co., for the purpose of having the shaft carried to Greenwich. The plaintiffs' servant told the clerk that the mill was stopped, and that the shaft must be sent immediately; and in answer to the inquiry when the shaft would be taken, the answer was, that if it was sent up by twelve o'clock any day, it would be delivered at Greenwich on the following day. On the following day the shaft was taken by the defendants, before noon, for the purpose of being conveyed to Greenwich, and the sum of £2 4s. was paid for its carriage for the whole distance; at the same time the defendants' clerk was told that a special entry, if required, should be made to hasten its delivery. The delivery of the shaft at Greenwich was delayed by some neglect; and the consequence was, that the plaintiffs did not receive the new shaft for several days after they would otherwise have done, and the working of their mill was thereby delayed, and they thereby lost the profits they would otherwise have received.

On the part of the defendants, it was objected that these damages were too remote, and that the defendants were not liable with respect to them. . . .

ALDERSON, BARON. We think that there ought to be a new trial in this case; but, in so doing, we deem it expedient and necessary to state explicitly the rule which the Judge, at the next trial, ought, in our opinion, to direct the jury to be governed by when they estimate the damages.

It is indeed, of the last importance that we should do this; for, if the jury are left without any definite rule to guide them, it will, in such cases as these, manifestly lead to the greatest injustice. . . .

Now we think the proper rule in such a case as the present is thus:— Where two parties have made a contract which one of them has broken, the damages which the other party ought to receive in respect of such breach of contract should be such as may fairly and reasonably be considered either arising naturally, i.e., according to the usual course of things, from such a breach of contract itself, or such as may reasonably be supposed to have been in the contemplation of both parties, at the time they made the contract, as the probable result of the breach of it. Now, if the special circumstances under which the contract was actually made were communicated by the plaintiffs to the defendants, and thus known to both parties, the damages resulting from the breach of such a contract, which they would reasonably contemplate, would be the amount of injury which would ordinarily follow from a breach of contract under those special circumstances so known and communicated. But, on the other hand, if these special circumstances were wholly unknown to the party breaking the contract, he, at the most, could only be supposed to have had in his contemplation the amount of injury which would arise generally, and in the great multitude of cases not affected by any special circumstances, from such a breach of contract. For, had the special circumstances have been known, the parties might have specially provided for the breach of contract by special terms as to the damages in that case; and of this advantage it would be very unjust to deprive them. Now the above principles are those by which we think the jury ought to be guided in estimating the damages arising out of any breach of contract. It is said, that other cases such as breaches of contract in the non-payment of money, or in the not making good title to land, are to be treated as exceptions from this, and as governed by a conventional rule. But as, in such cases, both parties must be supposed to be cognizant of that well-known rule, these cases may, we think, be more properly classed under the rule above enunciated as to cases under known special circumstances, because there both parties may reasonably be presumed to contemplate the estimation of the amount of damages according to the conventional rule. Now in the present case, if we are to apply the principle above laid down, we find that the only circumstances here communicated by the plaintiffs to the defendants at the time the contract was made, were, that the article to be carried was the broken shaft of a mill, and that the plaintiffs were the millers of that mill. But how do these circumstances show reasonably that the profits of the mill must be stopped by an unreasonable delay in the delivery of the broken shaft by the carrier to the third person? Suppose the plaintiffs had another shaft in their possession put up or putting up at the time, and that they only wished to send back the broken shaft to the engineer who made it; it is clear that this would be quite consistent with the above circumstances, and yet the unreasonable delay in the delivery would have no effect upon the intermediate profits of the mill. Or, again, suppose that, at the time of delivery to the carrier, the machinery of the mill had been in other respects defective, then, also, the same result would follow. Here it is true that the shaft was actually sent back to serve as a model for a new one, and that the want of a new one was the only cause of the stoppage of the mill, and that the loss of profits really arose from not sending down the new shaft in proper time, and that this arose from the delay in delivering the broken one to serve as a model. But it is obvious that, in the great multitude of cases of millers sending off broken shafts to third persons by carrier under ordinary circumstances, such consequences would not, in all probability, have occurred; and these special circumstances were here never communicated by the plaintiffs to the defendants. It follows, therefore, that the loss of profits here cannot reasonably be considered such a consequence of the breach of contract as could have been fairly and reasonably contemplated by both parties when they made this contract. For such loss would neither have flowed naturally from the breach of this contract in the great multitude of such cases occurring under ordinary circumstances, nor were the special circumstances, which, perhaps, would have made it a reasonable and natural consequence of such breach of contract, communicated to or known by the defendants. The Judge ought, therefore, to have told the jury, that, upon the facts then before them, they ought not to take the loss of profits into consideration at all in estimating the damages. There must therefore be a new trial in this case. . . .

NOTES AND QUESTIONS

1.   *Legal archaeology revisited.* In 1854, Gloucester was not a sleepy English village, but an important city and major inland port. Moreover, £300 was a significant sum, approximately $14,000 today. Extending that profit over a full year, the mill would have made an annual profit of roughly $1,400,000. See John Kidwell, "Extending the Lessons of *Hadley v. Baxendale*," 11 Tex. Wesleyan L. Rev. 421 (2005). Furthermore, the carrier was already nearly 200 years old at the time this case was tried and remained in existence for some time.   See   http://www.victorianturkishbath.org/6DIRECTORY/AtoZEstab/Animals/LonFinSF.htm

2.   *A tale of two rules in* Hadley I & II. The *Hadley* case characterizes damages into two categories. The first category ("*Hadley I*") includes damages " . . . such as may fairly and reasonably be considered either arising naturally, i.e., according to the usual course of things, from such a breach of contract itself. . . ." The second category ("*Hadley II*") includes damages " . . . such as

may reasonably be supposed to have been in the contemplation of both parties, at the time they made the contract, as the probable result of the breach of it." Both categories are repeated in Restatement (Second) of Contracts §§ 351(2)(a) [*Hadley I*] and (b) [*Hadley II*]. *Hadley I* damages are referred to as "general damages," whereas *Hadley II* damages are referred to as "special" or "consequential" damages. See Restatement (Second) of Contracts § 351, *cmt. b.*

3.   *Applicability to expectancy and reliance interests damages.* While *Hadley I* and *II* damages might frequent the expectancy interest more often than the reliance interest because of its lost profits from collateral contracts, the standards are clearly applicable to both categories. Restatement (Second) of Contracts § 351, *cmt. a* provides (suggesting that lost profits are consequential and *Hadley II* damages):

> Although the recovery that is precluded by the limitation of foreseeability is usually based on the expectation interest and takes the form of lost profits . . . the limitation may also preclude recovery based on the reliance interest. . . .

Lost profits are often regarded as consequential rather than general damages. However, whether lost profits are subject to the requirements of *Hadley I* or *II* depends more upon the nature of the transaction than upon labels such as "lost profits." Indeed, the proper characterization of damages as *Hadley I* or *II* is of critical importance because of the different standards applicable and because parties often attempt to eliminate *Hadley II* damages in the contract itself. Restatement (Second) of Contracts § 351, *cmt. b* provides:

> For example, a seller of a commodity to a wholesaler usually has reason to foresee that his failure to deliver the commodity as agreed will probably cause the wholesaler to lose a reasonable profit on it. See Illustrations 3 and 4. Similarly, a seller of a machine to a manufacturer usually has reason to foresee that his delay in delivering the machine as agreed will probably cause the manufacturer to lose a reasonable profit from its use, although courts have been somewhat more cautious in allowing the manufacturer recovery for loss of such profits than in allowing a middleman recovery for loss of profits on an intended resale.

Nonetheless, some would not apply *Hadley* to lost profits, whereas others might disagree. Compare Richard Posner, Economic Analysis of Law § 4.9 (5th ed. 1998), with Melvin A. Eisenberg, "Actual and Virtual Specific Performance, the Theory of Efficient Breach, and the Indifference Principle in Contract Law," 93 Cal. L. Rev. 975, 993 (2005).

4.   *The justice limitation applied to lost profits.* Restatement (Second) of Contracts § 351(3) provides that even if damages are foreseeable, a court may eliminate recovery for lost profits and confine the recovery to lesser reliance damages when justice requires such a result in order to avoid disproportionate forfeiture. Ordinarily, courts view disproportionate forfeiture as an unjust penalty and are hesitant to assess damages in such a case. The justice concept

carries this notion forward. Restatement (Second) of Contracts § 351, *cmt. f* explains:

> *f. Other limitations on damages.* It is not always in the interest of justice to require the party in breach to pay damages for all of the foreseeable loss that he has caused. There are unusual instances in which it appears from the circumstances either that the parties assumed that one of them would not bear the risk of a particular loss or that, although there was no such assumption, it would be unjust to put the risk on that party. One such circumstance is an extreme disproportion between the loss and the price charged by the party whose liability for that loss is in question. The fact that the price is relatively small suggests that it was not intended to cover the risk of such liability. Another such circumstance is an informality of dealing, including the absence of a detailed written contract, which indicates that there was no careful attempt to allocate all of the risks. The fact that the parties did not attempt to delineate with precision all of the risks justifies a court in attempting to allocate them fairly. The limitations dealt with in this Section are more likely to be imposed in connection with contracts that do not arise in a commercial setting. Typical examples of limitations imposed on damages under this discretionary power involve the denial of recovery for loss of profits and the restriction of damages to loss incurred in reliance on the contract. Sometimes these limits are covertly imposed, by means of an especially demanding requirement of foreseeability or of certainty. The rule stated in this Section recognizes that what is done in such cases is the imposition of a limitation in the interests of justice.

Does *Hadley I* still leave considerable scope for a jury to decide the quantum of damage recoverable under an instruction on that rule? *Hadley II* announces three distinct predicates for recovery: first, the damages must reasonably have been supposed to have been in the contemplation of both parties (courts now generally say contemplation of the defendant); second, at the time of contracting; and third, they must have contemplated such damage as the probable result of the breach. Finally, do these predicates restrict or expand the measure of damage recovery? See Melvin A. Eisenberg, "The Principle of *Hadley v. Baxendale*," 80 Cal. L. Rev. 563 (1992); Larry T. Garvin, "Disproportionality and the Law of Consequential Damages: Default Theory and Cognitive Reality," 59 Ohio St. L. J. 339 (1998); and William B. Harvey, "Discretionary Justice Under the Restatement (Second) of Contracts,"67 Cornell L. Rev. 666 (1982).

5. *Organizational liability from information directed to regular employees.* The *Hadley II* standard requires that liability attaches for consequential damages only when the breaching party "had reason to know" of special circumstances beyond the ordinary course of events. Restatement (Second) of Contracts § 351(2)(b). Importantly, the parol evidence rule does not preclude admission of evidence to establish that the breaching party had reason to know of special circumstances. Restatement (Second) of Contracts

§ 351(2)(b), *cmt. b.* However, when the breaching party involves a large organization, to whom must the injured party communicate the information regarding the special circumstances in order to charge the organization with the requisite *Hadley II* knowledge?

Restatement (Second) of Contracts § 351(2)(b) merely requires "reason to know" rather than actual knowledge. Therefore, proper notice to an agent of an organization will likely suffice. Restatement (Second) of Agency § 268 provides that notice to an agent (e.g., employee) is notice to the principal (e.g., employer) provided the agent had actual or apparent authority to receive the notice. Actual authority is determined by manifestations from the principal directly to the agent, but apparent authority is determined by manifestations from the principal to the third party as, for example, by placing the agent in a particular position. Compare Restatement (Second) of Agency §§ 26 (actual authority), with 27 (apparent authority).

6.   *The rejected tacit agreement test.* The tacit agreement test would require that at the time the contract was formed, the breaching party had actual knowledge of the special circumstances creating expanded consequential damages and consciously assumed that risk. The language of Restatement (Second) of Contracts § 351(2)(b)—"had reason to know"—clearly rejects that doctrine. Restatement (Second) of Contracts § 351, *cmt. a* provides:

> The mere circumstance that some loss was foreseeable, or even that some loss of the same general kind was foreseeable, will not suffice if the loss that actually occurred was not foreseeable. It is enough, however, that the loss was foreseeable as a probable, as distinguished from a necessary, result of his breach. Furthermore, the party in breach need not have made a "tacit agreement" to be liable for the loss. Nor must he have had the loss in mind when making the contract, for the test is an objective one based on what he had reason to foresee. There is no requirement of foreseeability with respect to the injured party.

As to be expected, both rules find scholarly support. Compare Richard A. Epstein, "Beyond Foreseeability: Consequential Damages in the Law of Contract," 18 J. Legal Stud. 105 (1989) (retain tacit agreement test), with Melvin A. Eisenberg, "The Principle of *Hadley v. Baxendale*," 80 Cal. L. Rev. 563 (1992) (reject test as exchange of information not likely to occur).

7.   *CISG consequential damages.* CISG art. 74 (ought to have foreseen at the conclusion of the contract) applies rules comparable to the common law rules of foreseeability, as do most civil law countries. See, e.g., Eric C. Schneider, "Consequential Damages in the International Sale of Goods: Analysis of Two Decisions," 16 U. Pa. J. Int'l. Bus. L. 615 (1995).

8.   *UCC version of general and consequential damages and foreseeability.* UCC § 2–714(1) allows a buyer to recover "general damages" that result from the "ordinary course of events from the seller's breach." UCC § 2–714(3) also permits the buyer to recover consequential damages. UCC § 2–715(2)

specifically addresses consequential damages, and UCC § 2–715(2)(a) confirms that consequential damage include any loss resulting from the buyer's general or particular requirements and needs that the seller at the time of contracting had reason to know. As a result, UCC §§ 2–714 and 2–715 follow the general and consequential paradigm, with the latter subject to a foreseeability standard.

The standard measure of "general damages" is measured by the difference in value between the goods as promised and when accepted or delivered. As with common law cases, care must be exercised to assign damages to one category or the other. Moreover, general damages may be consequential in another case. The point is to take care to assign names to the correct category in order to avoid double recovery, as well as to subject only the consequential damages to the foreseeability test. Characterization will also be required when the contract itself eliminates consequential but not general damages.

FLORAFAX INTERNATIONAL, INC. V. GTE MARKET RESOURCES, INC.

Supreme Court of Oklahoma
933 P.2d 282 (1997)

LAVENDER, Justice.

We consider the appropriateness of a jury award of lost profits over a two-year time period in favor of appellee/counter-appellant, Florafax International, Inc. against appellant/counter-appellee, GTE Market Resources, Inc., for breaching a contract requiring GTE to provide telecommunication and/or telemarketing services for Florafax. The profits were those Florafax claimed it stood to make from a collateral contract it had with a third party, but allegedly lost when the collateral contract was canceled purportedly because GTE breached its contract with Florafax. The Court of Civil Appeals reversed the lost profit award—remanding with instructions for a determination of lost profits incurred during a sixty (60) day period, a time frame chosen on the basis the collateral contract contained a clause allowing either party to it to terminate the collateral contract on sixty (60) days notice. Both parties sought certiorari, Florafax claiming error by the Court of Civil Appeals in limiting lost profits to a sixty (60) day period and GTE attacking the propriety of any lost profit award.

We previously granted both parties' petitions for certiorari and now hold the Court of Civil Appeals erred in limiting lost profits as it did. Instead, we hold the award of lost profits was consistent with our substantive law and was supported by competent evidence. Therefore, we vacate the Court of Civil Appeals' Memorandum Opinion to the extent it disturbed the jury's verdict and trial court's judgment as to the award of lost profits. Instead, we affirm that part of the judgment awarding lost profits based on the jury's verdict.

II. FACTS

Florafax is generally a flowers-by-wire company acting as a clearinghouse to allow the placement and receipt of orders between florists throughout the United States and internationally. Basically the system works as follows: retail florists become members of the Florafax network (apparently, thousands of retail florists join Florafax's wire service). Florafax maintains a list of the members and circulates a directory to them. The members are then able to send and receive orders among each other throughout the system. In other words, a consumer orders flowers at a retail florist at a certain location (e.g. Oklahoma City) to be delivered to someone in another location (e.g. Los Angeles). Florafax assists the transactions by collecting money from the florist taking the order from the customer and guarantying payment to the florist delivering the flowers. It processes the credit card activity on the transactions and charges a fee or fees for this service. Florafax also maintains a computer network whereby member florists can send and receive orders by computer—if they have such technology—without using the telephone. It also has a division that advertises floral products by the use of brochures, and other sales and promotional materials, allowing consumers to place a telephone order for floral products directly without going through a florist in their hometowns.

Evidence at trial showed at the time the agreements giving rise to this dispute were entered that Florafax was one of the largest floral wire services of its kind in the nation, and, in fact, certain evidence placed it third world-wide behind Florists' Transworld Delivery Association (FTD) and a company known as Teleflora. Evidence also showed Florafax had been headquartered in Tulsa, Oklahoma since, at least, 1979.

In addition to the above activities, Florafax solicits agreements with third party clients such as supermarket chains, American Express and other entities that advertise the sale of floral products by various methods (e.g. television, radio, newspapers, billing circulars, mass mailings to consumers) which allow a consumer to order floral arrangements via the use of a 1-800 telephone call, with Florafax agreeing to handle the actual inbound and outbound communication aspects of the transactions. In other words, when a consumer responds to an advertisement, it is not the advertiser that answers the telephone call to take the order, or that makes a telephone call or computer communication to a retail florist for fulfillment, but it is Florafax who handles these activities. Such orders would, of course, be fulfilled, if possible, by retail florist members taken from the Florafax directory maintained by it and, again, Florafax would handle the mechanics of processing the transactions, e.g. credit card processing. The advertiser would pay Florafax a certain fee or fees for its services.

One client that signed up for an arrangement like that described immediately above was Bellerose Floral, Inc., d/b/a Flora Plenty, a leading marketer of floral products advertising sales through use of the telephone number 1-800-FLOWERS. Florafax and Bellerose entered a contract in early October 1989 whereby Florafax and/or its designee would accept direct consumer orders (i.e. inbound calls and orders) placed via the 1-800-FLOWERS number and, of course, it also agreed to handle the outbound placement of orders either by telephone or computer transmission. The Florafax/Bellerose contract provided Florafax would be paid certain fee(s) per order. As we read the contract its initial term was for one year, to be automatically renewed from month to month thereafter, but that either party, with or without cause, could terminate the agreement upon sixty (60) days written notice.

GTE, on the other hand, was a company providing telecommunication and/or telemarketing services for other businesses. It provided for other businesses a call-answering center where telemarketing sales representatives (TSRs) physically answered telephones when orders from promotional activities came in from consumers and took care of transmitting the orders by telephone or computer for fulfillment. For certain management and business-related reasons Florafax subcontracted out much of the telecommunication and telemarketing services of its business.

In mid-October 1989, about two weeks after Florafax signed its agreement with Bellerose, the Florafax/GTE contract was entered. In essence, it provided GTE would via a call answering center (apparently located in the Dallas, Texas area) handle much, if not all, of the activities connected with taking incoming orders and placing outgoing calls or computer transmissions directed to it by Florafax associated with the purchase and fulfillment of floral orders throughout the United States and internationally. The agreement required Florafax to pay GTE certain fees for this service depending on the type of order.

The Florafax/GTE contract generally ran for a term of three years from the effective date the parties anticipated Florafax would begin directing calls to GTE for floral orders—a date anticipated to be in early December 1989. It also contained certain provisions that in essence might result in termination after a two-year period based upon application of a price/fee renegotiation clause. In answer to one of the questions submitted via a special verdict form, the jury determined the Florafax/GTE contract could be terminated after two years based on this clause.

The contract further contained a clause concerning lost profits providing in pertinent part:

20. Termination

a.   Termination for cause. Any non-defaulting party shall have the right to terminate this agreement at any date not less than forty-five (45) days after an event of default occurs and so long as it continues. In the event GTE ceases to perform its duties hereunder after a notice of termination is given or otherwise, Florafax may suffer tremendous damage to its business. GTE agrees to pay Florafax consequential damages and lost profits on the business lost.[2]

The contract also specifically noted GTE would be providing services not only for Florafax, but for others.

In addition to the above express contractual provisions, evidence was presented that officials with GTE knew prior to signing the contract that GTE would be providing its services not only directly for Florafax, but that Florafax had been soliciting business from entities such as Bellerose, business that was anticipated to be at least partially directed through GTE's call answering center. In fact, competent evidence exists in this record showing GTE specifically knew when it signed the contract with Florafax that Bellerose was considering turning over a portion of its inbound and outbound business to Florafax, and that Bellerose received somewhere between 100,000–200,000 orders annually. Evidence was also presented that showed GTE, prior to contract execution, considered it a positive aspect of entering the agreement that Florafax was constantly marketing and promoting its business by the addition of outside clients and that this addition of clients would lead to revenue increases. Evidence also existed that Bellerose was Florafax's largest customer and that it had been an ongoing business for at least sixteen (16) years prior to the date of trial.

Evidence was also submitted showing that before GTE entered the contract, its director of finance and administration did a financial analysis of the Florafax/GTE contract and determined GTE would make little or no money from it. His immediate supervisor (the general manager of GTE) was informed of the analysis. GTE, however, made the decision to enter the contract, apparently because it needed new customers and/or in the hope this financial analysis was wrong.

---

[2]   In at least one of its appellate submissions GTE has argued Florafax may not rely on the just quoted contract clause to support its claim to lost profits because Florafax never relied on the clause in the trial court. GTE is mistaken. First off, the entire contract between GTE and Florafax was admitted in evidence at trial. Second, Florafax did rely on the clause at trial. It was specifically referenced during the testimony of the first witness presented by Florafax, a Mr. Ron Fore, a vice-president and secretary of Florafax. Third, as will be seen in our analysis of this case, competent evidence existed, if believed by the jury, which was sufficient to show the clause was implicated. Essentially, the evidence was that during part of the life of the Florafax/GTE contract, GTE intentionally failed to perform its duties under the contract in an effort to force Florafax into renegotiating the pricing schedule contained in the contract.

Although from December 1989 through Valentine's Day in February 1990 certain problems surfaced in regard to the adequacy of GTE's performance, at some point after Valentine's Day the problems appeared to worsen. At some time after Valentine's Day and leading up to Mother's Day in May 1990, the latter holiday being described as the largest floral holiday of the year, the adequacy of GTE's performance became subject to serious question. What appears from the evidence to be the most glaring breach on GTE's part was a failure during the week leading up to Mother's Day to provide sufficient TSRs to answer calls anticipated to be directed to it by Florafax, including calls from Bellerose. Without adequate TSRs to take the calls, floral product orders would obviously be lost and Florafax income lost in the process.

Coupled with this evidence of a failure to adequately staff for anticipated calls, there was also evidence that during the term of the contract GTE's project manager for the Florafax account admitted to Florafax's off-site manager stationed at the GTE facility to look out for Florafax's interests there, that GTE no longer wanted the Florafax account—in essence, because GTE was not making money under the contract's pricing scheme. This same Florafax employee was also told by the same GTE project manager and another employee of GTE that GTE would not provide sufficient numbers of TSRs for the Florafax project essentially for the same reason, i.e. GTE was not making money on the project under the pricing terms in the contract. Evidence also showed that as early as April 1990 GTE was requesting from Florafax a change in the pricing terms of the contract, but that such change was never finally agreed to by Florafax. In effect then, there was both direct and circumstantial evidence tending to show that GTE intentionally failed to adequately perform its duties and obligations under its agreement with Florafax to provide telecommunication/telemarketing services in an effort to coerce Florafax into agreeing to a price renegotiation adjustment not required under the terms of the contract. Although other evidence from GTE disputed the evidence of Florafax that GTE intentionally failed to provide sufficient staffing for Florafax at its call answering center, as noted . . . as an appellate court we are in no position to weigh the evidence in such regard—that responsibility belonged to the jury.[4]

In addition, evidence was presented that GTE's failure to perform caused Bellerose to terminate its agreement with Florafax and Bellerose ceased its relationship with Florafax apparently some time in July 1990, directing no more calls from its 1-800-FLOWERS number through GTE after that time. The President of Bellerose essentially testified that he

---

[4] We caution to note that we do not mean to intimate that GTE never adequately performed its duties or obligations as per the terms of the Florafax/GTE contract. However, as noted in the text, there is sufficient competent evidence in the record to support a finding that at certain times—important times in the floral product industry by its nature—that GTE intentionally failed to adequately perform duties and obligations it was contractually required to perform.

anticipated his agreement with Florafax to be a long-term relationship if things worked out and, although his testimony was not absolute in such regard, that he pulled out of his relationship with Florafax because of the poor performance of GTE. In such latter regard, although the President of Bellerose acknowledged that he was also upset with Florafax, primarily because it did not manage the situation with GTE in such a way to insure adequate performance, we believe a reasonable conclusion from his testimony was that, the inadequate performance of GTE was the direct cause of Bellerose's decision to terminate the Florafax/Bellerose contract and that had GTE adequately performed, the relationship between Florafax and Bellerose would have been a long-term one, rather than being canceled in July 1990. Clearly, the evidence does not show any other major factor connected with Bellerose's termination of its relationship with Florafax other than the insufficient performance by GTE of duties and obligations it was required to perform under its contract with Florafax. In fact, the President of Bellerose testified that the most important issues leading to Bellerose's decision to terminate its relationship with Florafax were the performance issues—i.e., performance that was directly the responsibility of GTE under the Florafax/GTE agreement.

As a result of GTE's breach, in addition to losing Bellerose as a client, Florafax incurred costs primarily associated with taking steps necessary to set up its own call-answering center in Tulsa to perform the duties GTE was supposed to handle so that it would not lose other clients or business relationships as it had lost Bellerose. Florafax finally left the GTE facility at the end of September 1990.

In addition to seeking damages attributable to costs associated with performing the services GTE was supposed to perform, Florafax sought lost profits it claimed would have been realized from the Florafax/Bellerose contract. In support of and in opposition to the lost profit claim the parties presented conflicting economic projections through expert witnesses (Florafax through an economist, GTE through a Certified Public Accountant) as to how much profit, if any, Florafax would have made from the Bellerose contract over varying lengths of time. Although the two experts differed on certain aspects of their formulations (e.g. sale close ratios and percentage increase, if any, of Bellerose business) the projections were basically grounded on the pricing terms of the Florafax/GTE contract and projections of the number of Bellerose orders. A starting point for the latter projections had as their basis the number of calls actually received by GTE from Bellerose customers during the five to seven month period Bellerose calls and orders were actually being handled at the GTE facility.

One major difference between the experts' projections was that the Florafax expert increased the Bellerose sales volume from 1990 to 1991 one hundred percent (100%), while the GTE expert kept the call and order volumes flat in his projections. The one hundred percent (100%) increase was based on evidence the Bellerose sales volume increased about this percentage over the 1990-year levels. GTE's expert, in contrast, used a flat growth rate because a general floral industry survey indicated declining volumes in the floral industry from the late 1980s through 1991.

The Florafax expert estimated the Bellerose loss at $1,921,028.00 for a period extended out to three years, i.e. for the period of time that remained in the term of the Florafax/GTE contract at the time Bellerose canceled. The GTE expert estimated the Bellerose loss over the same time frame to be $505,731.00 if the fees to be paid to GTE by Florafax remained constant for this period of time. The GTE expert also gave an alternative figure that coincided with the remaining part of a two year period beginning in December 1989 based on the view the Florafax/GTE contract would be subject to termination at such time in view of the price renegotiation provisions of that contract. The loss of profits for this period was estimated to be $294,044.00. These figures of the two experts took into consideration that the fees Florafax had to pay to GTE for its services would have to be deducted from the income or revenue Florafax would have received from Bellerose orders.[5]

The jury determined GTE breached its contract with Florafax and, in addition to other damages, awarded Florafax $750,000.00 in lost profits that would have been earned under the Florafax/Bellerose contract over a two year period of time. Other damages awarded to Florafax included a little over $820,000.00, the majority of which reflected costs and expenses associated with setting up and/or expanding a call center in Tulsa, Oklahoma to perform those functions GTE was supposed to perform under the Florafax/GTE contract. On appeal, GTE, although not admitting liability—i.e. that it breached its contract with Florafax—does not contest the jury determination that it did breach the contract. We now turn to the lost profit damage issues to be reviewed.

---

[5] Although there was some dispute as to whether Florafax's expert properly deducted all of the expenses that should have been deducted to reach a net lost profit figure, it is clear from the evidence that the amounts reflected in the text from both experts did take into consideration the necessity of deducting the fees that Florafax would have had to pay to GTE for its services. Of course, only net profits—as opposed to gross profits—are recoverable and depending on the particular transactions involved, what does or does not have to be deducted to reach a net lost profit figure may vary. See H. HUNTER, MODERN LAW OF CONTRACTS, Breach & Remedies, § 7.03[4][c] at 7–20/7–23 (1986). GTE, on appeal, does not attack the lost profit award on the basis that it is not a net figure. We also note that the expert for GTE gave other alternative estimates of lost profits which included estimates that actually showed losses to Florafax in the second and third years of the Florafax/GTE contract. These estimates were based on the view that the fees paid to GTE by Florafax would have been subject to sharp increases because of provisions in the contract that might have resulted in either fee increases or reductions depending on whether anticipated talk times for taking telephone orders and/or fulfilling the orders taken varied by a certain percentage from the times anticipated for these services, the anticipated times being specified in the contract. At trial the parties disputed whether the anticipated talk times were actually exceeded so that a fee increase would actually have been appropriate.

III. LOST PROFITS FROM A COLLATERAL CONTRACT MAY BE RECOVERED AS A PROPER ELEMENT OF DAMAGE FOR BREACH OF CONTRACT

GTE raises two basic arguments on the propriety of the recovery of lost profits. These are: (1) lost profit damages cannot include profits from third-party collateral contracts or, if they are recoverable, Florafax failed to prove entitlement to them because it failed to show the prospect of profits from the Florafax/Bellerose contract or, conversely, the loss of such profits upon GTE's breach, were in the contemplation of GTE and Florafax at the time they entered the Florafax/GTE contract; and, (2) if lost profits from the Florafax/Bellerose contract are recoverable they must be limited to a sixty (60) day period, because profits beyond this time must be deemed too remote, speculative or uncertain, and Florafax could not be said to be reasonably assured of any profits from its relationship with Bellerose for any longer period, given the Florafax/Bellerose contract clause allowing either Florafax or Bellerose the right to terminate that contract upon sixty (60) days notice. In our view, each argument is without merit.

III(A). COLLATERAL CONTRACTS AND LOST PROFITS

GTE asserts Oklahoma jurisprudence has not squarely addressed the question of whether a party suing for breach of contract may recover lost profits arising from a collateral contract. Although this Court may not have used the exact phrase "lost profits from third-party collateral contracts" a review of Oklahoma law makes clear if such damages are properly proved they are recoverable. Thus, GTE's apparent view that lost profits from a collateral contract are never recoverable for breach of contract because as a matter of law they are inherently too remote, speculative and/or unforeseeable, is mistaken.

The time-honored general rules on recovery of damages for breach of contract are found in Hadley v. Baxendale, 9 Ex. 341, 156 Eng. Rep. 145 (1854)—rules this Court has generally followed. Coker v. Southwestern Bell Tel. Co., 580 P. 2d 151, 153 (Okla. 1978). They are: (1) where no special circumstances distinguish the contract involved from the great mass of contracts of the same kind, the damages recoverable are those as would naturally and generally result from the breach according to the usual course of things, and (2) where there are special circumstances in the contract, damages which result in consequence of the special circumstances are recoverable, if, and only if, the special circumstances were communicated to or known by both parties to the contract at the time they entered the contract. 22 AM.JUR. 2d Damages § 464 (1988). The lost profits involved here fall under the second branch of the Hadley v. Baxendale formulation.

Generally speaking, this Court has long espoused the view that loss of future or anticipated profit—i.e. loss of expected monetary gain—is recoverable in a breach of contract action: (1) if the loss is within the contemplation of the parties at the time the contract was made, (2) if the loss flows directly or proximately from the breach—i.e. if the loss can be said to have been caused by the breach—and (3) if the loss is capable of reasonably accurate measurement or estimate. Groendyke Transport, Inc. v. Merchant, 380 P. 2d 682 Second Syllabus (Okla. 1962). An award in the form of a loss of profits, in fact, is generally considered a common measure of damages for breach of contract, it frequently represents fulfillment of the non-breaching party's expectation interest, and it often closely approximates the goal of placing the innocent party in the same position as if the contract had been fully performed. H. HUNTER, MODERN LAW OF CONTRACTS, Breach & Remedies, § 7.02[2] at 7–5/7–6 (1986).

Our cases also recognize that where there is sufficient evidence presented on the issue of the recovery of special damages—including lost profits—what was or was not in the contemplation of the parties at the time of contracting is a question of fact to be determined by the trier of fact. Home-Stake Production Company v. Minnis, 443 P. 2d 91, 103 (Okla. 1968). Liability for lost profits arises where the loss of anticipated profits upon breach can reasonably be said to be in the contemplation of the parties at the time of contracting. Quincy Johnston, Inc. v. Wilson, 358 P. 2d 205, 208 (Okla. 1959).

The above rules were applied in the early case of Ft. Smith & Western Railroad Co. v. Williams, 30 Okla. 726, 121 P. 275 (1912), a case we deem to have clearly allowed recovery of lost profits that would have been gained by virtue of a collateral contract that had been entered into prior to the contract being sued upon. Williams involved a situation where an individual had purchased a right from a picnic committee located at Madill, Oklahoma to operate his merry-go-round during a two-day picnic to be held at Madill. After contracting with the picnic committee, the merry-go-round owner contracted with defendant railroad to ship the machine to the picnic. Because of delay by defendant it was not delivered to the picnic until the evening of the picnic's first day. Setting it up took until the morning of the picnic's second day. Plaintiff owner sued the railroad for the lost profits he claimed he would have made in selling rides during the first day of the picnic and the part of the second day that the merry-go-round was not operational prior to its set up.

This Court in Williams affirmed a jury verdict for lost profits where the evidence showed defendant had specifically been put on notice by plaintiff that the machine had to be delivered by a certain day so that it could be operational for use on the picnic's first day, had been informed of the use to which the merry-go-round would be put, had notice of the damage that would be suffered by plaintiff if it was not delivered in a timely manner and where there was evidence to support a reasonable estimate of the profits lost—evidence which included what plaintiff actually made during part of the picnic's second day. Id. 121 P. at 277–278. In other words, lost profit damages were allowed that would have been earned on the basis of the collateral contract the owner had previously entered with the picnic committee whereby he obtained the right to sell rides on the merry-go-round during the picnic. Thus, recovery for the loss of anticipated profits from collateral contracts are not per se off-limits in a breach of contract action. Instead, lost profits growing out of an existing collateral or subordinate agreement may be recovered where the possibility of profits was within the contemplation of the defaulting party when the main contract was made and such profits are proved with reasonable certainty. 22 AM.JUR. 2d Damages § 469 (1988); H. HUNTER, MODERN LAW OF CONTRACTS, Breach & Remedies, § 7.03[4][e]-[f] at 7–23/7–25 (1986).

Here, there is clearly sufficient competent evidence to show GTE had within its contemplation at the time of contracting the potential for profits from a Florafax association with Bellerose. As we noted in section II. FACTS above, GTE knew it would be providing services not only directly for Florafax, but for others on behalf of Florafax. It knew Florafax was soliciting other entities to use the services of a call answering center like GTE's and, in fact, GTE looked upon Florafax's solicitation of these other entities as a positive aspect of a contractual relationship with Florafax because of the potential for increased revenue.

Trial evidence also showed the Florafax/Bellerose contract was entered two weeks prior to the Florafax/GTE agreement and that GTE officials knew either before or contemporaneously with signing the latter contract that Bellerose was considering turning over a portion of its inbound and outbound business via its 1-800-FLOWERS network to Florafax-business GTE also knew consisted of 100,000–200,000 orders annually. Further, as already noted, a clause in the Florafax/GTE contract itself expressly reflects the parties' contemplation of the recovery of lost profits by Florafax should GTE cease to perform its duties and obligations during the term of the contract-and, as also noted, evidence exists in this record that GTE intentionally failed to perform during part of the term of the contract, a failure on its part we conclude would support a determination the lost profit clause of the Florafax/GTE contract was implicated.

In our view then, contrary to the arguments of GTE, lost profits from a collateral contractual relationship may be recovered in a breach of contract action if such damages can be said to have been within the contemplation of the parties at the time of contracting. Here, there is evidence in the record—if believed by the jury—that plainly would support a finding special circumstances were communicated to or known by GTE at the time of contracting, so that a reasonable conclusion would be that the prospect of profits and, conversely, their loss upon breach, were in the contemplation of the parties at the time of contracting and would be suffered by Florafax should GTE cease to adequately perform under the Florafax/GTE agreement. Therefore, GTE's apparent positions—that profits to be derived from a collateral contract are never recoverable or, even if otherwise recoverable, they are not so here because the prospect of such profits or damages from their loss cannot be said to have been in GTE's contemplation at the time of contracting—are without merit and provide no reason to disturb the award of lost profits by the jury. . . .

III(B).   THE SIXTY-DAY TERMINATION CLAUSE IN THE FLORAFAX/BELLEROSE CONTRACT DOES NOT PRECLUDE THE RECOVERY OF LOST PROFITS BEYOND THE SIXTY-DAY PERIOD

GTE, in addition to arguing no lost profits are proper, alternatively asserts that if their recovery is appropriate, they must be limited to a period of sixty (60) days because of the termination notice clause of the Florafax/Bellerose contract which allowed either party to that agreement to terminate that contract, with or without cause, upon sixty (60) days written notice. For this position prime reliance is placed on Osborn v. Commanche Cattle Industries, Inc., 545 P. 2d 827 (Okla. Ct. Civ. App. 1975), an opinion of the Oklahoma Court of Civil Appeals. Although we believe the rule of law laid down in Osborn is sound, the rule is not controlling here.

Osborn involved a situation where plaintiff had contracted with a feedlot to perform certain cleaning functions, stockpiling and disposal of manure and some other duties. The contract was for a term of three years, but contained a clause allowing either party to terminate the agreement by giving the other thirty-days advance notice. The feedlot was sold and the new owner, without knowing of the previous owner's contract with plaintiff, hired someone else to perform the duties plaintiff was to perform. Plaintiff, not knowing of the feedlot's sale, began to purchase equipment necessary to perform his duties under the contract. No formal notice was ever given to plaintiff by the feedlot that its contract with him was terminated. The breach in Osborn was a failure to give plaintiff thirty-days advance notice of the contract's termination. Plaintiff sued the previous owner to recover the profits he would have made over the three year-life of the contract, plus certain other damages. The trial court allowed the lost profit issue to go to the jury with instructions allowing their recovery for the entire three-year period, over defendant's objection only nominal damages were appropriate because either party to the contract had the right to terminate it upon thirty-days notice.

The Osborn court found error in submitting the lost profit issue to the jury for a longer period than the thirty (30) day notice time frame based on the following rule of law: no party to a contract may recover more in damages for a breach of the contract than might have been gained by full performance. Osborn, supra, 545 P. 2d at 831. Such rule of law is essentially codified at 23 O.S. 1991, § 96, which provides, with certain exceptions not applicable here, "no person can recover a greater amount in damages for the breach of an obligation, than he could have gained by the full performance thereof on both sides. . . . " The rule applied in Osborn because full or complete performance under the contract could have been supplied by defendant simply giving the agreed-to notice and, therefore, plaintiff's expectation interest could have been no greater than the prospect of profit over the length of the notice period. Osborn, supra, 545 P. 2d at 831. In that plaintiff was never assured of performance by the breaching party beyond the length of the notice period his prospect of net gain, likewise, could never extend beyond this period of time. \Id. Plaintiff could not recover more than thirty-days lost profits because he could not recover more in profits than he might have made from full performance. In other words, in Osborn it was absolutely certain plaintiff could not establish lost profits for any greater period of time because the defendant had an absolute right to terminate the contract upon giving the agreed notice and exercise of this right would have provided full performance on the defendant's part.

The situation here is quite different. First off, we must note that Florafax does not rely on any violation of the sixty-day notice provision by Bellerose to support its lost profit claim. It contends, instead, that it was the breach of GTE that caused Bellerose to terminate its relationship with Florafax when it did and its relationship with Bellerose would have continued as a long-term relationship generating profits to Florafax well into the future, had it not been for GTE's breach.

Secondly, GTE had no right to terminate either the Florafax/GTE or Florafax/Bellerose contracts upon any short specified notice provision. That right belonged only to Florafax and Bellerose, and only in relation to the latter contract. Thus, full performance could not have been supplied by the simple expediency of GTE giving sixty-days notice to Florafax that it was terminating their agreement. Instead, the Florafax/GTE contract, according to the unchallenged finding of the jury, had a minimum term of two years based on the effect of the price renegotiation provisions of the contract, i.e. Florafax was guaranteed performance by GTE for a full two years.

Thus, the rule of Osborn that a non-breaching party may not receive more in damages than he might or could have gained from full performance is inapplicable because this record contains competent evidence Florafax could have made profits from the Florafax/Bellerose contract for a period longer than the sixty (60) day notice period had GTE fully performed under the Florafax/GTE contract. In fact, competent evidence exists supporting the view it is probable some additional profits would have been made from the Bellerose relationship for a longer period of time. Further, application of the Osborn rule here would improperly allow GTE to benefit from a cancellation right it had no ability to exercise. Accordingly, the rule of

Osborn does not preclude Florafax's recovery of lost profit damages associated with the loss of the Bellerose relationship in excess of a sixty-day period. . . .

III(C).   COMPETENT EVIDENCE EXISTS TO SUPPORT THE AWARD OF LOST
PROFIT DAMAGES TO A REASONABLE CERTAINTY

Even though the rule of Osborn is inapplicable, GTE's arguments as to the termination notice clause of the collateral contract do, however, implicate the legal principle that before lost profit damages are recoverable it must be adequately shown such profits were reasonably certain to have been made by the non-breaching party absent breach. We believe the answer to the reasonable certainty question is not one subject to decision as a matter of law under this record, but was one of fact to be decided by the trier of fact—here the jury.

In order for damages to be recoverable for breach of contract they must be clearly ascertainable, in both their nature and origin, and it must be made to appear they are the natural and proximate consequence of the breach and not speculative and contingent. Chorn v. Williams, 186 Okla. 646, 99 P. 2d 1036, 1037 (1940). It is not necessary, however, for the recovery of lost profits shown to have been caused by a breach of contract, that the profits be established with absolute certainty and barring any possibility of failure, but it is only required that it be established with reasonable certainty that profits would have been made had the contract not been breached. Megert v. Bauman, 206 Okla. 651, 246 P. 2d 355, 358 (1952). In essence, what a plaintiff must show for the recovery of lost profits is sufficient certainty that reasonable minds might believe from a preponderance of the evidence that such damages were actually suffered. Cook Associates, Inc. v. Warnick, 664 P. 2d 1161, 1165 (Utah 1983); See also Camino Real Mobile Home Park Partnership v. Wolfe, 119 N.M. 436, 891 P. 2d 1190, 1200–1201 (1995) (fact of lost profit damage must be shown by preponderance of the evidence). . . . This requirement of proof applies to the fact of lost profits, the causation of lost profits and the amount of lost profits. Cook Associates, Inc. v. Warnick, supra, 664 P. 2d at 1165.

The above rules, at least in part, are essentially reflected in Oklahoma's statutory law found at 23 O.S. 1991, § 21, which provides:

> For the breach of an obligation arising from contract, the measure of damages . . . is the amount which will compensate the party aggrieved for all the detriment proximately caused thereby, or which, in the ordinary course of things, would be likely to result therefrom. No damages can be recovered for a breach of contract, which are not clearly ascertainable in both their nature and origin.

Once it is made to clearly appear that loss of business profits has been suffered by virtue of the breach, it is proper to let the jury decide what the loss is from the best evidence the nature of the case admits. Firestone Tire & Rubber Co. v. Sheets, 178 Okla. 191, 62 P. 2d 91, 93 (1936). When a breach of a contractual obligation with resulting damages has been established, although the amount of damages may not be based on mere speculation, conjecture and surmise alone, the mere uncertainty as to the exact amount of damages will not preclude the right of recovery. Larrance Tank Corporation v. Burrough, 476 P. 2d 346, 350 (Okla. 1970). It is sufficient if the evidence shows the extent of damage by just and reasonable inference. Id. We believe sufficient evidence was presented so that Florafax carried its burden to prove the fact, cause and amount of its lost profit damages with the requisite degree of reasonable certainty.

The fact of lost profit damage beyond merely a sixty-day period is shown by the testimony of Bellerose's President. Although not absolute, his testimony was, in essence, he considered the relationship with Florafax a long-term one had things worked out and that the most important issues to him in making the decision to terminate were issues concerning performance. This testimony showed the relationship in all probability would have continued long after it was terminated had GTE adequately performed. Although it is true—given the existence of the sixty-day notice provision—Bellerose might have terminated the Florafax/Bellerose contract at some point in time even had GTE performed, the state of this record does not require a conclusion Bellerose would have exercised its right of termination for some other reason.

We are also of the view the fact of damage is partially shown by the projections for profits of both the damage experts presented by the parties. Although they differed in their ultimate conclusions as to the extent or amount of lost profits, both presented estimates that Florafax could have made profits from the Florafax/Bellerose relationship had it survived.

Causation is also shown by sufficient competent evidence, evidence that partially overlaps with that of the fact of damage in this case. There is enough evidence to support a reasonable determination that Bellerose's decision to cancel or terminate its relationship with Florafax was the direct result of GTE's failure to render adequate performance and, that GTE's breach of the Florafax/GTE contract caused the cancellation. Therefore, there is sufficient evidence in this record upon which reasonable minds might rely that profits from the Florafax/Bellerose relationship would have actually been made by Florafax beyond a sixty-day period and that GTE's breach of its contract with Florafax caused the loss of Bellerose as a client.

As to the exact extent or amount of damages, the record contains sufficient evidence to take the matter out of the realm of mere speculation, conjecture or surmise. A track record existed which showed the calls coming to GTE from Bellerose during the five to seven months Bellerose business was actually being routed to GTE. There was also evidence that although the business relationship between Florafax and Bellerose was relatively new, Bellerose had been in business for a number of years, and it had experienced 100,000–200,000 orders annually. Such evidence clearly was appropriate to consider on the issue of the extent of lost profits. Although this case is not exactly like our cases dealing with the destruction of an established business by a breach of contract, it is sufficiently close to be analogized to the established business situation, where we have allowed the recovery of lost profits. See e.g. Firestone Tire & Rubber Co. v. Sheets, supra, 62 P. 2d at 93. . . .

Evidence also existed which showed that Bellerose, after terminating its relationship with Florafax, experienced a substantial increase in its sales volume in 1991. In other words, there was not only evidence tending to show a certain volume of orders prior to the breach, but evidence tending to show that level of sales would have in all probability increased substantially during part of the term of the Florafax/GTE contract had Bellerose continued its relationship with Florafax. This post-breach evidence is proper to be considered at arriving at a reasonable estimate of the loss caused by a breach of contract [Ft. Smith & Western Railroad Co. v. Williams, supra, 121 P. at 278] because all facts which would reasonably tend to make certain the amount of injury inflicted are admissible. Cloe v. Rogers, 31 Okla. 255, 121 P. 201, 208 (1912). Although the jury apparently did not totally credit the testimony or documentation presented by either Florafax's or GTE's experts as to their projections of profits lost, the $750,000.00 awarded for the two-year period was within the range of the estimates of the two experts. Accordingly, not only was the fact and causation of lost profit damages adequately shown to a reasonable certainty, but the amount of lost profit damages awarded was sufficiently shown through competent evidence contained in this record to take the matter out of the realm of mere speculation, conjecture and surmise.

IV. CONCLUSION

The award of the jury of lost profit damages associated with the Florafax/Bellerose contract was an appropriate remedy for GTE's breach of its contract with Florafax. It was consistent with our substantive law as to the recovery of lost profits for a breach of contract and was supported by competent evidence.

Accordingly, our previous grant of certiorari is limited to lost profit issues raised on certiorari; certiorari is withdrawn as improvidently granted on all other issues; the court of civil appeals' opinion is vacated as to its disposition of the lost profit award and is withdrawn from publication; and the trial court judgment is affirmed as to the award of lost profits.

NOTES AND QUESTIONS

1. *Breach of contract identification.* This case depends upon identifying and understanding the difference between two separate contracts. The first contract was between Florafax and GTE. On that contract, Florafax sought to recover damages for a GTE uncured material total breach. What damages were directly or generally caused by the breach of the GTE contract? Were those damages foreseeable? Florafax argued that since GTE's breach of contract with Florafax also caused Bellerose to terminate its contract with Florafax, damages should include losses Florafax suffered as a result of the termination of its contract with Bellerose. If Florafax had sought lost profits on its contract with GTE, would such damages be general or consequential? Since Florafax also sought damages from lost profits it would have made in its contract with Bellerose had GET not breached, are those damages general or consequential? Do you see why damage characterization makes a difference? Do you understand why lost profits on the contract breached by the defendant are not subject to the foreseeability standard? Only lost profits on so-called "collateral contracts" (those other than the breached contract between the plaintiff and defendant) are subject to the foreseeability standard. Do you understand why?

2. *Consequential damage assumption clause.* The Florafax-GTE contract contained a consequential damage clause (Clause 20) specifically making GTE aware that its breach could cause Florafax to suffer "tremendous damage to its business," and therefore GTE specifically agreed to pay Florafax for its resulting "consequential damages and lost profits on the business lost." Was this clause necessary to make GTE responsible for consequential damages? If not, is this clause as written necessary to make GTE liable for damages for lost profits on the Bellerose contract? Exactly what kind of knowledge of "special circumstances" is required under the *Hadley II* standard? Restatement (Second) of Contracts § 351(2)(b), *cmt b* provides that "[i]n the case of a written agreement, foreseeability is sometimes established by the use of recitals in the agreement itself." If you drafted the contract on behalf of Florafax, how would you modify Clause 20?

3. *Consequential damage elimination.* The Restatement (Second) of Contracts is silent with regard to contract provisions that attempt to reduce or eliminate a particular remedy. Thus, such a clause would be tested under other contractual doctrines, such as public policy and unconscionability. However, the UCC is quite specific regarding the elimination of remedies. UCC § 2–719(3) specifically permits a contract for the sale of goods to limit or exclude consequential damages. However, a clause limiting (or eliminating) consequential damages arising from a personal injury claim is *prima facie* unconscionable. Such clauses are valid where personal injury is not involved. Given this restriction, do think that common law contractual waivers of liability for personal injuries due to negligence should be enforceable, or should they also be *prima facie* unconscionable? Is there a policy reason justifying freedom of contract not involving the sale of goods that does not apply to negligent services causing personal physical injury? Generally, common law waivers of liability for personal injuries arising from mere negligence are

enforceable. See, e.g., *Sharon v. City of Newton*, 437 Mass. 99, 769 N.E.2d 738 (2002) (father capable of waiver school liability for negligent personal injuries suffered by his daughter).

4. *Parol evidence to establish foreseeability.* If Clause 20 was perfectly drafted, why was testimonial evidence necessary to prove that GTE knew (or should have known) about the Bellerose contract? If you represented GTE, would you object to the admission of such evidence by Florafax on the grounds that it violated the parol evidence rule? If so, would you likely be successful in preventing Florafax from admitting testimonial evidence to the jury for the purpose of establishing whether GTE knew or should have known about the collateral contract with Bellerose? Does the parol evidence rule apply? If so, would a merger clause help to exclude such evidence? See Restatement (Second) of Contracts § 351(2)(b), *cmt b* to the effect that "[t]he parol evidence rule (§ 213) does not, however, preclude the use of negotiations prior to the making of the contract to show for this purpose circumstances that were then known to a party." Can you explain why Restatement (Second) of Contracts § 213 does not preclude parol evidence for this purpose? What is the relevance of Restatement (Second) of Contracts § 214(e)?

5. *Non-economic losses as consequential or incidental damages.* American contract law generally does not permit recovery of non-economic losses, such as damages for emotional or mental distress, harassment, or injuries to personal or family relationships, that are caused by the breach of contract. See E. Allan Farnsworth, Contracts § 12.17 (4th ed. 2004). Restatement (Second) of Contracts § 353, however, permits recovery of losses for emotional disturbance in cases of bodily harm, or if "the breach is of such a kind that serious emotional disturbance was a particularly likely result." For an excellent survey of the impact of the *Hadley* foreseeability rules upon the development of this rule and the development of judicial exceptions to the general rule prohibiting such recovery, see generally Mara Kent, "The Common-Law History of Non-Economic Damages in Breach of Contract Actions Versus Willful Breach of Contract Actions," 11 Tex. Wesleyan L. Rev 481 (2005).

b. Mitigation Limitation

Restatement (Second) of Contracts § 347(d) provides that an injured party's loss in value (including lost profits) damages must be reduced by any other cost or loss avoided by not having to perform. The costs and losses avoided are most often referred to as "mitigation of damages" to imply that the failure to mitigate has negative consequences. As implied by Restatement (Second) of Contracts § 347, the injured party is expected to undertake reasonable steps to avoid increasing the breaching party's loss following a breach. The greatest potential for loss and cost avoidance occurs where the breaching party commits an uncured material total breach coupled with an election of the other party to terminate the contract. Concomitantly, the greatest potential for abuse or violation of this rule occurs where the injured party continues to perform following an uncured material total breach by the other party. Restatement (Second) of Contracts § 350(1) therefore simply states that damages are not recoverable for any loss that the injured party could have avoided without undue risk, burden, or humiliation.

As a consequence, the rule has two features, both explored in the two following cases. First, mitigation doctrine generally requires the injured party to stop or terminate performance under a contract once that party has reason to know performance by the other party will not be forthcoming. Second, the injured party has a positive duty to make reasonable efforts to redeploy resources devoted to the contract to other productive uses to mitigate the losses from the breach. While it is common to refer to the injured party's expected conduct in both cases as a "duty to mitigate," the phrase is misleading. The concept of a duty is that a breach gives the injured party a cause of action for breach of that duty. In the case of cost and loss avoidance, the breaching party does not have a cause of action against the injured party for the failure to mitigate. Rather, Restatement (Second) of Contracts § 347(c) (reduction) and Restatement (Second) of Contracts § 350(1) simply make clear that costs and losses incurred that could have been reasonably avoided may not be recovered under the loss in value or other loss formulations. To the same effect, see also UCC § 2–715(2)(a) (consequential losses may be recovered provided such losses "could not reasonably be prevented by cover or otherwise") and CISG Art. 77 (injured party must take "such measures as are reasonable in the circumstances to mitigate the loss").

While the mitigation doctrine is treated here in the traditional sense as a "limitation" on the expectancy interest, other explanations exist that justify mitigation as a normative measure of the expectancy interest. In each case, failure to mitigate confers a benefit on the injured party that justifies a reduction in the damage award to the breaching party. See Michael B. Kelly, "Living Without the Avoidable Consequences Doctrine in Contract Remedies," 33 San Diego L. Rev. 175, 177 (1996). In the following two cases, determine whether the defendant argued that damages were not mitigated because the injured party failed to stop (negative feature) or rather failed to redeploy resources to another contractual effort (positive feature). Notwithstanding the accepted nature of the doctrine, it remains riddled with many unanswered questions. See Charles J. Goetz & Robert E. Scott, "The Mitigation Principle: Toward A General Theory of Contractual Obligation," 69 Va. L. Rev. 967 (1983).

ROCKINGHAM COUNTY v. LUTEN BRIDGE CO.
United States Circuit Court of Appeals for the Fourth Circuit
35 F.2d 301 (1929)

PARKER, Circuit Judge.

This was an action at law instituted in the court below by the Luten Bridge Company, as plaintiff, to recover of Rockingham county, North Carolina, an amount alleged to be due under a contract, but [the county] contends that notice of cancellation was given the bridge company before the erection of the bridge was commenced, and that it is liable only for the damages which the company would have sustained, if it had abandoned construction at that time. The judge below refused to strike out an answer filed by certain members of the board of commissioners of the county, admitting liability in accordance with the prayer of the complaint, allowed this pleading to be introduced in evidence as the answer of the county, excluded evidence offered by the county in support of its contentions as to notice of cancellation and damages, and instructed a verdict for plaintiff for the full amount of its claim. From judgment on this verdict the county has appealed.

The facts out of which the case arises, as shown by the affidavits and offers of proof appearing in the record, are as follows: On January 7, 1924, the board of commissioners of Rockingham county voted to award to plaintiff a contract for the construction of the bridge in controversy. Three of the five commissioners favored the awarding of the contract and two opposed it. Much feeling was engendered over the matter, with the result that on February 11, 1924, W. K. Pruitt, one of the commissioners who had voted in the affirmative, sent his resignation to the clerk of the superior court of the county. The clerk received this resignation on the same day, and immediately accepted same and noted his acceptance thereon. Later in the day, Pruitt called him over the telephone and stated that he wished to withdraw the resignation, and later sent him written notice to the same effect. The clerk, however, paid no attention to the attempted withdrawal, and proceeded on the next day to appoint one W. W. Hampton as a member of the board to succeed him.

After his resignation, Pruitt attended no further meetings of the board, and did nothing further as a commissioner of the county. Likewise Pratt and McCollum, the other two members of the board who had voted with him in favor of the contract, attended no further meetings. Hampton, on the other hand, took the oath of office immediately upon his appointment and entered upon the discharge of the duties of a commissioner. He met regularly with the two remaining members of the board, Martin and Barber, in the courthouse at the county seat, and with them attended to all of the business of the county. Between the 12th of February and the first

Monday in December following, these three attended, in all, 25 meetings of the board.

At one of these meetings, a regularly advertised called meeting held on February 21st, a resolution was unanimously adopted declaring that the contract for the building of the bridge was not legal and valid, and directing the clerk of the board to notify plaintiff that it refused to recognize same as a valid contract, and that plaintiff should proceed no further thereunder. This resolution also rescinded action of the board theretofore taken looking to the construction of a hard-surfaced road, in which the bridge was to be a mere connecting link. The clerk duly sent a certified copy of this resolution to plaintiff.

At the regular monthly meeting of the board on March 3d, a resolution was passed directing that plaintiff be notified that any work done on the bridge would be done by it at its own risk and hazard, that the board was of the opinion that the contract for the construction of the bridge was not valid and legal, and that, even if the board were mistaken as to this, it did not desire to construct the bridge, and would contest payment for same if constructed. A copy of this resolution was also sent to plaintiff. At the regular monthly meeting on April 7th, a resolution was passed, reciting that the board had been informed that one of its members was privately insisting that the bridge be constructed. It repudiated this action on the part of the member and gave notice that it would not be recognized. At the September meeting, a resolution was passed to the effect that the board would pay no bills presented by plaintiff or any one connected with the bridge. At the time of the passage of the first resolution, very little work toward the construction of the bridge had been done, it being estimated that the total cost of labor done and material on the ground was around $1,900; but, notwithstanding the repudiation of the contract by the county, the bridge company continued with the work of construction.

On November 24, 1924, plaintiff instituted this action against Rockingham county, and against Pruitt, Pratt, McCollum, Martin, and Barber, as constituting its board of commissioners. Complaint was filed, setting forth the execution of the contract and the doing of work by plaintiff thereunder, and alleging that for work done up until November 3, 1924, the county was indebted in the sum of $18,301.07. . . .

[The court then held that the resolutions of the county board communicating repudiation of the contract to Luten were valid acts undertaken on behalf of the county.]

Coming, then, to the third question—i.e., as to the measure of plaintiff's recovery—we do not think that, after the county had given notice, while the contract was still executory, that it did not desire the bridge built and would not pay for it, plaintiff could proceed to build it and recover the contract price. It is true that the county had no right to rescind the contract, and the notice given plaintiff amounted to a breach on its part; but, after plaintiff had received notice of the breach, it was its duty to do nothing to increase the damages flowing therefrom. If A enters into a binding contract to build a house for B, B, of course, has no right to rescind the contract without A's consent. But if, before the house is built, he decides that he does not want it, and notifies A to that effect, A has no right to proceed with the building and thus pile up damages. His remedy is to treat the contract as broken when he receives the notice, and sue for the recovery of such damages, as he may have sustained from the breach, including any profit which he would have realized upon performance, as well as any other losses which may have resulted to him. In the case at bar, the county decided not to build the road of which the bridge was to be a part, and did not build it. The bridge, built in the midst of the forest, is of no value to the county because of this change of circumstances. When, therefore, the county gave notice to the plaintiff that it would not proceed with the project, plaintiff should have desisted from further work. It had no right thus to pile up damages by proceeding with the erection of a useless bridge.

The contrary view was expressed by Lord Cockburn in Frost v. Knight, L.R. 7 Ex. 111, but, as pointed out by Prof. Williston (Williston on Contracts, vol. 3, p. 2347), it is not in harmony with the decisions in this country. The American rule and the reasons supporting it are well stated by Prof. Williston as follows:

> There is a line of cases running back to 1845 which holds that, after an absolute repudiation or refusal to perform by one party to a contract, the other party cannot continue to perform and recover damages based on full performance. This rule is only a particular application of the general rule of damages that a plaintiff cannot hold a defendant liable for damages which need not have been incurred; or, as it is often stated, the plaintiff must, so far as he can without loss to himself, mitigate the damages caused by the defendant's wrongful act. The application of this rule to the matter in question is obvious. If a man engages to have work done, and afterwards repudiates his contract before the work has been begun or when it has been only partially done, it is inflicting damage on the defendant without benefit to the plaintiff to allow the latter to insist on proceeding with the contract. The work may be useless to the defendant, and yet he would be forced to pay the full contract price. On the other hand, the plaintiff is interested only in the profit he will make out of the contract. If he receives this it is equally advantageous for him to use his time otherwise.

The leading case on the subject in this country is the New York case of Clark v. Marsiglia, 1 Denio (N.Y.) 317, 43 Am. Dec. 670. In that case defendant had employed plaintiff to paint certain pictures for him, but countermanded the order before the work was finished. Plaintiff, however, went on and completed the work and sued for the contract price. In reversing a judgment for plaintiff, the court said:

> The plaintiff was allowed to recover as though there had been no countermand of the order; and in this the court erred. The defendant, by requiring the plaintiff to stop work upon the paintings, violated his contract, and thereby incurred a liability to pay such damages as the plaintiff should sustain. Such damages would include a recompense for the labor done and materials used, and such further sum in damages as might, upon legal principles, be assessed for the breach of the contract; but the plaintiff had no right, by obstinately persisting in the work, to make the penalty upon the defendant greater than it would otherwise have been.

And the rule as established by the great weight of authority in America is summed up in the following statement in 6 R.C.L. 1029, which is quoted with approval by the Supreme Court of North Carolina in the recent case of Novelty Advertising Co. v. Farmers' Mut. Tobacco Warehouse Co., 186 N.C. 197, 119 S.E. 196, 198:

> While a contract is executory a party has the power to stop performance on the other side by an explicit direction to that effect, subjecting himself to such damages as will compensate the other party for being stopped in the performance on his part at that stage in the execution of the contract. The party thus forbidden cannot afterwards go on and thereby increase the damages, and then recover such damages from the other party. The legal right of either party to violate, abandon, or renounce his contract, on the usual terms of compensation to the other for the damages which the law recognizes and allows, subject to the jurisdiction of equity to decree specific performance in proper cases, is universally recognized and acted upon.

This is in accord with the earlier North Carolina decision of Heiser v. Mears, 120 N.C. 443, 27 S.E. 117, in which it was held that, where a buyer countermands his order for goods to be manufactured for him under as executory contract, before the work is completed, it is notice to the seller that he elects to rescind his contract and submit to the legal measure of damages, and that in such case the seller cannot complete the goods and recover the contract price. . . .

We have carefully considered the cases of Roehm v. Horst, 178 U.S. 1, 20 S.Ct. 780, 44 L.Ed. 953, Roller v. George H. Leonard & Co. (C.C.A. 4th) 229 F. 607, and McCoy v. Justices of Harnett County, 53 N.C. 272, upon which plaintiff relies; but we do not think that they are at all in point. Roehm v. Horst merely follows the rule of Hockster v. DeLaTour, 2 El. & Bl. 678, to the effect that where one party to any executory contract refuses to perform in advance of the time fixed for performance, the other party, without waiting for the time of performance, may sue at once for damages occasioned by the breach. The same rule is followed in Roller v. Leonard. In McCoy v. Justices of Harnett County the decision was that mandamus to require the justices of a county to pay for a jail would be denied, where it appeared that the contractor in building same departed from the plans and specifications. In the opinions in all of these some language was used which lends support to plaintiff's position, but in none of them was the point involved which is involved here, viz., whether, in application of the rule which requires that the party to a contract who is not in default do nothing to aggravate the damages arising from breach, he should not desist from performance of an executory contract for the erection of a structure when notified of the other party's repudiation, instead of piling up damages by proceeding with the work. As stated above, we think that reason and authority require that this question be answered in the affirmative. It follows that there was error in directing a verdict for plaintiff for the full amount of its claim. The measure of plaintiff's damage, upon its appearing that notice was duly given not to build the bridge, is an amount sufficient to compensate plaintiff for labor and materials expended and expense incurred in the part performance of the contract, prior to its repudiation, plus the profit which would have been realized if it had been carried out in accordance with its terms. See Novelty Advertising Co. v. Farmers' Mut. Tobacco Warehouse Co., supra.

Our conclusion, on the whole case, is that there was error in failing to strike out the answer of Pruitt, Pratt, and McCollum, and in admitting same as evidence against the county, in excluding the testimony offered by the county to which we have referred, and in directing a verdict for plaintiff. The judgment below will accordingly be reversed, and the case remanded for a new trial.

NOTES AND QUESTIONS

1.   *Famous case.* The *Rockingham County* case is quite famous and as a result has generated a poem. Douglass G. Boshkoff, "Selected Poems on the Law of Contracts," 66 N.Y.U. L. Rev. 1542, 1543 (1991).

2.   *Legal archaeology revisited.* Judge John Parker's famous opinion and case may have been more about politics than the duty to mitigate, the doctrine for which it became famous. Barak Richman, Jordi Weinstock, and Jason Mehta, in a 2006 article, argue that the case was "more about the legitimacy of local government" than the duty to mitigate damages. See Barak Richman, Jordi Weinstock & Jason Mehta, "A Bridge, a Tax Revolt, and the Struggle to Industrialize: The Story and Legacy of *Rockingham County v. Luten Bridge Co.*, 84 N.C.L. Rev. 1841 (2006). As these authors argue, the dispute must be understood in the context of contemporaneous efforts to promote and build public infrastructure to facilitate industrialization of North Carolina in the 1920s. See id. Judge John Parker, the architect and author of the opinion, was

a respected jurist also caught up in the politically charged atmosphere surrounding the case. See Peter G. Fish, "Crossing Judge Parker's Luten Bridge: Partisan Politics, Economic Visions, and Government Reform in Retrospect and Prospect: A Commentary to Professor Richman," 84 N. C. L. Rev. 1913 (2006).

3. *American and English jurisprudence.* As Judge Parker fairly admits, the rule as to mitigation at the time was otherwise in England. He cites a contrary view by Lord Cockburn in *Frost v. Knight*, 7 L. R. Exch. 111 (1872). Why do you think Judge Parker chose a different path, given the early heavy reliance of American common law on English common law? See John V. Orth, "A Bridge, A Tax Revolt, and the Struggle to Industrialize: A Comment," 84 N. C. L. Rev. 1927 (2006).

4. *Who owns the bridge?* Assuming that Luten Bridge Co. (from Tennessee) found it more problematic and expensive to tear down the bridge after the case, what happens to the bridge and how does the case account for the future development? While the bridge was not then in use, does it have any value whatsoever to the county? What if three years later, the county builds roads to and from the bridge and the route serves a valuable public function? Did the county receive a bridge it did not currently want but may use in the future nearly free?

In their legal history of the case and its aftermath, Barak Richman, Jordi Weinstock, and Jason Mehta report that the Fishing Creek Bridge remained unconnected to any roads until 1935 when the North Carolina State Department of Transportation assumed ownership and constructed two dirt roads to the bridge. See Barak Richman, Jordi Weinstock & Jason Mehta, "A Bridge, A Tax Revolt, and the Struggle to Industrialize: The Story and Legacy of *Rockingham County v. Luten Bridge Co.*," 84 N.C. L. Rev. 1841, 1907–1908 (2006). At that time, Luten Bridge Co. filed another suit seeking payment from the state of $9800, but the action was dismissed when Luten Bridge failed to appear in court. See id. The bridge was permanently closed to traffic in 2003, but remains open to foot travel. See id.

PARKER V. TWENTIETH CENTURY-FOX FILM CORP.
Supreme Court of California
3 Cal.3d 176, 474 P.2d 689, 89 Cal.Rptr. 737 (1970)

BURKE, Justice.

Defendant Twentieth Century-Fox Film Corporation appeals from a summary judgment granting to plaintiff the recovery of agreed compensation under a written contract for her services as an actress in a motion picture. As will appear, we have concluded that the trial court correctly ruled in plaintiff's favor and that the judgment should be affirmed.

Plaintiff is well known as an actress, and in the contract between plaintiff and defendant is sometimes referred to as the "Artist." Under the contract, dated August 6, 1965, plaintiff was to play the female lead in defendant's contemplated production of a motion picture entitled "Bloomer Girl." The contract provided that defendant would pay plaintiff a minimum 'guaranteed compensation' of $53,571.42 per week for 14 weeks commencing May 23, 1966, for a total of $750,000. Prior to May 1966 defendant decided not to produce the picture and by a letter dated April 4, 1966, it notified plaintiff of that decision and that it would not 'comply with our obligations to you under' the written contract.

By the same letter and with the professed purpose "to avoid any damage to you," defendant instead offered to employ plaintiff as the leading actress in another film tentatively entitled "Big Country, Big Man" (hereinafter, 'Big Country'). The compensation offered was identical, as were 31 of the 34 numbered provisions or articles of the original contract. Unlike "Bloomer Girl," however, which was to have been a musical production, 'Big Country' was a dramatic "western type" movie. "Bloomer Girl" was to have been filmed in California; 'Big Country' was to be produced in Australia. Also, certain terms in the proffered contract varied from those of the original. Plaintiff was given one week within which to accept; she did not and the offer lapsed. Plaintiff then commenced this action seeking recovery of the agreed guaranteed compensation. . . .

The complaint sets forth two causes of action. The first is for money due under the contract; the second, based upon the same allegations as the first, is for damages resulting from defendant's breach of contract. Defendant in its answer admits the existence and validity of the contract, that plaintiff complied with all the conditions, covenants and promises and stood ready to complete the performance, and that defendant breached and "anticipatorily repudiated" the contract. It denies, however, that any money is due to plaintiff either under the contract or as a result of its breach, and pleads as an affirmative defense to both causes of action plaintiff's allegedly deliberate failure to mitigate damages, asserting that she unreasonably refused to accept its offer of the leading role in "Big Country."

Plaintiff moved for summary judgment under Code of Civil Procedure section 437c, the motion was granted, and summary judgment for $750,000 plus interest was entered in plaintiff's favor. This appeal by defendant followed. . . .

As stated, defendant's sole defense to this action which resulted from its deliberate breach of contract is that in rejecting defendant's substitute offer of employment plaintiff unreasonably refused to mitigate damages.

The general rule is that the measure of recovery by a wrongfully discharged employee is the amount of salary agreed upon for the period of service, less the amount which the employer affirmatively proves the employee has earned or with reasonable effort might have earned from other employment. . . . However, before projected earnings from other employment opportunities not sought or accepted by the discharged employee can be applied in mitigation, the employer must show that the other employment was comparable, or substantially similar, to that of which the employee has been deprived; the employee's rejection of or failure to seek other available employment of a different or inferior kind may not be resorted to in order to mitigate damages. . . .

In the present case defendant has raised no issue of reasonableness of efforts by plaintiff to obtain other employment; the sole issue is whether plaintiff's refusal of defendant's substitute offer of "Big Country" may be used in mitigation. Nor, if the "Big Country" offer was of employment different or inferior when compared with the original "Bloomer Girl" employment, is there an issue as to whether or not plaintiff acted reasonably in refusing the substitute offer. Despite defendant's arguments to the contrary, no case cited or which our research has discovered holds or suggests that reasonableness is an element of a wrongfully discharged employee's option to reject, or fail to seek, different or inferior employment lest the possible earnings therefrom be charged against him in mitigation of damages. . . .

Applying the foregoing rules to the record in the present case, with all intendments in favor of the party opposing the summary judgment motion—here, defendant—it is clear that the trial court correctly ruled that plaintiff's failure to accept defendant's tendered substitute employment could not be applied in mitigation of damages because the offer of the "Big Country" lead was of employment both different and inferior, and that no factual dispute was presented on that issue. The mere circumstance that "Bloomer Girl" was to be a musical review calling upon plaintiff's talents as a dancer as well as an actress, and was to be produced in the City of Los Angeles, whereas "Big Country" was a straight dramatic role in a "Western Type" story taking place in an opal mine in Australia, demonstrates the difference in kind between the two employments; the female lead as a dramatic actress in a western style motion picture can by no stretch of imagination be considered the equivalent of or substantially similar to the lead in a song-and-dance production.

Additionally, the substitute "Big Country" offer proposed to eliminate or impair the director and screenplay approvals accorded to plaintiff under the original 'Bloomer Girl' contract . . . and thus constituted an offer of inferior employment. No expertise or judicial notice is required in order to hold that the deprivation or infringement of an employee's rights held under an original employment contract converts the available 'other employment' relied upon by the employer to mitigate damages, into inferior employment which the employee need not seek or accept. . . .

In view of the determination that defendant failed to present any facts showing the existence of a factual issue with respect to its sole defense—plaintiff's rejection of its substitute employment offer in mitigation of damages—we need not consider plaintiff's further contention that for various reasons, including the provisions of the original contract set forth in footnote 1, Ante, plaintiff was excused from attempting to mitigate damages.

The judgment is affirmed.

SULLIVAN, Acting Chief Justice (dissenting).

The basic question in this case is whether or not plaintiff acted reasonably in rejecting defendant's offer of alternate employment. The answer depends upon whether that offer (starring in "Big Country, Big Man") was an offer of work that was substantially similar to her former employment (starring in "Bloomer Girl") or of work that was of a different or inferior kind. To my mind this is a factual issue which the trial court should not have determined on a motion for summary judgment. The majority have not only repeated this error but have compounded it by applying the rules governing mitigation of damages in the employer-employee context in a misleading fashion. Accordingly, I respectfully dissent.

The familiar rule requiring a plaintiff in a tort or contract action to mitigate damages embodies notions of fairness and socially responsible behavior which are fundamental to our jurisprudence. Most broadly stated, it precludes the recovery of damages which, through the exercise of due diligence, could have been avoided. Thus, in essence, it is a rule requiring reasonable conduct in commercial affairs. This general principle governs the obligations of an employee after his employer has wrongfully repudiated or terminated the employment contract. Rather than permitting the employee simply to remain idle during the balance of the contract period, the law requires him to make a reasonable effort to secure other employment. He is not obliged, however, to seek or accept any and all types of work which may be available. Only work which is in the same field and which is of the same quality need be accepted. . . .

It has never been the law that the mere existence of differences between two jobs in the same field is sufficient, as a matter of law, to excuse an employee wrongfully discharged from one from accepting the other in order to mitigate damages. Such an approach would effectively eliminate any obligation of an employee to attempt to minimize damage arising from a wrongful discharge. The only alternative job offer an employee would be required to accept would be an offer of his former job by his former employer.

Although the majority appear to hold that there was a difference 'in kind' between the employment offered plaintiff in "Bloomer Girl" and that offered in 'Big Country' . . . , an examination of the opinion makes crystal clear that the majority merely point out differences between the two films (an obvious circumstance) and then apodically assert that these constitute a difference in the kind of employment. The entire rationale of the majority boils down to this: that the 'mere circumstances' that "Bloomer Girl" was to be a musical review while "Big Country" was a straight drama "demonstrates the difference in kind" since a female lead in a western is not 'the equivalent of or substantially similar to' a lead in a musical. This is merely attempting to prove the proposition by repeating it. It shows that the vehicles for the display of the star's talents are different but it does not prove that her employment as a star in such vehicles is of necessity different in kind and either inferior or superior. . . .

It is not intuitively obvious, to me at least, that the leading female role in a dramatic motion picture is a radically different endeavor from the leading female role in a musical comedy film. Nor is it plain to me that the rather qualified rights of director and screenplay approval contained in the first contract are highly significant matters either in the entertainment industry in general or to this plaintiff in particular. Certainly, none of the declarations introduced by plaintiff in support of her motion shed any light on these issues.

Nor do they attempt to explain why she declined the offer of starring in "Big Country, Big Man." Nevertheless, the trial court granted the motion, declaring that these approval rights were 'critical' and that their elimination altered "the essential nature of the employment." . . .

The majority do not confront the trial court's misuse of judicial notice. They avoid this issue through the expedient of declaring that neither judicial notice nor expert opinion (such as that contained in the declarations in opposition to the motion) is necessary to reach the trial court's conclusion. Something, however, clearly is needed to support this conclusion. Nevertheless, the majority makes no effort to justify the judgment through an examination of the plaintiff's declarations. Ignoring the obvious insufficiency of these declarations, the majority announces that "the deprivation or infringement of an employee's rights held under an original employment contract" changes the alternate employment offered or available into employment of an inferior kind. . . .

In the instant case, there was nothing properly before the trial court by which the importance of the approval rights could be ascertained, much less evaluated. Thus, in order to grant the motion for summary judgment, the trial court misused judicial notice. In upholding the summary judgment, the majority here rely upon per se rules which distort the process of determining whether or not an employee is obliged to accept particular employment in mitigation of damages.

I believe that the judgment should be reversed so that the issue of whether or not the offer of the lead role in 'Big Country, Big Man' was of employment comparable to that of the lead role in 'Bloomer Girl' may be determined at trial.

NOTES AND QUESTIONS

1. *Pay-or-play provision and breach theory.* The court mentions but downplays the role of the "pay-or-play" provision of the contract. The specific provision in this contract provided as follows:

> We shall not be obligated to utilize your services in or in connection with the Photoplay hereunder, our sole obligation, subject to the terms and conditions of this Agreement, being to pay you the guaranteed compensation herein provided for.

Such provisions were common in studio contracts. Basically, under such a clause, the studio purchased an option on her time. The actress—Shirley MacLaine—agreed to be ready to make a particular film, but the studio had no obligation, merely the option, to use her in a film. Accordingly, when Fox decided to cancel the film, it did not breach a contract with Shirley MacLaine. Rather, Fox merely chose to exercise its option not to do the film or to use her. Therefore, Fox did not breach its option contract by canceling the film. Since Fox committed no breach of any contract with Shirley MacLaine, she was under no "duty" to mitigate Fox's damages. In fact, under the clause, Fox was obligated to pay her whether they used her or not and regardless of whether it cancelled the film. Victor P. Goldberg, "Bloomer Girl Revisited or How to Frame an Unmade Picture," 1998 Wis. L. Rev. 1051, 1055.

2. *MacLaine's acclaim as an actress.* Why would Fox agree to pay MacLaine so well? In fact, she was a hugely successful actress and had the film been a success, she would have earned far more than the $750,000 (nearly $3,000,000 by many estimates). Moreover, the director had already been selected—George Cukor—whose previous film, *My Fair Lady*, had also been highly successful. See Victor P. Goldberg, "Bloomer Girl Revisited or How to Frame an Unmade Picture," 1998 Wis. L. Rev. 1051, 1055–1056.

3. *Law and feminism.* In her early but critically important work in this field, Professor Mary Joe Frug was critical of contracts casebooks with two objectives. First, she sought to illustrate that a particular student's views about gender affect their understanding about a law casebook. Second, she sought to demonstrate that the gendered aspects of a casebook affect the understanding of the law and of the student. Professor Frug is quite critical that by emphasizing the "different or inferior standard," the case and casebooks remove context and significance that validate MacLaine's efforts and further suggest she was paid $750,000 to do nothing, a seemingly absurd result. The social significance of the *Bloomer Girl* movie was particularly compelling. See Mary Joe Frug, "Re-Reading Contracts: Feminist Analysis of a Casebook," 34 Am. U. L. Rev. 1065 (1985); see also Carol Sanger, "Feminism and Disciplinarity: The Curl of the Petals," 27 Loy. L. A. L. Rev. 225 (1993).

Mary Joe Frug was a Professor at the New England School of Law and married to a Harvard Law Professor when, at the age of 49, she was stabbed to death near their home in Cambridge on April 4, 1991. See Arthur Austin, "The Top Ten Politically Correct Law Review Articles," 27 Fla. St. U. L. Rev. 233, 237–238 (1999).

4.   *Mitigation burden of proof.* A wrongfully discharged employee must exercise reasonable efforts to locate other employment. The failure to do so means that the employee's damages are the salary for the remainder of the employment period reduced by the amount that such reasonable efforts would have produced.

Importantly, the burden of proof on mitigation is on the employer. The employee does not have to prove that he or she properly mitigated. The employer must prove the employee failed to properly mitigate and the reasonable amount that would have been available from the alternative employment. See Restatement (Second) of Contracts § 350, *cmt. c* and Boehm v. American Broadcasting Co., 929 F.2d 482 (9th Cir. 1991).

The court considers various factors controlling on the similarity question: location of job performance, type of acting role, hours of employment, status, and title. Do you consider the employer able to meet this difficult burden?

5.   *Effect of employer's offer to reemploy.* In *Ford Motor Co. v. E.E.O.C.*, 458 U.S. 219 (1982), the Supreme Court determined that an employer's unconditional offer to reemploy a wrongfully discharged employee in a new position terminates its liability for further Title VII damages if the employee refuses to accept the offer without justification. However, the offered position must be either the same job or one that is "substantially similar." See also Boehm v. American Broadcasting Co., 929 F.2d 482 (9th Cir. 1991).

6.   *Substantially similar employment.* The court makes clear that the employer must prove that the position refused by the wrongfully discharged employee must be substantially similar (whether arising from an offer of re-employment or potential employment with another employer). As a corollary, the employee's refusal to accept other employment that is different or inferior does not constitute a failure to properly mitigate.

c.   Certainty Limitation

Restatement (Second) of Contracts § 352 provides that "[d]amages are not recoverable for loss beyond an amount that the evidence permits to be established with reasonable certainty." In other words, the factfinder at trial cannot award purely speculative damages for a breach of contract. Instead, the plaintiff must prove the actual amount of damages caused by the breach. This does not require the plaintiff to prove damages with mathematical certainty, particularly since this may be impossible even in cases involving only simple contracts in well-developed markets. See Restatement (Second) of Contracts § 352 *cmt. a* and UCC § 1–305 *cmt. 1* (2001).

This requirement follows logically from the requirement of a chain of causation connecting damage to the breach. If the damage is not proven with sufficient certainty, the demonstration of required causal connection fails. The phrase "reasonable certainty" is vague. *Comment a* to § 352 provides a little further information and refinement of content. First, greater certainty of proof may be required in a breach of contract case than in a tort case. But as discussed above, courts may resolve doubts against the breaching party, especially where the breach was willful.

Certainty issues can apply to any item of claimed damages, but some types of damages are more susceptible to ascertainability problems than others. For example, while the certainty limitation applies equally to both reliance and expectancy damages, it is more likely that a nonbreaching party will be able to prove reliance costs and incidental damages than lost profits. See E. Allan Farnsworth, "Legal Remedies for Breach of Contract," 70 Colum. L. Rev. 1145, 1210–15 (1970). As Professor Farnsworth observed, damages for out-of-pocket reliance expenditures and "other losses" incurred in reliance on the contract can generally be determined with reasonable certainty. See id. at 1211; see also Restatement (Second) of Contracts § 352, *cmt. a.*

In contrast, lost profits are more likely to be difficult to ascertain. In some cases, where the contract takes place in the context of a well-developed and active market contract goods or services, the market provides a good indication of the amount of damages caused by a breach of contract. Alternatively, if the nonbreaching party is an established business, like the parties in the *Florafax* case discussed above, the court may use that party's long-term track record of profits to determine what the profit would have been on the contract at issue. Thus, the injury caused by a breach of a contract for the purchase of a late-model used car or for providing house painting services can be determined with relative certainty by comparing the contract price to the cost of obtaining substitute goods or services or by examining the seller's past record of profits and losses in similar transactions. See E. Allan Farnsworth, "Legal Remedies for Breach of Contract," 70 Colum. L. Rev. 1145, 1211–12 (1970); UCC § 2–713(1) (buyer's damages for nondelivery or repudiation by seller based on difference between the market price and the contract price plus incidental and consequential damages, minus expenses saved by reason of the breach).

In many cases, however, a well-developed market for the goods or services that can provide accurate price information from which to determine damages caused by the breach does not exist. See, e.g., John F. Shampton, "Statistical Evidence of Real Estate Valuation: Establishing Value Without Appraisers," 21 S. Ill. U. L.J. 113, 114 (1996). In such cases, courts must use alternative measures to attempt to determine the value of the promised performance with reasonable certainty. See, e.g., UCC § 2–

723(2) & *cmt.* ("Where the appropriate market price is not readily available the court is here granted reasonable leeway in receiving evidence of prices current in other comparable markets. . . . This section is not intended to exclude the use of any other reasonable method of determining market price or of measuring damages if the circumstances of the case make this necessary."). Thus, in comparison to contracts for readily available commodities or services, damages for breach of a contract for the purchase and sale of a rare painting or for the provision of artistic services will be relatively difficult to ascertain. Likewise, transactions involving the purchase and sale of a business firm, for instance, are notoriously difficult to value because the value of the underlying assets—the business entity at issue—depends upon many complex and variable factors. And new businesses, without established histories of similar contracts, likewise often experience difficulty in proving lost profits with reasonable certainty. See Bernadette J. Bollas, "The New Business Rule and the Denial of Lost Profits: [M]en Keep Their Promises When Neither Side Can Get Anything by the Breaking of Them," 48 Ohio St. L.J. 855, 856–59 (1987).

Finally, "[t]he most difficult sort of case in which to meet the requirement is that . . . in which a manufacturer or other entrepreneur claims that his supplier's failure to furnish capital goods, raw materials, land, or services has prevented him from realizing a collateral profit in a business venture for which they were indispensable." E. Allan Farnsworth, "Legal Remedies for Breach of Contract," 70 Colum. L. Rev. 1145, 1212 (1970). Such claims of collateral injuries caused by the breach of contract are inherently speculative and difficult to prove. Moreover, as with claims involving contracts in poorly developed markets or with respect to new business ventures, experts attempting to prove (or disprove) such damages may often offer radically different but nonetheless reasonable theories by which to measure the supposed losses. As you read the following case, consider whether the court adequately resolved the question of how to choose between competing theories of valuation in uncertain cases.

A-S Development, Inc. v. W.R. Grace Land Corporation

United States District Court for New Jersey
537 F.Supp. 549 (1982)

Anne E. Thompson, District Judge.

Introduction

This action began as a suit for specific performance of a real estate transfer. With the passage of time it became a claim for damages. On November 25, 1980, after a 12-day trial devoted exclusively to liability issues, this court rendered an opinion in favor of the plaintiff, A. S. Development, Inc. The opinion held that the defendant W. R. Grace Land

Corporation was liable for refusing to take title to Channel Club Tower, a Monmouth Beach condominium project, on March 13, 1975. Thereafter, on various days in September and November 1981, a damages trial was held. Subsequently, the parties submitted proposed Findings of Fact and Conclusions of Law. The parties submitted alternative damage schedules. I have carefully considered the thorough submissions of counsel and have drawn heavily upon them. The following Findings of Fact and Conclusions of Law are entered pursuant to Rule 52(a) of the Federal Rules of Civil Procedure as to the damages issues.

FINDINGS OF FACT

In 1974 A. S. Development, Inc. (hereinafter "A. S."), decided to terminate its real estate activities and to sell to the defendant W. R. Grace Land Corporation (hereinafter "Grace"), all of its substantial real estate holdings located in various parts of the United States. The parties drafted an agreement reciting the terms of that transfer dated June 30, 1974. Without the fault of the parties, one of the parcels in the transaction, Channel Club Tower, (hereinafter "CCT"), which was then under construction, became involved in a controversy regarding its electrical power supply. The parties agreed to remove the sale of CCT from the main agreement and to make it instead the subject of what was labeled a "supplemental agreement," also dated June 30, 1974. This supplemental agreement contained the specific conditions and contingencies relating to the transfer of CCT as well as to the transfer of A. S.'s interest in some undeveloped land not involved in this lawsuit.

The Sales Price

The supplemental agreement provided that the sales price for CCT was to be the book value of CCT as of the close of business on the day prior to closing. This book value ultimately was to be "determined as specified in a letter of instructions addressed . . . to Arthur Young & Co.," an accounting firm. Book value was defined in the trial testimony as historical cost. By letter of March 12, 1975, A. S. advised Grace that the book value was $9,632,364 subject to review and certification by Arthur Young & Co. Plaintiff obtained a review and certification of that figure in a report dated January 23, 1980. That report set forth a sales price of $9,721,754. . . .

When defendant refused to close title on CCT on March 13, 1975, plaintiff proceeded to sell the individual apartment units to "retail" buyers. The market was sluggish, such units were not in demand and it took almost five years to sell out the building. The cash receipts A. S. received from sales amounted to a total of $13,806,695 by June 1980. Defendant contends that this figure or the 1975 real estate tax assessment figure of $11,192,000 are indisputable evidence of the property's market value and should be used as a yardstick for the measure of damages. By comparing either figure to the contract price, defendant concludes that A. S. suffered no damages.

Defendant, however, disregards the fact that it took A. S. almost five years to sell out CCT, that plaintiff suffered the loss of the use of the nine million dollar sales price for nearly five years and that this lost time had money value.

Expert testimony was presented on behalf of the plaintiff by Edwin F. Thompson, an expert in real estate valuation and investment. He presented several alternative methodologies by which the damages in this case may be determined. Each methodology involved three factors: 1) the contract price of $9,721,754; 2) the monthly receipts for the sale of the units, less the cash disbursements for completion and marketing of the project.

The monthly receipts were, in essence, plaintiff's attempt at mitigation of damages. By comparing the monthly cash receipts and cash disbursements, a net monthly cash flow was calculated. If receipts exceeded disbursements in a given month, the cash flow for that month was considered positive. If disbursements exceeded receipts in a given month, the cash flow for that month was considered negative. Defendant does not dispute the figures showing the cash flow for the project. Plaintiff has offered its three methodologies to reflect the damages it claims to have suffered because the amounts it received for the units in CCT were provided in piecemeal fashion over a period of five years rather than in one lump sum on March 13, 1975.

Methodology No. 1. The Involuntary Loan Theory

The first theory construes defendant's failure to take title to CCT and to pay the purchase price on March 13, 1975 as an involuntary loan to Grace of $9,721,754, the book value purchase price. The theory contends Grace benefited by having the use of the money and by not having to pay the cost of a loan of that amount whereas A. S. suffered by not receiving the full purchase price on that date. The monthly net receipts which A. S. received from the sales of condominiums were viewed as payments on the "loan." Plaintiff calculated damages on the involuntary loan theory using an interest rate of four percentage points above the prime rate set by the Chase Manhattan Bank for commercial borrowers given the best credit rating. Documents and testimony in evidence showed that Grace had taken steps to apply for a commercial loan of $9,500,000 at this interest rate to finance its purchase. Furthermore, plaintiff's expert, Mr. Thompson, testified that 4% above Chase Manhattan's prime would represent a contemporary market rate of interest, assuming that a willing lender could be found.

Plaintiff's involuntary loan theory apportions the monthly net receipts from CCT as monthly payments on interest and principal to repay a loan at the above rate on the full purchase price of $9,721,754. Plaintiff introduced an amortization table (Plaintiff's Exhibit 137) showing the growth and reduction of the debt on a monthly basis from March 1975 to December 1981. Under this methodology, the balance due to A. S. representing the purchase price plus accumulated interest is $5,846,518 as of December 31, 1981.

Methodology No. 2. Alternative Capital Receipts

Another methodology presented by plaintiff's expert was intended to determine the amount of money A. S. and its parent American Standard, Inc. might have earned had A. S. had the benefit of the sales price of $9,721,754 on March 13, 1975. The theory utilizes the rate of return on capital earned by American Standard, Inc. on its operations from March 1975 to the present, and hypothesizes the investment of funds from March 1975 to December 1981. The measure of damages is the difference between the amount of money to which the contract price would have grown, compared with the amount of money to which the net cash receipts grew. Damages under this method were $7,598,412 as of the end of December 1981. This represented the amount of money A. S. was deprived of over the relevant time frame.

Methodology No. 3. Alternative Sales Price

The third methodology advanced by plaintiff's expert relies upon the principle of present value. Money to be received in the future is worth less than money received today simply because in order to hand over a set amount in a year's time, only something less than that amount need be invested today so that it will appreciate in value to the amount due. Starting from March 13, 1975, the future net cash flow receipts were discounted by using an interest rate to convert them to a single price as of March 13, 1975, thereby purportedly showing the difference between the price A. S. received and the contract price to which it was entitled (an alternative sales price). The difference was $2,646,823 and represents an estimate of damages as of that date. Since those damages were not paid as of that date, the damages of March 1975 were brought forward to the present time. The damages figure so obtained as of December 31, 1981 was $7,807,240. Under this methodology plaintiff's expert used an interest rate of 16%.

Mr. Thompson testified that there were no comparable sales of condominiums during this period of time from which to extract a market rate of interest. Therefore, he derived the 16% rate from a review of the yields to maturity on bonds of thirteen leading companies engaged in the business of real estate development at that time and whose bonds were traded publicly. The average yield on such bonds to maturity as of March 1975 was approximately 14%. To this 14% was added a two point increment to reflect the greater risk, the relative lack of liquidity and the added burden of management which plaintiff contends this condominium investment entailed. Thus the expert arrived at a 16% interest rate, an approximation of the rate of interest that real estate developers would supposedly demand for the use of their money.

One additional methodology was reviewed by plaintiff. Reference was made to a conventional market valuation (comparison of sales price with market price) performed by Landauer Associates, the real estate consulting firm with which plaintiff's expert, Edwin Thompson, was associated. That valuation resulted in a market value for CCT as of March 1975 of $5,500,000. Applying an interest rate of 16% compounded monthly from March of 1975 to the present time would, under this theory, result in damages to A. S. of approximately $10,000,000 as of September 1981.

Using the above methodologies, plaintiff supplied the court with the damage figures derived from various permutations of these formulae. Some were based on variations of simple interest, others were based on compounded interest. It was plaintiff's position that the use of compound interest rates is the more appropriate method, reflecting the actual practices of real estate investing. Furthermore, plaintiff contended that compounded interest is the most effective means of placing the parties in the positions each would be in if the contract had been performed. In conclusion, plaintiff projected a figure of $6,000,000 as the amount necessary to make A. S. whole as of the end of September 1981. In reaching this figure plaintiff's expert placed greatest reliance on Methodology No. 1, secondary reliance on Methodology No. 3 and the least reliance on Methodology No. 2. It was his view that Methodology No. 1 involved the least judgmental factors and was the most objective measure of plaintiff's damages. He regarded theory No. 2 as confirming his other two methods but he accorded it less weight than the other two methodologies.

Grace rejects A. S.'s methodologies as illogical theories having no precedent in statutory or decisional law and as fanciful attempts to create damages where none were present. However, defendant presented no expert witness to critique plaintiff's methodologies or to counter plaintiff's supposedly exotic theories.

Grace's initial thesis—that plaintiff suffered no damage or minimal damage by virtue of Grace's failure to buy CCT—is unsupportable in the context of practical investments. To completely ignore the passage of time during plaintiff's efforts at mitigation of damages is to overlook a most obvious aspect of plaintiff's injury. That plaintiff sought to sell this property to Grace as a departure from the real estate business and not as a profit-making transaction in and of itself is not dispositive of plaintiff's lost profits claim. There is no question but that had A. S. received the purchase price when it was due on March 13, 1975, it would have been in a position to invest the money in a potentially profitable undertaking. The time value of money due is a valid consideration to be used in measuring plaintiff's damages in this case.

Turning now to the three theories of damages advanced by plaintiff, the court will note their weaknesses and shortcomings and the arguments most heavily targeted by defendant. The involuntary loan theory, advanced as the least judgmental methodology, relies on certain assumptions which may or may not be completely valid. First, it is bottomed on an assumption that Grace was to borrow the funds to purchase CCT from a commercial lender at a rate of four percentage points over prime. Then it harnesses Grace to loan "repayments" paralleling the monthly net cash receipts plaintiff received during the nearly five years it took to sell out the project. No allowance is made for early repayment, which the Grace documents indicate was an expectation of Grace's loan application plan. The involuntary loan theory appears harsh inasmuch as the damages continued to grow even after the project was completely sold out. The theory places plaintiff in the highly favorable position of being a commercial mortgagee with a fail-safe mortgage despite the fact that A. S. might have taken the nine million dollar sale price it received from Grace on March 13, 1975 and deposited it in a less favorable investment.

The alternative capital receipts theory designated by plaintiff as Methodology No. 2 is vulnerable in that it does not necessarily reflect real estate rates of interest. Defendant attacks the fact that this theory is based upon the rate of return on investment earned by the parent company, American Standard, Inc., rather than the return rate of the plaintiff, A. S. Development, Inc. Further, Grace argues that no evidence was introduced showing that plaintiff or American Standard, Inc. contemplated any particular investment that would have earned the rates of return encompassed by this theory. Without commenting on these objections, I note that plaintiff offers this theory mainly as a corroboration of the reliability of the other two theories and, therefore, I, also, will accord it less consideration.

The alternative sales price theory was interesting but less satisfying than the involuntary loan theory. It relies upon yields to maturity of bonds not related to the subject matter of this lawsuit. The 16% interest rate employed in its calculations was the result of a professional judgment which was related in only a general way to the particular investment in this case. The theory has appeal because it targets the problem of the damage suffered by the loss of the time value of money but it is developed in a fashion which lends it less acceptability.

It is the court's duty to fashion an award of damages based upon a reasonable design for remedying the loss and putting the plaintiff in the position it would have been in had defendant not breached its contract. The court is persuaded that the methodology of the involuntary loan is, in the final analysis, the fairest design for compensating plaintiff for its loss. The court will mold a recovery based on this scheme. . . .

CONCLUSIONS OF LAW

The general rule for measuring damages for the breach of a contract for the purchase or sale of real property is that damages are assessed as the difference between the contract price and market value at the time of the breach. Corbin on Contracts, s 1098 A (p. 535). . . . Defendant urges application of that rule to this case. Grace points to the aggregate market price of the CCT units as prima facie evidence of market value. . . . Since plaintiff sold the property for an aggregate total of $13,806,695, the market price exceeded the contract price and defendant argues that no damages resulted. Using this measure, even allowing for the additional expense of $4,088,220 which plaintiff incurred to complete and market the property, plaintiff would appear to have suffered either damages of only $3,279 (using plaintiff's book value figure) or no damages (using defendant's book value figure).

Defendant calls the court's attention to the 1975 real estate tax assessment on CCT of over eleven million dollars as another indication of the market value of CCT and further demonstration that market value exceeded contract price.

None of defendant's arguments come to grips with plaintiff's rather unique injury in this case, however. They ignore the value of the loss of the use of a large sum of money for an extended period of time.

Courts have not been oblivious of the time value of money. One court acknowledged that "in our society today, money is a commodity with a legitimate price on the market and loss of its use . . . should be compensable." Shapiro v. Kansas Public Employees Retirement System, 216 Kan. 353, 532 P.2d 1081, 1084 (1975).

Though articulated in many different ways, the courts are mindful of the value of time in calculating the compensation for a damages award. As the court stated in U. S. v. Atlantic Refining Co., 85 F.2d 427, 429 (3d Cir. 1936), "delay in . . . (receiving) compensation is an element in determining the damages . . . and an award made on one date is not the equivalent of an award made at an earlier date." The delayed compensation is a greater figure and "delay . . . enters into the late award as an element of loss." See Harpum, Specific Performance With Compensation as a Purchaser's Remedy—A Study in Contract and Equity, 40 Camb.L.J. 47 (1981); Oakey, Pecuniary Compensation For Failure to Complete a Contract for the Sale of Land, 39 Camb.L.J. 58 (1980).

The aim of awarding damages is compensation. The goal is:

" . . . to put the injured party in as good a position as he would have had if performance had been rendered as promised. It goes without saying that this aim can never be exactly attained. The position that one would have occupied if history had been different is purely hypothetical. And yet that is the problem that the trial court . . . (is) required to solve." (It) must determine what additions to the injured party's wealth (expected gains) have been prevented by the breach and what subtractions from his wealth (losses) have been caused by it. Corbin on Contracts, § 992, pp. 5–6.

This case is difficult because the damages are not certain and the facts of the case do not provide guideposts to the proper techniques for the measurement of damages. The New Jersey Appellate Division faced the problem of uncertainty in damage awards in the recent case of Donovan v. Bachstadt, 181 N.J. Super. 367, 437 A.2d 728 (App. Div. 1981), which considered whether costs for increased mortgage interest was recoverable as damages. That court alluded to Sandler v. Lawn-A-Mat, 141 N.J. Super. 437, 454, 358 A.2d 805 (App. Div.) certif. den., 71 N.J. 503, 366 A.2d 658 (1976) where Judge Larner said that: Mere difficulty or lack of certainty in the proof or finding of the quantum of damages does not inhibit an award to the successful party. As noted by the Supreme Court in Tessman v. Grosner, 23 N.J. 193, 128 A.2d 467 (1957):

If the evidence affords a basis for estimating the damages with some reasonable degree of certainty, it is sufficient. Wolcott Johnson & Co. v. Mount, 36 N.J.L. 262, 272 (Sup.Ct., 1873), affirmed 38 N.J.L. 496 (ss A. 1875). The rule relating to the uncertainty of damages applies to the uncertainty as to the fact of damage and not to its amount, and where it is certain that damage has resulted, mere uncertainty as to the amount will not preclude the right of recovery. (citations omitted)

The Donovan court discussed the trend toward flexibility in assessing damages by referring to the approach discussed in Section 352 of the Second Restatement of Contracts, where it is stated that: Doubts are generally resolved against the party in breach. A party who has, by his breach forced the injured party to seek compensation in damages should not be allowed to profit from his breach. . . . Restatement (Second) of Contracts § 352 (1981).

Donovan also draws upon the "more flexible, less exact approach" of the Uniform Commercial Code in measuring damages. This approach is revealed in the Code's section on liberal administration of remedies, N.J.S.A. 12A:1–106(1), and in its language in Comment 4 to Section 2–715 that "(l)oss may be determined in any manner which is reasonable under the circumstances." N.J.S.A. 12A:2–715 (Comment 4). (omitted).

Thus it appears that uncertainty alone should not deter me from fashioning an award which would place plaintiff in as favorable a position as it would have been in had defendant not defaulted in its obligation. . . .

Defendant contends that plaintiff's damage claim is actually a claim for prejudgment interest which is governed by the applicable New Jersey prejudgment interest rule. Defendant argues that inasmuch as that rule was only recently amended in September 1981 increasing the statutory rate of interest from 8% to 12%, the plaintiff's damages, if any, should be assessed at 8% prior to September 1981 and 12% after that. Also, defendant points out that interest is to be calculated, according to the terms of the rule, as simple rather than compound interest.

I reject the contention that this rule controls the assessment of damages in this case. Certainly, the rule providing for prejudgment interest is a tool to be used to assure that any recovery by a prevailing party actually succeeds in making it whole. It indemnifies a "plaintiff for the loss of what the monies due him would presumably have earned if payment had not been refused." Rova Farms Resort v. Investors Insurance Co., 65 N.J. 474, 506, 323 A.2d 495 (1974). It also deters an obligor from delaying an offer of settlement in the hope that the delay will enable it to exploit the earning power of the money at stake. "The basic consideration is that the defendant has had the use, and the plaintiff has not, of the amount in question, and the interest factor simply covers the value of the sum awarded for the prejudgment period during which the defendant had the benefit of monies to which the plaintiff is found to have been earlier entitled." Id. Rova Farms, supra, 65 N.J. at 506, 323 A.2d 495.

Though this principle is applicable to the controversy between A. S. and Grace, its application in this case is different. The question here is whether an award for damages in a contract case can be fashioned in reliance on the time value of money when plaintiff has received the full contract price as the result of its efforts to mitigate the damages. I find that I must answer that question in the affirmative notwithstanding the guarantee of some imprecision in results. . . .

As discussed in my earlier opinion, I am satisfied that plaintiff's title was marketable, and that defendant's objections were false and contrived. Within the context of this investment transaction defendant wrongfully rejected title to CCT, and plaintiff's actions do not preclude its recovery in equity.

Accordingly, I find that plaintiff is entitled to damages in an amount to be calculated on the involuntary loan theory through the date judgment is entered. The involuntary loan theory will be calculated at an interest rate of 2% points above Chase Manhattan prime. This award provides fair and reasonable damages to plaintiff for defendant's use of the money over an extended period of time, yet it does not lock defendant into the fiction of the 1975 loan.

I have considered plaintiff's argument that post-judgment interest should be permitted on the final judgment at the Chase Manhattan prime rate compounded monthly. While I am not oblivious of the fact that a 12% post-judgment interest rate is less than a compensatory rate of interest on an award of this magnitude, there is nothing otherwise unusual about the facts of this case to warrant deviation from the promulgated court rule. Post-judgment interest is to be calculated at 12% simple interest.

NOTES AND QUESTIONS

1. *Reasonable certainty versus mathematical certainty.* The certainty limitation on damages does not require that the damages be ascertainable with mathematical certainty. Indeed, as the *A-S Development* opinion indicates, even the best models and calculations of the parties' experts will involve, to some extent, guesses and speculations. How does the court resolve the question of how to justify the application of one model over another? Likewise, does the court's eventual adoption of the involuntary loan theory at 2% over the prime rate (versus the 4% over prime rate measure proposed by plaintiff's expert) appear particularly reasoned and justifiable, or does the court appear to pull this number out of thin air? Also, note the wide range of possible damages given by the different models proposed by the plaintiff's expert. Why wouldn't such widely varying results indicate that damages were not reasonably ascertainable?

2. *Prejudgment interest on a "sum certain"?* How did the judge deal with "prejudgment" interest on a sum, which, at the time of suit, was "uncertain"? In this sense, prejudgment dates from the time the action is filed until judgment. Interest from the date of breach to the time the action is filed can only be recovered as damages. Would the plaintiff have recovered a true "expectancy" measure of damages without the inclusion of interest? Is the outcome suggested by Restatement (Second) of Contracts § 354 based on the relative uncertainty involved in calculating interest on a sum that remains unliquidated until entry of judgment? The "sum certain" aspect has ancient ties to the common law writ of "debt" that required the plaintiff prove it was owed a definite or certain sum of money. The action of debt was subject to the "wager of law" defense discussed in chapter 2. Ultimately, the action of debt was replaced by the action in assumpsit. After *Slade's Case,* assumption did not require a sum certain nor was it subject to the wager of law defense (oath-helpers testifying that defendant did not owe the debt).

3. *Certainty and valuation in complex transactions.* As noted above, complex transactions such as large-scale real property sales, corporate mergers and acquisitions, and many financial transactions present extraordinarily difficult issues with respect to valuation and determining damages with reasonable certainty. See e.g., Keith Sharfman, "Contractual Valuation Mechanisms and Corporate Law," 2 Va. L. & Bus. Rev. 53, 57–63 (2007). In such cases, there is no single valuation rule for determining the amount of damages caused by a breach of contract. See Jay W. Eisenhofer & John L. Reed, "Valuation Litigation," 22 Del. J. Corp. L. 37, 88–94 (1997) ("With regard to the actual valuation [of a target corporation], there is no methodology that is legally correct per se, but the method employed should be generally accepted in the financial community."). Based upon your reading of the case above, how

could counsel for W.R. Grace Land Corp. have better countered A-S Development's arguments regarding damages models? If damages do not include interest, is the contrast breaker encouraged to show recovery and judgment?

4. *Prejudgment interest, liquidation of claims, and ascertainability.* Historically, courts opposed awarding interest because they were hostile to the concept of interest itself. See, e.g., Patrick C. Diamond, "The Minnesota Prejudgment Interest Amendment: An Analysis of the Offer-Counteroffer Provision," 69 Minn. L. Rev. 1401, 1403 (1985). More recently, the law in many states changed, either by statute, court rule, or decision, permitting the recovery of interest if the claim was for a definite sum or one of ascertainable fixed value. So-called unliquidated claims, in many states, are supposedly not entitled to bear interest until converted into a judgment of the court. Restatement (Second) of Contracts § 354(1) appears to perpetuate this result. Demonstrably, this result fails to recognize the time value of money as applied to unliquidated claims, the apparent justification being that until the obligation is quantified by judgment, the defendant would not know how much to pay so as to avoid the interest cost. Moreover, would an award of pre-judgment interest adequately compensate injured promisees forced into bankruptcy because of the breach? See Royce de R. Barondes, "Rejecting the Marie Antoinette Paradigm of Prejudgment Interest," 43 Brandeis L. J. 1 (2004).

5. *Certainty as a limitation under the CISG.* The certainty limitation on contracts damages is primarily a creation of U.S. law. Importantly, the CISG does not contain any ascertainability limitation on contract damages. See Eric G. Schneider, "Consequential Damages in the International Sale of Goods: Analysis of Two Decisions," 16 U. Pa. J. Int'l Bus. L. 615 (1995); Note, "Unification and Certainty: The United Nations Convention on Contracts for the International Sale of Goods," 97 Harv. L. Rev. 1984 (1984).

E. EQUITABLE ALTERNATIVES WHEN MONETARY DAMAGES ARE INADEQUATE

1. INADEQUATE MONETARY REMEDY

The common law today in some ways comprises two separate systems for resolving disputes, law and equity. In England, the courts of the King's Bench and Queen's Bench had jurisdiction over all actions at law. These law courts generally only had the power to award damages, although limited exceptions such as a legal action for "replevin"—a judgment requiring actual delivery of goods to the buyer—existed. Over time, the chancellor—as the keeper of the king's conscience—began granting special relief in cases where the common law remedy of damages failed to provide adequate relief. See J.H. Baker, An Introduction to English Legal History 38–43 (1971). In such cases, the parties were summoned personally before the chancellor, and the chancellor then, in his discretion, ordered one party to take specific action. See id. By the fifteenth century, petitions to the chancellor had increased to the point that the Court of Chancery had become a separate system of courts charged with exercising equity jurisprudence and do justice in individual cases in which the forms of an action at law could not provide adequate relief. See id.

The separate courts of law and equity were merged in both England and the United States beginning in the late nineteenth century, so that law courts could hear actions that were available only in equity courts and grant equitable relief in those cases. Nonetheless, the distinction between the law and equity remains important, especially in the type of relief that may be awarded in equitable cases. In general, in contrast to actions at law, which are generally remediable only by an award of money damages, actions in equity may order injunctive relief, that is, an order that the defendant perform or refrain from performing some act. In contract law, a court order mandating that a party fulfill its obligations under a contract is called specific performance. An order that a party refrain from breaching a contractual obligation is a negative injunction.

Modern common law courts presume that damages will adequately compensate the injured party for losses caused by the other party's breach of contract. An injured party can obtain equitable relief only by proving by clear and convincing evidence that the party has no adequate remedy at law, that is, damages will not adequately compensate for the injury. Furthermore equitable claims are determined by the court, not the jury. A judge sitting in equity has broad discretion in fashioning equitable relief, or even denying such equitable relief altogether, to satisfy the fundamental goal of equity to achieve justice. See Restatement (Second) of Contracts § 358; UCC § 2–716(2); and David S. Schoenbrod, "The Measure of an Injunction: A Principle to Replace Balancing the Equities and Tailoring the Remedy," 72 Minn. L. Rev. 627 (1988). An equitable order of injunctive relief—whether specific performance, negative injunction, or other remedy—is enforceable by a contempt action for disobedience of the court's order. Finally, purely equitable defenses may be becoming less important over time. Equitable claims are subject to defenses not otherwise applicable to legal claims, including "unclean hands"—which prohibits equitable relief in favor of a wrongdoer—and "laches"—which denies relief where a plaintiff delays asserting a claim for an unreasonable amount of time, regardless of whether a statute of limitations has run. See Edward Yorio, "A Defense of Equitable Defenses," 51 Ohio St. L.J. 1201, 1205–08 (1990); Commentary, "An Increasing Role for Statute of Limitations in Courts of Equity—*Kahn v. Seaboard Corp.* and *In re USACafes*," 19 Del. J. Corp. L. 493, 493–96 (1994). Likewise, a court may refuse to order specific performance or an injunction where the contract is unfair, where the equitable relief would impose unreasonable hardship, where the performance required would contravene public policy, or where the defendant's compliance with the equitable order would be difficult to enforce or supervise. Restatement (Second) of Contracts §§ 364, 365, and 366.

The equitable relief analysis begins with the question of whether the plaintiff is entitled to raise an equitable claim. Common law generally bars equitable relief if "damages would be adequate to protect the expectation interest of the injured party." Restatement (Second) of Contracts § 359. "There is, however, a tendency to liberalize the granting of equitable relief by enlarging the classes of cases in which damages are not regarded as an adequate remedy," and the comments to § 359 suggest that courts should resolve doubts in favor of inadequacy of money damages. Id., *cmt. a.* Factors affecting the adequacy of damages in a particular case include the difficulty of proving damages with reasonable certainty, the difficulty of procuring a substitute performance, or the likelihood that a damages award would be uncollectable. Restatement (Second) of Contracts § 360.

Whether damages will adequately compensate the nonbreaching party for the injury also depends in part on judicial presumptions based upon the subject matter of the contract: sale of an interest in real property, sale of personalty, or personal services. First, a contract for the sale of an interest in real property is presumptively enforceable by an order of specific performance, although the breaching party may rebut that presumption in rare cases. See Restatement (Second) of Contracts § 360, *cmt.* e. As noted, this presumption arises as a peculiar holdover from the political and economic rights attendant upon property ownership in medieval England.

Second, damages do presumptively provide an adequate remedy for breach of contracts for the sale of personal property. Importantly, however, with respect to sale of goods contracts, the UCC significantly expands the situations in which a court may award specific performance in favor of a nonbreaching buyer, explicitly permitting such orders where the goods are "unique or in other proper circumstances." UCC § 2–716(1). The comments to § 2–716 emphasize that the buyer's inability to cover is strong evidence of the propriety of equitable relief. The proposed amendments to Article 2 would make specific performance available to sellers as well as to buyers. See Roy R. Anderson, "Of Hidden Agendas, Naked Emperors, and a Few Good Soldiers: The Conference's Breach of Promise . . . Regarding Article 2 Damage Remedies," 54 SMU L. Rev. 795, 836 (2001).

Third, a court may never order specific performance to enforce contracts for personal services. Restatement (Second) of Contracts § 367. But as discussed in the second case in this section, *Lumley v. Wagner,* contracts for personal services may be enforced by a negative injunction prohibiting a breaching employee from taking employment with a competitor if the employee's services are unique or extraordinary. Id., *cmt. c.*

As you read the following case, consider whether the presumptions discussed above make sense or whether specific performance should be available merely upon the election of the nonbreaching party. See Note, "The Changing Limits of Injunctive Relief," 78 Harv. L. Rev. 997, 1020–21 (1965). Would a rule permitting parties to seek specific performance as a matter of course or if their contract so provides more precisely compensate the nonbreaching party for their loss, overcompensate, or undercompensate? See Thomas S. Ulen, on the other hand, in "The Efficiency of Specific Performance: Toward a Unified Theory of Contract Remedies," 83 Mich. L. Rev. 341, 344 (1984); Alan Schwartz, in "The Myth That Promisees Prefer Supercompensatory Remedies: An Analysis of Contracting for Damages," 100 Yale L.J. 369 (1990); Jason S. Kirwan, "Appraising a Presumption: A Modern Look at the Doctrine of Specific Performance in Real Estate Contracts," 47 Wm. & Mary L. Rev. 697 (2005); and Nancy P. Spyke, "What's Land Got to Do With It?: Rhetoric and Indeterminacy in Land's Favored Legal Status," 52 Buff. L. Rev. 387 (2004). How would such a rule likely affect the willingness of parties to engage in willful breach, efficient breach, economic duress, or requests for bad faith modifications of the contract?

SEDMAK V. CHARLIE'S CHEVROLET, INC.

Missouri Court of Appeals, Eastern District, Division Four
622 S.W.2d 694 (1981)

SATZ, Judge.

This is an appeal from a decree of specific performance. We affirm.

In their petition, plaintiffs, Dr. and Mrs. Sedmak (Sedmaks), alleged they entered into a contract with defendant, Charlie's Chevrolet, Inc. (Charlie's), to purchase a Corvette automobile for approximately $15,000.00. The Corvette was one of a limited number manufactured to commemorate the selection of the Corvette as the Pace Car for the Indianapolis 500. Charlie's breached the contract, the Sedmaks alleged, when, after the automobile was delivered, an agent for Charlie's told the Sedmaks they could not purchase the automobile for $15,000.00 but would have to bid on it.

The trial court found the parties entered into an oral contract and also found the contract was excepted from the Statute of Frauds. The court then ordered Charlie's to make the automobile "available for delivery" to the Sedmaks.

Charlie's raises three points on appeal: (1) the existence of an oral contract is not supported by the credible evidence; (2) if an oral contract exists, it is unenforceable because of the Statute of Frauds; and (3) specific performance is an improper remedy because the Sedmaks did not show their legal remedies were inadequate.

This was a court-tried case. The scope of our review is defined by the well-known principles set out in *Murphy v. Carron,* 536 S.W.2d 30 (Mo. banc 1976). We sustain the judgment of the trial court unless the judgment is not supported by substantial evidence, unless it is against the weight of the evidence or unless it erroneously declares or applies the law. *Id.* at 32. In conducting our review, we do not judge the credibility of witnesses. That task quite properly rests with the trial court. Rule 73.01(c)(2). . . .

In light of these principles, the record reflects the Sedmaks to be automobile enthusiasts, who, at the time of trial, owned six Corvettes. In July, 1977, "Vette Vues," a Corvette fancier's magazine to which Dr. Sedmak subscribed, published an article announcing Chevrolet's tentative plans to manufacture a limited edition of the Corvette. The limited edition of approximately 6,000 automobiles was to commemorate the selection of the Corvette as the Indianapolis 500 Pace Car. The Sedmaks were interested in acquiring one of these Pace Cars to add to their Corvette collection. In November, 1977, the Sedmaks asked Tom Kells, sales manager at Charlie's Chevrolet, about the availability of the Pace Car. Mr. Kells said he did not have any information on the car but would find out about it. Kells also said if Charlie's were to receive a Pace Car, the Sedmaks could purchase it.

On January 9, 1978, Dr. Sedmak telephoned Kells to ask him if a Pace Car could be ordered. Kells indicated that he would require a deposit on the car, so Mrs. Sedmak went to Charlie's and gave Kells a check for $500.00. She was given a receipt for that amount bearing the names of Kells and Charlie's Chevrolet, Inc. At that time, Kells had a pre-order form listing both standard equipment and options available on the Pace Car. Prior to tendering the deposit, Mrs. Sedmak asked Kells if she and Dr. Sedmak were "definitely going to be the owners." Kells replied, "yes." After the deposit had been paid, Mrs. Sedmak stated if the car was going to be theirs, her husband wanted some changes made to the stock model. She asked Kells to order the car equipped with an L82 engine, four speed standard transmission and AM/FM radio with tape deck. Kells said that he would try to arrange with the manufacturer for these changes. Kells was able to make the changes, and, when the car arrived, it was equipped as the Sedmaks had requested.

Kells informed Mrs. Sedmak that the price of the Pace Car would be the manufacturer's retail price, approximately $15,000.00. The dollar figure could not be quoted more precisely because Kells was not sure what the ordered changes would cost, nor was he sure what the "appearance package"—decals, a special paint job—would cost. Kells also told Mrs. Sedmak that, after the changes had been made, a "contract"—a retail dealer's order form—would be mailed to them. However, no form or written contract was mailed to the Sedmaks by Charlie's.

On January 25, 1978, the Sedmaks visited Charlie's to take delivery on another Corvette. At that time, the Sedmaks asked Kells whether he knew anything further about the arrival date of the Pace Car. Kells replied he had no further information but he would let the Sedmaks know when the car arrived. Kells also requested that Charlie's be allowed to keep the car in their showroom for promotional purposes until after the Indianapolis 500 Race. The Sedmaks agreed to this arrangement.

On April 3, 1978, the Sedmaks were notified by Kells that the Pace Car had arrived. Kells told the Sedmaks they could not purchase the car for the manufacturer's retail price because demand for the car had inflated its value beyond the suggested price. Kells also told the Sedmaks they could bid on the car. The Sedmaks did not submit a bid. They filed this suit for specific performance.

Mr. Kells' testimony about his conversations with the Sedmaks regarding the Pace Car differed markedly from the Sedmaks' testimony. Kells stated that he had no definite price information on the Pace Car until a day or two prior to its arrival at Charlie's. He denied ever discussing the purchase price of the car with the Sedmaks. He admitted, however, that after talking with the Sedmaks on January 9, 1978,[1] he telephoned the zone manager and requested changes be made to the Pace Car. He denied the changes were made pursuant to Dr. Sedmak's order. He claimed the changes were made because they were "more favorable to the automobile" and were changes Dr. Sedmak "preferred." In ordering the changes, Kells said he was merely taking Dr. Sedmak's advice because he was a "very knowledgeable man on the Corvette." There is no dispute, however, that when the Pace Car arrived, it was equipped with the options requested by Dr. Sedmak.

Mr. Kells also denied the receipt for $500.00 given him by Mrs. Sedmak on January 9, 1978, was a receipt for a deposit on the Pace Car. On direct examination, he said he "accepted a five hundred dollar ($500) deposit from the Sedmaks to assure them the first opportunity of purchasing the car." On cross-examination, he said: "We were accepting bids and with the five hundred dollar ($500) deposit it was to give them the first opportunity to bid on the car." Then after acknowledging that other bidders had not paid for the opportunity to bid, he explained the deposit gave the Sedmaks the "last opportunity" to make the final bid. Based on this evidence, the trial court found the parties entered into an oral contract for the purchase and sale of the Pace Car at the manufacturer's suggested retail price.

Charlie's first contends the Sedmaks' evidence is "so wrought with inconsistencies and contradictions that a finding of an oral contract for the

---

[1]   According to Kells' testimony, both Mr. and Mrs. Sedmak visited Charlie's on January 9, 1978. Mrs. Sedmak testified only she visited Charlie's on that date.

sale of a Pace Car at the manufacturer's suggested retail price is clearly against the weight of the evidence." We disagree. The trial court chose to believe the Sedmaks' testimony over that of Mr. Kells and the reasonableness of this belief was not vitiated by any real contradictions in the Sedmaks' testimony. Charlie's examples of conflict are either facially not contradictory or easily reconcilable.

Although not clearly stated in this point or explicitly articulated in its argument, Charlie's also appears to argue there was no contract because the parties did not agree to a price. The trial court concluded "(t)he price was to be the suggested retail price of the automobile at the time of delivery." Apparently, Charlie's argues that if this were the agreed to price, it is legally insufficient to support a contract because the manufacturer's suggested retail price is not a mandatory, fixed and definite selling price but, rather, as the term implies, it is merely a suggested price which does not accurately reflect the market and the actual selling price of automobiles. Charlie's argument is misdirected and, thus, misses the mark.

Without again detailing the facts, there was evidence to support the trial court's conclusion that the parties agreed the selling price would be the price suggested by the manufacturer. Whether this price accurately reflects the market demands on any given day is immaterial. The manufacturer's suggested retail price is ascertainable and, thus, if the parties choose, sufficiently definite to meet the price requirements of an enforceable contract. Failure to specify the selling price in dollars and cents did not render the contract void or voidable. See, e.g., *Klaber v. Lahar*, 63 S.W.2d 103, 106–107 (Mo.1933); see also, § 400.2–305 RSMo 1978. As long as the parties agreed to a method by which the price was to be determined and as long as the price could be ascertained at the time of performance, the price requirement for a valid and enforceable contract was satisfied. *See Burger v. City of Springfield*, 323 S.W.2d 777, 783–84 (Mo.1959) . . . and § 400.2–305 RSMo 1978. This point is without merit.

Charlie's next complains that if there were an oral contract, it is unenforceable under the Statute of Frauds. The trial court concluded the contract was removed from the Statute of Frauds either by the written memoranda concerning the transaction or by partial payment made by the Sedmaks. We find the latter ground a sufficient answer to defendant's complaint. . . .

Finally, Charlie's contends the Sedmaks failed to show they were entitled to specific performance of the contract. We disagree. Although it has been stated that the determination whether to order specific performance lies within the discretion of the trial court, *Landau v. St. Louis Public Service Co.*, 273 S.W.2d 255, 259 (Mo.1954), this discretion is, in fact, quite narrow. When the relevant equitable principles have been met and the contract is fair and plain, " 'specific performance goes as a matter of right.' " *Miller v. Coffeen*, 280 S.W.2d 100, 102 (Mo.1955). Here, the trial court ordered specific performance because it concluded the Sedmaks "have no adequate remedy at law for the reason that they cannot go upon the open market and purchase an automobile of this kind with the same mileage, condition, ownership and appearance as the automobile involved in this case, except, if at all, with considerable expense, trouble, loss, great delay and inconvenience." Contrary to defendant's complaint, this is a correct expression of the relevant law and it is supported by the evidence.

Under the Code, the court may decree specific performance as a buyer's remedy for breach of contract to sell goods "where the goods are unique or in other proper circumstances." § 400.2–716(1) RSMo 1978. The general term "in other proper circumstances" expresses the drafters' intent to "further a more liberal attitude than some courts have shown in connection with the specific performance of contracts of sale." § 400.2–716, U.C.C., Comment 1. This Comment was not directed to the courts of this state, for long before the Code, we, in Missouri, took a practical approach in determining whether specific performance would lie for the breach of contract for the sale of goods and did not limit this relief only to the sale of "unique" goods. *Boeving v. Vandover*, 240 Mo.App. 117, 218 S.W.2d 175 (1945). In *Boeving*, plaintiff contracted to buy a car from defendant. When the car arrived, defendant refused to sell. The car was not unique in the traditional legal sense but, at that time, all cars were difficult to obtain because of war-time shortages. The court held specific performance was the proper remedy for plaintiff because a new car "could not be obtained elsewhere except at considerable expense, trouble or loss, which cannot be estimated in advance and under such circumstances (plaintiff) did not have an adequate remedy at law." *Id.* at 177–178. Thus, *Boeving*, presaged the broad and liberalized language of § 400.2–716(1) and exemplifies one of the "other proper circumstances" contemplated by this subsection for ordering specific performance. § 400.2–716, Missouri Code Comment 1. The present facts track those in Boeving.

The Pace Car, like the car in *Boeving*, was not unique in the traditional legal sense. It was not an heirloom or, arguably, not one of a kind. However, its "mileage, condition, ownership and appearance" did make it difficult, if not impossible, to obtain its replication without considerable expense, delay and inconvenience. Admittedly, 6,000 Pace Cars were produced by Chevrolet. However, as the record reflects, this is limited production. In addition, only one of these cars was available to each dealer, and only a limited number of these were equipped with the specific options ordered by plaintiffs. Charlie's had not received a car like the Pace Car in the previous two years. The sticker price for the car was $14,284.21. Yet Charlie's received offers from individuals in Hawaii and Florida to buy the Pace Car for $24,000.00 and $28,000.00 respectively. As sensibly inferred by the trial court, the location and size of these offers demonstrated this limited edition was in short supply and great demand. We agree, with the trial court. This case was a "proper circumstance" for ordering specific performance.

Judgment affirmed.

NOTES AND QUESTIONS

1.   *Unique or in other proper circumstances.* Historically, specific performance was available as a remedy for breach of a contract for the sale of goods usually only where the goods were truly unique, such as "heirlooms or priceless works of art." See UCC § 2–716, *cmt. 2.* UCC § 2–716 significantly expands the situations in which a nonbreaching plaintiff may be awarded specific performance by specifying that such relief is appropriate not just for unique goods, but also in other circumstances. See Harold Greenberg, "Specific Performance Under Section 2–716 of the Uniform Commercial Code: 'A More Liberal Attitude' in the 'Grand Style,'" 17 New Eng. L. Rev. 321 (1982); Wendy C. Lowengrub, Note, "Unique or Ubiquitous: Art Prints and the Uniform Commercial Code," 72 Ind. L.J. 595, 611–12 (1997). Was the car in Sedmak "unique" in any sense? Or was this case one of "other proper circumstances"? Would specific performance still be appropriate if the Sedmaks had merely ordered a car without specifying additional options?

2.   *Comparing the UCC "unique or in other proper circumstances" to the common law "no adequate remedy at law" standard for awarding specific performance.* Compare the UCC standard applied in Sedmak to the common-law standard that generally requires that the plaintiff may obtain the equitable relief of specific performance only where "no adequate remedy at law." The quintessential remedy at law is an award of damages, and consequently equity will step in only where damages cannot compensate the nonbreaching party for the loss caused by the breach. If this were a common-law case, could the Sedmaks have shown that they had no adequate remedy at law?

3.   *Replevin of goods.* In some cases, the parties may choose to "identify goods to the contract"—that is, the parties may identify existing goods as specifically the goods to which their contract applies, either explicitly or in limited circumstances implied by law. See UCC § 2–501(1). By identifying goods to the contract, "[t]he buyer obtains a special property and an insurable interest" in such goods. See id. UCC § 2–716(3) permits a nonbreaching buyer to maintain an action for replevin "for goods identified to the contract" under limited circumstances, such as, for instance, inability to effect cover after reasonable effort.

4.   *Specific performance of contracts for the sale of an interest in real property.* Because of the unique characteristics of land as the source of political and economic power in medieval England, contracts for the sale of an interest in real property have historically been presumably enforceable by an award of specific performance. See Lawrence M. Friedman, Contract Law in America: A Social and Economic Case Study 131 (1965). In the United States, this

presumption continued in force despite that land no longer carried with it the attendant political and class privileges that existed in England. See id. Nonetheless in many circumstances involving contracts for the sale of an interest in real property, the uniqueness of the interest becomes so tenuous that the presumption longer applies. In *Centex Homes Corp. v. Boag*, 128 N.J.Super. 385, 320 A.2d 194 (Ch. Div. 1974), for example, the Boags contracted to purchase a condominium unit in the plaintiff's housing project. When the Boags breached their contract, the plaintiff sought specific performance. The court held that specific performance was not appropriate:

> Here the subject matter of the real estate transaction—a condominium apartment unit—has no unique quality but is one of hundreds of virtually identical units being offered by a developer for sale to the public. The units are sold by means of sample, in this case model apartments, in much the same manner as items of personal property are sold in the market place. The sales prices for the units are fixed in accordance with schedule filed by Centex as part and the only variance as between apartments having the same floor plan (of which six plans are available) is the floor level or the building location within the project. In actuality, the condominium apartment units, regardless of their realty label, share the same characteristics as personal property. Id. at 198.

See also *Van Wagner Advertising Corp. v. S & M Enterprises*, 67 N.Y.2d 186, 501 N.Y.S.2d 628, 492 N.E.2d 756 (1986) (refusing to order specific performance for allegedly "unique" billboard location lease contract). Do you think that the presumption in favor of ordering specific performance of contracts for the sale of an interest in real property should continue to be eroded? See Jonathan Levy, "Against Supercompensation: A Proposed Limitation on the Land Buyer's Right to Elect Between Damages and Specific Performance as a Remedy for Breach of Contract," Jonathan Levy, "Against Supercompensation: A Proposed Limitation on the Land Buyer's Right to Elect Between Damages and Specific Performance as a Remedy for Breach of Contract," 35 Loy. U. Chi. L.J. 555 (2004); Jason S. Kirwan, Note, "Appraising a Presumption: A Modern Look at the Doctrine of Specific Performance in Real Estate Contracts," 47 Wm. & Mary L. Rev. 697 (2005). Or is there something unique and special about real property that justifies the continued presumption?

5. *Contracting for or prohibiting specific performance as a remedy.* Parties may occasionally attempt to specify in their contract whether a court may or shall award specific performance in the event of a breach of the contract. Courts are generally hostile to attempts by the parties to mandate equitable relief, although theoretically the parties may be able to draft their contract in such a way as to promote a finding that a breach of that contract cannot be remedied by an award of damages, and thus the parties have no adequate remedy at law. On the other hand, courts will enforce terms specifying that specific performance is not available as a remedy, although

such clauses will be narrowly interpreted. See Joseph M. Perillo, Calamari & Perillo on Contracts § 16.3 (5th ed. 2003).

6.   *Certainty of damages versus certainty of terms.* Restatement (Second) of Contracts § 362 provides that a court may not order specific performance or negative injunctive relief "unless the terms of the contract are sufficiently certain to provide a basis for an appropriate order." The comments further note that there may be cases in which the terms of a contract will permit a court to determine damages with reasonable certainty, but that are not certain enough to guide a court in ordering injunctive relief. See Restatement (Second) of Contracts § 362, *cmt. a.* How is that possible? If the terms of the contract are sufficiently definite to permit a court to determine with reasonable certainty the damages arising out of the parties' obligations, how could those same terms not be sufficiently definite to permit a court to order specific performance of those terms?

7.   *The indifference principle and specific performance.* Ideally, remedies for breach of contract should provide the amount and type of relief such that a nonbreaching party is indifferent to whether the other party breaches or performs the contract. See Melvin A. Eisenberg, "Actual and Virtual Specific Performance, the Theory of Efficient Breach, and the Indifference Principle in Contract Law," 93 Cal. L. Rev. 975, 979 (2005). But litigation costs and damages limitations generally cause damages remedies to undercompensate injured plaintiffs, meaning that most plaintiffs probably would rather have received performance than damages. Would a rule permitting the nonbreaching party an election between the remedies of specific performance or damages come closer to fulfilling the goal of the indifference principle? Why or why not? See Ronen Avraham & Zhiyon Liu, "Incomplete Contracts with Asymmetric Information: Exclusive Versus Optional Remedies," 8 Am. L. & Econ. Rev. 523 (2006).

8.   *Comparative law perspective on specific performance.* Unlike the common law, many civil law jurisdictions and the CISG permit the buyer to elect between damages and specific performance of the contract, without a showing that damages will not adequately compensate for the injury. See CISG Art. 46 ("The buyer may require performance by the seller of his obligations unless the buyer has resorted to a remedy which is inconsistent with this requirement."); 1999 Contract Law of the People's Republic of China Art. 107 ("Either party that fails to perform its obligations under the contract or fails to perform them as contracted shall bear the liability for breach of contract by continuing to perform the obligations, taking remedial measures, or compensating for losses."). See also Mo Zhang, Chinese Contract Law: Theory and Practice 296–98 (2006); Amy H. Kastely, "The Right to Require Performance in International Sales: Towards an International Interpretation of the Vienna Convention," 63 Wash. L. Rev. 607, 611 (1988).

2. PERSONAL SERVICE CONTRACTS

LUMLEY V. WAGNER

Court of Chancery of England
1 De G. M. & G. 604, 42 Eng. Rep. 687 (1852)

LORD CHANCELLOR LORD ST. LEONARDS.

The question which I have to decide in the present case arises out of a very simple contract, the effect of which is, that the Defendant Johanna Wagner should sing at Her Majesty's Theatre for a certain number of nights, and that she should not sing elsewhere (for that is the true construction) during that period. As I understand the points taken by the Defendant's counsel in support of this appeal they in effect come to this, namely, that a Court of Equity ought not to grant an injunction except in cases connected with specific performance, or where the injunction being to compel a party to forbear from committing an act (and not to perform an act), that injunction will complete the whole agreement remaining unexecuted.

I have then to consider how the question stands on principle and on authority, and in so doing I shall observe upon some of the cases which have been referred to and commented upon by the Defendants in support of their contention . . . .

The present is a mixed case, consisting not of two correlative acts to be done—one by the Plaintiff, and the other by the Defendants, which state of facts may have and in some cases has introduced a very important difference—but of an act done by J. Wagner alone, to which is superadded a negative stipulation on her part to abstain from the commission of any act which will break in upon her affirmative covenant; the one being ancillary to, concurrent and operating together with, the other. The agreement to sing for the Plaintiff during three months at his theatre, and during that time not to sing for anybody else, is not a correlative contract, it is in effect one contract; and though beyond all doubt this Court would not interfere to enforce specific performance of the whole of this contract, yet in all sound construction, and according to the true spirit of the agreement, the engagement to perform for three months at one theatre must necessarily exclude the right to perform at the same time at another theatre. It was clearly intended that J. Wagner was to exert her vocal abilities to the utmost to aid the theatre to which she agreed to attach herself. I am of the opinion that if she had attempted, even in the absence of any negative stipulation, to perform at another theatre, she would have broke the spirit and true meaning of the contract as such as she would now do with reference to the contract into which she has actually entered.

Whenever this Court has not proper jurisdiction to enforce specific performance, it operates to bind men's conscience, as far as they can be bound, to a true and literal performance of their agreements; and it will not suffer them to depart from their contracts at their pleasure, leaving the party with whom they have contracted to the mere chance of any damages which a jury may give. The exercise of this jurisdiction has, I believe, had a wholesome tendency towards the maintenance of that good faith which exists in this country to a much greater degree perhaps than in any other; and although the jurisdiction is not to be extended, yet a Judge would desert his duty who did not act up to what his predecessors have handed down as the rule for his guidance in the administration of such an equity.

It was objected that the operation of the injunction in the present case was mischievous, excluding the defendant J. Wagner from performing at any other theatre while this Court has no power to compel her to perform at Her Majesty's Theatre. It is true that I have not the means of compelling her to sing, but she has no cause of complaint if I compel her to abstain from the commission of an act which she has bound herself not to do, and thus possibly cause her to fulfill her engagement. The jurisdiction which I now exercise is wholly within the power of the Court, and being of opinion that it is a proper case for interfering, I shall leave nothing unsatisfied by the judgment I pronounce. The effect, too, of the injunction in restraining J. Wagner from singing elsewhere may, in the event of an action being brought against her by the Plaintiff, prevent any such amount of vindictive damages being given against her as a jury might probably be inclined to give if she had carried her talents and exercised them at the rival theatre; the injunction may also, as I have said, tend to the fulfillment of her engagement; though, in continuing the injunction, I disclaim doing indirectly what I cannot do directly. . . .

The authority of Clarke v. Price (2 Wils. 157) was much pressed upon me by the learned counsel for the Defendants; but that is a case which does not properly belong to their argument, because there was no negative stipulation, and I quite admit that this Court cannot enforce the performance of such an affirmative stipulation as is to be found in that case; there the Defendant having agreed to take notes of cases in the Court of Exchequer, and compose reports for the Plaintiff, and having failed to do so, the Plaintiff, Mr. Clarke, filed a bill for an injunction, and Lord Eldon, when refusing the injunction, in effect, said, I cannot compel Mr. Price to sit in the Court of Exchequer and take notes and compose reports; and the whole of his judgment shows that he proceeded (and so it has been considered in later cases) on the ground that there was no covenant.

NOTES AND QUESTIONS

1.   *Contracts for personal service or supervision will not be enforced.* The commentary to Restatement (Second) of Contracts § 367 proposes that an order of specific performance in the personal services context is unworkable for two reasons. First, an affirmative injunction requires supervision and enforcement

by the court, and courts are reluctant to attempt to evaluate whether the employee has complied with the injunction. See id., *cmt. a.* Second, an employer may enforce an order of specific performance against a recalcitrant employee by moving for an order of contempt against the employee. A court may fine or imprison the employee who resists such a contempt order, raising the spectre of state-enforced slavery and involuntary servitude. See id. Which of these propositions is more compelling in this case?

2. *Effectiveness of negative injunctions in enforcing employment agreements.* What did Lumley really win in this case? The court clearly hoped that its judgment would "tend to the fulfillment of [Wagner's] engagement," but explicitly disclaimed any ability to monitor Wagner's performance under the contract if she returned to her engagement with Lumley. What would happen if Wagner returned to Lumley's employment but provided services that, while within the letter of the employment agreement, fell below the parties' original expectations? At that point, Lumley would face a difficult choice—continue to employ the technically performing Wagner (and suffer possible business and reputational losses as customers became dissatisfied) or terminate Wagner and face a possible suit for breach of contract. See Geoffrey Christopher Rapp, "Affirmative Injunctions in Athletic Employment Contracts: Rethinking the Place of the Lumley Rule in American Sports Law," 16 Marq. Sports L. Rev. 261, 270–71 (2006). What incentives would Wagner have to avoid such conduct? Could Lumley structure the contract to protect himself against such substandard performance?

3. *The* Lumley *rule and gender bias.* Before *Lumley*, early nineteenth century American courts routinely refused to grant equitable relief against breaching employees. Importantly, however, these early cases involved only male employees. "Indeed, in the nineteenth century, all of the prominent cases in this line involved the services of women, and only women performers were subjected to permanent injunctions against performing elsewhere for the duration of the contract. In the corpus of reported cases, no male performer was ever permanently enjoined from quitting and performing elsewhere during the entire nineteenth century." Lea S. VanderVelde, "The Gendered Origins of the *Lumley* Doctrine: Binding Men's Consciences and Women's Fidelity," 101 Yale L.J. 775, 776–77 (1992). As Professor VanderVelde observes, American courts first applied the *Lumley* rule "in keeping with prevailing cultural biases" against female acting professionals, but later expanded these restrictions against employee freedom of contract to cover all providers of special or unique services, regardless of gender. Id. at 782. The effect of this rule was to legally subordinate those employees to their employers. Id.

F. REMEDIES SPECIFIED OR MODIFIED BY CONTRACT

The common law rules regarding the expectancy, reliance, and restitution interests and the foreseeability, avoidability, and certainty limitations provide base level default rules that govern where the parties' contract is silent. But, as with virtually all other aspects of their relationship, parties may decide to opt out of that system of default rules in favor of their own private ordering. This section considers situations in which parties specified through contract types, measures, or the availability of particular remedies for breach of contract. First, parties may attempt to specify *ex ante* the measure and method of calculation of damages that a court shall apply in the event of breach. Such "liquidated damages" clauses are generally enforceable under modern law, provided that they reasonably approximate possible damages caused by a breach of contract. Where the parties failed to reasonably approximate or predict their possible damages, however, courts will likely invalidate clauses specifying remedies as "penalty clauses."

Second, instead of specifying a particular measure of damages, the parties may also attempt to modify or exclude damages for certain types of injury, such as consequential damages or damages for personal injury. In some cases, such modifications and exclusions may have the effect of denying the injured party any possibility of relief.

1.   REMEDIES SPECIFIED BY CONTRACT

The default rules regarding damages interests and limitations cannot efficiently allocate remedies in every contract situation. Consequently, parties may attempt to specify at the time of contract formation the amount of damages for which the breaching party shall be liable. Restatement (Second) of Contracts § 356(1) provides that such liquidated damages clauses are enforceable, provided the amount is (1) "reasonable in light of the anticipated or actual loss caused by the breach;" and (2) the damages are difficult to prove or ascertain. UCC § 2–718(1) similarly provides that the parties may liquidate damages, "but only at an amount which is reasonable in light of the anticipated or actual harm caused by the breach, the difficulties of proof of loss, and the inconvenience or nonfeasibility of otherwise obtaining an adequate remedy." Contract terms providing for unreasonably large liquidated damages are unenforceable penalties. Restatement (Second) of Contracts § 356(1).

The touchstone of liquidated damages analysis is the reasonableness of the parties' attempt to estimate their damages. The reasonableness of this attempt is to be assessed both at the time of contracting and at the time of breach. The reasonableness standard is satisfied if the parties' estimate at the time of contracting is reasonable but does not approximate the actual loss. *or* if the liquidated damages clause approximates the actual loss even though it does not reflect other losses that might have been anticipated. For example, assume Able contracts with Baker for package delivery services and specifies that the liquidated damages for failure to deliver a package shall be $100. Baker fails to deliver a package worth $90. That $100 liquidated damages estimate will be reasonable if it either approximates the actual loss caused by the breach that occurred (regardless of whether other breaches might have caused greater or lesser amounts of damages) or if it approximates the loss the parties reasonably anticipated from a breach at the time of drafting (even if the actual loss is more or less than the anticipated loss). Importantly, however, under UCC § 2–718(1), some courts have interpreted this "reasonable in light of the anticipated or actual harm caused by the breach" element to require the parties' estimates of anticipated harm at the time of contracting to approximate the actual harm suffered at the time of breach. See Susan V. Ferris, "Liquidated Damages Recovery Under the Restatement (Second) of Contracts," 67 Cornell L. Rev. 862, 871–72 (1982).

The second prong is potentially more problematic. The injury that the parties attempt to resolve *ex ante* through the liquidated damages clause must be difficult to prove with reasonable certainty. Paradoxically, then, the parties must attempt to estimate the likely damages that would be caused by a breach to satisfy the first reasonableness prong. But if the parties can estimate their likely damages at the time of contracting, they should theoretically be able to ascertain those damages with reasonable certainty after the actual breach has occurred. The restatement comments attempt to resolve this dilemma by placing the certainty analysis on a sliding scale. "The greater the difficulty either of proving that loss has occurred or of establishing its amount with reasonable certainty . . . , the easier it is to show that the amount fixed is reasonable." Restatement (Second) § 356, *cmt. b.*

Liquidation of damages at the time of contracting provides substantial benefits in terms of reducing the costs and burdens of litigation on the parties and the legal system. Parties entering a contract in which the damages from breach will be potentially large but difficult to prove—such as lost business opportunities, damage to reputation and loss of good will, lost profits, and incidental and consequential damages—can estimate and consent to such damages at contract formation, thus avoiding problems of foreseeability, certainty, and mitigation at trial. See Restatement (Second) of Contracts § 362, *cmt. a.* Recognizing the potential benefits of a contractual agreement regarding remedies, courts began enforcing "liquidated damages" clauses where the parties had attempted in advance to reasonably estimate the damages that might result from a breach. See Susan V. Ferris, "Liquidated Damages Recovery Under The Restatement (Second) Of Contracts," 67 Cornell L. Rev. 862 (1982). But despite these benefits, courts remain highly suspicious of attempts by parties to specify damages in their contract terms and regularly invalidate clauses deemed to be "penalties." See Larry A. DiMatteo, "A Theory of Efficient Penalty: Eliminating the Law of Liquidated Damages," 38 Am. Bus. L.J. 633 (2001) (arguing that "the law of liquidated damages masks an unwarranted judicial intervention into freedom of contract").

Many commentators have argued that courts should enforce all liquidated damages provisions. See, e.g., Alan Schwartz, "The Myth That Promise[e]s Prefer Supracompensatory Remedies: An Analysis of Contracting for Damages," 100 Yale L.J. 369, 370 (1990). As Schwartz notes, "Courts sometimes mistake compensatory damage measures for penalties, and so have found that particular liquidated damages clauses would inevitably overcompensate promisees when those clauses only protected the expectation." Id. In Schwartz's view, both the *ex ante* and the *ex post* branches of the rule should be repealed because courts cannot easily know when a clause is supercompensatory. See id. at 387. Consequently, courts should presume the enforceability of such provisions rather than make every effort to strike them down. See Robert A. Hillman, "The Limits of Behavioral Decision Theory in Legal Analysis: The Case of Liquidated Damages," 85 Cornell L. Rev. 717, 732–33 (2000) ("Generally, overturning contract terms based on the degree of attention the parties paid to them seems too blunderbuss an approach to contract enforcement."). Rather than overturning such clauses based upon post hoc analyses of the reasonableness of the parties' private remedies provisions, some commentators have suggested policing liquidated damages provisions through other contract doctrines, such as unconscionability or duress. See id.; see also Charles J. Goetz & Robert E. Scott, "Liquidated Damages, Penalties and the Just Compensation Principle: Some Notes on an Enforcement Model and a Theory of Efficient Breach," 77 Colum. L. Rev. 554 (1977).

On the other hand, in some contexts heightened judicial scrutiny of attempts to liquidate damages may still be justified. Consumers, for example, often lack the sophistication to understand or avoid unfair liquidated damages terms, especially if producers obtain the consumers' apparent assent to liquidated damages through adhesive, standard form contracts. See, e.g., Melvin A. Eisenberg, "The Limits of Cognition and the Limits of Contract," 47 Stan. L. Rev. 211, 225–36 (1995) ("To begin with, bounded rationality and rational ignorance have a special bearing on liquidated damages provisions. . . . [A]ctors tend to be unrealistically optimistic . . . ."); Debora L. Threedy, "Liquidated and Limited Damages and the Revision of Article 2: An Opportunity to Rethink the U.C.C.'s Treatment of Agreed Remedies," 27 Idaho L. Rev. 427 (1991) (noting that UCC §§ 2–718 and 2–719 fail to distinguish between contracts negotiated between parties of relatively equal bargaining power and contracts of adhesion).

SP TERRACE, LP. v. MERITAGE HOMES OF TEXAS, LLC

Court of Appeals of Texas, Houston (1st Dist.)
334 S.W.3D 275 (2010)

OPINION ON REHEARING

JANE BLAND, Justice.

In this dispute over an earnest money contract to develop a plat of real estate, the trial court granted summary judgment in favor of Meritage Homes of Texas, LLC (Meritage) on its breach of contract claim against SP Terrace, LP, and Tyee Management, LLC (collectively, SP Terrace). The trial court summarily rejected SP Terrace's counterclaims for breach of contract against Meritage.

The contract called for SP Terrace to file a subdivision plat by December 31, 2005. SP Terrace concedes that it did not meet this deadline. But it argues that the contract extended the deadline, or alternatively that its compliance was excused. It claims fact issues exist on its affirmative defenses of oral modification, waiver, delay and interference by Meritage, on the amount of attorney's fees, and on its counterclaim against Meritage. We conclude that SP Terrace raises a fact issue on the issues of waiver and delay, but not as to contract modification or interference. We therefore reverse the trial court's summary judgment and remand the case for trial. We grant rehearing and withdraw our opinion and judgment dated May 6, 2010, to address an argument that SP Terrace raises in its motion for rehearing. Our disposition is unchanged.

Background

Underlying Facts

SP Terrace entered into an earnest money contract with Meritage to develop and sell ninety-six lots in a proposed Harris County subdivision. The development plan required small and narrow lots, and Meritage was one of a few builders who could construct houses to fit the particular lot sizes. The contract terms required SP Terrace to improve the overall subdivision. In particular, it required SP Terrace to file a subdivision plat with Harris County by a December 31, 2005 substantial completion deadline. After substantial completion, Meritage would then purchase the lots in a series of transactions. The total purchase price was $2,688,000. Meritage deposited ten percent of this price, $268,000, with SP Terrace as earnest money. If SP Terrace did not achieve substantial completion by December 31, 2005, Meritage could terminate the contract and recover its earnest money deposit. But, if Meritage delayed SP Terrace's performance of its contractual obligations, the substantial completion deadline would "be extended to the extent of any such delay."

On November 30, representatives from Meritage and SP Terrace met to discuss the project. At this point, SP Terrace was ready to file the subdivision plat. Meritage asked for changes to the plat, and it requested that SP Terrace postpone filing the plat to accommodate those changes. SP Terrace agreed, but informed Meritage that a six-month extension of the substantial completion deadline would be necessary to address these and any future changes to the development. According to Tyler Todd, the president of Tyee Management, SP Terrace's general partner, and Kelly Smalley, the project manager, the parties orally agreed to extend the substantial completion deadline, and the representatives of Meritage agreed to sign a written extension memorializing the oral modification. Smalley mailed a written agreement to Meritage before December 31, 2005. She never received a response.

The parties continued to work together to make changes and improvements to the development into early February 2006. But on February 3, Meritage informed SP Terrace that, due to SP Terrace's failure to meet the substantial completion deadline, Meritage was terminating the contract and demanding the return of its earnest money deposit.

Procedural History

After SP Terrace refused to return the earnest money deposit, Meritage sued for breach of contract. SP Terrace counterclaimed for breach of contract, alleging that Meritage (1) delayed SP Terrace's performance, (2) failed to cooperate with SP Terrace, and (3) breached their oral agreement to extend the substantial completion deadline by six months, all of which entitled SP Terrace to retain the earnest money deposit and recover actual damages in addition to the earnest money it kept.

Meritage moved for traditional and no-evidence summary judgment on its claims against SP Terrace and on SP Terrace's counterclaim. Meritage contended that the parties never agreed to extend the substantial completion deadline. Meritage argued that SP Terrace's counterclaim failed as a matter of law because it did not state a claim for affirmative relief and the liquidated damages provision in the contract precluded SP Terrace from recovering actual damages in excess of the earnest money deposit. Meritage contended that SP Terrace's waiver defense failed because Meritage never renounced its right to terminate the contract, and the forty-eight days that had passed between the substantial completion deadline and the date Meritage demanded the return of its earnest money deposit was not long enough to show that Meritage intended to yield its right to terminate. Meritage argued that any oral modification of the contract is unenforceable because it materially altered the obligations of the underlying written contract. Meritage also noted that SP Terrace failed to present any evidence that the amount of liquidated damages was an unreasonable forecast of the amount of its damages.

SP Terrace responded with the Todd and Smalley affidavits to show that fact issues existed regarding (1) an agreement to extend the substantial completion deadline; (2) whether Meritage, through its oral agreement to extend the deadline and its continued work with SP Terrace after December 31, 2005, waived the deadline; and (3) whether Meritage breached its duties to cooperate with SP Terrace and to not delay or interfere with SP Terrace's performance of its contractual obligations. SP Terrace also argued that the liquidated damages provision of the contract, which limited SP Terrace's recovery to retention of the earnest money deposit, was unenforceable penalty because it hypothetically would allow the forfeiture of the deposit due to any breach by Meritage, including a trivial one.

The trial court granted Meritage's motions. Shortly thereafter, Meritage moved for entry of a final judgment, asking the trial court to award it $268,000 in damages, $71,170.50 in attorney's fees incurred in prosecuting its claims in the trial court proceedings, $40,000 in attorney's fees if SP Terrace appeals to an intermediate appellate court, and an additional $27,500 in attorney's fees if Meritage ultimately prevails after full briefing and oral argument to the Texas Supreme Court.

SP Terrace moved the trial court to reconsider the summary judgment. SP Terrace attached excerpts from the deposition of Michael Pizzitola, taken after the original submission of the summary judgment motions, to further support its contentions. SP Terrace also attached the affidavit of its counsel of record opposing Meritage's requested amount of attorney's fees. The trial court's docket sheet includes the following entry for December 8, 2008: "D. (seller) Motion for leave of court to file additional evidence granted." The trial court did not memorialize the docket entry in any order, even though SP Terrace submitted a proposed order and requested that the trial court sign it. The trial court entered a final judgment in favor of Meritage, awarding the $268,000 earnest money deposit as damages and the full amount of attorney's fees requested by Meritage.

Discussion

Standard of Review

We review de novo the trial court's grant of a motion for summary judgment. . . .

When we construe a contract, we must "ascertain and give effect to the parties' intentions as expressed in the document." *Frost Nat'l Bank v. L & F Distribs., Ltd.,* 165 S.W.3d 310, 311–12 (Tex.2005) (per curiam). We consider the contract as a whole in order to give effect to all provisions of the contract. *See id.* at 312. We give contractual terms their plain, ordinary, and generally accepted meaning unless the contract shows that the parties intended a different meaning to control. *See Heritage Res. v. NationsBank,* 939 S.W.2d 118, 121 (Tex.1996).

[Eds.—The court considered SP Terrace's arguments regarding the affirmative defenses of oral modification and interference by Meritage. The court held that Meritage had not interfered with SP Terrace's contract performance and that the alleged oral modification was ineffective under the statute of frauds.]

* * *

Summary Judgment on SP Terrace's Counterclaim

SP Terrace also sues Meritage for breach of contract, and seeks damages beyond the earnest money deposit. The trial court rejected this claim, and SP Terrace appeals. Meritage responds that SP Terrace's counterclaim is not one for affirmative relief, but in any event, SP Terrace's recovery is limited to the earnest money contract.

A. Claim for Affirmative Relief

Meritage argues that SP Terrace's asserted contractual defense to the refund of Meritage's earnest money deposit is not an affirmative claim for relief. To qualify as a claim for affirmative relief, the defendant must allege a cause of action independent of the plaintiff's claim, on which the defendant can recover benefits, compensation, or relief, even though the plaintiff may abandon or fail to establish its claim. . . . If the defendant only resists the plaintiff's right to recover, then it does not state a claim for affirmative relief. . . .

In its "Second Amended Answer and First Amended Counterclaim," SP Terrace stated that Meritage's "actions, promises and representations" constituted a prior breach of the contract by Meritage, which excused SP Terrace from further performance and entitled SP Terrace to retain the earnest money deposit and recover actual damages, including lost profits, of at least $1,400,000.

Meritage argues that because SP Terrace always possessed the earnest money deposit, and if SP Terrace prevailed or Meritage abandoned its claim, SP Terrace would simply retain the earnest money. Therefore, SP Terrace's counterclaim, which asks the trial court to determine that SP Terrace is entitled to the earnest money, is essentially a claim for declaratory relief. We disagree. SP Terrace asked the trial court to determine it has a right to the earnest money deposit, but it also seeks actual damages beyond the earnest money deposit. *See Howell v. Mauzy,* 899 S.W.2d 690, 706 (Tex.App.-Austin 1994, writ denied) ("A court may allow a declaratory-judgment counterclaim, however, if it is something more than a mere denial of the plaintiff's claim and has greater ramifications than the original suit. A counterclaim has greater ramifications than the original suit if it seeks affirmative relief.") (internal citations omitted). We hold that SP Terrace's allegations state a claim for relief independent of Meritage's breach of contract claim. If the trier of fact concludes that Meritage has waived performance of the substantial completion deadline and was in breach of the agreement, then SP Terrace is entitled to pursue its claim for breach.

B. Earnest Money as Liquidated Damages

SP Terrace asked the trial court to set aside the earnest money liquidated damages provision for a breach by Meritage, contending that it penalizes Meritage because it requires Meritage to forfeit its earnest money no matter how trivial its breach. SP Terrace requests this interpretation of the contract so that its damages claim against Meritage can exceed the earnest money deposit it kept after Meritage terminated the contract. The clause in question provides that, upon default by Meritage, SP Terrace, as its sole remedy, may terminate the contract and retain the earnest money deposit.

We enforce a liquidated damages clause if (1) the harm caused by the breach is incapable or difficult of estimation, and (2) the amount of liquidated damages is a reasonable forecast of just compensation. . . . An assertion that a liquidated damages provision constitutes an unenforceable penalty is an affirmative defense, and the party asserting penalty bears the burden of proof. . . . Generally, that party must prove the amount of actual damages, if any, to demonstrate that "the actual loss was not an approximation of the stipulated sum." *Baker v. Int'l Record Syndicate, Inc.,* 812 S.W.2d 53, 55 (Tex.App.-Dallas 1991, no writ). If the amount stipulated in the liquidated damages clause is "shown to be disproportionate to actual damages," we should declare that the clause is a penalty and limit recovery to actual damages. *Johnson Eng'rs, Inc. v. Tri-Water Supply Corp.,* 582 S.W.2d 555, 557 (Tex.Civ.App.-Texarkana 1979, no writ); *see also* TEX. BUS. & COM.CODE ANN. § 2.718(a) (Vernon 2009) ("A term fixing unreasonably large liquidated damages is void as a penalty."). Whether a liquidated damages clause is an unenforceable penalty is a question of law for the court, but sometimes factual issues must be resolved before the court can decide the legal question. *See Phillips,* 820 S.W.2d at 788. For example, in *Phillips,* the Texas Supreme Court observed that "to show that a liquidated damages provision is unreasonable because the actual damages incurred were much less than the amount contracted for, a defendant may be required to prove what the actual damages were." *Id.*

SP Terrace adduced no evidence in the trial court that Meritage's forfeit of its earnest money operated as a penalty because Meritage's breach was a trivial one. Its aim was just the opposite—it was to prove that Meritage's breach caused damages far higher than the earnest money amount, although it offered no proof of that theory either. We decline to remove a limitation of remedy provision absent any evidence that the liquidated amount in the contract is unreasonably high or low in light of the alleged breach. . . .

SP Terrace relies on cases in which courts have disregarded liquidated damages provisions as unreasonable in their approximation of actual damages for trivial breaches. *See Stewart v. Basey,* 150 Tex. 666, 245 S.W.2d 484, 487 (1952) ("Our conclusion is that, since the contract provided the same reparation for the breach of each and every covenant, and since it would be unreasonable and a violation of the principle of just compensation to enforce it as to some of them, the provision for stipulated damages should be treated as a penalty."); *Community Dev. Serv., Inc. v. Replacement Parts Mfg., Inc.,* 679 S.W.2d 721, 727 (Tex.App.-Houston [1st Dist.] 1984, no writ) (holding that liquidated damages clause in earnest money contract was unenforceable penalty, because even though it provided reasonable damages for major breaches of the contract, it also allowed unreasonable damages for trivial breaches); *Bethel v. Butler Drilling Co.,* 635 S.W.2d 834, 837–38 (Tex.App.-Houston [14th Dist.] 1982, writ ref'd n.r.e.) (holding same). These cases are distinguishable in that either it was the breaching party who argued that the provision was a penalty, or in that the party seeking to set aside the provision adduced evidence that the liquidated damages clause was not a reasonable approximation of damages caused by the breach. *See Stewart,* 245 S.W.2d at 487 (where actual damages incurred by breaching party amounted to $38.50, "stipulation to pay several thousand dollars . . . would be so unreasonable that no court would lend its power to enforce it"); *Community Dev.,* 679 S.W.2d at 727 (jury findings and evidence supported claim that earnest money provision operated as penalty); *Bethel,* 635 S.W.2d at 843 (upholding trial court's determination that liquidated damages clause was penalty against breaching party, and limiting plaintiff's recovery to actual damages).

A liquidated damages provision is a penalty if it punishes the breaching party by subjecting it to a disproportionately high amount of damages relative to reasonably anticipated actual damages. Absent evidence that the earnest money amount here was not a reasonable approximation of an anticipated breach, limiting recovery to the earnest money deposit and preventing a party from recovering actual damages in excess of the bargained for liquidated amount does not constitute a penalty to the breaching party.[2] We decline to hold as a matter of law that the

---

[2] Other jurisdictions that have addressed this issue have held similarly, and refused to strike the liquidated damages provision on the ground that it is an unenforceable penalty. See, e.g., Mahoney v. Tingley, 85 Wash.2d 95, 529 P.2d 1068, 1070 (1975) ("A penalty exists where there is an attempt to enforce an obligation to pay a sum fixed by agreement of the parties as a punishment for the failure to fulfill some primary contractual obligation. In this case, it is not the party in default who seeks relief from an excessively high liquidated damages provision. Rather, the provision operates to limit the recovery of the party who incurred a loss as a result of the other parties' breach. There being no element of punishment involved, it cannot be said that plaintiff is being penalized in any sense.")(internal citations omitted); Margaret H. Wayne Trust v. Lipsky, 123 Idaho 253, 846 P.2d 904, 910 (1993) (following Mahoney and refusing to strike down liquidated damages provision as penalty when non-breaching party sought damages in excess of provision amount).

earnest money provision in this case is a penalty. *Cf. Phillips*, 820 S.W.2d at 788–89 (no fact issue that provision was penalty against breaching party because it provided that actual damages be determined and multiplied tenfold).

* * *

Conclusion

We hold that SP Terrace failed to raise a fact issue on its affirmative defenses of modification and interference by Meritage, but raises fact issues whether Meritage waived performance of the December 31 substantial completion deadline and whether Meritage caused delay that extended the time for performance. We further hold that SP Terrace's counterclaim states a claim for affirmative relief, but that SP Terrace fails to prove on this record that the earnest money provision of the contract is unenforceable as a matter of law. We therefore reverse and remand the case for further proceedings.

NOTES AND QUESTIONS

1.   *Is the classification of a clause as a "penalty" a question of law or fact?* The court notes that "[w]hether a liquidated damages clause is an unenforceable penalty is a question of law for the court, but sometimes factual issues must be resolved before the court can decide the legal question." What situations would likely create issues for the finder of fact? When would a court legitimately decide the penalty issue as a matter of law without first making findings of fact? Other courts have held that a court may invalidate a penalty clause as a matter of law where the punitive nature of the clause appears from the face of the document. *See, e.g., Board of Co. Comm. of Adams Co. v. City & Co. of Denver*, 40 P.3d 25 (2001) (ruling that the issue of penalty or not is one of law if the effect of the clause as a penalty is capable of determination on the face of the document; if not, the issue is one of fact.) Does this approach make sense? What evidence would be introduced to establish that the "liquidated damages" clause was a reasonable approximation of foreseeable damage and that quantification of any such damages would (from the perspective of the parties at the time of reaching agreement) be difficult in the event of breach?

2.   *Intent of the parties to liquidate damages in advance.* The *SP Terrace* court adopts a two-prong test for assessing the validity of the liquidated damages clause: "(1) the harm caused by the breach is incapable or difficult of estimation, and (2) the amount of liquidated damages is a reasonable forecast of just compensation." Other courts, such as the *Adams County* court referenced in Note 1, apply a three-prong test for assessing the validity of the liquidated damages clause: "(1) at the time the contract was entered into, the anticipated damages in case of breach were difficult to ascertain; (2) the parties mutually intended to liquidate them in advance; and (3) the amount of liquidated damages, when viewed as of the time the contract was made, was a reasonable estimate of the potential actual damages the breach would cause."

How do these standards compare to the elements of the Restatement (Second) of Contracts § 356 test? Is there room in the § 356 test for an intent element?

3.   *Labeling and disguising liquidated damages and penalty clauses.* Merely labeling a clause as "liquidated damages," a "penalty," or even a discount for early performance will not control a court's analysis of whether the clause in fact represents liquidated damages or is an impermissible penalty. The comments to Restatement (Second) of Contracts § 356 expressly provide that the parties' characterization has no significance in the liquidated damages/penalty clause analysis. "Although the parties may in good faith contract for alternative performance and fix discounts or valuations, a court will look to the substance of the agreement to determine whether this is the case or whether the parties have attempted to disguise a provision for a penalty that is unenforceable under this Section." Restatement (Second) of Contracts § 356, *cmt. d.*

4.   *The danger of "blunderbuss" drafting.* Suppose that a builder and an owner contract for $1,000 in liquidated damages in the event of any breach of their building contract. The common law standard requires that the liquidated damages reasonably approximate the anticipated or actual damages and that the damages be difficult to prove. Why would such a lump sum liquidated damages award potentially violate that standard? Which element of the common law standard would such a clause violate?

5.   *Liquidated damages and freedom of contract.* What, if anything, justifies the common law and UCC § 2–718 suspicion toward liquidated damages clauses? Is the judicial hostility to penalty clauses merely a holdover from ossified historical resistance to such contract terms? Or is it based upon jealousy regarding private parties attempting to encroach upon the damages-setting functions of the courts? Alternatively, do liquidated damages rules represent state paternalism and a lack of trust in the capacity of contracting parties to assess and consent to the damages they are willing to pay at the time of contract formation? See Anthony T. Kronman, "Paternalism and the Law of Contracts," 92 Yale L.J. 763, 776–77 (1983).

6.   *Liquidated damages and unconscionability.* Assume that courts are concerned with liquidated damages clauses because of the potential unfairness of penalties and the fact that contracting parties may not sufficiently appreciate the risks associated with such clauses. If that is the case, would unconscionability doctrine be a better tool for regulating and policing such clauses? See Larry A. DiMatteo, "A Theory of Efficient Penalty: Eliminating the Law of Liquidated Damages," 38 Am. Bus. L.J. 633, 655–57 (2001). Why or why not?

7.   *The "no actual damages" defense.* A number of courts have held that even if a liquidated damages clause reasonably estimates anticipated damages at the time of contracting, equity prohibits enforcement of such clauses if the nonbreaching party did not suffer any actual loss. See, e.g., Susan V. Ferris, "Liquidated Damages Recovery Under the Restatement (Second) of Contracts," 67 Cornell L. Rev. 862, 866–67 (1982). The commentary to § 356 supports this

rule: "If, to take an extreme case, it is clear that no loss at all has occurred, a provision fixing a substantial sum as damages is unenforceable." Restatement (Second) of Contracts § 356, *cmt. b.* Does this rule make sense? Alternatively, should courts apply this rule only in situations where the absence of actual damages was not foreseeable as a consequence of breach?

8.   *Should the presence of a "liquidated damages" clause in the contract preclude a grant of specific performance?* The terms of the contract themselves may affect the availability of equitable relief. Consider, for example, the implications of a valid liquidated damages clause. To be valid, the clause must be a reasonable approximation of the parties' damages at the time of execution and the time of breach or trial, but still be uncertain. Such a term then provides a schizophrenic implication with respect to the propriety of equitable relief. On the one hand, the mere existence of the liquidated damages clause impliedly represents an agreement by the parties that the liquidated money damages will compensate in the event of a breach. On the other hand, the requirements necessary for the validity of the liquidated damages clause are similar to the arguments necessary to show the unavailability of equitable relief. E. Allan Farnsworth suggested that a liquidated damages term, by itself, should not preclude a claim for equitable relief, but a contract provision prohibiting equitable relief should bar an order of specific performance, providing the parties clearly demonstrate that intent. See E. Allan Farnsworth, Contracts § 12.6 (4th ed. 2004) ("Nor does a provision for liquidated damages preclude the grant of specific performance or injunction instead of or in addition to the award of such damages, though a clear provision to the contrary will be given effect."); 25 Samuel Williston & Richard A. Lord, A Treatise on the Law of Contracts § 67:9 (4th ed. 2002). Restatement (Second) of Contracts § 361, perhaps not surprisingly, supports Farnsworth's position. Do you agree or disagree with Farnsworth's argument? Or should the parties' agreement to a valid liquidated damages clause be deemed conclusive proof that damages would adequately compensate the parties in the event of breach?

Unconscionability and Liquidated Damages

In December 2013, John and Jennifer Palmer—husband and wife—filed suit against Internet retailer KlearGear.com seeking damages for KlearGear's alleged bad faith attempt to collect a debt of $3,500. According to news stories and the Palmers' complaint, John, in December 2008, ordered from KlearGear a keychain and desk toy costing approximately $20. The goods never arrived, and by February 2009, Jennifer had made multiple unsuccessful attempts to contact KlearGear. She posted a short negative review of KlearGear on a consumer complaints website, RipoffReport.com. Three years later, in May 2012, KlearGear notified John that the RipoffReport.com review violated KlearGear's Terms of Use that John had accepted by clicking a box on KlearGear's website stating that he had read the terms. Specifically, the Terms of Use prohibited customers from "taking any action that negatively impacts KlearGear.com, its reputation, products, services, management or employees."

The nondisparagement clause further provided for liquidated damages of $3,500.

KlearGear rejected John's arguments that Jennifer (who did not accept the KlearGear terms) posted the negative review, rejected claims that the nondisparagement clause was not actually in the KlearGear.com Terms of Use until April 2012, and then informed John that he was also liable for an additional $50 dispute resolution fee. KlearGear referred the matter to a collection agency, allegedly causing injury to the Palmers' credit and reputation. In 2014, the Utah federal district court issued a default judgment against KlearGear for $306,750 for compensatory and punitive damages and attorneys fees. See Cyrus Farivar, "KlearGear must pay $306,750 to couple who left negative review," Ars Technica, June 25, 2014, http://arstechnica.com/tech-policy/2014/06/kleargear-must-pay-306750-to-couple-that-left-negative-review/; Palmer v. Kleargear.com, Complaint, Case No. 1:13-cv-00175, U.S. District Court for Utah, December 18, 2013.

Because of the default judgment, there was no judicial ruling on the enforceability of the nondisparagement, liquidated damages, and dispute resolution fee clauses. Are any of these clauses enforceable? What role might the doctrine of unconscionability play with respect to the enforceability of a liquidated damages clause such as those here? Does unconscionability provide any meaningful additional protection against abusive penalty provisions?

2. REMEDIES MODIFIED BY CONTRACT

Personal Injury. Under a system of contract law based upon principles of freedom of contract and private autonomy, parties should be able to modify, change, or contract out of default rules regarding recovery of damages for breach of contract. In non-coercive contexts, the parties should be free to prescribe, by mutual agreement, the scope and extent of any remedies to be available for breach. In short, for parties to a contract, contract will trump the tort of negligence, subject to important restrictions in the case of personal injury. While generally true, public policy considerations prohibit certain types of remedies modifications, such as the prohibition on penalties for breach of contract discussed above and, as discussed in this section, limits on damages for some types of personal injury claims resulting from a contractual relationship. See Todd D. Rakoff, "Contracts of Adhesion: An Essay in Reconstruction," 96 Harv. L. Rev. 1173, 1261 (1983); Larry A. DiMatteo, "Equity's Modification of Contract: An Analysis of the Twentieth Century's Equitable Reformation of Contract Law," 33 New Eng. L. Rev. 265, 276–77 (1999).

As a general rule, parties may agree by contract to act with respect to one another in a manner that would be tortious in the absence of such a contract. Likewise, the parties may also contract to limit their liability to one another for negligence in the course of their contractual relationship.

Consequently, to some extent, the parties may subordinate tort principles to contract through their voluntary agreements. See E. Allan Farnsworth, "Contracts Is Not Dead," 77 Cornell L. Rev. 1034, 1034–35 (1992). But public policy prohibits such limitations depending on the nature of the parties' business and/or the degree of intent involved in the tort. First, Restatement (Second) of Contracts § 195(1) provides that parties may not contract to limit or exclude liability for intentional or reckless torts. Thus, a contract between a racetrack owner and a driver purporting to exclude liability for personal injury is enforceable to the extent the driver suffers personal injuries caused by mere negligence. On the other hand, if the track owner intentionally or recklessly refused to clean up an oil slick, in the hopes of boosting revenues from crowds looking for more dangerous races, the clause would not bar claims for crash injuries resulting from the intentional or reckless tort.

Second, § 195(2) extends this public policy limitation on the right of parties to limit tort liability for personal injuries caused by negligence to providers of certain classes of contracts. These include clauses limiting or excluding (1) employer liability for injuries to employees in the course of their employment; (2) liability of persons "charged with a duty of public service" for injuries to persons to whom that duty is owed; and (3) liability "where the other party is a member of a class protected against the class to which the first party belongs." Restatement (Second) of Contracts § 195(2)(a)–(c). The first instance is relatively unambiguous. The class of persons "charged with a duty of public service," in contrast, varies and continues to develop in some jurisdictions. Five hundred years ago, the common law declared that an innkeeper would not be permitted to contract out of liability for negligence. Somewhat later, common carriers were similarly precluded from contracting out of liability. Innkeepers and common carriers were viewed as performing essential functions imbued with a strong public interest. See James F. Hogg, "Consumer Beware: The Varied Application of Unconscionability Doctrine to Exculpation and Indemnification Clauses in Michigan, Minnesota, and Washington," 2006 Mich. St. L. Rev. 1011. Other disciplines potentially charged with a duty of public service include hospitals, doctors, public utilities, public warehousemen, employers, and services involving extra-hazardous activities. See Schlobohm v. Spa Petite, Inc., 326 N.W.2d 920, 925 (Minn. 1982).

Finally, § 195(3) represents a potential conflict between contract and products liability tort law by permitting sellers to limit their special tort liability for physical injuries where "the term is fairly bargained for and is consistent with the policy underlying that liability." As Professor Farnsworth once quipped,

> [Under Restatement (Second) of Contracts § 195], a term
> exempting the seller of a product from special tort liability for

physical harm to a user or a consumer is enforceable if the term is "fairly bargained for and is consistent with the policy underlying that liability." If you think that is too cautious a statement of freedom of contract, take a look at comment m to section 402A of the Restatement (Second) of Torts, which says that you simply cannot disclaim the liability stated in that section. It took some diplomatic skill to get the American Law Institute to do a flip-flop and say in the black letter something that was the opposite of what they said in the torts comment.

E. Allan Farnsworth, "Contracts Is Not Dead," 77 Cornell L. Rev. 1034, 1034–35 (1992). "Under the 1964 Restatement Second [Torts], manufacturers had no power to disclaim strict liability for personal injury by contractual provisions accompanying the product's sale." Dan B. Dobbs, The Law of Torts § 371 (2001); see also Restatement (Third) of Torts: Products Liability § 18 (1998). While the Restatement (Second) of Contracts § 195(3) appears to provide a mechanism by which parties of relatively equal bargaining power can limit their strict tort product liability, most courts seem to have followed the position of the torts restatement. See David B. Gaebler, "Negligence, Economic Loss, and the U.C.C.," 61 Ind. L.J. 593, 627–28 & n. 176 (1986).

Terms designed to restrict or eliminate otherwise available common law remedies for breach of contract can take a variety of forms. They may start by negating the existence of a particular promise-based duty (such as by excluding warranties express or implied); they may expressly allocate any particular risk to one party or the other; they may impose a dollar cap on any liability; they may define a specific dollar amount as the sole and exclusive remedy for breach (liquidated damages); they may require the aggrieved party to indemnify or hold the breaching party harmless; or they may prescribe an exclusive remedy for breach, negligent or otherwise, such as repair or replacement. They may also contain a "forum selection" clause (see *Carnival Cruise Lines, Inc. v. Shute*, Chapter 3) or an arbitration clause (see *Hill v. Gateway 2000, Inc.*, Chapter 3). The law of "unconscionability" (discussed in Chapter 6) restricts the enforceability of remedies limitations that unfairly deprive the injured party of a remedy but has been slow and somewhat erratic in its development. See Blake D. Morant in "The Teachings of Dr. Martin Luther King, Jr., and Contract Theory: An Intriguing Comparison," 50 Ala. L. Rev. 63 (1998); Daniel D. Barnhizer analyzed these complexities in "Inequality of Bargaining Power," 76 U. Colo. L. Rev. 139 (2005). See also Melvin A. Eisenberg, "The Bargain Principle and Its Limits," 95 Harv. L. Rev. 741 (1982).

As you read the following case, consider the relationship between the doctrine of unconscionability and the standards relating to contract clauses excluding or limiting liability. Why do parties include such terms in their contracts? Is a contract term that provides the injured party no meaningful relief for breach or personal injury enforceable? See David S. Schwartz, "Understanding Remedy-Stripping Arbitration Clauses: Validity, Arbitrability, and Preclusion Principles," 38 U.S.F. L. Rev. 49 (2003). Is it possible for even a dickered liability limitation to produce substantive unfairness that renders the clause unconscionable?

SCHRIER V. BELTWAY ALARM COMPANY

Court of Special Appeals of Maryland
73 Md.App. 281, 533 A.2d 1316 (1987)

ALPERT, Judge.

Appellants, Eugene and Sheila Schrier, filed suit against the Beltway Alarm Co. in the Circuit Court for Prince George's County to recover damages for injuries Mr. Schrier sustained during a robbery of Veteran's Liquors, Inc., a liquor store conducted in corporate form in which appellants were principal shareholders. The trial court held valid and enforceable a $250.00 limitation of liability provision in the parties' contract and granted summary judgment in favor of Beltway for claims in excess of that amount. Pursuant to Md. Courts & Jud. Proc. Code Ann. § 4–402 (1984), the court also dismissed appellants' claim for lack of subject matter jurisdiction, the amount in controversy having been adjudicated as being less than $500. The pertinent facts are not in dispute.

In September 1977 Mr. Schrier, on behalf of Veteran's Liquors, entered into an "Alarm Protection Agreement" with Beltway Alarm Co. for the installation and maintenance of a "central station connected hold-up" system. Appellant agreed to pay a $287.00 installation fee, and $49.50 per month for a 3-year service contract. In November 1980, the parties entered into a second contract calling for monthly payments of $65.85 for continued maintenance of the system. Both contracts contained language limiting appellee's liability in the event of loss or damage due to a breach of contract or negligence in performance by Beltway. Specific pertinent language of the controlling 1980 contract will be provided in our discussion infra.

Mr. Schrier was shot and severely wounded on August 31, 1981 during the course of a hold-up of his liquor store. In the suit filed against Beltway subsequent thereto, Mr. Schrier alleged that he had activated two alarm buttons during the robbery but prior to the shooting. The Schriers filed counts in negligence, breach of contract, and breach of warranty, alleging that Beltway delayed 14 minutes in notifying the police department of the alarm, and that but for this delay Mr. Schrier would not have been shot.

In this appeal, Schrier contend that:

I. Paragraph 8 of the contract is an invalid liquidated damages clause.

II. The limitation of liability clause is void as a matter of public policy.

III. Appellants have a cause of action in negligence.

IV. Appellants are not bound by the liquidated damages provision of the contract.

We find no merit in any of appellants' theories; therefore, we affirm.

I.

Preliminarily, we note the parties' difficulty in characterizing the nature of Paragraph 8. Although the language appears to be standard in the alarm industry, Fireman's Fund Am. Ins. Cos. v. Burns Elec. Sec. Servs., Inc., 93 Ill. App. 3d 298, 417 N.E.2d 131, 417 N.E.2d 131, 132 (1981), the companies' desire to "cover all the bases" by characterizing the language as both liquidated damages and a limitation of liability has no doubt contributed to the problem. As we explain, however, "there is no real distinction for present purposes between a liquidated damage clause, a limited [liability] clause and an exculpatory clause." General Bargain Center v. American Alarm Co., 430 N.E.2d 407, 412 (Ind. App. 1982).

Paragraph 8 of the Agreement *sub judice* provided in part:

STATUS OF PARTIES, LIMITATION OF LIABILITY, LIQUIDATED DAMAGE PROVISION AND INDEMNITY AGREEMENT.

* * *

(b) Subscriber acknowledges that it is impractical and extremely difficult to fix the actual damages, if any, which may proximately result from a failure to perform any of the obligations herein or a failure of the system to operate because of, among other things: The uncertain amount or value of Subscriber's property or the property of others which may be lost or damaged; the uncertainty of the response time of the police or fire department; the inability to ascertain what portion, if any, of any loss would be proximately caused by Company's failure to perform any of its obligations or failure of its equipment to operate; the nature of the services to be performed by Company;

(c) Subscriber understand [sic] and agrees that if Company should be found liable for any loss or damage due from a failure to perform any of its obligations or a failure of the equipment to operate, Company's liability shall be limited to a sum equal to the total of six monthly payments or Two Hundred Fifty Dollars ($250.00) whichever is the lesser, as liquidated damages and not as a penalty and this liability shall be exclusive and shall apply if

> loss or damage, irrespective of cause of origin, results directly or indirectly to persons or property from performance or nonperformance of any of the obligations herein or from negligence, active or otherwise of Company, its employees or agents; . . .

Some courts have designated contract provisions similar to this as exculpatory, others as a limitation of liability, and still others label it as a liquidated damages clause. Regardless of the nomenclature, courts have uniformly upheld these contract clauses. . . .

Appellants first characterize paragraph 8 as a liquidated damages clause and argue that it is invalid because it provides for a penalty. Although we disagree with appellants' characterization of the disputed language, . . . we will address their argument because the enforceability of any type of limitation of damages clause with respect to a contract for a burglar alarm system is a question of first impression in Maryland. Exculpatory clauses and liquidated damages clauses have been upheld in other contexts, however, and are helpful to our determination of this case.

In the seminal case regarding exculpatory clauses, Winterstein v. Wilcom, 16 Md. App. 130, 293 A.2d 821, cert. den., 266 Md. 744 (1972), this court upheld an exculpatory agreement that relieved Wilcom of all liability for negligent conduct relating to activities at the "75–80 Drag-A-Way," a track where "automobile timing and acceleration runs were conducted on two racing lanes." Although Drag-A-Way had employees in a tower to detect any hazards on the track, no one warned Winterstein of a "cylinder head approximately 36" long, 6" wide and 4" high, weighing approximately 100 pounds . . . which was not visible to him when he commenced the race" but was visible to the employees in the tower. Winterstein hit the cylinder, lost control of the car, jumped a ditch, drove up an embankment and turned over. He sustained "serious, painful and permanent injuries." Id. at 133, 293 A.2d 821. Winterstein sued Wilcom, d/b/a Drag-A-Way for his injuries, alleging negligence. On the basis of the exculpatory "Release" signed by Winterstein, the trial court entered summary judgment for Drag-A-Way. Affirming the summary judgment, we explained:

> It is clear that the exculpatory provisions involved in the case before us whereby Winterstein expressly agreed in advance that Wilcom would not be liable for the consequences of conduct which would otherwise be negligent were under the general rule recognizing the validity of such provisions. There was not the slightest disadvantage in bargaining power between the parties. Winterstein was under no compulsion, economic or otherwise, to race his car. He obviously participated in the speed runs simply because he wanted to do so, perhaps to demonstrate the

superiority of his car and probably with the hope of winning a prize. This put him in no bargaining disadvantage. . . .

The short of it is that as to the releases here the effect of the exemptive clauses upon the public interest was nil. We find that each release was merely an agreement between persons relating entirely to their private affairs. In the absence of a legislative declaration, we hold that they were not void as against public policy. *Id.* at 138–39, 293 A.2d 821.

Likewise, it is well-settled that liquidated damage clauses are recognized and enforced in Maryland. *Blood v. Gibbons,* 288 Md. 268, 418 A.2d 213 (1980); *Cowan v. Meyer,* 125 Md. 450, 94 A. 18 (1915). The parties to a contract may stipulate to a specific amount of damages to be recovered by either for a breach of the agreement by the other. *Traylor v. Grafton,* 273 Md. 649, 332 A.2d 651 (1975). Breach of the contract, not an injury sustained by the other party, imposes the liability to pay the contractual damages. *Id.; Cowan, supra.* If, however, as appellants herein argue, the contract provision is actually intended as a penalty, it will not be enforced. *Id.* The following statement of the rule is still the law today:

[W]here the parties, at or before the time of the execution of the contract, agree upon and name a sum therein to be paid as liquidated damages, in lieu of anticipated damages which are in their nature uncertain and incapable of exact ascertainment, the amount so named in the agreement will be regarded as liquidated damages and not as a penalty, unless the amount so agreed upon and inserted in the agreement be grossly excessive and out of all proportion to the damages that might reasonably have been expected to result from such breach of the contract. And whether it is excessive or whether the damages are incapable of exact ascertainment should be determined from the subject matter of the contract considered in the light of all the surrounding facts and circumstances connected therewith and known to the parties at the time of its execution. That these questions should be considered and determined from the contract itself, its subject-matter and the surrounding facts and circumstances connected therewith with which the parties are confronted at the time of its execution, is made necessary in order to ascertain the intention of the parties, which is one of the essential factors in deciding whether the stipulation is for liquidated damages or is a penalty. It may afterwards be disclosed that the damages actually sustained are more or less than those anticipated at the time of the execution of the contract. If more, this fact would not characterize or stamp the stipulation as a penalty unless it was so exorbitant as to clearly show that such amount was not arrived at in a *bona fide* effort, made at or before the execution of the contract, to estimate the damages that might have been reasonably expected to result from a breach of it, and that it was named as a penalty for such breach. And on the other hand, if the amount stipulated was found to be inadequate, a greater amount could not be recovered for such breach, because of the agreement between the parties that the amount so named should be in lieu of the damages resulting therefrom. *Baltimore Bridge Co. v. United.*

Paragraph 8(b) of the agreement *sub judice* addresses the parties' inability to ascertain the extent of the damages that might be incurred as a result of a failure of the alarm system. . . . We . . . find no merit in appellants' argument that paragraph 8 is invalid as a penalty.

Its caption notwithstanding, we conclude that the contract clause at issue is a "limitation of liability" and not liquidated damages. Although every valid agreement for liquidated damages operates as a form of limitation, a contractual limitation of liability to an agreed maximum should be distinguished from a penalty or liquidated damages. 5A Williston on Contracts § 781A (3d ed. 1961). Liquidated damages is a "specific sum of money agreed upon as the amount of damages to be recovered for a breach of the agreement." Traylor, 273 Md. at 661, 332 A.2d 651. This distinction was also noted in Restatement of Contracts § 339, comment g (1932):

> An agreement limiting the amount of damages recoverable for breach is not an agreement to pay either liquidated damages or a penalty. Except in the case of certain public service contracts, the contracting parties can by agreement limit their liability in damages to a specified amount, either at the time of making their principal contract, or subsequently thereto.

Although paragraph 8 refers to "liquidated damages," the obvious purpose of the provision is clearly to limit Beltway's liability to the specified $250.00 amount. The controlling language is contained in subsection (c):

> if Company should be found liable for any loss or damage due from a failure to perform any of its obligations or a failure of the equipment to operate, *Company's liability shall be limited to* a sum equal to the total of six monthly payments or Two Hundred Fifty Dollars ($250.00) whichever is the lesser, as liquidated damages and not as a penalty.

Thus, unlike a true liquidated damages clause, under a "limitation of liability" clause: (1) damages, not merely breach of contract, must be proved; and (2) liability varies according to the extent of the injury up to the stated maximum. See Central Alarm v. Ganem, 116 Ariz. 74, 567 P. 2d

1203, 1207 (App. 1977) ("if the loss to the customer was $150, the expressed mutual assent was that recovery should be $150 and not $312," [the company's maximum liability under the contract]); accord General Bargain Center v. American Alarm Co., 430 N.E.2d 407, 411 (Ind. App. 1982); Vallance & Co. v. DeAnda, 595 S.W. 2d 587, 590 (Tex. Civ. App. 1980).

Unlike a liquidated damages clause, it is immaterial whether a limitation of liability is a reasonable estimate of probable damages resulting from a breach. 5A Williston on Contracts, § 781A (3d ed. 1961); Vallance & Co. v. DeAnda, 595 S.W. 2d at 590. A limitation of liability is not a penalty "in that it does not normally operate *in terrorem* to induce proper performance." Williston, supra; Restatement of Contracts § 339, comment g.

As we noted in our discussion on liquidated damages, the amount stated in the contract will be held invalid as a penalty only if it is "grossly excessive and out of all proportion to the damages that might reasonably have been expected to result from such breach of the contract." Baltimore Bridge Co. v. United Rwys. & Elec. Co., 125 Md. 208, 214–15, 94 A. 18 (1915). Rather than a harsh penalty, what we confront sub judice is "essentially the other side of the coin, to wit, a limitation of liability under circumstances clearly warranting such a limitation." Guthrie v. American Protection Indus., 160 Cal. App. 3d 951, 955, 206 Cal. Rptr. 834 (1984).

Appellants also contend that the disputed clause is unconscionable, in particular because personal injury is involved. Citing Md. Comm. Law Code Ann. § 2–719(3) and dicta in Fireman's Fund American Insurance Cos. v. Burns Electronic Security Services, Inc., 93 Ill.App.3d 298, 48 Ill.Dec. 729, 417 N.E.2d 131, 134 (1981) ("The case might be different had the alarm done or threatened personal injury, which has a special place in the law."), appellants argue that "the limitation [is] particularly abhorrent" in the face of personal injuries. Thus, appellants urge this court to adopt a dual standard: one for property damage and another for personal injury.

Clearly § 2–719(3) is inapplicable to the case at bar because consumer goods are not involved. Nor has the Maryland Legislature seen fit to declare invalid limitations on liability for personal injury except in agreements between landlord and tenant. See Md. Real Prop. Code Ann. § 8–105 (1981). This invalidation of some exculpatory clauses in residential leases was enacted in response to Eastern Ave. Corp. v. Hughes, 228 Md. 477, 180 A. 2d 486 (1962), in which the Court of Appeals upheld a lease clause which relieved the landlord of liability for injuries to the tenant and for damage to the tenant's property. The legislature to date has not extended this prohibition to agreements other than between landlords and tenants.

Nor do we find this limitation of liability unconscionable for any other reason. In affirming a summary judgment for the defendant alarm company in an analogous case, the Court of Appeals of Michigan reasoned:

> This is not an individual versus a monopoly. Here, both parties to the contract are corporations dealing at arms length. . . . The contract clause limiting defendant's liability to the aggregate of six monthly payments or $250 is manifestly reasonable under the circumstances of this case. Defendant is not in the insurance business. Rather, it provides an alarm service for a specific sum. That sum is not a premium for theft insurance.

St. Paul Fire & Marine Ins. Co. v. Guardian Alarm Co., 115 Mich. App. 278, 320 N.W. 2d 244, 247 (1982). Similarly, the Court of Appeals of California stated:

> [I]t is our opinion that it would be impossible in any case to prove, after the fact, that an operative alarm system would have prevented the crime. Consequently, it would be impossible to prove that the failure of an alarm system *caused any damage.*

> Most persons, especially operators of business establishments, carry insurance for loss due to various types of crimes. Presumptively insurance companies who issue such policies base their premiums on their assessment of the value of the property and the vulnerability of the premises. No reasonable person could expect the provider of an alarm service would, for a fee unrelated to the value of the property, undertake to provide an identical type coverage should the alarm fail to prevent a crime. Guthrie v. American Protection Indus., 160 Cal.App.3d 951, 954, 206 Cal.Rptr.3d 951 (1984) (emphasis in original).

The reasoning of both the California and Michigan Courts of Appeal is applicable equally to the limitation of liability clause at bar. Paragraph 8(a) provides:

> (a) It is understood and agreed by the parties hereto that Company is not an insurer and that insurance, if any, covering personal injury and property loss or damage on Subscriber's premises shall be obtained by the Subscriber; that the payments provided for herein are based solely on the value of the service as set forth herein and are unrelated to the value of Subscriber's property or the property of others located on Subscriber's premises; that Company makes no guarantee or warranty including any implied warranty of merchantability or fitness that the system or service supplied will avert or prevent occurrences or the consequence therefrom which the system or service is intended to detect or prevent; . . .

We conclude that the parties reached a "commercially sensible arrangement," and we will not rewrite their agreement to compel the appellee to act as an insurer. The agreement is not one "such as no man in his senses and not under delusion would make on the one hand, and no honest and fair man would accept on the other. Earl of Chesterfield v. Janssen, 2 Ves. Sr. 125, 28 Eng. Rpr. 82 (1750)." Abel Holding Co. v. American Dist. Tel. Co., 138 N.J. Super. 137, 350 A.2d 292, 303–04 (1975). . . . The agreement sub judice, therefore, is valid and binding on the appellants.

II.

Appellants argue next that the limitation clause is invalid as a "transaction affected with a public interest." In Winterstein v. Wilcom, 293 A.2d 821, 16 Md.App. 130 (1972), this court adopted, from the Supreme Court of California, the following six factor test to determine whether a particular transaction involves an invalid exculpatory provision. We quoted:

> [T]he attempted but invalid exemption involves a transaction which exhibits some or all of the following characteristics. It concerns a business of a type generally thought suitable for public regulation. The party seeking exculpation is engaged in performing a service of great importance to the public, which is often a matter of practical necessity for some members of the public. The party holds himself out as willing to perform this service for any member of the public who seeks it, or at least for any member coming within certain established standards. As a result of the essential nature of the service, in the economic setting of the transaction, the party invoking exculpation possesses a decisive advantage of bargaining strength against any member of the public who seeks his services. In exercising a superior bargaining power the party confronts the public with a standardized adhesion contract of exculpation, and makes no provision whereby a purchaser may pay additional reasonable fees and obtain protection against negligence. Finally, as a result of the transaction, the person or property of the purchaser is placed under the control of the seller, subject to the risk of carelessness by the seller or his agents. *Id.* at 137, 293 A.2d 821 quoting *Tunkl v. Regents of the Univ. of Calif.,* 60 Cal.2d 92, 32 Cal.Rptr. 33, 383 P.2d 441 (1963).

Appellants argue that "there is a strong public interest in protecting the innocent public from burglars by the use of properly operating alarm systems," and that "there is a strong public concern in protecting business establishments from being forced to accept contracts of adhesion offered by alarm companies." Our application of the *Winterstein* test to the facts at bar, however, leads us to conclude that paragraph 8 is not invalid for public policy reasons. First, the burglar alarm business is not one deemed suited for public regulation. The local Prince George's County regulations referred to by appellant regulate the electrical work involved in the installation of the system. As appellee notes, the underlying intent of the regulations appears to be compliance with electrical codes, and the avoidance of false alarms that result in the needless summoning of the police. *See* Prince George's County Code § 9–130 *et seq.*

We do not consider the installation and maintenance of a burglar alarm system an "essential" service, although we do not dispute its importance. The burglar alarm industry is not performing a police function or public service. Although a shopkeeper may desire additional protection from crime, other alternatives such as a security guard or a special bulletproof enclosure for employees are available. Furthermore, the shopkeeper may purchase insurance that will compensate him for property loss and personal injury. Indeed, even the policy at bar offered appellants an opportunity to purchase additional coverage. Paragraph 8(d) provides:

> In the event that the subscriber wishes Company to assume greater liability, Subscriber may, as a matter of right, obtain from Company a higher limit by paying an additional amount to Company, and a rider shall be attached hereto setting forth such higher limit and additional amount, but this additional obligation shall in no way be interpreted to hold Company as an insurer. . . .

Appellants chose not to avail themselves of this right.

We conclude, therefore, that the parties were not in an unequal bargaining position and the contract, although preprinted and standardized, was not one of adhesion. Appellants had alternatives, and they entered the contract after full opportunity to consider the alternatives and study the terms of the contract. In addition, the contract contained a disclaimer of warranties in paragraph 21 which appeared in bold-face type. Finally, we do not find that appellants were "under the control of" the appellee within the meaning of the *Winterstein* test.

We hold that a contract for the installation and maintenance of a burglar alarm does not enter the realm of public utilities, common carriers, and those businesses that have been held to "affect the public interest." The limitation of liability clause, therefore, is valid.

III.

Appellants next allege a separate cause of action in negligence. We conclude, however, that this issue is also controlled by the parties' contract. Paragraph 8(c) clearly limits appellee's liability to a maximum of $250 for personal injury or property loss resulting "from performance or nonperformance of any of the obligations herein or from negligence, active or otherwise of Company, its employees or agents. . . ."

Inasmuch as we have recognized that there is no public policy against a party's contracting against liability for damage caused by his ordinary negligence, Boucher v. Riner, 68 Md. App. 539, 514 A.2d 485 (1986); Winterstein v. Wilcom, 16 Md. App. 130, 293 A.2d 821 (1972), our discussion upholding the limitation of liability under parts I and II, supra, apply with equal force to the issue of negligence. Accord Central Alarm v. Ganem, 116 Ariz. 74, 567 P. 2d 1203 (App. 1977). . . .

IV.

In their final argument, appellants contend that they are not parties to the contract; the contract was between Veteran's Liquors and Beltway Alarm. They argue, therefore, assuming arguendo the limitation of liability is valid, they are not individually bound. We find no merit to this argument.

Appellants are the principal shareholders of Veteran's Liquors, they admitted in their brief that Veteran's Liquors is their privately owned company, and Mr. Schrier executed the contract on behalf of the company. Functionally and effectively, appellants are "Veteran's Liquors," and are individually bound by the terms of the contract. . . .

Judgment affirmed. . . .

NOTES AND QUESTIONS

1. *Limiting liability by negating the duty of care that would otherwise underlie negligent conduct.* As discussed in Chapter 4, contracting parties generally may agree to limit or exclude warranties as a means of avoiding liability. See, e.g., UCC § 2–316. A sale "as is, where is," excludes all warranties and leaves little room for, or need of, a liability limitation clause. Did the alarm company exclude any duty of care? What is the meaning of the contract term providing, "that the Company makes no guarantee or warranty including any implied warranty of merchantability or fitness that the system or service supplied will avert or prevent occurrences or the consequences therefrom which the system or service is intended to detect or prevent; . . . "?

2. *The difference between a liquidated damages clause, a limited liability clause, and an exculpatory clause.* The court used the following quotation, "[T]here is no real distinction for present purposes between a liquidated damages clause, a limited [liability] clause and an exculpatory clause." Do you agree? If you do not agree, what are the differences between these three methods of fixing or limiting liability? Should public policy apply in the same way to all three or differently to one or more?

3. *A "low-ball" liquidated damages clause.* Liquidated damages clause cases normally deal with situations in which the liquidated damages far exceed (at least in the defendant's estimate) the amount of actual damages. Can a

liquidated damages provision be challenged because it fixes an unduly low, rather than high, amount? Does an unduly low liquidated damages amount satisfy the "reasonable approximation" element of the test for distinguishing liquidated damages from penalties? In sale of goods cases, UCC § 2–718(1) provides that "[a] term fixing unreasonably large liquidated damages is void as a penalty," but contains no comparable provision for clauses fixing damages at an unreasonably low amount. The comment to this section suggests, however, that such clauses may be unconscionable. See UCC § 2–718, *cmt. 1.* See also Debora L. Threedy, "Liquidated And Limited Damages And The Revision Of Article 2: An Opportunity To Rethink The U.C.C.'s Treatment of Agreed Remedies," 27 Idaho L. Rev. 427, 452–57 (1991). But UCC § 2–719 may permit the parties to achieve the same results by limiting or eliminating liability for breach. See Roy R. Anderson, "Liquidated Damages Under the Uniform Commercial Code," 41 Sw. L. J. 1083, 1106 (1988). Is it possible to reconcile these two sections?

4. *Distinguishing between personal and economic injuries.* Should courts apply different public policy considerations to the enforceability of exculpatory clauses in cases of personal injury versus economic injury? As noted above, the Restatement (Third) of Tort: Products Liability § 1 provides that a seller or distributor of a defective product is liable for personal or property injuries caused by the defect. UCC § 2–719(3) accords with this principle by expressly defining limitations of liability for personal injury in the case of consumer goods (but not commercial goods) as unconscionable. Notably, the court in this case, dealing with common law principles, refused to treat personal injury as a category of harm protected against the effect of an exculpatory clause. Do you agree or disagree with this rule?

5. *The difference between a cap on liability and an exculpatory clause.* Functionally, a cap on liability simply establishes a ceiling on damages beyond which, if the provision is enforceable, an award cannot go. The plaintiff is not relieved of responsibility for proving liability, but any liability that is proven is limited by the cap. Can you see why a liquidated damages clause will be thrown out if not based on a reasonable approximation of the potential harm, while there is apparently no such predicate of enforceability for a damages cap? An exculpatory clause, if enforceable, precludes the plaintiff from establishing liability—it has an effect similar to the extinction of the duty necessarily underlying the charge of negligence.

6. *Bargaining power and exculpation clauses.* Generally, bargaining power appears as an explicit element in only a few contract doctrines, including unconscionability, public policy, and the enforceability of certain potentially adhesive contract terms, such as forum selection clauses and exculpatory clauses. See Daniel D. Barnhizer, "Inequality of Bargaining Power," 76 U. Colo. L. Rev. 139, 144–50 (2005). What about the bargaining power relationship in the exculpation clause context justifies such explicit scrutiny? See James F. Hogg, "Consumer Beware: The Varied Application of Unconscionability Doctrine to Exculpation and Indemnification Clauses in Michigan, Minnesota, and Washington,"2006 Mich. St. L. Rev. 1011.

7. *Public interest and exculpatory clauses.* The plaintiff in *Schrier* argued that the court should invalidate the exculpatory clause because the burglary alarm business was "affected with a public interest." How does the court distinguish between such transactions and other, presumably non-public businesses? Why should the validity of the exculpatory clause depend on whether the contract deals with a subject matter in the public interest (admission to a charitable hospital for instance) or simply a private deal between two parties?

8. *Nondisclaimable warranties and statutory preclusion of exculpatory clauses.* The court comments on the fact that the state legislature had precluded landlord exculpation in landlord and tenant leases, and other jurisdictions impose a mandatory, nondisclaimable warranty of habitability into residential lease contracts. See Anthony T. Kronman, "Paternalism and the Law of Contracts," 92 Yale L.J. 763, 766–774 (1983). And some jurisdictions also impose nondisclaimable tort liability upon landlords who fail to take reasonable measures to protect their tenants from criminal acts by third parties. See William K. Jones, "Private Revision of Public Standards: Exculpatory Agreements in Leases," 63 N.Y.U. L. Rev. 717, 738–45 (1988) and Corey Mostafa, Comment, "The Implied Warranty of Habitability, Foreseeability, and Landlord Liability for Third-Party Criminal Acts Against Tenants," 54 UCLA L. Rev. 971, 991–92 (2007). Likewise, UCC § 2–719(2) provides that "[l]imitation of consequential damages for injury to the person in the case of consumer goods is prima facie unconscionable. . . ." What factors would justify making warranties and liability for certain injuries nondisclaimable in some situations, but not others?

Economic Injury and Failure of Essential Purpose. Karl Llewellyn and the other authors of UCC Article 2 developed an elaborate framework into which the issues of the existence or non-existence of express or implied warranties were placed, together with the provision of or limitation on remedies for breach. This framework was discussed in Chapter 4. The inclusion or negation of warranties starts with UCC § 2–312 and § 2–313. The inclusion of implied warranties is covered in § 2–314 and § 2–315 and the exclusion or modification of warranties in § 2–316. Subsections (2), (3) and (4) of the latter section deal with the statutorily implied warranties. Thus, under UCC § 2–316(2), the implied warranty of merchantability can only be excluded by language mentioning "merchantability," and in the case of a writing, such language must be "conspicuous." The implied warranty of fitness for a particular purpose can be excluded only by a conspicuous writing. Subsection (3) permits the exclusion of all implied warranties by words such as "as is" or "with all faults." These provisions deal with the inclusion or exclusion of the implied warranties themselves.

UCC § 2–316(4), on the other hand, deals with the limitation of remedies for breach of any such warranties, citing the methodology found in UCC § 2–718 on liquidation or limitation of damages, and UCC § 2–719 on contractual modification of remedies. UCC § 2–719(1) provides for remedies in addition to or in substitution for those provided in Article 2. Thus, for example, a seller can limit the buyer's remedy to return of the goods and repayment of the price or repair and replacement of non-conforming goods. Section 2–719(1)(b) presumes such express remedies to be cumulative with other Article 2 remedies, unless the parties expressly agree to make that remedy exclusive.

In some cases, however, changed circumstances following contract formation can cause such an exclusive or limited remedy "to fail of its essential purpose." UCC § 2–719(2). In such cases, a court may refuse to enforce the exclusion or limitation and instead provide other remedies available under the UCC. Id. The buyer bears the burden of establishing such a failure of essential purpose. See White & Summers, Uniform Commercial Code § 12–11 (5th ed. 2000).

Clearly, § 2–719 contemplates that the parties may not wholly eliminate all remedies for breach through their exclusions or modifications. See UCC § 2–719, *cmt. 1* ("If the parties intend to conclude a contract for sale within this Article they must accept the legal consequence that there be at least a fair quantum of remedy for breach of the obligations or duties outlined in the contract."). But in some cases, as discussed in the case below, a combination of a remedy limitation—such as a term limiting the buyer's remedies to the seller's repair or replacement of nonconforming goods—together with a consequential damages limitation will leave the buyer without any remedy altogether if the seller refuses to perform. See Kathryn I. Murtagh, "UCC Section 2–719: Limited Remedies and Consequential Damage Exclusions," 74 Cornell L. Rev. 359, 359–60 (1989). Courts have split regarding whether a proven failure of essential purpose also renders an exclusion of consequential damages unenforceable, with some invalidating a consequential damages clause that fails of its essential purpose and others denying relief unless the consequential damages clause is also unconscionable. See id.; see also Howard Foss, "When to Apply the Doctrine of Failure of Essential Purpose to an Exclusion of Consequential Damages: An Objective Approach," 25 Duqesne L. Rev. 551 (1987).

Finally, UCC § 2–719(3) provides that consequential damages may be limited or excluded unless the limitation or exclusion is "unconscionable." Such a limitation for damages for injury to the person in the case of consumer goods is prima facie unconscionable, but the parties may limit damages for "commercial" losses. UCC § 2–719(3) is thus roughly compatible with the tort law principle of strict liability where a manufacturer or seller of a dangerous product is accountable for personal, but not economic, injury without proof of negligence. The "economic loss" doctrine is founded on the assumption and expectation that commercial entities can effectively negotiate contracts and warranties that allocate the risks of product failure. See, e.g., Steven C. Tourek, Thomas H. Boyd, and Charles J. Schoenwetter, "Bucking the 'Trend': The Uniform Commercial Code, the Economic Loss Doctrine, and Common Law Causes of Action for Fraud and Misrepresentation," 84 Iowa L. Rev. 875 (1999). Product failure, absent personal injury, is generally not protected by tort law, either strict liability or negligence. But product failure causing physical damage to other property may be covered under both strict liability and negligence. See David B. Gaebler, "Negligence, Economic Loss, And The U.C.C.," 61 Ind.L.J. 593, 599 (1986). Cortney G. Sylvester, "Economic Loss: Commercial Contract Law Lives," 27 Wm. Mitchell L. Rev. 417, 421–22 (2000). See also Anita Bernstein, "Keep It Simple: An Explanation of the Rule of No Recovery for Pure Economic Loss," 48 Ariz. L. Rev. 773 (2006); Jane Stapleton, "Comparative Economic Loss: Lessons from Case-Law-Focused 'Middle Theory,'" 50 U.C.L.A. L. Rev. 531 (2002). See also William K. Jones, "Product Defects Causing Commercial Loss: The Ascendancy of Contract over Tort," 44 U. Miami L. Rev. 731, 733 (1990) ("[I]n cases of commercial loss (not involving personal injury or property damage to ordinary consumers), the law of product liability should be confined to claims in contract.").

G. UCC BUYER AND SELLER REMEDIES

UCC remedies attempt to achieve the same general goal as the common law—to place the nonbreaching party in "as good a position as if the other party had fully performed. . . ." UCC § 1–305(a) (2001) (formerly UCC § 1–106). But in contrast to the relatively general approach toward party remedies under the common law, the UCC explicitly provides for different remedies depending upon whether the seller or the buyer breaches the contract and the circumstances of that breach. In general, a seller may breach a contract through anticipatory repudiation, delivery of goods that fail to conform to the terms of the contract, or repudiation of the contract altogether. Because the buyer's duties under a sale of goods contract primarily require only the payment of the purchase price, buyers typically breach their contracts through anticipatory repudiation before the time for performance, or a partial or total failure to perform at the time payment is due.

The remedies available to the buyer and seller vary with the different types of breaches, and the UCC provides non-breaching buyers and sellers with several options regarding their form of remedy. In general, however, UCC remedies provisions give both parties the option to terminate the contract and sue for money damages or to engage in "self-help" remedies such as demands for adequate assurances of performance, "cover," "cure," revocation of acceptance, and resale. See Celia R. Taylor, "Self-Help in Contract Law: An Exploration and Proposal," 33 Wake Forest L. Rev. 839, 868–77 (1998); Milton Copeland, "UCC Remedies for Breach of Contract in Agricultural Sales," 25 U. Memphis L. Rev. 899, 899–900 (1995).

1. BUYER'S REMEDIES

A seller can breach a contract for the sale of goods by anticipatory repudiation, non-delivery of goods, or delivery of non-conforming goods. Chapter 5 discusses the anticipatory repudiation and adequate assurances of performance in the context of both the common law and the UCC. See UCC §§ 2–609 (right to adequate assurance of performance) and 2–610 (anticipatory repudiation). In contrast, this section explores a buyer's remedies for a seller's breach caused by failure to deliver goods or delivery of non-conforming goods. See John A. Sebert, Jr., "Remedies Under Article Two of the Uniform Commercial Code: An Agenda for Review," 130 U. Pa. L. Rev. 360, 364–67 (1981). We emphasize that the purpose of this section is not to provide a detailed exegesis on the law of sale of goods, but rather to present some important provisions of the UCC Article 2, which contrast to some extent with common-law precedents.

a. Delivery of Non-Conforming Goods—The "Perfect Tender Rule" Versus Damages for Loss in Value

At common law, as discussed in Chapter 5, a performance that fails to conform constitutes either a substantial performance—which gives the nonbreaching party a right to sue for damages, but not to cancel the contract and terminate its own performance—or a material breach—which gives the nonbreaching party a right to terminate its performance, cancel the contract, and sue for damages for the breach. In contrast, the UCC requires that the seller's performance under a sale of goods contract must perfectly conform to the terms of the contract and, with important exceptions, gives the buyer a right to reject the goods for even minor nonconformities.

The basic outlines of the perfect tender rule appear in UCC § 2–601, which provides that if the seller delivers goods that "fail *in any respect* to conform to the contract," the buyer may reject or accept all or part of the delivery. (emphasis added). The only exception to the requirement of perfect tender occurs in installment contracts—contracts requiring or authorizing deliveries in separate lots—which permit rejection of nonconforming goods "if the non-conformity substantially impairs the value" of the nonconforming installment or contract. UCC § 2–612(2), (3). In rejecting goods under the UCC perfect tender doctrine, the buyer has a duty to specify the particular defect or defects justifying the rejection, and thereafter may not rely on other unstated defects to justify rejection or establish breach. See UCC § 2–605.

The timing of the delivery and rejection of nonconforming goods determines the rights of the seller to cure the nonconformity, depending on whether the time for performance has expired (UCC § 2–508(1)) and whether the seller reasonably believed any goods delivered would be acceptable under the contract (UCC § 2–508(2)). A seller who delivers nonconforming goods before performance is due has an absolute right to attempt to cure the defect before the time for performance expires. UCC § 2–508(1). If the time for performance has passed, a seller has a conditional right to cure the defect, provided that the seller "had reasonable grounds to believe" the performance would be acceptable "with or without a money allowance." UCC § 2–508(2). Thus, a computer seller who delivers a shipment of laptop computers to a purchasing law school knowing that a certain percentage are defective and offers the buyer a discount reflecting the percentage of probably defective machines would likely have a right to attempt to cure within a reasonable time even if the time for performance had passed. In contrast, if the seller knew that the shipment would be unacceptable even with the discount, then no right to cure arises.

After acceptance of nonconforming goods (see UCC § 2–606), a buyer has two options. First, even at that late date, a buyer may revoke acceptance of the delivery within a reasonable time after discovery of the non-conformity if the "non-conformity substantially impairs its value to him." UCC § 2–608(1), (2). But this option is only available if the buyer either reasonably assumed the seller would cure the non-conformity (and the seller actually has failed to cure), or if the buyer only discovered the defect after delivery and the defect was difficult to discern or the buyer relied upon the seller's assurances. UCC § 2–608(1)(a), (b). For example, assume that Phil enters a contract to buy a hovercraft from Watersports, Inc. for $14,000. Suppose that upon delivery, Phil discovers that the engine is smaller than promised and threatens to reject the hovercraft. If Watersports induces Phil to instead accept delivery by promising to install a conforming engine, Phil may later revoke his acceptance under § 2–608(1)(a) if Watersports fails to seasonably cure the defect. Suppose instead that two months after Phil accepts the hovercraft, a clamp in a sealed compartment breaks and causes the hovercraft to catch fire—if the defect was not discoverable before acceptance, Phil may again likely revoke his acceptance under § 2–608(1)(b). Importantly, however, the buyer must revoke acceptance and notify the seller of the revocation within a reasonable time after discovery of the defect or before "any substantial change in condition of the goods which is not caused by their own defects." UCC § 2–608(2).

After the buyer notifies the seller of rejection or revocation of acceptance of nonconforming goods, the seller must give instructions regarding disposition of such goods within a reasonable time. UCC § 2–604. Absent such instructions, or in the case of perishable goods, the buyer may store or resell the goods for the seller's account. UCC § 2–604. Although relatively straightforward, this rule can create problems for assessing damages where the buyer rejects or revokes acceptance of the goods, but nonetheless continues to control, possess, and use the rejected goods. Such actions may constitute an acceptance of the goods (see UCC § 2–606) or permit the seller to setoff the use value of the goods against the buyer's claim for damages. See John R. Bates, "Continued Use of Goods After Rejection or Revocation of Acceptance: The UCC Rule Revealed, Reviewed, and Revised," 25 Rutgers L. J. 1 (1993); Carolyn F. Lazaris, Note, "Article 2: Revocation of Acceptance—Should a Seller Be Granted a Setoff for the Buyer's Use of the Goods?," 30 New Eng. L. Rev. 1073, 1090–1101 (1996).

On the other hand, the buyer may also offset damages caused by the seller's breach against the purchase price. See UCC § 2–717 ("The buyer on notifying the seller of his intention to do so may deduct all or any part of the damages resulting from any breach of the contract from any part of the price still due under the same contract.").

Second, the buyer may keep the goods and sue for damages for the difference between the value of the goods as promised and the value of the goods as delivered, together with incidental and consequential damages, under UCC § 2–714. Importantly, a court may vary this damages measure in special circumstances where the difference between value promised and value received does not accurately reflect the damages caused by the seller's breach. See id. Under UCC § 2–607(3)(a), "the buyer must within a reasonable time after he discovers or should have discovered any breach notify the seller of breach or be barred from any remedy." See Michael F. Quinn, "Remedies," 502 PLI/Comm 41, 58 (1989).

b.   Buyer Monetary Damages for Seller Breach

If the seller repudiates or fails to deliver, or if the buyer rightfully rejects or revokes acceptance of any nonconforming delivery, UCC § 2–711 lists several options for remedying the seller's breach. First, the buyer may "cover"—that is, make a substitute purchase of comparable goods on the market and sue the buyer for the difference between the cost of cover and the contract price. See UCC § 2–712. Second, absent cover, the buyer may sue for damages based upon the difference between the market price and the contract price or, in the case of nonconforming goods, the difference between the value of the goods as promised and the value received. See UCC § 2–713 (damages for non-delivery or repudiation). Third, in proper cases, the buyer may obtain specific performance or replevin of the goods. See UCC §§ 2–502 (buyer's right to goods on seller's insolvency) & 2–716 (buyer's right to specific performance or replevin). Finally, a buyer in possession or control of properly rejected, nonconforming goods may resell them and offset the proceeds of resale against the buyer's damages. See UCC § 2–706. As discussed above, the parties may vary these default remedies through a liquidated damages clause. See UCC § 2–718. This section deals primarily with the first two options available to the nonbreaching buyer.

A nonbreaching buyer may elect *either* to cover and seek damages based upon the cost of making a substitute purchase under § 2–712 or, if the buyer cannot or chooses not to cover, to seek damages based upon the difference between the market price at the time the buyer learned of the breach and the contract price under § 2–713. These remedies are mutually exclusive. See John A. Sebert, Jr., "Remedies Under Article Two of the Uniform Commercial Code: An Agenda for Review," 130 U. Pa. L. Rev. 360, 380–83 (1981). In both situations, the buyer may seek incidental and consequential damages, as discussed previously in this chapter, but the buyer may not recover consequential damages that it could have reasonably prevented "by cover or otherwise." UCC § 2–715.

The right to cover under UCC § 2–712 reflects the business reality that a nonbreaching party must often actually receive the goods promised by the breaching seller to fulfill other obligations to its own customers. See Roy Ryden Anderson, "The Cover Remedy," 6 J. L. & Com. 155, 158–59 (1986). In such cases, it is not enough that the seller will eventually be liable for breach of contract damages, potentially including consequential damages if the breach causes the buyer to breach its own contracts to third parties. The buyer must have the goods *now*. While buyers technically have always had the right to make substitute purchases, UCC § 2–712 clarifies that the covering buyer's damages are based upon the cost of making the substitute purchase, not on the market price at the time of breach or some other potentially relevant time period. After the seller's breach, a covering buyer must make reasonable substitute purchases "in good faith and without unreasonable delay." UCC § 2–712(1). The buyer's damages in the case of cover are based upon the "difference between the cost of cover and the contract price together with any incidental or consequential damages . . ., but less expenses saved in consequence of the breach." UCC § 2–712(2). By expressly basing the buyer's damages upon the cost of cover, not the market price at the time of breach, this remedy comes close to putting the aggrieved buyer in the same economic position as actual performance would have and enables the buyer to achieve its prime objective, acquiring the needed goods. See James J. White & Robert S. Summers, Uniform Commercial Code § 6–3 (5th ed. 2006).

Despite clarifying the buyer's right to damages based upon the cost of cover, UCC § 2–712 provides only ambiguous guidance regarding how the court will assess the buyer's exercise of that right. As illustrated by the following case, terms such as "good faith," "without unreasonable delay," "reasonable purchase," and even "goods in substitution" may support a challenge to the buyer's attempts to approximate the performance promised by the seller.

DANGERFIELD V. MARKEL
Supreme Court of North Dakota
278 N.W.2d 364 (1979)

ERICKSTAD, Chief Justice.

This appeal arises as a result of our decision in Dangerfield v. Markel, 252 N.W.2d 184 (N.D.1977), in which we held that Markel, a potato grower, breached a contract with Dangerfield, a potato broker, to deliver potatoes, thus giving rise to damages under the Uniform Commercial Code. On remand the district court awarded Dangerfield $47,510.16 in damages plus interest and costs less an award to Markel of $3,840.68 plus interest. Markel appeals contending, among other things, that the district court made an erroneous award of damages to Dangerfield, and Dangerfield cross-appeals for an additional $101,675 in incidental and consequential damages. We affirm the district court judgment.

The facts in this case are stated in detail in two previous appeals to this court. By contract dated June 13, 1972, Markel (seller) contracted to sell Dangerfield (buyer) 25,000 cwt. of chipping potatoes during the 1972–1973 shipping season. The seller allegedly breached the contract by refusing to deliver 15,055 cwt. of potatoes during the contract period and the buyer was allegedly forced to purchase potatoes on the open market to fulfill a contract with potato processors. As a result of this alleged breach, the buyer claimed to have suffered severe financial hardship, shortage of capital, damaged business reputation, loss of business and lessened business growth. He prayed for general damages of $56,310 and consequential damages of $101,745, less a set-off of $3,840.68 withheld by the buyer from payments due the seller for potatoes delivered. The seller counterclaimed for the $3,840.68 withheld by the buyer and for additional damages allegedly suffered as a result of the buyer's alleged breach of contract. The trial court found for the seller and the buyer appealed to this court. . . .

The primary issue on this appeal is whether or not the trial court made an erroneous award of damages to the buyer under the Uniform Commercial Code. The trial court in essence found that the buyer was entitled to damages pursuant to Section 41–02–91, N.D.C.C. (s 2–712, U.C.C.) for the amount expended by the buyer to purchase the 15,055 cwt. of potatoes still due under the contract:

> "It appears to the Court that the Defendant (seller) . . . should be liable for the difference in price including freight, if any, between the quantity of the potatoes remaining to be delivered under the . . . contract after February 10, 1973 (date of breach), and the price including freight, if any, that the plaintiff (buyer) actually paid for potatoes to 'cover' the supply that the plaintiff, Dangerfield, had a right to expect to be delivered . . . under . . . (the) contract during the remainder of the 1972–73 potato shipping season."

The court determined that the buyer completed "covering" the contract on March 21, 1973, which was 38 days after the date of breach. During the first eighteen days of this cover period, the buyer's purchases averaged $4.41 per cwt. During the remaining twenty days, the buyer's purchases averaged over $5.41 per cwt., with many purchases made at $6.00 per cwt.

Seller argues in substance that thirty-eight days for the buyer to cover in a rapidly rising market is improper under Sections 41–02–90 and 41–02–91, N.D.C.C. (ss 2–711 and 2–712, U.C.C.); therefore, he submits that

Section 41–02–92, N.D.C.C. (s 2–713, U.C.C.) should have been used to compute damages.

Section 41–02–90, N.D.C.C., provides in part:

"Buyer's remedies in general Buyer's security interest in rejected goods. 1. Where the seller fails to make delivery or repudiates or the buyer rightfully rejects or justifiably revokes acceptance then with respect to any goods involved, and with respect to the whole if the breach goes to the whole contract (section 41–02–75), the buyer may cancel and whether or not he has done so may in addition to recovering so much of the price as has been paid

> a. 'cover' and have damages under the next section as to all the goods affected whether or not they have been identified to the contract; or
>
> b. recover damages for nondelivery as provided in this chapter (section 41–02–92)."

Section 41–02–91, N.D.C.C., provides:

"41–02–91. (2–712) 'Cover' Buyer's procurement of substitute goods.

"1. After a breach within the preceding section the buyer may 'cover' by making in good faith and without unreasonable delay any reasonable purchase of or contract to purchase goods in substitution for those due from the seller.

"2. The buyer may recover from the seller as damages the difference between the cost of cover and the contract price together with any incidental or consequential damages as hereinafter defined (section 41–02–94), but less expenses saved in consequence of the seller's breach.

"3. Failure of the buyer to effect cover within this section does not bar him from any other remedy."

Section 41–02–92, N.D.C.C., provides:

41–02–92. (2–713) Buyer's damages for nondelivery or repudiation.

1. Subject to the provisions of this chapter with respect to proof of market price (section 41–02–102), the measure of damages for nondelivery or repudiation by the seller is the difference between the market price at the time when the buyer learned of the breach and the contract price together with any incidental and consequential damages provided in this chapter (section 41–02–94), but less expenses saved in consequence of the seller's breach.

2. Market price is to be determined as of the place for tender or, in cases of rejection after arrival or revocation of acceptance, as of the place of arrival.

The seller submits that the market price at the time of the breach was between $3.75 and $4.25 per cwt. He argues that a proper measure of damages pursuant to Section 41–02–92, N.D.C.C., would be an average of $4.00 per cwt. minus the contract price at the time of the breach ($1.90), or damages of $31,615.50 as opposed to the present award of $47,510.16, a reduction of $15,894.66.

The buyer responds that due to the perishable nature of the product involved in this case and the installment nature of the contract, the cover period was not unreasonable pursuant to Section 41–02–91, N.D.C.C.; therefore, the damages are correct.

The pre-code measure of damages for a breach of contract for the sale of goods was to allow the aggrieved party the difference between his bargain (contract price) and the market price. Although this worked reasonably well in the majority of cases, practical problems arose in determining the market price as well as the related questions of "as of when" and "where." After the seller's breach, the buyer faced a dilemma, i. e. to ensure that he would be fully compensated for the seller's breach, the buyer had to make a substitute purchase that the finder of fact would later determine to be at the "market value." This "20-20 hindsight approach" by the factfinder produced questionable results. Therefore, Section 2–712, U.C.C., (Section 41–02–91, N.D.C.C.) was added to the buyer's arsenal of remedies. This section allows the buyer to make a substitute purchase to replace the goods that were not delivered by the seller and the damages are measured by the difference between the cost of the substitute goods and the contract price. See J. WHITE & R. SUMMERS, HANDBOOK OF THE LAW UNDER THE UNIFORM COMMERCIAL CODE 175–180 (1972. . . .

The official comment to Section 2–712, U.C.C., states that "the test of proper cover is whether at the time and place the buyer acted in good faith and in a reasonable manner, and it is immaterial that hindsight may later prove that the method of cover used was not the cheapest or most effective."

In order for Section 2–712, U.C.C., to apply, the buyer must make a reasonable purchase in good faith without unreasonable delay. If a buyer fails to cover or covers improperly, e.g. waits an unreasonable length of time or buys in bad faith, he may still be entitled to some relief.

The seller argues that the buyer's purchases did not satisfy the criteria of Section 2–712, U.C.C.; therefore, he is limited to the traditional measure of damages. Specifically, the seller argues that the buyer was obligated to purchase the entire cover on the date of the breach or shortly thereafter in order to mitigate his damages. . . .

The record indicates that the buyer could not cover the balance of the contract on the date of the breach:

> Q.   Once you learned you were not going to receive any more potatoes from Mr. Markel in February of 1973, did you attempt to buy potatoes to cover the shortage on the contract?
>
> A.   I did.
>
> Q.   Were you able to go out right at that time on February 12th or 13th, and buy quantity to cover the remaining balance on the contract?
>
> A.   No, I was not able to.
>
> Q.   Why was this?
>
> A.   Well, we were continuing on rising market, no one wanted to commit more than one or two loads at any one time, so would load on basis whatever day they got car, they would accept whatever market was at that day.
>
> Q.   If I understand what you are saying correctly, is that potatoes that were available at that time had to be bought and you would have to take delivery and ship them, that what you mean?
>
> A.   That's correct.
>
> Q.   That's correct?
>
> A.   Right.
>
> Q.   You were not able to buy potatoes in February for delivery in May?
>
> A.   No.
>
> Q.   Were you able to buy potatoes in middle of February for delivery say a month or two later?
>
> A.   No.
>
> Q.   Did you try to do this?
>
> A.   Yes.

Furthermore, the trial court was obviously of the opinion that the buyer acted in good faith under the circumstances:

> Based upon the foregoing facts and the Uniform Commercial Code as quoted above, the Court is of the opinion that the plaintiff having elected to 'cover' the defendant's breach was not obliged to purchase the entire cover as of the date of the breach since this contract called for installment deliveries over a period of months during the 1972, 1973 potato shipping season. In the absence of a showing of plaintiff so as to increase his damages against the

defendant, the Court will view as reasonable a course of purchases of cover stocks from time to time. This ruling is particularly called for in this case where the subject of the contract is a bulky perishable commodity and the quantities must be warehoused at carefully controlled temperatures to avoid freezing or undue deterioration in holding. It would be unreasonable under these circumstances to hold the covering buyer to a February 10, 1973, market price date for immediate delivery of the entire amount of cover necessary to complete the contract of sale. This is particularly true where, as here, the quantity and bulk of goods in question is large and where the goods normally would flow into commerce upon delivery rather than into storage.

It is generally accepted that if the buyer complies with the requirements of Section 2–712, U.C.C., his purchase is presumed proper and the burden of proof is on the seller to show that cover was not properly obtained. Kiser v. Lemco Industries, Inc., supra at 589. . . . We are mindful of the Code's basic remedial message in Section 41–01–06, N.D.C.C., (s 1–106 U.C.C.) to put the aggrieved party in the position performance would have. White and Summers, in their Hornbook series on the Uniform Commercial Code, comment on Sections 1–106 and 2–712:

> 2–712 is to be the remedy used by more aggrieved buyers than any other remedy, then the courts must be chary of finding a good faith buyer's acts unreasonable. The courts should not hedge the remedy about with restrictions in the name of 'reasonableness' that render it useless or uncertain for the good faith buyer. Indeed, one may argue that the courts should read very little substance into the reasonableness requirement and insist only that the buyer proceed in good faith. A question a lawyer might put to test his client's good faith under 2–712 is this: 'How, where, and when would you have procured these goods if you had not been covering and had no prospect of a court recovery from another?' If the client can answer truthfully that he would have spent his own money in the same way, the court should not demand more. J. White & R. Summers, Handbook of the Law under the Uniform Commercial Code, at p. 178.

We do not feel that the seller met his burden of showing that cover was improperly obtained in this case or that the district court's findings were clearly erroneous. Consequently, we affirm the district court judgment on this issue. . . .

The remaining issue to be considered is the buyer's cross-appeal for consequential damages pursuant to Section 41–02–94, N.D.C.C. (s 2–715 U.C.C.). Section 41–02–94 provides:

Buyer's incidental and consequential damages.

1.   Incidental damages resulting from the seller's breach include expenses reasonably incurred in inspection, receipt, transportation and care and custody of goods rightfully rejected, any commercially reasonable charges, expenses or commissions in connection with effecting cover and any other reasonable expense incident to the delay or other breach.

2.   Consequential damages resulting from the seller's breach include

    a.   any loss resulting from general or particular requirements and needs of which the seller at the time of contracting had reason to know and which could not reasonably be prevented by cover or otherwise; and

    b.   injury to person or property proximately resulting from any breach of warranty.

The buyer contends that as a result of the seller's breach, he suffered consequential damages in the amount of $101,675 due to his severe financial hardship, shortage of capital, damaged business reputation, loss of business, and lessened business growth.

The district court found that the buyer failed to prove these damages:

The Court finds that the plaintiff has otherwise failed in his burden of proof as to "incidental" or as to "consequential" damages as defined in Section 41–02–94 (2–715) N.D. Cent. Code, quoted in full above. It provides for recovery of consequential damages resulting from the seller's breach including, 'any loss resulting from general or particular requirements and needs of which the seller at the time of contracting had reason to know and which could not reasonably be prevented by cover or otherwise, * * * .'

Here "cover" was effected and plaintiff is entitled to recover for his excess costs as they were incurred therefor as general damages. He is not on this record entitled to more. The defendant cannot be held to be the guarantor of the plaintiff's subsequent standing as a potato broker, . . . or of the plaintiff's subsequent financial success, . . . particularly when the defendant's breach represents but a small fraction of the plaintiff's brokerage of activity in the Red River Valley for the subject season to say nothing of the volume of his operations in Arizona and Wisconsin.

The defendant's breach did not put the plaintiff out of business nor did it appear to materially impede his operations for the remainder of the shipping season. Conceivably he might have dealt even more actively in chipping potatoes during the remainder of the season had he not have had to obligate himself for higher than contract prices on cover stocks. However, it does not show affirmatively that he paid for his cover purchases until after receiving payment from his own processor customers. The sums received by Dangerfield from his sales of the 'cover' stock purchases itemized above shows that the plaintiff earned a $990.32 gain on these particular shipments. . . .

The Court has read and considered the entire transcript of the trial proceedings and has similarly examined all the exhibits and briefs of the parties from that record and arguments of counsel. The Court finds that the plaintiff is entitled to damages as shown above in the amount of $47,490.96 plus proven incidental damages of $19.50 and is not entitled to consequential damages in any amount. (Emphasis in original.)

Buyer has cited no authority that would allow consequential damages in the circumstances present here and we are not left with the definite and firm conviction that mistake has been made. Haugeberg v. Haugeberg, 258 N.W.2d 657 (N.D.1977). Consequently, we do not find the district court's findings to be clearly erroneous pursuant to Rule 52(a), N.D.R.Civ.P. The district court's judgment is affirmed in all respects.

SAND, PAULSON, PEDERSON and VANDE WALLE, JJ., concur.

NOTES AND QUESTIONS

1. *The reasonableness of buyer's "cover" purchases.* In a rapidly rising market, do you think that Dangerfield (the buyer) made reasonable and prudent efforts to cover? Could he have bought more potatoes than he did at the earlier lower prices? What was the significance of the fact that the underlying contract called for deliveries of potatoes in a series of installments?

2. *What would Dangerfield have recovered as damages under UCC § 2–713?* The market price of potatoes at the time of breach was much lower than some of the prices he paid in "covering." Markel argued that Dangerfield should be required to take his remedy under § 2–713 and not § 2–712. Do you see any reason why Markel's argument should be successful?

3. *Would a buyer faced with a seller's breach ordinarily select "cover" under § 2–712 as a preferred remedy?* Assuming that the buyer wants to and can accomplish a substitute purchase, "cover" will be the applicable remedy. Suppose, contrary to the facts in the case above, the market price of potatoes falls after the date of the seller's breach, and the buyer can buy potatoes at a price below that stated in the contract. May the buyer claim § 2–713 damages, and simply not treat his post-breach purchases as "cover"? Suppose that buyer finds it to her advantage not to cover and not to acquire substitute potatoes. In this situation, should buyer still be able to recover § 2–713 damages based on the difference between the contract price and market price at the time of

breach? Should her failure to cover break the "chain of causation" of buyer's loss? Suppose the only goods available meet the purposes of the goods contracted for, but have additional, and therefore more expensive, features. Should the buyer be able to treat such purchase of "better" goods as "cover" if that was the only choice available?

4. *Recovery of "incidental" damages.* What "incidental" damages do you think that Dangerfield should have been able to recover? Why is it necessary to recognize a class of damages separate from the cost of cover? Are such damages "direct" damages under the principle of *Hadley I*? Are "cover" damages also "direct" damages, or must they be proven to be reasonably foreseeable by the seller at the time of entering into the contract?

5. *Recovery of "consequential" damages.* What was the nature of the "consequential" damages that Dangerfield sought to recover? Should he have been able to recover these damages? A plaintiff who decides to "cover" may well have to pay up front to purchase a substitute product from a different seller in addition to any amounts already paid to the breaching seller. How would this affect the financial situation of a buyer like Dangerfield? Should such financial strain be a basis of recovery, assuming it is proven with adequate certainty? What difficulties would a court likely encounter attempting to determine damages resulting from "financial strain" caused by a seller's breach?

6. *Buyer's damages under the CISG.* Article 74 of the CISG protects the buyer's expectation interest, including lost profits. See Djakhongir Saidov, "Methods of Limiting Damages Under the Vienna Convention on Contracts for the International Sale of Goods," 14 Pace Int'l L. Rev. 307, 311 (2002). CISG Article 75 additionally preserves the right of both parties to mitigate their losses through cover or sale of non-accepted goods on the market: "If the contract is avoided and if, in a reasonable manner and within a reasonable time after avoidance, the buyer has bought goods in replacement or the seller has resold the goods, the party claiming damages may recover the difference between the contract price and the price in the substitute transaction as well as any further damages recoverable under article 74."

The CISG does not preserve the perfect tender rule. CISG Article 35(1) provides that "[t]he seller must deliver goods which are of the quantity, quality and description required by the contract and which are contained or packaged in the manner required by the contract." But as subsection (2) makes clear, the conformity of goods delivered under a contract subject to the CISG depends upon whether they are of equal quality to the goods described in the contract, not on whether they perfectly comply in every respect with the contract description. See CISG art. 35(2)(a) (defining conforming goods as "fit for the purposes for which goods of the same description would ordinarily be used") and art. (2)(c) (defining conforming goods as possessing "the qualities of goods which the seller has held out to the buyer as a sample or model"). For an analysis of the relationship between conformity and perfect tender of goods, see Catherine Piche, "The Convention on Contracts for the International Sale of Goods and the Uniform Commercial Code Remedies in Light of Remedial

Principles Recognized under U.S. Law: Are the Remedies of Granting Additional Time to the Defaulting Parties and of Reduction of Price Fair and Efficient Ones?" 28 N. Int'l & Com. Reg. 519, 520 (2003).

c. Seller's Remedies—UCC § 2–708 and the "Lost Volume Seller" Rule

The UCC limits the remedies available to a seller, compared to those available to a buyer, in several important respects. Most notably, there is no provision for a nonbreaching seller to obtain either specific performance or consequential damages. The specific performance limitation makes intuitive sense, given that the buyer's obligations under sale of goods contracts generally are limited to the payment of money—the breach of such payment obligations may easily be remedied by money damages. The justification for limiting seller recovery of consequential damages is less obvious. While the result is clear in cases involving suit for price, the denial of consequential damages in other situations raises, on occasion, significant obstacles in the way of sellers recovering their true "expectancy" measure of damages. In seeking to limit these obstacles, courts have given a generous interpretation to what can be claimed as "incidental" damages. See Roy Ryden Anderson, "In Support of Consequential Damages for Sellers," 11 J.L. & Com. 123 (1992).

Outside of these limitations, UCC § 2–703 lists six options for seller remedies for a buyer's anticipatory repudiation or breach of contract for the sale of goods, including:

- Withholding delivery of goods;

- Stopping delivery by bailee intermediaries;

- Reselling or salvaging the goods and recovering damages based upon the difference between the resale price and the contract price, plus incidental damages, minus expenses saved because of the breach (UCC §§ 2–704 & 2–706);

- Recovering damages for non-acceptance, including lost profits and overhead (UCC § 2–708);

- Maintaining an action for the contract price if the buyer has accepted or the seller cannot resell the goods (UCC § 2–709); or

- Cancelling the contract.

See also John A. Sebert, Jr., "Remedies Under Article Two of the Uniform Commercial Code: An Agenda for Review," 130 U. Pa. L. Rev. 360, 365–67 (1981). This section deals primarily with the seller's rights to resell, recover damages for non-acceptance of the goods, and maintain an action for the price. As the following case illustrates, the parties may further alter these default rules through liquidated damages and limitation of liability provisions. See UCC § 2–718.

UCC § 2–709 permits the nonbreaching seller to maintain an "action for the price" against a buyer that fails to pay the price as it becomes due. In such cases, the seller can sue for that price plus incidental damages as provided for in UCC § 2–710. An action for price under UCC § 2–709 is only available in explicitly defined circumstances: (1) the goods have been accepted by the buyer; (2) conforming goods have been lost or damaged after the risk of loss passed to the buyer; or (3) having "identified" goods to the contract the seller is unable to resell after "reasonable" efforts at a "reasonable" price or the circumstances "reasonably" indicate that such an effort will be unavailing. See James J. White & Robert S. Summers, Uniform Commercial Code § 7–2 (5th ed. 2006). Many of the cases dealing with an action for price thus turn on issues of acceptance or non-acceptance. Consequently, while students might well think that UCC § 2–709 is the usual remedy for a seller confronted with a breach by the buyer, this is not the case.

Where the buyer has rejected the goods, however, the seller may not maintain an action for price, even where such rejection is wrongful. In such situations, the seller has two options. First, the nonbreaching seller may resell or contract to resell the rejected goods pursuant to § 2–706. Provided the seller makes such a resale in good faith and in a commercially reasonable manner, the seller may sue for the difference between the contract price and the proceeds of resale, plus any incidental costs, less any expenses saved as a consequence of the breach. See UCC § 2–706.

Second, and alternatively, the seller may sue for lost profits under § 2–708. In general, the measure of seller lost profit damages is based upon "the difference between the market price at the time and place for tender and the unpaid contract price," plus incidental damages, less expenses saved in consequence of the breach. But as § 2–708(2) acknowledges, in many situations this measure will not fully compensate the seller, and in that case, the nonbreaching seller may claim damages based upon "the profit (including reasonable overhead) which the seller would have made from full performance by the buyer," plus incidental damages and "due allowance for costs reasonably incurred and due credit for payments or proceeds of resale." UCC § 2–708(2). This provision has become the primary mechanism under the UCC for determining seller damages. John A. Sebert, Jr., "Remedies Under Article Two of the Uniform Commercial Code: An Agenda for Review," 130 U. Pa. L. Rev. 360, 365–67 (1981); Roy R. Anderson, "Damages for Sellers Under the Code's Profit Formula,"40 Sw. L.J. 1021 at 1063 (1986) ("Under the Code's scheme the profit formula of section 2–708(2) is truly the dominant damage remedy for aggrieved sellers who suffer a breach prior to the time that the buyer accepts the goods.").

Section 2–708(1)—recovery of the difference between market and contract price—generally compensates the seller for the buyer's breach only where there is a market for the goods. In the case of goods sold by a retailer, distributor, or wholesaler, the goods are finished and in the custody and control of the retailer, wholesaler, or manufacturer as the case may be, and thus available for resale. But many sale of goods situations are not amenable to the remedy of resale and recovery of the difference between contract price and proceeds of the resale plus incidentals. For example, a "jobber," who merely acts as a conduit between the manufacturer or wholesaler and the buyer, or a "components" assembler, who accumulates parts from other sources and then sells the completed assembly, would both likely be undercompensated by the market price minus contract price formula. See Robert J. Harris, "A Radical Restatement of the Law of Seller's Damages: Sales Act and Commercial Code Results Compared," 18 Stan. L. Rev. 66, 82 (1965). Yet a third type of potentially undercompensated seller is the maker of goods that are not complete at the time of breach, leaving the seller with a challenge—whether to finish the goods, thus putting more time, effort, and expense, into the ultimate cost of the goods resold, or to sell the materials, as they stand, for scrap. Frequently, such goods will be "special order" with no ready market for the completed product. In such situations, the seller faces a choice between finishing manufacture of the goods and reselling the completed product or ceasing production and selling the incomplete product as scrap. Although Article 2 does not expressly address this problem, UCC § 1–103 incorporates common law standards that are not displaced by other UCC provisions, and thus courts may analyze the seller's actions under the more general common law duty to mitigate. The seller in each of these situations would likely be undercompensated by the UCC § 2–708(1) remedy. See James J. White & Robert S. Summers, Uniform Commercial Code §§ 7–9 & 7–10 (5th ed. 2006) ("Judges in pre-Code cases, writers, and Code drafters perceived that a contract market formula would not even grossly approximate the proper damage recovery for certain sellers.").

In resolving the problem of undercompensation in such cases, § 2–708(2) creates the "lost volume seller" rule. *Neri v. Retail Marine Corp.*, 30 N.Y.2d 393, 334 N.Y.S.2d 165, 285 N.E.2d 311 (1972), provides the paradigmatic illustration of this rule. Neri contracted to purchase a boat from Retail Marine for $12,500. After Retail Marine received the boat, Neri repudiated the contract. Retail Marine incurred some additional incidental expenses, such as storage costs, but later sold the boat to another buyer at the same price. From a strictly common law perspective, of course, this case is easy—Retail Marine successfully mitigated by reselling the boat at the contract price, resulting in some incidental damages but no lost profits. Likewise, under UCC § 2–706, contract price minus proceeds of resale, Retail Marine would have recovered at most its incidental expenses involved in arranging the resale.

But the lost volume seller rule under § 2–708(2), at least at first blush, appears to depart radically from the common law and definitely departs from the UCC § 2–706 standard. Despite that it appeared to permit a double recovery, the New York Court of Appeals awarded Retail Marine's lost profit on the Neri sale, notwithstanding the subsequent resale. The court reasoned that a seller like Retail Marine had an inexhaustible supply of such boats, and consequently if Neri had performed, Retail Marine would have made profits from two boat sales instead of just the profits from the second sale.

The lost volume seller rule applies only in limited circumstances. The seller must show that it had a sufficient supply of goods that it could have additionally performed the second sales contract and that it would have successfully solicited the ultimate purchaser, even if the original buyer had not breached its contract. See Robert J. Harris, "A Radical Restatement of the Law of Seller's Damages: Sales Act and Commercial Code Results Compared," 18 Stan. L. Rev. 66, 82 (1965). Nonetheless, the lost volume seller rule often appears to give sellers a windfall in terms of a double recovery of otherwise mitigated lost profits and has been heavily criticized. See, e.g., Victor P. Goldberg, "An Economic Analysis of the Lost-Volume Retail Seller," 57 S. Cal. L. Rev. 283 (1984). But courts have followed the "lost profits" approach with enthusiasm, and this subsection has been described as the seller's "pearly gates." See John M. Breen, "The Lost Volume Seller and Lost Profits Under UCC § 2–708(2): A Conceptual and Linguistic Critique," 50 U. Miami L. Rev. 779 (1996). As you read the following case, consider whether the compensation rule adopted by the court under-, adequately, or overcompensated Diasonics. Are there any alternative measures that would fully compensate a seller in Diasonics' position?

R.E. DAVIS CHEMICAL CORP. v. DIASONICS, INC.

Seventh Circuit Court of Appeals
826 F.2d 678 (1987)

CUDAHY, Circuit Judge.

Diasonics, Inc. appeals from the orders of the district court denying its motion for summary judgment and granting R. E. Davis Chemical Corp.'s summary judgment motion. Diasonics also appeals from the order dismissing its third-party complaint against Dr. Glen D. Dobbin and Dr. Galdino Valvassori. We affirm the dismissal of the third-party complaint, reverse the grant of summary judgment in favor of Davis and remand for further proceedings.

I.

Diasonics is a California corporation engaged in the business of manufacturing and selling medical diagnostic equipment. Davis is an Illinois corporation that contracted to purchase a piece of medical diagnostic equipment from Diasonics. On or about February 23, 1984, Davis and Diasonics entered into a written contract under which Davis agreed to purchase the equipment. Pursuant to this agreement, Davis paid Diasonics a $300,000 deposit on February 29, 1984. Prior to entering into its agreement with Diasonics, Davis had contracted with Dobbin and Valvassori to establish a medical facility where the equipment was to be used. Dobbin and Valvassori subsequently breached their contract with Davis. Davis then breached its contract with Diasonics; it refused to take delivery of the equipment or to pay the balance due under the agreement. Diasonics later resold the equipment to a third party for the same price at which it was to be sold to Davis.

Davis sued Diasonics, asking for restitution of its $300,000 down payment under section 2–718(2) of the Uniform Commercial Code (the "UCC" or the "Code"). Ill. Rev. Stat. ch. 26, § 2–718(2) (1985). Diasonics counterclaimed. Diasonics did not deny that Davis was entitled to recover its $300,000 deposit less $500 as provided in section 2–718(2)(b). However, Diasonics claimed that it was entitled to an offset under section 2–718(3). Diasonics alleged that it was a "lost volume seller," and, as such, it lost the profit from one sale when Davis breached its contract. Diasonics' position was that, in order to be put in as good a position as it would have been in had Davis performed, it was entitled to recover its lost profit on its contract with Davis under section 2–708(2) of the UCC. Ill.Rev.Stat. ch. 26, § 2–708(2) (1985). . . . Diasonics subsequently filed a third-party complaint against Dobbin and Valvassori, alleging that they tortiously interfered with its contract with Davis. Diasonics claimed that the doctors knew of the contract between Davis and Diasonics and also knew that, if they breached their contract with Davis, Davis would have no use for the equipment it had agreed to buy from Diasonics.

The district court dismissed Diasonics' third-party complaint for failure to state a claim upon which relief could be granted, finding that the complaint did not allege that the doctors intended to induce Davis to breach its contract with Diasonics. The court also entered summary judgment for Davis. The court held that lost volume sellers were not entitled to recover damages under 2–708(2) but rather were limited to recovering the difference between the resale price and the contract price along with incidental damages under section 2–706(1). Ill. Rev. Stat. ch. 26, § 2–706(1) (1985). . . .

Davis was awarded $322,656, which represented Davis' down payment plus prejudgment interest less Diasonics' incidental damages. Diasonics appeals the district court's decision respecting its measure of damages as well as the dismissal of its third-party complaint.

II.

We consider first Diasonics' claim that the district court erred in holding that Diasonics was limited to the measure of damages provided in 2–706 and could not recover lost profits as a lost volume seller under 2–708(2). Surprisingly, given its importance, this issue has never been addressed by an Illinois court, nor, apparently, by any other court construing Illinois law. Thus, we must attempt to predict how the Illinois Supreme Court would resolve this issue if it were presented to it. Courts applying the laws of other states have unanimously adopted the position that a lost volume seller can recover its lost profits under 2–708(2). Contrary to the result reached by the district court, we conclude that the Illinois Supreme Court would follow these other cases and would allow a lost volume seller to recover its lost profit under 2–708(2).

We begin our analysis with 2–718(2) and (3). Under 2–718(2)(b), Davis is entitled to the return of its down payment less $500. Davis' right to restitution, however, is qualified under 2–718(3)(a) to the extent that Diasonics can establish a right to recover damages under any other provision of Article 2 of the UCC. Article 2 contains four provisions that concern the recovery of a seller's general damages (as opposed to its incidental or consequential damages): 2–706 (contract price less resale price); 2–708(1) (contract price less market price); 2–708(2) (profit); and 2–709 (price). The problem we face here is determining whether Diasonics' damages should be measured under 2–706 or 2–708(2). To answer this question, we need to engage in a detailed look at the language and structure of these various damage provisions.

The Code does not provide a great deal of guidance as to when a particular damage remedy is appropriate. The damage remedies provided under the Code are catalogued in section 2–703, but this section does not indicate that there is any hierarchy among the remedies. One method of approaching the damage sections is to conclude that 2–708 is relegated to a role inferior to that of 2–706 and 2–709 and that one can turn to 2–708 only after one has concluded that neither 2–706 nor 2–709 is applicable. Under this interpretation of the relationship between 2–706 and 2–708, if the goods have been resold, the seller can sue to recover damages measured by the difference between the contract price and the resale price under 2–706. The seller can turn to 2–708 only if it resells in a commercially unreasonable manner or if it cannot resell but an action for the price is inappropriate under 2–709. The district court adopted this reading of the Code's damage remedies and, accordingly, limited Diasonics to the measure of damages provided in 2–706 because it resold the equipment in a commercially reasonable manner.

The district court's interpretation of 2–706 and 2–708, however, creates its own problems of statutory construction. There is some suggestion in the Code that the "fact that plaintiff resold the goods [in a commercially reasonable manner] does not compel him to use the resale remedy of § 2–706 rather than the damage remedy of § 2–708." Harris, "A Radical Restatement of the Law of Seller's Damages: Sales Act and Commercial Code Results Compared," 18 Stan. L. Rev. 66, 101 n. 174 (1965) (emphasis in original). Official comment 1 to § 2–703, which catalogues the remedies available to a seller, states that these "remedies are essentially cumulative in nature" and that "[w]hether the pursuit of one remedy bars another depends entirely on the facts of the individual case." See also State of New York, Report of the Law Revision Comm'n for 1956, 396–97 (1956).[7]

Those courts that found that a lost volume seller can recover its lost profits under 2–708(2) implicitly rejected the position adopted by the district court; those courts started with the assumption that 2–708 applied to a lost volume seller without considering whether the seller was limited to the remedy provided under 2–706. None of those courts even suggested that a seller who resold goods in a commercially reasonable manner was limited to the damage formula provided under 2–706. We conclude that the Illinois Supreme Court, if presented with this question, would adopt the position of these other jurisdictions and would conclude that a reselling seller, such as Diasonics, is free to reject the damage formula prescribed in 2–706 and choose to proceed under 2–708.

Concluding that Diasonics is entitled to seek damages under 2–708, however, does not automatically result in Diasonics being awarded its lost profit. Two different measures of damages are provided in 2–708. Subsection 2–708(1) provides for a measure of damages calculated by subtracting the market price at the time and place for tender from the contract price. The profit measure of damages, for which Diasonics is asking, is contained in 2–708(2). However, one applies 2–708(2) only if "the

---

[7] UCC comment 2 to 2–708(2) also suggests that 2–708 has broader applicability than suggested by the district court. UCC comment 2 provides:

> This section permits the recovery of lost profits in all appropriate cases, which would include all standard priced goods. The normal measure there would be list price less cost to the dealer or list price less manufacturing cost to the manufacturer.

The district court's restrictive interpretation of 2–708(2) was based in part on UCC comment 1 to 2–704 which describes 2–706 as the aggrieved seller's primary remedy. The district court concluded that, if a lost volume seller could recover its lost profit under 2–708(2), every seller would attempt to recover damages under 2–708(2) and 2–706 would become the aggrieved seller's residuary remedy. This argument ignores the fact that to recover under 2–708(2), a seller must first establish its status as a lost volume seller. See infra p. 667.

The district court also concluded that a lost volume seller cannot recover its lost profit under 2–708(2) because such a result would negate a seller's duty to mitigate damages. This position fails to recognize the fact that, by definition, a lost volume seller cannot mitigate damages through resale. Resale does not reduce a lost volume seller's damages because the breach has still resulted in its losing one sale and a corresponding profit. See Autonumerics, 144 Ariz. at 192, 696 P. 2d at 1341.

measure of damages provided in subsection (1) is inadequate to put the seller in as good a position as performance would have done. . . ." Ill.Rev.Stat. ch. 26, para. 2–708(2) (1985). Diasonics claims that 2–708(1) does not provide an adequate measure of damages when the seller is a lost volume seller. To understand Diasonics' argument, we need to define the concept of the lost volume seller. Those cases that have addressed this issue have defined a lost volume seller as one that has a predictable and finite number of customers and that has the capacity either to sell to all new buyers or to make the one additional sale represented by the resale after the breach. According to a number of courts and commentators, if the seller would have made the sale represented by the resale whether or not the breach occurred, damages measured by the difference between the contract price and market price cannot put the lost volume seller in as good a position as it would have been in had the buyer performed. The breach effectively cost the seller a "profit," and the seller can only be made whole by awarding it damages in the amount of its "lost profit" under 2–708(2).We agree with Diasonics' position that, under some circumstances, the measure of damages provided under 2–708(1) will not put a reselling seller in as good a position as it would have been in had the buyer performed because the breach resulted in the seller losing sales volume. However, we disagree with the definition of "lost volume seller" adopted by other courts. Courts awarding lost profits to a lost volume seller have focused on whether the seller had the capacity to supply the breached units in addition to what it actually sold. In reality, however, the relevant questions include, not only whether the seller could have produced the breached units in addition to its actual volume, but also whether it would have been profitable for the seller to produce both units. Goetz & Scott, Measuring Sellers' Damages: The Lost-Profits Puzzle, 31 Stan. L. Rev. 323, 332–33, 346–47 (1979).

As one commentator has noted, under the economic law of diminishing returns or increasing marginal costs [,] . . . as a seller's volume increases, then a point will inevitably be reached where the cost of selling each additional item diminishes the incremental return to the seller and eventually makes it entirely unprofitable to conclude the next sale. . . .

Thus, under some conditions, awarding a lost volume seller its presumed lost profit will result in overcompensating the seller, and 2–708(2) would not take effect because the damage formula provided in 2–708(1) does place the seller in as good a position as if the buyer had performed. Therefore, on remand, Diasonics must establish, not only that it had the capacity to produce the breached unit in addition to the unit resold, but also that it would have been profitable for it to have produced and sold both. Diasonics carries the burden of establishing these facts because the burden of proof is generally on the party claiming injury to establish the amount of its damages; especially in a case such as this, the plaintiff has easiest access to the relevant data. Finance America

Commercial Corp. v. Econo Coach, Inc., 118 Ill. App. 3d 385, 390, 73 Ill. Dec. 878, 882, 454 N.E.2d 1127, 1131 (2d Dist. 1983) ("A party seeking to recover has the burden not only to establish that he sustained damages but also to establish a reasonable basis for computation of those damages.") (citation omitted). . . .

One final problem with awarding a lost volume seller its lost profits was raised by the district court. This problem stems from the formulation of the measure of damages provided under 2–708(2) which is "the profit (including reasonable overhead) which the seller would have made from full performance by the buyer, together with any incidental damages provided in this Article (Section 2–710), due allowance for costs reasonably incurred and due credit for payments or proceeds of resale." Ill.Rev.Stat. ch. 26, para. 2–708(2) (1985) (emphasis added). The literal language of 2–708(2) requires that the proceeds from resale be credited against the amount of damages awarded which, in most cases, would result in the seller recovering nominal damages. In those cases in which the lost volume seller was awarded its lost profit as damages, the courts have circumvented this problem by concluding that this language only applies to proceeds realized from the resale of uncompleted goods for scrap. See, e.g., Neri, 30 N.Y.2d at 399 & n. 2, 334 N.Y.S.2d at 169 & n. 2, 285 N.E.2d at 314 & n. 2; see also J. White & R. Summers, Handbook of the Law under the Uniform Commercial Code § 7–13, at 285 ("courts should simply ignore the 'due credit' language in lost volume cases") (footnote omitted). Although neither the text of 2–708(2) nor the official comments limit its application to resale of goods for scrap, there is evidence that the drafters of 2–708 seemed to have had this more limited application in mind when they proposed amending 2–708 to include the phrase "due credit for payments or proceeds of resale." We conclude that the Illinois Supreme Court would adopt this more restrictive interpretation of this phrase rendering it inapplicable to this case.

We therefore reverse the grant of summary judgment in favor of Davis and remand with instructions that the district court calculate Diasonics' damages under 2–708(2) if Diasonics can establish, not only that it had the capacity to make the sale to Davis as well as the sale to the resale buyer, but also that it would have been profitable for it to make both sales. Of course, Diasonics, in addition, must show that it probably would have made the second sale absent the breach.

III. A.

Diasonics also appeals the district court's dismissal of its third-party complaint against Dobbin and Valvassori. The complaint alleged that the doctors tortiously interfered with Diasonics' contract with Davis and sought as damages Diasonics' lost profit. The district court dismissed the third-party complaint for failure to state a claim upon which relief could be granted. Fed.R.Civ.P. 12(b)(6).

A complaint should not be dismissed under Rule 12(b)(6) "unless it appears beyond doubt that the plaintiff can prove no set of facts in support of his claim which would entitle him to relief." Conley v. Gibson, 355 U.S. 41, 45–46, 78 S.Ct. 99, 102, 2 L.Ed.2d 80 (1957) (footnote omitted). The facts as alleged in Diasonics' third-party complaint are as follows. Dobbin and Valvassori are physicians who had agreed to perform professional services at a medical facility to be established by Davis. The equipment ordered by Davis from Diasonics was to be used at this facility. "Dobben [sic] and Valvassori were aware that Davis had entered into the . . . contract with Diasonics," and they "were further aware that the equipment would be of essentially no value to Davis if they failed to provide their services in connection with operating the equipment. . . ." Third-Party Complaint ¶¶ 8, 9. Dobbin and Valvassori breached their contract with Davis in order to establish their own facility, though they "knew that their conduct was reasonably certain to cause a breach by Davis of its contract with Diasonics. . . . " Id. ¶ 10.

The elements of the tort of interference with contractual relations under Illinois law are:

> a valid contract, defendant's knowledge of the existence of the contract, defendant's intentional and malicious inducement of the breach of the contract, breach of the contract caused by defendant's wrongful conduct and resultant damage to the plaintiff.

Swager v. Couri, 60 Ill.App.3d 192, 196, 17 Ill.Dec. 457, 460, 376 N.E.2d 456, 459 (3d Dist.1978). . . . The district court dismissed the complaint because it did not allege that the doctors intended to induce Davis to breach its contract with Diasonics. We agree. . . .

Accordingly, we affirm the district court's dismissal of the third-party complaint, reverse the grant of summary judgment in favor of Davis and remand for further proceedings consistent with this opinion.

NOTES AND QUESTIONS

1. *Subsequent proceedings.* Following remand, the district court found that Diasonics had adequately established damages for its lost profit amounting to $453,050 and entered judgment for Diasonics in the amount of $153,050 ($453,050 less the $300,000 deposit which Diasonics retained). Once again Davis appealed. The court of appeals held that: (1) the seller was not foreclosed from recovering lost profits, even though it was unable to specify for which particular unit buyer had contracted or to trace the exact resale buyer for that unit; and (2) the trial court's method of calculating damages on remand was not unreasonable. See *R.E. Davis Chemical Corp. v. Diasonics, Inc.*, 924

F.2d 709 (7th Cir. 1991). The sale agreement had provided that upon payment of the full purchase price, Davis was to be furnished a $225,000 research grant and also included an option to upgrade the system at an additional cost of $700,000. Once again the court remanded the case for further consideration of the evidence with respect to the research grant and the upgrade option. At this point, the trail of this case goes cold.

2. *The role and function of UCC § 2–718.* Subsection (1) of this section deals with liquidated damages. This case starts with subsection (2), which grants the buyer the right to recover (a) the portion of any down payment in excess of specified liquidated damages; or (b) of the amount by which the buyer's payment exceeds the lesser of $500 or 20% of the value of total performance. See UCC § 2–718(2). The buyer asserts this right as restitution, and it is available despite the buyer's breach. *Comment 2* to this section states: "Subsection (2) refuses to recognize a forfeiture unless the amount of the payment so forfeited represents a reasonable liquidation of damages as determined under subsection (1). A special exception is made in the case of small amounts . . . " Finally, subsection (3) provides for an offset to the extent that the seller establishes a right to recover under the provisions of Article 2 other than § 2–718(1). And thus the key to the decision here is the court's interpretation and application of § 2–708(2).

3. *Should § 2–706 be the primary or exclusive remedy?* The trial court held that Diasonic's recovery was required to be calculated under § 2–706— contract price minus proceeds of sale. As a result, that decision limited Diasonic's recovery to incidental damages since the machine had been resold at the same price as established in the Davis contract. How does the court resolve the potential inconsistency between the remedy granted under § 2–706 and that granted under § 2–708? How much weight should be accorded to § 2–704, *cmt.* 1, which describes § 2–706 as the aggrieved seller's primary remedy? See Footnote 2 to the case above. Some commentators, primarily those who consider the recovery of "lost profits" under the latter section unduly generous, criticize the court's construction of this potential inconsistency. But as the *R.E. Davis* opinion states, courts have generally granted plaintiffs discretion to choose between the two measures of remedy.

4. *When does UCC § 2–708(1) provide the appropriate remedy?* Subsection (1), subject to subsection (2), gives the seller the choice of a remedy measured by contract price less market price at the time and place for tender. The trigger for the recovery under subsection (2) of lost profits, including reasonable overhead, is a finding that the measure under subsection (1) "is inadequate to put the seller in as good a position as performance would have done." Under subsection (2), the seller is entitled to incidental damages, but is required to give "due credit for payments or proceeds of resale." Two things about this subsection that merit attention are the absence of any provision for consequential damages and the credit for any payments made by the buyer, including any proceeds from resale.

5. *"Due credit for . . . proceeds of resale."* The opinion in the case above intentionally ignores these words of UCC § 2–708(2) (enacted as a statutory provision). Do you think the court construed these words correctly? Courts must read the words and terms of a statute (or a contract) in the context of the whole work. Moreover, courts should also prefer interpretations of statutes and contracts that avoid, as much as possible, depriving words or clauses of any effect. Finally, the words or terms of a statute (or contract) should be interpreted in the light of the proven purpose of the parties. See, e.g., James F. Hogg, "The International Court: Rules of Treaty Interpretation II," 44 Minn. L. Rev. 5, 49–66 (1959–60). Critics of the "lost volume" approach have argued that the "due credit" words were included precisely to cover the case of incomplete goods sold as scrap and should not be ignored. Do you agree? The "lost volume" approach has been said to be inconsistent with the common law and UCC concept of duty to mitigate. Do you agree? How should the "lost volume" seller be treated under the common law?

6. *The tortious interference issue.* The court held that under Illinois law, to recover on a claim for tortious interference with contract, the plaintiff must show an intentional and malicious inducement to breach the contract. This burden of proof is somewhat relaxed in other jurisdictions.

7. *Are "lost profits" under UCC § 2–708(2) "direct" or "consequential"?* Did the court above treat the "lost profits" as direct (*Hadley I*) or consequential (*Hadley II*) damages? Do you agree with the court's treatment of this issue?

8. *The "lost volume" seller under the common law. Jetz Service Co., Inc. v. Salina Properties*, 19 Kan.App.2d 144, 865 P.2d 1051 (1993), is a "lost volume seller" case involving breach of a lease agreement, rather than a sale of goods contract. Jetz Service Co. supplied and maintained coin-operated laundry equipment in approximately 2,000 locations. Salina's predecessor leased 175 feet of space to Jetz to be used as a coin-operated facility. Jetz installed five washing machines and dryers. Salina later removed Jetz's machines in breach of the lease agreement. At first Jetz stored these machines in a warehouse and then relocated four sets to other income-producing space. Jetz sued for lost profits for the remainder of the lease period, but Salina argued that Jetz had failed to mitigate its damages, or in any case, had restored four sets of the machines to productivity. The trial court, reasoning by analogy to the UCC, determined that Jetz was entitled to lost profits as a "lost volume" seller. The Kansas Court of Appeals held, "We agree that Jetz Service does not sell goods, but the underlying concept is analogous; adequate authority exists to apply the lost volume rule to volume providers of services."

9. *The "lost volume" seller under the CISG.* It remains unclear whether the CISG incorporates the lost volume seller principle. See Djakhongir Saidov, "Methods of Limiting Damages Under the Vienna Convention on Contracts for the International Sale of Goods," 14 Pace Int'l L. Rev. 307 (2002) (concluding that Article 74 of the CISG protects the expectation interest including lost profits as well as the concept of costs avoided, and he thought that the lost volume principle should be recognized).

CHAPTER 10

RIGHTS AND DUTIES OF PERSONS NOT ACTUAL PARTIES TO THE CONTRACT

■ ■ ■

The term "party" to a contract literally means a person who forms a contract. While one person cannot form a contract without another person, more than two persons may form a contract. Most contracts are formed between two persons, each referred to as a "party" to that contract. When the contract is written, the writing itself identifies the parties.

The term "person" includes individuals, but is much broader. Accordingly, a contract may include organizations as parties. Restatement (Third) of Agency § 1.04(5). However, legal entities like business organizations cannot act for themselves and necessarily must act through individuals. When an individual acts on behalf of another person with that person's consent, an agency relationship is created. In an agency relationship, an individual agent acts on behalf of another party referred to as a principal. An agency relationship is a subset of a broader relationship, referred to as a fiduciary relationship, in which the agent owes the principal fiduciary duties to act fairly, in the best interests of the principal, and within the scope of the agency. Restatement (Third) of Agency §§ 1.01, 8.01. While the existence of a fiduciary relationship and the broader concept of trust and confidence may create special issues in contract law (see discussion Chapter 7), the focus of this section is simply on the proper identification of the parties of the contract.

Previous chapters focused nearly exclusively on the rights and duties the parties to the contract owed to and received from each other. Normatively, the contract is formed and enforceable because bargained-for consideration flows from each contract party to the other. Restatement (Second) of Contracts § 71. In this sense, the original parties to the contract are said to be in a relationship referred to as "privity in contract." As explored below, the concept of privity originally developed to allow the parties to the contract to sue each other, but to prevent other persons— collectively referred to as "third parties"—from suing either of the original parties. This chapter briefly explores the previously unchartered terrain concerning the extent to which such third parties may become engaged in the performance and enforcement of the contract.

The first section considers the rights of so-called "third-party beneficiaries" to enforce the terms of a promise against one of the actual contracting parties and addresses four main propositions. First, a contract creates third-party beneficiaries, if at all, at the time the actual parties form that contract. Second, third-party beneficiaries have standing to sue to enforce a benefit accruing to them as a beneficiary from the performances due to a party to the contract. Third, the rights of a third-party beneficiary are especially important, and are typically contested, when the original contractual promisee is no longer capable of, or sufficiently interested in, enforcing the terms of a promisor's promise. Fourth, once the third-party beneficiary's rights become vested, the original contracting parties remain free to amend the contract, but the amendment is not effective against the third-party beneficiary without its consent.

The second section considers the power of one or both of the actual contracting parties to "assign" or "delegate" to a third party some right to receive a performance due to them under the contract. The terms "assignment" and "delegation" technically refer to the transfer of rights and duties, respectively. Although assignments and delegations may occur in contracts between individuals, it is common in business reorganizations to transfer entire contracts as part of mergers or divestitures. In these circumstances, the entire contract is often purportedly transferred, including both an assignment of rights and delegation of duties. As a matter of economic and judicial policy, such post-contractual flexibility is encouraged, provided that the assignment or delegation does not materially affect rights and duties of the other party. But the effectiveness of such transfers is often affected by specific contract language protecting one of the parties from such a transfer. In the absence of protective language, the law generally favors the transfer as a natural commercial occurrence, again provided that the assignment or delegation does not materially affect the rights of the other party to the contract.

One important difference remains between assignment and delegation. In an assignment of a right, the assignor disappears from the contract and the assignee literally steps into the shoes of the assignor. In this sense, an assignment should be thought of as a transfer of a property interest. A delegation of duty is different. Even if a proper delegation occurs, the delegator remains contractually liable for any performance breach by the delegatee. This means that unless the obligor consents to a novation to release the delegator, the obligor actually retains the right to enforce the delegator's promise against the delegator. The delegator and delegatee must then adjust the consequences of the breach between themselves.

A. THIRD-PARTY BENEFICIARIES

The conceptual relationship between traditional contract and third-party beneficiary doctrine is awkward and yet explicable. Traditional contract doctrine determines the enforceability of the contract as a substantive matter. In contrast, third-party beneficiary doctrine examines whether a third party to the contract—i.e., someone who did not take part in the contractual manifestation of mutual assent and exchange of considerations—has rights under that contract and therefore the standing to enforce obligations created by that contract. Nonetheless, there are anomalies. For example, the Chapter 2 consideration discussion revealed that the modern bargain theory of consideration searches for any bargained-for exchange of legal detriments and largely rejects a fairness or equivalency test. As a result, the reason a contracting party seeks a promise is largely irrelevant for purposes of determining the enforceability of the promise. Paradoxically, once the promise is enforceable, the reason it was sought will become important to determine whether a third party should have standing to enforce the promise. Generally, courts must examine the relationship between the third party and the promisee to determine whether the promisee sought the promise primarily for the commercial or altruistic benefit of the third party. For example, A and B exchange promises to form a contract. Under traditional contract doctrine, B's reason for seeking A's promise is irrelevant to the substantive question of whether A's promise is enforceable. But if that promise is enforceable as a contract, B's reason for seeking A's promise is critical to the determination of whether C, a stranger to the contract, may enforce A's promise as a third-party beneficiary.

Medieval law had little regard for the right of a third party to enforce a promise under a separate contract because the third party was not "in privity" with the defendant. A.W. Brian Simpson, A History of the Common Law of Contract—The Rise and Fall of The Action of Assumpsit 184 (1996). The contractual privity limitation has historical roots in the assumpsit doctrine, originally an action to recover damages resulting from a deceitful promise. Only the promisee could bring the suit, and this limitation transferred into nineteenth century contract law. See id. at 475–85. One of the earliest English cases recognizing third-party beneficiary suit status was *Dutton v. Poole*, 2 Lev. 210, 83 Eng. Rep. 523 (K. B. 1677) (father's agreement not to sell wood that son would inherit if son would pay his sister's dowry was deemed enforceable by her). While English common law momentarily embraced the rights of third-party beneficiaries under Lord Mansfield in the latter part of the eighteenth century, England soon returned to medieval law's hostility to third-party beneficiary status. See Note, "Third Party Beneficiary Contracts in England," 35 U. Chi. L. Rev. 544 (1968). Finally, in 1999, the Parliament adopted third-party beneficiary status by legislation. See Joseph M. Perillo, Calamari and Perillo on Contracts § 17.1 (5th ed. 2003).

At least until the early part of the twentieth century, American common law was clearly antagonistic to third-party beneficiary status on grounds that the rights of such parties were beyond contractual imagination, the third party beneficiary stranger to the contract had no equivalent or mutual obligation to match the asserted right, and the beneficiary lacked privity because she was not a party to the contract. Anthony Jon Waters, "The Property in the Promise: A Study of the Third Party Beneficiary Rule," 98 Harv. L. Rev. 1109, 1112 (1985).

The seed of change was planted by the early, and now quite famous, New York Court of Appeals decision in *Lawrence v. Fox*, 20 N.Y. 268 (1859) (Gray, J). As noted below, *Lawrence* recognized the right of a creditor third-party beneficiary to bring an action against a promisor to pay a promisee a fixed monetary sum. The promisee was indebted to the third-party beneficiary at the time the promisor made the promise to the promisee to pay the third-party beneficiary directly.

The case drew the attention of Professor Samuel Williston, causing him to observe:

> In no department of the law has a more obstinate and persistent battle between practice and theory been waged than in regard to the answer to the question: Whether a right of action accrues to a third person from a contract made by others for his benefit? Nor is the strife ended; for if it be granted that the scale inclines in favor of practice, yet the advocates of this result are continually endeavoring to extend the territory which they have conquered and to apply the doctrines thereby established to cases which should be governed by other principles. Samuel Williston, "Contracts for the Benefit of a Third Person," 15 Harv. L. Rev. 767 (1902).

Williston thus thought the doctrine was a narrow exception, rather than the rule. While he thought justice required some limited remedy for a limited class of third-party beneficiaries, he thought the doctrine generally conflicted with classical contract theory. Melvin A. Eisenberg, "Third-Party Beneficiaries," 92 Colum. L. Rev. 1358, 1366 (1992). However, the privity and consideration arguments were largely deduced from classical contract theory and its older "meeting of the minds" approach. Neither doctrine, nor the meeting of the minds theory, reflects either practical notions inherent in modern objective contract theory or doctrines of fairness and equity. In many cases, the third-party beneficiary is the only party existing or sufficiently interested in the outcome to seek enforcement of the promise. See id. at 1370.

The Restatement (First) of Contracts, for which Professor Williston served as reporter, more comprehensively addressed the issue with its release in 1932. The text was heavily influenced by two factors. First, a second New York Court of Appeals case, *Seaver v. Ransom*, 224 N.Y. 233, 120 N.E. 639 (1918) (Pound, J.), extended the creditor third-party beneficiary rule of *Lawrence* to a donee third-party beneficiary. *Seaver* recognized the right of a donee third-party beneficiary to bring an action against the estate of a decedent–promisor to enforce a promise made to a decedent promisee. The decedent-promisee was the third-party beneficiary's aunt and was on her deathbed at the time she contracted with her husband that he would amend his own will to provide for an additional bequest to the third-party beneficiary. The aunt died, the uncle failed to amend his will, and the third-party beneficiary sued the uncle's estate to enforce his deathbed promise to her aunt. Equally compelling, an intervening series of path-breaking articles by Arthur Corbin addressed the topic following both the *Lawrence* and *Seaver* cases. See Arthur L. Corbin, "Contracts for the Benefit of Third Persons in Connecticut," 31 Yale L. J. 489 (1922); Arthur L. Corbin, "The Law of Third Party Beneficiaries in Pennsylvania," 77 U. Pa. L. Rev. 1 (1928); Arthur L. Corbin, "Third Parties as Beneficiaries of Contractors' Surety Bonds," 38 Yale L. J. 1 (1928); Arthur L. Corbin, "Contracts for the Benefit of Third Persons," 46 Law Q. Rev. 12 (1930); and Arthur L. Corbin, "Contracts for the Benefit of Third Persons in the Federal Courts," 39 Yale L. J. 601 (1930). Unlike Williston, Corbin thought the doctrine should be the rule and not the exception. See Anthony Jon Waters, "The Property in the Promise: A Study of the Third Party Beneficiary Rule," 98 Harv. L. Rev. 1109 (1985).

1. RESTATEMENT POSITIONS COMPARED

Recognizing the importance of comprehensively addressing the issue, Professor Williston reserved an entire chapter in the Restatement (First) of Contracts §§ 133–147. Not surprisingly, the Restatement (First) of Contracts explicitly distinguished between two types of third-party beneficiaries—the creditor beneficiary recognized in *Lawrence* and the donee beneficiary recognized in *Seaver*. Where performance of a promise in a contract will benefit a person other than the promisee, the benefactor is a "creditor beneficiary" if the terms of the promise do not show a purpose to make a gift and performance will satisfy a duty of the promisee to the beneficiary. Restatement (First) of Contracts § 133(1)(b). A "donee beneficiary" is a benefactor of a promise created by the promisee with the purpose of making a gift to the beneficiary. Restatement (First) of Contracts § 133(1)(a). Rather than rely on the common law as adopted and developed by the state judiciary, some states adopted legislation recognizing third-party beneficiary status by statute. Note, "The Third Party Beneficiary Concept: A Proposal," 57 Colum. L. Rev. 406, 414 (1957) (as noted above, the English Parliament followed suit in 1999).

Importantly, the creditor beneficiary was the dominant beneficiary status, with the donee beneficiary category becoming the "residual" category. This treatment comports with Williston's conception that third-party beneficiary status was conceptually a rational justice concept, but difficult to square with conventional, formalistic, and classical contract theory. Melvin A. Eisenberg, "Third-Party Beneficiaries," 92 Colum. L. Rev. 1358, 1377 (1992).

The critical and determinative test is the "intent" of the promisee to benefit the third party at the time the contract is formed. Restatement (First) of Contracts §§ 133(1)(a) ("purpose of the promisee" to benefit donee beneficiary); 133(1)(b) (no purpose to make gift, but rather to satisfy an obligation to creditor beneficiary). While some cases tend to analyze the broader intent of both parties, the language of the Restatement (First) of Contracts supports examining the intent of the promisee alone. Moreover, the issue requires an examination of why the promisee extracted the promise in the first instance. The promisor's intent is largely extraneous in these cases and largely isolated to self-interest. In any case, a plaintiff asserting third-party beneficiary status will have the burden to prove that status. The evidence will require the court to apply principles of interpretation to determine the intent of the promisee that may be unavailable because of death or other circumstances. The contract itself will control if it explicitly states the promisee's intent to create or not create a third-party beneficiary. Thus, if the contract either names a specific third-party beneficiary or states that there shall be no third-party beneficiary, the explicit contract language will be dispositive. Where the agreement is silent, but it is reasonably clear that the performance is to be rendered directly to the third party, that fact will often control. See Joseph M. Perillo, Calamari and Perillo on Contracts § 17.3 (5th ed. 2003). And the relationship between the promisee and the third party is often important for testing the promisor's intent to benefit.

Once a creditor or donee beneficiary exists, the promisor's promise may be enforced either by the original promisor or by the third-party beneficiary. Restatement (First) of Contracts §§ 135 (donee beneficiary); 136 (creditor beneficiary). However, two points should be obvious. First, full and complete performance of the promise discharges the duty to perform to both the promisee and the third-party beneficiary. Restatement (First) of Contracts § 133(1). Thus, even though the promise is enforceable by two parties, only a single performance is required. For instance, a promise to pay money to either the promisee or an intended creditor beneficiary is fully satisfied by payment to the promisee, and the creditor beneficiary cannot make a separate claim for payment against the promisor. Second, the promisor retains all the contract defenses otherwise available under the contract against the promisee as well as the third-party beneficiary. Restatement (First) of Contracts § 140. Accordingly, the third-party beneficiary receives the same right to enforce the promise as the promisee; if the promisee cannot enforce the promise, neither can the third-party beneficiary.

Finally, creation of a third-party beneficiary requires neither knowledge nor assent by the third-party beneficiary. Such a person may acquire rights without knowledge or notice. Restatement (First) of Contracts § 135, *cmt. a.* Consequently, once created, the third-party beneficiary's rights are generally fixed or "vested" at the time the contract is formed, not when the third party learns of the benefit. Restatement (First) of Contracts § 142. As a result, unless the contract provides otherwise, the parties to the contract may amend the contract, but the amendment is not effective against the donee beneficiary. However, a creditor beneficiary is more likely to be aware of the contractual undertaking for its benefit (because of its rights against the promisee), and as a result, the contract may be amended and the amendment is effective until the creditor beneficiary either brings suit upon or materially changes position on reliance on the promise. Restatement (First) of Contracts § 143.

While the Restatement (First) of Contracts made significant strides in advancing the contractual basis for third-party beneficiary status, its rigid two-category rule for classifying beneficiaries first as creditor beneficiaries and then only as residual donee beneficiaries reflected Williston's tempered tolerance for the doctrine. Many courts found the two-category approach too confining and incomplete to promote justice in appropriate cases. Indeed, perhaps reflecting Williston's intent, many, if not most, third parties failed to fit neatly into either category. David M. Summers, Note, "Third Party Beneficiaries and the Restatement (Second) of Contracts," 67 Cornell L. Rev. 880, 884 (1982).

Restatement (Second) of Contracts § 302 attempted to reject this rigid two-category approach by creating an arguably more practical and certainly more flexible "intent to benefit" test. A person may maintain a third-party beneficiary action on a contract provided the person is an "intended beneficiary." Restatement (Second) of Contracts § 302(1). An "intended beneficiary" means those persons necessary to reflect the intention of the parties to the contract, and either (i) performance will satisfy an obligation of the promisee to pay money to the beneficiary; or (ii) circumstances indicate the promisee intends to give the beneficiary the benefit of the promise. Restatement (Second) of Contracts § 302(1)(a)–(b).

While the Restatement (Second) of Contracts admirably avoids the rigidity of a rule requiring that a beneficiary must be either a creditor beneficiary or a donee beneficiary and adds an analysis of the intent of the "parties" rather than simply that of the "promisee," the improvements present their own unique problems. See Ernest M. Jones, "Legal Protection of Third Party Beneficiaries: On Opening Courthouse Doors," 46 U. Cin. L.

Rev. 313, 319–20 (1977) ("freedom of contract requires consideration of the common or shared intentions of both promisor and promise"). First, to discern the intent of the parties, the language reverts back to the language of the Restatement (First) of Contracts. This inevitably occurs because two "types" of intended categories are referenced. So, while the language purports to collapse donee and creditor beneficiaries into one category embracing all intended beneficiaries, the language links a "requirement" that the intended beneficiary must be of one style or the other. The commentary then notes the first style is "often referred to as a creditor beneficiary" (Restatement (Second) of Contracts § 302, *cmt. b*) and the second style is "often referred to as a donee beneficiary" (Restatement (Second) of Contracts § 302, *cmt. c*). Nonetheless, the intent to benefit test is clearly broader than the earlier two-category straightjacket, while at the same time maintaining the sense of the old common law distinctions. David M. Summers, Note, "Third Party Beneficiaries and the Restatement (Second) of Contracts," 67 Cornell L. Rev. 880, 889 (1982) and Note, "Third Party Beneficiaries and the Intention Standard: A Search for Rational Contract Decision-Making," 54 Va. L. Rev. 1166 (1968).

In a further expansion, the commentary contemplates creating third-party beneficiary status when the intended beneficiary "would be reasonable in relying upon on the promise." Restatement (Second) of Contracts § 302, *cmt. d*. The plaintiff in neither the *Lawrence* or *Seaver* cases was required to prove actual reliance. Because the beneficiary need not prove "actual reliance," the referenced reliance must simply include reasonable hypothetical reliance. Thus, this expansion does not appear to expand the doctrine significantly. Melvin A. Eisenberg, "Third-Party Beneficiaries," 92 Colum. L. Rev. 1358, 1383–84 (1992).

Importantly, the Restatement (Second) of Contracts § 310 eliminates the dual vesting rules inherent in Restatement (First) of Contracts § 142 (donee beneficiary) and Restatement (First) of Contracts § 143 (creditor beneficiary). Under the earlier rules, a donee beneficiary's rights vested immediately upon contract formation, but a creditor beneficiary's rights vested only upon bringing suit or incurring a material change in position. Restatement (Second) of Contracts § 310 rejects the donee beneficiary immediate vesting rule in favor of a reliance rule resembling the creditor beneficiary vesting rule. This change affects the enforceability of explicit terms prohibiting modification and the situations in which a modification is ineffective with respect to the rights of the third-party beneficiary. First, a term in the agreement itself may preclude modification of an intended beneficiary's rights. Restatement (Second) of Contracts § 310(1). The result would appear to negate the effectiveness of a later contract modification, rather than simply giving the intended beneficiary an action for damages for breach of the contract provision not to modify. Second, in the absence of such a term, the parties to the contract remain at liberty to amend the contract at any time. However, the modification is ineffective as to an intended beneficiary that (i) materially changes position in reliance on the contract prior to notice of the change; (ii) brings suit on the contract; or (iii) assents to the contract before amendment at the request of either contract party. Restatement (Second) of Contracts § 310(2)–(3). See David A. Rahnis, "Contracting Parties Retain Power to Discharge or Modify Duties Without Third-Party Beneficiary's Assent," 86 Ill. B. J. 103 (1998).

In effect, the changes on vesting moved from the old immediate done vesting rule to the creditor delayed vesting rule based largely on reliance. The vesting change reflected the fact that few cases had adopted the immediate vesting rule because it was unfair to the contracting parties. See William H. Page, "The Power of the Contracting Parties to Alter a Contract for Rendering Performance to a Third Person," 12 Wisc. L. Rev. 141 (1937).

In spite of the discussion and changes from the two restatements, common law may have been only incrementally affected. Some scholars argue that the language change has had very little impact on the rights of third-party beneficiaries. See Harry G. Prince, "Perfecting the Third Party Beneficiary Standing Rule Under Section 302 of the Restatement (Second) of Contracts," 25 B.C. L. Rev. 919 (1984).

2. THE PROBLEM OF INCIDENTAL BENEFICIARIES AND GOVERNMENT CONTRACTS

Privity or standing requirements attempt to assure the third party plaintiff has a sufficient nexus or interest in the promisor's performance to justify allowing a non-party to enforce the promise. Stated another way, the range of persons "interested" in one way or another in the performance of a contract can be and often is enormous. For example, employees are often vitally interested in their employer's critical supply contracts. Without the contract and supply, the company might fail and jobs lost.

The range of interested parties expands exponentially in the context of government contracts. Government contracts attempt to accomplish some public purpose to benefit persons served by that governmental unit. Consider, for example, the case of a government contract with a builder to construct a bridge into an office district: every commuter in the area will be personally concerned with timely completion of the contract. Do all the members of the public with a residual interest in the performance of the government contract have standing to enforce a breach, or does only the governmental party have standing to enforce the contract? The two restatements answered these questions differently. In all cases, competing policies exist. The third-party beneficiary law is conceptually justice-based, often allowing a third party to sue for enforcement when the original party cannot or chooses not do so. Of course, a specific state of federal statute may explicitly create a private cause of action. In those cases, the affected member of the public may maintain a direct cause of action under the statute, rather than seeking derivative enforcement as a third-party beneficiary.

Absent such a statutory direct cause of action, the rights of individual members of the public to enforce obligations created by a government contract depend largely upon whether the individual is an intended or an "incidental" beneficiary of the contract. Both restatements exclude incidental beneficiaries from any right to enforce. Restatement (First) of Contracts § 147 provides that an "incidental beneficiary" acquires no right against the promisor or the promisee by virtue of the promise. An incidental beneficiary is defined as a residual category, including all third parties deriving some benefit from a contract but not classified as either creditor or donee beneficiaries. Restatement (First) of Contracts § 133(1)(c). Similarly, Restatement (Second) of Contracts § 315 provides that an incidental beneficiary acquires no right against the promisor or the promisee by virtue of the promise. Likewise, an incidental beneficiary is defined as a residual category, including all third parties deriving some benefit from a contract but not classified as an intended beneficiary. Restatement (Second) of Contracts § 302(2). But, as discussed above, arguably the second restatement expanded the classes of third-party beneficiaries by rejecting the either/or distinction between creditor and donee beneficiaries in favor of intended beneficiaries. By expanding the classes of third-party beneficiaries entitled to enforce the contract, the second restatement reduces the class of incidental beneficiaries.

That said, the definitional requirements regarding third-party beneficiaries of government or public contracts have not shifted radically from the Restatement (First) of Contracts to the Restatement (Second) of Contracts. Any beneficiary of a government or public contract that is not regarded as either a creditor or donee beneficiary under the Restatement (First) of Contracts or an intended beneficiary under the Restatement (Second) of Contracts becomes an incidental beneficiary without any right to enforce the contract.

Restatement (First) of Contracts § 145 provides generally that a promisor in a contract with a governmental entity requiring service to members of the public served by the contract has no duty to such members for the consequences of a breach. Two exceptions exist. First, the member of the public served will obtain third-party beneficiary status if the contract itself reflects an intent that the promisor is directly responsible for damages to the public served. Restatement (First) of Contracts § 145(a). Second, when the nature and subject of the contract covers a matter that would create liability in the governmental contracting authority to the public for a failure to render the service, third-party beneficiary status will be granted. Restatement (First) of Contracts § 145(b).

That definition changed somewhat in the later restatement. Restatement (Second) of Contracts § 313(1) clarifies that the liability of a government contractor is not any broader than that of other contractors. Restatement (Second) of Contracts § 313(2) merely rephrases Restatement (First) of Contracts § 145(a)–(b).

Since both restatements begin with the negative proposition that members of the public generally cannot maintain an action directly against the government contractor, litigation in this area focuses on the two exceptions.

The first exception generally requires a determination of whether the contract language itself adequately implies that the member of the public is an intended third-party donee beneficiary. Contracts rarely state explicitly that a contractor is liable to the public. However, contract language routinely provides that the contractor is responsible for any damage to government or "private property" when carrying out the terms of the contract. Some courts interpret this to hold the contractor liable directly to the injured third party for property or personal injury damage. See e.g., *La Mourea v. Rhude*, 209 Minn. 53, 295 N.W. 304 (1940) (sewer construction contract provided contractor liable for personal property damage, thereby entitling homeowner to sue directly as result of damage). A contrary result was reached in an earlier New York case involving private homeowner damage due to a failure of a government contractor to provide fire hydrant water. See *H. R. Moch Co. v. Rensselaer Water Co.*, 247 N.Y. 160, 159 N.E. 896 (1928) (Cardozo, C. J.) (contract silent on liability of contractor to public).

The second exception essentially provides that a member of the public can sue the contractor directly when the contracting governmental unit itself was under a separate and independent duty to render the service to the public. The independent duty must arise other than from the contract itself, thus implicating both tort law and statutory interpretation. Where either tort law or a statute creates an implied duty, the member of the public may assert a third-party beneficiary action directly against the promisor. Robert S. Adelson, Note, "Third Party Beneficiary and Implied Right of Action Analysis: The Fiction of One Governmental Intent," 94 Yale L. J. 875, 879 (1985). Generally speaking, such a third-party beneficiary is either an intended or a creditor beneficiary. See Joseph M. Perillo, Calamari and Perillo on Contracts § 17.7 (5th ed. 2003). Given the limited governmental duties owed, this is a narrow exception and arises outside the contract itself.

The problem for government contractors, of course, is that the potentially large scope of government contracts may increase the promisor's liability well beyond that imagined by the promisor at the time the contract was formed. Consequently, the foreseeability rules embraced in the famous *Hadley v. Baxendale* case discussed in Chapter 9 are critical as limitations on government contractor liability. Absent such limitations, at some point, ballooning liability would increase the cost of performance and insurance, and potentially radically increase the cost of government contracts. Such a cost would simply be passed on to all members of the public. See Melvin A. Eisenberg, "Third-Party Beneficiaries," 92 Colum. L. Rev. 1358, 1407 (1992) and Anthony Jon Waters, "The Property in the Promise: A Study of the Third Party Beneficiary Rule," 98 Harv. L. Rev. 1109 (1985).

MARTINEZ V. SOCOMA COMPANIES, INC.

Supreme Court of California
11 Cal.3d 394, 521 P.2d 841, 113 Cal.Rptr. 585 (1974)

WRIGHT, Chief Justice.

Plaintiffs brought this class action on behalf of themselves and other disadvantaged unemployed persons, alleging that defendants failed to perform contracts with the United States government under which defendants agreed to provide job training and at least one year of employment to certain numbers of such persons. Plaintiffs claim that they and the other such persons are third party beneficiaries of the contracts and as such are entitled to damages for defendants' nonperformance. General demurrers to the complaint were sustained without leave to amend, apparently on the ground that plaintiffs lacked standing to sue as third party beneficiaries. Dismissals were entered as to the demurring defendants, and plaintiffs appeal.

We affirm the judgments of dismissal. As will appear, the contracts nowhere state that either the government or defendants are to be liable to persons such as plaintiffs for damages resulting from the defendants' nonperformance. The benefits to be derived from defendants' performance were clearly intended not as gifts from the government to such persons but as a means of executing the public purposes stated in the contracts and in the underlying legislation. Accordingly, plaintiffs were only incidental beneficiaries and as such have no right of recovery.

The complaint names as defendants Socoma Companies, Inc. ('Socoma'), Lady Fair Kitchens, Incorporated ('Lady Fair'), Monarch Electronics International, Inc. ('Monarch'), and eleven individuals of whom three are alleged officers or directors of Socoma, four of Lady Fair, and four of Monarch. Lady Fair and the individual defendants associated with it, a Utah corporation and Utah residents respectively, did not appear in the trial court and are not parties to this appeal.

The complaint alleges that under 1967 amendments to the Economic Opportunity Act of 1964 (81 Stat. 688–690, 42 U.S.C. §§ 2763–2768, repealed by 86 Stat. 703 (1972)) "the United States Congress instituted

Special Impact Programs with the intent to benefit the residents of certain neighborhoods having especially large concentrations of low income persons and suffering from dependency, chronic unemployment and rising tensions." Funds to administer these programs were appropriated to the United States Department of Labor. The department subsequently designated the East Los Angeles neighborhood as a "Special Impact Area" and made federal funds available for contracts with local private industry for the benefit of the 'hard-core unemployed residents' of East Los Angeles.

On January 17, 1969, the corporate defendants allegedly entered into contracts with the Secretary of Labor, acting on behalf of the Manpower Administration, United States Department of Labor (hereinafter referred to as the 'Government'). Each such defendant entered into a separate contract and all three contracts are made a part of the complaint as exhibits. Under each contract the contracting defendant agreed to lease space in the then vacant Lincoln Heights jail building owned by the City of Los Angeles, to invest at least $5,000,000 in renovating the leasehold and establishing a facility for the manufacture of certain articles, to train and employ in such facility for at least 12 months, at minimum wage rates, a specified number of East Los Angeles residents certified as disadvantaged by the Government, and to provide such employees with opportunities for promotion into available supervisory-management positions and with options to purchase stock in their employer corporation. Each contract provided for the lease of different space in the building and for the manufacture of a different kind of product. As consideration, the Government agreed to pay each defendant a stated amount in installments. Socoma was to hire 650 persons and receive $950,000; Lady Fair was to hire 550 persons and receive $999,000; and Monarch was to hire 400 persons and receive $800,000. The hiring of these persons was to be completed by January 17, 1970.

Plaintiffs were allegedly members of a class of no more than 2,017 East Los Angeles residents who were certified as disadvantaged and were qualified for employment under the contracts. Although the Government paid $712,500 of the contractual consideration to Socoma, $299,700 to Lady Fair, and $240,000 to Monarch, all of these defendants failed to perform under their respective contracts, except that Socoma provided 186 jobs of which 139 were wrongfully terminated, and Lady Fair provided 90 jobs, of which all were wrongfully terminated.

The complaint contains 11 causes of action. The second, fourth, and sixth causes of action seek damages of $3,607,500 against Socoma, $3,052,500 against Lady Fair, and $2,220,000 against Monarch, calculated on the basis of 12 months' wages at minimum rates and $1,000 for loss of training for each of the jobs the defendant contracted to provide. The third and fifth causes of action seek similar damages for the 139 persons whose jobs were terminated by Socoma and the 90 persons whose jobs were terminated by Lady Fair. The first, seventh, and eighth causes of action seek to impose joint liability on Socoma, Lady Fair, and Monarch as joint venturers, alleging that they negotiated the contracts through a common representative and entered into a joint lease of the Lincoln Heights jail building. The ninth, tenth, and eleventh causes of action seek to impose the liability of the corporate defendants upon their officers and directors named as individual defendants, alleging that the latter undercapitalized their respective corporations and used the same as their alter egos.

Each cause of action alleges that the "express purpose of the (Government) in entering into (each) contract was to benefit (the) certified disadvantaged hard-core unemployed residents of East Los Angeles (for whom defendants promised to provide training and jobs) and none other, and those residents are thus the express third party beneficiaries of (each) contract."

The general demurrers admitted the truth of all the material factual allegations of the complaint, regardless of any possible difficulty in proving them . . . , but did not admit allegations which constitute conclusions of law . . . or which are contrary to matters of which we must take judicial notice. . . . When a complaint is based on a written contract which it sets out in full, a general demurrer to the complaint admits not only the contents of the instrument but also any pleaded meaning to which the instrument is reasonably susceptible. . . . Moreover, where, as here, the general demurrer is to an Original complaint and is sustained without leave to amend, "the issues presented are whether the complaint states a cause of action, and if not, whether there is a reasonable possibility that it could be amended to do so." (MacLeod v. Tribune Publishing Co. (1959) 52 Cal.2d 536, 542, 343 P.2d 36, 38. . . .) Thus, we must determine whether the pleaded written contracts support plaintiffs' claim either on their face or under any interpretation to which the contracts are reasonably susceptible and which is pleaded in the complaint or could be pleaded by proper amendment. This determination must be made in light of applicable federal statutes and other matters we must judicially notice. (Evic. Code, §§ 451, 459, subd. (a).)

Plaintiffs contend they are third party beneficiaries under Civil Code section 1559, which provides: "A contract, made expressly for the benefit of a third person, may be enforced by him at any time before the parties thereto rescind it." This section excludes enforcement of a contract by persons who are only incidentally or remotely benefited by it. . . . American law generally classifies persons having enforceable rights under contracts to which they are not parties as either creditor beneficiaries or donee beneficiaries. (Rest. Contracts, §§ 133, subds. (1), (2), 135, 136, 147; 2 Williston on Contracts (3d ed. 1959) § 356; 4 Corbin on Contracts (1951) § 774; see Rest. 2d Contracts (Tentative Drafts 1973) § 133, coms. b, c.) California decisions follow this classification. (Southern Cal. Gas Co. v.

ABC Construction Co. (1962) 204 Cal. App. 2d 747, 752, 22 Cal. Rptr. 540; . . .)

A person cannot be a creditor beneficiary unless the promisor's performance of the contract will discharge some form of legal duty owed to the beneficiary by the promisee. (. . . Rest. Contracts, § 133, subd. (1)(b).) Clearly the Government (the promisee) at no time bore any legal duty toward plaintiffs to provide the benefits set forth in the contracts and plaintiffs do not claim to be creditor beneficiaries.

A person is a donee beneficiary only if the promisee's contractual intent is either to make a gift to him or to confer on him a right against the promisor. (Rest. Contracts § 133, subd. (1)(a).) If the promisee intends to make a gift, the donee beneficiary can recover if such donative intent must have been understood by the promisor from the nature of the contract and the circumstances accompanying its execution. . . . This rule does not aid plaintiffs, however, because, as will be seen, no intention to make a gift can be imputed to the Government as promisee.

Unquestionably plaintiffs were among those whom the Government intended to benefit through defendants' performance of the contracts which recite that they are executed pursuant to a statute and a presidential directive calling for programs to furnish disadvantaged persons with training and employment opportunities. However, the fact that a Government program for social betterment confers benefits upon individuals who are not required to render contractual consideration in return does not necessarily imply that the benefits are intended as gifts. Congress' power to spend money in aid of the general welfare (U.S. Const., art. I, § 8) authorizes federal programs to alleviate national unemployment. (Helvering v. Davis (1937) 301 U.S. 619, 640–645, 57 S. Ct. 904, 81 L. Ed. 1307.) The benefits of such programs are provided not simply as gifts to the recipients but as a means of accomplishing a larger public purpose. The furtherance of the public purpose is in the nature of consideration to the Government, displacing any governmental intent to furnish the benefits as gifts. (See County of Alameda v. Janssen (1940) 16 Cal. 2d 276, 281, 106 P.2d 11 . . . .)

Even though a person is not the intended recipient of a gift, he may nevertheless be "a donee beneficiary if it appears from the terms of the promise in view of the accompanying circumstances that the purpose of the promisee in obtaining the promise . . . is . . . to confer upon him a right against the promisor to some performance neither due nor supposed or asserted to be due from the promisee to the beneficiary." (Rest. Contracts, § 133, subd. (1)(a) (italics supplied. . . .) The Government may, of course, deliberately implement a public purpose by including provisions in its contracts which expressly confer on a specified class of third persons a direct right to benefits, or damages in lieu of benefits, against the private contractor. But a governmental intent to confer such a direct right cannot be inferred simply from the fact that the third persons were intended to enjoy the benefits. The Restatement of Contracts makes this clear in dealing specifically with contractual promises to the Government to render services to members of the public: "A promisor bound to the United States or to a State or municipality by contract to do an act or render a service to some or all of the members of the public, is subject to no duty under the contract to such members to give compensation for the injurious consequences of performing or attempting to perform it, or of failing to do so, unless, . . . an intention is manifested in the contract, as interpreted in the light of the circumstances surrounding its formation, that the promisor shall compensate members of the public for such injurious consequences. . . ." (Rest. Contracts § 145 (italics supplied);[2] see City & County of San Francisco v. Western Air Lines, Inc. (1962) 204 Cal. App.2d 105, 121, 22 Cal. Rptr. 216.)

The language omitted in this quotation and the quotation in the accompanying text relates to the creditor beneficiary situation in which the government itself would be liable for nonperformance of the contract. As noted earlier, plaintiffs do not claim to be creditor beneficiaries.

The present contracts manifest no intent that the defendants pay damages to compensate plaintiffs or other members of the public for their nonperformance. To the contrary, the contracts' provisions for retaining the Government's control over determination of contractual disputes and for limiting defendants' financial risks indicate a governmental purpose to exclude the direct rights against defendants claimed here.

Each contract provides that any dispute of fact arising thereunder is to be determined by written decision of the Government's contracting officer, subject to an appeal to the Secretary of Labor, whose decision shall be final unless determined by a competent court to have been fraudulent, capricious, arbitrary, in bad faith, or not supported by substantial evidence. These administrative decisions may include determinations of related questions of law although such determinations are not made final. The efficiency and uniformity of interpretation fostered by these administrative procedures would tend to be undermined if litigation such as the present action, to which the Government is a stranger, were permitted to proceed on the merits.

In addition to the provisions on resolving disputes each contract contains a 'liquidated damages' provision obligating the contractor to refund all amounts received from the Government, with interest, in the

---

[2] The corresponding language in the Tentative Drafts of the Restatement Second of Contracts (1973), section 145, is: "(A) promisor who contracts with a government or governmental agency to do an act for or render a service to the public is not subject to contractual liability to a member of the public for consequential damages resulting from performance or failure to perform unless . . . the terms of the promise provide for such liability. . . ."

event of failure to acquire and equip the specified manufacturing facility, and, for each employment opportunity it fails to provide, to refund a stated dollar amount equivalent to the total contract compensation divided by the number of jobs agreed to be provided. This liquidated damages provision limits liability for the breaches alleged by plaintiffs to the refunding of amounts received and indicates an absence of any contractual intent to impose liability directly in favor of plaintiffs, or, as claimed in the complaint, to impose liability for the value of the promised performance. To allow plaintiffs' claim would nullify the limited liability for which defendants bargained and which the Government may well have held out as an inducement in negotiating the contracts.[3]

It is this absence of any manifestation of intent that defendants should pay compensation for breach to persons in the position of plaintiffs that distinguishes this case from Shell v. Schmidt (1954) 126 Cal. App. 2d 279, 272 P. 2d 82, relied on by plaintiffs. The defendant in Shell was a building contractor who had entered into an agreement with the federal government under which he received priorities for building materials and agreed in return to use the materials to build homes with required specifications for sale to war veterans at or below ceiling prices. Plaintiffs were 12 veterans, each of whom had purchased a home that failed to comply with the agreed specifications. They were held entitled to recover directly from the defendant contractor as third party beneficiaries of his agreement with the government. The legislation under which the agreement was made included a provision empowering the government to obtain payment of monetary compensation by the contractor to the veteran purchasers for deficiencies resulting from failure to comply with specifications. Thus, there was "an intention . . . manifested in the contract . . . that the promisor shall compensate members of the public for such injurious consequences (of nonperformance)."[4]

---

[3]   Comment A of a section 145 of the Tentative Drafts of the Restatement Second of Contracts points out that these factors-retention of administrative control and limitation of contractor's liability-make third party suits against the contractor inappropriate: "Government contracts often benefit the public, but individual members of the public are treated as incidental beneficiaries unless a different intention is manifested. In case of doubt, a promise to do an act for or render a service to the public does not have the effect of a promise to pay consequential damages to individual members of the public unless the conditions of Subsection (2)(b) (including governmental inability to the claimant) are met. Among factors which may make inappropriate a direct action against the promisor are Arrangements for governmental control over the litigation and settlement of claims, the likelihood of impairment of service or of excessive financial burden, and the availability of alternatives such as insurance." (Italics supplied.)

[4]   In contrast to Shell, supra, is City & County of San Francisco v. Western Air Lines, Inc., supra, 204 Cal. App. 2d 105, 22 Cal. Rptr. 216. There, Western Air Lines claimed to be a third party beneficiary of agreements between the federal government and the City and County of San Francisco under which the city received federal funds for the development of its airport subject to a written condition that the airport 'be available for public use on fair and reasonable terms and without unjust discrimination.' Western Air Lines asserted that it had been charged for its use of the airport at a higher rate than some other air carriers in violation of the contractual condition, and therefore was entitled to recover the excess charges from the city. One of the reasons given by the court on appeal for rejecting this contention was the absence of any provision or indication of

Plaintiffs contend that section 145 of the Restatement of Contracts, previously quoted, does not preclude their recovery because it applies only to promises made to a governmental entity "to do an act or render a service to . . . the public," and, plaintiffs assert they and the class they represent are identified persons set apart from "the public." Even if this contention were correct it would not follow that plaintiffs have standing as third party beneficiaries under the Restatement. The quoted provision of section 145 "is a special application of the principles stated in §§ 133(1a), 135 (on donee beneficiaries)" (Rest. Contracts § 145, com. a), delineating certain circumstances which preclude government contractors' liability to third parties. Section 145 itself does not purport to confer standing to sue on persons who do not otherwise qualify under basic third party beneficiary principles.[5] As pointed out above, plaintiffs are not donee beneficiaries under those basic principles because it does not appear from the terms and circumstances of the contract that the Government intended to make a gift to plaintiffs or to confer on them a legal right against the defendants.

Moreover, contrary to plaintiffs' contention, section 145 of the Restatement of Contracts does preclude their recovery because the services which the contracts required the defendants to perform were to be rendered to "members of the public" within the meaning of that section. Each contract recites it is made under the "Special Impact Programs" part of the Economic Opportunity Act of 1964 and pursuant to a presidential directive for a test program of cooperation between the federal government and private industry in an effort to provide training and jobs for thousands of the hard-core unemployed or under-employed. The congressional declaration of purpose of the Economic Opportunity Act as a whole points up the public nature of its benefits on a national scale. Congress declared that the purpose of the act was to "strengthen, supplement, and coordinate efforts in furtherance of (the) policy" of "opening to everyone the opportunity for education and training, the opportunity to work, and the opportunity to live in decency and dignity" so that the "United States can

---

intent in the agreements between the government and the city to compensate third parties for noncompliance. The court said: The granting agreement in each instance entitles the (federal) administrator to recover all grant payments made where there has been any misrepresentation or omission of a material fact by the sponsor (i.e., the city). We find no other provision for recovery of funds by the administrator and none whatsoever permitting recovery of money or excess rates by a private party. Indeed the language of the granting agreement itself appears to us to point up that it is simply and entirely a financial arrangement between two parties. As the agreement states, it constitutes "the obligations and rights of the United States and the Sponsor with respect to the accomplishment of the Project. . . ." (204 Cal. App. 2d at p. 120, 22 Cal. Rptr. at p. 225.)

[5]   The same is true of the Tentative Draft of section 145 of the Restatement Second of Contracts which declares that the general rules on third party beneficiaries "apply to contracts with a government or governmental agency except to the extent that application would contravene the policy of the law authorizing the contract or prescribing remedies for its breach" and that "(i)n particular" the limitations of section 145, including those set forth in footnote 2, supra, apply to a government contractor's liability to a member of the public for nonperformance of a service to the public.

achieve its full economic and social potential as a nation." (42 U.S.C. § 2701.)

In providing for special impact programs, Congress declared that such programs were directed to the solution of critical problems existing in particular neighborhoods having especially large concentration of low-income persons, and that the programs were intended to be of sufficient size and scope to have an appreciable impact in such neighborhoods in arresting tendencies toward dependency, chronic unemployment, and rising community tensions. (42 U.S.C. former § 2763.) Thus the contracts here were designed not to benefit individuals as such but to utilize the training and employment of disadvantaged persons as a means of improving the East Los Angeles neighborhood. Moreover, the means by which the contracts were intended to accomplish this community improvement were not confined to provision of the particular benefits on which plaintiffs base their claim to damages—one year's employment at minimum wages plus $1,000 worth of training to be provided to each of 650 persons by one defendant, 400 by another, and 550 by another. Rather the objective was to be achieved by establishing permanent industries in which local residents would be permanently employed and would have opportunities to become supervisors, managers and part owners. The required minimum capital investment of $5,000,000 by each defendant and the defendants' 22-year lease of the former Lincoln Heights jail building for conversion into an industrial facility also indicates the broad, long-range objective of the program. Presumably, as the planned enterprises prospered, the quantity and quality of employment and economic opportunity that they provided would increase and would benefit not only employees but also their families, other local enterprises and the government itself through reduction of law enforcement of welfare costs.

The fact that plaintiffs were in a position to benefit more directly than certain other members of the public from performance of the contract does not alter their status as incidental beneficiaries. (See Rest. Contracts § 145, illus. 1:C, a member of the public cannot recover for injury from B's failure to perform a contract with the United States to carry mail over a certain route.) For example, in City & County of San Francisco v. Western Air Lines, Inc., supra, 204 Cal. App. 2d 105, 22 Cal. Rptr. 216, the agreement between the federal government and the city for improvement of the airport could be considered to be of greater benefit to air carriers using the airport than to many other members of the public. Nevertheless, Western, as an air carrier, was but an incidental, not an express, beneficiary of the agreement and therefore had no standing to enforce the contractual prohibition against discrimination in the airport's availability for public use. The court explains the distinction as follows:

> None of the documents under consideration confers on Western the rights of a third-party beneficiary. The various contracts and

assurances created benefits and detriments as between only two parties—the United States and the City. Nothing in them shows any intent of the contracting parties to confer any benefit directly and expressly upon air carriers such as the defendant. It is true that air carriers, including Western, may be incidentally benefited by City's assurances in respect to nondiscriminatory treatment at the airport. They may also be incidentally benefited by the fact that, through federal aid, a public airport is improved with longer runways, brighter beacons, or larger loading ramps, or by the fact a new public airport is provided for a community without one. The various documents and agreements were part of a federal aid program directed to the promoting of a national transportation system. Provisions in such agreements, including the nondiscrimination clauses, were intended to advance such federal aims and not for the benefit of those who might be affected by the sponsor's failure to perform. (204 Cal. App. 2d at p. 120, 22 Cal. Rptr. at p. 225.)

For the reasons above stated we hold that plaintiffs and the class they represent have no standing as third party beneficiaries to recover the damages sought in the complaint under either California law or the general contract principles which federal law applies to government contracts.

The judgments of dismissal are affirmed.

McCOMB, SULLIVAN, and CLARK, JJ., concur.

BURKE, Justice (dissenting).

I dissent. The certified hard-core unemployed of East Los Angeles were the express, not incidental, beneficiaries of the contracts in question and, therefore, have standing to enforce those contracts.

As the majority point out, we must reverse the order sustaining the demurrer in this case if we determine the written contracts incorporated into the complaint support plaintiffs' claim either on their face or under any interpretation to which the contracts are reasonably susceptible. . . . Furthermore, at this stage of the proceedings, the question of plaintiffs' ability to prove these allegations does not concern us, for plaintiffs need only plead facts showing they may be entitled to some relief. . . .

Civil Code section 1559 provides that "A contract, made expressly for the benefit of a third person, may be enforced by him at any time before the parties thereto rescind it." The general principles applicable to such contracts are set forth in Shell v. Schmidt, 126 Cal. App. 2d 279, 290–291, 272 P. 2d 82, 89, as follows: (A) third party beneficiary may maintain an action directly on such a contract. (Citation.) The promise in such a situation is treated as having been made directly to the third party. (Citation.) It is no objection to an action by the third party that the contracting party (here the government) could also sue upon the contract for the same breach. (Citation.) Of course, the beneficiary must be more than incidentally benefited by the contract. An incidental beneficiary cannot successfully maintain an action. (Citation.) Whether the beneficiary is or is not an incidental one, or a beneficiary for whose express benefit the contract was entered into, is a question of construction. (Citation.) It is not required that the third party beneficiary be specifically named as a beneficiary. All that section 1559 requires is that the contract be "made expressly for the benefit of a third person," and "expressly" simply means "in an express manner; in direct or unmistakable terms; explicitly; definitely; directly." (Citation.) Where the contract is for the benefit of a class any members or member of the intended class may enforce it. (Citation.) The fact that the government is one of the contracting parties does not change the rule. (Italics added.)

Applying the foregoing principles to the instant case I conclude that plaintiffs are express beneficiaries of the contracts between defendants and the government and are therefore entitled to enforce the contracts.

The majority contend that the congressional purpose in enacting the Economic Opportunity Act of 1964 (including the subsequent amendments thereto creating the Special Impact Program), and the government's purpose in executing the instant contracts with defendants pursuant to the Act, was to benefit only the general public and particularly the local neighborhoods where these programs were to be implemented. Although members of plaintiffs' class 'were among those whom the Government intended to benefit . . . ,' (maj. opn., p. 589) the benefits accruing to plaintiffs' class, according to the majority, were merely 'means of executing the public purposes stated in the contracts and in the underlying legislation.' (P. 587, italics added.)

The majority err in the above conclusion because the congressional purpose was to benefit *both* the communities in which the impact programs are established *and* the individual impoverished persons in such communities.[1] The benefits from the instant contracts were to accrue directly to the members of plaintiffs' class, as a reading of the contracts clearly demonstrates.[2] These direct benefits to members of plaintiffs' class

---

[1]   Evidence of Congress' purpose to aid the individual impoverished persons in such communities can be gleaned from 42 U.S.C.A. § 2701, wherein Congress declared that if our country is to achieve its full potential, "every individual" must be given "the opportunity for education and training, the opportunity to work, and the opportunity to live in decency and dignity." Congress implemented this general policy of assisting our impoverished citizens in various ways, including the Special Impact Program involved in this case. Yet, contrary to the majority, nothing indicates that Congress' Exclusive purpose in doing so was to assist the neighborhoods and communities in which these persons live. It seems clear that Congress intended both the communities and the individuals to be direct beneficiaries of the program. It is incorrect to label one as an intended direct beneficiary and the other as merely incidental.

[2]   In the contracts, the defendants agreed to provide training and jobs to a specified class of persons, whom plaintiffs represent. The government's express intent, therefore, was to confer a

were not merely the "means of executing the public purposes," as the majority contend (p. 589, italics added), but were the ends in themselves and one of the public purposes to which the legislation and subsequent contracts were addressed. Accordingly, I cannot agree with the majority that "the contracts here were designed not to benefit individuals as such but to utilize the training and employment of disadvantaged persons as a means of improving the East Los Angeles neighborhood." (pp. 592, 593, italics added.)

The intent of the contracts themselves is expressed in their preambles:

WHEREAS, the Secretary of Labor is authorized . . . to enter into contracts to provide for Special Impact Programs . . . directed to the solution of the critical problems existing in particular communities and neighborhoods within urban areas of the Nation having especially large concentrations of low-income persons and

WHEREAS, the President of the United States on October 2, 1967, launched a major test program to mobilize the resources of private industry and the Federal Government to help find jobs and provide training for thousands of the Nation's hardcore unemployed, or underemployed, by inviting private industry throughout the country to join with the agencies and departments of the Federal Government in assuming responsibility for providing training and work opportunities for such seriously disadvantaged persons.

NOW THEREFORE, pursuant to the aforesaid statutory authority, and the directive of the President, the parties hereto, in consideration of the mutual promises herein expressed, agree as follows: . . . (Italics added.) By these provisions, the contracting parties clearly state as one of their purposes their intent to find jobs for the hard-core unemployed.

In accord with this expressed intent, the substantive provisions of the contracts confer a direct benefit upon the class seeking to enforce them. The contracts call for the hiring of stated numbers of hard-core unemployed from the East Los Angeles Special Impact Area for a period of at least one year at a starting minimum wage of $2.00 per hour for the first 90 days and a minimum wage of $2.25 per hour thereafter, or for the prevailing wage for the area, whichever is higher. In addition to requiring appropriate job training for such employees, the contracts also require "that the Contractor will arrange for the orderly promotion of persons so employed into available supervisory-managerial and other positions, and will arrange for all contract employees to obtain a total ownership interest not exceeding thirty (30) percent in the Contractor through an appropriate

---

benefit, namely training and jobs, upon an ascertainable identifiable class and not simply the general public itself.

stock purchase plan. . . ." The scope of the stock purchase plans is detailed in each of the contracts.

In Lucas v. Hamm, 56 Cal. 2d 583, 590, 15 Cal. Rptr. 821, 364 P.2d 685, we noted that one of the usual characteristics of a third party beneficiary contract is that performance is to be rendered directly to the beneficiary. The direct benefits to accrue to the beneficiaries as enumerated above renders inescapable the conclusion that these are third party beneficiary contracts.

Although the contracts may also benefit particular communities and neighborhoods, this fact does not preclude the maintenance of the action by plaintiffs as intended beneficiaries of the contracts. It is not necessary under Civil Code section 1559, supra, that a contract be exclusively for the benefit of a third party to give him a right to enforce its provisions. . . . And, as will be discussed more fully, *infra*, nor does the existence of a liquidated damages clause running in favor of the government defeat plaintiffs' right to recover under the contract; the fact that the government may also being an action for the same breach does not bar the third party beneficiary from enforcing his rights. (Shell v. Schmidt, Supra, 126 Cal. App. 2d 279, 290, 272 P.2d 82.) All that is necessary is that the third party show he is a member of a class for whose benefit the contract was made. (Shell v. Schmidt, Supra; Ralph C. Sutro Co. v. Paramount, Supra.) Thus, plaintiffs have standing to bring an action for the breach of defendants' contracts with the government.

The majority, relying on Restatement of Contracts section 145, and City and County of San Francisco v. Western Air Lines, Inc., 204 Cal.App.2d 105, 22 Cal. Rptr. 216, contend that in the context of government contracts the intent to confer upon a third party a right of action against the promisor must be express; that intent "cannot be inferred simply from the fact that the third persons were intended to enjoy the benefits. . . ." (p. 589.) The majority insist that "The fact that plaintiffs were in a position to benefit more directly than certain other members of the public from performance of the contract does not alter their status as incidental beneficiaries." (p. 593.) The majority conclude (p. 592) that "section 145 of the Restatement of Contracts does preclude (plaintiffs') recovery because the services which the contracts required the defendants to perform were to be rendered to 'members of the public' within the meaning of that section." (Italics added by majority.)

The majority's reliance on Restatement of Contracts section 145, and City and County of San Francisco v. Western Air Lines, Inc., Supra, 204 Cal. App. 2d 105, 22 Cal. Rptr. 216, is misplaced. An analysis of section 145 of the Restatement (which also forms a part of the basis for the rule of Western Air lines) indicates that its provisions are not applicable to the case at hand. Section 145 provides in pertinent part that "A promisor bound to the United States or to a State or municipality by contract to do an act or render a service to some or all of the members of the public, is subject to no duty under the contract to such members to give compensation for the injurious consequences of performing or attempting to perform it, or of failing to do so, unless, (a) an intention is manifested in the light of the circumstances surrounding its formation, that the promisor shall compensate members of the public for such injurious consequences. . . ." (Italics added.)

The express language of this provision indicates that it applies only to a promise to do an act or render a service to "some or all of the members of the public." The section deals solely with the promisor's duty to give compensation to 'such' members of the public. The type of government contract to which section 145 applies is therefore distinguishable from the contracts in the instant case. Here, the contracts specify a particular class of persons who are to receive a direct benefit. The beneficiaries of these contracts are to receive the promised performance because of their membership in a particularly defined and limited class and not simply because they are members of the public in general. Defendants are not bound to 'do an act or render a service to some or all of the members of the public'; thus, by its own terms, section 145 of the Restatement is not applicable.

In addition, as indicated by comment (a) to section 145 of the Restatement, that section is merely a special application of the principles stated in Restatement section 133 which provides in part that "(1) Where performance of a promise in a contract will benefit a person other than the promisee, that person is, . . . (a) a donee beneficiary if it appears from the terms of the promise in view of the accompanying circumstances that the purpose of the promisee in obtaining the promise of all or part of the performance thereof is to make a gift to the beneficiary or to confer upon him a right against the promisor to some performance neither due nor supposed or asserted to be due from the promisee to the beneficiary. . . ."[3] Section 135 of the Restatement makes such a contract enforceable by the donee beneficiary.[4]

---

[3] Comment (c) to section 133 of the Restatement of Contracts states in part that "by gift is meant primarily some performance or right which is not paid for by the recipient and which is apparently designed to benefit him." Thus, section 133 states essentially the same rule as that enunciated in Shell v. Schmidt, Supra, 126 Cal. App. 2d 279, 290–291, 272 P. 2d 82. Section 133 has been followed by the California courts. (Hartman Ranch Co. v. Associated Oil Co., Supra, 10 Cal. 2d 232, 244, 73 P. 2d 1163; Southern Cal. Gas Co. v. ABC Construction Co., 204 Cal. App. 2d 747, 752, 22 Cal. Rptr. 540.)

[4] Section 135 of the Restatement of Contracts, Supra, provides: "Except as stated in § 140 (giving the promisor the protection against the third party beneficiary of any defenses he has against the promisee), (a) a gift promise in a contract creates a duty of the promisor to the donee beneficiary to perform the promise; and the duty can be enforced by the donee beneficiary for his own benefit; (b) a gift promise also creates a duty of the promisor to the promisee to render the promised performance to the donee beneficiary."

The language of section 133, standing alone, could reasonably suggest that members of the general public are 'donee beneficiaries' under any contract whose purpose is to confer a 'gift' upon them. Section 145 qualifies this broad language and treats the general public merely as incidental, not direct, beneficiaries under contracts made for the general public benefit, unless the contract manifests a clear intent to compensate such members of the public in the event of a breach. Section 145 does not, however, entirely preclude application of the 'donee beneficiary' concept to every government contract. Whenever, as in the instant case, such a contract expresses an intent to benefit directly a particular person or ascertainable class of persons, section 145 is, by its terms, inapplicable and the contract may be enforced by the beneficiaries pursuant to the general provisions of section 133. Thus, I would conclude that section 145 is consistent with the holding of Shell v. Schmidt, Supra, 126 Cal.App.2d 279, 272 P.2d 82, and the City and County of San Francisco v. Western Air Lines, Inc., Supra, 204 Cal.App.2d 105, 22 Cal. Rptr. 216.[5]

Comment C to the tentative draft of section 145 states further that "Government contractors sometimes make explicit promises to pay damages to third persons, and such promises are enforced. If there is no explicit promise, and no government liability, *the question whether a particular claimant is an intended beneficiary is one of interpretation, depending on all the circumstances of the contract.*" (Italics added.) Thus, under the tentative draft, section 145 is not an outright prohibition of the enforcement of government contracts by third parties absent the enumerated conditions. Comment C makes it clear that the question as to a particular claimant is one of interpretation, and that, where, as here, the contract manifests an intent to benefit a particular third party, liability is properly imposed upon the promisee in favor of such third party.

In City and County of San Francisco v. Western Air Lines, Inc., supra, 204 Cal. App. 2d 105, 22 Cal. Rptr. 216, defendant airline was held to be merely an incidental beneficiary of contracts providing that an airport "will operate . . . for the use and benefit of the public, on fair and reasonable terms and without unjust discrimination." (p. 118, 22 Cal. Rptr. p. 224,

---

[5]   The tentative draft of section 145 in Restatement 2d, Contracts (The American Law Institute, Restatement of the Law Second, Contracts, Tentative Draft No. 3 (April 18, 1967), p. 76), also supports the conclusion that this provision of the Restatement does not bar plaintiffs' action. The tentative draft states: "In particular, a promisor who contracts with a government or governmental agency to do an act for or render a service to the public is not subject to contractual liability to a member of the public for consequential damages resulting from performance or failure to perform unless (a) the terms of the promise provide for such liability; or (b) the promisee is subject to liability to the member of the public for the damages and a direct action against the promisor is consistent with the terms of the contract and with the policy of the law authorizing the contract and prescribing remedies for its breach." (Italics added.) Comment A to the draft of section 145 explains the rationale for the section in part as follows: "Subsection (2) applies to a particular class of contracts the classification of beneficiaries in § 133. Government contracts often benefit the public, But individual members of the public are treated as incidental beneficiaries unless a different intention is manifested." (Italics added.)

italics added.) Nothing in the various contracts and assurances involved in the case "shows any intent of the contracting parties to confer any benefit directly and expressly upon air carriers such as the defendant." (p. 120, 22 Cal. Rptr. p. 225.) The court stated that "to recover as a third party beneficiary, one must show that the contract in question was made expressly for his benefit. (Citations.)" (p. 120, 22 Cal.Rptr. p. 225.)

The rationale for the Western Air Lines rule is set out in Ukiah v. Ukiah Water and Imp. Co., 142 Cal. 173, 180, 75 P. 773, 775 (quoting from an earlier case) as follows, "The bar to such a recovery in each case is that *the contract was not for the protection of any particular property or person*, but was for the general benefit of all the property and persons within the municipal limits, and was entered into by the town as a public agency, solely for that purpose, and in the exercise of its power to furnish such general protection." (Italics added.)

Since in Western Air Lines the government contract at issue was not made expressly for the benefit of defendant but instead to benefit the general public, that case was correctly decided under Restatement of Contracts section 145. However, an interpretation to which the contracts in the instant case "are reasonably susceptible and which is pleaded in the complaint or could be pleaded by proper amendment" (maj. opn., p. 588), in light of the legislative intent and the language of the contracts themselves, is that they were made expressly for the benefit of a particular class of persons, namely the class consisting of the certified hard-core unemployed of East Los Angeles.

Western Air Lines holds that a member of the general public cannot recover under a contract made for the public benefit unless there appears an intent in the contract that the promisor shall compensate the public for injuries caused by the promisor's performance or failure to perform. (204 Cal. App. 2d at pp. 120–121, 22 Cal. Rptr. 216.) That case does not stand for the proposition that an *express* beneficiary, or a class of express beneficiaries, may not enforce the contract unless it expressly declares that the parties so intended. On the contrary, under the rules set forth in Shell v. Schmidt, Supra, 126 Cal. App. 2d 279, 290–291, 272 P. 2d 82, so long as the contract expressly declares an intent to benefit a particular individual or class of persons, such persons may enforce their rights under the contract notwithstanding the absence of a provision for damages for such beneficiaries in the event of breach. Therefore, the facts of the instant case are distinguishable from those of Western Air Lines and, furthermore, Restatement of Contracts section 145 is not applicable.

The majority contend that the inclusion of liquidated damages clauses in each of the contracts limits defendants' financial risks and was intended to preclude the assertion of third party claims. (p. 590.) Yet, these clauses simply provide for various refunds of monies advanced by the government in the event of a default. These so-called "liquidated damages" clauses nowhere purport to limit damages to the specified refunds. Nothing in the contracts limits the right of the government or, more importantly, plaintiffs' class, to seek additional relief. As I noted above, the fact that the government could also sue for breach of the contracts does not affect the rights of third party beneficiaries. (Shell v. Schmidt, Supra, 126 Cal. App. 2d 279, 290, 272 P. 2d 82.)

The majority also rely on the fact that, "the present contracts manifest no intent that the defendants pay damages to compensate plaintiffs or other members of the public for their nonperformance." (p. 590.) Therefore, it assertedly follows that giving plaintiffs the right to monetary benefits in lieu of performance would give to plaintiffs and the class they represent benefits never contemplated nor intended under the contracts. This argument disregards both the fact that the class was to receive a direct monetary benefit under the contracts in the form of wages, and that under well settled contract law, an aggrieved party is entitled to be compensated for all the detriment proximately caused by a breach of contract (Civ. Code § 3300).

A contract of employment ordinarily confers upon the employee the expectation that he will obtain the work bargained for. The measure of damages for the breach of such a contract, however, is not the award of the job, but is the amount of salary the employee would have earned for the agreed upon period of service less the amount which the employer affirmatively proves the employee has earned, or with reasonable effort might have earned, from other employment. (Parker v. Twentieth Century-Fox Film Corp., 3 Cal. 3d 176, 181, 89 Cal. Rptr. 737, 474 P. 2d 689.) Thus, the fact that plaintiffs' class has been promised only jobs and job training does not prevent them from recovering an amount of money which will compensate them for the loss of such jobs and training, i.e., the damages proximately caused by defendants' breach. (Civ. Code § 3300, supra.)

It is my conclusion, therefore, that the trial court erred in sustaining the demurrer without leave to amend. I would order the trial court to determine the propriety of plaintiffs' class action prior to proceeding upon the merits of the complaint.

TOBRINER and MOSK, JJ., concur.

NOTES AND QUESTIONS

1.   *Intent-to-benefit test.* Would the adoption of the "intent" standard of Restatement (Second) of Contracts change the result in the case?

2.   *Scholarly commentary.* The majority opinion has been criticized by scholars, but remains the law in California. See Ernest M. Jones, "Legal Protection Of Third Party Beneficiaries: On Opening Courthouse Doors,"46 U. Cin. L. Rev. 313 (1977). Mostly, the criticism is directed at the finding

regarding the promisor's intent. Under this interpretation, a finding of shared intentions that the beneficiaries receive the benefit of promisor's performances would be reasonable. This notion is based on general agreement that beneficiaries of government contracts should be protected when the promisor and promisee share intentions to provide such protection. Do you agree? See also Note, "*Martinez v. Socoma Companies*: Problems in Determining Contract Beneficiaries' Rights," 27 Hastings L. J. 137 (1976).

3.   *Implied right of private suit under statute.* One of the most famous situations where the United States Supreme Court has found an implied right of private action under a federal statute is § 10 of the Securities and Exchange Act, 1934. Robert S. Adelson, in "Third Party Beneficiary and Implied Right of Action Analysis: The Fiction of One Governmental Intent," 94 Yale L.J. 875 (1985), compared the implied right of action under a statute with the implied right of a third-party beneficiary under a public contract authorized by statute.

4.   *The UCC and Third-Party Beneficiary Status.* Most scholarly commentary addresses the common law development of third-party beneficiary status, while little is devoted to the same status under the UCC. See Gary L. Monserud, "Blending the Law of Sales with the Common Law of Third-Party Beneficiaries," 39 Duq. L. Rev. 111 (2000). The UCC itself is partially silent on direct third-party status, which means that common law standards will often apply. See UCC § 1–103(b) (2001) ("Unless displaced by the particular provisions of this Act, the principles of law and equity, including the . . . law relative to capacity to contract . . . supplement its provisions."). See generally, Robert A. Hillman, "Construction of the Uniform Commercial Code: UCC Section 1–103 and 'Code' Methodology," 18 B. C. L. Rev. 655, 659 (1977).

However, as the discussion of third-party beneficiary status developed in the context of privity, any discussion of the UCC and third-party beneficiary status must necessarily embrace privity because the UCC specifically adopts various privity provisions designed to clarify when a person who did not purchase goods from the manufacturer can sue. Indeed, UCC § 2–318 is titled "Third Party Beneficiaries of Warranties Express or Implied." Conceptually, the UCC could embrace two types of privity involving plaintiffs who did not purchase goods directly from the defendant. See James J. White & Robert S. Summers, Uniform Commercial Code § 11–2 (5th ed. 2000). First, so-called "vertical privity" involves a person who purchases goods from someone other than the manufacturer. An example includes a purchaser of a lawnmower from a department store who later sues the manufacturer for damages resulting from a breach of a product warranty. Second, so-called "horizontal privity" involves a person who does not purchase the product in question, but nonetheless suffers some form of personal injury or property damage resulting from a breach of a product warranty. An example includes a neighbor injured by a defective lawnmower borrowed from the purchaser. Under the UCC, the lack of privity is discussed by way of a defense to a claim of product warranty breach.

UCC § 2–318 is silent with respect to the purchaser's right to sue within the distribution chain. Therefore, under UCC § 2–318, three alternatives remove the privity barrier to a suit by a person who did not actually purchase the goods. Alternative A extends third-party beneficiary status to family and members of the household, as well as guests, who suffer personal injury. Alternative B extends third-party beneficiary status to any natural person reasonably expected to use or consume the product who is personally injured. Alternative C follows Alternative B, but also covers property damages as well as personal injury. Strictly speaking, these alternatives are traditional third-party beneficiary rules granting the third party who is injured or suffers damage from the consumption or use of a defective product the same rights that would have been available to the purchaser. The differences in the three stated alternatives relate to the nature of the relationship between the purchaser and the third party, and the nature of the injury. See UCC § 2–318, *cmt. 3.*

UCC § 2–318 is stated in the alternative. If a particular status does not fit any of the alternatives, the UCC becomes silent on third party beneficiary status, and the common law rules in the state must be used. See UCC § 1–103(b) (2001).

Finally, the UCC privity rules are not designed to displace tort law remedies based upon negligence or strict liability. Rather, the rules are designed to consider only contract claims. Of course, an injured plaintiff could plead the tort and contract actions in the alternative, but many facets might differ, including the appropriate remedy (expectation versus reliance), statute of limitations (normally four years under UCC § 2–725, but two years in torts), and defenses (applicability of contract duty and remedy limitations).

5.   *CISG third-party beneficiary rules.* The CISG does not state a specific rule regarding third-party beneficiaries. However, the Unidroit Principles of International Commercial Contracts 2004, published by Unidroit, Rome, 2004 ("UPICC") specifically extend third-party beneficiary status to all third-party beneficiaries as determined by the express and implied terms of the agreement. See UPICC art. 5.2 and Ole Lando, "CISG and Its Followers: A Proposal to Adopt Some International Principles of Contract Law," 53 Am. J. Comp. L. 379 (2005).

B. ASSIGNMENT AND DELEGATION

The third-party beneficiary discussion revealed that the term "party" to a contract generally refers to a person who formed the original contract. A "third-party beneficiary" never actually becomes a party to the contract, but rather derives standing to enforce a promise under a contract made for the benefit of that third party. Importantly, the determination of third party beneficiary status is made at the time the contract is formed and generally focuses on the intent of the promisee to benefit the third party. At the margins, often involving public contracts, the intent of the promisor may also becomes relevant to determine how far to extend the third-party concept without exposing the promisor to unwarranted risk and multiple suits.

Conceptually, assignment and delegation doctrine is different than third-party beneficiary doctrine. Like third-party beneficiary status, a third party does not become a "party" to the contract simply by virtue of an assignment of a right ("assignee") or a delegation of a duty ("delegatee"). Technically, a third party simply acquires rights or duties under the original contract, and the assigning ("assignor") or delegating ("delegator") party remains a party to the contract. For the third party to become an actual party to the contract and the delegator to step completely away from the contract, the parties must execute a "novation." With a novation, the other party to the contract consents to release a delegating party and substitute the third party, the delegating party is no longer a party, and the substituted party becomes a true party to the contract. Restatement (Second) of Contracts § 280. Conceptually, novation is a subpart of the larger concept of substituted contract between two original parties where an original obligee generally accepts an agreed substituted performance from the original obligor. See Restatement (Second) of Contracts § 279 ("substituted contract"). Thus, in a substituted contract, the original parties modify the original contract, whereas with novation, a third party is substituted for one of the original parties. Compare the Chapter 5 discussion of "accord and satisfaction" where the original contract remains in force until the "accord agreement" is "satisfied." Upon the failure of satisfaction, the original obligee may choose whether to sue on the original contract or the accord. See Restatement (Second) of Contracts § 281 ("accord and satisfaction").

A contract must have at least two parties, and each party has both a duty to perform to the other party and a correlative right to the performance of the other party. Although a contract will generally have multiple duties owed by each party, when speaking of a particular duty the party who is under an obligation to perform that duty is called the "obligor," and the party to whom the duty is owed is called the "obligee." The obligee may separately assign the right to receive the performance due under the contract, and the obligor's duty to perform may be separately delegated. Restatement (Second) of Contracts § 316(1). While courts tend to respect the intent of the parties when rights are assigned separately from a delegation of duties, it is also possible to "assign" or "transfer" the entire contract. When this occurs, the transfer is at once both an assignment and a delegation. Restatement (Second) of Contracts § 328(1). Especially in such cases, the term "transfer" is often used rather than "assignment" because the latter implies a voluntary assignment, whereas a transfer is broader and includes involuntary transfers that occur by operation of law (e.g., mergers and family court orders). See e.g. Revised Uniform Partnership Act (1997) § 101(14).

Unlike third-party beneficiary law, a person not a party to the original contract generally obtains rights and duties under that contract by assignment or delegation after the contract is formed, not at the time the contract is formed. Indeed, at the time of formation, neither contract party may have in mind a later assignment of a right or delegation of a duty. Where the contract does specifically consider the problem of assignment and delegation, most often the parties will attempt to confine the contractual relationship to the parties that formed the contract and restrict the ability to assign and delegate. Whether such prohibitive language is effective against third parties depends upon whether a delegation of duties alone is prohibited (always effective) or whether an assignment of a mere right alone is contemplated (almost never effective). In the absence of contrary terms, the law generally favors delegation and certainly favors assignment, provided the assignment or delegation does not have a material negative effect upon the other party to the contract.

1.   ASSIGNMENT OF CONTRACT RIGHTS

The term "assignment" has a non-intuitive aspect. By definition, when a right is effectively assigned, the assignor's right to enforce the right against the obligor is extinguished. At the same time, the assignee acquires the right to the obligor's performance. Restatement (Second) of Contracts § 317(1). As a result, the obligor's duty is switched from the assignor to the assignee without the consent of the obligor. Of course, this alteration might come as an unwelcome surprise to the obligor who anticipated dealing with the original contract party but now must render performance to a perhaps unknown and unwelcome assignee. Notwithstanding the "rights" substitution, technically the assignee does not become a party to the contract. Indeed, the assignor remains a party to the contract, with contract duties continuing to the other party. Upon breach by the assignor (who remains liable for performance), the other party may sue the assignor to enforce the contract, but not the assignee.

This often raises the difficult question concerning whether the other party may assert contract defenses against the assignee. For example, should the assignor materially breach the contract, is the other party's duty to pay the assignee "discharged" in the same manner as against the assignor? In the third-party beneficiary context, the promisor retains all defenses against the third-party beneficiary that exist against the promisee. Restatement (Second) of Contracts § 309. Does the same rule apply in the context of an assignment of a right? The answer is generally the same, but subject to important limitations. Restatement (Second) of Contracts § 338(1).

First, the third-party beneficiary rule is subject to a vesting exception that generally provides that the third-party beneficiary takes free of any modification of the contracting parties arising after the third-party beneficiary status vests. Restatement (Second) of Contracts § 311. Assignment law states a similar exception in that the assignee takes free of any modification of the contracting parties that arises after notice of the assignment. See Restatement (Second) of Contracts § 338(1) and UCC § 9–406(a). For example, should the obligor pay the assignor rather than the assignee after notice of the assignment, the payment would not discharge the obligor's duty to also pay the assignee.

Second, an obligor has two types of set-off rights against an assignee. For a claim of breach of the contract by the assignor prior to notice of assignment, the obligor may offset up to the full amount due, even after notice of the assignment. But a money judgment for breach cannot be obtained separately against the assignee for the assignor's breach, and the amount of the set-off cannot exceed the amount owed by the obligor. Restatement (Second) of Contracts § 336(2) and UCC § 9–404(a)(1). A set-off for a claim against the assignor arising not from the breach of the contract itself but another matter may also be set-off against the amount due the assignee provided, however, that the set-off accrues before the notice of assignment. See UCC § 9–404(a)(2). In all cases where the obligor is permitted a defense against payment to the assignee, the assignee will have a cause of action against the assignor for breach of any implied warranties attached to the assignment. Restatement (Second) of Contracts § 333. Consequently, whether set-off rights exist or not is only important where the assignor is insolvent or otherwise unable to compensate for its breach of either the contract or the warranty of assignment. In such cases, set-off rights will determine who bears the risk of loss attached to the assignor's breaches—the assignee or the obligor.

An important difference exists for assignees that achieve elevated status, immunizing them against all defenses and set-off claims of any nature that the obligor may have against the assignor. In these special cases, after the notice of assignment, the obligor must pay the assignee, but then can pursue the assignor for a remedy. This elevated status is referred to as the "holder in due course" doctrine and essentially means that, with some exceptions, the assignee as a holder in due course takes immunity from set-off claims and all other defenses. Under UCC § 3–302, a holder in due course is a (i) holder; (ii) of a negotiable instrument; (iii) who took the instrument for value; (iv) in good faith; and (v) without notice of specified problems. However, a Federal Trade Commission rule has substantially preempted and eliminated the state law holder in due course doctrine in consumer credit transactions. See FTC Holder in Due Course Regulations, 16 C.F.R. § 433.2 (1978). Financial institutions unhappy with this rule attempt to circumvent it by forcing retailers to include a provision whereby the consumer acknowledges the contract may be assigned and agrees that the assignee takes free of any defenses or set-offs. The UCC normatively validates such clauses, but many courts refuse to enforce them, and many statutes attempt to override them. See UCC § 9–403(b)(4). See discussion of waiver of defense clauses at Joseph M. Perillo, Calamari and Perillo on Contracts § 18.17 (5th ed. 2003).

Finally, just as courts view waiver of defense clauses and the holder in due course doctrine suspiciously, they are also hostile to clauses that attempt to prohibit assignment. This seeming inconsistency generally means that contract rights are freely assignable, but obligors maintain set-off rights in many cases against the assignee even after notice of the assignment. Cumulatively, these rights promote assignment and increase financing available to assignors in credit transactions with obligors. Nonetheless, limits exist. Language prohibiting assignment will be enforceable, but only when the substitution of the right of the assignee for that of the assignor (i) materially changes the duty of the obligor; (ii) materially increases the burden or risk imposed by the contract; or (iii) materially impairs the obligor's chance of obtaining return performance from the assignor. Restatement (Second) of Contracts § 317(2). These are very rare events since normally the first two requirements are satisfied because the payment already due is merely redirected to another party. The third condition is rarely satisfied because the assignor maintains an interest in good performance in order not to breach an implied warranty to the assignee. See discussion Joy Anderson, Note, "Contracts—Looking for 'Something': Minnesota's New Rule for Interpreting Anti-Assignment Clauses in *Travertine Corp. v. Lexington-Silverwood*," 32 Wm. Mitchell L. Rev. 1435 (2006).

Also, the UCC intervenes to further invalidate anti-assignment clauses in the case of certain contract rights to payments defined as "accounts." See UCC § 9–318. For a discussion of this doctrine, see Bryan D. Hull, "Harmonization of Rules Governing Assignments of Right to Payment," 54 SMU L. Rev. 473 (2001) and Grant Gilmore, "The Commercial Doctrine of Good Faith Purchase," 63 Yale L. J. 1057, 1067 (1954).

HERZOG V. IRACE

Supreme Court of Maine
594 A.2d 1106 (1991)

BRODY, Justice.

Anthony Irace and Donald Lowry appeal from an order entered by the Superior Court (Cumberland County, Cole, J.) affirming a District Court (Portland, Goranites, J.) judgment in favor of Dr. John P. Herzog in an action for breach of an assignment to Dr. Herzog of personal injury settlement proceeds[1] collected by Irace and Lowry, both attorneys, on

---

[1] This case involves the assignment of proceeds from a personal injury action, not an assignment of the cause of action itself.

behalf of their client, Gary G. Jones. On appeal, Irace and Lowry contend that the District Court erred in finding that the assignment was valid and enforceable against them. They also argue that enforcement of the assignment interferes with their ethical obligations toward their client. Finding no error, we affirm.

The facts of this case are not disputed. Gary Jones was injured in a motorcycle accident and retained Irace and Lowry to represent him in a personal injury action. Soon thereafter, Jones dislocated his shoulder, twice, in incidents unrelated to the motorcycle accident. Dr. Herzog examined Jones's shoulder and concluded that he needed surgery. At the time, however, Jones was unable to pay for the surgery and in consideration for the performance of the surgery by the doctor, he signed a letter dated June 14, 1988, written on Dr. Herzog's letterhead stating:

> I, Gary Jones, request that payment be made directly from settlement of a claim currently pending for an unrelated incident, to John Herzog, D.O., for treatment of a shoulder injury which occurred at a different time.

Dr. Herzog notified Irace and Lowry that Jones had signed an "assignment of benefits" from the motorcycle personal injury action to cover the cost of surgery on his shoulder and was informed by an employee of Irace and Lowry that the assignment was sufficient to allow the firm to pay Dr. Herzog's bills at the conclusion of the case. Dr. Herzog performed the surgery and continued to treat Jones for approximately one year.

In May, 1989, Jones received a $20,000 settlement in the motorcycle personal injury action. He instructed Irace and Lowry not to disburse any funds to Dr. Herzog indicating that he would make the payments himself. Irace and Lowry informed Dr. Herzog that Jones had revoked his permission to have the bill paid by them directly and indicated that they would follow Jones's directions. Irace and Lowry issued a check to Jones for $10,027 and disbursed the remaining funds to Jones's other creditors. Jones did send a check to Dr. Herzog but the check was returned by the bank for insufficient funds and Dr. Herzog was never paid.

Dr. Herzog filed a complaint in District Court against Irace and Lowry seeking to enforce the June 14, 1988 "assignment of benefits." The matter was tried before the court on the basis of a joint stipulation of facts. The court entered a judgment in favor of Dr. Herzog finding that the June 14, 1988 letter constituted a valid assignment of the settlement proceeds enforceable against Irace and Lowry. Following an unsuccessful appeal to the Superior Court, Irace and Lowry appealed to this court. Because the Superior Court acted as an intermediate appellate court, we review the District Court's decision directly. See Brown v. Corriveau, 576 A. 2d 200, 201 (Me. 1990).

STANDARD OF REVIEW

. . . We review the District Court's findings of fact based on stipulated facts and documentary evidence only for clear error.

VALIDITY OF ASSIGNMENT

An assignment is an act or manifestation by the owner of a right (the assignor) indicating his intent to transfer that right to another person (the assignee). See Shiro v. Drew, 174 F.Supp. 495, 497 (D. Me. 1959). For an assignment to be valid and enforceable against the assignor's creditor (the obligor), the assignor must make clear his intent to relinquish the right to the assignee and must not retain any control over the right assigned or any power of revocation. The assignment takes effect through the actions of the assignor and assignee and the obligor need not accept the assignment to render it valid. Palmer v. Palmer, 112 Me. 149, 153, 91 A. 281, 282 (1914). Once the obligor has notice of the assignment, the fund is "from that time forward impressed with a trust; it is . . . impounded in the [obligor's] hands, and must be held by him not for the original creditor, the assignor, but for the substituted creditor, the assignee." Id. at 152, 91 A. 281. After receiving notice of the assignment, the obligor cannot lawfully pay the amount assigned either to the assignor or to his other creditors and if the obligor does make such a payment, he does so at his peril because the assignee may enforce his rights against the obligor directly. Id. at 153, 91 A. 281.

Ordinary rights, including future rights, are freely assignable unless the assignment would materially change the duty of the obligor, materially increase the burden or risk imposed upon the obligor by his contract, impair the obligor's chance of obtaining return performance, or materially reduce the value of the return performance to the obligor, and unless the law restricts the assignability of the specific right involved. See Restatement (Second) Contracts § 317(2)(a) (1982). In Maine, the transfer of a future right to proceeds from pending litigation has been recognized as a valid and enforceable equitable assignment. McLellan v. Walker, 26 Me. 114, 117–18 (1896). An equitable assignment need not transfer the entire future right but rather may be a partial assignment of that right. Palmer, 112 Me. at 152, 91 A. 281. We reaffirm these well-established principles.

Relying primarily upon the Federal District Court's decision in Shiro, 174 F.Supp. 495, a bankruptcy case involving the trustee's power to avoid a preferential transfer by assignment, Irace and Lowry contend that Jones's June 14, 1988 letter is invalid and unenforceable as an assignment because it fails to manifest Jones's intent to permanently relinquish all control over the assigned funds and does nothing more than request payment from a specific fund. We disagree. The June 14, 1988 letter gives no indication that Jones attempted to retain any control over the funds he assigned to Dr. Herzog. Taken in context, the use of the word "request" did not give the court reason to question Jones's intent to complete the assignment and, although no specific amount was stated, the parties do not dispute that the services provided by Dr. Herzog and the amounts that he charged for those services were reasonable and necessary to the treatment of the shoulder injury referred to in the June 14 letter. Irace and Lowry had adequate funds to satisfy all of Jones's creditors, including Dr. Herzog, with funds left over for disbursement to Jones himself. Thus, this case simply does not present a situation analogous to Shiro because Dr. Herzog was given preference over Jones's other creditors by operation of the assignment. Given that Irace and Lowry do not dispute that they had ample notice of the assignment, the court's finding on the validity of the assignment is fully supported by the evidence and will not be disturbed on appeal.

ETHICAL OBLIGATIONS

Next, Irace and Lowry contend that the assignment, if enforceable against them, would interfere with their ethical obligation to honor their client's instruction in disbursing funds.[2] Again, we disagree.

Under the Maine Bar Rules, an attorney generally may not place a lien on a client's file for a third party. M. Bar R. 3.7(c). The Bar Rules further require that an attorney "promptly pay or deliver to the client, as requested by the client, the funds, securities, or other properties in the possession of the lawyer which the client is entitled to receive." M. Bar R. 3.6(f)(2)(iv). The rules say nothing, however, about a client's power to assign his right to proceeds from a pending lawsuit to third parties. Because the client has the power to assign his right to funds held by his attorney, McLellan v. Walker, 26 Me. at 117–18, it follows that a valid assignment must be honored by the attorney in disbursing the funds on the client's behalf. The assignment does not create a conflict under Rule 3.6(f)(2)(iv) because the client is not entitled to receive funds once he has assigned them to a third party. Nor does the assignment violate Rule 3.7(c), because the client, not the attorney, is responsible for placing the encumbrance upon the funds. Irace and Lowry were under no ethical obligation, and the record gives no indication that they were under a contractual obligation, to honor their client's instruction to disregard a valid assignment. The District Court correctly concluded that the assignment is valid and enforceable against Irace and Lowry.

---

[2]   Lowry and Irace rely upon Twin Valley Motors, Inc. v. John Morale et al., 136 Vt. 115, 385 A. 2d 678 (1978) to support their position on this issue. Whatever the merits of the Vermont court's decision in the context of that case and in the context of Vermont law regarding equitable assignments and professional ethics, the decision cuts against authority in Maine which clearly recognizes the validity and enforceability of equitable assignments by a client of all or part of his right to proceeds expected from pending litigation. McLellan v. Walker, 26 Me. at 117–18.

The entry is:

Judgment affirmed.

All concurring.

NOTES AND QUESTIONS

1. *Mode of assignment.* The *Herzog* court properly noted that the question of whether Jones made a valid legal assignment of his interest in the settlement proceeds involves interpretation of his purported intent. The particular intent required was to transfer his rights to the assigned amount permanently and without further action on his part. Restatement (Second) of Contracts § 324. The *Herzog* court phrased this intent in the reverse but similar manner—an intent to relinquish the right permanently. The particular words chosen by the assignor need not be formal, such as "permanently assign and relinquish," and indeed need not even be in writing. Restatement (Second) of Contracts § 324. However, where other law requires the contract itself to be in writing (e.g., land under common law or goods under the UCC), an equal dignity rule would require the assignment itself to be in writing. See Restatement (Second) of Contracts § 324, *cmt. b.* Unless the assignment language is chosen and written by a lawyer, the language is likely to be ambiguous on the question of intent to permanently relinquish. As a result, the court must utilize the rules of interpretation discussed in Chapter 4 to ascertain the assignor's intent. As reflected in the *Herzog* case, the matter of whether an "assignment" has occurred in the first instance is of primary importance. A notice of a "purported assignment" is of no consequence as to the obligor (law firm) unless Jones made a valid assignment in the first instance. Do you agree that Jones intended to make an assignment of his payment right to Dr. Herzog? If not, what would be Dr. Herzog's remaining remedies?

2. *Subrogation versus assignment.* The concept of subrogation is a legal concept normatively permitting a person who pays another's debt to exercise the rights and remedies of the other party whose debt was paid. For example, the terms of an insurance contract may obligate an insurance company to pay the insured's medical bills. The insurance company's payment ordinarily then subrogates the insurance company to exercise any rights or remedies of the insured relating to the amounts paid. Thus, if a third-party negligent tort caused the insured's physical injuries and associated medical bills, payment by the insurance company would subrogate the company to the insured's claims against the negligent tortfeasor, at least to the extent of the paid medical bills. In effect, this process shifts and allocates ultimate liability to the insurance company that accepted the particular risk—in this case the tortfeasor's insurance company. This "substitution" of the insurance company for the insured can occur in two ways. First, "equitable subordination" occurs by operation of law and is often compared to an equitable assignment of the insured's rights against the third party. It is based on concepts of justice and equity. Secondly, subrogation can occur by contract and is often used to supplement equitable subrogation. Most insurance contracts provide for

subrogation. See, e.g., Kaiser Foundation Health Plan v. Aguiluz, 47 Cal.App.4th 302, 54 Cal.Rptr.2d 665 (1996). In *Kaiser*, the attorney had notice of the client's contractual obligation to indemnify the insurance company from the proceeds of the lawsuit that generated the insurance company's payment of medical bills. That subrogation created a lien on the client funds, and the attorney was liable to the insurance company for payment of funds to the client without first payment of the insurance company lien.

3.   *Attorney professional responsibility and ethical issues.* A lawyer's obligations to clients flow from essentially three sources: professional standards, general law, and governing principles of ethics and morality. See Nathan M. Crystal, An Introduction to Professional Responsibility (Aspen Law & Business 1998). Nearly all states regulate the practice of law in that state, and the regulations are interpreted and enforced by the highest court in the state. Under the authority to regulate, courts issue rules of professional responsibility. Each state could, of course, simply write their own rules and standards, but given the similar nature of the practice of law from state to state, most states adopt some form of standard rules promulgated by the American Bar Association. Several iterations have occurred over the years. In 1908, the ABA released the Canons of Ethics, which were amended from time-to-time. In 1969, the ABA released the Model Code of Professional Responsibility. In 1983, the ABA released the Model Rules of Professional Conduct (MRPC). The MRPC were amended fourteen times between 1983 and 2000. In 2002, the MRPC adopted several amendments arising from an Ethics 2000 Commission comprehensive review of the MRPC. Thus, while these rules are intended to be a model, they remain in a constant state of flux. State adoption of the MRPC in various stages varies from state to state.

When adopted by a particular state, the MRPC bear the state name, such as in the *Herzog* case referring to the Maine Bar Rules. In Minnesota, the rules are referred to as the Minnesota Rules of Profession Conduct. Like the Restatement (Second) of Contracts, the MRPC adopts a blackletter rule supported by comments. The comments are intended only as interpretative guides. Most states have adopted some version of the MRPC, and many have varied some of the rules to some extent. State rules can usually be obtained from the website of the state supreme court, and the MRPC can be obtained from the ABA website.

When a lawyer receives funds on behalf of a client, regardless of the source, MRPC 1.15(a) requires the lawyer to hold that property separate from the lawyer's own property. MRPC 1.15(c) requires that a lawyer deposit legal fees paid by the client in advance into a trust account. Virtually every state now participates in the ABA Interest On Lawyers Trust Accounts (IOLTA) program, which requires that all such trust accounts be interest bearing, that the interest is not paid by or to the lawyer or the client, and that the interest is not taxable to either. Rather, the interest is used for public purposes to promote justice.

MRPC 1.15(d)(e) provides that if the lawyer trust account has funds over which third parties have or claim liens that are disputed, the lawyer must keep the property separate. Once separated, the lawyer assists in the resolution of the dispute and then promptly disperses the funds.

The attorney in *Herzog* argued that even an otherwise valid assignment by the client would violate rules of professional responsibility by requiring the lawyer to act adversely to the client's interest. The *Herzog* court dismissed this argument that since the funds belonged to the client, the client was free to assign those funds, and honoring that assignment was not an ethical violation. Did the court properly address the lawyer's concern? Did the client change his mind and direct his attorney not to make the payment to the physician? Why would the client do so? If the client disputes the assignment, and therefore the lawyer's right or obligation to pay the physician, how does the MRPC require the attorney to act with regard to the funds? See Charles M. Cork, III, "A Lawyer's Ethical Obligations When the Client's Creditors Claim A Share of the Tort Settlement Proceeds," 39 Tort Trial & Ins. Prac. L. J. 121 (2003); Sylvia Stevens, "The 'PUSHMI-PULLYU' Resolving Third-Party Claims To Client Funds," 60 SEP Or. St. B. Bull. 25 (2000).

4.   *Assignment of malpractice lawsuits and public policy.* The *Herzog* case involved the assignment of the proceeds of a lawsuit or settlement, but not the lawsuit itself. Can the lawsuit itself be assigned? At common law, the term "champerty" referred to an agreement between an officious intermeddler and a litigant whereby the intermeddler helps or takes over the litigant's lawsuit against the third party. Champerty is particularly troublesome when a lawyer's client "assigns" the right to pursue a claim and bring a malpractice action against the lawyer. There is a jurisdictional split in authority regarding the validity of such assignments. While the assignment satisfies the rigors of the assignment law, it may nonetheless violate the public policy doctrines discussed in Chapter 6. Consequently, the lawyer may often successfully pursue dismissal of a malpractice suit brought by an assignee on the basis of public policy. Compare, Wagener v. McDonald, 509 N.W.2d 188 (Minn. App. 1993) (public policy precludes the assignee's malpractice suit) and New Hampshire Ins. Co., *Inc. v.* McCann, 429 Mass. 202, 707 N.E.2d 332 (1999) (public policy does not preclude the assignee's malpractice suit). Scholarly debate has been likewise divided. See Kevin Pennell, Note, "On the Assignment of Legal Malpractice Claims: A Contractual Solution to a Contractual Problem," 82 Tex. L. Rev. 481 (2003) and Rosalie S. Walters, Note, "The Unwitting Attorney, The Desperate Client, and the Perpetuation of the New York Power Play: A Proposal to Ban Voluntary Assignments of Legal Malpractice Claims Via New York General Obligations Law Section 13–101," 3 Cardozo Pub. L. Pol'y & Ethics J. 543 (2005). For scholarly debate favoring the public policy ban, see Ronald E. Mallen, "Duty to Nonclients: Exploring the Boundaries," 37 S. Tex. L. Rev. 1147 (1996) (assignment chills the attorney's zeal in pursuing a client's claim and erodes confidence in the attorney-client relationship); Amy E. Douthitt, Note, "Selling Your Attorney's Negligence: Should Legal Malpractice Claims Be Assignable in Texas?," 47 Baylor L. Rev.

177 (1995) (risk of collusion and costs to the profession's credibility justify ban); John M. Limbaugh, Note, "The Sacrificial Attorney: Assignment of Legal Malpractice Claims," 65 Mo. L. Rev. 279 (2000). For scholarly debate favoring assignment, see Tom W. Bell, "Limits on the Privity and Assignment of Legal Malpractice Claims," 59 U. Chi. L. Rev. 1533 (1992) (legal malpractice claims should be assignable with limitations); Michael Sean Quinn, "On the Assignment of Legal Malpractice Claims," 37 S. Tex. L. Rev. 1203 (1996) (legal malpractice claims should be freely assignable); and Jennifer K. McDannell, Note, "Assignability of Legal Malpractice Claims," 14 Alaska L. Rev. 141 (1997).

5. *Partial assignments.* The common law was hostile to partial assignments, at least without the consent of the obligor (who would be required to make separate payments). As indicated in *Herzog,* modern law is more sympathetic. Partial assignments are now generally permitted, but require clarity as to amount. Restatement (Second) of Contracts § 326.

2. DELEGATION OF CONTRACT DUTIES

While parties can delegate duties separately from assignments of rights under a contract, it is more customary to assign rights separately than to delegate duties. Rights are most often assigned separately to finance performance of the duty preceding the right to payment for that performance. Duties, however, are seldom delegated without the attached right to payment because the right to payment is generally the reason the delegatee is willing to perform the delegated duty. Nonetheless, whether the duty is delegated separately, or more commonly, with an assignment of the rights or a transfer of the entire contract, the same principles apply. Attachment of the assigned rights to delegation does not alter the analysis of whether the duty may be delegated.

As discussed in the prior section, the determination of whether a right may be assigned is determined by focusing upon whether the assignment has a material effect on the other party to the contract or the obligor. Restatement (Second) of Contracts § 317(2). Similarly, the determination of whether a duty may be delegated is determined by focusing upon whether the delegation has a material effect on the other party to the contract or the obligee. Restatement (Second) of Contracts §§ 318(1)–(2). However, because the performance of a duty is much more likely to have a material effect on the obligee than an assignment is likely to affect an obligor, delegation is more restricted by the default rule, and contract language precluding delegation is more highly regarded.

Under the default rule, a contractual duty may be delegated to another without the consent of the obligee unless the delegation would be contrary to public policy or unless the terms of the agreement preclude delegation. Restatement (Second) of Contracts § 318(1). In addition, performance of a duty by the contracting party obligor is only required to the extent the obligee has a "substantial interest" in having that particular person render the performance. Restatement (Second) of Contracts § 318(2). An interest is substantial generally only when the contract involves (i) personal services of a particular individual (and not a company or business entity), or (ii) when the contract requires the exercise of personal skill or discretion. Restatement (Second) of Contracts § 318, *cmt. c* and UCC § 2–210(1). In these cases, the duty is said to be "non-delegable." For example, a singer contracts with a corporation to sing three songs over the radio to advertise the company's products. Since singing is a personal service with a unique skill, the singer may not delegate her obligation to sing to another singer without the company's consent. Restatement (Second) of Contracts § 318, *cmt. c, illus. 6.* However, the very use of the phrase "personal service contract" implies that the other party to the contract intends to rely specifically on the honesty, skill, reputation, character, ability, wisdom, and taste of the obligor. See Joseph M. Perillo, Calamari and Perillo on Contracts § 18.28 (5th ed. 2003). The phrase is nonetheless somewhat subjective and indeterminate. See Larry A. Dimatteo, "Depersonalization of Personal Service Contracts: The Search for a Modern Approach to Assignability," 27 Akron L. Rev. 407 (1994). Accordingly, a physician may not delegate her duty to her patient, a lawyer may not delegate her duty to her client, and an artist may not delegate her duty to perform.

An attempt to delegate a non-delegable duty constitutes an offer to waive the non-delegable feature of the duty. If the offer is refused because the obligee properly refuses to accept substitute performance, the failure of the delegator to perform constitutes a breach, and the obligee may bring suit for damages. However, even if the duty is non-delegable, if the obligee accepts the performance of the delegatee, then the delegation is proper by virtue of the implied consent. Restatement (Second) of Contracts § 323(1). However, the acceptance of the performance does not release delegator. Acceptance is not a novation. Restatement (Second) of Contracts § 318(3). Accordingly, if the delegatee's performance is defective, the delegator remains liable for the breach. Stated another way, simply because a delegatee assumes the liability to perform, that assumption does not operate as a novation to release the delegator.

3. ASSIGNMENT OF AN ENTIRE CONTRACT

In the purchase and sale of businesses, contracts become amalgamated with all other assets. All assets transfer together unless language in specific contracts effectively precludes that particular transfer. Language may manifest intent to assign or transfer the entire contract rather than simply assign rights or delegate duties independently. In such cases, the assignment or transfer of the contract constitutes both an assignment of the rights and a delegation of the duties. Restatement (Second) of Contracts § 328(1). The difference is significant. Contract rights are easily assigned, and assignment is difficult to preclude by contract language. Duties are not as easily delegated, and most often delegation is easily precluded by contract language.

Unfortunately, the two parties to a contract generally contemplate the continuance of the relationship. More importantly, they seldom contemplate the effect of the continuing relationship in the event one of the parties is acquired by a different business owner. For example, may the same two parties to a contract continue their contractual relationship despite a change in ownership and control of one of the parties? Does the mere fact that one of the contract business entities is owned by a different party have any impact on the transfer of the contract—even assuming the same parties will continue to perform as before the change in ownership?

SALLY BEAUTY CO. V. NEXXUS PRODUCTS CO.

United States Court of Appeal for the Seventh Circuit
801 F.2d 1001 (1986)

CUDAHY, Circuit Judge.

Nexxus Products Company ("Nexxus") entered into a contract with Best Barber & Beauty Supply Company, Inc. ("Best"), under which Best would be the exclusive distributor of Nexxus hair care products to barbers and hair stylists throughout most of Texas. When Best was acquired by and merged into Sally Beauty Company, Inc. ("Sally Beauty"), Nexxus cancelled the agreement. Sally Beauty is a wholly-owned subsidiary of Alberto-Culver Company ("Alberto-Culver"), a major manufacturer of hair care products and a competitor of Nexxus's. Sally Beauty claims that Nexxus breached the contract by canceling; Nexxus's asserts by way of defense that the contract was not assignable or, in the alternative, not assignable to Sally Beauty. The district court granted Nexxus's motion for summary judgment, ruling that the contract was one for personal services and therefore not assignable. We affirm on a different theory-that this contract could not be assigned to the wholly-owned subsidiary of a direct competitor under section 2–210 of the Uniform Commercial Code.

I.

Only the basic facts are undisputed and they are as follows. Prior to its merger with Sally Beauty, Best was a Texas corporation in the business of distributing beauty and hair care products to retail stores, barber shops and beauty salons throughout Texas. Between March and July 1979, Mark Reichek, Best's president, negotiated with Stephen Redding, Nexxus's vice-president, over a possible distribution agreement between Best and Nexxus. Nexxus, founded in 1979, is a California corporation that formulates and markets hair care products. Nexxus does not market its products to retail stores, preferring to sell them to independent distributors for resale to barbers and beauticians. On August 2, 1979, Nexxus executed a distributorship agreement with Best, in the form of a July 24, 1979 letter from Reichek, for Best, to Redding, for Nexxus:

Dear Steve:

It was a pleasure meeting with you and discussing the distribution of Nexus Products. The line is very exciting and we feel we can do a substantial job with it—especially as the exclusive distributor in Texas (except El Paso).

If I understand the pricing structure correctly, we would pay $1.50 for an item that retails for $5.00 (less 50%, less 40% off retail), and Nexus will pay the freight charges regardless of order size. This approach to pricing will enable us to price the items in the line in such a way that they will be attractive and profitable to the salons.

Your offer of assistance in promoting the line seems to be designed to simplify the introduction of Nexus Products into the Texas market. It indicates a sincere desire on your part to assist your distributors. By your agreeing to underwrite the cost of training and maintaining a qualified technician in our territory, we should be able to introduce the line from a position of strength. I am sure you will let us know at least 90 days in advance should you want to change this arrangement.

By offering to provide us with the support necessary to conduct an annual seminar (i.e. mailers, guest artists at your expense), we should be able to re-enforce our position with Nexus users and introduce the product line to new customers in a professional manner.

To satisfy your requirement of assured payment for merchandise received, each of our purchase orders will be accompanied by a Letter of Credit that will become negotiable when we receive the merchandise. I am sure you will agree that this arrangement is fairest for everybody concerned.

While we feel confident that we can do an outstanding job with the Nexus line and that the volume we generate will adequately compensate you for your continued support, it is usually best to have an understanding should we no longer be distributing Nexus Products—either by our desire or your request. Based on our discussions, cancellation or termination of Best Barber & Beauty Supply Co., Inc. as a distributor can only take place on the anniversary date of our original appointment as a distributor— and then only with 120 days prior notice. If Nexus terminates us, Nexus will buy back all of our inventory at cost and will pay the freight charges on the returned merchandise.

Steve, we feel that the Nexus line is exciting and very promotable. With the program outlined in this letter, we feel it can be mutually profitable and look forward to a long and successful business relationship. If you agree that this letter contains the details of our understanding regarding the distribution of Nexus Products, please sign the acknowledgment below and return one copy of this letter to me.

Very truly yours,
/s/ Mark E. Reichek
President

Acknowledged
/s/ Stephen Redding Date 8/2/79.
Appellant's Appendix at 2–3.

In July 1981 Sally Beauty acquired Best in a stock purchase transaction and Best was merged into Sally Beauty, which succeeded to Best's rights and interests in all of Best's contracts. Sally Beauty, a Delaware corporation with its principal place of business in Texas, is a wholly-owned subsidiary of Alberto-Culver. Sally Beauty, like Best, is a distributor of hair care and beauty products to retail stores and hair styling salons. Alberto-Culver is a major manufacturer of hair care products and, thus, is a direct competitor of Nexxus in the hair care market.[1]

Shortly after the merger, Redding met with Michael Renzulli, president of Sally Beauty, to discuss the Nexxus distribution agreement. After the meeting, Redding wrote Renzulli a letter stating that Nexxus would not allow Sally Beauty, a wholly-owned subsidiary of a direct competitor, to distribute Nexxus products:

As we discussed in New Orleans, we have great reservations about allowing our NEXXUS Products to be distributed by a company which is, in essence, a direct competitor. We appreciate your argument of autonomy for your business, but the fact remains that you are totally owned by Alberto-Culver.

Since we see no way of justifying this conflict, we cannot allow our products to be distributed by Sally Beauty Company.

Appellant's Appendix at 475.

In August 1983 Sally Beauty commenced this action by filing a complaint in the Northern District of Illinois, claiming that Nexxus had violated the federal antitrust laws and breached the distribution

---

[1]   The appellant does not appear to dispute the proposition that Alberto-Culver is Nexxus' direct competitor, see Reply Brief at 8–10; rather it disagrees only with Nexxus' contention that performance by Sally Beauty would necessarily be unacceptable. See infra.

agreement. In August 1984 Nexxus filed a counterclaim alleging violations of the Lanham Act, the Racketeer Influenced and Corrupt Organizations Act ("RICO") and the unfair competition laws of North Carolina, Tennessee and unidentified "other states." On October 22, 1984 Sally Beauty filed a motion to dismiss the counterclaims arising under RICO and "other states' law." Nexxus filed a motion for summary judgment on the breach of contract claim the next day.

The district court ruled on these motions in a Memorandum Opinion and Order dated January 31, 1985. It granted Sally's motion to dismiss the two counterclaims and also granted Nexxus's motion for summary judgment. In May 1985 it dismissed the remaining claims and counterclaims (pursuant to stipulation by the parties)[2] and directed the entry of an appealable final judgment on the breach of contract claim.

II.

Sally Beauty's breach of contract claim alleges that by acquiring Best, Sally Beauty succeeded to all of Best's rights and obligations under the distribution agreement. It further alleges that Nexxus breached the agreement by failing to give Sally Beauty 120 days notice prior to terminating the agreement and by terminating it on other than an anniversary date of its formation. Complaint, Count III, Appellant's Appendix at 54–55. Nexxus, in its motion for summary judgment, argued that the distribution agreement it entered into with Best was a contract for personal services, based upon a relationship of personal trust and confidence between Reichek and the Redding family. As such, the contract could not be assigned to Sally without Nexxus's consent.

In opposing this motion Sally Beauty argued that the contract was freely assignable because (1) it was between two corporations, not two individuals and (2) the character of the performance would not be altered by the substitution of Sally Beauty for Best. It also argued that "the Distribution Agreement is nothing more than a simple, non-exclusive contract for the distribution of goods, the successful performance of which is in no way dependent upon any particular personality, individual skill or confidential relationship." Appellant's Appendix at 119.

In ruling on this motion, the district court framed the issue before it as "whether the contract at issue here between Best and Nexxus was of a personal nature such that it was not assignable without Nexxus's consent." It ruled:

> The court is convinced, based upon the nature of the contract and the circumstances surrounding its formation, that the contract at issue here was of such a nature that it was not assignable without

---

[2] One of the two antitrust counts had already been dismissed by stipulation of the parties in May 1984.

Nexxus's consent. First, the very nature of the contract itself suggests its personal character. A distribution agreement is a contract whereby a manufacturer gives another party the right to distribute its products. It is clearly a contract for the performance of a service. In the court's view, the mere selection by a manufacturer of a party to distribute its goods presupposes a reliance and confidence by the manufacturer on the integrity and abilities of the other party. . . . In addition, in this case the circumstances surrounding the contract's formation support the conclusion that the agreement was not simply an ordinary commercial contract but was one which was based upon a relationship of personal trust and confidence between the parties. Specifically, Stephen Redding, Nexxus's vice-president, traveled to Texas and met with Best's president personally for several days before making the decision to award the Texas distributorship to Best. Best itself had been in the hair care business for 40 years and its president Mark Reichek had extensive experience in the industry. It is reasonable to conclude that Stephen Redding and Nexxus would want its distributor to be experienced and knowledgeable in the hair care field and that the selection of Best was based upon personal factors such as these. Memorandum Opinion and Order at 56 (citation omitted).

The district court also rejected the contention that the character of performance would not be altered by a substitution of Sally Beauty for Best: "Unlike Best, Sally Beauty is a subsidiary of one of Nexxus's direct competitors. This is a significant distinction and in the court's view, it raises serious questions regarding Sally Beauty's ability to perform the distribution agreement in the same manner as Best." Id. at 7.

We cannot affirm this summary judgment on the grounds relied on by the district court. Under Fed. R. Civ. P. 56(c) summary judgment may be granted only where there is no genuine issue as to any material fact and the moving party is entitled to judgment as a matter of law. The burden on the movant is stringent: "all doubts as to the existence of material fact must be resolved against the movant." Moore v. Marketplace Restaurant, Inc., 754 F.2d 1336, 1339 (7th Cir. 1985), quoting Dreher v. Sielaff, 636 F.2d 1141, 1143 n. 4 (7th Cir. 1980). Nexxus did not meet its burden on the question of the parties' reasons for entering into this agreement. Although it might be "reasonable to conclude" that Best and Nexxus had based their agreement on "a relationship of personal trust and confidence," and that Reichek's participation was considered essential to Best's performance, this is a finding of fact. See Phillips v. Oil, Inc., 104 S.W.2d 576, 579 (Tex.Civ.App.1937, writ ref'd n.r.e.) (question whether contract was entered into because of parties' "personal confidence and trust" is for the determination of trier of fact). Since the parties submitted conflicting affidavits on this question,[3] the district court erred in relying on Nexxus's view as representing undisputed fact in ruling on this summary judgment motion. See Cedillo v. Local 1, International Association of Bridge & Structural Iron Workers, 603 F.2d 7, 11 (7th Cir. 1979) ("questions of motive and intent are particularly inappropriate for summary adjudication").[4]

We may affirm this summary judgment, however, on a different ground if it finds support in the record. United States v. Winthrop Towers, 628 F.2d 1028, 1037 (7th Cir. 1980). Sally Beauty contends that the distribution agreement is freely assignable because it is governed by the provisions of the Uniform Commercial Code (the "UCC" or the "Code"), as adopted in Texas.[5] Appellants' Brief at 46–47. We agree with Sally that the provisions of the UCC govern this contract and for that reason hold that the assignment of the contract by Best to Sally Beauty was barred by the UCC rules on delegation of performance, UCC § 2–210(1), Tex.Bus & Com.Code Ann. § 2–210(a) (Vernon 1968).

III.

The UCC codifies the law of contracts applicable to "transactions in goods." UCC § 2–102, Tex. Bus. & Com. Code Ann. § 2–102 (Vernon 1968). Texas applies the "dominant factor" test to determine whether the UCC applies to a given contract or transaction: was the essence of or dominant factor in the formation of the contract the provision of goods or services? Montgomery Ward & Co., Inc. v. Dalton, 665 S.W. 2d 507, 511 (Tex. App. 1984) (contract for repair of roof predominantly involves services); Garcia v. Rutledge, 649 S.W. 2d 307, 310 (Tex. App. 1982) (contract for repair of truck predominantly a contract for services); Potts v. W.Q. Richards

---

[3] Reichek stated the following in an affidavit submitted in support of Sally Beauty's Memorandum in Opposition to Nexxus' Motion for Summary Judgment:

> At no time prior to the execution of the Distribution Agreement did Steve Redding tell me that he was relying upon my personal peculiar tastes and ability in making his decision to award a Nexxus distributorship to Best. Moreover, I never understood that Steve Redding was relying upon my skill and ability in particular in choosing Best as a distributor.

> I never considered the Distribution Agreement to be a personal service contract between me and Nexxus or Stephen Redding. I always considered the Distribution Agreement to be between Best and Nexxus as expressly provided in the Distribution Agreement which was written by my brother and me. At all times I conducted business with Nexxus on behalf of Best and not on my own behalf. In that connection, when I sent correspondence to Nexxus, I invariably signed it as president of Best.

> Neither Stephen Redding nor any other Nexxus employee ever told me that Nexxus was relying on my personal financial integrity in executing the Distribution Agreement or in shipping Nexxus products to Best. . . . Affidavit of Mark Reichek, ¶¶ 19–21, Appellant's Appendix at 189–190.

[4] It is also possible to read the district court's decision as ruling that all distribution agreements are as a matter of law personal services contracts and therefore nonassignable. For the reasons explained infra, we do not believe that this is an accurate statement of the law.

[5] The parties agree that the contract is governed by the law of Texas. See Zlotnick v. MacArthur, 550 F. Supp. 371, 373–74 (N.D. Ill. 1982).

Memorial Hospital, 558 S.W. 2d 939, 946 (Tex. Civ. App. 1977) (essence of hospital stay is the furnishing of services); Freeman v. Shannon Construction, Inc., 560 S.W. 2d 732, 738 (Tex. Civ. App. 1977) (sale of bulk cement in construction contract outweighed by predominant service of building structure). No Texas case addresses whether a distribution agreement is a contract for the sale of goods, but the rule in the majority of jurisdictions is that distributorships (both exclusive and non-exclusive) are to be treated as sale of goods contracts under the UCC.

Several of these courts note that "a distributorship agreement is more involved than a typical sales contract," Quality Performance Lines, 609 P.2d at 1342, but apply the UCC nonetheless because the sales aspect in such a contract is predominant. See Corenswet, 594 F. 2d at 134 ("Although most distributorship agreements, like franchise agreements, are more than sales contracts, the courts have not hesitated to apply the Uniform Commercial Code to cases involving such agreements."); Zapatha, 408 N.E.2d at 1374–75 n. 8 (courts have applied UCC to distribution agreements because the sales aspect is predominant). This is true of the contract at issue here (as embodied in the July 24, 1979 letter from Reichek to Redding). Most of the agreed-to terms deal with Nexxus's sale of its hair care products to Best. We are confident that a Texas court would find the sales aspect of this contract dominant and apply the majority rule that such a distributorship is a contract for "goods" under the UCC. . . .

IV.

The fact that this contract is considered a contract for the sale of goods and not for the provision of a service does not, as Sally Beauty suggests, mean that it is freely assignable in all circumstances. The delegation of performance under a sales contract (whether in conjunction with an assignment of rights, as here, or not) is governed by UCC section 2–210(1), Tex. Bus. & Com. Code § 2–210(a) (Vernon 1968). The UCC recognizes that in many cases an obligor will find it convenient or even necessary to relieve himself of the duty of performance under a contract, see Official Comment 1, UCC § 2–210 ("[T]his section recognizes both delegation of performance and assignability as normal and permissible incidents of a contract for the sale of goods."). The Code therefore sanctions delegation except where the delegated performance would be unsatisfactory to the obligee: "A party may perform his duty through a delegate unless otherwise agreed to or unless the other party has a substantial interest in having his original promisor perform or control the acts required by the contract." UCC § 2–210(1), Tex. Bus. & Com. Code Ann. § 2–210(a) (Vernon 1968). Consideration is given to balancing the policies of free alienability of commercial contracts and protecting the obligee from having to accept a bargain he did not contract for.

We are concerned here with the delegation of Best's duty of performance under the distribution agreement, as Nexxus terminated the agreement because it did not wish to accept Sally Beauty's substituted performance.[6] Only one Texas case has construed section 2–210 in the context of a party's delegation of performance under an executory contract. In McKinnie v. Milford, 597 S.W.2d 953 (Tex.Civ.App.1980, writ ref'd, n.r.e.), the court held that nothing in the Texas Business and Commercial Code prevented the seller of a horse from delegating to the buyer a pre-existing contractual duty to make the horse available to a third party for breeding. "[I]t is clear that Milford [the third party] had no particular interest in not allowing Stewart [the seller] to delegate the duties required by the contract. Milford was only interested in getting his two breedings per year, and such performance could only be obtained from McKinnie [the buyer] after he bought the horse from Stewart." Id. at 957. In McKinnie, the Texas court recognized and applied the UCC rule that bars delegation of duties if there is some reason why the non-assigning party would find performance by a delegate a substantially different thing than what he had bargained for.

In the exclusive distribution agreement before us, Nexxus had contracted for Best's "best efforts" in promoting the sale of Nexxus products in Texas. UCC § 2–306(2), Tex. Bus. & Com. Code Ann. § 2–306(b) (Vernon 1968), states that "[a] lawful agreement by either buyer or seller for exclusive dealing in the kind of goods concerned imposes unless otherwise agreed an obligation by the seller to use best efforts to supply the goods and by the buyer to use best efforts to promote their sale." This implied promise on Best's part was the consideration for Nexxus's promise to refrain from supplying any other distributors within Best's exclusive area. See Official Comment 5, UCC § 2–306. It was this contractual undertaking which Nexxus refused to see performed by Sally.

In ruling on Nexxus's motion for summary judgment, the district court noted: "Unlike Best, Sally Beauty is a subsidiary of one of Nexxus's direct competitors. This is a significant distinction and in the court's view, it raises serious questions regarding Sally Beauty's ability to perform the distribution agreement in the same manner as Best." Memorandum Opinion and Order at 7. In Berliner Foods Corp. v. Pillsbury Co., 633 F.Supp. 557 (D. Md. 1986), the court stated the same reservation more strongly on similar facts. Berliner was an exclusive distributor of Haagen-Dazs ice cream when it was sold to Breyer's, manufacturer of a competing

---

[6]   If this contract is assignable, Sally Beauty would also, of course, succeed to Best's rights under the distribution agreement. But the fact situation before us must be distinguished from the assignment of contract rights that are no longer executory (e.g., the right to damages for breach or the right to payment of an account), which is considered in UCC section 2–210(2), Tex. Bus. & Com. Code Ann. § 2–210(b) (Vernon 1968), and in several of the authorities relied on by appellants. The policies underlying these two situations are different and, generally, the UCC favors assignment more strongly in the latter. See UCC § 2–210(2) (non-executory rights assignable even if agreement states otherwise).

ice cream line. Pillsbury Co., manufacturer of Haagen-Dazs, terminated the distributorship and Berliner sued. The court noted, while weighing the factors for and against a preliminary injunction, that "it defies common sense to require a manufacturer to leave the distribution of its products to a distributor under the control of a competitor or potential competitor." Id. at 559–60. We agree with these assessments and hold that Sally Beauty's position as a wholly-owned subsidiary of Alberto-Culver is sufficient to bar the delegation of Best's duties under the agreement.

We do not believe that our holding will work the mischief with our national economy that the appellants predict. We hold merely that the duty of performance under an exclusive distributorship may not be delegated to a competitor in the market place—or the wholly-owned subsidiary of a competitor—without the obligee's consent. We believe that such a rule is consonant with the policies behind section 2–210, which is concerned with preserving the bargain the obligee has struck. Nexxus should not be required to accept the "best efforts" of Sally Beauty when those efforts are subject to the control of Alberto-Culver. It is entirely reasonable that Nexxus should conclude that this performance would be a different thing than what it had bargained for. At oral argument, Sally Beauty argued that the case should go to trial to allow it to demonstrate that it could and would perform the contract as impartially as Best. It stressed that Sally Beauty is a "multi-line" distributor, which means that it distributes many brands and is not just a conduit for Alberto-Culver products. But we do not think that this creates a material question of fact in this case. When performance of personal services is delegated, the trier merely determines that it is a personal services contract. If so, the duty is per se nondelegable. There is no inquiry into whether the delegate is as skilled or worthy of trust and confidence as the original obligor: the delegate was not bargained for and the obligee need not consent to the substitution.[9] And so here: it is undisputed that Sally Beauty is wholly owned by Alberto-Culver, which means that Sally Beauty's "impartial" sales policy is at least acquiesced in by Alberto-Culver-but could change whenever Alberto-Culver's needs changed. Sally Beauty may be totally sincere in its belief that it can operate "impartially" as a distributor, but who can guarantee the outcome when there is a clear choice between the demands of the parent-manufacturer, Alberto-Culver, and the competing needs of Nexxus? The risk of an unfavorable outcome is not one which the law can force Nexxus to take.

---

[9] Of course, the obligee makes such an assessment of the prospective delegate. If it thinks the delegated performance will be as satisfactory, it is of course free to consent to the delegation. Thus, the dissent is mistaken in its suggestion that we find it improper-a "conflict of interest"— for one competitor to distribute another competitor's products. Rather, we believe only that it is commercially reasonable that the supplier in those circumstances have consented to such a state of affairs. To borrow the dissent's example, Isuzu allows General Motors to distribute its cars because it considers this arrangement attractive.

Nor is distrust of one's competitors a trait unique to lawyers (as opposed to ordinary businessmen), as the dissent may be understood to suggest.

Nexxus has a substantial interest in not seeing this contract performed by Sally Beauty, which is sufficient to bar the delegation under section 2–210, Tex. Bus. Com. Code Ann. § 2–210 (Vernon 1968). Because Nexxus should not be forced to accept performance of the distributorship agreement by Sally, we hold that the contract was not assignable without Nexxus's consent.

The judgment of the district court is Affirmed.

POSNER, Circuit Judge, dissenting.

My brethren have decided, with no better foundation than judicial intuition about what businessmen consider reasonable, that the Uniform Commercial Code gives a supplier an absolute right to cancel an exclusive-dealing contract if the dealer is acquired, directly or indirectly, by a competitor of the supplier. I interpret the Code differently.

Nexxus makes products for the hair and sells them through distributors to hair salons and barbershops. It gave a contract to Best, cancellable on any anniversary of the contract with 120 days' notice, to be its exclusive distributor in Texas. Two years later Best was acquired by and merged into Sally Beauty, a distributor of beauty supplies and wholly owned subsidiary of Alberto-Culver. Alberto-Culver makes "hair care" products, too, though they mostly are cheaper than Nexxus's, and are sold to the public primarily through grocery stores and drugstores. My brethren conclude that because there is at least a loose competitive relationship between Nexxus and Alberto-Culver, Sally Beauty cannot—as a matter of law, cannot, for there has been no trial on the issue—provide its "best efforts" in the distribution of Nexxus products. Since a commitment to provide best efforts is read into every exclusive-dealing contract by section 2–306(2) of the Uniform Commercial Code, the contract has been broken and Nexxus can repudiate it. Alternatively, Nexxus had "a substantial interest in having his original promisor perform or control the acts required by the contract," and therefore the delegation of the promisor's (Best's) duties to Sally Beauty was improper under section 2–210(1).

My brethren's conclusion that these provisions of the Uniform Commercial Code entitled Nexxus to cancel the contract does not leap out from the language of the provisions or of the contract; so one would expect, but does not find, a canvass of the relevant case law. My brethren cite only one case in support of their conclusion: a district court case from Maryland, Berliner Foods Corp. v. Pillsbury Co., 633 F.Supp. 557 (D. Md. 1986), which, since it treated the contract at issue there as one for personal services, id. at 559 (a characterization my brethren properly reject for the contract between Nexxus and Best), is not helpful. Berliner is the latest in a long line of cases that make the propriety of delegating the performance of a distribution contract depend on whether or not the contract calls for the distributor's personal (unique, irreplaceable, distinctive, and therefore nondelegable) services. See, e.g., Bancroft v. Scribner, 72 Fed. 988 (9th Cir.1896) . . . By rejecting that characterization here, my brethren have sawn off the only limb on which they might have sat comfortably.

A slightly better case for them (though not cited by them) is Wetherell Bros. Co. v. United States Steel Co., 200 F.2d 761, 763 (1st Cir.1952), which held that an exclusive sales agent's duties were nondelegable. The agent, a Massachusetts corporation, had agreed to use its "best endeavors" to promote the sale of the defendant's steel in the New England area. The corporation was liquidated and its assets sold to a Pennsylvania corporation that was not shown to be qualified to conduct business in Massachusetts, the largest state in New England. On these facts the defendant was entitled to treat the liquidation and sale as a termination of the contract. The Wetherell decision has been understood to depend on its facts. See Jennings v. Foremost Dairies, Inc., 37 Misc. 2d 328, 235 N.Y.S. 2d 566, 574 (1962); 4 Corbin on Contracts, 1971 Pocket Part § 865, at p. 128. The facts of the present case are critically different. So far as appears, the same people who distributed Nexxus's products for Best (except for Best's president) continued to do so for Sally Beauty. Best was acquired, and continues, as a going concern; the corporation was dissolved, but the business wasn't. Whether there was a delegation of performance in any sense may be doubted. cf Rossetti v. City of New Britain, 163 Conn. 283, 303 A.2d 714, 718–19 (1972). The general rule is that a change of corporate form—including a merger—does not in and of itself affect contractual rights and obligations. United States Shoe Corp. v. Hackett, 793 F.2d 161, 163–64 (7th Cir. 1986).

The fact that Best's president has quit cannot be decisive on the issue whether the merger resulted in a delegation of performance. The contract between Nexxus and Best was not a personal-services contract conditioned on a particular individual's remaining with Best. Compare Jennings v. Foremost Dairies, Inc., supra, 235 N.Y.S. 2d at 574. If Best had not been acquired, but its president had left anyway, as of course he might have done, Nexxus could not have repudiated the contract.

No case adopts the per se rule that my brethren announce. The cases ask whether, as a matter of fact, a change in business form is likely to impair performance of the contract. Wetherell asked this. So did Arnold Productions, Inc. v. Favorite Films Corp., 298 F.2d 540, 543–44 (2d Cir. 1962) . . . Green v. Camlin, 229 S.C. 129, 92 S.E.2d 125, 127 (1956), has some broad language which my brethren might have cited; but since the contract in that case forbade assignment it is not an apt precedent.

My brethren find this a simple case-as simple (it seems) as if a lawyer had undertaken to represent the party opposing his client. But notions of conflict of interest are not the same in law and in business, and judges can go astray by assuming that the legal-services industry is the pattern for the entire economy. The lawyerization of America has not reached that point. Sally Beauty, though a wholly owned subsidiary of Alberto-Culver, distributes "hair care" supplies made by many different companies, which so far as appears compete with Alberto-Culver as vigorously as Nexxus does. Steel companies both make fabricated steel and sell raw steel to competing fabricators. General Motors sells cars manufactured by a competitor, Isuzu. What in law would be considered a fatal conflict of interest is in business a commonplace and legitimate practice. The lawyer is a fiduciary of his client; Best was not a fiduciary of Nexxus.

Selling your competitor's products, or supplying inputs to your competitor, sometimes creates problems under antitrust or regulatory law—but only when the supplier or distributor has monopoly or market power and uses it to restrict a competitor's access to an essential input or to the market for the competitor's output, as in Otter Tail Power Co. v. United States, 410 U.S. 366, 93 S.Ct. 1022, 35 L.Ed. 2d 359 (1973), or FTC v. Brown Shoe Co., 384 U.S. 316, 86 S.Ct. 1501, 16 L.Ed. 2d 587 (1966) . . . There is no suggestion that Alberto-Culver has a monopoly of "hair care" products or Sally Beauty a monopoly of distributing such products, or that Alberto-Culver would ever have ordered Sally Beauty to stop carrying Nexxus products. Far from complaining about being squeezed out of the market by the acquisition, Nexxus is complaining in effect about Sally Beauty's refusal to boycott it!

How likely is it that the acquisition of Best could hurt Nexxus? Not very. Suppose Alberto-Culver had ordered Sally Beauty to go slow in pushing Nexxus products, in the hope that sales of Alberto-Culver "hair care" products would rise. Even if they did, since the market is competitive Alberto-Culver would not reap monopoly profits. Moreover, what guarantee has Alberto-Culver that consumers would be diverted from Nexxus to it, rather than to products closer in price and quality to Nexxus products? In any event, any trivial gain in profits to Alberto-Culver would be offset by the loss of goodwill to Sally Beauty; and a cost to Sally Beauty is a cost to Alberto-Culver, its parent. Remember that Sally Beauty carries beauty supplies made by other competitors of Alberto-Culver; Best alone carries "hair care" products manufactured by Revlon, Clairol, Bristol-Myers, and L'Oreal, as well as Alberto-Culver. Will these powerful competitors continue to distribute their products through Sally Beauty if Sally Beauty displays favoritism for Alberto-Culver products? Would not such a display be a commercial disaster for Sally Beauty, and hence for its parent, Alberto-Culver? Is it really credible that Alberto-Culver would sacrifice Sally Beauty in a vain effort to monopolize the "hair care" market, in violation of section 2 of the Sherman Act? Is not the ratio of the profits that Alberto-Culver obtains from Sally Beauty to the profits it obtains from the manufacture of "hair care" products at least a relevant consideration?

Another relevant consideration is that the contract between Nexxus and Best was for a short term. Could Alberto-Culver destroy Nexxus by failing to push its products with maximum vigor in Texas for a year? In the unlikely event that it could and did, it would be liable in damages to Nexxus for breach of the implied best-efforts term of the distribution contract. Finally, it is obvious that Sally Beauty does not have a bottleneck position in the distribution of "hair care" products, such that by refusing to promote Nexxus products vigorously it could stifle the distribution of those products in Texas; for Nexxus has found alternative distribution that it prefers—otherwise it wouldn't have repudiated the contract with Best when Best was acquired by Sally Beauty.

Not all businessmen are consistent and successful profit maximizers, so the probability that Alberto-Culver would instruct Sally Beauty to cease to push Nexxus products vigorously in Texas cannot be reckoned at zero. On this record, however, it is slight. And there is no principle of law that if something happens that trivially reduces the probability that a dealer will use his best efforts, the supplier can cancel the contract. Suppose there had been no merger, but the only child of Best's president had gone to work for Alberto-Culver as a chemist. Could Nexxus have canceled the contract, fearing that Best (perhaps unconsciously) would favor Alberto-Culver products over Nexxus products? That would be an absurd ground for cancellation, and so is Nexxus's actual ground. At most, so far as the record shows, Nexxus may have had grounds for "insecurity" regarding the performance by Sally Beauty of its obligation to use its best efforts to promote Nexxus products, but if so its remedy was not to cancel the contract but to demand assurances of due performance. See UCC § 2–609; Official Comment 5 to § 2–306. No such demand was made. An anticipatory repudiation by conduct requires conduct that makes the repudiating party unable to perform. Farnsworth, Contracts 636 (1982). The merger did not do this. At least there is no evidence it did. The judgment should be reversed and the case remanded for a trial on whether the merger so altered the conditions of performance that Nexxus is entitled to declare the contract broken.

NOTES AND QUESTIONS

1. *Transfer versus assignment.* The contract in this case was transferred by operation of law under Texas corporate merger law. Once the shareholders of both corporations approve a plan of merger, all the assets and liabilities of the target corporation transfer by operation of law to the surviving corporation on the effective date specified in the plan of merger. Should it matter that the transfer occurred as a matter of law rather than by way of a "voluntary" assignment of the entire but isolated contract? If the delegation is not prohibited by the contract itself, what test does the common law apply to determine whether the delegation is effective? Although the court disapproved

of the delegation, could the rights have been assigned separately from the delegation of duties?

2.   *Terms prohibiting delegation.* The contract in *Sally Beauty* did not include language prohibiting a delegation of duties. If it had included such language, would the court have reached a different conclusion?

3.   *Posner's dissent.* Judge Posner makes a compelling argument that at least on this record, it is unclear that the delegation will have a material negative impact on Nexxus. In so doing, he attempts to analyze the essence of the Nexxus's argument—that the company that acquired Sally Beauty is a competitor. Judge Posner concludes they have very little in common in the competitive market place because of how and where the products are sold. Is that the only test? Regardless of where marketed, does Alberto-Culver sell substitute products similar to Nexxus? For an interesting analysis of Judge Posner's dissenting opinions in general (including *Sally Beauty*), see Robert F. Blomquist, "Dissent, Posner-Style: Judge Richard A. Posner's First Decade of Dissenting Opinions: 1981–1991—Toward An Aesthetics of Judicial Dissenting Style," 69 Mo. L. Rev. 73 (2004).

INDEX

References are to Pages